Handbook of Research on Redesigning the Future of Internet Architectures

Mohamed Boucadair
France Télécom, France

Christian Jacquenet
France Télécom, France

A volume in the Advances in Web Technologies and Engineering (AWTE) Book Series

Information Science REFERENCE
An Imprint of IGI Global

Managing Director:	Lindsay Johnston
Managing Editor:	Austin DeMarco
Director of Intellectual Property & Contracts:	Jan Travers
Acquisitions Editor:	Kayla Wolfe
Production Editor:	Christina Henning
Development Editor:	Brandon Carbaugh
Typesetter:	Michael Brehm, Tucker Knerr, & Lisandro Gonzalez
Cover Design:	Jason Mull

Published in the United States of America by
Information Science Reference (an imprint of IGI Global)
701 E. Chocolate Avenue
Hershey PA, USA 17033
Tel: 717-533-8845
Fax: 717-533-8661
E-mail: cust@igi-global.com
Web site: http://www.igi-global.com

Library of Congress Cataloging-in-Publication Data

Library of Congress Cataloging-in-Publication Data

Handbook of research on redesigning the future of internet architectures / Mohamed Boucadair and Christian Jacquenet, editors.
pages cm
Includes bibliographical references and index.
ISBN 978-1-4666-8371-6 (hardcover) -- ISBN 978-1-4666-8372-3 (ebook) 1. Computer network architectures. 2. Internet--Security measures. I. Boucadair, Mohamed, editor. II. Jacquenet, Christian, editor.
TK5105.5.H3663 2015
004.6'5--dc23
2015008170

This book is published in the IGI Global book series Advances in Web Technologies and Engineering (AWTE) (ISSN: Pending; eISSN: pending)

British Cataloguing in Publication Data
A Cataloguing in Publication record for this book is available from the British Library.

Advances in Web Technologies and Engineering (AWTE) Book Series

Ghazi I. Alkhatib
Princess Sumaya University for Technology, Jordan

David C. Rine
George Mason University, USA

ISSN: Pending
EISSN: pending

Mission

The **Advances in Web Technologies and Engineering (AWTE) Book Series** aims to provide a platform for research in the area of Information Technology (IT) concepts, tools, methodologies, and ethnography, in the contexts of global communication systems and Web engineered applications. Organizations are continuously overwhelmed by a variety of new information technologies, many are Web based. These new technologies are capitalizing on the widespread use of network and communication technologies for seamless integration of various issues in information and knowledge sharing within and among organizations. This emphasis on integrated approaches is unique to this book series and dictates cross platform and multidisciplinary strategy to research and practice.

The **Advances in Web Technologies and Engineering (AWTE) Book Series** seeks to create a stage where comprehensive publications are distributed for the objective of bettering and expanding the field of web systems, knowledge capture, and communication technologies. The series will provide researchers and practitioners with solutions for improving how technology is utilized for the purpose of a growing awareness of the importance of web applications and engineering.

Coverage

- Knowledge structure, classification, and search algorithms or engines
- Virtual teams and virtual enterprises: communication, policies, operation, creativity, and innovation
- Ontology and semantic Web studies
- Strategies for linking business needs and IT
- Web user interfaces design, development, and usability engineering studies
- Metrics-based performance measurement of IT-based and Web-based organizations
- Human factors and cultural impact of IT-based systems
- Competitive/intelligent information systems
- Case studies validating Web-based IT solutions
- Web Systems Architectures, Including Distributed, Grid Computer, and Communication Systems Processing

IGI Global is currently accepting manuscripts for publication within this series. To submit a proposal for a volume in this series, please contact our Acquisition Editors at Acquisitions@igi-global.com or visit: http://www.igi-global.com/publish/.

The Advances in Web Technologies and Engineering (AWTE) Book Series (ISSN Pending) is published by IGI Global, 701 E. Chocolate Avenue, Hershey, PA 17033-1240, USA, www.igi-global.com. This series is composed of titles available for purchase individually; each title is edited to be contextually exclusive from any other title within the series. For pricing and ordering information please visit http://www.igi-global.com/book-series/advances-web-technologies-engineering/37158. Postmaster: Send all address changes to above address.

Titles in this Series

For a list of additional titles in this series, please visit: www.igi-global.com

Artificial Intelligence Technologies and the Evolution of Web 3.0
Tomayess Issa (Curtin University, Australia) and Pedro Isaías (Universidade Aberta (Portuguese Open University), Portugal)
Information Science Reference • copyright 2015 • 422pp • H/C (ISBN: 9781466681477) • US $225.00 (our price)

Frameworks, Methodologies, and Tools for Developing Rich Internet Applications
Giner Alor-Hernández (Instituto Tecnológico de Orizaba, Mexico) Viviana Yarel Rosales-Morales (Instituto Tecnológico de Orizaba, Mexico) and Luis Omar Colombo-Mendoza (Instituto Tecnológico de Orizaba, Mexico)
Information Science Reference • copyright 2015 • 366pp • H/C (ISBN: 9781466664371) • US $195.00 (our price)

Handbook of Research on Demand-Driven Web Services Theory, Technologies, and Applications
Zhaohao Sun (University of Ballarat, Australia & Hebei Normal University, China) and John Yearwood (Federation University, Australia)
Information Science Reference • copyright 2014 • 474pp • H/C (ISBN: 9781466658844) • US $325.00 (our price)

Evaluating Websites and Web Services Interdisciplinary Perspectives on User Satisfaction
Denis Yannacopoulos (Technological Educational Institute of Piraeus, Greece) Panagiotis Manolitzas (Technical University of Crete, Greece) Nikolaos Matsatsinis (Technical University of Crete, Greece) and Evangelos Grigoroudis (Technical University of Crete, Greece)
Information Science Reference • copyright 2014 • 354pp • H/C (ISBN: 9781466651296) • US $215.00 (our price)

Solutions for Sustaining Scalability in Internet Growth
Mohamed Boucadair (France Telecom-Orange Labs, France) and David Binet (France Telecom, France)
Information Science Reference • copyright 2014 • 288pp • H/C (ISBN: 9781466643055) • US $190.00 (our price)

Adaptive Web Services for Modular and Reusable Software Development Tactics and Solutions
Guadalupe Ortiz (University of Cádiz, Spain) and Javier Cubo (University of Málaga, Spain)
Information Science Reference • copyright 2013 • 415pp • H/C (ISBN: 9781466620896) • US $195.00 (our price)

Public Service, Governance and Web 2.0 Technologies Future Trends in Social Media
Ed Downey (State University of New York, College at Brockport, USA) and Matthew A. Jones (Portland State University, USA)
Information Science Reference • copyright 2012 • 369pp • H/C (ISBN: 9781466600713) • US $190.00 (our price)

List of Contributors

Abba, Laura / *National Research Council, Institute for Informatics and Telematics, Italy* 32
Aghvami, Hamid / *King's College London, UK* 161
Altowaijri, Saleh / *Swansea University, UK* 531
Amann, Nathalie / *Orange, France* 500
Amenta, Valentina / *National Research Council, Institute for Informatics and Telematics, Italy* 32
Aranda, Pedro A. / *Telefónica I+D, Spain* 383
Bastide, Valéry / *Orange, France* 500
Bellagamba, Patrice / *Cisco Systems, France* 303
Binet, David / *Orange, France* 190
Borges, Isabel / *PT Inovação, Portugal* 409
Boucadair, Mohamed / *Orange, France* 190
Bursztynowski, Dariusz / *Orange, Poland* 68
Ceccarelli, Daniele / *Ericsson, Italy* 346
Chen, Yiping / *Orange, France* 500
Chochlidakis, Giorgos / *King's College London, UK* 161
Collange, Denis / *Orange, France* 190
Cruz, Tiago / *University of Coimbra, Portugal* 432
Cugini, Filippo / *CNIT, Italy* 237
Denazis, Spyros / *University of Patras, Greece* 364
Dohler, Mischa / *King's College London, UK* 161
Dzida, Mateusz / *Orange, France* 500
Faisal, Muhammad Ali / *COMSATS Institute of Information Technology, Pakistan* 531
Fieau, Frédéric / *Orange, France* 500
Fleming, Patrick / *Orange, France* 500
Franke, Michael / *Spinor, Germany* 68
Friderikos, Vasilis / *King's College London, UK* 161
Gouraud, Vincent / *Orange, France* 190
Gouta, Ali / *Orange, France* 500
Griffin, David / *University College London, UK* 68
Guillouard, Karine / *Orange, France* 190
Haleplidis, Evangelos / *University of Patras, Greece* 364
Jacquenet, Christian / *Orange, France* 190
Koufopavlou, Odysseas / *University of Patras, Greece* 364
L'Azou, Yves / *Orange, France* 190,500
Lazzaroni, Adriana / *National Research Council, Institute for Informatics and Telematics, Italy* 32

Table of Contents

Section 2
Novel Networking Approaches

Chapter 4
Service-Centric Networking 68
David Griffin, University College London, UK
Miguel Rio, University College London, UK
Pieter Simoens, University of Ghent, Belgium
Piet Smet, University of Ghent, Belgium
Frederik Vandeputte, Alcatel-Lucent Bell NV, Belgium
Luc Vermoesen, Alcatel-Lucent Bell NV, Belgium
Dariusz Bursztynowski, Orange, Poland
Folker Schamel, Spinor, Germany
Michael Franke, Spinor, Germany

Chapter 5
Power-Aware Networking 96
Mingui Zhang, Huawei Technologies, China
Hongfang Yu, University of Electronic Science and Technology of China (UESTC), China

Chapter 6
Application-Enabled Collaborative Networking 119
Tirumaleswar Reddy, Cisco Systems, India
Prashanth Patil, Cisco Systems, India
Anca Zamfir, Independent Researcher, Switzerland

Chapter 7
The Whole World is Going Mobile 137
Charles E. Perkins, Futurewei, USA

Chapter 8
Challenges of 5G Networking in Access and Core Networks 161
Vasilis Friderikos, King's College London, UK
Giorgos Chochlidakis, King's College London, UK
Hamid Aghvami, King's College London, UK
Mischa Dohler, King's College London, UK

Section 3
Advanced Transport Techniques & Traffic Forwarding and Routing Schemes

Chapter 9
Multipath TCP (MPTCP): Motivations, Status, and Opportunities for the Future Internet 190
David Binet, Orange, France
Mohamed Boucadair, Orange, France
Christian Jacquenet, Orange, France
Denis Collange, Orange, France
Karine Guillouard, Orange, France
Yves L'Azou, Orange, France
Luca Muscariello, Orange, France
Laurent Reynaud, Orange, France
Pierrick Seite, Orange, France
Vincent Gouraud, Orange, France

Chapter 10
A Top-Down Framework for Modeling Routing Design Complexity 214
Xin Sun, Florida International University, USA

Chapter 11
The Path Computation Element (PCE) 237
Francesco Paolucci, Scuola Superiore Sant'Anna, Italy
Filippo Cugini, CNIT, Italy

Chapter 12
Recent Advances in Traffic Forwarding Techniques 267
Quintin Zhao, Huawei Technology, USA
Zhenbin Li, Huawei Technologies, China

Chapter 13
Available Routing Construct (ARC) 303
Patrice Bellagamba, Cisco Systems, France
Pascal Thubert, Cisco Systems, France

Chapter 14
Asymmetric Extended Route Optimization (AERO)... 324
Fred L. Templin, Association for Computing Machinery (ACM), USA

Chapter 21
Recent Advances and Perspectives on Content Delivery Networks 500
Nathalie Amann, Orange, France
Valéry Bastide, Orange, France
Yiping Chen, Orange, France
Mateusz Dzida, Orange, France
Frédéric Fieau, Orange, France
Patrick Fleming, Orange, France
Ali Gouta, Orange, France
Yves L'Azou, Orange, France
Yannick Le Louédec, Orange, France
Nicolas Maréchal, Orange, France
Nathalie Omnès, Orange, France
Iuniana Oprescu, Orange, France
Vincent Thiebaut, Orange, France

Chapter 22
Future Networked Healthcare Systems: A Review and Case Study 531
Rashid Mehmood, King Khalid University, Saudi Arabia
Muhammad Ali Faisal, COMSATS Institute of Information Technology, Pakistan
Saleh Altowaijri, Swansea University, UK

Compilation of References 559

About the Contributors 601

Index 617

Detailed Table of Contents

The demographics of the Internet will experience significant changes in the near future. The developed countries are maximizing the number of citizens connected to the network while the developing countries, with the majority of the global population, increase their presence as the information technologies become more accessible. Leaders from the developed countries advocate the preservation of existing governance organizations regulating the network, such as the Internet Corporation for Assigned Names and Numbers (ICANN), on the basis of stability and security. New generations of Internet users are demanding new structures based on transparency, participation, accountability and legitimacy. In the absence of new agreements, uncoordinated changes to the existing governance structure could potentially affect the technical structure of the network and its functionality. Employing a Bayesian Belief Network model, this chapter analyzes the correlation between demographics, socio-economic factors and the feasibility of changes to the existing Internet governance structure. Favorable change conditions could initiate changes that could impact all Internet users. Results demonstrate that even when conditions for radical changes that could fragment the network are not present within the timeframe evaluated, conditions in support of changes increase with time, validating a need to modify the existing governance structure.

In this chapter, the analysis will focus on the concept of digital identity which is evolving and changing, based on the experiences that every individual lives. The chapter further highlights how the digital identity includes the fundamental human rights such as the right to a name, the right of reply, the right to protection of personal data and the right to an image. In translating the right to personal identity to

Energy consumption of networking infrastructures is growing fast due to the exponential growth of data traffic and the deployment of increasingly powerful equipment. Besides operational costs and environmental impacts, the ever-increasing energy consumption has become a limiting factor to long-term growth of network infrastructures. Operators, vendors and researchers have started to look beyond a single router or line card for network-wide solutions towards energy proportionality. Therefore, Power Aware Networking (PANET) has been proposed to improve network energy efficiency. A PANET-enabled network assumes that only a subset of devices will be involved in traffic forwarding when the network is lightly loaded, so as to improve global energy savings. PANET is introduced in this chapter. Promising solutions for PANET are also exposed. PANET features are also analyzed. The chapter also discusses the challenges and future work that needs to be done.

Identification and treatment of application flows are important to many application providers and network operators. They often rely on these capabilities to deploy and/or support a wide range of applications. These applications generate flows that may have specific characteristics such as bandwidth or latency that can be met if made known to the network. Historically, this functionality has been implemented to the extent possible using heuristics that inspect and infer flow characteristics. Heuristics may be based on port numbers, network identifiers (e.g., subnets or VLANs, Deep Flow Inspection (DFI), or Deep Packet Inspection (DPI)). However, many application flows in current usages are dynamic, adaptive, time-bound, encrypted, peer-to-peer (P2P), asymmetric, used on multipurpose devices, and/ or have different priorities depending on the direction of the flow, user preferences, and other factors. Any combination of these properties renders heuristic-based techniques less effective and may result in compromises to application security or user privacy. Application-enabled collaborative networking (AECN) is a framework in which applications explicitly signal their flow characteristics and requirements to the network. This provides network nodes with knowledge of the application flow characteristics, which enables them to apply the correct flow treatment and provide feedback to applications accordingly. This chapter describes how an application enabled collaborative networking framework contributes to solve the encountered problems.

The Internet is growing ever more mobile – meaning, that an ever greater proportion of Internet devices are mobile devices. This trend necessitates new designs and will produce new and even unpredictable conceptions about the very nature of the Internet and, more fundamentally, the nature of social interaction. The engineering response to growing mobility and complexity is difficult to predict. This chapter summarizes the past and the present ways of dealing with mobility, and uses that as context for trying to understand what needs to be done for the future. Central to the conception of future mobility is the notion of "always available" and highly interactive applications. Part of providing acceptable service in that conception of the mobile Internet will require better ways to manage handovers as the device moves around the Internet, and ways to better either hide or make available a person's identity depending on who is asking.

Chapter 8
Challenges of 5G Networking in Access and Core Networks 161
Vasilis Friderikos, King's College London, UK
Giorgos Chochlidakis, King's College London, UK
Hamid Aghvami, King's College London, UK
Mischa Dohler, King's College London, UK

The 5th Generation wireless and mobile communication is expected to provide ultrahigh data rates over wireless in the range of Gbps. But 5G will also be about providing consistency and supporting Quality of Experience in a personalized manner. We foresee an evolution in terms of physical layer enhancements to provide increased data rates, whereas a revolutionary step is required in terms of network orchestration and management to provide consistency and efficient utilization of the available resources at a minimum cost. In this chapter, key trends in wireless access technologies and thus-required network management strategies with respect to the core network are discussed. In the roadmap towards 5G networks, we envision an evolution of technologies for supporting Gbps wireless transmission, whereas a revolution would be required from the current modus operandi in the ways network orchestration and resource management is performed in these complex, hierarchical, heterogeneous and highly autonomous wireless networks.

Section 3
Advanced Transport Techniques & Traffic Forwarding and Routing Schemes

Chapter 9
Multipath TCP (MPTCP): Motivations, Status, and Opportunities for the Future Internet 190
David Binet, Orange, France
Mohamed Boucadair, Orange, France
Christian Jacquenet, Orange, France
Denis Collange, Orange, France
Karine Guillouard, Orange, France
Yves L'Azou, Orange, France
Luca Muscariello, Orange, France
Laurent Reynaud, Orange, France
Pierrick Seite, Orange, France
Vincent Gouraud, Orange, France

The Transmission Control Protocol (TCP) is one of the core components of the TCP/IP protocol suite. It has been extensively used for the past three decades (and counting) as the privileged connection-oriented transport mode for many Internet applications, including access to web contents. Nevertheless, experience with TCP can sometimes be rather poor for various reasons which include (but are not limited to) sub-optimized forwarding path capabilities. Because a TCP session can only be established over a single path (by definition), this restriction is not only unable to take into account the dramatic evolution of terminal technologies towards multi-interfaced devices, but also the ability to benefit from several yet potential forwarding paths for the sake of improved Quality of Experience (QoE).

Chapter 10
A Top-Down Framework for Modeling Routing Design Complexity 214
Xin Sun, Florida International University, USA

Networks with higher degrees of complexity typically require more effort to manage and are more prone to configuration errors. Unfortunately, complexity remains one of the least understood aspects of

networking. This chapter takes a first step toward bridging this gap, by presenting a top-down framework for modeling complexity in routing design, a critical and highly complex network design task. First, a set of abstractions is introduced for precisely defining objectives of routing design, and for reasoning about how a combination of routing design primitives will meet the objectives. Next, models are presented for quantitatively measuring the complexity of a routing design by modeling individual design primitives and leveraging configuration-derived complexity metrics. This modeling approach helps understand how individual design choices may impact the resulting complexity, and enables comparison of alternative routing designs and "what-if" analysis of the potential impact of a design change on complexity.

The Internet Engineering Task Force (IETF) has promoted the Path Computation Element (PCE) architecture to provide effective network resource utilization while guaranteeing advanced Internet applications with adequate quality of service (QoS). The PCE is a dedicated network entity devoted to path computation. This chapter presents the state-of-the-art of the PCE architecture for different networking scenarios including single-domain networks, optical networks, and multi-domain/layer networks. Relevant architectural and implementation aspects are analyzed and discussed, highlighting related benefits, limitations and open issues. Recent progresses and future directions are also addressed, including the PCE evolution to operate in the context of software defined networking.

Advanced service oriented routing and forwarding schemes are nurturing fast recently, thus paving the way to implementations that can overcome complications related to multi-vendor networking environments. Some of these proposals are improving and optimizing the existing traffic engineering functionalities where the forwarding planes are still under a distributed signaling control system, others are more network architecture level changes where the forwarding plane is totally centralized controlled through a centralized control plane. At the same time some of these proposals are the hybrid of the both. This chapter describes these advances by focusing on the aspects of forwarding scheme changes introduced in each of these areas.

Every computer network has been built in the last 30 years on the concept of routing tree to compute the path to be used to reach a given prefix or the border of a routing area. This chapter introduces the concept of Available Routing Construct (ARC), which is a two-end (or more) routing basic element that forms its own recovery domain. As it is dual ended, any failure in an ARC can be easily locally resolved by reversing the path toward the other end. A routing area can therefore be described in a graph of hierarchical ARCs. This new paradigm could be leveraged to improve the network resiliency and utilization for both unicast and multicast traffic.

Chapter 14
Asymmetric Extended Route Optimization (AERO).. 324
Fred L. Templin, Association for Computing Machinery (ACM), USA

Modern enterprise networks must accommodate mobile devices such as cell phones, tablets and laptop computers. When a mobile device moves to a new access network, it often receives a new Internet Protocol (IP) address. This can disrupt communication sessions and create challenges for locating and tracking mobile assets. The enterprise network should therefore provide each mobile device with a stable IP address or prefix that never changes, but this requires a new mobility architecture. Asymmetric Extended Route Optimization (AERO) supports mobility by modeling the enterprise network as a virtual link through a process known as encapsulation. The AERO system tracks mobile devices through control message signaling and an efficient routing system. AERO maintains optimal routes for roaming devices so that performance is maximized and congestion points are avoided. This chapter describes the AERO system for accommodating mobile devices within enterprise networks.

Section 4
New Approaches to (Automated) Network Services Design, Delivery and Operation

Chapter 15
Abstraction and Control of Transport Networks.. 346
Young Lee, Huawei Technologies, USA
Daniele Ceccarelli, Ericsson, Italy

Virtual network operation refers to the creation of a virtualized environment allowing operators to view the abstraction of the underlying multi-admin, multi-vendor, multi-technology networks and to operate, control and manage these multiple networks as a single virtualized network. Another dimension of virtual network operation is associated with the use of the common core transport network resources by multi-tenant service networks as a way of providing a virtualized infrastructure to flexibly offer new services and applications. The work effort investigating this problem space is known as Abstraction and Control of Transport Networks (ACTN). This chapter provides an ACTN problem description, identifies the scope of this effort, and outlines the core requirements to facilitate virtual network operation.

Chapter 16
Future SDN-Based Network Architectures.. 364
Evangelos Haleplidis, University of Patras, Greece
Spyros Denazis, University of Patras, Greece
Odysseas Koufopavlou, University of Patras, Greece

Networking has seen a burst of innovation and rapid changes with the advent of Software Defined Networking (SDN). Many people considered SDN to be something new and innovative, but actually SDN is something that has already been proposed almost a decade ago in the era of active and programmable networks, and developed even before that. Coupled with the fact that SDN is a very dynamic area with everyone trying to brand their architecture, research or product as SDN has defined a vague and broad definition of what SDN. This chapter attempts to put SDN into perspective approaching SDN with a more spherical point of view by providing the necessary background of pre-SDN technologies and how SDN came about. Followed by discussion on what SDN means today, what SDN is comprised of and a vision of how SDN will evolve in the future to provide the programmable networks that researchers and operators have longed for for many years now. This chapter closes with a few applicability use cases of the future SDN and wraps up with how SDN fits in the Future Internet Architectures.

Network Functions Virtualization (NFV) has emerged as a new paradigm for designing, deploying and operating network services. It is a natural evolution of the current trend of applying cloud technologies to Information Technology (IT) services, bringing them to network provider environments. While this is true for the most simple use cases, focused on the IT services network providers rely on, the nature of network services and the physical anchors of network themselves impose additional, unique requirements on the virtualization process in this environment. At the same time, NFV provides an opportunity to network providers, reducing operational costs and bringing the promise of dramatically easing the development of new services, reducing their time-to-market, and opening new possibilities for service provisioning. This chapter analyses these requirements and opportunities and the challenges NFV brings to network providers, and reviews the current state of the art in this new way of dealing with network services.

The combination of Software-Defined Networking (SDN) with Network Functions Virtualization (NFV) approaches is gaining momentum in the Industry as a new way of implementing, managing and controlling telecommunications networks. This chapter aims to go through SDN and lightly over NFV, presenting main characteristics and the standardization work on that technologies. SDN enables programming networks together with the ability to adapt to applications requirements and network dynamics. NFV aims at virtualizing network services by merging several network equipment types onto standard Information Technologies (IT) high volume virtualization technology (switches, servers and storage) located either in data centres, customer premises or network nodes. SDN and NFV interworking ambition is to bring on-demand resource provisioning, resource elasticity, among others with a centralized view of the overall network, able to automatically and dynamically honor service requirements.

The Residential Gateway (RGW) is a key device, located on the customer premises, that stands between the home network and the access network. It imposes a considerable cost for the NSP and constitutes a single point of failure for all the services offered to residential customers – such as Internet access, VoIP, IPTV and Video-on-Demand. As such, the RGW constitutes an ideal candidate for virtualization, potentially relieving the NSP from such problems while also providing benefits to end-users. This chapter discusses the rationale and proposes an architecture for a virtualized Residential Gateway (vRGW) that physically removes the RGW from the customer premises, moving it into the operator data center or other logical point-of-presence, as a virtualized entity. This solution potentially reduces deployment, maintenance and operation costs, whilst improving overall performance, flexibility, reliability and manageability – both for the access network infrastructure and for the services provided over this infrastructure.

The huge changes in multimedia and video consumption styles are leading to different challenges for the current Internet architecture in order to support the required quality of experience. A comprehensive solution to these would help the service providers and over-the-top players (OTT) to differentiate their services and the network operators to handle ever growing demands on network resources in an era of slower growth in revenues. This chapter discusses the requirements for and approaches to enhanced content delivery architectures, video delivery standards and current and future content transport mechanisms. The chapter also discusses the Quality of Experience (QoE) metrics and management for video content and introduces context-awareness in the video delivery chain. It also provides several examples for context-aware content delivery and personalized services.

This chapter provides an overview on the recent advances and perspectives on Content Delivery Networks. The first section, the introduction, sets the context. The second section identifies the different types of current CDNs and also insights on their evolution. The third section deals with CDN interconnection, reporting work status such as IETF and ETSI. The fourth section, on CDN and virtualization, describes the related initiatives in this area, in standardization bodies as well as in experimental deployments and evaluations. The fifth section focuses on the convergence of CDNs and clouds, presenting new business opportunities for the market players, as well as technical challenges. The sixth section addresses another trend, which is the extension of CDNs to home networking and terminal devices. The last section discusses content delivery for mobile, introducing solutions that operators can to optimize their networks and avoid being overwhelmed by ever growing traffic.

Chapter 22
Future Networked Healthcare Systems: A Review and Case Study 531
Rashid Mehmood, King Khalid University, Saudi Arabia
Muhammad Ali Faisal, COMSATS Institute of Information Technology, Pakistan
Saleh Altowaijri, Swansea University, UK

Future healthcare systems and organizations demand huge computational resources, and the ability for the applications to interact and communicate with each other, within and across organizational boundaries. This chapter aims to explore state-of-the-art of the healthcare landscape and presents an analysis of networked healthcare systems with a focus on networking traffic and architectures. To this end, the relevant technologies including networked healthcare architectures and performance studies, Health Level 7 (HL7), big data, and cloud computing, are reviewed. Subsequently, a study of healthcare systems, applications and traffic over local, metro, and wide area networks is presented using multi-hospital cross-continent scenarios. The network architectures for these systems are described. A detailed study to explore quality of service (QoS) performance for these healthcare systems with a range of applications, system sizes, and network sizes is presented. Conclusions are drawn regarding future healthcare systems and internet designs along with directions for future research.

Compilation of References 559

About the Contributors 601

Index 617

Preface

PREFACE

Not all the world population is connected. But the Internet is dramatically expanding. From the happy few who were able to exchange mails and access the Gopher servers of the early nineties to the 3+ billion of users who now generate large amounts of data, voice and video traffic regardless of where and how they are connected and whether they are in motion, the growth of the Internet is exponential and protean. The growth can be expressed as a function of the number of people who can access Internet-based facilities, but also as a function of the amount of Internet traffic, which currently doubles every three years. Also, the number of connected domains has been linearly increasing for the past 15 years.

It's not even about connecting more and more people anymore. It's about connecting everyone and everything to a multi-service Internet that has become the privileged infrastructure for global communications. Internet is not reduced to a global network that supports basic connectivity services anymore, but has rather become a global network that now supports a large variety of added value services.

The large variety of communication services, applications, device and networking technologies that are deployed over and connected to this global networking infrastructure generate various kinds of traffic that are different in terms of requirements, constraints and patterns. Such a protean development inevitably raises new challenges, so that the Internet remains the privileged communication infrastructure of the future, while trying to minimize the risk of a fragmented Internet that would be composed of a multitude of islands with no global reachability scope.

Stating that the Internet is a complex system is more than a tautology: it's an understatement. Introducing global changes and dictating how the Internet system as a whole should look like is at best utopic and very arbitrary at worst. The design and the deployment of Future Internet architectures assume the combination of very complex tasks, especially in light of the following:

- The benefits of implementing changes in existing networking infrastructures are not necessarily immediate for various reasons that include (but are not limited to) business development considerations, technical constraints and non-regression issues. Even worse, other networks can be impacted by "selfish" behaviors adopted by the networks they may not even be directly connected to: changes that affect a given network may sometimes propagate throughout the whole Internet.
- Conducting changes is not only about architectures and protocols; it is also about operational procedures, organizational methods, and other policies. Means to correlate all the impacting factors are yet-to-be-determined.

- Networking strategies are usually designed at the level of a network or a collection of networks, but changes are usually applied at lower levels, such as a routing area within a given domain. The impact of implementing these changes altogether is very hard to assess.
- The Internet of the future is very likely to be a complex mixture of heterogeneous techniques and technologies.
- The dilemma that consists at choosing a solution this is "fully" centralized or "fully" distributed is a false one! Actually, design choices are never black and white: gray zones are numerous and are often service-, technology- or culturally-inferred.
- Mastering the behavior of networks is critical for operators. Any solution that does not demonstrate how it can preserve the determinism of networking services will fail.
- Standard protocols and open interfaces are important but the semantics of the data conveyed by such protocols is equally critical. The format of the data should not be frozen but rather easily adapt to new requirements.
- Architecture and protocol extensions are generally proposed without assessing how they facilitate service troubleshooting (including failure detect and repair). Operational considerations are sometimes hardly taken into account when a new architectural design or a protocol candidate are nurturing.
- Introducing autonomous behaviors at the level of the Internet remains embryonic.

What This Book is About

The Internet is suffering from a large variety of technical, sometimes performance-degrading, issues which may eventually question its graceful evolution in light of the observed and foreseen exponential traffic growth. Some of these complications are key challenges that derive from the Internet growth, while others are likely to complicate the introduction of innovative services at large.

Various proposals have been made to maintain the original design principles of the Internet model (including simplicity, flexibility and extensibility principles) while allowing for more dynamicity in the way networks are designed and operated.

Such dynamics are manifold: introducing some intelligence in the networks facilitates the progressive automation of device configuration tasks and overall service procedures, whereas device autonomy improves decision-making processes and self-repair capabilities, thereby removing the constraints imposed by physical topologies.

Advanced context-based routing and forwarding schemes are also nurturing, thus paving the way to implementations that can overcome complications related to multi-vendor networking environments.

Some of these proposals are evolutionary, others are rather revolutionary.

A huge "buzz" around several concepts that include Software-Defined Networking (SDN) and Network Function Virtualization (NFV) has been observed in the recent years. Before the advent of SDN and NFV concepts, the research community investigated so-called "*clean slate*" proposals that have emerged, mostly thanks to important investment efforts (generally funded by public bodies) although hardly experimented (let alone deployed) at large scale.

We believe now is the time to clarify the landscape of these various approaches that may or may not shape the future of the Internet.

An in-depth analysis of the promises, pitfalls and other challenges raised by these initiatives should be conducted rigorously for the sake of clarity, while avoiding speculation on expected outcomes and technical benefits.

This book is an invitation to a journey through some of the challenges and how they can be addressed.

The challenges discussed in this book have been classified into the following areas.

Internet Governance, Regulatory Aspects and Privacy Considerations

There is no single entity that rules the Internet. The network of networks is not governed by some kind of control authority. Each network operator is free to enforce its own policies within the network it operates, including the interconnection policies that drive the connection of its network to other networks.

That said, communicating over the Internet often assumes the manipulation of critical information such as namespaces. In particular, the Domain Name System (DNS) service relies upon the establishment and the maintenance of a tree structure and any change in the root zone of the DNS is subject to the approval of a central administration that is placed under the responsibility of the US Department of Commerce.

Likewise, the management of the global IP address space and autonomous system numbers remains the responsibility of the Internet Corporation for Assigned Names and Numbers (ICANN). The ICANN is chartered to control the assignment of globally unique Internet identifiers that include domain names, IP addresses and port numbers in particular. Although governed by representatives from the academia, the industry and other non-commercial structures, the responsibility of ICANN is often challenged by some governmental bodies.

Generally speaking, the governance of the Internet remains a controversial debate that relates to the possible involvement of specific players like state governments in the manipulation of such critical data like domain names and IP addresses. Also, communicating over the Internet always assumes the transmission of personal data at the risk of jeopardizing privacy. Access to such data by undesired parties remains a major yet very likely risk, especially in light of the dramatic development of various social networks.

In particular, the manipulation of such data has recently provoked a major debate about the so-called right to be forgotten, so that the Internet becomes truly amnesiac for the benefit of its users. The future of the Internet is therefore highly conditioned by the progress of the debate on the Internet governance and the implementation of policies to prevent privacy leakages. The following chapters discuss what is at stake, and what options may make the Internet a safer place than it is today:

- The "*Future of Internet Governance*" chapter provides a detailed analysis of what Internet governance covers and discusses a model that depicts the dynamics of such governance, based upon a Bayesian Belief network approach.
- The "*Internet Identity and the Right to be Forgotten*" chapter provides an in-depth analysis of the notion of "online identity", where the right to personal identity implies a number of corollaries such as: the right to a name, the right of reply, the right to protection of personal data and the right to an image.
- Finally, the "*Towards Privacy Awareness in Internet Technologies*" chapter discusses the best balance between users' expectations and the practical level of privacy required to address user privacy needs. It also provides an analysis of some of the most popular protocols of the TCP/IP suite from a privacy angle.

Novel Networking Approaches

The efficiency of IP networking is now challenged by several factors that include the need to save energy and absorb the dramatic traffic growth, essentially because of a dramatic evolution of the Internet usage towards an always-on scheme of thought that yielded no less than an 81% global mobile data traffic growth in 2013.

The said efficiency, which can be expressed in terms of time to access services (*e.g.*, retrieve contents) or the amount of energy that can be saved is indeed exposed to the likely risk of performance, stability and scalability degradation that is further aggravated by the inability of the current Internet networking techniques to take into account service-specific traffic patterns or to gracefully deal with planned maintenance operations so that the end-to-end connectivity services that may be impacted by such operations will not be brutally disrupted.

The "*Service-Centric Networking*" chapter discusses a technique inspired from the Information-Centric networking (ICN) concept where networked software is dynamically deployed and invoked. Service-centric networking provides the mechanisms required to deploy replicated service instances across highly distributed networked cloud infrastructures and to route client requests to the closest instance while providing more efficient network infrastructure usage, improved Quality of Service (QoS) and new business opportunities for application and service providers.

The "*Power-Aware Networking (PANET)*" chapter discusses how energy consumption distorts the global Internet networking system because it is growing fast due to the exponential growth of data traffic and the deployment of increasingly powerful equipment. Besides operational costs and environmental impacts, the ever-increasing energy consumption has become a limiting factor to long-term growth of network infrastructures. Operators, vendors and researchers have started to look beyond a single router or line card for network-wide solutions towards energy proportionality. As a consequence, the concept of Power-Aware Networking (PANET) has been proposed to improve network energy efficiency.

The "*Application-Enabled Collaborative Networking (AECN)*" chapter introduces a new framework in which applications explicitly signal their flow characteristics and requirements to the network. This provides network nodes with knowledge of the application flow characteristics, which enables them to apply the correct flow treatment and provide feedback to applications accordingly. This approach is promising as existing heuristic-based solutions are currently challenged with the adoption of encryption.

Finally, the "*The World is Going Mobile*" chapter provides a detailed insight on the evolution of core mobile networking technologies. The engineering response to growing mobility and complexity is difficult to predict. Nevertheless, this chapter summarizes the past and the present ways of dealing with mobility, and uses that as context for trying to understand what needs to be done for the future.

The "*Challenges of 5G Networking in Access and Core Networks*" chapter discusses the key trends in wireless access technologies and thus-required network management strategies with respect to the core network. 5G networking is seen as an opportunity for supporting Gbps wireless transmission, whereas a revolution would be required from the current modus operandi in the ways network orchestration and resource management is performed in these complex, hierarchical, heterogeneous and highly autonomous wireless networks.

Advanced Traffic Forwarding and Routing Schemes

With nearly four billion of users and 21 billion of networked devices, Internet traffic is expected to reach an amount of 1.6 zettabytes (one zettabyte equals 1000 exabytes, *i.e.*, 10^{21} bytes) by the year 2018. Such dimensioning figures inevitably question the sustainability of the global Internet. The multi-service global network currently assumes a routing system that relies upon the maintenance of 500k+ IPv4 routes by the routers that belong to the so-called Default Free Zone (DFZ): the bigger the forwarding table, the longer it will take a router to make the appropriate forwarding decision.

The situation is further aggravated by the nature and the characteristics of the various applications that connect over the Internet: some of them are extremely QoS demanding, such as real time conversational services (that are delay-sensitive). Other applications may require hard guarantees about the routes that will be used to forward the corresponding traffic: a typical example is the large variety of applications that pertain to the development of the Internet of Things (IoT) or financial transactions.

Among such applications, the e-health service portfolio includes (but is certainly not limited to) the ability to dynamically monitor a set of biometric data so that the closest emergency services can be solicited in a timely manner whenever one of these data crosses a specific threshold. From a routing perspective, this kind of requirement assumes the computation and selection of robust, low latency paths to make sure that the statistics collected by biometric sensors can reach the nearest hospital facility in due time and with a minimized risk of losing packets or the integrity of the transmitted data.

In addition, sensor technologies that now belong to the family of Internet connected devices are often characterized by stringent Central Processing Unit (CPU) and energy constraints. Such constraints clearly affect the range of IP capabilities that can be supported by these devices. They are also very likely to distort the global routing system as we know it, not only because the current routing system that relies upon the combined activation of legacy Interior Gateway Protocols (IGP) with the Border Gateway Protocol (BGP) routing protocols fails to properly scale to accommodate networks of several tens of thousands of devices (typical of the size of wireless sensor networks deployed in urban environments for e-health, power or water metering, pollution metering, *etc*.), but also because such routing system is simply unable to address the aforementioned constraints.

The foreseen faulty scalability of the current routing system can be expressed as a function of the routing protocol's convergence time: the more the devices, the longer it will take to achieve a full synchronization of the routing tables maintained by all the devices of the network.

Likewise, the inability to address service-inferred, traffic pattern-derived requirements is mostly due to the fact that current routing algorithms can manipulate only one routing metric, which is usually the cost assigned to a given router's interface and which often reflects the bandwidth associated to the link that connects this interface to the network. Traffic engineering techniques have been investigated and standardized for quite some time, based upon the use of Constrained Shortest Path First (CSPF) routing algorithms that can take into account the information conveyed in IGP-specific messages that provide information about the available bandwidth or the amount of bandwidth that can be reserved over a given link.

Nevertheless, such techniques failed to be massively adopted mostly because of their inherent complexity from an operational standpoint, but also because they may question the scalability of the underlying routing system, expressed as a function of the number of additional states that need to be maintained by the participating routers. Such states reflect the active (bandwidth) reservations according to the completion of a signaling procedure that propagates bandwidth reservation requests and responses throughout the network, by means of a protocol like the Resource reSerVation Protocol (RSVP).

In addition, the massive development of (smart) terminals that can now be multi-interfaced (i.e., they can take advantage of several physical and/or logical interfaces to connect to one or multiple networks) strengthens the interest for establishing a communication over multiple, possibly distinct paths to either optimize network resource usage or consolidate the robustness of the said communication (*e.g.*, whenever a link fails, another link goes up without any perceived service disruption by the user).

This multi-path communication scheme has also been investigated for quite some time. The Equal Cost Multi-Path (ECMP) capability of link state routing protocols such as the Open Shortest Path First (OSPF) protocol is one example of a multi-path communication scheme where packets can be forwarded over multiple paths that have been assigned the same metric cost. Forwarding decisions over ECMP-labelled paths can rely upon various methods that include the hash-threshold (a router selects a key by performing a hash (a CRC16 for example) to select the next hop for each incoming packet).

ECMP is widely used in Wide Area Network (WAN) environments and basically activated by default when the networks run IGP such as OSPF. ECMP algorithms are agnostic to the upper transport layer protocols by nature, and can therefore be run for any kind of traffic balancing purposes.

But ECMP cannot take into account any traffic or performance metrics to accurately balance traffic between several, equal cost links: the next hop is only randomly selected through a hash code of packets header fields identifying the flows. Therefore, ECMP cannot achieve optimal traffic load balancing as it cannot exploit dynamic metrics for the sake of optimized resource management.

These issues, and others, are discussed in the following chapters, which also detail some of the technical options that are being investigated:

- The "*Multi-Path Transmission Control Protocol (MPTCP)*" chapter describes an extension of the connection-oriented transport protocol of the TCP/IP protocol suite that allows the establishment of a TCP connection that would be composed of several sub-flows over multiple paths. Although the MPTCP specification has been documented several years ago, it is now seen as a promising transport technique that can take full advantage of multi-interfaced device technologies. This chapter further discusses the foreseen evolutions of MPTCP that can better accommodate network or terminal device constraints, especially when the latter cannot support MPTCP features.
- The "*A Top-Down Framework for Modeling Routing Complexity*" chapter exemplifies a top-down framework for modeling and reasoning about complexity in routing design, a critical and highly complex network design task. This chapter promotes a framework that can be used to assess the complexity of routing configurations.
- The "*Path Computation Element*" chapter details the most recent evolutions of PCE architectures, including the so-called stateful approach that relies upon the maintenance of two databases, one that describes the set of Label Switched Paths (LSP) that have been established in a MPLS network, the other (the Traffic Engineering Database) that describes the network topology along with resource usage information. The stateful Path Computation Element can then be fed with impairment parameters for example to refine the path computation algorithm with extra information that best accommodates application requirements with the status of the network and the available resources.

- The "*Recent Advances in Traffic Forwarding Techniques*" chapter covers a set of forwarding and routing schemes that are meant to facilitate the enforcement of traffic engineering policies. Among these schemes, the Segment Routing (SR) and Service Function Chaining (SFC) approaches are currently highly debated within the Internet community at large and already attracted the interest of several large operators worldwide.
- The "*Available Routing Constructs (ARC)*" chapter describes the ARC techniques which basically consists in computing and selecting two-end (or more) routing basic elements that form their own recovery domain. Because ARC structures are dual ended, any failure in an ARC can be locally resolved by reversing the path toward the other end. A routing area can therefore be described as a graph of hierarchical ARCs. This new approach could be leveraged to improve the network resiliency and utilization for both unicast and multicast traffic.
- Finally, the "*Asymmetric Extended Route Optimization (AERO)*" chapter describes a technique that models the enterprise network as a virtual link that attaches all mobile devices through a procedure known as encapsulation. AERO then supports mobility through control message signaling so that network elements always know the current locations of the mobile devices. Each mobile device is assigned a stable IP address or prefix that never changes wherever the device roams. The network then allows mobiles to maintain optimal routes so that performance is maximized and network cost is reduced.

Improved Service Delivery Procedures

A wide range of service offerings can be accessed by Internet users, from web navigation to complex virtual private networks (VPN) services that rely upon the combination of several elementary functions, such as VPN traffic forwarding and routing, VPN traffic classification, marking, conditioning and scheduling, access control lists and filters (sometimes combined with VPN traffic encryption capabilities) and advanced management capabilities that often assume feedback mechanisms to make sure that the VPN service that has been delivered complies with what has been negotiated.

The broader the service portfolio, the more complex the service delivery procedure: from service parameter negotiation to resource allocation and policy enforcement, from configuration tasks to operational procedures, the production and the operation of any given service (even the simplest) become more and more prone to configuration errors, misallocated resources and potential security breaches.

The ability to introduce a high level of automation in the overall service procedure together with the availability of an adequate management toolkit have become of the utmost importance for most of the service providers and vendors, although for different reasons. There is a set of techniques that currently draw the attention of the Internet community, and which fall under the so-called "Software-Defined Networking" (SDN) umbrella:

- Techniques for the dynamic discovery of network topology, devices and capabilities, along with relevant information and data models that are meant to precisely document such topology, devices, and their capabilities.
- Techniques for exposing network services and their characteristics and for dynamically negotiating the set of service parameters that will be used to measure the level of quality associated with the delivery of a given service or a combination thereof.

- Techniques used by service-requirement-derived dynamic resource allocation and policy enforcement schemes, so that networks can be programmed accordingly. Decisions made to dynamically allocate resources and enforce policies are typically the result of the correlation of various inputs, such as the status of available resources in the network at any given time, the number of customer service subscription requests that need to be processed over a given period of time, the traffic forecasts, the possible need to trigger additional resource provisioning cycles according to a typical multi-year master plan, *etc.*
- Dynamic feedback mechanisms that are meant to assess how efficiently a given policy (or a set thereof) is enforced from a service fulfillment and assurance perspective. Such feedback mechanisms include features such as autonomic service diagnosis and repair, as well as self-tuning capabilities.

Some of these techniques have been investigated for quite some time; others like dynamic service parameter negotiation techniques are quite new, when considering their usage in large scale networking environments.

Also, the complexity of SDN and NFV architectures primarily resides in (1) the computation logic, which should have the ability to take into account various inputs of very different nature to make proper decisions in terms of resource allocation and policy enforcement schemes, and (2) means to ensure service verification.

For example, the ability to include a potentially large amount of service subscription requests over a potentially short period of time combined with resource allocation considerations dictated by five-year network planning policies and the actual status of the network expressed as a function of (un)available resources, link failures, traffic load, *etc.*, will inevitably affect the decision-making process.

Typically, this could even lead to multi-metric route calculation schemes so that the paths selected by the computation logic gracefully accommodate the requirements and constraints derived from the manipulation of the aforementioned input data.

Although automation techniques are meant to facilitate and improve the delivery of time-to-market services, they inevitably raise issues that are often linked to the nature and the number of services to be delivered: scalability comes to mind, especially considering the amount of signaling traffic that needs to be exchanged between the SDN computation logic that would typically reside in the control plane and the management (*e.g.*, information pertaining to the outcomes of a service parameter negotiation between a customer and a service provider) plane, let alone the data plane (*e.g.*, process notifications sent by network devices and which may affect the decision-making process, provisioning of configuration information to all the devices involved in the delivery of a service, *etc.*).

Another issue is what some literature calls the "*mad robot*" syndrome, where the SDN computation logic becomes out of control, at the risk of service degradation if not disruption.

These techniques and issues are further discussed in the following chapters:

- Speaking of virtualization techniques, the "*Abstraction and Control of Transport Networks*" chapter discusses another dimension of virtual network operation that is associated with the use of the common core transport network resources by multi-tenant service networks as a way of providing a virtualized infrastructure to flexibly offer new services and applications.
- The "*Future SDN-based Network Architectures*" chapter discusses what SDN means today and describes the foreseen evolution of SDN architectures.

- The "*Network Function Virtualization*" chapter discusses the opportunities brought by virtualization techniques that not only aim at improving the flexibility of resource allocation procedures but also facilitating the overall service delivery procedures regardless of the underlying and sometimes heterogeneous technologies involved. This chapter also provides a detailed insight on the work currently conducted by the ETSI (European Telecommunication Standards Institute) devoted to the promotion of Network Function Virtualization (NFV).
- "*Introducing Automation in Service Delivery Procedures: An Overview*" discusses how SDN and NFV interworking ambition can bring on-demand resource provisioning, resource elasticity, among others with a view of the overall network, able to automatically and dynamically honor service requirements.

Advanced Solutions for Delivering Contents and Other Services

Content Delivery Networks (CDN) have been deployed for a while, and are said to carry more than half of Internet traffic by 2018. Means to optimize the delivery and distribution of contents near the user's location while meeting context-aware load balancing requirements need to be investigated further. Note, these networks encouraged the development of cache techniques which somewhat complicated the design and the operation of Points of Presence that would no longer be seen as simple connection aggregation points.

Also, with an ever-growing number of CDN providers, the design of cascaded CDN networks raises new technical challenges (*e.g.*, access to some contents located several CDNs away from the user questions the optimization of traffic forwarding between "peering" CDNs, thereby raising CDN interconnection issues). Also, existing CDN providers are scaling up their infrastructure, while many network and enterprise service providers deploy their own CDN infrastructure, thus creating a need for interconnecting (local) CDNs so they can interoperate and collectively behave as a single delivery infrastructure.

As a consequence, interoperable CDN interconnection solutions based upon standard protocols for transport and message exchange as well as standard representations of CDN objects have become of primary importance for major stakeholders.

Another issue raised by a multi-service Internet is related to customer's quality of experience. Regardless of the nature of the content a user wants to access, it must be delivered according to the highest standards, especially for real time traffic such as video streaming. Being able to guarantee such as high standards for the sake of improved customer's quality of experience is another challenge of the future Internet.

Also, the said evolution of Points of Presence towards the hosting of various capabilities is sometimes seen as a first step towards the deployment of cloud resources at the edge of networks. With the observed expansion of cloud infrastructures to better accommodate various customers' demands, points of presence may become part of such infrastructures where virtual machines, CPU and storage resources could be dynamically allocated.

Such evolution is likely to distort the current access model where the residential gateways in the customer premises support a wide range of capabilities, from basic forwarding and routing features to network address translation and filtering capabilities.

These gateways also provide storage resources or typically connect specific storage resources, such as those used by Set Top Boxes (STBs) to download video files. There is now some consensus that suggests that these storage facilities as well as the companion residential gateway should become virtual resources located somewhere in the cloud infrastructure, at the cost of revisiting service production procedures and raising specific issues, especially in the area of personal data protection and privacy preservation.

These techniques and issues are further discussed in the following chapters:

- "*Context-Aware Content Delivery: Architectures, Standards and Transport*" focuses on the notion of context awareness and how it can infer networking techniques towards improved customer's quality of experience.
- The "*Optimizing the Delivery of Services Supported by Residential Gateways: Virtualized Residential Gateways*" chapter discusses the rationale and proposes an architecture for a virtualized Residential Gateway (vRGW) that physically removes the RGW from the customer premises, moving it as a virtualized entity into the operator data center infrastructure or any other logical point-of-presence. This approach potentially reduces deployment, maintenance and operation costs, whilst improving overall performance, flexibility, reliability and manageability – both for the access network infrastructure and for the services provided over this infrastructure.
- "*Recent Advances and Perspectives on Content Delivery Networks*" provides a detailed CDN state-of-the-art, which is complemented by a thorough discussion on the use of virtualization and cloud techniques for improved CDN performance. It also discusses the adaptation of CDN techniques to mobile networking environments.
- Finally, the delivery of healthcare services over IP infrastructures is the core subject addressed by the "*Future Networked Healthcare Systems: A Review and Case Study*" chapter. It explores the state-of-the-art of the healthcare landscape and presents an analysis of networked healthcare systems with a focus on traffic patterns and networking architectures. A detailed study of QoS performance related to the delivery of healthcare services based upon the use of several applications, and according to different system and network sizes is also presented.

WHAT THIS BOOK BRINGS: A BETTER UNDERSTANDING OF SOME OF THE CHALLENGES FACED BY THE FUTURE INTERNET

Given the amount of emerging ideas and proposals, an in-depth understanding and analysis of proposed solutions and hacks should be conducted so as to help Internet players in making appropriate design choices that would meet their requirements.

We believe this book can be useful to students, network engineers and technical strategists who want to get a partial picture of what the future Internet could look like. It addresses most if not all of the hottest topics that are currently being debated in the industry and various standardization bodies, by providing a detailed insight to some of the most promising techniques that will undoubtedly shape the Internet of the future.

It is certainly not some kind of crystal ball, but rather a comprehensive compilation of advanced, sometimes revolutionary solutions that are very likely to (positively) affect the evolution of the global Internet and which have been described by some of the experts of the domain who deserve our deepest gratitude for their invaluable contribution.

Acknowledgment

Many thanks to all the following reviewers who provided insightful comments and suggestions that greatly enhanced the overall quality of the chapters of this book (in alphabetical order): Acee Lindem, Alexandru Petrescu, Alisa Devlic, Andreev Sergey, Azeddine Gati, Brad Schoening, Brando Williams, Bruno Chatras, Christian Gallard, Christian Huitema, Daniel Abgrall, Daniel King, David Binet, Dean Cheng, Deniz Gurkan, Dhruv Dhody, Dirk von Hugo, Gang Chen, Heiner Hummel, Hosnieh Rafiee, Ian Farrer, Igor Bisio, Jacques Traore, James Uttaro, Joe Touch, Jon Crowcroft, Jouni Korhonen, Juergen Quittek, Ken Gray, Laurent Bloch, Linda Dunbar, Lothar Grimm, Lucian-Gheorghe Suciu, Lucy Young, Luiz Miguel Contreras Murillo, Mikael Abrahamsson, Mohammed Achemlal, Mohsen Souissi, Muhammad Zubair, Niall O'Reilly, Ning WANG, Panagiotis Georgatsos, Peter Willis, Philippe Fouquart, Qiang Duan, Qin Wu, Ray van Brandenburg, Robert Raszuk, Robin Wilton, Scott Brim, Sophie Durel, Stefan Poslad, Stéphane Litowski, Subramanian Moonesamy, Thierry Lejkin, Tom Taylor, Toni Janevski, Uwe Herzog, Wim Henderickx, Yann Adam, Yiu Lee, and Ziad Salem.

Section 1

Internet Governance, Regulatory Aspects, and Privacy Considerations

Chapter 1
The Future of Internet Governance:
Modeling the Dynamics of the Internet Governance – A Bayesian Belief Network Approach

Martin A. Negrón
George Washington University, USA

ABSTRACT

The demographics of the Internet will experience significant changes in the near future. The developed countries are maximizing the number of citizens connected to the network while the developing countries, with the majority of the global population, increase their presence as the information technologies become more accessible. Leaders from the developed countries advocate the preservation of existing governance organizations regulating the network, such as the Internet Corporation for Assigned Names and Numbers (ICANN), on the basis of stability and security. New generations of Internet users are demanding new structures based on transparency, participation, accountability and legitimacy. In the absence of new agreements, uncoordinated changes to the existing governance structure could potentially affect the technical structure of the network and its functionality. Employing a Bayesian Belief Network model, this chapter analyzes the correlation between demographics, socio-economic factors and the feasibility of changes to the existing Internet governance structure. Favorable change conditions could initiate changes that could impact all Internet users. Results demonstrate that even when conditions for radical changes that could fragment the network are not present within the timeframe evaluated, conditions in support of changes increase with time, validating a need to modify the existing governance structure.

INTRODUCTION

The collection of connections that make the network that we know as the Internet has become an essential resource for our society and the world. As we depend more on the advances provided by new communication technologies, we voluntarily and involuntarily accept the risks and challenges resulting from our reliance on a system whose stability depends on numerous factors, most of them outside the control of a single entity. Among the most notable challenges is the definition of

DOI: 10.4018/978-1-4666-8371-6.ch001

the laws that regulate the Internet, specifically the rules for the control of the network infrastructure. Due to its borderless nature, the control of the Internet or Internet governance has been marked by conflicts since its early days and those conflicts are becoming more complex as the Internet continues expanding.

The main cause of the Internet governance conflict results from the absence of a coordinated global agreement on how to manage the Domain Name System (DNS). The DNS is a critical component of the Internet infrastructure as it allows the location of connected systems. In the United States (US) the idea of the DNS evolved under the close supervision of the United States government's Department of Commerce. The Department of Commerce has maintained some control of the DNS in spite of numerous requests from the global community to embrace a global governance structure. The Internet Corporation for Assigned Names and Numbers (ICANN), a non-profit corporation under contract with the US Department of Commerce, is the current DNS authority. ICANN is not accountable to any intergovernmental body and is only regulated by the corporate laws of the state of California. Over the years, ICANN has proposed a number of structural changes to its organization in an attempt to establish a more inclusive structure, however; none of the proposed changes have addressed the oversight expectations of the stakeholders.

As the Internet continues its global expansion, stakeholders unsatisfied with the current governance structure have recommended alternatives to the current DNS governance and management structure. In the development of the 2014 "Marco Civil" law, the government of Brazil evaluated more than 2,000 contributions from civil society using a multi-sector approach to protect Internet neutrality, equal access, and freedom of expression that some experts believe could become a new model for global Internet governance (Pinheiro, 2014). Those alternatives vary from the integration of ICANN into an existing global organization or the transformation of ICANN into a truly global organization to the development of alternate DNS outside of ICANN. Decisions regarding the final outcome of the proposed changes could potentially result in significant impacts to the stability and functionality of the Internet. Even when the reactions derived from the Internet governance arguments have not produced any notable effects, some consider that the extreme case could be a fragmented Internet with multiple redundant and disconnected DNS structures. Note, a fragmented Internet would means that global connectivity over Internet wouldn't be a reality anymore. This would even lead to the emergence of multiple (isolated) Internets.

Previous research related to Internet Governance focused mainly on functional areas of the Internet governance such as domain name dispute resolution arbitration (Lindsay, 2007), the digital divide (Norris, 2001), and describing the evolution of the DNS. The history of the Internet governance dispute is well documented (Mueller, 2004; Mueller, 2010; DeNardis, 2009) from various perspectives and also the main causes of the disagreements are relatively well understood; in contrast, information about the potential consequences of the conflict is not abundant, mainly because the limited number of attempts to disengage from the existing DNS infrastructure has not been successful.

The importance of this type of analysis is validated by the impact that the conflict could have on a multitude of issues affected all Internet users around the world. Some of these issues include:

- There have been multiple attempts to include the representation of the community of users in the decision-making process; the decision-making process is still dominated by the ICANN stakeholders. In order to truly obtain representation from the constantly evolving Internet ecosystem, ICANN must actively identify methods to validate inclusion and representation of the community of users.

- Even when the ICANN structure includes representation of the global community as part of the At-Large Advisory Committee (ALAC), global representation is limited to citizens with existing access to the network and having the skills to productively participate in these forums. This condition deepens the effects of the digital divide.
- The international community of users (governments and citizens) has not legitimized the absolute control of the DNS by any single authority.

The most relevant concerns about DNS control and oversight expressed by the users are:

- Security concerns: The DNS could be used as a single entry point to access the Internet. In theory, control of the DNS could determine what is accessed, how, when and by whom.
- Traffic Data Mining: User data could be unwillingly exploited.
- Censorship: Social, political and cultural.
- The development of the DNS could be constrained by a reduced number of stakeholders who do not necessarily represent the interests of the broader Internet community, especially those who are not yet users due to conditions related to the digital divide such as availability, access and costs.

INTERNET GOVERNANCE CONFLICT

The Internet has become one of the most important global communication systems of the 21st century. This network is constantly changing the way we communicate with each other. It is in constant evolution in order to meet the constantly changing needs of its users. The rapid growth of the Internet in the 1970's and 1980's with its bottom-up development was driven mainly by private stakeholders; however, the development did not happen beyond governmental control (Kleinwächter, 2003). The evolution of the Internet is not advancing at the same speed and with the same effectiveness at all levels. One of the most controversial issues regarding the evolution of the Internet is the question of who should be responsible for developing policies for control and oversight of the DNS. Based on its multi-stakeholder nature, the Internet governance process requires a multicultural and multiuser approach promoting the collaboration of governments and the communications industry (Hart & Rolletschek, 2003).

Governance in this context refers to the rules and procedures that states and other involved parties agree to use to order and regularize their treatment of a common issue. It does not mean the same thing as "government;" in fact, the term was chosen specifically to differentiate (weaker) international ordering processes from (more binding) national ones (Mueller, 2004).

In his book Ruling the Root, Mueller (Mueller, 2004) presents the issues that define the Internet governance conflict as:

- The authority to set policy for and to manage the allocation and assignment of Internet Protocol addresses.
- The authority to add new names to the top level of the Internet domain name hierarchy.
- The responsibility for operating root servers that distribute authoritative information about the content of the top level of the domain name space.

Considering the extension of cyberspace and the complexity of regulating its access, the availability of a control system using DNS makes the governance of the DNS even more relevant to governments and citizens. Dr. Phillip Hallam-Baker, a former VeriSign's DNS expert, provided a relevant example to summarize these concerns (Hallam-Baker, 2007). For example, a small but vocal group of voters in the western southern peninsula of state A consider themselves to be political exiles from state B, an island in the vicinity of the peninsula. State A has a particular position of influence over the DNS and said voters lobby for the exclusion of state B. If such a thing were to happen today the result would be a temporary fracture of the DNS followed by the rapid emergence of an alternative DNS structure that was not subject to abusive influence from state A (Mueller, 2007).

The discussion of the Internet governance conflict should start with a definition of the Internet. The Internet Governance Project, a partnership of scholars at the Syracuse University, the Georgia Institute of Technology and the Wissenschaftszentrum Berlin für Sozialforschung, defined the Internet as "the global data communication system formed by the interconnection of public and private telecommunication networks using Internet Protocol (IP), TCP and the protocols required to implement IP Internetworking on a global scale, such as DNS and packet routing protocols" (Internet Governance Project, 2004). They also added that Internet based communication is non-territorial by nature, keeping it independent of political jurisdictions while connection costs are insensitive to distance and political boundaries, which has created a non-territorial arena for human interaction and thus for policy and governance. In terms of the technical elements of the Internet, an IP address is either a 32-bit number (for IPv4) or a 128-bit number (for IPv6) used to identify unique host computers on the network. For IPv4, this number is represented as a sequence of 4 decimal numbers separated by a dot, for example, 192.0.0.1. As for IPv6, and address is represented as a sequence of 8 hexadecimal numbers separated by a ':' character, for example, 2001:db8:cafe:deca:dead:beef:face:1. For ease of identification by the user, the IP addresses are matched with a text label called a domain name, for example www.un.org. Additionally, this type of arrangement allows the administrators to make changes to the IP addresses without affecting the corresponding domain names. The domain name system (DNS) is the tool used to match Internet protocol addresses (IP) and the domain names. The current domain name system was developed by Jon Postel and Paul Mockapetris, both members of the University of Southern California's Information Sciences Institute (Cranor, 2002; Mockapetris, 1987). Nowadays, it is impossible to determine whether the developers of the DNS were aware that the structure of their system was based on a supply-demand array. According to the basic laws of economics, as the demand for Internet resources increases, the value associated with the assignment and control of resources such as DNS root servers, the assignment of Top Level Domain (TLD), IP address allocation and assignment and Internet Service Provider (ISP) routing tables increases.

The origin of the Internet goes back to the beginning of the 1970's when the National Science Foundation (NSF) was funding and managing the non-military portion of the Internet. After the technical basis was established, the system that we know today as the Internet continued to be developed mainly by its users (Kleinwächter, 2000). The Internet itself became the instrument used by the developers to continuously improve the system. At the time, there were mainly two formal organizations supporting network development initiatives, the Internet Engineering Task Force (IETF) and the Internet Architecture Board (IAB). These organizations oversaw the technical aspects of the network. The non-technical areas were later coordinated by the Internet Society (ISOC), a non-governmental, not-for-profit organization broadly recognized as a representative of the Internet community. During the initial phases of the Internet, issues related to the management of the DNS were handled by bilateral agreements between the NSF and corporations such as the IANA and Network Solutions Inc (NSI) (Kleinwächter, 2000). NSI managed the services of domain name registration. Initially, domain name registration was free to the users but with the significant growth of registrations NSI removed the NSF as a funding source and started charging a $50 annual fee to registrants (Cranor, 2002). Registrants started complaining about the NSI monopoly. In addition, NSI used a first-come, first-served approach for the registrations of domain names within the .com, .net, and .org top-level domains (TLD) (Samuels 2003). The registration policy used by NSI created significant issues with trademark infringement since anyone could register any word as a web address. In reaction to the large number of disputes, in the mid 1990's, NSI created a dispute resolution policy to address the conflicts between the domain name registrants and the trademark owners. This policy did not satisfy the Internet community. The community reacted by creating the International Ad Hoc Committee (IAHC). The IAHC released a memorandum recommending a new method for registering TLD's (Samuels 2003). Meanwhile, the US government continued working on its own Internet policy.

Even when the US Government supported and promoted the evolution of the DNS and its oversight and control functions from its early stages, it was not until 1997 that they started collecting comments on shifting those functions to the private sector. The US government started the process against their will and without a defined plan, in part because of the growing conflicts between the ISOC, IANA and NSI. Experts expressed concerns about escalating conflicts affecting the stability of the network in the absence of formal arrangements to replace IANA and NSI. (Mueller, 1999b). The US government feared that a failure to reach an agreement with NSI allowing the continuation of name registrations in .com, .net, and .org could lead to the possibility of dissident users developing an alternative root server system outside of their control. A plan was finally outlined in June 1998 when the US Department of Commerce released a white paper written under the supervision of Ira Magaziner, President Clinton's Internet adviser.

The white paper proposed that, as part of the Clinton Administration's Framework for Global Electronic Commerce, the President direct the Secretary of Commerce to "privatize the domain name system (DNS) in a manner that increases competition and facilitates international participation in its management." (United States Department of Commerce, 1998). This statement could be understood as stating that the US government was planning to resign its control over the DNS; however, as a reaction to the white paper and after discussions with different Internet stakeholders, Jon Postel coordinated with the US Department of Commerce the incorporation on October 2nd of 1998 in the state of California of the Internet Corporation for Assigned Names and Numbers or ICANN. This new corporation was composed of representatives of different sectors of the communications industry. It was proposed that members of national governments or intergovernmental organizations were not able to serve on the ICANN board (Kleinwächter, 2000). Subsequent to evaluating public comments on the new corporation, the US government entered into a memorandum of understanding with ICANN. The first meeting of the original ICANN board of directors took place on November 14, 1998 in Cambridge, MA (Kleinwächter, 2000). The US government's objective was to delegate the DNS management functions to ICANN while maintaining a supervisory role. The creation of ICANN addressed a need to manage and stabilize a key global technical resource of the Internet. However, it exposed the need to develop global political and legal mechanisms to function outside of the established national boundaries (Kleinwächter, 2001). These conditions initiated the debate over ICANN fulfilling its functions of providing technical oversight while inherently managing a global asset as a new global governance system. Under these conditions, ICANN as a private organization with a contractual relationship with the US government was in a position to create global public policies and control a global information technology asset (Kleinwächter, 2001).

ICANN's responsibility for managing the DNS went beyond the original intent of limiting its scope to technical and administrative issues. "Observers view the White Paper process not as a bottom-up, consensus-driven exercise, but rather as a "sham" designed to shield "naked power politics" (Harvard Law Review, 1999). In areas such as the management of domain name allocations and root servers, it could not avoid dealing with policy issues such as property rights, competition policy, international law and the allocation of Internet resources. Considering that ICANN was engaged in developing public policy, the organization was similar to other global governance institutions in sectors like trade and finance (e.g., the World Trade Organization) (Klein, 2001).

The depth of the controversy over ICANN's legitimacy is reflected in the fact that even supporters of the ICANN idea questioned the legitimacy of their oversight functions. Hunter, an ICANN supporter, acknowledged that ICANN's regulatory actions raised legitimacy concerns that are foreign to entities functioning solely as corporations (Hunter, 2003). Discussing the importance of ICANN's legitimacy, Weinberg warned that if ICANN could not prove its legitimacy, stakeholders could migrate to alternative root systems and make ICANN's function superfluous (Weinberg, 2000). In 2006, the Canadian Internet Registration Authority (CIRA) presented an open letter to ICANN in which it expressed its concerns about ICANN's lack of legitimacy (CIRA, 2006). The letter made a series of recommendations to improve ICANN's legitimacy and transparency and the letter concluded by stating that CIRA planned to cease to support ICANN until their concerns were addressed. This action from CIRA could have created a precedent for more significant problems for ICANN. In response to CIRA's letter, ICANN only invited CIRA to an open discussion about their differences. ICANN failed to recognize a problem or any actions needed to clarify the legitimacy of their authority (Twomey, 2006).

The original policy document for ICANN promised to end US supervision after two years. US supervision, however, continued until 2006 under the subsequent contract. While this was not a major source of controversy within ICANN itself, it was a critical source of contention among other governments (Internet Governance Project, 2004). In general, a significant sector of the international community did not recognize ICANN as an independent entity. Abbott and Snidal emphasize the importance of independence for the effectiveness of an Independence Government Organization (IGO), "independence is highly constrained: member states, especially the powerful, can limit the autonomy of independent organizations, interfere with their operations, ignore their dictates, or restructure and dissolve them." (Abbott & Snidal, 1998).

The Internet Governance Project also identified other areas of disagreement with ICANN which included: the absence of a clear policy or process for the addition of new top-level domains; the degree to which ICANN is, or should be, accountable to individual users of the Internet; the degree to which ICANN is, or should be, accountable to or responsive to governments or independent of them (Internet Governance Project, 2004). The US government's idea to privatize the management of the DNS while influencing the process dismissed European demands for the participation of other government's in the decision making process (Mueller, 1999b).

The five major sources of controversy for ICANN were identified as (Kleinwächter, 2000):

1. Between private companies, who want to protect trademark interests and avoid patchwork legislation, and representatives of the civil society, who will try to keep the bottom-up culture of the Internet alive and

will defend human rights against one-sided commercial interests;

2. Between US Democrats, who started the ICANN process and will sell it as a success for them, the USA and the whole world, and US Republicans, who fear that ICANN will be beyond the control of the US Congress and blame the Democrats for not defending 'American interests' and for 'selling the Internet' to 'foreigners';
3. Between Americans who want to maintain control over key Internet assets and Europeans who are looking for a broader participation in decision-making processes, including the control of the root server system;
4. Between governments, who will refer to international law and try to keep their sovereignty at least over the TLDs under their national control known as ccTLDs, and non-governmental groups, who will reject the notion that the Internet is under governmental authority;
5. And within private industry itself, where the early starters, including NSI, will try to maintain their privileged position while late starters will refer to the principle of 'fair trade' to get better access to the market.

There are indirect discrepancies created by the Internet governance conflict that could significantly escalate the conflict in the future. As previously mentioned, ICANN's policy for the registration of TLD's is based on first possession rules meaning that the ownership of a domain name is awarded to the initial registrant. Furthermore, to actively participate in ICANN's procedures, participants are required to be Internet users since they need to be part of the "community at large". This suggests that people who are not currently Internet users will be considerably affected by the actions of the current users by the time they have access to the Internet, increasing the problem created by the digital divide. Some of the statistics related to the digital divide that should be considered in the discussion of the Internet governance conflict include (Bagchi, 2005):

- Social, economic, political, and linguistic factors have been cited as major factors governing Internet usage.
- Gross Domestic Product (GDP) per capita has been shown to be positively correlated to information and communication technology (ICT) infrastructure growth, and thus is expected to be negatively related to the digital divide.
- An increase in the level of education leads to an increase in computer investment of a nation.
- Nations with a low urbanization level can reflect a larger gap in the divide.
- Considering all nations, it was found that trust and personal wealth, in particular, help in bridging the gap between nations.
- Indicators that impact the digital divide are not the same for developing and industrialized nations in a given year.

Communication indicators have changed drastically in the last decade. According to the ITU (World Telecommunication/ICT Indicators Database Online, 2014), less than 20% of the global population has access to land-based telephone lines, however, the number of mobile users increased from 33% in 2005 to 96% in 2014. Conversely, the number of broadband subscriptions remains below 10%. These conditions narrow the digital divide gaps for mobile functions but maintains high levels of inaccessibility to broadband, limiting the type of data accessed.

Based on the impact of the Internet governance conflict on the digital divide, experts argue that domain names should figure into international law debates (Chander, 2003). Some of the justifications for the argument include:

- They determine who has global rights to geographic and cultural identifiers. As an example, the registration of SouthAfrica.com by an American corporation.
- Since the domain names represent a valuable resource of the Information Age, their international distribution has important wealth consequences. As useful domain names are controlled by current users, the domain name regime may help further entrench the existing worldwide misdistribution of wealth.

The new communications paradigm has evolved into a system of shared accountability and authority in which governments are just one of the stakeholders. In order to guarantee and guard their interests, the private industry and the Internet users are taking an active role in the development of the Internet governance system. This new system has been described as "trilateralism" (Kleinwächter, 2001). Even when governments represent the interest of the people, in cyberspace the private industry and the civil society have their own legitimacy and each of them has its own interests. In the process of developing this type of approach, the private sector will guard its business interests such as cost, value and return on investment while governments will be interested in public policy, stability, security and taxes and the end users will seek to maximize quality of service, value, privacy, freedom and human rights (Kleinwächter, 2001).

There had been various recommendations on how to reduce the scope of the Internet governance conflict and modify ICANN. Among the recommendations, the Internet Governance Project proposed a relatively simple vision (Internet Governance Project, 2005) on what they understood should be done. They proposed four recommendations:

- Limits on power and internationalized oversight.
- A legally binding International agreement narrowly defining ICANN's powers and replacing US Government supervision with internationalized supervision. This would allow abolition of ICANN's Government Advisory Committee.
- Democratization. Reinstatement and strengthening of the At Large membership of ICANN, especially a return to election of the At Large Board members and the granting of voting rights on ICANN's Generic Names Supporting Organization (GNSO) to At Large representatives.
- Competition. Coordinated sharing of responsibilities between ICANN and the International Telecommunications Union (ITU) in a way that would allow ccTLD managers and IP address users a choice of alternative governance arrangements.

These recommendations present alternatives on how to modify the existing mechanisms in order to meet the needs and requirements of a larger number of stakeholders, considering that satisfying the needs and requirements of all the stakeholders is an impossible task. The challenges associated with satisfying all stakeholders are validated by the ICANN Security and Stability Advisory Committee, "SSAC is skeptical that an all-inclusive root zone file could be created, maintained reliably, published in a timely and responsive manner, and be universally accepted" (SSAC Report, 2006).

There are others who propose a complete disengagement from the current system. The technology that serves as the backbone of the Internet could be modified by any user to develop a parallel DNS system or alternate top-level domains (TLD). The SSAC provides a definition for alternate roots (SSAC Report, 2006).

The phrases alternative roots and breakaway roots refer to entities that operate independently from ICANN to provide root name service and to control TLD name system management functions, including TLD label approval and registry services for second level labels registered under TLDs they create.

The Internet Society warns against the creation of alternate roots, "deploying multiple public DNS roots would raise a very strong possibility that users of different ISPs who click on the same link on a web page could end up at different destinations, against the will of the web page designers" (The Internet Society, 2000). Regardless of the potential consequences, the viability of a new system would depend mainly on the number of users it could attract, a generalization in agreement with Metcalfe's law. Countries that disagree with the United States' control over the DNS could potentially move to a different common database controlling domain names. That decision to develop segregated DNS could imply a significant negative risk and the willingness to accept that risk will depend on the willingness to accept US control over the system (Chander, 2003).

The SSAC defined five classes of alternative root name server and TLD name system operators (SSAC Report, 2006):

- Private (intra-organizational, institutional, and enterprise) name systems
- Experimental roots and TLD name system administration
- Commercial (for profit) TLD name system administration and "inclusive" root name service
- Protest (democratic, community access) roots and TLD name system Administration
- Politically motivated roots and TLD name system administration, including those established to support national and local character sets in top-level domain labels

The SSAC categorizes initiatives from sovereign governments who are not satisfied with ICANN and its relationship with the US government under the "politically motivated roots". The SSAC also justifies ICANN's actions and warns stakeholders who are considering options outside of the ICANN's realm against any initiative that could potentially fragment the DNS and the TLD systems.

The discussions on initiatives and considerations to develop an alternate root system are becoming more abundant. Chan argues that because of the control that the United States has over the domain system, a US-backed body controls Hong Kong's policymaking function for its ccTLD (Chan, 2005). Chan directly says that, "The Hong Kong Government may take control of ccTLDs by renouncing ICANN and its root server's authority" (Chan, 2005). Chan acknowledges the need to maintain a unified system nevertheless emphasizes that fairness takes precedence. Chan's statement recognizes the need to maintain an integrated system and demonstrates that the initiatives and proposals to develop alternate root systems are driven by the lack of democratic channels to govern the DNS. Perez labeled this condition as a democratic gap and asserted that the democratic gap risks the regime's legitimacy (Perez, 2004).

Later developments in the Internet governance dispute reflected some tendencies of relevant Internet stakeholders to disengage from the established system. During the summer of 2007, Liu Yenshan, China's top propaganda official at the time, supported the idea of "building a web culture with Chinese characteristics", specifying that the Internet in China is different from the Internet in other countries because it is catered to China's ideas, needs and language (Powell, 2007). The same year Liu made those comments, the Xinhua Financial Network News confirmed that the number of Internet users in China reached 162 million with a penetration of 12.3%, which meant that the number was expected to grow significantly (Xinhua Financial Network, 2007). By the end of 2008, China reached 210 million users according to an article published by The Economist which also describes China's uniqueness in Internet access based on the fact that the government controls the access to many foreign websites such as Wikipedia and EBay, saying that in China "the Internet is not truly a worldwide web: it is only as wide as China" (Alternative Reality, 2008). Also BBC news published an article highlighting the rapid growth of Internet users in Russia (Jackson, 2006). In addition to the developments in China and Russia, Brazil, a country where China's influence worries the United States (Hawksley, 2006), was requesting more participation in the management of the DNS, according to an article published in brazzilmag.com (Achmawi, 2008). The same article also mentioned that in addition to Brazil, Arab and African countries were making the same requests. In October 2010 during the Plenipotentiary Conference hosted by the United Nations International Telecommunication Union, representatives from multiple countries expressed their discontent with ICANN and the way the Internet governance is managed (Ermert, 2010). "All countries are in favor of having ICANN work under international and not under California law, the Saudi delegation said." Members of the ITU proposed the creation of an IP-address-registry within the ITU. The proposal was rejected by a group of western industrialized countries in support of increasing the oversight by the ICANN Governmental Advisory Committee (GAC) demonstrating that while a group of stakeholders were seeking a globalized approach, dominant groups managed to continue strengthening the status quo.

In May 2011, Republican and Democrat members of the House Judiciary Subcommittee on Intellectual Property, Competition, and the Internet came together to ask critical questions of ICANN during the ICANN Generic Top-Level Domain (gTLD) Oversight Hearing. The Coalition Against Domain Name Abuse (CADNA) actively participated in the hearings and recommended that Congress make an effort to understand the inner workings of ICANN. CADNA's President, Josh Bourne, told Congress, "you have to think about where the gTLD policy came from. More controversial policies like this one will come out of ICANN unless we take the time to thoroughly examine the organization as a whole...All of this is just a band-aid on a larger problem. We need to fix ICANN" (Bourne, 2011). Based on the information obtained at the hearing, the Subcommittee asked ICANN to postpone the launch of the new gTLDs in order for Congress to have a better understanding of its implications. The actions of the US Congress confirmed that ICANN was an organization that managed an international critical asset and it was only accountable to the US government.

The National Telecommunications and Information Administration (NTIA) of the US Department of Commerce issued a press release on March 14, 2014 expressing their intention to transition the DNS to the global multi-stakeholder community (National Telecommunications and Information Administration, 2014). The US House of Representatives developed multiple unsuccessful initiatives to stall the process (Manning, 2014) including the DOTCOM Act of 2014, a bill sponsored by Rep. John Shimkus (DOTCOM Act of 2014, 2014).

MODELING THEORY

Complex social systems are dynamic because the participants are constantly interacting with each other and their environment. Nowadays the social interactions, especially across geographical borders, are increased with the advances of technology (Latour, 2005). In extreme cases, the dynamics of the system based on those interactions could lead to a large degree of instability and unpredictability; however, those dynamics take place within stages that reflect detectable patterns and even within highly unstable systems; they allow the calculation of potential future conditions (Boulding, 1988). It is important to note that the actions of the participants are not typically assumed to be random. For example, game theory models for international relations assume that the actors are rational in relation to their objectives (Brams, 2004). This is based on the fact that by understanding the fundamentals of the system, the interactions of the participants with the system and within the system's boundaries are expected to maximize their own resources, protection and power (Keohane, 2005). Although participants will seek to maximize their utility, they are limited by their capacity to evaluate the complexity of a multiplayer sequential game. Informed participants are not irrational in their process of determining a strategy; however, they have a tendency to simplify the process based on their perception.

BAYESIAN BELIEF NETWORKS (BBN)

The idea of Bayesian Belief Networks (BBN) is based on a method developed by Rev. Thomas Bayes in the 1760's to update probabilities as new information becomes available (Pfister, 2012). Bayes' method serves as the foundation of a graphical tool employed for decision-making under uncertainty known as BBN. This graphical method maps out cause-and-effect relationships among key variables related to an event and the probabilities associated with those variables (Pershad, 2000). The network uses probabilities to represent the uncertainties that result from modeling real events. The probabilities allow the modeler to indicate the strength of each assertion clarifying not only the possible consequences of a situation but also the possible causes (Starr, 2004).

A BBN explicitly separates the knowledge of the independencies in the domain and the values of those independencies represented by variables capturing two discrete parts, a qualitative and a quantitative part (Van Duijnhoven, 2003). This property of BBN allows the modeler to define the causal relationships completely independent of the numerical probabilities affecting those relationships. In addition, the structure of the BBN allows the flexibility to reconfigure the network topology based on new information with minor modifications and minimum or no impact to the probabilities assigned to each variable. Changes in the environment could affect only a small number of nodes within the system leaving the rest of the system unchanged and making it simpler to reevaluate and estimate only those parameters affected by the changes rather than redesigning the complete system (Pearl, 2000).

The benefits of BBN may be summarized as follows (Neil, 2003):

- Provides a sound method of reasoning under uncertainty.
- Permits the combining of diverse data, including subjective beliefs and empirical data.
- Predictions can still be secured even when evidence is incomplete.
- Permits powerful "what-if" analysis to test the sensitivity of conclusions.
- Incorporates a visual reasoning tool, which aids documentation and explanation.

The basic concept is based on a conditional probability statement of the following kind: "Given the event B (and everything else known is irrelevant for A), then the probability of the event A is x" (Pershad, 2000).

Bayes Theorem follows from the basic conditional probability relationship:

$$P(A \mid B) = \frac{P(A \cap B)}{P(B)} \quad \text{Equation} \quad 1$$

and

$$P(B \mid A) = \frac{P(A \cap B)}{P(A)} \quad \text{Equation} \quad 2$$

where

$P(A \mid B)$ is the probability of A given B
$P(A \cap B)$ is the probability of the joint event A and B
$P(B \mid A)$ is the probability of B given A

These equations are the general formula for conditional probability.

Rearranging Equation 1 and 2 gives the Multiplication Rule:

$$P(A \cap B) = P(A \mid B) \times P(B) \quad \text{Equation 3}$$
$$P(A \cap B) = P(B \mid A) \times P(A) \quad \text{Equation 4}$$

From Equation 3 and 4 follows:

$$P(B \mid A) \times P(A) = P(A \mid B) \times P(B) \quad \text{Equation 5}$$

Note that if A and B are independent then Equation 5 becomes:

$$P(A \cap B) = P(A) \times P(B) \quad \text{Equation 6}$$

And rearranging the above equation 5 yields the well-known Bayes' Theorem:

$$P(B \mid A) = \frac{P(A \mid B) \times P(B)}{P(A)} \quad \text{Equation 7}$$

The Bayesian approach is characterized by three aspects: the subjective nature of the data used to define the network, the use of Bayesian reasoning; and the dual use capacity characterized by causal and evidential analysis (Darwiche, 2010). An advantage of using valid causal models over probability models is the fact that in addition to identifying changes based on iterations, causal models identify changes due to external inputs such as those influenced by policies, management approaches and varying activities (Pearl, 200). Those changes are not reflected when only considering joint distributions. In addition, classical statistics tools have limitations when dealing with uncertainty. Instead of only working with data obtained from observable events, Bayesian methods combine measurable data with subjective probabilities when no measurable data is available. Subjective probabilities are not obtained randomly; they are based on information sources such as opinions from experts or polls. The validity of the subjective information will depend on the knowledge and understanding of the system or event analyzed and the ability to make adjustments based on new information. The combination of statistical and subjective probabilities allows the inclusion of broader uncertain elements as part of the structured analysis (Starr, 2004). "BBN could also provide causal inference without redeveloping the network. Causal inference is the ability to reverse its logic" (Pershad, 2000).

The graphical structure of the BBN is described as a directed acyclic graph (DAG). The variables can have any number of states and are represented by interconnected nodes. For example, a variable can be represented by numerical values (the number of countries in a coalition) or the position of a country in reaction to a proposal (in favor, against, neutral). The use of BBN permits the assignment of discrete values to degrees of belief related to an event allowing the manipulation of those values based on the rules of probability calculus (Pearl, 2000). The variables in the model represent finite mutually exclusive discrete or continuous states.

The variables or nodes are connected by directional arcs. The arcs connecting the nodes are considered directed because they identify a specific directional effect (represented by arrows). A parent node illustrates an autonomous physical relation that represents the affecting node and is depicted by an arrow pointing away from it. The arrow represents that it is an influencing node. A child node, represented by an arrow pointing at the node, is influenced by parent nodes and captures a probability distribution for every combination of states of the parent variables (Starr, 2004). In developing a BBN model, the goal is to verify that the parent nodes represent all relevant causes, a process that is simplified by the qualitative structure of the model that ideally captures the essence of the causal conditions (Pearl, 2000). Nodes that are not connected by arrows are considered independent and provide the initial probability distribution of the variable. Acyclic means that the arrows may not form a directed cycle or loop in the network. This required property of a BBN is defined as d-separation. It is important to emphasize that the d-separation requirement does not imply that there can be only one possible path between two nodes (Pershad, 2000).

In the process of formulating the structure of a Bayesian network, the arcs do not necessarily follow a causal direction if the validity of the model's d-separation properties is verified and the model represents the actual perception of the conditional independence properties. The effectiveness of the model will depend on the accuracy in which real world relations are represented and improbable causal relations are excluded (Jensen, 2010).

Pearl identified three benefits for the use of graphs in probabilistic and statistical modeling:

- to provide convenient means of expressing substantive assumptions;
- to facilitate economical representation of joint probability functions; and
- to facilitate efficient inferences from observations. (Pearl, 2000).

A formal definition states that a Bayesian Belief Network over a set of variables X, is an ordered list of elements BN = G,T with:

1. G is a directed acyclic graph (DAG)

T = $Pr(X_i \mid p(X_i)) \mid X_i \in X$ is the set of local (conditional) probabilities, where $P(X_i)$ is a probability distribution over these states:

$$Pr\left(X_i\right) = \left(y_i, \ldots, y_n\right) 0^2 y_i{}^2 1, \sum_{i=1}^{n} y_i = 1$$

where y_i is the probability of X_i being in state X_i. (Duijnhoven, 2003).

The four stages in the lifecycle of a BBN can be distinguished as follows:

- Definition of the domain variables,
- Determination of a network structure
- Determination of conditional probabilities, and
- Usage in a knowledge-based system (Pershad, 2000).

A recommended approach to defining a BBN is to organize the data in three layers: causal variables (top layer), reasoning variables (middle layer) and the effects variables (bottom layer) (Pfister, 2012). In the process of defining the domain variables, the variables based on statistical data are identified and combined with the assumptions and inferences that will delineate the network structure. Each node must specify the joint probability distribution with respect to its parents.

TIMELINE

The origins of the conflict could be traced back to the creation of the DNS, however, for this analysis, the origin of the conflict is approximated to the definition of the original agreement between ICANN and the US Department of Commerce signed on December 24, 1998 and the initial set of data is from 2001.

The fast evolution of the Internet and the rapid growth of the user population create conditions in which time constraints are defined in relatively short time periods. The model developed using this analysis explores potential short-term outcomes from five to ten years in the future. To explore the future trends, the model is populated using projected values for the growth of Internet users in the countries evaluated for the analysis of the conditions in 2015. For the analysis of the conditions in 2020 only the values for per capita GDP and population were provided to the model and the analysis verified the effects of those two variables.

The data was divided in two groups; historical (prior to 2010), and target data (current data and projections). The model was adjusted and calibrated using historical data and after the calibration was completed, the target data was evaluated.

IDENTIFICATION OF THE REASONING VARIABLES

The strategy to develop the BBN model for the Internet governance conflict is to evaluate the existing governance structure as a regime. The definition of a regime applied to the model states that it consists of a formal or informal organization at the center of a political power and it is considered a more permanent form of government than a formal state government because it has a well-defined objective of using its power for the benefit of its participants. ICANN is not formally at the center of a political power; however, as presented in the evolution of the conflict, informally the organization has been historically influenced and dominated by the government of the United States.

A regime is characterized by three key elements (Figure 1) identified as socio-economic alliances, political-economic institutions, and a public policy profile (Ploberger, 2012).

These key elements are translated into the reasoning variables of the model by establishing an analogy between the key elements that characterize a regime and the variables that describe the Internet governance structure in order to identify the principal components of the model representing the primary decision problem. For the model representing the Internet governance conflict (Figure 2) the reasoning variables were defined

Figure 1. Key elements of a regime

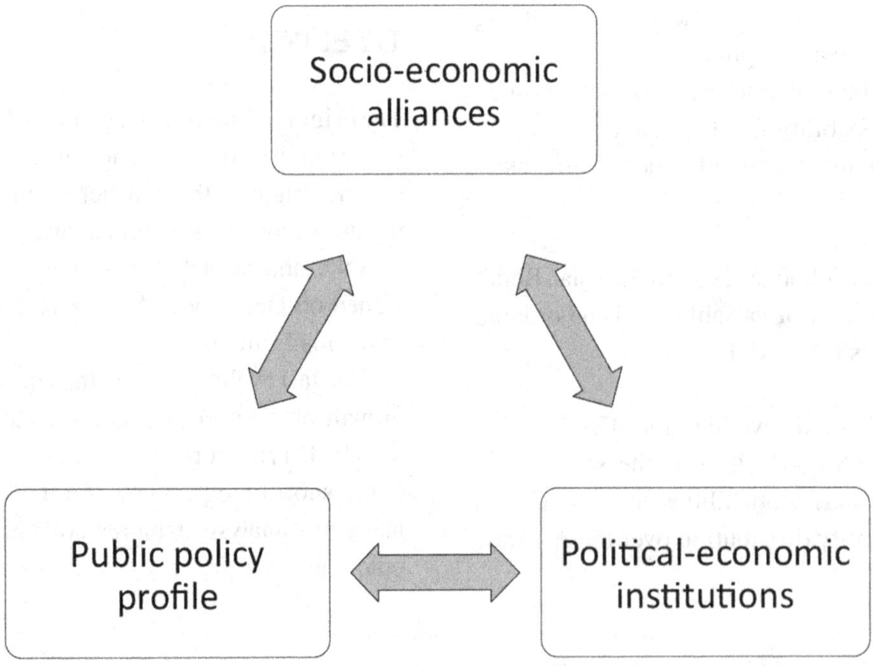

Figure 2. Reasoning variables representing the Internet Governance Conflict

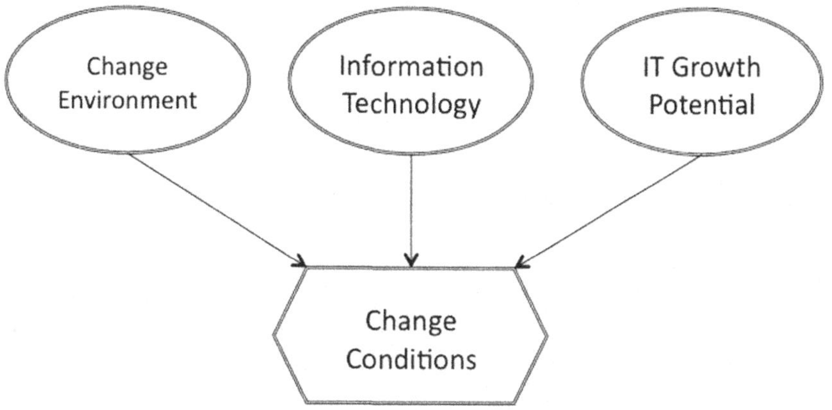

as change conditions, information technology and the IT growth potential. The following sections describe the parallels between the key elements of the regime and the reasoning variables considered.

REASONING VARIABLE: CHANGE ENVIRONMENT

In the case of Internet governance, the socio-economic alliances were represented by the factors that characterize the community of Internet stakeholders and were used to describe how those characteristics could influence a change in the existing governance structure. The Internet governance structure controls a system that will potentially be used by all the population of the world, making the global population the constituency of the regime. The socio-economic alliances element included variables related to language, age, education and income (Figure 3). These variables are obtained from reliable data sources and do not have any parent nodes.

Table 1 identifies the sources for the data used to populate the model. The table also identifies the references used to define the correlation among the different variables. The correlation of the variables was defined based on a detailed analysis of the results obtained from previous research related to Internet demographics and social capital. The sources used for the model validated a positive correlation between the selected variables and the reasoning variables defined. In the process of designing the Internet governance conflict model, parent nodes were considered the parent nodes influencing the reasoning variables as they represented the social, demographic and economic conditions that could facilitate or resist changes to the existing Internet governance system.

REASONING VARIABLE: INFORMATION TECHNOLOGY

The second key element that characterizes a regime, the political-economic institutions, is part of the functional organizational components that facilitate the operation of the regime. In the case of the Internet governance analogy, the political-economic institutions were determined to be equivalent to the functional element of the network. This is based on the information technology infrastructure that serves as both the network that connects all the stakeholders and also act as a component of the IT infrastructure, the DNS which is the asset managed and controlled by the existing governance structure.

Figure 3. Change Environment nature nodes

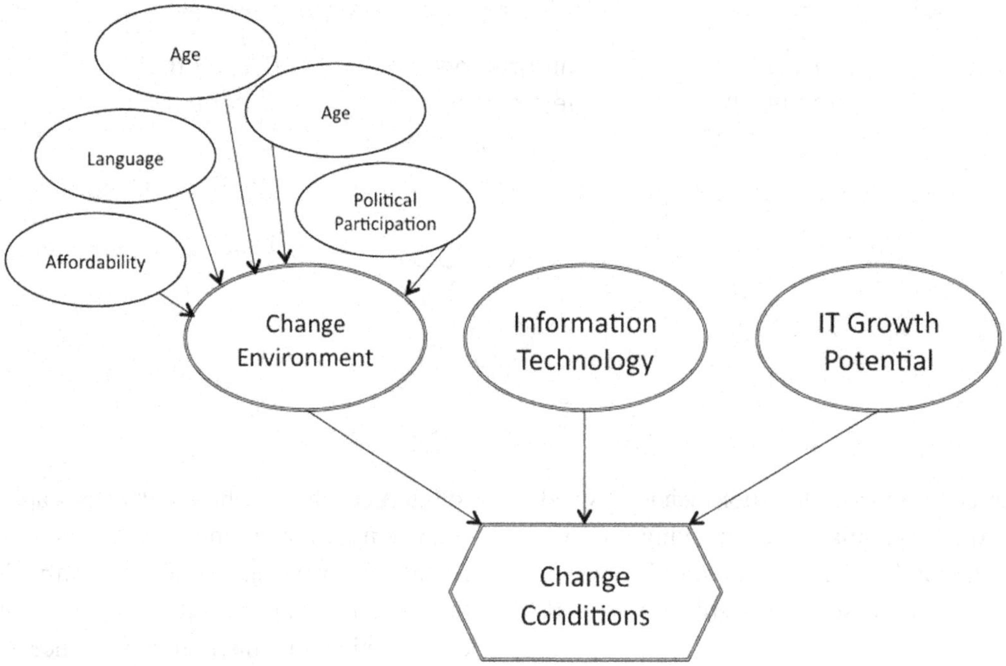

Table 1. Variable correlation and data source: Change Conditions

Variable	Correlation	Data
Affordability	(Czernich, 2012; Guillen, 2005; Dimaggio, Hargittal, Neuman and Robinson, 2001)	(Dutta and Bilbao-Osorio, 2012)
Language		(Central Intelligence Agency, 2011)
Age	(Boulianne, 2009; Bakker, 2011; Penard and Poussing, 2010; Dutta, Dutton and Law, 2011)	(Central Intelligence Agency, 2011)
Education	(Dunahee, 2012; Czernich, 2012) (Boulianne, 2009; Guillen, 2005; Penard and Poussing, 2010; Dimaggio, Hargittal, Neuman and Robinson, 2001; Dutta, Dutton and Law, 2011; Lebo, 2012; La Due Lake and Huckfeldt, 1998)	(Central Intelligence Agency, 2011)
Political participation	(Dunahee, 2012; Czernich, 2012; Postmes and Brunsting, 2002; Norris, 2001) (Boulianne, 2009; Pieterse, 2002; Bakker, 2011; Penard and Poussing, 2010; La Due Lake and Huckfeldt, 1998; Kittilson and Dalton, 2012)	(Economist Intelligence Unit, 2012)

The IT reasoning variable (P (IT)) of the model (Figure 4) evaluated the technical variables that validated the existence of the means to support the current structure, a change or options in between. The nature nodes that are part of the IT element included the use of electronic government systems (e-gov), the level of IT use within a country and IT as a government priority. The correlation references and the data sources are summarized in Table 2.

REASONING VARIABLE: IT GROWTH POTENTIAL

Public policy promotes the strengthening of government initiatives and institutions by developing and enforcing principles and actions in accordance with established laws and regulations. Public policy guides collective actions and provides the means to obtain tangible results. In the development of the BBN model, the equivalent to public policy within the Internet governance regime is also composed of the means by which the Internet governance system exists and evolves including the global population, the influence of globalization, the number of Internet users as well as the level of Internet use (Figure 5). The correlation references and the data sources are summarized in Table 3.

In the development of the BBN model, the number of users (U) was considered the main variable influencing potential future Internet governance change conditions (Guillen, 2005). Based on the statistics, developed countries are close to maximizing their presence in the network and the developing countries have a relatively low penetration rate, opening the possibility of significantly altering the demographics of the Internet. The growth of the Internet with the integration of new users from developing countries does not automatically influence change conditions since new users could drive new collective actions against the existing Internet governance authorities or they can strengthen the existing structure (Postmes, 2002).

In order to facilitate the organization of the data, the global population was divided in eight regions; North America, Central America, South America, Europe, Asia, Middle East, Africa and Oceania. The countries with the largest population within the regions defined were selected. For each region, the countries with the largest population were selected. The countries evaluated were the following: Nigeria, Egypt, South Africa, Kenya, Morocco, Algeria, India, China, Indonesia, Pakistan, Japan, Russia, Germany, France, United Kingdom, Italy, Spain, United States, Canada, Brazil, Colombia, Argentina, Peru, Venezuela, Mexico, Guatemala, Honduras, El Salvador, Iran, Saudi Arabia, Syria, Israel, Australia and New Zealand.

CONDITIONAL PROBABILITIES

The conditional probabilities were defined for each node based on the network topology derived from the history of the conflict, the information available about each variable and the causal links identified from the available data.

They were documented using the conditional probability tables (CPT) for each node. The CPT uses the data for the parent nodes and defines a state for the node under consideration. In the cases when the parent nodes are missing data, the software used defines probabilistic links based on the learned values. The DAG evaluated includes 61,922 conditional probabilities.

CHANGE ENVIRONMENT

The purpose of the conditional probability of the "change environment" (Figure 6) is to define the attitude towards change of the stakeholders based on the socio-economic alliances. The possible results of "activist", "engaged", "aware" and "dis-

Figure 4. Information Technology nature nodes

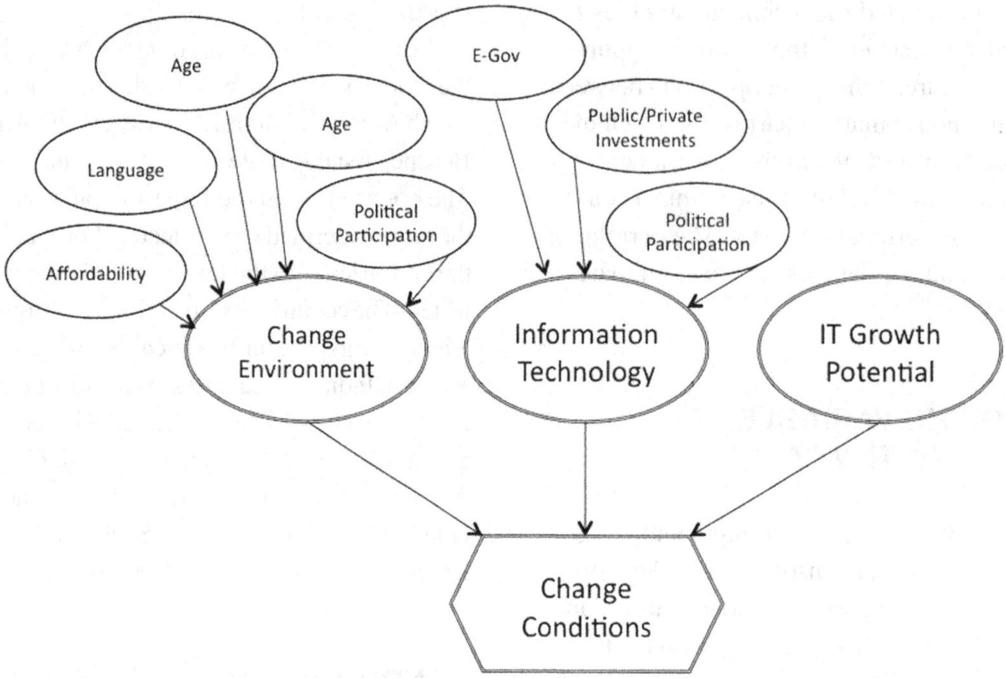

Table 2. Variable correlation and data source: Information Technology

Variable	Correlation	Data
E-Gov index		(United Nations E-Government Survey, 2012)
Public investment in IT	(Guillen,2005; DiMaggio, 2001)	(Atkinson, Ezell and Stewart, 2012)
Private investment in IT	(Guillen,2005; DiMaggio, 2001)	(Atkinson, Ezell and Stewart, 2012)
Technology use	(Bakker, 2011; Pieterse, 2002; Postmes and Brunsting, 2002)	(Lawrence, Hanouz and Doherty, 2012)

connected" captured the stakeholders anticipated condition based on their environment.

- Activist: active advocate supporting the existing governance structure or promoting a change
- Engaged: voicing opinions in favor or against the existing governance structure
- Aware: expresses and understanding of the relevance of the conflict but does not take any actions
- Disconnected: has not expressed any opinions or taken any actions

INFORMATION TECHNOLOGY

The "Information Technology" conditional probability captured the functional organizational components that facilitates the operation of the governance structure and determines the level of growth anticipated. The importance of this node was that it provided an idea of the level of stability of the network as it is with respect to the level of expansion that it could still experience within a country. A higher value indicated that there were a large number of technology resources available for the benefit of all stakeholders. Smaller values

Figure 5. IT Growth Potential nature nodes

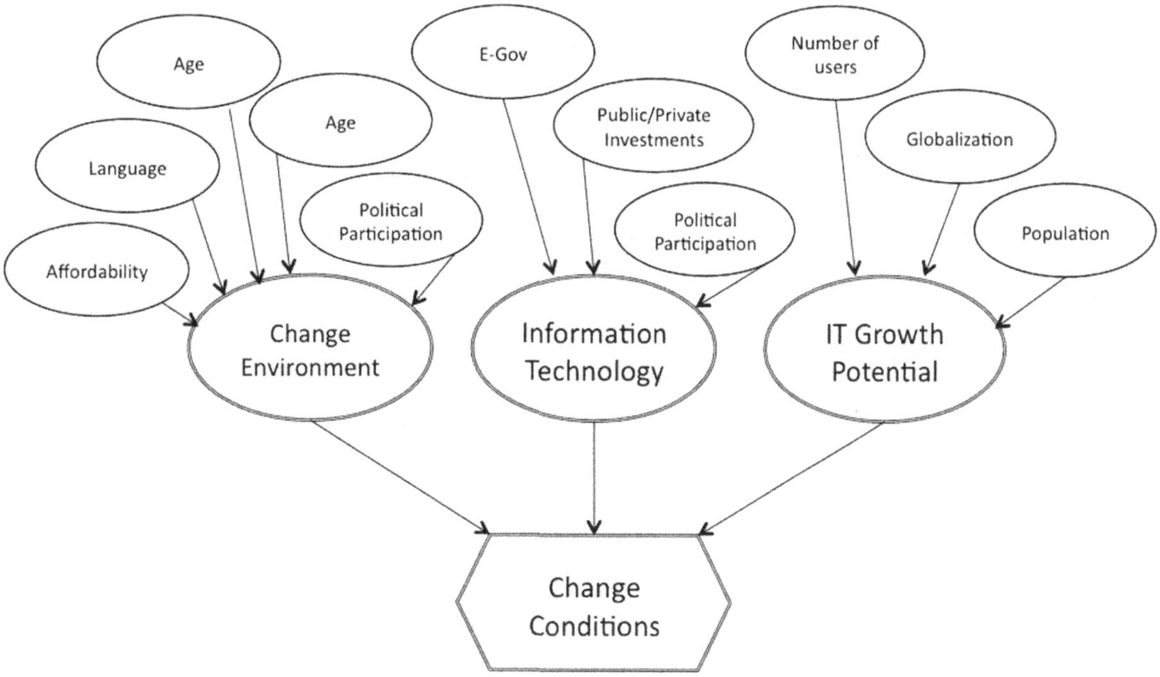

Table 3. Variable correlation and data source: IT growth potential

Variable	Correlation	Data
Number of users	(Norris, 2001; Boulianne, 2009; Bakker, 2011; Penard and Poussing, 2010; Kittilson and Dalton, 2011)	(International Telecommunication Union, 2012)
Globalization	(Pieterse, 2002)	(KOF Index of Globalization, 2012)
Population		(Central Intelligence Agency, 2011)

for this node represented a society that was still emerging technologically and might had other priorities.

IT GROWTH POTENTIAL

The "IT Growth Potential" node captures the influence of the means that strengthens the Internet and could either support a change or the existing systems depending on the influence of the countries increasing their participation in the network. If the result of the model showed that there was a reduced tendency towards change, the prevalence of that state depended on the growth potential of the global network because if there was a higher probability for the options between moderate and significant, the governance structure maintained a high probability of changing.

CHANGE CONDITIONS

The "Change Conditions" node determined the viability of the conditions to challenge the existing Internet governance structure.

Figure 6. Internet governance conflict conditional probabilities

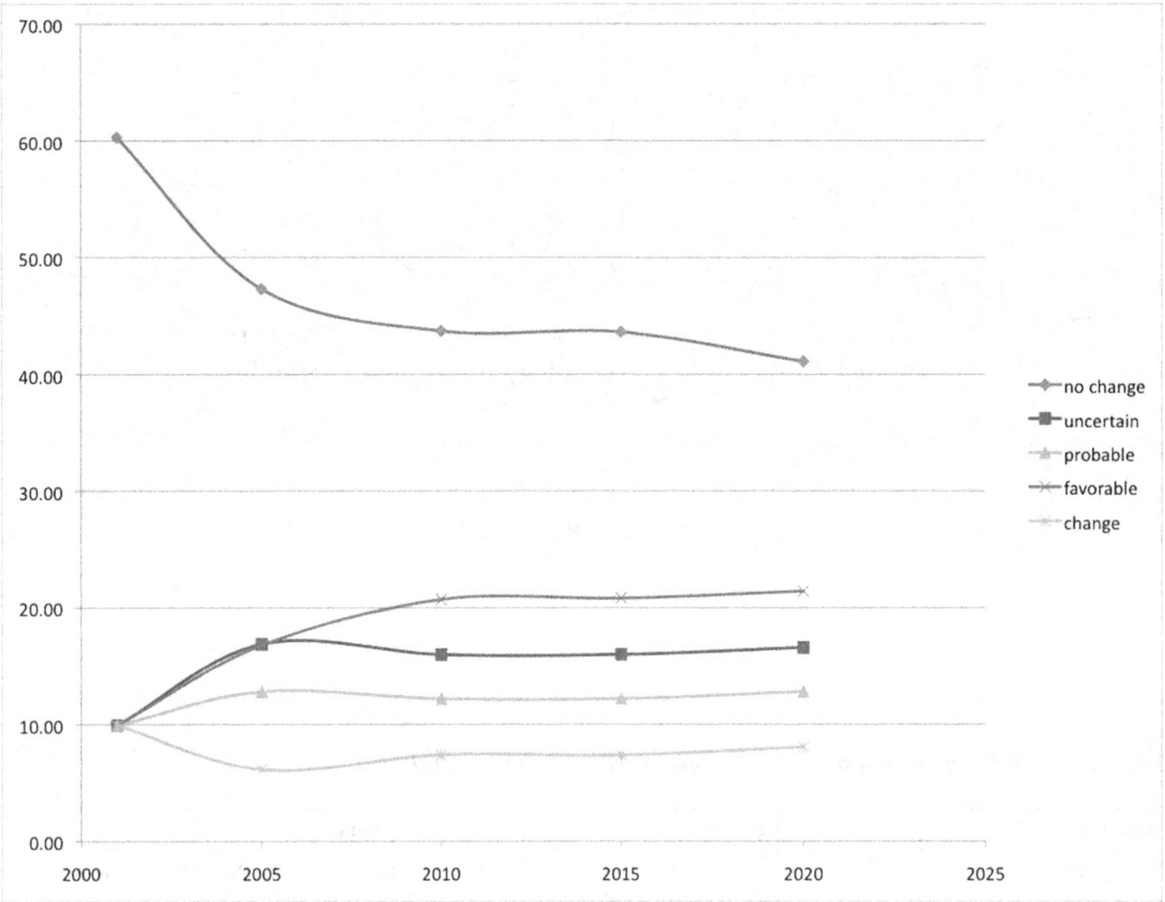

- **No change:** The country under evaluation considers that the Internet governance structure should remain as it is.
- **Uncertain:** The country under evaluation does not have a defined position regarding the future of the Internet governance structure.
- **Probable:** The country under evaluation expresses an inclination to support changes in the Internet governance structure or expresses concerns with the existing structure.
- **Favorable:** The country under evaluation openly expresses support for changes to the existing Internet governance structure.
- **Change:** The country under evaluation advocates changes to the Internet governance structure including the creation of a new governance system.

MODEL DATA

The data sources for the nature nodes are identified in the correlation tables: Table 1, Table 2 and Table 3. The data for the model was divided in two groups. The first group of the data is based on the historical values that are used for the model's learning and calibration process. This group includes values for 2001, 2005 and 2010.

The second group is the evaluation set and that includes data for years 2015 and 2020.

The model's learning process includes providing the model with fixed values for the reasoning variables in order for the model to learn the properties of the conflict at specific times. The fixed values are derived from the history of the conflict and reflect the information as it was documented for each of the years used for the learning process. A subset of countries with well-defined conditions and positions regarding the Internet governance conflict were selected out of the countries selected for the model for the learning process. The subset of countries selected includes Brazil, Canada, China, India, Russia, Saudi Arabia, South Africa, Syria and the United States. Table 4 includes the values used for each country for the learning process. The values in Table 4 are based on the values for the reasoning variables discussed earlier in this chapter.

DESCRIPTION OF POTENTIAL CHANGE CONDITIONS

The evaluation data explores the behavior of the model using projections for the variables related to GDP per capita, population and the number of Internet users. For 2015 and 2020, the values for population and GDP per capita were obtained from available projections from cited references. For 2015, the projections for the number of users were determined using high/low projection values defined as one standard deviation from the average projected growth in the number of users based on historical data. There are limitations in the use of additional projected variables because the values for those variables depend on a multitude of social, political and economic factors that could not be projected reliably using mathematical computations.

For the years 2015 and 2020 the "Change Environment" node continues displaying a trend of reduction in the category "disconnected" and a slight increase in the areas supporting changes with "aware" and "engaged" reflecting the largest increases. The environment and condition to support change in the Internet governance structure are expected to lag behind the categories reflecting the adoption of information technologies because the access and the knowledge of the system is needed before developing awareness about the Internet governance conflict. The fact that by 2020 the results show that "engaged" is the largest category could be interpreted as an increase in activism in reaction to both sides of the conflict. Table 5 summarizes the results of the "Change Environment" node for the years 2015 and 2020.

The "IT Growth Potential" shows a reduction in the lower categories related to minimum to small growth potential which means that as countries continue expanding their communication technologies the growth capacity stabilizes. The category of "significant" growth potential reflects an increase in 2020, which breaks from the downward trend expected for that category. A possible explanation for this change is that the stability in the growth potential is highly influenced by the advanced countries whose technologies grow at a slower rate due to the abundance of technology resources while developing countries benefit from the availability of those resources later in the process. Table 6 summarizes the results of the node "IT Growth Potential" for the years 2015 and 2020. The "Information Technology" does not reflect a variation in the evaluation years due to the limitations in the inputs used as the projected data for this node.

The "Change Conditions" node reflects a small decrease in support for "change" in 2015 and an increase for that category in 2020. The "no change" category continues a downward trend reaching almost 40%, which means that significantly more than half of the stakeholders expect some level of change. The "change" category does not reach 10%, which means that it does not become a viable option in the out years.

Table 4. Data identified for the model's learning process

Country	Growth			Environment			Change		
	2001	2005	2010	2001	2005	2010	2001	2005	2010
Brazil	large	large	small	disconnected	aware	engaged	nochange	uncertain	favorable
Canada	moderate	small	medium	aware	engaged	engaged	nochange	uncertain	uncertain
China	significant	significant	significant	disconnected	engaged	activist	nochange	favorable	change
India	significant	significant	significant	disconnected	aware	activist	nochange	probable	favorable
Russia	large	large	small	disconnected	engaged	activist	nochange	favorable	change
Saudi Arabia	moderate	moderate	small	disconnected	aware	engaged	nochange	uncertain	favorable
South Africa	large	large	moderate	disconnected	aware	engaged	nochange	uncertain	favorable
Syria	moderate	moderate	moderate	disconnected	aware	aware	nochange	probable	favorable

Table 5. Results for Change Environment node for 2015 and 2020

Change Environment	2015	2020
activist	21.30	21.70
engaged	27.20	27.60
aware	22.80	23.20
disconnected	28.70	27.50

Table 6. Results for IT Growth Potential node for 2015 and 2020

IT Growth Potential	2015	2020
significant	13.80	15.10
large	22.70	22.20
moderate	44.30	39.40
small	13.40	14.70
minimum	5.79	8.66

Considering that the added values of the "change", "favorable" and "probable" fail to reach at least 50% means that it is the "uncertain" category is the most relevant group. Depending on the direction they take after 2020 they could reinforce the existing scheme or promote modifications assuming that a change is highly unlikely based on the results. Table 7 summarizes the results of the "Change Conditions" node for the years 2015 and 2020. Figure 7 displays the results of the "Change Conditions" node.

CASE SCENARIOS: BRAZIL, RUSSIA, INDIA, CHINA (BRIC)

The evaluation of the case scenarios was performed by modifying the variables affected by the assumptions in order to define the conditions for the case scenario. In order to model the BRIC assumption, the values for the "Change Condition" node are set to "change" for the BRIC countries and to "no change" for the United States for 2015 and 2020. Figure 8 displays a graph of the values obtained from these assumptions. Based on the results obtained from the model, this scenario

Table 7. Results for "Change Conditions" node for 2015 and 2020

Change Conditions	2015	2020
no change	43.60	41.10
uncertain	16.00	16.60
probable	12.20	12.80
favorable	20.80	21.40
change	7.38	8.07

Figure 7. Change Conditions Node results

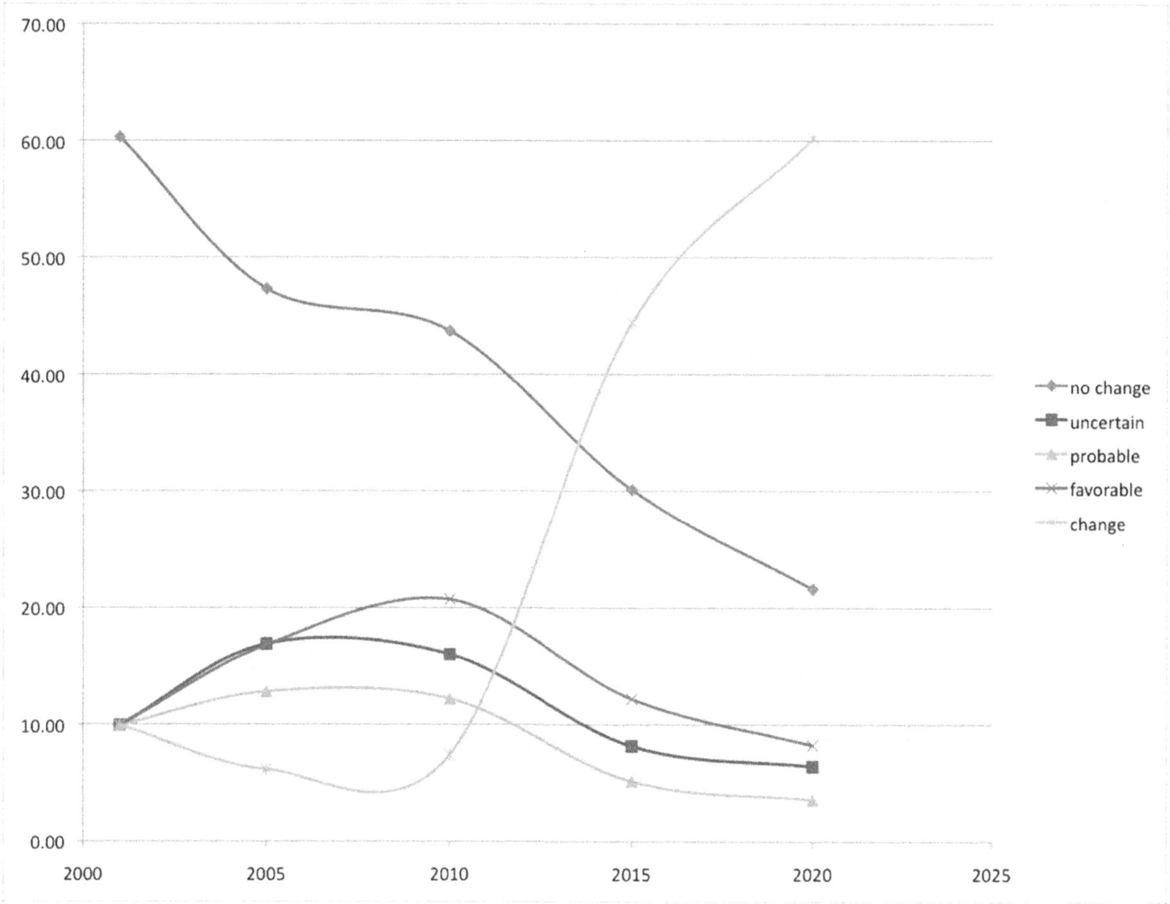

could significantly alter the Internet governance structure. The two extreme conditions of the "Change Conditions" node are polarized with the "change" category reflecting over 60% of the support and the "no change" category moving close to 20% of support and among the middle categories, "favorable" maintains the highest value adding to the trend to support a change.

These results show how the change of four highly influential countries in terms of social and economic factors could significantly alter the structure of one of the most important global technology assets. These conditions could represent a significant risk for the stability of the network because if the establishment does not support an initiative by the BRIC countries, then the evolution of the network in opposing directions could destabilize the system if the status quo remains in place while a potential coalition of BRIC countries develop a new structure. It is important to comment that a coordinated initiative by the BRIC countries in order to define a new Internet governance system is highly unlikely under the current social and political conditions of those countries.

Figure 8. BRIC Scenario - Change Conditions Node results

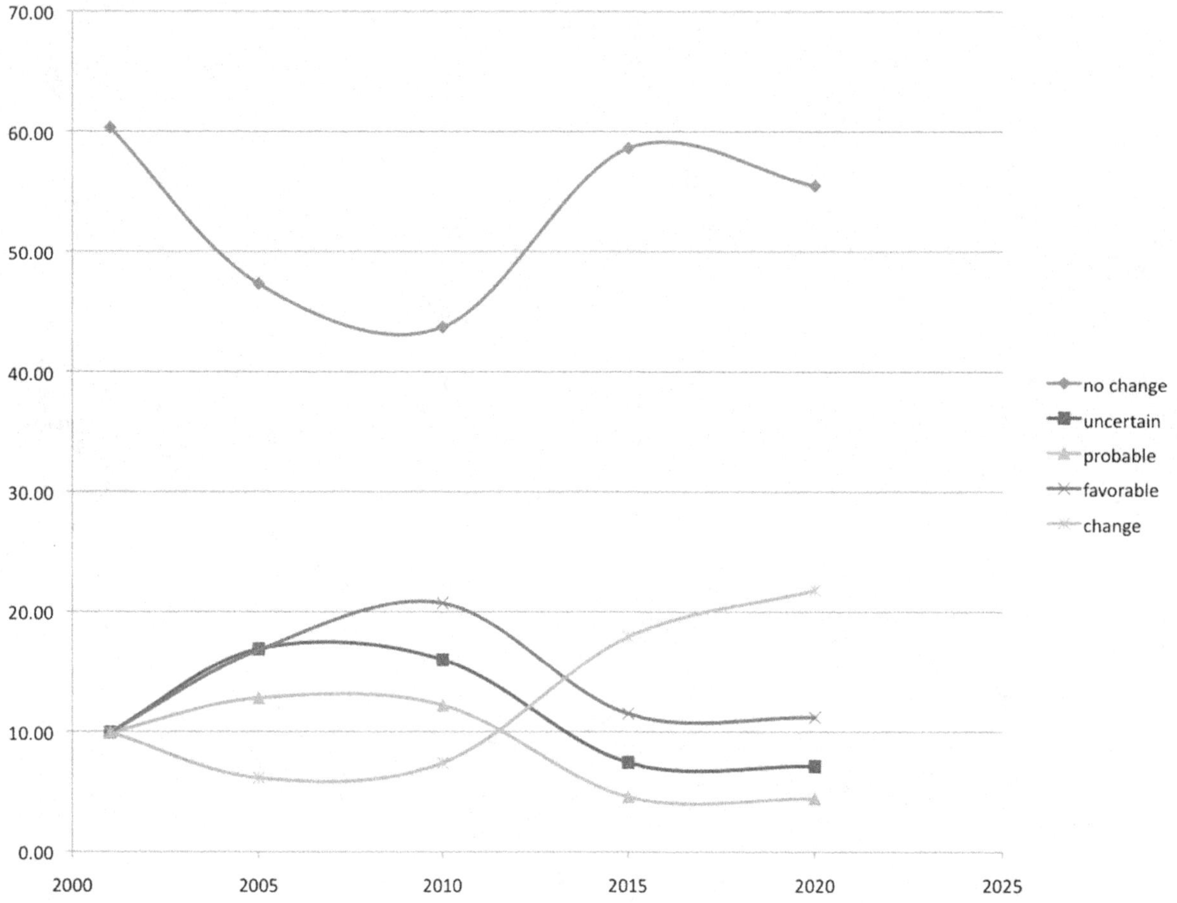

CASE SCENARIO: CHINA

The results for the China case scenario suggest that even when by 2020 the "change" category reflects a large increase with respect to the historical model, the value only moves slightly above 20% with the "no change" category maintaining more than 50% of the support. Even the "favorable" category reflects a considerable reduction from 2010 to 2015 reducing the probability of additional support for a change beyond 2020. From the results it can be assumed that based on the factors that define the model, China will not change the global Internet governance model if as a country it decides to develop its own DNS and Internet governance system. The condition could vary significantly if China manages to establish alliances with other influential countries as discussed in the BRIC case scenario. Figure 9 displays a graph of the results for this scenario.

ANALYSIS OF THE RESULTS

The large differences observed prior to developing the model between the Internet usage statistics from advanced countries and developing economies supported the assumption that the people without access to the Internet represent the majority of the potential Internet users. This assumption means that in a future breakdown of Internet users, those who are connected today will

Figure 9. China Scenario - Change Conditions Node results

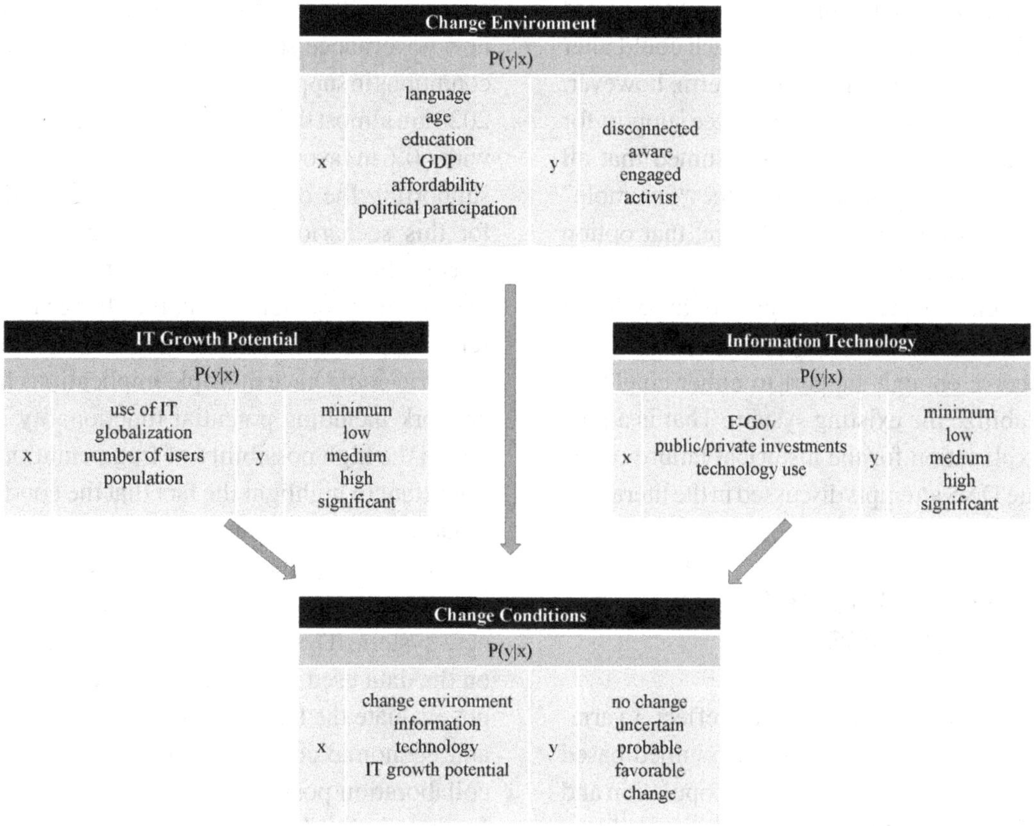

represent a minority with respect to those that will be connected but are not connected today. This information could lead to assume that as more people from developing countries obtain access to the network, the existing Internet governance system could be challenged. These conditions are feasible especially considering that some of the developing countries that represent the majority of those who are not connected have expressed formally and informally some level of disagreement with the existing structure as presented in the historical background of the conflict. The model developed as part of this research expanded the variables evaluated beyond just a population based analysis to evaluate the feasibility of the assumed changes. It demonstrated that although the perceived digital divide could influence changes, there are other factors that could reduce the influence of the perception that the new Internet users will automatically support changes to the Internet governance structure.

The results obtained from the model demonstrated that even when change is favored with time, the magnitude of the increase in support for change under standard conditions does not support the immediate creation of a new Internet governance structure. Conversely, the no change condition reflects values below 50% starting in 2005. This could be understood as a disagreement with the existing structure but the disagreement is not enough to provoke the creation of a new governance structure or to influence profound changes in the existing structure. As a result, the risks of a possible fragmentation of the network are minimized probably because the Internet users are willing to operate within the existing conditions but the need to modify and improve those conditions is maintained. Failure to recognize the need to develop a more inclusive approach could alter the change conditions in the long term, however, it would be difficult to project a large support for a change because even if it is assumed that all the stakeholders grouped under the "favorable" category move to support a change, that option would still remain below 30% by 2020. If a new DNS system outside of the control of the existing ICANN system is developed, it is unlikely that it will receive enough support to either challenge or destabilize the existing system. That is a possible explanation for the historical failure of the alternate DNS attempts discussed in the literature.

ANALYSIS OF THE RESULTS: CASE SCENARIOS

The results of the case scenarios reflect a variation from the anticipated results assumed based on the data available. Based on its population and the potential number of users, China could be considered the country of highest influence for the future of the Internet in many areas including the governance structure. The results demonstrate that an initiative by China to completely change the existing governance structure by developing a new system could potentially destabilize the network because it would polarize both extremes with less than 25% of the users supporting a new governance structure created by China and more than half of the users opposing any changes to the existing system. This represents a significant variation from the behavior of the model based on historical data, considering that for the model based on historical data, the group that fully supports the existing governance system only represents close to 40% of the users on a downward trend while the same group increases to 57% in 2015 and only by 55% in 2020 if China initiates a new governance structure starting in 2015.

The results obtained for the scenario evaluating an initiative from the BRIC countries to create a new governance structure reflect very favorable conditions in support of a change. The conditions in 2020 are almost the opposite of the China scenario with 60% in favor of a change and little over 20% supporting the existing system. The conditions for this scenario evolve at an accelerated rate starting in 2015 and even when the differences in 2020 are very significant, the change numbers reflect a potential upward trend after 2020. This scenario could have multiple implications for the network including potential functionality issues due to the high possibility of fragmentation. It is important to highlight the fact that the conditions modeled for this scenario assume full collaboration among the BRIC countries working towards a well-defined and shared goal of developing a new system. The assumptions are strictly based on the data used for the model. This analysis did not evaluate the feasibility of the political, social and economic conditions that would make that collaboration possible. The importance of these findings is the identification a possible combination of elements that could represent a strong challenge to the existing system. The results provide a tool to raise awareness of that possibility. In the best interests of the global Internet community, the identification of future conditions that could lead to a scenario similar to the one evaluated as part of this investigation should motivate the collaboration among the global Internet decision makers to minimize the possibility of a negative impact on the functionality of the system.

RECOMMENDATIONS

The global society is continually expanding the functionality of the communication systems. The ability of information and communication technologies to evolve based on multiple unrestrained contributions from around the world is what maintains and increases its robustness, however, as the dependence on the networks increase, it is important that as a society we understand the risks that we are accepting by relying on a system that evolves organically without an all-encompassing control system. Disputes related to the control of specific areas of the Internet could affect all of us. The results of this investigation offer an opportunity to continue defining and exploring social, political and economic conditions that could represent risks to the stability of the network. Although this investigation only focuses on Internet governance, factors similar to those evaluated could also influence other areas of the global communications network such as net neutrality, e-commerce and especially privacy and security. Unlike regular country constrained global issues such as trade and defense, communication technologies are controlled and influenced by a multitude of stakeholders. Even when this investigation does not evaluate the specific mechanisms that could promote changes to the governance system, the nature of the Internet allows a more user centered experience that could influence the future of the Internet and global communications more effectively than governments.

The influence of social, political and economic elements in the future Internet is not a novel idea since it is easily expected. However, the initial steps in the process of analyzing those dynamics provided by this investigation should motivate the expansion of this type of analysis in order to identify potential trends and expectations with respect to the future of global communications and the Internet. Our reliance on these global assets require that they continue expanding in a process that balances predictability and innovation allowing the influence of as many stakeholders as possible in order to maximize the stability of the system to promote that new developments are implemented using existing means rather than developing new segregated alternatives.

REFERENCES

Abbott, K. W., & Snidal, D. (1998). Why States Act through Formal International Organizations. *The Journal of Conflict Resolution*, *42*(1), 3–32. doi:10.1177/0022002798042001001

Achmawi, R. (2009). Brazil Wants Bigger Role for Emerging Nations in Internet's Management. *Brazzilmag.com*. Retrieved from: http://www.brazzilmag.com/index2.php?option=com_content&task=view&id=10204&pop=1&page=0&Itemid=1

Alternative reality - The internet in China. (2008, February 2). *The Economist*.

Atkinson, R. D., Ezell, S. J., & Stewart, L. A. (2012). *The Global Innovation Policy Index. Rep. N.p.* Information Technology and Innovation Foundation and the Kauffman Foundation.

Boulianne, S. (2009). Does Internet Use Affect Engagement? A Meta-Analysis of Research. *Political Communication*, *26*(2), 193–211. doi:10.1080/10584600902854363

Brams, S. J. (2004). *Game Theory and Politics*. Mineola, NY: Dover Publications.

Canadian Internet Registration Authority. (n.d.). *Open letter to the Internet Corporation for Assigned Names and Numbers (ICANN) from the Canadian Internet Registration Authority (CIRA)*. Retrieved from www.cira.ca

Chan, G. (2005). Domain name protection in Hong Kong: Flaws and proposals for reform. *International Journal of Law and Information Technology*, *13*(2), 206–242. doi:10.1093/ijlit/eai009

Chander, A. (2003). The new, new property. *Texas Law Review*, *81*(3), 715–797.

China's Internet users total 162 mln by end-June. (2007, July 18). *Xinhua Financial Network (XFN) News*.

Cranor, L. F., & Greenstein, S. (2002). *Communications Policy and Information Technology: Promises, Problems, Prospects*. The MIT Press.

Czernich, N. (2012). Broadband Internet and Political Participation Evidence for Germany. *Kyklos*, *65*(1), 31–52. doi:10.1111/j.1467-6435.2011.00526.x

Darwiche, A. (2010). Bayesian Networks. *Communications of the ACM*, *53*(12), 80–90. doi:10.1145/1859204.1859227

de Mesquita, B. B. (2004). Decision-Making Models, Rigor and New Puzzles. *European Union Politics*, *5*(1), 125–138. doi:10.1177/1465116504040448

DeNardis, L. (2009). *Protocol Politics: The Globalization of Internet Governance*. Cambridge, MA: MIT. doi:10.7551/mitpress/9780262042574.001.0001

DiMaggio, P., Hargittai, E., Neuman, W. R., & Robinson, J. P. (2001). W. Russell Neuman, and John P. Robinson. "Social Implications of the Internet. *Annual Review of Sociology*, *27*(1), 307–336. doi:10.1146/annurev.soc.27.1.307

DOTCOM Act of 2014, H.R. H.R. 4342, 113th Cong. (2014).

Dunahee, M. (2012). *World Internet Project International Report. Rep. Center for the Digital Future, 2012*. Retrieved from www.worldinternetproject.net

Dutta, S., & Bilbao-Osorio, B. (2012). *The Global Information Technology Report 2012, Living in a Hyperconnected World. Insight Report*. Geneva: World Economic Forum and INSEAD.

Dutta, S., Dutton, W. H., & Law, G. (2011). *The New Internet World: A Global Perspective on Freedom of Expression, Privacy, Trust and Security Online*. INSEAD Working Paper No. 2011/89/TOM. Retrieved from: http://ssrn.com/abstract=1916005

Ermert, M. (2011). UN And Internet Governance, Next Four Years: Better Cooperation Or Bigger Role?. *Intelectual Property Watch*.

Gleick, J. (1988). *Chaos: Making a New Science*. New York: Penguin.

Guillen, M. F., & Suarez, S. L. (2005). Explaining the Global Digital Divide: Economic, Political and Sociological Drivers of Cross-National Internet Use. *Social Forces*, *84*(2), 681–708. doi:10.1353/sof.2006.0015

Hallam-Baker, P. (2009). *RE: Last Call Comment on Draft-weiler-dnssec-dlv-iana-00.txt*. The Internet Engineering Task Force (IETF®).

Hart, T., & Rolletschek, G. (2003). The challenges of regulating the web. *The Journal of Policy, Regulation and Strategy for Telecommunications*, *5*(5), 6–24. doi:10.1108/14636690310500420

Hawksley, H. (2006). Chinese influence in Brazil worries US. *BBC News*. Retrieved from http://news.bbc.co.uk/go/pr/fr/-/2/hi/americas/4872522.stm

Hunter, D. (2003, Spring). ICANN and the Concept of Democratic Deficit. *Loyola of Los Angeles Law Review*, *36*, 1149–1183.

Index, D. (2011). (n.d.). Rep. N.p. *Economist Intelligence Unit*.

International Monetary Fund, World Economic Outlook Database. (n.d.). International Monetary Fund. Retrieved from http://www.imf.org/external/pubs/ft/weo/2012/01/weodata/weoselgr.aspx

Internet Governance Project. (2005). *The Future US Role in Internet Governance: 7 Points in Response to the US Commerce Dept.'s "Statement of Principles"*. Retrieved from www.internetgovernance.org

Internet Governance Project. (2004). *Internet Governance: The State of Play*. Retrieved from www.internetgovernance.org

Internet Governance Project. (2005). *Internet Governance:Quo Vadis? A Reponse to the WGIG Report.* Retrieved from http://www.internetgovernance.org/pdf/igp-quovadis.pdf

Internet Governance Project. (2005). *What to Do About ICANN: A Proposal for Structural Reform.* Retrieved from www.internetgovernance.org

Jackson, P. (2007). News fuels Russian internet boom. *BBC News.* Retrieved from http://news.bbc.co.uk/go/pr/fr/-/2/hi/europe/4880540.stm

Jensen, F. B., & Graven-Nielsen, T. (2010). *Bayesian Networks and Decision Graphs (Information Science and Statistics).* Springer.

Kauffman, S. A. (1996). *At Home in the Universe: The Search for Laws of Self-organization and Complexity.* New York: Oxford UP.

Keohane, R. O. (2005). *After Hegemony: Cooperation and Discord in the World Political Economy.* Princeton, NJ: Princeton UP.

Kittilson, M. C., & Dalton, R. J. (2012). Virtual Civil Society: The New Frontier of Social Capital? *Political Behavior, 33*(4), 625–644. doi:10.1007/s11109-010-9143-8

Klein, H. (2001). ICANN and the feasibility of global democracy: Understanding ICANN's at-large elections. *The Journal of Policy, Regulation and Strategy for Telecommunications Information and Media, 3*(4), 333–345. doi:10.1108/14636690110801996

Kleinwächter, W. (2000). ICANN as the 'United Nations' of the Global Information Society? The Long Road towards Self-Regulation of the Internet. *Gazette, 62*(6), 451–476. doi:10.1177/0016549200062006001

Kleinwächter, W. (2001). ICANN the silent subversive: ICANN and the new global governance. *The Journal of Policy, Regulation and Strategy for Telecommunications Information and Media, 3*(4), 259–278. doi:10.1108/14636690110801950

Kleinwächter, W. (2003). From Self-Governance to Public-Private Partnership: The Changing Role of Governments in the Management of the Internet's Core. *Loyola of Los Angeles Law Review, 36*, 1103–1126.

KOF Index of Globalization. (n.d.). *Eidgenössische Technische Hochschule Zürich.* Retrieved from http://globalization.kof.ethz.ch/

La Due Lake, R., & Huckfeldt, R. (1998). Social Capital, Social Networks, and Political Participation. *Political Psychology, 19*(3), 567–584. doi:10.1111/0162-895X.00118

Latour, B. (2005). *Reassembling the Social: An Introduction to Actor-network-theory.* Oxford: Oxford UP.

Lawrence, R. Z., Hanouz, M. D., & Doherty, S. (2012). *The Global Enabling Trade Report 2012 Reducing Supply Chain Barriers. Insight Report.* Geneva: World Economic Forum.

Lebo, H. (2012). *World Internet Project International Report. Rep* (3rd ed.). Los Angeles: University of Southern California.

Lindsay, D. (2007). *International Domain Name Law: ICANN and the UDRP.* Oxford: Hart Pub.

Manning, R. (n.d.). Obama's Internet Giveaway Threatened in House. *Breitbart.* Retrieved from: http://www.breitbart.com/Big-Government/2014/05/27/Obamas-Internet-GiveAway-Threatened-in-House

Mockapetris, P. (1987). *RFC 1035 - Domain Names - Implementation and Specification.*

Mueller, M. (1999a). ICANN and Internet Governance: Sorting through the debris of 'self-regulation'. *The Journal of Policy, Regulation and Strategy for Telecommunications Information and Media, 1*(6), 497–520.

Mueller, M. (1999b, June). "ICANN and Internet Regulation." Association for Computing Machinery. *Communications of the ACM*, *42*(6), 41–43. doi:10.1145/303849.303860

Mueller, M. (2007). The Politics of DNSSEC: The Light. *Internet Governance Project Blog*. Retrieved from http://blog.internetgovernance.org/blog/_archives/2007/9/9/3217425.html

Mueller, M. (2010). *Networks and States: The Global Politics of Internet Governance*. Cambridge, MA: MIT. doi:10.7551/mitpress/9780262014595.001.0001

Mueller, M., Mathiason, J., & McKnight, L. W. (2004). Making Sense of "Internet Governance:" Defining Principles and Norms in a Policy Context. *Internet Governance: Principles and Norms*, *2*, 1–22.

Mueller, M. L. (2004). *Ruling the Root*. The MIT Press.

National Telecommunications and Information Administration (NTIA). (n.d.). *United States Department of Commenrce. NTIA Announces Intent to Transition Key Internet Domain Name Functions*. Author.

Neil, M., Malcolm, B., & Shaw, R. (2003). *Modeling an Air Traffic Control Environment Using Bayesian Belief Networks*. Paper presented at the 21st International System Safety Conference, Ottawa, Canada.

NGO and Academic ICANN Study. (2001). *ICANN, Legitimacy, and the Public Voice: Making Global Participation and Representation Work*. Report of the NGO and Academic ICANN Study.

Norris, P. (2001). *Digital Divide: Civic Engagement, Information Poverty, and the Internet Worldwide*. Cambridge, UK: Cambridge UP. doi:10.1017/CBO9781139164887

Pearl, J. (2000). *Causality: Models, Reasoning, and Inferences*. Cambridge University Press.

Pershad, R. (2000). *A Bayesian Belief Network for Corporate Credit Risk Assessment*. (M.A.Sc. Thesis). University of Toronto.

Pfister, H., & Zalewski, J. (n.d.). *Bayesian Belief Networks*. Academic & Event Technology Services. Florida Gulf Coast University. Retrieved from http://itech.fgcu.edu/faculty/zalewski/CEN4935/BBN_Pfister_Zalewski.pdf

Pieterse, J. N. (2002). Globalization, Kitsch and Conflict: Technologies of Work, War and Politics. *Review of International Political Economy*, *9*(1), 1–36. doi:10.1080/09692290110102549

Pinheiro, M. (2014). *Brazil Assumes Leadership in Future of Internet Governance*. Inter Press Service News Agency. Retrieved from http://www.ipsnews.net/2014/04/brazil-assumes-leadership-future-internet-governance/

Ploberger, C. (2012). Analyzing Complex Political Change by Applying the Concept of Regime Change: Identifying the Transformations within the Japanese Political-bureaucratic-business Regime. *Asian Social Science*, *8*(15), 12–23. doi:10.5539/ass.v8n15p12

Postmes, T., & Brunsting. (2002). Collective Action in the Age of the Internet. *Social Science Computer Review, 20*(3), 290-301.

Powell, G. (2007). Promoting unique China Internet. *China Economic Review - Industries Updates*. Retrieved from: http://www.chinaeconomicreview.com

Rapoport, A. (1960). *Fights, Games, and Debates*. Ann Arbor, MI: University of Michigan.

Review, H. L. (1999). Developments in the Law. *The Law of Cyberspace*, *112*(7), 1574–1704.

Samuels, J. M., & Linda, B. (2003, Summer). Samuels "Internet domain names – The uniform dispute resolution policy.". *American Business Law Journal*, *40*(4), 885–904. doi:10.1111/j.1744-1714.2003.tb00312.x

Snidal, D. (1985). Coordination versus Prisoners' Dilemma: Implications for International Cooperation and Regimes. *The American Political Science Review*, *79*(4), 923–942. doi:10.2307/1956241

Starr, C., & Shi, P. (2004). *An Introduction to Bayesian Belief Networks and their Applications to Land Operations*. Land Operations Division, Systems Sciences Laboratory – Australian Government Department of Defense.

Sterman, J. D. (2000). *Business Dynamics: Systems Thinking and Modeling for a Complex World*. Irwin/McGraw-Hill.

The Internet Society. (2000). *IAB Technical Comment on the Unique DNS Root*. Retrieved from http://www.ietf.org/rfc/rfc2826.txt

The World Bank. (n.d.). *Data*. Retrieved from http://data.worldbank.org/

Thomas, L. (1978). *The Lives of a Cell: Notes of a Biology Watcher*. New York: Penguin.

Twomey, P. (2006). *ICANN letter to CIRA – Ref*. Retrieved from http://www.icann.org

UNESCO Institute for Statistics. (n.d.). Retrieved from http://www.uis.unesco.org/

Unit, E. I. Democracy Index 2011, Democracy Under Stress. Rep. (2011). *The Economist*. Retrieved May 2012 from: www.eiu.com

United Nations E-Government Survey 2012. (n.d.). United Nations, Economic & Social Affairs, United Nations. Retrieved from www.unpan.org/e-government

Van Duijnhoven, J. (2003). *Knowledge Assessment using Bayesian Networks – A case study in the domain of algebraic expectation*. Master's Thesis.

Weinberg, J. (2000). ICANN and the Problem of Legitimacy. *Duke Law Journal*, *50*(187), 187–260. doi:10.2307/1373114

Wendt, A. E. (1987, Summer). The agent-structure problem in international relations theory. *International Organization*, *41*(03), 335–370. doi:10.1017/S002081830002751X

Zgurovsky, M. Z., Boldak, A. A., & Pomerantseva, T. N. (2010). Analysis of the influence of global threats on the sustainable development of countries and regions of the world using Bayesian Belief Networks. *Cybernetics and Systems Analysis*, *46*(5), 822–832. doi:10.1007/s10559-010-9264-4

KEY TERMS AND DEFINITIONS

Bayesian Belief Networks: A graphical modeling method that maps out cause-and-effect relationships among key variables related to an event and the probabilities associated with those variables.

Domain Name System (DNS): It is considered a critical component of the Internet infrastructure as it allows the location of connected systems.

Internet Corporation for Assigned Names and Numbers (ICANN): A California based nonprofit organization created in 1998 that is responsible for managing the Domain Name System (DNS) including developing policy for internationalization of the system, introduction of new generic top-level domains (TLDs), and the operation of root name servers.

Internet Demographics: Statistical information related to Internet elements such as number of users, network availability and others.

Internet Governance: Rules and procedures that states and other involved parties agree to use to order and regularize their treatment of a common issue.

Modeling: The use of mathematical tools to explore future values of selected data based on defined assumptions.

Chapter 2
Internet Identity and the Right to be Forgotten:
International Trends and Regulatory Perspectives

Valentina Amenta
National Research Council, Institute for Informatics and Telematics, Italy

Adriana Lazzaroni
National Research Council, Institute for Informatics and Telematics, Italy

Laura Abba
National Research Council, Institute for Informatics and Telematics, Italy

ABSTRACT:

In this chapter, the analysis will focus on the concept of digital identity which is evolving and changing, based on the experiences that every individual lives. The chapter further highlights how the digital identity includes the fundamental human rights such as the right to a name, the right of reply, the right to protection of personal data and the right to an image. In translating the right to personal identity to our digitalized era, with its massive use of social networks, we have added to the related decalogue of rights the right to oblivion, equally called right to be forgotten. Given the complexity of the subject, the chapter develops an analysis of the actual international regulatory trends.

1. PRELIMINARY CONSIDERATIONS

The reflections that follow come from an overall view, the key issue in, on difficulties to identify what the right digital identity. Finding tiring and complex because of the difficulty to get to know the instrument in question; then that is itself the reason for the existence of this new law. After trying to define this right you will go to a careful and detailed analysis of one of the consequences that flow from it: the right to be forgotten. As we known, Internet is a strategic driver for the Information Society, designed by the European Community (EC), the objectives of social inclu-

DOI: 10.4018/978-1-4666-8371-6.ch002

sion and participation, having implications on the very essence of the individual, stimulate the development of new theories regarding personal identity on the Web. In fact, the advent of the Internet has meant a revolution for the contemporary era, having given rise to an impressive series of changes in social life and, above all, in terms of social relations. If the use of the network was merely associated, some time ago, with website browsing in order to acquire information, now this common approach has radically changed.

Internet is no longer a conglomeration of websites independent of one another, but must be considered as a combination of technological capabilities reached by man in the dissemination and sharing of information as regards general knowledge. We can look to the Internet as an environment that enables a user to experience new forms of contact, relationship and personal expression, such as through the social networks, which have become not just beaches for curious tourists passing through, but a habitat in constant expansion. In this way, the digital media have become contexts of the utilisation of information, as well as alternative spaces to daily reality for the use of a great range of services. Their introduction has redefined the concepts of space and time and now reflects the very essence of the individual.

The goal, then, would be to put the e-individual at the center of the information society in order to avoid/limit their exclusion from the technological evolution, proposing models of interaction and use capable of guaranteeing universal access to content and services offered over Internet.

If it is true that the Internet stands as the greatest instrument of social inclusion, it is also true that sollava inievitabilmente profiles problematic about the very nature of the individual. The technology change our habits and our lives, but in the face of the many benefits accruing from the application of these new techniques are beginning to manifest "special situations" defined by some authors as psychotechnologies. The use of new equipment interacts with our psychic apparatus and for the first time in the history of mankind, man has invented a device that forces him to adapt to "his" way of "thinking"; the use of the personal computer requires a real mental adaptation to its operation and consequently pushes the subject to adjust their cognitive functions to operation of the machine. The use of the network and the various applications is able to determine an expansion and a wrong perception of the boundaries of the self. Caught in the vortex of social relations, desperately divide our limited attention, allowing fragments of our consciousness to every person or thing that requires our time. In doing so, we risk losing slowly in the network of our identity.

Internet was celebrated as the site of a utopian social space where age, gender and ethnicity would be infinitely re-writable, allowing the subject to experience postmodern forms of identity fluid and multiple. In the social web, where social processes are organized right on the network, users have the opportunity to express themselves and expose themselves. The widespread use and importance of social networks has shifted so the online identity to a more real, blurring the boundaries between online and offline. It should, however, from a fundamental question: what is digital identity? It is defined as the identity consists of a user at the online virtual communities, often of a playful, focused on a virtual dimension, as opposed to the real one. Real and virtual are not in opposition, they are not good and the bad, the positive and the dangerous, the safe and the uncertain, but two types of experiences, modeling, knowledge of different realities. Digital identity has subsequently adopted a more general meaning of social identity, which the user sets on the Internet, becoming synonymous with the online identity. While some people use their real names digital identity, others prefer to remain anonymous, identifying themselves by means of pseudonyms. The term avatar, which is used just to indicate a size of digital imagery, in which a user provides a fantastic representation of itself, is also of type visual.

Much of the literature (Turkle, 2011) that argue the separation between virtual and real criticism of the social network claiming that people are swapping the face to face contact with the digital one. This duality arises from injury to see how to separate physical and digital environment, such as a zero-sum balance where the time and energy spent on a contact type are subtracted to another. There are digital and material realities, but only one actually composed of atoms and bits.

In essence, a person digital is the digital representation of an actual individual, which can be connected to this individual real and includes a sufficient amount of data (relevant) to be used, in a specific field and the purpose of its use, as delegation individual. An example is our Facebook profile that reflects who we know and what we do offline.

Roger Clarke (1994, pp. 77-92) has identified two types of digital identity: designed and sets, whose definitions are:

1. **Designed:** it is the one created by the same individual, which transfers it to the other by means of data (for example: creating a personal blog, a personal page on a social network, etc.).
2. **Sets:** that is projected onto the person by means of data from external agencies such as commercial companies or government agencies (eg, degree of solvency for the purpose of granting loans, health status for insurance or credit, etc.).

We could say, well, ultimately that the 'digital identity includes essential aspects from us: Some are generic (our nature as men), more specific (who we are, what we do etc..) And also comes complete with aspects related to the way we to use the web and other connected to them, also linked to the operation of the infrastructure

2. DIGITAL IDENTITY

The digital media (Comode, Krishnamurthy & Willinger, 2010) have become contexts of the use of information, as well as spaces alternative to everyday reality for leisure and free time. Facebook, Twitter (Humpreys, Gill & Krishnamurthy, 2013, pp. 843-857.) and YouTube have introduced a new way of conceiving digital identity, no longer as merely self-awareness but as cyber-sociality. In fact, the digital social groups to which the individual belongs represent a system of coordinates, where each new coordinate identifies the individual in a more precise way.

If we look at Second Life, it is a virtual world where anyone can build a second life, choosing their name, gender, self-image through the construction of their physical appearance. This social network is a virtual environment that can be accessed at the same time by thousands of different users who have an avatar, an identity that is represented by a character on the screen. The avatar has the ability and the opportunity to build a new communicative and relational set-up regardless of its origin and its real personality. At the same time the avatar has a relational space that is much wider than that of the real life of the user it represents. The avatar can in some cases become a mask to wear and remove when the interpretation is over, as theorized by Erving Goffman in 1969, according to whom each of us plays their part within a digital frame. In our era, however, that of the digital revolution, an interesting and new interpretation of the eternal question might be: who am I on the Web? The most cynical would probably say that on the Web we are nothing more than a few records in a large database, a username, a password and little more. However, these views can be added to the list of "unsatisfactory answers".

So, some additional key points to analyzing such a broad issue are: the vulnerability of our identity on the Internet and the implications it generates. The juridical issue at the basis of the digital identity of an individual is related to his or her protection, that is to say whether or not they are an autonomous legal entity. It is important to understand if there is a violation of the right to the personal identity of the individual of which the avatar is the expression. There are two practical Italian cases which could be useful to understand this issue:

1) The story of a young fifteen-year-old Sicilian, who in 2009 realized that on Badoo there was an account that she had never created, including photos of her and an accessible profile (SiciliaToday, 2009). Unknown computer users had in fact created an account and registered a profile on "Badoo" without her knowledge, also publishing photos depicting her in inappropriate behaviour. Following the initial investigation of the Caltagirone police, the locality of the registration was identified and further investigation identified another teenager of 16 years, rival in love of the unaware victim, whose objective was to denigrate the girl through the network, especially in the eyes of his "competitor".
2) Another example is the case of a famous Italian soccer player, Alessandro Del Piero, who discovered in 2009 the theft of his identity on Facebook (Zeus news, 2009). Besides the theft of identity, the thief clearly expressed neo-Nazi sympathies, which the original Del Piero categorically denied. In fact, fake celebrities on social networks are far from rare and can be a source of problems. The footballer took legal action against Facebook to protect his image.

Italian legislation protects the right of everyone to not have the authorship of his actions disclaimed and not to be attributed the authorship of someone else's actions (e.g., through untrue posts on Facebook), that is the right to not see his individual personality misrepresented. From this protection it is evident that personal identity is not only constituted by objective data, but also by the social projection of the personality of the individual. In this case the protected property is the social projection of personal identity (Dogliotti, 1980, pp. 965-974.). However, it should be noted that the social projection of a person is multiplied in the society we live in today, where social networks and, more generally, social relationships, become mass communication. By using Facebook, Twitter, YouTube, Second Life and other role play games, we see our identity fragmented into many small particles, which are beyond our control and which can bond with other particles of information created unbeknown to us. Biology teaches us that at the end of the process a new nucleus is formed that contains the DNA of the new personal identity.

An authoritative Italian doctrine states that: The spread of increasingly large and specialized collections of personal data, made for various purposes and by different subjects, produces various forms of dispossession and fragmentation, displacing oneself in diversified places ... the unity of people is broken and in its place we find many "electronic persons", just as many persons created by the market ... as there are interests that lead to the collection of information. We are becoming abstractions in cyberspace, we are dealing with a multiplied individual (Rodotà, 1997, pp. 615-619).

So the very identity itself is quite changeable, constantly evolving and transforming on the basis of the experiences of each individual. A well-known sociologist, Bauman (2009), has defined identity in the contemporary era by almost equating it to a garment which is worn until it is needed, while it suits the wearer. Considered in this way, the right to personal identity brings with it a number of corollaries such as: the right to a name (Ricci, 2008, pp. 77-99), the right to the protection of personal data (Buttarelli, 1997) and the right to personal image (Vercellone, 1959). If we translate the right to personal identity to our digitalized era, with its massive use of social networks, we need to add to the related Decalogue of rights the right to oblivion, equally called right to be forgotten. This is the right for natural persons to have information about them deleted after a certain period of time.

2.1 DIGITAL IDENTITY BETWEEN OLD AND NEW CONTINENT

In London, a decade ago, in 2003, two young English persons met each other in *Second Life*, they fell in love and got married. But when she found out that her husband's avatar had frequented an avatar call girl, she hired an avatar-detective. However, he discovered yet another virtual betrayal. In this case, the divorce attorney was absolutely real.

According to the Daily Mail (2008), the couple spent more time together on the Internet than they did in real life. And the lawyer was not at all surprised. He said it was the second case of divorce connected to Second Life that had happened in a week. The betrayed woman stressed that the Internet had not ruined her life, but whilst she had turned the page and started a new life with another husband, the Internet does not forget. The burden of betrayal, which she would like to forget, still remains through posts and situations of Second Life which reoccur.

On 25 January 2012, the European Commission officially unveiled its proposals for the new European legal framework in the field of data protection. The proposal consists of a Regulation, which will replace EU Directive 95/46/EC, and a Directive which will regulate the data treatment for purposes of law and order (currently excluded from the application field of Directive 95/46/EC). The procedure for final approval of the two regulatory instruments will involve the joint intervention of the European Parliament and the EU Council in accordance with the procedure known as co-decision (now defined by the Treaty of Lisbon as legislative procedure). Annex 53 of the EU Directive states that "every person shall have the right to rectify the data concerning him or her and the "right to be forgotten" if the retention of such data does not comply with this Regulation. In particular, individuals should have the right to have their data fully removed and no longer processed when it is no longer needed for the purposes for which it was collected or otherwise processed (...). Furthermore, pursuant to Article 17, the data controller has no obligation to proceed with the deletion of data, since the retention is necessary "(a) for the exercise of the right to freedom of expression under Article 80 (...)."

Nevertheless, this intervention by the EU represents a big step forward, although we are still far from a solution to the problem. According to Mayer Schonberger (2009), Professor of Internet Governance and Regulation at the Oxford Internet Institute, a solution should be sought in education and technology. The latter should allow the publication of content on the net with a pre-established expiry, while the former should involve convincing Internet users not to abandon for eternity fragments of their current life that are destined to become valuable pieces of the mosaic of their own digital identity.

In this direction, in Italy in 2009, a bill was presented which foresaw that after a certain period of time, varying according to the seriousness of the offense, and on condition that there is a written consent of the interested party, the images and data also of a juridical nature can no longer be diffused or maintained. In fact these would enable, directly or indirectly, the identification of the suspected or accused on the Internet pages freely accessible to users or by means of search engines external to the website source. California has enacted the so-called Eraser Law (Senate Bill No. 568, Chapter 336) for those under 18. A nickname was never so appropriate. From 2015, in fact, teenagers will be able to cancel their compromising digital past (such as embarrassing photos, untruthful comments or declarations of love entrusted to the network and destined to survive for ever). The law was enacted by the Governor of California Jerry Brown and will come into force on 1 January 2015, giving time for websites to adapt to the new legislation. This law requires operators to prepare the forms through which deletion of content may be requested. Furthermore, there is a clear obligation to publicize these forms.

Despite the good intentions, the law seems to be somewhat out of context because it does not consider the very nature of the Internet and above all the dynamics of information flow on the net. In fact, the content posted by a repentant minor, requesting its removal, could be bounced everywhere. It might very well have given rise to conversations, should they have been transformed and launched again on other sites, and the California law does not take this into account.

It would appear somewhat eccentric, though, that in addition to the need to know the age of the users, the sites will need to know whether or not the children live in California. This is as if to anchor the right to be forgotten to a right which is mostly sectorial and territorial. The attention is shifted from the protection of data to the safeguarding of minors. But then, for the Aristotelian syllogism, should this issue not be protected by the privacy code, but safeguarded as a fundamental right of the individual (be he young, adult, elderly)? But then, who am I and what safeguards can I obtain for the information about myself? This is the question that man has always posed at some stage of his existence. There are thousands of answers, but there is not one that fully satisfies us, since when we give an answer we have already changed again, and we have to reply to the same question with a different answer.

Herodotus might have commented that not only great and wondrous works, but also human events of common mortals deserve not to fade with time.

3. THE RIGHT TO BE FORGOTTEN: BACKGROUND AND SOCIAL IMPLICATIONS

If we translate the right to personal identity to our digitalized era, with its massive use of social networks, we need to add to the related Decalogue of rights the right to oblivion, equally called "*right to be forgotten*". This is the right for natural persons to have information about them deleted from online archives, even after a certain period of time, when the personal information may appear one-sided, unfair or may harm image or reputation. Note, techniques for enabling for an amnesic Internet are still a challenge.

If personal identity is a summary of the rights already mentioned through which the individual protects him/herself, it is certain that a variable which is not easily manageable on the Internet is *time*. As we all know, time plays a crucial role: the person is what she or he is at a particular historical moment and her or his identity changes with time. In fact, the events reported in posts, forums and videos on YouTube, related to a certain period, may no longer match the personality of a subject at a different historical moment. As is now well established, the Internet cancels space-time. Not only does the network change the amount, but also, and especially, the nature of communication. The information circulating is of a great quantity, but the difference lies in the easy availability of this information, which most of the time is deprived of source and is isolated from context. That is why it is felt that there is the need for a right to oblivion, intended as a right to be forgotten, i.e., the right for citizens to demand the deletion of any personal data that circulate on social networks and on the network in general.

It is undeniable that extension of the right to be forgotten to the world of the Web has turned out to be more complex than was foreseen, prompting numerous debates and controversy. But what if the pictures, data and personal information that it can pull out about you appear unfair, one-sided or just plain wrong? More and more people are claiming they have a right to be forgotten and are even trying to delete themselves from the Web. The issue appears poised to generate legal, technological and moral wrangling for years to come, putting in contrast the right to oblivion on the one hand and the right to information and transparency on the other. In fact, it is still difficult to define from a juridical point of view: (a) up to how many years from the fact can the individual exercise the right to obtain deletion of her or his data (b) what are the elements which, even after a certain amount of time, could justify the continuing existence of these data in online archives. On the other hand, it should be acknowledged that effectively there exist issues related to the publication of data and in search engines which would otherwise be difficult to find and to access.

3.1 The New European Legislation

The EU proposal of a new juridical framework regarding the protection of personal data is made up of two distinct legislative acts: a) a Regulation of the European Parliament and of the Council regarding the protection of individuals with regard to the processing of personal data and of the free movement of such data b) a Directive of the European Parliament and of the Council concerning the protection of individuals with regard to the processing of personal data by authorities for the purposes of prevention, investigation, detection and prosecution of criminal offenses or the execution of legal sanctions, and the free circulation of these data.

The Regulation, put forward on January 25, 2012 by Viviane Reding, the Vice President of the European Commission, was intended to be stricter than the 1995 Data Protection Directive 95/46/EC. The EU Regulation foresees the right to ask service providers to delete the personal information which is collected by data brokers under a users' consent clause in order to strengthen user information protection. The right to be forgotten also includes the notion of not to be searched for, and prescription of information. The regulation recommends service providers to request consent from their users when they deal with, their personal information such as medical history, criminal records, location and their orientation for implementing a marketing strategy. On failing to comply with the regulation, service providers would be fined up to €1 million or 2% of their sales figures. V. Reding explained that a change of regulations, related to the past Internet environment, is inevitable due to the changes of digital circumstances such as technological development and globalization. The proposal includes the following:

- Automated control of personal information
- Regulation to be applied not only to companies based in the EU area, but also to companies dealing with personal information of EU citizens. Even if the physical server of company processing data is located outside Europe. EU rules apply to search engine operators if they have a branch or a subsidiary in a Member State.
- Request of users' consent before collecting personal information
- Unified regulation applied to the entire EU
- Mandatory reporting when information leakage occurs
- Transferrable personal information when users change their Internet service providers.
- As a response to the EU proposal, there have been several objections to the Regulation. Corporations are opposed to it, claiming that the strict Internet standard would worsen the economic situation of the EU and delay the development of the Internet industry, which depends critically on the use of individual data to develop, improve, and fund services and content (Gross, 2012). Other people have raised doubts on how to implement the right to be forgotten, it being difficult to assume that

social networks like Facebook should have some form of control over what users do with information freely posted by other users (Warman, 2009). The Centre of Digital Democracy (CDD) has voiced that it would not be easy for the EU to reach an agreement with the Internet service providers. The General Data Protection Regulation will replace Directive 95/46/EC, putting in place a comprehensive reform for the protection of users' privacy on the Web that should be transposed into national law by all EU member states by 2015. In fact, it should be recalled that EU regulations have a general application and are binding in all their parts and directly applicable in national legislation. It might be interesting, with the aim of a thorough assessment of the proposal, to examine the institutional motives which inspired the EU legislator to put forward the proposal. These were:

- To address the regulatory fragmentation caused by divergent implementations of Directive 95/46/EC by Member States, establishing a more solid and coherent legal framework that guarantees individuals' control over their personal data and strengthens the legal and operational certainty for the economic actors and public authorities;
- To respond better to the challenges posed by the rapid evolution of new technologies (especially online) and the growing globalization which have transformed not only the economy but also social relations, changing the ways and means of processing personal data;
- To consequently establish a climate of trust in online environments, in order to stimulate economic development by providing the necessary drive for growth, employment and innovation in Europe.

The proposal encompasses the right to be forgotten and to erase data (Article 17), which will help stakeholders to better control information concerning them. They will be able to decide what information can continue to circulate and delete it if there are no legitimate reasons for its maintenance (e.g., legal obligations, the right to freedom of expression, public interest in the field of healthcare, for reasons of historical, statistical and scientific research, etc.). The online service providers will be forced to move from the opt-out rule (user data, unless on explicit request, belong to the supplier) to that of opt-in (the data belong only to the user, and it is for him/her to decide how to use them). The reform also foresees the obligation for social networks to prove that the retention of a certain piece of information is needed and to warn the user (alert within 24 hours) in case this information is stolen.

Many have criticized the reform launched by the EU and the underlying assumptions which are at the basis of the right to be forgotten, which in their opinion would deprive the network of its original essence. The Internet has become a huge repository of information, the only one of its kind, where everything is preserved and nothing is forgotten. The fact remains that this intervention by Europe represents a new way in which the old continent has interpreted the right to oblivion and made it operational on the Internet.

In this same context it is essential to mention the recent and much debated Judgment of the Court of Justice of the European Union 13 May 2014, in Case C-131/12, according to which an Internet search engine operator is responsible for the processing that it carries out of personal data which appear on web pages, published by third parties. Thus, if following a search made on the basis of a person's name, the list of results displays a link to a web page which contains information on the person in question, the very same data subject may directly approach the operator exercising the right to be forgotten. Where the operator does not grant the request, the data subject may bring the matter before the competent authorities in order to obtain, under certain conditions, the removal of that link from the list of results. The judgement of the Court of Justice of the European Union, for the first time, highlights some important key points:

- In operating their search service, Google is processing personal data and is acting as a data processor and controller under the terms of the European Data Protection Directive;
- Following this, search engines may have to remove links to web pages containing data which appear to be *inadequate*, *irrelevant*, or *no longer relevant*, or *excessive* in relation to the purposes for which they were processed and in the light of the time that has elapsed.
- A search provider can be required to consider removal regardless of the legal status of the personal information on the third party web pages.
- The judgement highlights the significance of interference to personal data rights that can be caused by the availability of the links associated with a name.
- The data subject's rights also override, as a general rule, the legitimate interest of Internet users to access information.
- A fair balance should be sought between these interests depending a) on the nature of the information in question and its sensitivity for the individual's private life and b) on the interest in communicating the information to the public, an interest which may vary, according to the role played by the data subject in public life.

The implications of the judgment, as confirmed by initial comments on it, are much more relevant than it seems, even for the supporters of the law itself. It enshrines in fact a principle that can be taken by the courts of each Member State, with problems of implementation and significant implications, not only for Google. Search engines will have to rethink the way they manage links and the way they display the contents of sites that they index.

The judgement practically makes Google and other search engines responsible for the visibility of personal data published online, even if they have simply gathered it together for inclusion in their indexes and in their results. When receiving from individuals the request to remove the link to specific content deemed *no longer relevant*, they must do so, even if the sites that actually host those contents continue to keep it online. More simply, the Court ruled that, under certain circumstances, some content or personal data may not be linked on the search engines, even if these contents are entitled to exist. As the judgement is fairly generic, it follows that many aspects of Internet identity could fall under the extended definition of "no longer relevant": links to photographs of teens, offensive comments on social networks, malicious comments, judicial penalties already served, business documents on recruitments and so on.

Furthermore, according to the EU judgment, the evaluation of these aspects will be made by the same user who seeks "de-indexation" of those contents, and if the search engine does not consent, he may apply to a national court. Many people wonder if it will ever be possible to put into practice what has been decided by the European Court of Justice, and if all this will inevitably lead to an endless series of inquiries and complaints by individuals who want to make it impossible to find old bits and pieces of their personal identity that they would rather keep hidden.

There is a further aspect, not least, of an ethical nature. Search engines could be put in the position of deciding what is of public interest and still relevant and what is not. The Court ruled that in the event that there are "public figures" involved, the search engines have the power to oppose the removal request and to refer the case to the national court or to the competent national authority for the protection of privacy. But even in this case there would still be an element of discretion: Google, or another search engine like Bing or Yahoo!, may decide to oppose some requests and not others, creating a *de facto* inequality of treatment. There are also implications regarding individual users. Making less accessible the "negative" information about the past of a person may raise a risk to those who have to interact with him. In fact, already in real life, we sometimes regulate our choices and decisions on the basis of information we have about other people. For example, should information about a conviction for violence be hidden or made accessible to those who have subsequent dealings with the convicted person?

In the coming months Google and the other search engines will have to find ways and means to address legal requirements similar to those that led to the judgment of the European Court of Justice. They will have to face the decisions of national courts which will act on the basis of the EU judgment, in a first implementation phase that promises to be very complex and hotly debated.

3.2 The International Context

Despite the enthusiasm of some European exponents, who have long recognized the need to regulate the right to be forgotten, among the observers and legal experts of communication rights there is considerable concern about the possible consequences of the judgment of the Court of justice of the European Union on the removal of links and the likely complications of its implementation.

The UK's data privacy watchdog has said that it would focus on "evidence of damage and distress to individuals" when reviewing complaints about Google and others' search results. The Information Commissioner's Office blog post (ICO) is the first official response to the EU ruling (Smith, 2014). The ICO will be responsible for resolving complaints in cases where a search engine refuses to remove links, but the body's director of data protection affirmed that ICO will not be ruling on any complaints until the search providers have had a reasonable time to put their systems in place and start considering requests.

As for Spain, it should be noted that already in 2011 the Spanish Data Protection Agency (*Agencia Española de Protección de Datos*) ordered Google to delete links on its search engine to any website containing out of date or inaccurate information about individuals and, thus, breaching their "right to be forgotten. As a consequence, Google challenged the AEPD's order in a Madrid Court, since, in Google's opinion, only publishers, and not search engines (which act as intermediaries), may be deemed responsible for contents published through their websites and on the Internet. Thus, only publishers should be forced to take action in order to guarantee users' privacy and, especially, their "right to be forgotten". Already at that time, this decision contributed to raising new questions on the balance between the right to be forgotten, on the one hand, and the freedom of speech and information on the other

In Brazil, on April 22 2014 the *Marco Civil*, the "charter of Internet," was finally approved by the Brazilian Senate as a law governing the rights and obligations of users of the network. After five years of work there was approval in São Paulo of the law that protects privacy, freedom of expression and ensures net neutrality. On the specific topic of the right to be forgotten the *Marco Civil* contains provisions against the attribution of liability to intermediaries. This states that providers are not responsible for the content posted online by users, an issue which has been debated for years in Europe, which Brazil had not yet legislated for. According to the new Brazilian legislation in fact, the service providers will be liable for the contents of third parties only if they do not remove the data pursuant to a court order.

In Italy, the principle of the right to be forgotten is dealt with by the DPA (Data Protection Authority). The Data Protection Commissioner, in 2005, attempted to identify a technical solution to ensure transparency regarding this issue and to avoid the creation, by means of search engines, of outright *electronic pillory*. The Ombudsman for privacy had examined an Italian case, in which a subject was sanctioned by a public body. On its website, the public institution had indicated the violation and the name of the violator. Consequently, the interested party had requested the removal of his name, claiming the right to privacy. The Ombudsman for privacy stated that the institution can continue to disclose on its website the legal decisions regarding the interested party and his company, but - after a reasonable period of time – the institution should relocate the legal decisions, dating to several years before, in a webpage of the site accessible only by means of the web address.

However, this page must be excluded from direct access by means of a common search engine. In practice, this case represented the recognition of the right to be forgotten and the prevalence of privacy legislation over the freedom of the press. Therefore, the court granted the claimant's claim, condemning the institution to pay damages, claiming that the news should have been cancelled because the persistence of the processing of personal data of the restaurant's owners and the name of the company, states the court, resulted both in infringement of the right to privacy and in a reputation damaged by systematic diffusion of the personal data.

In practice, the right to be forgotten existed in Italy before the judgment of the European Court of Justice on May 2014, which was extended to the Google search engine. In fact, already in 2012 the Italian Supreme Court had added an important contribution to the recognition of the right to be forgotten by stating that the information existing in the historical archives of online newspapers are to be considered *partial* since it does not report further developments of the facts, and therefore must be updated. The Court, in its judgment no. 5525/2012, imposed an obligation for publishers to update the online archives of the news published. Online newspapers have to provide their archives with a system designed to indicate (in the body or in the margin of the web page) the existence of a follow-up or development of the news, thus allowing quick and easy access by users for the purposes of going into more detail regarding the specific news item. This Court decision assigns a new value to the right to be forgotten within the context of the freedom of the press. It enshrines the principle according to which the public interest in the knowledge of a fact is contained in the space of time necessary to inform the community, whilst, as time goes by, it fades until it disappears. In practice, with the passage of time, the fact ceases to be news and it reassumes its original nature as a private matter (Di Ciommo, 2012, pp. 703-715.). Finally, in the United States, the concept of the right to be forgotten is alien to the American legal system and to the policies of major American companies. It is in fact a European law, originally, French and Italian, which is not applicable in the United States. According to some American exponents, the judgment of the EU Court is deemed to be short-sighted, because it gives merely a snapshot of the present situation. At present, in fact, doing a search online is basically equivalent to using only one search engine, Google, which owns about 90 percent of the European market (Lance, 2015). Preventing Google from linking a "no longer relevant" specific content may make sense, because it makes it practically impossible to find that content. But in a more open market what would happen? If in the future there are more competitors who want to remove certain links from the pages of results, says Meyer, will they have to submit a request to each search engine? And what will happen if in the future there appears a search engine that works in a distributed way, and not in a centralized manner, as Google does today? Who will become accountable as point of reference? Should there be a reference point for each country in which there is a search engine? The result is that, according to the case judged by the Court - if we try to find on Google the name of the person who made an appeal to the Court, we will not find that name listed, but if we look for it on the newspaper website then we will find it.

The judgement highlights wide-ranging and longstanding differences between how Europeans and Americans view fundamental values, including individual rights, privacy and the role of government and dominant telecom companies in information policy. Where Europeans see the "right to be forgotten," many Americans see George Orwell's memory hole. Where Europeans seem to have faith in the ability of regulators to protect the privacy of individual citizens, most Americans accept the fact that the Internet is an open door where anyone can enter and exit at anytime.

4. CONCLUSION

The reflections expressed so far become an important interpretation with reference to the centrality of the individual in an era of networks and also with regards to the concept of person, which is often underestimated. There is much debate on the mixture or blend between real and virtual universe, and here we are looking for questions and answers which are equally complex. A "journey in the virtual universe" leads to the formulation of questions that are centred not only on the network itself and for its own sake, but above all on the idea of person.

The Web knows very well that a great part of its fascination and attractiveness for end-users derives from its capacity to contain things *ad infinitum*, that is without limits of space and time, information and data of whatever kind (Schomberger, 2009). The person in the world of Internet is exposed to constant hazards in terms of his/her privacy and by using the social networks, jeopardizes his/her own private sphere. In fact, any piece of information uploaded to the Internet, escapes from the sphere of exclusive availability of its owner, in that it can be memorized by other application servers and picked up by a range of search engines. By means of "cache copy", many search engines operating on the Web make a copy of data available to users for each archived page, to be used when the original resource is no longer reachable. In this way search engines are carrying out, to all intents and purposes, an activity of memorization, aimed at making sure that the Internet forgets nothing.

As we have seen, the law has reawakened the debate on one of the most delicate themes of our time marked by global communication: that is the relationship between the so-called right to be forgotten on electronic communication networks and the freedom for anyone to use and access the Internet in order to freely express his or her identity. This is whether they are disabled or not. In this way, therefore, the right to protection of one's identity on the Web and of the consequent right to be forgotten becomes in our view, one of the constitutional bastions of the new Society of global Information.

As pointed out by Stefano Rodotà (2014), who has persistently underlined the importance of the right to be forgotten for a number of years, affirmation of the right to be forgotten as a fundamental right of the person is an important element for what every Constitutional Charter defines as constitutional freedom of personality. Naturally, the issues regarding application have no easy practical solution. Firstly, we must ensure that this right does not become an instrument of censorship. An important area regards blogs or online journalistic information, the true raw nerve of the relation between two equally important freedoms, freedom of information and freedom of control over one's own information. Secondly, there is the difficulty of practical application: once information enters the network its subsequent route is difficult to track.

Following the recent decision of the Court of Justice of the European Union, of which mention was made above, which ruled that users can ask to search engines to remove results related to their name, Google has released a new tool for require the removal of the content. Google announces that the removal request may be made by any citizen believes that the information in the results associated with a search of his name may be inadequate, irrelevant or no longer relevant, or excessive in relation to the purposes for which they were published.

During the implementation of this decision, Google will assess each request and will try to balance the privacy rights of the person with the right of all to learn and distribute information. During the evaluation of the request Google will determine if the results include outdated information about the user and if the information is in the public interest, for example in case of financial fraud, professional negligence, criminal convictions or the conduct of public officials.

The search engine giant has also announced that it is working on the formation of a committee of experts who can provide advice on how to manage the new feature dedicated to the right to be forgotten.

Every revolution, as we well know, has its price. The history of human evolution, like that of peoples and nations, in this regard, has no exceptions, and consequently does not admit romantic illusions. The transition from one condition to another implies unfailing relinquishments and losses. Exactly what man must sacrifice is not clear yet. In the way of an example, it is clear how man in the universe of the Internet is exposed to all kinds of hazards as regards his privacy, and how, above all through the use of the social networks, he is jeopardizing and perhaps every day bartering his own private sphere. It is naive to imagine that we can exactly foresee the nature and extend of this phenomenon.

The pervasiveness of the Internet and social networks has given a new dimension to the relationship between freedom and market, as it has between democracy and rights. The spheres of economic, political and social pluralism are witness to a constant growth, in the world of the Web, of new opportunities and also new risks. There exist new needs for the protection of rights and freedom and new rivalries constantly emerge in the exercising of rights that are disputed between innovation and protection. How can these processes be governed? How can they be faced in terms of rights and democracy? Can the world of the Web have rules, albeit mobile, which are without borders and in continuous mutation? Is there any need for a 'constitution' of Internet that gives new interdisciplinary answers and new policy orientations?

Without this awareness, which in philosophy has been referred to as "heterogenesis of currents", it is not possible today for the jurist to investigate with some hope of success the ways, the times and the locations of the Internet.

In this way, considering that the relationship between information and human memory has been deeply influenced by the diffusion of the Internet and in particular by Web search engines, it is necessary today to set out new equilibriums between protection of the right to inform (and be informed) and online protection of the personal identity of individuals. In this perspective, it would appear fair to have an obligation to integrate or update the piece of news that is no longer current, having it become a historical fact, but which is potentially damaging for the personal identity of the interested party, who has the right to the respect of their own personal and moral identity.

REFERENCES

Bauman, Z. (2009). *Intervista sull'identità*. Roma: Laterza.

Buttarelli, V. (1997). *Banche dati e tutela della riservatezza*. Milano: Giuffrè.

Clarke, R. (1994). The digital persona and its application to data surveillance. *The Information Society, 10*(2), 77-92.

Cormode, G., Krishnamurthy, B., & Willinger, W. (2010). A Manifesto for modelling and measurement in a social media. *First Monday*, *15*(9). doi:10.5210/fm.v15i9.3072

DailyMail. (2008). Retrieved November 14, 2008, from http://www.dailymail.co.uk/news/article-1085412/Revealed-The-woman-Second-Life-divorce--whos-engaged-web-cheat-shes-met.html

De Santis, F., & Liguori, L. (2011). *The "right to be forgotten" privacy and online news*. Retrieved March 8, 2011, from http://www.portolano.it/2011/03/the-"right-to-be-forgotten"-privacy-and-online-news

Di Ciommo, F. & Pardolesi, R. (2012). Dal diritto all'oblio alla tutela dell'identità dinamica. *Danno e Responsabilità*, 703-715

Dogliotti, M. (1980). Tutela dell'onore, identità personale e questioni di compatibilità. *Giustizia Civile*, 965-974.

Gross, G. (2012). Critic's: EU's proposed data protection rules could hinder Internet. *Computer World*. Retrieved September 5, 2012 from http://www.computerworld.com/article/2492101/data-privacy/u-s--privacy--consumer-groups-back-eu-s-proposed-privacy-rules.html

Humphreys, L., Gill, P., & Krishnamurthy, B. (2013). Twitter: A content analysis of personal information. *Information Comunication and Society Journal*, *17*(7), 843–857. doi:10.1080/1369118X.2013.848917

Lance, W. (2015). *Google advisers: Limit 'right to be forgotten' to Europe*. Retrieved February 6, 2015, from http://www.cnet.com/news/google-advisers-limit-right-to-be-forgotten-to-europe/

Ricci, A. (2008). Il diritto al nome. In Diritto dell'anonimato. Anonimato, nome e identità personale. Torino: Utet.

Rodotà, S. (1997). Persona, riservatezza e identità personale. Prime note sistematiche sulla protezione dei dati personali. *Rivista critica di diritto private*, 605-619.

Rodotà, S. (2014). *Il mondo nella rete. Quali diritti, quali I vincoli*. Roma: Laterza.

Schomberger, V. M. (2009). *Delete: The virtue of forgetting in the digital age*. USA: Princeton University Press.

SiciliaToday. (2009). Retrieved December 10, 2009, from http://siciliatoday.net/quotidiano/news/Rubata-identit-su-Badoo-a-ragazza-siciliana_17980.shtml

Smith, D. (2014). *Four things we've learned from the EU Google judgment*. Retrieved May 20, 2014, from https://iconewsblog.wordpress.com/2014/05/20/four-things-weve-learned-from-the-eu-google-judgment/

Turkle, S. (2011). *Alone together: Why we expect more from technology and less from each other*. Cambridge: MIT Press.

Vercellone, P. (1959). *Il diritto sul proprio ritratto*. Torino: Utet.

Warman, M. (2012). Government minister Ed Vaizey questions EU's "right to be forgotten" regulations. *The Telegraph*. Retrieved February 28, 2012, form http://www.telegraph.co.uk/technology/news/9109669/Government-minister-Ed-Vaizey-questions-EU-right-to-be-forgotten-regulations.html

Zeus News. (2009). Retrieved February 9, 2009, from http://www.zeusnews.it/n.php?c=9393

KEY TERMS AND DEFINITIONS

Bill of Right: literally means a bill on the rights, but the term has come to mean the use of the Declaration on the Rights.

Digital Identity: Digital identity is the data that uniquely describes a person or a thing and contains information about the subject's relationships. The social identity that an internet user establishes through digital identities in cyberspace is referred to as online identity.

European Union: The EU is an organization of supranational and intergovernmental, that from 1 July 2013 includes 28 member states independent and democratic.

Google: Google is an American company that offers online services, primarily known for the search engine Google, the Android operating system and a set of Web services like Gmail, Google Maps, YouTube.

Marco Civil da Internet: Marco Civil is the law that governs the use of the Internet in Brazil.

Right to oblivion: A concept that has been discussed and put into practice in the European Union (EU) and Argentina in recent years. The issue has arisen from the desires of some individuals to "determine the development of his life in an autonomous way, without being perpetually or periodically stigmatized as a consequence of a specific action performed in the past.

Social Networks: A social network is a social structure made up of a set of social actors (such as individuals or organizations) and a set of the dyadic ties between these actors.

Virtual Word: Virtual Word is a computer-based simulated environment. The term has become largely synonymous with interactive 3D virtual environments, where the users take the form of avatars visible to others.

Chapter 3
Towards Privacy Awareness in Future Internet Technologies

Hosnieh Rafiee
Huawei Technologies Duesseldorf GmbH, Hasso Plattner Institute, Germany

Christoph Meinel
Huawei Technologies Duesseldorf GmbH, Hasso Plattner Institute, Germany

ABSTRACT

With the increased use of the Internet to share confidential information with other users around the world, the demands to protect this information are also increasing. This is why, today, privacy has found its important place in users' lives. However, Internet users have different interpretations of the meaning of privacy. This fact makes it difficult to find the best way to address the privacy issue. In addition, most of the current standard protocols in use over the Internet do not support the level of privacy that most users expect. The purpose of this chapter is to discuss the best balance between users' expectation and the practical level of privacy to address user privacy needs and evaluate the most important protocols from privacy aspects.

INTRODUCTION

Today, Internet is used as a highway for exchanging data, data that might be confidential or sensitive for the owners who might be an individual, a company, an organization or a government. This is because there are thousands of Internet technologies (services) available to attract users to communicate through the Internet. Some examples of these technologies (services) are blogs, wikis, social networking and virtual worlds, online presentation tools and video and podcasting.

After Snowden's information leakage about NSA pervasive monitoring, unfortunately, Internet users are now aware of the fact that criminals are not the only people who are seeking to access their confidential data but also governments are trying to gather this information for different purposes.

This pervasive monitoring (Akko & Farrell, 2014) showed that the current Internet architecture and the whole TCP/IP protocol suite are not necessarily well designed to protect users' data from prying eyes.

DOI: 10.4018/978-1-4666-8371-6.ch003

This is why the Internet Engineering Task Force (IETF) recently started activities to investigate privacy awareness for the current standard protocols; such activities might require the redesign of some of the existing protocols. This is especially true when users and devices should be authenticated by other devices automatically so that they can be authorized to access some resources in visited networks.

The major focus of this chapter is the privacy status of the current authentication protocols as well as the evaluation of some of the standard communications protocols.

The remainder of this chapter is organized as follows:

It first focuses on the meaning of privacy, its status in different countries and possible attacks to jeopardize user's privacy. It then introduces existing standard organizations that formed the current Internet architecture by their cooperation. It also focuses on the description of some of the existing protocols. It then evaluates the current privacy status of these protocols. Since authentication and authorization protocols are really important, it then describes them in more detail. It is because a misconfigured system might allow an unauthenticated user to have an unauthorized access to some confidential data. This chapter concludes by making some recommendations.

WHAT IS PRIVACY?

The term privacy had come into existence when for the first time people declared themselves as owners of some items of physical property and wanted to protect them against intruders (Hirshleifer, 1980). Later, this term was used in a broader scope, especially in computer systems, and in combination with other terms such as anonymity, secrecy, etc.

Unfortunately, the broad scope of this term allowed it to be confused with other terms, such as security terms, whereby they were conceived to be the same, which is not true. This fact leads to disagreement on the privacy definitions.

In computer terms, privacy which considered being a social term gives one the ability to choose what data he/she wants to expose to others and what data he/she wants to keep from others. In other words, privacy gives users to control their data disclosure. But when interactions are done via computers and networks, privacy often relies on technical tools for data confidentiality and data integrity. Security, on the other hand, gives one the ability to protect these data and preserve their confidentiality. These important data can be anything including user's bank information, names, date of birth, medical information, user's address and any information that can give an attacker a possibility to track this user.

This information might be of different nature when we are talking about privacy in a company. The data can indeed be company's product details (confidential data that are hidden from competitors), codes, employees' personal information, etc.

Sometimes, privacy and security are conflicting. One example of this scenario is where a company records the location of its users in order to use it as part of the authorization process – perhaps some applications or datasets may only be accessed from inside company premises. But although this helps the company maintain security, tracking and recording employees' location could violate their privacy.

Privacy and Its Scope in Different Countries

The importance of protecting personal data motivated countries to work on an international privacy regulation. Finally, in 1970, the world's first data protection law was enacted in the Hesse in region of Germany (Rodrigues & et al., 2002). Since then, other countries have enacted their own national privacy regulations that describe the data protection during collection, storage and analysis.

Unfortunately, these countries had different understandings of this privacy regulation and defined different scopes for privacy and data protection.

In 1995, the European Commission proposed the first Data Protection Directive (DPD) (*Handbook on European Data Protection Law*, 2014) to protect individuals' personal data processing and the free movement of such data. This DPD was based on principles set out by the Organization for Economic Cooperation and Development (OECD) in 1980s (Shimanek, 2001). But European countries had different interpretations from this regulation. For example, some countries thought that only protecting a part of data was enough. Others considered the protection of only governmental data, and some countries thought to protect everything. This is among the reasons why in 2012, the European Commission proposed a new version of that Directive to try to achieve a unified meaning of privacy in European countries (European Commission, 2012).

Attacks on User's Privacy over the Internet

An attacker or a criminal might use different tools and mechanisms to obtain data about an individual -- a politician, a businessman or a regular user. He might then abuse such data and use them against an individual, a group of people, a company or a government for the purpose of blackmailing or damaging some investments and public resources. This is called harming privacy or privacy attack. The various layers of Internet protocol can each give rise to privacy risk and noting that one approach to "privacy by design" is to aim for minimization of identifiable data at each layer. That is, each layer should reveal only the information relevant to it. For instance, a MAC address is relevant to the transport layer, but should not, by default, be revealed to the application layer, which has no need for it. The following sections discuss some of these privacy attacks. (Physical privacy such as an attacker staring at your window is out of scope of this chapter)

Node Reconnaissance

The first step to harm user's privacy is usually to gather information about this user. This is why, in the Internet, any unique identity that might lead to assist an attacker to track an individual should be kept confidential. This might be a label, an IP address or any other unique identity.

In computer networks, this is done by finding the IP addresses of the nodes, and then, to run port scanning in order to find the available services running on the nodes. This is done in order to take advantage of the vulnerabilities of these services running on the node, which ends with the result that node's security is compromised. It helps an attacker to have access to the user's data stored on this node or abuse this node and use it as an entrance gate to a target network. In this case, the attacker already bypasses the network security devices and he/she is inside the network and can access many data exchanged among nodes in this network.

Location Based Tracking

This might be similar to node reconnaissance. If a node in different networks uses the same unique identity such as the same IP address, then an attacker might be able to track the node across the network. The reason for this is because it is very easy for an attacker to recognize that this node is the same node. Usually in computer networks, the network portion of an IP address may change overtime, but not the host identity part. For example, the network portion of an 128-bit Internet Protocol version 6 (IPv6) address is represented by the 64 leftmost bits, whereas the host identity portion (Interface Identifier, IID) of the IPv6 address is represented by the 64 rightmost bits. In other words, although the network portion of the

IP address may vary overtime, an interface of the node might keep the same IID. It might also generate an IID that is correlated to its previous one. In both scenarios, an attacker can technically track this user via this correlation and might be able to eavesdrop packet exchanges with other nodes in order to obtain some confidential information.

Privacy and Security

Many attacks that harm nodes' security might often lead to jeopardize user's privacy as well. This is because privacy is related to an entity such as an/a individual's/company's/government's information. This is why any attacks that are meant to obtain information about this entity might harm entity's privacy. It includes eavesdropping, spoofing, Man-in-the-middle (MITM), phishing attacks, water holing (planting a virus on a site that the target is known to visit), etc.

INTRODUCTION TO THE EXISTING STANDARDS

Standard protocols are the means to ensure interoperable implementations. One example of these standard protocols is the use of TCP/IP protocol suite standardized by the IETF. This protocol allows transparent communication of different services over the internet. One use case scenario for the standard protocols is where a user like Alice decides to have an online chat with her friend, Bob. She uses an Instance Messaging (IM) application as an Internet technology to do this without the need to care about how the communications take place. Everything for her, as a user, is transparent. In the background, there are many different protocols that work together to make sure the communications between Alice and Bob is properly established. Some examples of such protocols are the Transmission Control Protocol (TCP) (Information Science Institute, 1981), and the Internet Relay Chat (IRC) (Kalt, 2000).

Without protocols, the Internet could not exist as it is today. These standard protocols are the result of collaborations between several industries and individuals in different standard organizations. There are different standard organizations which are active in Telecommunication standards – International Telecommunication Union – Telecommunication (ITU-T), European Telecommunication Standards Institute (ETSI), Internet Engineering Task Force (IETF), International Organization for Standardization/International Electrotechnical Commission (ISO/IEC) JTC 1 (Information Technology), Institute of Electrical and Electronics Engineers (IEEE), World Wide Web Consortium (W3C), etc. These organizations annually propose thousands of standard protocols that function in different layers of the Open System Interconnection model (OSI) or other standard models. Domain Name System (DNS), Hypertext Transfer Protocol (HTTP) (Fielding & et al., 2014), Dynamic Host Configuration Protocol (DHCP), Internet Protocol (IP), Open Standard for Authorization (OAuth), Intermediate System to Intermediate System (IS-IS), Border Gateway Protocol (BGP) are some examples of these protocols that are proposed by IETF or ISO/IEC.

Domain Name System (DNS)

DNS (Mockapetris, 1987) is one of the widely used protocols over the Internet. One of the important functions of this protocol is to assist other protocols to translate user friendly names into IP addresses and vise versa. Unfortunately, DNS only supports basic protection mechanisms that check that the source address is the same as the address mentioned in the DNS configuration file and use a transaction ID. There are some mechanisms available to secure DNS protocols – DNS Security Extension (DNSSEC) (Weiler & Blacka, 2013), and Transaction SIGnature (TSIG) (Vixie & et al., 2000), are two examples of these mechanisms.

Dynamic Host Configuration Protocol version 6 (DHCPv6)

DHCPv6 (Droms et al., 2003) is a protocol that can be used to allow a DHCP server to automatically assign an IPv6 prefix or address to a network device.

Open Standard for Authorization (OAuth)

OAuth (Hardt, 2012) enables users to authorize a website or an application to access some resources on other websites or applications. It separates the role of clients from the resource owners. In other words, a user can have access to the resources located in another node without the need to have the username and password of the resource owner.

Intermediate System to Intermediate System (IS-IS)

IS-IS (ISO/IEC 10589, 2002) is a network layer routing protocol which allows the intermediate systems and the network layer forwarding systems, to exchange routing information.

Border Gateway Protocol (BGP)

BGP (Rekhter & et al., 2006) is a protocol that is used to exchange routing information between Autonomous Systems (AS). An AS is a collection of IP networks operated by one administrative entity. Unfortunately, an attacker can easily obtain unauthorized access to the data carried by the BGP protocol or spoof this information (Kent & et al., 2000). Secure BGP (S-BGP) has been specified as a possible solution to BGP's vulnerabilities. It uses Public Key Infrastructure (PKI) for key distribution and Internet Protocol security (IPsec) (Kent & Seo, 2005) to provide authenticity and integrity to packets. Since IPsec operated at the IP layer, it can also help prevent some TCP attacks such as TCP replay attacks. However, key exchange between all nodes would be a problem.

Open Shortest Path First (OSPF)

OSPF (Moy, 1998) is a dynamic routing protocol. Unlike BGP, it distributes routing information inside a single AS. It is flexible to the topology changes. Each router that uses this protocol maintains state information, including the network topology based upon a tree-based architecture derived from the set of shortest routes that have been computed to reach different neighboring nodes the router is attached to. This information is stored in the Link State Database (LSDB). OSPF is also vulnerable to several attacks. An attacker can manipulate the OSPF packets and cause the flushing of the routing tables maintained by target routers (Hartman & Zhang, 2013) (Cisco Security Advisory, 2013). One possible solution to protect OSPF against this kind of attack is the use of IPsec. However, this is not a very simple solution due to the fact that IPsec has a deploy-ability problem. This is because of complexity of configuring all routers to support IPsec as well as the support of Generic Routing Encapsulation (GRE). This is because IPsec does not support multicast traffic and it needs a tunneling to transport this traffic.

STATUS OF PRIVACY IN THE EXISTING STANDARDS

Today, millions of users have opportunities to use Internet. This is really an advantage for the companies who have services to offer. It is because they can easily reach millions of their customers simply by pressing a button and they can easily advertise their products. This is also an inexpensive way to reach their potential customers compared to postal mail, TV, or other broadcasting media.

Governments also found the use of Internet as an advantage to share data with their different offices around the world. One example is where an embassy stores applicants' information on a main database in its home country by the use of some intermediate software and exchange these data across the Internet using standard protocols.

Besides internet, this giant communication and information highway, emerge other concepts, like virtualization and clouds. It is attractive for many to have the ability to share data with multiple users, and access these data anywhere at any time using public storage, thereby reducing the cost of resources but at the same time increasing the computing power, decreasing complexity of management and administration of data centers, and decreasing the number of physical network resources such as a switch, a router, and using the Software Defined Network (SDN) (Chu, 2013) techniques to virtualize these resources.

Since every second there are terabytes of data exchanged via the Internet, many of which might be sensitive or confidential in nature, the security and privacy of these data are major concerns. There are some security standard protocols that provide some guarantees about data integrity and authenticity but many of them are not designed to protect users' data from prying eyes. In other words, the data might be exchanged in plain text although some of these data are confidential.

Since European countries are more and more concerned about privacy, in 2012, ETSI approved a standard regarding security, trust and privacy (ETSI - I, 2012) to specify privacy during authorization processes and communications. However, ETSI's solutions rely upon the use of many IETF and ISO/IEC standards for this purpose. One example is the use of Transport Layer Security (TLS) (Dierks & Rescorla, 2008) standardized by IETF. This standard organization also approved another document that details some requirements for monitoring users' data, storing these data and processing them (ETSI - II, 2012).

In 2013, IETF published a clear guideline (Cooper & et al., 2013) for considering privacy in Internet Protocols. In this document, the assumption is that the architectures of most of the current internet protocols are as flexible as they need to be in order to support privacy. This is, of course, to some extent true for some protocols but not for all. However, these approaches can be considered as a step towards users' privacy but this is still not enough since this document is informational and there is no implementations' enforcement. Furthermore, without the customers' demands, it is unlikely that manufactures would like to modify their existing products for privacy consideration. Since it might require both getting customers' agreement for the modification of their old products and also extra expenses for both customer and manufacture. Some old products also might not support any extensions and customers might not agree on buying new products.

In the following subsections, we evaluate the privacy status of some of the current standard protocols.

Routing Protocols

Routing protocols are used to exchange routing information between routers. The corresponding messages might contain unencrypted data and have a clear source and destination IP addresses. There are always attackers who are interested to receive these data. An attacker might try to fulfill his wicked plan by attacking a router and re-route all the packets/messages to his/her own destination in order to craft those data or only eavesdrop the data exchange between two communication endpoints. In other words, the attacker is interested to play a MITM. Unfortunately, most routing protocols, as explained earlier, either do not support any practical protection mechanisms or they only use IPsec for data authenticity and integrity but not for data confidentiality. In other words, they do not encrypt the messages/packets but they only sign them or use Message Authentication Code (MAC) to authenticate the routers that generate these messages.

The main disadvantage of IPsec is that all devices not only should support IPsec but there should also be a method to exchange keys among all players. This is also mentioned in last sections in more detail.

The use of virtualization, particularly the separation of controller plane from forwarding plane as it is considered in Software Defined Networking (SDN) approaches, seems to simplify the task of attackers. Before the evolution of OpenFlow devices, an attacker needed to attack every single router to forward traffic to him/herself or include him/her as a new hop to receive this traffic. With OpenFlow-enabled devices an attacker can spoof an OpenFlow message and propagate its attacks to other virtual devices in the network via this infected virtual device. This is easier when the network supports SDN-based approaches. This is because all flows are sent to a centralized controller which controls many virtual devices and can enforce configuration to all of these virtual devices. If one of these virtual devices is infected, it might allow the propagation of new configuration to all virtual devices by sending it to the controller (Shin & Gu, 2013) (Chu, 2013).

Although the data carried in each message might be encrypted by applications that submitted those messages, usually source and destination addresses as well as some other information that is used to forward these messages are unencrypted and not protected. Refer to privacy definition; any entity that might expose users' information should be protected. Since in digital communication, an IP address is an identity of a node (especially if it is fixed in a network), by obtaining an IP address of any node in any network, an attacker can try to correlate traffics to a node which configured a particular IP address or be able to eavesdrop communications by filtering the traffic based on this IP address. This might allow an attacker to obtain users' information. This is why, the IP addresses or other routing information might give the attacker some valuable information to harm users' privacy. Unfortunately, with the current Internet architecture, it appears that there is no solution to protect users on this attack, since, it is not possible to forward messages/packets based on anonymous IP addresses that not refer to any node or identify any node. This is also true when packet forwarding is based upon random labels. There is only an except in Multiprotocol Label Switching (MPLS) networks (Rosen & et al., 2001) where neighbor's node ID might not be known during sending initial path message (Berger, 2003). In this scenario, node might choose a random labet al. The good news is that Network Address Translation (NAT) (Audet & Jennings, 2007) that is a mechanism proposed to address the problem with IPv4 address pool exhaustion, might also be helpful to hide real IP addresses (network layer information – node's identity in the network) of the nodes where IP address can identify a node across a network. But this actually depends on the place of an attacker. If he/she is somewhere inside a Wide Area Network (WAN), then NAT cannot be helpful. NAT also is not widely used in IPv6 enabled networks.

Application Protocols

Email and World Wide Web (Web, 2014) are two popular applications used by most users. There are some protocols that enable applications to be used over the Internet. Some examples of these protocols are HTTP, Simple Message Transfer Protocol (SMTP) (Klensin, 2008), Internet Message Access Protocol (IMAP) (Crispin, 2003), DNS, etc. These protocols might use Secure Socket Layer (SSL) (Freier & et al., 2011) or Transport Layer Security (TLS) (Dierks & Rescorla, 2008) for security and data protection. However, if an attacker is a government who forces companies to give it access to the private keys or a company with high privilege on private keys' storage, then this information is no longer secret as it happened with NSA pervasive monitoring (Akko & Farrell, 2014).

Each of these protocols might contain sensitive information. The following sections explain these protocols in more detail.

DNS

DNS might often contain critical information. But current DNS standards are unable to provide DNS privacy. There are some research papers and works in progress (Rafiee & Meinel, 2013) that discuss a solution to this problem. However, none of the current proposed solutions are being standardized within the IETF or any other standard organization.

HTTP

HTTP transfers all data in plaintext. It is used for application layer communication over Internet. HTTP traverses over TCP/IP. This protocol (HTTP) cannot protect data from privacy attacks. To protect data, one might use HTTP over TLS (HTTPS) (Rescorla, 2000) which encrypts all the data in application layer but it does not encrypt data in network layer (node's identity). Using TLS also might not be able to protect data from pervasive monitoring. This is because it needs the use of DNS server that might be monitored by third parties. The security of DNS server also might lead to phishing attacks and privacy risks. Furthermore, certificates verification is also another place where an attack is possible on TLS. This is especially true when a server uses self-signed certificates. There is a risk of MITM attack especially for non-technical users. If the certificates are signed by CAs, there is a risk of CA databases to be accessible and monitored by unwanted people.

SMTP

SMTP is used to send an email from one Mail Transfer User (MTU)/Mail Transfer Agent (MTA) to another one. SMTP messages are sent in plaintext format. However, some other protocols like Secure Socket Layer (SSL) provide encryption for SMTP. Nevertheless, a problem with SMTP is that not all servers support protection mechanisms. So if one server supports some kind of protection mechanism but another does not, messages are then transferred in plain text which is not secure. In other words, some servers have already implemented opportunistic encryption. So, they encrypt the messages if it is possible (both server supports encryption) otherwise they switch to pain text. Therefore, an email that might contain confidential information about users, is prone to privacy attacks in sending and fetching processes. Furthermore, user adoption of client-side email encryption and signing remains extremely low. End to end encryption of webmail is hard to achieve with a seamless user interface. Secure mail infrastructures like PGP rely on the integrity of the key retrieval mechanism. Besides, the big webmail providers did not encrypt the traffic between their MTAs.

Monitoring and Control Protocols

Monitoring protocols such as Simple Network Management Protocol (SNMP) (Case, & et al., 1990) might carry critical information about resources of an enterprise or a company. This information is usually sent out in plain text without any protection. So, if an attacker can use the vulnerability of this network and bypass the firewalls or other security devices, he/she can easily eavesdrop and access this information. This information can be used later to attack a target user in this network and harm his/her privacy.

In our modern world, there are higher demands to use virtualized techniques. It is because virtualization techniques are said to increase flexibility and it is easier to add a policy dynamically. For example, many virtual machines (VMs) can be assigned to a group and a policy such as quota points or any security settings can be applied to this group. This feature (Apply policy to group) eliminates the needs of configuring each single host manually with new policy. It also does not need the hosts to be in a same domain supported by Microsoft Active Directory (AD) to apply such group policies on several host via the domain controller. In other words, the same VM configuration can be provided for different customers at once. Despite the many advantages of virtualization techniques, the orchestration of virtualized devices and services for the sake of proper operation assumes that different control messages need to be exchanged in the network: These messages might contain critical information about the network infrastructure and topology. By accessing this information, the attacker might be prone to attack a target user in this network and harm the privacy of this user.

AUTHENTICATION/AUTHORIZATION AND PRIVACY STATUS

Unauthorized access to data might lead to harm to a user's privacy. In other words, authentication and authorization protocols are keys to gain access to confidential data.

The last sections evaluated the current privacy status of a few Internet protocols. This section aims to evaluate the current authentication and authorization techniques. In other words, one must ask whether or not any of the current authentication protocols are also privacy-friendly.

Before answering this question, it is important to understand the differences between authentication and authorization. As illustrated in figure 1. (a), authentication is when a user provides his/her username and password or other authentication factor to login to a website or an application or a resource. The server checks this login information and if correct, it authenticates the user. This is usually done by assigning a session key or token to this user. This authenticated user can now access to some resources on this server, typically via a web interface. The server provides access to these resources by checking its access list to ensure whether or not this user is entitled to access resource x of this server. This is usually based upon policy and checking against an access list. This process is called authorization. In other words, this user is authorized to access resource x on the server. OAuth is one example of the authorization protocols. A username, password or a token might not itself reveal a lot of information to an attacker. But the use of this information on third party systems or correlating it to a certain server might authorize this attacker to access some confidential data and harm privacy of this user, an enterprise or even a government. In other words, this information (user ID or password) may not tell you much in themselves, but they are the key to other resources. When SSL or TLS are used to protect this access information and provide data authenticity and data confidentiality, then the protection level is tightly coupled to different factors such as self-certified certification vs. Public Certificate Authority (CA), private key protection, security of access devices and the ability of a user to protect his/her access data from prying eyes. The last three points are out of the scope of this document.

Self-certification usually disallows any third party to access the private key. This might avoid pervasive monitoring by governments but the user should be aware of key finger print so that the attacker does not have a chance to spoof the certification. On the other hand, using a public CA would provide a level of trust among users because the users' devices can already recognize such certifications that are signed and validated by a CA without any extra effort, but might allow data surveillance and harm user's privacy.

Unfortunately, end user adoption of public key technology scales poorly and has been slow to take off, except where the technology and the user have been carefully kept apart such as in mobile handsets and cable modems).

Besides, many authentication protocols carry identity in clear text – Radius being a good example. This allows third parties to observe who does what. Furthermore, many networks require authentication before access, which produces logs that can be exploited to compromise privacy.

Figure 1. a. Differences of authentication and authorization by the use of sample scenario b. Some of standard protocols (that reside in different OSI layers) involve in user requests

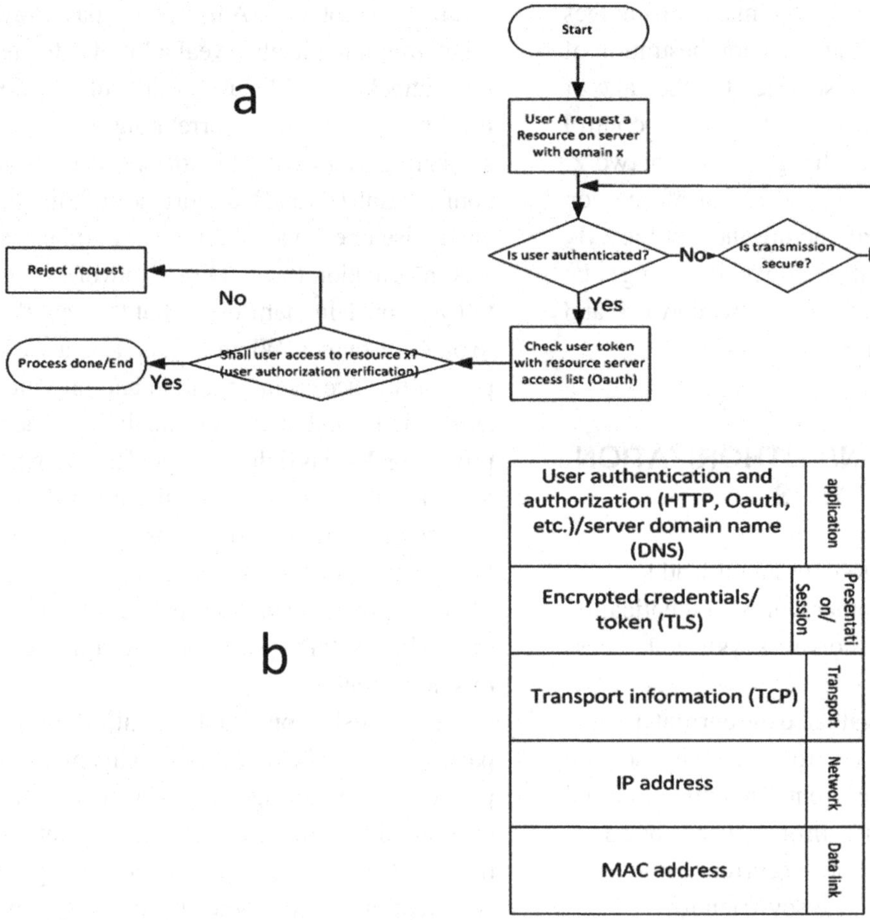

The following sections evaluate the privacy assurance of the current authentication and authorization protocols.

OAuth

OAuth (Hardt, 2012) allows a client to access some resources without sharing the resource owner's credentials. Figure 2 shows a simple example of using OAuth. Alice wants to access Bob's mathematic homework stored on a resource server. Alice asks Bob to give her his username and password to access those files. Bob stores some other files that he does not want to share with Alice. Bob adds Alice to the authorized users who can only access to mathematic homework. The resource server provides a credential to Alice that is a string token and can only be used to access mathematic homework for a semester. Alice uses that token to access Bob's mathematic homework. This example shows that this protocol also provides privacy to Bob, since it allows Bob to choose the data he wants to share with Alice. In case Alice's computer is compromised, an attacker can only access to mathematic homework but all Bob's resources.

Hardt evaluates the security and privacy of OAuth protocol in his specification. The assump-

Figure 2. OAuth in a simple example

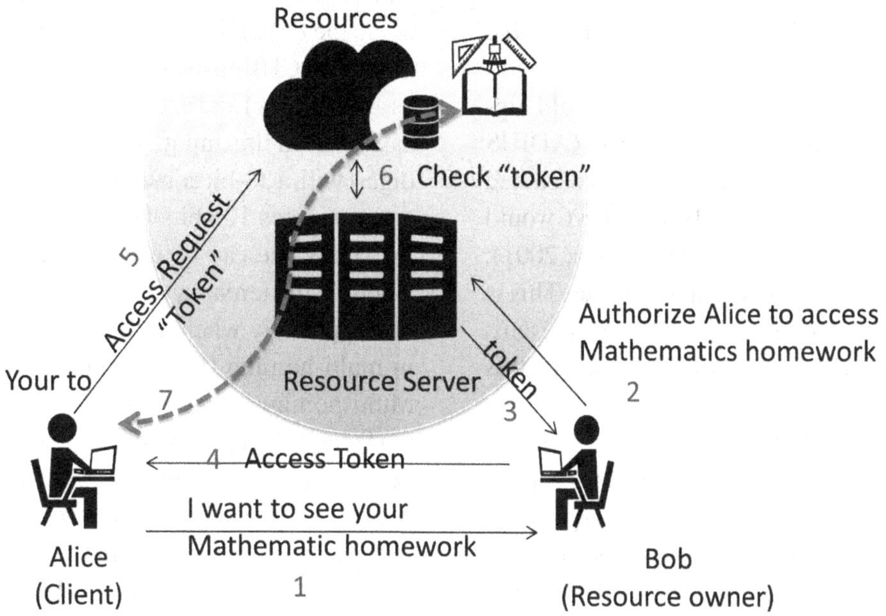

tion here is that the web application should use a mechanism to keep the client's data confidential. As explained in the last sections, usually TLS or SSL is in use to provide data confidentiality. In this case the problems are same as prior section.

Terminal Access Controller Access Control System (TACACS)

Terminal Access Controller Access-Control System (TACACS) (Finseth, 1993) is a remote authentication protocol to control dialup lines and used in older versions of UNIX. It uses UDP or TCP as the transport protocol. TACACS does not use any security mechanisms and all data are sent in plain text.

Later, Cisco enhanced this protocol to allow authentication, authorization and accounting and called it TACACS+ (Carrel, 1997). TACACS+ only uses TCP and encrypts all the traffic. Accounting is the process of measuring any relevant data for likely billing purposes – duration of a connection, amount of traffic exchanged between user and the internet, etc. This step comes after authentication and authorization steps. TACACS+ might encrypt packet data. If so, it usually uses a symmetric encryption algorithm. Encryption hides all the packet data from an attacker and protects the privacy.

Remote Authentication Dial-In User Service (RADIUS)

RADIUS (DeKok & Lior, 2013) is a client/server protocol that carries authentication and authorization information between a Network Access Server (NAS) that embeds a RADIUS client and a an access authentication server. This protocol uses a shared secret that is exchanged offline in order to authenticate the RADIUS client. The RADIUS server supports different authentication mechanisms to authenticate a user – Point-to-Point Protocol (PPP), Challenge-handshake authentication protocol (CHAP) (Simpson, 1996). This approach uses a MD5 hashing algorithm (Rivest, 1992) to protect passwords. However, MD5 is vulnerable to collision attacks (Tuner & Chen, 2011).

Since the assumption was that IPv6 would support IPsec, by default, another version of RADIUS was proposed which supports IPv6 and assumed that the mandatory support of IPsec in IPv6 would provide encryption for RADIUS (Aboba, 2001). Unfortunately this assumption is not true. This is because for deployability and complexity reasons, IPsec was not widely used in IPv6 and left this protocol alone with many security issues.

Therefore, RADIUS is not privacy friendly. This is because, firstly, it does not encrypt the packet contents and, as a result, it does not preserve data confidentiality. Secondly, an attacker can use a fake string that generates the same MD5 hash. It might allow an unauthorized access to some confidential resources. This is because MD5 hashes are collision vulnerable (Sotirov, et al., 2008).

Diameter

Diameter (Fajardo & et al., 2012) was proposed to address the issues raised by the RADIUS protocol. Some examples of these issues are scalability, reliability, security and flexibility. It is also an authentication, authorization and accounting protocol. It supports TLS/TCP and Datagram Transport Layer Security (DTLS)(Rescorla & Modadugu, 2012)/SCTP. The implementation might also support IPsec.

The privacy assurance of this protocol is tightly coupled to certification verification. In other words, it is either self-certified or it is issued by a public CA, as already mentioned in prior sections.

Host Identity Protocol (HIP)

The idea behind HIP (Moskowitz & et al., 2008) is that, to identify a host by a unique value that does not necessarily depend on IP addresses or domain names, this value might be associated with an IP address of a node. This value is usually generated using the ORCHID algorithm (Nikander & et al., 2007). ORCHID uses a unique random input (such as a public key) and executes a hash function such as SHA1 on this input. Then it concatenates this digest with a 28-bit constant prefix (2001:10::/28) and generates 128 bits Host Identity Tag (HIT).

This value can be used for authentication of a node in different systems. This is a good solution especially when nodes are highly mobile or in multi-homing (Liu & Xiao, 2007) scenarios. Multi-homing is a scenario where a node has more than one connection point (the node can therefore be attached to the same network or to different networks). The node might have different unique HIT but usually the one that is globally unique is used in different systems. When a node wants to check the uniqueness of the HIT value, it usually queries a DNS server (Nikander & Laganier, 2008). DNSSEC (Kolkman, & et al., 2012) can be used to provide integrity and authenticity of the query messages and the corresponding responses. However, DNSSEC is not designed to preserve data confidentiality (as mentioned in prior sections). To secure HIP communications, IPsec is used. IPsec uses Diffie-Hellman as one of the authentication mechanisms. However, for HIP, 384-bit Diffie-Hellman Group might be used. The 384-bit is not secure, it might be broken during run-time and it is recommended to use higher bits. But it might be used for the node with limited computational power.

When HIP relies upon IPsec, then the node's privacy is preserved during packet transfer but it might still be possible to obtain HIT values from a DNS server and harm users' privacy. In this case, a node is vulnerable to tracking attacks since it uses the same HIT value in different networks.

Extensible Authentication Protocol (EAP)

EAP (Aboba & et al., 2008) is an authentication framework that runs on data link layer protocols such as PPP or IEEE 802. It does not require an IP address for the communications. This protocol is usually in use in case IP layer connectivity is not available. It can support various authentication mechanisms – certificates, one-time passwords, public key encryption authentication. Figure 3 shows EAP communications. Alice tries to connect to a wireless network via an access point (AP). She sends her request to an AP. The AP requests Alice's identification data. Alice sends this identification data to AP. AP transmits this data to an authentication server. The authentication server verifies Alice's identity and sends the result back to AP. When authentication is successful, Alice can access to the network.

EAP provides data security by means of different mechanisms. One of the most popular mechanisms is the use of TLS. This is called EAP-TLS. This authentication method is used by different protocols. For instance dial-up, Virtual Private Network (VPN), 802.1x uses this method of authentication and still supported by some operating system such as Microsoft Windows.

RECOMMENDATIONS FOR FUTURE INTERNET ARCHITECTURES

The use of various standard protocols that work together to accomplish communications among different end nodes evolved Internet architecture. However, as explained in prior sections, the current architecture is not privacy-friendly. The aim of this section is to suggest possible options to consider privacy in Internet Protocols.

Authentication and Authorization

The following recommendations for user's authentication and authorization protocols can be applied:

- **It should not produce the same identity token to access to different systems:** Today, the use of single mechanisms such as the use of an open ID mechanism is preferable over the use of different accounts (username/password) in different systems.

Figure 3. Extensible Authentication Protocol

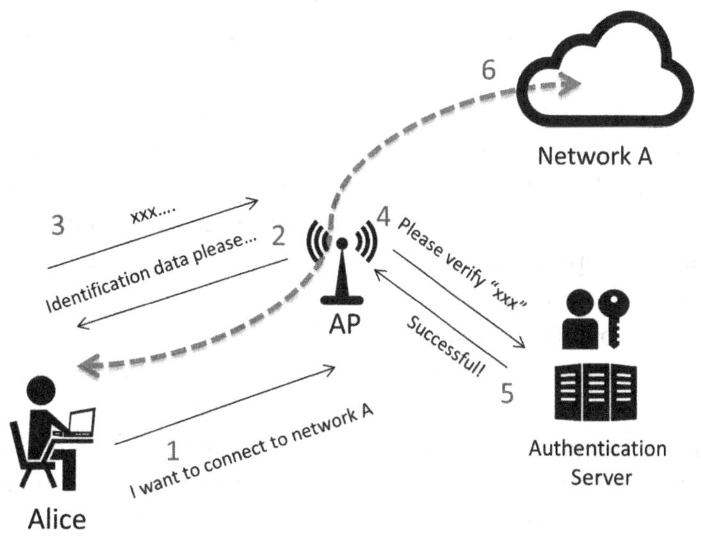

One example of Open ID mechanism is that a user can use its google account to access example.com website. On one hand, this mechanism appears to simplify the user's task by removing requirements for remembering several login/password pairs to access different systems. In other words, it federates authentication values used by variety of service providers. For example, one website might require an email address and a password. Another might require a username and a password. However, only the simplicity does not guarantee the preservation of privacy. So, any future protocols should consider both simplicity for the user and the use of changeable values over time to disallow any tracking or unauthorized access to user's data.

- **It is not recommended to use public servers to obtain the account values (especially for places that keep critical information such as financial services – banks, medical centers – hospitals, etc.):** The use of password reminder applications produced by third parties also increase the risk of unauthorized access to confidential resources and as a result harm user's privacy. It is also not recommended to use a public open ID. For example, when a user uses his x account information (from company x) to access cloud storage of another company (not company x), company x may be able to access this user information via the use of this open ID. Usually, this does not happen but the NSA scandal showed that this is doable.
- **It should support encryption:** Plain text data can be easily eavesdropped by attackers. Encryption is one of the requirements for authentication and authorization protocols.
- **It should avoid spoofing:** Spoofing in a sort of identity spoofing might allow an unauthorized user to access some resources. Spoofing can happen in different OSI layer -- IP spoofing (network layer), Identity spoofing (application layer), session ID spoofing (session layer), etc.

The authentication and authorization of a device might be different from the authentication/authorization of the device's user. Device authentication is widely used in different protocols to perform different operations such as the registration of a node in a server, updating some values on a server, peer-to-peer communications, authentication with proxy servers, authentication to control nodes, etc.

One example is where a node wants to update some records on a DNS server. Unauthorized update information on a zone file may result in compromised DNS and put the user's computer at a risk of infected computer via phishing attacks. This would allow an attacker to use this computer as an entry point for further attacks. Somewhat follows is a set of recommendations for node's authentication and authorization protocols

- It should support automation (this is not privacy-specific and applies also to security, etc.). It should be possible to perform this process (authentication and authorization) with minimal human interactions.
- It should support encryption
- It should avoid spoofing

One solution for a secure authentication and authorization is the combination of network layer security approaches with application layers. A node can generate a unique identity by the use of the following algorithm (Some steps are similar to the algorithm used to generate HIT values):

1. Generation of a public/private keys
2. Result = Concatenation of an IP address of the node with its public key
3. Digest = Execution of a hashing function on the result. By default it should be SHA256.

4. Unique Identity (UI): Taking 64 leftmost bits of the Digest

The UI should be exchanged with other nodes in a secure manner for any further communications. It can be hard copied on devices too, like what is done in Trusted Computing (TC) approaches. TC mechanisms might also consider encryption in chipsets (hardware).

For example, a node uses the Session Initiation Protocol (SIP) to establish a communication with a SIP server. There is a SIP proxy on the path to this SIP server. If there are no security approaches in use, an attacker can spoof the identity of this node (spoof one of its IP addresses) and establish a communication with the SIP server. One possible security solution would be the use of IPsec. But this would not work well in a scenario where SIP proxy exists. This is because SIP proxy breaks the communication and disallows end-to-end communication needed between client and SIP server.

Our proposed approach to provide a secure authentication is that to use UIs. As illustrated in figure 3, the UIs of SIP proxy and SIP server are stored manually in SIP server and SIP proxy server. Since the node wants to encrypt data, it sends its key to the SIP proxy and signs it with its private key (step 1, figure 4). The SIP proxy uses the same algorithm to re-generate the UI from the concatenation of this key and the node's source IP address (step 2, figure 4). It verifies the signature and when successful (step 3, figure 4), it compares the UI with the value available in its access list (step 4, figure 4). When there is a match, it sends its public key to the node and temporarily stores this node's public key in its cache (step 5, figure 3). The SIP proxy should clear the cache after some seconds. The node generates a random value and uses it as a session key. It encrypts this session key with the public key of a proxy server and signs it (step 6, figure 4). It then sends it to the SIP proxy. The SIP proxy again verifies the UI and signature. After a successful verification, SIP proxy request public key of SIP server (in case it does not already exist in its cache) (step 7, figure 4). After UI and signature verification, SIP server submits its public key (step 8, figure 4). SIP proxy encrypts client's session key with the public key of SIP server and submits it to SIP server (step 9, figure 4). Since then, SIP proxy accepts any packets from client and forwards it to SIP proxy (step 10, figure 4).

This is the same approach used by the SIP server to verify the SIP proxy. This approach provides both secure authentication and data confidentiality without the use of third parties.

This approach can be used in different mechanism such as SDN during authentication of a data plane to control plane. Therefore, the use of a secure authentication approach prevents unauthorized access to some resources that might contain user's confidential data. In other words, secure users' identification protects users' data from privacy attacks -- data disclosure, unauthorized access, etc.

Secure Transmission

Data that are exchanged across the networks need to be protected. This is because there are many intermediate devices that might have a possibility to eavesdrop these data on their way to the destination. This is why security during data transmission is one of the requirements to provide data privacy as well. In general, data protection is not possible unless we secure all routing protocols, the DNS protocol and other application layer protocols (It depends on scenario and network topology). For this data protection, we might need to encrypt data. If the keys for encryption are maintained securely, data encryption provides data confidentiality and data integrity which lead to a good data protection.

One solution is the use of tunneling approaches. However, as explained in prior sections, the key management might be a major issue. Tunnels are also prone to security attacks. The use of Certificates Authorities (CAs) might allow pervasive monitoring by governments. This is why it is not a

Figure 4. Authentication of SIP proxy server in SIP server using UI

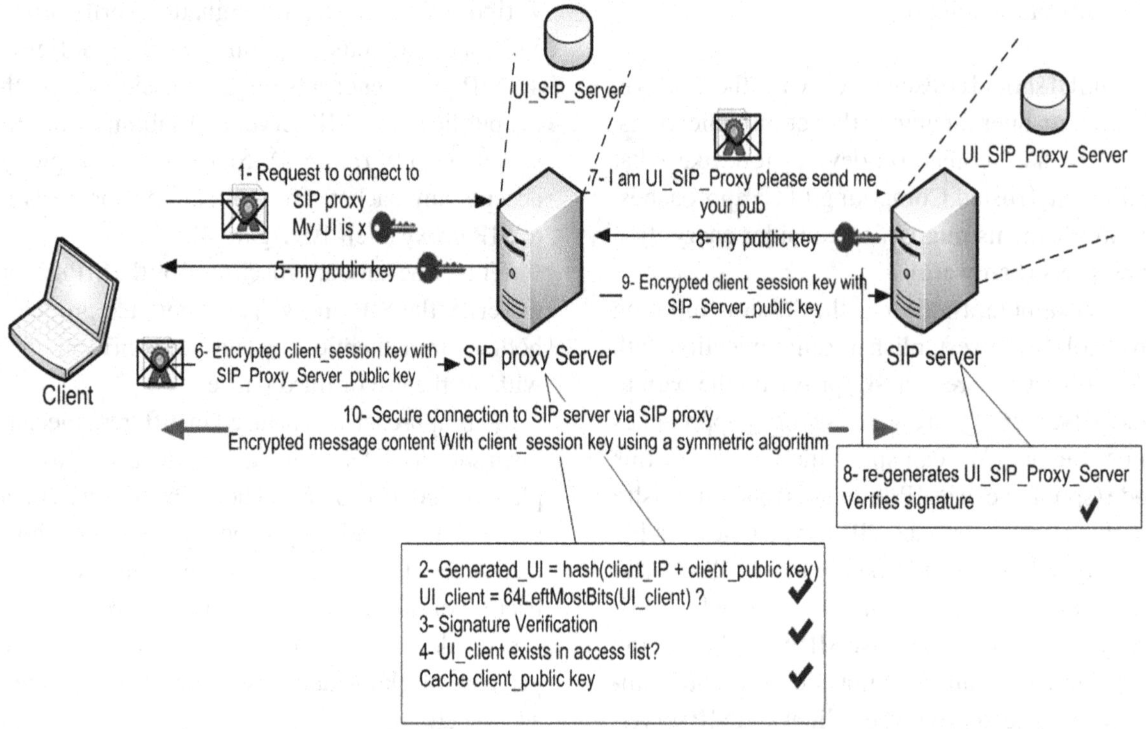

good choice for future protocols. Hardcopy of keys on the nodes might increase the likelihood of key exposure to an attacker by node compromising.

The question of what solution can be used for both automation and easy key management needs to be addressed. The easiest answer would be the hardcopy of the keys in the node and the use of so called Trusted Computing (TC) approaches. These approaches were proposed/are proposed by the Trusted Computing Group (TCG). In this approach, critical information can be encrypted in hardware. Server and clients in this approach are pre-configured with the keys and whenever the software request for the private key to sign something, the chipset generates a random key that is associated to the key value stored in hardware (the keys stored in chipset). The software which communicates with this hardware is also protected by different approaches such as detecting any misbehavior of any software on this node in order to prevent the access to this critical information. This approach is supposed to provide protection in case a node is compromised.

Randomization

The use of random labels and values instead of meaningful names help to prevent exposing device information and as a result exposing vulnerabilities of this device. It would also help protecting user's privacy since it minimizes the risk of device compromise. Randomization mechanisms can be used by protocols for different purposes. Three practical examples of randomization is in mDNS/DNSSD, Bluetooth low energy standards and IP address generation scenarios.

For considering performance or in case the nodes in the network are so dynamic (join and leave the network and might also have dynamic IP addresses), it might not be possible to encrypt all data exchanged between nodes. One example is a scenario where multicast DNS (mDNS) and DNS Discovery protocols (DNSSD) are in use. A node might use a random label to avoid an attacker to detect the detailed information about the service provider (e.g., a printer). The combination of authentication and randomization would help to protect privacy in mDNS/DNSSD designs.

If both client and server need to hide its identity, then the same pairing mechanisms used in Bluetooth can be considered. In other words, resource provider can agree on some random labels with nodes in the network and start using them. This is, of course, might not be applicable to DNSSD example scenario.

Another example is the configuration of an IP address. As explained earlier, an attacker might try to find an IP address to track a node over a network or perform further attacks against this node. To prevent this attack, a node should use pseudo random functions to generate its IID or the host part of an IP address. In IPv4, this does not really help since the address space is really small and the attacker can easily scan the network. But in IPv6, the large IID space, i.e., 2^64, is an advantage. So, by using random IID, an attacker cannot easily find a node's IP address and as a result, does not have a possibility to track this node and eavesdrop the packets exchanged between this node and other nodes. This randomization techniques should be implemented by ISPs for their users, or added to consumer products like routers,

SUMMARY

Usually, there is no agreement on the definition of privacy. It is because it might cover a wide scope and might be confused with other terms such a security. Here we explained these scopes and introduced the privacy regulations in some countries around the world.

We then tried to address many of the existing privacy problems of Internet protocols that may affect the operation of the nodes of a network. There are many standard organizations that work together to propose different specifications. Implementations of these specifications have created the current Internet architecture. This chapter introduced some of these protocols and evaluated their privacy status. It also focused on one of the most important functions of the Internet, i.e., authentication and authorization. It evaluated various authentication and authorization mechanisms by considering the possibility for pervasive monitoring and data surveillance. It also provided some recommendations to consider for future Internet Protocols.

REFERENCES

Aboba, B., Simon, D., & Eronen, P. (2008, August). *Extensible Authentication Protocol (EAP) Key Management Framework*. Retrieved from http://tools.ietf.org/html/rfc5247

Aboba, B., Zorn, G., & Mitton, D. (2001, August). *RADIUS and IPv6*. Retrieved from http://tools.ietf.org/html/rfc3162

Akko, J., & Farrel, S. (2014, April 7). *Pervasive Monitoring*. Retrieved from http://www.internet-society.org/sites/default/files/IETF%20Update-Pervasive%20Monitoring.pdf

Audet, F., & Jennings, C. (2007, January). *Network Address Translation (NAT) Behavioral requirements for Unicast UDP*. Retrieved from http://tools.ietf.org/html/rfc4787

Berger, L. (2003, January). *Generalized Multi-Protocol Label Switching (GMPLS) Signaling Functional Description*. Retrieved from https://tools.ietf.org/html/rfc3471

Carrel, D. (1997, January). *The TACACS+ Protocol - Work in Progress*. Retrieved from http://tools.ietf.org/html/draft-grant-tacacs-02

Case, J., Fedor, M., Schoffstall, M., & Davin, J. (1990, May). *A Simple Network Management Protocol (SNMP)*. Retrieved from https://tools.ietf.org/html/rfc1157

Chu, Y. H. (2013, September). *SDN Architecture and Service Trend*. Retrieved from http://event.nchc.org.tw/2013/sdn/upload/content_file/525770e4007ba.pdf

Cisco Security Advisory. (2013, August 1). *OSPF LSA Manipulation Vulnerability in Multiple Cisco Products*. Retrieved from http://tools.cisco.com/security/center/content/CiscoSecurityAdvisory/cisco-sa-20130801-lsaospf

Cooper, A., Tschofenig, H., Aboba, B., Peterson, J., Morris, J., Hansen, M., & Smith, R. (2013, July). *Privacy Considerations for Internet Protocols*. Retrieved from http://tools.ietf.org/html/rfc6973

Crispin, M. (2003, March). *Internet message access protocol - Version 4rev1*. Retrieved from http://tools.ietf.org/html/rfc3501

DeKok, A., & Lior, A. (2013, April). *Remote Authentication Dial-In User Service (RADIUS) Protocol Extensions*. Retrieved from http://tools.ietf.org/html/rfc6929

Dierks, T., & Rescorla, E. (2008, August). *The Transport Layer Security (TLS) Protocol Version 1.2*. Retrieved from http://tools.ietf.org/html/rfc5246

ETSI - I. (2012). Intelligent Transport Systems (ITS); Security; Trust and Privacy Management. *ETSI TS 102 941 V1.1.1*. Retrieved from http://www.etsi.org/deliver/etsi_ts/102900_102999/102941/01.01.01_60/ts_102941v010101p.pdf

ETSI - II. (2012). Security and privacy requirements for collaborative cross domain network monitoring. *ETSI GS INS 009 V1.1.1*. Retrieved from http://www.etsi.org/deliver/etsi_gs/INS/001_099/009/01.01.01_60/gs_ins009v010101p.pdf

European Commision. (2012, January 25). *The protection of individuals with regard to the processing of personal data and on the free movement of such data (General Data Protection Regulation)*. Retrieved from http://ec.europa.eu/justice/data-protection/document/review2012/com_2012_11_en.pdf

Fajardo, V., Arkko, J., Loughney, J., & Zorn, G. (2012, October). *Diameter Base Protocol*. Retrieved from http://tools.ietf.org/html/rfc6733

Fielding, R., & Reschke, J. (2014, June). *Hypertext Transfer Protocol (HTTP/1.1): Message Syntax and Routing*. Retrieved from http://tools.ietf.org/html/rfc7230

Finseth, C. (1993, July). *An Access Control Protocol, Sometimes Called TACACS*. Retrieved from http://tools.ietf.org/html/rfc1492

Freier, A., Karlton, P., & Kocher, P. (2011, August). *The Secure Sockets Layer (SSL) Protocol Version 3.0*. Retrieved from http://tools.ietf.org/html/rfc6101

Handbook on European Data Protection Law. (2014). Luxembourg: Publications Office of the European Union.

Hardt, D. (2012, October). *The OAuth 2.0 Authorization Framework*. Retrieved from http://tools.ietf.org/html/rfc6749

Hartman, S., & Zhang, D. (2013, March). *Analysis of OSPF Security According to the Keying and Authentication for Routing Protocols (KARP) Design Guide*. Retrieved from http://tools.ietf.org/html/rfc6863

Hirshleifer, J. (1980). Privacy: Its origin, function and future. *The Journal of Legal Studies*, *9*(4), 649–664. doi:10.1086/467659

Information Science Institute. (1981, September). *Transmission Control Protocol*. Retrieved from http://tools.ietf.org/html/rfc793

ISO. IEC 10589. (2002, November 15). *Information technology -Telecommunications and information exchange between systems — Intermediate System to Intermediate System intra-domain routeing information exchange protocol for use in conjunction with the protocol for providing the connectionless-mode network service (ISO 8473)*. Retrieved November from http://webstore.iec.ch/preview/info_isoiec10589%7Bed2.0%7Den.pdf

Kalt, C. (2000, April). *Internet Relay Chat: Server Protocol*. Retrieved from http://tools.ietf.org/html/rfc2813

Kent, S., Lynn, C., Mikkelson, J., & Seo, K. (2000). Secure Border Gateway Protocol (S-BGP)—Real World Performance and Deployment Issues. In *Proceedings of the Network and Distributed System Security Symposium (NDSS 2000)*. Retrieved from http://users.ece.cmu.edu/~adrian/731-sp04/readings/KLMS-SBGP.pdf

Kent, S., & Seo, K. (2005, December). *Security Architecture for the Internet Protocol*. Retrieved from http://tools.ietf.org/html/rfc4301

Klensin, J. (2008, October). *Simple Mail Transfer Protocol*. Retrieved from http://tools.ietf.org/html/rfc5321

Kolkman, O., Mekking, W., & Gieben, R. (2012, December). *DNSSEC Operational Practices, Version 2*. Retrieved from https://tools.ietf.org/html/rfc6781

Liu, X., & Xiao, L. (2007). A Survey of Multihoming Technology in Stub Networks: Current Research and Open Issues. *IEEE Network*, *21*(3), 32–40. doi:10.1109/MNET.2007.364256

Mockapetris, P. (1987, November). Domain names - Concepts and facilities. *RFC*. Retrieved November 1987, from http://www.ietf.org/rfc/rfc1034.txt

Mockapetris, P. (1987, November). Domain names - Implementation and specification. *RFC*. Retrieved November 1987, from http://www.ietf.org/rfc/rfc1035.txt

Moskowitz, R., Nikander, P., Jokela, P., & Henderson, T. (2008, April). *Host Identity Protocol*. Retrieved from http://tools.ietf.org/html/rfc5201

Moy, J. (1998, April). *OSPF Version 2*. Retrieved from http://tools.ietf.org/html/rfc2328

Nikander, P., & Laganier, J. (2008, April). *Host Identity Protocol (HIP) Domain Name System (DNS) Extension*. Retrieved from http://tools.ietf.org/html/rfc5205

Nikander, P., Laganier, J., & Dupont, F. (2007, April). *An IPv6 Prefix for Overlay Routable Cryptographic Hash Identifiers (ORCHID)*. Retrieved from http://tools.ietf.org/html/rfc4843

Rafiee, H., & Meinel, C. (2013). A Secure, Flexible Framework for DNS Authentication in IPv6 Autoconfiguration. In *Proceedings of IEEE Conference on Network Computing and Applications (NCA 2013)* (pp. 165 – 172). IEEE. doi:10.1109/NCA.2013.37

Rekhter, Y., Li, T., & Hares, S. (2006, January). *A Border Gateway Protocol 4 (BGP-4)*. Retrieved from http://tools.ietf.org/html/rfc4271

Rescorla, E. (2000, May). *HTTP Over TLS*. Retrieved from http://tools.ietf.org/html/rfc2818

Rescorla, E., & Modadugu, M. (2012, January). *Datagram Transport Layer Security Version 1.2*. Retrieved from http://tools.ietf.org/html/rfc6347

Rivest, R. (1992, April). *The MD5 Message-Digest Algorithm*. Retrieved from https://tools.ietf.org/html/rfc1321

Rodrigues, R. J., Wilson, P., & Schanz, S. J. (2002). The Regulatory Framework. In *The Regulation of Privacy and Data Protection in the Use of Electronic Health Information* (pp. 34–38). Washington, DC: Pan American Health Org.

Rosen, E., Viswanathan, A., & Callon, R. (2001, January). *Multiprotocol Label Switching Architecture*. Retrieved from http://tools.ietf.org/html/rfc3031

Shimanek, A., (2001). Do you Want Milk with those Cookies?: Complying with Safe Harbor Privacy Principles. *Iowa J. Corp. L., 455*, 462–463.

Shin, S., & Gu, G. (2013). Attacking Software-Defined Networks: A First Feasibility Study. *Proceedings of HotSDN'13 Conference in China*. Retrieved from http://conferences.sigcomm.org/sigcomm/2013/papers/hotsdn/p165.pdf

Simpson, W. (1994, July). *The Point-to-Point Protocol (PPP)*. Retrieved from http://tools.ietf.org/html/rfc1661

Simpson, W. (1996, August). *PPP Challenge Handshake Authentication Protocol (CHAP)*. Retrieved from http://tools.ietf.org/html/rfc1994

Sotirov, A., Stevens, M., Appelbaum, J., Lenstra, A., Molnar, D., Osvik, D. A., & Weger, B. D. (2008, December). *MD5 considered harmful today*. Retrieved from http://www.win.tue.nl/hashclash/rogue-ca/

Status of implementation of Directive 95/46 on the Protection of Individuals with regard to the Processing of Personal Data. (2013, July 16). Retrieved from http://ec.europa.eu/justice/data-protection/law/status-implementation/index_en.htm

Tuner, S., & Chen, L. (2011, March). *Updated Security Considerations for the MD5 Message-Digest and the HMAC-MD5 Algorithms*. Retrieved from https://tools.ietf.org/html/rfc6151

Vixie, P., Gudmundsson, O., Eastlake, D., III, & Wellington, B. (2000, May). Secret Key Transaction Authentication for DNS (TSIG). *RFC*. Retrieved May 2000, from http://www.ietf.org/rfc/rfc2845.txt

Web. (2014). *World Wide Web Consortium*. Retrieved from http://www.w3.org/Consortium/

Weiler, S., & Blacka, D. (2013, February). *Clarifications and Implementation Notes for DNS Security (DNSSEC)*. Retrieved from tools.ietf.org/html/rfc6840

KEY TERMS AND DEFINITIONS

Authentication: Act of verifying identity of an entity.

Authorization: act of determining whether requesting entity is allowed access to a resource.

DHCPv6: A protocol that can be used to allow a DHCP server to automatically assign an IP address to a host from a defined range of IP addresses configured for that network.

DNSSEC: An extension to DNS which secures the DNS functions and verifies the authenticity and integrity of query results from a signed zone.

Host Identity Protocol (HIP): Provides a unique identity for a node. This protocol used in scenarios such as multihoming or when a user is dynamic and mobile.

IPsec: provides access control, data authentication, integrity, and confidentiality for the data that is sent between communication nodes across IP networks.

Open Standard for Authorization (OAuth): Provides user's authorization without a need for the resource owners to share his credentials.

Privacy: The ability to choose what data to expose to others and what data to keep from others.

Standard Protocols: Agreements between international organizations concerning computer communications, networking and Internet architecture.

Section 2
Novel Networking Approaches

Chapter 4
Service-Centric Networking

David Griffin
University College London, UK

Miguel Rio
University College London, UK

Pieter Simoens
University of Ghent, Belgium

Piet Smet
University of Ghent, Belgium

Frederik Vandeputte
Alcatel-Lucent Bell NV, Belgium

Luc Vermoesen
Alcatel-Lucent Bell NV, Belgium

Dariusz Bursztynowski
Orange, Poland

Folker Schamel
Spinor, Germany

Michael Franke
Spinor, Germany

ABSTRACT

This chapter introduces a new paradigm for service centric networking. Building upon recent proposals in the area of information centric networking, a similar treatment of services – where networked software functions, rather than content, are dynamically deployed, replicated and invoked – is discussed. Service-centric networking provides the mechanisms required to deploy replicated service instances across highly distributed networked cloud infrastructures and to route client requests to the closest instance while providing more efficient network infrastructure usage, improved QoS and new business opportunities for application and service providers.

INTRODUCTION

There is an emerging trend for more demanding services to be deployed across the Internet and in the cloud. Applications such as virtual and augmented reality, vehicle telematics, self-navigating cars/drones and multi-user ultra-high-definition telepresence are envisioned beyond the social and office-based applications such as email and photo sharing applications common in today's cloud computing world. While future deployments such as 5G and all-optical networks are aiming to reduce network latency to below 5ms and increase throughput by up to 1000 times (Huawei, 2013) over both fixed and mobile networks, new techniques for efficiently deploying replicated services close to users and the means for selecting between them at request/invocation time are required. Deploying such highly demanding services and providing the network capabilities

DOI: 10.4018/978-1-4666-8371-6.ch004

to access them requires a focused approach, combining the features of service management and orchestration with dynamic service resolution and routing mechanisms leading to *Service-centric Networking*, the subject of this chapter. The focus of this chapter is how to deploy low latency, high bandwidth services on today's IP infrastructures, but as the next generation of wireless and optical networks are rolled out, service-centric networking techniques for the localisation of processing nodes and the selection of running instances will become even more crucial for supporting the vision of the tactile Internet (Fettweis, 2014).

The Internet was originally conceived as a data communications network to interconnect end-hosts: user terminals and servers. The focus was on delivering data between end points in the most efficient manner. All data was treated in the same way: as the payload of packets addressed for delivery to a specific end-point. In recent years, since the development of the world-wide web, the majority of traffic on the Internet originates from users retrieving content. The observation that many users were downloading the same content led to the development of content delivery/distribution networks (CDNs). CDNs cache content closer to the users to reduce inter-provider traffic, and improve users' quality of experience by reducing server congestion through load balancing requests over multiple content replicas. In a content-centric world, communications are no longer based around interconnecting end-points, but are concerned with *what* is to be retrieved rather than *where* it is located. CDNs achieve this by building overlays on top of the network layer but recent research in the domain of Information-Centric Networking has taken matters a stage further by routing requests for named content to caches that are dynamically maintained by the network nodes themselves, rather than having predefined locations of the content, pushed a priori based on predicted demand. Such an approach represents a basic paradigm shift for the Internet.

Although content/information centric networking has received significant attention recently, the approach, like classical CDNs, was originally designed for the delivery of non-interactive content and additional means are needed to support distributed interactive applications. Cloud computing on the other hand has been developed to deliver interactive applications and services in a scalable manner to cope with elasticity of demand for computing resources, exploiting economies of scale in multi-tenancy data centres. However today's typical cloud-based applications tend to be deployed in a centralised manner and therefore struggle to deliver the performance required by more demanding, interactive and real-time services. Furthermore, deploying cloud resources in highly distributed network locations presents a much more complex problem than those faced in individual data centres or cloud infrastructures with only a handful of geographical locations.

Service-centric networking (SCN) is a new networking architecture which aims at supporting the efficient provisioning, discovery and execution of service components distributed over the network. Today's cloud computing architectures are centralised and agnostic of wide-area network performance outside of the data centre. This makes them unfit for geographically distributed services with tight QoS constraints and high bandwidth and computation demands. SCN combines service instantiation and network routing at a fine granularity. Dynamic instantiation of services close to the consumers will naturally adapt to variations in demand. An important dimension includes lightweight interactions between layers for service placement and in-network instance selection without overburdening the latter layer with service-specific logic.

In SCN, we build upon the current trend for edge and fog computing (Cisco, 2014) and envision large numbers of service execution environments distributed throughout the Internet: in access points close to the users; co-located with routers within an ISP's network; in local data centres owned and operated by ISPs; and in traditional data centres and service farms operated by cloud and service providers. As an example, Figure 1 shows three interconnected Autonomous Systems (ASes)/Internet Service Providers (ISPs), each has one or more data centres acting as service execution environments. A service has been instantiated in two locations. From a service management and placement perspective, the orchestrator logic needs to decide in which service execution environment a service should be instantiated. Given this rich set of resources, SCN aims to optimise the location of individual service component instances according to the performance requirements of the application, the location of its users and according to the experienced demand. Replicas of service components may be provisioned according to predicted load levels and furthermore they can be instantiated on-the-fly to deal with demand elasticity. The service placement logic needs to trade-off the costs of instantiating services everywhere in terms of the quantity of data-centre resources required to host these instances against the expected performance of the intervening network which will affect the quality of experience of the users.

The service instance placement problem can be formalised as provisioning service component instantiation points, given the location and capabilities of infrastructures, varying demand patterns and the QoS requirements of the service. A key challenge of service-aware networking is the routing and load-balancing of service requests to the best instances given the existence of many different service replicas in the network that could serve the request. To support dynamic service instantiation, lightweight component-based virtualisation technology with reliable isolation properties is required, as well as service description and orchestration languages that can be used to describe an application in terms of service components and interactions.

To meet the service performance targets as well as to support resilience in case of service node failure or network or service-level congestion there will be many replicas of the same service component instance running throughout the Internet. The users, the service providers or the network itself must be able to select an appropriate one. SCN requires a service-anycast capability for resolution in the network so that service instance selection can be optimised on the grounds of proximity, network performance metrics and server load. For instance, with reference to Figure 1, User_1 will receive better network performance from selecting instance X rather than Y, however, if the execution environment hosting instance X is overloaded it may be better for User_1's requests to be resolved to instance Y, or for the SCN system to create an appropriate service instance close to the user on the fly. The user/end host should simply request the service by name, with the binding to instance X or Y being determined by the name resolution/routing system according to a combination of network and service metrics (further details are contained in the section on Service Resolution and Routing, below).

Figure 1. Service-centric networking: Network level view

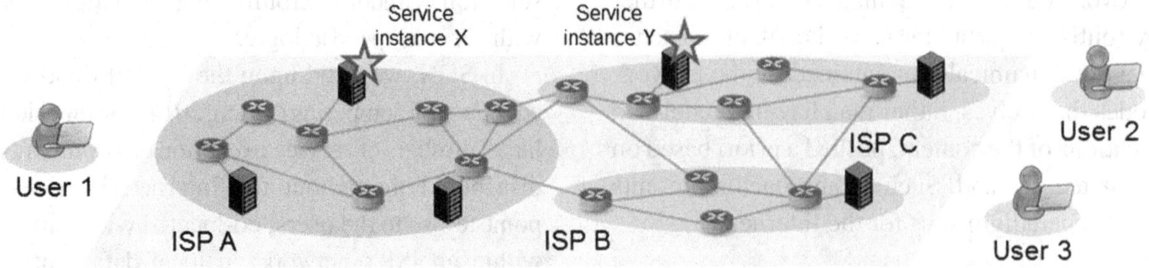

The remainder of this chapter is organised as follows: First related work and background technologies are discussed, followed by the SCN-specific requirements. The problem of service management and orchestration is introduced highlighting the necessary functionality. Then the role of the networking functions for service resolution and routing are discussed. The chapter goes on to describe one possible overall architecture being studied in the FUSION project for bringing together the necessary service and network layer capabilities for SCN operations. The practicalities of designing services for being deployed and dynamically managed in SCN are presented in the next section. Practical system deployment considerations are discussed from the perspectives of the overall business model issues, the software developer and network operator. Finally conclusions on SCN are drawn and future research directions are highlighted.

BACKGROUND

Over more than a decade, Content Delivery Networks (CDNs) have become one of the most important technologies commonly used throughout the Internet in support of scalable delivery of content including rich media, web acceleration/caching/small file delivery and large file/software delivery. CDNs cache content closer to the users to reduce traffic in interconnection links, and improve the quality of experience by providing higher downloading speed, lower delays and improve availability of content compared to what is achievable with standalone servers. To this end CDNs perform optimisations on different levels of system architecture. At the network level, they intelligently optimise the allocation of content among data centres, and route requests so as to assign clients to optimal servers. In addition, multiple content delivery mechanisms are used including such features as Web application acceleration, IP acceleration, Web application streaming, secure content delivery, large file optimisation, download manager, to mention a few (Akamai, 2014b; Conboy, 2014; Deutsche Telekom, 2014; Edgecast, 2014; Incapsula, 2014). Accordingly, a high-level functional architecture of a typical CDN consists of three main building blocks, namely content deployment (responsible for policy-based replication and caching), content delivery (including request routing and lower level content delivery mechanisms), and monitoring (providing measurement data for the purposes of two former blocks) (Buyya, Pathan, & Vakali, 2008). Other functions such as accounting are typically employed by CDNs but are omitted from this discussion as they are secondary in this context. At the heart of CDN is the request routing system, which typically uses customised Domain Name System (DNS)-based resolution to direct client requests to optimal servers in compliance with CDN provider policies. To offer advanced optimisation capabilities such as those mentioned before, CDN solutions are often being combined with network appliances to form application delivery networks (ADN). In such a setting, application delivery controllers (ADC) of ADN optimise the delivery of application traffic from/to distributed data centres at the transport level and load balance traffic within data centres, while the CDN is responsible for routing user requests to data centres hosting appropriate instances of the application.

Application delivery networks (ADN) mentioned above share many principles with CDNs, and the basic difference between them is that ADNs are able to recognise multiple applications on-the-fly and optimise their performance by using different forms of application acceleration and employing layer 4-7 switches to load balance traffic over a pool of servers located in a single data centre. In fact, while CDNs are strongly oriented towards optimal delivery to large populations of clients using CDN resources distributed in many sites, most ADNs operate locally at the level of a single data centre. The latter provides an explanation why merging both technologies becomes a natural evolutionary step for CDN providers. A simpler, yet still distributed scenario assumes Geo DNS- based resolution of client requests among multiple instances of the application with ADCs playing the role of reverse proxies, for example see (Aiscaler, 2014).

The concept of SCN builds on CDNs and ADNs which provide partial solutions to the problems targeted by SCN. In particular, SCN, accounting for service-level information, fills the gaps in network-wide service orchestration and introduces service routing to provide intersection with traffic engineering in transport network and data centres.

Information Centric Networking (ICN) has attained significant attention in recent years (Aranda & Zitterbart, 2010), (Trossen, 2011), (Sail, 2011), (Named Data Networking, 2013), (GreenICN, 2013). A dedicated research group in IRTF has been established (ICNRG, 2014). Representative ICN proposals include such designs as CCN, PSIRP/PURSUIT, DONA, Curling and NetInf, to mention a few. As noted in (Ghodsi, Shenker, Koponen, Singla, Raghavan, & Wilcox, 2011), all these architectures share three main design principles, namely use of Publish-Subscribe primitives, adoption of universal (in network) caching, and content-oriented security model tightly coupled with the naming scheme adopted by the design. The Pub/Sub communication model makes the provider and the user mutually invisible and allows them to be online independently of each other. This feature also opens the door to the use of ubiquitous caching with the aim of optimising performance and saving network resources. To allow ubiquitous caching, all ICN designs introduce content-oriented security in place of classical models based on securing the connection. For a comprehensive comparative survey of all recent ICN designs the reader is referred to (Xylomenos et al., 2013). From our perspective, an important fact about ICN is that the introduction of this paradigm by itself does not provide explicit solutions to many problems related to future services. The first explicit attempt to extend ICN from content to services (Named Function Networking, 2013) contributes to the task of sequencing the services in a service chain, but it leaves open several problems including optimal instance selection, which require more sophisticated coordination than that needed for caching of static content.

Cloud computing has been developed to deliver applications and services in a scalable manner to cope with elasticity of demand for computing resources, exploiting economies of scale in multi-tenancy data centres. Just as with CDN services in the past, cloud resources are now being deployed in local ISPs and other distributed network locations, presenting a much more complex problem than can be solved with generalised resource assignment algorithms in individual data centres or cloud infrastructures with only a handful of geographical locations. While new networking paradigms for intra-data centre communications have been developed to facilitate the distribution of data-processing intensive applications over a flexible number of computing devices within the same data centre, these techniques and technologies are limited to specific data centres and services, and have not been rolled out to the wider-area Internet. Although cloud federation has received a lot of attention in recent years the techniques have been aimed at improving scalability for cloud-based applications and they do not address the problem of fine-grained localisation of processing nodes in the network between the federated clouds. Similar conclusions apply also to the converged use of NaaS and cloud technologies despite a lot of research that has been done in this domain (Qiang, Yuhong, Vasilakos, 2012.). The latter refers in particular to related activities undertaken recently in the context of NFV (ETSI, 2013) where the joint use of network and data centre resources is key for the realisation of distributed network services.

Several distributed service management architectures have been proposed with IRMOS,

NGSON and PADIS being representative recent examples, discussed in the following paragraphs.

The goal of Interactive Real-time Multimedia Applications on Service Oriented Infrastructures (IRMOS) (Menychtas, 2010) is to enhance SLAs in a grid/cloud computing platforms with providing strict quality guarantees in the transport network. Automatic deployment and instantiation of a service using resources distributed in a network is based on an abstract description of all the execution environment requirements of the service (given in the form of Virtual Service Network, VSN), including the description of the connectivity requirements between service components and their individual QoS demands. To this end IRMOS integrates the orchestration of network resource management and allocation functions for cloud services based on VSN specification. IRMOS relies on strict QoS guarantees so it fits best to managed networks and needs adoptions for wide area Internet.

Next Generation Service Oriented Network (NGSON) (IEEE, 2011) identifies several individual architectural components and functionalities, however, restricted basically to service routing and composition. NGSON provides capabilities for service composition/orchestration which take the form of ordering the invocation of possibly multiple basic services in response to a single request. It also adopts the concept of centralised controller for network resource and QoS control which conceptually corresponds to traditional resource managers and can easily be extended to the form of an SDN controller. NGSON does not cover resource management in data centres and service placement. Extensions to NGSON should thus include service orchestration capable of allocating and load balancing among service instances through active cooperation with distributed execution environment. As of today, only the functional architecture of NGSON has been standardised, but no interface specifications are available. A proof-of-concept implementation was based on the RESTful protocol for service routing and the use of Business Process Execution Language (BPEL) notation for composite service orchestration (Lee & Kang, 2012).

PaDIS (Provider-Aided Distance Information System) (Poese at al., 2012a) is designed as an ISP-operated system to improve server selection for users' requests in the context of CDNs. PaDIS works at the level of local DNS. It intercepts DNS responses for client queries from the authoritative CDN DNS server and rewrites the CDN surrogate server address provided in the A/AAAA record with the address of the surrogate considered optimal for this query. Optimal surrogate selection by PaDIS is based on the local knowledge of ISP about network conditions and topological diversity of CDN surrogate servers learned through sniffing DNS traffic. Conceptually, PaDIS thus allows ISPs to enter the request routing loop of a CDN in order to improve delivery performance based only on server selection without explicitly changing routing in the network. This general idea of cooperation between ISPs and CDNs has subsequently been enhanced by allowing ISPs to (1) rank CDN surrogate servers pre-selected by the CDN instead of rewriting DNS responses on its own (Poese at al., 2012b) and (2) get involved in the process of allocating CDN surrogate servers by automated on-demand negotiation and deployment of new CDN surrogates based on an IaaS model (Frank et al., 2013).

One of the requirements for service-centric networking is the ability of the platform to take network state information into account for the purposes of both the orchestration and service routing. In this context we note that in addition to using raw monitoring data, service-centric networking may potentially benefit from concepts originally developed for overlay applications. A notable example of such a solution is the concept of Application Layer Traffic Optimization (ALTO) (Seedorf & Burger, 2009) which provides network information in the form of abstractions like network map and cost map based on modelling the network as a set of equivalence classes known as Provider-defined Identifier (PID) being collections of end-point addresses. Moreover, ALTO extensions to cover data centre information have also been proposed recently (Lee, Bernstein, Dhody, & Choi, 2014). Despite known proof-of-concept implementations of ALTO (Scharf et al., 2012) and a first commercial product being available (Dharwadkar, 2011), practical adoption of ALTO has been slow. Considering the successful use of (partially) similar services like Radar offered by Cedexis (Cedexis, 2014) one can expect that ALTO additionally needs extensions to multi-domain environments.

Summarising the above discussion, we conclude that while the integration of CDNs, ADNs, NGSON and other known solutions like ALTO is possible at a conceptual level, it is hard to just take existing technologies in order to achieve the goals of SCN. The most important missing parts are network-wide service orchestration and support for the implementation and propagation of network policies to allow service resolution taking account of server load, data centre resources and network conditions. The SCN approach is holistic in addressing these problems as outlined in the remainder of this chapter.

REQUIREMENTS FOR SERVICE-CENTRIC NETWORKING

In this section, the requirements for orchestrating and managing demanding interactive services and execution resources across a distributed set of heterogeneous execution environments are introduced, covering the high-level non-functional service and business requirements that impact SCN.

Service-Related Requirements

The services that could benefit from a service-centric networking infrastructure share a number of key properties and requirements that potentially have a huge impact on the overall SCN architecture.

Network Sensitivity

By network sensitivity, we imply that the functional behaviour of these services is sensitive with respect to the network bandwidth, latency and/or jitter characteristics. Placing these services too far from the end users (e.g., in distant centralised cloud environments) can result in bad QoS, eventually bad QoE, or increased service cost. This is a key necessary property for all distributed SCN architectures, since non network-sensitive services can easily be deployed on classic cloud infrastructures.

Real-Time Services

Along with the network sensitive nature of services comes the real-time nature of the services, as these envisioned services need to deliver data or a data stream within a specific deadline or at a particular rate. Real-time services will also be sensitive to factors such as computational capacity or storage resources within a data centre (DC).

User Session Longevity

We envision that services with possibly long active sessions can benefit from service-centric networks. For example, a personalised video transcoding service or game rendering service can be active for several minutes to hours. During this period, potentially large amounts of compute and networking resources may be consumed. Proper service placement, deployment and selection strategies are needed to meet these service requirements.

Resource Intensity

The combination of the above service requirements on real-time behaviour and long user sessions necessitates that demanding services must be deployed and managed very efficiently. Many of these services will have very specific resource requirements (e.g., compute-bound, memory-bound, I/O-bound, network-bound, etc.) and may rely on particular accelerators for efficient and effective operation (e.g., a 3D live rendering service typically requires a GPU). Careful selection of appropriate cloud environments and execution nodes is essential for the intended service classes.

Distributed Service Graphs

Complex services typically consist of a graph of service components that together perform complex functions. Each of these service components in a service-centric network can be deployed in one or more execution environments depending on the various interconnection and execution requirements and constraints. Such services require a more complex orchestration and service selection/routing considering the overall end-to-end performance of the service across multiple domains.

Instant On-the-Fly Deployment

Accurately predicting service demand patterns is not trivial, especially combined with the fact that services need to be deployed across a potentially large number of execution environments, resulting in a fragmented deployment of services across the Internet. In case of unanticipated load patterns, services may need to be deployed instantly to be able to serve new incoming requests with similar QoS. Secondly, in a universal service-centric networking system where tens of thousands of services can be managed, there will be a long tail of services for which pre-deployment of some instances in all locations is not cost-effective. Under these circumstances, the service-centric networking system should be able to immediately deploy new instances on-the-fly in order to handle these infrequent or unpredictable service requests. As a result, a service-oriented networking system should incorporate on-demand service placement and deployment mechanisms in addition to service selection mechanisms.

Security

Due to the dynamic management and orchestration mechanisms, security (including integrity) regarding service management and service selection are crucial. For example, a service-centric networking system should be able to guarantee that misbehaving entities cannot pretend to be other services and that requests do not arrive at the wrong service instance. Proper service authorisation and authentication mechanisms should be in place.

Business-Related Requirements

Business-related requirements can also drive and constrain service-centric networks for a number of reasons:

- First, service-centric networks must simplify service deployment without having to deal with the complexities of a highly distributed infrastructure.
- Secondly, service oriented networks should allow for ISPs to provide improved service and network QoS/QoE by leveraging their detailed network information as well as reduce their network bandwidth costs thanks to smart placement and service selection.

SERVICE LEVEL MANAGEMENT AND ORCHESTRATION

This section discusses a number of candidate high-level architectures for Management and Orchestration (MANO) for service-centric networking, followed by an enumeration of the key service management and orchestration functions. We discuss how these functions are impacted by the specific service requirements and how they can be implemented in a flexible and scalable manner in a distributed execution environment.

Challenges

The requirements outlined in the previous section impose a number of key challenges for any service-centric networking MANO architecture. We briefly elaborate on these challenges.

Scalability and Flexibility

SCN architectures need to manage large amounts of service instances of many different service types across numerous execution environments of various types. This means that on one hand, the overall SCN architecture should be able to efficiently scale with increasing amounts of services that are deployed in such architecture. On the other hand, due to the specific requirements and capabilities of the services and available infrastructures, the SCN architecture should also be able to provide enough flexibility so that the various services can be deployed efficiently on the various execution environments. In the next section, we will describe various high-level MANO architectures and discuss their effectiveness with respect to scalability and flexibility.

Heterogeneity

As previously indicated, the services of interest could have drastically different requirements with respect to resources, operations and orchestration. Similarly, in a completely distributed service-centric networking architecture, the various execution and networking environments can be quite heterogeneous in nature as well, from a resource, infrastructure and management platform point of view. More specifically, execution environments will range from standard centralised general purpose cloud environments to highly distributed, small size and specialised execution environments that are located very close to the edge or even within the home, with tight resource and management constraints.

Scalable Distributed High-Level MANO Architecture

Mapping the service-centric networking requirements as specified in the previous section to possible architectures, we see a number of candidate architectures.

- One centralised cloud, possibly including a number of distributed execution environments or zones that are all fully managed by the central cloud orchestrator.
- Collaborative or federated clouds, where each cloud environment operates completely independently but can interact with other cloud environments without one central coordinator.
- Hierarchical cloud, incorporating a global orchestrator which has a high-level view and control of multiple decentralised lower-level cloud environments. Each of these lower-level cloud environments is treated mostly as a black box with respect to the high-level orchestrator and provide their own service management and orchestration functions.

Each of these solutions has a number of advantages and disadvantages regarding scalability, level of control, multi-cloud-provider support, etc. For example, a single centralised cloud architecture has the advantage of ultimate level of visibility and control, as all services and execution nodes are under the immediate control of a centralised orchestrator who has full visibility. However, this solution is prone to scalability issues in case tens or hundreds of thousands of services must be managed across hundreds or thousands of distributed execution environments. A single centralised cloud environment also typically implies only a single-cloud-provider model, which can constrain the possible geographical deployment locations for the services.

With a completely decentralised approach, scalability can be handled more easily. However, this model implies that service providers need to register, deploy and manage their services with multiple cloud providers and in multiple locations, making the configuration and management of widely deployed services more complex.

A hierarchical architecture tries to combine the best of both worlds. In this approach, the advantages of the decentralised cloud architecture (i.e., independent MANO operations and multi-cloud-provider support) can be combined with global service orchestration and management functions. The reduced level of control can be largely mitigated using special techniques such as the concept of evaluator services as proposed in the FUSION architecture, discussed later in the chapter.

In the next sections, we focus on describing the challenges and requirements for managing demanding network-sensitive services in a hierarchical cloud architecture. Two examples of hierarchical cloud architectures are IRMOS (Menychtas, 2010) and FUSION (discussed later in this chapter), where the concept of orchestration domain and execution zones (or nodes) is introduced. Note that both approaches allow inter-domain service orchestration and management that can be modelled either as a decentralised set of clouds or as an extended form of hierarchical clouds with two or more levels.

Key Service Management and Orchestration Functions

This section discusses the role and expectations of the key service MANO functions in a service-centric network system.

Service Registration

A key service management function is the service registration that handles all registrations of new service types, provides updating with respect to their deployment parameters, and ultimately decommissioning of a particular service in the orchestration domain. Registering a new service may involve a subsequent automatic deployment of a number of service component instances within an orchestration domain, as described in a service manifest. The service manifest identifies the components of a service, the requirements for provisioning in terms of the computational requirements of the infrastructure and the network performance targets for interconnecting users to the service endpoints and between the service components forming the service graph. Service names are assigned at registration time and form part of the service manifest, with the domain orchestrator being responsible for ensuring that names are globally unique. The service manifest is of crucial importance, as a service-centric networking system needs to be able to automatically deploy, manage and interconnect service instances across a distributed set of heterogeneous execution environments. The service manifest needs to capture all necessary information regarding the service graph, its deployment and platform dependencies, lifecycle management, monitoring, automatic scaling as well as various security, business and other policies.

Service Placement

Due to the various service requirements, load patterns and heterogeneous execution environments, it is essential to find the optimal execution environments when deploying new instances of particular services. In a hierarchical cloud environment, the service placement problem can be divided in two sub-problems, namely finding an optimal execution environment for hosting the service components, and finding an optimal host within the selected execution environment for effectively deploying and running each service component, not necessarily in this order. A key requirement for this mechanism to work efficiently is that at the domain level the service placement function should have enough information to appropriately assess and rank different execution environments. To avoid scalability or even confidentiality issues, this should not require every execution environment to expose their full resource capabilities and system information to the domain level. Secondly, service requirements can be very application and hardware specific, making it extremely difficult for capturing this in a set of static requirements that need to be specified and understood by a service placement function. Thirdly, as some of the execution environments could be close to the edge, they will likely be less powerful in terms of processing and storage capabilities and therefore only have a constrained set of potentially very specific resources. These resources need to be distributed across the services in a cost-efficient manner. Key trade-offs to be made here will be QoS/QoE and profitability.

One way of assessing the suitability of an execution environment to run a specific service is to make use of an associated evaluator service that can assess and score the efficiency of deploying a service in that environment. Execution environments can apply local policies and preferences by wrapping these scores into offers that remain valid for a period of time. This technique/solution allows for very service specific requirements (potentially incorporating historical data), execution environment capabilities such as GPU support as well as execution environment specific policies to be incorporated at the expense of additional overhead in the execution environments for hosting these service evaluators and preparing the corresponding offers.

To effectively deal with environments that are resource constrained and for which there are multiple independent alternatives, the concept of auctioning has been proposed, in which orchestrators representing different services can bid for specific resources in the execution environments for their service components based on the estimated QoS/QoE their users will receive.

Service placement algorithms operate at several epochs: firstly in a static fashion for the initial service deployment and secondly in a more dynamic mode whenever there is a significant change in user demand patterns or the availability of execution environments as they are added or removed. Dynamic service scaling is discussed further in the following subsection.

Service Scaling

Service scaling goes beyond service placement. Whereas service placement mainly involves the selection of what execution environments should host a service, service scaling refers to the number of instances that should actually be deployed in each of the selected execution environments.

Instance-scaling algorithms typically balance resource usage with application performance. Upscaling the number of service instances will improve application-level performance metrics such as response delay, but incurs additional costs (energy, renting). Downscaling is needed to avoid unnecessary capacity costs when the service demand is low.

In a hierarchical architecture, service scaling can occur at the various layers, both at the domain orchestration layer as well as within each execution environment, each implementing their own scaling algorithms based on a combination of service requirements and internal scaling policies. We will refer to these scaling functions as inter-zone and intra-zone scaling, respectively. By zone we refer to a logical representation of a data centre where a service can be deployed.

Regarding intra-zone scaling, a number of options are available. A first option is to leave the intra-zone scaling decision authority to the service itself. In this case, the intra-zone scaling is completely opaque to the orchestration layers.

The advantage of this scenario is that application-specific elasticity rules can be applied without exposing Key Performance Indicators to other components. Two main drawbacks are (i) that a standardised scaling interface to the intra-zone orchestrator is needed, and (ii) that each service needs to provide and implement its own scaling mechanism.

In a second intra-zone scenario, all scaling decisions are made by the intra-zone orchestrator. Service instances report Key Performance Indicators (KPIs) to this entity, which will then automatically scale up and down, based on service and other scaling rules and policies. In case this intra-zone orchestrator cannot further upscale, it may notify the domain-level inter-zone orchestrator, which can subsequently take necessary actions.

At the domain level, the inter-zone orchestrator can implement global scaling decisions to ensure resources for a particular service are available across multiple zones. As an example there may be insufficient resources in a specific zone to meet the predicted load of anticipated user demand which require inter-zone orchestration algorithms to identify that additional service component instances should be deployed in alternative zones that meet the required user QoE for the service. Inter-zone scaling can take into account service-specific elasticity rules and policies, load pattern predictions, internal elasticity rules and policies as well as potential explicit triggers from either the lower-layer intra-zone orchestrators or even manual triggers (e.g., from a service provider to identify expected demand spikes or to modify over/under-provisioning policies). These inter-zone scaling decisions will subsequently trigger placement and corresponding deployment decisions.

Service Deployment

In a hierarchical architecture, service deployment takes place at the level of the orchestration domain and that of individual execution zones. The domain-level service deployment function involves triggering and coordinating the deployment functions at the selected execution environments to start deploying new instances within their execution environments. How the latter is implemented and enforced is up to the execution environment. This decoupling improves both scalability as well as flexibility, as each execution environment can customise and optimise its service deployment function with respect to the execution environment specifications and policies. A crucial factor here is that the service placement and scaling functions at the domain and execution environment levels need to provide all necessary service and resource deployment specifications so that the execution environment can efficiently and automatically deploy the new service component instances within the execution environment.

Service and Resource Monitoring

Capturing, aggregating and propagating state and runtime information for both resources and services is a key MANO function in a service-centric networking architecture. It provides valuable feedback information to various parties, enables real-time or longer automated or manual feedback and control loops to improve the system and its services. Monitoring functions typically incorporate at least the following set of metrics:

- Data centre or execution infrastructure related metrics
- Networking related metrics
- Service execution related metrics
- Application related metrics
- Service-oriented networking architectural related metrics

Given the potential scale of service-centric networking architectures, a crucial trade-off is how much information should be captured at the lowest layers and how much information should or could be propagated and aggregated to higher layers to keep the amount of monitoring information manageable. Security, privacy or business incentives could restrict the amount of information that can be exposed or interpreted to higher orchestration layers.

Service Resolution and Routing

The SCN routing sub-system needs to provide a new *anycast primitive* that combines network and service metrics. Names need to be converted to the best instance and the service routing system needs to be able to trade-off network quality with server quality. Whilst implementing this decision the service routing needs to try to accommodate service specific requirements to provide good quality of experience to the user at the same time that it load balances the service load amongst all the replicas. Obviously, service instance quality needs to be conveyed to the routing sub-system accurately and efficiently.

An intuitive way of implementing this sub-system of SCN, would be to retrofit the Domain Name System (DNS) with a small set of features that would enable the finding of the best closest replica of a given service. This however would have limitations on what could be achieved, namely:

- DNS is tied to a particular name space which is organised hierarchically. Different applications may want to use different name spaces, either flat (e.g., Magnet links), different hierarchies (e.g., ISBN), more expressive name spaces, randomly allocated names, full URLs, etc. Retrofitting these in DNS would only be possible by completely changing IP-level information routing and the client access protocol.
- Service Anycasting could not be retrofitted in DNS without a major overhaul. One needs a significant amount of service routing information to be propagated, including both network and service metrics. This will need a new protocol and is important to tie it to the resolution/invocation component so that a feedback cycle can be achieved.
- The only result returned by a standard DNS query for a service is a single IP address. However, a composite service could be constructed from different components executed on different servers or make use of multiple transport sessions, using different ports and possibly different transport protocols. A service-centric network will need to be able to return more complex structured results.
- DNS does not allow for clear implementation and propagation of network policies. ISPs can "hijack" DNS queries and return preferential results but this is not done in a formal way and does not allow for collaboration implementing traffic engineering policies. In addition, network providers may want to prioritise some services to some clients. A SCN control plane should have a well-designed intersection with traffic engineering and traffic prioritisation. These capabilities can be significantly increased with recent developments in software defined networking (SDN).
- The ability for services to restrict access to their services is becoming crucial in an increasing adversarial Internet. Denial of service is a top concern for the Internet ecosystem and a SCN should be able to restrict access at the edge of the network. This would enable the deployment of more secure services. Exposing IP addresses to the outside world limits this capability.
- DNS allows for very little client parameterisation when a query is issued. A SCN will enable parameters to be passed at query/invocation type where the client can indirectly control the response it receives. For example, a client might only be interested in service instances in a radius of 5ms. Another important option is for the client to request for more than one instance

and then choose which one to contact. This can be used for parallelism and resilience purposes.

Another dimension to be explored is the amount of disruption a SCN may and should cause to the Internet architecture. In particular a choice needs to be made between a clean slate architecture or an overlay solution that works over an unmodified IPv4/IPv6 Internet. Although a clean slate approach would potentially provide a slightly more efficient control plane (since the queries/request would follow a more optimal path) this is not a sufficient argument to propose a complete overhaul of the Internet fabric. Changing network layer functionality has proven incredibly difficult in the last decades. IPv6 transition is the classical example but there are lots of good ideas proposed by the research community that stumble due to the ossification of the Internet.

An overlay solution that aims to complement the Domain Name System is much easier to deploy. It will consist of software running on commodity servers which is easy to replace, update and deploy. Memory becomes much less critical allowing for a more feature-rich service-centric architecture where meta-data for each service can contain many attributes.

Given the above context the networking requirements of a Service-centric Network are as follows:

- Each service is identifiable by a globally unique name. Apart from an overall convention preventing naming clashes, each service can choose the naming scheme that it wishes.
- Service instances may have to be authenticated.
- Services are supported by the existing IPv4/IPv6 architecture where the data plane is not changed.
- A composite service may be formed of multiple service components that may be running on more than one server, in different ports and using different transport protocols.
- The service-centric network overlay needs to resolve names to locators or to directly send messages to service instances without exposing their IP addresses to the users.
- End users' clients should be able to report Quality of Experience back to the overlay and that information should be used to inform future service resolution/routing decisions taken by the overlay.
- The service overlay should provide authentication at the edge so that services can choose to only be contacted by authorised clients to mitigate denial of service attacks without unwanted traffic being propagated far into the network.
- A network provider running a service resolver/router as part of the service overlay should be able to influence the service resolution decisions according to its preferences and policies, for example according to the network costs to reach different instances of the same service.

Although the network layer of SCN could be implemented using a variety of primitives, the following messages illustrate a possible set for meeting the requirements outlined above:

1. REGISTER: This message is used to register service component instance(s) with the local service router. It is potentially authenticated to certify that the service is legitimate.
2. UNREGISTER: This message is used to unregister service instance(s) when these stop being available.
3. SERVICE_UPDATE: Message sent from the execution zone to local service router and between service routers for conveying the known service instances and their associated metrics.

4. RESOLVE: This message is issued by a user's client, or a service component in the case of a composite service. It requests the service routing/resolution system to resolve a given name to one or more network locators.
5. INVOKE: This message is also issued by a client/service component. Rather than requesting that a name is resolved to a locator, the service routing overlay forwards the service invocation request directly to the best server instance through the overlay.
6. QOE_REPORT: Report sent by the client to the local router about a particular flow
7. ROUTING_UPDATE: Message sent between service routers to establish the overlay. It is not service specific.

In the following sub-section we present an overall architecture integrating the resolution and routing functionality as discussed in this subsection with the service management and orchestration functions as presented in the preceding subsection.

FUSION ARCHITECTURE

FUSION (Future Service Oriented Networks) is an EU FP7 project developing a new networking architecture designed to support efficient provisioning, discovery and execution of service components distributed over the Internet.

The FUSION framework can be seen in Figure 2. In comparison with Figure 1, two layers are added above the routing plane to accommodate the service routing and execution planes for enabling SCN functions. Functionality is divided into 3 layers. At the lower layer IP routing forwards packets using traditional end-to-end protocols. At the upper layer the execution plane consists of all the execution zones where the service instances will run. In the middle the service router layer will forward requests from clients to the appropriate service instances.

The basic operation of the FUSION system is that orchestration domains – consisting of a potentially large number of geographically distributed execution zones – deploy services on behalf of application developers or service providers in one or more execution zones according to the expected demand by service users. This is depicted in the upper layer of Figure 2. Service routing domains, consisting of one or more service routers, are responsible for matching service requests referring to a service by serviceID to execution zones containing running instances of the requested service. This is depicted in the middle layer of Figure 2. Service routing is anycast in nature – the user simply requests a service and it is the responsibility of the service routing plane to find the "best" available instance for that request. Once a specific service instance in a specific execution zone has been selected for the user request data plane communications take place in the data forwarding plane depicted by "IP Routing" in the lower layer of Figure 2. Note that the physical data centres are depicted in the lower IP routing layer as the data plane communications will be directly established between users and service instances running in physical data centres, while execution zones – logical representations of a data centre – are shown in the upper execution plane.

FUSION Architecture Overview

The main functional entities in the FUSION architecture are depicted in Figure 3. The three main entities are the orchestrator, execution zone and service router.

The *orchestrator* manages its orchestration domain resources including execution zones and services which it manages on behalf of application developers (or service providers). The orchestrator is responsible for service management functions including service registration, server placement (selecting appropriate execution zones to execute service instances), service lifecycle management and monitoring.

Figure 2. FUSION framework

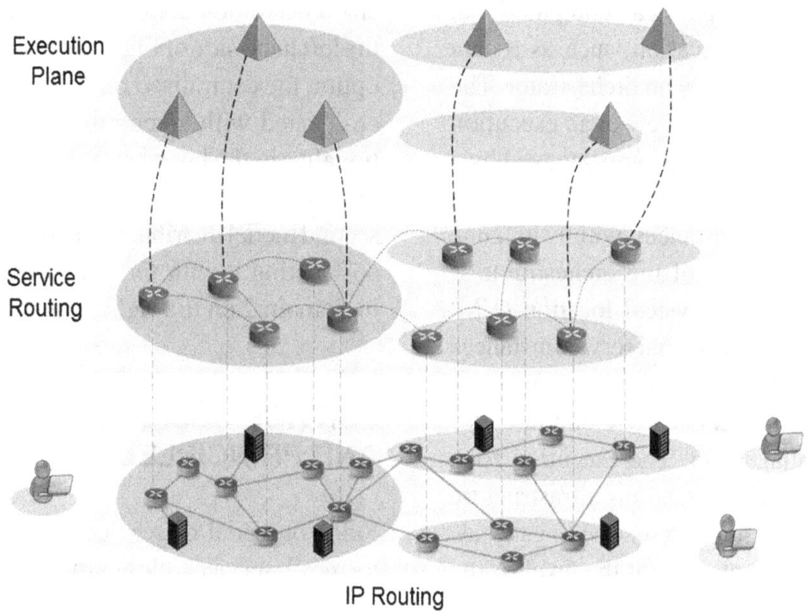

Figure 3. FUSION high level functional architecture

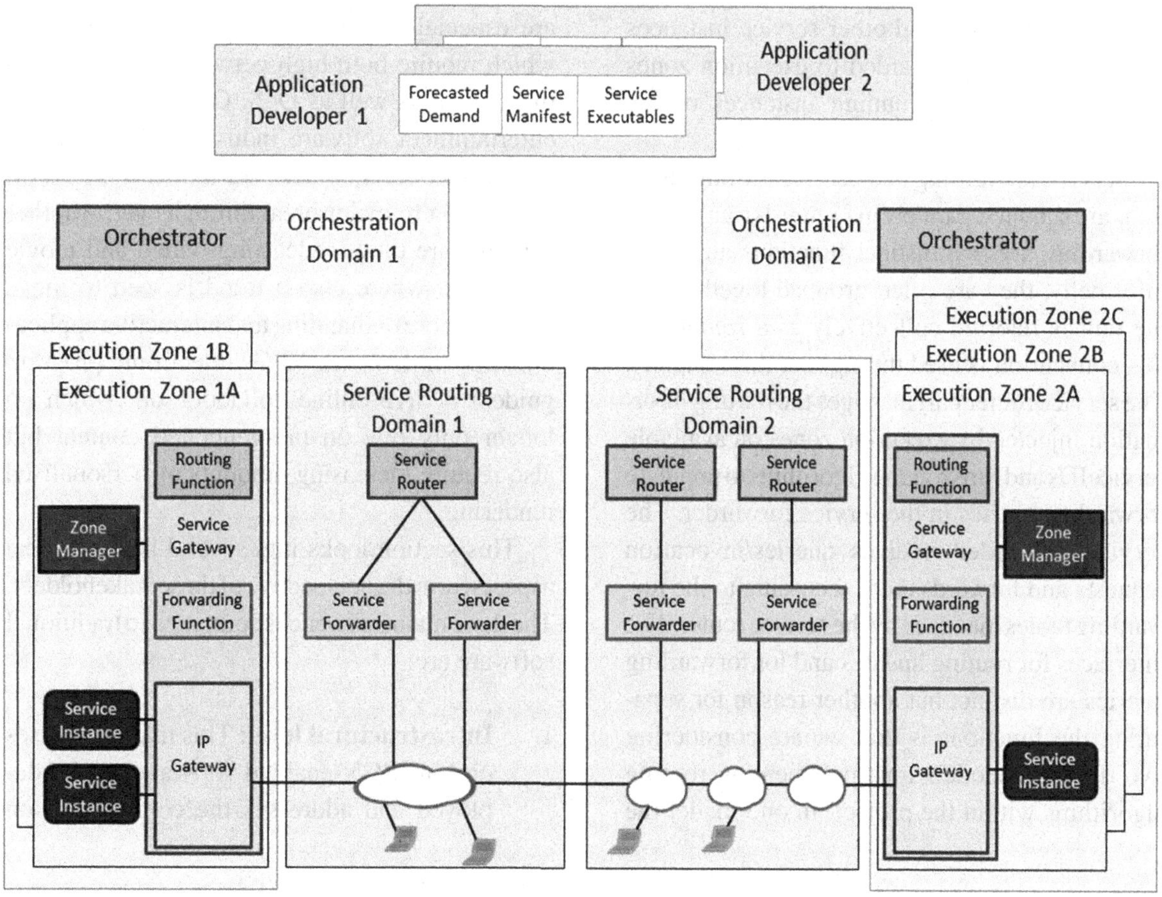

The *execution zone* is the logical representation of a collection of physical computational resources in a specific location, such as a data centre, which is managed by an orchestrator. The orchestrator has an abstract view of an execution zone and the detailed internals are managed by a *zone manager*. The zone manager is responsible for managing service instances within its zone but under the instruction of the orchestrator. It will select the specific physical location (VM, machine, rack, etc.) of individual service instances and interact with the local infrastructure management platform of the data centre/cloud node for VM lifecycle management. The execution zone interacts with the communications infrastructure of the outside world through a service gateway. The service gateway interacts at the level of the service routing and forwarding planes and IP.

The *service router* is responsible for maintaining and managing service routing information to create forwarding paths for queries/invocation requests from users and other service instances to be resolved or forwarded to execution zones containing available running instances of the specified serviceID.

Service forwarding and service routing functions are shown separately in Figure 3 (routing and forwarding are two distinct functions although, informally, they are often grouped together and the unit is referred collectively as a *router* and this convention is used throughout this chapter). The service router part manages the routing information injected by execution zones on available serviceIDs and runs routing algorithms to populate forwarding entries in the service forwarder. The service forwarder receives queries/invocation requests and forwards them according to the forwarding tables managed by the service router. The interfaces for routing updates and for forwarding queries are distinct but another reason for separating the functions is that we are considering two different models for implementing routing algorithms within the project. In one model the service routing functions are centralised within an orchestration domain as shown in domain 1 on the left hand side of Figure 3 – in this architectural option the centralised routing algorithms may be co-located with a centralised orchestrator functionality in the business model case of combined orchestration and service routing domains. The second model distributes the routing functionality, co-locating it with service forwarding as shown in domain 2 on the right hand side of Figure 3.

SERVICE DESIGN REQUIREMENTS AND PRINCIPLES

Since one goal of service-centric networking is to move services closer to the user running on distributed execution environments, interactive applications can be deployed more optimally across the network, optimising both networking and execution behaviour. These new possibilities are especially interesting for software vendors which require both high network and execution throughput as well as QoS. One example is the entertainment software industry, where similar efforts have recently been started, however without leading to major breakthroughs yet. Another example are the broadcasting, video and movie industries, where also a trend is seen to move towards more demanding and interactive applications, i.e., interactive EPGs (electronic program guides) or live online collaboration, which no longer only rely on pre-generated content but also require increasing amounts of personalised rendering.

This section looks into several key technical aspects from the perspective of these stakeholders. The three main differences compared to traditional software are:

1. **Infrastructural level:** This mainly focuses on how SCN-enabled software can be deployed and addresses the communication

interfaces of the deployed components with the network. Changes to existing software may be required. However, with appropriate application wrappers and manifests existing services could also be adapted to the SCN environment.

2. **Architectural level:** increased network throughput enables new ways of separating software modules. Traditionally, synchronisation for interactive internet applications was done by exchanging small amounts of data such as position vectors of objects and synthesising this information separately on each client, which required the client to perform its own calculations. With the new possibilities provided by SCN, especially regarding better networking performance due to service replication and optimal service selection, interactive media applications can move functionality from the client to the server, e.g., perform rendering on the server resulting in very thin client applications for the users.

In the following paragraphs, the above mentioned challenges are described in more detail.

Running Media Software on a Service-Centric Networking Infrastructure

One important task of many media software vendors is to adapt their software to service-centric networking infrastructures. Porting software to the underlying operating system environment involves packaging it in a way it can be installed, run and terminated in a standardised way, for example by packaging it in a container or virtual machine. The virtualisation of the underlying hardware is important because the strengths of software oriented networking applications is that the exact hardware and hence its specification is not known in advance. Additionally – as today's servers are running multiple virtual machines – isolation of different applications from different vendors and customers is a requirement. One possible approach is the use of Docker or similar light-weight container technology.

Classical interactive media software usually runs as a fat client or as a stand-alone application on consumer platforms which are optimised for such applications, for example Microsoft Windows. Because of the widespread usage in the consumer sector, GPU driver support for Windows is much better than for Linux. However, today's cloud infrastructures are often based on Linux for good reasons, since Linux-based platforms are well suited and proven for large-scale administration and tend to be more lightweight which makes deployment easier. The open source paradigm also allows faster incorporation of new technologies, like, for example, the integration of virtualisation functionalities in kernel modules. Last but not least, easier licensing and cost reduction play an important role for software, which will be deployed to a pool of compute resources where it is not always clear how many instances of this software are running at a given time.

For multi-media applications like entertainment software or any other software incorporating real time rendering, access to highly parallelised vector arithmetic hardware, such as GPUs is crucial. Additional research is required to solve challenges regarding efficient and light-weight GPU access without having to carry a full graphical windowing environment on different platforms. For example, in Linux environments, accessing a GPU without a full X environment is still an issue. Research and development in this area is currently a very active topic. Based on the above we envision that first services without specific hardware accelerator requirements will be deployed in SCN.

As more data centres become equipped with such hardware accelerators, (e.g., Amazon EC2 amongst other currently provide VM instances with GPU support), more demanding applications will be able to leverage SCN.

Input and Output Channels

Many applications fall into one of the following categories:

1. Standalone applications running on a device.
2. Server-client based applications with standard clients (usually a web browser).
3. Server-client based applications with proprietary clients that implement application specific logic, for example performing calculations locally before sending the results to the server or performing calculations on the data received from the server. Such clients can be considered as fat clients.
4. Server-client based applications with proprietary clients that perform application-independent functions. An example is cloud-based gaming where the client implements simple tasks such as input forwarding and video streaming the output. Such clients can be considered as thin clients.

Standalone applications and fat clients often have drawbacks with respect to mass-deployment across many different devices, which often have a wide variety of hardware and software platforms with varying capabilities and constraints. This not only results in huge porting efforts but it can also result in different QoE, as some devices may support particular features, whereas others do not. For example, mobile devices, set-top-boxes and other upcoming devices often have very restricted hardware, allowing only a subset of these applications to be deployed efficiently on these devices. Furthermore, offline software is prone to software piracy because all of the relevant data is shipped to the end user, where software is subject to possible illegal copies.

One example of a thin client model is the cloud gaming service provider Onlive, which is running its games in specialised data centres, which can be accessed by the users using custom thin client applications. Another example is Sony's PS4, which addresses the problem of the PS4 hardware not being compatible with legacy PlayStation games by integrating their services with Gaikai delivering video stream-based gaming. Another advantage of running the applications in the network is that software maintenance and upgrades are largely simplified.

This leads to a trend towards thin, general purpose clients, which mainly forward user I/O to the respective server. The question remains whether the output from the server should be performed using a higher level output description, like HTML or the X-Server protocol, or if the output is readily prepared as a video stream. While HTML or X-Server are often already considered as thin clients, these approaches have many of the disadvantages discussed above, for example requiring suitable hardware to run parts of the software on client-side, especially complex output generation operations. Service-centric networking optimises the placement and selection of service components to meet target QoS/QoE metrics for the services/users to improve the performance of client-server interactions, thereby enabling more services to be deployed in the cloud rather than as stand-alone applications. Applications can benefit from the advantages discussed with even thinner clients making this approach suitable for many advanced applications.

In addition to the above architectural changes, higher level changes and challenges have to be faced. There are already protocols for remote desktop connections (like VNC, RDP and so on), which are optimised for delivering desktop video output over large distances. The disadvantage of these technologies is that their compression algorithm is largely based on the fact that at standard graphics output on desktop PCs, only small parts of the screen change with every frame. This does not normally work as well for multimedia applications due to greater volume of picture changes to be delivered. Classical video streaming, as used for video-on-demand services, is, on the other hand, optimised for the compression of rapidly changing pictures; however, these protocols do not typically support return channels for conveying user input. Therefore a combination of desktop capturing and video streaming approaches need to be developed and possibly standardised for implementing and deploying interactive media applications. In addition, video codecs add a significant computation overhead, which often requires specialised hardware. Developers need to be able to assess the capabilities of cloud resources before deploying components that depend on specialised hardware capabilities.

Session Slots

In today's highly interactive media applications, for example entertainment software, the rendering part is primarily designed to generate output for a single user, mainly because this was the main use-case when running such software on an end-user device. Therefore today the most commonly used approach for porting such applications into the cloud is to run a separate process instance or even dedicate a VM for each user. However, this approach is obviously inefficient since multiple user sessions cannot share common data and instantiating a new session can take a significant amount of time.

For cloud computing this approach may be sufficient because scaling can be achieved by increasing the number of machines instantiated. However this does not solve the problem of longer start-up times. In service-centric networking however, the hardware at the optimal location (based on network metrics) cannot be increased at short notice. To make full use of the new possibilities introduced with service-centric networking it is therefore necessary to think about possible optimisations do not dilute the advantages achieved. Therefore a special focus is placed on the question of how to serve multiple users with a single process. A single running software instance will now be able to support multiple users which are logically distinct but share the resources allocated to that software. Rather than dealing with the implementation complexity of each service a service developer will identify the quantity of *session slots* an instance can support. This is a service-independent way of identifying the resources available to serve multiple users simultaneously. Service placement and scaling algorithms, as introduced earlier in the chapter, can manage the quantity of session slots supported by the service component instances running in a zone without being concerned with the implementation details.

SYSTEM DEPLOYMENT CONSIDERATIONS

Business Considerations

Today ISPs are confronted with an increasing multiplicity of services that have to be deployed, updated and managed. These services, with their compute and networking requirements, and the ever increasing speed of service deployment time have an important impact on ISPs' business models and business parameters such as target addressable market, revenues and total cost of ownership amongst others.

ISPs hosting real-time-aware services are confronted with choices whether to host these services using:

1. Hardware appliances on customer basis,
2. Dedicated service offerings using centralised cloud
3. A SaaS-like solution.

In the SaaS-like case applications could be offered as part of a central application store whereby services are rolled out automatically, incurring increasing costs due to hardware and software investments caused by the automation itself but carrying potential revenue increases. Each of these options implies a different compute and network architecture whereby the investments in compute platforms (hosting these services) need to be balanced against network related investments.

Along with the growing number of customer oriented applications to be supported, the fast-pacing progress in the NFV area opens a window of opportunity for ISPs and service providers to virtualise their core services and co-host these services with personalised customer services thereby optimising compute resources and operational benefits in a unified management platform.

Specifically due to the automated service deployment and service routing capabilities of SCN, ISPs are presented with a specific set of questions and trade-offs. A key question being "centralised vs. distributed" whereby investments in "compute" platforms need to be balanced against network related investments at the level of their backbone, aggregation or access networks.

The economical optimum for service deployment is service specific and should be determined by the geographical and time distribution of the services usage patterns along with its specific networking and QoS requirements and the possible statistical multiplexing benefits of running multiple services on the same infrastructure.

Developer Considerations

In the past, developers of server-client software had two, very clearly distinguishable options: Implementing logic of their service on the server or on the client side. Either choice had some implications:

1. If the required processing was highly computation intensive, placing them on the server was a good choice if not all clients (e.g., consumer PCs or mobile devices) have the required computational power.
2. If low latency was needed (especially for immediate feedback from users), a short network distance was preferable. If this collided with the first item (heavy calculations with immediate feedback needed, e.g., physics simulations in virtual worlds), as a compromise it was possible to approximate the computation on the client side with very short feedback time and overriding these results with the final and more accurate server computation results when these were available (resulting in physics objects snapping to their correct position some milliseconds after an impact occurred, for example).

Service-centric networking however enables a smoother model, where centralisation can now be traded against network performance with fine granularity. However, this raises several considerations for the service orchestration functions of placement and scaling algorithms and on the request resolution/service routing functions at service access time. These include:

1. Which computation power is available at a given execution environment? With distributed, localised execution environments it may no longer always be the case that a server with the required resources is located in a central location remote from the client.
2. Are there specific hardware requirements that must be fulfilled? For example, GPU support is a common requirement in media applications.
3. What are the costs of running a service instance at a given execution environment?
4. What are the network performance metrics from the client to the server and between service components running in a distributed fashion?

The above questions have to be answered by the orchestration logic which decides where to place a service and the service resolution/routing functions which select dynamically between running service component instances. Service providers do not necessarily have to care about the specific deployment decisions made by the orchestration functions. However, if they are aware of these questions, this can help developing the service software in a way that optimal placement can be facilitated.

ISP Considerations of Technical Aspects of System Deployment

There are several recent trends that indicate possible deployment scenarios of SCN. Of particular importance is the growing interest of ISPs in adopting virtualisation techniques in order to optimise their infrastructure and broaden business opportunities. Some ISPs have been running relatively small data centres for several years to offer services like hosting, utility computing or cloud computing to their customers (AT&T, 2014; Deutsche Telekom, 2012). Such data centres have also hosted appliances used for internal purposes of the ISP like, e.g., CGNAT and DPI. Recently, several ISPs have deployed CDN infrastructures on their own to reduce network traffic and improve QoE for their customers (CDN Planet, 2011; Telecompetitor, 2011; Deutsche Telekom, 2014), and some of them have subsequently established alliances with major CDN providers (Akamai, 2012, 2013a, 2013b, 2014a; Orange, 2012), often in order to extend their service offerings, e.g., (Bartley, 2014; Campbell, 2014). Obviously, existing data centres of the ISPs are natural candidates for the placement of CDN servers inside the ISP domain. The active role of major ISPs in multiple NFV proof-of-concepts (ETSI, 2014) confirms their growing interest in migrating their infrastructures assuming the use of virtualisation techniques for the implementation of many network functionalities. Migration strategies to be adopted by individual ISPs will of course depend on their unique preferences. However, there are good reasons to expect that options of particular interest to many ISPs will be based on aggregating current access and edge functions and collocating them together with moderate-size (mini) data centres given sufficient degree of geographical distribution of such new points-of-presence. In fact, the number of such locations in a single ISP domain may be quite large (for example, AT&T claimed to have 38 data centres around the globe with 23 of them located in North America, AT&T, 2008) which gives an ISP a lot of flexibility in configuring its virtualised infrastructure.

The above facts, together with business considerations provided previously, suggest that ISPs are important candidates able to host SCN-enabled execution zones in direct proximity of users and efficiently operate the service routing plane based on their knowledge of the network. The deployment facilities for SCN functions can be based on the mini-data centres of the ISPs meaning that dedicated large data centre infrastructures may not need to be deployed. We note also that in this scenario, service routers of a given ISP can additionally route requests to external data centres not hosted by the ISP. Under these assumptions, the details of deployment scenarios for the service routing plane in a given ISP domain may depend on specific requirements of future services with regard to delays of the resolution process. A preferred option is to have a central service router (or cluster of routers) handling all queries in a given ISP domain. However, given stringent requirements for delays and using similar arguments as those provided in (Poese at al., 2012b) regarding the deployment of Content-aware Traffic Engineering (CaTE) resolvers, the ISP can decide to distribute service routers among its points-of-presence. Such distributed service routers still could constitute a logically centralised entity, i.e. there would be no forwarding of messages between them. Yet, we admit that explicit use of forwarding capability of service routers would be justified in case of attaching technologically closed subdomains such as the Evolved Packet Core (EPC) part of the LTE (Long-term Evolution) architecture. The latter option fits well scenarios for large ISPs operating both fixed and mobile domains.

CONCLUSION AND FUTURE RESEARCH DIRECTIONS

Today's centralised cloud infrastructure does not provide the required flexibility for fine-grained deployment of real-time, interactive applications. In this chapter we presented a novel service-centric networking paradigm that aims to optimise bandwidth and response time of such services by combining advanced service placement, replication and in-network selection at fine granularity. We described several aspects of the architecture; the orchestration, service routing, service design and service deployment. For each aspect we listed the building blocks, component interactions and considerations for future development.

Users will benefit from the bandwidth and response time optimisation potential of balancing service loads at the network level. Moreover, the suggested anycast routing and late binding network primitives increase resilience to congestion and failures as service requests are forwarded to geographically distributed instances at run-time.

Software service providers and software vendors face new challenges but also new opportunities by service-centric networking infrastructures. The main challenge is to port their software to these new deployment platforms, which often requires not only to port to different operating systems and support interaction with the network (infrastructural changes), but also to change the distribution of application components between servers and clients (architectural changes). A main opportunity for software service providers and software vendors is access to a service-centric infrastructure (formed by orchestration, placement and scaling algorithms, service replication and dynamic instance selection on a combination of server and network metrics) which uses resources much more efficiently provides a much higher QoS to the end user.

ISPs will no longer serve as "dumb pipe" providers to over-the-top services, but may directly offer service hosting capacity with additional advantages like flexibility, geolocality and low-latency access compared to today's cloud providers. As service-oriented-networking enables on-demand deployment, scaling and load balancing, ISPs can lower their costs for service operation and maintenance while guaranteeing network and execution platform performance. In turn, this will lower the barrier for smaller application developers to roll out advanced services with tight networking constraints. Application developers will be able to describe complex deployment constraints including dynamic aspects.

The service routing plane goes hand in hand with the development of a novel service orchestration layer. Appropriate service placement and scaling mechanics must take into account both short-term (current demand) and long-term (cost, policy) metrics. Given the heterogeneity and stringent requirements of the targeted services, traditional techniques used in centralised clouds must be augmented with novel capabilities like just-in-time deployment and provisioning (even triggered at service-request time). Service placement within a zone must exploit appropriate accelerators (GPUs, encoders, etc.) and efficiently share sources and resources (stored 3D objects, textures, decoded video frames, GPU buffers, transcoding function, subtitling service, etc.)

To realise this new service-centric networking paradigm, many research challenges lie ahead. Future work includes detailing the service routing plane to enable routing based on a number of metrics including network characteristics, server load and operational costs for a multitude of services. The forwarding tables are managed by network components to be able to redirect requests to the best instances based on changing server load and network characteristics. Selection agility is required, as server and network characteristics may rapidly change over time and space. A major research topic is how the in-network selection can quickly adapt to these changing conditions. Here we must find a trade-off between frequent monitoring to allow accurate predictions and the bandwidth which this background traffic consumes. A further consideration is how routing across multiple service routing domains is achieved, considering the trade-off between the granularity of announcements of the availability and load of service instances/execution zones versus the overhead and complexity of maintaining large amounts of state information in service routers. Another avenue of future research is the development of on-demand service deployment. Service management functions can detect the need for additional service instances to be deployed or for instances to be migrated between execution zones. At the domain level, orchestrators might wish to sub-contract execution zones of other domains. Developing an inter-domain orchestration protocol, considering the complexities of dynamic service placement and scaling is one of the research challenges that is still open. Finally, the requirements and designs must be validated in targeted test cases and large-scale prototypes.

REFERENCES

Aiscaler. (2014). *Product overview*. Retrieved from http://aiscaler.com/product-overview#ADN

Akamai. (2012). *Akamai and AT&T Forge Global Strategic Alliance to Provide Content Delivery Network Solutions*. Retrieved from http://www.akamai.com/html/about/press/releases/2012/press_120612.html

Akamai. (2013a). *KT and Akamai Expand Strategic Partnership*. Retrieved from http://www.akamai.com/html/about/press/releases/2013/press_032713.html

Akamai. (2013b). *Swisscom and Akamai Enter Into a Strategic Partnership*. Retrieved from http://www.akamai.com/html/about/press/releases/2013/press_031413.html

Akamai. (2014a). *Akamai and Telefonica Enter into Global Content Delivery Alliance*. Retrieved from http://www.akamai.com/html/about/press/releases/2014/press-032514.html

Akamai. (2014b). *Web Application Accelerator*. Retrieved from http://www.akamai.com/html/solutions/web_application_accelerator.html

Aranda Gutiérrez, P., & Zitterbart, M. (Eds.). (2010). Final Architectural Framework. 4WARD. In *Architecture and Design for the Future Internet FP7-ICT-2007-1-216041-4WARD Deliverable D-2.3.1*. Retrieved from http://www.4ward-project.eu/

AT&T. (2014). *Products & services*. Retrieved from http://www.business.att.com/enterprise/business-solutions/

Bartley, T. (2014). *Orange is Glad they Chose Akamai for Live Video & Events*. Retrieved from https://blogs.akamai.com/2014/06/orange-is-glad-they-chose-akamai-for-live-video-events.html?utm_source=feedburner&utm_medium=feed&utm_campaign=Feed%3A+TheAkamaiBlog+%28The+Akamai+Blog%29

Buyya, R., Pathan, M., & Vakali, A. (Eds.). (2008). *Content Delivery Networks*. Berlin: Springer-Verlang. doi:10.1007/978-3-540-77887-5

Campbell, T. (2014). *Orange: "OTT services bring new revenue growth opportunities"*. Retrieved from http://www.iptv-news.com/2014/06/orange-ott-services-bring-new-revenue-growth-opportunities/

Cedexis. (2014). *Cedexis Radar*. Retrieved from http://www.cedexis.com/radar/

Cisco. (2014). *Cisco Technology Radar Trends*. Retrieved from http://www.cisco.com/c/dam/en/us/solutions/collateral/trends/tech-radar/tech-radar-trends-infographics.pdf

Conboy, C. (2014). *Front End Optimization for Developers*. Retrieved from https://developer.akamai.com/stuff/Optimization/Front_End_Optimization.html

Deutsche Telekom. (2012). *Strategic partnership for Cloud Computing: T-Systems to offer customers VMware vCloud Datacenter Services*. Retrieved from http://www.telekom.com/media/enterprise-solutions/129772

Deutsche Telekom. (2014). *CDN solution*. Retrieved from http://www.telekom-icss.com/cdnsolution

Dharwadkar, P. (2011). *Network Positioning System, Cisco on-line presentation*. Retrieved from http://www.ausnog.net/sites/default/files/ausnog-05/presentations/ausnog-05-d02p01-pranav-dharwdkar-cisco.pdf

Edgecast. (2014). *Application delivery network*. Retrieved from http://www.edgecast.com/services/adn/

ETSI. (2013). *Network Function Virtualisation: Architectural Framework. ETSI GS NFV 002, V1.1.1*. Sophia Antipolis, France: ETSI.

ETSI NFV Wiki. (2014). *Ongoing PoCs*. Retrieved from http://nfvwiki.etsi.org/index.php?title=Ongoing_PoCs

Fettweis, G. P. (2014). The Tactile Internet: Applications and Challenges. *IEEE Vehicular Technology Magazine*, *9*(1), 64–70. doi:10.1109/MVT.2013.2295069

Frank, B., Poese, I., Lin, Y., Smaragdakis, G., Feldmann, A., Maggs, B., & Weber, R. et al. (2013). Pushing CDN-ISP Collaboration to the Limit. *SIGCOMM Computer Communications Review*, *43*(3), 34–44. doi:10.1145/2500098.2500103

Ghodsi, A., Shenker, S., Koponen, T., Singla, A., Raghavan, B., & Wilcox, J. (2011). Information-centric networking: seeing the forest for the trees. In *Proceedings of the 10th ACM Workshop on Hot Topics in Networks (HotNets-X)* (pp. 1-6). New York: ACM. doi:10.1145/2070562.2070563

Green, I. C. N. (2013). *Architecture and Applications of Green Information Centric Networking*. Retrieved from http://www.greenicn.org/

Huawei. (2013). *5G: A Technology Vision*. Retrieved from http://www.huawei.com/5gwhitepaper/

ICNRG. (2014). *Information-Centric Networking Research Group (ICNRG)*. Retrieved from https://irtf.org/icnrg

IEEE. (2011). IEEE Standard for the Functional Architecture of Next Generation Service Overlay Networks. In *IEEE Std. 1903-2011*. New York, NY: IEEE.

Incapsula. (2014). *Application delivery from the cloud*. Retrieved from http://www.incapsula.com/cloud-based-application-delivery.html

Lee, S., & Kang, S. (2012). NGSON: Features, state of the art, and realization. *IEEE Communications Magazine*, *50*(1), 54–61. doi:10.1109/MCOM.2012.6122533

Lee, Y., Bernstein, G., Dhody, D., & Choi, T. (2014). ALTO Extensions for Collecting Data Center Resource Information. In IETF draft-lee-alto-ext-dc-resource-03.

Limelight. (2014). *Orchestrate performance*. Retrieved from http://www.limelight.com/services/orchestrate-performance.html

Menychtas, A. (Ed.). (2010). Updated Final version of IRMOS Overall Architecture. In *Interactive Realtime Multimedia Applications on Service Oriented Infrastructures Deliverable D3.1.4*. Retrieved from http://www.irmosproject.eu/Files/IRMOS_WP3_D3_1_4_NTUA_v1_0.pdf

Named Data Networking. (2013). *What is NDN?* Retrieved from http://named-data.net/2013/07/03/what-is-ndn/

Named Function Networking. (2013). Retrieved from http://named-function.net

Orange. (2012). *Orange and Akamai form Content Delivery Strategic Alliance*. Retrieved from http://www.orange.com/en/press/press-releases/press-releases-2012/Orange-and-Akamai-form-Content-Delivery-Strategic-Alliance

CDN Planet. (2011). *Telefonica*. Retrieved from http://www.cdnplanet.com/cdns/telefonica/

Poese, I., Frank, B., Ager, B., Smaragdakis, G., Uhlig, S., & Feldmann, A. (2012). Improving Content Delivery with PaDIS. *IEEE Internet Computing*, *16*(3), 46–52. doi:10.1109/MIC.2011.105

Poese, I., Frank, B., Smaragdakis, G., Uhlig, S., & Feldmann, A. (2012). Enabling content-aware traffic engineering. *SIGCOMM Computer Communications Review*, *42*(5), 21–28. doi:10.1145/2378956.2378960

Qiang, D., Yuhong, Y., & Vasilakos, A. V. (2012). A Survey on Service-Oriented Network Virtualization Toward Convergence of Networking and Cloud Computing. *IEEE eTransactions on Network and Service Management*, *9*(4), 373–392. doi:10.1109/TNSM.2012.113012.120310

SAIL - Scalable and Adaptive Internet Solutions. (2011). *Network of Information*. Retrieved from http://www.sail-project.eu/about-sail/netinf/

Scharf, M., Voith, T., Roome, W., Gaglianello, B., Steiner, M., Hilt, V., & Gurbani, V. K. (2012). Monitoring and Abstraction for Networked Clouds. In *Proceedings of the 16th International Conference on Intelligence in Next Generation Networks (ICIN)* (pp. 80-85). Berlin: IEEE.

Seedorf, J., & Burger, E. (2009). Application Layer Traffic Optimization (ALTO) Problem Statement. In IETF RFC 5693.

Telecompetitor. (2011). *AT&T Intros New Cloud Based CDN Services*. Retrieved from http://www.telecompetitor.com/att-intros-new-cloud-based-cdn-services/

Trossen, D. (Ed.). (2011). Conceptual Architecture: Principles, Patterns and Sub-components Descriptions. In *Publish Subscribe Internet Technology FP7-INFSO-ICT-257217 Deliverable D2.2*. Retrieved from http://www.fp7-pursuit.eu/PursuitWeb/

Xylomenos, G., Ververidis, C., Siris, V., Fotiou, N., Tsilopoulos, C., Vasilakos, X., & Polyzos, G. et al. (2013). A Survey of Information-Centric Networking Research. *IEEE Communications Surveys and Tutorials*, *16*(2), 1024–1049. doi:10.1109/SURV.2013.070813.00063

KEY TERMS AND DEFINITIONS

Evaluator Service: the computational entity running in an execution zone that is able to score and rate the execution zone and the execution points within that execution zone on various aspects of the service manifest – for example availability of specialised hardware, network and computational metrics for QoS estimation, the performance measured to nearby service instances.

Execution Point: the specific physical or virtual environment in which a service instance is deployed within an execution zone.

Execution Zone: a logical representation of a collection of physical computational resources in a specific location such as a data centre.

Orchestration Domain: an orchestration domain consists of an orchestration entity and one or more execution zones where the orchestrator may deploy and execute service instances. An orchestration domain may own the computing resources forming the execution zone or it may contract resources from a third party, e.g. a public cloud provider.

Service Instance: A single instantiation of an atomic or composite service running in an execution zone and identified by a service identifier. There will usually be multiple instances of the same service running in the same execution zone and across many execution zones, all identified by the same service identifier.

Service Orchestrator: the entity responsible for service management functions including service registration, server placement, service lifecycle management and monitoring.

Service Placement: the mechanism for selecting appropriate execution zones to instantiate service instances.

Service Resolution and Routing: the system responsible for maintaining and managing service routing information to create forwarding paths for queries/invocation requests from users and other service instances to be resolved or forwarded to execution zones containing available running instances of the specified service.

Service-Centric Networking: a new networking architecture which aims at supporting the efficient provisioning, discovery and execution of service components distributed over the Internet combining network-level and service-level information.

Session Slot: a service and application independent metric identifying the number of simultaneous sessions that can be handled by a specific service instance or group of instances in an execution zone.

APPENDIX: ACRONYMS

5G: Fifth Generation
ADC: Application Delivery Controller
ADN: Application Delivery Network
ALTO: Application Layer Traffic Optimization
AS: Autonomous System
BPEL: Business Process Execution Language
CCN: Content Centric Network
CDN: Content Distribution Network
CGN: Carrier Grade NAT
DNS: Domain Name System
DPI: Deep Packet Inspection
EC2 (Amazon): Elastic Compute Cloud
EPC: Evolved Packet Core
EPG: Electronic Program Guide
FUSION: Future Service Oriented Networks
GPU: Graphics Processing Unit
ICN: Information Centric Networking
IMS: IP Multimedia Subsystem
I/O: Input/Output
IRMOS: Interactive Real-time Multimedia Applications on Service Oriented Infrastructures
IRTF: Internet Research Task Force
ISP: Internet Service Provider
LAN: Local Area Network
LTE: Long Term Evolution
MANO: Management and Orchestration
NaaS: Network as a Service
NAT: Network Address Translation
NFV: Network Function Virtualisation
NGSON: Next Generation Service Oriented Network
PaDIS: Provider-Aided Distance Information System
PID: Provider-defined Identifier
QoE: Quality of Experience
QoS: Quality of Service
RDP: Remote Desktop Protocol
SaaS: Software as a Service
SCN: Service-centric Networking
SDN: Software Defined Networking
ServiceID: Service Identifier
SLA: Service Level Agreement
VM: Virtual Machine
VNC: Virtual Network Computing

Chapter 5
Power-Aware Networking

Mingui Zhang
Huawei Technologies, China

Hongfang Yu
University of Electronic Science and Technology of China (UESTC), China

ABSTRACT

Energy consumption of networking infrastructures is growing fast due to the exponential growth of data traffic and the deployment of increasingly powerful equipment. Besides operational costs and environmental impacts, the ever-increasing energy consumption has become a limiting factor to long-term growth of network infrastructures. Operators, vendors and researchers have started to look beyond a single router or line card for network-wide solutions towards energy proportionality. Therefore, Power Aware Networking (PANET) has been proposed to improve network energy efficiency. A PANET-enabled network assumes that only a subset of devices will be involved in traffic forwarding when the network is lightly loaded, so as to improve global energy savings. PANET is introduced in this chapter. Promising solutions for PANET are also exposed. PANET features are also analyzed. The chapter also discusses the challenges and future work that needs to be done.

1. INTRODUCTION

Energy consumption of networking infrastructures is growing fast due to the exponential growth of data traffic and the deployment of increasingly powerful equipment. There are emerging needs for power-aware routing and traffic engineering (TE), which adapt routing paths to traffic load in order to reduce energy consumption network-wide. Today's Internet Service Provider (ISP) networks have redundant routers and links, over-provisioned link capacity, and sometimes enforce load balancing-based traffic engineering policies. As a result, routers and links operate at full capacity all the time with low average usage, typically less than 40% of link utilization (Guichard, Faucheur, & Vasseur, 2005). This practice makes networks resilient to traffic spikes and component failures, but also leaves networks far from being energy-efficient.

Power-aware routing and traffic engineering have been proposed to improve the energy efficiency of networks, for example, by aggregating traffic onto a subset of links and putting other

DOI: 10.4018/978-1-4666-8371-6.ch005

links with no traffic into sleep. Observations have shown that line cards are a significant source of router's power consumption, accounting for 40% - 70% of total power consumption (Cisco, 2009). Most of the energy is consumed even if the router is in standby state, and forwarding packets at full speed only increases the energy consumption by a small percentage. This implies that being able to put links into sleep mode can potentially save a lot of energy. Designing practical protocols, however, has been challenging, because making routing protocols power-aware brings significant changes to the routing system and the entire network: it implies dramatic changes in hardware support, protocol design, network monitoring, and operational practices. These issues often depend on the specific network environments.

The Power Aware Networking (PANET) initiative has been proposed to investigate how network energy efficiency can be improved. The idea of PANET is that forwarding path computation can take into account the energy information for the sake of optimized, energy-efficient, network resource usage. For example, the design of a PANET-enabled network may assume that only a subset of devices will be involved in traffic forwarding when the network is lightly loaded. Those devices that are not involved in traffic forwarding operations can thus enter sleep state and save power accordingly, so that important energy savings can be achieved.

The chapter is organized as follows: Section 2 describes several PANET use cases. Section 3 presents the most representative feasibility studies of PANET conducted by the academic and industry, and which aim at addressing energy efficiency in networking infrastructures. Section 4 presents a set of requirements, and challenges for building a PANET-enabled network. Section 5 introduces PANET effort within Standards Developing Organizations (SDOs), such as the IETF EMAN WG (Internet Engineering Task Force Energy MANagement Working Group) and GAL (Green Abstraction Layer standard) of ETSI (European Telecommunications Standards Institute). Section 6 suggests some future work.

2. USE CASES

This section investigates PANET use cases which cover both backbone and data center networks. As for the energy efficiency of backbone networks, only intra-domain use cases are considered. Trying to be energy efficient at the inter-domain scale seems technically feasible, but it can easily end up with lack of business motivation. Inter-domain use cases are left for future study.

2.1. Power Awareness in Backbone Networks

The IETF EMAN WG focuses on the energy management of networking devices. For example, networking devices following the specification of the EMAN MIB (Management Information Base) can report their power states; the energy management of the network can therefore make use of these states. However, there is a gap on how to make use of this kind of data to achieve energy efficient networks. With a power control plane, it becomes possible to make use of these measurements and power control ability to achieve the energy efficiency of a whole network. This section lists several use cases for backbone networks.

For example, the bootstrapping time of a router may take several minutes and the stabilization of it (acquisition of the data to populate the topology database, for example) may take much longer. It is unrealistic to switch off and on a whole node in backbone networks frequently to achieve energy efficiency, so this section only investigates the cases in which links (i.e., links' attached components) are shut down or put into sleeping state for energy conservation purposes.

2.1.1. Sleeping Links

The power draw on line-cards occupies a great portion in the total power consumption of a whole routing system. For high-end routers, this portion may be higher than 50% (M. Zhang, Yi, Liu, & B. Zhang, 2010, pp. 20-30).

Network devices and their processing capacity are provisioned for worst cases such as traffic burst and busy hours. Most of the time, many networks are lightly loaded. Unfortunately, the power consumption of network devices is not proportional to their traffic load. An extreme case is that even if there is no load, there is still considerable base power consumption. Unlike PCs which can be shut down or enter power saving modes (such as sleeping), network devices are powered on and running even when there is no load. This reality means that the network is wasting lots of power.

The conception that "a link is put into sleep state" is frequently mentioned in various technical documents. In this chapter, this conception is formalized as follows. The coupled end-points (such as interfaces, network process units (NPU) or the entire line card) attached to an idle link enter the sleeping mode to save energy. Similarly, the wake up of a link (done by endpoint) also means the wake up of those coupled end-points. Traffic Engineering is used to create the opportunity for more links to become idle. This process can be automated through the control plane. Take Fig.1 as an example: suppose R1, R2, R3 and R4 are sending traffic to R3, R4, R1 and R2 respectively. In Fig.1 (a), paths R1-R2-R3, R2-R3-R4, R3-R4-R1 and R4-R1-R2 are being used. All links are active. In Fig.1 (b), paths R1-R2-R3, R2-R3-R4, R3-R2-R1 and R4-R3-R2 are being used. Link R1-R4 is idle, therefore it can be put into sleeping state to save energy.

Different from traditional Traffic Engineering techniques which aim to balance traffic load around the whole network to avoid hot spots, green Traffic Engineering aims at creating more idle links which can be put into sleeping state. However, green Traffic Engineering should not achieve energy conservation at the expense of possibly degrading the network performance. It is recommended that QoS metrics, such as availability, throughput, delay and loss, should be taken into consideration as constraints for green

Figure 1. Aggregate traffic to create opportunities for link sleeping

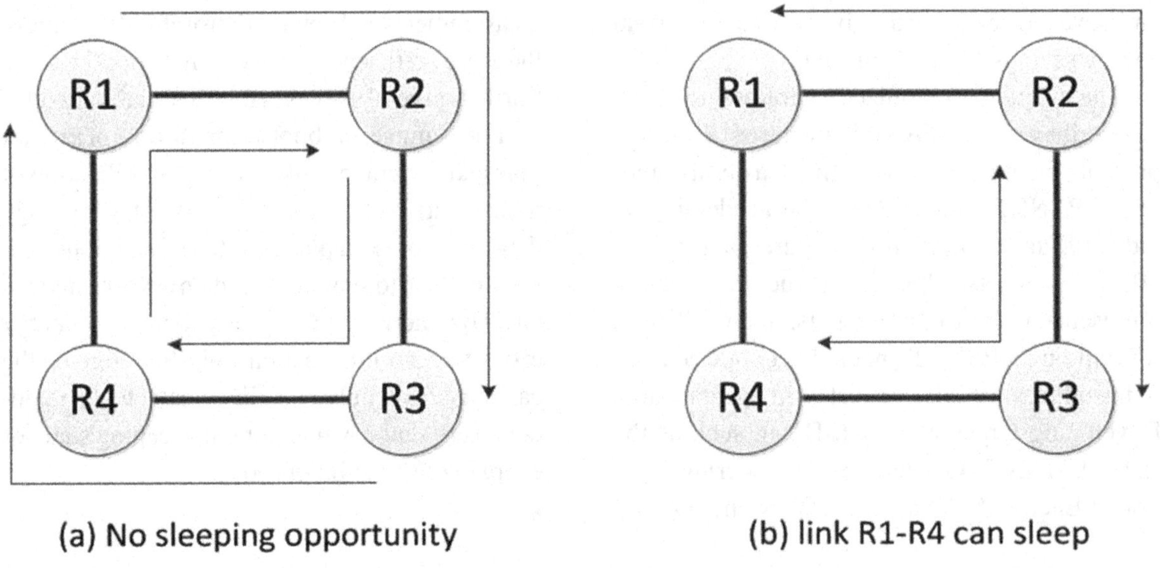

Traffic Engineering path computation purposes. Any traffic engineering policy that may violate these constraints should be avoided.

With the traffic load fluctuating, the green Traffic Engineering should be periodically performed. When the network is lightly loaded, the GreenTE should be able to put more links in idle state (M. Zhang et al., 2010, pp. 21-30). When the network is heavily loaded, Green TE should keep more links in active state to absorb more traffic in order to avoid any traffic jam. Requirements for green Traffic Engineering are listed below.

2.1.2. Be Aware of Sleeping Links at the Management Plane

It is possible to wake up a link or put it into sleeping state based upon management plane operations. The state change impacts the data plane of the network.

Take Fig.1 as an example: if link R1- R4 is sleeping, it will cut off the R3-R4-R1 and R4-R1-R2 paths. Therefore, the paths in Fig.1 (b) should be used. Take Fig.2 as an example: in order to avoid any impact due to the sleeping link, the multicast tree in Fig.2 (b) should be used rather than that in Fig.2 (a). It requires a knob to achieve the adjustment of data plane via the control plane.

Sleeping links are different from failed links since they can be awake to relieve the traffic jam (e.g., high delay, packet loss and congestion indication) whenever it becomes necessary. This difference creates the necessity for the network to remember these links in order to make decisions to wake them up at a proper time.

2.1.3. Gather Information for Decision Making

Wherever the decision point is located, the traffic of the network is the necessary input for Traffic Engineering. This information should be measured and maintained. For example, network elements (routers and switches) can gather flow data and export them to collectors, by using Netflow (Claise et al., 2013). For another example, Simple Network

Figure 2. Multicast Forwarding Plane

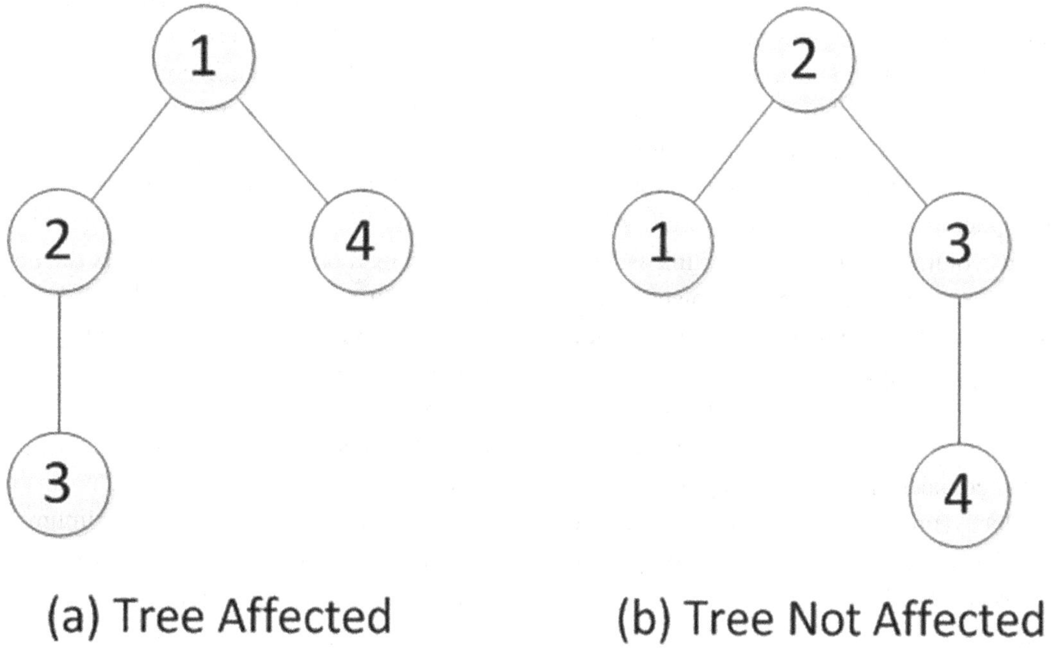

Management Protocol (SNMP) interface counters can also be used as an input to green Traffic Engineering. The Network Management System (NMS) may periodically poll these counters to compute the links' load. The traffic matrix of the network can then be derived from the results of this computation.

Compared to traditional Traffic Engineering (TE), power-aware TE additionally requires the information about the power consumption of network devices. It requires for instance a MIB module for monitoring energy consumption and power states of devices (Energy Management, 2010).

The essentials of this use case are as follows:

1. Entities to be power-controlled: Routers, etc.
2. What actions to take: Network Management System (NMS) polls traffic load counters and power consumption profiles for each link; Routers execute the green TE algorithm; Routers send signals to trigger the sleeping/wake-up transition of a NPU on a line card accordingly.

2.1.4. Composite Links

A composite link is a logical link composed of multiple physical links. The endpoints of a composite link are responsible for mapping traffic onto the component links and maintaining the state of the composite link. Power awareness can be applied to composite links as well. When the traffic volume on a composite link is low, some component links can be shut down to limit energy consumption. When the traffic volume becomes high, the sleeping component links can be awake to absorb the traffic load. The advantage of performing energy savings for composite links is that the connectivity of the composite link is hardly affected unless all the component links are sleeping. Thus, the control plane of the component link is not disrupted.

The essentials of this use case:

1. Entities to be power-controlled: Composite links attached end-points.
2. What actions to take: NMS measures the traffic load and power profile of component links; Attached end-points adaptively put component links into sleeping state or wake them up according to the traffic load on the composite link.

2.2. Energy-Efficiency in Data Center Networks

Servers and network devices (ICT equipment) are intensively placed in data centers, which can consume a huge amount of energy every day, while a large part (as high as 85%) is actually wasted (Abts, Marty, Wells, Klausler, & Liu, 2010). The growing amount of energy consumed by a data center has led to high operating costs. The workload of a data center fluctuates greatly every day. There is a significant opportunity to limit the energy consumption by means of right-sizing the ICT infrastructure when the workload is low at night.

Although non-ICT equipment, such as lighting, in a data center consume quite a large amount of energy as well, this section concentrates on right-sizing the ICT infrastructure for energy conservation. Energy conservation of non- ICT equipment are out of the scope of this section.

Traffic load of a data center is generated by the workload on servers and affects the network infrastructure. The changing workload determines that the traffic load varies as a function of time. However, network devices are always powered on even though the traffic load fluctuates, which inevitably wastes energy when traffic load is low. Ideally, the network infrastructure is elastic and can fit the traffic patterns with minimum subset to minimize the energy consumption. For now, data center networks generally work at layer 2.

The essentials of this use case:

1. Devices to be power-controlled: All network equipment in a data center.
2. What actions to take: Network devices report their traffic load and power consumption profile to the orchestrator. The orchestrator of a data center network adaptively establishes the switching paths over the network infrastructure. The idle links are put into power saving mode (e.g., sleeping), so that the network infrastructure becomes energy efficient.

As shown in Fig.3, when servers are idle and put into sleeping state, the switches they connect to may also become "idle".

3. RELATED WORK

This section discusses the most representative feasibility studies of PANET in the academic and industry sectors that address energy efficiency in networking infrastructures.

3.1. Academic Studies

Flow Optimization-based framework for request-Routing and Traffic Engineering (FORTE) (Gao, Curtis, Wong, & Keshav, 2012, pp. 211-222) dynamically controls the fraction of user traffic directed to each datacenter in response to changes in both request workload and carbon footprint. It allows an operator to navigate the three-way tradeoff between access latency, carbon footprint, and electricity costs and to determine an optimal datacenter upgrade plan in response to increases in traffic load.

GreenTE, an intra-domain traffic engineering mechanism, maximizes the number of links that can be put into sleep under given performance constraints such as link utilization and packet delay (M. Zhang et al., 2010, pp. 21-30). GreenTE can reduce line cards' power consumption by 27% to 42% under constraints that the maximum link utilization remains below 50% and the network diameter remains the same as in shortest path routing.

Donadio, Russo, Canonico and Ventre (2013) provides a green extension to the GMPLS network control plane, called O-Gene (Open GrEen network control plaNE), which can minimize power consumption under QoS constraints and a uniform way for the network resource orchestration to access devices with green networking capabilities. Path Computation Element (PCE) architectures can compute end-to-end paths to meet QoS and maximize energy efficiency in networks. The aforementioned authors plan to implement the Green OSPF-TE by extending OSPF in the future.

General Distributed Routing Protocol for Power Saving (GDRP-PS) (Ho & Cheung, 2010, pp. 1-6), a distributed routing protocol compatible with existing core networks, coordinates the process for routers to enter sleep mode for power saving purposes in wired core networks without significantly affecting service quality and network connectivity during non-peak hours. It is designed to be built on top of any existing distributed Internet routing protocol without any compatibility problems.

(Bolla, Bruschi, Carrega. & Davoli, 2011) focuses on energy-aware devices and proposes an analytical model to accurately represent the impact of green network technologies (i.e., low power idle and adaptive rate) on network- and energy-aware performance indexes. It can effectively represent energy- and network-aware performance indexes. They also propose an optimization procedure based on the model which aims at dynamically adapting the energy-aware device configuration to minimize energy consumption, while coping with incoming traffic volumes and meeting network performance constraints.

Figure 3. Elastic Data Center ICT Infrastructure

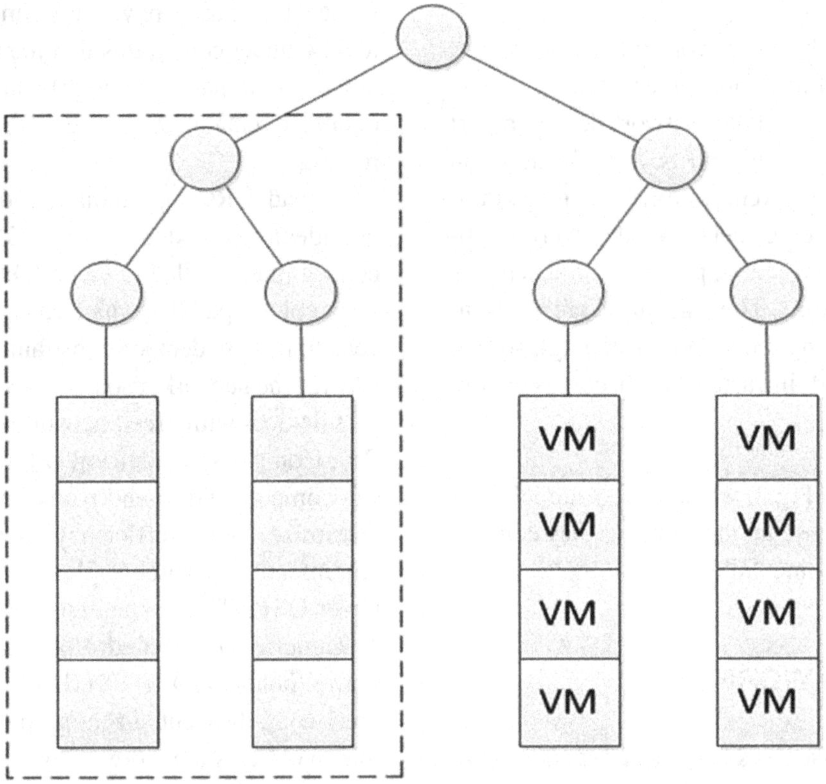

3.2. Industry Studies

Current generation products are increasingly constrained by the availability of power in both the developed and developing markets. While the unit power consumption (i.e., functionality per watt) continues to decrease, the rate of the decrease is much lower than the explosion of bandwidth. Because of economics and environmental impact, Cisco have discussed topics related to power consumption in high-end routing/switching systems (Wobker, 2012). It indicates that many papers in labs are feasibility studies that can hardly apply to the real Internet routing system, and a balance between performance and power savings should be found.

A power management framework, called "Cisco EnergyWise Suite" (Cisco, 2013) is designed to monitor, optimize and control energy consumption of all connected devices and support strategies in order to achieve more efficient power utilization. EnergyWise is a new feature embedded in Cisco switches and routers, providing communication and control capability for terminal devices connected to Cisco networks managed by Cisco EnergyWise devices to monitor their power consumption, and take actions to reduce the power consumption based upon business rules, for example.

GreenTouch (GreenTouch, 2014) announced that it is possible to reduce the net energy consumption in communication networks by up to 90% by 2020, by combining technologies, architectures, components, algorithms and protocols. This dramatic net energy reduction in the mobile, fixed access and core networks, while taking into account the dramatic increase of traffic, is fueled by significant improvements in the energy efficiencies of the component networks (including a factor of 1043 for mobile networks, a factor of 449 for fixed access networks and a factor of 64 for core networks). Deploying these technologies would have a significant economic impact (because of reduced operational expenses) as well as an environmental impact (through reduced energy consumption and carbon emissions) for operators and service providers, while at the same time providing value to consumers and businesses as well as revenue-generating opportunities through the delivered applications and services.

EEE SG (Energy Efficient Ethernet Study Group, 2007) is a set of enhancements to the twisted-pair and backplane Ethernet family of computer networking standards that allow for less power consumption during periods of low data activity. EEE capabilities will enable new system level energy management techniques that will save energy beyond the network interface. EEE will address interface changes required to improve energy efficiency. Ethernet equipment vendors and customers can then achieve an optimal cost balance between the network infrastructure components and the attached stations. In view of technical feasibility, energy efficiency techniques based upon capabilities that aim at reducing power consumption have been broadly deployed and used; in view of economic feasibility, EEE will not materially impact component or installation costs, and may provide cost savings opportunities.

3.3. PANET Work in SDOs

3.3.1. PANET Initiative within IETF

Network capacity is usually over-provisioned to better accommodate traffic bursts. Resiliency designs usually assume a waste of energy, because not all resources are always solicited. There is therefore a need to optimize the energy consumption as a function of time, so that off-peak periods yield significant energy savings.

In the recent years, vendors have made a significant effort to develop energy-efficient network devices that can dynamically adapt their power consumption as a function of the traffic load. However, network devices are far from fully power proportional to traffic load. In other words, network devices keep guzzling a high-level of power even in the absence of data traffic, because of the activation of routing and management protocols that assume some CPU activity. For example, typical line card technologies consume no less than 80% of the full power even if they are idle.

Chips widely support various system power states, which allow them to go asleep and wake up without requiring a system reboot. Just like laptops that can save energy during their sleeping phase, network devices should also be able to go through sleeping phases for the sake of energy savings. Many studies have been conducted in the past few years to demonstrate the feasibility of energy-efficient networking techniques without compromising the overall quality of the networking infrastructure (e.g., in terms of resource availability). Compared to the conventional wired network which typically requires only link and node states to set up the forwarding paths, such energy-aware networking techniques assume the ability to exchange additional information between energy-efficient network devices. Such information can be manifold: energy status, energy resource availability, energy resources that can be reserved, etc. This information influences traffic forwarding schemes and related routing policies. Protocols are assumed to exchange and take into account this information for path computation purposes. However, most of the existing routing protocols are currently unable to use energy information as a metric for path computation purposes. The IETF should be involved to specify such protocol extensions.

The idea of the PANET initiative is that forwarding path computation can take into account the aforementioned energy information for the sake of optimized, energy-efficient, network resource usage. For example, a PANET-enabled network may assume that only a subset of devices will be involved for forwarding traffic during the night. Those devices that are not involved in traffic forwarding operations during night time can thus enter an idle state and save power accordingly.

Means to dynamically trigger the devices to behave in the power-low mode are yet-to-be investigated. PANET takes into account traffic demand, network topology and network devices power states as inputs for path computation purposes and energy state management.

PANET can benefit to any region of a network: core network, access networks, data center networks, home networks, etc. The PANET effort is intended to be generic and not specific to a given deployment use case. In particular, PANET can be used in a variety of contexts.

3.3.2. EMAN on Energy MIB

Managed objects are accessed via a virtual information store, termed the Management Information Base or MIB (Energy Management, 2010). MIB objects are generally accessed through SNMP. Objects in the MIB are defined using the syntax of the Structure of Management Information (SMI).

The EMAN standards provide a specification for Energy Management. EMAN defines a subset of MIBs for use with network management protocols for Energy monitoring of network devices and devices attached to the network and possibly extending to devices in the industrial automation setting with a network interface. The focus of the MIB modules is the identification of Energy Objects and reporting the context and relationships of Energy Objects. The module addresses Energy Object identification, Energy Object context, and Energy Object relationships.

3.3.3. IEEE 802.3az

IEEE 802.3az specifies a set of standards on enhancements to the twisted-pair and backplane Ethernet family (IEEE 802.3az). These enhancements allow for energy saving during periods of low data activity. The work of the P802.3az Energy Efficient Ethernet Task Force was completed in September 2010.

Energy is used to keep the physical layer transmitters on all the time. It could be saved if links could be put into "sleep" mode when no data needs to be sent. When the controlling software or firmware finds that, it can issue a Low Power Idle (LPI) request to the Ethernet controller physical layer PHY. The PHY will then send LPI symbols for a specified time onto the link to disable its transmitter (Spurgeon & Joann, 2014).

Green Ethernet technology was a superset of the 802.3az standard. It detects link status, allowing each port on the switch to power down into a standby or 'sleep' mode when a connected device is not active. Moreover it detects cable length and adjusts the power accordingly. Green Ethernet was first employed on home products. Projected power savings of up to 45 - 80 percent were estimated using Green Ethernet switches (D-Link, 2007), translating into a longer product life due to reduced heat dissipation.

3.3.4. ETSI GAL

The ETSI Standard (ES) is produced by ETSI Technical Committee Environmental Engineering (EE) (ETSI, 2014). GAL is a novel way for managing and monitoring energy and performance profiles of device hardware. The GAL is an interface between data and control planes for exchanging information regarding the power status of a device. This interface is specifically conceived to hide the implementation details of energy-saving approaches, as well as to provide methodologies for interactions between heterogeneous "green" capabilities and Hardware (H/W) technologies, on one hand, and control and monitoring frameworks, on the other hand. With "green" capabilities, we refer to any type of mechanisms that implement appropriate optimization policies aimed at reducing the power consumption of a resource. Indeed, this interface provides flexible access to the power management capabilities of the future energy aware telecommunication fixed network nodes to effectively adapt the energy consumption of the network nodes with respect to the load variations.

By means of the GAL, control applications will be allowed to get information on how many power management settings are available at the data plane, and on the potential effect of using such settings. Likewise, control applications will be capable of performing several certain power management configuration tasks on the device. It is worth noting that, in order to provide the information needed by control applications to reduce the energy consumption while meeting QoS constraints, the GAL explicitly represents the impact on network performance when different power management settings are applied.

The main objective of the GAL is to standardize the interface between the Network Control Policies (NCPs, for energy efficiency purposes) and the power modulation capabilities of network devices. There are three key aspects that have to be addressed by the GAL:

1. To make explicit the trade-off between consumption and network performance;
2. To map the consumption of hardware blocks with virtual/logical network resources; and
3. To hide the details/complexity of internal power modulation mechanisms.

ES defines the GAL general architecture, the interoperable interface (GSI) between the energy-aware control processes (NCPs and LCPs - Local Control Policies) and the power management capabilities of the fixed network devices and the EASes describing the different configurations and corresponding performance with respect to the energy consumption of the devices.

4. ISSUES, REQUIREMENTS AND CHALLENGES

With the increase of network services and exponential traffic growth, the network operators are expanding their infrastructures with more high-capacity, full-featured network devices, which also leads to the increase of network energy consumption. Besides, today's service provider networks are mostly designed for high performance and reliability, without much consideration about energy efficiency. These networks usually have redundant routers and links, over-provisioned link capacity, and multiple paths for load-balancing and protection purposes, which make the networks far from being energy efficient. As the price of energy continues to rise, the increasing network energy consumption becomes a significant portion of the network operational costs. While energy consumption has become an important issue, network operators are very cautious about energy conservation solutions due to the concerns about the potential impacts on the network performance and resiliency.

4.1. Requirements for PANET

This section presents a set of requirements for building a PANET network while meeting operators' requirements on performance and resiliency.

4.1.1. Requirements on Network Elements

Today's network elements are mostly designed for high throughput and availability. With the increase of throughput capacity, the energy consumption of network elements is also rising accordingly. Since most of time the network elements would not work in fully loaded state, if their energy consumption could be proportional to the traffic load, energy conservation could be achieved. Typically, after a network element is turned on, the base energy consumption is relatively high, and the energy consumption of the device does not vary a lot from zero load state to fully loaded state. While there has been a lot of effort aiming at making the energy consumption of network devices proportional to the traffic load, this objective is unlikely to be achieved in the near term due to technology limitations, etc. For near term energy savings, the network elements should meet the following requirements:

1. Network elements should support a set of energy saving modes (e.g., sleeping mode, etc., as defined by the IETF EMAN working group). The energy consumption under energy saving modes should be much lower than under nominal operation.
2. Network elements should support the report of energy consumption and state information.
3. The transition between different energy modes should not cost a lot of energy; otherwise there will not be much benefit of transiting between different energy modes.
4. Network elements should support the transition between different energy modes within an acceptable time, e.g., in the sub-second range.
5. Network elements should support some method for reducing the risk of losing packets while transiting from an energy mode to another.

4.1.2. Requirements on the Whole Network

While energy awareness and conservation of individual network element is fundamental, currently there are many limits in reducing the energy consumption at a network element level. Besides, different from terminal devices like PC and mobile phones, network elements usually cannot be shut down arbitrarily as this may affect the services carried in the network. Thus mechanisms which could reduce the energy consumption from the whole network point of view should also be considered.

Most of the existing networks are over-provisioned for better service performance and redundancy, which means they are not energy efficient by default. In order to save energy, the entire network should become power aware, and then it can make appropriate decisions to save energy whenever possible. Since the network does not carry high traffic volumes most of the time of operation, this means there is chance for the network to coordinate network elements and encourage some of the network elements to enter energy saving modes. Meanwhile, reducing the energy consumption of the network should not undermine the performance of services carried by the network. For energy conservation of the whole network, the network should meet the following requirements:

1. The network should try to keep all the active network elements with a reasonable utilization rate, network elements with low utilization should be instructed to enter energy saving modes. For example, the network elements with utilization lower than a specific threshold may be put into low rate mode to reduce energy consumption, or the traffic carried by these network elements may be migrated to other paths such that these network elements could be put into sleeping mode.
2. With energy conservation, the network should retain enough network availability and resiliency against node and link failures. In other words, the redundancy of the network should be kept at a reasonable level, e.g., 2-connected.
3. Energy savings of the network should not induce latency increase nor traffic loss at the cost of degrading service performance. QoS metrics such as end-to-end delay, loss and jitter should be kept at a desired level.
4. The network should be able to dynamically adapt resource usage to traffic demand, by awakening sleeping nodes whenever and

wherever required, as a function of the statistical data collected on a regular basis.
5. The network stability should be preserved. Particularly, route oscillation should be avoided.

4.1.3. Requirements on the Control Plane

Most of the existing network control protocols are not designed with an objective that includes energy efficiency, and some protocols may not work properly when some of the network elements are in energy saving modes. For example, when a network link is put into sleeping mode, the protocols run on this link will be impacted. For energy saving of the whole network, the control plane should meet the following requirements:

1. The control plane should be able to work properly when some of the network elements are in energy saving mode. For example, the RIB databases maintained by the routers of the network should provide a consistent view of the network topology at any given time, including sleeping nodes and links.
2. The control plane should support the advertisement and computation of energy-related information (e.g., current energy saving mode) by network elements.
3. The control plane should be able to coordinate the energy saving operations of network elements to achieve the overall network energy saving.
4. The control plane should be able to maximize the opportunity for network elements to enter an energy saving mode.

4.1.4. Requirements on the Management Plane

The management plane is also necessary for building a power aware network. The IETF EMAN working group has defined requirements and mechanisms for energy management, see (Quittek et al., 2013). Such management requirements include the identification of energy-managed devices and their components, monitoring of a series of power states and power properties. It further includes the control of the power supply and power states of the managed devices.

4.2. Support from Hardware/ Control Plane

In order to save power, routers and switches should support low power states, and make control primitives available to enter or leave low power states. To reduce the impact on network performance, routers and switches should have the ability to change power states quickly. What follows is the hardware/control plane support needed by power-aware protocols.

4.2.1. Support from Hardware

Sleeping State

Most sleeping-based approaches require routers and switches, or a component of them such as a line card, to support sleeping state. While some approaches may choose to turn off a device, this would often impact network resilience because booting a device takes a significant amount of time. A sleeping device or component should be able to wake up quickly. Moreover, entering and leaving sleeping state should not incur too much power.

Multiple Data Rates

CMOS-based silicon supports Dynamic Voltage Scaling (DVS), so clocking an interface at a lower frequency, and operating at lower data rates can save considerable amounts of energy. This calls for router interfaces to support multiple data rates. If an interface could support more data rates and incur low penalty power on a change, there are more opportunities to save energy. Furthermore, some approaches like the Adaptive Link Rate (ALR) may become attractive if an interface could have different sending and receiving data rates (Gunaratne, Christensen, Nordman, & Suen, 2008).

Electrical Damage

Many electronic devices are not designed to be turned on and off frequently. When a device is awake, the in-rush current may damage or destroy a component and its related circuits. Hardware that is friendlier to power management is needed.

Optical Component Support

Electrical components consume much more energy than optical components in network routing infrastructures. Therefore, many power-aware routing or traffic engineering approaches are designed with electrical devices in mind. However, the number of optical components in ISP networks can also be large. Care should be taken when adopting existing approaches to optical networks. For example, optical receivers cannot be turned off when Wake-on-Arrival (WoA) is needed. Furthermore, there is room for more power saving when optical components are explicitly considered in the approach. It is possible to turn off an optical receiver while maintaining the ability to wake it up when needed.

4.2.2. Support from Control Plane

Congestion after Traffic Surges

Traffic engineering approaches usually take into account traffic information as measured at a given time, and that the resulting computed path is meant to accommodate such traffic so that it is forwarded over a topology that now includes some links that are either in a sleeping mode or which operate at lower rates. This route computation scheme usually keeps link utilization under certain thresholds, so that there is some safe margin in case traffic increases. However, because a route is computed periodically, congestion is still possible when traffic increases to a level that exceeds the safe margin within one adjustment period. To address this issue, some method of fast readjustment is needed. When a traffic increase is observed, the routing scheme should be slightly altered to accommodate this traffic, probably by waking up some links or increasing rates of other links.

Network Partition on Link or Node Failure

Many sleep-based approaches will result in a topology with very low redundancy level. These constrained topologies are vulnerable to link and node failures, which are quite common in large networks. Those approaches should be improved by adding a constraint of redundancy level. A redundancy level of 2, which could protect the network from a single link failure, is a reasonable target from an energy saving standpoint. It's possible to incorporate power aware features into Maximum Redundancy Tree (MRT) to achieve energy savings while keeping the network 2-disjoint. Once a partition is detected, it's easy to repair by waking up all sleeping links. But this causes a sudden increase of power consumption, which is sometimes undesirable. A local algorithm to select a subset of sleeping links that could repair the partition is needed. The selection doesn't need to be optimal, because waking up a small subset of links is much better than waking up all sleeping links.

Sleeping Link State in Routing Protocols

Sleeping links should be handled separately in routing protocols. A sleeping link should be advertised as up, probably with a tag stating its sleeping. No HELLO messages should be sent over a sleeping link, so no HELLO messages could be received from a sleeping link. Missed HELLO messages on a sleeping link should not cause the link to be treated as down. As a consequence, if a sleeping link fails, the failure would not be detected until the router attempts to wake it up. To proactively detect a failure, it may be desirable to wake up the link and probe it periodically (using a long interval, for example every hour). No control message should be sent over a sleeping link. This may cause the network to converge slower than usual, because LSA packets are flooded across a whole area or even a whole domain. Fortunately, most power-aware approaches have network diameter constraints, so convergence times should be comparable.

IP Multicast on Power-Aware Constrained Topologies

IP Multicast works by building one or more trees on available links. If any link in a multicast tree goes to sleep, some receivers may not be able to receive multicast packets for a noticeable period of time, until IP multicast automatically repairs the tree. So, if a link is part of a multicast tree, it should not be put into sleeping mode. One solution consists in keeping all links that compose a multicast tree active. If there are many multicast trees that don't have much overlap, a major portion of links would be forced active by multicast, and, as a consequence, the power saving potential is greatly limited. Another solution consists in explicitly modifying multicast trees in a power-aware fashion. This is not an easy way to go. There should be a delay constraint on each multicast tree, while there may be a large number of multicast trees. After a multicast tree is modified, utilization of multiple links will change. A third solution consists in making IP multicast power-aware. When a multicast tree is being built, energy consumption is taken into account, such that IP multicast would attempt to use as few links as possible as long as delay constraints could be satisfied. The resulting multicast distribution tree will be composed of links that will not go to sleep.

Network Monitoring

Network operators demand network and device monitoring solutions. The most important indicators are: "How much energy is saved?", "How does energy saving impact network performance?", and "How much energy is consumed?"? The IETF EMAN WG is chartered to define energy objects for network devices, as well as state monitoring and controlling solutions. When a device is running on full power state, the power demand is recorded as full power demand. When a power-aware approach is deployed, actual energy consumption is measured. The amount of saved energy is the full power demand multiplied by the elapsed time during the measurement of actual energy consumption subtracted by actual energy consumption.

In centralized periodical adjustment approaches, the centralized server should have the knowledge of the currently applied solution (which is based upon previous traffic information) and the current traffic information. It can then calculate what link utilization and delay become when traffic is forwarded according to the currently applied solution, as well as the performance as if this traffic were forwarded without any power-aware consideration. It's not trivial to measure the impact in other cases.

MIBs are needed to standardize the data and variables to monitor, regardless of the underlying technology. Management software for network operation needs to integrate power-aware routing and traffic engineering information into the existing IT architecture.

4.3. Challenges

The high-level idea of power-aware networks is to adjust forwarding paths based on traffic level. When traffic level is high, use more links to carry the traffic; when traffic level is low, merge traffic onto a subset of links so that other links can be put into sleep mode or reduce link rates in order to save power. This needs to be done without significantly impacting network QoS, resiliency, and interoperation with other protocols.

4.3.1. How to Shorten the Time Needed for State Transition

Common energy management schemes at the component level (such as a line card) are based upon the notions of Sleep-on-Idle (SoI) and WoA. When a link is idle for a short period of time, it goes into sleep; when a packet arrives, it wakes up. Most components can go to sleep very quickly, and they also need to be able to wake up quickly. Besides, entering and leaving sleeping states often incurs extra energy draw, which needs to be kept as small as possible. Different designs may have different requirements for the transition time between power states. In an uncoordinated sleeping approach, upstream routers intentionally buffer packets for a very short period of time to allow downstream routers sleep longer. This approach can only allow a component to sleep for a few milliseconds; otherwise the buffering may cause too much extra delay. Hence this approach requires a very short transition time and low penalty power. In coordinated sleeping approaches, where routers coordinate about which paths to use and when to put links into sleep mode, a component usually can sleep much longer, for example seconds, minutes or even longer. Therefore, their requirement on transition time and power is more relaxed.

Most Ethernet cards supports auto-negotiation of data rate, which happens when a cable is plugged in and takes hundreds of milliseconds. This negotiation usually takes hundreds of milliseconds. Auto-negotiation is not suitable for changing data rates to save energy, because buffers would be filled up during the negotiation period and likely lead to packet loss. A faster mechanism for initiating and agreeing upon a link data rate change is necessary. A data rate change is expected to be completed within 100 microseconds for a 1Gbps link.

4.3.2. How to Enlarge the Percentage of Power Saving from Sleep

By introducing hardware support for Wake-on-Packet, longer sleeping periods could be achieved, thereby saving more energy.

Sleeping modes are the most likely approach to save energy in routers and switches. When a component enters a sleeping state, it consumes only a little amount of power. If there is a need to use a sleeping interface or line card, it could be awaken and become usable after a transition time. To wake up a sleeping interface or line card, some approaches simply use a timer: during the sleeping period, all packets towards it are lost; after a predetermined period, the interface or line card is awaken. Thus, the sleeping period cannot be longer than a few seconds; otherwise packet loss may occur in case of sudden traffic increases, which fill up the buffer. To achieve longer sleeping periods, some approaches propose Wake-on-Packet: when a packet arrives at a sleeping interface or line card, the component will be awaken by the packet. The specific requirements vary from one approach to another:

1. A dummy packet wakes up the interface or line card, and is then lost. Actual packets could be accepted after transition time is elapsed.
2. An actual packet wakes up the interface or line card, and is buffered. This packet is processed as soon as the component becomes active.
3. When one or more interfaces are sleeping on a line card, a shadow port will receive and buffer one actual packet arriving at any of those sleeping interfaces, and wake up the sleeping interface then handover the packet. If multiple packets arrive at sleeping interfaces simultaneously, all of them are lost.

4.3.3. How to Save Power from Monitoring Temperature Sensors and Traffic Load

Here is an example about temperature, fan speed and power-saving. For a router, every control board, switch fabric, and line card have several temperature sensors in strategic locations. During the design phase of a board, the safe temperature range and other parameters of each sensor are decided according to the tolerance of related chips.

Fans keep router cool and ensure continuous operation, but a fan running at full speed consumes lots of power. Fan speed, with the default configuration of automatic adjustment, is determined by the current reading of temperature sensors. Every temperature sensor determines a demanded fan speed according to its parameters, and the fan speed is set to the highest speed as required by the sensors. This means that, when there is one sensor demanding 75% fan speed while all other sensors demand 40% fan speed, the actual fan speed would be 75%. In our experiments, the change in temperature between idle and full load is not big enough to impact fan speed. Fan speed is always 40% regardless of load; this is still true when eight line cards are installed and 40G traffic is running. However, whenever an older line card is installed, one sensor on those line cards would push fan speed up to 75%.

In addition, the relationship between the fan power that is required and the ambient temperature is not linear (L. J. Wobker, 2012). There is a change point that needs to be considered. The relationship between the router power supply efficiency and its load is also non-linear. Therefore, it is an effective way to achieve reasonable power supply efficiency by keeping temperature and load under certain level.

5. PROMISING SOLUTIONS

The PANET approach has been extensively studied and many efforts have been conducted. However, the gap analysis shows there still remains much work to be conducted for PANET. This section exposes the directions that PANET should take, as far as the following aspects are concerned: network planning policies based upon PANET solutions; how to use PANET information for Traffic Engineering; power-aware SDN-based management.

5.1. Network Planning Policies Based on PANET Solutions

Nowadays, many researchers are studying network planning policies based upon PANET solutions. In particular, there is a power-aware network planning tool under study, named GreenPlan, which is said to reduce network power consumption while still maintaining network performance at desired levels.

5.1.1. Basic Idea

The combination of high path redundancy and low link utilization provides a unique opportunity for power-aware network planning as illustrated by the example in Fig.4. Traditional traffic engineering tools spread traffic evenly in a network, trying to minimize the risk of congestion induced by traffic bursts. However, energy efficient network planning tools can free some links by moving traffic onto other links, so that links without traffic can go to sleep for an extended period of time. For example, the traffic between P1 and P4 are sent over the path P1-P2-P3-P4 while links P1-P5, P4-P5 can be idle. Idle links can be shut down for the next days or months for the purpose of energy saving.

Figure 4 shows a bundling link between P2 and P3. Bundling links are widely used in real networks for the purpose of increasing link capacity. If these bundling links are in low utilization, some of their component links can also be shut down without breaking the connectivity of attached devices.

5.1.2. Traffic Matrix Gathering

The controller in the network collects network topology and traffic matrix from OSPF's Link State Advertisements (LSAs). In OSPF, each router floods LSA packets whenever link states change. Thus, the controller can readily collect all the link state information and compile the up-to-date network topology.

Directly measuring a traffic matrix in real-time is still expensive in the case of large networks. Instead, the GreenPlan controller collects link load information from routers and computes the traffic matrix locally. The link load information is part of the Traffic Engineering Link State Advertisement (TE-LSA). TE-LSA packets are also flooded in the network. TE-LSA packets report a link's maximum bandwidth and unreserved bandwidth, and the difference between them is the link load. A router sends out TE-LSA packets when there is a significant change in bandwidth usage, as perceived by the router (and according to specific thresholds that are configured explicitly on each router). Once the link load information is collected, the controller computes the network traffic matrix. For example, the tomogravity method defined in Zhang, Roughan, Duffield and Greenberg (2003) can be used. The essential of tomogravity is to find a traffic matrix among all possibilities that best fit the observed link load and network routing and configuration data. Tomogravity is proved to be lightweight, accurate, and can be done within a few seconds for large ISP networks.

Both the network topology and link load information are collected by the controller passively. The controller does not poll any specific router, nor has any explicit point-to-point conversation with any individual router. All information is announced via LSAs. This design choice is compatible with existing mechanisms, simplifies operations, and also inherits the delivery reliability provided by LSA flooding.

5.1.3. Flow Distribution

With the network topology and traffic matrix, the controller solves the GreenPlan problem to determine which links need to be turned on or off, and distributes this information to routers via the Traffic Engineering Metric (TE-Metric) attribute. The GreenPlan convention is that if a link's TE-Metric is set to be equal to its OSPF weight, the

Figure 4. Example of Energy Efficient Network Planning

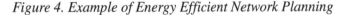

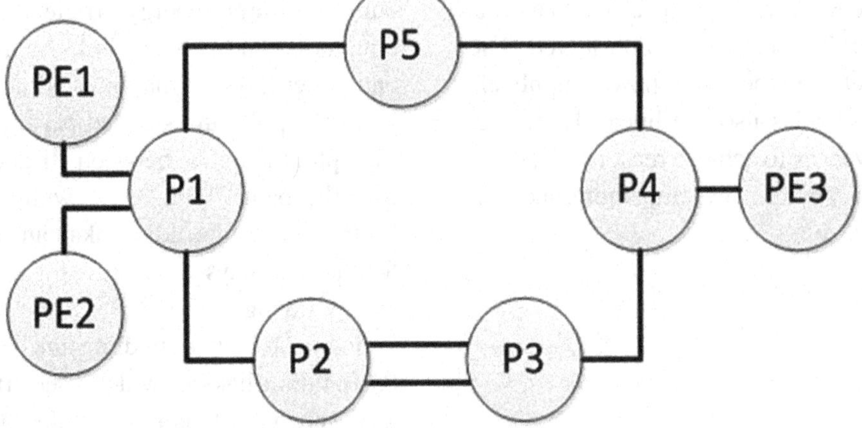

link should to be turned on; if a link's TE-Metric is set to be the maximum value allowed, it should be turned off. Note that both TE-LSA and TE-Metric messages are flooded in the network as regular OSPF Opaque LSA packets; therefore, they can reach all routers as long as the network is connected and require no separate interfaces or links to be reserved. The flow conservation constraints of the GreenPlan formulation guarantee that the solution does not partition the network.

To minimize packet loss during routing transitions, extra care is needed when routers are turning on/off links. When a router has a link to turn off, it should not do so immediately, because otherwise some on-the-fly packets may be lost. Ideally, it should wait for all the alternative paths to be set up before actually turning off a link, in a make-before-break fashion. In practice, a router may turn off a link after the link has been idle for more than a certain period of time. The network diameter can serve as a rough threshold for this purpose. When a router has a link to wake up, it should turn on the link immediately but not transmit data onto this link until both ends of the link are ready. Two routers can exchange messages to confirm that they are ready. Such messages can be MPLS signaling messages, OSPF Hello messages, or simple messages designed specifically for this purpose. An alternative is to simply use a timer.

5.2. How to Quick up PANET Solutions for Traffic Engineering

The goal of power-aware traffic engineering is to try to concentrate traffic to a subset of links, namely to save as much energy as possible by making links idle, and to achieve energy conservation without significantly affecting network performance and reliability.

The PANET solutions for Traffic Engineering aim at switching off the line cards (network links) while accommodating QoS constraints in a hybrid MPLS/OSPF scheme. This problem can be formulated as a Mixed Integer Programming (MIP) problem with the total power saving as the objective to be maximized. Performance requirements such as maximum link utilization (MLU) and network delay are considered as constraints in the problem based on a MIP formulation. Generally speaking, MIP problems are NP-Hard, thus their computation time for networks of medium and large sizes is a concern. Therefore, some optimization methods are needed to develop PANET solutions for Traffic Engineering.

Heuristics are the most widely used methods to replace optimization algorithms when attempting to solve large dimensional optimization problems. Heuristics provide a lower rate for each node bifurcation to solve specific problems for each search tree, so they have a better computational efficiency. Thus, different heuristic methods can be developed (e.g., local search, genetic algorithm, ant algorithms) to develop PANET solutions for Traffic Engineering. The practical constraints (e.g., maximum link utilization, packet delay, energy model) can be used to develop heuristic. However, the choice of iterative stopping condition of heuristic is crucial and varies with cases: if the iterative stopping condition is too simple, the heuristic will miss the feasible solutions and if the iterative stopping condition is too strict, the heuristic will be too slow. Thus, efficient iterative stopping condition of heuristic is not easy to get. And the convergence rate of heuristic must be acceptable. Therefore, how to smartly design heuristics that can gracefully contribute to the development of PANET solutions for Traffic Engineering needs much more effort.

Furthermore, "divide-and-conquer" is an excellent strategy to reduce the solution scale and the computational complexity. The basic idea is to partition the large network into several smaller areas, which are independent or do not overlap, while enforcing the same routing policy as the original network. Then, the areas can be solved efficiently. Eventually, a solution for the whole network can be obtained by combining the solutions of all areas in a very short period of time. Clearly, the total amount of work required to solve the problem is decided by the number of areas, the work of each area and the workload related to the combination of all the area-specific solutions. However, how to properly partition the network is tricky. Considering that the divide-and-conquer method can speed up PANET solutions for Traffic Engineering, it is necessary to design an effective algorithm based on the divide- and-conquer method.

Moreover, branch-and-bound method can be in conjunction with PANET solutions to accelerate the solving process. Branch-and-bound methods adopt "pruning" operation for the solution space tree of the problem to reduce the search of the solution space tree. The question is: how to "prune"? In the branch-and-bound method, the role of bound is used to stop the search for non-viable branches. When the solution space tree is deep (leaf nodes being the solutions), if the algorithm knows in advance what are the suboptimal solutions, it can stop investigating some branches of the solution tree. Thus, the efficiency of the algorithm can be greatly improved by narrowing the search space. However, due to the difficulty of delimitation, how to use the branch-and-bound method in PANET solution requires careful design.

5.3. SDN-based Power Aware Networking

SDN architectures usually separate data and forwarding planes (Boucadair & Jacquenet, 2014), and assume a logically centralized computation logic. Those features enable the SDN controller to allocate resources and schedule resource allocation in a unified manner, implement flexible bandwidth-on-demand services, optimize network usage to maximize and improve resource utilization, etc. Thus, SDN-based power-aware networking is promising. This section presents future work for SDN-based power aware networking, including the following aspects that should be addressed: i) how to generate the green topology; ii) how to migrate traffic from nominal topology to the green one.

5.3.1. How to Generate the Power-efficient Topology

The realization of power-saving is usually done by putting network devices, such as routers, into sleeping mode, based upon static or dynamic power models, which is the same for ISPs SDN networks. While the generation method of green topology for ISPs can be used to produce the power-efficient topology for SDN, many researchers have provided their green topologies for different purposes, such as GreenTE.

5.3.2. How to Migrate Traffic from Nominal Topology to the Power-efficient One

While some on-the-fly packet loss can be prevented by exchanging messages between two routers, some packets may still be lost during routing transitions. Actually, routing transitions may trigger network-wide traffic migrations. If the traffic migrations are not carefully planned to implement, network congestion may occur. Although the controller can easily issue the migration command to all network nodes in a one-shot manner, the time that all network nodes execute the migration varies greatly. After the network nodes receive the upgrade signal issued by the controller, some nodes will forward packets based on the new path, while other network devices are still acting according to the old network route. During this period of time, the link load during traffic migrations could get significantly higher than before or after the migration. This problem may be further aggravated when the traffic is fluctuating. As a result, operators are completely in the dark about how severely links could be congested during traffic migration, not to mention how to come up with a feasible workaround to fix up packet loss.

The following section gives an example of the congestion problem and shows promising solutions.

5.3.3. Congestion Problem Description

Whenever a router has a link to turn off, it should not do so immediately, because otherwise some on-the-fly packets may be lost. Ideally, it should wait for all the alternative paths to be set up before actually turning off a link. In practice, a router may turn off a link after the link has been idle for more than a certain period of time.

Establish alternate paths in advance is a method to guarantee the consistency of per-packet/per-flow, which means every packet traversing the network is forwarded along an explicit path - either the original one or the new one but never a mixture of the two. In addition, network-wide traffic migration caused by routing transition could lead to severe link congestion if not done properly. We illustrate this problem using a simple example depicted by Fig. 5.

Figure 5 shows transient congestion has happened during network transition in a small network. To simplify the example, a link is regarded as a congested one as long as the traffic load exceeds its available/physical bandwidth. In Fig. 5, a circle denotes ingress where traffic flows into the network, while each ligature connecting two circles denotes the correspondence link.

The number on each link denotes the traffic load and the arrow indicates the traffic direction. Three traffic flows enter the network from ingress S1, S2 and S4 respectively. The traffic from S1 to S3 is 900, while traffic from S2 to S3 is 200, and traffic from S4 to S3 is 350. In order to deal with the shutdown of link S4-S3, the routing rules on S1, S2 and S4 must be transformed from the initial state to the final one. However, due to the overwhelming difficulty of altering routing paths on S1, S2 and S4 simultaneously, link S1-S3 will be congested for carrying the aggregate traffic of two flows if S4 and S2 are changed before S1, as illustrated in Fig. 5 (c). This example represents the link that can be congested for some time due to a chaotic traffic migration.

ISPs host many interactive applications such as search and advertisement which require very low latency. Even small losses and queuing delays could dramatically impair the user-perceived performance. Thus, congestion avoidance is essential when networks implement power-aware routing.

Performing zero-loss network-wide traffic migration can be highly tricky in ISP environments, because it often involves changes to many ingress routers, and its impact can ripple throughout the network. To avoid congestion, operators have to develop a thoughtful migration plan ahead of time.

In order to ensure the consistency of the transition, a two-phase commit mechanism is leveraged to move traffic during each round. In the first phase, all the alternative paths have been set up before actually moving traffic flows. In the second phase, ingress routers perform routing transition according to the migration plan.

Progressively and orderly traffic migration can be formulated as an Integer Linear Programming (ILP) with the number of migration rounds as the objective to be achieved. In this problem, maximum link utilization must be considered as a constraint; each ingress switch should be updated in one and only one round; and the ingress switches selected in the same round should satisfy timing independent requirements, which means whatever the actual update order among these ingress nodes is, congestion will not happen. However, ILP problems are NP-Hard, thus the computation time for large scale networks is a concern. Therefore, some speedup algorithms for traffic migration problems deserve to be studied. If the size of the ILP problem could be reduced, the computational efficiency would be improved remarkably. In fact,

Figure 5. The illustration of transient congestion

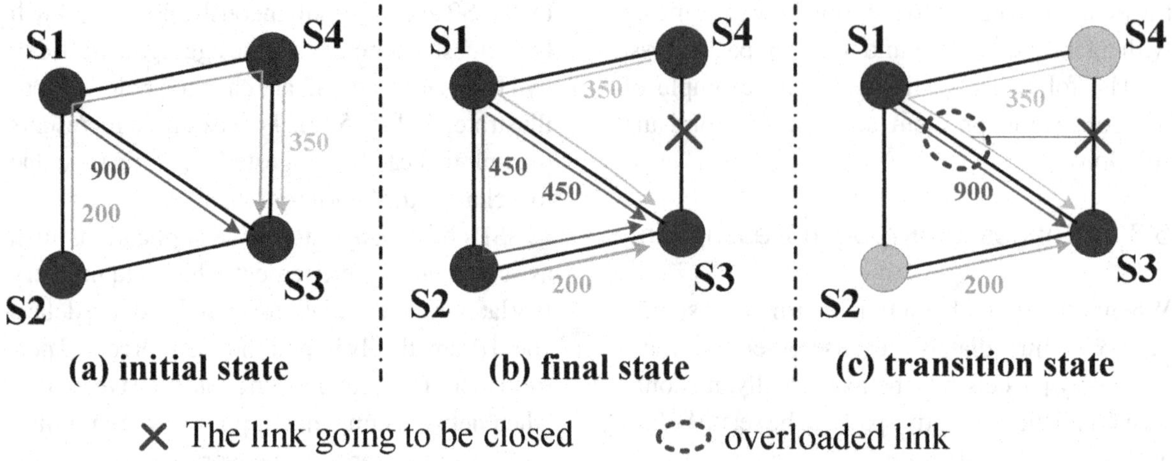

by virtue of the characteristics of flow migration (for example, some flow migration could release bandwidth of heavy loaded links and never incur any congestion, the computing scale can be greatly reduced.

Other heuristic algorithms (e.g., local search, genetic algorithm, ant algorithms) can also be used to solve traffic migration problems. But, how to design an efficient algorithm is not so simple.

CONCLUSION

The chapter describes some basic potential use cases of Power Aware NETworking, and lists several studies in academics and industry as well as work progress in SDOs. While energy consumption has become an important issue, network operators are very cautious about energy conservation solutions due to the concerns about the potential impacts on the network performance and resiliency. The chapter then presents a set of requirements for building a PANET while meeting operators' requirements on performance and resiliency. Power-aware routing and traffic engineering can reduce energy consumption in network infrastructures without dramatically affecting performance and resilience. This goal depends on certain support from hardware and control plane, and may raise new issues. Different power-aware approaches have different requirements and challenges. Future work, such as how to quick up PANET solutions for traffic engineering and how to build SDN-based Power Aware Networking are yet-to-be investigated.

REFERENCES

Abts, D., Marty, M. R., Wells, P. M., Klausler, P., & Liu, H. (2010). Energy Proportional Datacenter Networks. In *Proceedings of the 41st International Symposium on Computer Architecture (ISCA '10)*. New York, NY: ACM.

Bolla, R., Bruschi, R., Carrega, A., & Davoli, F. (2011). Green Network Technologies and the Art of Trading-Off. In *Proceedings of the 30th IEEE Conference on Computer Communications Workshops on Green Communications and Networking (INFOCOM WKSHPS '11)*. New York, NY: IEEE. doi:10.1109/INFCOMW.2011.5928827

Boucadair, M., & Jacquenet, C. (2014). *Software-Defined Networking: A Perspective from within a Service Provider Environment, RFC 7149, March 2014*. Retrieved from http://www.rfc-editor.org/rfc/rfc7149.txt

Cisco. (2009). *Power Management for the Cisco 12000 Series Router*. Retrieved from http://www.cisco.com/c/en/us/td/docs/ios/12_0s/feature/guide/12spower.html

Cisco. (2013). *Cisco EnergyWise Suite*. Retrieved from http://www.cisco.com/c/en/us/products/switches/energywise-technology/index.html

Claise, B. (Ed.). (2004). *Cisco Systems NetFlow Services Export Version 9, RFC 3954, October 2004*. Retrieved from http://www.rfc-editor.org/rfc/rfc3954.txt

D-Link. (2007). *D-link first company to offer 'green ethernet™' technology for network connectivity, embrace energy-saving initiatives*. Retrieved from http://www.dlinkgreen.com/press.asp?pressrelease_id=6

Donadio, P., Russo, S., Canonico, R., & Ventre, G. (2013). O-Gene: Towards an Open Green Network Control Plane. In *Proceedings of the 8th IEEE symposium on Computers and Communications (ISCC '13)*. New York, NY: IEEE. doi:10.1109/ISCC.2013.6754941

Energy Efficient Ethernet Study Group. (2007). *IEEE 802.3 EEESG Objectives* [PDF document]. Retrieved from http://www.ieee802.org/3/eee_study/eee_objectives.pdf

European Telecommunications Standards Institute. (2014). *ETSI ES 203 237 V1.1.1*. [PDF document]. Retrieved from http://www.etsi.org/deliver/etsi_es/203200_203299/203237/01.01.01_60/es_203237v010101p.pdf

Gao, P. X., Curtis, A. R., Wong, B., & Keshav, S. (2012). It's not Easy Being Green. In *Proceedings of the ACM Special Interest Group on Data Communication (SIGCOMM) on the applications, technologies, architectures, and protocols for computer communication (SIGCOMM '12)*. New York, NY: ACM.

GreenTouch. (2014). *Global Study by Greentouch Consortium Reveals How Communications Networks Could Reduce Energy Consumption by 90 Percent by 2020*. Retrieved from http://www.greentouch.org/index.php?page=green-meter-research

Guichard, J., Faucheur, F. L., & Vasseur, J. P. (2005). *Definitive MPLS Network Designs*. Indianapolis, IN: Cisco Press.

Gunaratne, C., Christensen, K., Nordman, B., & Suen, S. (2008). Reducing the Energy Consumption of Ethernet with Adaptive Link Rate (ALR). *IEEE Transactions on Computers*, *4*, 447–461.

Ho, K. H., & Cheung, C. C. (2010). Green Distributed Routing Protocol for Sleep Coordination in Wired Core Networks. In *Proceedings of the 6th International Conference on Networked Computing (INC '10)*. New York, NY: IEEE.

Internet Engineering Task Force, Energy Management Working Group. (2010). *Charter for "Energy Management" WG (charter-ietf-eman-01)*. Retrieved from https://datatracker.ietf.org/wg/eman/charter/

Quittek, J. (Ed.). (2013). *Requirements for Energy Management, RFC 6988, September 2013*. Retrieved from http://www.rfc-editor.org/rfc/rfc6988.txt

Spurgeon, C. E., & Joann, Z. (2014). *Ethernet: The Definitive Guide*. Sebastopol, CA: O'Reilly Media.

Wobker, L. J. (2012). *Power consumption in high-end routing systems* [PDF document]. Retrieved from http://www.nanog.org/meetings/nanog54/presentations/Wednesday/Wobker.pdf

Zhang, M., Cheng, Y., Liu, B., & Zhang, B. (2010). GreenTE: Power-Aware Traffic Engineering, In *Proceedings of the 18th IEEE International Conference on Network Protocols (ICNP '10)*. New York, NY: IEEE. doi:10.1109/ICNP.2010.5762751

Zhang, Y., Roughan, M., Duffield, N., & Greenberg, A. (2003). Fast Accurate Computation of Large-Scale IP Traffic Matrices from Link Loads. In *Proceedings of the ACM Special Interest Group on Performance Evaluation (SIGCOMM '03)*. New York, NY: ACM. doi:10.1145/781027.781053

KEY TERMS AND DEFINITIONS

Backbone Network: A part of network infrastructure that interconnects various pieces of network, providing a path for the exchange of information between different LANs or sub-networks. A backbone can tie together diverse networks in the same building, in different buildings in a campus environment, or over wide areas.

Data Center Network: The part of network infrastructure that are used to connect a large amount of servers in a data center of an enterprise, Internet Service Provider, etc.

Network Topology: The mathematical arrangement of the various links and nodes of a network.

Quality of Service (QoS): It is the idea that transmission rates, error rates, and other characteristics can be measured, improved, and, to some extent, guaranteed in advance.

Sleep: A state of the network devices. When a network device enters the sleep mode, it consumes less power, transports no traffic while preserves state information in the memory or somewhere.

Software Define Network: The network architecture to allow network administrator to manage the network on a central controller. This controller acts as an oracle which has the full knowledge of the network state.

Traffic Engineering: Telecommunication network engineers or programs use the knowledge of statistics including the nature of traffic, measurements and simulations to make predictions and to plan telecommunication networks.

Traffic Matrix: A mathematical matrix giving the traffic volumes for a certain time interval between origin and destination in a network.

Chapter 6
Application-Enabled Collaborative Networking

Tirumaleswar Reddy
Cisco Systems, India

Prashanth Patil
Cisco Systems, India

Anca Zamfir
Independent Researcher, Switzerland

ABSTRACT

Identification and treatment of application flows are important to many application providers and network operators. They often rely on these capabilities to deploy and/or support a wide range of applications. These applications generate flows that may have specific characteristics such as bandwidth or latency that can be met if made known to the network. Historically, this functionality has been implemented to the extent possible using heuristics that inspect and infer flow characteristics. Heuristics may be based on port numbers, network identifiers (e.g., subnets or VLANs, Deep Flow Inspection (DFI), or Deep Packet Inspection (DPI)). However, many application flows in current usages are dynamic, adaptive, time-bound, encrypted, peer-to-peer (P2P), asymmetric, used on multipurpose devices, and/ or have different priorities depending on the direction of the flow, user preferences, and other factors. Any combination of these properties renders heuristic-based techniques less effective and may result in compromises to application security or user privacy. Application-enabled collaborative networking (AECN) is a framework in which applications explicitly signal their flow characteristics and requirements to the network. This provides network nodes with knowledge of the application flow characteristics, which enables them to apply the correct flow treatment and provide feedback to applications accordingly. This chapter describes how an application enabled collaborative networking framework contributes to solve the encountered problems.

INTRODUCTION

Networks today, whether public or private, are challenged by demands to support rapidly increasing amounts of traffic. New channels for originating and consuming rich media are deployed at a rapid pace. Pervasive video and access on demand are becoming second nature to consumers. Applications make extensive use of rich media, placing unprecedented quality of experience (QoE)

DOI: 10.4018/978-1-4666-8371-6.ch006

demands on the underlying network. These trends present challenges for network forecast and planning operations.

Now more so than ever before, identification and differential treatment of flows are critical for the successful deployment and operation of applications. These applications use a wide range of signaling protocols and are deployed by a diverse set of application providers that are not necessarily affiliated with the network providers across which the applications are used.

Historically, identification of application flows has been accomplished using heuristics that infer flow characteristics based on port ranges, network separation, or inspection of the flow itself. Inspection techniques include:

- Deep packet inspection (DPI), which matches against characteristic signatures (e.g., key string, binary sequence).
- Deep flow inspection (DFI), which analyzes statistical characteristics (e.g., packet length statistics like ratio of small packets, ratio of large packets, small payload standard deviation) and connection behavior of flows.

Each of these techniques suffers from limitations, particularly in the face of the challenges outlined previously.

Heuristic-based approaches may not be efficient and require continuous updates of application signatures. Port-based solutions suffer from port overloading and inconsistent port usage. Network separation techniques like IP sub-netting are error prone and increase network management complexity. DPI and DFI are computationally expensive, prone to error, and become more challenging with greater adoption of encrypted signaling and secured media. An additional drawback of DPI and DFI is that any insights developed at one network node are not available, or need to be recomputed, at nodes further down the application flow path.

The goal of the Application Enabled Collaborative Networking (AECN) framework is to offer mechanisms that allow applications to request differential network treatment for their flows and to learn what the network can do for them while preserving flow encryption practices. The intent is for the applications to have the ability to initiate information exchanges in order to provide a more precise allocation of network resources and thus a better user experience, while ensuring security for the flow data. The underlying logic is that a network that is prepared in advance with applications flow treatment requirements will select and enable the appropriate means to offer the differentiated forwarding and traffic management behaviors matching those requirements. Typical requirements clauses are described in Boucadair, M., Jacquenet, C. & Wang., N. (2014).

Background

Evidently, media bandwidth requirements always depend on the service being used. Common services like e-mail require less bandwidth. By contrast, other services such as cloud-hosted virtualized desktops can place heavy per-user demands on an Internet connection, especially in deployments with high resolution desktops or multimedia. Some tasks can be highly variable. Cloud storage services, whether straightforward file sharing such as Box and Dropbox or more complex document management such as SharePoint, end up using a variable amount of bandwidth. Photographs and video files can be huge and uploading these resources could consume a fair amount of the available bandwidth, creating problems like congestion, especially problematic on shared connection. Perhaps the biggest consumer of bandwidth in recent times has been the use of real time video and audio over the Internet.

On top of bandwidth, latency considerations are also very important. Some applications, such as e-mail, are latency insensitive. Real-time applications require small latencies. For example voice over IP (VoIP) applications become unusable in the presence of high end-to-end latency; even short delays of a few tens of milliseconds are enough to make a poor audio experience while hundreds of milliseconds can render them almost unlistenable, with 150 milliseconds generally regarded as the limit for tolerable voice calls.

Determining the bandwidth requirements for an application, or the services that can be used given the available bandwidth can be non-trivial. Available required bandwidth is not the only important consideration as making good use of the bandwidth is also important. The one way to overcome this is for the network to be able to identify traffic flows in order to provide differential treatment to flows based on their requirements. Current common approach to identify traffic flows of applications in a network is to rely on dedicated content-aware devices. These devices not only parse fields on the IP and transport layers but also recognize application-related information above the transport layer. Content awareness is mainly realized through DPI functionality, which inspects characteristic signature (e.g., key string, binary sequence, etc.), and DFI, which analyzes statistical characteristic and connection behavior of traffic flows, to identify applications. However, there are limitations when deploying and operating these tools. IP applications, their characteristics and requirements change frequently and it takes time to complete application traffic analysis and update signature database after a new application or version appears. This results in time windows where these new applications are unusable and identification is not accurate. In addition there are investment costs that cannot be neglected. Sometimes the cost to identify the traffic is no less than that of forwarding the traffic. Operational cost of the additional identifying nodes is also an important issue. More potential failure points and possible optical power split may affect network quality and user experience.

AECN addresses these problems by allowing applications to request differential treatment for their flows in the access network. The network responds according to policies and may take actions to accommodate the request.

AECN

Issues, Controversies, Problems

For successful application deployment and operation, networks require visibility into traffic in order to troubleshoot, plan capacity, and perform accounting and billing. This is currently implemented by exporting observed traffic analysis via dedicated protocols such as Internet Protocol Flow Information Export (IPFIX) and Simple Network Management Protocol (SNMP) as well as other proprietary protocols and methods.

In addition, policy-based networking can be enabled using techniques that include traffic classification, policing and shaping, providing admission control, impacting routing, and permitting passage of specific traffic (e.g., firewall functions).

These techniques, visibility and differentiated network services, are critical in many networks. However, the reliance on inspection and observation limits their deployment. Reasons for this include:

- Identification based on IP addresses/prefixes is difficult to manage. The addresses may be numerous and may change; they may be dynamic, private, or otherwise not meant to be exposed. With Content Delivery Network InterConnection (CDNI, Bertrand et al., 2012), content could be served from an upstream CDN or any of a number of downstream CDNs, and it would not be possible to manually track the IP addresses of all the CDN surrogates. Even in cases where identification by IP addresses is possible, more granular identification of individual flows is not possible (e.g., audio vs. video vs. data).

- Classification based on TCP/UDP port numbers often result in incorrect behavior due to port overloading, i.e., ports used by applications other than those claiming the port with IANA (Internet Assigned Numbered Authority).
- More and more traffic is encrypted, rendering DPI and DFI impossible, inefficient, or much more complex, and sometimes done at the expense of privacy or security (e.g., applications might be required to share encryption keys with an intermediary proxy performing DPI/DFI).
- Visibility generally requires inspecting applications' signaling traffic. Signaling traffic may flow along a different path than the actual application data traffic. Attempts to apply differentiated network services are not effective in this scenario.
- There is a trend toward multipathing, allowing both signaling and data traffic to follow multiple paths, so that the entire flow is visible on any path.
- Extensions to signaling protocols and changes in the ways applications use them can result in false negatives or false positives during inspection.
- Inspection techniques are completely non-standard, so the ability and accuracy to identify traffic varies across vendors, and different implementations are likely to give different results for the same traffic.
- Inspection techniques that require parsing the payload of packets (e.g., DPI) impact performance due to additional processing but also impact memory due to the growing number and size of signatures to identify new protocols.
- Network services leveraging heuristic-based classification have a negative effect on the application behavior by impacting its traffic while not providing explicit feedback to the application. This results in lost opportunity for the application to gain insight and adjust its operation accordingly.

Sample AECN Use Cases

This section covers a number of use cases that are relevant in the context of AECN, including the details and challenges for each use case.

Efficient Capacity Usage

Network traffic is bursty and often follows diurnal usage patterns such that there are times of day where traffic levels are at a peak, and other times of day where they are at a valley. Proper network and capacity planning should be able to cater to traffic services at peak. Maintaining a network with consistent demand and usage patterns requires building capacity at a faster rate than the growth of the peak while satisfying requirements for diversity, fault tolerance and performance; this may result in traffic being forwarded, prioritized or dropped during periods of congestion.

There are several problems to consider in this context:

- Simply building enough capacity for peak usage is not always efficient and cost-effective, because not all traffic needs to transit the network at the exact moment it is queued. For example, streaming video, real time communication, and head-to-head gaming need immediate access, while data synchronization with the cloud for backups, downloading software updates, or preloading content onto a CDN could be deferred to times when more capacity is available. Today, all of the traffic competes for the same capacity at the same time. Few tools exist to provide applications with the information they need to make more intelligent decisions on demand, and thus they mostly default to “as soon as possible”.

- Queue management is not a substitute for capacity, and often a network designed for long periods of congested operation provides a poor user experience, since queue management is ultimately a method to identify which traffic should be dropped first.
- A network that is not at peak usage has idle capacity. A well managed network where capacity is added in increments may observe idle capacity, for example if bandwidth is added in increments of 10G or 100G, with only a small fraction of it being used before growth catches up. This inefficiency is magnified when one considers the spare capacity designed into most networks to tolerate failures in the network with minimal traffic impact. In many cases, the idle capacity even at peak may be up to 50%, and at off peak, it could be much higher.
- Few networks have consistent demand and usage patterns. While the average usage may follow a rough pattern, this does not always provide for flash demands, where a large number of users are simultaneously downloading an OS update, watching the same event via streaming video, more heavily using the network during weather events like snowstorms. Typical usage patterns also do not take into account the effects of outages like shifting large volumes of traffic around in the network, and so managing these exception events either requires further spare capacity, or acknowledgement that some traffic will be dropped due to congestion, with a noticeable impact to end user experience.

Firewall Traversal and Identification of New Applications

Modern firewalls use application-layer gateways (ALGs) to perform policy enforcement. For example firewalls may implement a SIP-aware ALG function that examines the SIP signaling and manages the appropriate pinholes for the Real-Time transport Protocol (RTP) media. In particular, a firewall extracts media transport addresses, transport protocol and port numbers from session description (potentially for each direction in/out), and creates a dynamic mapping for media to flow through. This model does not work when firewalls fail to identify the application and therefore the ALG for policy enforcement. For example, application media may be dropped in any of the following cases (see also Figure 1):

1. Session signaling is end-to-end encrypted, e.g., using TLS (Dierks, T., Rescorla, E., 2008).
2. The firewall does not understand the session signaling protocols or extensions that are used by the endpoints (e.g., WebRTC as defined by Bergkvist et al., 2013).
3. Session signaling and media traverse different firewalls (e.g., signaling exits a network via one firewall whereas media exits a network via a different firewall).
4. Session signaling and/or media is split across multiple paths (e.g., using MultiPath TCP (MPTCP, see Chapter “*Multipath TCP (MPTCP): Motivations, Status & Opportunities for the Future Internet*”) or Concurrent Multipath using Transfer Stream Control Transmission Protocol (CMT-SCTP)) so that a full exchange is not visible to any individual firewall.

Figure 1. Failure to identify new application resulting in media drop

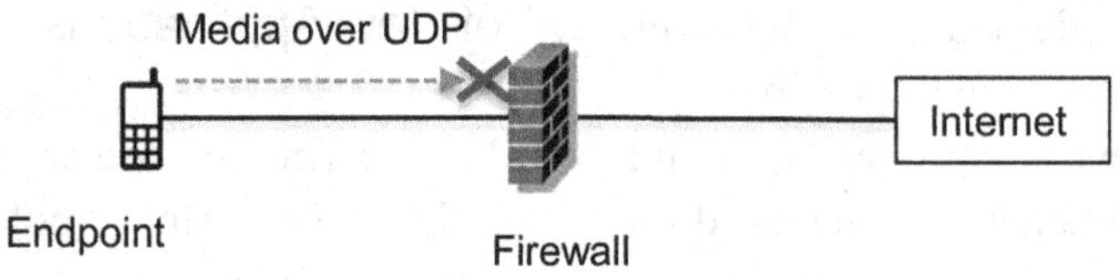

Video Bit Rate Adaptation

HAS, (HTTP Adaptive Streaming, n.d) is an umbrella term for various HTTP-based streaming techniques that allow a client to switch between multiple bit rates, depending on current network conditions.

A HAS client requests and receives a manifest file that contains information about the available streams at different bit rates and the segments of the streams. After parsing the information encoded in this file, the client proceeds to sequentially request the chunks listed in the manifest file, starting from the lowest bit rate stream. If the client determines that the download speed is greater than the bit rate of the segment downloaded, then it requests the next higher bit rate segments. If later it finds that the network throughput has deteriorated by observing lower downstream speed, then it will request a lower bit rate segment. In Figure 2 examples of clients with high, low and varying bandwidth and playback conditions are shown.

The problems with HAS are as follows:

- A HAS client selects the initial bitrate without knowing current network conditions. This could cause start-up delay and frame freezes while a lower bitrate chunk is being retrieved. A HAS client does not have a mechanism to learn current network conditions, or to signal the flow characteristics and flow priority to the network.
- A HAS server can mark the packets appropriately but setting a DSCP has limitations. The DSCP value may not be preserved or honored over the Internet and the hosting operating system may not allow setting DSCP values.
- An ISP can use DPI to prioritize one-way video streaming content but this tech-

Figure 2. HTTP adaptive streaming

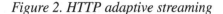

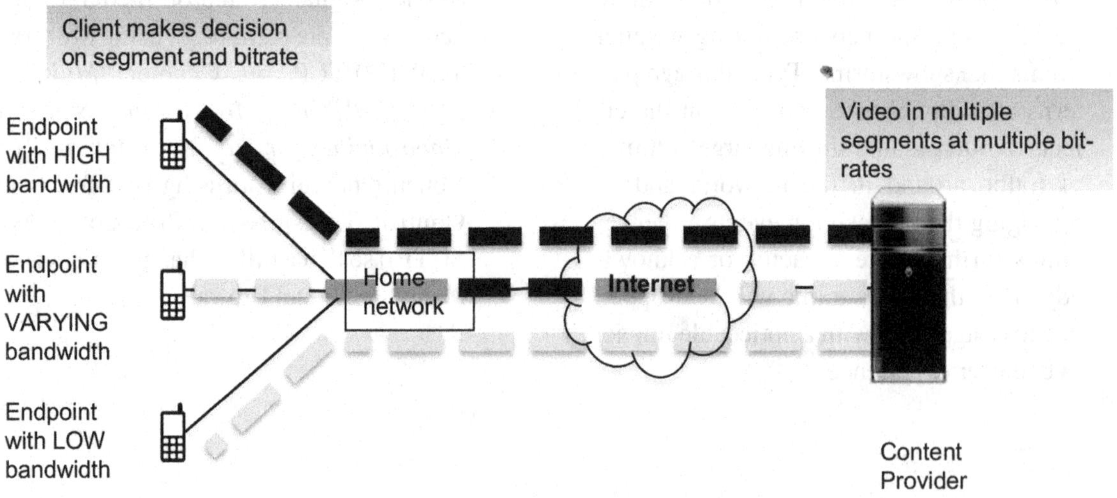

nique is expensive and fails if the traffic is encrypted.

- An application always knows better than DPI what its requirements are. Content Providers may need a mechanism to convey the flow characteristics and desired treatment to the ISP. Existing mechanisms and the associated limitations are:
  - An ISP can be informed of the IP addresses used by content providers to identify the traffic originating from those servers. As with any configuration, this is prone to human error and requires timely updates when changes occur. With CDNI, content could be served either from the upstream CDN or any of a number of downstream CDNs and it is not possible to manually track the IP addresses of all the CDN surrogates. There is also no way to differentiate content that could be available in different bitrates.
  - If a HAS client is behind a NAT and a content provider uses a RESTful API (such as OneAPI, n.d.) to install differentiated QoS, then the ISP needs to find the pre-NAT information. The content provider also needs to be aware of the ISP to which the client is attached and the IP address of the Policy Decision Point (PDP) in the ISP to which it needs to signal the flow characteristics.

Multi-Interface Selection

An increasing number of hosts are operating in multiple-interface environments. For each communication, a host with multiple interfaces needs to choose the best interface to be used. Oftentimes, this decision is based on a static configuration and does not consider the link characteristics of that interface, resulting in negative user experience. The network interfaces may have different link characteristics; however, in the absence of data about the upstream and downstream characteristics of the access link, the host and/or application may select the least fit interface. The application would also benefit from knowing the end-to-end path characteristics.

In Figure 3, a typical example of a mobile device with two network interfaces, WLAN (typically a Wi-Fi interface) and 3G, is shown. Since applications running on the device are not aware of network conditions, they may end up using an interface with lower bandwidth, higher delay and jitter.

SOLUTIONS AND RECOMMENDATIONS

The goal of AECN is to offer mechanisms that allow applications to request network services for better user experience. Following techniques and solutions are proposed to address the issues described previously.

- Efficient capacity usage:
  - AECN is a mechanism for the network to provide applications with information about network resource availability, so that individual applications can manage their demand. This demand management will help to smooth traffic by redirecting some of the demand to off-peak, and has an analog in the power industry where demand-based pricing or smart grid technology signals devices that use a large amount of power so that they can be intelligent about their demands and reduce the burden on the available capacity of the electrical grid.
  - Similarly, AECN provides a means for applications to communicate their required performance envelope. This information can be used by the net-

Figure 3. Host in multi-interface environment

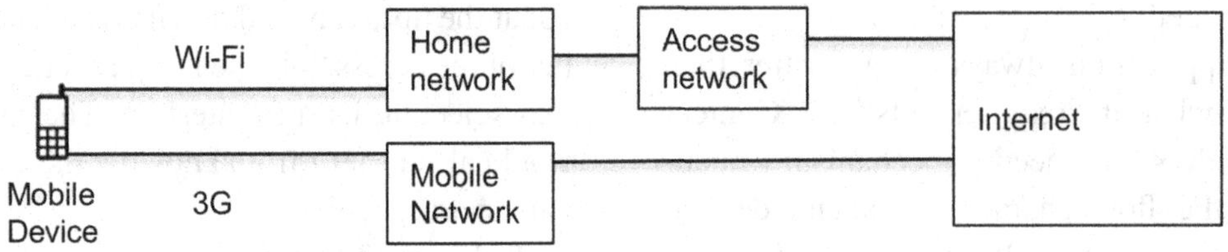

work to determine the best way to deliver the requested service.
  - Provide a means for "below best effort" or scavenger class data transmission so that traffic marked as scavenger will be carried in periods of no congestion, but may be discarded during periods of congestion due to either peak usage or outages.
  - This solution could also be used in conjunction with engineered paths through the network as constructing with techniques like Traffic Engineering (Auduche et al., 2001) and Segment Routing (Filsfils et al., 2014) in order to provide capacity for traffic that has specific performance requirements, or that could use sub-optimal path. For example, if capacity exists on a longer backup path and since some traffic is not affected by a few 10s of milliseconds of additional latency, it should be marked to use the non-optimal path even if that path is not seen as best by the routing protocol.
- Identification of new applications for firewall traversal:
  - The host provides the authorization it received from an application server, to a server that is trusted by the network to authorize flows and associated actions (e.g., policies). This is achieved by sending a cryptographic token as part of signaling which authorizes the firewall mapping for the media.
- Video Adaptation: use client metadata to help with video bit rate selection:
  - A HAS client can use third party authorization to request access to network resources. At a high level, the client first obtains a cryptographic token from the authorizing network element, and then includes that token in the request along with relevant flow characteristics. The ISP validates the token and grants the request accordingly.
- Multi-interface selection by using client metadata to help with interface selection, prioritization and aggregation:
  - The problem can be solved if a mechanism is provided for applications to communicate required flow characteristics with the available interfaces, and to know about the network conditions of each interface, or to what extent the application flow requirements can be met by each interface. The application can then prioritize the interfaces based on information gathered and select interfaces that best meet its requirements.

The remaining of the section covers the details of the AECN approach and describes some of the techniques and protocols that it uses.

High Level AECN Approach

In the previous sections the need of communication between application and network was identified. In order to provide an implementable solution, the following needs to be considered:

- Identify the protocol(s) best fit to solve the problem depending on the use case, the application that is going to use it, connectivity and network type and trust level present in the running environment.
- Provide the specification on how the protocol is used to solve the problem and describe the required extensions.

Applications continue to grow in number, type and diversity. They are running on a multitude of host types and operating systems and following different delivery models (native, web, cloud). Many use peer-to-peer (P2P) or client-server models and open standard protocols for establishing connectivity.

Applications run in diverse environments such as enterprises, home networks, home automation environments, factory floors, hospital setting, and utilities. Devices hosting the applications may connect to the network in diverse ways, using different technologies, having multiple interfaces to the same or different network devices, connecting over diverse technologies such as cable, digital subscriber line (DSL), fiber to the home (FTTH), cellular, and wireless,. In order to operate in these environments, some applications already run lightweight client-server network protocols. One example of such protocols is the Session Traversal Utilities for NAT (STUN) to discover public addresses when behind NAT devices or (Rosenberg et al., 2008). Another is the Port Control Protocol (PCP) detailed in the work of Wing et al. (2013) and used to create explicit port forwarding rules.

The AECN solution requires a protocol to be used for signaling the application flow characteristics to the network and getting feedback from the network. At the time of writing this book, few existing protocols with new extensions are being considered:

1. Client-server network protocol: PCP with flow metadata extensions. . Handles both TCP and UDP flows, but also other transport protocols (SCTP).
2. On-path application protocol: STUN with flow metadata extensions between hosts. Handles UDP flows (media streams).
3. On-path network protocol: RSVP (Braden et al., 1997) with flow metadata extensions. Handles all TCP, UDP and raw IP flows. RSPV is limited to controlled environments.

Flow Metadata Processing

In AECN, applications signal the flow characteristics and service required. The network responds back to applications with the result of processing the request.

Depending on its nature and needs, the application may request different services (e.g., bandwidth accounting, report of available bandwidth within service class, notification on certain events). As the application requirements change, the flow characteristics communicated to the network may be revised. When network state changes or when different events occur, if needed, network elements can send updates.

For example, at startup, an application may send bandwidth, delay and jitter requirements. The network performs bandwidth accounting against the matching service class and sends a response to the application. In another example, an application requests the bandwidth available for a class with certain delay and jitter guarantees. The network responds and the application adjusts the rate to the available bandwidth. If the available bandwidth changes, the application is notified and can read just the bit-rate.

Port Control Protocol (PCP)

Port Control Protocol (PCP, Wing et al., 2013a) provides a mechanism to describe a flow to the network. The primary driver for PCP has been creating port mappings on NAT and firewall devices. When doing this, PCP pushes flow information from the host into the network (specifically to the network's NAT or firewall device), and receives information back from the network (from the NAT for firewall device). PCP allows applications to create mappings from an external IP address, protocol, and port to an internal IP address, protocol, and port. These mappings are required for successful inbound communications destined to machines located behind a NAT or a firewall. Figure 4 illustrates the PCP messages exchanged to create a mapping on the PCP controlled device.

This simple bi-directional communication of flow information using PCP makes PCP a very suitable candidate to signal other interesting flow information, useful for AECN, from a client to a server.

PCP FLOWDATA Option

The FLOWDATA option (Wing et al., 2013b) described in this document allows a host to signal the bi-directional characteristics of a flow to its PCP server. A few examples are minimum and maximum bandwidth, delay and loss tolerance for upstream direction. Downstream direction characteristics can also be signaled.

After signaling, the PCP server determines if it can accommodate that flow, making any configuration changes if necessary to accommodate the flow, and returns information in the FLOWDATA option indicating its ability to accommodate the described flow.

Usage and Processing

A host may want to indicate to the network the priority of a flow after the flow has been established (typical if the host is operating as a client) or before the flow has been established (typical if the host is operating as a server). Both of these are supported and depicted in the following diagrams.

Figure 5 shows a connection being first established and then the flow being prioritized. This allows for the fastest connection setup time with the server.

The diagram in Figure 6 shows first the client asking the network to prioritize a flow, then establishing a flow. This is useful if the priority of the flow is more important than establishing the flow quickly.

Figure 7 shows a PCP client getting a PCP MAP mapping for incoming flows with priority. This ensures that the PCP client has a mapping

Figure 4. PCP Generic client-server interaction

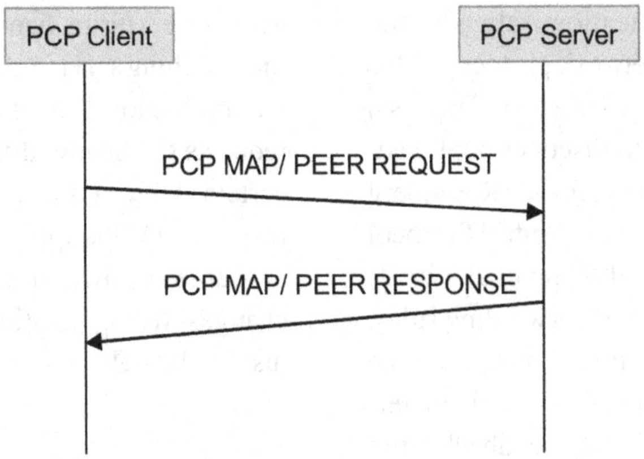

Figure 5. Client initiated connection before flow prioritization

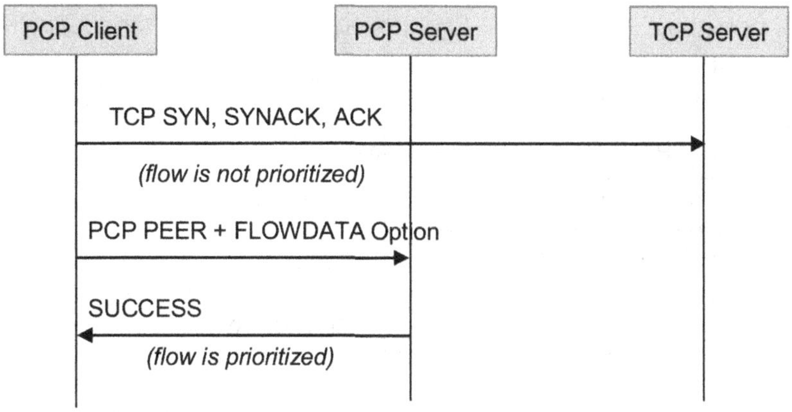

and all packets associated with the incoming TCP connections matching that mapping are prioritized. The PCP Client in this case could be a video server in a data center.

The diagram in Figure 8 shows how two separate connections, where only one is active at a time, use the same instance identifier.

Traversal Using Relay NAT (TURN)

Traversal Using Relay NAT, TURN, (Mahy et al, 2010) is a protocol that is often used to improve the connectivity of P2P applications. By providing a relay service, TURN ensures that a connection can be established even when one or both sides are incapable of a direct P2P connection. A client can choose to signal flow characteristics of a relay channel to the TURN server, so that the TURN server is aware of the flow characteristics of the channel. The TURN server can potentially signal back to the client that it can (fully or partially) accommodate the flow. This sort of signaling will be useful for long-lived flows such as media streams or WebRTC data channels, traversing through the TURN server. The TURN server can further communicate the flow information to a number of on-path devices in its network using a Policy Decision Point (e.g., a SDN controller). Thus, the network hosting the TURN server can accommodate the flow. With this mechanism,

Figure 6. Client initiated connection after flow prioritization

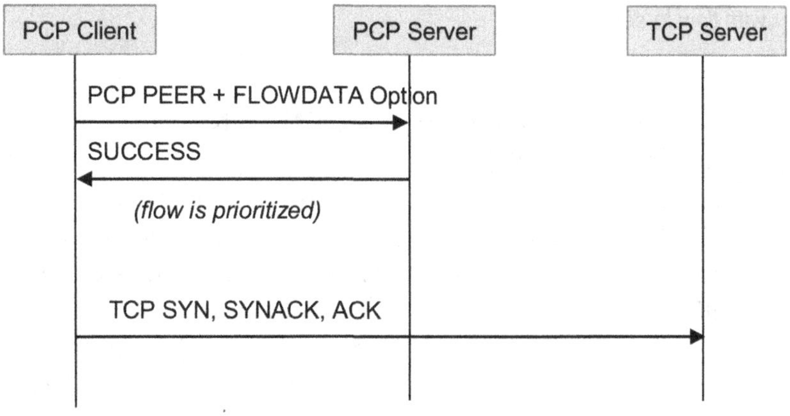

Figure 7. Server initiated connection after flow prioritization

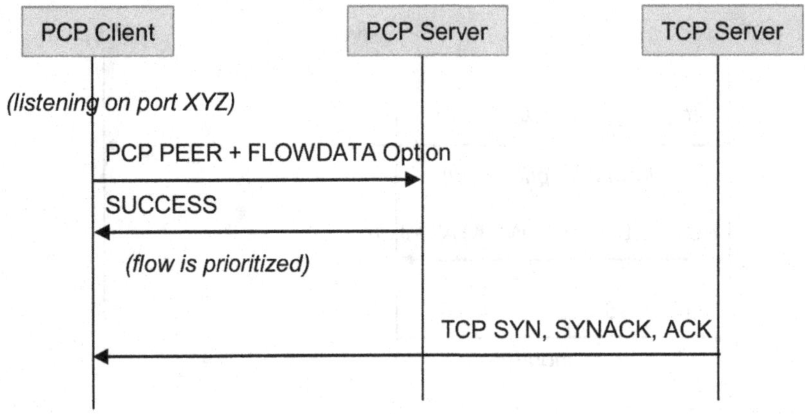

Figure 8. Two server connections with same instance ID

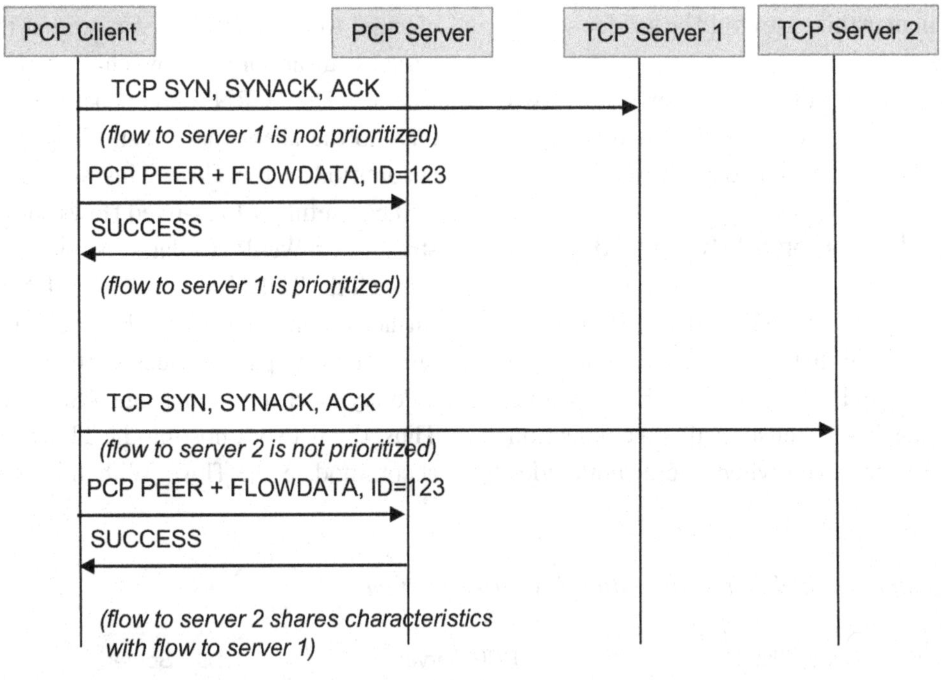

a TURN client can request the TURN server to provide certain characteristics for the relayed channel on both legs (client-to-server, server-to-peer).

Figure 9 depicts a TURN client signaling the desired flow characteristics to a TURN server over the TURN ChannelBind request.

AECN SDN

One of the goals of SDN is to define a set of techniques, existing or new, that allows for easy automation and offer means to interact with network resources dynamically in order to ensure optimized resource usage. A comprehensive overview of the SDN landscape and the functional taxonomy of

Figure 9. Message diagram, operating a server

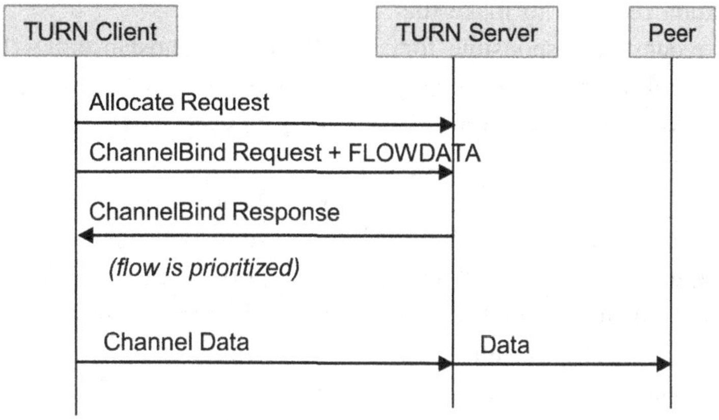

the techniques used can be found in the work of Boucadair & Jacquenet (2014).

There are several proposals on how the network can be programmed with flow information in order to enable different service policies (e.g., traffic prioritization). Typically this involves a controller that collects flow information by receiving copies of flow data packets or performing DPI if on-path. Many flows today are very dynamic, time-bound (short lived), encrypted and asymmetric, and require different priorities depending on network conditions, direction, time of the day, and other factors. Therefore, this means that controller examination of the flow packets cannot be used successfully to infer flow and metadata information (Penno et al., 2014).

Architecture

In order to automate the resource allocation and usage, AECN proposes the following SDN architecture and message flow as illustrated in Figure 10 (Penno et al., 2014)

1. Applications running on the end points (e.g., User Equipment, Data Center Servers, CPE routers) signal associated metadata to Network Elements. This can be achieved by using PCP (Wing et al. 2013a) with the PCP Flow Extension (Wing et al., 2013b) which allows a PCP Client to signal flow characteristics to the network, and the network to signal its ability to accommodate that flow back to the host.
2. The Policy Decision Point (PDP, Yavatkar et al., 2000) manages resources and triggers configuration operations based on applicable policies. To achieve this, a protocol that has built-in primitives for reliable real-time messages and that, ideally, shares information about network availability between the network device and the PDP is required. REST, Extensible Messaging and Presence Protocol (XMPP) (Saint-Andre, 2011) or similar protocols are good candidates.
3. PDP installs the flows in routers or switches and assigns them a series of actions, modify flow actions, collect statistics, or (more importantly) extend the provisioning of these flows end-to-end. PCP with THIRD_PARTY option, NETCONF (Enns et al., 2011), COPS-PR (Chan et al., 2001), or any similar protocols.

In Figure 10, the middlebox is any flow-aware device (e.g., edge router, switch, CPE router).

Some advantages of the AECN SDN architecture are:

- Host driven: The host/ application, which has the information required to make the correct service request is responsible for communicating the flow metadata according to the application needs. The approach works with encrypted and multi-party flows.
- Network Authorization: When network access control is required, the host gets authorization from the Application Server trusted by the network in order to install flows and associated actions (e.g., policies). The Application Server could be deployed in a third party network. This is important for networks that do not trust the host.
- Immediate incremental value for endpoints and applications in an end-to-edge manner: once a AECN CPE router is installed, applications could signal flow characteristics to the network for both directions and benefit from traffic prioritization, firewall pinholes and other services without other changes to the network.

Message Flow

When an end host installs a flow in the middlebox through a PCP message a call is made to the PDP. This message carries the following information:

- Match condition elements, including source/destination IP, source/destination port, L4 Protocol, VLAN Id.
- Metadata conveyed in PCP FLOWDATA option.
- Lifetime in PCP response which is mapped to the OpenFlow's idle_timeout (Openflow, 2013). This way, the PCP client is aware when the flow entry is removed.

The PDP uses any relevant protocol, e.g. NETCONF (Enns et al., 2011), COPS-PR (Chan et al., 2001) or OpenFlow (Openflow, 2013) to add, delete and modify flows and their metadata. For example, an OpenFlow controller could get the information of configured queues and their properties. The OpenFlow controller either associates the flow with appropriate queue or instructs the OpenFlow-enabled network device to rewrite the DiffServ Code Point (DSCP) bits

Figure 10. AECN signaling flow with SDN

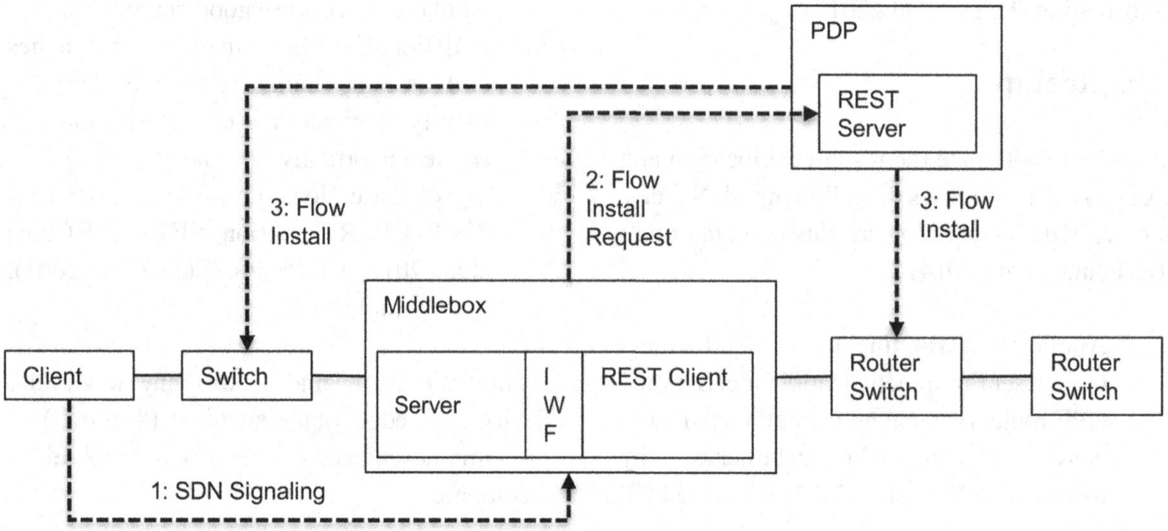

for the flow based on the metadata conveyed in the REST message.

When an application-driven flow times out or is explicitly deleted, if required, a REST API call is generated and the controller is notified. This allows the PDP to delete the flow from other devices in the network.

The PDP could also decide on its own to remove the installed flow. In this case, a PCP unsolicited response is sent to the PCP Client owner of such flow.

Deployment Considerations and Challenges

There are a few challenges with enabling the AECN technique. The selection and extensions of the signaling protocol(s) is one. In many cases, the use of an existing protocol limits the deployment to the use cases that were targeted by the initial protocol specification.

The other challenge with the signaling protocol is path congruency with the associated flow (path-coupled vs. path-decoupled). With client-server signaling protocols (out of band signaling), the application needs to contact the server on a node that is on the forwarding path. In some cases, e.g., dual homing or when a server is not directly connected, this may not always be possible.

Path-coupled (also known as On-path) protocols try to guarantee that signaling messages follow the same path as the data packets. They typically do this by encapsulating the messages they initiate with the same header as the data packets. Intermediate nodes are enabled to inspect and intercept these packets. In addition they probe routing or forwarding with a locally created dummy data packet and then pre-route the packet accordingly. One example is RSVP. Path congruency with data flow is ensured as long as all devices on path are enabled. But this is rarely the case and the reality is that these types of protocols are only deployed today in small controlled environments, never in the public Internet.

In-band signaling protocols carry the signaling messages in packets that are, for the purpose of routing or switching, identical with the data packets. STUN is one such protocol. There are no congruency issues with these types of protocols. However, as in the case of on-path signaling, they open up security holes.

A network device receives application messages either because they are addressed to the device or the device is configured to intercept them. Most requests need to be processed and some create state. A request message will consume network resources such as CPU, memory, hardware entries required for classification, and bandwidth. To prevent denial of service attacks, it is important that non-authenticated and non-authorized messages are dropped early in the processing chain. Also, network devices should allow operator selection for the type of processing (e.g., process, drop or forward only).

There are cases where a signaling message specifies flow data for either or both directions of the flow and it is possible for network devices to receive conflicting flow data for a given direction of the flow. Appropriate conflict resolution is important in this case and needs to be clearly specified by the standards.

FUTURE RESEARCH DIRECTIONS

Some of the challenges to deploy AECN are listed below:

- Update applications to support AECN.
- Update some network elements to support AECN.
- Support from browser, OS to provide appropriate AECN API to applications.
- Provide UI to change the priority of flows on an endpoint.

AECN must consider security and privacy implications to provide protection again false claims, leakage of private information, and unwarranted differentiated treatment of flows. For example, the network may need to validate application provided flow information before using it to provide differential treatment of the application's flows. Similarly, an application may need assurance of confidentiality protection before providing potentially sensitive information.

A basic security requirement of AECN is that there must be a mechanism for mutual authentication between the application signaling flow information and the network entity that uses this flow information to provide differential treatment for flows as well as feedback to applications about such treatment. Without this, the solution is open for attacks with fake applications falsely claiming to be legitimate applications that require special treatment, i.e., the network infrastructure is at risk of being misused. Should the network entity be spoofed, applications could be misled that the network has accommodated the requested flow characteristics.

AECN is being actively pursued within the IETF standardization community and has gathered momentum and interest from service providers, vendors and application providers alike.

CONCLUSION

The goal of AECN is to provide a programmable network that allows applications to signal flow characteristics that help service providers with identification and treatment of application flows. This is a very important step in moving towards a model where a host, based on application use, can demand appropriate treatment anywhere and anytime. This will also serve as an important step for network monetization.

REFERENCES

Adaptive Streaming, H. T. T. P. (n.d.). *Wikipedia*. Retrieved November 25, 2014, from http:// https://en.wikipedia.org/wiki/Adaptive_bitrate_streaming

Awduche, D., Berger, L., Gan, D., Li, T., Srinivasan, V., & Swallow, G. (2001). RSVP-TE: Extensions to RSVP for LSP Tunnels. *IETF*. Retrieved November 25, 2014, from https://tools.ietf.org/html/rfc3209

Bergkvist, A., Burnett, D. C., Jennings, C., & Narayanan, A. (2013). WebRTC 1.0: Real-time Communication Between Browsers. *World Wide Web Consortium*. Retrieved November 25, 2014, from www.w3.org/TR/webrtc/

Bertrand, G., Stephan, E., Burbridge, T., Eardley, P., Ma, K., & Watson, G. (2012). Use Cases for Content Delivery Network Interconnection. *IETF*. Retrieved November 25, 2014, from https://tools.ietf.org/html/rfc6770

Boucadair, M., & Jacquenet, C. (2014). Software-Defined Networking: A Perspective from within a Service Provider Environment. *IETF*. Retrieved November 25, 2014, from https://tools.ietf.org/html/rfc7149

Boucadair, M., Jacquenet, C., & Wang, N. (2014). IP Connectivity Provisioning Profile (CPP). *IETF*. Retrieved November 25, 2014, from https://tools.ietf.org/html/rfc7297

Braden, R., Zhang, L., Herzog, S., Berson, S., & Jamin, S. (1997). Resource ReSerVation Protocol (RSVP). *IETF*. Retrieved November 25, 2014, from https://tools.ietf.org/html/rfc2205

Chan, K., Seligson, J., Durham, D., Gai, S., McCloghrie, K., Herzog, S., . . . Smith, A. (2001). COPS Usage for Policy Provisioning (COPS-PR). *IETF*. Retrieved November 25, 2014, from https://tools.ietf.org/html/rfc3084

Dierks, T., & Rescorla, E. (2008). The Transport Layer Security (TLS) Protocol Version 1.2. *IETF*. Retrieved November 25, 2014, from https://tools.ietf.org/html/rfc5246

Enns, R., Bjorklund, M., Schoenwaelder, J., & Bierman, A. (2011). Network Configuration Protocol (NETCONF). *IETF*. Retrieved November 25, 2014, from https://tools.ietf.org/html/rfc6241

Filsfils, C., Previdi, S., Decraene, B., Litkowski, S., Horneffer, H., Milojevic, I., . . . Crabbe, E. (2014). Segment Routing Architecture. *IETF*. Retrieved November 25, 2014, from https://tools.ietf.org/html/draft-filsfils-spring-segment-routing-04

Mahy, R., Matthews, P., & Rosenberg, J. (2010). *Traversal Using Relays around NAT*. TURN.

OneAPI. (n.d.). *GSM Association*. Retrieved November 25, 2014, from http://www.gsma.com/oneapi/

OpenFlow. (2013). OpenFlow Switch Specification Version 1.4. *OpenNetworking Foundation*. Retrieved November 25, 2014, from https://www.opennetworking.org/images/stories/downloads/sdn-resources/onf-specifications/openflow/openflow-spec-v1.4.0.pdf

Penno, R., Reddy, T., Boucadair, M., & Wing, D. (2013). Application Enabled SDN (A-SDN). *IETF*. Retrieved November 25, 2014, from http://tools.ietf.org/html/draft-penno-pcp-asdn-00

Relay Extensions to Session Traversal Utilities for NAT (STUN). (n.d.). *IETF*. Retrieved November 25, 2014, from https://tools.ietf.org/html/rfc5766

Rosenberg, J. (2010). Interactive Connectivity Establishment (ICE): A Protocol for Network Address Translator (NAT) Traversal for Offer/Answer Protocols. *IETF*. Retrieved November 25, 2014, from https://tools.ietf.org/html/rfc5245

Rosenberg, J., Mahy, R., & Wing, D. (2008). Session Traversal Utilities for NAT (STUN). *IETF*. Retrieved November 25, 2014, from https://tools.ietf.org/html/rfc5389

Saint-Andre, P. (2011). Extensible Messaging and Presence Protocol (XMPP): Core. *IETF*. Retrieved November 25, 2014, from https://tools.ietf.org/html/rfc6120

Wing, D., Cheshire, S., Boucadair, M., Penno, R., & Selkirk, P. (2013). Port Control Protocol (PCP). *IETF*. Retrieved November 25, 2014, from https://tools.ietf.org/html/rfc6887

Wing, D., Penno, R., Reddy, T., & Selkirk, P. (2013). PCP Flowdata Option. *IETF*. Retrieved November 25, 2014, from https://tools.ietf.org/html/draft-wing-pcp-flowdata-00

Yavatkar, R., Pendarakis, D., & Guerin, R. (2000). A Framework for Policy-based Admission Control. *IETF*. Retrieved November 25, 2014, from https://tools.ietf.org/html/rfc2753

Yavatkar, R., Pendarakis, D., & Guerin, R. (2000). A Framework for Policy-based Admission Control. *IETF*. Retrieved November 25, 2014, from https://tools.ietf.org/html/rfc2753

KEY TERMS AND DEFINITIONS

ALG: Application-level gateway is a security component deployed on firewall or NAT boxes to allow customized traversal filters in order to support address and/ or port translation for certain application layer protocols.

CDN: Content Delivery (or Distribution) Network is a set of servers deployed in multiple data centers across the Internet in order to serve content to end users while also offering high performance and high availability.

DFI: Deep flow inspection is a packet filtering technique that analyzes statistical characteristics like packet lengths, ratio of large packets and small payload standard deviation, and connection behavior of flows, to determine the actions to be applied to application flow or session packets (e.g. classify, mark, redirect, block, drop)

DPI: Deep packet inspection is another form of computer network packet filtering that examines the packet content to decide on the actions to be taken on the packets or for the purpose of collecting statistical information.

PCP: Port Control Protocol is a computer networking protocol that allows hosts on IPv4 or IPv6 networks to control how the incoming IPv4 or IPv6 packets are translated and forwarded by an upstream router that performs Network Address Translation (NAT) or packet filtering.

SDN: Software defined networking is a network architecture that allows network administrators to manage network services through abstraction of lower-level functionality. This is achieved through mechanisms that allow decoupling of the control and forwarding planes.

TURN: Traversal using relays around NAT, is a protocol that enables a client behind NATs or firewalls to receive incoming data over TCP or UDP connections. It is most useful for clients behind symmetric NATs or firewalls that wish to be on the receiving end of a connection to a single peer.

Chapter 7
The Whole World is Going Mobile

Charles E. Perkins
Futurewei, USA

ABSTRACT

The Internet is growing ever more mobile – meaning, that an ever greater proportion of Internet devices are mobile devices. This trend necessitates new designs and will produce new and even unpredictable conceptions about the very nature of the Internet and, more fundamentally, the nature of social interaction. The engineering response to growing mobility and complexity is difficult to predict. This chapter summarizes the past and the present ways of dealing with mobility, and uses that as context for trying to understand what needs to be done for the future. Central to the conception of future mobility is the notion of "always available" and highly interactive applications. Part of providing acceptable service in that conception of the mobile Internet will require better ways to manage handovers as the device moves around the Internet, and ways to better either hide or make available a person's identity depending on who is asking.

INTRODUCTION

Technology marches forward and provides ever more useful (and complicated) wireless devices for our entertainment and profit. Handheld devices commonly have more storage and computing power than the roomful of equipment popularized as futuristic in so many science fiction movies. Even more impressive is the capacity for convenient wireless access to information around the world, at the click of a finger. And yet, the wireless revolution has just begun. Both licensed and unlicensed band communications have been growing at a prodigious rate, and, to the surprise of many industry experts, the IEEE 802 Wireless family now appears to be the dominant wireless family if measured by total traffic over the air (Brodkin, 2012; Brustein, 2014). If measured by direct profit from subscribers, however, licensed-band cellular wireless channels have a tremendous advantage.

Users are confronted with a confusing array of applications, configuration choices, underlying technologies, pricing schedules, product features, and upgrade options. Unfortunately, it is often the case that applications such as voice or interactive video that work on one radio technology may fail

DOI: 10.4018/978-1-4666-8371-6.ch007

on another radio technology, or have prohibitive cost. More often than not, applications work differently or fail entirely depending upon the underlying operating system, but aside from this "bug", the main reason typical customers/users care about the operating system is because of some perceived status imputed to it. That status is not really based on technology. We observe that these "bugs" of inconsistent user interface and availability are mostly built-in to the application suite offered with the products, and vendors perceive that fixing such bugs would enable the customer to use competitive products. In other words, these bugs are seen as a way to segment the market, presenting a competitive advantage, forcing customers to choose one product that seems least inconvenient for the desired uses. This effect is even more prominent when considering uses for licensed-band communication technologies and products (i.e., smartphones for cellular networks).

There are several technology vectors that will work against this enforced market segmentation.

- Multifunction / multiradio devices will dominate the market, and users will be frequently confronted by the abovementioned bugs
- Conservation of battery power is one of several issues motivating the dynamic selection of the closest access point as well as reductions in signaling requirements during "idle" times. Note that "always-on" applications generating frequent "keepalive" messages have severe impact on battery consumption.
- The availability of "media-independent" protocols which can provide wireless communication and handover services that are not closely tied to the specific wireless technology.

Wireless devices naturally provide continuous opportunities for user mobility, and people love the freedom provided by radio communications. The natural feeling of freedom and convenience afforded by wireless Internet access has raised customer expectations, and one result will be the continued increase in the number of Internet access points. We can expect to see near-ubiquitous coverage of urban areas by both licensed and unlicensed-band radio access points, with the choice increasingly made based on convenience, rather than dictated by application limitations or contract limitations.

Unfortunately, what seems natural to the user is not very naturally provided by traditional Internet protocols. As a result, there have been numerous attempts to provide a natural user experience with the assistance of the application. In particular, applications running on unlicensed band radio channels have been instrumented with features to help with handover and session continuity from one access point (or base station) to the next. This trend has been driven particularly because of the lack of operating system support for mobility management, which would typically eliminate the need for the disparate application-layer mobility management solutions. The result is that some applications can survive movement to new locations (i.e., new network attachment), and other applications cannot. When the application does survive, the results are still quite variable, including temporary lock-up, request for reauthorization, loss of streaming video, and restarting transfers for files and webpages.

As real-time applications (such as virtual reality) become popular, this handover behavior will increasingly be seen as amateurish and annoying. Application-based mobility management is typically different for each application, with different characteristics and surprises. Vendor-centric mobility management (i.e., mobility management not interoperable and supported only for sessions while running on a particular vendor's equipment), as practiced in today's cellular networks, can respond somewhat more quickly, but is usually encumbered with accounting protocol gadgetry that limits performance. Moreover, suitable handover performance is strictly limited to the particular operator's network.

It is the thesis of this chapter that wireless is the future of the Internet, and high-performance mobility management is crucial for enabling a satisfactory user experience. Just as we have become accustomed to beautiful imagery that was infeasible on the web at 2400 baud, we will soon become accustomed to smooth and convenient streams of data uninterrupted by artifacts related to handovers.

REVIEW OF INTERNET MOBILITY MANAGEMENT

Early Days and Dreams

Even in the early 80's, there was a dream to enable mobile devices to run everywhere in the global Internet as identified by their globally unique IP address (C. Sunshine, 1980). The elements of the Sunshine/Postel scheme were remarkably prescient compared to later designs over the last 30 years. Various new ideas have come under consideration, but (if we consider encapsulation to be a variety of lazy source routing) many of the ideas present can be found even in today's client-based solutions. Notably, work in the early Mobile IP working group of the IETF (IETF, 1992) never referenced the Postel note, as if the Working Group (WG) members were simply unaware of the work.

By the time wireless interfaces were becoming more popular in the late 1980's, several research and standardization groups (e.g., from Panasonic, Columbia, CMU, and IBM) were investigating the possibilities for handling mobile wireless devices as part of the Internet. Our group at IBM was excited about the educational possibilities as well as the convenience for hospital applications, public safety, and disaster relief. Military applications, while obvious, were intentionally out of scope for the research group due to company policy; nevertheless we often did consider the strategic importance of including those applications as part of our design space. Also during those years, groups at MIT and Columbia expressed willingness to collaborate with us and we had many fruitful interactions (Ioannidis, Maguire, Ben-Shaul, Levedopoulos, & Liu, 1990; Ioannidis & Maguire, 1993; Ioannidis, 1993).

These groups and others from Carnegie Mellon, Matsushita, Xerox PARC, and elsewhere formed the nucleus of the IETF Mobile IP working group which formed in 1992. Initial ideas for solutions were based on source routing, multicast, and encapsulation. At the time these solutions were developed, wireless links were quite slow -- in fact the major use for wireless was to transmit short messages for pagers. Consequently, saving bits was a high priority, as evidenced by specifications such as "Minimal Encapsulation" (Perkins, 1996), which by now are mostly ignored.

Basics

Mobility management has several component technologies that are typically present, regardless of the particular physical medium or protocol suite employed at the point of attachment. The fundamentals are:

- Identity management (including authentication)
- Binding location address to routing address
- Rerouting

In addition, depending upon the application, the following may be desirable.

- Preserving the subnet fiction (as if the mobile device were connected to a home subnet)
- Capability advertisement

Finally, for increased performance, we often find the following additional improvements:

- Local forwarding between access points
- Context transfer

The next subsections present a brief summary of each of these functional components along with the reason for their importance and some examples.

Identity Management, Authentication, and Authorization

In commercial networks, connectivity is granted to a device based on identifying the device as the electronic agent of a subscriber, often by requiring the subscriber to enter a password or other uniquely identifying information by way of the device. This naturally leads to a large overlap between mobility management and various techniques of verifying the subscriber's identity. Since a mobile device is typically not located in the same network as the information database required to verify the subscriber's identity, this verification requires a protocol between the device and the network, as well as a protocol between the network infrastructure elements that must cooperate to enable the exchange of credentials between the mobile device and the authentication/authorization service platform(s).

There are quite many different designs for enabling authentication, far too many to provide even a representative sampling. Most systems rely on cryptography to inhibit identity theft or misappropriation of resources. Since for many service providers, the subscriber database is considered to be a major business asset, access to the credential information in the subscriber database is tightly controlled along with almost all the other information about the subscriber. This naturally leads to centralization for authentication, which can lead to significant performance degradations for any such centralized design. The more difficult, or the more delay, inserted by protocol operations between a local point of attachment and a remote authentication service, the less likely the subscriber will enjoy speedy access to the Internet, and the more likely that handovers between points of attachment will introduce annoying glitches in application interactivity.

These points will be revisited later during discussion about future Internet design points.

Address Binding

If a mobile device is to be accessible from the Internet, it needs an IP address known to its communication partner. For communications initiated from the Internet towards the mobile device, that device needs to provide a globally unique identifier that can be resolved to an IP address, so that packets can be forwarded to the mobile device. There are many namespaces for globally unique identifiers that can be made available for this purpose:

- IP addresses
- MAC addresses
- DNS names
- URLs
- NAI (Network Access Identifier, which looks like an email address)
- IMSI (International Mobile Subscriber Identity), TMSI (Temporary Mobile Subscriber Identity),
- IP address plus port number (for address sharing schemes, including NAT44-based, NAT64-based, A+P -based communications (Bush et al., 2011))
- RFID
- ... and numerous others

If communication is to be maintained with the mobile device as it changes its point of attachment to the Internet, in most designs an association is created between a local address (the address at the point of attachment), and the above-mentioned globally unique identifier. In the IETF, this association is typically called a "binding". Using that terminology, a mobile device that requires continuity in its communication with a partner would then require a "binding update" to associate a new local address with its global address. The protocol mechanisms for accomplishing a binding update are even more numerous and varied as the number of namespaces. See for instance: (Wedlund & Schulzrinne, 1999; R. Shacham, 2009; Maltz & Bhagwat, 1998) various layer-2 schemes (Mishra, Shin, & Arbaugh, 2003; Snoeren & Balakrishnan, 2000)

Future mechanisms for managing binding updates will likely become even more complicated. Notably, a binding update typically will require interaction with the identity management features of the mobility management design, to avoid spurious handovers. Otherwise, a malicious user might trigger a handover to gain unauthorized control over the communication streams of a victim (mobile) device.

There are, at least, two ways by which a mobile device may avoid the need for address binding (and binding update):

- Routes to the global address can be disseminated to all the infrastructure routers between the mobile device and its communication partners.
- The mobile device can simply interrupt and restart any communications whenever movement occurs.

The first of these methods is not scalable. In limited deployments, the method has proved effective. But mobile devices are likely to access dozens or hundreds of Internet destinations on a continual basis, especially given the propensity for advertisers to fetch numerous display ads on many web pages. A billion devices accessing that many destination addresses through an average Internet path length of about 10 hops would produce tens of billions of route updates every day. This is widely thought to be an unacceptable burden on the routing structure of the Internet.

The second one seems unlikely to satisfy anyone who might desire reasonable interactivity with their mobile applications.

Rerouting

As mentioned in the last section, following the association between global and local address requires some kind of rerouting for the packets. In the degenerate case, where there is no local address separate from the global address, the need for rerouting is quite a bit greater, and this approach is usually considered unscalable unless it is somehow caused to be limited in scope. This leads to interesting design possibilities, generally within the design space known as "micromobility" (Ramjee, Porta, Thuel, & Varadhan, 2002; Campbell & Gomez, 2002).

Otherwise, re-routing may be done either by encapsulation (also known as tunneling) or by source routing, and the two approaches can easily be combined as may be necessary. Both methods require solid security protection – otherwise a malicious source route (or a malicious tunnel setup) could cause traffic to the mobile device to be rerouted either for improper observation and recording, or else to be completely disrupted.

The source routing can be either loose or strict, although most designs rely on loose source routing. The number of tunneling protocols is quite large, much larger than one might expect just based on the actual needs of tunneling. Much of the diversity stems from evolution from previous network investments. Some of the tunneling protocols incorporate various directives for quality of service, charging identification, traffic classification, and so on. The tunneling can occur at almost any layer of the protocol stack, leading to explosive growth of the design space. Tunnel setup and maintenance can be done by a completely separate protocol, or directly be inclusion of information elements along with the tunneled data. In other words, control of the tunneling may be isolated from the flow of tunneled packets through the data plane, or the control traffic may flow alongside the data traffic.

Service Features

Identity management and rerouting are fundamental functions required for mobility management, but other features can also be of prime importance in certain situations. Two such features are subnet management and capability exchange.

Subnet Management

IP networks have for many years been organized around the concept of subnets. The original design of IP allowed for class A, class B, and class C networks for unicast data transmission. Upon rapid adoption of the World Wide Web (WWW) running over IP networks, the demand for newly allocated subnetworks accelerated, motivating the adoption of Classless Inter-Domain Routing (CIDR) (Huitema, 1993) because it enabled allocation of subnets of many more sizes than just three. This greatly slowed down the consumption of the IP address space. Roughly speaking, the determining characteristic of a subnet is that packets can be broadcast to every host in the subnet without requiring routers to retransmit the packet. This feature was very natural when subnets could be closely associated with Ethernets, even as the physical medium of Ethernet was itself evolving to a non-broadcast medium. Features such as neighbor discovery and local file exchange depend upon subnet addressing, and yet mobility makes it much more difficult for individual hosts on a subnet to send and receive broadcasts.

Mobility management technologies have been designed to maintain the appearance of subnets (for instance, Mobile IP (Perkins, 2001), although the concepts surrounding neighborliness seem less relevant now than they were when Ethernet was the dominant physical medium for most Internet end-host connectivity. If current trends continue, it seems that end hosts will continue to be less and less concerned with determining whether or not a communication partner is on the same subnet.

Capability Exchange / Advertisement

When a mobile device has several choices for connectivity to the Internet, determining which choice will offer the best features for the needs of the applications may become important. This can be done by gathering service advertisements for the multiple points of attachment, by comparing network identifiers (e.g., SSIDs) to configured lists of identifiers and looking for a match, by special protocol -- e.g., Service Location Protocol (SLP) (Veizades, Guttman, Perkins, & Kaplan, 1997; Guttman, Perkins, Veizades, & Day, 1999) or in many cases by simply inferring the likely Quality of Service (QoS) from the nature of the physical wireless medium. For instance, one can expect higher bandwidth from 802.11g than from 802.11b. When comparing access points for best service, higher received power levels or lower interference levels can be preferred.

New work within the IEEE 802 Wireless group aims at making this choice more efficient even before the wireless device associates with a candidate access point. Other work in the IETF from the seamoby WG (IETF Seamless Mobility (seamoby) Working Group, 2000) has had similar goals, but this work has not seen significant adoption. Use of the SRV records with DNS (Gulbrandsen, Vixie, & Esibov, 2000) is a way to contact general services, but this is done long after the point of attachment has completed the establishment of the wireless link; thus, this method can't really be used to determine which wireless link might be most suitable. Other methods exist (e.g., Apple's Bonjour, 3GPP's ANDSF (Karlsson, 2008)) with similar design goals, and similarly not suitable for selecting the best point of attachment. This is an area ripe for improvement in future Internet designs.

Localized Signaling

The advantage of localized signaling should be clear; if protocol operations happen mostly local to the point of attachment, response time can be orders of magnitude better. Unfortunately, identity management is often done in a manner that is inhospitable to signal localization. For instance, if subscriber data used for authentication is located on a remote server somewhere else on the Internet, interaction with that remote server is necessary to verify the identity of the mobile device. Immediately one might consider design ideas aimed at locating the subscriber credentials closer to the point of attachment, but this approach has new pitfalls. Maintaining database consistency is tricky when the subscriber database is spread out over dynamically changing points of attachment. Moreover, as the number of entities involved with maintaining security increases, the opportunities for penetrating the network security also increases. Finally, security protocols are already quite complicated, and the new complications arising from database distribution lead directly to new vulnerabilities to programming errors (including data synchronization and replication issues). Nevertheless, as the need for better handover performance increases, the advantage of localized signaling may well motivate deployment of such performance improvements. Work done in the IETF hokey WG (IETF Handover Keying WG (hokey), 2006) (closed in 2012) is relevant to this purpose.

Closely related to localized signaling is the idea of locally maintaining a collection of information relevant to the mobile device. This collection of relevant information is typically known as a context (or mobile context). As the mobile device moves from one network attachment to the next, the mobile context can be made to follow it from one point of attachment to the next. The context can then be used to re-establish local state (for instance, multicast group membership, or header compression state). This would usually allow much better feature response at the new point of attachment, compared to re-running various protocols to re-establish the necessary state.

The following sections will describe some mobility management designs that will illustrate the above features and show how the features work together as a system.

Mobile IPv4

At the time of final publication for Mobile IPv4 in 1996, the state of the wireless world was far different than today. Since wireless speeds would always lag the speed of wired networks, many people were confident that wireless devices would always be considered inadequate for "real work". Nowadays we see that the wireless links are "fast enough" so that most people prefer wireless whenever available for normal workloads. On the other hand, the cellular telephone companies were not at all interested in IP anyway, and so they did not participate in the IETF standardization process. This divide persisted for many years, with traditional cellular engineers being viewed within the IETF as having "bell-shaped heads" -- referring to the continued dominance of Bell Telephone and its progeny in the business of wireless communications.

Mobile IPv4 (Perkins, 1996; Perkins, 2010) was the first Internet-based mobility management protocol to be standardized within the IETF. As illustrated in Figure 1, the Home Agent (HA) is forwarding data from the correspondent node to the Foreign Agent (FA). The FA then sends the data directly to the Mobile Node (MN). Data from the MN to the correspondent node is sent directly from the FA without necessarily requiring additional service from the HA.

As the Internet continued its rapid growth, it became obvious that Internet communications were a force to be reckoned with. And yet it was still not for quite many years that mobile wireless data commanded very much attention. It took the spread of IEEE 802.11 before that would happen.

Figure 1. Mobile IPv4

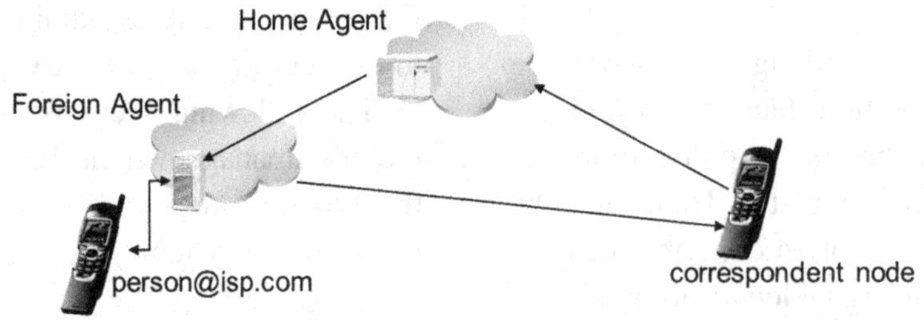

Mobile IPv4 can be understood as a somewhat minimalistic approach to providing the three fundamental functions of identity management, address binding, and rerouting. The identity management was handled by maintaining a set of security associations, one per mobile user (more accurately, one per IP address in use on a mobile device). While not really a subscriber database, this directory of security associations plays an analogous role by enabling the mobile device's credentials to be checked upon every notification sent by the mobile device.

The re-routing function was specified to make use of encapsulation. The current address of the mobile node (its so-called "care-of address") and the global address of the mobile node (its "home address") are the tunnel endpoints of the encapsulated traffic. Packets arriving at the home network are delivered to the care-of address, and packets from the mobile node can be tunneled from the care-of address to the home network for subsequent delivery to the rest of the Internet. The original design of Mobile IPv4 provided the appearance of the home network as a broadcast subnet, but usually only for devices actually residing on the home network. It was viewed that mobile devices would sometimes be "at home" on a subnet, and other times be "away" on a visited network at the "care-of address". There was not any provision for capability advertisement or the abovementioned performance improvement features. . In Mobile IPv4, the address binding function was enabled by *registration* of the care-of address with the home agent (HA). Importantly for vehicular networking, almost the exact same protocol operations can be put into use for supporting mobile routers as well as mobile hosts (Devarapalli, Wakikawa, Petrescu, & Thubert, 2005; Leung, Dommety, Narayanan, & Petrescu, 2008).

Mobile IPv4 formed the basis for several important but non-compliant network protocols for systems including CDPD (Cellular Digital Packet Data), CDMA (Code Division Multiple Access), and Nextel's "push-to-talk" service. These systems essentially copied Mobile IP and made proprietary modifications without bringing their work into the IETF. Of course the IETF has no enforcement power, and any system designer can make modifications, albeit at the expense of interoperability. Unfortunately, the designers of the mobile networks just mentioned were not concerned about interoperability, and in fact would typically prefer if their customers were not able to switch to different networks (owned by the competition). The designers of commercial mobile networks did not participate in the IETF, and the IETF standards were seen as not meeting the business objectives of the commercial network operators.

As a result, the vision of Mobile IP did not fully materialize, due to the following factors:

- No desire for wireless operators to promote inter-network compatibility

Figure 2. Mobile IPv6 (RFC 6275)

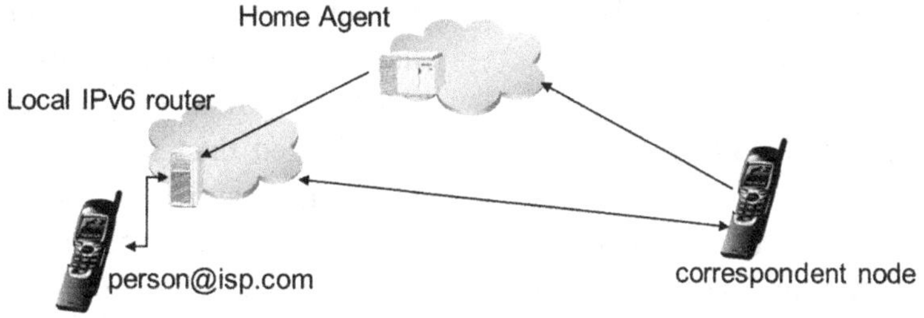

- Lack of availability of Mobile IP on connected devices (including laptops)
- Inability to map Mobile IP operational requirements into the normal operational practices and subscriber databases of commercial networks.

These difficulties persist even today. As long as subscriber revenue continues to drive the current business models of wireless network operation, it is not clear whether Mobile IP will ever live up to its daring promise of inexpensive, pervasive, and transparent connectivity to the wireless Internet.

Mobile IPv6

Soon after the standardization of Mobile IPv4, it was recognized that before too long the global supply of IPv4 addresses would be exhausted. Work immediately started on a replacement protocol, eventually to be known as IPv6. Since Mobile IPv4 was hot off the presses, it seemed quite clear that a variation should be considered for use with IPv6. In fact, the charter of the IPv6 Working Group called for mobility support as an essential component of the protocol.

The design of Mobile IPv6 (Perkins, Johnson, & Arkko, 2011) (illustrated in Figure 2) manifests the two fundamental features of mobility management, namely identity management and rerouting. As with Mobile IPv4, rerouting occurs by encapsulating data traffic for delivery from the home network to the visited network. In the case of Mobile IPv6, it was more efficient to use IPv6's loose source route feature. Indeed, source routing designs were submitted for Mobile IPv4 as well, but rejected due to inherent security concerns. Since IPv6 was chartered to mandate the availability of IPsec, source routing was again able to be considered.

The design of Mobile IPv6 involved several innovative features. The use of randomized IP addresses was considered to enable a certain level of privacy, although to be effective in the wireless Internet this would have to be combined with MAC address randomization. The triangle routing problem of Mobile IPv4 was to be resolved by enabling binding updates at correspondent nodes as well as with the home agent. No identity management is required by the correspondent nodes, and the protocol design is scalable to the projected scale of the IPv6 Internet. This scalability was achieved by relaxing identity management to a simple verification that the mobile node supplying the binding update to a correspondent node was the same as the mobile node that first initiated communications with that correspondent node, by means of return routability tests. Strictly speaking this is also true regarding binding updates supplied by the mobile node to its home agent. However, the home agent has to be equipped with a security association with the mobile node, which typically depends on some kind of identity management.

In order to maintain compatibility with existing Internet services, DSMIPv6 (Dual-Stack Mobile IPv6) (Soliman, 2009) was designed to allow

MIPv6 hosts to interact with MIPv4 home agents (and the IPv4 Internet) as may be required during the transition period from IPv4 to IPv6.

GPRS Tunnel Protocol (GTP)

No discussion of tunneling protocols would be complete without at least some mention of GTP, which in modern cellular telephone networks is used to carry traffic from the mobility anchor to the current point of attachment of a mobile device. In fact, GTP is much more than a tunneling protocol, and has many many extensions for a variety of control purposes. In LTE networks (Pudney, 2006), GTP (Tamura, 1999; Milton, 2008) is used to carry data within the core network elements for delivery to and from the Internet.

In the figure 3, functional modules Packet-Data Gateway (P-GW), Serving Gateway (S-GW), Mobility Management Entity (MME), Evolved NodeB (eNodeB) (i.e., LTE base station), and User Equipment (UE) are shown. The UE establishes a radio link to the eNodeB. The MME, S-GW, and P-GW form the nucleus of the Evolved Packet Core (EPC), indicating that the EPC is an evolution from previous packet core designs from 3GPP. The packet core has historically been the routing domain of the cellular network service provider, and typically has only wireless computers. The actual network architecture is significantly more complicated than shown in the figure, but the additional features are not directly relevant to mobility management as described in this chapter.

Compared to earlier 3GPP designs, the EPC offers advantages including the separation of the control plane (signaling with the MME) from the data plane, which is established using GTP between the P-GW and the S-GW and between the S-GW and the eNodeB. This separation between control plane and data plane enables separate optimizations to be applied for control signals and for data flows, which have significantly different traffic characteristics.

In the EPC, the anchor function is concentrated at the P-GW, and the address of the UE is topologically correct for the connection between the P-GW and the Internet. Re-routing occurs as the UE moves between different eNodeBs and, for larger movements, between S-GW domains; it is accomplished by modifying the tunnel endpoints of the GTP tunnels as made necessary for delivery

Figure 3. LTE

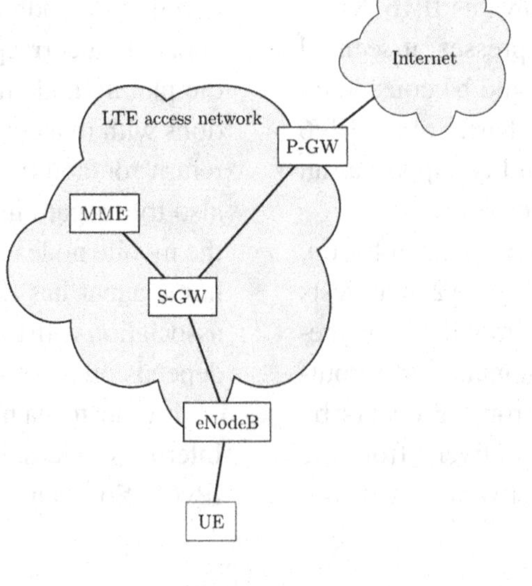

of packets to the eNodeB supplying wireless connectivity to the UE.

Proxy Mobile IP (PMIP)

In order to avoid requiring that all mobile devices have Mobile IP software installed, a modified version of Mobile IPv6 was designed in which the network infrastructure handles all mobility management signaling. In fact, the protocol for binding updates is identical to Mobile IPv6 except for the addition of a single bit to the control signaling to indicate that Proxy Mobile IP (PMIP) (Gundavelli, Leung, Devarapalli, Chowdhury, & Patil, 2008) is in use. Although the protocol is the same, there is a new network function (analogous to the Foreign Agent in Mobile IPv4) called the Mobility Access Gateway (MAG), which performs localized mobility management signaling on behalf of the mobile node.

As shown in Figure 4, the Home Agent is renamed to be the Local Mobility Agent (LMA). The LMA receives binding updates from the MAGs as a mobile node moves from one point of attachment to the next. Since the intention motivating PMIP is to ensure that the mobile node does not require additional software, all IP address changes must be hidden from the mobile node. This requires that all MAGs, acting as local access routers, must supply the same IP address to the mobile node – and, in fact, even the same MAC address.

These requirements, taken together, usually are met by strict administrative control over the infrastructure mobility management elements. As a result, the mobile node is automatically restricted to roam over a single administrative domain. While useful and widely deployed in various cellular networks, this still provides only a very limited subset of what might be considered Internet mobility management.

Seamoby

Early on, soon after the main design of Mobile IPv6 was completed, the need for improved handovers motivated the formation of a new working group for Seamless Mobility (seamoby). Several features useful for seamless mobility and localized signaling were identified:

- Localized handover signaling
- Context transfer
- Paging
- Network selection

By some measures, seamoby was considered to be a failure. The protocols that were designed and published were not deployed, and the working group was chaotic and divisive. However, the basic

Figure 4. Proxy Mobile IPv6 (RFC 5213)

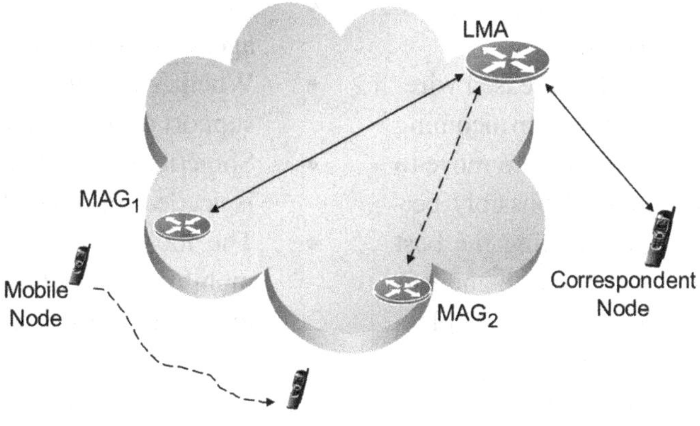

precepts were quite correct; in the opinion of the author, the difficulties were mostly political and not due to technical infeasibility.

Fast Mobile IP (FMIP) (Koodli, 2009) was the protocol designed for localized handover signaling. The basic idea is to enable neighboring access routers to cooperate during handovers so that a mobile node could quickly reattach to the network without waiting for signaling to/from its home agent. Experiments in Nokia Research Center labs showed that local handovers could be completed in less than 10 milliseconds, typically far less time than required for carrying out binding update and binding acknowledgement between the mobile node and the home agent. It was seen that this could allow seamless reception of even high-definition television at very low signaling cost, and FMIP operations could complete at the same time as the global Mobile IP protocol signaling was proceeding, usually completing tens or hundreds of milliseconds after FMIP had already completed the handover.

Context transfer extensions were designed to accompany the FMIP signaling. In this way, important bits of context necessary for smooth handling of communications with the mobile node could be transferred to the mobile node's new point of attachment. For instance, multicast group memberships could be maintained with optimal local delivery. Compression state for wireless communications could even be transferred between neighboring basestations, enabling almost perfect resumption of compressed operations. QoS indications for bandwidth reservation could also be transferred without renegotiation.

When a mobile node detects increased wireless interference or reduced power from incoming bits over the air, it should take action to move to another point of attachment with possibly better signal characteristics. Determining the best neighboring network is far from trivial, and it is still a matter of ongoing design in various wireless standards organizations such as IEEE and 3GPP. The seamoby working group developed CARD (Candidate Access Router Discovery) for this purpose. Unfortunately, the CARD effort seems to have had somewhat less success, and relies on signaling packets containing a potentially large amount of information that might never be used.

Lastly, it should be mentioned that seamoby also considered paging for Mobile IP and Internet mobility management. Paging, as applied in cellular networks, provides a way for a mobile device to save power by interrupting (for perhaps long periods of time) mobility management signaling. Then, when service is once again needed, the device re-establishes its presence in the network. The problem to be solved, then, is how the mobile node might be notified to receive incoming communications. For this purpose, *paging areas* are defined in which the mobile node may be found, essentially by local broadcast requesting the mobile node to restart mobility management. Due to the contentious nature of the working group, and because paging was perceived (perhaps rightly so) to be less important than the other efforts, the paging design effort was tabled for later consideration. But that never happened.

Distributed Mobility Management (DMM)

More recently, the DMM Working Group (dmm) has been formed to design mechanisms for distributed mobility management. The work of dmm rests on several observations:

- Not all mobile nodes need mobility management support at all times
- Whether or not a mobile node needs such support depends on the applications it runs
- Sometimes mobility management support is needed for only a brief time
- The mobile nodes should make use of a mobility anchor (e.g., home agent) that is located as close as possible for IP routing

The location of the home agent is largely determined by the address used by the mobile node. In other words, the mobility management required by the mobile node partially depends on the address chosen by the mobile node as the communication endpoint for the application in use. This means that there is a close connection between mobility management requirements and source address selection (see for example (Gont, 2011).

Pushing the mobility anchor down the topological hierarchy of the Internet has been called "flattening" the access network. This has the effect of reducing signaling latency, but is limited by scalability considerations. Data may also reach a mobile device considerably faster if its mobility anchor point is nearby, instead of within a possibly distant home network. Finally, when the mobility anchor point is under the same administrative domain as the roaming network of the mobility device, middleboxes such as firewalls and traffic shapers are more likely to be properly configured for enabling access by the mobile node. Not coincidentally, this aspect of flattening also aligns with the administrative requirements necessary for the use of Proxy Mobile IP.

On the other hand, such flattening techniques may work against simple integration with the Internet of Things, simply because of the greater need for scalability and proper gateway architecture. Vehicular networking may present additional difficulties unless the roadside networks are constructed very carefully to avoid introducing numerous administrative boundary crossings. Alternatively, it may be determined that flattening and some other techniques from dmm are not closely compatible with the needs of vehicular networking or the larger-scale Internet of the future. On the other hand, the "just in time" nature of dmm mobility management is likely to enhance scalability independently of flattening.

Media-Independent Handover

As mentioned in earlier sections, IEEE 802 Wireless technologies currently are carrying a preponderance of the world's wireless data. Practically all of this wireless data is carried over 802.11 and its variations (802.11a, b, g, n, ac, etc.) but Zigbee (802.15) makes a contribution -- and, previously, WiMAX (802.16) was a serious contender for serving the world's needs for wide-area ("4G") communications. As time progresses, it is likely that additional wireless technologies will be needed for longer range, better battery life, and perhaps easier integration with systems using cognitive radio. The past and future concerns about continuing heterogeneous radio systems was a strong motivator for the creation of 802.21, a task group within IEEE 802 Wireless to enable media-independent handovers. This group has developed a general handover protocol, and more recently several amendments, for just this purpose.

The 802.21 protocol has several components:

- Command Service
- Information Service
- Event Service (e.g., delivery of notifications and trigger conditions)

These media-independent services enable various handover preparations as shown in Figure 5. For instance, an event can be established to notify the handover management application whenever signal strength dips below a useful level. Preferably, the level would be set before the deteriorating link would be useless, so that handover preparations can be made even before the new radio interface is made active, minimizing any downtime during a break-before-make handover. Usually, new credentials for the mobile node should be established at the target access network so that network-reentry at the new point of attachment does not incur authentication latency.

Figure 5. Scope of Media Independent Handover (MIH)

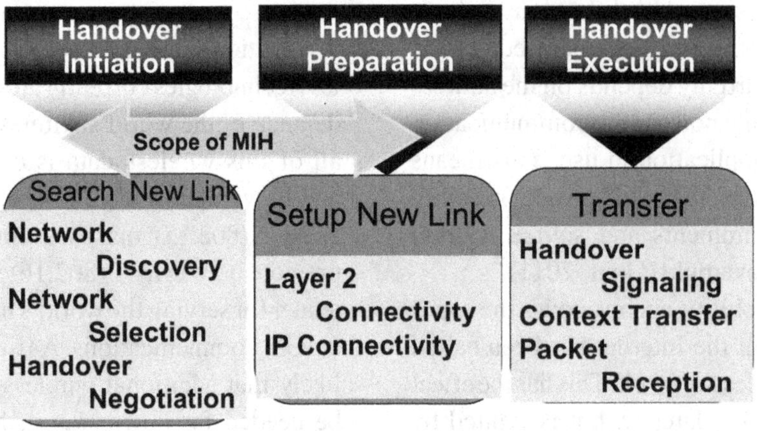

MPTCP

More recently, multipath TCP (MPTCP) (Ford, Raiciu, Handley, & Bonaventure, 2013) has been developed for certain types of mobility management. For mobile devices with multiple radios, a new subflow can be added for an application when it is detected that an existing radio interface has started to exhibit poorer performance or more bit errors. For this purpose, identity management and rerouting can be considered to operate at the application layer (or in some implementations directly at the transport layer). Keys for identity management are exchanged during MPTCP initialization and can be used to add or delete subflows. In this way, the multi-radio device can get a new IP address on a radio interface before its previous IP address loses contact, and arrange for a smooth handover.

It remains to be seen whether MPTCP will gain significant non-proprietary deployment. It has the advantage of enabling mobility without requirement for a home agent, but the reasons for this advantage are exactly the same reasons why applications running TCP only cannot gain the benefit. See the section "Multipath considerations" for more about MPTCP.

Future Internet Design Directions (Especially, Distributed Mobility Management)

Estimates for 5G speeds and performance characteristics are becoming more popular lately. On the one hand, 4G equipment is becoming much more widely available, and has enabled a new class of user experiences. For instance, many people are comfortable relying on 4G network connectivity for traffic reports, map services, shopping, sharing pictures, social media interactions, and finding instant answers to whatever topics might arise during conversations with friends. Many people are *unsatisfied*, however, because 4G has done much to raise peoples' expectations and it is often obvious where performance and/or coverage improvements are needed.

One recent commentator from a large equipment vendor simply suggests that 5G will fix this problem by providing *everything* somehow *better*:

- High data rates
- High capacity
- Low latency
- Massive number of devices: 7B --> 50B --> ?5000B?

- Low battery consumption
- Low cost
- High reliability
- "Affordable and sustainable"

While it is difficult to argue with this approach, it is the purpose of this chapter to provide some deeper insight into just how such a better network might be engineered. Moreover, mobility management is noticeably absent from the above list; perhaps it is implicit as part of the presumed improvement in user experience. A similar but much better exposition of 5G requirements has been developed as part of the METIS 2020 (Mobile and wireless communications Enablers for the Twenty-twenty Information Society) project (METIS Consortium, 2013).

By now there has been 20 years of design work in the IETF for general mobility management. Commercial networks have been expanding rapidly, and offer continual decrease in the price of carrying wireless data. However, the price reduction is counterbalanced by a continual increase in the volume of data to be carried. These trends have put pressure on the commercial networks to utilize less expensive communications channels. Many operators have turned to (unlicensed) IEEE 802 Wireless (and, in particular, 802.11) for use as an auxiliary communications channel. They want to use 802.11 to offload wireless data from their core networks (which support data transmitted over expensive licensed spectrum).

Unlicensed band / 802.11*

Even without the addition of wireless offload, IEEE 802 Wireless technologies already carry the great majority of the world's wireless traffic. This trend is likely to persist into the indefinite future unless impeded by new regulations. The possibility of regulatory action cannot be disregarded, as we have already seen communities where common deployment of 802.11 for general citizen use has been outlawed. In other jurisdictions overseas, it has been made illegal to carry Voice over IP (VoIP) over 802.11, in order to preserve the revenue model of the wireless operators in those countries.

The cost of 802 Wireless equipment is remarkably low. It has become the wireless physical medium of choice in most homes, businesses, conferences, hotels, airports, and most other venues where the relatively short range of the wireless link is not unduly inconvenient. Nevertheless, there have been analyses showing that the total cost of coverage over square miles of area would be higher using popular WiFi technologies than with, for instance, LTE. This suggests that WiFi may continue to dominate in areas not requiring great range, and LTE may continue to grow as the technology more likely to work everywhere. This evolution will probably mainly depend on pricing, but could also depend on perceived differences in user experience. If new WiFi technologies lose their cost advantage, or if LTE equipment and subscription pricing drop dramatically, then the future outlook of WiFi will become far less rosy. Other variants such as 802.11p do offer longer range communications and could grow in importance especially for vehicular applications.

Recently, there has been interest in an unlicensed-band version of LTE known as LTE-U. Although standards are not expected to be complete for several more years, LTE-U and its follow-on LTE-AA could have a substantial impact on the future role of WiFi. Within the IEEE, discussions with 3GPP are in progress with both organizations agreeing on the need to avoid interference in unlicensed band communications.

Unfortunately, there has been somewhat less success with providing handovers between the plentiful WiFi access points. This, again, results from the requirements for identity management and rerouting. For systems of WiFi access points under the administration of an enterprise network domain, handover can be made quite transparent by various techniques, mostly performed at layer

2. For residential WiFi or even WiFi access points at hotels or conferences, not much effort is made to provide smooth handovers. This could change if more reliance is made upon VoIP using WiFi connections. As it is, most non-voice smartphone applications don't need mobility management, and wireless operators are happy to maintain voice connectivity over licensed-band communication channels.

In the future, people may learn to expect smoother performance from their wireless handsets. What is needed is a sort of trans-operator identity management service – that is, a generalized roaming service. Alternatively, network operators could band together to offer identity management for WiFi customers at any WiFi hotspot (or access point). There is no technical barrier for network operators to offer a service. The only thing lacking is a common purpose to offer wireless users the best possible performance and handover service.

Similar comments apply to enabling handovers between WiFi access points and LTE (either macro cell or small cell). In the best scenarios, LTE operators would offer (for perhaps a small fee per transaction) to quickly identify WiFi users, thus enabling very fast link setup as well as high-performance handovers between WiFi and LTE, or even just between neighboring WiFi hotspots owned by different establishments. Such services are already starting to become available.

Differentiating Mobility Sessions

As the volume of wireless data grows inexorably year over year, the extra traffic caused by rerouting it through a home network has been viewed as an unacceptable business expense. As mentioned in the section about DMM design considerations, we expect applications to be differentiated by the mobility needs. On the one hand, many web-based applications can rely on TCP retransmission for a sufficient level of reliability. On the other hand, people love photography and video, and interactive video places stringent time requirements on packet delivery. It is possible that more and more emphasis will be placed on real-time delivery, which then would promote mobility management solutions as have been developed in the IETF. Roughly speaking, there are perhaps five varieties of mobility support:

- none
- short-term (e.g., file transfer)
- medium (e.g., streaming video)
- real-time (e.g., interactive video, Skype voice/video/chat)
- long-term (e.g., mobile servers)

Another way to get better performance is to increase the number of available points of attachment. Even better would be to enable simultaneous use of multiple communication paths. If each application could use a separate communications channel, the mobile device could produce and consume a much greater volume of data. For this to work properly there should be some interactions between the various access domains so that sessions could be initiated and handed over properly.

For each of the points of attachment, the same fundamental mobility functions must be available -- identity management and rerouting. For best performance, typically necessary for real-time applications on mobile devices, the identity management function must be optimized in some way to prevent dependence upon remote services. This can be done by augmenting the mobile's local context with some derived credentials that can be verified locally. Here, these derived credentials will be called a mobile security context. Roughly speaking, the way this works is as follows.

Initially, the mobile device and its network point of attachment agree on some local credentials. As the mobile device moves, the network point of attachment provides derived credentials to a neighboring point of attachment, and then the mobile device provides its credentials (or its newly derived credentials) to its new point of attachment. These derived credentials are available without protocol interactions between the mobile and remote authentication services.

This handover optimization can work equally well between heterogeneous wireless media, and between points of attachment operated by different network operators. In the latter case, however, protocol operations are typically inhibited due to lack of cooperation or desire of network operators to charge for, and maintain control over, end-user communications. It is to be hoped that in the future, user convenience will begin to outweigh adherence to authentication policies geared to restricting user choice.

Dynamic Anchoring

Dynamic anchoring is related to the concept of application differentiation based on the type of mobility service required, as suggested in the last section. The anchor point associated with application flows on the mobile device can be dynamically situated depending on which flows are currently active. This is highly nontrivial, and it depends on protocols which have not yet been defined. The problem will be to find a standard way to do the following protocol operations:

- identify anchor points serving each classification of application mobility support (e.g., static, medium, streaming, real-time)
- negotiate the proper re-routing technique (from numerous possibilities) = properly characterize and situate the mobile device's context (including security context)
- carefully identify both start and end conditions for application mobility support needs

If inter-operator cooperation can be established, as mentioned in the previous section, then dynamic anchoring can be better provided by allowing service continuity between neighboring operators even for dynamically chosen anchors and medium or even short-term mobility support needs.

Multipath Considerations

Given that terrestrial wireless media is far more vulnerable to disruption and bit errors than wired or optical fiber media, it makes sense to consider redundancy in packet transmissions. This can be done in quite many ways. Multipath TCP (mentioned earlier) and related work in the IETF was designed for this purpose. MPTCP offers some compatibility with TCP, as well as some resiliency to allow retransmissions of packets over alternate "subflows". MPTCP builds upon earlier work done for Stream Control Transmission Protocol (SCTP) (Stewart, et al., 2000) which is another multipath transport protocol designed in the IETF. SCTP was adopted for use within 3GPP but has not otherwise seen much adoption, perhaps because of its incompatibility with TCP.

But this is certainly not the end of the story. For better performance, multipath flows could carry redundantly encoded packets which enable payload construction as long as the percentage of dropped packets does not exceed a threshold limit. Some of the flows could be tunneled or encrypted separately from other flows. On the other hand, if the flows have unequal delays, much of the performance improvement can be negated; in extreme circumstances the performance can be worse than that of traditional TCP (Arzani, Gurney, Cheng, Guerin, & Loo, 2014).

Other hybrid approaches are possible, and if history is any guide, all different approaches will be tried.

Ownership of Location Information

A user's location should be owned by the user – not Google, or Verizon, or the NSA. And yet, breaches of user privacy and location information have seemingly become almost routine. In the future, we must strive for much better management of this information.

Location services have become much more important as it has become possible to discover where a user is by the simple device of associating the user device's current IP address (or care-of address) with a location within range of the point of attachment offering that IP address. For instance, insertion of advertisements (e.g., in search engine results) should be relevant to a user's current location. Coupons can be offered for the user's favorite items.

This practice relies on treating the user's current location as an asset owned by the network operator. In the future, as people discover the myriad opportunities for misuse of this data, much more personalized and configurable procedures will have to be developed and made available. What is currently an aggravation can easily turn into an intrusion and even into a threat, once the information falls into the wrong hands. As one simple example, once a person is located at the shopping mall, thieves could target a home and be done within fifteen minutes. Of course similar strategies are already in use, but if data concerning a user's location is mistreated, thieves and other criminals would not even need to be local to monitor the movements of their victims.

Future Technology Trends

Small Cell

One way to increase capacity is to increase the number of network points of attachment, taking care to avoid interference between neighboring points (e.g., base stations or access points). Assignment of frequencies in such a way that neighbors use different frequency arrangements is helpful (and a ubiquitous part of industry practice), but soon the area cannot sustain the addition of any more base stations unless the power of each station is decreased. Since the need for increased capacity will continue into the indefinite future, it seems likely that range for base stations and access points will decrease, often to only a fraction of that available from today's base stations. Such points of attachment with reduced range are called "small cells".

Strictly, speaking, "small cell" is not a future technology. Already, IEEE 802 Wireless technologies typically qualify for that designation. Moreover, there are plenty of small cells deployed for cellular radio transmission, as an alternative to the "macro cell" typically used today. Future trends indicate that over 50% of newly deployed radio heads will be indoor small cells (Scf, 2013).

One result of increased deployment of small cells will be a corresponding increase in the importance of smooth handovers. This is simply because the time duration between annoying glitches will become smaller, so that the glitches can no longer be easily ignored. Put another way, the number of applications, that could withstand typical disconnection and reconnection patterns without user annoyance, will decrease. Another result will be a strong increase in the need for operators to coordinate traffic between small cells, perhaps even to reassign mobile devices to less congested neighbors. This operation behind the scenes really needs to be done smoothly.

More Unlicensed Spectrum

The most direct way to provide increase capacity is to free up more spectrum. During recent years there has been additional licensed spectrum offered at auction, but as mentioned most of the traffic growth has happened over unlicensed spectrum. If additional unlicensed spectrum is made available, the fundamental nature of the communications industry could change.

Of course, unlicensed spectrum is more vulnerable to misuse and congestion than licensed spectrum, and this may eventually prove to be the downfall of IEEE 802 Wireless technologies or LTE-U. However, such a negative outcome is currently purely speculative, and up until now the vulnerabilities have rarely been cause for serious user concerns. Instead, deployment continues unabated.

It has often been observed that the creative use of unlicensed band spectrum -- using Bluetooth as well as IEEE 802 Wireless and other radio technologies -- has led to many innovations and new businesses. This observation, along with the fact that unlicensed band carries far more data than wireless band bearers, makes a powerful argument for the allocation of additional unlicensed band spectrum. In fact, persuasive arguments have been made to change the rules of use for even some existing blocks of spectrum, in order to improve utilization and serve the greater need. Whether or not these arguments, which seem sound technically, are able to overcome the economic arguments made by licensees for existing cellular communication bands, remains to be seen.

If indeed more unlicensed band spectrum is made available, that would also provide additional motivation for the development of so-called cognitive radio for detecting the availability and nature of nearby communication channels. Insofar as such new developments would encourage development of quite many new physical layer technologies, we would likely see a corresponding increase in the number of network access providers. This would then naturally drive further development of improved and more widespread handover techniques as have been proposed earlier in this chapter.

Personal IoT

The Internet of Things is expected to add another order of magnitude of addressable devices to the population of the Internet -- including sensors of many types, vehicles, home automation, visual displays, lighting, process control, and so many others. This huge enlargement of the Internet population is almost certain to bring along with it new expectations, new mechanisms for congestion, new traffic characteristics, and even a new understanding of global communications. Already, even at the coarsest level of granularity, mapping programs and scene visualization have substantially changed the nature of travel and deepened our understanding of the world around us. Even now, except for the very basic matter of wireless coverage, there is no technical barrier to prevent our experience of the whole world to be enhanced in the same way that an automated tour guide enhances our understanding of artwork. Indeed, without exaggeration we may expect to become much more aware of the fabulous artwork provided to us almost everywhere by Mother Nature. For example, we may expect to see much closer the beauty of the mountains, the dense jungle undergrowth, and the aerial dances of birds.

The nature of the specific sensors will dictate the real time characteristics for service to and from applications which interact with the sensors. As has been discussed earlier, these characteristics will impose certain requirements on traffic handling to and from our mobile devices. We may hope to be guided by interactive applications offering video and audio services. With truly ubiquitous and variable communication channels as has been discussed in previous sections, each service interruption can well be viewed simply as a programming error, or else a failure of the network operator to provide for the needs of the user.

Once the Internet of Things starts to get personal, there will be strong motivation to exert access control so that one user's mobile device should not be able to gain unauthorized access to another user's collection of Things. After initial authorization, this will again impel careful distribution of access credentials to the neighborhood of the Internet of Things for ready access by the user (and the user's mobile devices). Balancing the need for interactivity, economical connectivity, convenient access, and timely delivery of services is likely to occupy the attention of network designers who wish to usher in the Internet of Things.

Vehicular: Self-Driving, Calendar Integration, and Special Events

Ubiquitous and convenient wireless access will enable and motivate many changes to work and office connectivity -- so many that it might well be unpredictable and, in any case, would prevent any attempt to make a representative (much less complete) enumeration. To pick just one, consider the implications of self-driving cars.

First of all, there is a need for real-time interactivity, and mobility management must be designed with this in mind. Since the path for the mobile "device" is highly constrained to remain on the roadways, predictive techniques are likely to succeed. Information contained within the onboard maps can be supplemented in real time with updated road information as well as details of traffic congestion. Course corrections can easily be handled from user controls, and user preferences can be used to suggest interesting side trips or opportunities for unscheduled visits.

An Internet-enabled car has to be considered as a major appliance within the global Internet of Things. It will interact with other widely accessible devices as well as many personal devices, and other cars, and consequently needs the pertinent authorizations. Since a car will often have multiple drivers, provision must be made to enable the car to have its own basic set of capabilities and authorizations, but also to acquire permissions and context from the driver. Passengers should, when allowed by the driver, be able to make use of neighboring services from the Internet of Things as well as the bounteous resources offered by the automobile as it travels along the road. The "always-on" reachability features offered by the Mobile IP family of protocols allow novel self-driving applications such as valet parking ("car go park yourself", "car wake up come look for me, I don't care where you are"). The same features help with enhanced reliability – the car stays connected throughout widest geographical areas covered by most heterogeneous wireless access links. These features are likely to motivate a huge variety of novel applications whose impact might equal that of the arrival of the Internet.

All of this is in addition to process control and local signaling which will be required for improving traffic safety. Of course pertinent traffic information must be shared without disclosing private information, but also information must be prioritized so that traffic safety information takes precedence over entertainment or social media. This will require careful attention to caching, localized signaling, distributed context maintenance, and proper authentication, all of which interact and have effects on other protocols. High performance mobility management would enable applications to operate transparently with similar performance as during static (non mobile) periods of operation. Applications written to request level of mobility support from the operating system (e.g., no support needed, short-term connectivity only, real-time, etc.) will be preferred, but traditional applications should also be supported.

Access to personal information such as calendars, home automation, and so on will enable more efficient response to unexpected situations that may arise. Many attractive scenarios have been developed and some of them probably seemed at the time like science fiction. Nevertheless, as far as communications aspects are concerned, we have the technology to realize even more today than most people envisioned only 50 years ago. Much of what will actually be developed will depend more on the perceived business cases of the large wireless providers, than on the technical feasibility of the applications.

Need for Eternal Vigilance / Privacy Threatened

No discussion about the future Internet would be complete without discussion of the need for citizens to be forever vigilant about protecting their privacy and preventing unauthorized use of their personal credentials or data (see for example (Cooper, 2012)). Recent revelations have described the compromise of *billions* of password-protected accounts, as well as the collection of vast storehouses of private data and metadata. These revelations have come as a complete surprise to most people, but even so there still has not been sufficient action to avert future wrongdoing. Imagine for a moment that, with a flick of a switch, someone thousands of miles away could insert malicious automotive directives and cause high-speed collisions along major urban freeways. Many traffic deaths would occur, and the resulting impenetrable traffic jams would cause additional catastrophic damages.

This is just one example, based on self-driving automobiles deployed with insufficient security features. The Internet is an achievement hardly dreamed of until 50 years ago, and has irrevocably changed the course of human history. Like most technology, Internet communications are morally neutral, and can be used to bring joy into many lives, or to bring misery. It is up to all of us to shape the future of this immense endeavor. The same comments apply especially to more sophisticated methods for high performance mobility management, in many more scenarios than just the abovementioned disasters that could result from poor automotive security. Since smooth mobility management enables perfect application control regardless of location, we might see that misguided authority activities could lead to growing risks of trespassing citizen rights, unprecedented within known history of human society. It's up to us to shape this future.

CONCLUSION

The future of the Internet is difficult to predict; even given the historical facts, it is difficult to create a sensible narrative about why things have turned out as they have. Even the growing dominance of mobile wireless devices in the Internet is not assured, as we may well find that the majority of nodes in the Internet of Things are not mobile. Nevertheless, it is certain that mobile wireless devices will continue to place ever increasing demands on the capacity of the Internet, and that video and audio applications (especially video) will grow to consume a still larger proportion of the data to and from wireless devices.

The total traffic demand to and from wireless devices is confidently projected to exceed that from wired devices, regardless of the relative numbers of wireless versus wired endpoints. It also seems pretty likely that advances in electronic, optical, and materials technologies will continue to enable impressive new features and performance.

It is not at all certain that existing mobility management infrastructures can expand to handle this growth. We can project the need for the following improvements:

- Provide distributed mobility management for localized signaling and avoidance of remote points of failure
- In particular, advances in handover keying and authentication to reduce disruptions for real-time mobile applications
- Increases in raw capacity for wireless technologies
- Better privacy protections (see, for instance, Apple's new policies)
- Better access network selection
- Better classification of traffic flows based upon support requirements for mobility management.

Combining these improvements with the parallel improvements in platform storage, speed, virtual reality, and cross-device operation, it seems very likely that our freedom of action and access to life-simplifying information will continue to improve, as long as we pay attention to the dangers of global integration.

REFERENCES

Arzani, B., Gurney, A., Cheng, S., Guerin, R., & Loo, B. T. (2014). Impact of Path Characteristics and Scheduling Policies on MPTCP Performance. *The 4th International Workshop on Protocols and Applications with Multi-Homing Support (PAMS 2014)*. Victoria/Canada: IEEE CS Conference Publishing Service.

Brodkin, J. (2012, May 30). WiFi, cellular data to account for 60% of all Internet traffic by 2016. *Ars Technica*. Retrieved from http://arstechnica.com/information-technology/2012/05/wifi-cellular-data-to-account-for-60-all-internet-traffic-by-2016/

Brustein, J. (2014, Sep 18). Wi-Fi Should Scare the Hell out of Verizon and AT&T. *Business Week*. Retrieved from http://www.businessweek.com/articles/2014-09-08/wi-fi-should-scare-the-hell-out-of-verizon-and-at-and-t

Bush, R. (2011). *The Address plus Port (A+P) Approach to the IPv4 Address Shortage (RFC 6346)*. IETF. doi:10.17487/rfc6346

Campbell, A., & Gomez, J. (2002). IP Micromobility Protocols. *ACM SIGMOBILE Mobile Computer and Communication Review (MC2R)*, 45–54.

Cooper, A. (2012). *Report from the Internet Privacy Workshop (RFC 6462)*. IETF.

Devarapalli, V., Wakikawa, R., Petrescu, A., & Thubert, P. (2005). *Network Mobility (NEMO) Basic Support Protocol (RFC 3963)*. IETF. doi:10.17487/rfc3963

Ford, A., Raiciu, C., Handley, M., & Bonaventure, O. (2013). *TCP Extensions for Multipath Operation with Multiple Addresses (RFC 6824)*. IETF. doi:10.17487/rfc6824

Gont, F. (2011). *Security Assessment of the Internet Protocol Version 4 (RFC 6274)*. IETF. doi:10.17487/rfc6274

Gulbrandsen, A., Vixie, P., & Esibov, L. (2000). *A DNS RR for specifying the location of services (DNS SRV) (RFC 2782)*. IETF. doi:10.17487/rfc2782

Gundavelli, S., Leung, K., Devarapalli, V., Chowdhury, K., & Patil, B. (2008). *Proxy Mobile IPv6 (RFC 5213)*. IETF. doi:10.17487/rfc5213

Guttman, E., Perkins, C., Veizades, J., & Day, M. (1999). *Service Location Protocol, Version 2 (RFC 2608)*. IETF. doi:10.17487/rfc2608

Huitema, C. (1993). *IAB Recommendation for an Intermediate Strategy to Address the Issue of Scaling (RFC 1481)*. IETF. doi:10.17487/rfc1481

IETF. (1992). *IP Routing for Wireless/Mobile Hosts (mobileip)*. IETF.

IETF Handover Keying WG (hokey). (2006). Retrieved from Handover Keying (hokey): http://datatracker.ietf.org/wg/hokey/history/

Ioannidis, J. (1993). *Protocols for Mobile Internetworking* (PhD Thesis). New York: Columbia University.

Ioannidis, J., & Maguire, G. Q. (1993). The design and implementation of a Mobile Internetwork Architecture. *USENIX Winter 1993 Technical Conference* (pp. 491-502). USENIX Association.

Ioannidis, J., Maguire, G. Q., Ben-Shaul, I. Z., Levedopoulos, M., & Liu, M. (1990). *Porting AIX onto the Student Electronic Notebook*. New York: Columbia University Computer Science Technical Reports.

Karlsson, M. (2008, Oct). *Access Network Discovery and Selection Function (ANDSF)*. Retrieved from 3GPP TS 24.312: http://www.3gpp.org/dynareport/24312.htm

Koodli, R. (2009). *Mobile IPv6 Fast Handovers (RFC 5568)*. IETF. doi:10.17487/rfc5568

Leung, K., Dommety, G., Narayanan, V., & Petrescu, A. (2008). *Network Mobility (NEMO) Extensions for Mobile IPv4 (RFC 5177)*. IETF. doi:10.17487/rfc5177

Maltz, D., & Bhagwat, P. (1998). MSOCKS: An Architecture for Transport Layer Mobility. *INFOCOM '98. Seventeenth Annual Joint Conference of the IEEE Computer and Communications Societies*. (pp. 1037 - 1045). IEEE.

METIS Consortium. (2013). *METIS 2020*. Retrieved from https://www.metis2020.com/

Milton, L. (2008, Mar). *3GPP Evolved Packet System (EPS); Evolved General Packet Radio Service (GPRS) Tunnelling Protocol for Control plane (GTPv2-C); Stage 3*. Retrieved from 3GPP TS 29.274: http://www.3gpp.org/DynaReport/29274.htm

Mishra, A., Shin, M., & Arbaugh, W. (2003). An Empirical Analysis of the IEEE 802.11 MAC Layer Handoff Process. *SIGCOMM Comput. Commun. Rev*, 93-102.

Perkins, C. (1996). *IP Mobility Support (RFC 2002)*. IETF. doi:10.17487/rfc2002

Perkins, C. (1996). *Minimal Encapsulation within IP (RFC 2004)*. IETF. doi:10.17487/rfc2004

Perkins, C. (2010). *IP Mobility Support for IPv4, Revised (RFC 5944)*. IETF. doi:10.17487/rfc5944

Perkins, C., Johnson, D., & Arkko, J. (2011). *Mobility Support in IPv6*. IETF. doi:10.17487/rfc6275

Pudney, C. (2006, Dec). *General Packet Radio Service (GPRS) enhancements for Evolved Universal Terrestrial Radio Access Network (E-UTRAN) access*. Retrieved from 3GPP TS 23.401: http://www.3gpp.org/DynaReport/23401.htm

Ramjee, R., Porta, T., Thuel, S., & Varadhan, K. (2002). HAWAII: A Domain-based Approach for Supporting Mobility in Wide-area Wireless Networks. *IEEE/ACM Transaction on Networking*.

IETF Seamless Mobility (seamoby) Working Group. (2000). *Context Transfer, Handoff Candidate Discovery, and Dormant Mode Host Alerting (seamoby) charter*. IETF.

Shacham, R., Schulzrinne, H., Thakolsri, S., & Kellerer, W. (2009). *Session Initiation Protocol (SIP) Session Mobility (RFC 5631)*. IETF.

Small, C. F. R. (2013). *Market status statistics Q1 2013*. Author.

Snoeren, A. C., & Balakrishnan, H. (2000). *TCP Connection Migration*. IETF Internet Draft.

Soliman, H. (2009). *Mobile IPv6 Support for Dual Stack Hosts and Routers (RFC 5555)*. IETF. doi:10.17487/rfc5555

Stewart, R., Xie, Q., Morneault, K., Sharp, C., Schwarzbauer, H., & Taylor, T. (2000). *Stream Control Transmission Protocol (RFC 2960)*. IETF. doi:10.17487/rfc2960

Sunshine, C. (1980). *Addressing Mobile hosts in the ARPA Unternet Environment*. J. P.: IETF.

Tamura, T. (1999, Apr). *General Packet Radio Service (GPRS); GPRS Tunnelling Protocol (GTP) across the Gn and Gp interface*. Retrieved from 3GPP TS 29.060: http://www.3gpp.org/DynaReport/29060.htm

Veizades, J., Guttman, E., Perkins, C., & Kaplan, S. (1997). *Service Location Protocol (RFC 2165)*. IETF. doi:10.17487/rfc2165

Wedlund, E., & Schulzrinne, H. (1999). Mobility Support using SIP. In *WOWMOM '99 Proceedings of the 2nd ACM international workshop on Wireless mobile multimedia* (pp. 76-82). New York: ACM.

KEY TERMS AND DEFINITIONS

Care-of-Address: An IP address associated with a mobile node while visiting a foreign link. A packet addressed to the mobile node which arrives at the mobile node's home network when the mobile node is away from home and has registered a Care-of Address will be forwarded to that address by the Home Agent in the home network.

Handover: The process by which an active mobile node changes its point of attachment to the network.

Home Address: An IP address assigned to a mobile node, used as the permanent address of the mobile node. This address is within the mobile node's home link.

Home Agent: A router on a mobile node's home link with which the mobile node has registered its current care-of address. While the mobile node is away from home, the home agent intercepts packets on the home link destined to the mobile node's home address, encapsulates them, and tunnels them to the mobile node's registered care-of address.

Mobile Host: A mobile node that is an end host and not a router. A Mobile Host is capable of sending and receiving packets. A mobile host can be a source or destination of traffic, but not a forwarder of it.

Mobile Network: A network, moving as a unit, which dynamically changes its point of attachment to the Internet and thus its reachability in the topology.

Mobile Node: An IP node capable of changing its point of attachment to the network. A Mobile Node may either be a Mobile Host or a Mobile Router.

Mobile Router: A router capable of changing its point of attachment to the network, moving from one link to another link.

Chapter 8
Challenges of 5G Networking in Access and Core Networks

Vasilis Friderikos
King's College London, UK

Hamid Aghvami
King's College London, UK

Giorgos Chochlidakis
King's College London, UK

Mischa Dohler
King's College London, UK

ABSTRACT

The 5th Generation wireless and mobile communication is expected to provide ultrahigh data rates over wireless in the range of Gbps. But 5G will also be about providing consistency and supporting Quality of Experience in a personalized manner. We foresee an evolution in terms of physical layer enhancements to provide increased data rates, whereas a revolutionary step is required in terms of network orchestration and management to provide consistency and efficient utilization of the available resources at a minimum cost. In this chapter, key trends in wireless access technologies and thus-required network management strategies with respect to the core network are discussed. In the roadmap towards 5G networks, we envision an evolution of technologies for supporting Gbps wireless transmission, whereas a revolution would be required from the current modus operandi in the ways network orchestration and resource management is performed in these complex, hierarchical, heterogeneous and highly autonomous wireless networks.

1. INTRODUCTION AND BACKGROUND

The key challenge for mobile and wireless networks for the decade to come will undoubtedly be to support the anticipated thousand-fold mobile traffic increase, while at the same time efficiently support the ever increasing diverse set of requirements from different applications. With 4G technologies (LTE-A) not fully deployed yet (as of 2014) research and innovation efforts have commenced on the development of the next generation wireless systems. Generally referred to as 5G, it will need to encompass breakthrough technologies and architectures, which will be able to match the unprecedented rise in quantity and heterogeneity of wireless traffic. This has repercussions on both access and core networks, which will be the discussion point of this chapter. We will dwell on latest emerging design paradigms, notably network densification and split-architectures, distributed mobility support and network visualization. These

DOI: 10.4018/978-1-4666-8371-6.ch008

items are discussed bearing in mind the general requirements of wireless design, i.e. cost, scalability, robustness and availability, unprecedented delay allowing for control application, and peak rates aiming to match those of wired networks.

Prior to this, let us revise some of the lessons learn from prior cellular designs and deployments. 3G will be remembered as the first mobile network which was largely IP enabled, i.e. packet-switching technologies have been designed into the network. That was important for the exponential uptake of data-driven applications, which eventually would drive the smart phone revolution. On the downside, 3G will be remembered as performing relatively poorly in the Radio Access Technology (RAT) and Radio Access Network (RAN) side – contrary to all promises made on the ease of using a single-frequency network. A positive side-effect of the radio network management becoming so complex, however, was the emergence of self-organizing networking (SON) techniques which would pave the way for proper management of heterogeneous networks in 4G and now 5G networks. 3G was also the first system to introduce more advanced multi-antenna systems, such as space time coding, among others, and prove it would work in a commercial setting.

4G learned from the lessons of designing and rolling out 3G. Notably, the core was made lighter and flatter and was entirely packet-switched; the RAN was enjoying advanced concepts such as Coordinated Multipoint (CoMP) reception and carrier aggregation (CA); more SON features – mainly related to RAN management – appeared; and a much simpler yet powerful and scalable air interface was introduced in form of OFDMA. 4G engineers tried less to come even closer to the Shannon bounds, rather than building a cost efficient system able to meet capacity needs of the emerging smartphone revolution. Techniques such as CoMP for example seem to be complex for efficiently implementing them in real networks. Two major constituents in the design were the availability of more spectrum (leading to CA protocols) and denser networks (leading to the first highly heterogeneous cellular networks). On the other hand, 4G networks can be considered as "islands" where sharing and innovation on the control and management plane are very much limited since all functions are based on proprietary hardware and software. This is a significant limiting factor to ensure network sustainability and integration of various different heterogeneous networks.

With above lessons in mind, the community is currently gauging the design requirements for 5G networks, where some trends are outlined in below sections of this book chapter. To this end, the rest of the chapter is organized as follows. In the next section, we discuss trends and opportunities related to 5G RAT/RAN designs, which includes mm-Wave, machine-type communication (MTC), phantom cells as well as decoupled up and downlinks. In the subsequent section, the emerging issue of softwarization of the end-to-end communication is introduced that includes both Software-defined Radio (SDR), Software-defined Networking (SDN) and Network Function Virtualization (NFV). This is followed by the emerging trend of network sharing via virtualization where recent works and challenges are discussed. The chapter is closed with a set of 5G design visions, hopefully enabling future avenues of research.

2. TOWARDS 5G: RAT EVOLUTION AND RAN REVOLUTION

In this section, we outline issues related to RAT and RAN designs. Notably, we outline some of the lessons learned from previous design efforts of 3G and 4G networks. Then, we discuss emerging trends and how they are reflected in the RAT and RAN designs.

2.1 Heterogeneous Access Network: Challenges and Opportunities

Based on emerging data traffic growth and increased penetration of mobile technology in a number of traditional data markets but also new market segments such as Machine-to-Machine (M2M), device to device and vehicular communications, there is a significant pressure for further evolution of the current cellular access network technologies and architectures to accommodate the data growth. To this end, 5G networks are expected to provide increased data rates, with smaller cell radius and be highly heterogeneous. In the mixture of technologies beyond the support of 3G, 4G and WiFi networks, it is expected to have a new interface in the mmWave range and possibly a new air interface for machine-type communications (MTC). As for the support of Wifi-like systems, the emerging IEEE 802.11ac standard (Bejarano et al. 2013) is an enhanced version of the IEEE 802.11n with wider bandwidth (up to 160 MHz), MIMO with up to 8 streams, multi-user MIMO, higher level modulation (up to 256-QAM) and beam-forming also capability. Currently, work has been initiated towards the IEEE 802.11ax standard. The focus for 802.11ax is on the current 2.4 GHz and the 5 GHz unlicensed bands, but further spectrum between 1 GHz and 6 GHz might be included as they become available. As articulated by the High Efficiency WLAN (HEW) IEEE group, the aims are (a) improving spectrum efficiency & area throughput, and (b) improving real world performance in indoor and outdoor deployments both in the presence of interfering sources, dense heterogeneous networks as well as in moderate to heavy user loaded access points. The current consensus and expectations is that the IEEE 802.11ax will not be standardized and ratified before 2019. In such diverse access ecosystem, in order to provide ubiquitous services, some of the fundamental notions existing in previous generations such as control and data forwarding from the same BS will inevitably be relaxed as will be explained in the sequel. In such 5G post-cellular network scenario where there is a plethora of small cells, most probably shared from a number of different operators, the emphasis will be on how to support QoE aware allocation of available resources taking into account contextual information from the mobile user (Quadros et al. 2012). Such contextual information could be highly diverse ranging from user device, mobility pattern, to the actual application in use and other relevant parameters related to the location of the user and/or the environment. For such multi-service architectures QoE would be handled through a flexible management of shared resources, i.e. spectrum as well as infrastructure, among operators. The ever-increasing level of miniaturization of computing units will yield smarter and more capable mobile devices with even greater demand for capacity. Addition of many small cells, with different architectural variations, emerged as a major solution for enhancing capacity but only if interference and mobility are properly managed. Optimizing resource allocation over the whole range of available spectrum and small cells from all operators through logical RAN (Radio Access Network) sharing would bring unprecedented improvement in the QoE/energy efficiency trade-off which can be mapped into proportional gains for sharing operators.

A graphical representation of a more "flattened" and heterogeneous mobile network is shown in Figure 1 below. As can be seen in the figure, there is an inevitable convergence between high speed optical and wireless networks, and the key differentiation and challenge for 5G and beyond networks would be to provide an increased percentage of traffic flows to be routed locally and avoiding core network handling that would increase overall end-to-end delays. Until now the focus has mainly been placed on inter-BS communication (for example through the X2 interface in LTE) and fiber deployment to the BSs ("Fiber-To-The-Cell" as it is broadly called now) to provide increased levels of mobility support (Parkvall et al. 2011). But, integration of advanced caching technologies and more user-centric resource management and allocation of wireless resources require a rethinking of how traffic is handled at the edge of the converged wireless-optical network in order to provide optimal traffic handling and reduction of the end-to-end latency as well as congestion on the core network. As shown in the Figure 1, the expectation is that content will be located closer to the user through adaptive caching technologies and the expectation is that caching will reach to the level of access points and even terminals (Golrezaei et al. 2012). Such intelligent distribution of popular content at the edge of the network in a user-centric manner will allow for significant de-congestion of the core network and for increased performance in terms of latency.

2.2 Architectural Perspectives on the Integration of mmWave Technologies

Currently, mobile operators are trying to cope with the increasingly high demand for Internet applications in cellular networks by utilizing fragmented bandwidth with carrier frequencies that broadly speaking range between 700 MHz and 2.6 GHz. Available spectrum at these carrier frequencies can now be deemed as limited for the expected increase of traffic and as a result in order to increase aggregate transmission rates and to cope with the ever increasing user demand there is a need to move higher in the spectrum. To this end, wireless technologies for 5G envision the use of the currently very much underutilized millimeter wave (mm-wave) frequency spectrum such as for example the usage of 28GHz and 38GHz (Fettweis, 2013), (Rappaport et al. 2013) or even the unlicensed 60GHz as pictured by the Wireless Gigabit Alliance (Cordeiro, 2010). Clearly, at these frequencies, signal attenuation is significant and as a result high-speed broadband access to the Internet can be considered only for pico cells with radius of up to 200 meters for example. When moving from frequencies 3GHz to 30GHz the path loss increase by almost 20 dB (using Friis Law for free space path loss). Therefore, for dense mmWave wireless networks new tools are required in order to understand capacity and coverage limitations in different settings – with special attention being placed on providing seamless user experience by minimizing the probability of coverage holes (Bai et al. 2013). Also, in these carrier frequencies the power amplifier has an efficiency of less than 10%; therefore, energy consumption is a key issue. A major challenge would thus be to support a homogeneous user experience by utilizing information regarding the elasticity of a large number of Internet applications and the actual mobility of users. In such frequencies, special attention should also be placed on MAC design due to short frame length and range as well as antenna directivity. Despite the fact that directional antennas exhibit

Figure 1. Illustration of a 5G mobile network depicting the access, core and backbone networks and the evolution of increased traffic flow towards the edge of the network (left hand side), driven by the caching mechanisms to keep content closer to the user (right hand side)

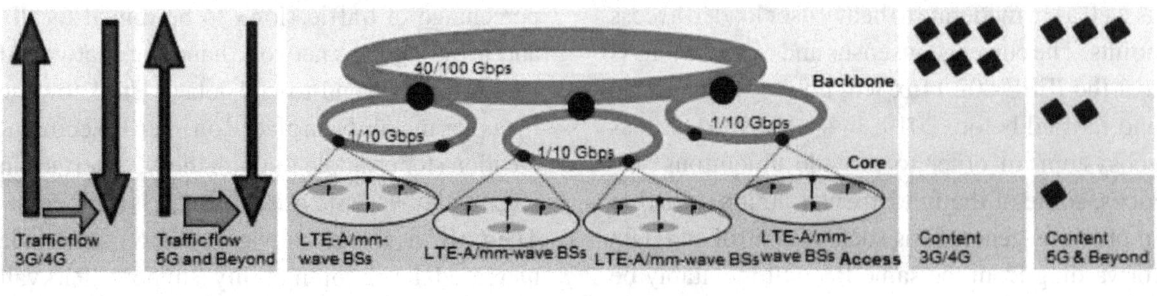

many advantages compared to traditional omnidirectional transmission, wide deployment creates a number of challenges for both the MAC as well as the network layer when some form of IP QoS need to be supported. The most critical challenge in that setting is node mobility since to establish (and maintain) directional connections, nodes are expected to be aware of the direction/location of their communicating peers.

Figure 2 shows a hierarchical future cellular network topological setting with 3 LTE-A cells and a couple of mm-wave Gbps pico cells. Seamless mobility is supported by the LTE-A cells where ultra high-speed connectivity is provided by the Gbps pico cells. As shown in the figure, connectivity to the core network is supported by ultra high capacity fiber to all base stations but in the general case there are also wireless point-to-point and multi-hop links as shown in the figure. Another candidate architecture has been presented in (Sakaguchi, 2013) where the authors introduce the concept of cloud cooperated heterogeneous cellular network (C-HetNet). In C-HetNet the central idea is that small power pico basestations (BSs) overlaid on a macrocell are connected to cloud radio access network (C-RAN) to operate cooperatively with the macro BS. In terms of frequencies, it is expected to operate around 3GHz/60GHz pico BSs and around the carrier of 2GHz for the macro BS. Both macro and outdoor pico cells will be connected to cloud radio access network (C-RAN) as enhanced remote radio heads (RRHs).

2.3 Architectural Perspectives on the Integration of MTC Technologies

Machine-type communication (MTC) is a wireless transmission paradigm where devices send their data to remote servers or to other machines (e.g., actuators) without human intervention. MTC was shown to have a set of unique characteristics, which includes power-efficient communications, support of group functionalities, mostly no mobility support, among many others. This, in turn, requires technically advanced protocols and architecture designs if to be successful in 5G. It is, however, considered to be a major value-add in emerging 5G systems; the business opportunities for operators in MTC are ample, including markets such as transport and logistics, e-health, smart grids, e-health, etc.

Figure 2. An envisioned 5G integration scenario of macro cells (such as LTE-A) and high speed mmWave connected via ultra high capacity fiber optic network

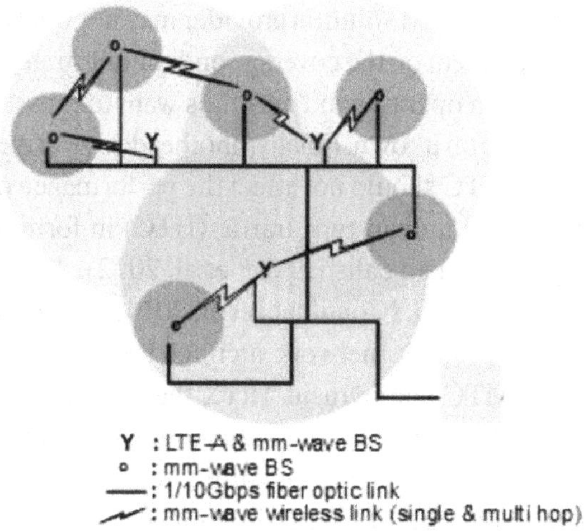

A major technical challenge is the sheer scale of the number of devices, which is unpredictable whilst many devices may access the cellular system simultaneously leading to congestion and overloading of radio access and core networks. This, in turn, constitutes a major challenge towards low-latency and low-power MTC with low impact onto the core. Another important issue is related to the observation that many machines are geographically located in a very confined and coverage-limited area (e.g., sensors/actuators in a hospital or a refinery). As a consequence, the radio access network of Beyond LTE-A should be able to efficiently manage several hot-spots, many of which might be located in challenging positions (e.g., indoors or at the cell-edge). Above mentioned issues are exacerbated by the strict requirements on the design of MTC terminals which should be low cost (i.e., low complexity and computational capabilities) and with low energy consumption in order to guarantee extended lifetimes. Furthermore, the M2M solution provider may not want to be dependent on the coverage and rollout strategy of a given operator and may thus want to provide coverage on its own. Finally, another design driver is that MTC should not affect the performance of traditional human-type traffic (HTC) in form of e.g., voice/data calls (Zheng et al, 2012).

To this end, (Condoluci et al, 2014), proposed a truly scalable network architecture for ultra-dense MTC deployment. Here, the high number of machines is presumed to be mainly located in challenging position within the macrocell. These are assumed to simultaneously access the network, e.g. due to a triggered alert, which poses several serious design issues so as to be able to guarantee the requirements of ubiquitous connectivity. The thus proposed evolved 3GPP architecture with the aim to efficiently support MTC is shown in Figure 3. In this architecture, LTE-capable MTC devices communicate directly with a Home-evolved NodeBs (HeNBs). HeNBs are effectively cellular-enabled low-cost femto-cells communicating at low-power transmission (less than 100mW). Non-3GPP devices access is also catered for through trusted non-3GPP access points (APs) that are operator controlled, and are managed by the HeNB-Gateway (HeNB-GW) like legacy HeNBs. The HeNB-GW aggregates traffic from a large number of HeNBs and trusted non-3GPP APs into the existing core network. The architectural embodiment was shown to yield very high reliability with outages lowered by orders of magnitude compared to traditional macro cellular approaches (Condoluci et al, 2014). The resilience is an important feature for MTC communications as it enables industry-grade MTC deployments, in addition to saving energy due a decreased number of retransmissions.

Some interesting features are worthwhile pointing out:

First, the proposed RAN architecture suggests having HeNBs use a separate frequency band. This may seem capacity sub-optimal but has recently been shown to be the best tradeoff in terms of ease of deployment, throughput and reliability. Indeed, licensed spectrum below 3 GHz has already been widely exploited for cellular services via Macro-cell eNBs (MeNBs); however, additional higher frequency bands (such as 3.5 GHz and above) have recently become available. Such frequencies are challenging for macro-cell deployments due to propagation characteristics, while they are very suitable for HeNBs communicating over relatively short range. This proposed frequency-separated deployment avoids inter-cell interference and relaxes the RF requirements with a consequent reduction of equipment costs.

Second, the architecture makes much more use of the X2 interface. Notably, it handles the exchange of control traffic between eNB(s) and HeNBs for system parameters configuration/reconfiguration (e.g., frequency band selection). The X2 interface can be further exploited as a low-latency interface to exchange data traffic for time-critical events; this is useful when e.g. a sensor reports an alert, which needs to be acted upon with an actuator.

Third, the architecture stipulates the use of the Home eNB Gateway (HeNB-GW) which overcomes significant 3GPP inefficiencies in terms of MME/S-GW overload when the number of HeNBs as well as the number of MTC connections per HeNB are large. In the proposed architecture, the HeNB-GW – part of the backhaul and securely connected to the core – has the key role of being a concentrator of several HeNBs for both control and user planes which aids system scalability.

The advantages of consciously running MTC over HeNBs are as follows:

- The first, and foremost, is that coverage is significantly improved. That is very handy

Figure 3. Enhanced network architecture for ultra-dense MTC access to the 3GPP LTE-A core via HeNBs/HeNB-GWs and trusted non-3GPP APs; curtesy of (Condoluci et al, 2014).

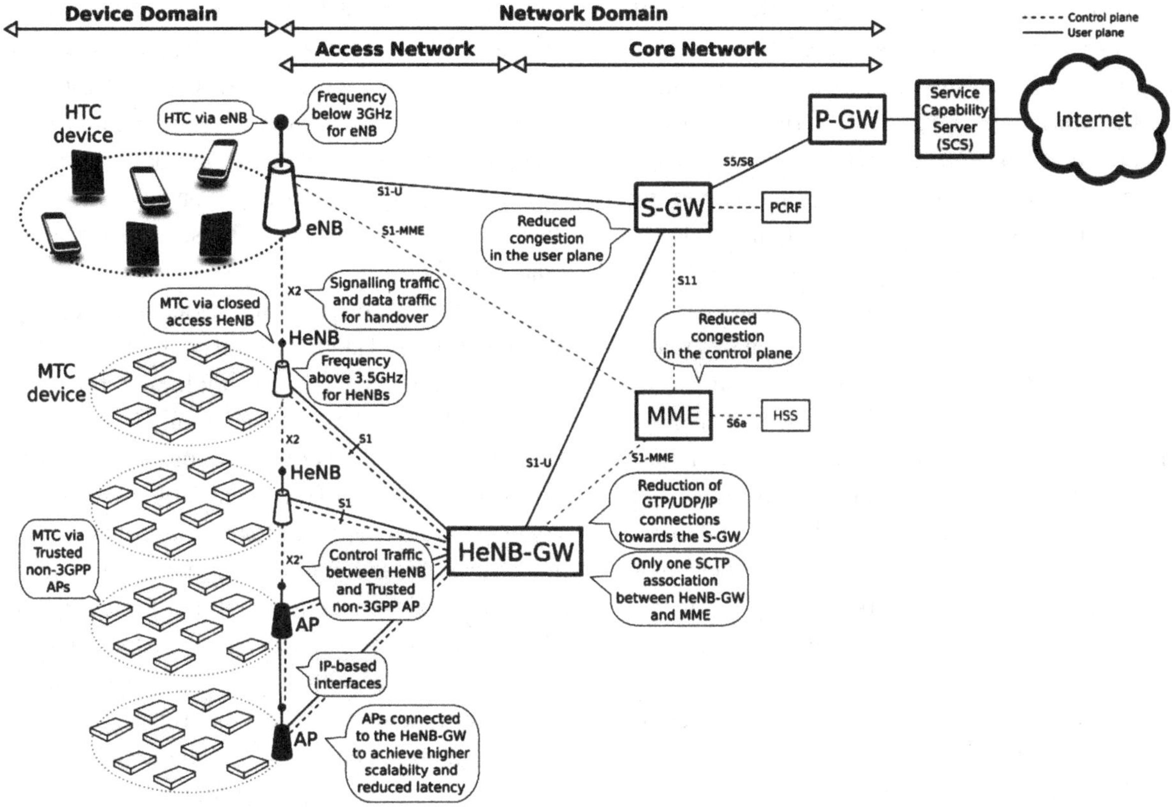

in challenged environments which are typical for B2B MTC deployments in indoor-deployments, smart meters in the basements of the buildings, etc.

- Another advantage pertains to security and protection which can be achieved by using the closed subscriber group of HeNBs where only MTCs registered with the system are allowed to access the networks.
- Furthermore, the separation ensures that HTC is well separated from MTC which is to the benefit of both systems, thereby guaranteeing critical performance of MTC and minimizing churn for HTC systems.
- Then, in terms of core network improvements, it aids the S-Gateway scalability since the number of GPRS Tunneling Protocol (GTP), UDP and IP connections between HeNB-GW and S-GW are drastically reduced compared to a direct HeNBs connection. Furthermore, the heartbeat messages via the Stream Control Transmission Protocol (SCTP), used during association between the HeNB-GW and MME, are drastically reduced.

The trend in 5G networking design will thus undoubtedly be to handle MTC traffic locally, which is useful for closing control loops; and to strive for protocol designs which minimize the control traffic, such as heartbeat messages.

In terms of resource management, the move towards the Cloud RAN (C-RAN) concept is worth pointing out which is based around the idea that baseband processing of a number of – possible heterogeneous – cells is centralized (cloud) leaving only basic RF functionalities at the base stations. C-RAN is attracting significant attention because it can potentially ease coordination of radio resources across distributed access nodes compared to the current practices of the macro cell centric architectures. In fact, in heterogeneous macro and high density small cells environments the traditional paradigm of coordination via the X2 interface will become challenging. C-RAN can play a key role here by providing a centralized view on the network allowing for more efficient management and reduction of the interference as well as allocation of available resources. In terms of 5G, such approaches look increasingly desirable since they will allow a straightforward step towards virtualized basebands, and advanced solutions for network sharing. Having said that a number of challenges still pertain to the design of cloud based wireless networks especially in terms of fronthaul requirements in terms of capacity as well as decreasing delays to less than 5msec to enable a wide set of new applications including M2M and vehicular to vehicular (V2V) and Vehicular 2 Infrastructure (V2I).

2.4 Split Wireless Architectures

To support emerging RAT/RAN paradigms, such as mm-Wave or MTC, novel ways of handling network control are required, motivated by a clear need to move beyond current cellular networking paradigms and separate the aspects of capacity gains and coverage increase via a logical, and/or physical, decoupling of the data and control or signaling transmissions/planes in future wireless networks. Current emerging architectural paradigms are proposing the so-called split control and data-forwarding paradigm and towards this directions are the cell on-demand (Capone et al. 2012) and Phantom cell (Nakamura et al. 2013) architectures and their ramifications. In such emerging networking paradigms signaling nodes which are in essence macro-BSs covering a large geographical area provide coverage and always-on connectivity are designed for low rate services (system access and paging) and data nodes (small cells) used on demand based and depending on the actual spatial-temporal characteristics of traffic to provide increased data rates. In that case scenario advanced network level algorithms need to be devised to provide near-optimal utilization between the data forwarding, control nodes and backhaul traffic handling. The scenario is illustrated in Figure 4.

The efforts towards the logical decoupling of signaling and data transmissions are still in an embryonic stage and it is not known how this split would affect the actual QoE and/or QoS performance of the network. In order to provide consistency with non-fluctuating QoE there should be an integrated approach for mobile connectivity which provides exceptional opportunity of centralized interference management and logical RAN sharing for various small cells owned by different operators in an area through a low-power macro BS, called macro-controller (Zaidi et al. 2014). An integrated approach will allow the orchestration of the heterogeneous wireless access technologies (such as for example IEEE 802.11n, IEEE 802.11ac and mmWave) so that better spatial capacity can be achieved in the network. An area that has received less attention is how to integrate device-to-device (D2D) communication (3GPP, 2014) under such split-architecture. In D2D communications, two close-ranged mobile nodes are eligible to connect directly and communicate between them by utilizing either the cellular spectrum (inband communications) or the unlicensed spectrum (outband communications), unlike the traditional communication in cellular networks where the communication has to be established via the BS (Doppler et al. 2009). D2D resource management mainly depends on the actual spectrum sharing technique (i.e. underlay or overlay) and can take place in a centralized (Lee D. H. et al., 2013) or fully-distributed (Wen et al. 2013) manner. Current emphasis has been mainly placed on resource allocation algorithms for D2D com-

Figure 4. Illustration of the concept of split architectures (such as the on-demand, or Phantom cell concept) where there is a physical decoupling between control and forwarding planes. Small cells and macro-BS are connected also via fiber as shown.

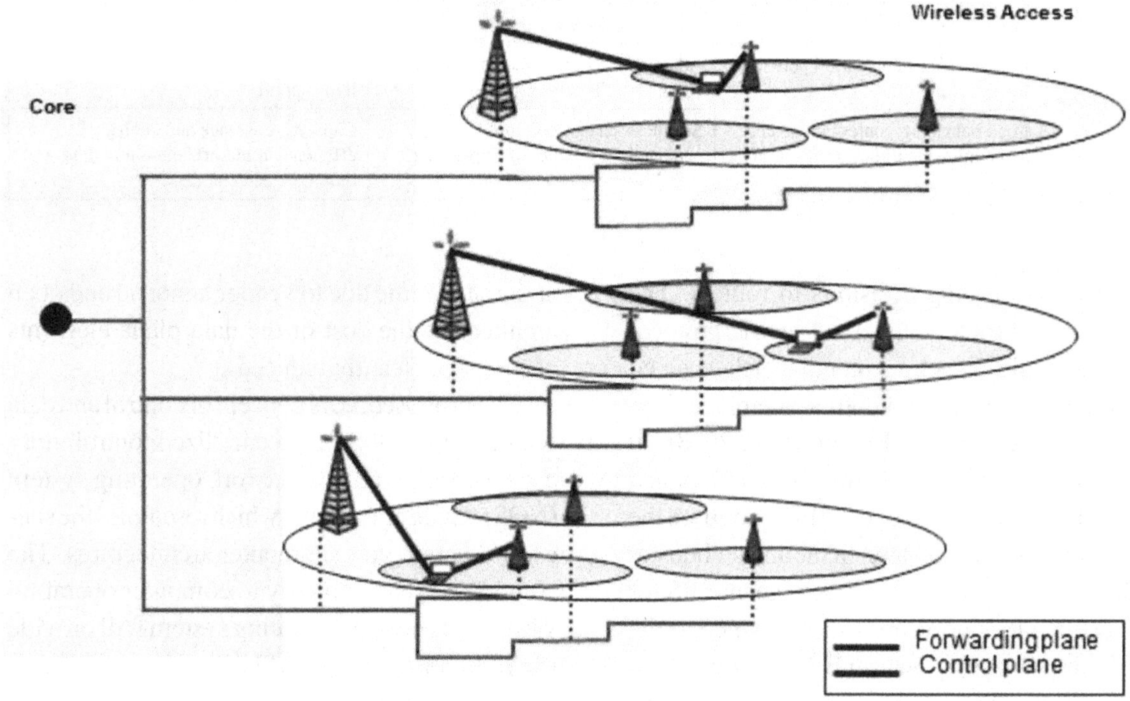

munications under the traditional multi-cell setting with pre-defined fractional frequency re-use being deployed. However, integration techniques for D2D communications under a split-architecture scenario are still in early stage and further work is needed in that direction. For example in split architectures with small cells it might be the case that one of the participating node in the D2D link might not be within the range of the closest small cell and therefore off-loading use of D2D link and/or cases where access to content is required by the transmitter or received of the D2D link require further extensions in order to be applied in such emerging architectures. Some key challenges for split architectures are summarized in Table 1.

In separate efforts, the problem of control and data forwarding separation has been explicitly targeted in what is now called split architectures, which led to the era of Software Defined Networking (SDN). The rational of decoupling control and data planes in SDN has been mainly propelled from a very different set of problems compared to the reasons that led to the cell on demand and Phantom cell concepts. In wide area networks the traditional tight coupling of forwarding and control planes resulted in overly complicated control planes and complex network management implemented mainly via black boxes. Therefore, because of the high complexity and vendor specific implementations both equipment vendors as well as network operators have been resistant to allow for innovative changes. Hence, such architectures that are based on tight coupling provided a barrier for experimentation of new protocols and technology developments. On the other hand, in the so-called split architectures, dedicated controllers collect required information from routers, and based on gathered information compute and

Table 1. Key challenges for the emerging split-architectures in wireless networks

	Decoupling control and data forwarding plane		
Challenges	Optimal cell selection algorithms to minimize potential outages from mobile nodes	Data offloading "as a service", associated mechanisms with minimal overhead policies	Integration to support Device to Device (D2D) communications (single and/or multi hop)
	Energy efficient operation policies for switching-off data BS	Adaptive fractional frequency reuse in Phantom cells settings	Control message aggregation for multi hop support
	Load balancing, context aware cell association algorithms transmissions	Seamless service continuity and personalized Quality of Experience (QoE) support	Capacity, coverage and energy efficiency trade-offs including data-only BSs sleep modes.

distribute forwarding decisions to routers. The controller and routers utilize a specific protocol and an example of such a protocol which received significant interests from both academic and industry is OpenFlow (McKeown et al., 2008). In a similar line of research to the above mentioned works, the authors in (Li et al., 2013) proposed the anchor-booster architecture. In the anchor booster architecture the macro eNB acts as anchor BS for C/U-plane information transmission whereas the small cell eNB act as a booster BS for U-plane data transmissions. This partial decoupling will allow for a more simplified small cell eNB processing while at the same time the role of the macro eNB will facilitate mobility management.

The general architecture of an OpenFlow enabled network segment is shown in Figure 5. The figure also shows how such an SDN based approach can be utilized in conjunction with cell on demand and Phantom cell concepts in order to provide a programmable and scalable solution for data and control plane separation. Clearly, such de-coupled control platform setting simplify the task of modifying the overall logic of network control and in addition to that provides the required abstraction and isolation as a programmable interface where vendors as well as third parties can create a wide variety of new protocols and management applications. Therefore, within a software defined networking model both the data and the control planes can evolve and scale in an independent manner, while at the same time due to vendor agnostic and open architecture the cost of the data plane elements can be significantly reduced.

The proposed SDN concept of control and data separation via a logically-centralized control entity can be considered as a network operating system (NOS) (Gude et al. 2008), which resembles the successful paradigm in computer architectures. The core idea is that, similarly to computer operating systems, a network operating system will provide the right abstractions (APIs) to allow a plethora of different network applications to be developed.

From the above discussion, it becomes evident that that decoupling of the control and forwarding plane happened by two different communities almost in parallel: the fixed networking community in the form of SDN and the wireless community in form of Phantom cells for example. Hence, current trends in access network design are in-line with the SDN concepts and techniques. Therefore, SDN can be considered as the enabling technology to allow for quick roll-outs of architectures such as cell on demand and Phantom cells. There are on-going efforts utilizing SDN concepts in wireless access networks such as the CloudMAC (Vestin et al. 2013) which enables virtualized access points (explained further in the sequel) and the work in (Guimaraes et al. 2013) that allows SDN-aware vertical handover techniques. But, significant further work is required to allow such an integration with wireless specific requirements. Worth pointing out is that for example the

Figure 5. Split Architecture: (left) Generic setting of an SDN/OpenFlow type data and control plane separation in a wide area network, (right) a distributed SDN architecture to enable control and data forwarding spiting in future wireless networks.

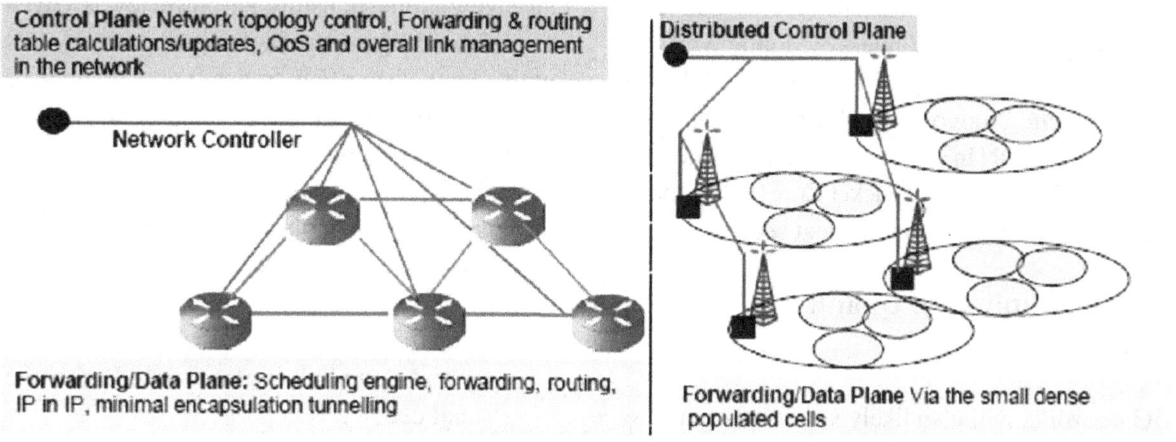

native OpenFlow protocol suite supports a wide set of possible rules to handle packets but this is based on the traditional TCP/IP available header fields. Hence, for wireless networks the packet handling strategies need to be augmented to take into account the special characteristics of wireless transmission and the heterogeneity of the wireless access networks. In addition, mobility support functionalities need to be considered from the outset for an SDN enabled wireless access network. With respect to performance, though, SDN should be considered as an enabler – rather than a solution that will increase the performance. It ought to allow for programability and orchestration of the radio access networks where new control and resource management functionalities can be quickly set-up, tested and implemented.

Split architectures and SDN networks could also be viewed as an enabler and facilitating technologies for moving towards a cloud-based radio access networks (C-RAN) that have been recently proposed as an efficient way of managing and deploying small cells (Bhaumik et al. 2012), (Bernardos et al. 2013), (Guan et al. 2010). The core idea in C-RAN – being another method of decoupling compared to split architectures and SDN - is to decouple baseband processing units (BBUs) from the actual remote radio head (RRH), which allows for centralized operation of BBUs and scalable deployment of light-weight RRHs as small cells. In essence, SDN would enable virtualization at the access network and via centralized resource orchestration (baseband pool) an operator would be able to dynamically allocate resources to a set of different virtualized base stations (utilizing possibly different air-interfaces). The key challenge in such operation is the provision of a high capacity access/core network to allow for small latencies from the passive elements on the edge (RRH) to the data-center for processing of the BBU pool.

Therefore, in emerging cellular networks concepts stem from SDN and OpenFlow will potentially allow greater flexibility by enabling fully programmable BS and hence controlling in a dynamic way data paths and transmissions. In addition to that and as will be discussed further in the next section, programmability will also enable dynamic policies for logical RAN sharing frameworks to provide resource management for optimal QoE/energy efficiency trade-off among multiple mobile operators. As mentioned above the emphasis should be placed on QoE criteria compared to QoS measures not only because they incorporate elasticity of different services, e.g., delay tolerant sessions but because they can facilitate the provision of resource management schemes to enable consistent service delivery. Currently, within the Wireless & Mobile Working Group within the Open Networking Foundation (ONF) there is ongoing work on furthering the adoption of SDN in wireless environments focusing on cellular Evolve;d Packet Core (EPC), these issues will be detailed in the next section.

2.5 Decoupling of Uplink and Downlink

5G networks will also likely witness a complete redesign on the flow of uplink and downlink data streams. This issue has been started to be studied rigorously by (Elshaer et al, 2014), leading to some interesting first system design guidelines. The study has been driven by the observation that cell association in cellular networks has traditionally been based on the downlink received signal power only, despite the fact that up and downlink transmission powers and interference levels differed significantly. This approach was adequate in homogeneous networks with macro base stations all having similar transmission power levels. Given an exponential growth of heterogeneous networks with a large disparity in transmit power and very heterogeneous interference "temperatures", this approach was shown to be highly inefficient. As illustrated in Figure 6, a more efficient approach is to rigorously decouple up and downlinks where three zones are distinguished:

1. when the user is close to the small cell, both up and downlink are associated with the small cell;
2. when the user is far from any small cell, both up and downlink are associated with the macro cell;
3. and in-between, where the optimal solution is to have the uplink go via the small cell and the downlink via the macro cell.

Figure 6. An illustration of how up/downlink decoupling (DUDe), and of the different association zones; curtesy of (Elshaer et al, 2014)

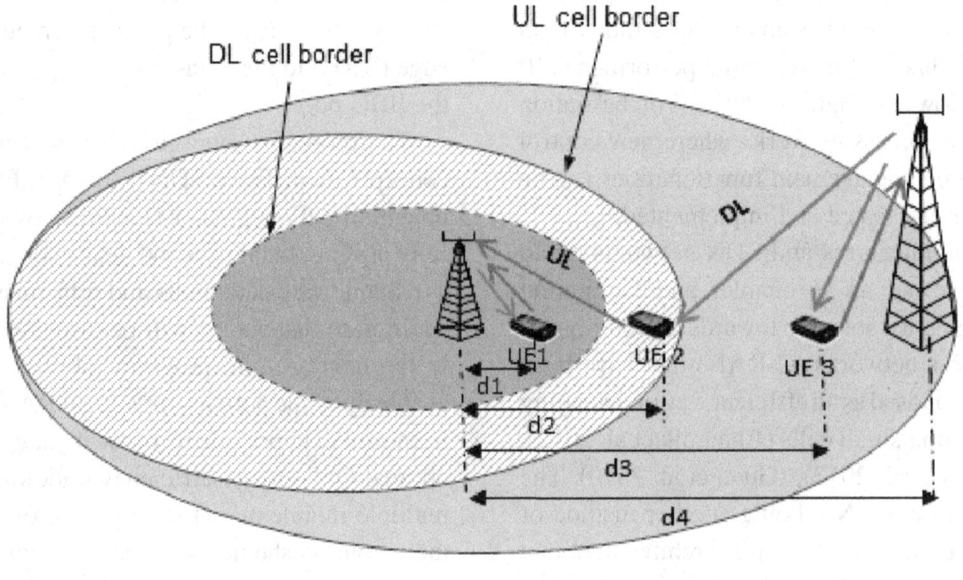

This shift is due to cellular networks shifting from a single-tier homogeneous network to multi-tier heterogeneous networks (HetNets). HetNets are today composed of macro, micro, pico and femto cells. Traditional cellular networks, i.e. those presuming the existence of macro cells only/mainly, have been designed based on the downlink (DL) which is due to the fact that network traffic is mostly asymmetric in a way that the throughput required in the downlink is higher than the one required in the uplink. Cell association has thus normally been based on the downlink received signal power only. Despite differing UL and DL transmission powers and interference levels, this approach was sufficient in a homogeneous network where all the BSs are transmitting with the same or similar average power level. However, in HetNets there is a large disparity in the transmit power of the different layers; and thus this approach is highly inefficient in terms of the uplink. This is further amplified by the fact that uplink is becoming more and more important with the growth of high-rate uplink video applications as well as data/time critical MTC applications.

As HetNets become denser and small cells smaller, the transmit power disparity between macro and small cells is increasing and, as a consequence, the gap between the optimal DL and UL cell boundaries increases. For the sake of improving efficiency in 5G, this necessitates a new design approach which is the Downlink and Uplink Decoupling (DUDe) where the UL and DL are basically treated as separate network entities and a UE can connect to different serving nodes in the UL and DL. Whilst performance is significantly improved with an increasing amount of heterogeneity, significant research challenges lay ahead. Notably, the support of mobility needs to be designed carefully and likely approaches from CoMP will need to be borrowed where a given eNB acts as an anchor point for communications during handover procedures. Furthermore, the decoupling concept can be applied to emerging paradigms, such as carrier aggregation (CA) and/or CoMP, thus allowing for a completely flexible assignment of the UL and DL across eNBs and carriers. Finally, the decoupling is likely most efficient on a per-flow basis, i.e. very bursty traffic will not necessarily see the improvements unless the decoupling can be applied on a per-packet basis.

3. TOWARDS 5G: Core Network Revolution

This section deals with core networking issues where we believe some major design changes are required to ensure competitiveness and meeting 5G performance requirements.

3.1 Core Network Challenges and Opportunities

In 5G networks, the design of the core network is of fundamental importance since the support of ultra low latency applications and ubiquitous seamless mobility support require strong support from the core/backbone network. This includes dynamic application-aware per-flow and/or per-class routing decision making, advanced multi-homing approaches, and distributed mobility support under growing heterogeneity. Indeed, the increased heterogeneity of wireless access and the need for high speed ubiquitous/seamless access to a variety of different Internet applications calls for efficient mobility management schemes at the IP layer. Furthermore, the introduction of programmability at the network level is changing the landscape of networking and even though such techniques have been mainly considered in data centers extensions for wireless/mobile networks is becoming the next frontier attracting significant research efforts worldwide.

Mobility management has been considered as a functionality to support vertical handovers (Tamijetchelvy et al., 2012) (Hongyan et al.,

2003) but there has been little effort to optimize its performance, especially for small cells, HetNets and split-architectures where the notion of cell is disappearing. Hence, **efficient solutions** for mobility aware network slicing/sharing and virtualization are completely open areas of research. The aim is thus to shed further light on the trade-offs between host and session mobility, optimized routing in virtualized infrastructures and opportunistic adaptation to full or hybrid decentralization of the mobility functionalities based on network and traffic conditions.

3.2 From Centralized to Distributed Mobility Management in 5G

During the last years, the number of the mobile Internet users tends to increase steadily and the data traffic follows an exponential increase. In addition, according to predictions an explosive growth of data demand is going to take place over the next few years. However, due to the current flat rate model that has been in use in mobile services, mobile operators have been turned into 'dumb pipes' for the application providers, watching in this way the average revenue per user (ARPU) decreasing in a fast rate.

In order to increase the margin and increase their profit, mobile operators have to find solutions and techniques in order to increase the utilization of the limited physical resources as well as to make the traffic delivery more efficient. Among others, main emphasis has been given in IP mobility management as a way to improve the QoS for end-service and the total performance of the core and access network. Below, there is a description of the main all-IP mobility management schemes that have been proposed so far.

The Internet Engineering Task Force (IETF) standards organization proposed Mobile IP in order to support IP hosts mobility. The main concept is to give to the MN two different addresses: the home address (HoA), which is the fixed address to identify it and the care of address (CoA), which is used in order to track the MN's location (current subnet). In Mobile IPv4 (MIPv4) (Perkins, 2010), a network entity called home agent (HA) is responsible of mapping the HoA and the CoA and forwarding flows towards and from the MN. In particular, when a Correspondent Node (CN) is about to send packets to a MN, it will actually try to reach the home address of the MN. Then, locally this flow will be tunneled through the HA to the MN or a foreign agent with direct link to the MN, by IP-in-IP encapsulation.

In Mobile IPv6 (MIPv6) (Perkins et al., 2011), the mapping of the HoA and the CoA can be done, also, by each CN as long as it has stored to its cache the binding updates for the Mobile Nodes (MNs) with which they communicate. This enhanced feature of MIPv6 avoids the suboptimal (triangle) routing via the HA, because CNs can send packets directly to the MNs, using IPv6 routing header option, if they have recent entries for their statuses. In the case that a CN has no entry for an MN, the flow will be forwarded to the MN through the HA, but when the MN receives the encapsulated packets, it will send back to the HA and/or the CN a Binding Update (BU) about its current CoA, using either extension headers or piggybacking on data packets (Figure 8(a)).

In cases with high mobility, the fast changes of MN's point of attachment can decrease the QoS, mainly due to signaling overhead and delay. For this reason, IETF proposed Fast Handovers for Mobile IPv6 (Koodli, 2008), which manages to decrease the triggering time of handover procedure. More specifically, when a MN detects that it is about to migrate to a new Access Router (AR) domain, as long as it has information for this domain, it prepares the binding update signaling and the flow forwarding in order to minimize the handover delay. In this way, the MN manages to move, while having an open session, within different AR domains without being affected by the handover procedure.

Hierarchical Mobile IPv6 (HMIPv6) (Soliman et al., 2008), is another mobility support

Figure 7. Mobility Management in (a) MIPv6 and in (b) PMIPv6

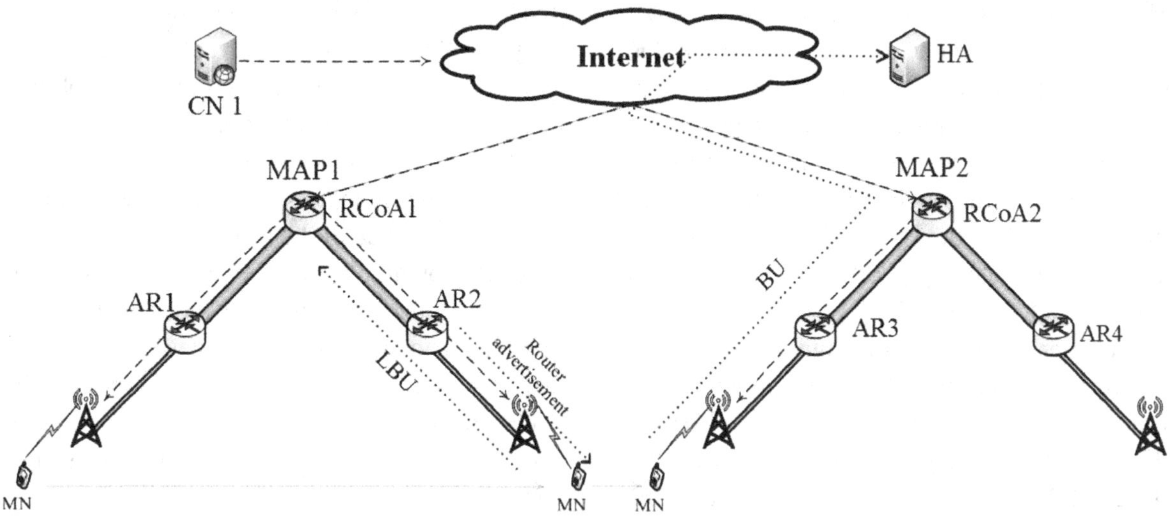

Figure 8. Mobility Management in Hierarchical MIPv6

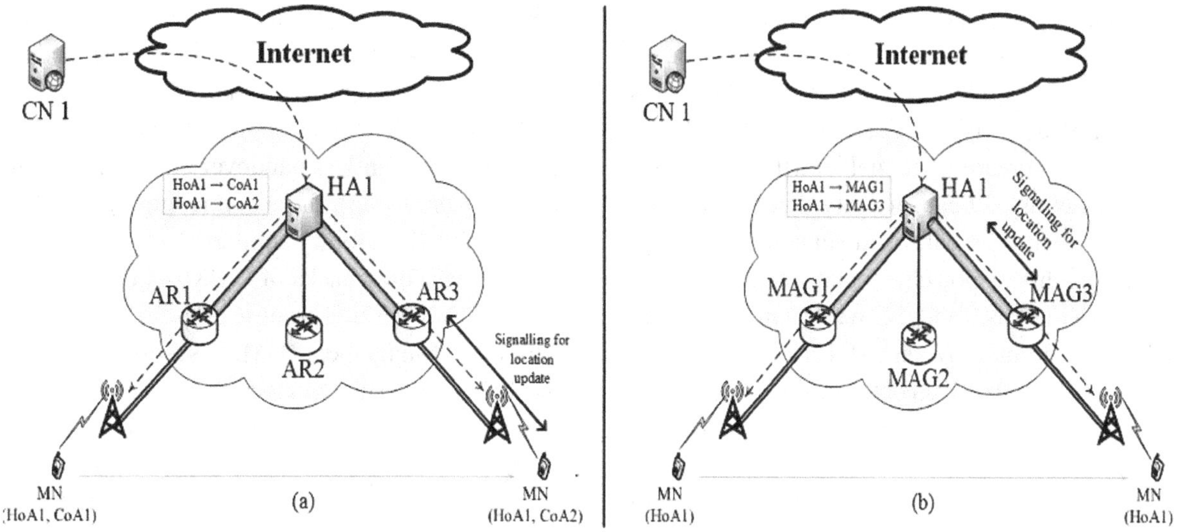

scheme proposed by IETF as an extension to MIPv6, mainly suitable for scenarios where a lot of handovers take place and the MNs are located far away from their home domains. According to HMIPv6 (Figure 7), the mobility of the users is handled locally by network entities called Mobility Anchor Points (MAPs), which serve certain AR domains and act like local HAs. In this way, most of the handovers are handled locally in an efficient and fast way. On the other hand, when an MN migrates to a different MAP domain, MIPv6 handles the mobility support as it was described above. More precisely, when a MN is located inside a MAP region, it obtains a Regional Care of Address (RCoA) and the HA and the CNs are update their entry. From now on, every flow towards the MN will be routed through the MAP, which serves this area using the on-Link Care of Address (LCoA). While the MN moves within the same MAP area, its MAP is responsible of tunneling the flow to the AR which serves the MN, avoiding in this way high signaling and making the handover procedure fast. In the more rare cases of global handovers (between different MAP domains), the BU has to be sent back to the HA and/or CN of the MN in order to update the RCoA and to forward the flow through the new MAP.

In order to decrease the signaling overhead and to avoid the requirement of mobility software at the MN, Proxy Mobile IPv6 (PMIPv6) (Gundavelli et al., 2008) was proposed. PMIPv6 (Figure 8(b)) is a network-based mobility solution, where in contrast to the previous mobility management schemes there is no need to install any-mobility related software on the MN, while the mobility management is assigned to specific network entities. More precisely, Mobility Access Gateway (MAG) is a network entity, which runs on the AR, and it is responsible for tracking MN's location and creating a tunnel with the other basic network entity, Local Mobility Anchor (LMA). LMA, which is an enhanced version of MIPv4's HA, is mainly responsible for ensuring the reachability of the MN's address, while it moves within a PMIPv6 domain. When a MN is located inside a PMIPv6 domain, MAG obtains MN's profile and then it sends a Proxy Binding Update (PBU) to LMA, which after an authentication process sends back a Proxy Binding Acknowledgment (PBA) and sets up a route for the MN's home network prefix using the tunnel with the MAG. After receiving the PBA, MAG is able to emulate the MN's home network can send a Router Advertisement (RA) message to MN in order for it to configure its home prefix accordingly. At this moment, all data will be forwarded via this MAG-LMA tunnel, saving bandwidth from the MN by excluding it from mobility-related signaling (so, the MN is unaware of the mobility support procedure).

All of the above mentioned mobility management schemes share the common feature that they are strongly centralized and for this reason we will refer to them as Centralized Mobility Management (CMM) schemes. As summarized in (Lee et al., 2013), the main disadvantage of CMM is the suboptimal or 'triangle' routing, which means that all the flows have to be routed through potentially unnecessarily longer paths via a centralized mobility anchor. In this way, mobility anchors become points of congestion causing high delay and degradation of the QoS. In addition, the centralized anchors can also become single points of failure affecting in a greater degree the robustness of the whole network. Moreover, CMM schemes lack per se of dynamic mobility support as well as scalability because of the fact that they turn out to be a bottleneck for the whole network, especially when MNs tend to increase. For this reason, core networks are dimensioned to support peak data traffic. Finally, in CMM there is a waste of network resources because even in cases where seamless handover is not important (Internet browsing), there is tracking of the MN and 'blind' IP mobility support.

All these drawbacks of CMM schemes motivated IETF's working group to propose Distributed Mobility Management (DMM) scheme (Chan et al., 2014), a mobility management scheme, where the mobility function is distributed at the edge of the core network. In (Chan et al., 2014) the main requirements that DMM had to meet and the motivations were defined. According to (Zuniga et al., 2013) the main classes of solutions for distribution of the mobility management are the client, the network and the routing based solutions.

In the client-based approach, the anchoring is distributed at the edge of the core network and the MN uses additional IP address at each visited AR. In this way, for each new flow the MN will use the locally anchored address but each time it migrates to another AR it keeps reachability for the previous IP address of the domain where the flow was set up. In order to do so, the MN has to bind the addresses of the active sessions with the local address of its current domain allowing the data to be forwarded from the previous HA to the new one. This approach needs software intelligence from the side of the MN because it has to update the entries of the current and previous addresses, use the right one to start new sessions, track the addresses which need mobility support and take care of the binding, signaling and tunneling.

Regarding the network-based approach, there are two subclasses: the fully distributed and the partially distributed solution, depending on whether or not the control plane is decoupled from the data plane. According to the former one both the data and the control plane are distributed to the edge of the network and network entities (LMA and MAG in PMIPv6 approach) are responsible for data forwarding and mobility related signaling. In partially distributed solution only the data plane is distributed while the control plane is managed by network entities (e.g. 3GPP's MME), which are located hierarchically higher across the network.

In Figure 9 we visualize the two different schemes by depicting a comparison of routing and tunneling between DMM (shown as Case 1) and CMM (shown as Case 2). For the case of DMM when the MN is connected to MAR 1 the routing path is optimal and the tunneling cost is minimal since it only take place between the MAR 1 and the AR where the MN is connected to. On the other hand, in the case of a handover then the routing path becomes sub-optimal since the flow has to be tunnelled to the new MAR (MAR 2) via MAR 1. As can be seen in the figure for more handovers the sub-optimality of the routing path can further deteriorate and in that specific setting the number of hops when connected to MAR 3 will be 7 instead of the optimal path that requires 3 hops. On the other hand, for the case of CMM (in the figure we consider PMIPv6) the routing cost even in the case of multiple handovers can remain close to optimal (depending on the location of the LMA) but there is a significant tunneling cost since all flows need to be encapsulated between the LMA towards the MN. Figure 10 focus on the issue of tunneling cost between DMM and CMM approaches when taking into account cell residence times and session duration times. Both of these can be considered as independent random variables that have a direct effect on the performance of the different mobility support schemes. The figure depicts the cases where during session duration time there are zero (P_0) up to three (P_3) handovers. As can be seen in the figure CMM always results in tunneling overhead whereas in the case of DMM tunneling overhead only take place when there is a handover. Therefore, in the cases where the session duration time is significant less than the cell residence time DMM can entail significant less overhead compared to CMM schemes.

Therefore, it becomes evident that the performance of DMM schemes are very much topology dependent since there can be instances where a more centralized approach might perform better especially in terms of routing. These design trade-offs need to be carefully taken into account for supporting seamless mobility under DMM solutions.

Finally, in the routing-based approach (P. McCann, 2013) the routers are connected in mesh-like structure and not in a hierarchical one (i.e. core, aggregation and access). The main difference is that during a handover, the flow will not be tunneled from the former AR to the new AR, but each time an optimal route will be deployed via routing updates. However, this implementation has some disadvantages comparing to the other two. The main are the limitations by the routing convergence of the handover delay and the scalability issues due to potential storms of routing updates.

In current 3GPP Release 12, although DMM is not yet deployed, there have already been some remarkable efforts in terms of traffic relieving and dynamic mobility management. Two of the

Figure 9. Comparison of routing and tunneling between DMM (Case 1) and CMM (Case 2) mobility support.

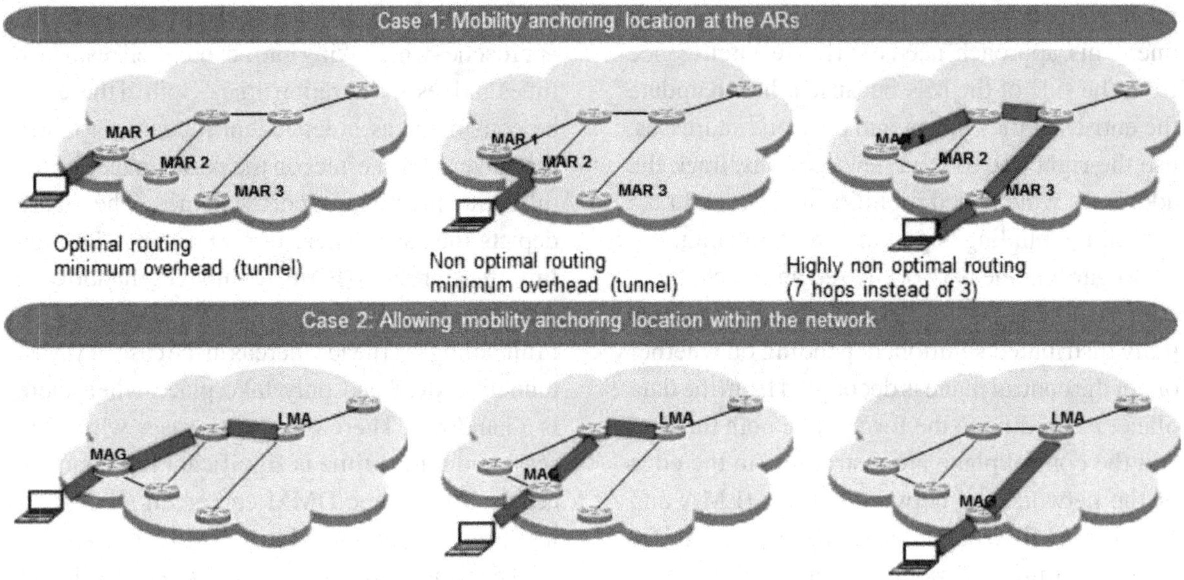

Figure 10. Tunneling cost of DMM and CMM (PMIPv6) for different instances of cell residence time and session duration

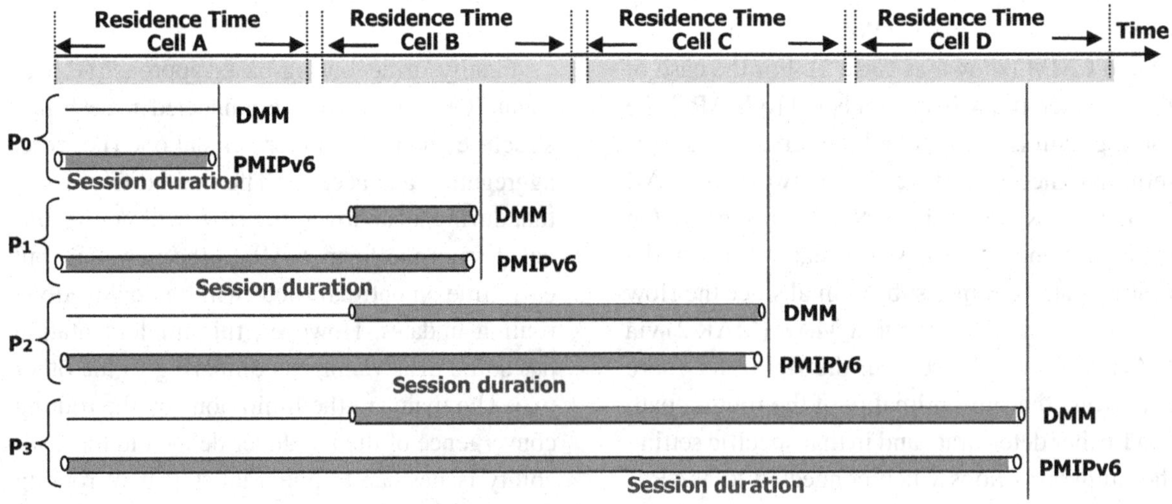

most remarkable of them are Selected IP Traffic Offloading (SIPTO) and Local IP Address (LIPA) (3GPP TS 23.401, 2011). SIPTO's concept is to allow traffic offloading at a network node close to the UE's point of attachment to the access network by selecting a set of gateways, which are located geographically close to it. LIPA allows a UE to connect to other IP-capable entities in its local network without the involvement of the rest of the network.

Several other works towards the improvement of current 3GPP mobility management have been proposed the last years. In (Hahn, 2011a), (Hahn, 2011b) there is a proposal for distribution of the data plane in 3GPP Evolved Packet Core (EPC) networks. Particularly, the author studies the potential gain from the relocation of GWs in order to optimize the routing of the flows to the users and to get rid of non-optimal routing. The authors in (Bernardos et al., 2012) motivated by the disadvantages of centralized mobility management and by the lack of mobility support of SIPTO and LIPA, they present an evolved 3GPP architecture that supports fully distributed mobility management, which is also compatible with current solutions. Their approach introduces a new mobility support entity, the distributed gateway, which is located at the edge of the network and it is responsible of supporting the mobility and forwarding the data during handovers.

In (Guo et al., 2013a), the authors propose efficient local mobility management schemes for 3GPP LTE-A networks, where instead of dealing with path switching at the core network for each handover they introduce the idea of local traffic forwarding chain construction in order to use the existing Internet backhaul and the local path between the local anchor femtocell and the next femtocell for active sessions. The results show that the proposed schemes manage to reduce the signaling cost and relieve the processing burden of mobile core networks, where femtocells are deployed. They can also enable fast session recovery after a handover allowing in this way to adapt to the self-deployment nature of the femtocells.

In (Chochlidakis G. et al., 2014) the authors propose a hybrid distributed mobility management scheme for next generation networks. In particular, firstly an optimization framework for optimal deployment of mobility agents in CMM is presented. Then, the DMM scheme as proposed by IETF is modeled and the two schemes are compared to each other. Based on this comparison, a hybrid DMM schemes is presented, where delay-sensitive flows are handled by mobility anchors located hierarchically higher across the network, in cases where the handover delay might be highly dependent on the network topology. The simulation results show that there can be achieved a significant improvement on the achieve QoS for these flows.

Finally, the authors in (Xenakis et al., 2013), firstly provide the main aspects and challenges of mobility management in mobile networks with deployment of femtocells classified according to the cell identification, the access control, the cell search and selection, and the handover decision and execution. Then they present the accurate landscape of the so far existent in the literature algorithms and techniques according to the class they belong to, mainly focusing on the handover decision phase.

In conclusion, future mobile networks, in order to address the limitation of physical resources and to increase the capacity to deal with high future demand, they are expected to make extended use of femtocells. One of the important issues of the deployment of smaller cells is the increased number of handover and the need of efficient and reliable mobility support. For this reason, a distributed mobility management approach is strongly believed that is going to be deployed by next generation networks. As stated above, such deployment will allow the mobile operators to move from centralized architectures to more flexible distributed architectures, where the mobile function will move towards the edge of the network as well as anywhere across the network (Chochlidakis G. et al., 2014), depending on desired QoS, types of delivered services and overall performance requirements.

3.3 Network Virtualization in Mobile Networks

Broadly speaking, virtualization is the process of creating virtual entities, which have the same characteristics with physical resources and emulate their function. This is by far not a new concept since the idea of virtualization was firstly introduced in computer systems in the early 60's through multi-programming techniques. Since then, and under the same concept, different resources, like memories, CPUs etc. have been virtualized and used in order to increase the utilization, the flexibility and the total efficiency of computer systems. Currently, virtualization can be classified into three main categories, which are by themselves areas that attracted significant research: storage virtualization, which refers to creation of virtual memories using resources from a single or multiple physical memories, server virtualization, where different virtual machines can be created from one or more physical machines and network virtualization, the technique of forming virtual networks (VNs) by combining physical resources. An example of the later one is shown in Figure 11 where two different clients negotiate with an ISP (physical infrastructure) for the creation of two virtual networks. Assuming an SDN enabled infrastructure, the mobile operator or ISP needs to define the topology (this is called virtual network embedding), which must have the requirements as specified by the client.

Enablers towards this direction will be both software-defined networking techniques in which control and forwarding planes are logically decoupled as well as Network Function Virtualization (NVF) where different mobile network functions can be decoupled from a specific hardware which

Figure 11. A scenario of physical mobile wireless network infrastructure (belonging for example to an ISP) and the creation of two Virtual Networks representing two different requests by different clients

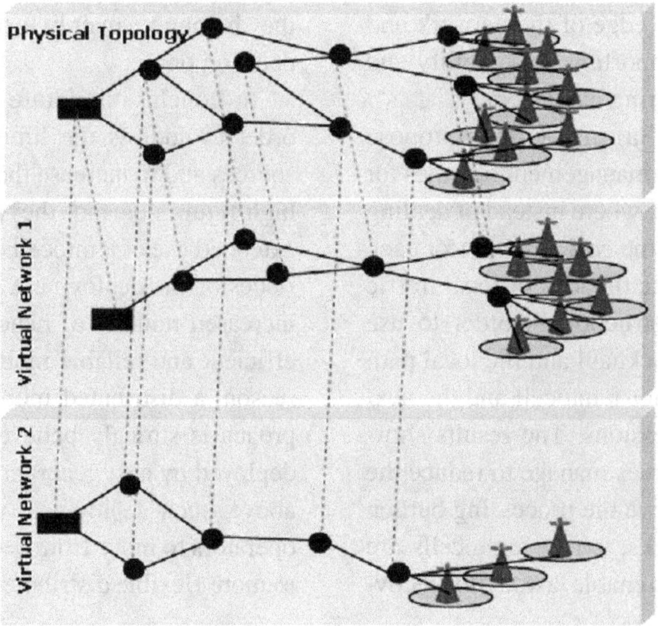

in current networks are mainly proprietary (ETSI, 2013). Therefore, broadly speaking, NFV can be considered as the idea of implementing network functions from software-specific hardware to software-based applications (hardware agnostic) on widely used off-the-shelf systems. Still it can be deemed as rather early to foresee the actual direction in terms of impact that SDN and NFV will have on the infrastructure and operation of the network even though key players have already intensify the efforts in that scope area. It is worth pointing out that there are more than 200 member companies including operators within the ETSI NFV initiative. For example the Internet Multimedia Subsystem (IMS) might quickly move from an all-in-one black box to hardware agnostic virtualized functions which might also be implemented in the cloud. Despite that, network virtualization is emerging as an important architectural item for emerging wireless network, hence we discuss this further in the sequel.

As already eluded above, over the last few years, mobile operators have to deal with the problem of exponential traffic demand and to come up with solutions in order to improve their QoS and their overall sustainability. Taking into consideration that physical resources are limited and expensive, the increase of their utilization is a high-priority problem. For this reason, it comes as no surprise that network virtualization becomes more and more a prominent solution (Khan et al., 2011).

The main advantages of network virtualization are the fact that increases the flexibility and the utilization of the resources and thus it is energy efficient. Thanks to network virtualization, it is much easier for a mobile operator to redesign dynamically the network by adding and removing network elements as well as to recover much faster and reliably from network failures. In addition, network virtualization gives the chance to more operators to enter the market by leasing resources and setting up virtual networks, without owning large and expensive infrastructures. This leads to a more competitive market with better quality of service and better choices for the end-user.

The main plan of network virtualization in mobile networks consists of three basic roles. Firstly, the infrastructure providers own, manage and virtualize the physical resources. The virtual network providers act like brokers between the infrastructure providers and the network operators by combining the physical resources in order to form the virtual networks. Finally, the virtual network operators are responsible of running the virtual networks and provide service to the end-users.

The virtualization techniques in current mobile networks can be classified into virtualization of physical infrastructure (i.e. nodes, links etc.) and virtualization of the air-interface (access control and spectrum). Regarding spectrum virtualization, the main problem that has to be addressed is how radio physical resources can be partitioned and shared among different network providers. In (Costa-Perez et al., 2013) the authors provide a preview on the state-of-the-art on RAN sharing techniques and then they present their proposal, Network Virtualization Substrate (NVS), a slice scheduler and a flow scheduling framework. Their approach aims to provide isolation between shared resources, customization in order to achieve dynamic allocation and improved utilization of the resources. In (Kokku et al., 2013) the authors present CellSlice, which is an innovative system for slicing wireless physical resources, enabling efficient RAN sharing. CellSlice is a gateway-level solution, which remotely controls the scheduling decisions without the modification of the BS schedulers, making it easier to be adopted. The results show that CellSlice's performance is close to NVS's, being access-technology independent, hence can be considered suitable for various networks. The authors in (Panchal et al., 2013) perform a study and evaluation of different sharing options, from simple to more complex methods. Then they compare, via a simulation testbed, capacity sharing, spectrum sharing and virtualized spectrum sharing under different scenarios in order to conclude that capacity sharing, a generalization of traditional roaming, is the best performing as well as the simplest option while spectrum sharing is least effective. In (Guo et al., 2013b), the authors propose a partial resource reservation, which is a flexible active RAN sharing technique allowing each operator to have a minimum percentage of the physical resources and also having access to a common resource pool with a first-come-first-serve scheme. Their proposal, adapted for LTE networks, manages to address both the scheduler and admission control aspects. After system-level simulation, they show that, in comparison to full reservation schemes, their proposal can dynamically and efficiently allocate the physical resources among different operators according to the demand and traffic priorities and in this way to increase the spectrum utilization.

Regarding the virtualization of the core network, a major problem that attracted significant research attention over the last few years is finding efficient (or optimal if possible in some instances) ways to map a virtual network over a physical infrastructure. Virtual network embedding deals with the allocation of virtual resources both in nodes and links and it can be divided in virtual node mapping and virtual link mapping. The authors in (Fischer et al., 2013) provide the landscape of the research work that has been done so far on the area of algorithms and techniques, which address the virtual network embedding problem. Then, they create a taxonomy of major algorithmic efforts which exist in the literature. One clear message which is becoming now apparent is that more effort should be placed on the design of distributed virtual network embedding algorithms, since centralized ones have not only the problem of single-point of failure but they might increase overall signaling load from the access to the core network in areas which are particularly prone to congestion. Distributed approach might be more effective to "hide" their operation across the network since decision making might take place locally decreasing in that sense overall signaling load in the network. In addition, energy efficiency and security are aspects that should be kept in mind in future research. This is an important issue since with greater degree of programmability in the network the vulnerabilities will only tend to increase in the network hence special attention should be place in protecting a software-defined network from sophisticated malicious attacks. Network control and decision making in 5G networks should be able to handle a very heterogeneity of requirements from current, emerging and future applications. In terms of only delay for example these should range from millisecond (tactile Internet) to hundreds of milliseconds (mobility, resource allocation) and hours (network slicing, topology configuration). Hence, in this emerging environment orchestration of the control plane is becoming significantly important due to the high heterogeneity of the time scales in terms of decision making. Therefore, we might need to devise dedicated scheduling and control plane optimization algorithms to enable efficient "smart" decision making using an ever increasing information set from the network hence creating networks that are able to adapt efficiently to internal (i.e., failures) and external (i.e., traffic, mobility) events.

4. CONCLUSION AND FUTURE OUTLOOK

To resolve the challenges stemming out of the increased traffic demand and heterogeneity of that traffic, research towards 5G will inevitably have to put in the epicentre some big questions surrounding the future of mobile communications. The proliferation of small base stations towards the vision of HetNets and network densification creates by itself a set of complex management issues ranging from uses such as spectrum re-use to coverage, consistency on the service delivery and QoE support. In this significant more complex environment the notion of hexagonal cells will be decreasing and mobile nodes will participate more actively on overall network management and control. Bearing that in mind, we have discussed emerging architectural paradigms such the cell on demand and the phantom cell concept that aim to split control and data planes physically in order to ease network management. We have also described that in separate efforts SDN/NVF in essence allows for logical separation of control and data forwarding planes as well as decoupling between hardware and software of various network functionalities to allow for further innovation in networks. Hence combining these two emerging paradigms is an area of significant interest for future research. Furthermore, we comprehensively elaborate on some fundamental issues on supporting seamless mobility under a heterogeneous wireless access environment focusing on both the centralized as well as the emerging distributed mobility management schemes. Network virtualization has been considered as an enabler to provide quick roll outs of new techniques, reduce cost via infrastructure sharing while at the same time we have identified some key challenges with respect to network virtualization as pertain to wireless networks. In the path towards 5G, there is an urgent need to explore revolutionary approaches in terms of network orchestration and management compared to the current paradigms in order to allow for service consistency as well as efficient utilization of the available resources. On the other hand, an evolution is envisioned on lower layer techniques that will aim to further increase capacity by mainly exploring higher radio frequencies. Finally, some key open ended research problems have been discussed.

Further paradigm changes however will likely be the norm in the upcoming 3GPP releases towards 5G or even beyond:

- **Optional Core.** With mobility and RRM managed at the very edges, i.e. mainly by the context-aware UE; billing and authentication virtualized; and QoS/QoE provided by SDN paradigms; the core will essentially lose its importance and thus likely be an optional feature in 3GPP on the long run. This, in turn, will aid the tightest possible integration between 3GPP and non-3GPP technologies.
- **System Component Decoupling.** We have briefly discussed decoupled data and control channels which are seen as an enabler of multi-RAT HetNets; this enables an eNB to provide phantom-like control channel coverage to handle data transfer via 3GPP and non-3GPP RATs in a completely equal and transparent fashion. We also dwelled on a trend likely to persist, which is to completely decouple up and downlinks; again, properly designed HetNets will be core to such developments since the downlink can be provided by a 3GPP-compliant RAT whereas the uplink via a non-3GPP RAT. We will further experience the decoupling of addressing and forwarding; and the decoupling of RF from baseband; just to mention a few. This decoupling trend will enormously increases the flexibility and thus performance of the overall wireless system.
- **Disappearance of the Cell.** The cell, as known to 2G-4G system designers, will disappear in 5G and beyond. That is, a UE will not be associated by some coverage area but rather by some selection decision. Therefore, association decisions and related planning will completely change over the coming years.

We hope that the vision outlined in this chapter will be of substantial use in the discussion and design of emerging 5G systems.

ACKNOWLEDGMENT

This work is partially funded by the European Commission Framework Programme 7 Marie Curie Initial Training Networks (ITN) CROSSFIRE project. The authors would also like to thank their collaborators in providing material related to MTC in femtocells and the decoupled up and downlinks.

REFERENCES

3 GPP TS 23.703. (2014). Technical Specification Group Services and System Aspects; Study on architecture enhancements to support Proximity-based Services (ProSe). *Technical Report 3rd Generation Partnership Project.*

3GPP TS 23.401. (2011). General Packet Radio Service (GPRS) Enhancements for Evolved Universal Terrestrial Radio Access Network (E-UTRAN) Access". *Technical Report 3rd Generation Partnership Project.*

Bai, T., & Heath, R. W. (2013). Coverage in dense millimeter wave cellular networks. *Asilomar Conference on Signals, Systems and Computers* (pp. 2062-2066). Asilomar.

Bejarano, O., Knightly, E. W., & Park, M. (2013). IEEE 802.11ac: From channelization to multi-user MIMO. *IEEE Communications Magazine*, *51*(10), 84–90. doi:10.1109/MCOM.2013.6619570

Bernardos, C. J., Zunniga, J.C., & Reznik, A. (2012). Towards flat and distributed mobility management: A 3GPP evolved network design. In *Communications (ICC), 2012 IEEE International Conference on*. IEEE.

Bernardos, C. J., De Domenico, A., Ortin, J., Rost, P., & Wübben, D. (2013). *Challenges of designing jointly the backhaul and radio access network in a cloud based mobile network*. Lisbon, Portugal: Future Networks Summit.

Bhaumik, S., Chandrabose, S. P., Jataprolu, M. K., Kumar, G., Muralidhar, A., Polakos, P., . . . Woo, T. (2012). CloudIQ: A Framework for Processing Base Stations in a Data Center. ACM MobiCom, August 22-26, Istanbul, Turkey.

Bing, H., He, C., & Jiang, L. (2003), Performance analysis of vertical handover in a UMTS-WLAN integrated network. *Personal, Indoor and Mobile Radio Communications, PIMRC, 14th IEEE Proceedings on.*

Capone, A., Filippini, I., Gloss, B., & Barth, U. (2012). Rethinking cellular system architecture for breaking current energy efficiency limits. IEEE Sustainable Internet and ICT for Sustainability (SustainIT), Pisa, Italy.

Chan, H., Liu, D., Seite, P., Yokota, H., & Korhonen, J. (2014). Requirements for Distributed Mobility Management, *Internet Draft: draft-ietf-dmmrequirements-15 (work-in-progress)*. IETF. [Online]. Available: http://datatracker.ietf.org/doc/draft-ietf-dmm-requirements/

Chochlidakis, G., & Friderikos, V. (2014). Hybrid Distributed Mobility Management for Next-Generation Wireless Networks. *International Conference on the Network of the Future (NoF'14)*, Paris, France.

Condoluci, A., Dohler, M., Araniti, G., Molinaro, A., & Zheng, K. (2014, August). (accepted). Towards 5G DenseNets: Architectural Advances For Effective Machine-Type Communications over Femtocells. *IEEE Communications Magazine*.

Cordeiro, C., Akhmetov, D., & Park, M. (2010). *IEEE 802.11ad: introduction and performance evaluation of the first multi-gbps wifi technology. ACM international workshop on mmWave communications: from circuits to networks (mmCom '10)*. New York, NY, USA: ACM.

Costa-Perez, X., Swetina, J., Guo, T., Mahindra, R., & Rangarajan, S. (2013, July). Tao Guo; Mahindra, R.; Rangarajan, S., "Radio access network virtualization for future mobile carrier networks. *Communications Magazine, IEEE, 51*(7), 27–35. doi:10.1109/MCOM.2013.6553675

Doppler K., Rinne M., Wijting C., Ribeiro C.B., Hugl, K. (2009). Device-to-device communication as an underlay to LTE-advanced networks. *IEEE Communications Magazine, 47*(12).

Elshaer, H., Boccardi, F., Dohler, M., & Irmer, R. (2014). Downlink and Uplink Decoupling: a Disruptive Architectural Design for 5G Networks. IEEE Globecom 2014, Austin, TX.

ETSI. Network Function Virtualization: Architectural Framework, white paper (available online) 2013

Fettweis, G. (2013). 5G What Will it Be: The Tactile Internet. *Keynote talk at ICC 2013*. Retrieved from http://goo.gl/DJhg8E

Fischer, A., Botero, J. F., Till Beck, M., de Meer, H., & Hesselbach, X. (2013). Virtual Network Embedding: A Survey. Communications Surveys & Tutorials, IEEE, 15(4), 1888-1906.

Golrezaei, N., Shanmugam, K., Dimakis, A. G., Molisch, A. F., & Caire, G. (2012). *FemtoCaching: Wireless video content delivery through distributed caching helpers*. Orlando, FL: IEEE INFOCOM.

Guan, H., Kolding, T., & Merz, P. (2010). *Discovery of Cloud RAN*. C-RAN International Workshop, Bejing, China.

Gude, N., Koponen, T., Pettit, J., Pfaff, B., Casado, M., McKeown, N., & Shenker, S. (2008). NOX: Towards an operating system for networks. *ACM SIGCOMM Computer Communications Review, 38*(3), 105–110. doi:10.1145/1384609.1384625

Guimaraes, D., Corujo, R. L., Aguiar, F., Silva, & Rosa. (2013),. Empowering Software Defined Wireless Networks Through Media Independent Handover Management. IEEE Globecom, Atlanta, GA.

Gundavelli, S., Leung, K., Devarapalli, V., Chowdhury, K., & Patil, B. (2008). *Proxy Mobile IPv6," RFC 5213 (Proposed Standard), IETF, updated by RFC 6543*. Retrieved from: http://www.ietf.org/rfc/rfc5213.txt

Guo, T., & Arnott, R. (2013b), Active LTE RAN Sharing with Partial Resource Reservation, *Vehicular Technology Conference (VTC Fall), 2013 IEEE 78th*, pp.1-5 doi:10.1109/VTC-Fall.2013.6692075

Guo, T., Ul Quddus, A., Wang, N., & Tafazolli, R. (2013a, January). Local Mobility Management for Networked Femtocells Based on X2 Traffic Forwarding, *Vehicular Technology. IEEE Transactions on, 62*(1), 326–340.

Hahn, W. (2011a). 3GPP Evolved Packet Core support for distributed mobility anchors: Control enhancements for GW relocation. *ITS Telecommunications (ITST), 2011 11th International Conference on.*

Hahn, W. (2011b). Flat 3GPP Evolved Packet Core. *Wireless Personal Multimedia Communications (WPMC), 2011 14th International Symposium on.*

Khan, A., Kellerer, W., Kozu, K., & Yabusaki, M. (2011, October). Network sharing in the next mobile network: TCO reduction, management flexibility, and operational independence. *Communications Magazine, IEEE, 49*(10), 134–142. doi:10.1109/MCOM.2011.6035827

Kokku, R., Mahindra, R., Zhang, & Rangarajan, S. (2013). CellSlice: Cellular wireless resource slicing for active RAN sharing. *Communication Systems and Networks (COMSNETS), 2013 Fifth International Conference on.*

Koodli, R. (2008). *Fast Handovers for Mobile IPv6', RFC 5268 (Proposed Standard).* IETF.

Lee, D. H., Choi, K. W., Jeon, W. S., & Jeong, D. G. (2013). *Resource Allocation Scheme for Device-to-Device Communication for Maximizing Spatial Reuse.* IEEE Wireless Communications and Networking. doi:10.1109/WCNC.2013.6554548

Lee, J., Bonnin, J.-M., Seite, P., & Chan, H.A. (2013). Distributed IP mobility management from the perspective of the IETF: motivations, requirements, approaches, comparison, and challenges. *IEEE Wireless Communications, 20*(5), 159-168.

Li, Q.C., Niu, Wu, & Hu, R.Q. (2013). Anchor-booster based heterogeneous networks with mmWave capable booster cells. *Globecom Workshops (GC Wkshps), 2013 IEEE.*

Liu, D., Zuniga, J., Seite, P., Chan, H., & Bernandos, C. (2014), Distributed Mobility Management: Current practices and gap analysis. *Internet Draft: draft-ietf-dmm-best-practices-gap-analysis- 03, IETF, 2014.* Retrieved From: http://datatracker.ietf.org/doc/draft-ietf-dmm-best-practices-gap-analysis

McCann, P. (2012). Authentication and Mobility Management in a Flat Architecture. *Internet Engineering Task Force Internet Draft: draft-mccann-dmm-flatarch-00.* Retrieved from: http://tools.ietf.org/html/draft-mccann-dmm-flatarch-00

McKeown, N., Anderson, T., Balakrishnan, H., Parulkar, G., Peterson, L., Rexford, J., & Turner, J. et al. (2008). Openflow: Enabling innovation in campus networks. *ACM SIGCOMM Computer Communications Review, 38*(2), 69–74. doi:10.1145/1355734.1355746

Nakamura, T., Nagata, S., Benjebbour, A., Kishiyama, Y., Hai, T., Xiaodong, S., & Nan, L. et al. (2013). Trends in small cell enhancements in LTE advanced. *IEEE Communications Magazine, 51*(2), 98,105. doi:10.1109/MCOM.2013.6461192

Osseiran, A., Braun, V., Hidekazu, T., Marsch, P., Schotten, H., Tullberg, H., & Schellman, M. et al. (2013). The Foundation of the Mobile and Wireless Communication System for 2020 and Beyond. In *Proc. IEEE Vehic. Tech Conf.* Dresden, Germany: IEEE.

Panchal, J. S., Yates, R. D., & Buddhikot, M. M. (2013, September). Mobile Network Resource Sharing Options: Performance Comparisons. *Wireless Communications, IEEE Transactions on, 12*(9), 4470–4482. doi:10.1109/TWC.2013.071913.121597

Parkvall S., Furuskar A., Dahlman E. (2011). Evolution of LTE toward IMT-advanced. *IEEE Communications Magazine, 49*(2), 84-91.

Perkins, C. (2010). *IP Mobility Support for IPv4, Revised, RFC 5944 (Proposed Standard), IETF.* Retrieved From: http://www.ietf.org/rfc/rfc5944.txt

Perkins, C., Johnson, D., & Arkko, J. (2011). Mobility Support in IPv6, RFC 6275 (Proposed Standard). *IETF.* Retrieved from: http://www.ietf.org/rfc/rfc6275.txt

Quadros, C., Cerqueira, E., Neto, A., Riker, A., Immich, R., & Curado, M. (2012). *A mobile QoE Architecture for Heterogeneous Multimedia Wireless Networks*. Anaheim, CA: IEEE Globecom Workshops. doi:10.1109/GLOCOMW.2012.6477724

Rappaport, T. S., Sun Shu, R., Mayzus, Z. H. Z., Azar, Wang, Wong, Schulz, Samimi, & Gutierrez. (2013). Millimeter Wave Mobile Communications for 5G Cellular: It Will Work!. IEEE Access, 1.

Rost, P., Bernardos, C. J., De Domenico, A., Di Girolamo, M., Lalam, M., Maeder, A., & Wübben, D. et al. (2014). Cloud technologies for flexible 5G radio access networks. *IEEE Communications Magazine, 52*(5), 68–76. doi:10.1109/MCOM.2014.6898939

Sakaguchi, K., Sampei, S., Shimodaira, H., Rezagah, R., Tran, G. K., & Araki, K. (2013). *Cloud cooperated heterogeneous cellular networks*. Intelligent Signal Processing and Communications Systems (ISPACS), 2013 International Symposium on.

Soliman, H., Castelluccia, C., El-Malki, K., & Bellier, L. (2008). Hierarchical Mobile IPv6 (HMIPv6) Mobility Management, RFC 5380 (Proposed Standard). *IETF.* Retrieved from: http://www.ietf.org/rfc/rfc5380.txt

Tamijetchelvy, R., & Sivaradje, G. (2012). An optimized fast vertical handover strategy for heterogeneous wireless access networks based on IEEE 802.21 media independent handover standard. *Fourth International Conference on Advanced Computing (ICoAC).* doi:10.1109/ICoAC.2012.6416817

Vestin, J., Dely, P., Kassler, A., Bayer, N., Einsiedler, H., & Peylo, C. (2013). CloudMAC: Towards software defined WLANs. *ACM SIGMOBILE Mobile Computer Communications Review, 16*(4), 42–45. doi:10.1145/2436196.2436217

Wen, S., Zhu, X., Lin, Z., Zhang, X., & Yang, D. (2013). Distributed Resource Management for Device-to-Device (D2D) Communication Underlay Cellular Networks. *IEEE 24th International Symposium on Personal Indoor and Mobile Radio Comm. (PIMRC).*

Wubben, D., Rost, P., Bartelt, J., Lalam, M., Savin, V., Gorgoglione, M., & Fettweis, G. et al. (2014, May). Benefits and impact of cloud computing on 5G signal processing, *IEEE Signal Processing Magazine, Special Issue on 5G. Signal Processing.*

Xenakis, D., Passas, N., Merakos, L., & Verikoukis, C. (2014). Mobility Management for Femtocells in LTE-Advanced: Key Aspects and Survey of Handover Decision Algorithms. Communications Surveys & Tutorials, IEEE, 16(1), 64-91.

Yousaf, F. Z., Lessmann, J., Loureiro, P., & Schmid, S. (2013). SoftEPC Dynamic Instantiation of Mobile Core Network Entities for Efficient Resource Utilization. *IEEE International Conference on Communications*, Budapest, Hungary.

Zaidi, Z., Friderikos, V., & Ali Imran, M. (2014). An integrated approach for future mobile network architecture. *IEEE International Symposium on Personal, Indoor and Mobile Radio Communications (PIMRC)*, Washington, DC.

Zheng, K., Hu, F., Wang, W., Xiang, W., & Dohler, M. (2012). Radio Resource Allocation in LTE-Advanced Cellular Networks with M2M Communications. *IEEE Communications Magazine, 50*(7), 184–192. doi:10.1109/MCOM.2012.6231296

Zuniga, J.C., Bernardos C. J., De La Oliva A, Melia, T., Costa, R., Reznik, A, (2013). Distributed mobility management: A standards landscape. *IEEE Communications Magazine, 51*(3).

KEY TERMS AND DEFINITIONS

HetNets: The use of a wide range of different technologies - base stations, radio access networks, including WLANs - as well as multiple cell sizes and transmission power levels.

mmWave Communications: The use of spectrum bands between 30 and 300 GHz, in which available bandwidth can be much wider than today's cellular networks where spectrum use is in the vicinity of 3GHz.

Network Virtualization: The process of uniting hardware (and software) network resources and network functionalities into isolated, software-based administrative entities that allows the creation of virtual networks on top of the (shared) physical network infrastructure.

Phantom Cells: Small cells that are controlled by a macro-cell BS controller in wireless split based architectures.

Split-Architectures: Physical decoupling on the wireless access between the user-plane and control-plane. In split-architectures, small cells provide high data rate communication to the users whilst network orchestration take place via a macro-Base Station that act as the control plane for efficient wireless resource management.

Uplink/Downlink Decoupling: Differentiating mobile user cell association for downlink and uplink traffic in different wireless access points depending on overall network conditions and mobile user location.

Vertical/Horizontal Handover: Providing service continuity upon changing the point of attachment of a mobile user in the case of same radio access network technology (horizontal handover) or different radio access technology (vertical handover).

Section 3

Advanced Transport Techniques, and Traffic Forwarding and Routing Schemes

Chapter 9

Multipath TCP (MPTCP): Motivations, Status, and Opportunities for the Future Internet

David Binet
Orange, France

Mohamed Boucadair
Orange, France

Christian Jacquenet
Orange, France

Denis Collange
Orange, France

Karine Guillouard
Orange, France

Yves L'Azou
Orange, France

Luca Muscariello
Orange, France

Laurent Reynaud
Orange, France

Pierrick Seite
Orange, France

Vincent Gouraud
Orange, France

ABSTRACT

The Transmission Control Protocol (TCP) is one of the core components of the TCP/IP protocol suite. It has been extensively used for the past three decades (and counting) as the privileged connection-oriented transport mode for many Internet applications, including access to web contents. Nevertheless, experience with TCP can sometimes be rather poor for various reasons which include (but are not limited to) sub-optimized forwarding path capabilities. Because a TCP session can only be established over a single path (by definition), this restriction is not only unable to take into account the dramatic evolution of terminal technologies towards multi-interfaced devices, but also the ability to benefit from several yet potential forwarding paths for the sake of improved Quality of Experience (QoE).

DOI: 10.4018/978-1-4666-8371-6.ch009

CONTEXT, ISSUES AND RATIONALE

Motivation

Devices are more and more multi-interfaced (i.e., can mount multiple logical interfaces bound to the same or distinct physical interfaces). As such, multiple addresses may be assigned from various network types (e.g., wired network, mobile network, WLAN hot-spot, etc.). These addresses may be of distinct address families (IPv4, IPv6 or both) and may have different scopes (e.g., private IPv4 address, IPv6 ULA, IPv6 GUA, etc.). They may be bound to the same physical interface or different interfaces. A host may use a service to advertise all available IP addresses so that a remote host can make use of one of these addresses to establish a communication with the multi-interfaced device.

Some networks (e.g., enterprise networks) are multi-homed (i.e., a given corporate site is connected to the network by at least two distinct links). These networks may use the same node to connect to the provider's network or connect to a specific node for each link. A network may also be connected to the same network provider but through several interconnection links. A multi-homed device that is assigned one address (in the provider independent mode) or many addresses (provider assigned mode), may be configured to balance both incoming and outgoing traffic through available links. Even when multiple links are used, some failures are encountered when an interface is out of service.

Because TCP (transport control protocol) connections are identified by an IP address and a port number, any change of the connection conditions will disrupt the TCP connection and therefore the service. This change is particularly harmful:

- When the host is assigned a new IP address because of a renumbering event in the network side
- Because the host is connected to another network (e.g., handover to WLAN)
- When the interface to which the address is bound, is unavailable.

Means to notify the remote peer about the unavailability of an address would be helpful to restore an existing connection (e.g., long TCP sessions).

Various techniques have been proposed in the past to make use of multiple paths to establish a connection between two hosts or to optimize network resource usage by means of traffic balancing capabilities. Some of these techniques (Villamizar, C., 1999)) only rely upon the routing protocol machinery, and may therefore be useless for a TCP host, unless this host participates to the route computation procedures.

As a consequence, means for a TCP host to make use of available resources, enhance robustness and be able to automatically recover from any connection condition change without disrupting the TCP service are likely to improve the user's quality of experience.

On The Complexity of Aggregation at L1/L2 Level Background

3GPP initiated an effort to aggregate several radio resources for the sake of increasing bitrates (denoted as Carrier Aggregation (CA) (Wannstrom, J., 2013)). Aggregation is achieved at the radio level by combining the set of allocated contiguous or non-contiguous component carriers. This extension requires modification at the radio interface level of UE (User Equipment) and some tuning at the network side.

Carrier Aggregation (CA) is specific to radio-based environment and, as such, it is not convenient for other deployments cases such as wired networks or enforcing advanced TE (Traffic Engineering) features in core networks. Furthermore, Carrier

Aggregation does not target the same design objectives as MPTCP.

This document does not exclude the activation of MPTCP and ca to further increase data transfer rates.

MPTCP Background

MPTCP was originally proposed in 1995 by C. Huitema to address requirements raised by a multi-homing context, including address (seamless) mobility and resiliency requirements. The proposal was called Multi-homed TCP (Huitema, 1995) and was based upon a new TCP identifier for connections to make them independent of IP addresses.

The multi-homed TCP idea was revived in the early 2000's when IETF was discussing IPv6 multi-homing issues (*multi6* WG). Host-centric proposals using legacy transports (e.g., TCP-MH (TCP Multi-Home Options, (Matsumoto & all, 2003))) were promoted…but failed to be adopted. In the meantime, new protocols have been designed with these constraints in mind, such as SCTP (Stream Control Transmission Protocol (Stewart, R. et al., 2007)).

SCTP is a promising transport protocol that supports advanced features such as path recovery but, unfortunately, this protocol is not widely adopted. The basic reason is almost the same failure factor which handicapped the evolution of core TCP/IP protocols: the massive proliferation of middle-boxes, such as NATs and firewalls.

The *MPTCP* IETF working group was chartered in 2009 to specify the required TCP extensions to be multi-address aware. The WG charter has been updated in mid-2012 to revisit the MPTCP specifications and produce documents on the Standards Track.

Network and Application Constraints

MPTCP was designed to fulfil the following requirements:

- Like typical TCP flows, MPTCP flows must be seen by intermediary nodes.
- MPTCP must be backward compatible with legacy TCP hosts and must accommodate existing applications.
- The use of MPTCP must not lead to a degraded perceived QoE (quality of experience) compared to legacy TCP.
- MPTCP must not induce failures compared to legacy TCP.

More details on MPTCP design principles are provided in the following section.

MPTCP DESIGN PRINCIPLES

MPTCP design assumes that multiple paths that can be used by a multi-interfaced device to establish a TCP connection are available. Although this assumption may be questionable in some scenarios (e.g., a host connected to the same CPE but using two distinct interfaces), this assumption simplifies the design as it does not require that fully disjoint paths are actually available in the network (e.g., no need for means to explore available path and detect wither these paths are disjoined or not). As such, MPTCP sub-flows may be established over different paths that may share one or more nodes.

MPTCP assumes each path is identified by *{local IP address, local port number, remote IP address, remote port number}* tuples. Altering one of these parameters leads to another path. In particular, a MPTCP endpoint may bind its IPv4 and IPv6 addresses to the same MPTCP connection.

MPTCP introduces the concept of "sub-flow" to designate a TCP flow over an individual MPTCP path, which is one of the components of a MPTCP connection (Figure 1).

A MPTCP connection is composed of one or more sub-flows. These sub-flows can be used simultaneously (e.g., in order to maximum resource usage) or sequentially (e.g., allows for session handover during failure events) (Figure

Figure 1. MPTCP Sub-flows

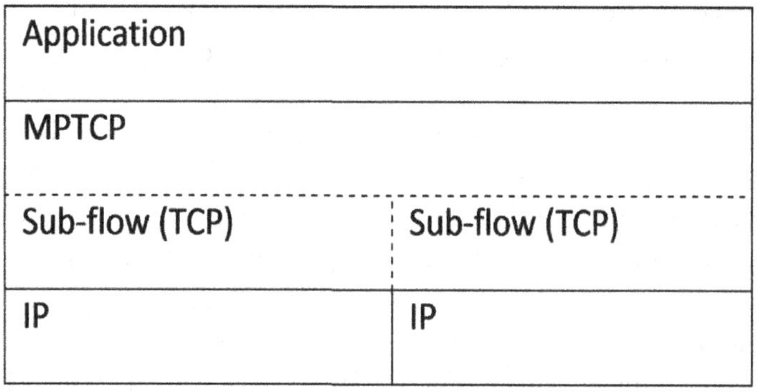

2). A sub-flow can be terminated by a MPTCP endpoint like any regular TCP connection (i.e., send a FIN message).

MPTCP is designed to be backward compatible with TCP, robust in the presence of middle-boxes (e.g., NAT, Firewalls, etc.) and should not alter the end user's Quality of Experience compared to regular TCP operation. Obviously, to make use of MPTCP, both endpoints must be MPTCP-aware. Triggers to fall back to TCP are supported

Figure 2. MPTCP initialization

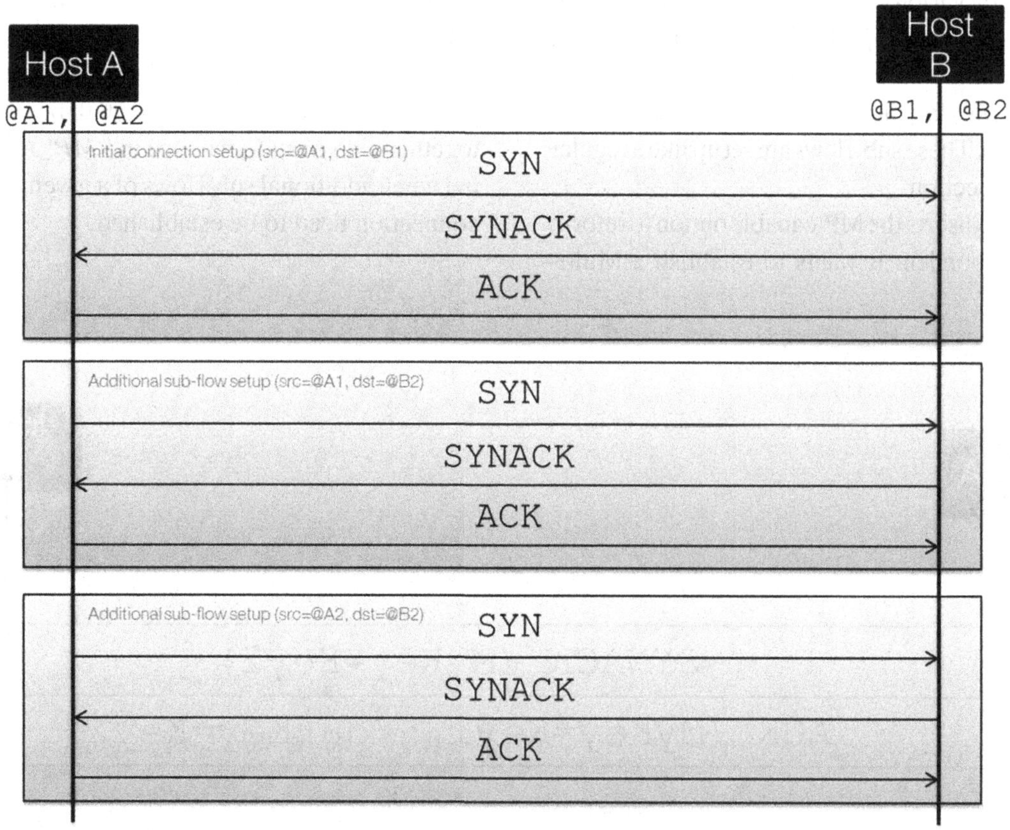

by MPTCP (e.g., fall back to regular TCP when communicating with a remote legacy TCP speaker or when involved middle-boxes remove MPTCP signals from TCP messages).

Various designs can be adopted. Some MPTCP connections can be established between end nodes if these ones are MPTCP compliant or through some proxies if one end node or both of them do not support MPTCP feature.

The support of multiple paths in TCP could have been achieved with a simple TCP option (e.g., (Huitema, 1995)), but due to the presence of middle-boxes, the MPTCP design is more complex than expected. MPTCP defines a new TCP option which is used for various purposes. Each of these purposes is identified by a sub-type

MP-Capable

This option is carried in SYN, SYN/ACK and ACK packets when initializing a TCP session and is used for various purposes. Firstly, it checks if the remote host supports MPTCP and is used for the exchange of information between MPTCP peers to validate the establishment of additional sub-flows. These sub-flows are set up like a regular TCP connection.

A host inserts the MP-capable option to inform its correspondent it wants to establish a Multi-Path TCP session. The option carries a 64-bit key that is used to authenticate subsequent sub-flow establishment.

Each MPTCP peer must indicate if it is MPTCP capable by means of this option. If a sender inserts the MP-Capable option in a SYN packet but does not receive any MP-Capable option in the corresponding SYN/ACK packet, a regular single path TCP connection is established. If a sender does not include the MP-Capable option in the SYN packet, the correspondent must not insert the MP-Capable option in SYN/ACK response. If the third ACK packet does not include any MP-Capable option, a single path TCP session is established.

The MP-capable option is only used in the first sub-flow of a connection. Other sub-flows of this connection will use the MP-Join option that is described in Section 2.5.

The *MP_CAPABLE* handshake allows to check whether both endpoints support MPTCP and also to exchange a 64-bit key that will be used to authenticate the establishment of additional sub-flows (Figure 3).

Concretely, this security key is used by each endpoint to generate a token that will be signalled together with a random nonce in a *MP_JOIN* signal when additional sub-flows of a given MPTCP connection need to be established.

Figure 3. MPTCP Key Exchange

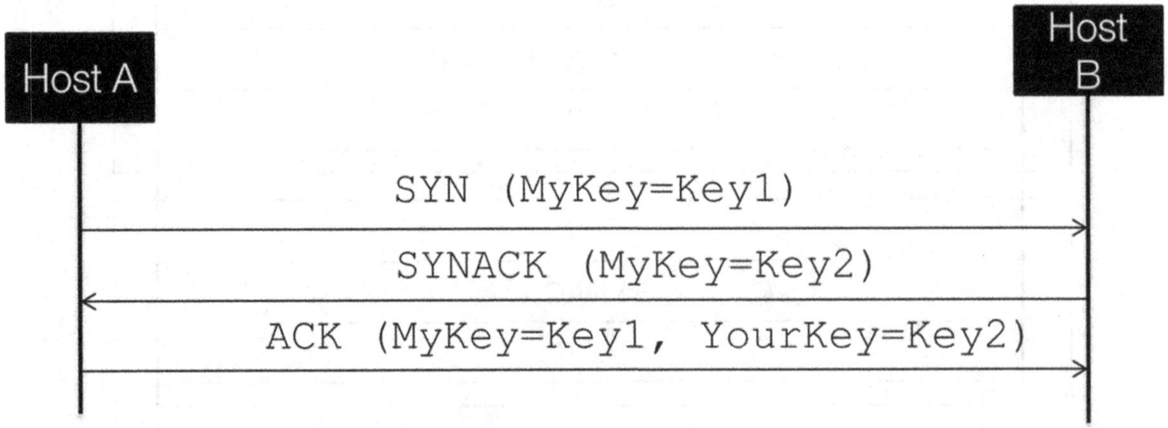

ADD_ADDR

A Host may want to inform its correspondent about another potential address that may be used for the establishment of an additional sub-flow, for example. It can be the case when a middle-box (e.g., a NAT device) does not authorize any sub-flow setup in a given direction. In this case, a host will use the ADD_ADDR TCP option to inform its correspondent about the availability of a new address (possibly the availability of additional ports). Then, the correspondent node can establish additional sub-flows by using this new address. The IP addresses that a host learns from its correspondent node by means of the ADD_ADDR and MP_JOIN options must be stored by this node.

A MPTCP endpoint may signal to a remote endpoint the availability of an additional IP address by means of the *ADD_ADDR* signal without creating a specific sub-flow. Signaling multiple IP addresses that are available at an endpoint may lead to session failures because external IP addresses perceived by remote peers may not be the same as those available locally.

For example, an IPv6-only node may be aware of its IPv6 prefix although its IPv4 endpoint peer will perceive that IPv6-only host with an IPv4 address.

As a consequence, the *ADD_ADDR* signal includes an address identifier that will be used to uniquely identify a candidate IP address for the local endpoint, hence avoiding issues raised by the presence of NATs in the path. The *ADD_ADDR* signal can also be used to convey a port number in case an endpoint does not use the same port number for all available IP addresses. Signaling distinct port numbers may not be a typical usage of MPTCP.

The host must also store the Address ID, a data structure that uniquely identifies an address that can be used by MP_JOIN exchanges and also when an IP address is being removed. It must be noticed that address advertisement messages can be disregarded by the receiver if, for example, a host informs its correspondent about available IPv6 addresses although the correspondent is an IPv4-only node.

REMOVE_ADDR

While a MPTCP connection is set up, some addresses used for this connection may become unavailable. In case an address becomes invalid, the host should inform its peer about this unavailability by means of the REMOVE_ADDR option, so that the peer can remove the sub-flows attached to this IP address. For security reasons,

Figure 4. DSS (Data Sequence Signal) option format

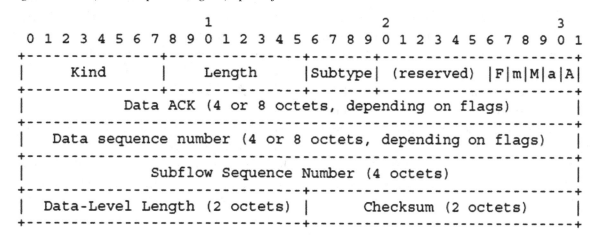

```
                     1                   2                   3
 0 1 2 3 4 5 6 7 8 9 0 1 2 3 4 5 6 7 8 9 0 1 2 3 4 5 6 7 8 9 0 1
+---------------+---------------+-------+----------------------+
|     Kind      |    Length     |Subtype| (reserved) |F|m|M|a|A|
+---------------+---------------+-------+----------------------+
|          Data ACK (4 or 8 octets, depending on flags)        |
+--------------------------------------------------------------+
|   Data sequence number (4 or 8 octets, depending on flags)   |
+--------------------------------------------------------------+
|              Subflow Sequence Number (4 octets)              |
+-------------------------------+------------------------------+
|  Data-Level Length (2 octets) |      Checksum (2 octets)     |
+-------------------------------+------------------------------+
```

a host, when receiving a REMOVE_ADDR option, should send a TCP Keepalive message to its peer so that it can check whether sub-flows can be withdrawn or not. Some RST messages should be sent by both peers when closing a sub-flow.

MP_PRIO

During the initialization process, hosts may want to indicate if a sub-flow is a regular or a backup path that will be used only if some regular paths are not available, yielding a notion of prioritizing the use of sub-flows. While a connection is established, a host can inform its peer about a change regarding this priority thanks to MP_PRIO option. Depending on the use case, different prioritization policies may be enforced. In most cases, all available paths will be used to maximise throughput. In some other cases, there may be a need to forward all traffic over a given path and use another path for backup purposes only. Other policies may then privilege the use of a specific path for some traffic, and the use of others paths for other traffic. The MP_PRIO option can be used to modify priority and inform the peer about this modification.

MP_JOIN

This option is used to set up other sub-flows for a given MP-TCP connection. The Initial MP-TCP connection is set up thanks to the MP_Capable option while subsequent sub-flow establishment assumes the use of the based on MP_JOIN option. This option is also carried in SYN, SYN/ACK, ACK messages.

A given host can inform its correspondent about other addresses to be used to establish additional sub-flows by using the MP_JOIN option or the ADD_ADDR option.

In order to initiate additional sub-flows for a MPTCP connection, a node will use the key exchanged during the MPTCP handshake, and carried in the MP_Capable option. Any of the two MPTCP hosts can set up additional sub-flows but, in practice, this is the initiator of the MPTCP connection that adds sub-flows.

MP_FAIL

Issues may arise during the lifetime of a MPTCP connection, which may require the termination of a sub-flow or the entire TCP connection. In this case, fall-back procedures are needed to return to safe operation conditions. Various solutions have been specified to make MPTCP solutions reliable and be sure that sub-flows are operational. Some situations may require the use of the MP_FAIL option. If checksums have been negotiated between peers, each portion of data is protected by a checksum. The checksum computation will fail if any device on the path modifies the payload. The modification of the length of data or sub-flow is also detected. If a segment checksum computation fails, all following segments cannot be trusted. If the checksum process has not been negotiated, there is no possibility that other layers are informed about the modification of the payload. In case such issue arises on a given sub-flow, it may impact the data stream of the multi-path connection itself. So, in this case, the MP_FAIL option that carries information about the first data sequence number that encountered the checksum computation failure is used. The receiver must discard all data following the sequence number specified in the MP_FAIL option. This MP_FAIL option affects only one direction, since the reverse direction may not be affected at all.

MP_FASTCLOSE

The MP-FASTCLOSE option is used to abruptly close MPTCP connection. RST messages that have the same usage as TCP connections cannot be used as a RST message may only concern a sub-flow of the whole MPTPCP connection. The

MP_FASTCLOSE option is meant to inform the peer that all sub-flows of a given MPTCP connection will be interrupted and that no other data should be sent on this connection. This option is sent in a given sub-flow and carried by an ACK message, while RST information is sent in other sub-flows of the MPTCP communication. The peer will send back a TCP RST and close other sub-flows. When the initial sender receives the TCP RST message in the remaining sub-flow, it can close the entire MPTCP connection. A re-transmission process with associated timers can be set up in case RST messages are not received within a given time.

MP_DSS

If the same TCP sequence space is used by all individual MPTCP sub-flows, a firewall may discard some packets because "holes" in the exchanged sequence numbers may be observed. As a consequence, MPTCP assumes that the regular TCP sequence numbers in the TCP header are specific to each sub-flow, while the MPTCP connection data sequence mapping and the MPTCP connection-level ACK are signaled in *DSS* (Data Sequence Signal) signals (Figure 4). DSS is used to "glue" individual sub-flows that belong to the same MPTCP connection.

Data exchanged between two peers are forwarded along various paths when a MPTCP connection is set up. Means to ensure packet reassembly and reordering, as well as reliable packet delivery are required. The data sequence mapping as well as Data Ack are signalled in the MP_DSS option. The data sequence mapping is used to map sub-flow sequences for a connection. It provides a mapping between the sub-flow sequence number and the data sequence number. It is used by a receiver to ensure the data stream sent to the application layer is composed of properly (re)ordered data. A Data Ack is a connection level acknowledgement and is quite similar to standard TCP cumulative ACK. A Data Ack also indicates the next data sequence number it expects to receive. So, there are sub-flow-level ACKs and Data-level Acks. Sub-flow ACKs are meant to acknowledge the reception of data over a given sub-flow, while Data-level ACKs are meant to acknowledge the reception of data at the connection level, thereby indicating that all MPTCP options and data has been well received and accepted by the peer.

The use of sub-options is motivated by the limited available TCP option space and also to reduce chances that only a subset of MPTCP signals are accepted by some firewalls and NATs. *Note, that NATs and firewalls may be designed to filter some MPTCP sub-types.*

MPTCP can be enabled in various modes:

- Native MPTCP: Two MPTCP endpoints establish and make use of all sub-flows that correspond to the available addresses/port numbers. This mode is enabled to optimize data throughput.
- Active/Backup MPTCP: Two MPTCP endpoints enable multiple sub-flows, but only a subset of these sub-flows is actually in use for data transfer. MPTCP endpoints can use the MP_PRIO signal to change the priority for each sub-flow.
- Single sub-flow MPTCP: Two MPTCP endpoints use one single sub-flow and when a failure is observed, an additional sub-flow is enabled so that traffic is forwarded along the newly established sub-flow.

These modes are not to be confused with the deployment use cases elaborated hereafter.

MPTCP CANDIDATE USE CASES

Various MPTCP use cases can be considered. Examples of such use cases are listed below:

- Traffic handover among multiple WLAN hotspots.

- Traffic Offload from a mobile network to WLAN.
- Traffic Offload to a radio interface when wired access is unavailable.
- Radio and wired line aggregation.
- Traffic balancing among multiple paths.
- Network resource usage optimization in general.
- These use cases can target one or several of the following objectives:
- Maximize bandwidth usage.
- Ensure session continuity during failure events (e.g., temporary failure of an interface).
- TE (Traffic Engineering) (including load-balancing).

  The following sub-sections elaborate on these deployment objectives.

Bandwidth Aggregation

Description

The main objective of aggregating bandwidth is to optimize both downlink (e.g., for HD TV and video services) and uplink (e.g., picture or cloud-based services) bandwidth. Bandwidth usage can be optimized between two MPTCP endpoints by forwarding data over multiple TCP paths. Depending on the network segment subject to the bandwidth aggregation, various MPTCP designs can be considered:

- **End-to-end MPTCP:** both endpoints support MPTCP and manage data forwarding over the different end-to-end MPTCP paths.
- **Full proxy MPTCP:** both endpoints are unaware of MPTCP, but two MPTCP proxies are inserted in between. For instance, a first proxy may be located in the access router while the second one may be embedded in the edge router or in a dedicated platform. Both proxies manage data forwarding between these proxies. Note that different TCP ports on a single host can use disjoint paths, such as through Equal Cost Multi-Path (ECMP) implementations (Hopps, 2000), meaning that the MPTCP proxy scenario can also benefit from an ECMP-capable environment.
- **Partial proxy MPTCP:** one of the endpoints (e.g., the user terminal) supports MPTCP while a MPTCP proxy is inserted in the path (e.g., located in the edge router). This is a kind of flavour of the previous scenario, where only one of the hosts has to support MPTCP.

Analysis

The above deployment scenarios share the following characteristics:

- Bandwidth aggregation is an interesting feature since it is likely to improve end user's perceived Quality of Experience. Nevertheless, this is feasible only if available alternative paths provide equivalent throughput and latency; otherwise it may be insignificant and is insufficient to justify a MPTCP design. Without fine tuning MPTCP parameters (e.g., packet scheduling, path management and congestion control), observed performances may even be degraded since high latency differences between two paths generate more buffered traffic and complex reordering tasks at the transport level with a likely impact on transmission delays and packet loss rates.
- MPTCP is by definition reserved to TCP traffic and cannot consequently handle other kinds of traffic such as UDP traffic. However, bandwidth resource optimization is essentially worthwhile for QoS-demanding applications such as video streaming applications, which usually assume a TCP transport.

Besides, the deployment scenarios present specific characteristics:

- The "End-to-End MPTCP" scenario is not viable at the scale of the Internet because it requires all endpoints support MPTCP.
- The "Full Proxy MPTCP" deployment scenario has no impact on endpoints. However, it relies on MPTCP proxies implemented in network nodes which intercept all traffic from endpoints and forward it over appropriate paths. Such aggregation points must implement a NAT function. Depending on the design, devices that embed a MPTCP proxy may become single points of failure and may suffer from congestion under some circumstances (e.g., low overprovisioning factor is used). Moreover, this scenario requires implementing a MPTCP proxy in the CPE for providing a bandwidth increase of the network access segment, thus yielding extra cost and possibly complexity.
- The "Partial MPTCP Proxy" scenario may be the most realistic as it addresses higher bandwidth requirements over the last mile. It avoids the impact on the correspondent endpoints, particularly on application servers. However it still requires an aggregation point in the network and MPTCP support at the level of user terminals. This last requirement cannot be guaranteed in all smartphones. A variant deployment scheme would be the activation of MPTCP in the CPE. A MPTCP CPE would be able to aggregate its WAN connections (e.g., DSL and LTE). This deployment scenario avoids the constraint of MPTCP support in the user terminal endpoint but requires a CPE upgrade, yielding extra cost and possibly complexity.

The proxy can be managed by a third entity or by one of the access network providers. If both access networks are managed by the same service provider, managing the MPTCP proxy may be simplified. Note that:

- The use of MPTCP to enhance robustness can be achieved using some routing features in the CPE without requiring any involvement of another device in the network. This benefit will apply for all transport protocols; not only TCP. Nevertheless, such solution to enhance the serviceability of CPE devices does not offer seamless mobility and requires companion means to notify the remote party an address change has occurred.
- The hosts need to discover and acquire proxy reachability information.

MPTCP may drain the battery of the terminal device, which may become rapidly critical for mobile hosts.

Session Continuity

Description

MPTCP may also be used to guarantee session continuity when traffic needs to be re-forwarded over different paths, e.g., from cellular access to WLAN (Wireless LAN), in case congestion or any other issue that is likely to impact a given access network is detected.

Thanks to session continuity solutions, an IP session can be moved from one access to another without any service disruption or impact for the user.

Various options are possible to enable such session mobility. Most of these options rely upon some network layer functions (Mobile IP (Perkins, 2010), PMIP (Gundavelli & all, 2008) or event GTP (http://www.qtc.jp/3GPP/Specs/29060-690.pdf) while others like MPTCP operate at the transport layer or the application layer (e.g., SIP).

Whatever the solution retained for session mobility, it generally relies upon some kind of anchor point located in the network. The anchor point is meant to hide to the correspondent that a host handover has occurred between a given access network to another. This is something that has been documented for 4G networks for example, where the ePDG is designed to connect non-3GPP networks to 3GPP networks.

Besides the need for an anchor point, session continuity requires

- Means for a host to detect it must transfer some flows from a given access network to another
- Security solutions to authenticate the mobility anchor point
- Some optimization to avoid any impact on the QoE as perceived by the end-users
- Means to optimize power consumption on terminals

Analysis

For session continuity purposes, the involvement of a MPTCP proxy is likely. For such use case, the MPTCP proxy acts as a mobility manager. This means it redirects downlink traffic to the right end user terminal interface when the end user terminal requires to handover from one access network to another. It hides the change of access network to the peer endpoint.

The applications embedded in the user terminal do not have any knowledge about the access network used to transmit a given flow.

However, other solutions for session continuity exist, and are more mature than MPTCP even if one advantage of MPTCP is to enable a make-before-break process as access networks are available at the same time and some new communication path is ready before some leakage happens on existing one. But the drawback of MPTCP is that it affects the terminal's power consumption and battery draining if the terminal is a mobile node

Session continuity may not be the only driver to motivate the deployment of MPTCP and it is likely that such use case should be combined with other use cases to justify some MPTCP deployment in a given environment.

Moreover, MPTCP session continuity is limited to TCP traffic only.

It implies that both end user terminal and proxy sides are able to identify and select traffic that may be redirected to another path without disrupting the TCP connection. A control function is then required to map specific application/IP flows to the appropriate paths (i.e., to physical interface at the end user terminal side).

Finally, security issues, those are typical of scenarios that involve third parties (especially in mobile environments), may be encountered if the MPTCP proxy cannot authenticate the user terminal which requests traffic redirection.

TRAFFIC ENGINEERING PURPOSES

Load Balancing

Description

Equal Cost Multi-path (ECMP) (Hopps, 2000) is a technique used by typical link state routing protocols so that packets can be forwarded over multiple paths that have been assigned the same metric cost. Forwarding decisions over an ECMP-labeled path can rely upon various methods that include the hash-threshold (a router selects a key by performing a hash (a CRC16 for example) to select the next hop for each incoming packet).

ECMP is widely used in WAN environments and basically activated by default when the networks run protocols like OSPF (Open Shortest Path First). ECMP algorithms are agnostic to the upper transport protocols by nature, and can therefore be run for any kind of traffic balancing purposes.

According to (Kandula & all, 2009) the most frequent overloads observed in data centers are either long-lived and localized or short-lived and widespread. Usual congestion control mechanisms such as those implemented by regular TCP implementations may be solicited to reduce short-lived widespread congestions. But there is still a need for traffic balancing to move traffic of long-lived localized congestions. MPTCP can be used in DC environments for the sake of traffic balancing between servers or Virtual Machines (Raiciu & all, 2011).

MPTCP could also be a solution to the often identified problem of TCP incasts(Krevat & all, 2007 (Chen, 2009) observed with many typical cloud applications such as distributed storage (e.g., BigTable or Hbase), data-intensive computing (e.g., MapReduce, Dryad, Spark n2n or n21), partition/aggregation workflow, etc. (Zhang, J., Ren, F., Lin, C., 2013).

Analysis

Many reasons explain the relative inefficiency of ECMP (Equal Cost Multi-Paths):

- The first one is that until recently(Cai et al., 2012), it did not take into account any traffic or performance metrics to balance the traffic. The next hop was only randomly selected through a hash code of packets headers fields identifying the flows(Hopps, 2000). It is still the version implemented in data centers according to (CEF, 2013) (Al-Fares and al, 2010) (Van der Pol, R., Bredely, M., Barczyky, A., 2013) (Raiciu et al., 2011). Randomized load balancing (RLB) where each flow is assigned a random path from the set of possible paths is indeed the simplest solution, but not the most efficient. The problem is that often a random selection causes hot-spots to develop, where an unlucky combination of random path selection causes a few links to be under-loaded and links elsewhere to have little or no load (Raiciu et al., 2010). Even if(Cai et al., 2012) proposes to take into account dynamic metrics to select the next hop, it does not specify which metrics nor how they are measured. The efficiency of the modification on data center congestions still requires further studies.
- A second drawback of ECMP, L2 protocols such as TRILL (Touch, J., Perlman, R., 2009) or IEEE 802.1aq (Shortest Path Bridging) (IEEE, 2012) and most of widespread load balancing mechanisms is their flow-level granularity. Splitting traffic with (large) flow-granularity can cause load imbalance across paths resulting in poor utilization of network resources(Dixit, 2011)(Raiciu et al., 2010) (Van der Pol et al, 2012). A key limitation of this scheme is that two or larger, long-lived flows can collide on their hash and end up on the same output port, creating an avoidable bottleneck (Al-Fares and al, 2010). On the contrary, MPTCP chooses the best path for each TCP packet based on the most recent end-to-end information received from each path through the last acknowledgments. Actually, per packet load balancing is possible with Cisco Express Forwarding (CEF) for example but it is not recommended for services sensitive to packet reordering like data traffic over TCP or VoIP. Indeed a TCP endpoint receiving out-of-order packets from different paths will consider many of them as lost while a MPTCP connection is able to reorder packets from its various sub-flows.
- A third drawback of ECMP is it applies independently at each hop, while MPTCP balances the load globally on end-to-end paths, based on end-to-end traffic metrics (packet loss and round-trip time). Other methods than MPTCP have been proposed to optimize globally the forwarding of the flows, such as Hedera (Al-Fares et al., 2010) using a centralized flow scheduler. But (Raiciu et al., 2010) has shown that such scheduler has to run frequently to

keep up with flow arrivals and departures, and it may need a non-negligible information rate, which can affect the throughput in overload conditions.

MPTCP should then improve the load balancing in data center, compared to ECMP and other current load balancing mechanisms. A remaining point is the possible coexistence of MPTCP with these or similar (local, random, flow-grained) load balancing mechanisms in future data center networks.

It has been shown in (Raiciu & all, 2011) that MPTCP with ECMP works fine, and is better than single path TCP with ECMP. An outstanding investigation track is to compare the efficiency of MPTCP alone and over lower level load balancing mechanism, depending on the relative proportion of single TCP and non-TCP traffic.

Dynamic Traffic Engineering

Description

Traffic engineering (TE) a backbone network requires the knowledge of the demand, i.e., the traffic matrix and provides the best possible routing to serve the predicted traffic, whereas high variability and unpredictable demand is neglected. Dynamic routing allows designing robust networks in terms of resiliency and against congestion, typically due to highly variable traffic matrices. However early experimental experiences discouraged the deployment of such advanced feature for almost thirty years. Recent advances in the area have shown that actually dynamic, yet stable, traffic engineering is possible and desirable by jointly optimizing routing and traffic flow control.

MPTCP is a protocol implementation realizing joint optimization of routing and congestion control by flow controlling traffic sources between two end points as reported in the Figure 5. MPTCP objective is to maximize the data transfer throughput whereas for traffic engineering purposes it is frequently required to also reduce latency or path length. In this section we focus on analyzing how dynamic TE can be implemented by using MPTCP.

Analysis

MPTCP may serve to TE objectives by managing large flow aggregates representing the data flowing from an ingress router towards an egress router of the network. Such Origin-Destination (OD) pairs fits to MPTCP flow definition, while MPTCP sub-flows serve traffic splits among the multiple available routes in the networks from the Origin to the Destination. The simplest way to make routes available to the ingress router is using source routing. The implementation choices depend mostly on the particular network segment and available technologies implemented in the routers. For all implementations, the main protocol knobs required are the following:

- Routes calculation entity: given a network of routers and the set of all OD pairs, the entity computes the routes, all possible or a subset, among the OD pairs. This operation can also be distributed into the different ingress routers.
- Routes advertisement: the ingress node might not be allowed to use all routes according to some policy implemented in the network. Such policies must be advertised to the route computation entity.
- Rate control: flow controllers in ingress routers, one per destination, implementing sub-flow rate control.
- Congestion feedback: egress routers must implement a congestion feedback signal to be sent to the associated ingress router. Every OD pair cooperate to keep traffic load balancing stable: the origin by load balancing arriving traffic along the sub-flows whereas the destination send per sub-flow feedbacks used to manage per

Figure 5. Path control and path state notification

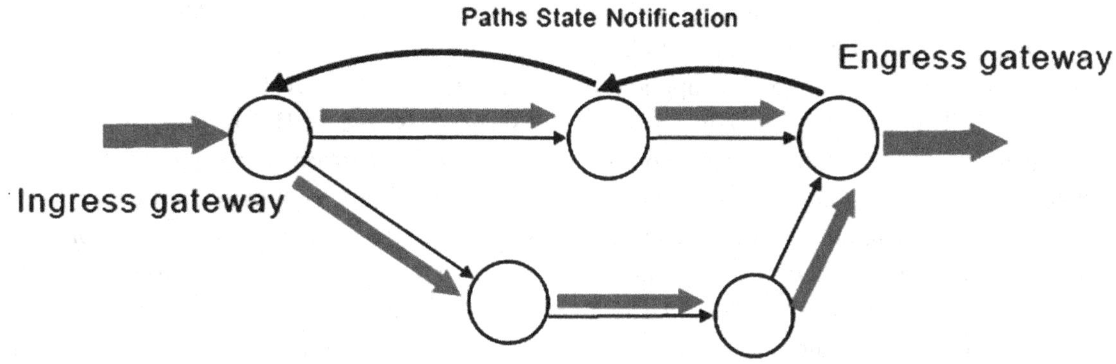

sub-flow rate control in the ingress. The congestion feedback must be implemented as an additional protocol data unit in substitution to TCP acknowledgements. Such PDUs do not need to follow the sub-flow path: the shortest path only toward the origin can be used.

CURRENT STATUS

MPTCP API Operation and Foreseen Extensions

From an application point of view, the forwarding of data sent by a given application is split into one or several sub-flows and transmitted on available paths towards the MPTCP-capable peer. But the MPTCP protocol does not require any change in existing applications and a TCP API can still be used, considering MPTCP capability could not be available for such applications. A non MPTCP-aware application will behave like a normal TCP application while some extended APIs (Scharf, M., Ford, A., 2013) can provide additional capabilities to MPTCP-aware applications.

In particular, the MPTCP API allows to:

- Enable/disable MPTCP,
- Bind MPTCP to a set of local addresses, or add a set of new local addresses to an existing MPTCP connection, remove a local address from an MPTCP connection,
- Get the pairs of addresses currently in use by the MPTCP sub-flows, or get the local connection identifier for this MPTCP connection

The MPTCP API can be extended in the future to support advanced features such as the initialization of a MPTCP session without using any IP address as a locator but a name instead. Another feature is the control of the level of redundancy by indicating whether segments should be sent on more than one path in parallel.

Implementation Status

As a result of a survey conducted by the *MPTCP* Working Group (Eardley, 2013), the following observations can be made:

- MPTCP is implemented in Apple iOS 7 (Apple, 2014) MPTCP is used as follows: A primary connection is set up over the WLAN network, and a backup connection is set up over the cellular access network. The Siri application (Caviglione, 2013) uses MPTCP and will try to establish a connection over the WLAN network. If any issue arises on the WLAN access, the mobile phone will switch over the cellular access without disrupting the Siri application. MPTCP is used by iOS 7 to enable seamless service continuity based upon a kind of make-before-break handover facility. This implementation is the first large scale use of MPTCP. According to preliminary Apple feedback (Notes, 2013), it seems that few middle-boxes drop out unknown options, such as those used by MPTCP. Most issues are due to corporate firewall filtering rules.

- A distribution has been released for an Android device.
- Both a Linux and FreeBSD implementations are available.
- A Netscaler Firmware implementation is available from Citrix Systems.

The FreeBSD implementation supports IPv4 only, while remaining implementations claim to support both IPv4 and IPv6. This claim should be questioned given that one of these implementations does not support IPv6.

MPTCP signals are not all supported by these implementations (e.g., *FAST_CLOSE*, *ADD_ADDR*).

A commercial offering using MPTCP is available since 2012 (MPN, 2012). This offering relies on specialized hardware together with the use of tunnels and proxies to aggregate traffic.

Specifications Are Not That Frozen

The IETF is planning to move the MPTCP specifications to the standards track. Updates of the MPTCP specification will need to be taken into account based on the initial outcomes from implementers and experiments, as well as further studies about security risks and solutions.

The revision of the specification (Ford & all, 2014) updates the ADD_ADDR option to mitigate hijack attacks, and this new option has been renamed ADD_ADDR2. Implementers reported a security risk induced by the use of *ADD_ADDR* and as such this option is not supported by many of the available implementations. Instead, *MP_JOIN* signal is used immediately without any prior signaling to the remote endpoint. More discussions on this attack vector (and others) are included in (Bagnulo, 2013). A fix to this security vector attack is to include the token of the connection in the ADD_ADDR signal.

These implementations accept sending *REMOVE_ADDR* but ignore it when received from a remote party. All these implementations assume only the endpoint that initiates the MPTCP connection is allowed to establish subsequent sub-flows.

These implementations do not follow the same behavior for both receiver and sender buffers. Some of them use automatic buffer tuning while others use an active/backup mode.

The revision of MPTCP specifications aims at strengthening the security of the protocol, based upon the use of SSL.

Focus on Power Consumption Considerations

Enabling MPTCP is energy consuming (hence likely to affect overall service performance when 3G/4G interfaces are involved in the MPTCP session, for example). Indeed, a significant aspect of the use of multiple interfaces is the additional energy consumption a device supporting MPTCP is likely to require in this regard. The MPTCP process itself does not consume energy, but the activation of several interfaces at the same time is power consuming.

Experiments with a Nokia N950 Smartphone embedding a Linux kernel implementation of MPTCP (Paasch, 2012) confirm that in the context of concurrent 3G/WLAN usage to perform bandwidth aggregation, since 3G and WLAN have different energy active and saving state patterns, the overall consumption varies with the traffic type: for repeated downloads of a small file of 100 kB with 5 seconds idle time between each download, MPTCP, when using both interfaces concurrently, achieves similar energy consumption levels compared to that of single TCP over 3G, but consumes about twice as many Joules per bit, compared to single TCP over WLAN.

However, for larger data transfers (in this case through repeated downloads of 1MB files with no significant idle time between transmissions), MPTCP over 3G and WLAN has an intermediate energy consumption, halfway between exactly single TCP over WLAN (lower bound) and single TCP over 3G (upper bound), with the benefit of about a doubled throughput, compared to WLAN-only and 3G-only.

In any case, traffic clearly influences MPTCP energy consumption and it is therefore suggested in (Paasch, 2012) to use MPTCP based bandwidth aggregation when the device is actively used for transmission, and to fall back to the use of a single interface, possibly the most energy efficient, when the device enters an idle phase. *Trade-off between redundancy and energy consumption should be fixed.*

In this regard, an active research domain for MPTCP is the elaboration of a flexible strategy to contextually switch flows between interfaces in order to improve the protocol's overall energy efficiency. This objective is not trivial, since depending on the radio access technologies used, the related energy states may be numerous and difficult to consistently consider in a simple interface-switching scheme.

An approach, as presented in (Pluntke, C., Eggert, L. and Kiukkonen, 2011), is to design and run on the device an energy-efficient MPTCP scheduler that dynamically controls interface switching. Based on locally monitored information such as measured throughput, energy states per interface and on a table of scheduling rules pre-computed and stored on the device, the scheduler can then determine on which interface(s) the set of active MPTCP connections should be shifted, through standard MPTCP dialogs.

While valuable in the context of simple interface handover, the chosen design (i.e., use of a Markov decision process-based scheduler, requiring as many scheduling rules as needed to cover all the possible switching cases) is not scalable.

In this context, allowing the scheduler, for flexibility purposes, to take additional local information besides throughput, would therefore have a detrimental impact on the number of state variables and eventually on the size of the pre-computed scheduling rules.

Moreover, an additional scheduling function does not seamlessly integrate with the existing MPTCP design. Other approaches (Tuan, A. L. et al., 2012) therefore avoid the definition of a new scheduling function and focus instead on the design of a MPTCP backward-compatible congestion control function on the basis of an energy measurement model exchanged between MPTCP endpoints through the active network interfaces.

This strategy is based on the underlying assumption that, as previously observed for 3G and WLAN interfaces, different radio access technology have different energy consumption patterns depending on the transmitted traffic. It is therefore sought to perform an energy-aware load balancing, hereby privileging interfaces with low energy consumption measurements.

The efforts documented in (Paasch, 2012) (Pluntke, C., Eggert, L. and Kiukkonen, N., 2011) (Tuan, A. L. et al., 2012) have the common objective to obtain a practical trade-off between available path diversity and energy consumption. Most of this effort remains at the early modelling and simulation stages, and still require *MPTCP* working group consensus and exhaustive performance evaluation through experimentations.

Strategies that use multiple interfaces for bandwidth aggregation will inevitably face increased energy consumption, possibly mitigated however by a smart energy-aware load balancing scheme. Significant gains, on the other side, are to be expected from energy-aware schemes that are able to finely monitor interfaces and aggressively switch MPTCP connections to the most energy efficient path(s).

Pending Issues

The following observations can be made:

- Early experiments demonstrated that MPTCP works. In particular, an application can recover from an address change without any intervention from the user.
- Simple congestion algorithms are designed; nevertheless, the efficiency of these algorithms is yet-to-be assessed (as a function of the testing conditions).
- Activating MPTCP may alter the service observed by TCP users without any perceived impact for MPTCP hosts. In some configuration, it was reported this degradation is 50-60% (Khalili & all, 2012).
- MPTCP hosts may be aggressive to TCP hosts (Khalili & all, 2012).
- Randomly flipping the traffic among (equal) paths may have undesired effect.
- A slow path can significantly degrade the overall throughput of the MPTCP session.
- Checksum computation may affect the overall performance. The throughput may even be reduced by 30% (Raiciu & all, 2012).
- TCP buffer is important to consider. It was reported that TCP over WLAN provides better performance compared to MPTCP over 3G or WLAN when the buffer is less than 400 KB. Note that, according to some experiments (Raiciu & all, 2012), the observed throughput when MPTCP is enabled, is even doubled when the buffer is 500 KB for instance.
- Up to 30% of performance degradation is observed when the best sub-flow experiences frequent timeouts.
- Depending on the number of established MPTCP sub-flows, CPU usage may be increased by the activation of MPTCP (Raiciu & all, 2012).
- A small latency is observed when MPTCP is enabled. A candidate solution would be to consider initiating both a legacy TCP connection and a MPTCP one; the one from which an answer was receive wins.
- Most of TCP sessions are short-lived and the use of MPTCP is not required for these sessions. Applications should be able to interact with the MPTCP API to disable/enabled MPTCP whenever required.

EVOLUTION PERSPECTIVES

Other Approaches

Interface Bonding

The "bonding" feature which is available in all Linux and Android terminal distribution allows the interface aggregation of a multi-interfaced terminal. It consists in a logical interface grouping performed at the terminal side which hides the presence of different physical interfaces to the application. This feature relies on the terminal capability to use the same external IP address over the available interfaces.

A first "bonding" operation mode is the fallback interface by configuring one of the interfaces as the preferred one; as soon as it fails, IP packets are immediately redirected to the backup configured interface.

Bandwidth aggregation is another "bonding" operation mode: it consists in sending IP packets, one by one, alternatively over the different physical interfaces.

However, experimentations on Linux-based interface bonding have shown very poor performances, particularly when latencies between two alternative paths differ, disrupting TCP functioning.

Note that some issues which justified the design of MPTCP will be experienced if this feature is used: if no SYN message is received by a firewall, subsequent packets will be dropped, etc.

Multi-Homed Terminal Combined With Connection Manager and Policy Based Routing

An alternative solution is based upon end-user terminal capabilities combining multi-interfaced and routing support: the user terminal is able to simultaneously attach to at least two different network interfaces and applies policy based routing to forward given IP flows to appropriate interfaces.

This solution has some impacts on global architecture and in particular, requires specific functions to be implemented in terminals. Such solution has been specified by the 3GPP with the publication of ANDSF (Access Network Discovery and Selection Function) and ISRP (Inter System Routing Policy) specifications.

Even if this solution provides means to improve bandwidth availability for end-users, the first goal of an ANDSF-based system is to forward traffic through the "best" interface, according to various parameters. As a consequence, an ANDSF design can optimize the usage of available resources. It requires traffic identification and selection capabilities at the level of the user terminal in order to apply different forwarding policy decisions. Therefore, ANDSF does not actually improve the bandwidth on a per application basis, but rather it allows the user terminal to improve the usage of network resources overall.

Network Layer Solutions

For IP session continuity, standardized IETF IP level solutions (e.g., Mobile IP suite) may be more appropriate solutions compared to MPTCP. They enable seamless IP flow transferring between different network paths including heterogeneous accesses.

This solution flavor is natively independent of traffic type but requires some anchor point in the network. But obviously, the use of MPTCP may raise some limitations if Apple wants to extend the multi-interface solution to other applications than Siri, and specifically for applications that do not use TCP as the transport protocol.

Network mobility solutions rely on a mobility agent implemented in the network. The use of such mobility agents are detailed in the 3GPP EPC Multi-flow based on Multi Access Packet Data Network Connectivity/MAPCON and IP Flow Mobility/IFOM Release 10 specifications.

Some extension of these network solutions (IP Flow Mobility/IFOM) can select and bind IP flows of a user terminal to differentiated paths between the user terminal and its mobility agent (i.e., one path via 3GPP accesses and another one via non-3GPP accesses). These solutions have an impact on user terminal which shall implement specific IP mobility protocols, except in particular network-based implementation (e.g., PMIP). But architectural issues remain identical whatever the network solution retained for seamless service continuity requirements.

For aggregation bandwidth purposes, proprietary solutions like multiple VPN bonding are also available (e.g., Viprinet). These solutions support any type of traffic (e.g., UDP or TCP packets) and require two tunnel termination points: one at the customer side (e.g., Multichannel VPN Router) and the other at the service platform level (e.g., Multichannel VPN Hub in the data center), to manage data stream encryption/decryption and splitting/reassembling. Tunnel termination points shall implement NAT or equivalent mapping functions.

Application- Or Session-Based Solutions

Aggregation bandwidth solutions may rely on specific mechanisms developed at the application level. For instance, video streaming applications may implement the standardized SVC (Scalable Video Services) which is a video encoding solution "slicing" streaming flows into several layers and that may be sent over different paths. The video player reconstructs the original streaming flows from the different received layers. This solution was abandoned a few years ago due to poor performance. Its successor may gain interest.

Other proprietary solutions are available such as Aviwest, a commercial product used for mobile video report and implemented in professional wireless cameras.

Also Airplug today markets its proprietary solution deployed by KT Telecom and addressing mass market devices. Video and audio streaming aggregation as well as session continuity is announced. This product does not require any change in the network side. It relies on specific software agents running at the application level and implemented in multi-interfaced user devices. Optionally, servers may be installed at platform service level to enhance the service quality. However software agents only work with Android devices.

Concerning session continuity, standardized session based solutions (e.g., SIP) may also be more appropriate compared to MPTCP. They may be implemented with or without dedicated mediator located in a service control platform (e.g., a "Service Centralization and Continuity Application Server" in the IMS platform) between endpoints. The mobility management is application specific, i.e. one specific end-to-end mobility session shall be initiated per application.

Extensions have been proposed to allow multipath RTP (e.g., (Singh, V. et al., 2013)).

Optimized Multi Path (OMP)

Description

As mentioned in the previous ECMP section, ECMP cannot achieve optimal traffic load balancing as it cannot exploit dynamic metrics for the sake of optimized resource management. Optimized Multi-Path (OMP, (Villamizar, C., 1999)) is an attempt to better utilize link resources, where the routing protocol is used to (1) identify congested links and (2) distribute traffic load statistics accordingly. Traffic is then dynamically moved away from congested paths, and traffic injection becomes a function of the link utilization (Figure 6).

Link load information is conveyed in an OSPF Opaque LSA (Link State Advertisement) (or its IS-IS equivalent TLV), and is derived from the SNMP counters that have been documented in the Interface Management Information Base (IF MIB) and which are polled every 15 seconds.

From these SNMP counters, a fractional link utilization (in both directions) is computed and the flooding decision is based upon the current value of the load for a given link, the difference between current and previous loads and the elapsed time since the last flooding.

The input and output link utilizations are expressed as fractions using the *ifInOctets*, *ifOutOctets*, *ifInSpeed* and *ifOutspeed* SNMP counters. Packet loss is computed from the sampling of the *InLoss* and *OutLoss* SNMP counters. The load computation will then provide an input to the flooding decision made by the router, as per the example below (Figure 7):

The opaque information also conveys a measure of the packets that have been dropped because of a queue overflow (expressed as a fraction), as well as the link capacity expressed in kbit/s.

This computation scheme obviously suggests a trade-off between the flooding frequency and

Figure 6. Optimized multi-path model (Traffic engineering context).

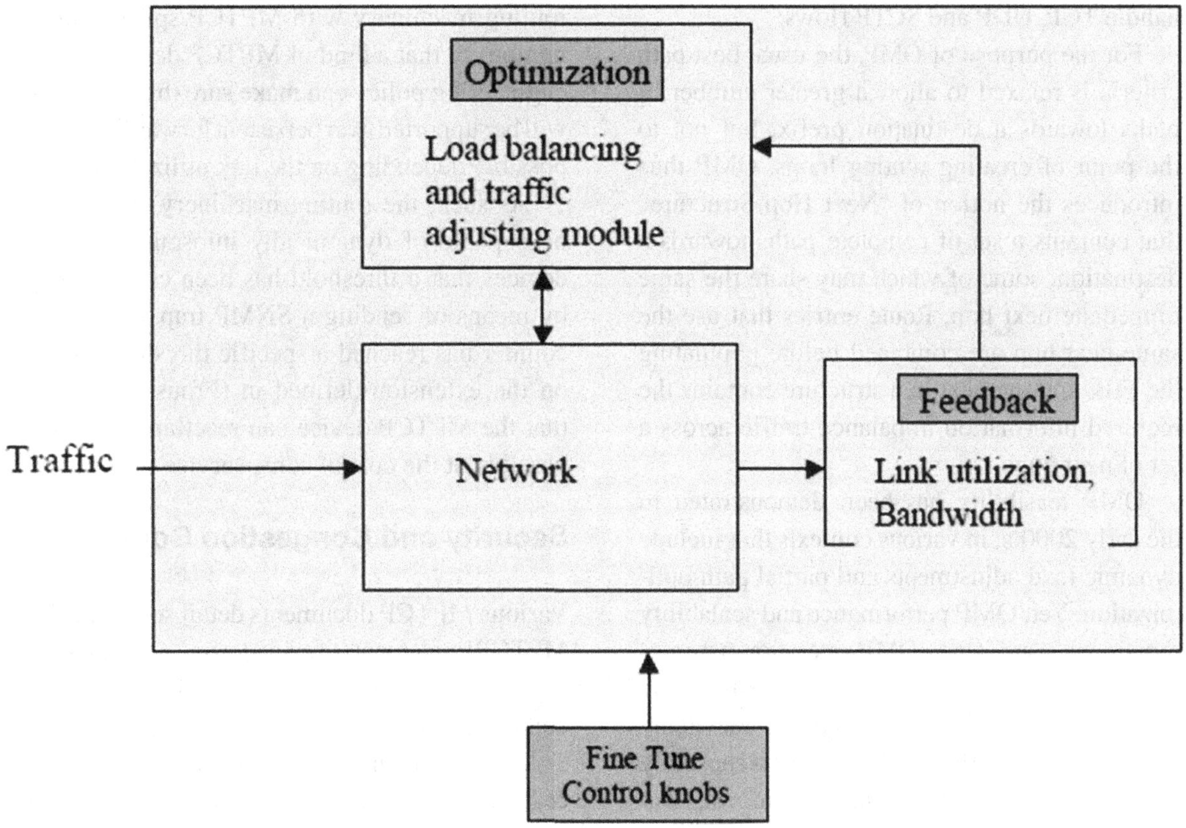

Figure 7. Sample Load Computation Algorithm.

```
PrevEquivLoad = EquivLoad;
if (Loss < 0.005) {
    EquivLoad = FilteredUtil;
} else {
    if (Loss <= 0.09) {
        LossComp = 10 * sqrt(Loss);
    } else {
        LossComp = 3;
    }
    EquivLoad = FilteredUtil * LossComp;
}
```

the traffic overhead. Like ECMP, OMP is agnostic to the upper transport protocol and can therefore handle TCP, UDP and SCTP flows.

For the purpose of OMP, the usual best path criteria is relaxed to allow a greater number of paths towards a destination prefix, but not to the point of creating routing loops. OMP thus introduces the notion of "Next Hop Structure" that contains a set of complete paths towards a destination, some of which may share the same immediate next hop. Route entries that use the same next hop are combined before populating the FIB, and the next hop structure contains the required information to balance traffic across a set of next hops.

OMP feasibility has been demonstrated in the early 2000's, in various contexts that include dynamic load adjustments and partial path optimization. Yet, OMP performance and scalability remain an issue, since OMP operation assumes significant CPU resources to store the next hop structures, while flooding decisions inevitably raise signaling overhead considerations caused by the generation of updated link load information.

Other approaches have been investigated since then, such as the Adaptive Multi-Path Routing (AMP, (Gojmerac & all, 2003) for dynamic traffic engineering purposes. AMP optimizes OMP in that it restricts the need to store next hop structure information to a local scope (compared to the global topology information maintained by OSPF routers, for example), so that signaling overhead is optimized.

Analysis

Dynamic traffic balancing capabilities by means of advanced routing protocol machineries like ECMP or OMP algorithms can never guarantee that any TCP flow will always be forwarded over the exact same path, as long as the TCP connection is established. Therefore, there may be some room for further investigation so that MPTCP capable devices (that is, devices that can dynamically master the establishment and the maintenance of sub-flows as per the MPTCP logic) can feed the routing machinery with MPTCP specific information, so that a kind of MPTCP derived traffic engineering policy can make sure that sub-flows will be supported over persistent forwarding paths, possibly depending on the link utilization.

As such, the routing machinery should also be capable of dynamically informing MPTCP devices that a threshold has been crossed (e.g., by means of sending a SNMP trap whenever a counter has reached a specific threshold or rely on the extension defined in (Proust, 2004), so that the MPTCP device can react appropriately, possibly at the cost of some service disruption.

Security and Congestion Control

Various MPTCP documents detail some specific MPTCP implementations or design, possible security issues and recommendations and congestion control mechanisms.

Two documents (Deng et al., 20014) and (Wei & Xiong, 2014) detail the mechanisms to be supported by a MPTCP proxy in the situation where a MPTCP-device communicates with a non-MPTCP device. These MPTCP proxy-related documents mainly deal with mobile contexts, where scarcity of cellular resources is an issue for service availability and QoE in general. MPTCP-proxy model requires that the proxy is on the path of every sub-flow and also is likely to become a Single Point Of Failure (SPOF) for customer's sessions. Various functions must be enabled by the MPTCP proxy such as the detection of MPTCP capability for terminals and the anchoring of sub-flows.

Operational MPTCP experience has been documented in (Bonaventure, 2014). The experiment used a Linux-based MPTCP implementation activated by thousands of users in the world. One first feedback discusses the interference of middle-boxes for MPTCP traffic. From the analysis carried out by various researchers, MPTCP can accommodate some of such interference. Some use cases including Data centers environment and the interaction with load balancing solutions (ECMP, LAG) and cellular/WLAN offload are also of interest. Congestion control is an important issue for MPTCP and various IETF documents deal with such issue. Single path algorithms are not adapted to a multi-path context and running some TCP congestion control on each sub-flow is not enough and some management of all sub-flows belonging to a flow must be considered in congestion control. The final of a congestion control design is to dynamically use the least congested path for data transmission. Standardized congestion control is specified in (Raiciu, C., Handly, M., Wischik, D., 2011) and some optimization has been proposed in (Khalili, 2014) and in (Xu, 2014). (Bonaventure, 2014) provides some results of congestion control based upon various solutions.

Some interaction with the DNS system and consequences on agreement signed by ISPs with CDN providers are also of interest. It could be the case if some specific CDN servers are used for WLAN and 3g. If MPTCP is used, and specific contracts are signed between ISPs and CDN providers, its usage can impact these agreements.

REFERENCES

Al-Fares, M., Radhakrishnan, S., Raghavan, B., Huang, N., & Vahdat, A. (2010). *Hedera: Dynamic flow scheduling for data center networks*. Academic Press.

Apple. (2014, October). *iOS: Multipath TCP Support in iOS 7*. Retrieved March 16, 2015 from http://support.apple.com/kb/ht5977

Bagnulo, M., Paasch, C., Gont, F., Bonaventure, O., & Raiciu, C. (2013). *Analysis of MPTCP residual threats and possible fixes*. Academic Press.

Bonaventure, O., & Paasch, C. (2014). *Experience with Multipath TCP*. Academic Press.

Cai, Y., Wei, L., Ou, H., Arya, V., & Jethwani, S. (2012). *Protocol Independent Multicast Equal-Cost Multipath (ECMP)*. Redirect. doi:10.17487/rfc6754

Caviglione, L. (2013). A first look at traffic patterns of Siri. *Transactions on Emerging Telecommunications Technologies*.

Chen, Y., Griffith, R., Liu, J., Katz, R.H., & Joseph, A.D. (2009). *Understanding TCP Incast Throughput Collapse in Datacenter Networks*. Academic Press.

Dixit, A., Prakash, P., & Kompella, R. (2011). *On the Efficacy of Fine-Grained Traffic Splitting Protocols in Data Center Networks*. Academic Press.

Eardley, P. (2013). *Survey of MPTCP Implementations*. Academic Press.

Ford, A., Raiciu, C., Handley, M., & Bonaventure, O. (2013). *TCP Extensions for Multipath Operation with Multiple Addresses*. Academic Press.

Gojmerac, I., Ziegler, T., Ricciato, F., & Reichl, P. (2003). *Adaptive Multipath Routing for Dynamic Traffic Engineering*. Academic Press.

Gundavelli, S., Leung, K., Devarapalli, V., Chowdhury, K., & Patil, B. (2008). *Proxy Mobile IPv6*. Academic Press.

Hopps, C. (2000). *Analysis of an Equal-Cost Multipath Algorithm*. Academic Press.

Huitema, C. (1995). *Multi-homed TCP*. Academic Press.

IEEE. (2012, January). *Bridges and Virtual Bridged Local Area Networks – Amendment 9: Shortest Path Bridging*. Academic Press.

Kandula, S., Sengupta, S., Greenberg, A., Patel, P., & Chaiken, R. (2009). *The Nature of Data Center Traffic: Measurements and Analysis*. Academic Press.

Khalili, R., Gast, N., Popovic, M., & Le Boudec, J.Y. (2012). *Non-Pareto Optimality of MPTCP: Performance Issues and a Possible Solution*. Academic Press.

Khalili, R., Gast, N., Popovic, M., & Le Boudec, J.Y. (2014). *Opportunistic Linked-Increases Congestion Control Algorithm for MPTCP*. Academic Press.

Krevat, E., Vasudevan, V., Phanishayee, A., Andersen D. G., Ganger, G. R., Gibson, G. A., & Seshan, S. (2007). *On Application-level Approaches to Avoiding TCP Throughput Collapse in Cluster-Based Storage Systems*. Academic Press.

Matsumoto, A., Kozuka, A., Fujikawa, K., & Okabe, Y. (2003). *TCP Multi-Home Options*. Academic Press.

Multipath Networks, M. P. N. (2012). Retrieved from http://multipathnetworks.com/

Notes. (2013, November). Retrieved from http://www.ietf.org/proceedings/88/minutes/minutes-88-mptcp

Paasch, C., Detal, G., Duchene, F., Raiciu, C., & Bonaventure, O. (2012). *Exploring Mobile/WiFi Handover with Multipath TCP*. Academic Press.

Perkins, C. (2010). *IP Mobility Support for IPv4*. Academic Press.

Pluntke, C., Eggert, L., & Kiukkonen, N. (2011). *Saving Mobile Device Energy with Multipath TCP*. Academic Press.

Proust, C. (2004). *An approach for Routing at Flow level*. Academic Press.

Raiciu, C., Handley, M., & Wischik, D. (2011). *Coupled Congestion Control for Multipath Transport Protocols*. Academic Press.

Raiciu, C., Paasch, C., Barre, S., Ford, A., Honda, M., Duchene, F., … Handley, M. (2012). *How Hard Can It Be? Designing and Implementing a Deployable Multipath TCP*. Academic Press.

Raiciu, C., Pluntke, C., Barre, S., Greenhalgh, A., Wischisk, A., & Handley, M. (2010). *Data center networking with multipath TCP*. Academic Press.

Raiciu, C., Pluntke, C., Barre, S., Greenhalgh, A., Wischisk, A., & Handley, M. (2011). *Improving datacenter performance and robustness with Multipath TCP*. Academic Press.

Scharf, M., & Ford, A. (2013). *Multipath TCP (MPTCP)*. Application Interface Considerations. doi:10.17487/rfc6897

Singh, V., Karkkainen, T., Ott, J., Ahsan, S., & Eggert, L. (2013). *Multipath RTP*. Academic Press.

Stewart, R., Xie, Q., Tuexen, M., Maruyama, S., & Kozuka, M. (2007). *Stream Control Transmission Protocol (SCTP)*. Dynamic Address Reconfiguration. doi:10.17487/rfc4960

Touch, J., & Perlman, R. (2009). *Transparent Interconnection of Lots of Links (TRILL): Problem and Applicability Statement*. Academic Press.

Tuan, A. L., Kyung, H., Choong, S.E., Razzaque, M.A., & Sungwon, L. (2012). *ecMTCP: An Energy-Aware Congestion Control Algorithm for Multipath TCP*. Academic Press.

Van der Pol, R., Boele, S., Dijkstra, F., & Barczyk, A. (2012). *Multipathing with MPTCP and Openflow*. Academic Press.

Van der Pol, R., Bredel, M., Barczyky, A., Overeinder, B., Van Adrichem, N., & Kuipers, F. (2013). *Experiences with MPTCP in an intercontinental multipathed OpenFlow network*. Academic Press.

Villamizar, C. (1999). *OSPF Optimized Multipath*. OSPF-OMP.

Wannstrom, J., (2013). *Carrier Aggregation Explained*. Academic Press.

Xu, M., Cao, Y., & Fu, X. (2014). *Delay-based Congestion Control for MPTCP*. Academic Press.

Zhang, J., Ren, F., & Lin, C. (2013). *Survey on Transport Control in Data Center Networks*. Academic Press.

KEY TERMS AND DEFINITIONS

Bandwidth: Amount of data the can be carried on a network during a period of time.

Congestion: Congestion happens when bandwidth on a link or node capacity are too much limited to transmit data traffic.

Path: Sequence of links between a sender and a receiver.

Proxy: An intermediary program which acts both as a server and a client for the purpose of making request on behalf of other clients.

Session continuity: Capability for a node to maintain its ongoing IP sessions while changing its (IP) point of attachment.

Sessions: Interactive communication between two or more devices.

Sub-flows: A flow of TCP segments operating over an individual path.

Transmission Control Protocol: Layer 4 protocol that is widely supported in IP networks. TCP provides several features such as reliability and order delivery.

Chapter 10
A Top-Down Framework for Modeling Routing Design Complexity

Xin Sun
Florida International University, USA

ABSTRACT

Networks with higher degrees of complexity typically require more effort to manage and are more prone to configuration errors. Unfortunately, complexity remains one of the least understood aspects of networking. This chapter takes a first step toward bridging this gap, by presenting a top-down framework for modeling complexity in routing design, a critical and highly complex network design task. First, a set of abstractions is introduced for precisely defining objectives of routing design, and for reasoning about how a combination of routing design primitives will meet the objectives. Next, models are presented for quantitatively measuring the complexity of a routing design by modeling individual design primitives and leveraging configuration-derived complexity metrics. This modeling approach helps understand how individual design choices may impact the resulting complexity, and enables comparison of alternative routing designs and "what-if" analysis of the potential impact of a design change on complexity.

INTRODUCTION

Ad-hoc design decisions made during organic growth (e.g., company mergers, expansion to new markets) and incremental evolution (e.g., user mobility, department reorganizations) have caused many enterprise networks to become unnecessarily complex and increasingly difficult and costly to operate. Operator interviews and anecdotal evidence suggest that networks with higher degrees of complexity in their design and implementation generally require more manual intervention to manage, are more difficult to reason about, predict and troubleshoot, and are more prone to configuration errors. For many complex enterprise networks, the amount of management effort required has become the dominant cost of operation (Kerravala, 2004). Despite this investment, configuration errors account for 50%-80% of network outages (Juniper, 2008), 80% of Air Force network vulnerabilities (CSIS, 2008), and 65% of all successful cyber-attacks (Pescatore,

DOI: 10.4018/978-1-4666-8371-6.ch010

2003). Further, the significant amount of time, effort and risk involved in upgrading complex networks has forced many operators to be extremely reluctant to adopting new and innovative architectures (e.g., software defined networking, cloud computing), and thus poses a fundamental barrier to innovation in the long term.

Unlike network performance, resiliency and security which have all been extensively studied and for which models, algorithms and tools have been successfully developed, complexity remains the least understood part of computer networks. While part of the complexity in network design is inherent, given the wide range of operational objectives that these networks must support, to include security (e.g., implementing a subnet level reachability matrix), resiliency (e.g., tolerating up to two component failures), safety (e.g., free of forwarding loops), performance, and manageability. There is also evidence, however, to suggest that some of the network design complexity may have resulted from a semantic gap between the high-level design objectives and the diverse set of routing protocols and low-level router primitives for the operators to choose from. Often, for the same target network multiple designs exist to meet the same operational objectives, and some designs are significantly easier to implement and manage than others. For example in some cases, route redistribution may be a simpler alternative to BGP (Border Gateway Protocol) for connecting multiple routing domains. However, the reasoning about complexity remains qualitative and objective, and essentially a black-art. Today we do not have a scientific model to characterize the degree of complexity in a given network design, or to compare two design proposals in terms of their complexity. Lacking an analytical model to guide the operators, the current routing design process is mostly ad hoc, prone to creating designs more complex than necessary. This lack of research on network complexity has been more recently recognized by both academia and industry.

As a first and important step towards bridging this gap, this chapter seeks to quantitatively model the complexity associated with a network design, with a view to developing alternate designs that are less complex but meet the same set of operational objectives. In doing so, it focuses on routing design as a concrete application, given its prevalence and high complexity. More specifically, the chapter presents a top-down approach to characterizing the complexity of enterprise routing design given only key high-level design parameters, and in the absence of actual configuration files. The model takes as input abstractions of high-level design objectives such as network topology, reachability matrix (which pairs of subnets can communicate), and design parameters such as the routing instances, and choice of connection primitive (e.g., static routes, redistribution, etc.).

The overall modeling approach is to (i) formally abstract the operational objectives related to the routing design which can help reason about whether and how a combination of design primitives will meet the objectives; and (ii) decompose routing design into its constituent primitives, and quantify the configuration complexity of individual design primitives using the existing bottom-up complexity metrics.

A top-down approach such as this has several advantages. By working with design primitives directly (independent of router configuration files), the model is useful not only for analyzing an existing network, but also for "what if" scenarios analysis capable of optimizing the design of a new network and similarly, a network migration, or evaluating the potential impact of a change to network design. Further, the presented models help provide a conceptual framework to understand the underlying factors that contribute to configuration complexity. For example, reachability restrictions between subnet pairs may require route filters or static routes, which in turn manifest as dependencies in network configuration files.

BACKGROUND

This section briefly reviews the state of the art in complexity metrics, operational practice and tools for network design and configuration, and top-down network modeling and design.

Configuration-Derived Metrics for Quantifying Management Complexity

There has been a lack of quantitative, objective metrics for measuring network management complexity, and this area has only recently started receiving attention in the research community. The most notable work by Benson, Akella and Maltz (2009) introduced a family of complexity metrics that are derived from the device configuration files. More specifically, two major metrics were presented: *number of referential links*, and *number of router roles*.

The first metric, number of referential links, captures the amount of dependencies in the device configurations. Such dependencies may exist both among the configuration of multiple devices and among the configuration of multiple components of a single device. Basically a referential link is created when a network object (e.g., a route filter, a subnet) is defined in one configuration block, and is subsequently referred to in another configuration block, in either the same configuration file or a different file.

As an example, consider Figure 1 that shows configuration snippets from two routers. The referential links are shown in italics. In line 5 of Router 1's configuration, a route filter named TO-SAT is applied to the interface GigabitEthernet1/1 to filter two routes in the outgoing direction. This line introduces two referential links: one to the name of the filter (defined in lines 7-8), and the other to the name of the interface (defined in line 1). Moreover, the definition of the route filter (lines 7-8) introduces two referential links to the two subnet prefixes, which are defined in Router 2's configuration (line 10 and 13).

The intuition behind using referential links as a complexity metric is that, such dependencies typically require manual effort to maintain as the network evolves organically. For example, in Figure 3, if the two subnet addresses configured on "Router 2" are changed to different IP prefixes (such changes could be the result of the subnets moving to a different physical location such as

Figure 1. Configuration snippets of two routers.

Router 1
```
1.  interface GigabitEthernet 1/1
2.    ip address 10.1.0.1 255.255.255.252
3.  !
4.  router eigrp 10
5.    distribute-list prefix TO-SAT out GigabitEthernet1/1
6.  !
7.  ip prefix-list TO-SAT seq 5 permit 192.168.1.0/24
8.  ip prefix-list TO-SAT seq 10 premit 192.168.5.0/24
```

Router 2
```
1.  interface FastEthernet1/1
2.    ip address 192.168.1.1 255.255.255.0
3.  !
4.  interface FastEthernet2/1
5.    ip address 192.168.5.1 255.255.255.0
6.  !
```

a new building), then the route filters defined on "Router 1" must be manually updated to use the new prefixes. More systematically, through empirical studies mainly consisting of operator interviews and measurement of configuration data of operational enterprise networks, Benson et al. (2009) have found that, when operators need to change the design of their networks, the number of steps they need to take to modify configuration increases monotonically with the number of referential links, though the metric is not directly proportional to the number of steps.

The second metric, number of router roles, captures the implicit roles played by routers in implementing policies At a high level, a router role is a section of configuration that implements a common function or policy, such as a routing instance or a filter permitting specific packets. Intuitively, the more distinct roles that routers need to simultaneously play in the network, the more complex it would be to manage and update configurations. As a simple example, a network that only needs to implement a single packet filter is understandably easier to manage than another network that needs to implement multiple different packet filters on different routers, with other things being equal. The empirical study performed by Benson et al. (2009) has shown that this metric can qualitatively reflect the network management complexity.

Operational Practice and Tools for Network Design and Configuration

Network operators need to perform a variety of design and management tasks, and meet a wide range of security, resilience, and performance requirements in doing so. Example tasks include, but not limited to, grouping user hosts into virtual local area networks (VLANs) to ease the management of different user groups, the setting up routing domains and inter-connecting multiple routing domains (e.g., to support company merger), assigning IP addresses to subnets and end hosts, and the installation of packet filters to perform ingress filtering and to control access to privileged databases.

The operational community has a rich history of crafting the art of network design and reconfiguration. Nonetheless, the state of the practice by operators is still defined predominantly by ad-hoc, manual decision making. Notable efforts to simplifying network design involve template-based approaches that codify and promote best practices and abstract languages to specify configurations in a vendor-neutral fashion. There are also tools such as PRESTO (Enck et al. 2007) to convert a network design into device-vendor-specific configuration commands. These approaches merely focus on the low-level mechanisms and their configuration. They do not model network-wide operator intent such as reachability and manageability. Similarly, Narain (2005) presents a logic-based approach to configuration generation based on model-finding, and the focus is on the generation of configuration parameters conforming to correctness rules distilled from best practices. Finally, various design guidelines including those for a top-down network design approach can be found in the literature, e.g., Oppenheime (2010). These guidelines provide practical insights into the trade-offs of different design choices regarding topology, hardware and protocols. However, considerable manual effort is required to determine how to apply these guidelines to the design of a network of medium to large size.

Top-Down Network Modeling and Systematic Network Design

Systematic network design has emerged as a potential solution to the challenges facing the operational community. Such design is characterized by the use of formal models to capture the design requirement, constraints, and considerations. As such the design is guaranteed to be correct and additionally optimizes certain performance metrics. Most efforts on this front focus on developing abstractions and models to formulate individual network protocols and mechanisms, such as BGP, OSPF (Open Shortest Path First), route redistribution, VLAN, packet filters, MPLS (MultiProtocol Label Switching) class of service, just to name a few. The formal models can then be used to reason about how different designs of the individual protocols/mechanisms being modeled can impact the end-to-end network performance, security, etc., and algorithms and heuristics can be developed to automate this reasoning process. There is also recent progress on modeling the interaction between multiple routing algorithms deployed in the same network (Alim and Griffin, 2011). However, those works focus on the performance, security, safety and resiliency behavior of network protocols and mechanisms, but none of them take complexity into account.

MODELING COMPLEXITY OF ENTERPRISE ROUTING DESIGN

Motivation and Overview

Networks with higher degrees of complexity in their design and implementation generally require more manual intervention to manage, are more difficult to reason about, predict and troubleshoot, and are more prone to errors. Thus operators often want to minimize the management complexity of their networks by identifying the underlying factors that contribute to the existing complexity and finding out the most effective ways to reduce the complexity. Furthermore, operators often face "what-if" questions of how a potential change in the network design (e.g., adopting new technology, migrating to a different architecture) may impact the overall complexity of the network. While such design changes are typically motivated by potential improvement in performance, availability and/or costs, their impact on complexity must be carefully understood and controlled to ensure the desired level of manageability.

Conceivably, an operator could enumerate all possible designs, translate each into configurations, and finally quantify the design complexity from the configurations using the available complexity metrics as those discussed in the previous section. However, such a brute-force approach may only work for small networks where the design space is relatively small. Additionally, this approach still requires a model to determine which design candidates actually meet the design objectives.

Thus a practical modeling approach must be able to operate on high-level design objectives and parameters and in the absence of actual configuration files, and quantitatively estimate the resulting network complexity from the given specifications. Further, the model should also provide a conceptual framework to understand the underlying design factors that contribute to complexity and shed direct light on the intricate choices faced by the operators while designing a network.

This section presents such a top-down modeling approach, which has the following three major components:

1. Decompose the given design task into its constituent primitives;
2. Formally abstract the operational objectives related to the given design task, which can help reason about whether and how a combination of design primitives will meet the objectives;
3. Quantify the management complexity of individual design primitives using the available metrics

Furthermore, this section applies the above modeling methodology to a concrete design task: enterprise routing design. This particular design task is chosen given that it is both prevalent (required in virtually every enterprise network) and highly challenging (involving selecting and configuring multiple elements).

Dimensions of Routing Design

This section provides an overview of the requirements and challenges in routing design. The goal is to identify the general sources of its complexity by exposing the major design choices that operators must make. In doing so, a toy example illustrated in Figure 2 is used. In this example, a hypothetical company has three subnets (Sales, Support and Data Center) in the main building and two additional subnets in "building 2".

Reachability Requirements of Policy Groups

An integral part of almost every enterprise's security policy is to compartmentalize the flow of corporate information in its network. For the example network, there are two categories of users: Sales and Support. Suppose the Data Center subnet contains accounting servers that should be accessible only by the Sales personnel. A corresponding requirement of routing design would be to ensure that only the Sales subnets have good routes to reach the Data Center subnet.

The concept of a "policy group" is introduced to refer to the set of subnets that belong to one user category and have similar reachability requirements. A primary source of complexity for routing design is to support the fine-grained reachability requirements of policy groups. This is particularly challenging since business stipulations often imply that subnets of a policy group may need to be distributed across multiple buildings, multiple enterprise branches, or even multiple continents.

A Single Routing Instance vs. Multiple Routing Instances

The operator faces several choices in designing networks to meet the reachability requirements described above. Perhaps the most fundamental design choice is the number of routing protocol instances, or simply *routing instance*, to be created for the target network. A routing instance refers to a connected component of the network where all member routers run the same routing protocol, use matching protocol parameters, and are configured to exchange routes with each other.

One common strategy that the operator may choose is to deploy a single Interior Gateway Protocol (IGP) routing instance over the entire network, to allow full reachability among all subnets. The operator then places filters (either packet filters, or route filters, or both) on selected router interfaces to implement the required reachability policy. This is a viable solution for small networks. However, for medium to large networks, a large number of filtering rules need to be configured, and on many router interfaces. In addition, according to a recent study by Sung et al. (2011), proper placement of filters in itself

Figure 2. Example enterprise network spanning two offices

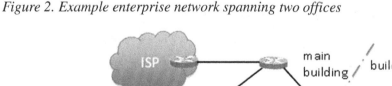

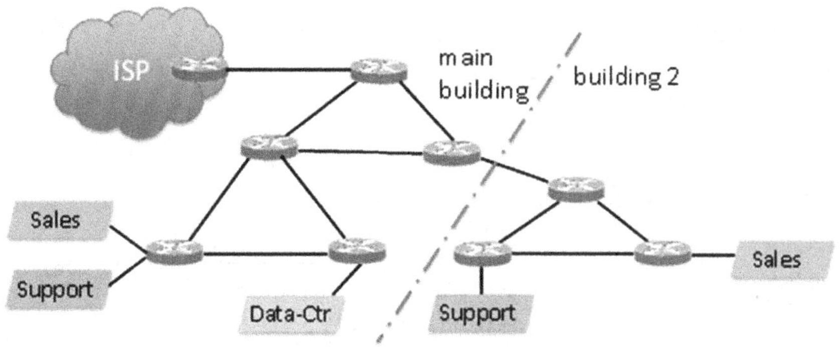

is a complex task, particularly when the solution must be resilient against link failures and other changes in the network topology. Finally, in the case of packet filters, a design with a large number of such filters will likely introduce performance problems because they incur per packet processing.

Alternatively, as another common design strategy, the operator may choose to deploy a separate routing protocol instance to connect the subnets of each policy group. To illustrate, suppose the operator of the example network has created a routing design with three routing instances, as shown in Figure 3. Each office building has its own routing instance ("OSPF 10" or "OSPF 20") while the EIGRP 10 instance serves as the backbone of the network. The operator has chosen to use BGP to connect to the Internet. It is straightforward to configure an external BGP (eBGP) peering session and route redistribution between the EIGRP and BGP instances to allow routes to be exchanged between the enterprise network and its service provider The complexity increases significantly, however, if the operator needs to configure route filters to reject certain incoming and/or outgoing routes. The problem would be compounded for multi-homed enterprise networks because of additional policy requirements such as the designation of primary and backup or load balancing policy.

For connecting the routing instances of OSPF 10 and the backbone, the operator has chosen to use a single border router (i.e., XZ1) that participates in both routing instances. (For brevity, the resiliency requirement is not considered in this example.) This removes the need for BGP peering to advertise routes across the boundaries of the instances. However, the operator must still configure route redistribution and possibly route filters to allow the injection of routes between the two instances. Another complication is that multiple routing instances may simultaneously offer routes to the same destination at a border router. The operator must implement the correct order of preference between the instances, sometimes requiring an override of some protocols' default Administrative Distance (AD) values on a per border router basis.

For connecting the routing instances of "OSPF 20" and the backbone, the operator has adopted a different approach. Two border routers (i.e., Y3 and Z2) are used as in the case of the ISP connection. However, instead of using a dynamic protocol, the operator has configured two sets of static routes, on the two border routers respectively, to achieve reachability across routing instances. This design incurs considerable amount of manual configuration on a per destination prefix basis. For example, on Y3, static routes are required for destination prefixes not only within "EIGRP 10" but also within "OSPF 10". Clearly, due to its static nature, the design may not bode well when the subnet prefixes frequently change or dynamic re-routing is required. However, it has one advantage over

Figure 3. A design with multiple IGP instances for the example network

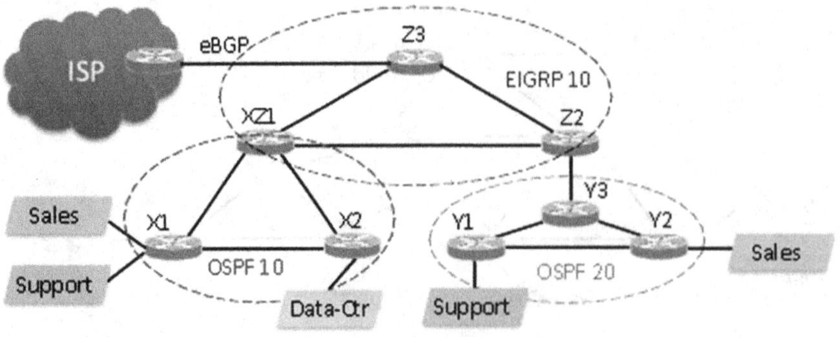

dynamic mechanisms like BGP or co-location of routing processes in one border router: the packet forwarding paths across routing instances are much easier to predict when hardcoded. In contrast, both BGP and route redistribution can result in routing anomalies in ways that are difficult to identify from their configurations (Le, Xie and Zhang, 2008).

Abstractions for Modeling Routing Design

This section presents a set of formal abstractions that capture the routing design primitives, and design objectives and constraints. These abstractions form the foundation for modeling design complexity.

Abstracting Essential Elements of Routing Design

At the routing layer, a network consists of subnets, routers, and links. Each subnet connects to a router and uses that router as its gateway (i.e., the router forwards all the packets generated (or destined to) by the subnet). A "route" is considered as an IP prefix, plus additional attributes (e.g., weight) that may be used for calculation of a next-hop for the route. A router always has routes to all the connected subnets for which it is the gateway. In addition, routes may be manually injected into a router via configuration of static routes. Routers may exchange routes by running one or more dynamic routing protocols. To participate in each routing protocol, a router must run a separate routing process. Each routing process maintains a separate Routing Information Base (RIB). The RIB contains all the routes known to the routing process, each associated with one or more next-hops. A router also maintains a global RIB, and uses selection logic to select routes from its routing process RIBs, as well as routes to connected subnets and statically configured routes, to enter the global RIB. The global RIB is a major component of the Forwarding Information Base (FIB) which is used to make forwarding decisions. A router R_i is said to have a route to a subnet S_j if the prefix of S_j matches a valid route in the global RIB of R_i. Furthermore, a subnet S_i is said to be routable from another subnet S_j if the gateway router for S_j has a valid route to S_i. Finally, since this section concerns only the routing design and uses routing as the only mechanism to implement reachability, the terms "reachable" and "routable" are therefore used inter-changeably.

Let $\{I_1, I_2, ...\}$ denote the set of routing instances. As described above, routing processes in the same routing instance exchange all their routes freely. As a result, all the routing processes share the same set of routes. To change this behavior, route filters are typically used to filter route updates between routing processes. On the other hand, routing processes in different routing instances do not exchange any route. To change this behavior, *connecting primitives* must be used (e.g., static routes, route redistribution and BGP). The routers where connecting primitives are implemented are termed *border routers*. In modeling the design complexity, it is assumed that the set of routing instances and their member routers and routing processes are given as an input. It is also assumed that Each cell $\mathbf{M}_C(i,j)$ specifies the connecting primitive used by routing instances I_i and I_j to allow routes to be advertised from I_i to I_j. Note that it is possible to use a different connecting primitive to advertise routes in the other direction from I_j to I_i.

Abstracting Routing Design Objectives and Constraints

Three fundamental objectives and constraints of enterprise routing design are considered in this chapter: reachability, resiliency, and path policies.

First, the reachability matrix $\mathbf{M_R}$ is introduced to capture the reachability requirements. Each cell $\mathbf{M_R}(i, j)$ denotes whether the subnet S_i can reach the subnet S_j. Note that this chapter follows the common practice that only uses routing design to implement reachability at the subnet level. The host-level reachability is not considered here as it is typically implemented by data plane mechanisms such as packet filters.

Second, the border-router matrix $\mathbf{M_B}$ is introduced to capture the resiliency requirement. Each cell $\mathbf{M_B}(i,j)$ specifies the set of border routers of routing instance I_i that enable I_i to advertise routes to another routing instance I_j . Note that a routing instance may use different border routers to communicate with different neighboring routing instances.

Third, the route-exchange matrix $\mathbf{M_X}$ is introduced to capture the path policies. Each cell $\mathbf{M_X}(i,j)$ specifies the set of routes that the routing instance I_i should advertise to another routing instance I_j to meet the reachability requirement. We assume that the routes in the matrix are already in the most aggregated form. Clearly the set of *external* routes that Ii has may be calculated as $\cup_j \mathbf{M_X}(j,i)$. Let T_i denote the set of *internal* routes that I_i has (i.e., routes originated by subnets inside I_i). Let W_i denote the entire set of routes that I_i has, which may be calculated as follows:

$$W_i = \left(\bigcup_j \mathrm{M_X}(j,i) \right) \bigcup T_i$$

Leveraging Referential Links for Measuring Complexity

The metric of referential links introduced in the Background section is leveraged for measuring the routing design complexity. As discussed above, this is a quantitative, fine-grained metric that measures the amount of dependencies in the device configurations. This metric has been validated by Benson et al. (2009) and it reflects the operators perceived complexity (measured by the number of steps they take to perform typical management tasks) reasonably well. This metric also shows the most variation across designs, making it particularly useful in facilitating comparisons. Other metrics proposed by previous works (e.g., the number of router roles) are coarser grained, do not show as much variation, and are straightforward to estimate from the design, and thus is not used in this work.

Modeling Intra-Instance Complexity

This section presents a framework for estimating complexity that exists within a routing instance. For simplicity, it focuses on distance vector routing protocols. It first shows that such complexity results from the need to install route filters inside a routing instance, in order to implement the different reachability requirements of different subnets. It then presents models to quantify the complexity associated with such route filters. In doing so, the models determine the route filter placement and the filter rules.

Source of Intra-Instance Complexity

The complexity within a routing instance primarily comes from the route filters installed inside the instance. By definition, all routing processes of the same routing instance maintain the same routing tables. This means that all the subnets connecting to those routing processes will have the same reachability scope. If this is not desired, route filters must be installed to restrict the reachability within a routing instance. As an example, consider the network shown in Figure 4. Routers R_1-R_7 and subnets S_1-S_4 are placed in routing instance I_1. Border router R_2 runs eBGP with another autonomous system AS_2 and injects eBGP-learned routes to I_1. The figure also shows the desired reachability matrix. To implement the reachability matrix, route filters must be carefully placed. For example, to prevent S_1 and S_2 from reaching S_4, while permitting S_3 to reach S_4, route filters must be installed between R_3 and R_5, and between R_3 and R_6. Similarly, a route filter must be installed between R_1 and R_4 to prevent S_4 from reaching S_1 and S_2. In addition, another route filter must be installed between R_3 and R_7, to prevent S_3 from reaching the external routes of routing instance I_2.

In general, the degree of diversity in terms of reachability among subnets of the same routing instance directly impacts the amount of filtering required, which in turn determines the complexity inside that routing instance. To capture this degree of diversity, we leverage the concept of policy groups introduced earlier. Formally, let $\{Z_1, Z_2, ...\}$ denote the set of policy groups in a network. A policy group Z_i is a set of subnets that (i) can reach each other, and (ii) are subject to the same reachability treatment toward other subnets (e.g., if a subnet $S_a \in Z_i$ can reach another subnet $S_b \in Z_j$, then all subnets in Z_i must be able to reach S_b as well). Clearly, policy groups divide the set of all subnets, and each subnet belongs to one and only one policy group. The set of policy groups of a given network can be easily derived from the reachability matrix $\mathbf{M_R}$. In the example in Figure 4, S_1 and S_2 form a policy group, while S_3 and S_4 each constitutes a separate policy group.

By definition, there is no need for filtering within a policy group. Thus, if a routing instance contains only a single policy group, the intra-instance complexity is zero. On the other hand, if a routing instance contains subnets of multiple policy groups, route filters must be installed among them to implement their different reachability constraints, and thus incur complexity.

Modeling the Complexity

Intuitively, the degree of complexity of a given routing instance I_a depends on two factors:

1. The number of route filters installed inside I_a as each installation of a filter creates a referential link to the name of that filter (e.g., line 5 of Router 1 in Figure 1);
2. The complexity associated with each route filter, which is measured by the number of rules in each filter, as each rule creates a referential link to an IP prefix address (e.g., lines 7-8 of Router 1 in Figure 1).

Figure 4. An example network to illustrate the new complexity for route filters. The reachability matrix shown has one row (column) per subnet, and each cell denoted as Y (N) indicates the corresponding subnets can (cannot) reach each other.

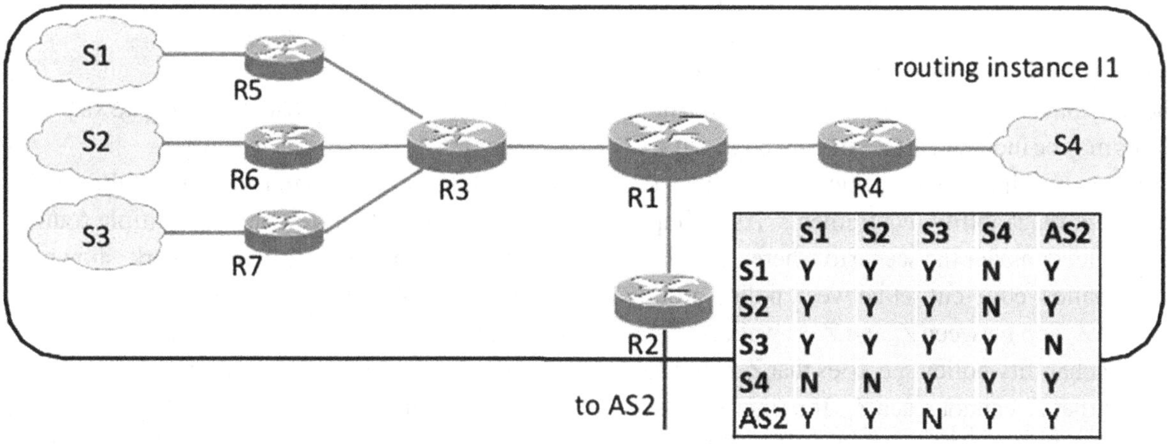

	S1	S2	S3	S4	AS2
S1	Y	Y	Y	N	Y
S2	Y	Y	Y	N	Y
S3	Y	Y	Y	Y	N
S4	N	N	Y	Y	Y
AS2	Y	Y	N	Y	Y

Below the two factors are modeled separately.

Estimating the Number of Filters

Consider the router filters needed to implement the reachability requirement of a policy group Z_i *toward* other subnets. If another policy group Z_j contains one or more subnets that Z_i cannot reach, then a route filter must be placed on every possible layer-three path between Z_i and Z_j, to filter out routing updates corresponding to those subnets of Z_j before they reach any gateway router of Z_i. (For brevity, if a router is a gateway router for any subnet in a policy group, it is simply called a gateway router of that policy group.). Similarly, consider every external network (i.e., external autonomous systems) E_k. If there exist one or more subnets in E_k that Z_i must not reach, a route filter must be placed on every possible path between Z_i and E_k to filter routing updates corresponding to those external subnets as well.

In both cases described above, the *upper* bound on the number of route filters needed for a policy group Z_i is the total number of paths between Z_i and Z_j (E_k), summed over all Z_j and E_k for which filtering is needed. The upper bound can always be achieved by placing the filters on the gateway routers of Z_i (to prevent the unwanted routing updates to be used by those gateway routers of Z_i). The *lower* bound is the number of links in the smallest edge-cut set between Z_i and Z_j (E_k), summed over all Z_j and E_k for which filtering is needed. However, it is worth noting that the lower bound may not always be achievable, as some links may be included in the smallest edge-cut sets between multiple pairs of policy groups that have different reachability requirements. As a simple example, consider the scenario where a link is in the smallest edge-cut set between policy groups Z_a and Z_b and between Z_b and Z_c as well. Assume the reachability policy specifies that Z_a can reach Z_b but that Z_c cannot reach Z_b. If a filter is placed on this link and filters out routing updates corresponding to Z_b, it would wrongfully prevent Z_a from getting those updates.

Estimating the Number of Rules in Each Filter

Consider using a route filter to implement a policy group Z_i's reachability constraint toward another policy group Z_j. The number of rules in this filter depends on the number of routes to be blocked from Z_j to Z_j, as one route translates to one filter rule (refer to Figure 1 for an illustration of a route filter with two rules). For example, for the toy network described above (Figure 4), a route filter must be installed to prevent the routes of S_1 and S_2 from being advertised to S_4. The number of rules in this filter will be two, as there are two prefixes to be blocked. (Note that the number of rules may be reduced, if several prefixes can be aggregated into a larger prefix. For simplicity, such route aggregation is not modeled in this work, and can be separately considered before applying the framework presented here.)

Modeling Inter-Instance Complexity

This section presents a framework for estimating the inter-instance complexity, which results from the use of connecting primitives. Models will be presented for estimating the complexity of the three typical connecting primitives: route redistribution, static and default routes, and BGP.

Source of Inter-Instance Complexity

The inter-instance complexity is resulted from the use of primitives to connect multiple routing instances. Consider the toy network shown in Figure 5 as an example. There are two routing instances: I_1 running OSPF with process ID 10, and I_2 running EIGRP with process ID 20. I_1 contains subnets S_1 and S_2, and I_2 contains S_3. The reachability policy specifies that S_1 and S_2

can reach each other and so do S_2 and S_3, but S_1 and S_3 must not communicate. Given the network as such (i.e., without the use of any connecting primitive), I_1 and I_2 cannot exchange any route, and thus cannot communicate at all. To implement the reachability between I_1 and I_2, one or more border routers must be deployed to physically connect the two routing instances, and in addition, a connecting primitive must be configured on the border routers to enable route exchange.

An important factor that impacts the degree of inter-instance complexity is the resiliency requirement, which specifies the number of border routers each routing instance should have. While having more border routers improves resiliency, doing so also introduces potential anomalies (e.g., routing loops, infinite forwarding loops) and complicates the configuration. Preventing such anomalies will introduce additional complexity and will be modeled explicitly.

Route Redistribution

Using route redistribution to connect two routing instances requires having a common border router that runs routing processes in both routing instances. The border router then may be configured to redistribute routes from one routing instance to the other, and vice versa. (Note that route redistribution must be separately configured for each direction.) For example, Figure 6a illustrates the design using route redistribution for the network shown in Figure 5. Router R_4 is the border router and is configured to redistribute routes between I_1 and I_2. Figure 6b shows the relevant configuration snippet of R4 in Cisco IOS syntax, with referential links highlighted in italics. Lines 1 and 4 create two routing processes, one participating in each routing instance. Lines 2 and 5 redistribute routes from I_2 to I_1 and from I_1 to I_2 respectively.

By default, route redistribution will redistribute all the active routes (i.e., routes that are installed in the FIB). For example, R_4 in Figure 6a will redistribute routes of both S_1 and S_2 to I_2. This enables S_3 to reach both S_1 and S_2, which does not conform to the reachability policy as shown in Figure 4. To change the default behavior, a route filter (e.g., in the form of a route-map) must be used in conjunction with route redistribution, as shown in line 5 in Figure 6b. The route filter permits a subset of routes to be redistributed as specified by the filtering rules (lines 7 and 8), and blocks the rest of the routes.

Modeling Complexity with a Single Border Router

Consider route redistribution from a routing instance I_i to another routing I_j. Route redistribution in the other direction may be modeled similarly and separately. As shown above, the configuration may include two components: (i) configuration of the route redistribution itself, which has a constant complexity; and (ii) configuration of a route filter, which is needed if only a subset of I_i's routes can be redistributed to I_j. Let K_{rr} denote the complexity of configuring the route redistribution itself. Let the function f(x) denote

Figure 5. A toy network with two routing instances.

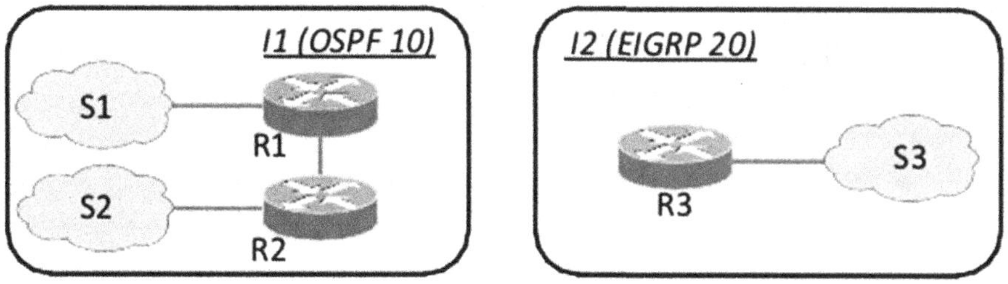

	S1	S2	S3
S1	Y	Y	N
S2	Y	Y	Y
S3	N	Y	Y

Figure 6. Design using route redistribution for the network shown in Figure 5

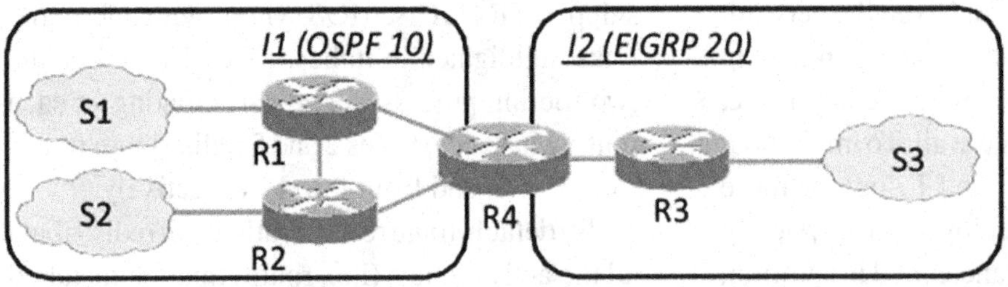

	S1	S2	S3
S1	Y	Y	N
S2	Y	Y	Y
S3	N	Y	Y

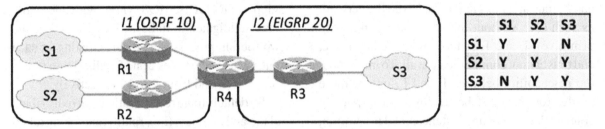

(a) The network design using route redistribution and a single border router.

Router 4

```
router ospf 10
   redistribute eigrp 20
!
 router eigrp 20
   redistribute ospf 10 route-map OSPF-TO-EIGRP
!
route-map OSPF-TO-EIGRP permit 10
   match ip address 1
!
access-list 1 permit S2
```

(b) Configuration snippet of the border router R4.

the complexity of configuring and installing a route filter with x rules (i.e., the filter permits x routes). Note that f (x) includes: (i) the complexity of defining the route filter, which is linear to the number of rules to be defined, and (ii) the complexity of installing the filter by referring to its name, which is a constant factor. In addition, let h(i, j) be the following binary function that denotes whether a filter is needed: (Recall that a filter is not needed if all the routes that I_i has, i.e., W_i as defined earlier, can be redistributed into I_j.)

$$h(i,j) = 0, \text{ if } \mathrm{M_X}(i,j) = W_i;$$
$$h(i,j) = 1, \text{ otherwise.}$$

The overall complexity denoted by $C_{rr}(i,j)$ can be calculated as follows:

$$C_{rr}(i,j) = K_{rr} + f\left(\mathrm{M_X}(i,j)\right) h(i,j)$$

Modeling Complexity with Multiple Border Routers

Now consider the design scenario where route redistribution is configured on multiple border routers to redistribute routes from I_i to I_j, as illustrated in Figure 7. The complexity of this design depends on what connecting primitive is used to send routes in the reverse direction (i.e., from I_j to I_i), as being discussed below.

On the one hand, if no connecting primitive or a different connecting primitive than route redistribution is used in the reverse direction, the complexity C_{rr} is simply the complexity in the single border-router case multiplied by the number of border routers, i.e.,

$$C_{rr}(i,j) = \left(K_{rr} + f(\mathbf{M}_{\mathbf{X}}(i,j)h(i,j)\right)\left|\mathbf{M}_{\mathbf{B}}(i,j)\right|$$

Recall that $\mathbf{M}_{\mathbf{B}}(i, j)$ denotes the set of border routers that I_i uses to reach I_j, which is an input to the framework. $|\mathbf{M}_{\mathbf{B}}(i,j)|$ denotes the size of this set, i.e., the number of border routers.

On the other hand, if route redistribution is also used in the reverse direction, then a potential anomaly called route feedback may occur. Route feedback happens when a route is first redistributed from I_i to I_j by one border router, but then is redistributed back from I_j to I_i by another border router. For example, in the network in Figure 7, the route of S_1 may be first redistributed from I_1 (RIP) to I_2 (OSPF) by router R_4. So router R_5 may learn S_1 from both RIP and OSPF. If R_5 prefers the OSPF-learned route, it will redistribute the route back to RIP. Route feedback can lead to several problems such as routing loops and route oscillations, as demonstrated in the previous work by Le, Xie and Zhang (2007). Clearly route feedback can happen only when *mutual* route redistribution is conducted by multiple border routers between two routing instances.

As a common conservative solution to this issue, a route filter is used in conjunction with

Figure 7. A design where route redistribution is configured on multiple border routers. Assume full reachability among all subnets.

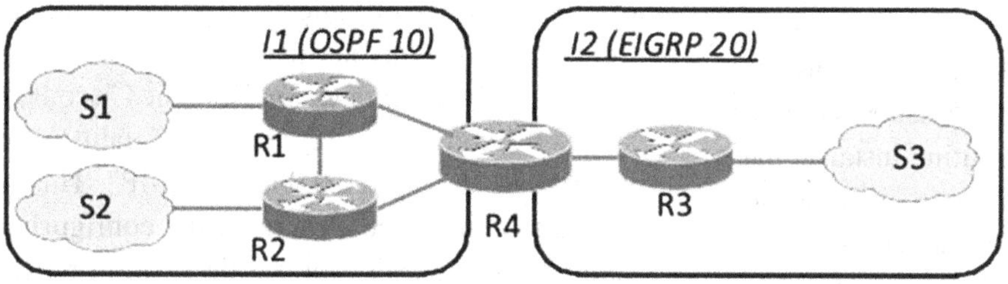

	S1	S2	S3
S1	Y	Y	N
S2	Y	Y	Y
S3	N	Y	Y

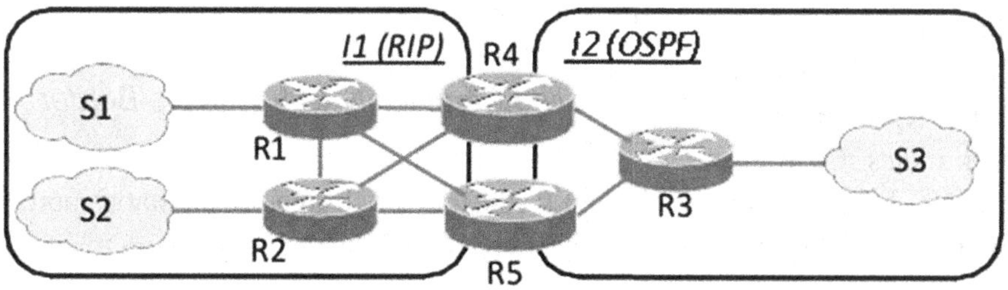

route redistribution to prevent any route from re-entering a routing instance that it's originally from. In the above example, a route filter should be installed on R_4 and R_5 to allow only the route S_3 to enter I_1, and prevent the routes S_1 and S_2 from re-entering I_1. Note that such a filter may be already in place to implement reachability as described earlier (i.e., to permit only a subset of I_j's routes to be redistributed to I_i, and block all other routes). In such case, there is no additional complexity introduced. Only in the case where the filter is not needed otherwise (i.e., when $\mathbf{M_X}$ (j, i) = W_j), a route filter needs to be configured for the sole purpose of preventing route feedback. To summarize, in the mutual route redistribution case, the total inter-instance complexity of using route redistribution to advertise routes from I_i to I_j is:

$$C_{rr}(i,j) = \left(K_{rr} + f\left(\mathbf{M_X}(i,j)\right)\right)\left|\mathbf{M_B}(i,j)\right|$$

The complexity on the reverse direction may be similarly modeled.

Static Routes

Static routes provide a mechanism for manually entering routing table entries. A design using static routes for the network in Figure 5 is shown in Figure 8a. In such designs, each routing instance must have its own border router that participates in only that routing instance. Static routes are configured on the border routers to point to destination subnets in the other routing instance. One static route is needed for every destination subnet. Further, the static routes are redistributed into the respective routing instance so that internal routers in the routing instance also have those routes.

Figure 8. b shows the relevant configuration snippets of the two border routers R_4 and R_5, with referential links highlighted in italics. On R_4, a static route is configured in line 4. The static route points to S3 as the destination, and specifies R_5 as the next-hop to reach the destination. This static route enables R_4 to have a route to S_3. Further, line 2 redistributes the static route into I_1, so that other routers of I_1 (i.e., R_1 and R_2) also have a route to reach S_3. Similarly, a static route to S_2 is configured on R_5 (line 8) and redistributed to I_2 (line 6).

Modeling Complexity with a Single Border Router

Consider using static routes to allow a routing instance I_j to reach a set of subnets in another routing instance I_i, as specified by $\mathbf{M_X}$(i, j). Let $|\mathbf{M_X}$(i, j)$|$ denote the size of $\mathbf{M_X}$(i,j), i.e., the number of subnets in I_i that can be reached by I_j. Since one static route is needed for each subnet in $\mathbf{M_X}$(i, j), in total $|\mathbf{M_X}$(i, j)$|$ static routes need to be configured on the border router of I_j. Let K_{sr} denote the complexity of configuring one static route, which is a constant factor. The total complexity denoted by C_{sr}(i, j) can be calculated as follows:

$$C_{sr}(i,j) = \left|\mathbf{M_X}(i,j)\right| K_{sr}$$

A default route may be viewed as a special case of static routes, which injects a default gateway to the router. A default route has a constant complexity denoted by K_{dr}. For example, in the Cisco IOS syntax the command to configure a default route is "ip route 0.0.0.0 0.0.0.0 next-hop-IP". This is essentially the same command for configuring static routes, except that the destination prefix takes the special form "0.0.0.0 0.0.0.0", which will match any IP address. Clearly the complexity of this command is one (i.e., a constant), as it creates a single referential link to the address of the next-hop router.

Modeling Complexity with Multiple Border Routers

Figure 9 illustrates a design where static routes are configured on multiple border routers to inter-

Figure 8. Design using static routes for the network shown in Figure 5.

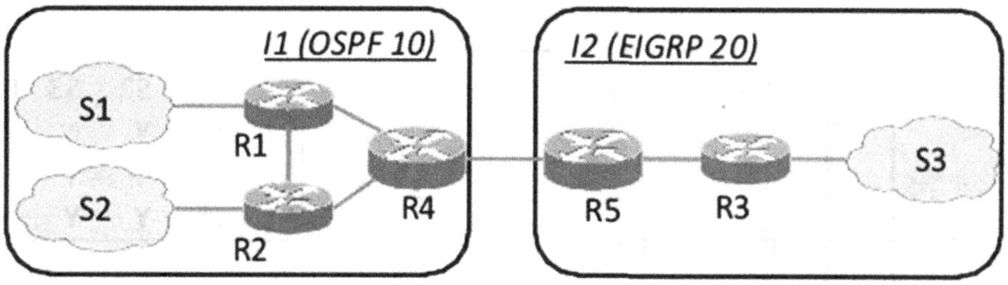

	S1	S2	S3
S1	Y	Y	N
S2	Y	Y	Y
S3	N	Y	Y

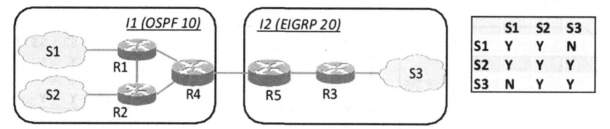

(a) The network design using route redistribution and a single border router for each routing instance.

<u>*Router 4*</u>

1. router ospf 10
2.   redistribute static
3. !
4. ip route *S3 R5*

<u>*Router 5*</u>

5. router eigrp 20
6.   redistribute static
7. !
8. ip route *S2 R4*

(b) Configuration snippet of the border routers R4 and R5.

connect the two routing instances. Consider the general scenario where a routing instance Ij uses static routes to reach a set of subnets in Ii. On each border router of Ij, and for each destination subnet in Ii, multiple static routes may be configured, each using a different border router of Ii as the next-hop. For example, in Figure 9. two static routes may be configured on R_6 to reach S_2, one using R_4 as the next-hop and the other using R_5. It is assumed that an arc matrix $\mathbf{M}_A$ is also given as input to the modeling framework. Each cell $\mathbf{M}_A$(i,j) specifies the set of arcs from the set of border routers in Ij to the set of border routers in Ii. An "arc" is said to exist from one border router Rb$\in\mathbf{M}_B$(j, i) to another border router Ra$\in\mathbf{M}_B$(i, j), if there exists a static route on Rb that uses Ra as the next hop.

One limitation with static routes is that they may not be able to automatically detect the failure of the next-hop router or the link in between, and will continue to try to forward traffic to the bad path, even when other valid paths exist. This will result in packets being dropped. For example, in Figure 9, when there is no failure, R_6 will load balance the two static routes and use both R_4 and R_5 to forward traffic to I_1. R_7 will do the same thing. However, if R_4 fails, R_6 and R_7 will not be able to detect the failure or remove the corresponding

Figure 9. Static routes are configured on all border routers R4-R7. Assuming full reachability among all subnets.

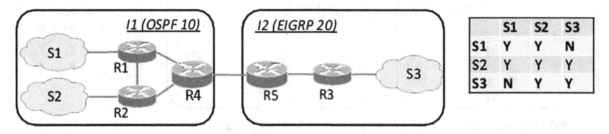

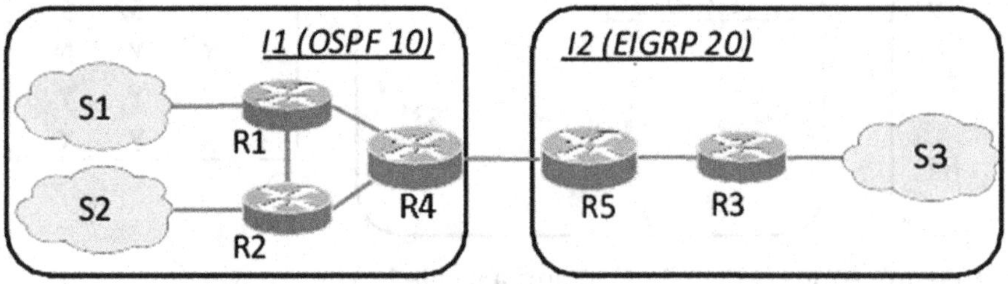

	S1	S2	S3
S1	Y	Y	N
S2	Y	Y	Y
S3	N	Y	Y

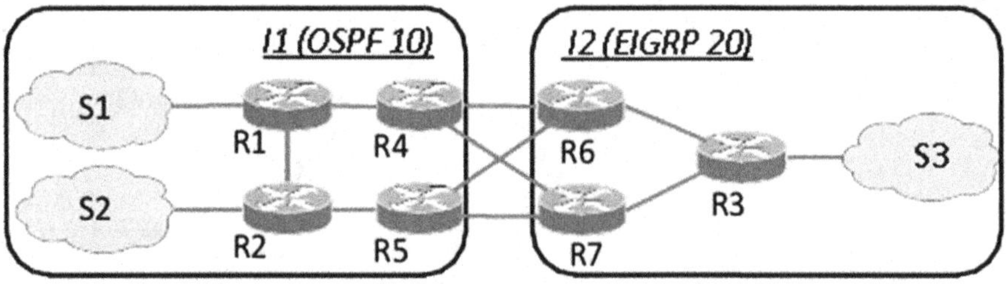

static route that uses R_4 as the next-hop. Instead, they will continue to try to forward half of the traffic to R_4, resulting in those packets being dropped.

Some vendors have provided proprietary solutions to address this issue. A representative solution is Cisco's Object Tracking. An Object Tracking module may be created on each border router and for each destination, and each static route can be configured to refer to an object tracking module. At a high level, object tracking will periodically ping the destination subnet of the static route, using the same next-hop router as specified in the static route. When a failure occurs and the destination is no longer reachable via the particular next-hop, the static route will be removed from the RIB at that point. Clearly, the use of Object Tracking introduces additional complexity.

Let K_{obj} denote the complexity of installing object tracking to one static route. The total complexity of using static routes to enable I_j to reach I_i can be modeled as follows, assuming each arc contains static routes to reach all subnets in $\mathbf{M_X}(i, j)$:

$$C_{sr}(i,j) = |\mathbf{M_A}(i,j)||\mathbf{M_X}(i,j)|(K_{sr} + K_{obj})$$

That is, the total complexity is the single-arc complexity (which includes both the complexity of configuring the set of static routes and the complexity of installing object tracking to each static route), multiplied by the total number of arcs from I_j to I_i (denoted by $|\mathbf{M_A}(i,j)|$).

Border Gateway Protocol (BGP)

As a routing protocol, BGP enables routes to be exchanged among routing instances. BGP typically requires each routing instance to have its own border router(s). For the toy network shown in Figure 5, the design using BGP is illustrated in Figure 10a. Again R4 and R5 are the border routers for routing instances I1 and I2 respectively. In addition to running the respective IGP routing processes, R4 and R5 each also run a separate BGP routing process. A BGP interconnection relationship is established between R4 and R5, so that R4 can advertise S2 to R5, and R5 can advertise S3 to R4. R4 and R5 also redistribute the BGP-learned routes to their respective routing instance, so that other routers in the routing instance have those routes too.

Figure 10. b shows the relevant configuration snippets of R4 and R5. Configuring R4 involves: (i) starting a BGP routing process (line 4); (ii) redistributing routes from the IGP into the BGP process (line 7); (iii) establishing a BGP peering session with the neighboring border router R5 and exchanging routes with it (line 5); (iv) installing an optional route filter to restrict the routes to be advertised (line 6); and (v) redistributing the BGP-learned routes into IGP (line 2). Similar configuration is done on R5 too. Note that the BGP process does not have any route by default, hence routes must be explicitly redistributed from the IGP to the BGP, i.e., the step (ii) above. Also note that BGP advertises all its routes to neighbors by default. If this is not desired, a route filter must be used to restrict routes to be advertised, i.e., the step (iv) above.

Modeling Complexity with a Single Border Router

Consider that a routing instance I_i advertises through BGP a set of routes to another routing instance I_j. The complexity of configuring BGP on I_i's border router consists of three components: (i) the complexity of configuring the BGP session itself, including configuring the BGP process and the peering relationship with the neighbor; (ii) the complexity of configuring mutual route redistribution between the IGP and the BGP processes; and (iii) the complexity of configuring a route filter, if it is needed (i.e., if only a subset of I_i's routes should be advertised to I_j).

Let K_{bgp} denote the complexity of configuring the BGP session itself, which is a constant factor. Let f (x) and h(i, j) be the same functions as above. The total complexity denoted by $C_{bgp}(i, j)$ can be calculated as follows:

$$C_{bgp}(i,j) = K_{bgp} + 2K_{rr} + f\left(\mathbf{M_X}(i,j)\right)h(i,j)$$

Modeling Complexity with Multiple Border Routers

Now consider the design scenario where multiple BGP-speaking border routers are used by each routing instance to exchange routes among them. In such scenario, typically each border router runs external BGP (eBGP) peering sessions with one or more border routers of the other routing instance, and runs internal BGP (iBGP) peering sessions with each border router of the same routing instance. Figure 11 illustrates one such design. For example, R4 in Figure 11 runs eBGP peering sessions with R6 and R7, and an iBGP peering session with R5. Similar configuration applies to the other three border routers as well.

It is assumed that an eBGP-peering matrix $\mathbf{M_P}$ is given as input, where each cell $\mathbf{M_P}$(i,j) specifies the set of eBGP peering sessions between border routers of Ii and Ij. For the example network shown in Figure 11, $\mathbf{M_P}$(1,2) is 4. In addition, it is assumed that each border router runs an iBGP session with every other border router in the same routing instance, which is required for iBGP to work correctly. Hence each border router of Ii runs $|\mathbf{M_B}(i,j)|-1$ iBGP sessions.

The complexity of configuring I_i's border routers to exchange routes with another routing instance I_j consists of three parts: (i) the complexity of configuring the eBGP sessions with border routers of I_j, which includes configuring route filters if needed to restrict routes to be advertised; (ii) the complexity of configuring the iBGP sessions

Figure 10. Design using BGP for the network shown in Figure 5.

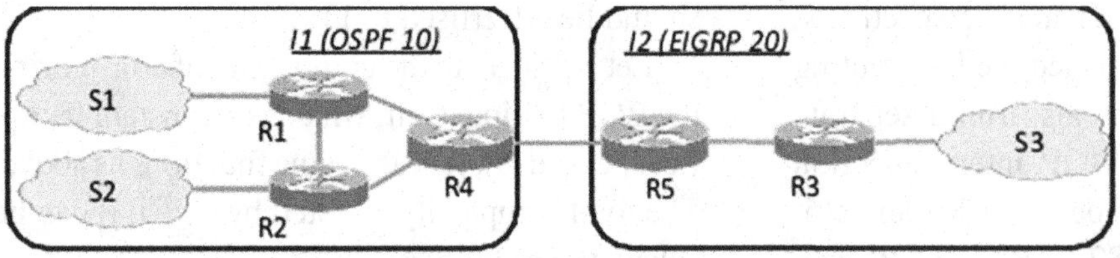

	S1	S2	S3
S1	Y	Y	N
S2	Y	Y	Y
S3	N	Y	Y

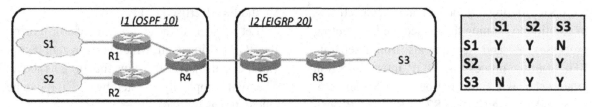

(a) The network design using BGP and a single border router for each routing instance.

Router 4

```
router ospf 10
   redistribute bgp 64501
   !
router bgp 64501
   neighbor R5 remote-as 64502
   neighbor R5 distribute-list 1 out
   redistribute ospf 10
!
access-list 1 permit S2
```

Router 5

```
router eigrp 20
   redistribute bgp 64502
!
router bgp 64502
   neighbor R4 remote-as 64501
   redistribute eigrp 20
!
```

(b) Configuration snippet of the border routers R4 and R5.

among border routers of I_i; and (iii) the complexity of configuring the route redistribution between the BGP process and the IGP process. Hence the total complexity may be calculated as follows:

$$C_{bgp}(i,j) =$$
$$\left(K_{bgp} + f\left(\mathbf{M_X}(i,j)\right)h(i,j)\right)\left|\mathbf{M_P}(i,j)\right|$$
$$+\left(K_{bgp}\left(\left|\mathbf{M_B}(i,j)\right|-1\right)+2K_{rr}\right)\left|\mathbf{M_B}(i,j)\right|$$

FUTURE RESEARCH DIRECTIONS

This section discusses important future directions for advancing the state of the art in network complexity research.

Comprehensive and Accurate Complexity Metrics

Ideal complexity metrics should directly and accurately quantify the degree of difficulty and the amount of manual effort required in managing a network. However, current complexity metrics are entirely derived from device configurations. As such, they are only an indirect measure as they try

Figure 11. BGP is configured on all border routers R4 - R7. Assuming full reachability among all subnets.

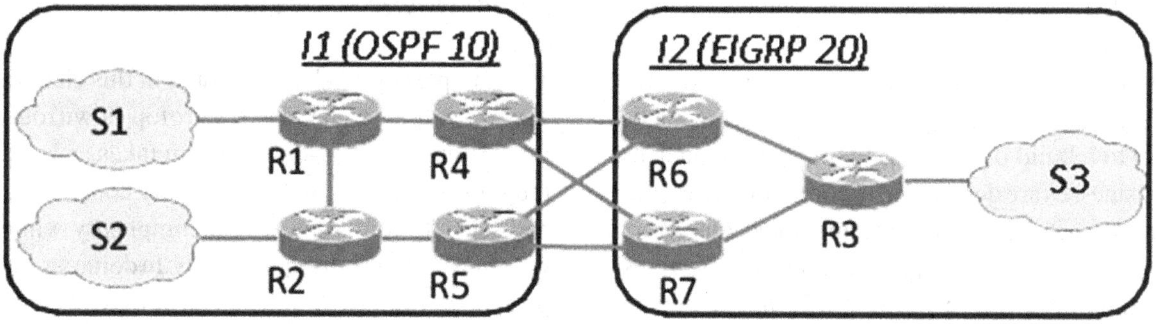

to use the characteristics in the configuration to infer the complexity in management. While this is a reasonable first step, it clearly suffers from several fundamental limitations. First, metrics derived from configurations make it difficult to correlate the observed complexity with the underlying root cause in the design and architecture of the network. Second, configuration-based metrics only capture a small portion of the complexity space, as much of the complexity in reasoning about and predicting the network behavior is not reflected by the configuration. In fact, in many cases complex designs are disguised by simple configurations. For example, recent empirical studies reveal that while route redistribution creates less configuration dependencies than static routes, it is considerably harder to understand and predict, and is thus more prone to errors. As another example, much of the complexity exists in choosing appropriate protocol parameters (e.g., local preference for BGP, administrative distance for route redistribution); however such complexity is not captured by existing configuration-based metrics as the parameters do not create explicit dependency.

Thus an important future research direction is to develop metrics that can quantify the network complexity in an accurate and comprehensive way. Such metrics should be able to directly measure the amount of effort required in managing a network, which includes parameterizing various protocols and mechanisms, troubleshooting, etc. Such complexity metrics can guide the design and development of future networking technologies, e.g., new specification languages, new architectures, and new management systems. They also enable developers to reason about and quantify potential management complexity in their new architectures or systems, allowing them to make careful, complexity-aware design decisions.

Identifying the Root-Cause of Complexity

An overly complex network can exhibit a variety of symptoms that hinder operation. Such symptoms include labor intensity, i.e., excessive numbers of steps are required to perform a simple operation, and un-predictability, i.e., the end-to-end effect of the network is difficult to understand and predict, to name a few. However, multiple complexity symptoms can be the result of a single underlying root cause. Such root causes can lie in the network design and architecture. For example, compared to a well-structured hierarchical topology, a flat mesh-like topology makes it harder to both perform filtering between two nodes (as there could exist many possible paths between them), and to predict how traffic flows through the network (which is needed for implementing traffic engineering and for troubleshooting).

Enterprises want to simplify their networks to cut operational costs. However it is often impractical to rebuild the entire network from scratch, as businesses are dependent on continuous networking services and cannot be interrupted. Operators instead want to identify incremental modifications to their networks that can significantly lower the complexity, while only requiring moderate effort (as operators are already busy with maintaining the status quo). Hence operators wish to be able to answer the following questions: (i) What is the degree of complexity in the design and implementation of my network? How does this complexity impact key management tasks? (ii) What are the top N causes of complexity? and (iii) If we can only invest a fixed amount of money and/or time, where should the investment be spent to maximize the reduction in complexity? Unfortunately today none of these questions could be answered, as there is currently no way to quantitatively characterize the symptoms of complexity or correlate the observed symptoms to underlying root causes. Hence an important future work will be to develop diagnostic techniques to effectively correlate the characterized complexity to the common underlying root cause. In doing so, it might be useful to leverage techniques similar to the concept of Shared Risk Link Groups (SRLG), which has been applied to identify the root causes of IP network faults. Furthermore, merely identifying the root causes of complexity is often not sufficient, as there could be multiple causes and the operators may not have the time to fix all of them. Hence it is also important to develop ranking techniques to identify the set of complexity causes to fix, such that the total costs of fixing the causes are within the time/effort budget specified by the operators, while maximizing the potential benefits of complexity reduction.

Complexity-Aware Top-Down Network Design

The complexity models presented in this chapter pave the way for complexity-aware top-down routing design. Such top-down design takes as input the high-level design objectives and constraints, and seeks to minimize design complexity while meeting other design requirements. In doing so, the presented complexity models can be used to guide the search of the design space to systematically determine (i) how policy groups should be grouped into routing instances; (ii) optimum placement of route filters; and (iii) what primitives should be used to connect each pair of routing instances.

In a broader scope, the overall network design process may be decomposed into four distinct stages: (i) wiring and physical topology design; (ii) addressing plan management (including VLAN design and IP address allocation); (iii) routing design; and (iv) deployment of services such as Voice over IP and IPsec. The task of routing design can be further broken down into two sequential steps: (1) creating routing instances and determining the set of routes to be exchanged between each pair of these instances, and then (2) configuring policy groups and the necessary glue logic. Step (1) is relatively straightforward, typically influenced by factors such as the proximity of routers (e.g., in the same building, city, etc.), administrative boundaries (e.g., different network segments are man- aged by different operators), and equipment considerations (e.g., EIGRP is available only on Cisco routers). Therefore, this work focuses on the second step while assuming that the first step has been accomplished. In the future, it should be beneficial to consider multiple design stages and steps in one framework and explore ways to improve routing design further through joint optimization of all pertinent design choices.

Complexity and Automation

Automation is widely considered the Holy Grail in network management. The emerging software-defined networking (SDN) is a major step toward this direction by enabling a programmable control plane. While automation can potentially reduce a large amount of configuration complexity, the complexity might manifest itself in other forms. For example, while SDN has the potential to automatically translate a given objective (e.g., load balancing) into device configurations, human effort may still be required to deal with the complexity in detecting and resolving potential conflict(s) among multiple objectives (e.g., load balancing and power saving) as pointed out by Volpano, Sun and Xie (2014). As another example, programming is still largely a manual effort and software bugs are not uncommon. As such, programming-based automation like the SDN model may shift from configuration complexity to programming complexity (and subsequently the complexity in dealing with network failures and anomalies caused by software bugs). In general, while automation is much needed and can potentially significantly reduce network management complexity, future work is needed to fully understand the interaction between automation and complexity.

CONCLUSION

This chapter introduced a top-down modeling framework for systematically characterizing the complexity of enterprise routing design. The framework requires only key high-level design parameters as input and works in the absence of actual configuration files. The overall modeling approach is to (i) formally abstract the routing specific operational objectives which can help reason about whether and how a combination of design primitives will meet the objectives; and (ii) decompose routing design into its constituent primitives, and quantify the configuration complexity of individual design primitives, using the number of referential links as the complexity metric. More specifically, abstractions are presented for capturing operational objectives in reachability, resiliency and safety; and models are presented for estimating complexity of implementing reachability policy inside a single routing instance, and for estimating complexity of connecting multiple routing instances using route redistribution, static routes and BGP. This modeling approach makes the presented framework useful not only for analyzing an existing network, but also for "what if" analysis capable of optimizing the design of a new network and similarly, a network migration, or evaluating the potential impact of a change to network design. Overall, this is an important first step towards enabling systematic top-down routing design with minimizing design complexity being an explicit objective. Future work includes developing more comprehensive and accurate complexity metrics, developing algorithms for automatically producing complexity-optimized routing designs in a top-down fashion, and using similar models to capturing complexity of other enterprise design tasks.

REFERENCES

Alim, M., & Griffin, T. (2011). On the interaction of multiple routing algorithms. In *Proceedings of ACM CoNEXT*. New York, NY: ACM. doi:10.1145/2079296.2079303

Benson, T., Akella, A., & Maltz, D. (2009). *Unraveling the complexity of network management*. In *Proceedings of USENIX NSDI*. Berkeley, CA: USENIX Association.

Center for Strategic and International Studies (CSIS). (2008). *Securing cyberspace for the 44th presidency*. Retrieved from http: //csis.org/files/media/csis/pubs/081208_securingcyberspace_44.pdf

Enck, W., McDaniel, P., Sen, S., Sebos, P., Spoerel, S., Greenberg, A., & Aiello, W. et al. (2007). Configuration management at massive scale: System design and experience. In *Proceedings of USENIX Annual Technical Conference*. Berkeley, CA: USENIX Association.

Juniper Network. (2008). *What's behind network downtime? Proactive Steps to Reduce Human Error and Improve Availability of Networks.* Retrieved from https://www-935.ibm.com/services/au/gts/pdf/200249.pdf

Kerravala, Z. (2004). *As the value of enterprise networks escalates, so does the need for configuration management*. The Yankee Group Report.

Le, F., Xie, G., & Zhang, H. (2007). Understanding route redistribution. In *Proceedings of International Conference on Network Protocols*. Piscataway, NJ: IEEE.

Le, F., Xie, G., & Zhang, H. (2008). Instability free routing: Beyond one protocol instance. In *Proceedings of ACM CoNEXT*. New York, NY: ACM. doi:10.1145/1544012.1544021

Narain, S. (2005). Network configuration management via model finding. In *Proceedings of USENIX LISA*. Berkeley, CA: USENIX Association.

Oppenheime, P. (2010). *Top-Down Network Design* (3rd ed.). Indianapolis, IN: Cisco Press.

Pescatore, J. (2003). *Taxonomy of software vulnerabilities*. The Gartner Group Report.

Sung, E., Sun, X., Rao, S., Xie, G., & Maltz, D. (2011). *Towards systematic design of enterprise networks.* IEEE/ACM Trans. *Networking, 19*(3), 695–708. doi:10.1109/TNET.2010.2089640

Volpano, D., Sun, X., & Xie, G. (2014). *Towards Systematic Detection and Resolution of Network Control Conflicts. In Proceedings of ACM HotS-DN*. New York, NY: ACM.

KEY TERMS AND DEFINITIONS

Border Routers: Routers where the connecting primitives are implemented to connect multiple routing instances.

Connecting Primitives: Routing mechanisms that inter-connect multiple routing instances, including route redistribution, static and default routes, and BGP.

Inter-Instance Complexity: Complexity arises from the need to implement reachability among multiple routing instances, for example though the use of connecting primitives.

Intra-Instance Complexity: Complexity arises from the need to implement reachability within a single routing instance, for example though the use of route filters.

Policy Groups: A policy group abstracts the set of user hosts that have the same reachability requirements towards all other hosts.

Reachability Matrix: A matrix that captures the reachability requirements. Each row/column of the matrix denotes a subnet, and each cell specifies whether the subnet of the row can reach the subnet of the column.

Referential Links: Dependencies among configuration of different routers and among different parts of the configuration of the same router.

Routing Instances: A routing instance refers to a connected component of the network where all member routers run the same routing protocol, use matching protocol parameters, and are configured to exchange routes with each other.

Chapter 11
The Path Computation Element (PCE)

Francesco Paolucci
Scuola Superiore Sant'Anna, Italy

Filippo Cugini
CNIT, Italy

ABSTRACT

The Internet Engineering Task Force (IETF) has promoted the Path Computation Element (PCE) architecture to provide effective network resource utilization while guaranteeing advanced Internet applications with adequate quality of service (QoS). The PCE is a dedicated network entity devoted to path computation. This chapter presents the state-of-the-art of the PCE architecture for different networking scenarios including single-domain networks, optical networks, and multi-domain/layer networks. Relevant architectural and implementation aspects are analyzed and discussed, highlighting related benefits, limitations and open issues. Recent progresses and future directions are also addressed, including the PCE evolution to operate in the context of software defined networking.

INTRODUCTION

Multi-Protocol Label Switching with Traffic Engineering extensions (MPLS-TE, Awduche et al, 1999) and Generalized MPLS (GMPLS, Mannie, 2004) provide the Traffic Engineering (TE) capability to forward traffic flows along explicit routes, namely Label Switched Paths (LSPs). The TE capability allows to perform path computation subject to additional QoS constraints typical of such networks, e.g., guaranteed bandwidth in MPLS networks, spectrum continuity constraint in optical networks. TE relies on resource availability and topology information collected through routing protocols, such as Open Shortest Path First with TE extensions (OSPF-TE, Katz, Kompella, & Yeung, 2003) or Intermediate System to Intermediate System with TE extensions (ISIS-TE, Li T. & Smith H. (2008). In LSPs provisioning, the path computation process represents one of the crucial steps to achieve TE objectives, including optimizing network resource utilization.

Within a given domain, the path computation is usually determined by the routing information collected at the head-end node, while resources are reserved during the signaling phase, exploited

DOI: 10.4018/978-1-4666-8371-6.ch011

through distributed protocols, such as the Resource reSerVation Protocol with TE extensions (RSVP-TE, Awduche et al, 2011). The separation between the routing and signaling operations may lead to sub-optimal TE solutions generally inducing a waste of network resources. In optical networks, the impairment-aware spectrum assignment process, may introduce additional potential TE inefficiencies (e.g., worst case impairment assumptions). Moreover, distributed path computation may require heavy processing at each source (control plane) node, especially when based on multiple constraints. Moving from single-domain single-layer scenarios to multi-layer/technology, multi-vendor and inter-domain, additional issues arise, such as restricted topology visibility due to scalability reasons and/or administrative constraints among others. For example, when the source and destination of a traffic request belong to different administrative domains, the need to preserve operator- and policy-specific information confidentiality and integrity across domains prevents the open advertisement of detailed intra-domain network resources. Such limitations considerably complicate path computation and affect the inter-layer/inter-domain TE performance in terms of the overall network resource utilization.

The aforementioned path computation restrictions for provisioning end-to-end connections are at the basis of a significant research and engineering activity carried on in the last years and still active nowadays in the context of core network control plane developments.

The Internet Engineering Task Force (IETF) has proposed a set of techniques defined under the umbrella of the Path Computation Element (PCE) architecture (Farrel, Vasseur, & Ash, 2006). Such techniques rely on path computation, performed by dedicated network entities (i.e., the PCEs).

The PCE collects link-state information from network nodes and performs path computation on behalf of network nodes. In addition, it may resort to other information sources, such as the network management system (NMS), to retrieve detailed information about resource utilization or physical network parameters (e.g., link/span length and impairments in optical networks). The PCE provides the additional advantage that network nodes can avoid highly CPU-intensive multi-constraint path computations and effective TE solutions are achievable also in case of legacy network nodes. For example, NMS can be used as Path Computation Client (PCC) to communicate with PCE to get path information and then supply head-end node with full explicit path (e.g. using the management interface, like the TE management information base (MIB) module (Srinivasan, Viswanathan & Nadeau, 2004).

Communication between a PCC (i.e., a network element or an NMS willing to request a path), and the PCE is implemented using the Path Computation Element communication Protocol (PCEP, Vasseur & Le Roux, 2009). The PCE is responsible for the path computation in its own layer/domain, where it has full visibility and updated information on available network resources. Cooperation between PCEs takes place in multi-layer/domain scenarios by sharing the result of each (intra-domain) path computation expressed as, for example, border node(s) to traverse, intra-domain path segments, metric values. The combination of these results provides the entire source-destination path, and no additional information is exchanged among different domains. Specific techniques and procedures have been proposed and defined for each specific scenario.

This chapter discusses the main activity efforts in utilizing the PCE architecture in the context of single-domain, multi-layer and multi-domain networks, including a specific focus on optical networks. The role of PCE is analyzed and discussed for what concerns LSP provisioning and also reliability aspects.

In the following sections we first provide a general overview of the PCE architecture. The main PCEP messages, objects and operations are also detailed. Then, we analyze the PCE applicability in various network scenarios, starting from the simplest, the single domain single-layer network, and going through increasing complexity scenarios, such as multi-layer, multi-domain, and multi-domain multi-carrier scenarios. Both packet-switched and lambda/spectrum -switched networks have been considered for the PCE applicability. Furthermore the PCE architecture is considered in the context of Software Defined Networking (SDN). Finally, conclusions and future directions are highlighted and discussed.

PCE ARCHITECTURE

PCE is defined as a network functional element devoted to the TE-based path computation of LSPs (Farrel, Vasseur, & Ash, 2006). The PCE can be either a dedicated network device (e.g., a server) or a module located inside an existing network element (e.g., PCE-equipped controller, PCE-equipped node). The PCE has the responsibility of path computation on a specific and well-defined network domain (e.g., Autonomous System (AS), group of domains). The capabilities and efficiency of path computation is strictly related to the network resource information and to the path computation algorithms available at the PCE.

The PCE architecture is designed within a client-server framework, in which the PCE operates as a server and a Path Computation Client (PCC) operates as a client. The PCE service then comprises a PCE receiving path computation requests from a number of PCCs. Typically, depending on the considered scenario, the PCC is either a network node, an NMS, or another PCE. PCC and PCE interact by means of PCEP, which will be hereafter detailed.

The general internal architecture of the PCE is depicted in Figure 1 and includes:

- the Traffic Engineering Database (TED), storing the topology of the controlled network and TE information (e.g., per-link available bandwidth).
- the path computation module, actually performing path computation based on selected algorithms and procedures.
- the communication module, mainly collecting path computation requests and providing path computation replies to clients, as well as mechanisms to update the TED.

Figure 1. PCE general internal architecture

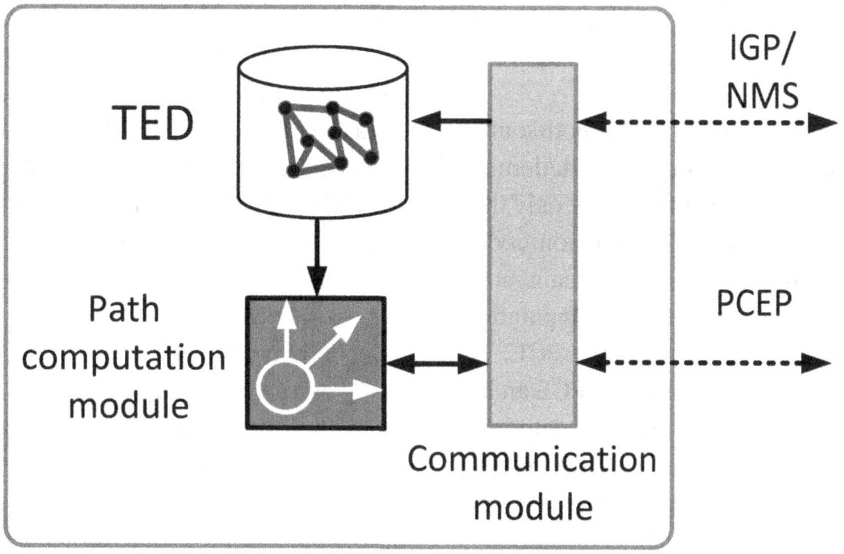

The TED is continuously populated by means of different possible procedures. The most considered update procedures rely on:

1. Peering instance (possibly in passive mode) with the Interior Gateway routing Protocol (e.g., OSPF-TE or IS-IS TE) running in the controlled network.
2. Updates provided by the NMS (e.g. relying on TE MIBs sent through SNMP and translated into TED info or adopting vendor-specific proprietary solutions).

Alternative or mixed procedures have been proposed in the literature addressing specific scenarios and will be described later.

The path computation module utilizes the TED information to perform path computation. A number of algorithms available in the literature (Garroppo et al, 2010) have been proposed and applied, having the TED information as input. The most important considered algorithms belong to the Djikstra shortest-path and constraint-shortest-path algorithm family, to the Suurballe-Tarjan disjoint path algorithm family, Steiner Tree for point-to-multipoint (Paolucci et al, 2013).

The communication module provides an interface used to handle messages between the PCE and the connected PCCs, through a number of PCEP sessions. It also includes, in an independent fashion, the communication channel used to update the TED.

A path computation request having both source and destination nodes in one area/network/domain controlled by a PCE will be handled by only that PCE. However, if source and destination nodes belong to two different areas/layers/domains controlled by different PCEs, the path computation process cannot be handled by a single PCE. To solve this issue, as described later, the PCE architecture comprises multi-PCE path computation.

With a single PCE, path computation is performed in a single step providing the end-to-end path route. With multiple PCEs, the computation is performed in multiple steps. In the latter case, different procedures can be adopted: independent path segment computation, or inter-PCE computation.

In the independent path segment computation (Vasseur, Ayyangar, & Zhang, 2008), the path is computed on per-domain basis. For each direction, the entry boundary node of each domain relies on the PCE to compute a segment towards the next area/layer/domain, then the entry boundary node reserves resources up to the exit boundary node of the same domain. The procedure is then iterated up to the destination in the destination domain. In this case path computation and resource reservation steps are inter-laced. In the inter-PCE computation (King, & Farrel, 2012, Vasseur, et al, 2009), the entire end-to-end path route is computed by means of cooperation among multiple PCEs. Such cooperation may be implemented through either a peer or a hierarchical procedure. Both procedures will be described in the multi-domain/layer section.

The PCE can be classified in terms of the amount of network information and on the kind of operation that it can trigger. Basically, the general PCE architecture includes the sole TED as the network information source, detailing a per-link resource reservation, with no association with the LSP that has reserved such resources. Whereas, the state of the LSP (i.e., the resources occupied by a specific LSP) is typically maintained at the LSP source node, which is the owner of the LSP. The PCE that meets these conditions is referred to as the generic stateless PCE. However, the PCE can be fed with additional information enabling proactive procedures in the network. The PCE can then be classified as follows:

- Stateless,
- Passive Stateful,
- Active Stateful, or
- Active Stateful with instantiation capabilities.

The stateless PCE is not aware of the LSPs operating in the network.

The stateful PCE (Crabbe et al, 2014), besides the TED, is aware of the LSPs operating in the network. For this purpose, the PCE internal architecture is enriched with an additional database: the LSP database (LSP-DB), as shown in Fig. 2. The LSP-DB stores the list of the LSPs and their attributes (i.e., including the route and the reserved resources). With such additional information, the PCE is able to perform a wider range of planning and optimization path computation procedures with greater efficiency. For example, stateful capabilities enable efficient shared path protection computation. The LSP-DB is populated and maintained by the PCEP. The maintenance is assured by the PCC-PCE synchronization, which imposes the exchange of LSP status updates. Three operation modes are defined for a stateful PCE: passive, active, and active with instantiation.

A passive stateful PCE receives path computation requests for new LSPs or update/re-optimization requests for existing LSPs. In this case the PCC is not forced to include information on the current routes of the LSP, since such information is already available at the PCE.

An Active stateful PCE, besides synchronization, enables LSP delegation functions. In this case, LSP ownership is delegated by the PCC to the PCE. In this way, the PCE has the capability to directly update the attributes of an existing LSP. Delegation can be temporary or assumed as permanent (subject to possible revocation).

Active stateful PCE with instantiation capabilities has the additional capability to drive the initiation and the removal of an LSP.

The PCE architecture requires that each PCC should be aware of the presence and the location of a PCE in the controlled domain and the definition of its path computation domain and capabilities. In addition to static configurations on the PCC, DNS-based discovery has been proposed. PCE discovery mechanisms have been standardized in (Le Roux, 2006) and extensions to IGP protocols (e.g., OSPF and IS-IS) allow the flooding of PCE information and location. They implement auto-

Figure 2. Stateful PCE

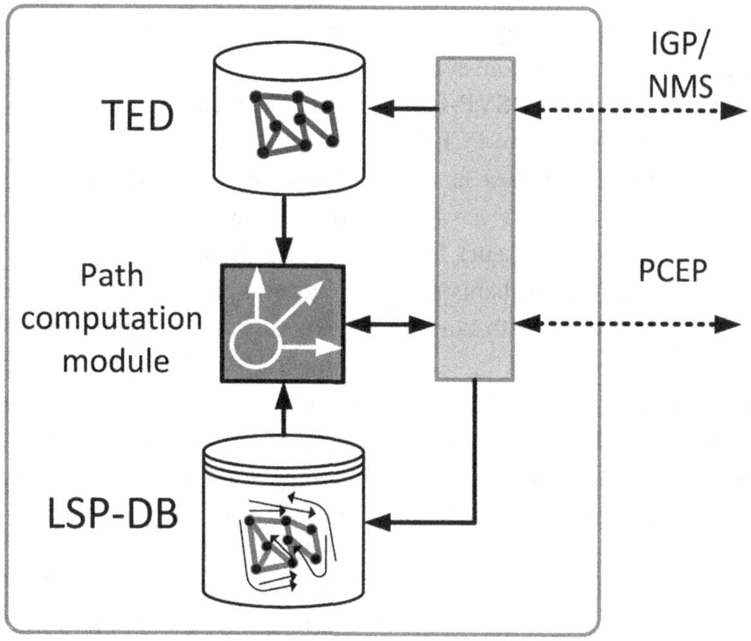

matic and dynamic detection of PCEs along with additional information about supported capabilities and target area/domain, in order to perform the most suitable PCE selection for a given path computation request. In the case of PCE failure, discovery mechanisms have also the scope of advertising alternate PCE (i.e., backup PCE).

Additional functionalities have been specified to enable effective, secure and monitored path computation service:

- *Policy-enabled path computation.* (Bryskin et al, 2008) describes the impact of policy-based decision making when incorporated into the PCE architecture and provides additional details on applying policy within the PCE architecture.
- *Diffserv-aware TE path computation extensions.* (Sivalaban et al, 2009) defines a new PCEP object which carries the Class-Type of the LSP in the path computation request. During path computation, a PCE uses the Class-Type to identify the bandwidth constraint of the LSP.
- *Confidentiality*: (Bradford et al, 2009) defines a mechanism to hide the contents of a segment of a path, called the Confidential Path Segment (CPS). The CPS may be replaced by a path-key that can be conveyed in the PCEP and signaled within RSVP-TE explicit route object (ERO). Secure PCEP communication is defined in Lopez et al (2014).
- *PCE monitoring functions.* (Vasseur, Le Roux, & Ikejiri, 2010) defines mechanisms to check aliveness, congestion, path computation execution time, etc.
- *Vendor-specific constraints and attributes* (Zhang & Farrel, 2014) defines "vendor-specific" attributes that can be used to carry arbitrary, proprietary information (e.g., objective functions operating on non-standard constraints or metrics)
- *Point-to-Mulitpoint (P2MP)* (Zhao Q. et al, 2010) extends PCEP messages enabling full support of P2MP LSP, including multiple destination endpoints, secondary ERO and destination unreach information
- *Objective functions* (Le Roux, Vasseur & Lee, 2009) defining PCEP encoding of standard optimization criteria for path computation (e.g., request of path computation minimizing aggregate bandwidth consumption)

PCE COMMUNICATION PROTOCOL

PCEP is a client-server protocol running on TCP (IANA port 4189) between PCC and PCE. Messages are defined to initiate, maintain and terminate a PCEP session. PCC and PCE first open a PCEP session. The PCEP session establishment includes the exchange of Open and Keepalive messages in order to be aware of the PCE path computation capabilities and agree on session parameters, such as timers for session refresh messages. The core of the protocol interaction is realized through the exchange of two messages: the Path Computation Request (PCReq) message and the Path Computation Reply (PCRep) message. Additional messages are also defined to handle specific events and communication errors (e.g., Error (PCErr) and Notification (PCNtf) messages). The PCEP session terminates upon the reception of a Close message.

The PCReq message is sent by the PCC to request a path computation. The mandatory objects of the message are the Request Parameter object (RP), identifying the request, and the END-POINTS (source and destination of the requested LSP). Optional objects are used to indicate path computation constraints, such as the METRIC, the BANDWIDTH, the exclusion/inclusion of nodes in the path (XRO, IRO), the objective function to utilize (OF), the LSP attributes, such as priority and fast-reroute options (LSPA).

The PCRep message is sent by the PCE once path computation is completed. The result of path computation may be positive (i.e., a path satisfying the requested constraints have been found) or negative (i.e., there are no paths satisfying the constraints). In the former case, the PCRep mandatorily includes the RP object with the same identifier (ID) of the request (so that the PCC can match request to corresponding reply) and the Explicit Route Object (ERO). The ERO encodes the computed path in terms of list of nodes/links/domains (e.g., IPv4/IPv6 addresses, unnumbered interfaces, AS numbers), depending on the considered scenario, the switching capabilities of the nodes and on PCE internal policies. The ERO may be strict (i.e., specifies the sequence of all the nodes of the path) or loose (i.e., indicates only a sequence of some nodes or abstract nodes of the path). Additional objects are used to indicate the path METRIC, if requested. In the latter case of negative reply, the PCRep includes the RP and the NO-PATH object, detailing the reasons of the path computation failure. Additional objects can be included to identify the constraint that caused the failure (e.g., the BANDWIDTH object is included if bandwidth was the bottleneck), thus suggesting the PCC to relax that specific constraint.

The PCEP allows the handling of complex path computation procedures, such as multiple path computation, point to multi-point LSP and re-optimization.

Multiple path computation is performed when a number of LSPs have to be provisioned and some of them are required to have mutual dependency. Typical cases are represented by the deployment of a service comprising LSPs (e.g., a full mesh VPN) and LSPs with protection. In a single PCReq, a number of LSP requests, each identified by a single RP object, can be bundled, however each request will be computed independently. To enable combined and synchronized path computation, the Synchronized Vector (SVEC) object is utilized, detailing the list of involved requests and the relationship among them. For example, node/link/SRLG (Shared Risk Ling Group) disjoint path computation are requested by means of specific flags within the SVEC. Even without specific disjoint path constraints, the SVEC can be followed by the OF object, thus indicating a multiple joint path computation with a global objective function to be achieved.

Multicast path computation request/reply is enabled by PCEP through the extension of the END-POINTS object (including more than one destination) in PCReq and the introduction of UNREACH and Secondary Sub-ERO (SERO) objects in the PCRep. The reply specifies the path expressed as a tree with a ERO and a number of SEROs departing from one element of the ERO or another SERO. The UNREACH object specifies which destinations are not reached with path computation (Zhao Q. et al, 2010).

Re-optimization of existing LSPs can be achieved by specifying in the PCReq, besides the aforementioned constraints, the path currently associated to each LSP. Record Route Object (RRO) associated to each LSP is then submitted for re-optimization. Moreover, if global joint re-optimization is required, a Global Concurrent Optimization (GCO) object is used to indicate the type of requested optimization and to specify whether an ordered list of replies should be provided (e.g., to minimize service disruption) (Lee et al, 2009).

The stateful PCE (Crabbe, Minei, Medved &Varga, 2014) introduces novel functionalities, such as the proactive update of LSP attributes and the direct initiation/removal of LSPs. The stateful PCE introduces the LSP object, univocally identifying an LSP established in the network. Each request associated with such LSP includes the LSP object. Passive stateful PCE is then able to run re-optimization without the need of RRO information. The functions related to the stateful capabilities are the following:

- LSP state synchronization (active or passive): the stateful PCE receives by the PCC the state of an established LSP (i.e., typically, the LSP source node) and stores it in the LSP-DB.
- LSP update request (active): active stateful PCE requires the modification of some attributes of a selected LSP to the related PCC (i.e., the source node).
- LSP state report (active or passive): The PCC provides the stateful PCE with the outcome of the update request and the actual updated attributes of an LSP, after LSP modifications.
- LSP control delegation (active): The PCC grants to the stateful PCE the right to update LSP attributes on one or more LSPs. The PCE becomes the right owner of those LSPs. The PCC may withdraw the delegation. The PCE may release the delegation.
- LSP instantiation (active with instantiation): The PCE is able to trigger the establishment of a new LSP and the removal of an existing LSP.

Synchronization is realized through the exchange of a PCEP Report (PCRpt) message, including the LSP object and the attributes of such LSP (i.e., ERO, BANDWIDTH). Update requests are done by means of PCEP Update messages (PCUpd), including the Stateful Request Parameter (SRP) object to identify the update request, the LSP Object and the modified ERO and/or attributes. For each PCUpd, a set of state report messages (PCRpt) with the same SRP are sent by the PCC to acknowledge the outcome and/or the current steps of modifications (e.g., LSP active, LSP up, LSP down). Control delegation is realized with PCRpt messages. Instantiation is realized by means of PCEP Initiation message (PCInitiate), which specifies all the attributes of the path to be instantiated (including the ERO). The PCInitiate can also be used to suggest the removal of an existing LSP.

PCE APPLICATION

The PCE architecture has been designed to address several networking scenarios and use cases.

A basic use case consists in single domain owned and maintained by a single administrative entity, e.g., a network operator. Single layer networks are based on a unique switching capability. The consequence of the aforementioned two assumptions is that the routing protocol can exchange the whole network topology without any restriction or summarization (e.g., within OSPF-TE areas). In this context, the adoption of a PCE could provide several benefits. For example, based on the desired QoS level offered to customers, the network operator may choose to adopt complex path computation algorithms in order to satisfy multi-constraint Service Level Agreement (SLA) profiles (Boucadair, Jacquenet & Wang, 2014), or a set of synchronized paths that are part of the same service instance (also referred to as path computation bundling), or perform a global re-optimization of a set of provisioned paths.

The PCE can operate on a full topology with a desired level of granularity. Additional information may be taken into account to improve the path computation, depending on the data-plane technology. For example, in optical networks, the set of information typical of the management plane (i.e., signal quality measurements, alarms) can be used by the PCE.

Provisioning and Re-Optimization

Path computation in meshed networks requires a careful treatment depending on the kind of services utilized by connections. For some services (e.g., virtual private networks (VPNs) serving multiple sites), a single VPN instance may require the setup of multiple LSPs (e.g., a full mesh). Nonetheless, QoS-guaranteed services may require protection mechanisms, made available by two (or more) dependent LSPs with specific constraints (e.g., link and node disjoint). To all these extents, the

PCE architecture and PCEP allow the bundling of multiple requests onto either a single synchronized vector (SVEC) object, in which many LSPs are required to be setup are subject to a single global optimization parameter (e.g., minimize the maximum link load) or a synchronized dependent path computation requests (e.g., disjointness for primary and backup paths).

The bundling selection may occur either at the network management system or at the PCE, as shown in Fig. 3. In the former case (Fig. 3a), the NMS is responsible for service provisioning and submits synchronized requests to the PCE. In the latter case, the PCE receives generic requests and is responsible for (optional) service differentiation and bundling operation. In Fig. 3b, a PCE architecture comprising service differentiation and bundling is shown. A number of parameters such as request inter-arrival time, time spent in the request queue, number of pending requests are considered in the bundling selection algorithm. Typically, bundling selection should achieve a reasonable trade-off between efficient TE performance and setup delay.

For example, the work in Ahmed et al (2012) evaluates bundling effects in optical network scenarios with service differentiation. The PCE is equipped with a counter of path computation requests, triggering concurrent path computation upon overcoming a given threshold. Results show that the blocking probability, defined as the probability that an LSP demand is refused due to unavailable resources, decreases linearly as the counter threshold increases, while the LSP setup time, defined as the time required to perform both path computation and resource reservation, increases exponentially.

Bulk path computations are also required in the case of network re-optimizations (Lee, Le Roux, King & Oki, 2009)(Dhody & Wu, 2014) (Gifre et al., 2014).

In the case of a stateless PCE, the re-optimization of network resource usage can be performed only upon request from a PCC. In particular, a PCC has to send a request to the PCE together with detailed route and bandwidth information of the LSPs that are requested to be concurrently optimized. This represents an inefficient and time-consuming procedure. Moreover, and most importantly, the PCC has to be able to determine when and which LSPs should be optimized. However, this capability is typically not available at PCCs, making this procedure extremely inefficient.

On the other hand, the capability provided by the stateful architecture to exploit both unreserved traffic engineering resources (maintained at the PCE TED) and LSP routes (maintained at the PCE LSP-DB) enables the PCE to evaluate the fragmentation level of the controlled optical infrastructure.

Specifically designed algorithms (Wang & Mukherjee, 2013) can be applied to assess potential benefits provided by network re-optimization procedures. These evaluations can be performed upon network events potentially inducing network fragmentation, such as tear-down of one/many LSPs, LSPs re-routing upon failure occurrence, after failure repair operation. In addition, the potential benefits of network re-optimization (i.e., de-fragmentation) could be evaluated also asynchronously, i.e., periodically or during off-peak traffic conditions.

Then, when the active functionality is introduced, the PCE is also able to directly trigger network optimization. Indeed, if the potential benefits highlighted by the evaluation phase are considered adequate, the active PCE can operate on selected or all LSPs, by providing the new LSP attributes through PCEP PCUpd messages. Moreover, the PCE can consider specific sequences of operations, thus limiting or avoiding dead-lock conditions and traffic disruption.

Network Recovery

The (G)MPLS control plane is also responsible for network reliability. Indeed, since each network link can be traversed by a huge amount of data,

Figure 3. Bundling of (bulk) path computation: (a) NMS-driven; (b) PCE-driven

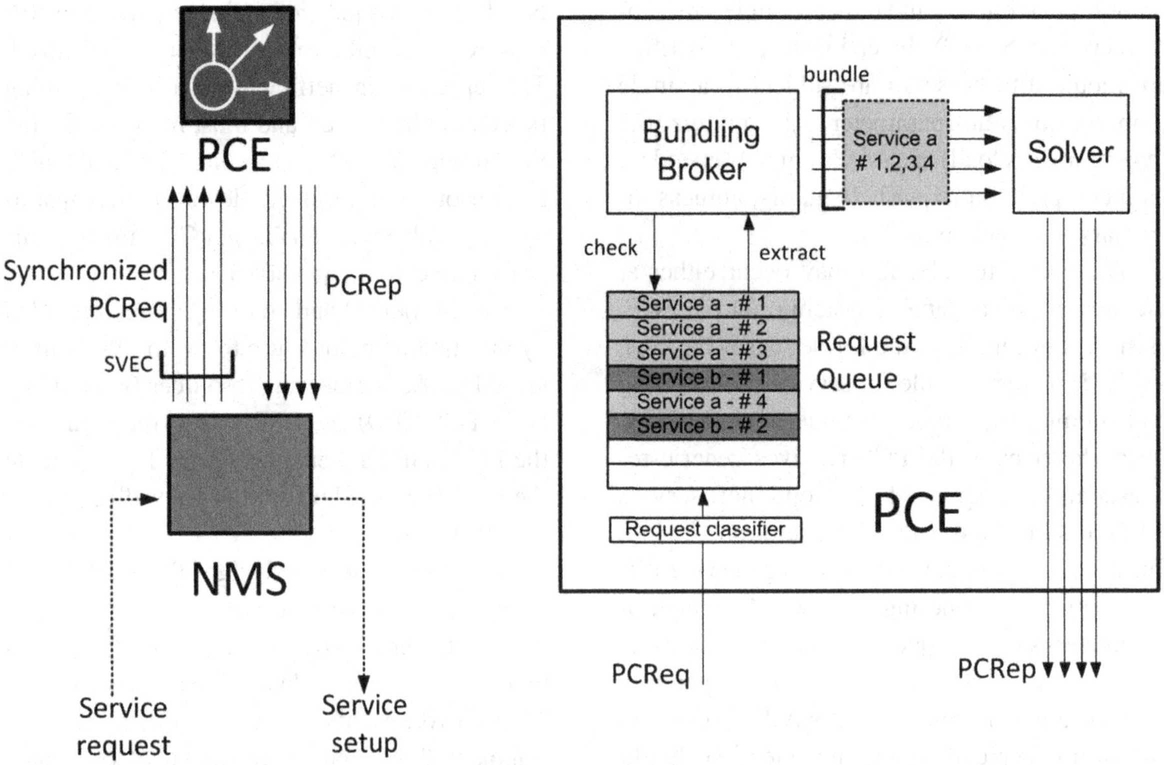

a single failure (e.g., link failure) can generate a significant service degradation. Two different types of reliability mechanisms have been mainly proposed in literature: protection and restoration mechanisms. In the former type, backup bandwidth is reserved upon connection establishment. In the latter type, backup bandwidth is reserved only upon failure occurrence.

Most research work on protection mechanisms aims at reducing the amount of reserved backup bandwidth (Andriolli, Giorgetti, Valcarenchi & Castoldi, 2007) (Tornatore et al., 2009). In particular, shared path protection, based upon the introduction of backup bandwidth sharing among LSPs that cannot be disrupted by the same failure, emerged as a very attractive protection mechanism. Although several distributed implementations of shared path protection have been proposed, it is clear that a centralized view as provided by a stateful PCE storing the working and backup paths of all established LSPs can help in achieving higher sharing ratios and improve resource utilization.

Research work on restoration mechanisms mainly considered two performance parameters: recovery blocking probability and recovery time (Giorgetti, Valcarenghi, Cugini & Castoldi, 2010) (Munoz, Casellas & Martinez, 2010). Indeed, if restoration is used, a burst of messages is typically generated on the control plane upon failure occurrence because all the disrupted connections try to be restored as fast as possible. Recovery blocking probability is therefore degraded because a number of recovery attempts may be blocked due to resource contention. Therefore, a centralized PCE can be effectively used for coordinating the recovery attempts (through bulk computations) achieving a significant reduction of blocking due to resource contention. On the other hand, the PCE utilization implies additional PCEP communications and possibly longer computation times, significantly degrading the recovery times. This trade-off has to be carefully considered when proposing the utilization of PCE for restoration.

In the case the PCE is requested to provide alternative routes to recover network failures, different procedures can be applied according to the considered PCE architecture. The procedures, shown from the PCE perspective in Fig. 4, are applied in a network scenario including three different ingress nodes operating as PCCs and controlling failed LSPs.

In the first case, shown in Fig. 4a, a stateless PCE is considered. Upon failure occurrence, the nodes detecting the failure generate routing protocol updates to advertise all network nodes about the failed resources (e.g., a link). The PCE, by listening to routing protocol advertisements, can become aware of the failed resources. Moreover, each upstream node detecting the failure sends a GMPLS Error message to notify the ingress node about the LSP failure. Each ingress node, operating as PCC, immediately triggers a PCReq to the PCE. Thus, the stateless PCE receives multiple independent requests for path computations. Once each path computation is completed, the PCE sends PCRep messages to every PCC. This concludes the recovery process from the perspective of the PCE architecture (then ingress nodes will perform the signaling over the newly computed paths, if successfully identified).

In the second case, shown in Fig. 4b, a stateful PCE is considered. Different from the previous case of the stateless PCE architecture, once the PCE becomes aware of the failed resources, it is immediately able to identify the failed LSPs. Indeed, the routes of all established LSPs are stored within the LSP-DB available at the stateful PCE. Thus, the stateful PCE can immediately perform all needed path computations, without waiting for all PCReq messages. Once the PCReq messages are actually received from the involved ingress nodes, the stateful PCE can be ready to reply with PCRep messages. Thus, the overall recovery time can be reduced. Moreover, in this case, the path computation can be also performed in a joint (bulk) way, with relevant benefits in terms of path computation efficiency and probability to successfully identify alternative routes to failed LSPs.

In the third case, shown in Fig. 4c, an active stateful PCE is considered. As in the previous case, once the PCE becomes aware of the failed resources, it is immediately able to identify the failed LSPs and perform bulk path computation. However, different from the previous case of stateful PCE architecture, in the case of active stateful, the PCE is also subsequently able to provide the ingress nodes with alternative routes, without waiting for PCReq messages to be received. Thus, as soon as the bulk path computation is completed, PCUpd messages are immediately sent to the

Figure 4. Recovery procedure from PCE perspective in the case of: (a) Stateless PCE; (b) Stateful PCE; (c) Active Stateful PCE

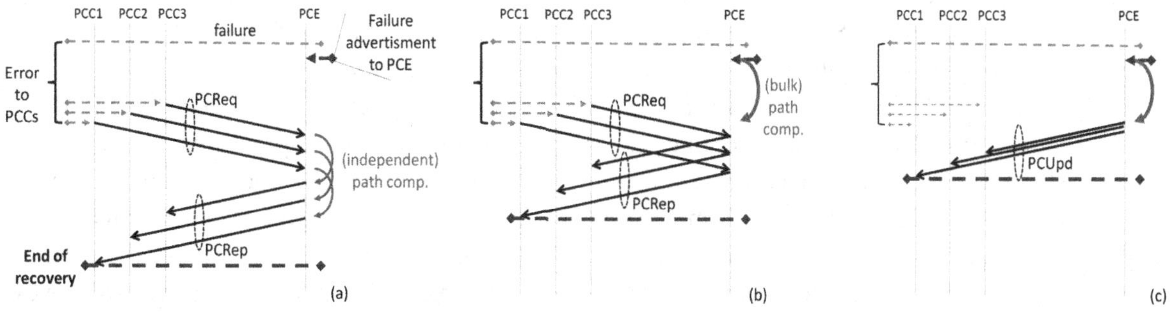

PCCs. Thus, the overall recovery time can be further reduced.

PCE IN OPTICAL NETWORKS

In optical networks, light paths are provisioned by solving the well-known routing and wavelength/ spectrum assignment (RWA/RSA) problem (Paolucci et al., 2011; Lee, Bernstein & Imajuku, 2011). Optimal joint solutions have been demonstrated to be NP-complete, so a large number of heuristics have been investigated and proposed. In the traditional source-based routing scheme, the source node is responsible for performing routing. Such selection is based on the topology and the TE information that are made available by distributed routing protocols (e.g., OSPF-TE). In the context of transparent wavelength switched optical network (WSON), the additional spectrum continuity constraint is considered to provision a single light path from source to destination.

Spectrum assignment is typically performed during signaling through a distributed scheme. The set of available spectrum resources is carried by the signaling protocol (i.e., by RSVP-TE Path message) up to the destination and skimmed at each node. The destination node then selects the frequency slot, based on given policies (e.g., first-fit, random-fit, best-fit). Spectrum reservation is then enforced backwards up to source (i.e., by RSVP-TE Resv messages).

Possible inefficiencies of the aforementioned scheme rely on functional, traffic engineering and temporal segregation between routing and spectrum assignment. Functional segregation prevents an accurate joint RSA leading to sub-optimal solutions. TE segregation derives from applying routing and spectrum assignment on different information databases (e.g., routing on global OSPF-TE TED, spectrum assignment on local RSVP-TE path state database). Temporal segregation occurs by performing routing and spectrum assignment at different times, thus incurring in temporally misaligned databases. In addition, spectrum assignment is spread in time and intrinsically subject to information de-synchronization (e.g., leading to collisions). All these aspects are further complicated by the need to account for physical impairments. A number of end-to-end physical parameters have to be considered to assess the expected Quality of Transmission (QoT). For example, signal attenuation, amplified spontaneous emission (ASE), polarization mode dispersion (PMD), chromatic dispersion, self-phase modulation (SPM), and cross-phase modulation (XPM) may need to be specifically considered. However, physical impairments are currently not even included within the standard distributed GMPLS protocol suite.

The PCE architecture has been proposed to address impairment-aware RSA (IA-RSA). Indeed, a centralized path computation may help to reduce, and even remove, the inefficiencies due to functional segregation and de-synchronization. Moreover, a centralized path computation may efficiently address the intrinsic IA-RSA complexity, including the computational effort to perform impairment estimation.

Several PCE-based architectures for IA-RSA have been proposed and successfully validated (e.g., Gonzales de Dios et al, 2014):

- *Combined IV and RSA Process (IV&RSA)*: the processes of impairment validation and RSA are aggregated into a single PCE. In this case the same PCE exploits routing and spectrum availability information as well as physical parameters. Thus, RSA may be jointly performed accounting for impairments (Fig. 5-a).
- *IV-Candidates + RSA Process (IV-candidate+RSA)*: the impairment validation and RSA processes are separated and performed by two different PCE entities. In this case, the IV PCE provides the RSA PCE with a set of validated candidate routes, i.e., each route and each frequency

slot along these routes with guaranteed QoT. Thus, the IV PCE, exploits physical parameter information besides routing information. Then, the RSA PCE performs RSA on the set of validated candidate routes without accounting for physical parameters and QoT (Fig. 5-b).

- *Routing + Distributed Spectrum Assignment and IV*: a PCE, unaware of spectrum resource availability information and physical parameters, is assumed. Spectrum assignment and impairment validation are performed in a distributed way by exploiting either signaling or routing protocol extensions (Fig. 5-c).

In the case of distributed IV, all network nodes are required to store network physical parameters. Instead, when centralized IV is considered, only the PCE has to store and maintain physical parameter information. Thus, IV&RSA and IV-candidate+RSA relax the amount of information stored in the nodes. Moreover, in these centralized cases, network resources are typically better utilized. On the other hand, the network is not able to fully operate autonomously (e.g., in the case of a PCE failure).

Other alternatives to the aforementioned three PCE architectures for IA-RSA have been also presented and discussed in the literature. For example, (Zhao Y. et al, 2012) describes and evaluates eight different approaches just focusing on RWA with no IV: A double cooperating PCE architecture is presented and demonstrated. Similarly to IV-candidate+RSA, it is composed of two PCEs, but differently from IV-candidate+RSA, a candidate or a set of candidates are computed by the PCE RSA without accounting for physical parameters. Then, the candidates are passed to the IV PCE for impairment validation which sends back the validated candidates to the RSA PCE. However, this architecture may suffer from increased delay with respect to IV-candidate+RSA if no candidate presents an acceptable QoT and the RSA PCE has to compute other candidates.

An experimental comparison among several PCE architectures for IA-RSA has been reported in (Paolucci et al, 2011). In this study, two cases are first identified. When simplified QoT models are adopted by the PCE, the IV-candidate+RSA architecture typically experiences a larger delay than IV&RSA because of the communication between IV PCE and RSA PCE. However, when more complex and accurate QoT models and algorithms are adopted, IV&RSA may experience a larger delay to compute RSA than IV-candidate+RSA. However, in this case, the larger complexity of IV&RSA may be justified due to better traffic engineering performance (e.g., in terms of lower achieved light path blocking probability). Indeed, with IV-candidate+RSA, the IV PCE has to provide the RSA PCE with candidate routes which satisfy QoT for any central frequency. For scalability reasons, this is typically done by treating non-linear impairments according to a worst-case scenario (e.g., assuming maximum induced cross-phase modulation). However, this worst-case approach of the IV-candidate+RSA may estimate some source-destination pairs as unreachable, thus causing lightpath blocking even if the worst-case scenario does not actually occur. Conversely, IV&RWA is able to perform a more accurate impairment validation, also specifically accounting for non-linear impairments (e.g., estimating the actual cross-phase modulation), thereby overcoming these blocking problems. Generally, if wavelength-dependent impairments (e.g., cross-phase modulation) are particularly relevant in a network scenario (such as multi-rate networks) IV&RSA typically presents better performance than IV-candidate+RSA in terms of blocking probability, but it requires a larger delay for path computation. Finally, IV-candidate+RSA may even achieve lower path computation delays if the set of candidate routes are pre-computed by the IV PCE and stored by the RSA PCE. Thus, the communication between the two PCEs oc-

Figure 5. Impairment-aware RSA architectures in optical networks

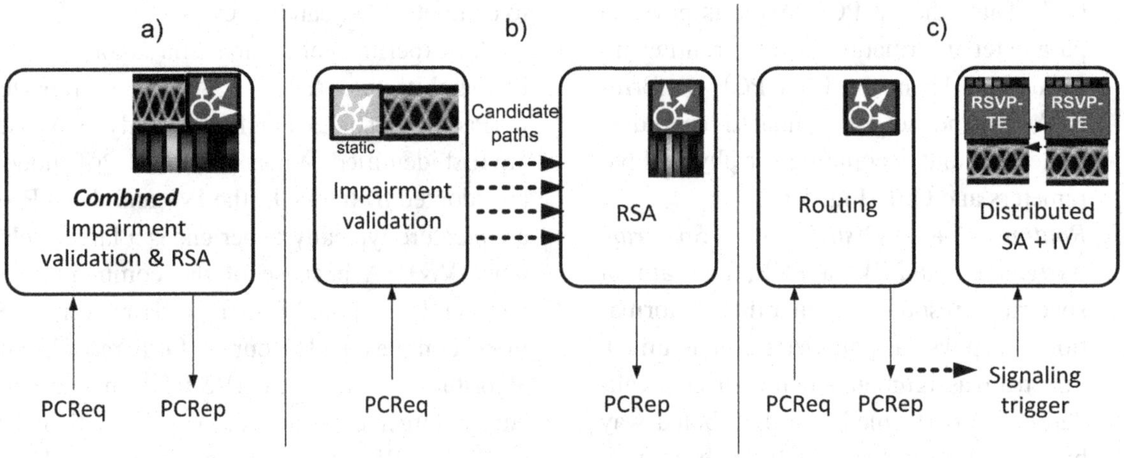

curs off-line and, upon computation request, the RSA PCE may promptly exploit candidate route information.

The aforementioned considerations and scalability issues are further complicated in the case of network nodes supporting bandwidth-variable transponders, i.e., including the capability to adapt transmission parameters (e.g., modulation format and coding), according to the necessary optical reach. An important consideration lies on the fact that RSA is strictly related to the impairment validation and the modulation format selection. Indeed, given a bit-rate, the more efficient the modulation format in terms of occupied spectrum, the less robust the signal in terms of QoT (which in turns determines the overall optical reach). As an example, 16-quadrature amplitude modulation (16-QAM) halves the required spectrum occupancy with respect to quadrature phase shift keying (QPSK), but 16-QAM presents a limited optical reach with respect to QPSK.

To guarantee adequate QoT on a specific path, a proper modulation format has to be computed, determining a corresponding frequency slot width to be considered for spectrum assignment. Thus, differently to traditional optical networks where the modulation format is a constraint of the source node (the PCC), in flex-grid optical networks with bandwidth-variable transponders, the modulation format and other transmission parameters may be an output of the RSA (Cugini et al, 2012). Thus, the PCEP protocol should include modulation format information, not only in the PCReq message as in traditional optical networks, but also in the PCRep. Works (Cugini et al, 2012) and (Casellas et al., 2013a) report experimental results on the aforementioned proposed approach, evaluated in optical network testbeds employing coherent detection applied on single carrier and orthogonal frequency division multiplexing (OFDM) signals, respectively.

Different performance can also be experienced according to the stateless or stateful condition.

For example, in the case of stateless PCE controlling a multi-rate optical network (e.g., including 100Gb/s polarization-multiplexing QPSK (PM-QPSK) and 10Gb/s On-Off Keying (OOK)), as sketched in Fig. 6a, path computation is not aware about bit-rate and modulation format of existing light paths. Thus, the stateless PCE has to consider the worst case scenario and to always include guard bands (e.g., implicitly considered within the frequency slot of each computed light path), even if not necessary (e.g., when adjacent light paths have the same bitrate and format). This leads to a dramatic waste of spectrum resources.

In the case of stateful PCE, the LSP-DB can store and maintain the state of the transmission parameters of the existing light paths, including the modulation format. This enables the PCE to implement specifically designed IA-RSA, which can avoid worst case implementation with guard bands implicitly included (as in Fig. 6c) and place guard bands only if strictly necessary (as in Fig. Fig. 6b). Thus, a stateful PCE can provide effective spectrum utilization in the case of light path provisioning.

Moreover, thanks to the active functionality, the PCE can perform network re-optimization on reserved spectrum resources by operating on existing lightpaths, in such a way that the waste of spectrum resources dedicated to guard bands is minimized (e.g., by creating pools of contiguous light paths of the same type).

De-Fragmentation in Optical Networks

Finally, a thematic in flex-grid optical networks is the de-fragmentation problem. Especially in dynamic networks, after some light path release, the spectral efficiency is compromised due to the fragmentation of the available spectrum into small non-contiguous spectral bands, decreasing the probability of finding sufficient contiguous spectrum along the whole route for new lightpath requests. However, thanks to lightpath re-routing or spectrum re-assignment (Cugini et al., 2013), it is possible to reduce the fragmentation and to improve the spectral efficiency. Thus, several defragmentation (i.e., re-optimization) solutions have been recently proposed for flex-grid optical networks.

PCE IN MULTI-DOMAIN/ LAYER NETWORKS

In single area/layer/domain networks, the dissemination of TE information is always enforced. However, in multi-area/layer/domain networks, this is inhibited by the difficulty of having different switching capabilities, and to preserve control plane scalability as well as the confidentiality of domain-specific policy information, thus limiting the amount of information exchanged among area/layers/domains. As a consequence, the TED is restricted to a single area/layer/domain. Therefore, effective path computation of LSPs traversing several areas/domains/layers requires a coordination among the PCEs responsible for those areas/domains/layers. An additional issue is the selection of the areas/domain/layers sequence, in the case multiple sequences are available.

Multi-Domain Networks

In multi-domain networks, TE is inhibited by the difficulty of preserving scalability and the confidentiality of domain-specific policy information (in a multi-provider scenario) across domains. Mainly due to scalability problems, inter-domain routing protocols (e.g., Border Gateway Protocol, BGP) only exchange reachability information without detailing the network resource availability. The PCE architecture is able to extend the TE-based path computation in scenarios where resource information flooding is limited. In such scenario, it is assumed that a single PCE is responsible for path computation inside each domain, while the inter-domain path computation is achieved by means of a coordinated communication process among PCEs, using the procedures defined by PCEP.

The most considered inter-domain path computation procedures are the per-domain computation, the Backward Recursive PCE-based Computation (BRPC, Vasseur et al., 2009) and the Hierarchical PCE (H-PCE, King & Farrel, 2012) approach.

The per-domain computation is the simplest procedure, since it does not involve inter-PCE computation. The sequence of domains is assumed determined a-priori. For each domain, the PCE is queried for intra-domain path computation

Figure 6. Example of IA-RSA strategies: stateless RSA worst case (a), stateful RSA requiring guard bands (b), stateful RSA not requiring guard bands (c).

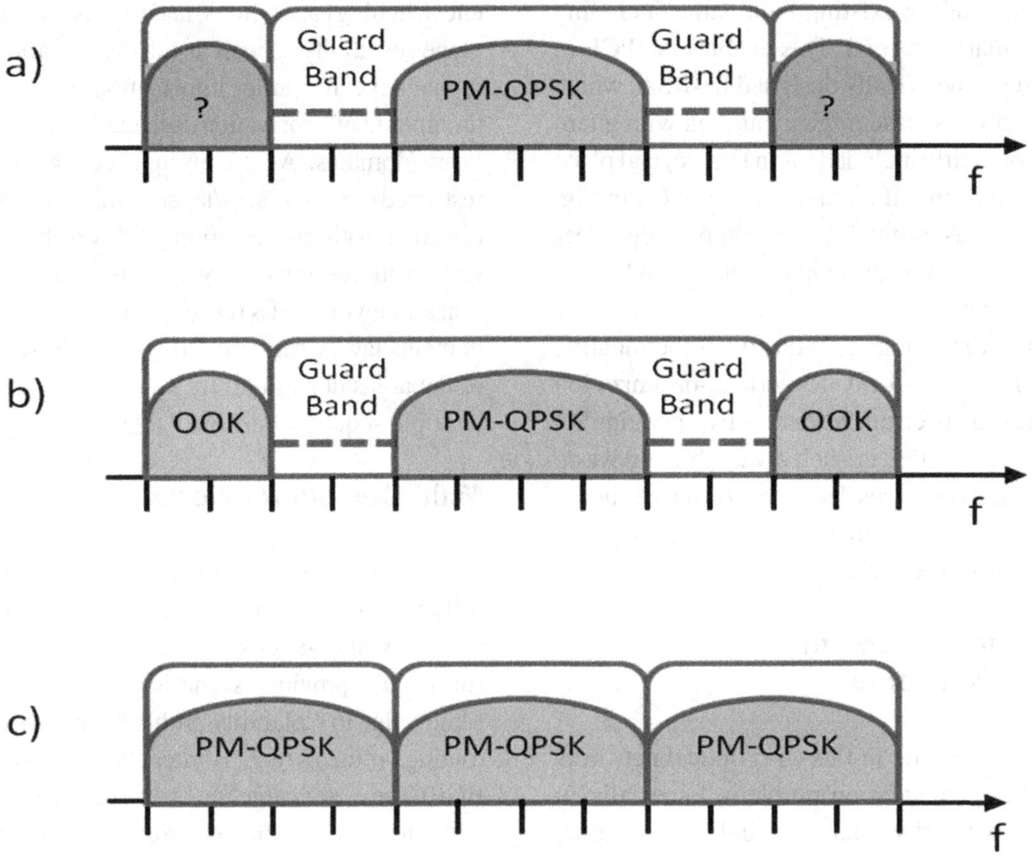

segment towards one of the border nodes (BN) connected to the next domain. Signaling procedures (e.g., RSVP-TE) are then triggered until the edge node is reached. The procedure is then iterated until the destination domain is reached. The end-to-end path is then the result of independent path computations inside each domain and, as a consequence, may not reflect the optimal path in terms of metrics.

In the inter-PCE path computation, coordination among PCEs of different domains is introduced. This strategy enables the end-to-end path computation of inter-domain LSPs, allowing the decoupling between path computation and resource reservation. Each PCE computation is performed based on the segment computation results provided by the contiguous PCE through PCEP.

Among the possible strategies enabling inter-PCE path computation, BRPC is primarily considered. BRPC (Vasseur et al, 2009) is an inter-PCE path computation procedure that computes an end-to-end constrained shortest path, in a reverse fashion, from the destination domain towards the source domain. The BRPC procedure assumes that the sequence of domains is known. According to the domain path, it is possible to define the entry (exit) border nodes (BN) as the set of BNs that are connected to the upstream (downstream) domain.

To compute the inter-domain path, it is assumed that a consistent metric is used in each domain. The BRPC mechanisms are shown in

Fig. 7. The PCC (i.e., node A) requests an inter-domain path computation to the source PCE (i.e., PCE1), by sending a PCReq message. The PCReq is forwarded to the PCEs along the domain path through the client-server chain with the BRPC flag set (in the PCReq RP object). The destination PCE (i.e., PCE3) computes a tree of potential paths, referred to as *virtual shortest path tree* (VSPT), from each entry BN in its domain to the destination node. VSPT paths are included in a strict or loose fashion (i.e., by indicating only the entry BNs) in the ERO object (i.e., branches T-V-Z and W-Y-Z).

The corresponding segment weights are included in the Metric object of PCRep messages. The PCRep message is then forwarded to the upstream PCE. In turn, each PCE computes the VSPT from its own entry BNs to the destination by stitching downstream PCE VSPT branches and forwards the PCRep message with updated information to the upstream PCE.

As an example, PCE2 computes I-J-K-T-V-Z and P-Q-R-S-O-W-Y-Z branches (note that it is not mandatory to stitch both branches provided by PCE3). Upon receipt of the PCRep message, the source PCE computes the end-to-end path using the VSPT and returns the result to the PCC. The A-Z path with the shortest accumulated metric is computed. This is due to the VSPT propagation mechanism, which allows the selection of BNs by the upstream PCE based on alternative cumulated metrics. The BRPC application achieves optimal path computation on the considered metric. The BRPC procedure avoids the sharing of domain-related information: only aggregate information about the possibility and the weight to reach the destination from a BN is flooded.

The H-PCE (King & Farrel, 2012) approach, a further case of inter-PCE communication, defines the procedures for combining end-to-end path computation with effective domain sequence computation. In the H-PCE, a single *parent PCE* (pPCE) is responsible for inter-domain path computation, while in each domain a local *child PCE* (cPCE) performs intra-domain path computation. The pPCE resorts to the Hierarchical TED (H-TED) that stores the list of the domains and inter-domain connectivity information (e.g., inter-domain links with wavelength availability information), to determine the sequence of domains.

Moreover, in order to perform more effective inter-domain path computation, the pPCE is allowed to ask cPCEs for the path computation of the several edge-to-edge segments of inter-domain LSPs. In Fig. 8, a path computation request from source node A to destination node Z is forwarded to the cPCE of domain 1. Since the destination node does not belong to domain 1, cPCE1 forwards the request to the pPCE. Then, pPCE resorts to the domain topology map in its H-TED and selects the involved domains to be crossed.

To retrieve the domain segments, the pPCE performs parallel path computation requests that are sent to the involved cPCEs. Such requests can be single or multiple requests, depending on the level of intra-domain information summarization (Paolucci et al., 2010) provided by H-TED. In the case of no summarization, the pPCE asks for each segment combination.

In the example of Fig. 7, pPCE asks cPCE2 for I-K, I-O, P-K, P-O segment computation. In the case intra-domain topology summarization is applied, each domain is described through a weighted abstract topology (e.g., one node, full-mesh of border nodes, star topology). In the example, if full-mesh summarization is utilized and shortest hop count is considered as the weight metric, the virtual intra-domain link I-K that has weight 3 is shortest among the others.

Hence, the pPCE will ask only the I-K detailed computation. Segment computations are returned to the pPCE, which combines the obtained results and computes the end-to-end path, returning the result to cPCE1. Procedures have been proposed to minimize the number of segment requests to the pPCE and to provide additional intra-domain information to the pPCE during the segment

Figure 7. Example of Backward Recursive PCE-based computation procedure.

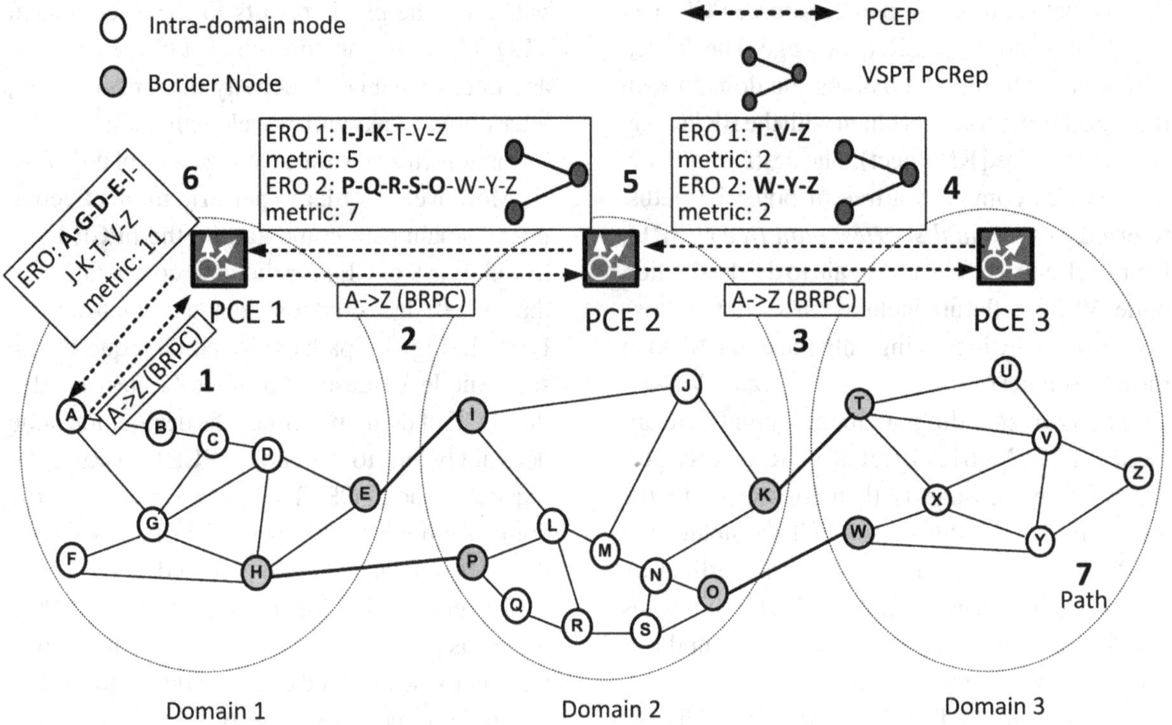

computation (Giorgetti et al 2011, 2012). Moreover, efficient H-TED population and update mechanisms have been investigated. One of the most attractive techniques that are currently being considered refers to the utilization of the BGP with Link State Extensions (BGP-LS) (Gredler et al., 2014).

The BGP protocol is enriched with Link State attributes and objects typical of IGPs (e.g., OSPF-TE, IS-IS-TE). A BGP speaker for each domain is responsible for exporting the topology and the intra-domain information (with the desired summarization level) to the BGP speaker located at the pPCE. The H-TED is then built upon information provided by the BGP speaker. Thus, Link State information is available at the pPCE with the desired level of accuracy and confidentiality, without incurring in scalability issues as in the case of a large single domain governed by IGP flooding procedures.

Multi-Domain Multi-Carrier Scenarios

The possibility offered by the PCE architecture to achieve effective TE solutions may be replicated in multi-provider scenarios, in which peering providers agree upon sharing network resources to provide QoS-based services and form a confederated TE-based multi-domain network and adopt service composition strategies to achieve end-to-end QoS. In such scenario, the most suitable architectures are those that enable peer relationships among PCEs, as, for example, BRPC. However, additional issues, typical of the inter-provider scenario, have to be carefully considered. In fact, enhanced interoperation raises a huge challenge for what concerns policies, security and confidentiality. Moreover, not only TE, but also economical and business reasons drive inter-carrier path computation strategies (Farrel et al., 2014).

Figure 8. Example of inter-domain path computation based on Hierarchical PCE.

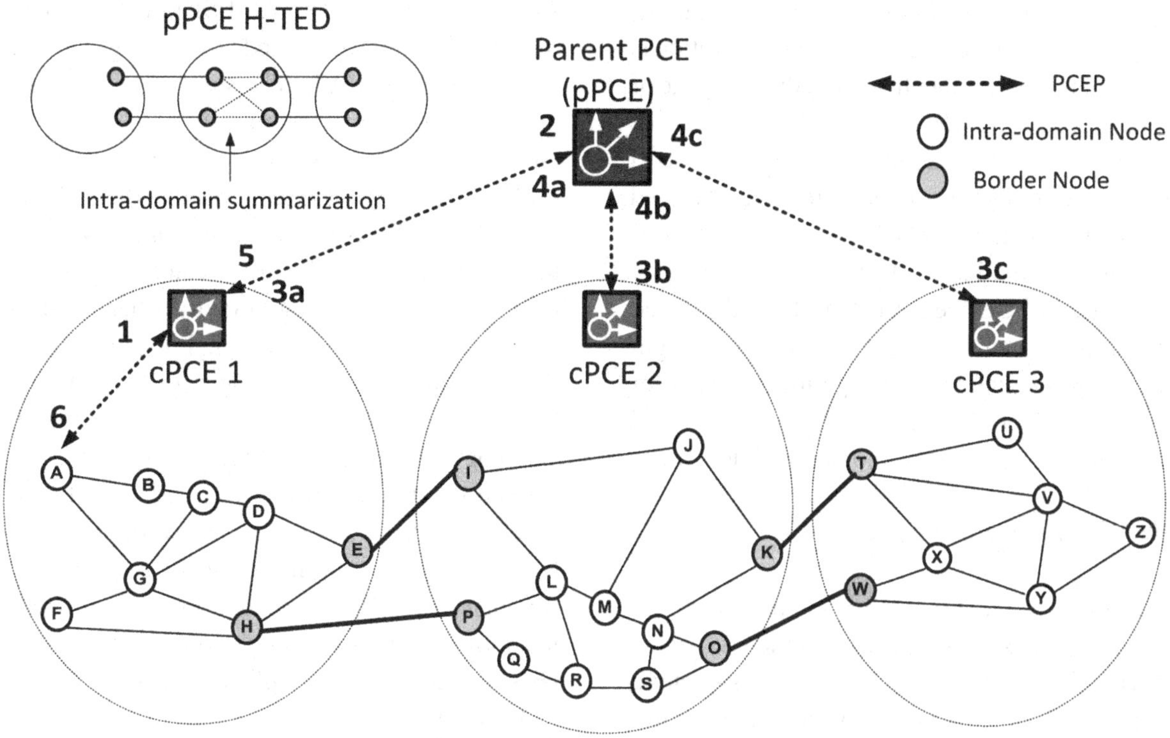

Inter-carrier TE has the potential to become one of the reference business models for the Internet. However, its deployment has encountered some reluctance so far, essentially due to economic and security issues. Models of business-driven PCE have been proposed, e.g. in (Djarallah, 2011), based on the introduction of business metrics, such as SLA matching and pricing, in order to select either the domain sequence or the BRPC end-to-end path. Additional business and QoS databases, populated by resorting to economical and SLA policies, are linked to the TED in order to select the next peer PCE of the BRPC chain.

Security and confidentiality should also be preserved. Breaking confidential information is a serious threat to the exchange of data between operators. It can be carried out in many ways, such as intrusion attempts during the data transfer, injection of modified control messages, spoofing, or more sophistically, cross-analysis of the information provided by a domain through the use of an authorized and authenticated protocol sessions. Typically, to limit the disclosure of confidential information, domains establish secure communications (e.g., Dierks, 2008) and enforce policies assuring and a given SLA including identification, authentication and authorization mechanisms.

Concerning PCEP, one adopted mechanism to preserve confidentiality discourages PCEs and PCCs to exchange strict explicit lists of traversed intra-domain hops, whereas paths are expressed in the form of an encrypted key (i.e., path key). However, this basic level of trust agreement may not guarantee the required level of confidentiality. Differently from connection requests triggered during signaling, PCEP-based computations do not imply the subsequent setup of the required connection, thus potentially enabling a malicious utilization of the PCE Architecture.

Security mechanisms have been proposed enabling authentication, authorization and accounting (AAA) functions by integrating path computation and reservation (Jacob & Davie, 2005 and Fang et al, 2005. In particular, the relationship between path computation and reservation is kept secured and authenticated by the exchange of verified path keys, realized with the utilization of secure tokens (Polito et al, 2011). Indeed, beyond AAA, smart mechanisms allowing an authorized and authenticated peer PCE to infer critical intra-domain information of adjacent domains through a set of licit PCEP requests have been discussed (Gharbaoui et al, 2013). This security leak might represent a valuable advantage for a competitor to gain market shares, leveraging on potential failures and weaknesses in other peer domains.

Multi-Layer Networks

A multi-layer network consists of transport nodes with interfaces operating at multiple data plane layers of either the same or different switching technology and controlled by a single control plane instance (Shiomoto et al, 2008). Each node interface switching technology is identified by a specific Interface Switching Capability (ISC). Examples of ISC are Packet Switching Capable (PSC) or Lambda Switching Capable (LSC).

An LSP starts and ends in the same layer (i.e., ISC), and may cross one or more lower layers. Once an LSP is established within a layer from one layer border node to another, it can be used as a data link in an upper layer. Furthermore, it can be advertised as a TE Link and exploited in the path computation of LSPs originated by different nodes. Such TE Link is referred to as Forwarding Adjacency LSP (FA-LSP).

A FA-LSP has the special characteristic that it does not require the set up of a routing adjacency (peering) between its end points. A Virtual TE Link (VL) is defined as a lower-layer LSP that is advertised to the upper layer as if it were fully established (i.e., as an FA-LSP), but differently from FA-LSPs, it is not established (i.e., it is just computed but it is neither signaled nor cross-connections are performed).

Figure 9. shows a an example of a packet switching capable (PSC) FA-LSP (and the related installed lower-layer lambda switching capable (LSC) LSP) and a VL. The support of VL does not require any routing extension. Thus, both VLs and FA-LSPs are advertised to the upper layer as TE links without distinguishing them. If an upper-layer LSP is set up by utilizing a VL, the underlying LSP must be immediately signaled in the lower layer. Signaling can start either dynamically (i.e., triggered by the signaling at the upper layer) or upon specific configuration performed by a management entity (e.g., Virtual Network Topology Manager – VNTM, Oki et al, 2009).

The latter solution is privileged by network operators since it allows the control of the lower layers, thus preventing an unconditional and frequent LSP set up or tear down (i.e., network instability). Some of the motivations that drive the possible set up of VLs in place of pre-established LSPs, are the following.

First the pre-provision of lower layer LSPs may be disadvantageous since it might reserve bandwidth that could be used for other LSPs in the absence of upper-layer traffic. In addition the utilization of VLs makes the lower layer data and control plane more stable, since it avoids to pre-provision LSPs that in the absence of upper-layer traffic could be torn down for re-optimization purposes. With VLs, the re-optimization implies just the path computation and it does not trigger any LSP set up or data plane modification. This is particularly important for example in the LSC data plane where node configuration (i.e., OXC cross-connections) may affect the optical quality of transmission of active LSPs, e.g., inducing cross-talk on adjacent channels or triggering complex optical power equalizations.

At the upper layer, the combination of the FA-LSPs and the VLs defines the Virtual Network Topology (VNT) provided by the lower layer. The VNT facilitates the path computation of LSPs in multi-layer networks since it describes the resources at a single layer (both actually avail-

Figure 9. Example of PCE application in multi-layer networks

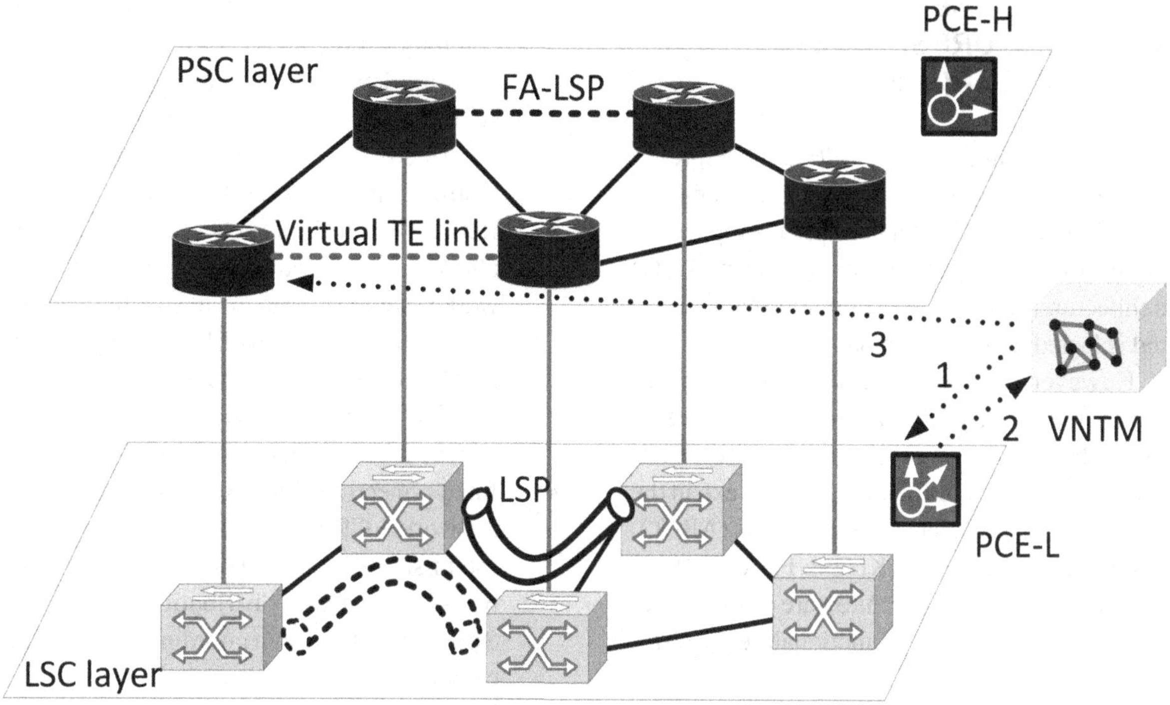

able through FA-LSPs and potentially available through VLs).

A PCE per layer can rapidly perform LSP path computations without considering the large TED including the detailed resources available in the whole multi-layer network, necessary in a single multilayer PCE. The VNTM is defined as the functional element that manages and controls the VNT (Oki et al, 2009), e.g., it configures the set up and tear down of VLs.

Thus, the cooperation between the VNTM and the PCEs allows the effective set up of LSPs. In particular, many use cases consider the presence of two PCEs: a layer-2 PCE (or, in general, PCE-H), co-located at the VNTM, and a layer-0 PCE (or, in general, PCE-L). The layer-2 PCE is responsible for path computation in the PSC layer and to trigger requests to the layer-0 PCE. At this regard, the use of stateful PCE extensions is currently under study.

In particular, the use of the PCInit message is particularly suitable, since the upper layer has the ability of directly driving the instantiation of a lower-layer LSP (see message 1 of Fig. 8). The detailed path computation can be handled by the L0-PCE (if available). Indeed, it can be achieved by sending a loose ERO with the only L0 LSP endpoints. Thus, the L0-PCE can compute the L0 LSP path and report its establishment by means of a PCRpt message (message 2 of Fig. 8). The same mechanism allows the coordinated tear down of L0 LSP by means of the VNTM. The VNTM- and PCE-based architectures also enable the practical utilization of the grooming and multi-layer provisioning strategies largely investigated in the last 15 years.

HOW PCE CAN FOSTER THE DEPLOYMENT OF SDN ARCHITECTURES: ASSETS AND CHALLENGES

The recent evolution of the PCE architecture, as discussed in the previous sections, has enabled the PCE to evolve from a pure path computation engine towards a more complex and powerful architecture, supporting instantiation capabilities and selected network automations.

However, to guarantee adequate network management and virtualization capabilities, a comprehensive network control requires additional components and modules. To this extent the Application-based Network Operations (ABNO) architecture is proposed (King & Farrel, 2014).

ABNO is a modular architecture primarily defined to provide advanced functionalities, such as:

- Network service virtualization and optimization of traffic flows between applications to create overlay networks, e.g., to support content delivery networks, video streaming and real-time communications. This is achieved through northbound interfaces, e.g., Application Programming Interfaces (APIs).
- Direct communication and programmability of network nodes through southbound interfaces, such as PCEP, Interface to the Routing System (I2RS) and the OpenFlow protocol.
- Network resource coordination to fully automate provisioning, facilitate grooming and de-grooming, Virtual Private Network (VPN) planning, bandwidth scheduling, network maintenance and global optimization.

ABNO can provide the following types of service to applications by coordinating the components that operate and manage the network:

- Optimization of traffic flows between applications to create an overlay network for communication in use cases such as file sharing, data caching or mirroring, media streaming, or real-time communications described as Application Layer Traffic Optimization (ALTO) [RFC5693].
- Remote control of network components allowing coordinated programming of network resources through such techniques as Forwarding and Control Element Separation (ForCES) [RFC3746], OpenFlow [ONF], and the Interface to the Routing System (I2RS) I-D.ietf-i2rs-architecture].
- Interconnection of Content Delivery Networks (CDNi) [RFC6707] through the establishment and resizing of connections between content distribution networks. Similarly, ABNO can coordinate inter-data center connections.
- Network resource coordination to automate provisioning, facilitate grooming and regrooming, bandwidth scheduling, and global concurrent optimization [RFC5557].
- Virtual Private Network (VPN) planning in support of deployment of new VPN customers and to facilitate inter-data center connectivity.

The main components of the ABNO architecture, as shown in Figure 10, include:

- PCE. In this scenario, it is considered as a pure path computation engine.
- TED and LSP-DB Databases. Additional databases may also be included, e.g., to store and maintain information useful for the application layer or about policies, predicted or scheduled traffic demands, links and node failure and repair history.
- Provisioning Manager. It enables the direct communication and programmability of network nodes. The following proto-

Figure 10. General ABNO architecture (King & Farrel, 2014)

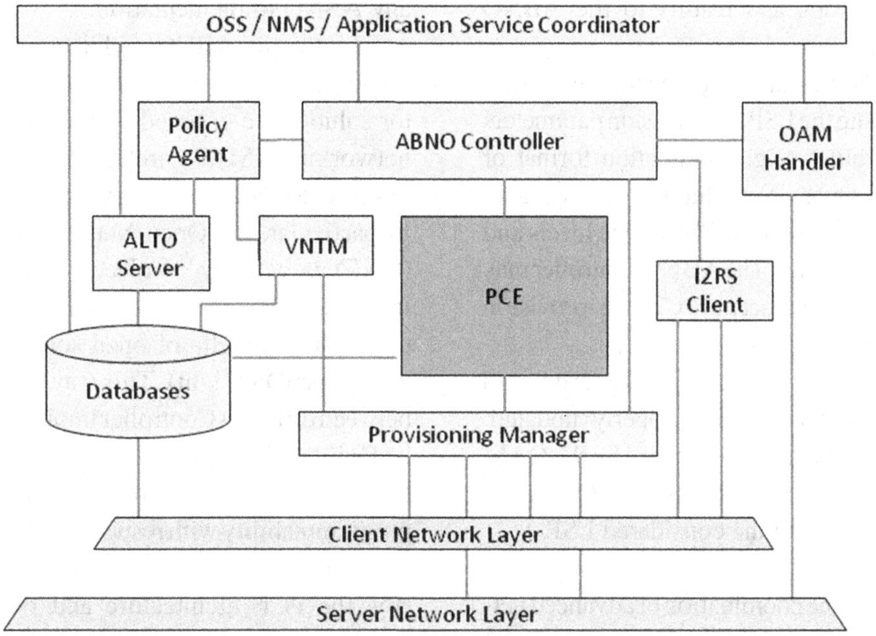

cols and solutions are typically supported: PCEP, I2RS and OpenFlow.

- Operation Administration and Maintenance (OAM) Handler. Collects network monitoring information and performs alarm correlation. The OAM Handler may also trigger other ABNO components to preserve or recover network services.
- Policy Agent. Configured by the NMS/OSS, it enables the overall control to account for policies.
- Virtual Network Topology Manager (VNTM). It handles the virtual topology in multi-layer networks, facilitating the automatic and coordinated creation/removal of LSPs at different network layers.
- ALTO (Application Layer Traffic Optimization) server. Provides an abstracted view of network information that is used by the application layer to select service resources aware of network utilization and performance.
- ABNO controller. It is in charge of the coordination of ABNO components in response to changing network conditions and in accordance with application network requirements and policies.

A stateless PCE within ABNO is achieved by relying on the TED database and the provisioning manager for PCEP. An (active) stateful PCE is implemented within ABNO by additionally considering the LSP database.

The intervention of the other ABNO modules is required to perform more complex networking operations (Gifre et al, 2014). For example, a possible use case involving the ABNO Controller, the OAM Handler and, possibly, the Policy manager is related to a transmission degradation (e.g., due to minor failures) that affects an LSP operated over an optical network:

1. The OAM Handler receives alarm notifications and performs proper correlation procedures.

2. The OAM Handler reports the relevant OAM considerations and results to the ABNO Controller.
3. The ABNO Controller triggers the PCE to re-compute the LSP transmission parameters and attributes (e.g., modulation format or even the route). Note that the Policy Agent may be involved to verify service levels and available policies. The ABNO controller may also directly instruct the PCE to re-provision the LSP.
4. Network operations are triggered and involved databases are properly updated. Specific tests may be triggered by the OAM Handler to check the status (e.g., Quality of Transmission) of the considered LSP.

In addition to the coordination of advanced networking and configuration functionalities, ABNO also tries to target the support of network function virtualization solutions. Indeed, in addition to a Network Management System (NMS), also more recent Operations Support System (OSS) architectures and Application Coordinators are considered on top of the ABNO architecture. However, so far, virtualization aspects in the context of ABNO have not been adequately investigated.

Moreover, among all ABNO components, only the PCE has reached an adequate level of stability and maturity, while the other components and interfaces have not been completely defined and assessed.

Furthermore, the ABNO architecture has been defined as a pure functional architecture, with no indications on implementation aspects. On the one hand, this approach enables implementations to choose which features to include and allows multiple functional components to be either grouped together into one software component or to be distributed across distinct processes or hardware components. On the other hand, this flexibility complicates the development of a clearly defined solution, significantly delaying any ABNO implementation.

Finally, the ABNO architecture may have to compete against different controller/orchestrator solutions, e.g. based on the software defined networking (SDN) architecture (see Chapter "Future SDN-based Network Architectures"). In particular, the Open Networking Foundation (ONF) is actively involved in the design and implementation of common SDN solutions, even under the umbrella of open source frameworks (e.g., OpenDayLight). This way, interoperability between different Controller implementations will be facilitated, providing potentially better access to network function virtualization and network programmability with respect to ABNO solutions.

Given the good level of stability and maturity, the PCE architecture and PCEP are also successfully included within the (current) SDN implementations (Casellas et al., 2013b). Indeed, this facilitates the adoption of SDN. For example, PCEP can be maintained for the southbound communication to edge nodes, thereby avoiding the extremely expensive and disruptive replacement of network nodes. Moreover, several extensions (e.g., for optical parameters, objective functions, etc.) are well defined within PCE/PCEP and there are relevant benefits to simply re-use these available mechanisms and functionalities.

However, this may change in the long term, given the general goal to avoid the support of many different protocols for network programmability. Indeed, too many other candidate protocols can be currently considered for the configuration of forwarding functions including, besides OpenFlow, the Network Configuration Protocol (NETCONF, Enns et al, 2011), COPS Usage for Policy Provisioning (COPS-PR, Chan et al, 2001), Routing Policy Specification Language (RPSL, Alaettinoglu, 1999), etc. (Boucadair & Jacquenet, 2014).

CONCLUSION, DEPLOYMENTS, AND FUTURE DIRECTIONS

This chapter presented the state-of-the-art and main activities carried out in the recent years in the context of the Path Computation Element (PCE) architecture, with specific focus on core networks running the (G)MPLS control plane. Both packet-switched (e.g., MPLS networks) and optical networks can take advantage of PCE, in terms of overall integrated control plane stability, resource utilization, TE solutions in multi-layer and multi-domain networks.

The following topics were covered by the chapter: the PCE architecture description and motivations, the PCE in single domain, multi-layer, multi-domain and multi-carrier networks, with specific focus on bundling and synchronization, provisioning and protection/restoration techniques, and optically impairment-aware computation also in the context of flexi-grid networks.

The PCE architecture has nowadays reached a good level of maturity and stability. So far, the PCE has been implemented within many network management systems. In most of the cases, particularly in the context of optical networks, its implementation is hidden within the overall network control system and not available as stand-alone interoperable network element. In these cases, the PCEP protocol is rarely supported and proprietary solutions or software APIs are typically used to access the path computation functionalities.

The complete PCE architecture including the PCEP protocol has been adopted by most router manufacturers. So far, the support of PCEP has been limited to top level routers, i.e., those designed for core networks and providing very high throughput (hundreds of Gigabit/s). In these cases, dedicated solutions for PCE implementations are available on the market (also called independent control plane solutions). These PCE platforms are typically implemented within a high-density rack-mounted solution including multiple routing engines and high-performing redundant servers.

The actual deployment of stand-alone PCE platforms by Network Operators is still quite limited. The main reason stands in the fact that equipment within a network domain are typically supplied by a single vendor, which also provides its vendor-specific control and management system, including a proprietary PCE module which often remains hidden within the overall system. Moreover, to provide adequate and comprehensive network control, the sole path computation functionality is not satisfactory, and stand-alone vendor-independent orchestration platforms are required.

For this reason, the recent evolution of the PCE architecture has moved to also support active and instantiation capabilities. However, this seems insufficient too, and new architectures are emerging to satisfy the requirement of comprehensive network control and management. These new architectures, including the ABNO proposals, fall within the umbrella of the Software-Defined Networking (SDN) techniques, where the capability to perform effective path computation still represents a key component. In the next years, the PCE technology is then expected to be fully integrated within a comprehensive controller architecture efficiently supporting all relevant network control capabilities as well as network function virtualization.

REFERENCES

Ahmed, J., Cavdar, C., Monti, P., & Wosinska, L. (2012). A dynamic bulk provisioning framework for concurrent optimization in PCE-based WDM networks. *Journal of Lightwave Technology*, *30*(14), 2229–2239. doi:10.1109/JLT.2012.2195296

Alaettinoglu, C., Villamizar, C., Gerich, E., Kessens, D., Meyer, D., Bates, T., . . . Terpstra, M. (1999). Routing policy specification language (RPSL) (pp. 1-56). RFC 2622.

Andriolli, N., Giorgetti, A., Valcarenghi, L., & Castoldi, P. (2007). Idle protection capacity reuse in multiclass optical networks. *Journal of Lightwave Technology*, *25*(5), 1152–1162. doi:10.1109/JLT.2007.893928

Awduche, D.; Berger, L., Gan, D., Li, T., Srinivasan, V., & Swallow, G. (2001). *RSVP-TE: extensions to RSVP for LSP tunnels*. RFC 3209.

Awduche, D.; Malcom, J.; Agogbua, J.; O'Dell, M.; McManus, J. (1999). *Requirements for traffic engineering over MPLS*. RFC 2702.

Boucadair, M., & Jacquenet, C. (2014). *Software-Defined Networking: A Perspective from within a Service Provider Environment*. RFC7149.

Boucadair, M., Jacquenet, C., & Wang, N. (2014). *IP Connectivity provisioning Profile (CPP), RFC 7297*. IETF. doi:10.17487/rfc7297

Bradford, R., Vasseur, J. P., & Farrel, A. (2009). Preserving Topology Confidentiality in Inter-Domain Path Computation Using a Path-Key-Based Mechanism. RFC5520.

Bryskin, I., Papadimitriou, D., Berger, L., & Ash, J. (2008). *Policy-Enabled Path Computation Framework, RFC5394*. IETF.

Casellas, R., Martinez, R., Munoz, R., Vilalta, R., Liu, L., Tsuritani, T., & Morita, I. (2013b). Control and management of flexi-grid optical networks with an integrated stateful path computation element and OpenFlow controller. *Optical Communications and Networking, IEEE/OSA Journal of, 5*(10).

Casellas, R., Munoz, R., Fabrega, J.M., Moreolo, M.S., Martinez, R., Liu, L., … Morita, I. (2013a). Design and Experimental Validation of a GMPLS/PCE Control Plane for Elastic CO-OFDM Optical Networks. *Selected Areas in Communications, IEEE Journal on, 31*(1), 49-61.

Chan, K., Seligson, J., Durham, D., Gai, S., McCloghrie, K., Herzog, S., & Smith, A. (2001). *COPS usage for policy provisioning* (COPS-PR). RFC3084.

Crabbe, E., Minei, I., Medved, J., & Varga, R. (2014). *PCEP Extensions for Stateful PCE, draft-ietf-pce-stateful-pce-10*. IETF.

Cugini, F., Meloni, G., Paolucci, F., Sambo, N., Secondini, M., Gerardi, L., & Castoldi, P. et al. (2012, March 1). Demonstration of flexible optical network based on path computation element. *Journal of Lightwave Technology*, *30*(5), 727–733. doi:10.1109/JLT.2011.2180361

Cugini, F., Paolucci, F., Meloni, G., Berrettini, G., Secondini, M., Fresi, F., & Castoldi, P. et al. (2013). Push-pull defragmentation without traffic disruption in flexible grid optical networks. *Journal of Lightwave Technology*, *31*(1), 125–133. doi:10.1109/JLT.2012.2225600

Dhody, D., & Wu, Q. (2014). *Path Computation Element communication Protocol extensions for relationship between LSPs and Attributes, draft-dhody-pce-association-attr-01, IETF*. PCE Working Group.

Dierks, T. (2008). *The transport layer security (TLS) protocol version 1.2*. RFC5246.

Djarallah, N. B., Pouyllau, H., Le Sauze, N., & Douville, R. (2011). Business-driven PCE for inter-carrier QoS connectivity services. In *Future Network & Mobile Summit*. FutureNetw.

Enns, R., Bjorklund, M., Schoenwaelder, J., & Bierman, A. (2011). *Network configuration protocol* (NETCONF). Internet Engineering Task Force, RFC6241.

Fang, L., Bita, N., Le Roux, J. L., & Miles, J. (2005). Interprovider IP-MPLS services: Requirements, implementations, and challenges. *Communications Magazine, IEEE*, *43*(6), 119–128. doi:10.1109/MCOM.2005.1452840

Farrel, A., Drake, J., Bitar, N., Swallow, G., Ceccarelli, D., & Zhang, X. (2014). *Problem Statement and Architecture for Information Exchange Between Interconnected Traffic Engineering Networks, draft-farrel-interconnected-te-info-exchange-07, Network Working Group*. IETF.

Farrel, A., Vasseur, J. P., & Ash, J. (2006). *A Path Computation Element (PCE)-based Architecture, RFC 4655*. IETF. doi:10.17487/rfc4655

Garroppo, R. G., Giordano, S., & Tavanti, L. (2010). A survey on multi-constrained optimal path computation: Exact and approximate algorithms. *Computer Networks*, *54*(17), 3081–3107. doi:10.1016/j.comnet.2010.05.017

Gharbaoui, M., Paolucci, F., Giorgetti, A., Martini, B., & Castoldi, P. (2013). Effective Statistical Detection of Smart Confidentiality Attacks in Multi-Domain Networks. *Network and Service Management, IEEE Transactions on*, *10*(4), 383-397.

Gifre, L., Paolucci, F., Velasco, L., Aguado, A., Cugini, F., Castoldi, P., & Lopez, V. (2014). First Experimental Assessment of ABNO-driven In-Operation Flexgrid Network Re-Optimization. *IEEE Journal of Lightwave Technology*.

Giorgetti, A., Paolucci, F., Cugini, F., & Castoldi, P. (2011). Hierarchical PCE in GMPLS-based multi-domain Wavelength Switched Optical Networks. *OFC Conference*. doi:10.1364/NFOEC.2011.NTuC4

Giorgetti, A., Paolucci, F., Cugini, F., & Castoldi, P. (2012). Impact of intra-domain information in GMPLS-based WSONs with hierarchical PCE. *OFC Conference*. doi:10.1364/NFOEC.2012.NTu2J.2

Giorgetti, A., Valcarenghi, L., Cugini, F. & Castoldi, P. (2010). PCE-based dynamic restoration in wavelength switched optical networks. *ICC conference, 2010*.

Gonzalez de Dios, O.; et al., (2014). *Framework and Requirements for GMPLS based control of Flexi-grid DWDM, draft-ietf-ccamp-flexi-grid-fwk-01, Feb 2014*. IETF.

Gredler, H., Medved, J., Previdi, S., Farrel, A., & Ray, S. (2014). *North-Bound Distribution of Link-State and TE Information using BGP, draft-ietf-idr-ls-distribution-06, IDR Working Group*. IETF.

Jacob, P., & Davie, B. (2005). Technical challenges in the delivery of interprovider QoS. *Communications Magazine, IEEE*, *43*(6), 112–118. doi:10.1109/MCOM.2005.1452839

Katz, D., Kompella, K., & Yeung, D. (2003). *Traffic engineering (TE) extensions to OSPF version 2*. RFC 3630.

King, D., & Farrel, A. (2012). *The Application of the Path Computation Element Architecture to the Determination of a Sequence of Domains in MPLS and GMPLS*. RFC6805.

King, D.; Farrel, A.; (2014). A *PCE-based Architecture for Application-based Network Operations, IETF draft, draft-farrkingel-pce-abno-architecture-13, Oct 2014*. IETF.

Le Roux, J. L. (2006). *Requirements for Path Computation Element (PCE) Discovery, RFC 4674*. IETF.

Le Roux, J. L., & Papadimitriou, D. (2008). *Evaluation of Existing GMPLS Protocols against Multi-Layer and Multi-Region Networks (MLN/MRN), RFC 5339*. IETF. doi:10.17487/rfc5339

Le Roux, J. L., Vasseur, J. P., & Lee, Y. (2009). *Encoding of Objective Function in the Path Computation Element Communication Protocol (PCEP), RFC 5541*. IETF. doi:10.17487/rfc5541

Lee, Y., Bernstein, G., & Imajuku, W. (2011). *Framework for GMPLS and Path Computation Element (PCE) Control of Wavelength Switched Optical Networks (WSONs), RFC 6163*. IETF. doi:10.17487/rfc6163

Lee, Y., Le Roux, J. L., King, D., & Oki, E. (2009). *Path Computation Element Communication Protocol (PCEP) Requirements and Protocol Extensions in support of Global Concurrent Optimization, RFC 5557*. IETF. doi:10.17487/rfc5557

Li, T. & Smith, H. (2008). *IS-IS Extensions for Traffic Engineering*. RFC5305.

Lopez, D., Gonzales De Dios, O., Wu, Q., & Dhody, D. (2014). *Secure Transport for PCEP, draft-ietf-pce-pceps-00, IETF draft*. IETF.

Mannie, E. (2004). *Generalized multi-protocol label switching (GMPLS) architecture*. RFC3945.

Munoz, R., Casellas, R., & Martinez, R. (2010). Experimental evaluation of dynamic PCE-based path restoration with centralized and distributed wavelength assignment in GMPLS-enabled transparent WSON networks. *ECOC Conference*, 2010. doi:10.1109/ECOC.2010.5621587

Oki, E., Takeda, T., Le Roux, J. L., & Farrel, A. (2009). *Framework for PCE-based Inter-Layer MPLS and GMPLS Traffic Engineering, RFC 5623*. IETF. doi:10.17487/rfc5623

Paolucci, F., Cugini, F., Giorgetti, A., Sambo, N., & Castoldi, P. (2013). A survey on the path computation element (PCE) architecture. *IEEE Communications Surveys and Tutorials*, *15*(4), 1819–1841. doi:10.1109/SURV.2013.011413.00087

Paolucci, F., Cugini, F., Iovanna, P., Bottari, G., Valcarenghi, L., Castoldi, P. (2010). Delay-Bandwidth-aware Metric Abstraction Schemes for OIF E-NNI Multidomain Traffic Engineering. *IEEE/OSA Journal of Optical Communication and Networking*, *2*(10), 782-792.

Paolucci, F., Sambo, N., Cugini, F., Giorgetti, A, & Castoldi, P. (2011). Experimental Demonstration of Impairment-Aware PCE for Multi-Bit-Rate WSONs. *Optical Communications and Networking, IEEE/OSA Journal of*, *3*(8).

Polito, S.G., Zaghloul, S., Chamania, M., & Jukan, A. (2011). Inter-Domain Path Provisioning with Security Features: Architecture and Signaling Performance. *Network and Service Management, IEEE Transactions on*, *8*(3).

Shiomoto, K., Papadimitriou, D., Le Roux, J. L., Vigoreaux, M., & Brungard, D. (2008). *Requirements for GMPLS-based Multi-Region and Multi-Layer Networks (MRN/MLN), RFC 5212*. IETF. doi:10.17487/rfc5212

Sivalaban, S., Parker, J., Boutros, S., & Kumaki, K. (2009). *Diffserv-Aware Class-Type Object for the Path Computation Element Protocol*. RFC 5455.

Srinivasan, C., Viswanathan, A., & Nadeau, T. (2004). *Multiprotocol label switching (MPLS) label switching router (LSR) management information base (MIB)*. RFC 3813.

Tornatore, M., De Grandi, F., Munoz, R., Martinez, R., Casellas, R., & Pattavina, A. (2009). Effects of outdated control information in control-plane enabled optical networks with path protection. *IEEE /OSA Journal of Optical Communication and Networking*, *1* (2), A194-A204.

Vasseur, J., Ayyangar, A., & Zhang, R. (2008). *A per-domain path computation method for establishing inter-domain traffic engineering (TE) label switched paths (LSPs)*. RFC5152.

Vasseur, J. P., & Le Roux, J. L. (2009). *Path Computation Element (PCE) Communication Protocol (PCEP), RFC 5440*. IETF. doi:10.17487/rfc5440

Vasseur, J. P., Le Roux, J. L., & Ikejiri, Y. (2010). *A set of Monitoring Tools for Path Computation (PCE)-based Architecture, RFC 5886*. IETF. doi:10.17487/rfc5886

Vasseur, J.P., Zhang, R., Bitar, N., & Le Roux, J.L. (2009). *A Backward-Recursive PCE-based Computation (BRPC) Procedure to Compute Shortest Constrained Inter-Domain Traffic Engineering Label Switched Paths, RFC 5441*. IETF.

Wang, R., & Mukherjee, B. (2013). Provisioning in elastic optical networks with non-disruptive defragmentation. *Journal of Lightwave Technology*, *31*(15), 2491–2500. doi:10.1109/JLT.2013.2268535

Zhang, F., & Farrel, A. (2014). *Conveying Vendor-Specific Constraints in the Path Computation Element Communication Protocol, RFC 7150*. IETF. doi:10.17487/rfc7150

Zhao, Q., King, D., Verhaeghe, F., Takeda, T., Ali, Z., & Meuric, J. (2010). *Extensions to the Path Computation Element Communication Protocol (PCEP) for Point-to-Multipoint Traffic Engineering Label Switched Paths, RFC 6006*. IETF. doi:10.17487/rfc6006

Zhao, Y., et al. (2012). Routing and wavelength assignment problem in PCE-based wavelength-switched optical networks. *Optical Communications and Networking, IEEE/OSA Journal of 2*(4), 196-205.

KEY TERMS AND DEFINITIONS

Application-Based Network Operations (ABNO): Modular architecture providing advanced networking functionalities, such as network service virtualization, coordination and optimization between applications and network resources, programmability of network elements.

Flexi-Grid or Elastic Optical Network (EON): Evolution of the WSON technology where spectrum resources are reserved over a flexible grid.

Path Computation Element (PCE): Dedicated network entity devoted to path computation.

Path Computation Element Protocol (PCEP): Client-server communication protocol to issue path computation requests to PCE and return computed paths in responses.

Quality of Service (QoS): Service performance experienced by a network user.

Software Defined Networking (SDN): A technology that allows network administrators to manage network services through abstraction of lower-level network functionalities.

Traffic Engineering: Process of mapping traffic demand onto a network.

Wavelength Switched Optical Network (WSON): Type of telecommunication network where data traffic flows through end-to-end optical connections (lightpaths) that are switched at the wavelength granularity over a fixed grid.

APPENDIX

Table 1. Acronyms

AAA	Authentication Authorization and Accounting
ABNO	Application-based Network Operations
API	Application Programming Interface
AS	Autonomous System
ASE	Amplified Spontaneous Emission
BGP	Border Gateway Protocol
BGP-LS	Border Gateway Protocol with Link State extensions
BN	Border Node
BRPC	Backward Recursive PCE-based Computation
ERO	Explicit Route Object
FA-LSP	Forwarding Adjacency LSP
GCO	Global Concurrent Optimization
GMPLS	Generalized Multiprotocol Label Switching
IRO	Include Route Object
LSC	Lambda Switching Capability
LSP	Label Switched Path
LSPA	LSP Attributes
LSP-DB	Label Switched Path Database
HPCE	Hierarchical PCE
HTED	Hierarchical Traffic Engineering Database
IANA	Internet Assigned Numbers Authority
IA-RSA	Impairment-aware RSA
IETF	Internet Engineering Task Force
IGP	Interior Gateway Protocol
ISC	Interface Switching Capability
IS-IS-TE	Intermediate System to Intermediate System protocol with TE extensions
IV	Impairment Validation
MPLS	Multiprotocol Label Switching
NMS	Network Management System
OAM	Operation Administration and Maintenance
OF	Objective Function
ONF	Open Networking Foundation
OSPF-TE	Open Shortest Path First with Traffic Engineering extensions
PCC	Path Computation Client

continued in following column

Table 1. Continued

PCE	Path Computation Element
PCEP	Path Computation Element Protocol
PCErr	Path Computation Error message
PCInit	Path Computation Initiation message
PCNtf	Path Computation Notification message
PCReq	Path Computation Request
PCRep	Path Computation Reply
PCRpt	Path Computation Report message
PCUpd	Path Computation Update message
PMD	Polarization Mode Dispersion
PSC	Packet Switching Capability
QoS	Quality of Service
QoT	Quality of Transmission
RRO	Record Route Object
RP	Request Parameter
RSA	Routing and Spectrum Assignment
RSVP-TE	Reservation Protocol with Traffic Engineering extensions
RWA	Routing and Wavelength Assignment
SDN	Software Defined Networking
SLA	Service Level Agreement
SNMP	Simple Network Management Protocol
SPM	Self-Phase Modulation
SRLG	Shared Risk Link Group
SVEC	Synchronized Vector
TCP	Transmission Control Protocol
TE	Traffic Engineering
TED	Traffic Engineering Database
VL	Virtual Link
VNT	Virtual Network Topology
VNTM	Virtual Network Topology Manager
VPN	Virtual Private Network
VSPT	Virtual Shortest Path Tree
XPM	Cross-Phase Modulation
XRO	Exclude Route Object

Chapter 12
Recent Advances in Traffic Forwarding Techniques

Quintin Zhao
Huawei Technology, USA

Zhenbin Li
Huawei Technologies, China

ABSTRACT

Advanced service oriented routing and forwarding schemes are nurturing fast recently, thus paving the way to implementations that can overcome complications related to multi-vendor networking environments. Some of these proposals are improving and optimizing the existing traffic engineering functionalities where the forwarding planes are still under a distributed signaling control system, others are more network architecture level changes where the forwarding plane is totally centralized controlled through a centralized control plane. At the same time some of these proposals are the hybrid of the both. This chapter describes these advances by focusing on the aspects of forwarding scheme changes introduced in each of these areas.

INTRODUCTION

To build the service-oriented and application-aware Traffic Engineering (TE) paths, there are a lot of new challenges and requirements that need to be considered. The list of these requirements is still extending as new services are to be deployed. A non-exhaustive list of requirements is provided below: The new traffic forwarding solutions should have a structure that can cope with emerging "agile" requirements.

1. The new traffic forwarding solutions should have a structure that scale better instead of providing only a portion of the functionalities needed by the users/operators.
2. The new traffic forwarding solutions should have a structure that has better performance.
3. The new traffic forwarding solutions should require changes on the existing hardware as less as possible.
4. The new traffic forwarding solutions should enhance the security of the network instead of weakening the security of the network.

DOI: 10.4018/978-1-4666-8371-6.ch012

5. The new traffic forwarding solutions should have a structure which provides a practical and smooth transition strategy from the existing network architecture to the new architecture.

By improving and optimizing the existing distributed networking solutions, some of these new requirements can be met, but some of the new requirements need a centralized controlled system to implement a complete solution. For example, Entropy Label (EL) is a technique where the existing network architecture principle is kept intact and the new load balancing functionality is provided through adding a new layer of labels to be used in the traffic forwarding path. The Software-Designed Networking (SDN) is a typical example for the cases where a centralized controller is needed to dynamically build the service-oriented traffic engineering paths with a claim of ensuring simplicity and scalability. In some cases, a hybrid scheme (i.e., distributed system and centralized controlled system) can also satisfy certain new requirements nicely. For example, a source routing based traffic engineering path is a hybrid approach, where the basic routing and forwarding information can be propagated through distributed IGPs (Interior Gateway Protocols), and the path can be calculated through a centralized controller.

This chapter first describes new advances in forwarding schemes which are focused on improving and optimizing existing traffic forwarding functionalities, and then presents reasons why service-oriented routing and forwarding features are needed. The chapter also describes the new requirements for the traffic forwarding, once the forwarding paths (e.g., tunnels) are built to be service-driven instead of reachability oriented. The chapter also describes how the new forwarding schemes satisfy these new requirements. Also, this chapter discusses the challenges that arise when the new forwarding schemes are deployed during the transition from a reachability-based routing network to a context-based routing network.

The recent advances in traffic forwarding areas which are covered in the later sections of this chapter are:

a) MPLS (Multi-Protocol Label Switching) Multiple Topology (MPLS-MT)
b) Entropy Label (EL)
c) Network Virtualization Overlay (NVO3)
d) Segment Routing (SR)
e) Using PCE as the Central Controller of Traffic Engineering Tunnels (PCECC)
f) Service Function Chaining (SFC)
g) Open Flow
h) Protocol Oblivious Forwarding/Protocol Independent Forwarding (POF/PIF)

The immediate goal of the above techniques is to satisfy the new requirements that result from service-driven traffic engineering paths. At the same time, these solutions ambitions to make the control plane as simple as possible while minimizing the changes in the forwarding plan as much as possible.

To achieve the final goal of improving the performance of the network and reducing the complexity of the network from the point view of forwarding, these new forwarding techniques evolve the forwarding architectures to make them scale, to provide higher granularity/flexibility of steering, to provide easier manageability/operation, and to provide better security.

Each of the advanced forwarding technologies introduced in this chapter enriches the current set of networking solution tools from different angles so that the aforementioned final goal can be achieved with a smooth transition from today's network to tomorrow's network and a flexibility of deployment for the existing and new users.

For example, MPLS-MT can address the security issue by providing service separation through end-to-end disjoined topologies corresponding to each service with strict security requirements. Still, how to actually enforce polices to realize this separation is a very sensitive and may have incidences on the experienced security level. When the load balancing issue is a major concern, then EL can be considered as a good candidate to consider. When an "intelligent" traffic engineered forwarding path is the key requirement for the users in a legacy network, then SR/PCECC can be a nice tool to address those requirements, while the existing data plane needs few changes. For the scenarios where the complexity of the network and vendor dependency need to be addressed, Open Flow based SDN could be considered.

BACKGROUND

Traditional traffic forwarding schemes have evolved upon the traditional distributed routing schemes, where routes are distributed among the network nodes dynamically. Many efforts have focused on the enhancement of the efficiency of the forwarding plane and the stability of the traffic tunnel. These forwarding schemes include GRE (Generic Routing Encapsulation) tunnel, MPLS LDP (Label Distribution Protocol) and RSVP-TE (Resource Reservation Protocol with Traffic Engineering) tunnels, etc. Since the routes are based on the reachability of the destination nodes and the traffic forwarding paths which constrain satisfaction of the path from the origin of the forwarding path to the destination of the forwarding path, these forwarding schemes give users stable and unified traffic paths to be used to forward the traffic. But these existing forwarding schemes have their own drawbacks, since the traffic forwarding paths usually require complex configuration operations beforehand, and they are not flexible enough and not dynamic enough among different services. Also, the forwarding paths are managed and maintained among all the nodes in the distributed network, and these forwarding paths are also dependent on network topology. Once the new user cases are added, such as application-aware traffic engineering paths, service function chains, etc., the existing network topology with pre-built traffic forwarding paths will not be flexible enough to satisfy the new services.

MPLS MULTIPLE TOPOLOGY

Issues, Controversies, Problems Which MPLS-MT Addresses

There are increasing requirements to support multi-topology in the service aware network. For example, service providers may want to assign different levels of service(s) to different topologies so that the service separation can be achieved from end-to-end. It is also possible to have an in-band management network on top of the original network topology, maintain separate routing and MPLS domains for isolated multicast or IPv6 islands within the backbone, or force a subset of an address space to follow a different MPLS topology for the purpose of security, QoS (Quality of Service) or simplified management and/or operations.

OSPF (Open Shortest Path First) and IS-IS (Intermediate system to intermediate system) use MT-ID (Multi-Topology Identification) to identify different topologies. For each topology identified by a MT-ID, IGP computes a separate SPF (Shortest Path First) tree independently to find the best paths to the IP prefixes associated with this topology.

IGP-MT requires additional data-plane resources maintain multiple forwarding for each configured MT. On the other hand, MPLS-MT does not change the data-plane system architecture, if an IGP-MT is mapped to an MPLS-MT. In case MPLS-MT, incoming label value itself can determine an MT, and hence it requires a single NHLFE (Next Hop Label Forwarding Entry) space. MPLS-MT requires only MT-RIBs (MT Routing Information Bases) in the control-plane, no need to have MT-FIBs (MT Forwarding Information Bases). Forwarding IP packets over a particular MT requires either configuration or some external means at every node, to maps an attribute of incoming IP packet header to IGP-MT, which is additional overhead for network management. Whereas, MPLS-MT mapping is required only at the ingress-PE (Provider Edge) of an MPLS-MT LSP, because each node identifies MPLS-MT LSP switching based on the incoming label, hence no additional configuration is required at every node.

Solutions and Recommendations

Since the forwarding plan needs to be changed in IGP-MT solution, Zhao (2014) introduces the MPLS-MT solution. For FECs (Forwarding Equivalent Classes) that are associated with a specific topology, Zhao (2014) proposes to use the same MT-ID of this topology in LDP (Label Distribution Protocol). Thus the Label Switching Path (LSP) for a certain FEC may be created and maintained along the IGP path in this topology.

Maintaining multiple topologies for MPLS network in a backwards-compatible manner requires several extensions to the label signaling encoding and processing procedures. When a label is associated with a FEC, the FEC includes both the IP address and topology it belongs to.

There are two possible solutions to support MT-aware MPLS network from MPLS forwarding point of view. The first one is to map a label to both IP address and the corresponding topology. The alternate one is to use label stacks. The upper label maps to the topology, the lower label maps to the IP address. The first option does not require changes to the data plane, and it could use multiple labels for the same address even on different topologies. The second option requires two lookup operations on the data forwarding plane but it can use the same label for the same address on different topologies.

MT-based MPLS in general can be used for a variety of purposes such as service separation by assigning each service or a group of services to a given topology, where the management, QoS and security of the service or the group of the services could be simplified and guaranteed, in-band management network "on top" of the original MPLS topology, maintain separate routing and MPLS forwarding domains for isolated multicast or IPv6 islands within the backbone, or force a subset of an address space to follow a different MPLS topology for the purpose of security, QoS or simplified management and/or operations.

As illustrated in Figure 1, the default topology is virtualized into star, ring and diamond topologies and each topology is used for a specific service by categorizing the incoming packages into each service type. One of the uses of the MT-based MPLS is where one class of data requires low latency links, for example Voice over Internet Protocol (VoIP) data. As a result such data may be sent preferably via physical landlines rather than, for example, high latency links such as satellite links. As a result an additional topology is defined as all low latency links on the network and VoIP data packets are assigned to the additional topology. Further possible examples are File Transfer Protocol (FTP) or Simple Mail Transfer Protocol (SMTP) traffic which can be assigned to an additional topology comprising high latency links, Internet Protocol version 4 (IPv4) versus Internet Protocol version 6 (IPv6) traffic which may be assigned to different topology (Cheng, Boucadair & Retana, 2013).

There are a few possible ways to apply the MT-ID of a topology in LDP. One way is to dedicate a new TLV for MT-ID and insert the TLV into messages describing a FEC that needs Multi-Topology information. Another approach is to expand the FEC TLV to carry MT-ID if the FEC needs Multi-Topology information.

Other than the service separation, there are a few other application scenarios for MPLS-MT. These scenarios are listed as below:

Figure 1. Virtualization Using Multiple Topologies

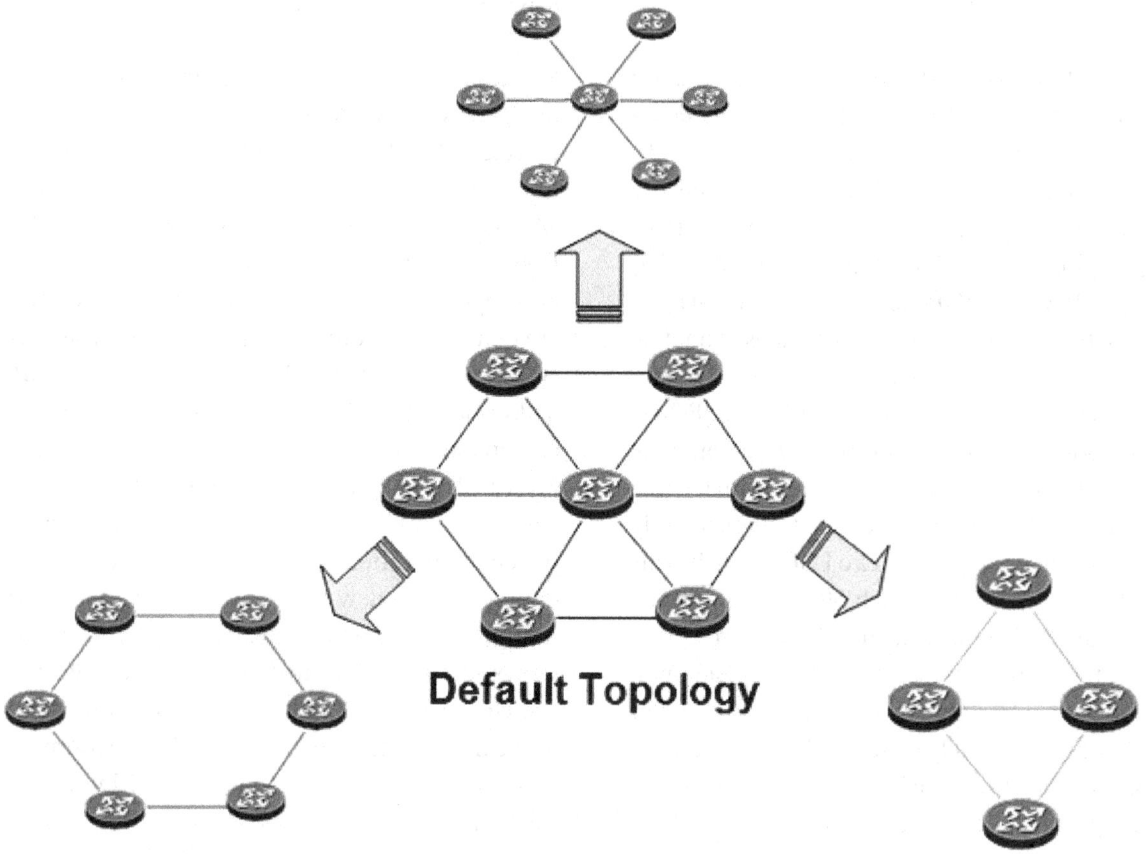

Application Scenario-1: Using MT for P2P Protection

IP MT-based FRR (Fast ReRouting) can be used for configuring alternate paths via backup MT, such that if the primary link fails, then the backup topology can be used for forwarding. However, such technique requires special marking of IP packets that needs to be forwarded using the backup topology. MPLS-LDP-MT procedures simplify the forwarding of the MPLS packets over backup-MT, as MPLS-LDP-MT procedure distributes separate labels for each MT. How backup paths are computed depends on the implementation, and the algorithm. One example is the Maximum Redundant Tree (MRT) algorithm (Enyedi, 2014) where the backup path is computed dynamically by signaling the primary path and secondary path belong to two mutual protective topologies. The micro loop issue which exists by using the IP/LDP FRR backup path computation algorithm is solved when MRT algorithm is used. The MPLS-LDP-MT in conjunction with IGP-MT and backup path computing algorithms such as MRT could be used to separate the primary traffic and backup traffic dynamically without the need to modify forwarding plane and at the same time have a better coverage for failure protections. For example, service providers can create a backup MT that consists of links that are meant only for backup traffic. Service providers can then establish bypass LSPs, standby LSPs, using backup MT, thus keeping un-deterministic backup traffic away from the primary traffic.

Application Scenario-2: Using MT for mLDP Protection

For the P2MP (Point-to-MultiPoint) or MP2MP (MultiPoint-to-MultiPoint) LSPs setup by using mLDP (Multicast Label Distribution Protocol), there is a need to setup a backup LSP to ensure an end-to-end protection for the primary LSP for applications such as IPTV. Since the mLDP LSP is setup following an IGP-computed route, the second LSP setup by following the IGP routes cannot be guaranteed to have the link and node diversity from the primary LSP. By using MPLS-LDP-MT, two topologies can be configured with complete link and node diversity, where the primary and secondary LSPs can be established independently within each topology. The two LSPs setup by this mechanism can protect each other end-to-end.

Figure 2 illustrates the mLDP local protection where the primary and secondary backup paths will use the same link between router "A" and router "C" if no MPLS-MT is used. When the multiple topologies are used as it illustrates in Figure 3, the backup path will be setup in a disjointed topology comparing to the primary path.

Application Scenario-3: Service Separation for Traffic Isolation

MPLS-MT procedures allow establishing two distinct LSPs for the same FEC, by advertising separate labels for each configured topology. Service providers can implement CoSes (Classes of Services) using MPLS-MT procedures without requiring creating separate FEC address for each class. MPLS-MT can also be used to separate multicast and unicast traffic, and it can also be used to create specific topologies for certain services so that the specific topology is only used for the dedicated service and not shared with other services.

Application Scenario-4: Simplified inter-AS VPN Setup

When an LSP is crossing multiple domains for the inter-AS (Autonomous System) VPN (Virtual Private Networks) scenarios illustrated in Figure 4, the existing solutions can use the so-called option "A" where the inter-domain ASBRs (AS Border Routers) are connected through IGP using IP tunnels, option "B" where the inter-domain ASBRs are connected through MP-BGP (Multiprotocol-Border Gateway Protocol) using a single layer LSP, and option "C" where the inter-domain ASBRs are connected through MP-BGP using double layer LSPs. The inter-domain LSP setup process can be simplified by configuring a set of routers which are in different domains into a new single domain with a new topology ID using the LDP multiple topology as it illustrates in Figure 5. All the routers that belong to this new topology will be used to carry the traffic across multiple domains. Since these routers are in a single logical domain identified with the new topology ID, LDP-based LSP set up can be achieved without the complex inter-AS VPN solution's option "A".

When MPLS-MT is used in the application scenarios discussed above, the ingress and egress nodes should implement the mapping functionality to map FEC(s) to the desired topology accordingly.

ENTROPY LABEL

Issues, Controversies, Problems Which Entropy Label Addresses

Load balancing, or multi-pathing, is an attempt to balance the traffic across a network by allowing the traffic to use multiple paths. Load balancing has several benefits: it optimizes network resources usage; it can help absorb traffic surges by spreading them across multiple paths, and it allows better resilience by offering alternate paths in the event of a link or node failure.

Figure 2. mLDP Local Protection without Using MPLS Multiple Topologies

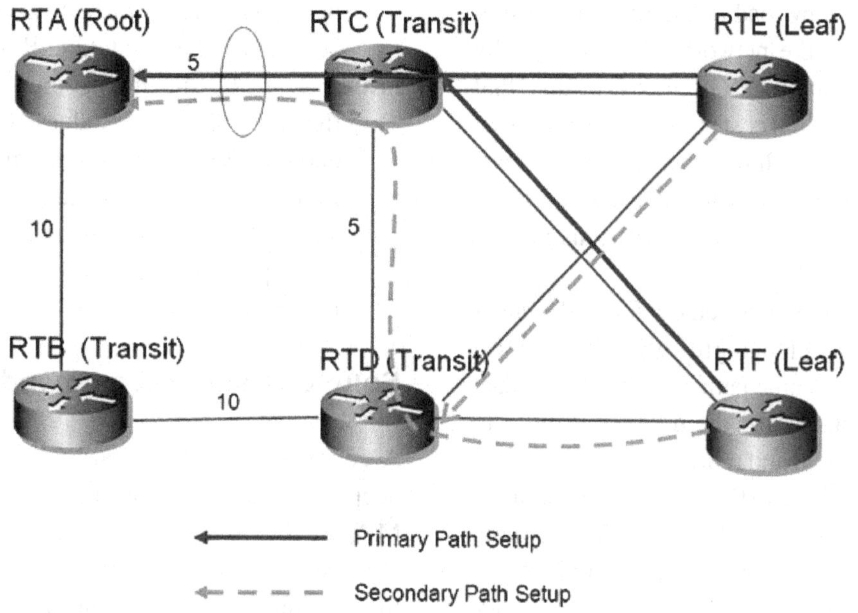

Figure 3. mLDP Local Protection by Using MPLS Multiple Topologies

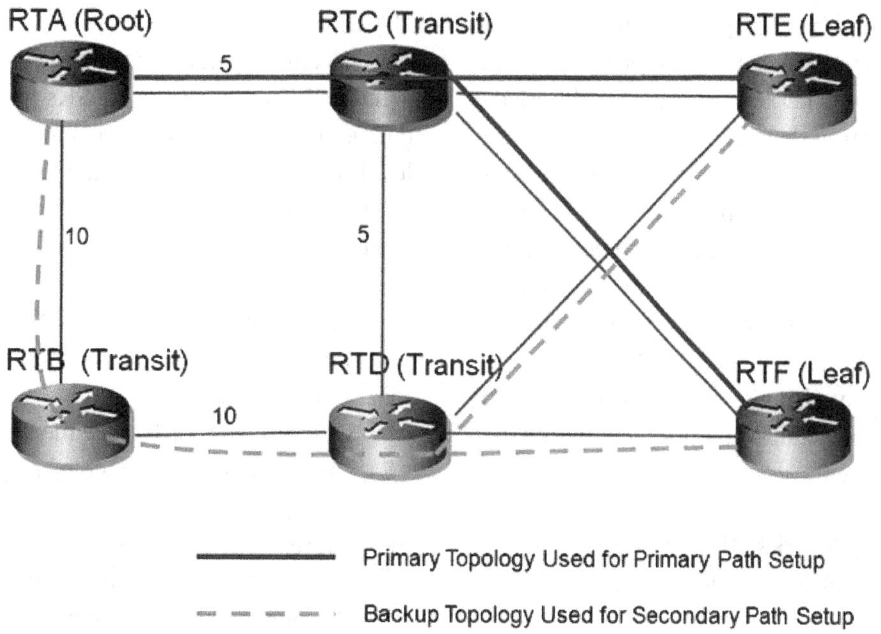

As providers scale their networks, they use several techniques to achieve greater bandwidth between nodes. Two widely used techniques are: Link Aggregation Group (LAG) and Equal Cost Multi-Path (ECMP). LAG is used to bond together several physical circuits between two adjacent nodes so they appear to higher-layer protocols as a single, higher-bandwidth "virtual" pipe. ECMP is used between two nodes separated by one or more hops, to allow load balancing over several shortest paths in the network. This is typically obtained by arranging IGP metrics such that there are several equal cost paths between source-destination pairs. Both of these techniques may, and often do, coexist in differing parts of a given provider's network, depending on various choices made by the provider.

A very important requirement for load balancing is that packets belonging to a given "flow" must be mapped to the same path, i.e., the same exact sequence of links across the network. This is to avoid jitter, latency, and reordering issues for the flow. What constitutes a flow varies considerably. A common example of a flow is a TCP session. Other examples are a Layer 2 Tunneling Protocol (L2TP) session corresponding to a given broadband user or traffic within an ATM virtual circuit.

To meet this requirement, a node uses certain fields, termed "keys", within a packet's header as input to a load-balancing function (typically a hash function) that selects the path for all packets in a given flow. The keys chosen for the load-balancing function depend on the packet type; a typical set (for IP packets) is the IP source and destination addresses, the protocol type, and (for TCP and UDP traffic) the source and destination port numbers. An overly conservative choice of fields may lead to many flows mapping to the same hash value (and consequently poorer load balancing); an overly aggressive choice may map a flow to multiple values, potentially violating the above requirement.

For MPLS networks, there are few challenges to be tackled:

Issue1: Finding useful keys in a packet for the purpose of load balancing can be more of a challenge.

Issue2: MPLS encapsulation may require fairly deep inspection of packets to find these keys at transit Label Switching Routers (LSRs).

Issue3: Transit LSRs, not having the full context that an ingress LSR does, have the hard choice between potentially misinterpreting fields in a packet as valid keys for load balancing (causing packet-ordering problems) or adopting a conservative approach (giving rise to sub-optimal load balancing).

Solutions and Recommendations

A candidate solution to eliminate the need for deep inspection is to have the ingress LSR of an MPLS Label Switched Path extract the appropriate keys from a given packet, input them to its load-balancing function, and place the result in an additional label, termed the "entropy label", as part of the MPLS label stack it pushes onto that packet. This solution is specified in (Kompell, 2012).

The entire label stack of the MPLS packet can then be used by transit LSRs to perform load balancing, as the entropy label introduces the right level of "entropy" into the label stack.

There are five key reasons why this is beneficial:

a) At the ingress LSR, MPLS encapsulation hasn't yet occurred, so deep inspection is not necessary.
b) The ingress LSR has more context and information about incoming packets than transit LSRs.
c) Ingress LSRs usually operate at lower bandwidths than transit LSRs, allowing them to do more work per packet.
d) Transit LSRs do not need to perform deep packet inspection and can load balance effectively using only a packet's MPLS label stack.

Figure 4. Inter Domain VPN Setup Needs Complex Solutions such Option A/B/C

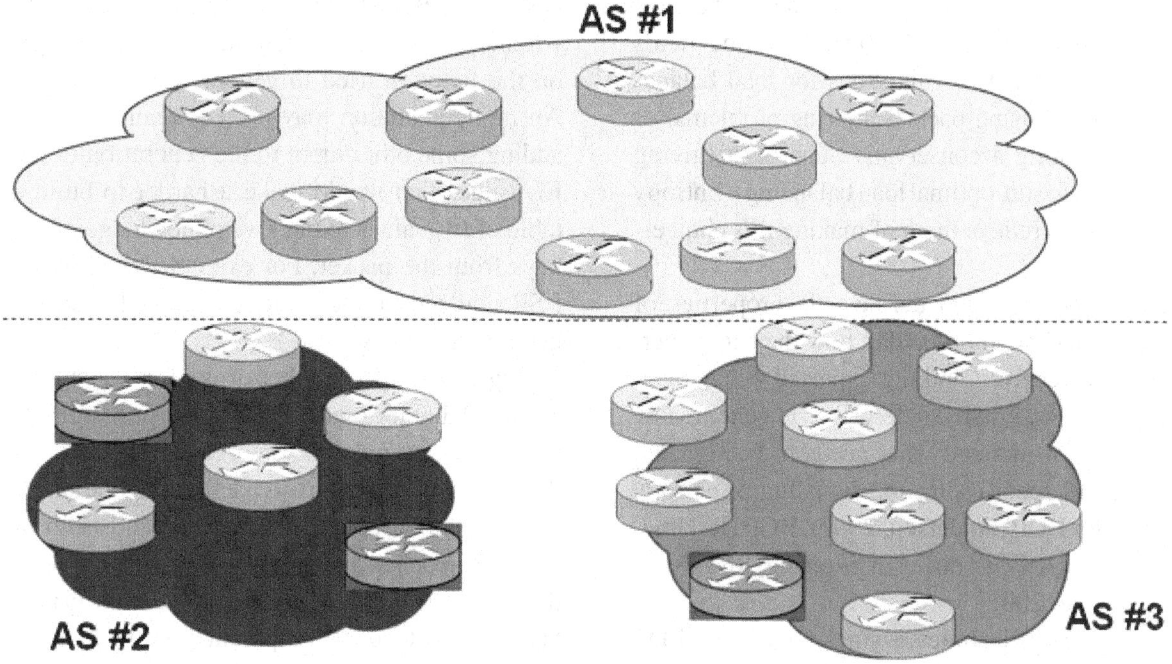

Figure 5. Inter Domain VPN Setup Using MPLS Multiple Topology

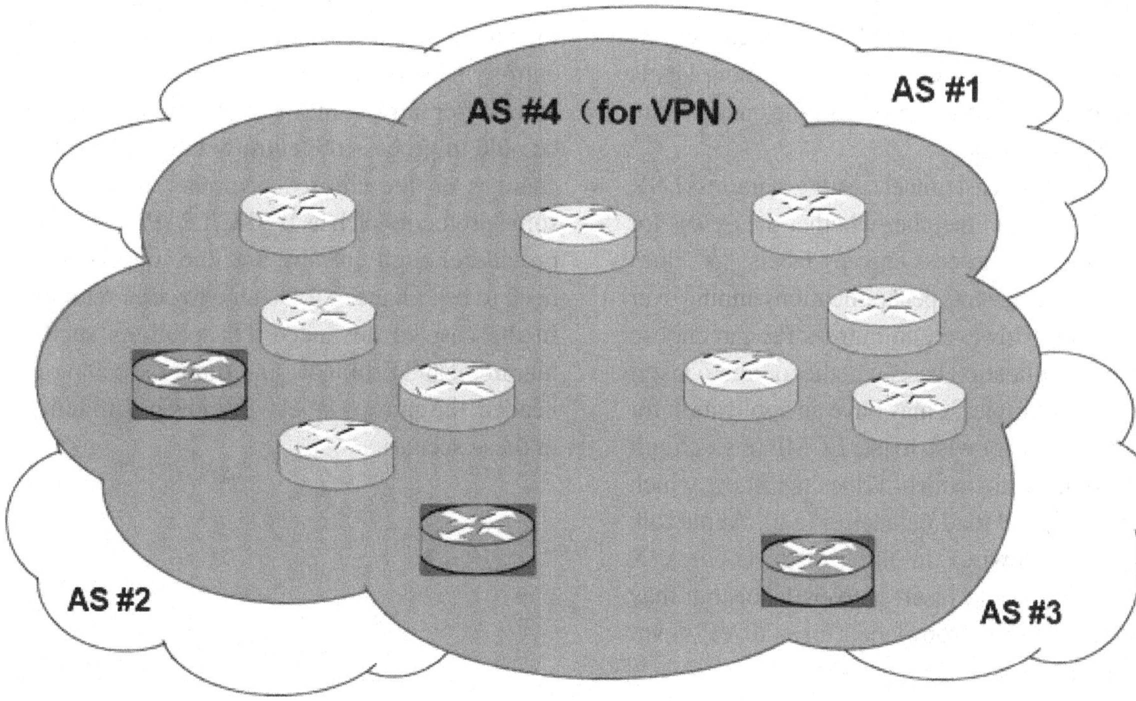

e) Transit LSRs, not having the full context that an ingress LSR does, have the hard choice between potentially misinterpreting fields in a packet as valid keys for load balancing (causing packet-ordering problems) or adopting a conservative approach (giving rise to sub-optimal load balancing). Entropy labels relieve them of making this choice.

Kompella (2012) defines the properties of entropy labels, in particular, how they are generated and received and the expected behavior of transit LSRs. Finally, it describes in general how signaling works and what needs to be signaled as well as specifics for the signaling of entropy labels for LDP (Anderson, 2007), BGP (Rekhter, 2006), and RSVP-Traffic Engineering (RSVP-TE) (Awduche, 2001).

Figure 6 illustrates a simple intra-AS LDP tunnels where the EL and AL (which could, for example, be a VPN label) are generated and inserted by the ingress LSR, received and processed by the transit LSP. Figure 6 shows ultimate hop popping (UHP) with the egress LSR.

Note that, the MPLS application does not matter; it may be that "X" pushes some more labels (e.g.; for a VPN or VPLS) below the ones shown, and "Y" pops them.

For each unicast tunnel starting at ingress LSR "X", "X" must remember whether the egress for that tunnel can process entropy labels. "X" does not have to keep state per application running over that tunnel. However, an ingress PE can choose on a per-application basis whether or not to insert ELs. For example, X may have an application for which it does not wish to use ECMP (e.g., circuit emulation) or for which it does not know which keys to use for load balancing (e.g., AppleTalk over a pseudowire). In either of those cases, X may choose not to insert entropy labels but may choose to insert entropy labels for an IP VPN over the same tunnel.

Note that if the EL value is calculated only based on packet headers, then a relatively efficient wiretapping interface could be added depending on the function used to generate the EL value. An implementation may protect against this by adding some other input to the generation of the EL values that would make it harder to build a table of EL values to tap given knowledge of the keys from the packet. For example, the ingress LSR could generate a random input to the EL generation process.

Figure 7 shows another example of using the entropy label for load balancing purposes. In the wholesale services of some carriers, traffic of thousands of xDSL ports is packed into one single PW (Pseudowire); it is makes the bandwidth of this PW reached to several Gbytes, the PW in this scenario are called FAT PW. FAT PW brings heavy traffic load for equipment through the path.

FAT PW can be cut into several "data flows" and identified by entropy label. After that, data flows will be forwarded in different paths by load-sharing mode.

When entropy label is implemented, the following issues need to be considered. Since the entropy label requires the chipsets to process the label differently, some vendors' chipset may not be able to process the entropy label without the changes on the chipsets. Another issue is that some protocols such as IPSEC/L2TP/GTP do not provide enough entropy and the ingress nodes need to be enhanced to be able to cope with this. In the case of advanced TE solutions such as hierarchical TE tunnels and tunnel stitching are needed, the entropy label will show its limitations in these scenarios.

Figure 6. LDP with UHP: Ingress Inserts ELs with the UHP by the Egress LSR

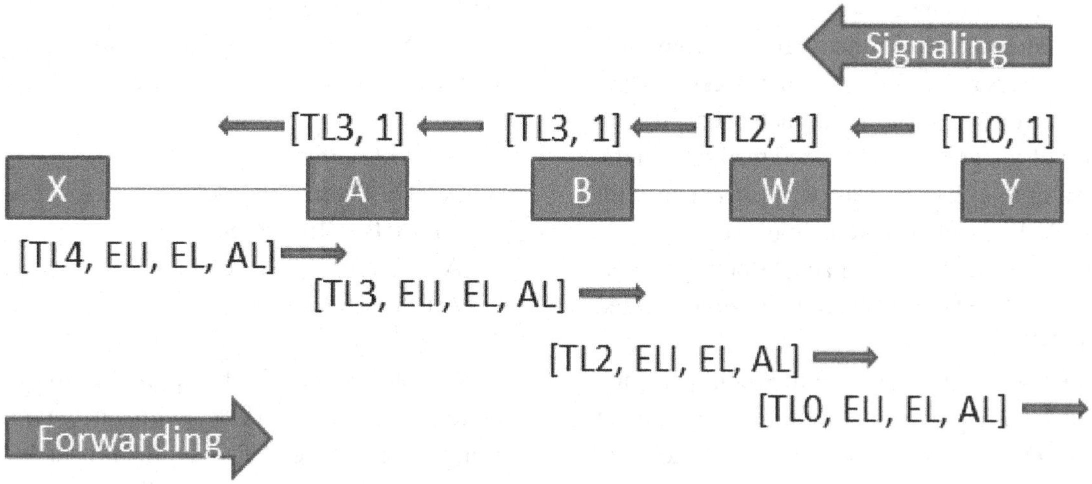

Figure 7. Using Entropy Label in FAT PW for Load Balancing

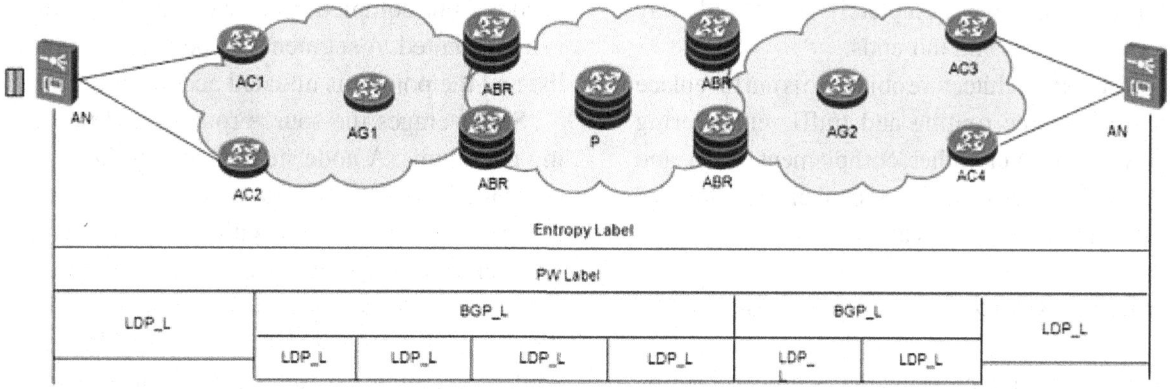

SEGMENT ROUTING

Issues, Controversies, Problems Which Segment Routing Addresses

The ability for a node to specify a unicast forwarding path, other than the normal shortest path, that a particular packet will traverse, benefits a number of network functions, for example:

a) Some types of network virtualization techniques, including multi-topology networks and the partitioning of network resources for VPNs
b) Network, link, path and node protection such as fast re-route
c) Network programmability
d) OAM techniques
e) Simplification and reduction of network signaling components
f) Load balancing and traffic engineering

Source-based routing mechanisms have previously been specified for network protocols, but have not seen widespread adoption other than in MPLS traffic engineering.

The aforementioned network functions may require greater flexibility and per packet source imposed routing than can be achieved through the use of the previously defined methods. In the context of this charter, 'source' means 'The point at which the explicit route is imposed'.

In this context, Source Packet Routing in Networking (SPRING) architecture is being defined within IETF.

SPRING architecture should allow incremental and selective deployment without any requirement of Flag Day or massive upgrade of all network elements.

SPRING architecture should allow optimal virtualization: put policy state in the packet header and not in the intermediate nodes along the path. Hence, the policy is completely virtualized away from midpoints and tail-ends.

SPRING architecture objective is not to replace existing source routing and traffic engineering mechanisms but rather complement them and address use cases where removal of signaling and path state in the core is a requirement.

Solutions and Recommendations

Filsfils (2014) documents the Segment Routing (SR) solution, where a node steers a packet through an ordered list of instructions, called segments. A segment can represent any instruction, topological or service-based. A segment can have a local semantic to an SR node or global within an SR domain. SR allows enforcing a flow through any path and service chain while maintaining per-flow state only at the ingress node of the SR domain.

Segment Routing can be directly applied to the MPLS architecture (Rosen, 2001) with no change on the forwarding plane. A segment is encoded as an MPLS label. An ordered list of segments is encoded as a stack of labels. The active segment is on the top of the stack. A completed segment is popped off the stack. The addition of a segment is performed with a push.

In the Segment Routing MPLS instantiation, a segment could be of several types:

a) An IGP segment,
b) A BGP Peering segments,
c) An LDP LSP segment,
d) An RSVP-TE LSP segment,
e) A BGP LSP segment.

Segment Routing can be applied to the IPv6 architecture (Deering, 1998), with a new type of routing extension header. A segment is encoded as an IPv6 address. An ordered list of segments is encoded as an ordered list of IPv6 addresses in the routing extension header. The active segment is indicated by a pointer in the routing extension header. Upon completion of a segment, the pointer is incremented. A segment can be inserted in the list and the pointer is updated accordingly.

SR leverages the source routing and tunneling paradigms. A node steers a packet through a controlled set of instructions, called segments, by pretending the packet with an SR header. A segment can represent any instruction, topological or service-based. SR allows enforcing a flow through any topological path and service chain while maintaining per-flow state only at the ingress node of the SR domain.

The SR example (Daqupta, 2014) in Figure 8 illustrates that traffic engineering path from router A to router Z is set up by using the combination of node adjacency and link adjacency segments. The package oriented from node "A" has the label stack of [72 78 65]. When node "B" receives the package, it forwards the package to next hop which is node "C" by looking up its forwarding table. Node "C" receives the package and finds out that the label 72 is for itself, then label 72 is removed and the next label is a local label 78 for local link adjacency, then the package is forwarded through the corresponding link to its next hop. Eventually

Figure 8. SR Example

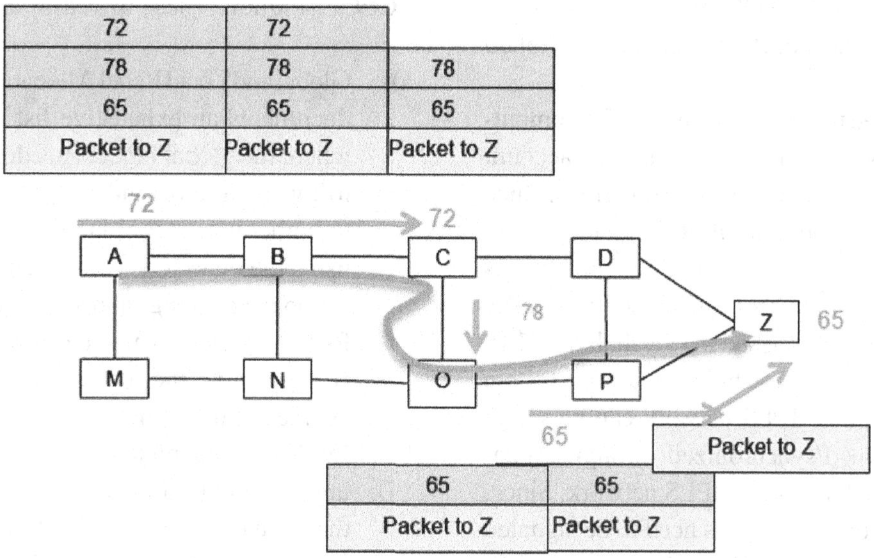

node Z receives the package through the engineering tunnel which goes through ABCOPZ.

Since SR alone does not provide the means to do full TE, Service/flow mappings are needed to be able to leverage the value of segment routing.

Since SR is suitable for the P2P (Point-to-Point) traffic engineering tunnels where the engineering tunnel doesn't have the bandwidth guarantee requirement, this solution is for certain deployment scenarios.

For the deployments where the SR is required for P2P engineering tunnels and also multicast tunnels are also needed at the same time, the operator can deploy the PCE centralized controller based solution, which is introduced in the later part of this chapter.

PCE+

Issues, Controversies, Problems Which PCE+ Addresses

In certain network deployments, service providers would like to dynamically adapt to a wide range of customer's requests for the sake of flexible network service delivery. SDN techniques ambition to provide additional flexibility regarding how the network is operated compared to legacy networks

Taking the smooth transition between traditional network and the new SDN enabled network into account, especially from a cost impact assessment perspective, using the existing PCE (Path Computation Elements) components from the current network to function as the central controller of the SDN network is a candidate deployment option, which not only achieves the goal of having a centralized controller to provide the functionalities needed for the central controller, but also leverages the existing PCE network components.

The PCE communication Protocol (PCEP) provides mechanisms for PCEs to perform route computations in response to Path Computation Clients (PCCs) requests. PCEP Extensions for PCE-initiated LSP setup in (Crabbe, 2014) describes a set of extensions to PCEP to enable active control of MPLS-TE and GMPLS tunnels.

Crabbe (2014) describes the setup and teardown of PCE-initiated LSPs under the active stateful PCE model, without the need for local configuration on the PCC, thus allowing for a dynamic MPLS network that is centrally controlled and deployed.

It is possible to use a stateful PCE for computing one or more SR-TE paths taking into account various constraints and objective functions. Once a path is chosen, the stateful PCE can instantiate an SR-TE path on a PCC using PCEP extensions specified in (Filsfils, 2014) using the SR specific PCEP extensions described in (Sivabalan, 2014).

By using PCE and SR-based solutions, LSP in both MPLS and GMPLS network can be setup/delete/maintained/synchronized through a centrally controlled dynamic MPLS network. Since, in these solutions, the LSP is need to be signaled through the head end LER to the tail end LER, there are either RSVP-TE signaling protocol need to be deployed in the MPLS/GMPLS network, or extend IGP with node/adjacency segment identifiers signaling capability to be deployed.

Solutions and Recommendations

The PCE Based Central Controller (PCECC) solution proposed in (Zhao, 2014) allows for a dynamic MPLS network that is eventually controlled and deployed without the deployment of RSVP-TE or extended IGP with node/adjacency segment identifiers signaling capability while providing all the key MPLS functionalities needed by the service providers. These key MPLS features include MPLS P2P LSP, P2MP/MP2MP LSP, MPLS protection mechanism etc. In the case that one LSP path involves legacy network nodes and the new network nodes which are centrally controlled, the PCECC solution provides a smooth transition step for users.

PCECC not only removes the existing MPLS signaling totally from the control plane without losing any existing MPLS functionalities, but it also achieves this goal through utilizing the existing PCEP without introducing a new protocol into the network.

Zhao (2014) documents the use cases for the PCECC solution. These use cases are:

a) Global and Local Label Allocation: Li (2014) documents an exhaustive list of use cases where the global label is needed. Instead of using offline tools and manual configuration to come up a global label range statically, using the PCECC is convenient to negotiate a global label range and assign a global label for each device. While the global label range is negotiated, the local label range is also decided at the same time for each device.
b) FIB/LFIB Download: To empower networking with centralized controllable modules, there are many choices for downloading the forwarding entries to the data plane, one way is the use of the OpenFlow protocol, which is used to populate forwarding tables according to a set of instructions to the data plane. There are other candidate protocols to convey specific configuration information towards devices also. Since the PCEP is already deployed in some of the service network, to leverage the PCEP to populate the MPLS forwarding table is a possible good choice.
c) SR Support: To support the source routing based forwarding similar to SR, the node and link adjacency IDs can be negotiated through the PCECC with each PCECC clients and these IDs can be just taken from the global label range which has been negotiated already.
d) P2P LSP Protection: With the capability of supporting SR within the PCECC architecture, all the P2P forwarding path protection use cases described in (Francois, 2014) will be supported to within the PCECC network. These protection alternatives include end-to-end path protection, local protection without operator management and local protection with operator management.

Figure 9. PCECC Architecture

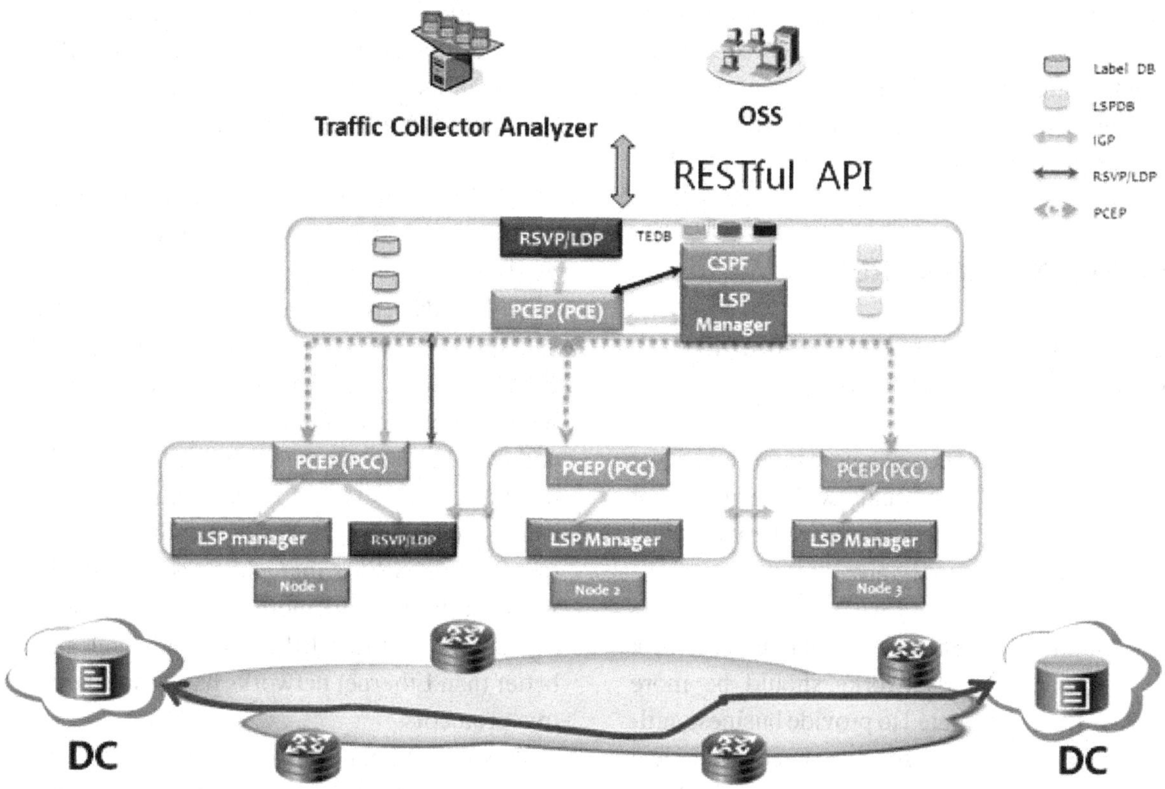

e) P2MP/MP2MP LSP Support: With the capability of global label and local label existing at the same time in the PCECC network, PCECC will use compute, setup and maintain the P2MP and MP2MP LSP using the local label range for each network nodes.

f) P2MP/MP2MP LSP Protection: With the capability of setting up/maintaining the P2MP/MP2MP LSP within the PCECC network, it is easy to provide the end-end managed path protection service and the local protection with the operation management in the PCECC network for the P2MP/MP2MP LSP, which includes both the RSVP-TE P2MP based LSP and also the mLDP based LSP.

For the centralized architecture, the performance achieved through distributed system cannot be easily matched if the entire forwarding path is computed, downloaded and maintained by the centralized controller. The performance can be improved by supporting part of the forwarding path in the PCECC network through the segment routing mechanism except that the adjacency IDs for all the network nodes and links are propagated through the centralized controller instead of using the IGP extension.

The PCE+ based solution can be deployed in a totally new network where each node in the network are centralized controlled by the PCE+ controller. In this scenario, the centralized controller doesn't need to enable any MPLS related signaling module.

When the PCE+ based solution is used in a mixed network where current existing MPLS signaling protocols are still running for certain parts of the network, then the MPLS signaling protocol related module needs to be enabled for the PCE+ controller so that the PCE+ controller can be functioning as a MPLS signaling proxy module to automatically stitch the LSP segments together among the traditional LSP segments and new LSP segments setup by the PCE+ central controller.

NVO3 (VXLAN/NVGRE)

Issues, Controversies, Problems Which NVO3 Addresses

Multi-tenancy has become a core requirement for data centers (DC), especially with the advent of cloud computing. The key requirements needed to support multi-tenancy are:

a) Support on-demand, instant tenant network provisioning: Networks should be more service- orientated to provide business agility and efficient use of resources. Classical network systems focus on building large scale and static IP network, they are less considerate application. The modern cloud data center must be able to deploy applications rapidly, using any and all resources (compute, storage, and network) available in the data center at any time.
b) Support traffic isolation and address independence among different tenant networks: Underlay network can be partitioned to be different domains. Network isolation techniques should provide enough segments for large cloud deployments; traditional IEEE 802.1Q VLAN provides 4096 LAN segments (through a 12-bit VLAN identifier) which limits the scalability of cloud networks beyond 4K VLANs.
c) Support the placement and migration of VMs (Virtual Machines) anywhere within the data center, without being limited by DC network constraints such as the IP subnet boundaries of the underlying DC network. Layer 2 connectivity among different VMs belonging to a given tenant segment (subnet) can be extended across different PODs (Points of Delivery) within a data center or between different data centers.

TRILL (Transparent Interconnection of Lots of Links) and SPB (Shortest Path Bridging) are two Ethernet technologies which can overcome the above VLAN network shortcomings. Both TRILL and SPB can be used for creating a cloud with a flat Ethernet address, so that nodes can move around within the cloud and not need to change their IP address. The advantage with TRILL or SPB is that links will be used more efficiently than when using spanning tree protocols. Another advantage of TRILL or SPB is that adding additional links will make the network more resilient and efficient. TRILL or SPB based Ethernet clouds scale much better than Ethernet networks based on spanning tree protocols.

Network Virtualization Overlay (NVO) is an IP based technique also used to solve the above VLAN network issues. Compared to TRILL and SPB, it can be incrementally deployed, without necessarily requiring upgrade of the entire network. IETF NVO3 WG document (Narten, 2013) defines the specific issues in cloud data center, including VM mobility, address separation, auto provisioning and configuration, etc. NVE (Network Virtualization Edge) encapsulates/decapsulates the frame from/to tenant system in certain overlay protocol format. NVGRE and VXLAN are two of the most popular overlay protocols in market. (Mahalingam, 2014) encapsulation is based on UDP, with an 8-byte header following the UDP header. The encapsulation described in (Sridaharan, 2014) is based on end encapsulation described in (Farinacci, 2000) and it mandates the inclusion of the optional GRE Key field which carries the VSID (Virtual Subnet Identifier).

Compared to traditional VLAN, NVO3 offers the following benefits:

Figure 10. NVO3 Generic Reference Model

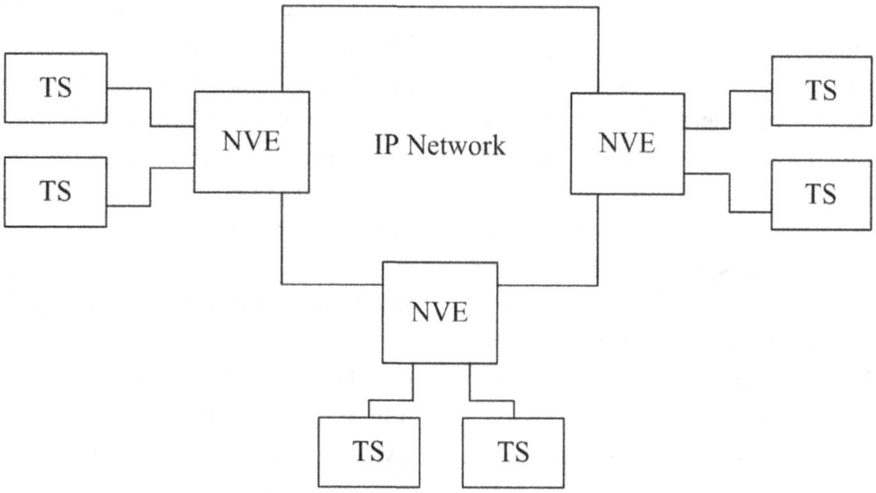

1. Flexible placement of multi-tenant segments throughout the data center: NVO3 provides a solution to extend Layer 2 segments over the underlying shared network infrastructure so that tenant workload can be placed across physical pods in the data center. Traditional VLAN and switching boundaries are not flexible or easily extended; VM placement and migration normally are restricted in a POD.
2. Higher scalability to address more Layer 2 segments: Both VXLAN and NVGRE include the identifier of the specific NVO instance, Virtual Network Identifier (VNI) in VXLAN and Virtual Subnet Identifier (VSID), NVGRE, in each packet. VLANs use a 12-bit VLAN ID to address Layer 2 segments, which results in limiting scalability of only 4096 VLANs.
3. Better utilization of available network paths in the underlying infrastructure: VLAN uses the Spanning Tree Protocol for loop prevention, which ends up not using half of the network links in a network by blocking redundant paths. In contrast, VXLAN and NVGRE packets are transferred through the underlying network based on its Layer 3 header and can take complete advantage of Layer 3 routing, equal-cost multipath (ECMP) routing, and link aggregation protocols to use all available paths. Underlay network devices can use VXLAN UDP source port and GRE key field in NVGRE header as ECMP HASH factor to improve load balancing granularity.

NVO3 overlay network normally works together with SDN controller to provide a centralized NVE-NVA architecture. Overlays give us network agility by separating the location of a device from its identity, the logical network provisioning for each tenant is decoupled from physical network, VM can be freely placed and migrated without limitation by network constraints. The centralized controller of NVA gives us consistent network behavior wherever an application is deployed, the application centric abstraction of the network, and a single point of control.

Controversies

NVE may co-locate with server hypervisor or external to server. If NVE resides in the hypervisor, it is software based solution, the representative solutions are VMWare NSX, Microsoft Hyper-V, etc. If NVE resides in a TOR device, it is hardware based solution; the representative solution is Cisco ACI. Also there is hybrid solution, NVO3 layer 3 gateways are implemented in aggregation devices to enhance forwarding capacity, NVO3 layer 2 translation gateways are implemented in TOR to interconnect between virtualized devices and non-virtualized devices, other NVEs are still resides in software hypervisor.

Compared to software-based solutions, hardware-based solutions can provide more forwarding capacity and heterogeneous network connectivity, but it lacks innovation agility because it needs chipset, switch vendors and SDN controller collaborative efforts and normally more innovation cycle is likely to be required. The comparison between hardware-based and software-based solution is as follows:

Solutions

Layer 2 Unicast Traffic Forwarding

In Figure 12, TS1 and TS3 in VN 10 communicate with each other through NVO3 tunnel between NVE1 and NVE2. This example assumes that address learning has been done on both sides, and corresponding MAC-to-NVE mappings exist on both NVEs.

When TS1 sends traffic to TS3, it forms Ethernet frames with MAC-B address of TS3 as the destination MAC address and sends them out to NVE-1. NVE-1, with a mapping of MAC-B to NVE-2 in its mapping table, performs NVO3 encapsulation on the packets. In the outer IP address header, the source IP address is the IP address of NVE-1, and the destination IP address is the IP address of NVE-2. NVE-1 then performs an IP address lookup for the IP address of NVE-2 to resolve the next hop in the transit network and subsequently uses the MAC address of the next-hop device to further encapsulate the packets in an Ethernet frame to send to the next-hop device. The packets are routed toward NVE-2 through the transport network based on their outer IP address header, which has the IP address of NVE-2 as the destination address. After NVE-2 receives the packets, it strips off the outer Ethernet, outer IP tunnel headers, and forwards the packets to TS3, based on the original destination MAC address in the Ethernet frame.

Multicast Traffic Forwarding

Besides the need to support the Address Resolution Protocol (ARP) and Neighbor Discovery (ND) in overlay network, there are also other several applications that require the support of multicast and/or broadcast in data centers, such as the multicast heartbeats among cluster server nodes. With NVO3, there are many possible ways that multicast may be handled in such networks.

a) Head-end replication: A multicast or broadcast transmission is achieved by replicating the packet at the source NVE, and making copies, one for each destination NVE that the multicast packet must be sent to.
b) Centralized replication at multicast service node: With this method, all multicast packets would be sent using a unicast tunnel encapsulation to a multicast service node. The multicast service node, in turn, would create multiple copies of the packet and would deliver a copy, using a unicast tunnel encapsulation, to each of the NVEs that are part of the multicast group for which the packet is intended.
c) IP multicast in the underlay: Multicast traffic in overlay network often makes the use of the underlay network multicast capability, e.g., use the mapping between overlay and underlay multicast group. In this method, the underlay supports IP multicast and the ingress NVE encapsulates the packet with the appropriate IP multicast address in the

Figure 11. NVE Software Based and Hardware Based Solution

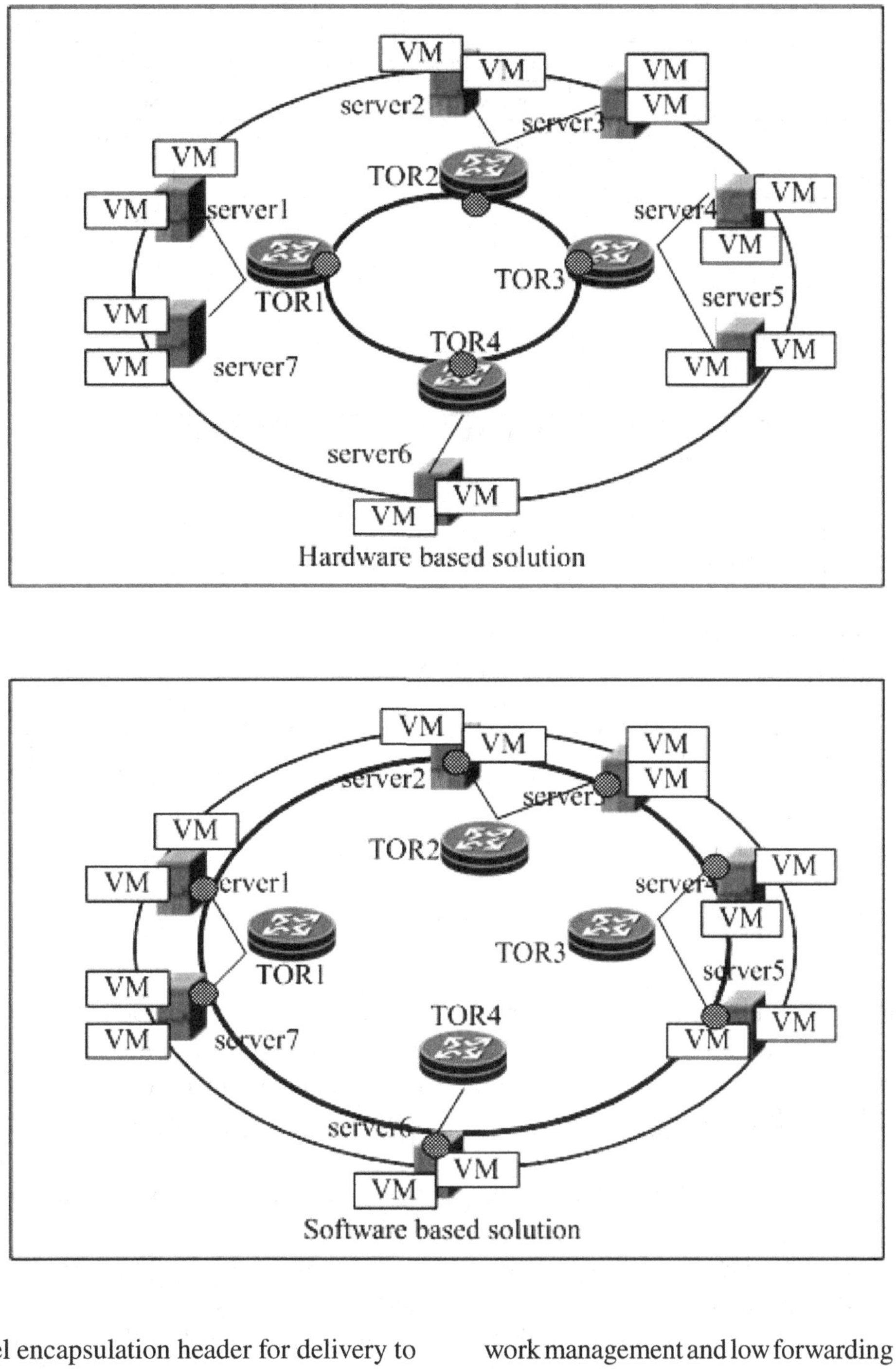

tunnel encapsulation header for delivery to the desired set of NVEs.

PIM may be used for the underlay multicast tree construction. However it has issues of poor scalability, long convergence time, complex network management and low forwarding efficiency. Therefore an IS-IS based control plane tree construction mechanism (Lucy, 2014) is used in the underlay network.

In this method, the NVE would be required to participate in the underlay as a host using IGMP/

Table 1. Differences between Software Based Solution and Hardware Based Solution

	CT Solution	IT Solution
NVE location	Network edge device	Server
Heterogeneous access	Supported	Not supported
VM migration	Complex	Simple
Forwarding performance	High	Low
Innovation cycle	Slow	Fast

Figure 12. NVO3 Example

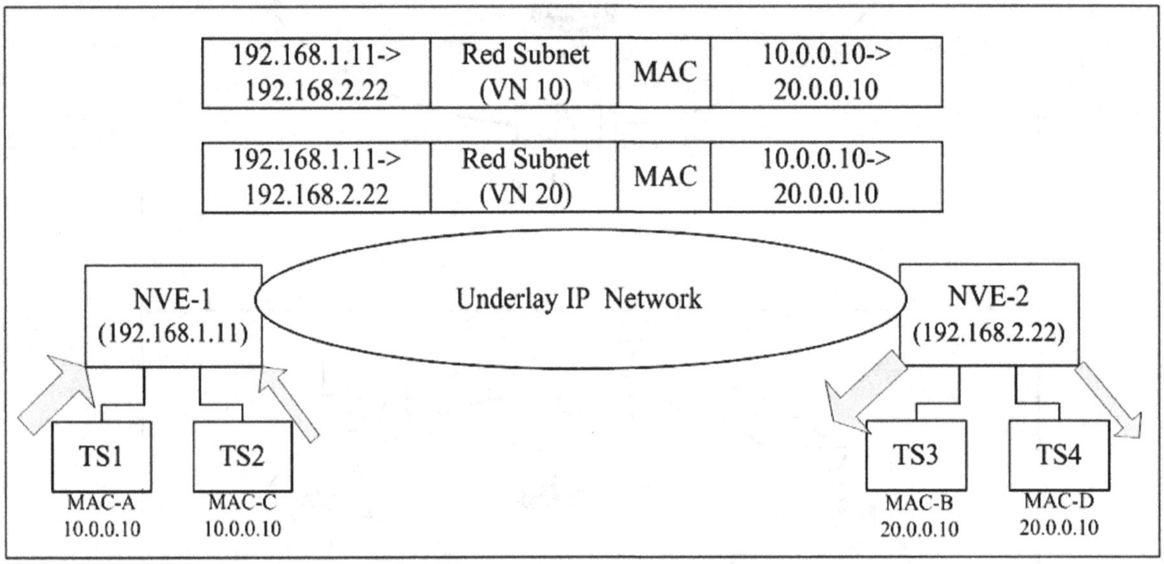

MLD in order for the underlay to learn about the groups that the NVE participates in.

Distributed Layer 3 Gateway

The relaying of traffic from one VN to another will pass through the DC gateways. If such gateways are centralized, traffic between TSes (Tenant Systems) on different VNs can take suboptimal paths, i.e., triangular routing results in paths that always traverse the gateway. As an optimization, individual NVEs can be part of a distributed gateway that performs such relaying, reducing or completely eliminating triangular routing. In a distributed gateway solution, each ingress NVE can perform such relaying activity directly, so long as it has access to the policy information needed to determine whether cross-VN communication is allowed. Having individual NVEs be part of a distributed gateway allows them to tunnel traffic directly to the destination NVE without the need to take suboptimal paths.

In the distributed gateway scenario, a NVE must perform Layer 2 routing for the TSes that are on the same subnet and IP routing for the TSes that are on the different subnets of same tenant.

As IP address space in different routing domain can be overlapped, so VRF should be created on each edge NVE to isolate IP forwarding process among different routing domain. If a routing domain spreads over multiple NVEs, routing information of the routing domain should be synchronized among these NVEs to ensure the reachability to all TSes in that routing domain.

When a NVE receives inter-subnet traffic from local TS whose destination MAC is gateway MAC, the NVE will perform Ethernet header termination and look up IP forwarding table to forward the traffic to IP next hop. If destination TS is connected to a remote NVE, the remote NVE will be the IP next hop for traffic forwarding. Ingress NVE will perform NVO3 encapsulation for such inter-subnet traffic and forward it to the remote RBridge through IP network. When the remote NVE receives the traffic, the NVE will decapsulate NVO3 header and then looks up IP forwarding table to forward it to the destination TS. Through this solution, NVO3 can provide pair-wise data frame routing for inter-subnet traffic.

Anycast Layer3 Gateway

All tenant system traffic going in/out DC will pass through the DC GWs. For a large DC and supporting many tenant networks, such GWs can be the pain point for the scalability. Although VRRP (Knight, 2998, Hinder, 2004, Nadas, 2010) may be used at the GWs to provide link/node redundancy, it does not resolve the scalability issue. Distributed GW may be implemented on NVEs (Black, 2014), which may reduce the traffic passing through these GWs; however all the traffic going in/out DC still have to go through these GWs.

Anycast Layer 3 Gateway means that multiple GW network devices support GW functions between overlay VNs and external networks and have the same GW IP and MAC address for each overlay VN, these gateways share same gateway IP and MAC address for each VN, the GW IP and MAC address is called gateway anycast IP and MAC address. To ensure NVO3 traffic load balancing from ingress NVEs to these gateways, these gateways also share same outer IP address, this address is called as device underlying anycast IP address in the document.

Gateway anycast IP address is used as the default gateway's IP address for all TSs in the corresponding VN. As different VNs are allowed to have overlapping MAC address space, different anycast gateway IP addresses can map to the same anycast MAC. When sending traffic toward a VN gateway on GW devices, ingress NVEs use the device underlying anycast IP address as outer IP destination address on NVO3 packets. The VN may be an L2 VN or L3 VN.

Each GW network device announces device underlying anycast IP address in underlying IGP network. If these gateways have same routing cost to ingress NVE, the underlying equal-cost multi-path (ECMP) approach will distribute the NVO3 traffic from the ingress NVE to one of GW devices.

When sending traffic toward a tenant system in a VN, a VN GW on a GW device obtains the mapping of the tenant system and attached NVE from a table lookup. If the VN is an L3 VN, the GW device encapsulates the packet with the NVE IP address as outer destination IP address and its device underlying anycast IP address as the outer source IP address. If the VN is an L2 VN, the GW device inserts inner MAC header with its anycast MAC address as the source MAC address and tenant MAC address as the destination MAC address; then encapsulates the packet with the NVE IP address as outer destination IP address and its underlying anycast IP address as the outer source IP address.

NVO3 and MPLS VPN Network Interconnection

To provide cloud service to external data center client, data center networks should be connected with WAN networks. BGP MPLS/IP VPN has already been widely deployed at WAN networks. Normally internal data center and external MPLS/IP VPN network belongs to different autonomous system (AS). This requires the setting up of inter-as connections at Autonomous System Border Routers (ASBRs) between NVO3 network and external MPLS/IP network.

Currently, a typical connection mechanism between a data center network and an MPLS/IP VPN network is similar to Inter-AS Option-A of RFC4364, but it has scalability issue if there is huge number of tenants in data center networks. To overcome the issue, inter-as Option-B can be used to enhance the scalability.

Two ASBRs involves in the option B. One is at WAN side (ASBR-w); one is at DC side (PE/ASBR or ASBR-d). Similar to the solution described in section 10, part (b) of (Rosen, 2006) (commonly referred to as Option-B) peering ASBRs are connected by one or more sub-interfaces that are enabled to receive MPLS traffic. An MP-BGP session is used to distribute the labeled VPN prefixes between the ASBRs. In data plane, the traffic that flows between the ASBRs is placed upon MPLS tunnels; traffic separation among different VPNs between the ASBRs relies on MPLS VPN Label.

As for the routing distribution process from DC to WAN side, MPLS VPN Label is allocated on ASBR-d per VN per NVE. As for the routing distribution process from WAN to DC side, VN ID is allocated per MPLS VPN Label receiving from ASBR-w on ASBR-d. From data plane perspective, VN ID and MPLS VPN Label switching is performed on ASBR-d, ASBR-w has no difference with traditional RFC4364 based Option-B behavior, no VRF is created on the ASBR-d. If there is a VRF which has much VPN prefixes, EBGP VPN connection can be terminated on ASBR-d, which means the ASBR doesn't allocate new VN IDs for each MPLS VPN Label and advertise it to peer NVE in local AS, VRF is created on the ASBR-d and the VPN route from WAN side populates to local VRF. For the traffic from DC to WAN side, IP forwarding process is performed, VRF is selected based on VN ID, and then the traffic will be MPLS encapsulated and send to peer ASBR.

GENEVE Encapsulation

VMware, Microsoft, Red Hat and Intel have proposed a new encapsulation protocol that would standardize how traffic is tunneled over the physical infrastructure by network overlay software.

The encapsulation is called Generic Network Virtualization Encapsulation (GENEVE) (Sridhar, 2016). In theory, GENEVE would replace three similar but competing protocols: Microsoft's NVGRE and VMware's VXLAN and Stateless Transport Tunneling (STT).

GENEVE includes extensions that would allow network overlays to insert metadata into encapsulated frames to share additional information about network state; it can be used for service chaining applications such as specialized forwarding or stitching firewalls and load balancers.

GENEVE will bring more interoperability to the network overlay market. But there are still some controversies in IETF about metadata use case and where should it be included.

Recommendations

In cloud computing era, NVO3 technologies can satisfy the key requirements of multi-tenancy in data center network. NVGRE and VXLAN are two typical NVO3 technologies. NVO3 can solve data center virtualization issues including VM mobility, address separation, auto provisioning and configuration, etc. It is being deployed in an increasing number of data center networks. In the future, generic encapsulation schemes maybe designed to replace VXLAN and NVGRE; it can carry more system state or metadata between NVEs.

When NVO3 is deployed in a data center networks, distributed gateway, centralized anycast gateway, underlay network multicast solution and inter-as connection solution between NVO3 and MPLS VPN network are important aspects and should be deliberately considered to provide a complete solution.

a) In homogeneous environment, NVE can be deployed on host server. In heterogeneous environment, NVE can be deployed on TOR physical switch, VXLAN, NVGRE and native Ethernet encapsulation translation can be performed on physical switch.
b) Distributed layer 3 gateway is suggested to be deployed for east-west inter-subnet traffic forwarding.
c) Anycast layer3 gateway is suggested to be deployed at DC exit point to forward north-south bound traffic between data center and WAN network.
d) If underlay network doesn't support multicast, head-end replication at ingress NVE or centralized replication can be used to convey multicast traffic in overlay network. If underlay network support multicast, one or more VNs can be mapped to one multicast group address in underlay network.
e) For large scale data center network, inter-as option-B can be used to interconnect NVO3 and IP/MPLS VPN network. For small or medium data center network, inter-as option-A can be used to interconnect NVO3 and IP/MPLS VPN network.

SERVICE FUNCTION CHAINING (SFC)

Issues, Controversies, Problems Which SFC Addresses

IP networks rely more and more on the combination of advanced functions for the delivery of added value services. Typical examples of such functions include firewall such as the one which is described in (Woodyatt, 2011), DPI (Deep Packet Inspection), NAT, load balancer, etc. Such advanced functions are denoted SF (Service Function). Current service function deployment models are relatively static and are often coupled to network topology; this will greatly reduce, and in many cases, limit the ability of an operator to introduce new services and/or service functions. Because network topology dependency, the following problems are easily induced while the current service function deployment models are used (Quinn, 2014):

a) **Topological Dependencies:** Network service deployments are often coupled to network topology, whether it can be physical or virtualized, or a hybrid of the two. Such dependency imposes constraints on the service delivery, potentially inhibiting the network operator from optimally utilizing service resources, and reduces the flexibility. This limits scale, capacity, and redundancy across network resources.
b) **Configuration Complexity:** A direct consequence of topological dependencies is the complexity of the entire configuration, specifically in deploying service function chains. Simple actions such as changing the order of the service functions in a service function chain require changes to the topology.
c) **Constrained High Availability:** An effect of topological dependency is constrained service function high availability. Worse, when modified, inadvertent non-high availability or downtime can result. Since traffic reaches many service functions based on network topology, alternate, or redundant service functions must be placed in the same topology as the primary service.
d) **Consistent Ordering of Service Functions:** Service functions are typically independent; service function_1 (SF1)...service function_n (SFn) are unrelated and there is no notion at the service layer that SF1 occurs before SF2. However, to an administrator many service functions have a strict ordering that must be in place, yet the administrator has no consistent way to impose and verify the ordering of the service functions that

are used to deliver a given service. Service function chains today are most typically built through manual configuration processes. These are not only slow but also error prone. With the advent of newer service deployment models the control and policy planes provide not only connectivity state, but will also be increasingly utilized for the creation of network services. Such control/ management planes could be centralized, or be distributed.

e) **Application of Service Policy:** Service functions rely on topology information such as VLANs or packet (re) classification to determine service policy selection, i.e. the service function specific action taken. Topology information is increasingly less viable due to scaling, tenancy and complexity reasons. The topological information is often stale, providing the operator with inaccurate placement that can result in sub-optimal resource utilization. Furthermore topology-centric information often does not convey adequate information to the service functions, forcing functions to individually perform more granular classification.

f) **Transport Dependence:** Service functions can and will be deployed in networks with a range of transports, including under and overlays. The coupling of service functions to topology requires service functions to support many transport encapsulations or for a transport gateway function to be present.

g) **Elastic Service Delivery:** Given that the current state of the art for adding/removing service functions largely centers on VLANs and routing changes, rapid changes to the service deployment can be hard to realize due to the risk and complexity of such changes.

h) **Traffic Selection Criteria:** Traffic selection is coarse, that is, all traffic on a particular segment traverse service functions whether the traffic requires service enforcement or not. This lack of traffic selection is largely due to the topological nature of service deployment since the forwarding topology dictates how (and what) data traverses service function(s). In some deployments, more granular traffic selection is achieved using policy routing or access control filtering. This results in operationally complex configurations and is still relatively inflexible.

i) **Limited End-to-End Service Visibility:** Troubleshooting service related issues is a complex process that involves both network-specific and service-specific expertise. This is especially the case when service function chains span multiple DCs, or across administrative boundaries. Furthermore, the physical and virtual environments (network and service), can be highly divergent in terms of topology and that topological variance adds to these challenges.

j) **Per-Service Function (Re)Classification:** Classification occurs at each service function independent from previously applied service functions. More importantly, the classification functionality often differs per service function and service functions may not leverage the results from other service functions.

k) **Symmetric Traffic Flows:** Service function chains may be unidirectional or bidirectional depending on the state requirements of the service functions. In a unidirectional chain traffic is passed through a set of service functions in one forwarding direction only. Bidirectional chains require traffic to be passed through a set of service functions in both forwarding directions. Many common service functions such as DPI and firewall often require bidirectional chaining in order to ensure flow state is consistent. Existing service deployment models provide a static approach to realizing forward and reverse service function chain association most often requiring complex configuration of each network device throughout the SFC.

l) **Multi-vendor Service Functions:** Deploying service functions from multiple vendors often require per-vendor expertise: insertion models differ, there are limited common attributes and inter-vendor service functions do not share information.

SFC aims to address the aforementioned issues associated with service deployment. Each service function path defines an ordered set of service functions that must be applied to packets and/or frames selected as a result of classification. It tries to provide a mechanism to dynamically enforce a SF-derived, adequate forwarding policy for packets entering a SFC-enabled domain. A SFC-enabled domain includes the functional elements of SFC classifier, SFC Ingress Node, SF Node and SFC Egress Node. To provide explicit information used to identify each SFP and to share metadata/context information between SFs, a new data plane encapsulation should be designed.

Solutions and Recommendations

The SFC architecture described in (Halpern, 2014) consists of the following logical elements:

a) Service Overlay: Service function chaining utilizes a service specific overlay that creates the service topology. The service overlay provides service function connectivity and is built "on top" of the existing network topology and allows operators to use whatever overlay or underlay they prefer to create a path between service functions, and to locate service functions in the network as needed. Within the service topology, service functions can be viewed as resources for consumption and an arbitrary topology constructed to connect those resources in a required order. Adding new service functions to the topology is easily accomplished, and no underlying network changes are required. Lastly, the service overlay can provide service specific information needed for troubleshooting service-related issues.

b) Service Classification: Classification is used to select which traffic enters a service overlay. The granularity of the classification varies based on device capabilities, customer requirements, and service offered. Initial classification determines the service function chain required to process the traffic. Subsequent classification can be used within a given service function chain to alter the sequence of service functions applied. Symmetric classification ensures that forward and reverse chains are in place. Similarly, asymmetric -- relative to required service function -- chains can be achieved via service classification.

c) Dataplane Metadata: Data plane metadata provides the ability to exchange information between logical classification points and service functions (and vice versa) and between service functions. As such metadata is not used as forwarding information to deliver packets along the service overlay. Metadata can include the result of antecedent classification and/or information from external sources. Service functions utilize metadata, as required, for localized policy decisions. In addition to sharing of information, the use of metadata addresses several of the issues raised in the previous section, e.g., decouple the policy from the network topology, and the need for per-service function classification (and re-classification). A common approach to service metadata creates a common foundation for interoperability between service functions, regardless of vendor. Service function chaining utilizes a service specific overlay that creates the service topology. The service overlay provides service function connectivity and is built "on top" of the existing network topology and allows operators to use whatever overlay or underlay they prefer to create a path between service functions, and to locate service functions in the network as needed.

SFC Ingress Node

The SFC Classifier is embedded in SFC Ingress Node. When an ingress node receives an interface of the SFC Ingress Node that connects to the outside of the SFC domain, the ingress node should get SF Map Index firstly relying on SFC Classifier.

The SFC Classifier Check whether the received packet matches an existing classification rule, If no rule matches, forward the packet to the next hop according to legacy forwarding behavior.

The SFC Classifier classifies packets based on (some of) the contents of the packet. Particularly, it classifies packets based on the possible combination of one or more header fields, such as source address, destination address, DS field, protocol ID, source port and destination port numbers, and any other information. Each SF Map Classification Rule must be bound to one only one SF Map Index.

Then the ingress node retrieves the corresponding SF Map from the SFC Policy Table and gets the locator of the first SF as indicated in the SF Map Entry. If multiple locators are available, the selection can be based on local criteria (e.g., the closest/best path). Finally the ingress node sends the packet to the first SF node.

SF Node

This section assumes the default behavior is each SF Node does not embed a Classifier. When a packet is received by a SF Node, the SF Node must check whether the packet conveys a SF Map Index.

a) If no SF Map Index is included, forward the packet according to legacy forwarding policies.
b) If the packet conveys a SF Map Index, retrieve the corresponding SF Map from the SFC Policy Table. If no entry is found in the table, forward the packet according to legacy forwarding policies. Otherwise, the packet is de-capsulated (if needed) and then presented as an input to the local SF. In case several SFs are co-located in the same node, the packet is processed by all SFs indicated in the SF Map. Once the packet is successfully handled by local SF(s), the packet is forwarded to the next SF Node in the list or to an intermediate node (if the local SF Node is the last element in the SF Map). If the local SF node is not the last one in the SF Map, it retrieves the next SF Node from the list, retrieves its locator for the SFC Policy Table, and forwards the packet to the next hop. If the local SF Node is the last element in the SF Map, it forwards the packet to the next hop according to legacy forwarding policies.

SFC Egress Node

When a packet is received through an interface that connects the SFC Egress Node to its SFC domain, the Egress Node must:

1. Strip any existing SF Map Index.
2. Forward the packet according to legacy forwarding policies.

A full marking mechanism is suggested to be deployed. Ingress nodes perform the classification and marking functions. Then, involved SF Nodes process received packets according to their marking. SF node mechanism isn't suggested, in which every SF Node embeds also a classifier, and the ingress node only decide the first node to forward to. Packets are forwarded at each node according to local policies. No marking is required when all SFs are collocated with a classifier.

Packets are forwarded to the required Service Functions in service-inferred forwarding planes which is independent from transport network. SFC can automate the overall process of generating and enforcing policies to accommodate a set of network

Figure 13. SFC Logical Architecture

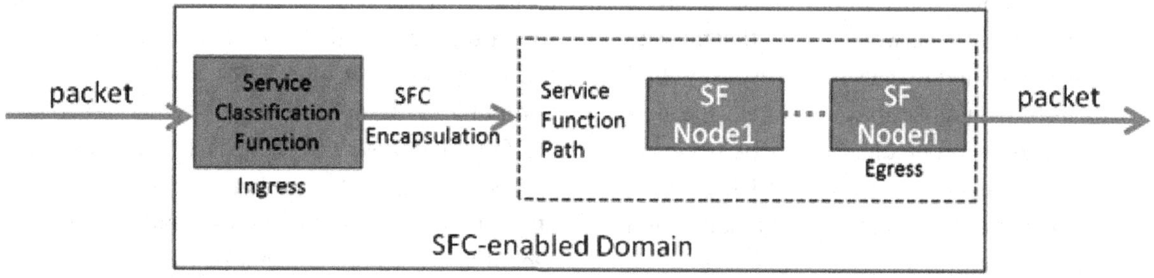

connectivity service objectives, so management of Service functions can be greatly eased.

There are several forwarding methods for SFC; these methods can be classified into certain categories in terms of distribution of information for setting the paths and decision of the paths. The methods used to distribute the information and the patterns used to decide the paths will affect the mechanism of Service Chaining as well as service flexibility. Homma (2014) analyses these forwarding approaches in details.

OPENFLOW

Issues, Controversies, Problems Which OpenFlow Addresses

Traditional network architectures are ill-suited to meet the requirements of today's enterprises, carriers, and end users. In the SDN architecture, the control and data planes are decoupled, network intelligence and state are logically centralized, and the underlying network infrastructure is abstracted from the applications. As a result, enterprises and carriers gain unprecedented programmability, automation, and network control, enabling them to build highly scalable, flexible networks that readily adapt to changing business needs.

Limitations of Current Networking Technologies:

1. Complexity that leads to stasis: Protocols tend to be defined in isolation, however, with each solving a specific problem and without the benefit of any fundamental abstractions. This has resulted in one of the primary limitations of today's networks: complexity. For example, to add or move any device, IT must touch multiple switches, routers, firewalls, Web authentication portals, etc. and update ACLs, VLANs, QoS, and other protocol-based mechanisms using device-level management tools. In addition, network topology, vendor switch model, and software version all must be taken into account. Due to this complexity, today's networks are relatively static as IT seeks to minimize the risk of service disruption.
2. Inconsistent policies: To implement a network-wide policy, IT may have to configure thousands of devices and mechanisms. For example, every time a new virtual machine is brought up, it can take hours, in some cases days, for IT to reconfigure ACLs across the entire network. The complexity of today's networks makes it very difficult for IT to apply a consistent set of access, security, QoS, and other policies to increasingly mobile users, which leaves the enterprise vulnerable to security breaches, non-compliance with regulations, and other negative consequences.
3. Inability to scale: As demands on the data center rapidly grow, so too must the network

grow. However, the network becomes vastly more complex with the addition of hundreds or thousands of network devices that must be configured and managed. IT has also relied on link oversubscription to scale the network, based on predictable traffic patterns; however, in today's virtualized data centers, traffic patterns are incredibly dynamic and therefore unpredictable.

4. Vendor dependence: Carriers and enterprises seek to deploy new capabilities and services in rapid response to changing business needs or user demands. However, their ability to respond is hindered by vendors' equipment product cycles, which can range to three years or more. Lack of standard, open interfaces limits the ability of network operators to tailor the network to their individual environments.

Solutions and Recommendations

SDN is a dynamic and flexible network architecture that protects existing investments while future-proofing the network. With SDN, today's static network can evolve into an extensible service delivery platform capable of responding rapidly to changing business, end-user, and market needs.

OpenFlow is one of the standard communications interfaces defined between the controllers and forwarding layers of SDN architecture. OpenFlow allows direct access to and manipulation of the forwarding plane of network devices such as switches and routers, both physical and virtual (hypervisor-based). It is the absence of an open interface to the forwarding plane that has led to the characterization of today's networking devices as monolithic, closed, and mainframe-like. No other standard protocol does what OpenFlow does, and a protocol like OpenFlow is needed to move network control out of the networking switches to logically centralized control software.

OpenFlow can be compared to the instruction set of a CPU. As shown in Figure 2, the protocol specifies basic primitives that can be used by an external software application to program the forwarding plane of network devices, just like the instruction set of a CPU would program a computer system.

The OpenFlow protocol is implemented on both sides of the interface between network infrastructure devices and the SDN control software. OpenFlow uses the concept of flows to identify network traffic based on pre-defined match rules that can be statically or dynamically programmed by the SDN control software. It also allows IT to define how traffic should flow through network devices based on parameters such as usage patterns, applications, and cloud resources. Since OpenFlow allows the network to be programmed on a per-flow basis, OpenFlow-based SDN architecture provides extremely granular control, enabling the network to respond to real-time changes at the application, user, and session levels. Current IP-based routing does not provide this level of control, as all flows between two endpoints must follow the same path through the network, regardless of their different requirements.

The OpenFlow protocol is a key enabler for software-defined networks and currently is the only standardized SDN protocol that allows direct manipulation of the forwarding plane of network devices. While initially applied to Ethernet-based networks, OpenFlow switching can extend to a much broader set of use cases. OpenFlow-based SDNs can be deployed on existing networks, both physical and virtual. Network devices can support OpenFlow-based forwarding as well as traditional forwarding, which makes it very easy for enterprises and carriers to progressively introduce OpenFlow-based SDN technologies, even in multi-vendor network environments.

By decoupling the network control and data planes, OpenFlow-based SDN architecture abstracts the underlying infrastructure from the applications that use it, allowing the network to become as programmable and manageable at scale as the computer infrastructure that it increasingly resembles. An SDN approach fosters network virtualization, enabling IT staff to manage their servers, applications, storage, and networks with a common approach and tool set. Whether in a carrier environment or enterprise data center and campus, SDN adoption can improve network manageability, scalability, and agility.

The OpenFlow is designed primarily with fixed function switches in mind. Fixed function switches recognize a predetermined set of header fields and process packets using a small set of predefined actions. As a consequence, expanding the capability of OpenFlow to control additional network technologies leads to continual modification of the OpenFlow protocol specification. As SDN becomes more widely adopted, there is pressure to evolve the OpenFlow protocol, to extend the protocols it supports, the packet headers it recognizes, and the way in which packets are processed.

OpenFlow-based SDN is currently being rolled out in a variety of networking devices and software, delivering substantial benefits to both enterprises and carriers.

One deployment example of SDN is in Google's B4 network. B4 network is a private WAN connecting Google's data centers across the planet. B4 has a number of unique characteristics: i) massive bandwidth requirements deployed to a modest number of sites, ii) elastic traffic demand that seeks to maximize average bandwidth, and iii) full control over the edge servers and network, which enables rate limiting and demand measurement at the edge. These characteristics led to a Software Defined Networking architecture using OpenFlow to control relatively simple switches built from merchant silicon. B4's centralized traffic engineering service drives links to near 100% utilization, while splitting application flows among multiple paths to balance capacity against application priority/demands.

In summary, the advantages of the SDN solutions include:

a) Centralized management and control of networking devices from multiple vendors;
b) Improved automation and management by using common APIs to abstract the underlying networking details from the orchestration and provisioning systems and applications;
c) Rapid innovation through the ability to deliver new network capabilities and services without the need to configure individual devices or wait for vendor releases; Programmability by operators, enterprises, independent software vendors, and users (not just equipment manufacturers) using common programming environments, which gives all parties new opportunities to drive revenue and differentiation;
d) Increased network reliability and security as a result of centralized and automated management of network devices, uniform policy enforcement, and fewer configuration errors;
e) More granular network control with the ability to apply comprehensive and wide-ranging policies at the session, user, device, and application levels; and
f) Better end-user experience as applications exploit centralized network state information to seamlessly adapt network behavior to user needs.

The risks associated with SDN include:

Software defined networks will lead to higher security risks and lower reliability levels for all users. For telecom operators it could also result in a loss of control of the network.

a) The service interruption risk: The existing network has been deployed through the word for many years and the SDN solution is totally changed the architecture of the existing network. The deployment of the SDN solution must be done gradually where the existing network solution and SDN solution should be xo-existed for a certain period

Figure 14. Example of OpenFlow Instruction Set

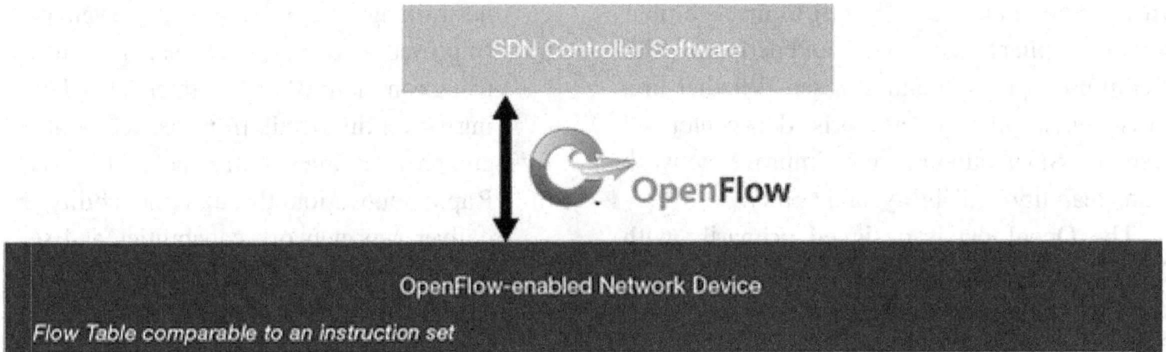

MAC src	MAC dst	IP Src	IP Dst	TCP dport	...	Action	Count
*	10:20:.	*	*	*	*	port 1	250
*	*	*	5.6.7.8	*	*	port 2	300
*	*	*	*	25	*	drop	892
*	*	*	192.*	*	*	local	120
*	*	*	*	*	*	controller	11

of time. During this transition period, the interoperability between these two solutions is necessary. There is a challenge for deploying out the SDN solution while the services from the existing network can't be interrupted.

b) Cyber-security risk: SDNs transfer the intelligence currently held in a network equipment box to a software layer, enabling the network to be centrally controlled. Like many areas of the digital world, that means physical protection barriers are replaced by cyber-security protection barriers. But it means that anyone, anywhere in the world, can potentially hack into the telecom network. Whilst hacking of telecom customers is commonplace today, SDNs could make hacking of the telecom network itself more likely, effectively enabling an enemy of the state to take over control of a country's telecom network.

c) Lower reliability: Traditionally, telecom networks were famed for their "five-nine" reliability levels – that is, that communication links have a 99.999% probability of working as expected. The advent of IP networking technology introduced some degree of open standards to telecom networks and reliability levels have fallen as a result. But SDN technology will open up interfaces much more, reducing equipment hardware to commodity boxes and raising the likelihood of hardware failures. That means network applications are less likely to work as well as they do today because a single vendor no longer takes responsibility for them.

d) Loss of control: Today network operators make money by charging large corporations to reserve dedicated bandwidth and to charge for a range of network services. SDNs will allow customers to program the network themselves and make more efficient use of the bandwidth they consume. Third party software developers will also be able to sell their customers more innovative network services, bypassing the network operator entirely. Operators therefore risk losing control of their network to industry outsiders.

PROTOCOL OBLIVIOUS FORWARDING (POF)

Issues, Controversies, Problems Which POF Addresses

The OpenFlow 1.x is protocol-specific semantics that forces the forwarding elements (FE) to understand the packet formats and retain the specific packet processing knowledge. The reactive evolving path needs incessant standard revisions to accommodate new features and new protocols.

The current OpenFlow based SDN promotes the programmability of network devices by downloading flows into devices from the controller but it cannot support new protocols automatically. The programmability can only apply to the existing protocols. If one service based on a new protocol needs to be implemented, the operator has to ask the device vendor to modify the code of the devices to support the new service. A packet is composed of multiple protocol headers and payload. The protocol headers are parsed and modified by NP micro code or ASIC logic during the forwarding process. The position of each protocol field, such as the IPv4 source address, is calculated by the code that is preloaded into the devices according to protocol format by the device vendor. If one new protocol needs to be supported, the code must be modified. This will lead to a long deployment cycle for new services based on new protocols. The current OpenFlow based SDN cannot resolve the aforementioned problem. In the OpenFlow specifications, the protocol field is only identified by the field type. The position of the protocol fields cannot be derived from the flow's forwarding instructions. So the position of each protocol fields must be calculated by the code, which means the code of the devices must be modified for processing new protocol headers

Solutions

A POF forwarding element does no need to understand the packet format. In POF, flow table search keys are defined as {offset, length} tuples, and instructions access data using {offset, length} tuples. The figure below is a basic IPv4 process flow used for demonstrating how POF works. The 'Type' is denoted with {12B, 2B}, the 'Destination IP Address' is denoted with {30B, 4B}, etc.

In order to demonstrate the capability of POF and evaluate the possibility of using the existing hardware to support POF, we have developed two prototypes in parallel. One is an open-source software prototype. The other is based on one of our NP-based router platforms. The POF software-based switch is published on this website, and any person and community can play with it, expand it, optimize it, and run innovative services on top of it. It is our hope that our efforts can stir interests in both industry and academia.

How can POF benefit Service Providers & Network Operators?

Protocol Oblivious Forwarding (POF) aims to be a groundbreaking technology that will shape the future SDN forwarding plane infrastructure. POF enhances the current SDN forwarding plane with the following advantages:

a) Enable fast innovation and new source of revenue. POF-enabled FEs can support any existing or new protocols and network services without vendor-supported FE upgrades. Users can implement proprietary protocols easily to meet forwarding, security, and OAM requirements. It can significantly accelerate the new service introduction.
b) Enable OPEX reduction. POF provides a stable and future-proof forwarding plane and a standard southbound interface for sustainable SDN evolvement. New services

are deployed in the form of standard or customized software offered by third parties. Users have full controllability and visibility to their networks.

c) Enable CAPEX reduction. POF makes standard-based software and hardware possible. The open market helps users avoid vendor lock-in. The white-box devices and the standard forwarding ASICs can be used to offer better performance at lower cost.

Recommendations

a) POF thoroughly decouples the SDN control plane and the forwarding plane. Software can construct flexible applications without any underlying constraints. Controller applies high level languages and compilers to program the FEs through the standard instruction set
b) POF advocates a standard, flexible and future-proof forwarding plane. Allow FEs to focus on performance rather than functionality. FE will become simpler and more flexible
c) POF calls for continuous research to improve. Standardize the corresponding interface and the FIS.

FUTURE RESEARCH DIRECTIONS

Future solutions should focus more on the simplicity of the network operation, maintenance and the flexibility for adding new services in a timely manner (i.e., shorten Time to Market cycles). Some challenges are listed below:

1. New services should be added more easily:
    a. More benefits for Users.
        i. Better performance.
        ii. Better scalability
        iii. Minimal configuration operations.
    b. Agnostic to the underlying network topology
2. Mix of traffic engineering paths where portion of the paths are controlled in a distributed manner while other part of the tunnels are controlled in a centralized manner.
3. More openness of the network.

NVO3

Current VXLAN and NVGRE encapsulation can't satisfy all network virtualization requirements; system state is often needed to be carried along with the packet data. When compared to the tags used to exchange metadata between line cards on a chassis switch, 24-bit VN ID is not enough and should be extended to carry more system state or metadata. There are nearly endless uses for this metadata, ranging from storing input ports for simple security policies to service based context for interposing advanced middle boxes.

GENEVE is being designed to support all network virtualization use cases, where tunnels are typically established to act as a backplane between the virtual switches residing in hypervisors, physical switches, or middle boxes or other appliances. The new encapsulation should consider following restrictions:

a) The data plane is generic and extensible enough to support current and future control planes.
b) Tunnel components are efficiently implementable in both hardware and software without restricting capabilities to the lowest common denominator.
c) High performance over existing IP fabrics.

SFC

Service Functions process the traffic flows which traverse the SFC-enabled domain. In additional to the data which is in the processed traffic flow itself, the Service Functions may also benefit from

Figure 15. POF Message Format and Processing Sequence

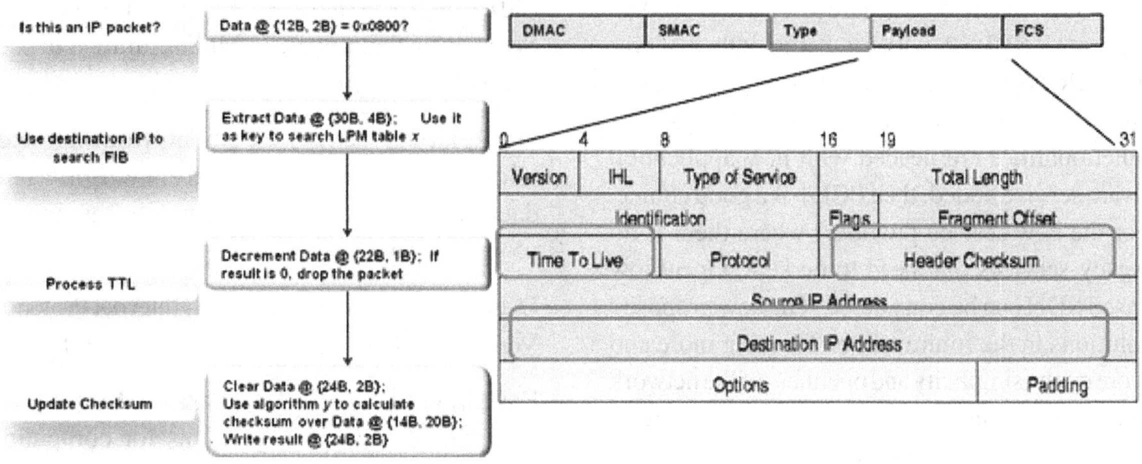

additional contextual information about the traffic flows. This additional contextual information is referred to as metadata. Metadata use cases, interconnection between metadata-unaware Service Functions and metadata-aware Service Functions, and the approaches for signaling metadata are all needed to be further investigated in the future.

Segment Routing

Future solutions are focusing on how to support more of the current traffic engineering tunnels' functions and solve the issue of limitations on the number of layers of the label stacks which can be encapsulated on a packet.

SDN

The enrichment of the functionalities of Open Flow protocol within shorten cycles is one of the challenges Open-Flow based SDN faces. Another challenge is to find better solutions to speed up the flow programming for a lager SDN network.

CONCLUSION

While the existing forwarding schemes evolve to have better efficiency to satisfy the existing requirements, at the same time, as the service-oriented routing schemes are nurturing, there are more new use cases and requirements coming out of the new services identified. This requires the network to support new forwarding schemes in a revolutionary way so that the complexity of the existing network can be solved while the new services are provided with efficiency. Since the current distributed networking architectures have been deployed for so many years and for so many users, the smooth transition from the current network architecture to the new service-oriented architectures is a must, so all the new architecture and solutions should consider the backward compatibility. Especially for an efficient and practical solution for the traditional service providers, hybrid solutions where distributed and central controlled solutions are mixed together naturally are the way to go.

Since the deployment environments are so diverse, the solutions which address each individual application scenario's problem with simplicity will be chosen. MPLS multiple topology is a promising tool for the end-to-end network virtualization if the forwarding plane must not be changed. For the service providers where they only need to support P2P LSP without bandwidth reservation, SR is a candidate worth to be considered, and for the service providers where all the MPLS functionalities are needed with new application aware service added, then PCE+ is a good choice. For the new service providers where there is no legacy services that need to be kept, OpenFlow based SDN can be considered. The new proposed solutions in the future will be focusing more and more on the simplicity and openness of the network operation, maintenance and flexibility of adding new services. For the users who want enable their network functions rapidly with flexibility, SFC is an interesting tool.

Since most of the new techniques introduced in this chapter are in the initial development stage and some of them are in the initial deployment stages. The advantages and disadvantages for these techniques can be future justified once there are more deployments in the near future.

REFERENCES

Anderson, L. AB, A., Minei, I, Thomas, B. (2007) LDP Specification, RFC5036.

Awduche, D., Berger, L., Gan, D., Li, T., Srinivasan, V. (2001) RSVP-TE: Extensions to RSVP for LSP Tunnels, RFC3209.

Black, D., Hudson, J., Kreeger, L., Lasserre, M., Narten, T. (2015) An Architecture for Overlay Networks (NVO3), draft-ietf-nvo3-arch-01.

Cheng, D., Boucadair, B., Retana, A. (2013) Routing for IPv4-Embedded IPv6 Packets, RFC6992.

Crabbe, E., Minei, I., Medved, J., Varga, R. (2014) PCEP Extensions for Stateful PCE, draft-ietf-pce-stateful-pce-10.

Crabbe, E., Minei, I., Sivabalan, S., Varga, R. (2014) PCEP Extensions for PCE Initiated LSP Setup in a Stateful PCE Model, draft-ietf-pce-pce-initialed-lsp-03.

Daqupta, D. (2014) Segment Routing. Retrieved from https://conference.apnic.net/data/37/apnic2014-segment-routing_santanu_v5_1393404956.pdf

Deering, S., & Hinden, R. (1998) Internet Protocol, Version 6 (IPv6) Specification. RFC2460

Enyedi, G., Csaszar, A., Atlas, A., Bowers, C., Gopalan, A. (2015) Algorithms for computing Maximally Redundant Trees for IP/LDP Fast-Reroute, draft-ietf-rtgwg-mrt-frr-algorithm-03.

Farinacci, D., Li, T., Hanks, S., Myer, D., Traina, P. (2000) Generic Routing Encapsulation (GRE), RFC2784.

Filsfils, C., Francois, P., Previdi, S., Decraene, B., Litkowski S., Horneffer, M., ... Crabbe, E. (2014). Segment Routing Use Cases, draft-filsfils-spring-segment-routing-use-cases-01.

Filsfils, C., Previdi, S., Bashandy, A., Decraene, B., Litkowski S., Horneffer, M., ... Crabbe, E. (2014) Segment Routing Architecture, draft-ietf-spring-segment-routing-mpls-00.

Francois, P., Filsfils, C., Decraene, B., Shakir, R. (2014) Use-cases for Resiliency in SPRING, draft-ietf-spring-resiliency-use-cases-00.

Garg, P., Wang, Y. (2014) NVGRE: Network Virtualization using Generic Routing Encapsulation, draft-sridharan-virtualization-nvgre-07.

Gross, J., Sridhar, T., Garg, P., Wright, C., Ganga, I., Agarwal, P., ... Hudson, J. (2015) Geneve: Generic Network Virtualization Encapsulation, draft-gross-geneve-02.

Halpern, J., & Pgnataro, C. (2015) Service Function Chaining (SFC) Architecture, draft-ietf-sfc-architecture-07.

Halpern, J., & Pignataro, C. (2015) Service Function Chaining (SFC) Architecture, draft-quinn-sfc-arch-07.

Hao,W., Yong, L., Hares, S., Fang, L., Davari, S. (2014) Inter-AS Option B between NVO3 and BGP/MPLS IP VPN network, draft-hao-l3vpn-inter-nvo3-vpn-01.

Hao, W., Yong, L., Li, Y., Shao, W., Liu, V. (2014) NVO3 Anycast Layer 3 Gateway, draft-hao-nvo3-anycast-gw-00.

Hinden, R. (2004) Virtual Router Redundancy Protocol, RFC2004.

Homma, S., Naito, K., Lopez, D. R., Stiemerling, M., Dolson, D. (2015) Analysis on Forwarding Methods for Service Chaining, draft-homma-sfc-forwarding-methods-analysis-01.

Knight, S. (1998) Virtual Router Redundancy Protocol, RFC2338.

Kompella, K., Drake, J., Amante, S., Henderickx, W., Yong, L. (2012) The Use of Entropy Labels in MPLS Forwarding, RFC6790.

Lasserre, M., Balus, F., Morin, T., Bitar, N., Rekhter, Y. (2014) Framework for DC Network Virtualization, RFC7365.

Li, R., Zhao, Q., Yang, T., Raszuk, R. (2014) MPLS Global Label Use Cases, draft-li-mpls-global-label-usecases-03.

Mahalingam, M., Dutt, D., Duda, K., Agarwal, P., Kreeger, L., Sridar, T., ... Wright, C. (2014) VXLAN: A Framework for Overlaying Virtualized Layer 2 Networks over Layer 3 Networks, RFC7348.

Narten, T., Gray, E., Black, D., Fang, L., Kreeger, L., Napierala, M. (2013) Problem Statement: Overlays for Network Virtualization, draft-narten-nov3-overlay-problem-statement-04.

Nasdas, S. (2010) Virtual Router Redundancy Protocol (VRRP) Version 3 for IPv4 and IPv6, RFC5798.

Quinn, P., & Nadeau, T. (2014) Service Function Chaining Problem Statement, draft-ietf-sfc-problem-statement-13.

Rekhter, R., Li, T., Hares, S. (2006) A Border Gateway Protocol 4 (BGP-4), RFC4271.

Rijsman, B., & Moisand, J. (2014). Metadata Considerations, draft-rijsman-sfc-metadata-considerations-00.

Rosen, E., Rekhter, Y. (2006) BGP/MPLS IP Virtual Private Networks (VPNs), RFC 4364.

Rosen, E., Viswanatan, A., Callon, R. (2001) Multiprotocol Label Switching Architecture, RFC 3031.

Sivabalan, S., Medved, J., Filsfils, C., Crabbe, E., Raszuk, R., Lopez, V., Tantsura, J. (2014) PCEP Extension for Segment Routing, draft-sivabalan-pce-segment-routing-03.

Song, H. (2013) Protocol-Oblivious Forwarding: Unleash the Power of SDN through a Future-Proof Forwarding Plane. In proceeding of sigcomm 2013.

Sushant, J., & Alok, A. (2013) B4: Experience with a Globally-Deployed Software Defined WAN. In *Proc. SIGCOMM* (2013), 3-14.

Woodyatt, J. (2011) Recommended Simple Security Capabilities in Customer Premises Equipment (CPE) for Providing Residential IPv6 Internet Service, RFC6092.

Yong, L., Hao, W., Eastlake, D., Qu, A., Hudson, J., Chunduri, U. (2014) ISIS Protocol Extension For Building Distribution Trees, draft-yong-isis-ext-4-distribution-tree-02.

Zhao, Q., Raza, K., Zhou, C., Fang, L., Li, L., King, D. (2014) LDP Extensions for Multiple Topology, RFC7307.

Zhao, Q., Zhao, K., Li, R., Dhuody, D., Palle, U., Zhang, B. (2015) PCEP Procedures and Protocol Extensions for Using PCE as a Central Controller (PCECC) of LSPs, draft-zhao-pce-pcep-extension-for-pce-controller-01.

Zhao, Q., Zhao, K., Li, R., Ke, K. (2014) The Use Cases for Using PCE as the Central Controller (PCECC) of LSPs, draft-zhao-pce-central-controller-user-cases-01.

KEY TERMS AND DEFINITIONS

Active Segment: the segment that MUST be used by the receiving router to process the packet. It is identified by a pointer in the IPv6 architecture. It is the top label in the MPLS architecture.

ECMP: Equal Cost Multi-Path.

EL: Entropy Label.

ELI: Entropy Label Indicator.

FEC: Forwarding Equivalence Class.

IGP Segment: the generic name for a segment attached to a piece of information advertised by a link-state IGP, e.g. an IGP prefix or an IGP adjacency.

IGP: Interior Gateway Protocol. Either of the two routing protocols, Open Shortest Path First (OSPF) or Intermediate System to Intermediate System (IS-IS).

IGP-Adjacency: an IGP-Adjacency Segment is an IGP segment attached to an unidirectional adjacency or a set of unidirectional adjacencies. By default, an IGP-Adjacency Segment is local (unless explicitly advertised otherwise) to the node that advertises it.

LAG: Link Aggregation Group.

LER: Label Edge Router.

LSP: Label Switched Path.

LSR: Label Switching Router.

MT Topology: A topology that is built using the corresponding MT-ID.

MT-ID: A 16-bit value used to represent the Multi-Topology ID.

NVA: Network Virtualization Authority.

NVE: Network Virtualization Edge.

PCC: Path Computation Client- any client application requesting a path computation to be performed by a Path Computation Element.

PCE: Path Computation Element. An entity (component, application, or network node) that is capable of computing a network path or route based on a network graph and applying computational constraints.

PDP: Policy Decision Point.

PE: Provider Edge.

PW: Pseudowire.

Segment: a segment identifies an instruction.

SF: Service Function.

SFC: Service Function Chain.

SFP: Service Function Path.

TE: Traffic Engineering.

TOR: Top of Rack.

TS: Tenant System.

TTL: Time to Live.

UHP: Ultimate Hop Popping.

VN: Virtual Network.

VPN: Virtual Private Network.

Chapter 13
Available Routing Construct (ARC)

Patrice Bellagamba
Cisco Systems, France

Pascal Thubert
Cisco Systems, France

ABSTRACT

Every computer network has been built in the last 30 years on the concept of routing tree to compute the path to be used to reach a given prefix or the border of a routing area. This chapter introduces the concept of Available Routing Construct (ARC), which is a two-end (or more) routing basic element that forms its own recovery domain. As it is dual ended, any failure in an ARC can be easily locally resolved by reversing the path toward the other end. A routing area can therefore be described in a graph of hierarchical ARCs. This new paradigm could be leveraged to improve the network resiliency and utilization for both unicast and multicast traffic.

INTRODUCTION

The traditional routing model is based on a greedy approach that defines a cost metric and then ensures that a packet always progresses so as to monotonically decrease that metric. Link State IGPs (Interior Gateway Protocols) typically describe a routing area using trees as construct, but a tree offers only one solution for a next hop to a given destination. Several tricks are under work to compute multiple trees to allow fast re-routing and/or load repartition.

The "Available Routing Construct (ARC)" proposal introduces a totally disruptive approach where topology is described as a graph of local multi-ended entities called ARCs.

In a space that is dual to the physical domain of links and routers, ARCs form a Directed Acyclic Graph (DAG) so going from an ARC to the next is effectively greedy and ensures progress of the packet being forwarded. But in the physical domain, the operation of forwarding inside an ARC does not need to be greedy. It can be any form of loop-less walk that may explore the ARC

DOI: 10.4018/978-1-4666-8371-6.ch013

structure and attempt to exit an ARC towards any other ARC that is downstream in the ARC domain. In other words, an ARC is a micro domain where any operation such as transmission failure recovery and load balancing can be attempted.

The ARC approach is adapted to any routing environment as it is offering natively in one compute micro-loop less Fast-ReRouting (FRR) / Spread load balancing / Bicasting for video traffic.

ARC proposes a split-in between the global path topology that defines the hierarchy of ARCs, and the local topology within an ARC where decision is taken locally to execute local repair or congestion control. In addition, an ARC is by concept dual-ended and offer a support for dual replication of key multicast traffic such as video, where two independent paths must be offered to the replica of the flow, in a concept called: BiCasting.

There are several possible algorithms to build the graph of ARCs, the one proposed in this chapter is a computation that derives from SPF (Shortest Path First); but most interesting benefits are obtained with a centralized approach that may be implemented using a Software-Defined Networking (SDN) controller, a Path Computation Element (PCE) or a Network Management Entity (NME), or with a hybrid approach.

ARC can be positioned in the boundary between SDN and classical distributed routing schemes. Some SDN/NME/PCE techniques will build an ARC set but then the ARC set can live on its own like classical routing and adapt to variations in the network like link-downs and various congestions, without a need for the (centralized) controller to perform continuous adjustments. ARC ambitions to be a factor of efficiency and simplification.

ARCs are particularly efficient in circular topology as of MPLS-TP (MPLS Transport Profile) where it solves, for instance, the hierarchical ring requirement.

By concept, ARC is working as a native SDN protocol where a controller computes the global topology but the data-plane is responsible for ensuring real time operations like convergence and repartition without involving the controller, which could be too slow.

ARC is an opportunity to leverage existing OSPF & IS-IS and be effective in the SDN arena. ARCs apply to operational networks that require ultra-high availability, as well as to networks that would rely on FRR (Fast Re-Route) and MPLS-TP techniques today.

It is also adapted in IoT (Internet of Things) to Low-power Lossy Networks (LLNs) where links constantly expose transient failures and where a retry through an alternate next hop is usually a preferable strategy.

To improve current IGPs, especially in the domain of the loop-less FRR, two tracks have been taken by IETF and Cisco/Juniper: One approach is Loop-Free Alternates (LFA) with an improvement denoted Remote-LFA (RLFA) while the other one is Maximally Redundant Trees (MRT). Both approaches are good and quite efficient, but they do not solve the inherent problem of IGPs, which is the single next hop choice to a given destination based on tree computation and establishment. These enhancements (LFA and MRT) require the computation of multiple disjoint trees to establish backup paths that are physically disjoint of the primary path. LFA by itself covers only a subset of the potential network topology, while its extension RLFA requires a tunnel technology like label path to extend the coverage. On its side, MRT computes a sub-optimum alternate path. Compared to these techniques, ARC works as well as with IP/MPLS, and always computes the next optimum SPF path as alternate.

Regarding other Directed Acyclic Graph (DAG) techniques, for most nodes, DAGs enable multiple forwarding solutions to a given destination for a number of nodes in the DAG. So for most nodes, if an adjacency is lost, there is an alternate that can be used instead, by a local decision that does not require any control exchange at the time of failure. But it is impossible to generate a DAG that provides at least two forwarding solutions for each and every node and so will not enable the full redundancy scheme that is required. RPL (Thubert and al., 2012) improves on DAG and adds the concept of sibling links that are not oriented and uses loop detection at packet forwarding time. That is fine for the low traffic but in the context of data centers the goal is a proactive method that guarantees loop avoidance.

Link Reversal enables to fix a DAG. Again this can be used in several situations where it is acceptable for a fix to take some time, but as the reversal of a link might cascade, the technique by itself is not sufficient to guarantee the instantaneous convergence that is targeted and transient loops will occur.

ARC improves the generic link reversal technique by making sure that each individual step of reversing a link moves the graph from a loop-free situation into another loop-free situation.

Some SDN proposals control all flows individually, and when the number of flows grows, this might become cumbersome, the optimization is "NP-Complete", and there is a limit to what controllers can bear. ARC allows some of the benefits of SDN such as path computation, but can perform for a bulk of flows from multiple sources going to a same destination. SDN also mandates the controller to have a permanent reachability to all devices to control them. ARCs enable a semi-distributed computation that is done per destination (e.g., a set of border routers) as opposed to per flow. Each destination may compute its own topology and distribute it from itself, thus recovering any damage on the way. The performances of an ARC fabric will be less deterministic than a per flow computation but the computation is faster and allows for huge amounts of best effort flows that SDN cannot handle effectively. ARCs will dynamically recover packet or link losses, and will load balance.

Each ARC can be its own independent domain for high availability and load balancing purposes. This is a major change of paradigm, which allows recovering from multiple breakage events. Advanced studies on ARCs are still needed but ARCs are a promising approach to address issues that are currently unsolved, including the so-called "Olympic Rings", the Shared Risk Link Group (SRLG), or the oscillation-free network based load balancing.

CREATING A TOPOLOGY BASED ON ARCS

Generating a Loop-Free Routing Topology Using Routing Arcs

ARC is a method that consists in creating, in a computing network, a loop-free routing topology comprising a plurality of routing arcs for reaching a destination device; each routing arc comprising a first network device as a first end of the routing ARC, a second network device as a second end of the routing ARC, and at least a third network device configured for forwarding any traffic along the routing ARC toward the destination device via any one of the first or second ends of the routing arc; and causing the network traffic to be forwarded along at least one of the routing arcs to the destination device (see Figure 1).

ARC revisits the traditional concept of path so as to overcome its intrinsic limitations. An ARC is a new routing construct, made of a bidirectional sequence of nodes and links with ingress at any point but egresses only at the edges; a cursor delineates the high point away from which packets are directed in normal operations. An ARC fabric, a.k.a., an ARC set, is built as a directed acyclic graph (DAG) of ARCs; as a result, forwarding from an ARC down to another is a greedy operation; but forwarding inside an ARC does not have to be greedy, and a packet is entitled to exit the ARC by either of the two (or more) edges. Due to the innate way an ARC is built, each node can still reach one of the egress edges upon a single

Figure 1. Forwarding along ARC

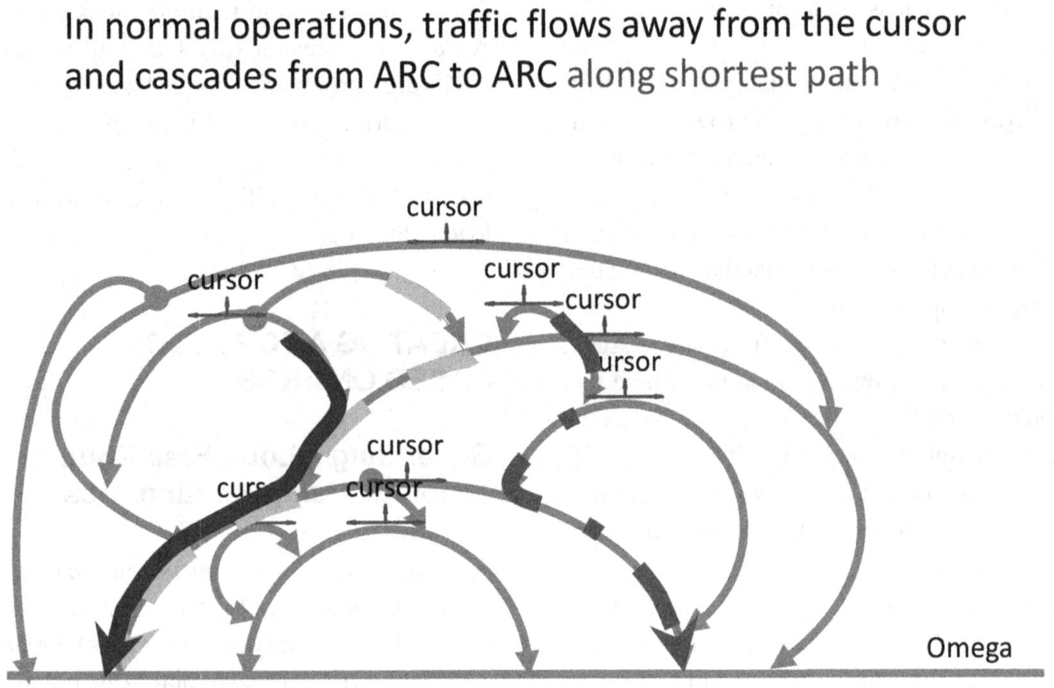
In normal operations, traffic flows away from the cursor
and cascades from ARC to ARC along shortest path
cursor
cursor
cursor
cursor
cursor
cursor
Omega

breakage within the ARC. An ARC thus provides its own independent domain of fault isolation and recovery and an ARC topology is resilient to one breakage per ARC with no traffic interruption.

The routing graph to reach a certain destination is expressed as a cascade of ARCs, each ARC providing its own independent domain of fault isolation and recovery.

Main Concepts

The main ARC concepts are listed below (see Figure 2):

1) Root: A root is a node that is a single point to access a resource, for instance an external prefix. Because it is a single point, there is no way around a root. So there cannot be a second path to bypass the root and reach the destination. All of the root links are oriented inwards and resolved.

In case of multiple nodes accessing the same resource, a virtual root is created representing the unique "Omega" node.

2) Heir: An heir is directly connected to the root.
3) Leaf: A leaf is a node with a single link. The link is oriented outwards and resolved.
4) Junction: A Junction is a node that has two paths to the root in such a fashion that there is no single point of failure that can cut off the junction from the root. We accept that a node is a junction even if it means turning a link to get the alternate path.
5) Safe Node: A Safe node is a Root, a heir or a junction.
6) Arc: An arc is a dual ended reversible path between two safe nodes.

Edge nodes have one link oriented outwards. All other links are an intermediate node that terminates two reversible links.

Figure 2. ARC concepts

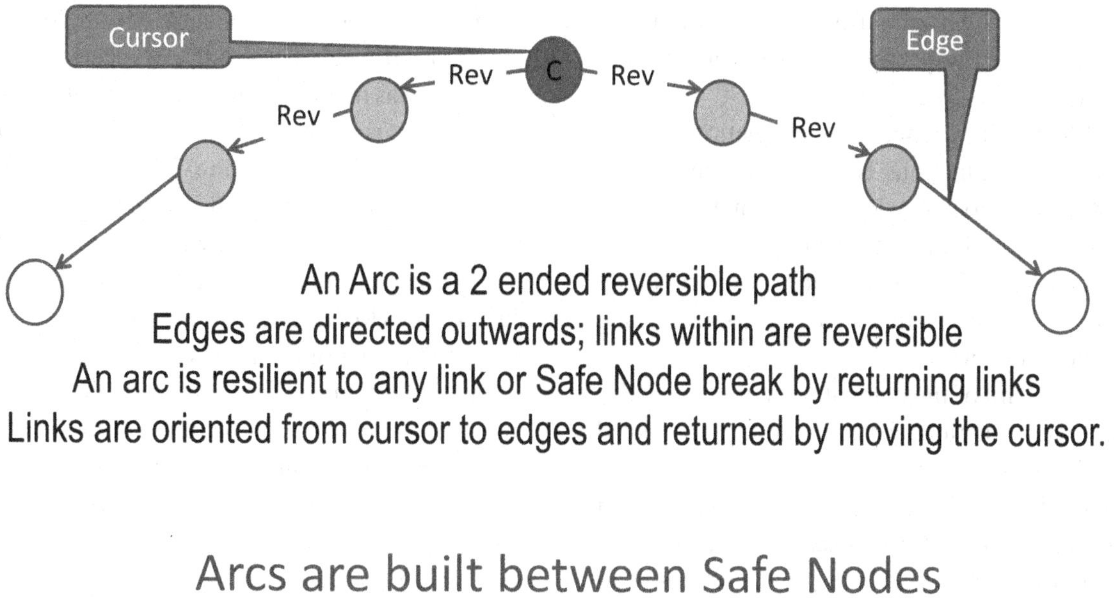
Cursor
Edge
Rev
C
Rev
Rev
Rev
An Arc is a 2 ended reversible path
Edges are directed outwards; links within are reversible
An arc is resilient to any link or Safe Node break by returning links
Links are oriented from cursor to edges and returned by moving the cursor.
Arcs are built between Safe Nodes

7) Edge Junction: An Edge Junction is a router within an arc that has one reversible link. An Edge Junction can have multiple links oriented inwards or outwards.
8) Intermediate Junction:

An Intermediate Junction is a router within an arc that has two reversible links. All other links are oriented inwards to avoid loops. A link can be safely reversed towards an Intermediate Junction.

Properties

ARC properties are listed below:

1) a node connected to a heir and the root is a junction
2) a node connected to two different heirs is a junction
3) a node connected to a heir and a junction is a junction
4) a node connected to two different junctions is a junction

Heirs and junctions are Safe Nodes, then:

5) A node connected to two different Safe Nodes is a junction.
6) A node that has non-congruent paths to at least two different Safe Nodes is a junction. A junction sees two Safe Nodes and hides them as long as they are only reachable from via that junction.
7) A node that can only see one junction is in the sub-dag of that junction and can be tracked as such.

The objective is to run SPF as part of a protocol that allows every node that is not yet safe to become a junction, so that every node has a shortest path and a backup path. This is achieved by building arcs that end in Safe Nodes.

With a DAG, some nodes will be junctions by simply observing the rules above. But some will not. To make all nodes behave as junctions, some links have to be reversed upon detection of a local problem.

The art is to determine a DAG that computes which links can be turned as a response to a link down, and which links from the DAG must be reversed right away to enable each single turn to result in a loop-free topology.

When children nodes of a junction are not immediately junctions because they do not see another junction, the DAG computation is not completed until it hits a second junction that is a descendant of the first junction. An Arc is then built of these two junctions making nodes along the arc junctions.

At the end of the computation, if some nodes are still not junctions (because they are connected to only one safe node), it means that this junction is actually a single point to access the destination and thus the algorithm is executed again considering now this node as root. This ends when all nodes are roots, leaves or Junctions.

Generating a Loop-Free Routing Topology Based On Merging Buttressing Arcs Into Routing Arcs

ARC is a method that consists in creating a loop-free routing topology comprising a plurality of routing arcs for reaching a destination device. Traffic is forwarded along the routing arc toward the destination device via any one of first or second ends of the corresponding routing arc. This results in the creation of a buttressing arc (Figure 3) having an originating end joined to a first of the routing arcs and a terminating end joined to a second end of the routing arcs.

Loop-free arc topology is accomplished via the following rules:

- Rule 1: A new arc must terminate in existing arcs or a final destination.
- Rule 2: A new arc is made of nodes that are not already in an arc.

Lemma: Arbitrary ARCs following rules 1 and 2 will lead to a loop-free topology.

Demonstration:

Assign the number "N" to each ARC that represents the sequence in which ARCs are formed. The first ARC gets 1, the Nth ARC gets N.

If this was making a loop, then it would have a suite of arcs such that: ARCx ends in ARCy that end in ARCz ... that ends in ARCx

But then by applying rules 1 and 2, Nx > Ny > Nz ... > Nx so Nx > Nx, which is impossible.

A concept of height and UP/DOWN is introduced. An ARC is a height that must be strictly greater than that of the ARCs it terminates into.

A "flying buttress" is a split-ARC that merges into an existing ARC to form a Comb. This allows Intermediate Junctions with outgoing edges DOWN. A path DOWN ends in a lower ARC. Links DOWN can be outgoing while other links must be pruned outgoing.

- Rule 3: The height of an ARC must be strictly greater than that of the ARCs it terminates into.
- Rule 4: A new ARC may become a flying buttress by merging with an existing ARC or Comb at its upper end if its other end terminates in an ARC or Comb that has a strictly lower height than the 1st one.
- Rule 5: The height of the resulting comb structure is that of the ARC merged into.

Lemma: one can form arbitrary ARCs and ARC- buttress following rules 1 to 5, and the topology will be loop-free.

Demonstration:

The new ARC- buttress is a new ARC so traffic can safely be injected from the ARC- buttress into the ARC because rules 1 and 2 apply.

The difference is that traffic can also be injected from the merged ARC.

But with rules 3 and 4 that traffic can only end up in an ARC that is below the merged ARC so it cannot come back into the merged ARC.

It is guaranteed to form loop-free structures as long as it picks H> Max(H1, H2) when a new

Figure 3. Special case of a Buttressing ARC

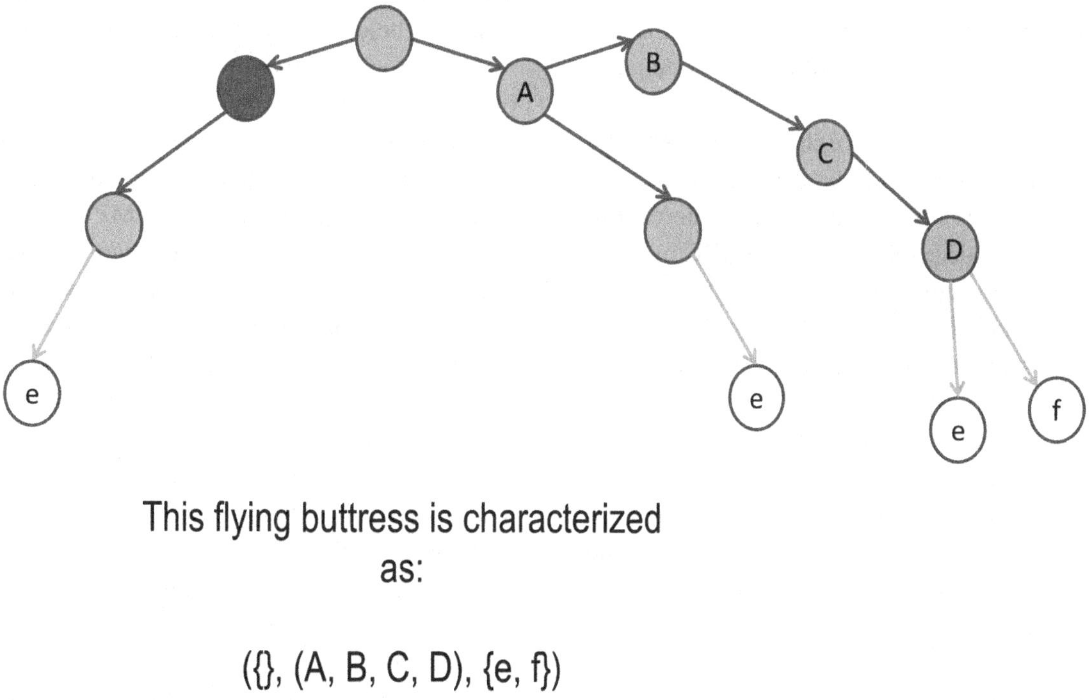

ARC is built and that terminates in existing ARCs of heights H1 and H2.

A junction can connect an ARC-Buttress to an existing ARC, as long as the new buttress terminates strictly below H. The benefit is that the link between the existing junction and the arc-buttress is now reversible.

Building a flying buttress topology starts with a Safe Set of nodes that has only the final destination. Then recursively:

1. Pick arbitrary connected nodes that are not in the Safe Set to form an ARC that terminates in the Safe Set.
2. The Height of the ARC is an arbitrary number H that must be greater than that of the Combs the arc terminates in.
3. An ARC being formed that ends in an ARC at height H can be merged at the other end into any existing ARC of height > H. The resulting ARC inherits the height of the ARC it is merged into.
4. If the ARC does not merge into an existing one, then it becomes a Comb Backbone by itself.
5. Links from the Comb that terminate in the Safe Set in Combs of lesser height are '"DOWN" thus oriented outwards from this Comb. The other links are pruned outwards.
6. The nodes in the new Comb are added to the Safe Set.
7. Following a Comb ends at an edge. Following an edge always ends in a lower Comb.
8. Recursively cascading Combs always ends at a destination.

Reliable Dissemination Along an ARC Fabric

Available Routing Construct (ARC) describes the computation on an arc topology by a computation engine.

There are three approaches to compute the ARC set topology. One is greedy, where each node computes for each destination the overall topology and determines to which ARC element it belongs too, including its two neighbors; this is not the approach that is taken in this chapter. The second way is to have the destination to compute the topology and disseminate it over the area; with an option that induces the third approach, which is to have an external PCE (Path Computation Element) that performs the computation and injects it in the area via the destination node that disseminates it from there. This chapter will focus on the second proposal, but keeping in mind that the third one is just a kind of SDN (Software Defined Network) evolution of it.

OMEGA is defined as the destination of an arc topology. This is not necessarily the destination of a packet but simply the node where packets in an arc topology converge, like the root of a DODAG. This OMEGA can be a virtual node, representing the destination prefixes that are multi-homed to the topology.

In other words, this computation of the ARC topology can happen in:

1. a centralized PCE associated to a Network Management System (NMS),
2. the destination OMEGA of the ARC topology (a server or a Border Router), or
3. any node computing the ARC topology for a number of destinations in its Autonomous System (AS), for instance border routers that can reach a same set of external prefixes.

In case (1), the PCE can reliably communicate with the destination of the ARC topology, so it ends up in situation (2) as there is no need for the controller to access every devices, the propagation of the topology being disseminated from the destination OMEGA node. The mechanism that is described below enables in case (2) the destination OMEGA to share/disseminate the relevant piece of the ARC topology with the members of the topology, and activate that new topology as if it is being flooded, with no loss of packet, either as routing table entries or labels in an MPLS fashion.

A basic version of case (3) ignores multi-homing, and builds an ARC topology per border router. If multiple BRs are to be used to reach an external prefix, it is up to the node that injects the packet in the ARC topology to select which ARC topology and thus which OMEGA BR will send the packet out of the network. This model enables to apply policies to load balance outgoing traffic.

Case (3) can also include multi-homing considerations. In that case, we define OMEGA as a virtual node for all border routers. One approach would be to have one of the nodes performing the computation and then distribute the information to all other border routers, and then case (3) is back to case (2) as well. This multi-homing border election and synchronization as well as backup could rely on a protocol like ICCP (Inter-Chassis Communication Protocol) that is described in RFC 7275.

The mechanism can also be used to flood other information, and measure the activity of the routing structure through LSB (Link State Bees).

LSB is a forwarding-plane mechanism that explores the possible paths along a DAG or an ARC set and computes dynamic costs for load balancing purposes. LSB are flooded OAM frames, that would explore paths that are set up by routing and aggregate metrics such as load, that are not used in routing plane (because of oscillations/Arpanet syndrome), but may use in forwarding plane.

More information can be found in the US Patent UPSTO 7,693,064

The following steps are illustrated below:

- **Step 1:** the destination computes the ARC structure, using the proposed algorithm, though other methods could be applied. One ARC topology is built to describe the full set of prefixes belonging to the same ultimate OMEGA node. Alternatively, two sets of ARCs could have been built to ensure a multiple ARC set approach. Optionally, obtain the topology from a PCE or NMS.
- **Step 2:** Each ARC is serialized by naming it by its cursor, and listing the nodes in the arc in order as a list L, with a specific metadata to indicate the cursor. Then for each edge (Left and Right) of the arc, the sets Sl and Sr of exit nodes are attached to the list in order to represent the location of the arc in the topology.
- **Step 3:** the destination OMEGA injects the topological information, for instance as a Label Distribution Protocol (LDP) PDU, at each end of the arcs that ends up in it. The topological information is associated with a unique identifier of OMEGA, so that multiple messages regarding this topology may be correlated. Recursively, every junction forwards the information along the ARC, and copies any edge node of a parent ARC if this junction happens to be an exit point for that parent ARC. So the serialized topology ends up being injected from each end of any given arc, somewhat asynchronously. If a label switch topology is to be built, this causes to build a label in both directions, correlated by the unique identifier of OMEGA.
- **Step 4:** When a junction gets a topology from a node, it means that this node is already down the arc path towards the destination: this path is usable. The junction digests the topology and passes it along the arc towards the other side and sets up routing along the arc towards the source of the packet. So the routing is always set towards a node that is already ready, and recursively towards the destination.
- **Step 5:** A junction that is an exit for an incoming ARC injects the message to the edge in the incoming ARC, like OMEGA did already.
- **Step 6:** If the junction is the cursor, then it will forward the topology along the arc only if it is a new topology. This will cause a new topology arriving at one end to flow: a) till the other end and install routes and label switched paths all along the arc in the same direction, or b) till it hits a node that already acquired the topology from the other side if we only setup routing and no LSP. In case b), when the propagation collides, it flows back towards the cursor and overwrites the routes so they go away from the cursor. When the cursor gets the topology again from the other side, it does not propagate it anymore.

In a restatement, the ARC topology is injected backward from the destination and flows along the ARC set. As soon as a node receives the new topology, it can make usage of it in a loop-free fashion as every node below belongs to the new topology.

In the ARC itself the concept of cursor is enabled only when the new topology has been received by both ends of the ARC, until then one exit of the ARC is used by all nodes in the ARC.

Protecting a Topology Using ARCS

Repair of Failed Network Routing Arcs Using Data Plane Protocol

SDN and PCE approaches separate the control plane from the data plane. This means that control actions will be delayed and sometimes impossible if the connectivity to the SDN controller is broken. Tens of seconds of interruption on a 100 Gbps link can represent a whole library sent to the sink.

This means that more than ever, the network must be self-healing and self-optimizing, without any intervention from the controller. SDN will ultimately force the move of some intelligence from the control place to the data plane. Fast reroute is an example of reflex actions that can be taken at the forwarding layer. FRR is a local decision of rerouting, there is no protocol exchange with neighbors or with a central point to take the alternate at failure time, and action has been pre-computed.

A network includes multiple routing arcs for forwarding traffic to a destination. Each arc is comprised of nodes connected in sequence by reversible links. The arc is oriented away from a node initially holding a cursor toward one of first and second edge nodes through which the network traffic exits the arc. Each node includes a network device. The nodes in the arc detect a first failure in the arc. Responsive to the detection of the first failure, the nodes exchange first management frames over a data plane within the arc in order to transfer the cursor from the node initially holding the cursor to a first node that is close to the first failure and reverse links in the arc as appropriate so that traffic in the arc is directed away from the first failure toward the first edge node of the arc through which traffic can exit the arc.

This is performed using a novel form of OAM frames that enable a recursive forwarding plane solution to the SRLG problem in an ARC system.

This novel form of OAM frames called (Joint Operation and Automation of the Network) enables the repair of extensive damage in the data plane with limited packet loss with no need to solicit a PCE or a SDN controller.

JOAN frames are contained within an ARC and usually go from one end to the other.

Let's analyze the behavior in three different cases:

1. Single failure in ARC: its purpose is to capture the cursor at the breakage point. The interesting piece is that it shows how the Joan frame that goes from one side of an ARC to the other can both transport the cursor handoff and reorient the ARC links away from the new position of the cursor at the breakage point.
    1. A point of failure becomes a broken edge of the ARC. It sources a JOAN frame towards the other end of the ARC that requires transfer of cursor-ship.
    2. If the other edge is still passing traffic, it accepts and echoes JOAN back that carries response
    3. On the way back the cursor gives away cursor-ship by placing a token in the JOAN frame
    4. The token causes next nodes return their links towards the old cursor away from the new cursor. All links are now reoriented away from the breakage point.
    5. The edge cursor is in fact a split cursor oriented inwards
2. Dual SRLG failure: Statistically, if a dual error occurs, it should affect two different and independent ARCs, and the problem is then solved locally in each ARC as described in the previous paragraph. But in case the dual failure occurs on the same ARC, it uses Joan frames to solve the problem. At a high level, the technique is an evolution of link reversal as used in the TORA (Temporally Ordered Routing Algorithm) protocol, considering that in an ARC set, ARCs form a directed acyclic graph. Using Joan frames, in the incoming links of an isolated segment are first frozen (blocked) and then reverted.
    1. Failure location becomes JOAN source, sends JOAN that requires cursor-ship.
    2. Remote edge is already a failure point, it cannot accept, sends a negative JOAN back.

3. Incoming edge nodes on the way back freeze incoming ports, stopping incoming flows.
4. Freezing and returning are both breakages in the parent ARC, so in parallel process is recursive, and parents try to get cursors on their own ARC
5. The new failure location receives a negative JOAN frame and becomes a sink, meaning that it will drop incoming packets.
6. It sends a second JOAN frame to turn around all incoming links. On the way, incoming links are turned outgoing (whether still frozen or not)
7. Parents that obtained cursor unfreeze the edge link, the others recursively freeze incoming links.
8. The unfrozen node for the incoming link that was returned to outgoing triggers JOAN allowing both broken edges to become cursor which orients all links towards self, attracting all traffic to the newly found exit. This message and the associated action are similar to the cursor transfer in the above case with one failure only, but now both broken ends of the ARC can be cursors towards the ARC.
9. Traffic injected inside the broken segment can now exit via the ex-parent ARC and flow over the other end of that ARC. Traffic in other ARCs was unaffected.

3. Multiple errors in multiple ARCs: This is the real SRLG case with a number of failures that appear unrelated but which may correspond to a same bundle of fibers being cut through by mistake during some excavation or it could be a wave perturbation in a WLAN network. The algorithm will be recursive and find a way through if any. This case is a recursion of the two others that have been analyzed in previous paragraphs.

1. The result of a first pass of JOAN frames as discussed above is that some links are frozen, and the associated edges have become sinks. Other breakages are repaired when only one breakage would happen in a given ARC.
2. With a recursion of the process described in part 2, it must be noted that when an ARC returns incoming into outgoing links, all links must be returned, including that from a child ARC that was just returned the other way.
3. Then the grand-parent ARC provides an issue, and unfreezing happens on the ARC-to-ARC way back. Unfreezing triggers another link reversal in an isolated segment.
4. At the end, the resulting situation is that most of the traffic can be forwarded to destination. A zone could be completely blocked and could not be reconnected if it has no alternative solution and is completely isolated, but this is a case that no algorithm can recover.

ARC Reversal

In addition to the previous paragraph, this part emphasized more on how to reverse arc so as if an arc is doubly broken, incoming arcs can be transformed as outgoing, in a fashion similar to link reversal techniques, albeit controlled and predictable unlike link reversal.

The link from all incoming ARCs between the breakages are reversed making each of the incoming ARCs buttressing ARCs for the broken sub-ARC that acts as the backbone of the resulting comb structure. The height of the broken sub-ARC is incremented to be higher than any of the buttressing ARCs thus formed. Transient loops may form after the first incoming reversed till all are reversed so this control operation must be prioritized.

Note that, as a result, an incoming ARC might be isolated, whenever it ends on both sides in the broken sub-ARC. The incoming ARC must in turn augment its own height to flow back into the broken ARC. If there is an exit left (a reversed link on the broken sub-ARC), then, the connectivity is restored. If there is no exit on the sub-ARC, it needs to augment its height and the process might count to infinity (being a maximum height increment). It might happen, though, that the incoming ARC also had incomings which end up elsewhere, in which case we do not reach infinity but use that incoming of incoming as exit.

After that, we are back to earlier work: packets can flow along the comb using the traditional labyrinth walk, taking the next best path at an intersection.

Repair of Failed Network Routing Arcs Using MPLS

In case of MPLS networks, the imposition of the alternate path toward a failure is making usage of a pre-set backup LSP in the ARC.

Finally, one pair of path labels is laid along each ARC, each label being the backup for the other for fast reroute purposes. It is important to note that this FRR is only executed at points of failure, and is not relying on any link reversal method that would require data-plane driven reversion detection.

This proposal relies on the same approach than FRR with regard to routing around failure, meaning that the control plane does prepare the alternate label to go around the failure; but it also diverges from FRR in that it is not relying on a tunnel approach.

Substituting the backup label pre-computed by the control plane to the primary one, allowing FRR, will instantaneously cover any single failure in an ARC. This approach supports multiple failures, as long as each failure occurs in a different ARC. In case of isolation due to an unexpected dual error in the same ARC, the data plane will cover flow handling reduction by means of Time to Live (TTL), until the control becomes aware, and the point of local repair installs a sink to stop the FRR swap to avoid permanent loops due to dual rerouting (Figure 4).

Load Repartition Over ARCS

Recursive Load Balancing in a Loop-Free Routing Topology Using Routing Arcs

Using OAM Frames Combined with Control Loops to Load Balance in an ARC

This part describes how OAM frames between edge and cursor can control the load at the cursor with an automation loop that is entirely located in the forwarding plane, and does not impact the PCE that computes the routes.

Each edge of the ARC emits JOAN frames towards the cursor. These frames may contain multiple metrics including a concept of bandwidth used, available, node latency, etc. that can be used in a control loop to load balance. At the simplest, though, that can be only one bit, a Backward Explicit Congestion Notification.

High level:

In normal operations, the cursor is located at the high point of an ARC, so that on both sides the adjacent nodes are nearer than the cursor to the destination. This position ensures that all traffic flows away from the cursor.

JOAN (OAM) frames that are sent periodically from both edges gather the congestion levels of intermediate nodes. The Joan frame arrives finally at the cursor where it is read and processed.

Based on early levels of congestion on one side, the cursor will send more traffic away from the congested side (that can be the edge or in between the cursor and the edge as gathered by the JOAN frame). If it is sending 100% on one side and that

Figure 4. Backup labels along an ARC.

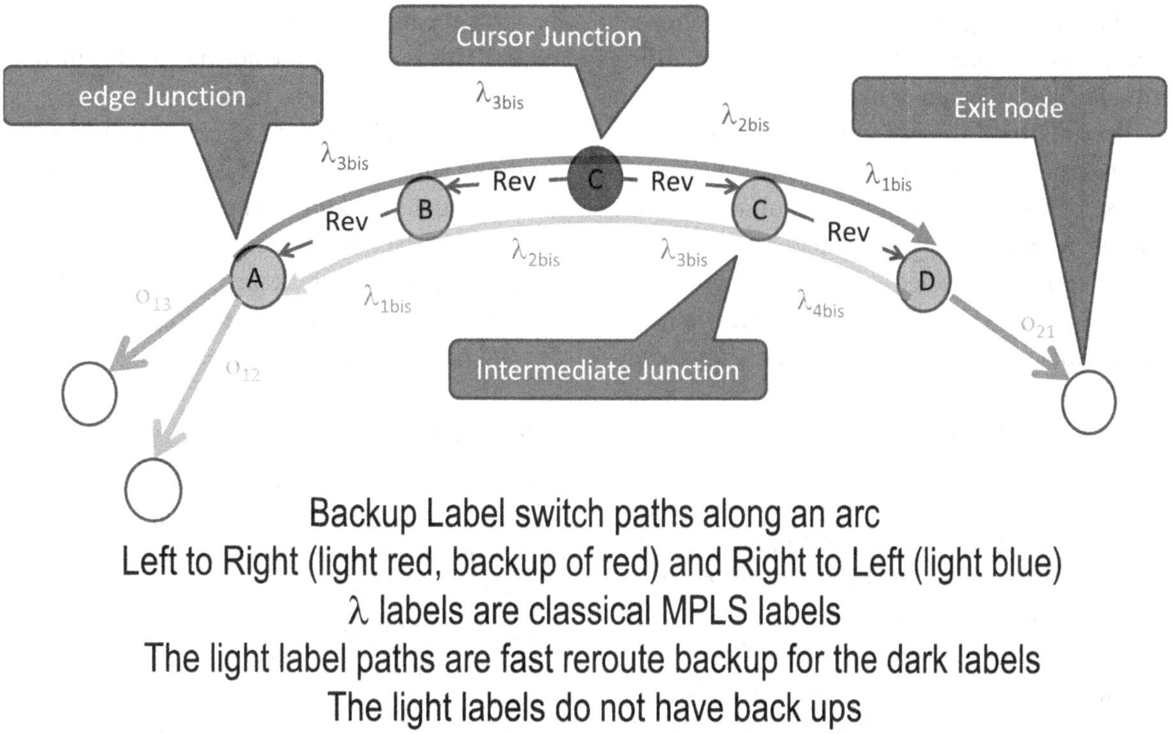
Cursor Junction
edge Junction
Exit node
Intermediate Junction
A
B
C
C
D
Rev
Rev
Rev
Rev
Backup Label switch paths along an arc
Left to Right (light red, backup of red) and Right to Left (light blue)
λ labels are classical MPLS labels
The light label paths are fast reroute backup for the dark labels
The light labels do not have back ups

is not enough, then it uses another JOAN frame to transfer the cursor role to the next node towards the congestion point.

In turn, the new cursor can load balance, and the cursor can move forward towards the congestion point until balancing is achieved or both sides now indicate congestion. In the latter case, the cursor now responds back to the JOAN frame with another JOAN frame indicating a global congestion of the ARC (for the particular flows). Nodes with incoming ARCs pass the JOAN frame to the edges of the incoming ARCs, and that information is assimilated as a congestion state. This way, the traffic from incoming ARCs is pushed back.

The interesting aspect of this approach is that, unlike legacy packet-switched networks like the Internet, the load balancing is performed in the forwarding plane. The control plane and the associated routing protocols and metrics are not involved. Instead, a control loop is put in place between the congestion point and the cursor over the JOAN frames that aim at converging towards a level that is acceptable by the congested node.

The control loop is a trade-off between:

1) The position of the cursor is elastic in that in the absence of indication of congestion, it always tends to return to its original position.
2) An indication of congestion tends to augment the level of diverted traffic and then moves the cursor away towards the congestion.

To achieve the balance between those opposite goals, the JOAN frame is emitted at a rate that is sufficiently low to validate the result of a previous adaptation before making a new one. This can be set to a number of times the round trip delay of a JOAN frame along the full ARC.

Upon receipt of an indication of congestion, the percentage of diverted traffic is augmented, typically in a geometric fashion, for instance Percent(t+1) = Percent(t) + 2^n where n is the number of contiguous congestion indications. When Percent reaches 100% and congestion is still indicated, the cursor moves.

It results that, in case of subsequent indications of congestion, the percentage grows exponentially. In case of a subsequent indication of no congestion, we reset n and restore the percentage to that of the earlier congested situation Percent(t+1) = Percent(t-1). From there, we can grow a new exponential that will stay almost flat around the appropriate value.

In a similar fashion, subsequent indications of no congestion with the cursor away from the normal position will cause Percent(t+1)=Percent(t) - 2^n where n is the number of contiguous non-congestion indications, and when 100 percent of the traffic is restored towards the ex-congested place, the cursor may move back one hop.

An intermediate information of high but acceptable load can be passed in the JOAN frame, in which case the cursor would not change its position even if it was displaced.

ARC and MPLS

Label Distribution and Route Installation in a Loop-Free Routing Topology using Routing Arcs

The data plane can be slow and for applications such as MPLS TP, we might want a model whereby the automatic action at the breakage fixes the issue. A simple u-turn is not enough because the second breakage inside an ARC will cause a loop.

They are two proposals to solve that loop, one version with one additional label and one with two additional labels along the ARC.

1-label version

This version applies when there is no need to move the cursor around for purposes such as load balancing. A label path is set up in both directions, and they do not have a backup. Additionally, we lay a label path from the fixed cursor towards the edges. This is actually the normal label path, and the other two label paths back up this one.

In this model, the main label is followed away from the cursor towards the edge and in case of a breakage the backup label path that goes along the ARC in the other direction backs it up.

In case of double breakage, the packet, if placed from primary label path into backup, reaches the second breakage and is dropped.

2-label version

This model allows moving the cursor, at the expense of an additional label. Basically two labels are lawn in each direction (a main and a backup) so that the other label backs up a main label running in one direction. Then again, as a backup label has no backup itself, in case of breakage, packets are dropped.

Labels are used to mark an ARC topology as opposed to a simple (linear) path. A new LDP format is introduced, that contains non-linear source route information to reflect the ARC topology. The propagation of the message and the installation of routes and labels happens at virtually no loss of packets when the topology changes.

ARC and RING Topology

Hierarchal Label Distribution and Route Installation in a Loop-Free Routing Topology Using Routing Arcs at Multiple Hierarchal Levels for Ring Topologies

Recursive ARC is a method that consists in creating a loop-free routing topology comprising a plurality of routing arcs for reaching a destination network node, each routing arc comprising a first network node as a first end of the routing arc, a second network node as a second end of the routing arc, and at least a third network node configured for forwarding any traffic along the routing arc toward the destination node via any one of the first or second ends of the routing arc. At least one of the first, second, or third network nodes are implemented as a ring-based network having a prescribed ring topology (e.g., Figure 5); and establishing loop-free label switched paths for reaching the destination network node via the routing arcs of the loop-free routing topology, the label switched paths independent and distinct from any attribute of the prescribed ring topology.

Here, the ARC technology is used in a fractal fashion. It will build small arcs (iota level) that can be abstracted as single super-node to make a complex ring look like a simple ring (of iota arcs). Following an iota ARC leads to the next ARC along a ring.

Then it will make lambda arcs along those rings, and then again abstract them to represent the connectivity between a ring and the next. Following a lambda arc leads to the next lambda arc, which belongs to the next ring along a path.

Then it will build omega level arcs that lead to a destination. Only omega calculations depend on a destination. The lambda computation depends on the connectivity of a ring and the iota computation depends on the complexity of that ring.

At the iota level the algorithm picks a node that is interconnecting the inner and outer rings and runs an algorithm named "Olaf", once clockwise ignoring counter-clockwise links and a second time the other way around. It ends up building two chains of arcs that this node completes. This can be done as soon as a ring is assembled, regardless of its connectivity to other rings. For each ARC it is making usage of 4 (iota) labels.

At the lambda level the algorithm builds an ARC-set that joins any two contiguous connections to another ring. The ARC-set comprises only one ARC that goes all around the ring if there is only one connection between the two rings, two arcs if there are two connections, etc. Those arcs are built of super nodes that are in fact iota level arcs. Arcs that lean to a next ring along a ring impersonate the connectivity between those two rings. As a result, every node of a ring belongs to an arc of the ARC-set that leads to any connected ring.

Then each ring is abstracted as a node, and ring interconnection as a link, or a set of links and nodes, depending on the inner complexity of the connection point to build a super topology.

Then the algorithm computes ARCs on the super topology. These are ARC of ARCs of ARCs, each level allowing a degree of high availability at its level of the hierarchy. And then again, at that level it uses (again) laid of 4 (Omega).

Omega labels are switched at the connection points and encapsulated in a lambda label within a ring. If the ring is complex, lambda is again encapsulated in iota. In case of breakage, the alternate iota path is tried in order to follow the same ring in the same direction. If that iota path also is broken, this iota arc cannot help anymore (i.e., normal forwarding along the lambda does not work). The iota label is popped and the lambda is switched to its backup, which means sending the packet back along the ring to the next exit towards the next ring, which is the other end of the lambda arc. If that fails too (which means an iota is doubly broken the other way too or that the next ring is really unreachable), lambda is popped and omega is switched to its backup, which means going back along an ARC of rings, or using an alternate exit if this ring is the end of its arc of rings.

This recursion describing ARC of ARCs of ARCs can be seen as a fractal approach to route computation where each level provides a degree of high availability that covers more and more extensive damage.

Note that any tagging can be used, including VLAN (1Q) tagging for carrier Ethernet interconnection.

Figure 5. Olympic style rings

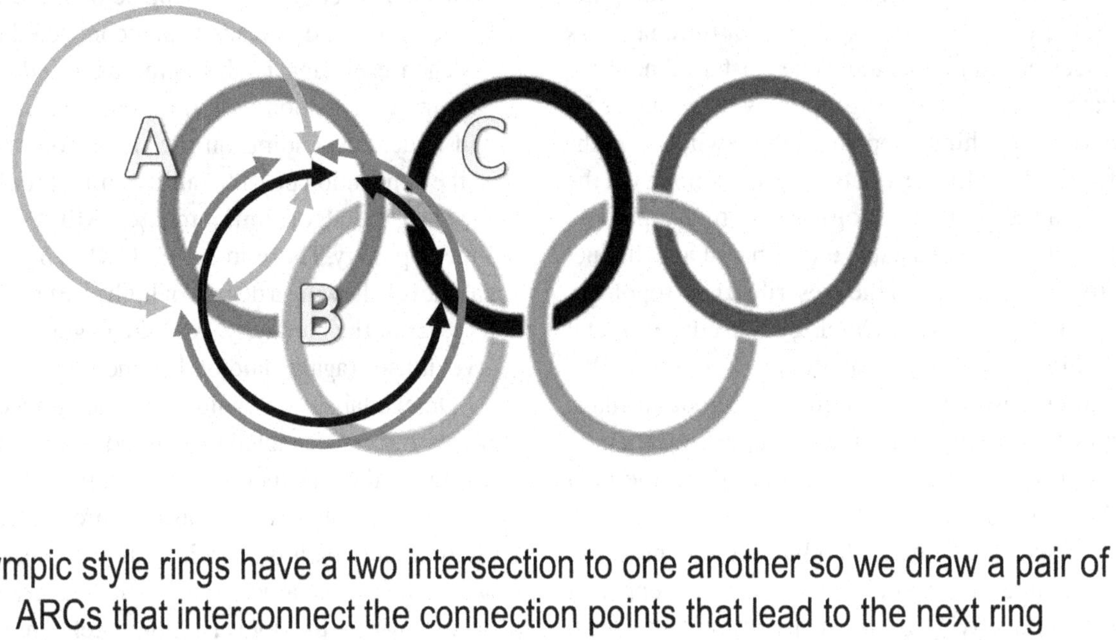
A
C
B
Olympic style rings have a two intersection to one another so we draw a pair of ARCs that interconnect the connection points that lead to the next ring

ARC-Based Forwarding in an MPLS-TP Environment

Arc forwarding consists in constructing arcs, deciding where the cursor sits on the arc and then forward packets along the arc. To implement this on a MPLS network, the arc is mapped on the outer labels while the inner label(s) stick to their traditional definition. Specifically for an MPLS-TP network where every tunnel is implemented by 2 LSPs this is a straightforward operation.

To facilitate the deployment of MPLS-TP, the NMS computes the working and protected paths based on arcs. Because MPLS-TP has already most of the required features in the control plane, this computation is better computed in the NMS and hands-off activation requests to the network elements. From there, it's normal label switching.

ARC and Multicasting

Flooding and Multicasting in a Loop-Free Routing Topology Using Routing ARCS

Multicast ARC is a method that consists in creating, in a computing network, a loop-free routing topology comprising a plurality of routing arcs for reaching multicast listeners from a multicast source, each routing arc comprising a first network device as a first end of the routing arc, a second network device as a second end of the routing arc, and at least a third network device configured for receiving from each of the first and second network devices a copy of a multicast packet originated from the multicast source; and causing the multicast packet to be propagated throughout the loop-free routing topology based on the first and second ends of each routing arc forwarding the corresponding copy into the corresponding routing arc.

ARC reuses the forwarding method whereby a copy of a packet is injected from each end of an ARC and duplicated into other incoming ARCs. Each packet flows along this ARC counter-arc-wise and arc-wise until they meet or until they reach the cursor.

Flooding is used in the description below for the broadcast of information that the routers can understand the packets at least to the point where a duplicate can be recognized and pruned. The benefit in ARC topologies is that in case of a breakage, the packet will flow till the breakage point from both ends and loss is avoided.

Multicasting is used here to propagate information that a router cannot interpret or recognize as duplicate. As opposed to the case above, packet replication cannot be stopped by the router at any node in the ARC that would need to recognize a same flooded packet coming from the other direction. Instead, the cursor ends the forwarding of multicast packets in both directions. The drawback is that at the time of a breakage, there will be a loss for all nodes between the breakage point and the cursor till the cursor is moved to the breakage point. So when a breakage happens, the cursor has to be moved quickly, which can be done for instance by generating a control packet from the breakage point towards the cursor (JOAN), or by some external management automation.

An ARC topology is built for a multicast group and rooted at a Rendezvous point or a source. The number of transmissions of a multicast packet is minimized as follows:

The reasoning is that there are M+N+n-1 transmissions for a given ARC where M is the number of routers with no listener that are present in the arc set, N is the number of nodes in the ARC and n the number of exits.

- Minimizing M: This ARC topology reaches a minimum of routers that do not have listeners attached. An additional cost is associated to such routers that we do not want to incorporate in the ARC structure. The cost can be adjusted, made dependent on the number of listeners, etc., but the overall idea is to make it equivalent to the cost of several hops. So nodes without listeners will be FAR by nature and will be mostly avoided by the lowest ARCs. So routers with no listeners will mostly be either not visited yet or collapsed when the algorithm terminates, that is, when all the routers with listeners are part of the ARC topology.
- N is incompressible. All Ns must be incorporated in the ARC topology
- Minimizing "n": The ARCs are organized in long ARCs as opposed to collapsed ARCs. The junction of a collapsed ARC will get a copy per exit, that is 2 copies for a simple collapsed ARC; a network of 3 nodes would thus require 6 copies if it is organized as simple collapsed ARCs whereas it will require only 4 if the 3 nodes are organized as a single ARC. There is a trade-off to find because more ARCs reduce the reliability of the system. So the selected behavior is:
    - Prune excess exits, that is keep only one exit per edge when there are multiple exits.
    - Merge connected ARCs when possible. For instance, if a Flying buttress connects to an existing ARC and the rest of the way along the original ARC has no router with listener, then that leg can be removed, and a longer ARC is obtained. That's typically the case of a collapsed ARC next to one another forming one that can be absorbed as a Flying buttress. Instead of forming a classical Flying buttress, it can be merge into a single ARC of 2 nodes and with only 2 exits, by pruning an exit from the original col-

lapsed ARC. Then recursively it absorbs additional forming collapsed ARCs so instead of forming a comb a long ARC is built.

- Once all the routers with listeners have joined the ARC topology for a given RDV point, the resulting topology is trimmed of all the ARCs that are not used to reach routers with listeners. This is done by building a hierarchy of ARCs and starting with the higher levels till it reaches an ARC with a listener. As long as there is an ARC that has no incoming ARC and no listener, then that ARC is pruned from the topology.
- If a router that is not in an ARC gets a first listener, it will insert itself in an existing ARC if it has 2 neighbors that are consecutive in an ARC (classical in ad-hoc radio networks) or it will attempt to become the edge of an ARC by extending that ARC in a buttressing Arc.

Bicasting Using Non-Congruent Paths in a Loop-Free Routing Topology Having Routing ARCS

The concept of bi-casting already exists in networking. It is used a lot in industrial wireless networks where not only reliability but also timeliness must be guaranteed.

For instance "HoneywellOne" uses a backbone and promiscuous listening and duplication to ensure that if a node fails a transmission to its main Access Point (AP), then another collocated AP will sniff that packet and send a copy to the main AP, which will sort out duplicates. Finally, bi-casting Reverse Path Check (RPF) is used in video distribution.

The concept of bi-casting is already known but this paragraph describes the method to leverage ARCs to build bi-casting paths, and the way it is used heirs to define East and West concepts.

ARCs propose a loop-free routing topology providing first and second non-congruent paths; and forwarding bi-casting data, comprising a data packet in a first direction from a network node and a bi-cast copy of the data packet in a second direction from the network node, concurrently to the destination node respectively via the first and second non-congruent paths.

Here, ARC technology is used to allow bi-casting so that any failure will not prevent a packet to be delivered, as at least one copy of a packet makes it through. In case of full delivery of the duplicated packets, the root is in charge of filtering duplicates.

Different to the current state-of-the-art is the way ARC ensures the use of divergent, mostly non-congruent paths.

First, is defined a concept of south (the root), and as many as nodes directly connected to the root, aka heirs, dubbed as either easts or wests.

As is built an ARC fabric towards the root, the ends of each ARC is oriented depending if the arc ends towards a different Heir. In case of a collision, that is both ends of an ARC terminate on an ARC segment that is associated to the same heir, then the side of the arc that has the longest path to that heir picks the alternate heir in the arc it terminates into.

For bi-casting, a source will prepare two packets, tagged with the pair of heirs that are associated to the location where the packet is duplicated (Called EAST and WEST). As a packet goes through the ARC fabric, the E packet will always follow an ARC towards its EASTern end whereas the W packet will always go WEST. As opposed to classical ARCs, a packet that experiences a breakage is not reversed.

Bi-casting can also apply to the way back, for instance when the way in is traced by a reservation protocol for a video stream. In that case, single points of failure can be avoided, to make the path fully non congruent.

Marking the ARC's in East and West is a key feature that can be used for Protocol Independent Multicast (PIM) and mLDP (Multicast LDP) redundant tree building. For Live-Live and Multicast only Fast Re-Route (MoFRR), PIM and mLDP need to build divergent trees across the network. It is possible for PIM/mLDP to follow the ARC's towards the root and send Join/Label Mappings over each leg of the ARC when it enters a new ARC. This will provide redundancy, but more is needed. End-to-end connection just needs two paths in the network (spanning multiple ARC's) that are divergent. In order to achieve this, bi-casting can be used. As explained above, the ARCs are divided in East and West, which spills over into each connected ARC. PIM and mLDP will be modified to include an identifier in the PIM Join/mLDP Label Mapping to indicate if either East or West has to be followed when forwarded over the ARC's towards the root.

A bi-casting example is provided in Figure 6.

Also ARC corrects the collisions when building mLDP/PIM paths. There are 2 sorts of collisions: Collision type 1 is when a western path crosses an eastern path along a same ARC. Pruning the crossing routes along the arc solves this. In effect at the points of the collisions, the packets will switch from a path that was traced by the east mLDP/PIM to a path that was traced by the west mLDP/PIM, or the other way around. The second case of collision is when an eastern end of an arc terminates at the same node as the western end of another arc and the mLDP/PIM control packets for both east and west go through that node (bad luck really!). The second mLDP/PIM control packet is sent back to avoid that node and will leave the incoming arc at its other end. This may result in a collision type 1 later, to be solved by pruning as discussed above. Finally, if a zone of the topology is not bi-connected, the unique link that reaches that zone is colored either way, east or west, and as in the case of a collision type two (2), the mLDP/PIM control packet with the other color will have to use that exit as well. Effectively, the paths that are traced by both colors will converge on that link, but they will split again afterwards.

ARCs Based SDN Path Protection for Livelive

Live-live for time sensitive flows requires the establishment of (usually two) node-disjoint (i.e., non-congruent) paths from one (or possibly more) sources (e.g., CDNs streaming video) to a particular destination. Live-live improves the reliability of the delivery with a minimum jitter: a same stream can be injected along both paths so a loss or a breakage along one path does not prevent the reception of a stream within an acceptable latency. An alternate use is when only one path is live with data and the other is in hot standby, ready to take over. MPLS-TP has similar requirements, and uses OAM frames to switch from the live to the backup path.

Wireless Deterministic Networking takes this requirement one step further, and requires that parallel paths be segmented so as to be merged and split again every few hops. The desired outcome would be that the streams can be matched at the end of each segment, and if a packet was lost on one path in one segment, it is re-injected at the end of the segment from a copy on another path in that segment.

CONCLUSION

ARC is a research domain that aims to renew the domain of the Internal Gateway Protocol (IGP), and in spite of some academic interest, it is still today a research item. This is mainly due to the fact that the existing Shortest-Path-First (SPF) approaches are tuned and retuned to improve their own reliability, offering not so much space to innovation.

ARC is a micro domain where any operation such as transmission failure recovery and load balancing can be attempted. A routing area is

Figure 6. Bi-casting example

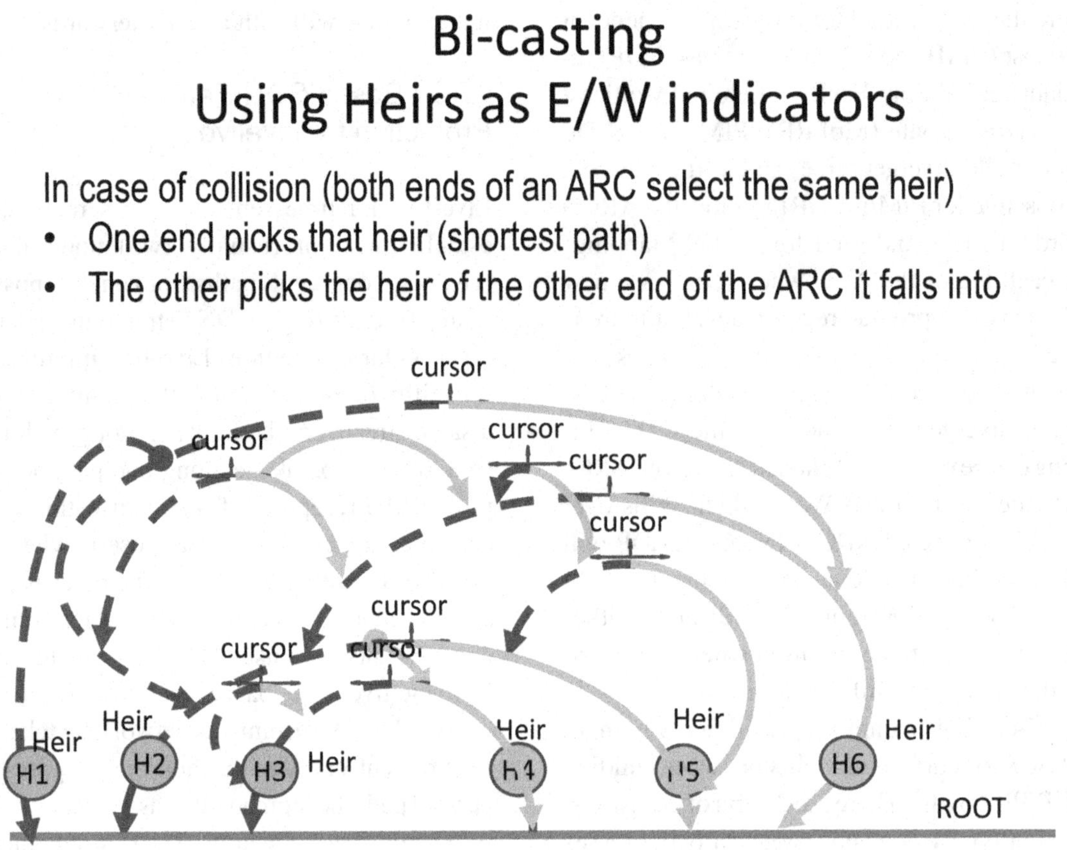
Bi-casting
Using Heirs as E/W indicators
In case of collision (both ends of an ARC select the same heir)
• One end picks that heir (shortest path)
• The other picks the heir of the other end of the ARC it falls into
cursor
cursor
cursor
cursor
cursor
cursor
cursor
Heir
Heir
Heir
Heir
Heir
Heir
H1
H2
H3
H6
ROOT

now described in a graph of hierarchical ARCs. An ARC is inherently, in the simplest case, bi-connected, and it offers not only FRR but also load balancing and bi-casting.

ARC is at the boundary between SDN and classical distributed routing, the ARC itself is a self-repair area, with local piloting of the key behaviors that cannot rely on an external device, while the global graph topology, composed of a set of ARC, is computed by a central controller and diffused seamlessly over the existing topology.

ARC is particularly efficient in circular topology as of MPLS-TP where it solves elegantly the hierarchical ring requirement, and is probably the only technic as of today to propose a solution to this complex case.

Advanced studies on ARCs are still needed but ARCs are a promising approach to address issues that so far do not have a solution at all, including the so-called Olympic Rings, the Shared Risk Link Group, or the Oscillation-free network based load balancing.

REFERENCES

Atlas, A., Kebler, R., Bowers, C., Enyedi, G., Csaszar, A., Tantsura, J., & White, R. (2015). *Maximally Redundant Trees (MRT)*. Retrieved March 15, 2015 from https://datatracker.ietf.org/doc/draft-ietf-rtgwg-mrt-frr-architecture/

Atlas, A., & Zinin, A. (2008). *IP fast re-route*. Retrieved March 15, 2015 from https://datatracker.ietf.org/doc/rfc5286/

Bocci, M., Bryant, S., Frost, D., Levrau, L., & Berger, L. (2010). *MPLS-TP Framework*. Retrieved March 15, 2015 from https://datatracker.ietf.org/doc/rfc5921/

Bryant, S., Filsfils, C., Previdi, S., Shand, M., & So, N. (2014). *Remote-LFA (RLFA)*. Retrieved March 15, 2015 from https://datatracker.ietf.org/doc/draft-ietf-rtgwg-remote-lfa/

Melakessou, F. (2014). *Towards a New Way of Reliable Routing: Multiple Paths over ARCs*. Retrieved March 15, 2015 from https://www.scilab.org/content/download/1718/15085/file/UniversityLuxembourg_ScilabTEC2014.pdf

Melakessou, F., Palatella, M., & Engel, T. (2014). *Towards-a-new-way-of-reliable-routing-multiple-paths-over-arcs*. Retrieved March 15, 2015 from http://www.iot-butler.eu/news/towards-a-new-way-of-reliable-routing-multiple-paths-over-arcs

Thubert, P., & Bellagamba, P. (2014). *Available Routing Construct (ARC)*. Retrieved March 15 2015, from https://datatracker.ietf.org/doc/draft-thubert-rtgwg-arc/

Winter, T., Thubert, P., Brandt, A., Hui, J., Kelsey, R., Levis, P., … Vasseur, J. P. (2012). *RPL: IPv6 Routing Protocol for Low-Power and Lossy Networks*. Retrieved March 15, 2015 from https://datatracker.ietf.org/doc/rfc6550/

KEY TERMS AND DEFINITIONS

ARC Set: A global topology composed of a graph of ARCs.

Available Routing Construct (ARC): A local construct that handles locally failure and load balancing.

Cursor: Point in the ARC determining data flow direction. East of the ARC the data is flowing the opposite of West side.

Fast ReRouting (FRR): A technic that happens locally in the routing area, allowing diverging traffic from a failure without waiting for a global recomputation of routing path.

Joint Operation and Automation of the Network (JOAN): Local messages to the ARC that allow to handle cursor dynamic placement and load balancing behavior.

Micro-Loop: During a failure recovery, topology changes locally but not globally, most of recovery technics induce temporary but heavy loop for data. ARC is loopless by concept.

Multi-Failures Protection: Most of local repair technologies do not allow repairing multiple failures at the same time without data loop. Some advanced approaches allow considering Shared Risk Link Group (SRLG) where some form of multiple failures are considered when they are related to the same error source. With ARCs, multi-failures are supported either when occurring in different ARCs, or even in the same ARC.

Software-Defined Networking (SDN): In the context of ARC, an approach where the topology is computed in an external controller and downloaded on every node. In ARC, this topology is diffused bottom to top to allow loopless installation.

Chapter 14
Asymmetric Extended Route Optimization (AERO)

Fred L. Templin
Association for Computing Machinery (ACM), USA

ABSTRACT

Modern enterprise networks must accommodate mobile devices such as cell phones, tablets and laptop computers. When a mobile device moves to a new access network, it often receives a new Internet Protocol (IP) address. This can disrupt communication sessions and create challenges for locating and tracking mobile assets. The enterprise network should therefore provide each mobile device with a stable IP address or prefix that never changes, but this requires a new mobility architecture. Asymmetric Extended Route Optimization (AERO) supports mobility by modeling the enterprise network as a virtual link through a process known as encapsulation. The AERO system tracks mobile devices through control message signaling and an efficient routing system. AERO maintains optimal routes for roaming devices so that performance is maximized and congestion points are avoided. This chapter describes the AERO system for accommodating mobile devices within enterprise networks.

INTRODUCTION

The Internet was designed long before the advent of modern mobile networked devices. The Internet Protocol (IP) therefore includes no provisions for a device to move between different network points of attachment while still maintaining a stable IP address or prefix. Instead, each mobile device is assigned an IP address that is topologically-inferred, i.e., bound to its current access network point of attachment. This address is called a Topologically-Fixed Address (TFA). If the device moves to a new access network, it must relinquish its former TFA address and obtain a new one. In some instances, this may disrupt ongoing communication sessions and complicate mobile device tracking. A means of maintaining a stable IP address or prefix across mobility events would therefore result in a more flexible architecture.

In addition to the mobility challenges, the Internet is currently undergoing growing pains since there are now billions of networked devices worldwide with many more on the way. This exponential growth has exhausted the IP version 4 (IPv4) (Postel et al., 1981) address space that is physically constrained to support at most 4 bil-

DOI: 10.4018/978-1-4666-8371-6.ch014

lion addresses. To remedy this address run-out condition, the Internet Engineering Task Force (IETF) has designed IP version 6 (IPv6) (Deering & Hinden, 1998) with sufficient address space for the forseeable future. Moreover, mobile devices often require not just a single address but a mobile network prefix that can address multitudes of additional devices and services. Since all public IPv4 prefixes have already been consumed (and since private IPv4 addresses are not routable outside the enterprise) this can only be cleanly accommodated by the expanded address space offered by IPv6.

Modern enterprise networks appear as Autonomous Systems (ASes) in the Internet's Border Gateway Protocol (BGP) routing system (Rekhter, Li, & Hares, 2006), but they are internally organized as an Internet unto themselves. These enterprise networks have an internal routing system and addressing architecture that must be capable of providing pervasive connectivity to ensure the smooth operation of enterprise services. More and more, mobile enterprise network devices connect through multiple diverse wireless (e.g., Wireless LAN or "WLAN") and wired-line (e.g., Ethernet) access technologies. However, each time the mobile device transitions from one access network to another it receives a new TFA and discontinues the use of its old TFA. Without specific mitigations, this can disrupt ongoing communication sessions and can make tracking and locating devices based on IP address challenging.

It has long been known that a technique called tunneling can present a mobile device with a stable Topology-Independent Address (TIA) (or TIA prefix) even if its TFA changes frequently. Tunneling involves the encapsulation of an inner IP packet with a TIA source and/or destination address within an outer IP header that uses TFA addresses. The enterprise network routing system then bases its packet forwarding decisions on the outer TFA address instead of the inner TIA address, i.e., the TFA and TIA address spaces are kept separate. Tunneling introduces additional header bytes that reduce the amount of space available for user data and consume network bandwidth resources. However, tunneling is seen in widespread and ever-growing use throughout the Internet since the benefits often outweigh the costs.

Tunnels have an ingress endpoint and one or more egress endpoints, but the discovery of an egress endpoint nearest the packet's destination (also known as "route optimization") is required to provide optimum performance and reduce network cost. The selection of an egress endpoint must also be securely coordinated with mobility events to defeat encapsulation-based attacks. Asymmetric Extended Route Optimization (AERO) was therefore designed to address these needs.

The following sections present the AERO routing, addressing and mobility management system. The reader will be introduced to the features that make AERO a natural fit for mobility management and address stability in enterprise networks. AERO is based on a Non-Broadcast, Multiple Access (NBMA) tunnel virtual link model, where all nodes appear as neighbors the same as if they were attached to the same physical link. Enterprise networks will increasingly need to provide support for mobility, route optimization, IPv6 transition, multiple interfaces, security, traffic engineering and many others. They can therefore benefit from adopting the AERO technology as part of their long-term architectural evolution.

BACKGROUND

The NBMA tunnel virtual link model is not new. It was introduced in "6over4" (Carpenter & Jung, 1999), where multicast mapping between the IPv6 and IPv4 multicast address spaces were also required. Since many enterprise networks still do not support multicast, however, a unicast-only variant was introduced in ISATAP (Templin, Gleeson & Thaler, 2005). However, these approaches only connect hosts (not routers) and do not support mobility. Their applicability has therefore been limited primarily to experimental use. Other approaches have also considered Virtual LAN (VLAN) switching (Chown, 2006) as an alternative to the NBMA tunneling approach, but these require explicit programming of Layer 2 (L2) devices which may or may not be easily coordinated within large and/or complex enterprise networks.

More recently, the Internet Research Task Force (IRTF) Routing Research Group (RRG) studied alternatives for managing growth and stability in the Internet global routing tables. A principal requirement was to avoid exposing the routing system to the de-aggregated IP prefixes of mobile routers. To address these requirements, the RRG studied new routing and addressing architectures, including the Internet Routing Overlay Network (IRON) (Templin, 2011).

IRON provided an architectural sketch of how an NBMA tunnel virtual interface model could support large-scale mobile networking as well as tunneling of any network layer protocol within any other network layer protocol. The IRON effort led to the development of the original AERO specification (Templin, 2012) which is now undergoing significant revisions in a second edition (Templin, 2014). The goal of this effort is to move AERO to an IETF proposed standard that can be widely adopted and implemented by major computing and networking equipment product manufacturers.

Throughout its development, AERO has investigated mobility use cases similar to those addressed by Internet Mobile IPv6 (MIPv6) protocol suite (Perkins, Johnson, & Arkko, 2013) and Proxy Mobile IPv6 (PMIPv6) (Gundavelli, Devarapalli, Chowdhury & Patil, 2008). A further effort on Network Mobility (NEMO) (Devaraplli, Wakikawa, Petrescu & Thubert, 2005) supports mobile networks attached to a MIPv6 host. While AERO has similarities with these approaches, the NBMA tunnel virtual link model provides a natural architecture for route optimization, mobility and security for mobile routers. Fundamentally speaking, the MIPv6 archetype is a mobile host that wanders away from its home link, while the AERO archetype is a mobile router that always stays connected to its home network. This distinction presents new opportunities that are subject for ongoing investigations.

THE AERO VIRTUAL LINK MODEL

AERO views the enterprise network as a connected network routing region that supports IP networking. When tunneling is used, the ingress and egress tunnel endpoints are seen as link-layer peers through encapsulation. This gives rise to a virtual link model in which all potential tunnel endpoints in the enterprise network appear as single hop neighbors. (This is in contrast to the common understanding of point-to-point tunnels that have only a single ingress point and a single egress point.) Unless explicitly blocked along some paths, e.g., by packet filtering, an enterprise network can therefore be modeled as a Non-Broadcast Multiple Access (NBMA) virtual link.

An AERO virtual link has the properties that each device on the link can address other devices via unicast (i.e., single-destination) link-layer addressing. These "link-layer" addresses are actually the TFA addresses in the outer IP header which can be routed within the enterprise network such that encapsulated packets may travel over many routers, bridges, switches, etc. while the network layer sees only a single logical IP hop. With respect to this property, it is then possible to use IP for normal data message exchanges over the AERO link, and to use the IPv6 Neighbor Discovery (ND) protocol (Narten, Nordmark, Simpson & Soliman, 2007) and the Dynamic Host Configuration Protocol for IPv6 (DHCPv6) (Droms, Bound, Volz, Lemon, Perkins & Carney, 2003) for control message signaling. We therefore consider the operation of IP, the IPv6 ND protocol and DHCPv6 over an AERO virtual link (or, more simply, an AERO link).

Figure 1 depicts an AERO link configured over an enterprise network:

Figure 1. AERO virtual link model

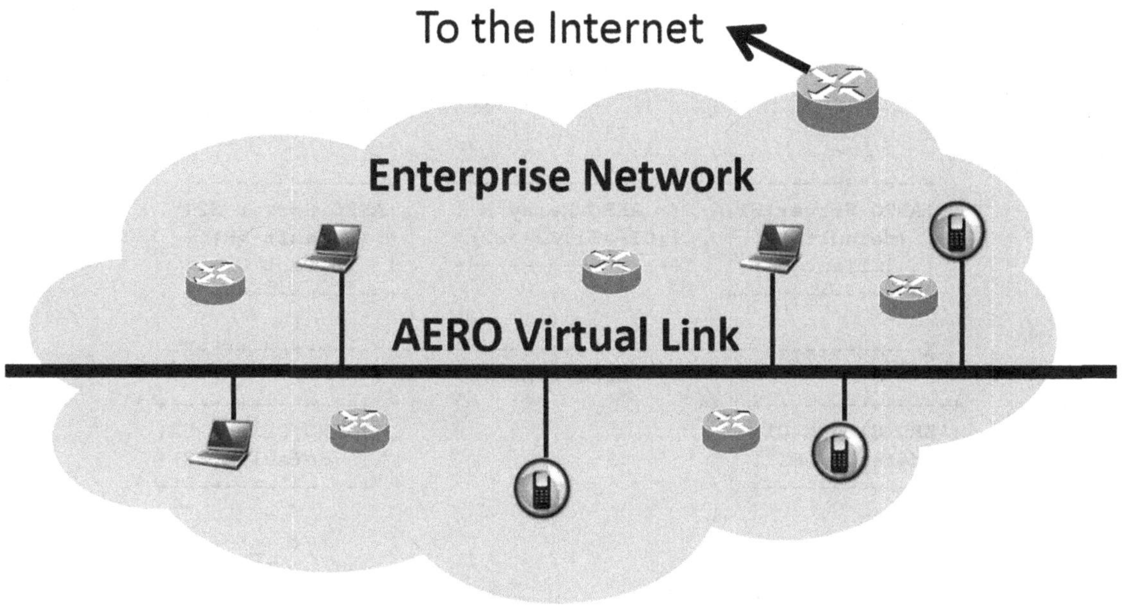

In Figure 1, the enterprise network connects to the Internet via border routers that provide firewalling, proxying or other packet filtering services to protect the enterprise from Internet-based attacks and to prevent exfiltration of sensitive enterprise information. Within the enterprise network, the inter-connected interior routers, bridges, switches, etc. (depicted as small blue disk icons) provide a backbone over which the AERO link is supported. Then, enterprise mobile devices (depicted as laptop computers and cell phones) can connect to the AERO link over which they can communicate directly with one another as though they were all connected to the same physical link.

The AERO link provides a seamless TIA service to mobile devices so that service continuity and stable addressing can be maintained across mobility events. For example, a corporate laptop computer user could begin a day by attaching the laptop to a docking station connected to a wired Ethernet LAN. The user may then need to carry the laptop to a conference room where the network connectivity changes over from Ethernet to a WLAN or other wireless service. Later in the day, the user may leave the enterprise network campus and connect via a cellular wireless service. Throughout these movements, the device should be able to retain its same stable TIA.

The AERO link spans the enterprise network via a set of AERO nodes that are deployed without needing to upgrade or replace any existing enterprise network assets. These nodes are known as AERO Clients, AERO Servers and AERO Relays as shown in Figure 2:

For simplicity, Figure 2 shows a single Relay, two Servers and two Clients. In practical deployments, however, there may be tens of Relays, hundreds of Servers and many thousands of Clients or more. The simple figure illustrates the relationship between AERO link elements.

First, Relays connect the AERO link to the rest of the enterprise network routing system, and serve as transit nodes for communicating with correspondents outside the AERO link. Relays advertise one or more AERO Service Prefixes (ASPs) into the enterprise network routing system. Each ASP is a TIA prefix from which AERO Client Prefixes (ACPs) are delegated to AERO Clients.

Figure 2. AERO link clients, servers and relays

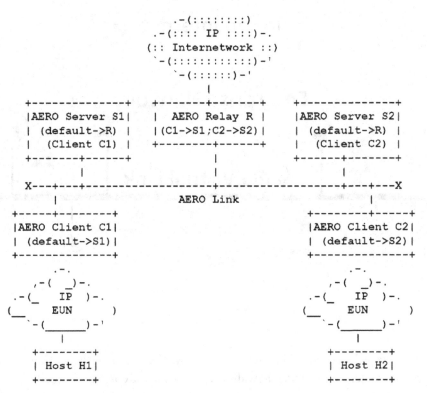

```
                        .-(::::::::)
                     .-(:::: IP ::::)-.
                    (:: Internetwork ::)
                     `-(::::::::::::)-'
                        `-(::::::)-'
                             |
  +--------------+  +-------+-------+  +--------------+
  |AERO Server S1|  | AERO Relay R  |  |AERO Server S2|
  | (default->R) |  |(C1->S1;C2->S2)|  | (default->R) |
  |  (Client C1) |  +-------+-------+  |  (Client C2) |
  +-------+------+          |          +------+-------+
          |                 |                 |
  X---+---+-----------------+-----------------+---+---X
      |                 AERO Link                 |
+-----+--------+                          +--------+-----+
|AERO Client C1|                          |AERO Client C2|
| (default->S1)|                          | (default->S2)|
+--------------+                          +--------------+
       .-.                                       .-.
    ,-(  _)-.                                 ,-(  _)-.
 .-(_   IP  )-.                            .-(_   IP  )-.
(__    EUN     )                          (__    EUN     )
   `-(______)-'                              `-(______)-'
        |                                         |
    +--------+                                +--------+
    | Host H1|                                | Host H2|
    +--------+                                +--------+
```

For example, the Relays could be provisioned with an IPv6 ASP such as 2001:db8::/32 from which longer ACPs such as 2001:db8:1:0::/56, 2001:db8:5:1::/64, etc. are derived (Huston, Lord, & Smith, 2004) (Kawamura & Kawashima, 2010).

Relays maintain complete knowledge of all Servers and their associated Clients via a routing protocol that operates over the AERO link. For this purpose, a private BGP dynamic routing protocol instance is used to connect all Relays to all Servers. Servers report their list of associated Clients to the Relays via routing protocol updates. Since there may be many Clients, this may represent a very large amount of routing information. Changes to the routing system should therefore occur only occasionally. Servers therefore only send BGP updates when they encounter a new ACP or withdraw an existing ACP; they do not send BGP updates when the link-layer address for an existing ACP changes.

Second, Servers configure a default route for each of the Relays for reaching destinations for which they do not have a more-specific route. This means that the Server will pass all packets for which it does not have firsthand routing knowledge to a Relay where full topology knowledge is maintained. Servers participate in the BGP routing protocol instance to report their list of associated Clients to the Relays, but they do not report this information to other Servers. When a new Client associates with a Server, the Server injects a route for this Client's ACP into the BGP routing system so that it will be discovered by all Relays. When an existing Client disassociates with the Server, the Server withdraws the ACP from the BGP routing system.

Servers in turn act as default routers for their associated Clients. They maintain a list of all ACPs keyed by a Client Identifier that was registered when the Client was enrolled in the service.

When a Client associates with a Server, the Server delegates the ACP to the Client. The Server also notes the Client's TFA so that it has a correct address to use for encapsulating the packets it sends to the Client. If the Client's TFA changes, the Server updates its local TFA mapping for the Client's ACP but does not announce the change in the routing system. Most mobility events are therefore coordinated by each individual Server and are not propagated to other Servers or Relays.

Finally, Clients are the mobile devices themselves (e.g., laptop computers, cell phones, tablets, airplanes, etc.) that connect via an enterprise network access link where they receive a link-layer TFA. Clients can also connect End User Networks (EUNs) to the AERO link in a manner that is consistent with the emerging "Internet of Things" vision. Clients can therefore act as mobile routers that connect potentially large end user networks to the rest of the AERO link. The Client's entourage of EUN devices can then travel with the Client wherever it goes and still maintain pervasive connectivity to the rest of the network.

Clients discover a list of nearby Servers and choose one or more to associate with through a process known as Prefix Delegation (PD). In this process, the Client receives the same ACP PD from each Server (i.e., the Client receives the same service regardless of which Server(s) it associates with). The Client then configures a default route via its associated Servers and can then use the ACP to assign an addressing plan for its attached EUNs. The Client further monitors its access network connections to detect any changes. If the Client moves, for example from a 4G cellular service to a WLAN link, its TFA will change. The Client then immediately reports this change to its associated Servers where the mobility event will be registered. Initially, each Client has only a default route via its associated Servers. If the Client wishes to communicate directly with another Client (for example, if Client C1 in Figure 2 wishes to communicate directly with Client C2) it initiates a process known as route optimization.

Conceptually, the AERO link is analogous to the MIPv6 home link, AERO Relays are analogous to the "enterprise network-facing" portion of the MIPv6 Home Agent, AERO Servers are analogous to the "home link-facing" portion of the MIPv6 Home Agent, and AERO Clients are analogous to MIPv6 Mobile Nodes. However, the AERO link spans the entire enterprise network while the MIPv6 home link is a single physical link located somewhere within the enterprise. Also, unlike the MIPv6 Home Agent, AERO Servers are redundantly replicated across the enterprise and need not attach to the same physical link. The AERO link Relays and Servers combined can therefore be likened to a MIPv6 Home Agent broken up into a multitude of component pieces and spread throughout the enterprise to provide a distributed mobility architecture.

AERO LINK TRUST MODEL

AERO Servers and Relays are deployed through the explicit administrative actions of the enterprise network engineering staff. The staff is responsible for network integrity, and therefore ensures that the devices are deployed in a secured manner on secured networks. Therefore, Servers and Relays have naturally in-built trust relationship.

Client devices that connect to the enterprise network must authenticate themselves to the access network link admission agent. For wired-line connections such as Ethernet, the physical security of the protected wiring provides sufficient link-layer authentication for the connected device. For WLAN and other on-campus wireless connections, an additional link-layer authenticating service such as 802.1x is needed. For cellular service Access Point Networks (APNs), an IPsec tunnel from the service provider into the enterprise network is used.

However, authentication at the link-layer does not prevent an authorized Client from launching network-layer attacks over the AERO link. For example, an authorized Client could attempt to cancel another Client's ACP delegations. The Client also could try to convince a Server that another of its Clients has moved, it could attempt to siphon traffic destined to another Client, it could pretend to be a Server itself, etc. These "insider attacks" must be guarded against since an attacker could be located in a far distant corner of the enterprise network where traffic flows and traces alone may not be sufficient to detect and capture the incident.

A first aspect of the AERO link trust model involves the Client's ability to trust its Servers. This is supported through the publication of Server TFAs in the enterprise network name service. The Client must then trust that the name service cannot be subverted and that the Server's TFAs cannot be spoofed by another node. These accommodations are naturally supported given sound enterprise network engineering practices, which must be assumed if enterprise network integrity is properly managed.

A second aspect of the AERO link trust model involves the Server's ability to trust its Clients. For this reason, Servers should authenticate DHCPv6 messages before creating or updating a Client neighbor cache entry. The authenticated DHCPv6 exchanges prove that the Client is not only authorized at the link-layer but also at the network layer.

A final aspect of the AERO link trust model involves a Client's ability to trust other Clients. This aspect requires a "chain of trust" in which the Clients initially exchange messages via trusted Servers and Relays until a secured route optimization can provide the trust needed to allow them to exchange packets directly. Clients then must use periodic IPv6 ND message exchanges to maintain this brokered trust.

AERO LINK ENCAPSULATION

The AERO virtual link model is supported through a technique known as tunneling which entails encapsulation of an (inner) IP packet within an (outer) IP packet header and any other encapsulation headers. Any IP-in-IP combination can be used, including IPv4-in-IPv4, IPv6-in-IPv4, IPv4-in-IPv6, and IPv6-in-IPv6. AERO by default also includes a User Datagram Protocol (UDP) header (Postel, 1980) in addition to the outer IP header. The UDP header allows AERO packets to traverse network paths that filter packets with unknown transport-layer headers.

The outer IP packet header includes a TFA destination address that can be routed through the enterprise network routing system. This means that ordinary routers, bridges, switches, etc. throughout the enterprise network can recognize the TFA and understand how to direct the packet to its final destination. The inner IP packet header containing a TIA address is typically not examined by network elements in the path, and is only examined by the final destination.

Figure 3 shows an example of AERO Client A sending an encapsulated IPv6 packet to AERO Client B across an IPv4 enterprise network. In this example, Host A creates an IPv6 packet with source address 2001:db8:0:1::1 and destination address 2001:db8:0:2::1. Host A sends the packet to Client A (i.e., its IPv6 default router) where Client A has an IPv6 route for the target destination prefix via Client B.

Client A then encapsulates the packet by wrapping it in an outer UDP and IPv4 header. The IPv4 header uses a TFA source address taken from one of Client A's access links and a TFA destination address taken from one of Client B's access links. The UDP header uses the AERO reserved port number (i.e., 8060). Client A then admits the packet into the enterprise network routing system, where it may undergo many IPv4 routing hops on the path to Client B. This IPv4 path is often referred to as the tunnel (and for this particular example, an IPv6-in-IPv4 tunnel).

When Client B receives the encapsulated packet, it removes the outer headers and processes the inner packet as though it had arrived on a physi-

Figure 3. AERO link encapsulation

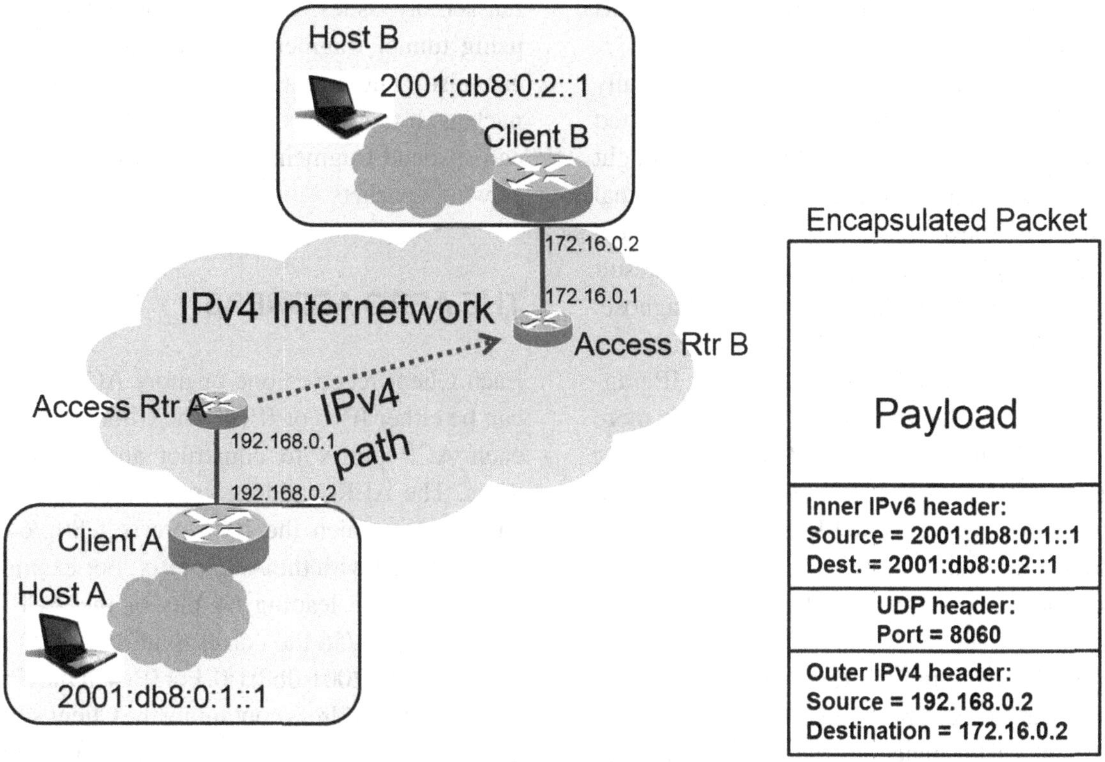

cal network interface. Client B finally forwards the packet to Host B as an ordinary IP packet. During this process the inner IP "hop count" field was not decremented within the tunnel, so that Client A and Client B appear to be attached to the same physical link, i.e., a single IP "hop". This single-hop behavior is the essence of why the tunnel can be modeled as a virtual link even though the packet may have traveled over many enterprise network hops.

Encapsulation of an inner IP packet within an outer IP header reduces the amount of space available for payload data. This is seen as a reduction in the Maximum Transmission Unit (MTU) on the path from Host A to Host B. Both IPv4 and IPv6 provide a service known as Path MTU Discovery whereby a source is informed that it must reduce the size of the packets it sends (Mogul & Deering, 1990)(McCann, Deering & Mogul, 1996). Unfortunately, this mechanism has several well-known issues that are further exacerbated by encapsulation.

First, the point at which a packet is determined to be too large to traverse the path is known as a restricting link (where each link in the path has a fixed link MTU). The router at the head end of the restricting link is responsible for dropping the too-large packet and returning a "Packet Too Big (PTB)" message to the original source. However, network devices such as packet filtering gateways, firewalls, etc. are often configured to discard such messages.

Second, if the restricting link is within the tunnel, the PTB message will be returned to the tunnel ingress and not directly to the original source. The tunnel ingress is then responsible for translating the PTB message into a corresponding message to send to the original source. However,

PTB messages sent by routers within the tunnel often include insufficient information to support this translation.

Finally, PTB messages can be artificially created by adversarial devices in unprotected networks. In that case, the PTB message might report a degenerate size that leads the original source to believe that the path MTU is much smaller than is actually the case. This can result in poor performance that is difficult to diagnose.

An alternative to using PMTUD is known as IP fragmentation. When the source uses IP fragmentation, it splits the packet into two or more pieces. This eliminates the need for the network to return any PTB message feedback, however IPv6 and IPv4 both have a fixed-length Identification field that limits the number of packets that can be sent. For example, the IPv4 Identification field is only 16 bits in length which means that the source can only send up to 2^{16} different packets into the network at a time. This number is far too small to match the performance characteristics of modern data link technologies.

A new path MTU probing mechanism described in (Mathis, Heffner, 2007) addresses the issues for both standard path MTU discovery and IP fragmentation, but requires assistance from tunnels in the path. The tunnel ingress therefore must do a small amount of fragmentation and probing on its own to provide a consistent MTU the same as for any link on the path from the source to the destination.

The minimum MTU for IPv6 is 1280 bytes, and AERO recommends the same size for IPv4. Since the vast majority of links in the Internet support an MTU of at least 1500 bytes, the tunnel ingress uses these two sizes as thresholds for MTU mitigation. In particular, the tunnel ingress uses tunnel fragmentation if necessary to ensure that packets that are between these thresholds can be accommodated while allowing smaller and larger packets into the tunnel without fragmentation. Tunnel fragmentation occurs at a mid-layer above the outer IP layer and below the inner IP layer, and therefore avoids IP fragmentation and reassembly issues. While sending initial packets using tunnel fragmentation, the tunnel ingress can also send unfragmented 1500 byte probe packets. If the probes succeed, the tunnel ingress can suspend fragmentation and send all packets as whole packets.

THE AERO ADDRESS

Each Client receives one or more ACPs, which can be either IPv6 or IPv4. The Client then uses each ACP prefix to construct an AERO address. The AERO address is an IPv6 link-local address for which the IPv6 prefix fe80::/64 is concatenated with the ACP prefix. For example, for IPv6 if the leading 64 bits of the ACP is: 2001:db8:1:0::/56 the corresponding AERO address is: fe80::2001:db8:1:0. For IPv4, if the IPv4-mapped IPv6 address containing the Client's IPv4 prefix is: ::ffff:192.0.2.0 the corresponding AERO address is: fe80::ffff:192.0.2.0. The AERO address also has an associated prefix length which is not encoded within the address itself but is carried as ancillary data, e.g., in a link-layer address option.

The AERO address format enables several important aspects of the AERO architecture. First, since the AERO system always assigns a unique ACP to each Client, the Client can always create a unique IPv6 link-local address for IPv6 ND and DHCPv6 messaging. Second, since the AERO address embeds an IP prefix, it can be used both for IPv6 neighbor discovery and IP route determination. It is therefore not necessary for Servers to maintain IP routes for Clients (or for Clients to maintain IP routes for other Clients), since the AERO address already encodes sufficient information. Finally, the AERO address can be derived from the source and/or destination addresses of IP packets with no need for any form of address resolution. The AERO address structure therefore provides the basis for packet forwarding and neighbor coordination within the AERO system.

Figure 4. AERO service routing system

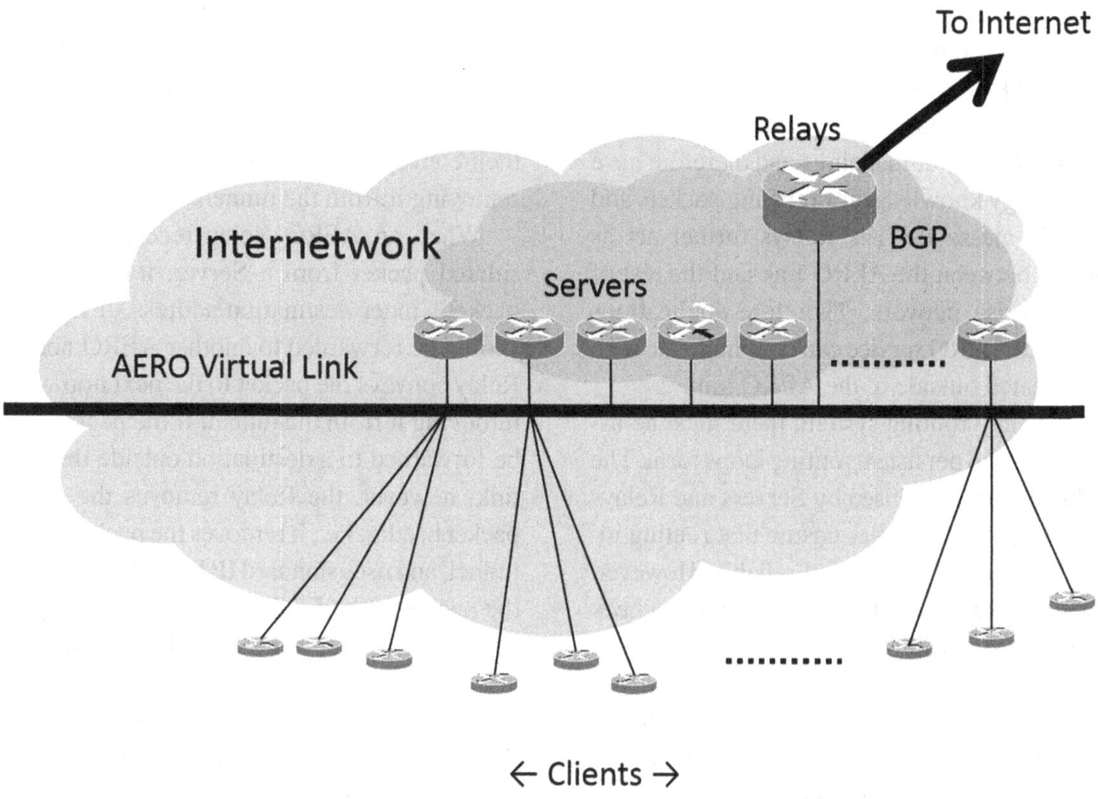

AERO ROUTING SYSTEM

The AERO routing system is coordinated between AERO Relays and Servers and is responsible for tracking all active ACPs throughout their operational lifetime. The AERO routing system is depicted in Figure 4 below:

In order to support routing protocol control messaging, each Relay establishes a permanent IPv6 neighbor cache entry for each Server, and each Server establishes a permanent IPv6 neighbor cache entry for each Relay. Servers further consider each Relay as a default router for forwarding packets to destinations for which they do not have more-specific forwarding information.

The AERO routing system is based on an interior and dedicated instance of the Border Gateway Protocol (BGP) that is kept separate from all other enterprise network dynamic routing protocol instances. In this system, all AERO Servers act as stub ASes and peer with each Relay in the AERO system. The Relays in turn peer with each Server in the AERO system but do not peer with other Relays. The Relays further inject the ASP(s) for the AERO system into the enterprise network dynamic routing system.

When a Server delegates an ACP to a Client, it injects the ACP into the BGP routing system. When a Server releases an ACP, it withdraws the ACP from the BGP routing system. When the Server injects or withdraws an ACP, it performs a reliable BGP message exchange with each Relay.

Relays may be configured to report or suppress some or all ACP updates to their peering Servers. If the Relays report ACPs, the Servers will have more-specific forwarding information that can be used for Server-to-Server forwarding in the data plane. If the Relays do not report ACPs, the amount of BGP routing protocol messaging is reduced but Servers will only have partial topology information and may need to make use of Relays for default forwarding services.

In this way, Relays become aware of all AERO link ACP-to-Server mappings and therefore have full topology knowledge for relaying packets and IPv6 ND messages. The Relays further act as conduits between the AERO link and the rest of the enterprise network. Therefore applications that use the AERO service can communicate with peers located outside of the AERO link.

As for any routing system, there must be assurance that no persistent routing loops form. The reliable connections used by Servers and Relays to exchange BGP updates ensure that routing information will be propagated reliably. However, Servers and Relays must implement a simple check to defeat any possible looping. Namely, a Server that receives a data packet from a Relay must not forward the packet back to the same or a different Relay, and a Server or Relay that receives a data packet from a Server must not forward the packet back to the same Server.

AERO PACKET FORWARDING AND ND MESSAGE RELAYING

Clients connect EUNs to the AERO link, i.e., they provide mobile router services for devices on (downstream-attached) EUNs. When a Client receives an IP packet from an EUN source, it encapsulates the packet and admits it into the AERO link where it may be conveyed to either a Server or another Client. Once the packet has been admitted into the AERO link, however, it travels "in the tunnel", i.e., it is forwarded by enterprise network devices towards to the end of the tunnel based on information carried in its outer IP header.

When a Server receives an encapsulated packet, it examines the packet's inner destination address without ever removing it from the tunnel. If the Server determines that the packet should be forwarded to another AERO node, it changes the outer IP source address to its own address and changes the outer IP destination address to the address of the next hop AERO node. The Server then conveys the packet to the next hop without removing it from the tunnel.

When an AERO Relay receives an encapsulated packet from a Server, it examines the packet's inner destination address. If the packet should be forwarded to another AERO node, the Relay conveys the packet to the next hop without removing it from the tunnel. If the packet should be forwarded to a destination outside the AERO link, however, the Relay removes the outer IP packet header, i.e., it removes the packet from the tunnel, and uses standard IP forwarding to convey the packet to the final destination.

The same procedure described above applies also to IPv6 ND and DHCPv6 messages. In that case, Relays and Servers make their forwarding decisions based on the IPv6 destination address whether they are searching for the address in the neighbor cache or in the IP forwarding table. They then convey the IPv6 ND message to the next hop without decrementing the hop count and thus preserving the appearance of an ordinary link.

The above processes obscure the distinction between network-layer routing and link-layer bridging, but can best be understood as a natural characteristic of the AERO link. Namely, IP packets as well as IPv6 ND and DHCPv6 messages may be re-encapsulated and pushed along several "segments" of the AERO link before they reach their final destination.

AERO CLIENT/SERVER INTERWORKING

Servers are deployed in a distributed fashion throughout the enterprise network. Enterprise buildings and campuses that experience a greater

Client load may require more Servers than at other locations. Therefore, a strictly uniform distribution is not required, but rather a commensurate number of Servers can be deployed in each location based on the expected Client load. Each Server acts as both a default router and a DHCPv6 server for its associated Clients.

Each Server is provisioned with a directory of ACP to Client ID mappings that are established when Clients are enrolled in the AERO system. The directory is typically available as an online service that is managed by the enterprise network engineering staff. The Client ID is supplied in the DHCPv6 option of the same name, and is typically an asset tag number, a serial number, a MAC address, or any other type of identification value.

Servers register their TFAs in the enterprise name service (typically, the Domain Name System (DNS)) under a Fully-Qualified Domain Name (FQDN) appropriate for their attached link (Mockapetris, 1987). Each FQDN has a suffix appropriate for the attached link (e.g., "example.com") and uses the well-known prefix "linkupnetworks". Clients can then query the DNS for the FQDN "linkupnetworks.example.com" to discover the TFAs of nearby Servers.

Clients use DHCPv6 PD (Troan & Droms, 2003) to request delegation of their ACPs from the Server or Servers they have selected. When the Client issues a DHCPv6 Request, the Server first authenticates the message, then searches the directory to match the Client's claimed Client ID with the correct ACP. When the Server issues the ACP via a DHCPv6 Reply, it also creates a static IPv6 neighbor cache entry based on the Client's AERO address as the network-layer address, the Client's TFA as the link-layer address and with a lifetime based on the DHCPv6 PD lifetime. The Server also injects a route for the ACP into the AERO service routing system.

When the Client receives the ACP delegation, it creates a static IPv6 neighbor cache entry for the Server's TFA and IPv6 link-local address (taken from the DHCPv6 Reply message source address) with a lifetime based on the DHCPv6 PD lifetime. The AERO Client also uses the ACP to assign an addressing plan to its attached EUNs. In some cases, the Client may already know the exact ACP it will receive from the AERO service and may have already pre-provisioned the ACP to its EUNs.

After the Client has established and propagated its ACP as described above, EUN applications can begin sending packets that use an address taken from the ACP as the source address. If the Client moves to a new access network, it issues a DHCPv6 Rebind message to the Server to report the change in TFA. The Server authenticates the message then changes the TFA mapping in the IPv6 neighbor cache entry for the Client. If the Client associates with multiple Servers, it issues a DHCPv6 Rebind message to each Server. Note that none of these mobility events are propagated beyond the Client's associated Server(s), and therefore do not disturb other Servers or Relays.

If the Client moves a significant topological and/or geographical distance from its current Server, it can issue a new DHCPv6 PD Request through a new Server as described above. After it has received the ACP prefix delegation, it can release its association with the former Server by issuing a DHCPv6 Release. When the old Server receives the DHCPv6 Release message, it authenticates the message then deletes the IPv6 neighbor cache entry for the Client if authentication succeeds. It also withdraws the ACP from the AERO service routing system.

After receiving ACP delegations, Clients can send unicast IPv6 ND Router Solicitation (RS) messages to their Servers at any time to receive unicast Router Advertisement (RA) message replies. This can provide a vital keepalive mechanism, e.g., to keep state alive in network middleboxes. For example, when Network Address Translators (NATs) are in the path keepalives may be necessary to maintain address and port mappings.

AERO ROUTE OPTIMIZATION

Clients can always communicate with peers by sending their packets through a Server as a default forwarding agent. However, unnecessary use of AERO service resources may create traffic congestion and also result in sub-optimal routes with poor performance. For example, with reference to Figure 2 since Clients C1 and C2 are both attached to the same AERO link it would be more efficient for them to communicate with each other directly instead of involving Servers and Relays. In some environments, it may also be more cost effective since the Clients may be billed for the use of the AERO service resources. It is therefore in the best interest of Clients to use route optimized paths whenever possible.

To perform route optimization, when host H1 sends a packet destined to host H2, the packet is forwarded through the EUN until it reaches Client C1. Client C1 examines the packet's destination address and determines that host H2 can be reached via an AERO link neighbor since the address is covered by the ASP. However, Client C1 does not yet know the TFA of Client C2, i.e., the Client with the EUN on which host H2 is located. Client C1 therefore initiates a route optimization message exchange as outlined in Figure 5 below:

To initiate route optimization, Client C1 forwards both the data packet and a "Predirect" message (i.e., a route optimization request) to Server S1. Server S1 forwards both the packet and the Predirect to Relay R, which in turn forwards them to Server S2 which in turn forwards them to Client C2.

When Client C2 receives the packet, it forwards the packet to host H2. When Client C2 receives the Predirect, it creates a neighbor cache entry for Client C1 in the ACCEPT state so that it can accept encapsulated packets directly from the TFA of Client C1. Client C2 then sends a "Redirect" message (i.e., a route optimization reply) to Server S2. Server S2 forwards the Redirect to Relay R, which in turn forwards it to Server S1 which in turn forwards it to Client C1.

When Client C1 receives the Redirect, it creates a neighbor cache entry for Client C2 in the FORWARD state so that it can send packets directly to the TFA of Client C2. However, there is a question in point as to whether the direct path from C1 to C2 is usable without involving Servers and Relays. This is due to the fact that enterprise network elements in the path may refuse to pass encapsulated packets due to packet filtering configurations, etc. Therefore, Client C1 should test the direct path either before or while it forwards ordinary data packets.

To test the path, Client C1 sends an IPv6 ND Neighbor Solicitation (NS) message directly to Client C2. If C2 receives the NS message, it sends a Neighbor Advertisement (NA) message back to C1 via S2 (note that this is not depicted in the figure). C1 then receives positive confirmation that the direct path is working. If the direct path from Client C1 to Client C2 cannot be used, Client C1 simply deletes the neighbor cache entry for Client C2 and allows packets to flow through Server S1 again. Client C1 can then attempt to establish a route optimized path again at some point in the future.

Note that this procedure is asymmetric, meaning that only the forward path from Client C1 to Client C2 is enabled. If Client C2 similarly wishes to perform route optimization to receive a direct route to Client C1, it issues the same Predirect/Redirect message exchange procedure as described above. This asymmetric procedure has the useful side effect that unidirectional paths can be used and still result in optimal routes.

Following route optimization, if either Client C1 or C2 change their TFAs (e.g., due to changing to a new access link) the Client with the changed TFA sends a DHCPv6 Rebind message to its Server. It then sends unsolicited NA messages to each of its current correspondent Clients to inform them of the update. This method is the

Figure 5. AERO route optimization detailed message exchange

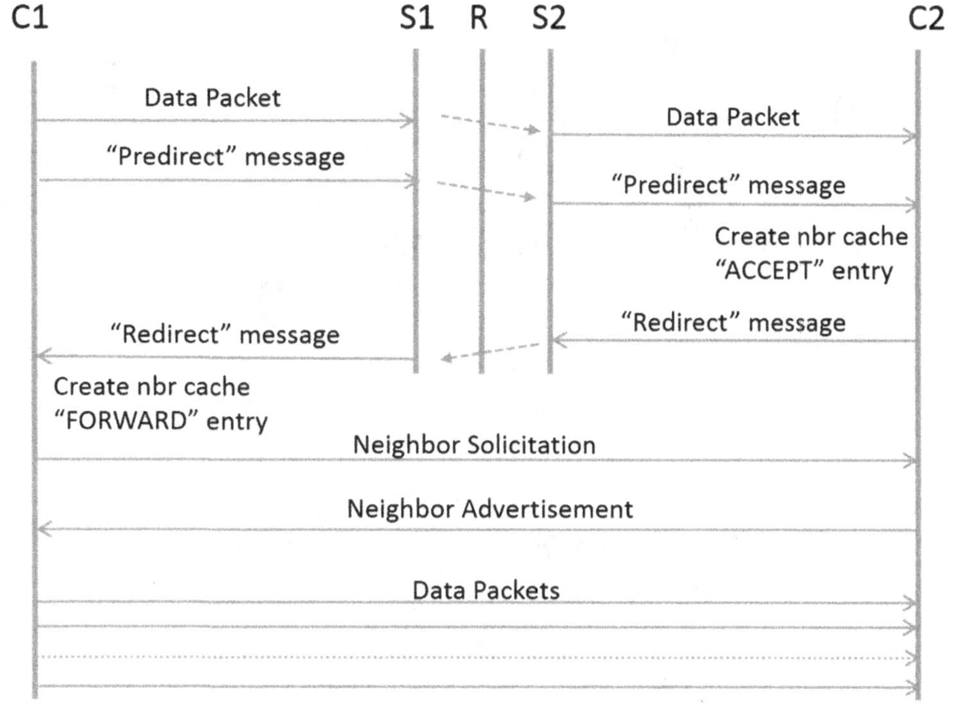

same as described for an IPv6 host changing its link-layer address as described in (Narten, Nordmark, Simpson & Soliman, 2007).

MOBILE VPN CONSIDERATIONS

Enterprise network mobile device users frequently move to off-campus locations, e.g., to attend off-site meetings, to travel by air to a customer site, to return home after work, etc. When a mobile device leaves an enterprise network campus, it naturally moves outside of the operational range of on-campus access networks. When the mobile device disconnects from the enterprise network (e.g., when the signal from the on-campus wireless technology fades), it enables an Internet-based access technology such as 4G cellular wireless. The device is now "on the Internet" and no longer "on the enterprise network". Figure 6 depicts a major enterprise network in which some mobile devices are connected to on-campus access links and others are connected to Internet access links:

In order to reach back into the enterprise network, the mobile device first discovers the Internet-based TFA of the security gateway for the enterprise network Virtual Private Network (VPN), and that serves as an endpoint for a VPN link established by the mobile. The mobile device then establishes a security association with the VPN gateway to set up an encrypted tunnel over the Internet. In order to supply the mobile device with the same ACP it would receive if it were entering the enterprise from an on-campus access link, the VPN gateway must also act as an AERO Server. Then, the mobile device (acting as an AERO Client) can issue DHCPv6 messages to the VPN gateway the same as if it were speaking to an ordinary Server.

Note that the Internet-based mobile device receives an Internet-based TFA instead of an enterprise network-based TFA. This address is

Figure 6. Enterprise network world view

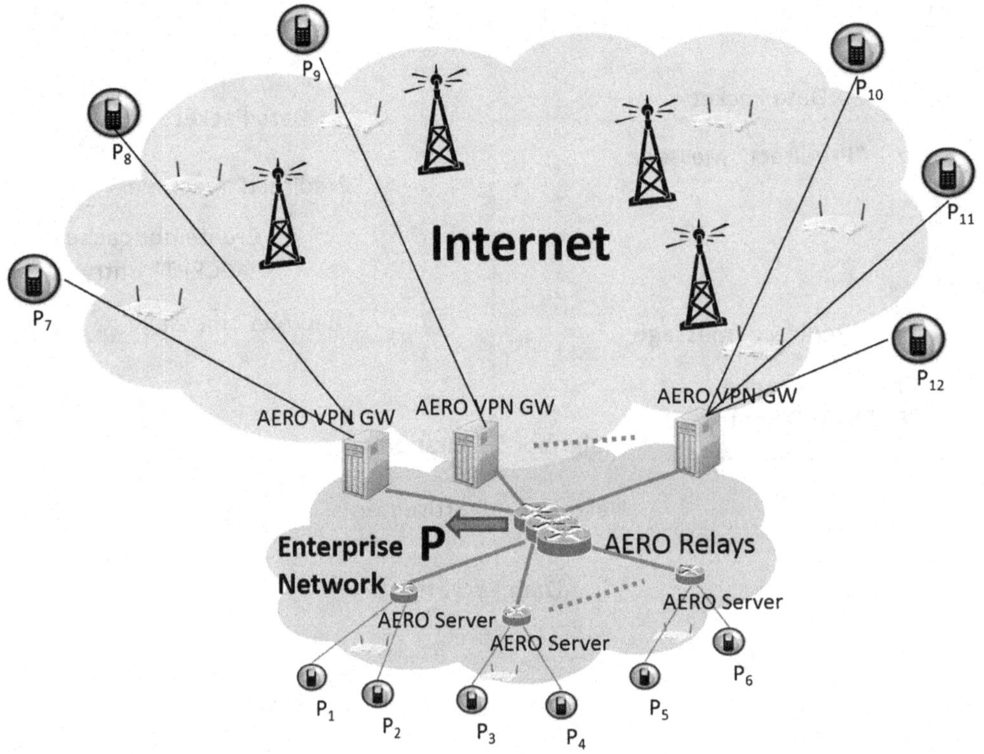

foreign to the enterprise network routing and addressing system and must therefore not be exposed inside the enterprise. The VPN gateway (acting as an AERO Server) therefore must also act as a proxy for the mobile device when speaking to other nodes on the AERO link. This requires the creation of a neighbor cache entry with Internet mobile device' AERO address as the network-layer address and the enterprise interior TFA of the VPN gateway as the link-layer address. The mobile device then continues to use AERO signaling in the same manner as if it were located within the enterprise network, but the signals are proxied by the VPN gateway.

In this way, the mobile device can change between Internet access links in the same way as it can change between access links within an enterprise campus. For example, a mobile device accessing the Internet via a 4G cellular wireless provider could change over to a WLAN hotspot in an airport terminal. The mobile device can register this change in Internet TFAs with the VPN gateway by sending a DHCPv6 Rebind message the same as if it were located within the enterprise. When the mobile device returns to an enterprise campus from the Internet, it can once again associate with an enterprise network access link and shut down the VPN link.

MULTICAST CONSIDERATIONS

While the AERO link basic service model is NBMA (i.e., Non-Broadcast, Multiple Access), there may be cases in which partial or full multicast services can be provided. At a minimum, AERO interfaces map the IPv6 "All_DHCP_Relay_Agents_and_Servers" link-scoped multicast address to the link-layer address of a Server. However, AERO interfaces can also map other multicast groups to the link-layer address of a Server in the same fashion to achieve a unicast-mapped multicast capability. The Server is then responsible for acting as a multicast proxy for its Clients.

Some enterprise networks offer a native multicast capability that spans the entire enterprise. In that case, the AERO interface can use multicast-mapped multicast services so that the multicast destination address in the inner packet header is algorithmically mapped to a multicast destination address in the outer packet header. The enterprise network multicast routing system then propagates the multicast packet to all network elements that subscribe to the group.

IMPLEMENTATION AND DEPLOYMENT CONSIDERATIONS

Each AERO node requires either a user-level AERO service daemon or an in-kernel implementation of the AERO interface and neighbor cache. When an AERO service daemon is used, no kernel changes are necessary and the daemon handles all user application packets via an abstraction known as the TUN/TAP interface. In that case, the AERO interface and neighbor cache serve as an intermediate conduit between the TUN/TAP interface and the underlying network interface, while user applications bind to the TUN/TAP interface as though it were a real network interface. Figure 7 below shows the architectural placement of the AERO service daemon with reference to the operating system kernel (depicted by the block diagram):

When an in-kernel implementation is used, no AERO service daemon is needed and user applications bind directly to the AERO interface via the socket layer. In that case, the AERO interface is an intermediate conduit between the socket layer and the underlying network interface. Figure 8 below shows the placement of the AERO interface and neighbor cache within the operating system kernel:

Clients such as cell phones, tablets, laptops, etc. typically implement the AERO service as a user-level AERO service daemon. The AERO service daemon forwards packets and coordinates DHCPv6 and IPv6 ND message exchanges over the tunnel. An early version of an AERO service daemon has been developed and tested, and will soon be released.

Servers can use either an AERO service daemon or an in-kernel implementation. They further require an online directory service for accessing Client ID to ACP mappings. Servers use BGP to communicate their Client constituencies to Relays. An open public domain BGP implementation can be used for this purpose. In terms of deployment, Servers can be realized in virtual machines, lightweight network appliances, or larger special-purpose server hardware. In some environments, a dense deployment of many lightweight servers might be preferable to a sparse deployment of a few powerful servers.

Relays are typically configured on enterprise router platforms. They form BGP peerings with all AERO Servers and can use a commercial or public domain BGP package for this purpose. Relays require very little in the way of special-purpose AERO software, since they do not take part in DHCPv6 or IPv6 ND messaging. Instead, the Relay simply relays packets within the tunnel at the link-layer while rewriting source and destination addresses as necessary. This function can be realized in a very small code footprint.

FUTURE RESEARCH DIRECTIONS

Mobile devices often have multiple data link technology interfaces. For example, modern mobile phones typically have both WLAN and 4G Cellular interfaces, and airplanes have many wireless data link interfaces that may or may not be available during all phases of flight. These interfaces are typically used "one at a time", with one interface active while the other is held in cold or warm

Figure 7. User-level AERO service daemon implementation

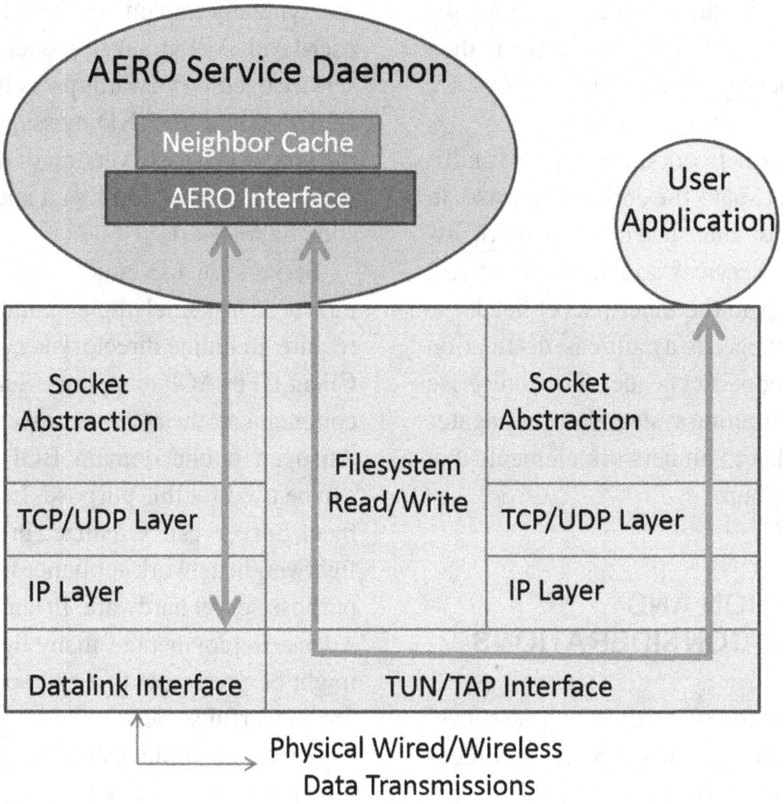

standby. A future use may enable more than one active interface simultaneously while using the same ACP. In that case, the Client would use multiple TFAs to communicate with their relevant AERO Servers and other correspondent Clients.

AERO has an in-built facility for the Client to indicate the specific link to which its current TFA applies. This indication is encoded in the IPv6 ND Source/Target Link Layer Option (S/TLLAO) as well as the DHCPv6 Client Link Layer Address Option (CLLAO). AERO link neighbors that receive IPv6 ND and DHCPv6 messages with these options can then map the Client's TFA to the correct link.

Coordination of multiple active network interfaces on a single device presents several challenges. The service providers that supply each interface with TFAs also often supply additional provisioning information such as the default router's address, the DNS name server address, etc. So, if the multiple active network interfaces are enabled within multiple provisioning domains, it may be difficult for the Client to keep the provisioning information separate.

In addition to handling of multiple active interfaces, application of AERO to networks with ad-hoc structures is another area for active investigation. For example, Clients may need to operate over networks where there may be no Servers. In that case, the Client requires some other form of egress tunnel endpoint discovery for correspondent Clients on the AERO link. This is especially true for mobile VPN Clients that need to establish destination-specific VPNs, e.g., when Client A forms a VPN link to Client B based on an out-of-band TFA resolution database and Internet securing protocols.

Figure 8. In-kernel AERO interface implementation

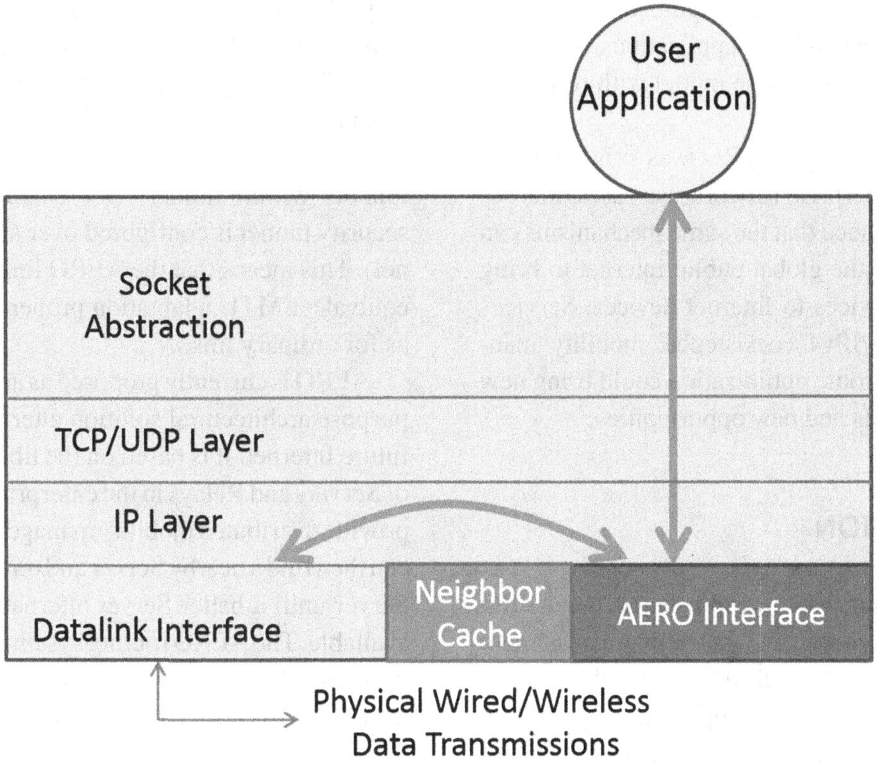

AERO has been extensively studied as an enterprise network-interior routing and addressing system. Mobility management and route optimization have therefore mainly considered the case of mobile devices roaming only within the enterprise network domain or via a VPN link to the enterprise across the public Internet. However, the same mechanisms employed for this "intra-network" route optimization and mobility management can also be applied when the source and destination nodes are associated with different home networks. In that case, mobility and route optimization signaling would be coordinated in an Internet-wide fashion very similar to the MIPv6 return routability procedure.

PMIPv6 provides a service where network access routers coordinate the movements of unmodified mobile nodes that do not participate in any specialized mobility signaling protocols. Future investigations will study the application of AERO in a similar scenario in which Clients become fixed infrastructure elements to be used in a similar fashion as for PMIPv6 access routers.

AERO provides a natural virtual link model for separating control and data plane functions. For example, when a Client associates with a Server, the Server can use an out-of-band signaling protocol to populate forwarding information for the Client in a companion Forwarding Agent. When the Client subsequently sends packets via the Server, the Server can return an RA message that directs the Client to send future packets via the Forwarding Agent. Future studies will focus on whether this control/data plane separation can improve performance.

Although the basic AERO model envisions the AERO link as spanning the entire enterprise network, it is also quite possible to compartmentalize the enterprise into multiple AERO link domains. A sketch of what such compartmentalization for

NBMA enterprise network applications might look like is found in (Templin, 2013). Future research will investigate applications of a compartmentalized enterprise model with respect to the AERO service.

Finally, although AERO was originally designed for enterprise network use cases, there is growing evidence that the same mechanisms can be applied to the global public Internet to bring advanced services to Internet devices. Services such as IPv6/IPv4 coexistence, mobility management and route optimization could bring new service models and new opportunities.

CONCLUSION

In this chapter, we have presented the AERO routing, addressing and mobility management system. The system applies to traditional enterprise networks, but can also be applied in civil aviation air traffic control networks, airline fleet management networks, disaster relief and humanitarian aid networks, operator networks and many others. AERO is designed to operate over diverse data link types including Ethernet, WLAN, cellular wireless, satellite communications, etc. By incorporating mobile VPN services, AERO also allows mobile nodes to switch between Internet-based and on-campus access links.

AERO Clients may be any kind of mobile device, including laptop computers, cell phones, tablets, airplanes, vehicles, etc. Both mobile hosts and mobile routers are supported; therefore, mobile devices can connect arbitrarily complex EUNs with large numbers of associated networked devices. AERO is based on DHCPv6 PD and IPv6 ND messaging, but supports operation of both IPv4 and IPv6 based Clients. This provides a useful solution for enterprise network administrators that need to support either one or both IP protocol versions independently.

AERO is based on encapsulation of an inner IP packet within an outer IP header. Encapsulation has the well-known issue that a reduction in the path MTU is made visible to end systems. Fortunately, AERO includes mechanisms for MTU adaptation even in the presence of nested tunnels within tunnels (for example, when a security tunnel is configured over an AERO tunnel). This means that the AERO link will display equivalent MTU adaptation properties the same as for ordinary links.

AERO is currently proposed as an IETF multipurpose architectural solution alternative for the future Internet. It is based on the liberal insertion of Servers and Relays in the enterprise network to provide distributed mobility management. Clients can then find a nearby Server and remain with that Server until a better Server alternative becomes available. The AERO routing system can also support considerable deployments of Clients within the enterprise, e.g., 10^6 Clients or more. Limiting factors include the number of Servers and Relays deployed as well as BGP routing table sizes.

AERO provides many benefits in addition to maintaining a TIA that remains stable across mobility events. In particular, AERO can coordinate mobile VPNs, accommodate tunnels over multiple underlying interfaces, support traffic engineering, provide nested mobile networks within networks, and many others. Many of these features become even more important in "non-traditional" enterprise networks such as air traffic management networks, emergency response and disaster relief networks, vehicular networks and many others.

AERO is easily implemented on Client, Server and Relay devices. Using common public domain application software packages, the AERO functions can often be implemented without changing the operating system kernel.

Finally, AERO is intended as an open standard for vendors to use in developing products for their customers. Publication in the IETF will provide a path to ensure vendor product interoperability. As more use cases for AERO are discovered, it is expected that products targeted for specific deployment environments will also support AERO. The desired end-state is a distributed mobility management service for enterprise networks of all shapes and sizes to support a new Internetworking paradigm.

REFERENCES

Carpenter, B. & Jung, C. (1999). Transmission of IPv6 over IPv4 Domains without Explicit Tunnels, *Internet Engineering Task Force (IETF) RFC 2529.*

Chown, T. (2006). Use of VLANs for IPv4-IPv6 Coexistence in Enterprise Networks, *Internet Engineering Task Force (IETF) RFC 4554.*

Clark, D., Sollins, K., Wroclawski, J., & Braden, R. (2005). Tussle in Cyberspace: Defining Tomorrow's Internet [TON]. *IEEE/ACM Transactions on Networking*, *13*(3), 462–475. doi:10.1109/TNET.2005.850224

Deering, S. & Hinden, R. (1998). Internet Protocol, Version 6 (IPv6) Specification, *Internet Engineering Task Force (IETF) RFC 2460.*

Devaraplli, V., Wakikawa, R., Petrescu, A., & Thubert, P. (2005). Network Mobility (NEMO) Basic Support Protocol, *Internet Engineering Task Force (IETF) RFC 3963.*

Droms, R., Bound, J., Volz, B., Lemon, T., Perkins, C. & Carney, M. (2003). Dynamic Host Configuration Protocol for IPv6 (DHCPv6), *Internet Engineering Task Force (IETF) RFC 3315.*

Gundavelli, S., Devarapalli, V., Chowdhury, K., & Patil,B. (2008). Proxy Mobile IPv6, *Internet Engineering Task Force (IETF) RFC 5213.*

Huston, G., Lord, A., & Smith, P. (2004). IPv6 Address Prefix Reserved for Documentation, *Internet Engineering Task Force (IETF) RFC 3849.*

Kawamura, S., & Kawashima, M. (2010). A Recommendation for IPv6 Address Text Representation, *Internet Engineering Task Force (IETF) RFC 5952.*

Mathis, M. & Heffner, J. (2007). Packetization Layer Path MTU Discovery, *Internet Engineering Task Force (IETF) RFC 4821.*

McCann, J., Deering, S., & Mogul, J. (1996). Path MTU Discovery for IP version 6, *Internet Engineering Task Force (IETF) RFC 1981.*

Mockapetris, P. (1987). Domain names - Implementation and specification, *Internet Engineering Task Force (IETF) RFC 1035.*

Mogul, J., & Deering, S. (1990). Path MTU Discovery, *Internet Engineering Task Force (IETF) RFC 1191.*

Narten, T., Nordmark, E., Simpson, W. & Soliman, H. (2007). Neighbor Discovery for IP version 6 (IPv6), *Internet Engineering Task Force (IETF) RFC 4861.*

Perkins, C., Johnson, D., & Arkko, J. (2013). Mobility Support in IPv6, *Internet Engineering Task Force (IETF) RFC 6275.*

Postel, J. (1980). User Datagram Protocol, *Internet Engineering Task Force (IETF) RFC 768.*

Postel, J. (Ed.). (1981). Internet Protocol, Internet Engineering Task Force (IETF) RFC 791.

Rekhter, Y., Li, T., & Hares, S. (2006). A Border Gateway Protocol 4 (BGP-4), *Internet Engineering Task Force (IETF) RFC 4271.*

Templin, F. (2011). The Internet Routing Overlay Network (IRON), *Internet Engineering Task Force (IETF) RFC 6179.*

Templin, F. (2012). Asymmetric Extended Route Optimization (AERO), *Internet Engineering Task Force (IETF) RFC 6706.*

Templin, F. (2013). Operational Guidance for IPv6 Deployment in IPv4 Sites Using the Intra-Site Automatic Tunnel Addressing Protocol (ISATAP), *Internet Engineering Task Force (IETF) RFC 6964.*

Templin, F. (2014). Asymmetric Extended Route Optimization (AERO) (Second Edition), Internet Engineering Task Force (IETF) work-in-progress (draft-templin-aerolink).

Templin, F., Gleeson, T., & Thaler, D. (2005). Intra-Site Automatic Tunnel Addressing Protocol (ISATAP), *Internet Engineering Task Force (IETF) RFC 5214.*

Troan, O. & Droms, R.. (2003). IPv6 Prefix Options for Dynamic Host Configuration Protocol (DHCP) version 6, *Internet Engineering Task Force (IETF) RFC 3633.*

KEY TERMS AND DEFINITIONS

AERO Address: an IPv6 link-local address with an embedded IP prefix and assigned to a Client's AERO interface.

AERO Client Prefix (ACP): an IP prefix taken from an ASP and delegated to a Client.

AERO Client: a node that assigns AERO addresses to an AERO interface and receives IP prefixes via a DHCPv6 Prefix Delegation (PD) exchanges with one or more AERO Servers.

AERO Interface: a node's attachment to an AERO link.

AERO Link: a Non-Broadcast, Multiple Access (NBMA) tunnel virtual overlay configured over an enterprise network.

AERO Node: a node that configures an AERO interface on an AERO link.

AERO Relay: a node that configures an AERO interface to relay IP packets between nodes on the same AERO link and/or forward IP packets to correspondents on other networks.

AERO Server: a node that configures an AERO interface to provide default forwarding and DHCPv6 services for AERO Clients.

AERO Service Prefix (ASP): an IP prefix associated with the AERO link and from which AERO Client Prefixes (ACPs) are derived (for example, the IPv6 ACP 2001:db8:1:2::/64 is derived from the IPv6 ASP 2001:db8::/32).

End User Network (EUN): an internal virtual or external edge IP network that an AERO Client connects to the rest of the network via the AERO interface. More specifically, the Client acts as a mobile router on behalf of its (downstream-attached) EUNs.

Link-Layer Address: a TFA address along with the UDP port number used for encapsulation. Link-layer addresses are used as the encapsulation header source and destination addresses.

Network Layer Address: the source or destination address of the encapsulated IP packet.

Topologically-Fixed Address (TFA): an IP address assigned to an AERO node's access network connection to the enterprise network.

Topology-Independent Address (TIA): an address provided to an AERO Client by the AERO service and that can be used from any enterprise network point of attachment.

Section 4

New Approaches to (Automated) Network Services Design, Delivery and Operation

Chapter 15
Abstraction and Control of Transport Networks

Young Lee
Huawei Technologies, USA

Daniele Ceccarelli
Ericsson, Italy

ABSTRACT

Virtual network operation refers to the creation of a virtualized environment allowing operators to view the abstraction of the underlying multi-admin, multi-vendor, multi-technology networks and to operate, control and manage these multiple networks as a single virtualized network. Another dimension of virtual network operation is associated with the use of the common core transport network resources by multi-tenant service networks as a way of providing a virtualized infrastructure to flexibly offer new services and applications. The work effort investigating this problem space is known as Abstraction and Control of Transport Networks (ACTN). This chapter provides an ACTN problem description, identifies the scope of this effort, and outlines the core requirements to facilitate virtual network operation.

1. INTRODUCTION

Transport networks have a variety of mechanisms to facilitate separation of the data plane from the control plane including distributed signaling for path setup and protection, centralized path computation for planning and Traffic Engineering (TE), and a range of management and provisioning protocols to interact with network resources. These mechanisms represent key technologies for enabling flexible and dynamic networking. Dynamic networking refers to network capability that allows on-line path computation, dynamic discovery of real-time resource information and provisioning based on real-time network resource information.

Transport networks in this chapter refer to a set of different type of connection-oriented networks, primarily Connection-Oriented Circuit Switched (CO-CS) networks and Connection-Oriented Packet Switched (CO-PS) networks. This implies that at least the following transport networks are in scope of the discussion of this chapter: Layer 1 optical networks (e.g., Optical Transport Network (OTN) and Wavelength Division Multiplexing (WDM)), Multi-Protocol Label Switching – Trans-

DOI: 10.4018/978-1-4666-8371-6.ch015

port Profile (MPLS-TP), Multi-Protocol Label Switching – Traffic Engineering (MPLS-TE), as well as other emerging connection-oriented networks. One of the characteristics of these network types is the ability of dynamic provisioning and traffic engineering such that service guarantees can be fulfilled.

One of the main drivers for Software Defined Networking (SDN) is a physical separation of the network control plane from the data plane. This separation of the control plane from the data plane has been already achieved with the development of MPLS/Generalized Multi-Protocol Label Switching (GMPLS) [GMPLS] and Path Computation Element (PCE) [PCE] for TE-based transport networks. In fact, in transport networks, such separation of data and control plane was dictated at the onset due to the very different natures of the data plane (circuit switched TDM or WDM) and a packet switched control plane. The physical separation of the control plane from the data plane is a major step towards allowing operators to gain the full control for optimized network design and operation. Moreover, another advantage of SDN is its logically centralized control regime that allows a global view of the underlying network under its control. Centralized control in SDN helps improve network resource utilization with distributed network control plane capabilities. For TE-based transport network control, PCE can be deployed for centralized control for path computation purposes.

As transport networks evolve, the need to provide network abstraction has emerged as a key requirement for operators; this implies in effect the virtualization of network resources so that the network is "sliced" for different uses, applications, services, and customers each being given a different partial view of the physical underlying network and each considering that it is operating with or on a single, stand-alone and consistent network. Moreover, particular attention needs to be paid to the multi-domain case. The work effort investigating this problem space is known as Abstraction and Control of Transport Networks (ACTN). ACTN can facilitate virtual network operation via the creation of a single virtualized network. This supports operators in viewing and controlling different domains (at any dimension: applied technology, administrative zones, or vendor-specific technology islands) as if they would deal with a single virtual network.

Network virtualization, in general, refers to allowing the customers (and services/applications) to utilize a certain amount of network resources as if they own them and thus control their allocated resources in a way most optimal with higher layer or application processes. This empowerment of customer control facilitates introduction of new services and applications as the customers are permitted to create, modify, and delete their virtual network services. Customers are not necessarily limited to external entities with respect to the network providers. Customers can be an internal entity that may coordinate different domains (at any dimension: applied technologies, administrative zones, or vendor-specific technology islands). A virtual network control coordinator is a form of customer with respect to physical networks and their domain controllers. A virtual network control coordinator is a customer of domain networks in multi-domain scenarios such that the generated network abstraction is received by each domain's physical network controller.

This virtual network control coordinator can be an internal entity with respect to the operator's control domain as it facilitates virtual network operation. On the other hand, this virtual network control coordinator can be a third party entity such as bandwidth brokers that coordinate bandwidth services between networks and customers.

The granularity level of virtual control given to the customers can vary from a tunnel connecting two end-points to virtual network elements that consist of a set of virtual nodes and virtual links in a mesh network topology. More flexible, dynamic customer control capabilities are added to the traditional VPN along with a customer specific virtual network view. Customers control a view of virtual network resources, specifically allocated to each one of them. This view is called an abstracted network topology. Such view may be specific to the set of consumed services as well as to a particular customer.

As the customer controller is envisioned to support a plethora of distinct applications, there would be another level of abstraction from the customer to individual applications.

The virtualization framework described in this chapter is named Abstraction and Control of Transport Network (ACTN). This framework aims to facilitate the following:

- Abstraction of the underlying network resources to higher-layer applications, services and users (customers);
- Slicing infrastructure to meet specific application and users requirements;
- Creation a virtualized environment allowing operators to view and control multi-domain (i.e., multi-subnet, multi-technology, multi-vendor islands, etc.) networks into a single virtualized network;
- A computation scheme, via data models, to serve various customers that request network connectivity and properties associated with it;
- A virtual network controller that maps customer requests to the virtual resources (allocated to them) to the supporting physical network control and performs the necessary mapping, translation, isolation and security/policy enforcement, etc.;
- The coordination of the underlying transport topology, exposing it as an abstracted topology to the customers via open and programmable interfaces.

The organization of this chapter is as follows. Section 2 provides a discussion for business actors, Section 3 a Computation Model, Section 4 a Control and Interface model and Section 5 Design Principles.

2. BUSINESS ACTORS IN ACTN

The traditional Virtual Private Network (VPN) (Callon & Suzuki, 2005; Andersson, & Rosen, 2006) and Overlay Network (ON) (Templin, 2011) models are built on the premise that one single network provider provides all virtual private or overlay networks to its customers. This model is simple to operate but has some disadvantages in accommodating the increasing need for flexible and dynamic network virtualization capabilities. Inter-domain VPN service would presumably suggest coordination between virtual controllers but with limited network virtualization capabilities.

The ACTN model is built upon business roles that reflect the current landscape of network virtualization environments. There are three key business roles in the ACTN model.

- Customers
- Service Providers
- Network Providers

2.1. Customers

Within the ACTN framework, different types of customers may be involved, depending on the type of their resource needs, on their number and type of access. As an example, it is possible to group them into two main categories:

- "Basic" Customers: include fixed residential subscribers, mobile subscribers and small enterprises. This is traditionally called "Mass-market." Usually the number of basic customers is high; they require small amounts of resources and are characterized by steady requests (relatively time invariant). A typical request for a basic customer is for a bundle of voice service and internet access. Connectivity guarantees requested by this category is "loose" (Howarth, et al, 2006).

- Advanced Customers: typically include enterprises, governments and utilities. Such customers can request for both point-to-point and multipoint connectivity with high resource demand significantly varying in time and from one customer to another. This is one of the reasons why a bundled service offer is not enough but it is desirable to provide each of them with customized virtual network services. Unlike the previous category, connectivity guarantees for this type are "hard" ones.

As customers are geographically spread over multiple network provider domains, the necessary control and data interfaces to support such customer needs is no longer a single interface between the customer and one single network provider. With this premise, customers have to interface multiple providers to get their end-to-end network connectivity service and the associated topology information. Customers may have to request multiple virtual network services with differing service objectives and QoS requirements. For flexible and dynamic applications, customers may want to control their allocated virtual network resources in a dynamic fashion. To allow that, customers should be given an abstracted view of the network topology on which they can perform their own control decisions and take the corresponding actions. Customers of a given service provider can in turn offer a service to other customers in a recursive way. An example of recursiveness with two service providers is shown in Figure 1 below.

- Customer (of service B)
- Customer (of service A) & Service Provider (of service B)
- Service Provider (of service A)
- Network Provider

2.2. Service Providers

Service providers are the providers of virtual network services to Customers. Service providers may or may not own physical network resources. When a service provider is the same as the network provider, this is similar to traditional VPN models. This model works well when the customer maintains a single interface with a single provider. When customer location spans across multiple independent network provider domains, then it becomes challenging to facilitate the creation of end-to-end virtual network services with this model.

A more interesting case arises when network providers only provide infrastructure while service providers directly interface their customers. In this case, service providers themselves are customers of the network infrastructure providers. One service provider may need to keep multiple independent network providers as its end-users span geographically across multiple network provider domains. Any service disruption needs to be escalated to service provider as network providers are invisible to the customers. It is service provider's responsibility to mitigate connectivity issues directly with network providers.

The ACTN network model is predicated upon this three tier model and is summarized in Figure 2.

There can be multiple types of service providers:

- Data Center providers: can be viewed as a service provider type as they own and operate data center resources to various WAN clients that need Data Center Interconnect (DCI) WAN links, they can lease physical network resources from network providers.
- Internet Service Providers (ISP): can be a service provider of internet services to their customers while leasing physical network resources from network providers.
- Mobile Virtual Network Operators (MVNO): provide mobile services to their

Figure 1. Recursiveness

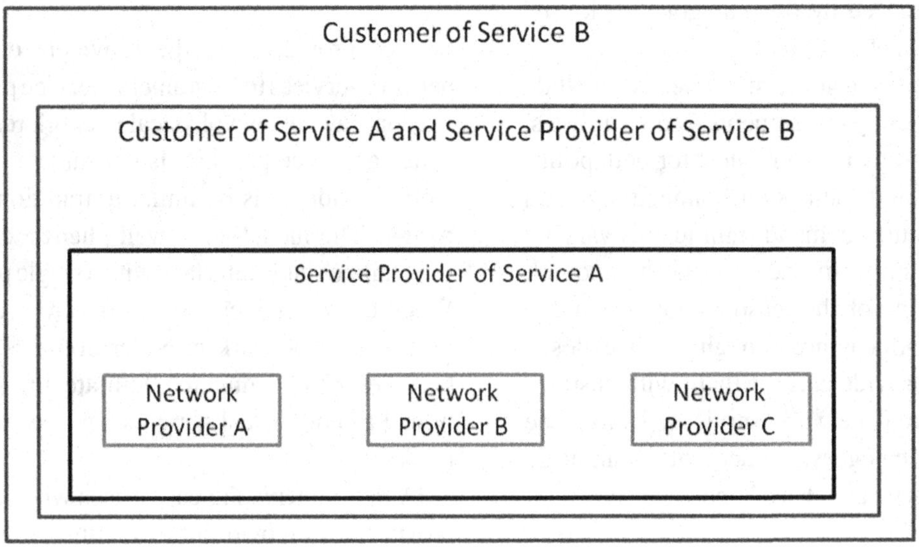

Figure 2. Three tier model

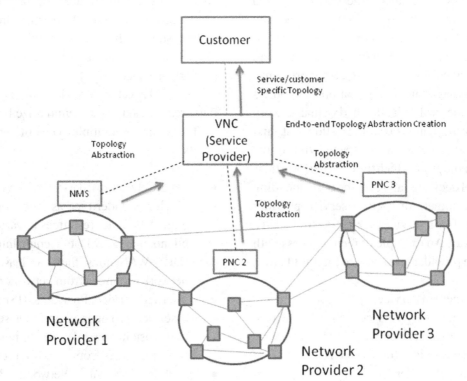

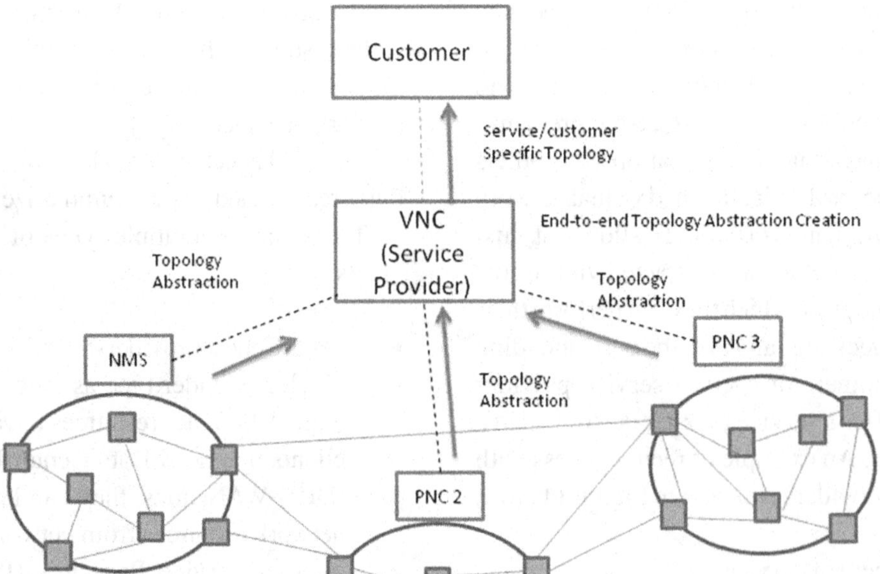

end-users without owning the physical network infrastructure.

2.3. Network Providers

Network Providers are the infrastructure providers that own the physical network resources and provide network resources to their customers. The layered model proposed by this chapter separates the concerns of network providers and customers, with service providers acting as aggregators of customer requests.

3. MULTI-DOMAIN MANAGEMENT

Network operators build and operate multi-domain networks that may be multi-technology, administrative or vendor-specific (vendor islands). Interoperability for dealing with different domains is a perpetual problem for operators. Due to these multi-domain issues, the introduction of new service offerings, often requiring connections that traverse multiple domains, need significant planning, and several manual operations to interface different vendor equipment and technology.

The creation of a virtualized environment allowing operators to view and control multi-subnet, multi-technology networks into a single virtualized network highly facilitates network operators and will accelerate service deployment, including more dynamic and elastic services, and improve overall network operations and scaling for existing services.

Figure 3 depicts a common scenario in which two different domains can be managed by a single Virtual Network Controller (VNC), which is in charge of acting as an orchestrator between them and presenting them as a single entity to its clients.

In this figure, the case of packet and optical domains controlled by different Physical Network Controllers (PNCs) is shown but any combination can be considered, like e.g., a single PNC controlling the packet domain 1 and another PNC controlling the optical domain 2, etc.

4. COMPUTATION MODEL OF ACTN

This section discusses ACTN framework from a computational point of view. As multiple customers run their virtualized network over a shared infrastructure, making efficient use of the underlying resources requires effective computational models and algorithms. This general problem space is known as Virtual Network Mapping or Embedding (VNM or VNE). Refer to (Boucadair & Jacquenet, 2014) for further discussion on this topic.

As VNM/VNE issues impose some additional compute models and algorithms for virtual network path computations, this section discusses key issues and constraints for ACTN context.

4.1. Request Processing

This is concerned about whether a set of customer requests for Virtual Network (VN) creation can be dealt with in real-time or off-line, and in the latter case, simultaneously or not. This depends on the nature of applications the customer supports. There are applications and use cases, like e.g., management of catastrophic events or real time Service Level Agreement (SLA) negotiation that requires a real-time VN creation. If the customer does not require real-time instantiation of VN creation, the computation engine can process a set of VN creation requests simultaneously to improve network efficiency.

4.2. Types of Network Resources

When a customer makes a VN creation request to the substrate network, what kind of network resources is consumed is of concern of both the customer and service/network providers. The customer needs to put constraints (e.g., TE param-

Figure 3. Multi domain management

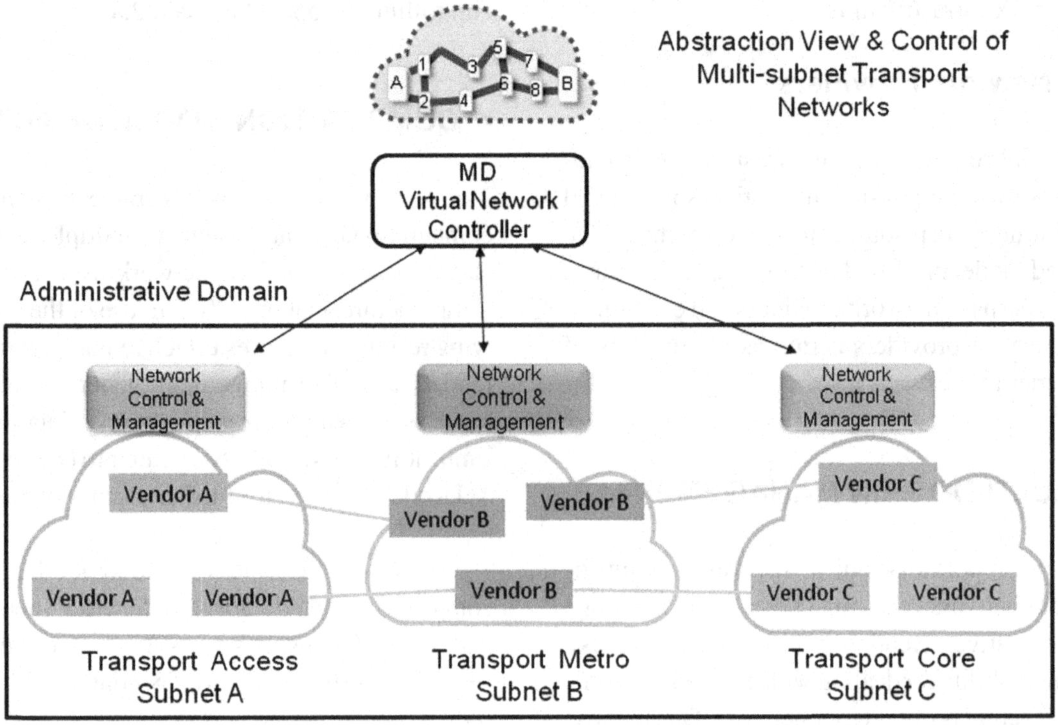

eters, resiliency) for the provisioning of the VN, while the service and network providers need to choose which resources meet such constraints and possibly have minimal impact on the capability of serving other customers. This negotiation between the customer and the provider may necessitate an interface between them to communicate the terms of the negotiation. This interface can be either a static interface which is a part of SLA negotiation or a dynamic interface with communication protocols that automate the negotiation process. For transport network virtualization, the network resource consumed is primarily network bandwidth that the required paths would occupy on the physical link(s). However, there may be other resource types such as CPU and memory that need to be considered for certain applications. These resource types shall be part of the VN request made by the customer. Refer to (Boucadair, Jacquenet, & Wang, 2014) for detailed discussions on the resource types.

4.3. Accuracy of Network Resource Representation

As the underlying transport network may consist of a layered structure, how to represent these underlying physical network resources and topology into a form that can be reliably used by the computation engine that assigns customer requests into the physical network resource and topology, is challenging.

4.4. Resource Sharing and Efficiency

Related to the accuracy of network resource representation is resource efficiency. As a set of independent customer VNs is created and mapped onto physical network resources, the overall network resource utilization is the primary concern of the network provider.

In order to provide an efficient utilization of the resources of the provider network, it should be possible to share given physical resources among a number of different VNs. Whether a virtual resource is sharable among a set of VNs (and hence of customers) is something the service provider needs to agree with each customer. Preemption and priority management are tools that could help provide an efficient sharing of physical resources among different VNs.

4.5. Guarantee of Client Isolation

While network resource sharing across a set of customers for efficient utilization is an important aspect of network virtualization, customer (and traffic) isolation has to be guaranteed. Admission of new customer requests or any changes of other existing customer VNs must not affect any particular customer in terms of resource guarantee, security constraints, and other performance constraints.

4.6. Computing Time

Depending on the nature of applications, how quickly a VN is instantiated from the time of request is an important factor. For dynamic applications that require instantaneous VN creation or VN changes from the existing one, the computation model/algorithm should support this constraint.

4.7. Admission Control

To coordinate the request process of multiple customers, an admission control will help maximize the overall ACTN efficiency.

4.8. Path Constraints

There may be some factors of path constraints that can affect the overall efficiency. Path Split can lower VN request blocking if the underlying network can support such capability. Path Split refers to the creation of several paths to accommodate the traffic demand that cannot be provided with a single path. A packet-based TE network can support path split while circuit-based transport may have limitations.

Path migration is a technique that allows changes of nodes or link assignments of the established paths in an effort to accommodate new requests that would not be accepted without such path migration(s). This can improve overall efficiency, yet additional care needs to be applied to avoid any adverse impacts associated with changing the existing paths.

Re-optimization is a global process to reshuffle all existing path assignments to minimize network resource fragmentation. Again, an extra care needs to be applied for re-optimization.

5. CONTROL AND INTERFACE MODEL FOR ACTN

This section provides a high-level control and interface model of ACTN.

5.1. A High-level ACTN Control Architecture

To allow virtualization, the network has to provide open, programmable interfaces, in which customer applications can create, replace and modify virtual network resources in an interactive, flexible and dynamic fashion while having no impact on other customers. Direct customer control of transport network elements over existing interfaces (control or management plane) is not perceived as a viable proposition for transport network providers due to security and policy concerns among other reasons. In addition, as discussed in the previous section, the network control plane for transport networks has been separated from the data plane and, as such, it is not viable for the customer to directly interface with transport network elements.

While the current network control plane is well suited for control of physical network resources via dynamic provisioning, path computation, etc., a virtual network controller needs to be built on top of physical network controllers to support network virtualization. On a high-level, virtual network control refers to a mediation layer that performs several functions:

- Computation of customer resource requests into virtual network paths based on the global network-wide abstracted topology;
- Mapping and translation of customer virtual network slices into physical network resources. This is the results of the negotiation specifics given the resource availability represented by the global network-wide abstract topology. ;
- Creation of an abstracted view of network slices allocated to each customer, according to customer-specific objective functions, and to the customer traffic profile.

In order to facilitate the above-mentioned virtual control functions, the virtual network controller (a.k.a., "virtualizer") needs to maintain two interfaces:

- One interface with the physical network controller functions which is termed as the VNC-PNC Interface (VPI).
- Another interface with the customer controller for the virtual network, which is termed as Client-VNC Interface (CVI).

Figure 4 depicts a high-level control and interface architecture for ACTN.

Figure 4 shows that there are multiple customer controllers, which are independent to one another, and that each customer supports various business applications over its Northbound Interface NBI. This NBI is with respect to the customer controller. Any customer interfaces situating above the controller are referred to as NBI and these interfaces support specific applications of the customers. There are layered client-server relationships in this architecture. As various applications are clients to the customer controller, it also becomes itself a client to the virtual network controller. Likewise, the virtual network controller is also a client to the physical network controller. This layered relationship is important in the protocol definition work on the NB API, the CVI and VPI interfaces as this allows third-party software developers to program client controllers and virtual network controllers independently.

There are several ways in which the Physical Network Controller manages the network elements, e.g., via management protocols such as SNMP (Presuhn, 2002), PCEP (Vasseur & Le Roux, 2009; Farrel, Vasseur, & Ash, 2006) and GMPLS (Manning, 2004), or any other type of protocol. In other words, the ACTN architecture both applies to physical networks controlled by control plane protocols (e.g., PCEP and GMPLS) or management plane protocols.

5.2. Customer's Controller

A Virtual Network Service is instantiated by the customer controller via the CVI. As the customer controller directly interfaces the application stratum, it understands multiple application requirements and their service needs. It is assumed that the customer controller and the VNC have a common knowledge of the end-point interfaces based on their business negotiation prior to service instantiation. End-point interfaces refer to customer-network physical interfaces that connect customer premise equipment to network provider equipment.

Figure 5 shows an example physical network topology that supports multiple customers.

In this example, customer A has three end-points A.1, A.2 and A.3. The interfaces between customers and transport networks are assumed to be 40G OTU links. For simplicity's sake, all network interfaces are assumed to be 40G OTU links and all network ports support ODU switching and grooming on the level of ODU1 and ODU2. Customer controller for A provides its

Figure 4. Control and interface architecture for ACTN.

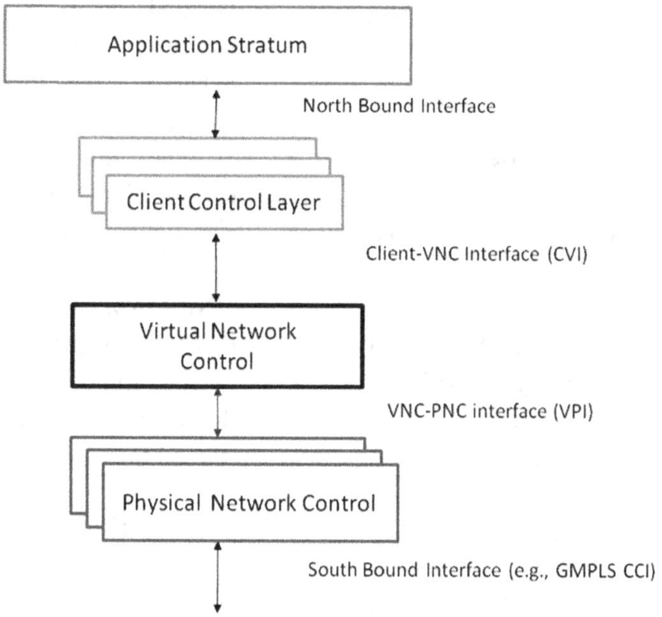

Figure 5. Multi-tenant ACTN architecture example

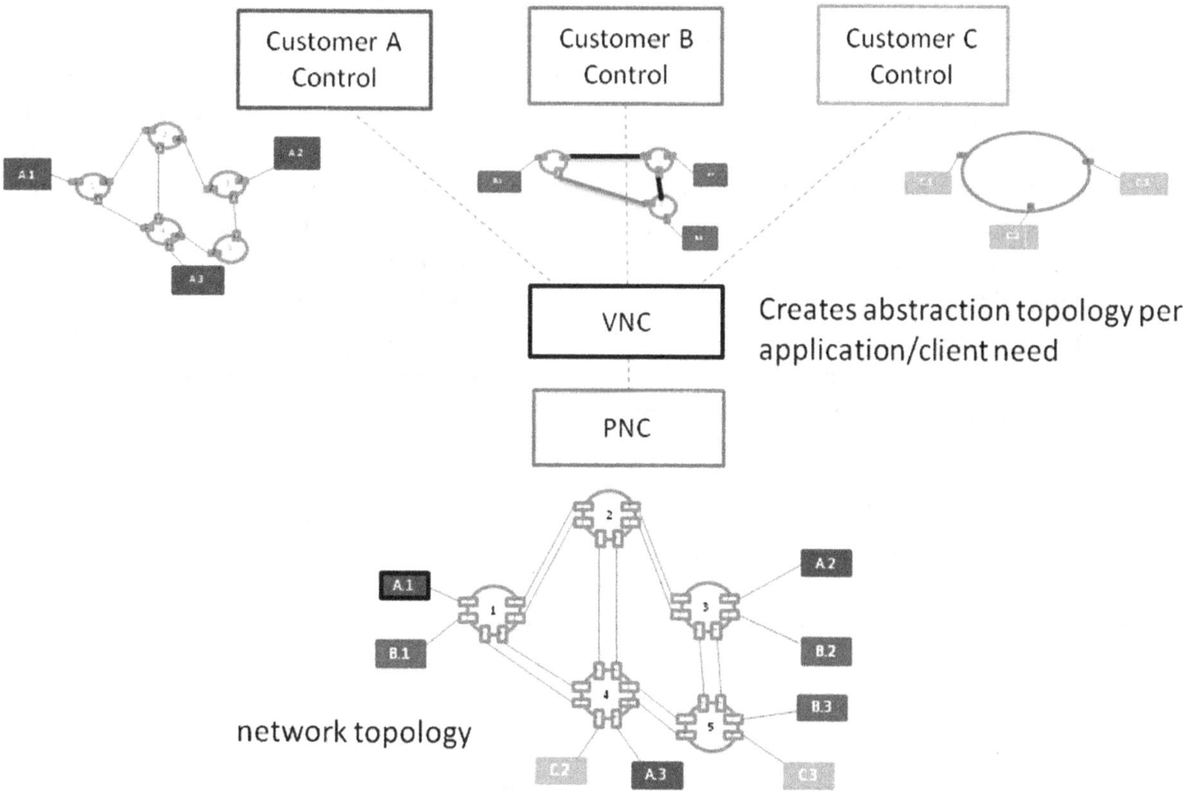

traffic demand matrix that describes bandwidth requirements and other optional QoS parameters (e.g., latency, diversity requirement, etc.) for each pair of end-point connections.

5.3. Virtual Network Controller

The virtual network controller sits between the consumer controller (the one issuing connectivity requests) and the physical network controller (the one managing the resources). The Virtual Network controller can be collocated with the physical network controller, especially in those cases where the service provider and the network provider are the same entity.

The virtual network controller is composed by the following functional components in Figure 6:

- VNS proxy: is the functional module in charge of performing policy management and AAA (Authentication, authorization, and accounting) functions. It is the one that receives VN instantiation and resource allocation requests from the Customer controllers.
- Abstract Topology DataBase: This is the database where the abstract topology, generated by the VNC or received from the PNC, is stored. A different VN instance is kept for every different customer.
- Resource Manager: The resource manager is in charge of receiving VNS instantiation requests from the customer controller and, as a consequence, triggering a concurrent path computation request to the PCE in the PNC based on the traffic matrix. The Resource manager is also in charge of generating the abstract topology for the customer.
- vConnection Agent: This module is in charge of mapping VN setup commands into network provisioning requests to the PNC.
- VNC OAM handler: The VNC OAM handler is the module that is in charge of understanding how the network is operating, detecting faults and reacting to problems related to the abstract topology.

5.4. Physical Network Controller

The physical network controller is the one in charge of configuring the network elements, monitoring the physical topology of the network and passing it, either raw or abstracted, to the VNC.

It is composed by the following functional components in Figure 7:

- VNC proxy: The VNC proxy is the functional module in charge of performing policy management and AAA (Authentication, authorization, and accounting) functions on requests coming from the VNC.
- PCE: This is the stateful PCE performing the path computation over the physical topology and that provides the vConnection agent with the network topology.

Figure 6. Virtual network controller components

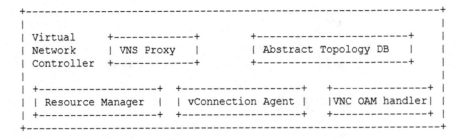

```
+----------------------------------------------------------------+
|                                                                |
| Virtual      +-------------+      +------------------------+   |
| Network      | VNS Proxy   |      | Abstract Topology DB   |   |
| Controller   +-------------+      +------------------------+   |
|                                                                |
| +-------------------+ +-------------------+ +---------------+  |
| | Resource Manager  | | vConnection Agent | |VNC OAM handler|  |
| +-------------------+ +-------------------+ +---------------+  |
+----------------------------------------------------------------+
```

Figure 7. Physical network controller components

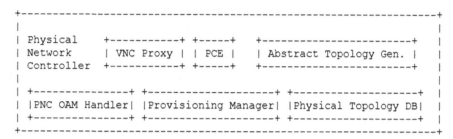

```
+--------------------------------------------------------------+
|                                                              |
| Physical     +-----------+ +-----+  +------------------------+ |
| Network      | VNC Proxy | | PCE |  | Abstract Topology Gen. | |
| Controller   +-----------+ +-----+  +------------------------+ |
|                                                              |
| +---------------+ +--------------------+ +--------------------+ |
| |PNC OAM Handler| |Provisioning Manager| |Physical Topology DB| |
| +---------------+ +--------------------+ +--------------------+ |
+--------------------------------------------------------------+
```

- Abstract topology generator: the network topology can be passed to the VNC as raw or abstract. In case the topology is passed as abstract topology, this module is in charge of generating it from the physical topology DB. The module is optional.
- ONC OAM handler: it verifies that connections exist, implements monitoring functions to see if failures occur. It is the proxy to an OSS/NMS system but does not duplicate any of OSS/NMS functionalities.
- Physical topology database: The physical topology database is mainly composed by two databases: the Traffic Engineering Database (TED) and the LSP Database (LSP-DB).
- Provisioning manager: The Provisioning Manager is responsible for making or channeling requests for the establishment of LSPs. This may be instructions to the control plane running in the networks, or may involve the programming of individual network devices. In the latter case, the Provisioning Manager may act as an OpenFlow Controller (Hood, 2014).

5.5. Abstracted Topology

There are two levels of abstracted topology that need to be maintained and supported for ACTN. Customer-specific Abstracted Topology refers to the abstracted view of network resources allocated (shared or dedicated) to the customer. The granularity of this abstraction varies depending on the nature of customer applications.

Figure 5 illustrates how three independent customers A, B and C provide their respective traffic demand matrix to the VNC. The physical network topology shown in Figure 5 is the provider's network topology generated by the PNC topology creation engine such as the link state database (LSDB) and Traffic Engineering DB (TEDB) based on control plane discovery functions. This topology is internal to PNC and not available to customers. What is available to them is an abstracted network topology (a virtual network topology) based on the negotiated level of abstraction. This is a part of VNS instantiation between a client control and VNC.

Figures 8-10 depict illustrative examples of different levels of topology abstractions that can be provided by the VNC topology abstraction engine based on the physical topology database maintained by the PNC. The level of topology abstraction is expressed in terms of the number of virtual network elements (VNEs) and virtual links (VLs). For example, the abstracted topology for customer "A" shows there are 5 VNEs and 15 VLs. This is by far the most detailed topology abstraction with a minimal link hiding compared to other abstracted topologies.

As different customers have different control/application needs, abstracted topologies for customers B and C, respectively show a much higher degree of abstraction. The level of abstraction is determined by the policy (e.g., the granularity level) placed for the customer and/or the path com-

Figure 8. Abstracted topology for customer A (5 VNEs and 15 VLs)

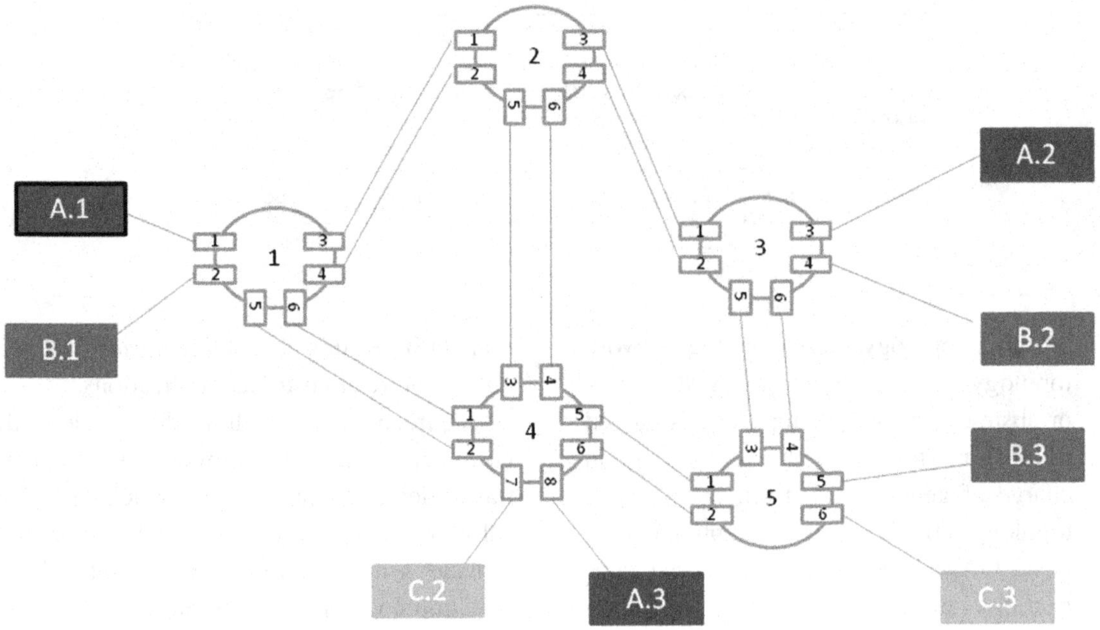

Figure 9. Abstracted topology for customer A (1 VNEs and 3 VLs)

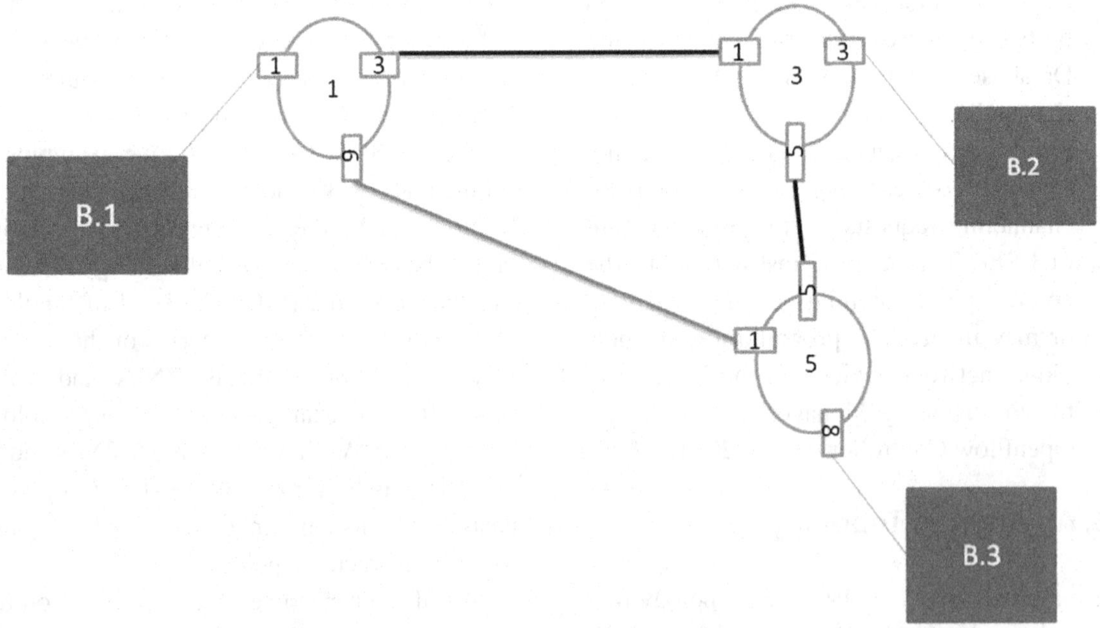

Figure 10. Abstracted topology for customer A (3 VNEs and 6 VLs)

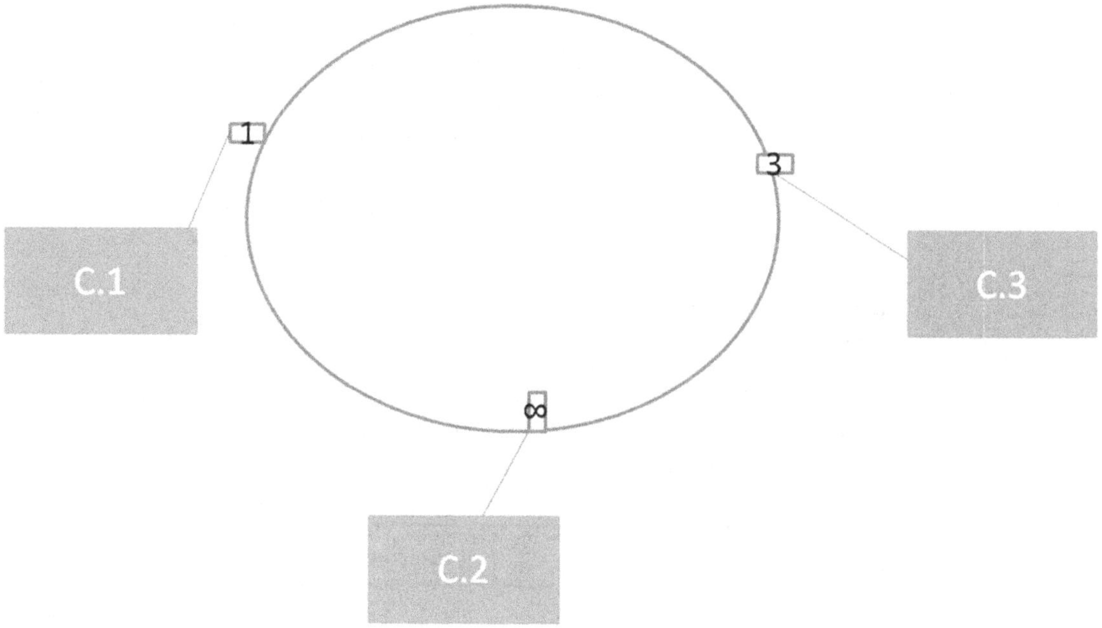

putation results by the PCE operated by the PNC. The more granular the abstraction topology is the more control is given to the customer controller. If the customer controller has applications that require more granular control of virtual network resources, then the abstracted topology shown for customer A may be the right abstraction level for such controller. For instance, if the customer is a third-party virtual service broker/provider, then it would desire much more sophisticated control of virtual network resources to support different application needs. On the other hand, if the customer were only to support simple tunnel services to its applications, then the abstracted topology shown for customer C (one VNE and three VLs) would suffice.

5.6. Workflows of ACTN Control Modules

Figure 11 shows workflows across the customer controller, VNC and PNC for the VNS instantiation, topology exchange, and VNS setup.

The customer controller "owns" a VNS and initiates it by providing the instantiation identifier with a traffic demand matrix that includes path selection constraints for that instance. This VNS instantiation request from the Customer Controller triggers a path computation request by the Resource Manager in the VNC after VNC's proxy's interlay of this request to the Resource Manager. PCA sends a concurrent path computation request that is converted according to the traffic demand matrix as part of the VNS instantiation request from the Customer Controller. Upon receipt of this path computation request, the PCE in the PNC block computes paths and updates network topology DB and informs the Resource Manager of the VNC of the paths and topology updates.

It is assumed that the PCE in PNC is a stateful PCE (Crabbe et al, 2014). PCA abstracts the physical network topology into an abstracted topology for the customer based on the agreed-upon granularity level. The abstracted topology is then passed to the VNS control of the Customer Controller. This controller computes and assigns

Figure 11. ACTN workflows

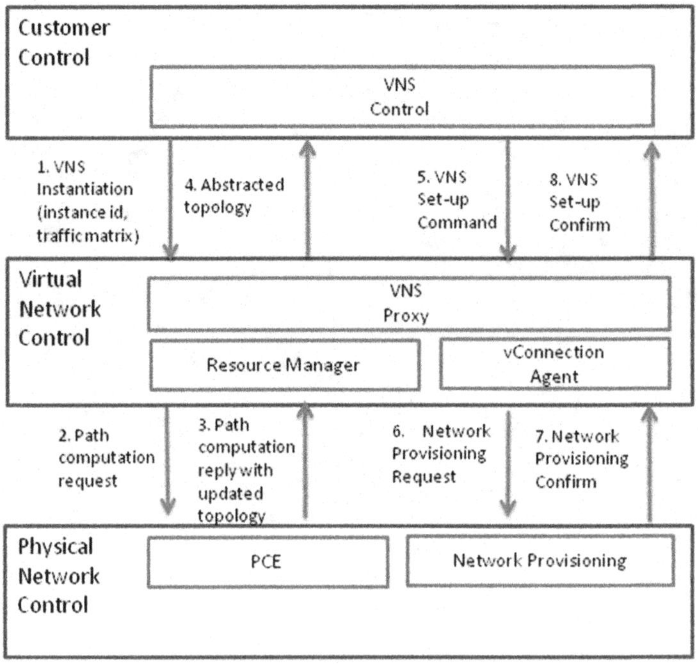

virtual network resources for its applications based on the abstracted topology and creates VNS setup command to the VNC. The VNC vConnection module turns this VN setup command into network provisioning requests over the network elements.

5.7. Programmability of the ACTN Interfaces

From Figure 11, we have identified several interfaces that are of interest of the ACTN model. More precisely, ACTN concerns the following interfaces:

- Customer-VNC Interface (CVI): an interface between a customer controller and a virtual network controller.
- VNC-PNC Interface (VPI): an interface between a virtual network controller and a physical network controller.

The NBI interfaces and direct control interfaces to NEs are outside of the scope of ACTN.

The CVI interface should allow programmability, first of all, to the customer so they can create, modify and delete virtual network service instances. This interface should also support open standard information and data models that can transport abstracted topology.

The VPI interface should allow programmability to service provider(s) (through VNCs) in such ways that control functions such as path computation, provisioning, and restoration can be facilitated. Seamless mapping and translation between physical resources and virtual resources should also be facilitated via this interface.

6. DESIGN FEATURES OF ACTN

6.1. Network Security

Network security concerns are always one of the primary principles of any network design. ACTN is no exception. Due to the nature of heterogeneous VNs that are to be created, maintained and deleted flexibly and dynamically and the anticipated interaction with physical network control components, secure programming models and interfaces have to be available beyond secured tunnels, encryption and other network security tools.

6.2. Privacy and Isolation

As physical network resources are shared with and controlled by multiple independent customers, isolation and privacy for each customer has to be guaranteed.

Policy should be applied per client.

6.3. Scalability

As multiple VNs need to be supported seamlessly, there are potentially several scaling issues associated with ACTN. The VN Controller system should be scalable in supporting multiple parallel computation requests from multiple customers. New VN request should not affect the control and maintenance of the existing VNs. Any VN request should also be satisfied within a time-bound of the customer application request. The invocation of VN resources allocated to customer/application

Interfaces should also be scalable as a large amount of data needs to be transported across customers to virtual network controllers and across virtual network controllers and physical network controllers.

There should also be a scalable means to identify flows belonging to a customer/service.

6.4. Manageability and Orchestration

As there are multiple entities participating in network virtualization, seamless manageability has to be provided across every layer of network virtualization. Orchestration is an important aspect of manageability as the ACTN design should allow orchestration capability.

ACTN orchestration should encompass network provider multi-domains, relationships between service provider(s) and network provider(s), and relationships between customers and service/network providers.

Ease of deploying end-to-end virtual network services across heterogeneous network environments is a challenge. Atomic network management capability and life cycle management of VNs should be supported to fulfill service assurance.

6.5. Programmability

As discussed earlier in Section 5.5, the ACTN interfaces should support open standard interfaces to allow flexible and dynamic service creation. At a minimum, the ACTN interfaces should support VN create/modify/delete/monitor functions. See also Section 5.7 for the discussion of programmable primitives.

6.6. Network Stability

As multiple VNs are envisioned to share the same physical network resources, combining many resources into one should not cause any network instability. Provider network oscillation can affect readily both on virtual networks and the end-users.

Part of network instability can be caused when virtual network mapping is done on an inaccurate or unreliable resource data. Database synchronization is one of the key issues that need to be ensured in an ACTN design.

FUTURE RESEARCH DIRECTIONS

One of the important on-going and future research areas is virtual network mapping. For ACTN to take on the real transport networks of the operators, the creation of abstracted topology that can be mapped into physical network resources with efficiency is of critical component. This is an algorithmic research that is predicated upon scalable resource abstraction of multi-layer networks.

CONCLUSION

In this chapter, the problem space called Abstraction and Control of Transport Network (ACTN) in which the creation of a virtualized environment would allow operators to manage their underlying multi-admin, multi-vendor, multi-technology networks as a single virtualized network. This would improve the network resource efficiency as well as new service introduction, especially the connectivity services traversing these multi-domain networks. In addition, the ATCN principles can also help operators create new applications and services allowing external multi-tenant customers to share their transport network resources.

REFERENCES

Andersson, L., & Rosen, E. (2006). Framework for Layer 2 Virtual Private Networks (L2VPNs). RFC 4664.

Boucadair, M, & Jacquenet, C. (2014). Software-Defined Networking: A Perspective from within a Service Provider Environment, *RFC 7149.*

Boucadair, M., Jacquenet, C., & Wang, N. (2014). IP Connectivity Provisioning Profile (CPP). RFC 7297.

Callon, R. & Suzuki, M. (2005). A Framework for Layer 3 Provider-Provisioned Virtual Private Networks (PPVPNs). RFC 4110.

Farrel, A., Vasseur, J.P., & Ash, J. (2006). A Path Computation Element (PCE)-Based Architecture. RFC 4655.

Hood, D. (2014). *SDN Architecture. Issue 1. Open Networking Foundation.* ONF.

Howarth, M., Boucadair, M., Flegkas, P., Wang, N., Pavlou, G., Morand, P., & Georgatsos, P. et al. (2006). End-to-end Quality of Service Provisioning through Inter-provider Traffic Engineering. *Computer Communications (Elsevier)*, *29*(6), 683–702. doi:10.1016/j.comcom.2005.07.022

Presuhn, R., Case, J., McCloghrie, Rose, M., K., & Waldbusser, S. (2002). Version 2 of the Protocol Operations for the Simple Network Management Protocol (SNMP). RFC 3416.

Vasseur, J. P., & Le Roux, J. L. (2009). *Path Computation Element (PCE) Communication Protocol (PCEP). RFC 5440. Crabbe, E., Minei, I., Medved, J., Varga, R. (2014), PCEP Extensions for Stateful PCE, draft-ietf-pce-stateful-pce-10.* IETF.

ADDITIONAL READING

Chowdhury, N., & Boutaba, R. (2009). Network virtualization: State of the art and research challenges. *IEEE Communications Magazine*, *47*(7), 20–26. doi:10.1109/MCOM.2009.5183468

Chowdhury, N., & Boutaba, R. (2010). *A survey of network virtualization.* Elsevier Computer Networks.

KEY TERMS AND DEFINITIONS

Customers: Customers are users of virtual network services. They are provided with an abstract resource view of the network resource (known as “a slice”) to support their users and applications. In some cases, customers may have to support multiple virtual network services with different service objectives and QoS requirements to support multiple types of users and applications. Customers can be internal trusted parties with respect to the provider such as wholesale service department, etc. Customers can also be trusted external parties with respect to the provider.

Network Providers: Network Providers are the infrastructure providers that own the physical network resources and provide transport network resources to their customers. Service Providers can be the customers of Network Providers or can be the Network Providers themselves. A Network Provider owns and administers one or many transport domain(s) (typically Autonomous System (AS)) composed of IP switching and transmission resources (e.g., routing, switching, forwarding, etc.). Network Providers are responsible for ensuring connectivity services (e.g., offering global or restricted reachability). Connectivity services offered to Customers are captured in contracts from which are derived the technology-specific clauses and policies to be enforced by the components involved in the connectivity service delivery. Offered connectivity services are not restricted to IP.

Network Virtualization: Network virtualization refers to allowing the customers to utilize certain network resources as if they own them and thus allows them to control their allocated resources in a way most optimal with higher layer or application processes. This customer control facilitates the introduction of new applications (on top of available services) as the customers are given programmable interfaces to create, modify, and delete their virtual network services.

Service Providers (also Virtual Network Service Provider): Service Providers are the providers of virtual network services to their customers. Service Providers typically lease resources from single or multiple Network Providers' facilities to create virtual network services and offer end-to-end services to their customers. A Virtual Network Service Provider is a type of Service Provider, except that they may own no physical equipment or infrastructure, or have limited physical infrastructure and will require virtual resources for offering the final service, and only provide services built upon virtual network infrastructure. In general, this chapter does not distinguish between a Virtual Network Service Provider and Service Provider.

Transport Networks: Transport networks are defined as network infrastructure that provides connectivity and bandwidth for customer services. They are characterized by their ability to support server layer provisioning and traffic engineering for client layer services, such that resource guarantees may be provided to their customers. Transport networks in this chapter refer to a set of different types of connection-oriented networks, which include Connection-Oriented Circuit Switched (CO-CS) networks and Connection-Oriented Packet Switched (CO-PS) networks. This implies that at least the following transport networks are in scope of the discussion of this chapter: Layer 1 (L1) optical networks (e.g., Optical Transport Networks (OTN) and Wavelength Switched Optical Networks (WSON)), MPLS-TP, MPLS-TE, as well as other emerging network technologies with connection-oriented behavior.

Chapter 16
Future SDN-Based Network Architectures

Evangelos Haleplidis
University of Patras, Greece

Spyros Denazis
University of Patras, Greece

Odysseas Koufopavlou
University of Patras, Greece

ABSTRACT

Networking has seen a burst of innovation and rapid changes with the advent of Software Defined Networking (SDN). Many people considered SDN to be something new and innovative, but actually SDN is something that has already been proposed almost a decade ago in the era of active and programmable networks, and developed even before that. Coupled with the fact that SDN is a very dynamic area with everyone trying to brand their architecture, research or product as SDN has defined a vague and broad definition of what SDN. This chapter attempts to put SDN into perspective approaching SDN with a more spherical point of view by providing the necessary background of pre-SDN technologies and how SDN came about. Followed by discussion on what SDN means today, what SDN is comprised of and a vision of how SDN will evolve in the future to provide the programmable networks that researchers and operators have longed for for many years now. This chapter closes with a few applicability use cases of the future SDN and wraps up with how SDN fits in the Future Internet Architectures.

INTRODUCTION AND HISTORICAL BACKGROUND TO SDN

Network research has gained a burst of activity and innovation for the past couple of years, with the advent of what is called, Software Defined Networking (SDN). SDN, as a term, was introduced in 2008 by Stanford University researchers (McKeown et al. 2008) as an attempt to enable researchers to operate network in a more programmable fashion in order to run their experiments such as new protocols, interfaces or algorithms on real production networks.

DOI: 10.4018/978-1-4666-8371-6.ch016

Simulations and emulations can only provide insights of whether a proof of concept may be applicable. To actually deploy new protocols or architectures on real hardware, the students would either have to convince hardware manufacturers to adopt them, but they are very reluctant to do so, as the design cycle of a new device could take a lot of time and yet generate a limited monetary incentive. Or they would have to develop the hardware themselves, using custom-based hardware as described by Lockwood et al. (2007). This custom-based hardware was soon embraced by the networking community.

However, based on research and demonstration of SDN-enabled technologies, the industry realized that by utilizing the concepts proposed by the SDN proponents, they could solve real-world problems. In environments such as data centers where it is crucial to optimize resources and thus the capability to customize the behavior of the network, till then constrained to the decision of a distributed control plane, and the capability of automation of configuration in environments was a key factor.

SDN initially begun with the precept of separating the forwarding plane from the control plane (these terms will be elaborated further in this chapter) to allow applications to program the network. The separation is achieved by abstracting the forwarding plane and providing an open interface to the control plane. Such a separation incurs many benefits to both planes as it allows research and innovation to occur independently in each plane.

However the concept of separating the control plane from the forwarding plane, or in other words, separating the signaling from the data path, has been present in the networking world for a long time documented by Feamster et al. (2013) and Mendonca et al.(2013). As discussed in Feamster et al. (2013) and later in this chapter, the main reasons for adoption was the urgent need for programmability, especially in DCs, while using open standard interfaces and utilizing existing switch chipsets to require as little change as possible.

SDN dates even back with ITU's SS7 (ITU 1993) networks where the signaling of telephone calls was separated from the actual phone call in order to setup and tear down phone calls, but that enabled new services to be formed such as local number portability and number translations. In addition ITU's ATM technology (ITU 1990) has been based on the concept of separating signaling and datapath, the signaling being used to set up the connections.

Next came the era of Active and Programmable Networks (A&PN), as surveyed by Tennenhouse et al. (1997) and Campbell et al. (1999) where network programmability was the focus. A&PN was based upon on a richer model than programmability and presented two alternatives: the in-band and out-of-band control.

In-band control was the most representative approach of the active networking school of thought from those years, where the concept was that code was actually traversing the network alongside the packets and was executed at specific nodes in the network such as Active Node Transfer System (ANTS) discussed by Wetherall et al. (1998). However it was the out-of-band control, the programmable networks approach, which dominated the research results and the experimentations that were carried out. The programmable networks concept was to allow software to control how the devices manipulate packets, the exact concept that current SDN proponents are advocating for.

There is a couple of interesting research projects that came out of the era of A&PN such as the P1520 (Biswas et al 1998), and Tempest (Rooney et al. 1998) projects. The IEEE P1520 standardization effort addressed the need for a set of standard software interfaces for programming networks in terms of rapid service creation and open signaling by defining a set of levels of abstraction and their respective interfaces similar to SDN concepts. The Tempest project, taking a cue from the advances of network virtualization enabled multiple virtual networks to coexist on the same set of physical switches and allowing software controllers to control how network devices handle the traffic.

Network virtualization and the results of Tempest were also picked up and the experimentation research trend manifested itself in national programs and initiatives such as the Global Environment for Network Innovations (GENI) in USA, and Future Internet REsearch (FIRE) in Europe has involved the majority of research labs and teams of the A&PN era.

Born out of the vision of network programmability and driven by the Network Processing Forum (NPF) in 2001, the Forwarding and Control Element Separation (ForCES) working group was chartered in the IETF. ForCES (RFC 3746), in a few words provides a modelling language (RFC 5812) to describe network resources as blocks, called Logical Functional Blocks (LFBs) which, when interconnected create a graph of resources. ForCES also specified an open protocol (RFC 5810) that can be used query and control the LFBs.

Followed by a couple of research projects such as the 4D project (Greenberg et al. 2005) and the Routing Control Platform (RCP) (Caesar et al. 2005), the Ethane project (Casado et al. 2007) led to OpenFlow (McKeown et al. 2008). OpenFlow provides a specific abstraction of an OpenFlow switch and includes a protocol that is used to query and control the switch. OpenFlow was initially developed by Stanford, but was soon handed to the Open Networking Foundation organization which has continued to extend it. It has undergone a number of versions and iterations since its inception.

It is not coincidental that SDN and the concept of network programmability have strongly reemerged with the advent of cloud computing, virtualization and data center technologies. The lack of network programmability in a clear and uniform approach is still a challenge that is being overcome. SDN's overall motivation, in addition to solving network cloud provisioning is driven by the desire to deploy, control and manage networks, devices and services, e.g. load balancers, firewalls, virtual networks by introducing a high level of automation in the overall service delivery and operation procedures. Virtualization and data center technologies have increased tenfold the number of devices, physical and virtual that a data center IT team needs to manage and maintain, as well as considering Virtual Machine (VM) migrations, multi-tenancy and custom services, all these add up to an ever increasing operational load on network administrators.

The aforementioned problem was usually addressed with scripts, or manual configurations, but SDN provides a clean and deterministic approach into solving these problems. By abstracting the forwarding plane and empowering applications to control and manage the network, it provides a very appealing toolset for network administrators. In addition, it provides a software-based approach to virtualize the network, as discussed in Sherwood et al. (2009), to allow researchers to take control of a portion of the actual hardware for experimentation. SDN had a very fertile ground where there was a specific need to be covered, such as a data center as discussed earlier, the level of technological maturity was right, which led to SDN's success where earlier attempts on network programmability failed to move ahead.

One of the most notable SDN examples is Google's SDN-based WAN (Jain 2013) for interconnecting data centers using OpenFlow. Google showcased that using SDN concepts for WAN interconnection can greatly improve performance in link utilization, and that centralizing a controller to aggregate link topologies the system load is reduced and higher availability.

SDN has come a long way, but during its course since 2008 and due to the increased interest of the community, it has undergone many changes, e.g. OpenFlow evolved through several iterative versions, from 1.0 to 1.4. SDN was also embraced in different ways by standardization organizations (SDOs) and every stakeholder attempted to brand their product, architecture or research as SDN. This has inadvertently led to a fragmented and disjoint view of what SDN is, what is the architecture, what layers and planes it encompasses, what are the abstractions and interfaces.

This chapter attempts to provide a more general view of what SDN is by taking a step backwards and put SDN in perspective by taking in the history of network programmability and see how it affected SDN, the current view as it is defined by SDOs and the literature and finally provide a vision of how SDN will interact with future SDN-based network architectures based upon the discussion about a few use cases.

A BROAD AND CURRENT VIEW OF SDN

RFC7426 provides a detailed description of the SDN layers architecture, aiming to provide a clearer view of the emerging paradigm. By dividing the SDN architecture into distinct planes, abstraction layers and interfaces, the draft aims to clarify SDN terminology and establish some commonly accepted ground across the SDN community. Figure 1 takes SDN into perspective and visualize the architecture, the layers and the interfaces that take part in the overall picture.

It must be noted that Figure 1 provides an abstract view, meaning that implementations may vary. For example many implementations in the past have opted for placing the management plane on top of the control plane. This can be interpreted as having the control plane acting as a service to the management plane. Also while not shown explicitly in the figure, these planes can be placed in a recursive manner, for example multiple control planes one on top of the other, or services and applications may span multiple layers such as both the control and management.

A network device, as shown in Figure 1, is an entity that receives packets on its ports and performs one or more network functions on them. The sum of network devices in a network is otherwise known as the infrastructure layer. Network devices are composed of resources, simple such as a port, or complex comprised of multiple individual resources. The network device is also considered a complex resource. Resources are not limited to networking but also include CPU, memory and ports. It is important to notice that in this abstract view there is no distinction between physical or virtual devices, or whether such devices are implemented in hardware or software.

There are two distinct planes associated with network devices, the forwarding and the operational plane. The forwarding plane provides switching, routing and filtering functions. Resources of the forwarding plane include but are not limited to meters, queues and classifiers. The Operational Plane on the other hand is responsible for the operational state of the network device, for instance, with respect to status of network ports and interfaces. Operational plane resources include, but are not limited to, memory, CPU, ports, interfaces and queues.

In SDN, the resources of these two planes are abstracted and exposed by the Device and Resource Abstraction Layer (DAL). The DAL may be expressed by multiple abstraction models. For example ForCES LFBs or the OpenFlow's switch specification is an instantiation of a DAL. The ForCES LFB model, YANG model (RFC 6020) or SMI are examples of modeling semantics that can be used to define DAL abstractions (data models). Having a common set of abstractions, or a way to define abstractions in a unified approach is paramount in SDN, as it is important for the upper planes to view all devices in the same manner. Specific SNMP MIBs for example where such DAL instances that are still being used.

It is worth discussing the DAL since having the right abstractions is paramount to the success of SDN. A lot of effort is being directed towards defining the DAL. While OpenFlow in itself provides only a specific instance of an OpenFlow's switch DAL, the ONF has chartered the Forward-

Figure 1. High Level View of SDN Architecture

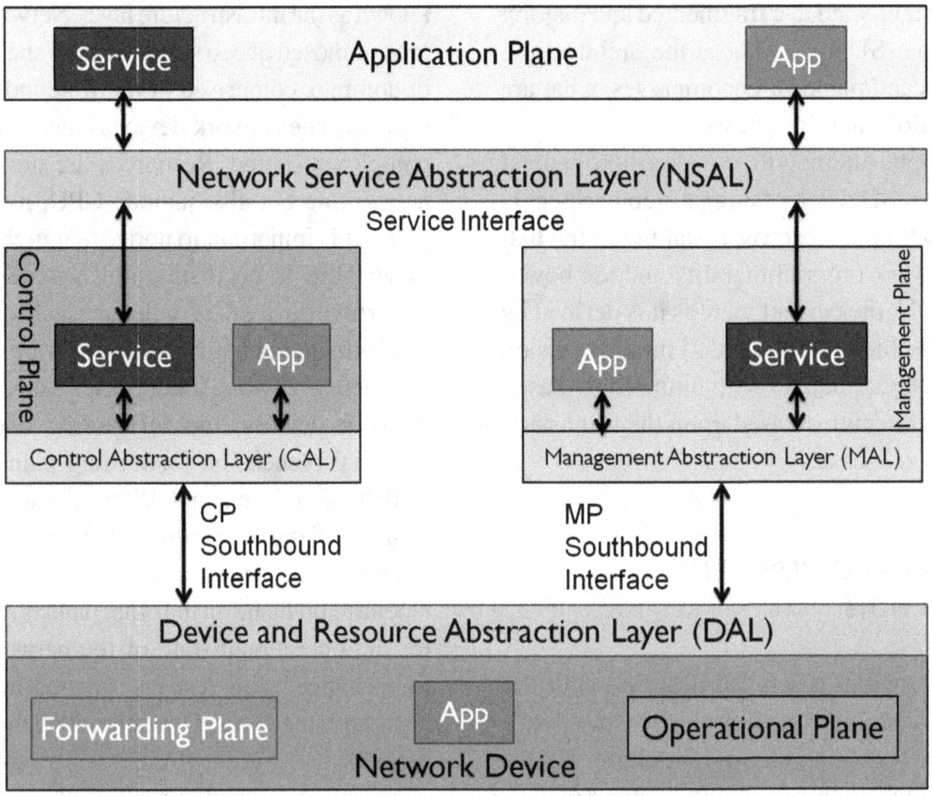

ing Plane Abstractions working group and has recently published the first white paper for Table Type Patters (ONF 2014 TTP). Nakao (2012) and Song (2013) follow the example of OpenFlow but differentiate from the fact that they allow flexible match patterns for classifying packets. Another school of thought consist in applying a common set of abstractions based upon various versions of OpenFlow, as described in Parniewicz et al. (2014).

Above the devices there are two distinct planes, the control and the management plane. The control plane is responsible for making decisions on how packets should be manipulated by one or more network devices and pushing such decisions down to the forwarding plane of the network devices for execution. Since the control plane's main focus is to instruct the forwarding plane about how it should process packets, it also requires operational plane information to influence the decision-making process. Such information includes the current state of a particular port or its capabilities, for example.

The management plane is responsible for monitoring, configuring and maintaining network devices and its main focus is on the operational plane of the device and less on the forwarding plane. The management plane may also configure the forwarding plane, but it usually does so infrequently and in a batched approach. At the introduction of SDN, the management plane was considered out of scope (ONF 2012 and ONF 2013) and indeed the earlier definitions of SDN suggested that SDN is all about the separation of forwarding from control. Recently ONF (ONF 2014) and ITU (ITU SG13 2014) have also included the management plane as part of SDN.

The control plane and management plane manipulate the network device and its resources through respective interfaces, the Control Plane Southbound Interface (CPSI) and the Management Plane Southbound Interfaces (MPSI). These interfaces have their own distinct characteristics depending on the respective planes.

The first characteristic is timescale. Timescale specifies how fast a plane responds and needs to respond. For example the control plane needs to respond in a very small timescale as packets may wait for the being forwarded while the control plane decides where to forward them. The management plane on the other hand may not necessarily need to react fast to changes.

The second characteristic is persistency. Persistency refers to how long the state of the device will remain stable. Control plane state may fluctuate and change rapidly in a matter of milliseconds and thus are more ephemeral, whilst management plane state is usually more stable and may remain static for a longer period of time.

The third characteristic is locality. Usually control plane functionalities were collocated with the forwarding and operation planes and distributed, whilst management plane functionalities were more centralized and off the device. Locality is an interesting characteristic as with the concept of SDN to separate the control plane and have a more centralized architecture, the control plane tends to act more as a management plane. It is important therefore for SDN controllers to take into account issues that used to be addressed for the management plane, such as availability.

The final characteristic is the CAP theorem. The CAP theorem states that for a distributed system, between three characteristics, Consistency, Availability and Partitioning tolerance, a designer can only select two at best. For example if partitioning tolerance is given, then a designer can choose between consistency or availability. In the context of SDN that means that a centralized management system has consistency, knows all the states but not availability as it may lose connectivity. A distributed controller on the other hand has availability as it is connected directly to devices but loses consistency as propagation of state takes some time. Since SDN proponents initially discussed a centralized controller CAP provides a good tool to specify the issues that this may bring. Panda et al. (2013) discussed approaches on how to alleviate issues raised by CAP when applied to SDN.

Both Control and Management Plane have their respective abstraction layers, the Control Abstraction Layer and the Management Abstraction Layer that abstract their respective southbound interface. The control and management planes may support more than one interface and the CAL and MAL abstract the interface functionalities.

The interfaces between the control and the management planes and the device are also important for SDN and are usually know as southbound interfaces. These interfaces formalize the interaction between the controllers and managers and the devices: command operations such as query, config and subscribe for events go through such interfaces. Each respective interface has its own characteristics, for example the control plane southbound interface needs to react fast to changes and support multiple events per second, whilst the management plane southbound interface needs to be more user friendly as it is likely to be solicited by network administrators. Examples of control plane southbound interfaces include the ForCES protocol, OpenFlow and SNMP, while examples of management plane southbound interfaces include NETCONF, SNMP, OVSDB and PCEP, amongst others.

Finally the application plane is where user applications and services reside that use services from the control and management plane. Applications differ from services as services provide functionality to other services or applications, where applications only consume services. The application plane host applications and services that are not related to control or management plane activities but only make use of them.

The Network Service Abstraction Layer (NSAL) abstract services, control and management as well as application plane services to other services and applications to consume them. The NSAL is also known as the SDN northbound interface and is currently not specified. In fact the NSAL is under research as to what abstractions are the best to describe the underlying services. SDN proponents suggest RESTful or RPC APIs for NSAL. RESTful are designed according to the representation state transfer design paradigm that includes resource identification, self-descriptive messages and no connection state. RPCs are APIs where a client need to know the procedure and the associated parameters a priori before using it.

ONF (ONF 2014) has also specified an SDN architecture depicted in Figure 2. The ONF architecture also introduces the data plane, the control plane, the application plane as well as management. The architecture, and especially the definition of control and management, resembles the SDNRG discussion (RFC7426). Similarly the ONF architecture provides an abstract view devoid of implementation details.

There are some differentiations between the ONF and SDNRG definitions. The ONF architecture document provides more internal view of the control plane and takes into account more interfaces between recursive planes as well as discussed virtualization in greater detail. The ONF architecture provides an interesting view of how multi-technology, multi-domain and multi-tenancy networks operate following an SDN approach.

For the purposes of the ONF, the DAL, as defined in (RFC7426), is considered to be OpenFlow and OF-CONFIG. OF-CONFIG is actually NETCONF with the OpenFlow network element being described in several YANG modules.

ITU (ITU SG13 2014) has also defined a relevant architecture which is similar to Figure 2. The ITU includes the resource layer instead of the data plane, the SDN control layer, the application layer and multi-layer management functions. The SDN control layer in ITU (ITU SG13 2014) includes resource abstractions, such as the DAL in (RFC7426), but introduces the concept of orchestration as the means to provide control and management of network resources covering, for example, management of physical and virtual network topologies, network elements, and data traffic.

Having discussed all the necessary layers of an SDN architecture, there is common ground

Figure 2. ONF SDN architecture

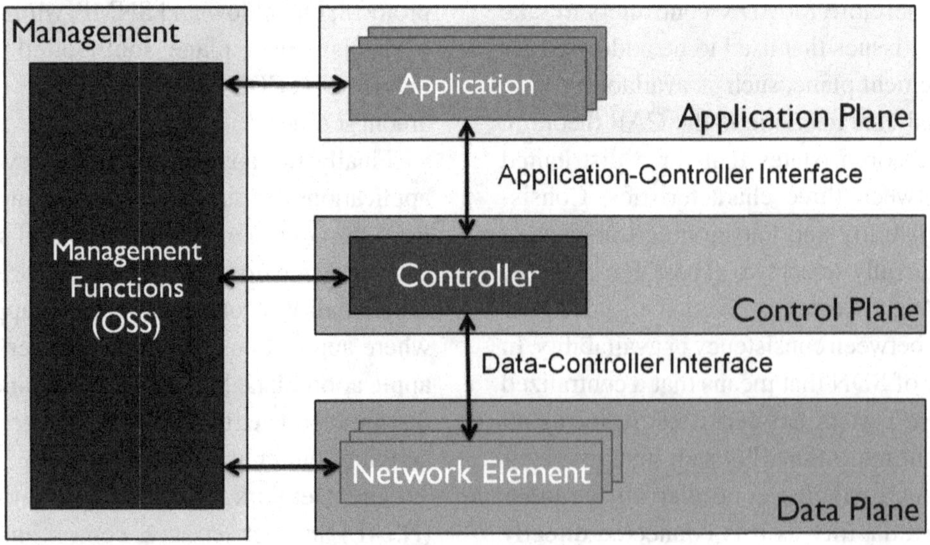

upon which all further discussion can be placed upon. For example, common SDN controllers such as Beacon (Erickson et al. 2013), NOX (Gude et al. 2008), are control plane services that use OpenFlow as a protocol that carries information through the Control plane southbound interface and provide services to other application and services. Flowvisor (Sherwood et al. 2009) is actually a control plane service that provides service to other control plane services, since it is actually a proxy controller.

Inspired by software programming languages, researchers such as Monsanto et al. (2012), Foster et al. (2011) have created their own programming languages and compilers that abstract the network and form a foundation for formal languages as discussed by Guha et al. (2013). Formal verification and other tools such as network debugging (Handigol 2012), integrated development environments (IDE) such as NetIDE discussed by Facca et al (2013) are but a few of the recent toolkit that the SDN community is currently realizing.

SDN REALIZATION AND IMPLEMENTATION CHALLENGES

SDN has the potential to accrue several benefits to implementers, such as automated error recovery, higher link utilization and customizing network behavior. However up till now, SDN has not yet been adopted globally, with few or none deployments in production networks. There are a couple of issues that account for this lack of adoption.

The first issue is the maturity of the SDN technology, including abstractions, architecture, tools and applications. Earlier in this chapter three SDN architecture definitions were introduced by three standardization organization (SDO). While these three have many in common, it can be expected that other SDO's will want to have their own SDN definition which will not help advance a common view and will not help to advance technical aspects nor will it solve deployment concerns.

The maturity of abstractions is yet another issue that proves to be a difficult challenge. SDN, as also depicted in Figure 1, involves at least two abstraction layers. These two are the DAL, where the resources of the network devices are abstracted, required for the southbound interface and the NSAL where network services are abstracted, required for the northbound interface.

In regards to the DAL, work has already been done but it has not yet solidified. OpenFlow provided some specific abstractions which were enhanced and changed as new versions were being defined with attempts to provide more generic abstractions in concepts like discussed in Bosshart et al. (2013) and Song (2013). However one of the issues with OpenFlow, is that it requires to reinvent all current network functions, such as discovery using LLDP or ARP handling without the ability to utilize hardware that already support that function. If a hybrid solution is used, the state of the non-OpenFlow portion of the switch is unavailable to the OpenFlow Controller.

As discussed earlier, besides OpenFlow there are other solutions that can be utilized for the DAL, such as the ForCES model, YANG, SMI. The latter provide language constructs with which DAL resources can be abstracted. The issue with this approach is that there can be multiple different abstractions, proprietary or conflicting, that may hinder adoption. The best current practice to avoid this pitfall is the creation of standardized data models, such as MIBs, LFB libraries and YANG modules. In addition controllers that can abstract this kind of different models may be one approach to resolve these issues, such as discussed in Medved (2014) which attempts to provide homogeneity for such heterogeneous abstractions.

While there has been significant research and implementation for the DAL, there is little progress on the NSAL abstractions. The two leading interfaces as discussed earlier are RESTful or RPC interfaces. However there is little work done on what abstractions are going to be used and how services that both the control and/or management plane are going to be available to applications. Since most of the added value of SDN is the ability of applications to modify network behavior, the lack thereof of commonly accepted NSAL abstractions hinders the deployment of SDN.

On the other hand building SDN solutions is not an easy task; there are a number of SDN challenges that need to be addressed. Sezer et al. (2013) discuss four fundamental issues in building an SDN solution. The first is performance versus flexibility and how SDN networks can achieve high-throughput, security and performance in a scalable fashion. With the sometimes necessary packet redirection to the controller, performance becomes an issue. However recent advances in networking hardware and the performance achieved by new processors, better overall performance can be achieved.

The second is scalability and how a controller can maintain a consistent view of the network. This problem can also be viewed with the CAP theorem in mind. Should a controller be centralized or distributed? How would state between controllers be distributed and how fast would the network state converge? These are the questions an SDN network designer needs to keep in mind when designing an SDN network.

The third is security. Security is of paramount importance in networks but also in SDN environments where more interfaces are introduced thereby exposing more targets for potential attacks. In addition, since the SDN controller is usually defined as a logically centralized entity, it is easier to focus attacks on the controller as well as to perform DoS and DDoS attacks. When the controller is taken down, the network will either stop working or will not be updated, as a consequence, become incosistent with the information maintained by the SDN controller. Kreutz et al. (2013) provides also another view on the SDN security aspects and identifies potential points of attack on SDN architectures, for example the interface between controller and the network devices and between controllers.

The final issue discussed by Sezer et al. (2013) is interoperability and how existing legacy solutions can interact with SDN-enabled network devices. Should legacy equipment being treated as black boxes where typical forwarding is enforced while the rest of the network is SDN-enabled? Sezer et al. (2013) discuss this issue and proposes PCE and also further development on other solutions that will alleviate this problem and provide backwards compatibility with IP and MPLS technologies.

Additionally, Hakiri et al. (2014) introduced more challenges such as inter SDN communications. How can different SDN domains exchange information? The ONF (ONF 2014) architecture introduces such an interface. Such a challenge will need to be address in order for SDN to be used in larger networks than individual autonomous systems. Ideas such as the Software defined internet exchange discussed by Feamster et al. (2013) may be applicable to solve such issues.

Finally Jammal et al. (2014) introduced the issues of reliability and controller placement. In the case of reliability the controller must be able to configure and validate network topologies and configurations to prevent and mitigate errors. In addition if connection with the controller is lost what will happen if problems occur within the network? The other issue is controller placement. Jammal et al. (2014) discusses that for wide-area SDN deployments, controller placement is crucial as multiple SDN controllers are required and their placement affect many metrics in the network such as latency, fault tolerance and performance. Considering the fact that every packet the device does not know what to do with is sent to the controller, the placement of controllers is crucial.

A VISION OF SDN FOR NETWORK ARCHITECTURES

A few years after the emergence of SDN and because of the advances of virtualization, on October

2012 some of the major operators got together in Darmstadt (Germany) and published the first white paper that discusses Network Functions Virtualization (NFV) (ETSI NFV 2014). The goal was simple yet powerful and is three-fold. Firstly to attempt to reduce the Capital Expenses (CAPEX) cost of purchasing physical, dedicated and sometimes expensive network equipment such as firewalls. Such equipment may be sparsely used as the purchase is often based upon perceived use and in effect underused, thereby increasing the overall energy consumption among other issues. Secondly to allow quick innovation and deployment cycles of new devices to provide new services for users. Finally, to reduce the overall Operational Expenses (OPEX) cost of management required for a large and always evolving number of such devices by automation.

NFV's solution is to virtualize network functions, such as firewalls and routers, and deploy them as software on virtual platforms, e.g. Virtual Machines (VM), residing in high volume devices on a per-need basis. NFV is applicable to any data plane packet processing and control plane function in mobile and fixed networks. Such an approach will allow operators to design, implement, deploy and destroy network functions at will and reduce energy consumption by utilizing only the necessary amount of infrastructure resources. As such NFV must provide flexibility, adaptability to new user requirements for services and elasticity.

In tandem with NFV, the newly formed IETF Service Function Chaining (SFC) working group's charter specifies that the working group will "produce an architecture for service function chaining that includes the necessary protocols or protocol extensions to convey the Service Function Chain and Service Function Path information to nodes that are involved in the implementation of service functions and Service Function Chains, as well as mechanisms for steering traffic through service functions".

SFC introduces a new problem, that of the SFC resource allocation and deployment and is concerned with mapping an SFC onto the underlying physical infrastructure and assigning resources to SFC nodes and edges (e.g., bandwidth, computing and storage) and involves four steps. The first step is the mapping of SFC nodes (i.e., Virtual Network Functions (VNFs)) onto multiple distributed data centers. The second step includes the deployment of VNFs allocated to the same data centre onto servers and allocating resources to them. The third step entails the deployment a virtual network infrastructure in the form of Service Graph to interconnect the VNFs. The final step is the mapping SFC edges onto network paths on top of the virtual network infrastructure.

Taking a different point of view, NFV relates to network resource management which includes reservation, allocation, instantiation and withdrawal, SFC relates to resource chaining and SDN relates to control and management of resources. All the three techniques, SDN, NFV and SFC may be combined to facilitate the overall service delivery and operation procedures for the lifecycle of networks. This concept is illustrated in Figure 3. Haleplidis, Salim et al. (2014) discuss how a common abstraction model for SDN and NFV is applicable using ForCES to achieve the aforementioned concept.

A possible future of network architectures are completely elastic and on demand as an overlay on top of a base infrastructure. A developer using a VNF app store will be able to select the necessary VNFs, create the interconnections that will be required, or simply define a policy of what interconnections should look like and click a button. The rest will be done automatically with all the toolset that SDN, NFV and SFC provide. This is a research direction that is considered in the literature such as John (2013) specifically in a unified network approach.

SDN is not only applicable in such a future network architecture scenario, but is one of the key components. SDN provides the toolkit that can accommodate the rapid changes that NFV introduces in the network. With NFV, new func-

Figure 3. SDN, NFV, SFC and the network lifecycle

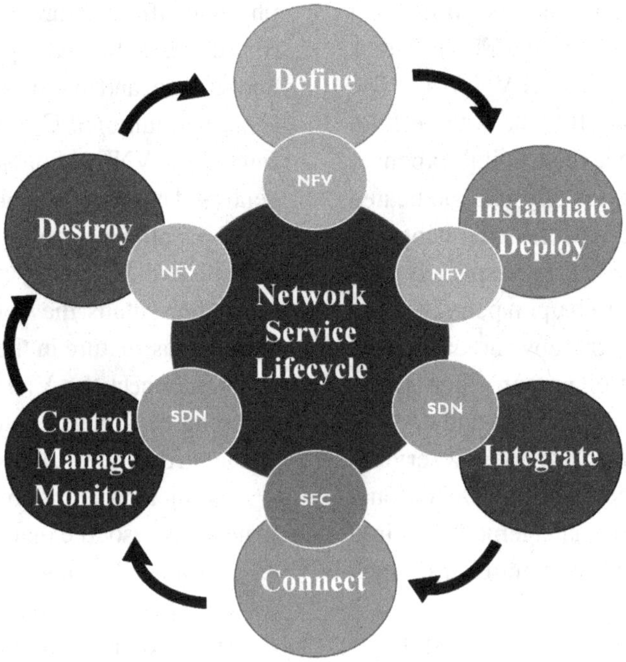

tions can be instantiated into the network and it is up to SDN to interconnect these functions that reside on virtual environments without the need for manual configuration which may jeopardize the time to deliver a service, depending on the number and the complexity of the configuration tasks.

SDN's DAL, the resource abstraction layer, provides a unified approach on how resources are modeled and controlled, applicable to the NFV domain as well. The use of formal languages also suggests that in the future, network architectures may as well become software-defined, thus a developer may simply describe in a more high-level overview what the required network configuration is. This will then be translated a few levels below into a set of configuration commands that will be processed by the participating devices to provide the requested network architecture. Thus SDN may transform a base underlay network into fully fledged overlay network architecture as depicted in Figure 4.

Such a transformation is realized with the accrued benefits that SDN provides such as optimization, automation and network virtualization. Having a logically centralized controller with a complete network resource visibility allows the controller to optimize paths and orchestrate better resource utilization. Applications on top of or inside the controller can automate processes such as failovers, high availability and load sharing. In addition new network virtualization techniques are emerging, allows multiple users to run on the same infrastructure with additional isolation. These techniques existed prior to SDN, however SDN provides a programmatic approach to reaping their full potential without resorting to custom scripts, command line interfaces and telneting into multiple devices to monitor, configure and manage.

SDN APPLICABILITY ON FUTURE NETWORK ARCHITECTURES

SDN has been applied on multiple network domains, from the classical wired technologies, to wireless (Yap 2010) (Dely 2011) (Pentikousis

Figure 4. SDN as key building block for future network architectures

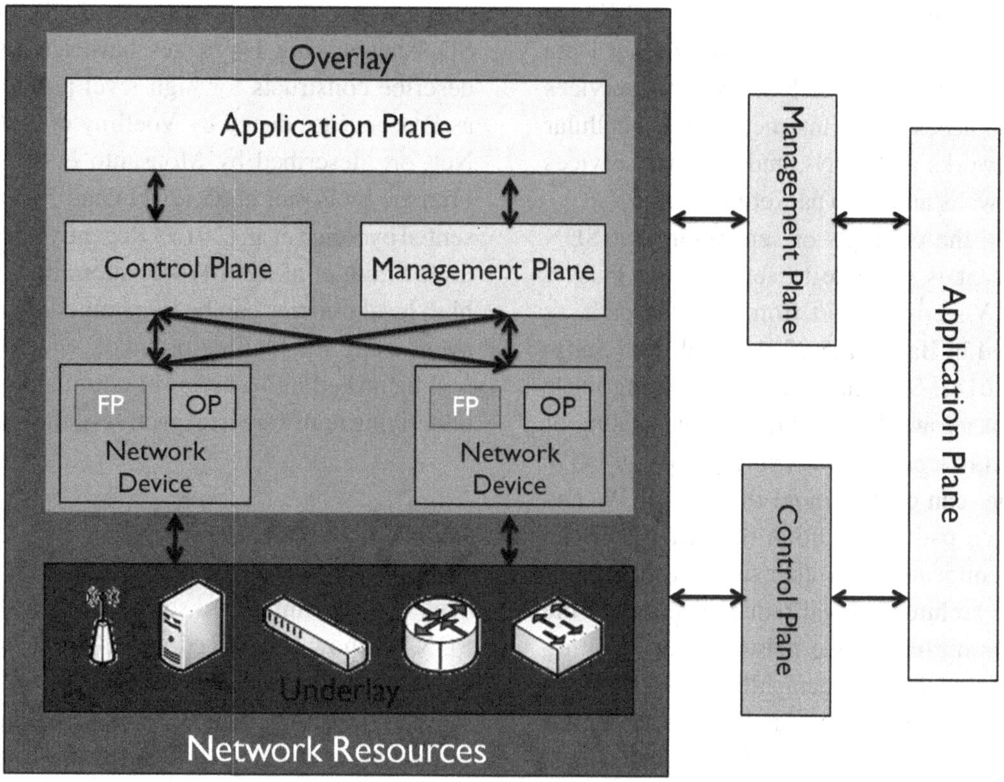

2013) (Bernardos 2014), optical (Channegowda 2013) (Gringeri 2013) and even IoT (Valdivieso 2014) (Qin 2014). By creating DAL instances for each domain, SDN controllers can be used and provide access to applications to interact and manage resources for each domain.

Currently, there is no SDN solution that has attempted to unify all domains under a single DAL, but recently a UK project called Towards Ultimate Convergence of All Networks (TOUCAN) has been chartered for that specific purpose. It is expected that results from such a project will have a significant impact to network architectures. Providing the necessary abstractions to applications irrespective of the underlying network substrate and allowing applications to request network paths, make use of combined architectures to solve resource, efficiency and high utilization requests will empower applications.

Adapting current architectures to SDN is also another aspect of how SDN affects network architectures. A specific applicability scenario for SDN, NFV and SFC that illustrates some of the previous discussion relates to the 3GPP's Long Term Evolution (LTE) Evolved Packet Core (EPC). The Evolved Packet Core (EPC) as described also in Olsson (2009) is the core network architecture of LTE's wireless communication networks. The user equipment (UE) connects to a base station, which directs traffic through a serving gateway (SGW) over a GPRS Tunneling Protocol (GTP) tunnel and through a packet gateway (PGW) and then to the internet.

The SGW forwards user data packets, while also acting as the mobility anchor for the user plane during handovers. The Packet Gateway (PGW) enforces quality-of-service (QoS) policies by signaling with the Policy and charging rules function (PCRF) and monitors traffic to perform billing by signaling to the Online (OCS) and Offline charging systems (OFCS). The PGW also filters packets and connects to the Packet Data Network (PDN). PDN includes network services as well as access to the Internet and other cellular data networks and PDNs, and includes services like firewalls and deep packet inspection.

Using the concepts of separation that SDN assumes, it is possible to separate the PGW's and SGW's control part from the data path, as described in Basta et al. (2013) and Hadi Salim et al. (2014). Separating and virtualizing these functions allows the instantiation and scaling of each part independently. A single SGW or PGW controller can control more than one SGW and PGW data path. In addition the controllers can now be collocated with other signaling entities of the LTE architecture and reduce latency for the signaling portion of the network, thus creating separate signaling and datapath networks. Figure 5 depicts a concept of separation of the control and data path network in the 3GPP architecture.

Grey boxes are the control network and purple boxes the data path portion of the network. Using SDN concepts, the architecture is transformed, yet still remain 3GPP compliant. This separation allows each domain to scale as required. Control plane entities can be collocated to reduce latency and improve network experience and data plane entities can be reduced to simply perform forwarding at fast rates.

Taking this concept one step further with the concepts of virtualization discussed in the previous subsection and in other chapters of this book, control plane entities can be instantiated to support more customers or data path plane entities could be instantiated to provide each user with a personalized (to a very extreme scenario) data path network using NFV and virtualization techniques.

Already SDN has started to affect new designs and concepts. Taking as a given the concepts of a centralized, or logically centralized, controller and the programmability of devices, the focus is now on applications. Specifically how to define high level policies and how these will be translated into a series of commands towards the devices. SDN networking languages have attempted to describe constructs for high level policies such as Procera introduced by Voellmy et al. (2012), NetCore described by Monsanto et al. (2013), Frenetic by Foster et al. (2011) and Pyretic presented by Reich et al. (2013). Recently an internet draft Smith et al. (2014) was submitted on how high level policies can be transmitted to a policy agent using the OpFlex protocol, which in turn will be turned into a series of commands for the underlying hardware irrespective of the interface.

CONCLUSION

This chapter initially discussed the history of SDN and how it emerged as well as the current views on the architectures, layers and interfaces that an SDN implementation may be comprised of. Having defined such architecture to provide a common base for discussion, this chapter followed with how SDN relates to other networking technologies, specifically NFV and SFC and concluded with a few examples of applicability on future network architectures.

To sum the chapter up, it is easy to see that SDN, or programmability becomes an attractive toolkit for network design and operation. With its current incarnation, SDN has several key roles to play on future network architectures.

First by completely separating signaling from the actual datapath it is possible to redefine how a network can be designed. For example a network designer may choose to create a completely separate network for signaling alone, to optimize the usage of the (data path) network.

Second, by providing a common DAL, it is now possible to unify all the heterogeneous network domains such as wired, wireless and optical under a common controller. Unifying all domains will empower SDN and allow the use in networks that are comprised of various infrastructures.

Figure 5. Concept of separation in the 3GPP LTE's architecture

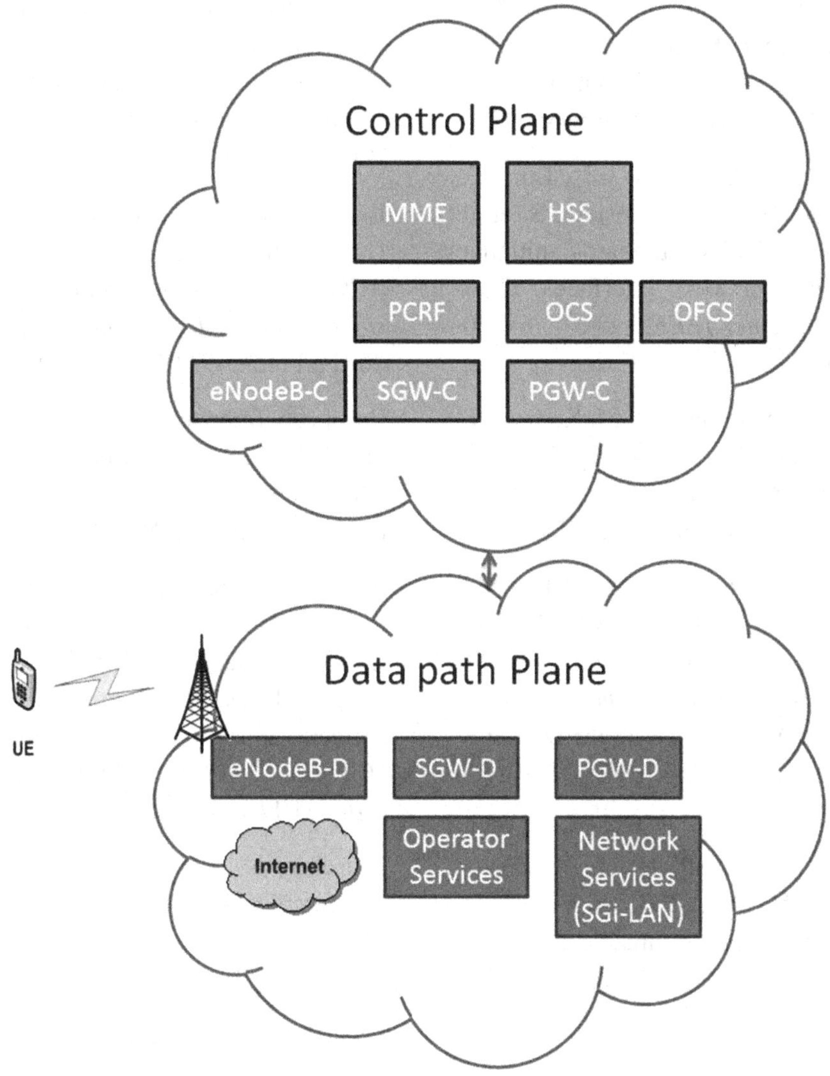

Finally, by combining SDN, NFV and SFC, it will be possible to use software resources to manage the network lifecycle and to allow software applications to actually define the network infrastructure and then control and manage it.

This chapter will close with an attempt to provide a tentative and general definition of what exactly SDN is in a few words. SDN is a programmable networks approach, which allows software applications to program the network.

REFERENCES

Basta, A., Kellerer, W., Hoffmann, M., Hoffmann, K., & Schmidt, E. D. (2013, November). A Virtual SDN-enabled LTE EPC Architecture: a case study for S-/P-Gateways functions. In Future Networks and Services (SDN4FNS), 2013 IEEE SDN for (pp. 1-7). IEEE.

Bernardos, C. J., de la Oliva, A., Serrano, P., Banchs, A., Contreras, L. M., Jin, H., & Zúñiga, J. C. An Architecture for Software Defined Wireless Networking. IEEE Wireless Communications Magazine. doi:10.1109/MWC.2014.6845049

Biswas, J., Lazar, A. A., Huard, J. F., Lim, K., Mahjoub, S., Pau, L. F., & Weinstein, S. et al. (1998). The IEEE P1520 standards initiative for programmable network interfaces. *Communications Magazine, IEEE*, *36*(10), 64–70. doi:10.1109/35.722138

Bosshart, P., Daly, D., Izzard, M., McKeown, N., Rexford, J., Talayco, D., . . . Walker, D. (2013). Programming protocol-independent packet processors. *arXiv preprint arXiv:1312.1719*.

Caesar, M., Caldwell, D., Feamster, N., Rexford, J., Shaikh, A., & van der Merwe, J. (2005, May). Design and implementation of a routing control platform. In *Proceedings of the 2nd conference on Symposium on Networked Systems Design & Implementation-Volume 2* (pp. 15-28). USENIX Association.

Campbell, A. T., De Meer, H. G., Kounavis, M. E., Miki, K., Vicente, J. B., & Villela, D. (1999). A survey of programmable networks. *Computer Communication Review*, *29*(2), 7–23. doi:10.1145/505733.505735

Casado, M., Freedman, M. J., Pettit, J., Luo, J., McKeown, N., & Shenker, S. (2007). Ethane: Taking control of the enterprise. *Computer Communication Review*, *37*(4), 1–12. doi:10.1145/1282427.1282382

Channegowda, M., Nejabati, R., & Simeonidou, D. (2013). Software-defined optical networks technology and infrastructure: enabling software-defined optical network operations [Invited]. *Optical Communications and Networking, IEEE/OSA Journal of*, *5*(10), A274-A282.

Dely, P., Kassler, A., & Bayer, N. (2011, July). Openflow for wireless mesh networks. In *Computer Communications and Networks (ICCCN), 2011 Proceedings of 20th International Conference on* (pp. 1-6). IEEE. doi:10.1109/ICCCN.2011.6006100

Erickson, D. (2013, August). The beacon openflow controller. In *Proceedings of the second ACM SIGCOMM workshop on Hot topics in software defined networking* (pp. 13-18). ACM. doi:10.1145/2491185.2491189

European Telecommunications Standards Institute. (2012). *Network Functions Virtualisation*. white paper. Retrieved March 12, 2015, from http://portal.etsi.org/NFV/NFV_White_Paper.pdf

Facca, F. M., Salvadori, E., Karl, H., López, D. R., Gutiérrez, P. A. A., Kostic, D., & Riggio, R. (2013, October). NetIDE: First steps towards an integrated development environment for portable network apps. In *Software Defined Networks (EWSDN), 2013 Second European Workshop on* (pp. 105-110). IEEE.

Feamster, N., Rexford, J., Shenker, S., Clark, R., Hutchins, R., Levin, D., & Bailey, J. (2013). *SDX: A software-defined internet exchange*. Open Networking Summit.

Feamster, N., Rexford, J., & Zegura, E. (2013). The road to SDN. *Queue*, *11*(12), 20–40. doi:10.1145/2559899.2560327

Foster, N., Harrison, R., Freedman, M. J., Monsanto, C., Rexford, J., Story, A., & Walker, D. (2011, September). Frenetic: A network programming language. ACM SIGPLAN Notices, 46(9), 279-291. doi:10.1145/2034773.2034812

Future Internet REsearch (FIRE). (n.d.). Retrieved March 12, 2015, from http://www.ict-fire.eu/home.html

Global Environment for Network Innovations (GENI). (n.d.). Retrieved March 12, 2015, from http://www.geni.net/

Greenberg, A., Hjalmtysson, G., Maltz, D. A., Myers, A., Rexford, J., Xie, G., & Zhang, H. et al. (2005). A clean slate 4D approach to network control and management. *Computer Communication Review*, *35*(5), 41–54. doi:10.1145/1096536.1096541

Gringeri, S., Bitar, N., & Xia, T. J. (2013). Extending software defined network principles to include optical transport. *Communications Magazine, IEEE*, *51*(3), 32–40. doi:10.1109/MCOM.2013.6476863

Gude, N., Koponen, T., Pettit, J., Pfaff, B., Casado, M., McKeown, N., & Shenker, S. (2008). NOX: Towards an operating system for networks. *Computer Communication Review*, *38*(3), 105–110. doi:10.1145/1384609.1384625

Guha, A., Reitblatt, M., & Foster, N. (2013). *Formal Foundations For Software Defined Networks*. Open Net Summit.

Hadi Salim, J., Joachimpillai, D., Martin, J., Lopez, D., & Haleplidis, E. (2014). *ForCES applicability for NFV and integrated SDN, ETSI NFV PoC, April 2014*. Retrieved March 12, 2015, from http://docbox.etsi.org/ISG/NFV/PER/05CONTRIBUTIONS/2014//NFVPER(14)000046r2_ForCES_Applicability_for_NFV_and_integrated_SDN.docx

Hakiri, A., Gokhale, A., Berthou, P., Schmidt, D. C., & Thierry, G. (2014). Software-defined Networking: Challenges and Research Opportunities for Future Internet. *Computer Networks*, *75*, 453–471. doi:10.1016/j.comnet.2014.10.015

Haleplidis, E., Pentikousis, K., Denazis, S., Salim, J. H., Meyer, D., & Koufopavlou, O. (2014). *RFC 7426 Software Defined Networking: Layers and Architecture Terminology*. IRTF SDNRG.

Haleplidis, E., Salim, J. H., Denazis, S., & Koufopavlou, O. (2014). Towards a Network Abstraction Model for SDN. *Journal of Network and Systems Management*, 1–19.

Handigol, N., Heller, B., Jeyakumar, V., Mazières, D., & McKeown, N. (2012, August). Where is the debugger for my software-defined network? In *Proceedings of the first workshop on Hot topics in software defined networks* (pp. 55-60). ACM. doi:10.1145/2342441.2342453

ITU-T Study Group 13. (2014). *Y.3300, Framework of software-defined networking*. Retrieved March 12, 2015, from http://www.itu.int/ITU-T/recommendations/rec.aspx?rec=12168

Jain, S., Kumar, A., Mandal, S., Ong, J., Poutievski, L., Singh, A., & Vahdat, A. et al. (2013, August). B4: Experience with a globally-deployed software defined WAN. In *Proceedings of the ACM SIGCOMM 2013 conference on SIGCOMM* (pp. 3-14). ACM. doi:10.1145/2486001.2486019

Jammal, M., Singh, T., Shami, A., Asal, R., & Li, Y. (2014). Software-Defined Networking: State of the Art and Research Challenges. *Computer Networks, 72*, 74–98.

John, W., Pentikousis, K., Agapiou, G., Jacob, E., Kind, M., Manzalini, A., . . . Meirosu, C. (2013, November). Research directions in network service chaining. In Future Networks and Services (SDN4FNS), 2013 IEEE SDN for (pp. 1-7). IEEE. doi:10.1109/SDN4FNS.2013.6702549

Kreutz, D., Ramos, F., & Verissimo, P. (2013, August). Towards secure and dependable software-defined networks. In *Proceedings of the second ACM SIGCOMM workshop on Hot topics in software defined networking* (pp. 55-60). ACM. doi:10.1145/2491185.2491199

Lockwood, J. W., McKeown, N., Watson, G., Gibb, G., Hartke, P., Naous, J., . . . Luo, J. (2007, June). NetFPGA--An Open Platform for Gigabit-Rate Network Switching and Routing. In *Microelectronic Systems Education, 2007. MSE'07. IEEE International Conference on* (pp. 160-161). IEEE.

McKeown, N., Anderson, T., Balakrishnan, H., Parulkar, G., Peterson, L., Rexford, J., & Turner, J. (2008). OpenFlow: Enabling innovation in campus networks. *Computer Communication Review, 38*(2), 69–74. doi:10.1145/1355734.1355746

Medved, J., Varga, R., Tkacik, A., & Gray, K. (2014, June). OpenDaylight: Towards a Model-Driven SDN Controller architecture. In *A World of Wireless, Mobile and Multimedia Networks (WoWMoM), 2014 IEEE 15th International Symposium on* (pp. 1-6). IEEE.

Mendonca, M., Nunes, B. A. A., Nguyen, X. N., Obraczka, K., & Turletti, T. (2013). *A Survey of software-defined networking: past, present, and future of programmable networks.* hal-00825087.

Monsanto, C., Foster, N., Harrison, R., & Walker, D. (2012). A compiler and run-time system for network programming languages. *ACM SIGPLAN Notices, 47*(1), 217–230. doi:10.1145/2103621.2103685

Monsanto, C., Reich, J., Foster, N., Rexford, J., & Walker, D. (2013, April). *Composing Software Defined Networks.* NSDI.

Nakao, A. (2012). *Flare: Open deeply programmable network node architecture.* Author.

Olsson, M., Rommer, S., Mulligan, C., Sultana, S., & Frid, L. (2009). *SAE and the Evolved Packet Core: Driving the mobile broadband revolution.* Academic Press.

Open Networking Foundation. (2012). *Software-Defined Networking: The New Norm for Networks.* ONF White Paper.

Open Networking Foundation. (2013). *SDN Architecture Overview.* Retrieved March 12, 2015, from https://www.opennetworking.org/images/stories/downloads/sdn-resources/technical-reports/SDN-architecture-overview-1.0.pdf

Open Networking Foundation. (2014). *SDN Architecture, Issue 1.* Retrieved March 12, 2015, from https://www.opennetworking.org/images/stories/downloads/sdn-resources/technical-reports/TR_SDN_ARCH_1.0_06062014.pdf

Open Networking Foundation. (2014). *OpenFlow Table Type Patterns Version 1.0.* Retrieved March 12, 2015, from https://www.opennetworking.org/images/stories/downloads/sdn-resources/onf-specifications/openflow/OpenFlow%20Table%20Type%20Patterns%20v1.0.pdf

Panda, A., Scott, C., Ghodsi, A., Koponen, T., & Shenker, S. (2013, August). CAP for Networks. In *Proceedings of the second ACM SIGCOMM workshop on Hot topics in software defined networking* (pp. 91-96). ACM. doi:10.1145/2491185.2491186

Parniewicz, D., Doriguzzi Corin, R., Ogrodowczyk, L., Rashidi Fard, M., Matias, J., Gerola, M., & Pentikousis, K. et al. (2014, August). Design and implementation of an OpenFlow hardware abstraction layer. In *Proceedings of the 2014 ACM SIGCOMM workshop on Distributed cloud computing* (pp. 71-76). ACM. doi:10.1145/2627566.2627577

Pentikousis, K., Wang, Y., & Hu, W. (2013). Mobileflow: Toward software-defined mobile networks. Communications Magazine, IEEE, 51(7).

Qin, Z., Denker, G., Giannelli, C., Bellavista, P., & Venkatasubramanian, N. (2014) A Software Defined Networking Architecture for the Internet-of-Things. *Network Operations and Management Symposium (NOMS).* IEEE. doi:10.1109/NOMS.2014.6838365

Reich, J., Monsanto, C., Foster, N., Rexford, J., & Walker, D. (2013). Modular SDN Programming with Pyretic. *USENIX Login, 38*(5), 128-134.

Rooney, S., van der Merwe, J. E., Crosby, S. A., & Leslie, I. M. (1998). The Tempest: A framework for safe, resource assured, programmable networks. *Communications Magazine, IEEE, 36*(10), 42–53. doi:10.1109/35.722136

Sezer, S., Scott-Hayward, S., Chouhan, P. K., Fraser, B., Lake, D., Finnegan, J., . . . Rao, N. (2013). Are we ready for SDN? Implementation challenges for software-defined networks. Communications Magazine, IEEE, 51(7).

Sherwood, R., Gibb, G., Yap, K. K., Appenzeller, G., Casado, M., McKeown, N., & Parulkar, G. (2009). Flowvisor: A network virtualization layer. *OpenFlow Switch Consortium, Tech. Rep.*

Smith, M., Dvorkin, M., Laribi, Y., Pandey, V., Garg, P. & Weidenbacher, N. (2014). OpFlex Control Protocol. *IETF individual draft, draft-smith-opflex-00.*

Song, H. (2013, August). Protocol-oblivious forwarding: Unleash the power of SDN through a future-proof forwarding plane. In *Proceedings of the second ACM SIGCOMM workshop on Hot topics in software defined networking* (pp. 127-132). ACM. doi:10.1145/2491185.2491190

Song, H. (2013, August). Protocol-oblivious forwarding: Unleash the power of SDN through a future-proof forwarding plane. In *Proceedings of the second ACM SIGCOMM workshop on Hot topics in software defined networking* (pp. 127-132). ACM. doi:10.1145/2491185.2491190

Telecommunication Standardization sector of ITU. (1990). *CCITT Recommendation 1.361, B-ISDN ATM Layer Specification*, Geneva, Switzerland: Author.

Telecommunication Standardization sector of ITU. (1993). *ITU, Q.700: Introduction to CCITT Signalling System No. 7.* Geneva, Switzerland: Author.

Tennenhouse, D. L., Smith, J. M., Sincoskie, W. D., Wetherall, D. J., & Minden, G. J. (1997). A survey of active network research. *Communications Magazine, IEEE, 35*(1), 80–86. doi:10.1109/35.568214

Valdivieso Caraguay, Á. L., Benito Peral, A., Barona López, L. I., & García Villalba, L. J. (2014). SDN: Evolution and Opportunities in the Development IoT Applications. *International Journal of Distributed Sensor Networks*, 2014.

Voellmy, A., Kim, H., & Feamster, N. (2012, August). Procera: a language for high-level reactive network control. In *Proceedings of the first workshop on Hot topics in software defined networks* (pp. 43-48). ACM. doi:10.1145/2342441.2342451

Wetherall, D. J., Guttag, J. V., & Tennenhouse, D. L. (1998, April). ANTS: A toolkit for building and dynamically deploying network protocols. In Open Architectures and Network Programming, 1998 IEEE (pp. 117-129). IEEE. doi:10.1109/OPNARC.1998.662048

Yap, K. K., Kobayashi, M., Sherwood, R., Huang, T. Y., Chan, M., Handigol, N., & McKeown, N. (2010). OpenRoads: Empowering research in mobile networks. *Computer Communication Review, 40*(1), 125–126. doi:10.1145/1672308.1672331

ADDITIONAL READING

Boucadair, M., & Jacquenet, C. (2014). Software-Defined Networking: A Perspective from within a Service Provider Environment. RFC 7149

Google. 2012. Inter-Datacenter WAN with centralized TE using SDN and OpenFlow: https://www.opennetworking.org/images/stories/downloads/sdn-resources/customer-case-studies/cs-googlesdn.pdf

IETF SFC working group. Retrieved March 12, 2015, from https://datatracker.ietf.org/wg/sfc/charter/

IRTF NFV research group. (proposed). Retrieved March 12, 2015, from http://trac.tools.ietf.org/group/irtf/trac/wiki/nfvrg

IRTF SDN research group. Retrieved March 12, 2015, from https://irtf.org/sdnrg

King, D., & Farrel, A. (2013). A PCE-based architecture for application-based network operations.

Kreutz, D., Ramos, F., Verissimo, P., Rothenberg, C. E., Azodolmolky, S., & Uhlig, S. (2014). Software-Defined Networking: A Comprehensive Survey. arXiv preprint arXiv:1406.0440.

Nadeau, T. D., & Gray, K. (2013). *SDN: Software Defined Networks*. O'Reilly Media, Inc.

OpenDaylight project. Retrieved March 12, 2015, from http://www.opendaylight.org

KEY TERMS AND DEFINITIONS

Abstraction Layer: A layer that abstracts one or more layers below to a layer above.

Control Plane: Network functionality that assigns one or more network devices on how to treat packets.

Forwarding Plane: Resources of network devices that relate to the data path.

Management Plane: Network functionality responsible for maintaining and managing the network.

Network Device: A device that performs one or more network operations.

Resource: A component available within a system.

Software Defined Networks: A programmable networks approach that allows software to programs to manipulate the network.

Chapter 17
Network Functions Virtualization:
Going beyond the Carrier Cloud

Diego R. López
Telefónica I+D, Spain

Pedro A. Aranda
Telefónica I+D, Spain

ABSTRACT

Network Functions Virtualization (NFV) has emerged as a new paradigm for designing, deploying and operating network services. It is a natural evolution of the current trend of applying cloud technologies to Information Technology (IT) services, bringing them to network provider environments. While this is true for the most simple use cases, focused on the IT services network providers rely on, the nature of network services and the physical anchors of network themselves impose additional, unique requirements on the virtualization process in this environment. At the same time, NFV provides an opportunity to network providers, reducing operational costs and bringing the promise of dramatically easing the development of new services, reducing their time-to-market, and opening new possibilities for service provisioning. This chapter analyses these requirements and opportunities and the challenges NFV brings to network providers, and reviews the current state of the art in this new way of dealing with network services.

ENTER THE SOFTWARE-DEFINED ERA

The integration of Information Technologies and Communications, commonly referred as ICT, has been more a long-term goal than a reality for a long time. Roughly speaking, networking and computing knew an evolution at comparable pace till the global availability of the Internet and the almost pervasive application of its base protocols to any networking problem. Not surprisingly, the very success of these basic principles made the evolution of network technologies more and more difficult, precisely because they were the base for the radical changes that were taking place in the IT arena, around the ideas of Internet-based services and, most of all, the cloud.

DOI: 10.4018/978-1-4666-8371-6.ch017

IT evolution and, in particular the evolution of Internet-based services, have been rooted on the successive revolutions in software development practices, and in more and more powerful abstractions easing the conception, creation and operation of these services. This software-based nature has allowed business actors in the IT services arena to become agile in terms of satisfying new requirements and deploying new solutions, best exemplified by the DevOps paradigm in Loukides (2012) a set of best practices gaining strong momentum in the IT industry, and focused on the tight communication (and even integration) of the activities related to development, operations, and quality assurance.

Network infrastructures, on the other side, became tied to their topologies and the requirements on using open, standardized interfaces among the different nodes in these topologies. While the development of network nodes became certainly software intensive, the evolution of network services was tied to longer innovation cycles, requiring the agreement on standards among node producers. What is more, the generalization of the network node as the basic functional unit implied an enormous degree of heterogeneity in network elements and their management procedures, what translated in additional problems for any attempt to make infrastructure evolution agile or able to satisfy evolving user requirements.

On the Internet arena we had on the one hand network service providers, dealing with highly-heterogeneous and difficult to evolve infrastructures, and unable to address in a timely manner specific user requirements or to cover long-tail demand at any reasonable cost, while on the other hand there were the IT service providers, much more agile, relying on an almost uniform infrastructure, and able to adapt and evolve their software at a much faster pace, therefore being able to increase their value while network infrastructures were becoming more and more ossified.

The advent of cloud computing was not only a forward step in IT service virtualization, as they did not need to be hosted at a physical infrastructure operated by the IT service provider anymore, but at the same time it implied some additional requirements on the network infrastructure that could not be solved by means of the usual techniques applied so far. These additional requirements on flexibility (the network had to adapt to the ever-changing cloud configuration) and abstraction (applications needed to interact with the network as a resource among others) brought the need for a different conceptual framework for networks, beyond the usual concepts so far. Furthermore, the idea of running IT services on virtualized infrastructures made some researchers think on the possibility of doing the same for the functions performed at the nodes of the network, what we will be refer in the following as network functions. These two orthogonal directions constituted the basis for the current trends in network "softwarisation".

Network softwarisation is a general term referring to all techniques oriented towards the application of two main and related principles:

- Providing a general interface for the provisioning, management, control and invocation of network resources, by means of software abstractions that hide complexity and deployment details of actual network infrastructures.
- Decoupling the different planes conforming the network, and using open interfaces between them, in order to make the supporting infrastructure as much regular and homogeneous as possible, and relying on software mechanisms to support specialized functionalities.

With this approach, network services are provided by a layered structure, grounded on general-purpose, homogenous hardware, with one or several software layers running on top of it and defining network behaviour and functionalities in general. Everything running on the network, from basic functionalities to user applications, and including management and operation elements, becomes software modules that use the open interfaces exposed by each layer.

There are two essential directions for network softwarisation that can be applied independently, though they greatly benefit from their simultaneous application, to the degree of being suitable to be considered essentially intertwined. Software Defined Networking (SDN) goes for the decoupling of the control and data planes in a network to gain programmability and simplify data plane elements, while Network Functions Virtualization (NFV) goes beyond, advocating for the general separation of functionality (on software) and capacity (on a general virtualization layer running upon standard regular hardware), increasing network elasticity and drastically reducing the heterogeneity of the supporting infrastructure. SDN and NFV are not competing technologies, but complementary. NFV goals can be achieved using non-SDN mechanisms, relying on the techniques currently in use in many datacentres, but approaches relying on the separation of the control and data forwarding planes as proposed by SDN can enhance performance, simplify compatibility with existing deployments, and facilitate operation and maintenance procedures. Given a network environment based on virtualized functions, the provision of the different virtual appliances and, particularly, the logical connectivity among them would need to be as flexible and natural as possible. It would be hard to understand that a flexible environment where virtual network nodes could be created and expanded on demand were possible but setting up the connectivity among these virtual appliances required semi-manual provision. Furthermore, NFV is able to support SDN by providing the infrastructure upon which the SDN software can be run.

This chapter is dedicated to the description and analysis of NFV and its main features. The NFV essential concepts and its expected benefits will be discussed in the following section, followed by a brief history of the idea and its main milestones: the history is necessarily brief as the NFV concept was coined in formal terms around three years ago. We will follow with a description of the main drivers and use cases for NFV, plus a definition of the different fundamental elements that constitute the NFV architecture framework: the virtualized infrastructure, the functional components and their design patterns, and the management of orchestration required to put infrastructure and components to work so they can build the intended network infrastructure services. Since a new technology like this cannot be free of (important) challenges we will end the chapter with a description of the most salient ones.

THE NFV CONCEPT, BENEFITS, AND RISKS

NFV is a technology (or set of technologies) aimed to build network infrastructure services the same way IT services are constructed relying on current cloud infrastructures. NFV advocates a homogeneous supporting infrastructure providing computing, storage and connectivity mechanisms, which are expected to be accessed through a common virtualization interface by involved software elements that implement the actual network functions. It is important to note the double role of network facilities. There is a layer of homogeneous, virtualized network mechanisms used to support the interconnection of the elements (hardware and software) required by the software modules implementing the second, upper layer of network functions running on the infrastructure.

Figure 1 illustrates the general model for NFV showing its different layers:

These layers are:

1. The NFV Infrastructure (NFVI), able to provide a set of virtual resources for computing, storage and networking through a virtual-

Figure 1. The general NFV model

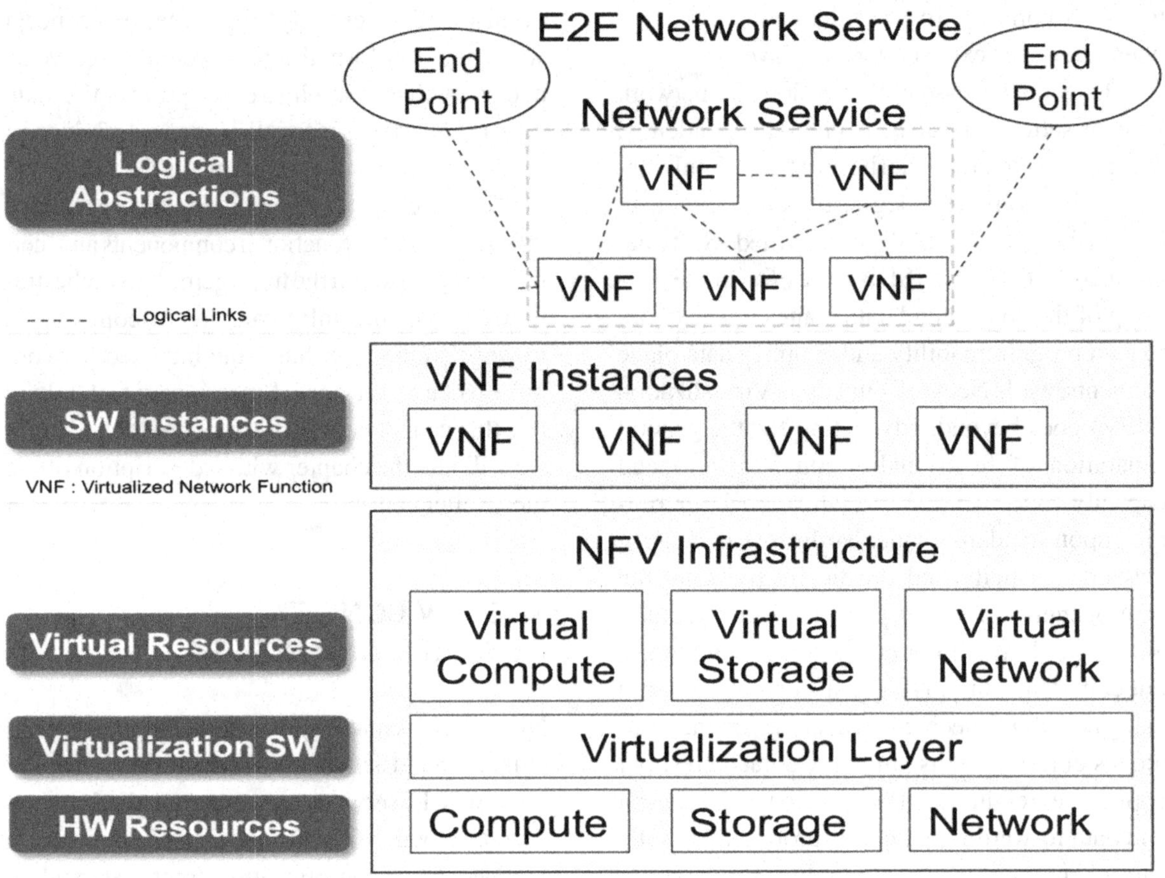

ization layer that abstracts actual hardware resources that provide the required support to the computing, storage and networking mechanisms.

2. The set of software instances implementing the Virtualized Network Functions (VNFs, think of virtualized intrusion detection systems, virtualized Evolved Packet Core elements, virtualized home gateways…). Each of these software instances are deployed on top of the NFVI and, as such, are suitable for relocation, replication, deletion, and any other kind of operation required to maintain the appropriate performance and reliability of the functions they provide.
3. The network services: Actual network services are created by composing several of these VNFs in a Forwarding Graph and attaching them to network endpoints.

In common practice, we can consider the NFVI as composed by a cloud-like infrastructure of physical computing and storage servers running hypervisors, interconnected by a regular switching fabric able to support common network virtualization mechanisms such as overlays or VLANs, possibly with detached data and control planes by using OpenFlow by McKeown et al. (2008) or an equivalent protocol. NFVI can be distributed, i.e. located at different points of presence, and this implies that WAN links and their control are to be considered within NFVI as well in most cases.

The realization of a VNF can be seen as one or more Virtual Machines (VMs), each one executing the software performing all or a certain set of the whole VNF functionality on the NFVI hypervisors. These VMs are usually termed VNF Components (VNFC) and are interconnected by means of NFVI network mechanisms to guarantee the functional (equivalent to their non-virtualized counterparts) and non-functional requirements (in terms of performance, security, reliability,...) of the associated network function.

The VNFs built this way become part of network services constructed by composing them in a service forwarding graph. It is worth noting that this architecture is essentially recursive: the network services built this way can constitute the underlying network layer supporting a VNF in an upper layer.

More than Carrier Clouds

In several points above we have used the term "cloud-like infrastructures" to refer to the NFVI, and implicitly made reference to usual cloud characteristics like resilience or elasticity by replication. Looking at this, it would seem natural to consider that NFV could be achieved by a direct application of cloud technologies to substitute the physical network elements by virtual implementations running on the current cloud infrastructures, probably enhanced to support additional requests on resiliency and reliability according to what has come to be called "carrier cloud".

While this was probably an initial guess in many cases, there are three essential aspects that distinguish NFV from the direct application of cloud technologies to provide network infrastructure services, and therefore require going beyond carrier clouds to implement NFV.

First of all, the kind of workloads that NFV implies is completely different from the kind of workloads considered by the current cloud practice. VNFs are extremely dependent on direct I/O and memory operations, and much less on direct computing or storage access. And this not only has impact on VNF performance when deployed directly following "classical cloud" mechanism, but also (and even most significantly) on the portability of VNF instances across the cloud infrastructure. Available experimental evidence shows high performance deviations among workload distributions that were considered completely equal by classical cloud VM placement mechanisms in ETSI-NFV-ISG (2014). To properly achieve performance and portability goals, it is necessary to improve cloud orchestrators, hypervisors, kernels and even hardware drivers to support finer-grained placement policies, provide better control of direct memory communication among software instances, and override the virtualization layer for direct I/O to network interfaces. Many of the required techniques are inspired by those currently applied in high-performance computing, like NUMA in Cong & Wen (2013).

Secondly, network services need to adapt to network shape. While the classical cloud applications are endpoints in a communication (the archetypal web server in many cases), most network infrastructure services are middle-points (for example, a router or a firewall) and many of them are subject to stringent delay requirements and/or similar constraints. That implies that infrastructures and VM placement strategies must adapt to the network shape and support both highly centralized and consolidated datacentres in the cases they can be used and their economies of scale applied, and much more decentralized schemas, where the cloud becomes close to the fog concept presented in Bonomi et al. (2012). The important point here is not only to support both kinds of deployments but also to be able to seamlessly integrate them.

Finally, when it comes to the orchestration and management of the resources, it is worth noting again that we are dealing with networks at two layers: the supporting infrastructure already present in the current clouds, and the upper network service layer provided by VNFs and their composition into services. To guarantee performance, upper network services may need to directly manipulate the underlying network infrastructure well beyond the limits of usual northbound interfaces exposed by the SDN controllers that are being deployed within current cloud datacentres.

Actors in NFV and the Interfaces between Them

Figure 2 illustrates the different actors that can intervene in a fully virtualized network infrastructure, according to the layered model we discussed above for NFV:

1. NFVI Providers offer access to the rest of the actors: they provide access to datacentre and communication links that constitute the NFVI, mostly using the access models already described for cloud, like IaaS and PaaS, but additional ones as well, as it is the case of NaaS (Network-as-a-Service).
2. VNF Tenants run their VNFs on top of the NFVI, and can provide VNFs to potential users on an individual basis (VNFaaS), or together with additional tooling kits supporting higher-level integration and management (VNPaaS).
3. Admins of different enterprises integrate the VNFs into their network services, either for internal use or for actively providing them to third parties.
4. Network Service Providers assemble VNFs and attach them to a public network accord-

Figure 2. Actors in the NFV ecosystem

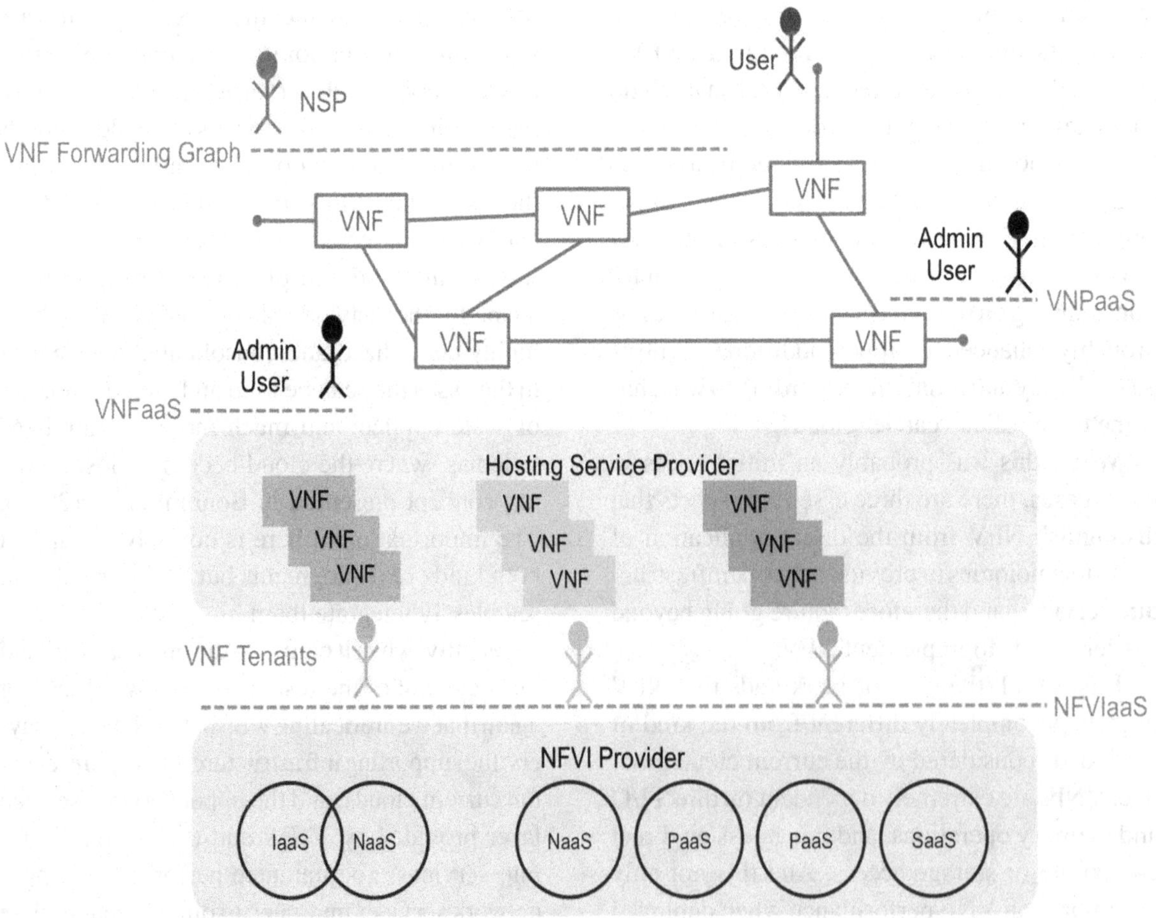

ing to a VNF Forwarding Graph, creating a virtualized network service. These services will imply in many cases the integration of virtualized and non-virtualized elements.

5. Finally, Users consume the services offered by NSPs or their Admins.

It is obvious that any two or more of the roles described in points 1 to 4 above can be merged, and that the most likely scenario for the initial phases will consist of a full integration of all roles by the network service provider, with a coming stage where independent NFVI providers will emerge and their NFVI offer will be utilized by network operators to run (part of) their VNFs and services. Mixed scenarios, where high integration is applied for certain kinds of functions, while other specialized ones are provided by specific tenants are foreseeable as well.

Another important point is that any of the four degrees of freedom described above can be split into additional layers according to the state of the network infrastructure market and even because of regulatory reasons requiring to guarantee or enhance open competition in that market.

The Expected Benefits of NFV

The original whitepaper in Chiosi et al. (2012) that we can consider as the founding manifesto of NFV, states an initial list of potential direct benefits from applying virtualization to network functions:

- *Reduced equipment costs and reduced power consumption through consolidating equipment and exploiting the economies of scale of the IT industry.*
- *Increased speed of Time to Market by minimizing the typical network operator cycle of innovation. Economies of scale required to cover investments in hardware-based functionalities are no longer applicable for software-based development, making feasible other modes of feature evolution. Network Functions Virtualization should enable network operators to significantly reduce the maturation cycle.*
- *Availability of network appliance multi-version and multi-tenancy, which allows use of a single platform for different applications, users and tenants. This allows network operators to share resources across services and across different customer bases.*
- *Targeted service introduction based on geography or customer sets is possible. Services can be rapidly scaled up/down as required.*
- *Enables a wide variety of eco-systems and encourages openness. It opens the virtual appliance market to pure software entrants, small players and academia, encouraging more innovation to bring new services and new revenue streams quickly at much lower risk.*

Beyond this, NFV proponents foresee a great business value in applying NFV in terms of cost savings and additional revenue sources for network operators, new opportunities for solution providers and, most importantly, in opening new business models and innovation opportunities. Let us consider the most compelling breakthroughs that NFV brings to network operation and management while we identify their main implications in terms of emerging business models.

First of all, when building the infrastructure, a network operator (or another party willing to become an infrastructure provider) can invest in a pool of general resources that are configured on-demand for specific purposes when needed, rather than investing in multiple pools of specific network devices with tailored functions. These pools can be:

- Shared by different business units within an operator, bringing new internal business organization and planning.
- Shared by different operators, paving the way for much deeper and more flexible mechanisms for infrastructure sharing.
- Provided by third parties, which implies new business opportunities for infrastructure providers and new potential models for network service providers to operate.

To provide network functionality, a virtual function can be instantiated on-demand wherever it is needed in the network, rather than only at those points where the dedicated device is located. This decoupling of function and location brings possibilities for:

- Independent providers to offer network functions as a service to network service providers, following similar technology and charging patterns to those currently in use in cloud infrastructures.
- Network operators to provide long-tail services that are practically impossible to address with current infrastructures, covering new market niches, expanding their service and charging options, and enabling a new breed of application services relying on them.
- Entrepreneurs in Over-the-top (OTT) services to become able to compete in quality-of-experience with established providers at reasonable costs by means of agreements with network service providers for specialized services.

Taking advantage of the virtualization layer, the pool of servers can be updated in a much easier way. Therefore, network service providers can benefit more quickly from advances in hardware and translate them into gains for all their network functions and services. This enhanced update capability allows for:

- Shorter innovation cycles in hardware infrastructures, enabling innovative agents to gain market momentum at a much faster pace, and reducing the entry barrier for new players.
- A more open competition among infrastructure vendors, infrastructure providers, and network service providers themselves.

Furthermore, new functions can be added or improved by updating a software image, rather than waiting for a vendor to develop and manufacture a dedicated appliance. This is probably the most revolutionary aspect of NFV and it implies:

- Breaking the current vertical integration silos that link network hardware, network software, and network management elements.
- Bringing open-source development and business models to network design, operation and management.
- Simplifying the evaluation and adoption of new solutions, enhancing the market applicability of research and innovation results.
- Opening the field for new service models, integrating network and application services.
- Allowing the application of well-known software development principles and tools to network planning, design, development, and operation.

Finally, management and operation can be performed by means of software image configuration and orchestration, reducing the complexity of managing a myriad of dedicated, heterogeneous devices. This characteristic is very much connected with the one just discussed. However, the management and operation aspects have interesting implications to current network business models, as they:

- Allow a much easier support for network multi-tenancy and slicing, supporting new mechanisms for managed services in both directions: either managed by the operators for customers, or managed by third parties for the operators.
- Enable the application of DevOps principles in network management, aligning them with the practices that have made IT service providers so agile in addressing user requests and incorporating innovation results.

And the Risks

As any significant change in the base network technologies, the evolution towards NFV implies risks that can translate into higher costs and performance degradation. The major risk factors are related to potential gaps derived from technology immaturity and the required changes in operational models.

NFV defines (actually is still defining) a new set of standards that imply a deep reshaping of the concepts that have guided the creation of network infrastructures, and the development of the hardware and software implementing network functionality, bringing new principles for essential properties like redundancy, resiliency and security. Furthermore, the changes in operational models will not only deeply affect the structure of network provider operations at all levels (business process, support systems, staffing…) but also bring a new definition of the relationships between operators and vendors.

From a general risk management perspective, NFV deployments shall consider maintaining a high level of pre-integration where possible and to closely follow, evaluate, and test the matureness of technology and standards. Furthermore, it also makes sense to start by migrating selected services in early phases, starting for well-controlled scenarios focused on specific geographical areas, end user profiles or target application environments. This approach may limit the complexity of troubleshooting and also serve as an isolated system where technology, tools and methodology for troubleshooting can be refined and evaluated in parallel to building competence.

A practical example of the combination of the risks mentioned above, that may mostly affect early deployments, is the initial lack of the appropriate combination of sufficiently powerful tools and the years-long expertise currently available in network operations, from testing and validation procedures to fault diagnosis and troubleshooting. This could imply much higher costs in terms of fault management and performance degradation assessment. Lack of tooling support could translate mostly into higher rates of escalation to second-line management, while lack of a widespread expertise could result in errors in root cause detection and longer response time. This can have a great impact on OPEX and even translate into poor end-user performance if the number and severity of second-line incident reports increase beyond the capacity of the second-line management. Any realistic NFV deployment plan will require both the infrastructure technology and the virtualized network functions to be equipped with good tracing capabilities and whatever other troubleshooting tools ready from day one. Similarly the technology transformation has to be matched with a sufficient level of staff competence – either provided in-house through hands-on training or brought in from external sources.

A SHORT HISTORY OF NFV

Network operators and some network equipment manufacturers had been working on technologies related to network virtualization for some years, and in particular on the ideas around running network functions on general-purpose servers and cloud infrastructures, mostly inspired by the impact of cloud technologies in all fields of IT. By the beginning of this decade, encouraging results on the performance of these solutions for real-world network workloads were attained. Some informal discussions began to take place, mainly among operators, and there was a general will of seeking a common understanding and facilitating industry progress in this area.

A meeting of several of the world largest network operators in Paris in June 2012 not only coined the term "Network Functions Virtualization" to label the technology, but also was the starting point for convening a wider industry forum and starting the preparation of a joint whitepaper intended to define the vision and goals of NFV, and to galvanize the community about what the group was sure was a radical paradigm shift in the networking industry. The whitepaper, with the contribution of 13 network operators worldwide, was made public on October 2012, as a "call to action".

One of the first decisions to foster the development of the just named NFV was to make the industry forum supporting it as open as possible, so the decision was to follow the principles of open standards. A second decision, to root the forum at an existing standards organization, was taken in order to shorten the time necessary to formally establish it. After the consideration of several choices, an Industry Specification Group (ISG) under ETSI was created. The ETSI ISG formula provided a rather flexible and open umbrella for the NFV activities. First of all, it was open to any organization willing to participate, independently of its being full member of ETSI or not: only an agreement has to be signed, basically acknowledging the open nature of the results, and the procedures for producing and agreeing on them defined by the ISG Terms of Reference. Given the importance of swiftly producing a sound set of documents that could act as reference for the industry, flexibility was as important as openness to achieve the NFV goal. The ISG model appeared as the right combination of flexibility and formal guarantees for this goal, and experience has confirmed this impression.

The first plenary of the NFV ISG took place in January 2013. The group elected a chairman and a vice-chairman, and the work was structured around five groups, coordinated by a Technical Steering Committee (TSC):

- INF, in charge of defining the supporting NFV infrastructure (NFVI) elements and interfaces.
- SWA, focused on the architecture and design patterns for the virtualized network functions (VNFs) running on top of the NFVI.
- MANO, with the mandate of defining how the orchestration and management of the network services based on the VNFs should be performed.
- REL, aimed at considering how the stringent reliability requirements of network services could be satisfied by means of this new approach to build them.
- PER, centred on providing best practices to support sustainable performance and guaranteed portability of VNFs and the services based on them.
- SEC, dedicated to the analysis of the potential security issues introduced by the new NFV approach of mobile software running on a virtualized infrastructure.

Since its creation, the ISG has released several documents and produced a second joint operator whitepaper, discussing the perspectives of network operators on the progress of the NFV approach. The first batch, dealing with end-to-end issues, was delivered after only 10 months. This batch included the reference architecture framework shown in Figure 3, that has become the essential reference for any further activity around NFV. The group has also created a framework to define and run Proof-of-Concept (PoC) experiments. These experiments are intended to both explore technology options in the NFV space, and to contribute to demonstrate the feasibility of the NFV approach and create awareness on it. At the moment of this writing, the ISG has more than 200 participating organizations, and is mostly involved in producing a comprehensive document release, due by the end of its initial two-year term, as well as discussing the future evolution of the group once this initial term comes to its end.

The activities around NFV have not been limited to the ETSI ISG, but have spawned into other Standards Defining organizations (SDOs). To just name a few, these other bodies include the IETF/IRTF (with initiatives like VNFPOOL and the proposed NFVRG), TMForum and its ZOOM project, BBF, DMTF, and the ONF. The obvious connection between NFV and cloud technologies has translated into direct contributions to open-source projects, with OpenStack as main focus, as well as the recently initiated OPNFV project.

Furthermore, practically all the major network operators have announced their participation in different kinds of PoCs, and even started real-service pilots, like Telefónica in Brazil. All major network equipment manufacturers have made announcements regarding their new platforms for NFV, while other players including IT manufacturers, academia and a great number of small-size companies and start-ups have gathered under the NFV banner and are actively contributing to its consolidation and further evolution.

DRIVERS AND USE CASES

Both Software Defined Networking (SDN) and NFV have been made possible by the growth in computing power and the extension of virtualization-specific support functions in mainstream processors we have experienced in the last years. Current commercial-off-the-shelf (COTS) servers have enough computing power to implement network functions with high throughput requirements. In addition, cloud computing has delivered tools to automate and control high-volume deployments in datacentres. In contrast, network equipment has been based on extremely specialized hardware and software platforms. From the point of view of a network operator, this has resulted in vendor lock-in, practically no possibility of reusing equipment as their service portfolio evolves and very long time-to-market and innovation cycles. With strong competitive pressures, due to the emergence of OTT service providers with radically different cost structures and the increase in competition, network providers regard NFV as an opportunity to reduce vendor lock-in, improve reusability and, in general, reshape their cost structure in order to improve their profit margins.

NFV capitalizes on the *softwarisation* of the network: network functions are implemented as programs that run on standardized software and when a certain service is not demanded anymore, the resources (i.e., the servers) where it was implemented can be easily repurposed for new services.

The ETSI NFV ISG has produced a use case specification document ETSI-NFV-ISG (2013c) that motivates different use cases of the NFV architectures to highlight the benefits of the introduction of NFV for the network architecture and for the services. The architectural use cases are rooted in the concept of *everything as a Service* (XaaS) introduced in the cloud computing world. The ETSI NFV ISG provides the following architectural use cases:

- Network Functions Virtualization Infrastructure as a Service
- Virtual Network Function as a Service
- Virtual Network Platform as a Service
- VNF Forwarding Graphs

And a series of service-related use cases that highlight different challenges:

- Mobile core network and IMS
- Mobile base stations
- Home environment
- Content Delivery Networks (CDNs)
- Fixed access network

Figure 3. The NFV Reference Architecture Framework as in ETSI-NFV-ISG (2013a)

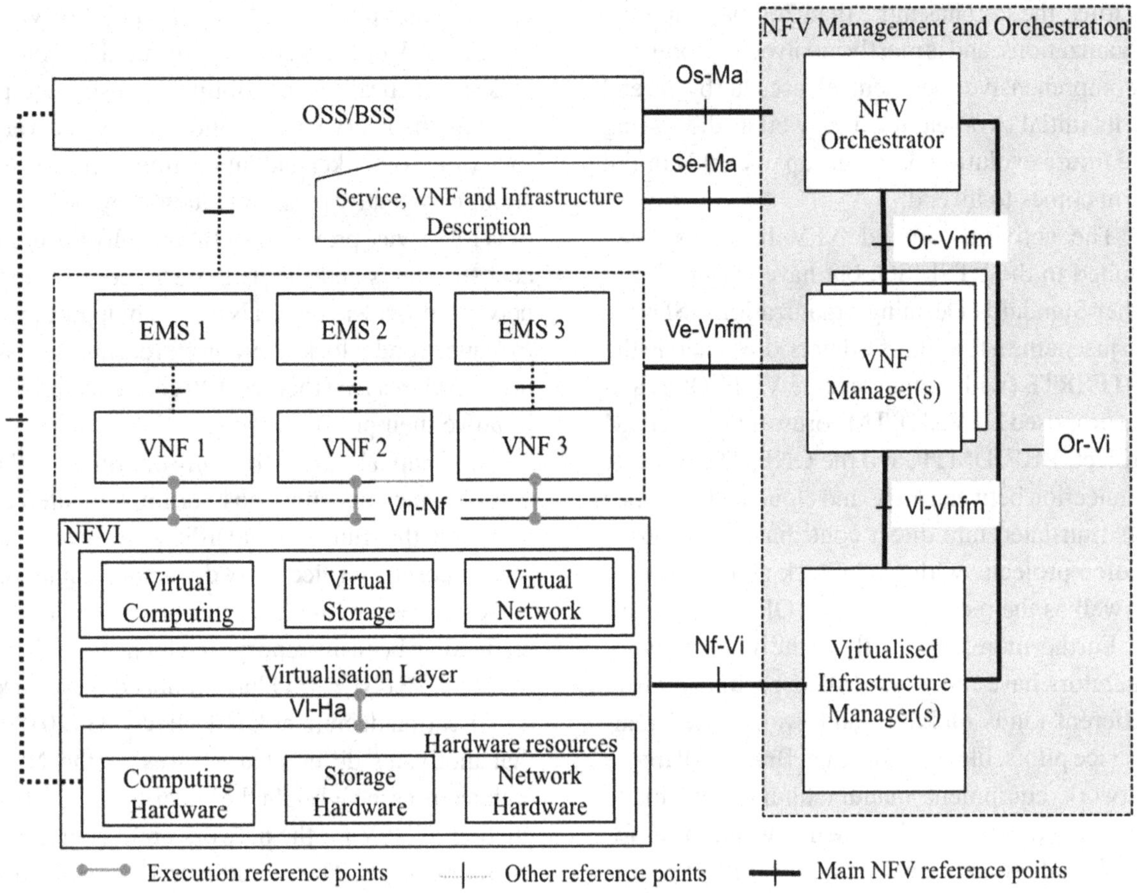

Extending and building on the concepts and lessons learnt from the *Infrastructure as a Service* (IaaS) concept in the Cloud world, NFV has introduced the notion of Network Function Virtualization as a Service (NFVIaaS). If IaaS allowed datacentre providers to offer their infrastructure to clients who are not in a position to implement their own full-fledged datacentres in the form of virtual datacentres, NFVIaaS foresees the emergence of big NFV Infrastructure providers that resell their resources to clients who want to implement their services based on NFV but are not able to implement their own infrastructure.

Also based on prior experience in the cloud work, the ETSI NFV ISG proposes a use case where a provider runs this VNF on his NFV Infrastructure and offers it to the end customer as a service. The VNF envisaged in the use case deals with the emerging services a business user is confronted with by trends like *Bring Your Own Device* (BYOD), etc. Instead of furnishing the (business) end user with a complex device that needs frequent updates, etc., the network operator implements the complex functions on a VNF he offers to the user. This concept is equivalent to the *Software as a Service* (SaaS) concept in the cloud world. The next step in the cloud world was to allow a client to mix and match offerings from several providers in what is known as the *Platform as a Service* (PaaS) paradigm. In the NFV use cases, it translates into the *Virtual Network Platform as a Service* (VNPaaS). This use case illustrates the sharing of an infrastructure by several clients and the need for authorization as well as resource control in order to guarantee the correct functioning of the infrastructure. It shows how multi-tenancy can be implemented at the VNF level.

In addition to translating the lessons learnt in Cloud environments, the ETSI NFV ISG also shows how VNF graphs can be used to compose services end-to-end. It is based on a catalogue of VNFs that have a set of published, standardized interfaces at different layers. The VNFs implement the same functionalities as equivalent physical network functions that are readily available in the market. It then compares both solutions and shows the benefits introduced by the VNF solution. This comparison, shown in Table 1, holds for VNFs in general and not only for a specific use case.

Comparison of Physical and Virtualized Network Functions

The service-oriented use cases present the case of virtualizing different components of the network and the positive aspects of doing so. The mobile core virtualization is a realistic target: a network infrastructure with a significant number of functions which mainly implement the control plane of the network and which are currently distributed in different boxes. These functions can be easily virtualized and deployed on a datacentre-alike infrastructure. The Open IMS Core project in *Open IMS Core* shows how the Call Session Control Functions (CSCFs) and the Home Subscriber Server (HSS) can be implemented as virtualized functions. It also demonstrates a side-effect of the virtualization trend: by removing the dependence on proprietary hardware and relying on a software-only solution, new entrants can more easily offer their products, some with Open Source licensing schemes. The same stands for the Open EPC project *OpenEPC - Open Evolved Packet Core*, which furnishes implementations for all functional components for an Evolved Packet Core.

INFRASTRUCTURE

The objective of NFV is essentially to separate the software that defines the network functionality (the Virtualized Network Function, VNF) from the hardware and generic software providing its capacity to function (the NFV Infrastructure, NFVI). It is therefore a requirement that the VNFs and the NFVI be separately specified.

The NFV architecture framework defines the term NFVI as the totality of the hardware and software components constituting the environment in which VNFs are deployed and run. The NFVI is deployed as one or more nodes that collectively

Table 1.

	Physical Appliance	Virtual Appliance
Efficiency	Dedicated (rigid) and sized for peak load (underutilized)	Function and size depending on current load
Resilience	Backup on specific hardware and dedicated resources. Requires additional network capacity	Backup may share resources and network capacity.
Flexibility	Lengthy deployment cycles, upgrade sometimes not possible	Shorter cycles and easier deployment, since functions are SW based
Complexity	Graph depends/can only be deployed on a given physical network layer	Virtualized networking layer can be adapted easily to forwarding graphs
Deployability	Requires physical boxes when deployed on another provider's premises/infrastructure	Virtualization eases the deployment of a given function on another provider's infrastructure

implement the required functionality to support the execution environment for VNFs. A location where a NFVI node is deployed is an NFVI Point of Presence (PoP). A PoP may contain one or more nodes as well as other network elements. The NFVI PoPs form a distributed infrastructure able to support the locality (in terms of network topology) and latency requirements of the particular functions and their flexible deployment and operation. NFVI nodes and PoPs build the dynamically reconfigurable platform for the execution of the VNFs, according to the requirement of the different actors in the NFV ecosystem we described in a previous section.

Cloud Computing and the NFVI

Cloud computing is clearly an essential enabler for NFV, and it is at the root of the NFV concept itself. NFV has to leverage on technologies that are currently applied in cloud computing. At the core of these technologies are hardware virtualization mechanisms by means of hypervisors, and the usage of virtual Ethernet switches for transferring traffic between virtual machines and physical interfaces (though other possible virtualization mechanisms could be applicable, the current focus of the NFV community is on these techniques). Furthermore, current cloud approaches provide methods to enhance resource availability and usage by means of orchestration and management mechanisms, applicable to the automatic instantiation of VNFs, resource management, re-initialization of failed VMs, creation of VM state snapshots, migration of VMs, etc.

In terms of the NIST definition of cloud computing in Mell & Grance (2011), NFV can be seen as a type of Private Cloud IaaS where VNFs are executed in support of the services that a network operator provides. The execution environment for VNFs is provided by the distributed NFVI, which implies a challenge to the common understanding about management centralization as a relevant benefit of cloud computing, as we noted above when talking about adapting NFV to the network shape.

The NIST definition of cloud computing identifies five essential characteristics of cloud services. Since NFV encompasses these five characteristics, it could be considered as an application of cloud technology and it is clear that a NFVI should provide equivalent support of these essential characteristics:

1. **On-demand self-service**. The consumer of the NFVI expects to be able to unilaterally provision and allocate existing deployed NFVI resource capacity (server time, storage capacity…). In many cases, this resource allocation will be made directly by the VNFs or, more properly, by the management and orchestration functions coordinating them. Allocation shall follow the patterns required to provide a sustainable and predictable VNF performance.
2. **Broad network access**. NIST describes broad network access in cloud computing as providing capabilities that are available over the network and can be accessed through standard mechanisms that promote use by heterogeneous thin or thick client platforms. The NFVI PoPs are to be accessed remotely, and VNFs will handle the network traffic of a variety of existing network elements and terminal types. The network access capacity required at a particular PoP will depend on the fields of application of the VNFs instantiated at that PoP, which is also related to the requirement to adapt the NFVI to the shape of the network.
3. **Resource pooling**. While a single VNF might be deployed at a single PoP, in general, the NFVI is expected to support multiple VNFs from different service providers in a multi-tenant model. Resource demands on the NFVI are expected to change dynamically with the service load processed by the VNFs. Location independence is an objec-

tive in that specific VNFs should not be constrained to only run on dedicated NFVI hardware resources, beyond requirements related to their semantics, such as latency or resiliency.

4. **Rapid elasticity**. VNF operation will request rapid elasticity along with automated provisioning and release of the computing, storage and communication resources of the NFVI. In most cases these requests should be triggered in response to events related to the service load processed by the VNF, to the rearrangement of resources for optimization of NFVI usage by the management and orchestration mechanisms, as well as to failover and recovery procedures.
5. **Measured service**. The management and orchestration of VNFs will normally require the automatic control and optimization of NFVI resource usage by the VNFs. This optimization implies that the use of those resources by individual VNFs is metered in some fashion appropriate to each particular resource.

In the light of the service models applicable to cloud, the advent of NFV provides different opportunities, not only for network operators but also to other potential new actors in the network service arena. VNFs are software applications running on cloud-like infrastructures, offering functions that can process data and control plane traffic for a network operator rather than just web services:

- In IaaS, the capability provided is the provisioning of compute, storage and communication resources so that applications can be run on them. Here, the VNFs are the applications intended to be run and the virtualization infrastructure in which they are executed provides an IaaS for the network operator. The NFVI should provide the appropriate security mechanisms to ensure that only authorized entities have access to NFVI resources.
- NFV provides an opportunity to significantly improve the speed with which new services and applications are developed and deployed. The PaaS model provides a service model consistent with deployment of services constructed by the composition of multiple VNF instances.
- While many VNFs are expected to be typically executed according to a private cloud model by the network operator, some categories may be amenable to be executed in a third party cloud infrastructure and utilized in a SaaS model.

Finally, let us consider the different deployment models for cloud infrastructures and their applicability to the NFV case. In a first stage, most (if not all) of the NFVI and VNF instances will be deployed and operated by the same network operator using them. Hence, this initial deployment will be essentially aligned with the private cloud model. A possible next step could be the constitution of collaboration models among operators, or even among operators and software or service vendors. These models could lead to the deployment of community clouds, though the scope and extension of such community clouds remain to be seen. While it seems rather unlikely that VNFs and the services using them will integrally be hosted in current public clouds, a model based on an evolution of this public cloud approach could see the light as NFV matures and a clearer understanding of Service Level Agreements (SLAs) and security requirements becomes available. Finally, operators may be interested from the initial stages in a hybrid cloud deployment model where they maintain an IaaS private cloud for their own services. However, this infrastructure is offered on a wholesale basis to host VNFs from other service providers, and extended to provide VNFs-as-a-Service for enterprises, or other operators.

The NFVI Domains

In order to deal with the complexity of the infrastructure, the ETSI NFV has identified three domains within the NFVI, which are clearly differentiated at a functional and a practical levels: the compute domain (including both computing and storage resources), the hypervisor domain and the infrastructure network domain. Each of these domains deals with specific problems that can be treated independently. So, for example, the selection of the computing infrastructure is largely unaffected by the selection of the underlying infrastructure network. These domains allow for largely autonomous supply and evolution of each one.

The role of the compute domain is to provide the computational and storage resources (supported by COTS hardware) needed to host individual components of VNFs. The use of industry standard high volume servers is a key element in the economic case for NFV. An industry standard high volume server is a server built using standardized IT components (for example x86 or ARM architectures) and sold at a massive scale. A common feature of industry standard high volume servers is that there is competitive supply of the subcomponents that are interchangeable inside the server. The computing domain considers a functional 'unit of compute' basically integrated with the computational hardware device. This unit of compute is functionally defined as consisting of:

- An entity capable of executing a generic computational instruction set (the CPU)
- An entity able to hold state (the storage)
- An element in charge of reading and writing data to the network (the NIC)
- Other "acceleration" hardware, such as elements for encryption and decryption or "enhanced" packet forwarding. However, the value of this acceleration hardware needs to be carefully assessed, because it reduces the portability of the VNFs based on it and implies a cost of prior provision.

The hypervisor domain mediates the resources of the computer domain to the virtual machines implementing the VNFs. In essence, the hypervisor can emulate every piece of the hardware platform, even to the point, in some cases, of completely emulating a CPU instruction set. Even when not emulating a complete CPU architecture, there can still be aspects of emulation which cause a significant performance hit.

In addition, as there may be many virtual machines all running on the same host machine, they are likely to be connected one to the other. The hypervisor provides emulated virtual NICs for the VMs. However, there is also the need for a virtual Ethernet switch to provide connectivity between the VMs and between the VMs and the physical NICs. This is handled by the hypervisor virtual switch (vSwitch). The vSwitch may also be a significant performance bottleneck.

There is a number of features available in current and immediately forthcoming server hardware greatly improving the performance of VMs, including multicore processors, system-on-chip processors that integrate multiple cores and interfaces, specific CPU enhancements/instructions to control memory allocation and direct access on I/O, and PCI-e bus enhancements. These allow high performance VMs to run effectively as if they were running natively on the hardware, while under the full control of the hypervisor.

The resulting hypervisor architecture is one of the primary foundations of the NFV infrastructure, providing the full performance of 'bare metal' while supporting the full orchestration and management provided by the hypervisor. The NFV community is actively developing the necessary enhancements for the realization of this architecture and contributing them to the relevant open-source projects in this area.

The infrastructure network domain performs a number of essential roles, supporting the communication channels required for:

- The VNFCs in a distributed VNF
- The different VNFs building a service
- Any VNF and its orchestration and management
- Orchestration and management to interact with the NFVI components
- Remote deployment of VNFs
- The interconnection with the existing network where the network service is to be attached

The role of the infrastructure network is to provide a large number of discrete connectivity service instances. In general, it is a fundamental requirement that these services are separate from each other and not accessible to each other. This is the antithesis of the universal networking in the wider Internet. These essential roles imply that the infrastructure network must predate any VNF but must provide sufficient network connectivity to carry out its roles. In order to achieve this, it must have all the essential elements needed for providing connectivity already self-contained with the domain, including an addressing scheme, routing and bandwidth allocation processes, and the necessary operational mechanisms to assess the reliability, availability, and integrity of the connectivity services. Many active players within the NFV community is that SDN constitutes the basic technology for providing these elements.

VNFS, COMPONENTS, AND DESIGN PATTERNS

A VNF is a network function that is capable of running in a NFV Infrastructure (NFVI), being orchestrated by an NFV Orchestrator and a VNF manager as shown in Figure 4. Each VNF may be controlled by an Element Management System (EMS). In addition to interfacing to the VNF Manager and the EMS, the VNF provides well-defined interfaces to other VNFs.

In the same way a Network Service might be a composition of several VNFs, the VNF provider may choose to use one VNF Component (VNFC) or use VNFC composition to implement a VNF. In this context, the work of the Service Function Chaining (SFC) working group (Guichard & Narten (2013)) in the IETF is also significant.

VNFs may or may not need to store state during their lifetime. Examples of this are a stateful firewall, a stateless tunnel termination function, etc. The VNF Architecture specification document ETSI-NFV-ISG (2013a) describes alternatives for how VNF state is stored and handled depending on the VNF type. In addition, it identifies other design patterns that include patterns to deal with traffic evolution. Thus, for example, VNFs may or may not be instantiated in parallel within a VNF to scale in and out as a response to changes in traffic, resource allocation, etc. When VNFs are instantiated in parallel, the VNF provider will have to specify how many instances may be instantiated in parallel within a VNFC, what kind of scaling models may be used and what are the alternatives to implement load balancing within a VNF and between VNFs.

VNFs are software components that have specific life-cycle management requirements in order to implement network functions. The lifecycle of a VNF is inspired both by current best practices in network management and in the datacentre worlds. One of the main opportunities of NFV is the fact that some types of network functions implemented in software can, in specific cases, be scaled in and out, i.e. the network function can be instantiated with different resource requirements depending on the throughput it is expected to provide. Scaling can be implemented with well-known techniques applied to virtual machines in the data-centre world. However, these techniques cannot be generally applied, since there are VNFs that require a careful consideration before deployment within

Figure 4. VNF Functional architecture

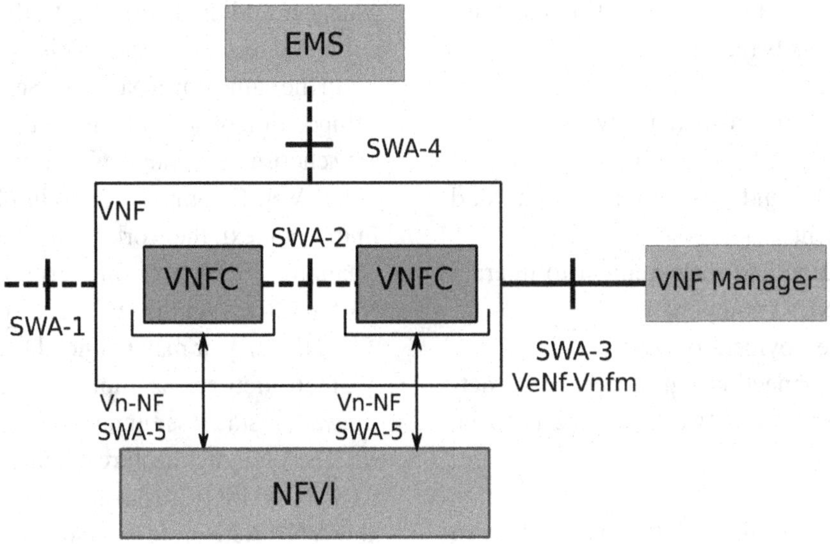

the VNFI in order to guarantee adequate levels of performance. Factors like underlying hardware (i.e., CPU type, Network Interface Cards (NICs), memory, internal buses, etc.), virtualization layer (i.e., hypervisor, virtualization mode, etc.) and operating system can have a severe impact on the performance that can be achieved for a given VNF. The ETSI NFV ISG has issued a document on "Performance Considerations and Best Practices" in ETSI-NFV-ISG (2014) analysing the different factors and providing guidelines and specific descriptors to capture the requirements for both of the NFVI and the VNFs.

NFV deployment should be transparent to the end-user and, therefore, similar levels of service availability to those provided by traditional, discrete networks are to be expected. In other words, the NFV system has to be designed to be as resilient as traditional networks. However, the paradigm shift from hardware- to software-based systems implies that instead of a design that is meant to guarantee a given uptime, NFV suppliers design their technology to minimize the impact of failures on the service. An NFV system will be provided with automated recovery from failures. The main challenge in an NFV environment is threefold:

1. An underlying architecture needs to be provided that does not exhibit a single point of failure.
2. All designs have to be applicable to a multi-vendor environment.
3. The infrastructure will be hybrid, with components that are implemented in portable software and components that come from the discrete network and that will be gradually phased out.

The ETSI NFV ISG has issued a resiliency requirements document in ETSI-NFV-ISG (2013d) that analyses the resiliency problem in NFV environments. Resilience is tightly coupled with security. VNFs are network functions running on a virtual machine, a network built of VNFs is exposed to the same threats as the physical network functions plus the threats that apply to virtualization. In addition, new threats arise from the mere fact of combining virtualization and networking. ETSI-NFV-ISG (2013b) analyses such threats with the objective of providing the problem statement as well as further insight to be incorporated into security accreditation processes for NFV-based products. Despite the additional threats, virtualization also furnishes some interesting tools like secure boot and/or trusted boot that allow operators to check the validity of VNF images before they are executed on an NFV platform and avoid the introduction of forged VNFs.

The IETF is also working on related areas: the creation of services from VNFs by composition can be generalized as the creation of services as service function chains (SFCs). The SFC working group is studying the mechanisms to create and operate service function chains. The need to monitor the operational state of the VNFs composing a service and to be able to pinpoint points of failure is being discussed and different Operations and Management (OAM) frameworks are being considered. How VNF instances can be pooled is also being explored along with the debate about the creation of the VNFPOOL working group (see Zong et al. (2014)) at the time of writing this chapter.

MANAGEMENT AND ORCHESTRATION: MANO

In the environment of telecommunications networks, network functions must be able to support remote configuration and management. For this purpose, network functions provide an interface to the management and orchestration (MANO) mechanisms used by the operators. This interface is often denoted as their "Northbound interface". Given the objective of NFV of separating capacity (NFVI) from functionality (VNFs) it is natural that this separation includes their management and orchestration. On the one hand, VNFs are not any longer required to deal with the management of the infrastructural aspects, while on the other hand, efficient VNF lifecycle management has to be provided to support the new features brought by virtualization (fast delivery and recovery, auto-scaling, etc.) The goal of NFV management and orchestration is to provide a high level of common MANO functionality with a common interface for it to be utilized by the network provider's business and operational support systems.

MANO functions are structured by means of three layers that group the management and orchestration functions at the infrastructure, VNF and service levels. At each layer, a functional entity is defined by the NFV MANO architecture, ensuring the exposure of services that provide access to these functions in an open, well-known abstracted manner. These services can be consumed by other authenticated and properly authorized NFV MANO functions, and by the business and operation support systems applied by the network operator.

The management of any element in the network is associated to mechanisms defined according to FCAPS (Fault, Configuration, Accounting, Performance, Security). Beyond these Specific Management Functional Areas (SMFAs), specific aspects introduced by virtualization must be considered for NFV MANO. Fault and performance management are functionalities required by any networking framework, and especially sensitive in the case of NFV, as it requires a radically new approach to any kind of fault processing, from notification to root-cause analysis, as well as new mechanisms for performance metrics collection, metrics calculation and aggregation. In addition, policy definition and enforcement mechanisms have to incorporate support for the specific issues associated to virtualization and the new operations permitted by it.

ICT resource allocation is a complex task in general, given the number of (even conflicting) requirements and constraints that need to be satisfied at the same time. For the NFVI, the specific requirements for network allocation and performance add new complexity compared to the resource allocation strategies applied so far in current cloud environments. While the management and orchestration functions at the NFVI level must be necessarily oblivious to the VNFs it hosts, resource allocation and release will be likely requested throughout these VNF lifetimes if we want to take advantage of the NFV ability to dynamically adapt VNF capabilities to load fluctuations. The NFV MANO functions that coordinate virtualized resources are grouped under the name of the Virtual Infrastructure Manager (VIM).

At the VNF level, MANO aspects must contemplate the newer aspects introduced by the virtual nature of the supporting infrastructure, which require a set of management functions focused on the creation and lifecycle management of the resources used by the VNF. In the NFV architecture, this lifecycle management corresponds to the functional entity known as the VNF Manager (VNFM), responsible for operations such as instantiation, scaling, updating, upgrading and terminating a VNF. The VNFM must rely on a VNF deployment template describing the attributes and requirements necessary to realize such a VNF and to manage its lifecycle. Though most of the VNFM functions can be considered generic common functions applicable to any type of VNF, the NFV MANO architecture considers the case where certain VNFs may need specific functionality for their lifecycle management. The architecture does not assume any predefined mapping among a given VNFM and the number and classes of VNFs it can manage: A VNFM may be in charge of a single VNF instance, or the management of multiple VNF instances of the same class or of different classes. What is more: VNFs can be classified according to their particular purpose, the type of service they participate in, or their provider just to name a few possibilities. During the lifecycle of a VNF, the VNFM can monitor the performance of the VNFs under its control, according to their deployment template, and use this information for triggering management operations, most typically scaling ones.

The MANO function in charge of network service lifecycle use the service deployment templates describing them and performs tasks related to:

- On-boarding the services by registering their templates in the service catalogue, including those required by the composing VNFs.
- Instantiating the services by means of the artefacts provided in their deployment templates.
- Scaling the services, growing or reducing their whole capacity.
- Updating the services by supporting configuration changes, such as inter-VNF connectivity or the particular instances of the composing VNFs.
- Creating and updating the inter-VNF connectivity and their attachment to the general network infrastructure through the service's VNF Forwarding Graph (VNFFG).
- Terminating the services, including the de-provisioning of their VNFFG, the termination of the composing VNFs, and the release of the NFVI resources in use.

A network service deployment template typically includes the description for managing the associations between different network functions (either virtualized or not: a service can have heterogeneous components), and the VNFFGs associated with the Network Service. These tasks are performed by a functional block named NFVO (NFV Orchestrator), which is also in charge of the orchestration of NFVI resources across multiple VIMs.

This dual nature of the current NFVO role is related to the foreseeable situation of separated administrative domains. As discussed before, reasonably mature scenarios for NFV will not have a single organization controlling and maintaining the whole NFV system. Administrative domains can be mapped to different organizations and therefore can exist within a single service provider or distributed among several service providers. At least two basic domains can be initially foreseen: the infrastructure domain and the tenant domain. An infrastructure domain can be generally defined by the NFVI resources under a single administration, and may provide infrastructure to a single or multiple tenant domains. Infrastructure domains are oblivious to the VNFs and services its tenants deploy on it, and in charge of the necessary VIM(s) and the NFVO resource orchestration functions. A tenant domain can use the NFVI in a single or multiple infrastructure domains, and it will be concerned with general service and VNF management, including FCAPS aspects, VNFM(s) and the service orchestration functions of the NFVO.

THE CHALLENGES AHEAD

We believe that the paradigm shift that NFV brings to network design and operation has become clear along the previous sections. Such a paradigm shift implies great challenges, not only in what relates to the technical aspects but to organizational and even cultural aspects. Given the scope of this book, we will not elaborate on the latter, though we think it would be interesting to make a few reflections on them as well. In parallel to addressing these organizational challenges, and in many cases before organizations deal with them, there are a number of technology aspects to be considered. Most of them have already been characterized by the NFV community and are subject to active research.

Many of the challenges presented below can be mitigated by limiting initial NFV deployments to a single NFV Infrastructure in a single administration domain limiting its offerings to only network services (VNF Graphs) sold to end-users. As the challenges are addressed NFV deployments can become more sophisticated offering a richer range of services across different NFV infrastructures and administrations. This strategy will allow network operators, customers and VNF vendors, to gain immediate benefits.

Functional and Service-Level Considerations

NFV will induce new design patterns at all network levels, from the elements themselves to service inception. Breaking the "box boundaries" opens new ways for element componentization, as well as infrastructure and service abstractions that should allow translating the infrastructure virtualization into more powerful network virtualization. To support these virtualization patterns, new mechanisms for infrastructure and service function description will be required, especially declarative languages and tools for supporting the design flows. Finally, these design patterns will require the application of system-wide optimizations at all levels, from the physical infrastructure up to the composite services.

Orchestration is the key element for achieving the goals of operation automation and elasticity that constitute the core of the NFV benefits. We have insisted all along the text on the need for going beyond current cloud practice to cover the requirements of NFV, and this is especially relevant when it comes to orchestration. This implies the availability of network-aware orchestration methods that can support features like the automation of network function chaining and autonomous service behaviour such as self-configuration, self-diagnostic, and self-healing. Another relevant aspect is related to the possibility of applying analytics methods to enhance orchestration, so NFV can benefit of the great amount of data that the simpler deployment of software probes can feed into cloud-based analytics engines. Thus, analytics (or big data, if you allow us to use another hyped word) could be put in the management loop allowing a much more flexible and efficient network operation. Probably the most important consequence of the availability of these advanced orchestration mechanisms will be the simplification of operational procedures, allowing for a tighter integration of business process and network management that will bring the expected service development agility to the levels envisaged by the NFV concept. Note that many of the concepts we have identified here are not new and are being explored in the broader world of Software Defined Networking (SDN). In fact, SDN and NFV enjoy a symbiotic relationship where each of them benefits from the advances in the State-of-the-Art of the other.

Security Considerations

Security issues constitute one of the most important challenges for the success of NFV. We must bear in mind that a great part of current network security is based on the physical security that prevent insider attacks, but this will no longer hold when virtualization becomes commonplace, and network functions will become essentially executed on off-the-shelf hardware and software, which implies more reported and unreported (zero-day) vulnerabilities, more attack tools (such as virus and rootkits), and an increased motivation for attackers, as they could exploit NFV-based networks to cause larger scale disruption.

It is therefore required to reduce the combined attack surface, and with that goal a first set of measures can be derived from the current security practice in IT virtualization, taking advantage of enlarged mitigation mechanisms provided by hypervisors via techniques like introspection and containment. Beyond that, there are specific aspects that must be addressed to guarantee a secure development of NFV, mostly connected to the fact that NFV faces the combination of the network as an infrastructure and the network as an application. A first item among these aspects is related with image and infrastructure attestation: there must be ways to guarantee the installed software corresponds to the intended function and is provided by a trusted origin and, conversely, a given function must be assured it is running on the appropriate environment. While models like TPM [TPM] have been proposed for these procedures, it is necessary to test their ability to scale up to the requirements of dynamic network service provisioning.

A second front is related to topology validation and enforcement, so that VNFs can be assured of being connected according to the appropriate functions in the service chain and not going through any potential data leakage or man-in-the-middle. There are incipient techniques applied in SDN deployments for that purpose, but apart from them and their required maturity, procedures are required above the infrastructure network.

The introduction of NFV brings new security issues when it comes to Authentication Authorisation and Accounting (AAA) as discussed in Vollbrecht et al. (2000), as it implies using identity and accounting facilities at two or more layers: the network and virtualization infrastructure (e.g., identifying the tenant or guest service providers) and the network function (e.g., identifying the end-users). A generalized AAA schema for identifying users utilizing a particular tenant infrastructure and/or a tenant acting on behalf of a user is required to support these patterns and the new operational and business models they will bring. Current AAA mechanisms assume there will be a single identity, single policy decision and enforcement points, a single level of policy, and a single accounting infrastructure. Even if a strict separation by encapsulation (as current practice seems to suggest) would be feasible without breaking some of the promised NFV enhancements in what relates to scalability, agility and resilience, there exist risks related to each one the three components in AAA. Authentication procedures can imply privacy breaches associated to the disclosure of user information at layers that are not intended to consume certain identity attributes. Authorization risks are mostly related to privilege escalation produced by wrapping unrelated identities that cannot be verified at a given layer. Finally, accounting needs to be performed at all the underlying infrastructure layer(s), and they will not only require accounting at the granularity of virtualized applications that use the infrastructures, but also at the coarser granularity of the tenants running virtualized network functions.

Deployment Considerations

Although there are already solutions available that can be tagged as "NFV", the final push is yet-to-come. While the industry is providing Proofs of Concept (PoCs) for specific scenarios, large-scale deployments are not yet available. As shown above, NFV needs to be integrated in a framework that provides the orchestration with the networking layer. As Sato et.al. (2013) describe, it is the combination of both technologies that will deliver the tools for a more flexible and cost-effective network, based on a unified end-to-end model for the network comprising the end user. A crucial aspect of NFV is the infrastructure onto which NFV will be deployed. A general misconception is that state-of-the-art datacentres will suffice. The networking layer and the virtual machine placement algorithms need to be redesigned from scratch. Current datacentres are designed with north-south and east-west traffic profiles in mind, which correspond to a virtualization paradigm that does not take into account where the virtual machines are placed and how they interact. The NFV datacentre, in contrast, needs to have a precise knowledge of where the different VNFs are placed and how the network traffic between them is flowing. Additionally, the placement of the NFV datacentres themselves has to be considered. Basta et.al. evaluate the influence of the network topology on the network load overhead introduced by the fact of decomposing the LTE network stack into different functions and placing them on a reduced number of datacentres in a disperse geography like the USA, while having to cope with service limitations like the delay budget (Basta et al. (2014)).

A real hurdle can come from the incumbent equipment vendors that see NFV as a threat to their current business model. [SEZER-2013] presents a serious, but somewhat biased view of the challenges of SDN. Many of the assertions in [SEZER-2013] also apply to NFV deployments, due to the symbiotic relationship of NFV and SDN. However, it is puzzling why NFV is not mentioned in the article. Incumbents use Fear, Uncertainty and Doubt (FUD) tactics to slow down the pace of NFV evolution and adoption. By using these tactics, they expect to gain some time to try to regain control of a market they are losing. Some of them play the card of operational complexity as claimed in *cisco-blog-tailf*. Acquiring successful start-up companies in order to control the evolution of the SDN/NFV landscape is another tactic that is used by some big equipment providers. Another threat comes from the claim of using "Open and Standard" interfaces. In many cases, this claim just translates into the use of standard transport protocols or basic coding (e.g., XML, YANG, NETCONF, etc.) and hides the fact that proprietary extensions are needed to perform any sensible control function. A well-known precedent of this tactic is SNMP, where standard MIBs have limited functionality and proprietary MIBs are often needed to effectively control network elements.

And a Few Organizational Considerations

The networking industry (operators, manufacturers, integrators…) has been largely organized around the idea of physically distinguishable nodes providing well-identified services, and almost physically distinguishable links connecting them. To put it in plain words, boxes and cables connecting them. These boxes have been extremely intensive in software for quite a long time, but this software could not go beyond the limits of the box it was intended to run on. NFV opens a completely new set of possibilities, where software is not only confined to a particular "box", and can even be used to implement the "cables" connecting it to other elements.

These changes will require all kinds of actors to change almost every aspect. To start with, working methodologies must become closer to the current DevOps practices and shorter times to market. Second, organizational structures will have to contemplate shorter paths between business management and engineering (or development, that is). We cannot forget that commercial relationships between these actors shall change as well, as virtualized infrastructures allow for much more fluid business models. And, over all, organizations and the individuals that compose them will have to adjust their culture to a new way of thinking of their products (whatever they are: services, network nodes, technologies…) and their skills.

REFERENCES

Basta, A., Kellerer, W., Hoffmann, M., Morper, H. J., & Hoffmann, K. (2014). Applying NFV and SDN to LTE Mobile Core Gateways, the Functions Placement Problem. In *Proceedings of the 4th workshop on all things cellular: Operations, applications, & challenges* (pp. 33–38). New York, NY, USA: ACM; http://doi.acm.org/10.1145/2627585.2627592 doi:10.1145/2627585.2627592

Bonomi, F., Milito, R., Zhu, J., & Addepalli, S. (2012). Fog computing and its role in the internet of things. In *Proceedings of the first edition of the mcc workshop on mobile cloud computing* (pp. 13–16). New York, NY, USA: ACM. doi:10.1145/2342509.2342513

Chiosi, M., Clarke, D., Willis, P., Reid, A., López, D., …. A. M. (2012, October). *Network Functions Virtualisation. An Introduction, Benefits, Enablers, Challenges and Call for Action.* Retrieved March, 6, 2015 from http://portal.etsi.org/NFV/NFV_White_Paper.pdf

Clemm, A. (2007). Network Management Fundamentals (1 ed.). CiscoPress.

Cong, G., & Wen, H. (2013). (2013). Mapping Applications for High Performance on Multithreaded, NUMA Systems. In *Proceedings of the acm international conference on computing frontiers* (pp. 7:1–7:4). New York, NY: ACM. http://doi.acm.org/10.1145/2482767.2482777

ETSI-NFV-ISG. (2013a, Oct). *Network Functions Virtualisation (NFV); Architectural Framework* (Tech. Rep.). ETSI. Retrieved March, 6, 2015 from http://www.etsi.org/deliver/etsi_gs/NFV/001_099/002/01.01.01_60/gs_NFV002v010101p.pdf

ETSI-NFV-ISG. (2013b, Oct). *Network Functions Virtualisation (NFV); NFV Security; Problem Statement* (Tech. Rep.). ETSI. Retrieved March, 6, 2015 from http://docbox.etsi.org/ISG/NFV/Open/Latest_Drafts/NFV-SEC001v021-NFV_Security_Problem_Statement.pdf

ETSI-NFV-ISG. (2013c, Oct). *Network Functions Virtualisation (NFV); Use Cases* (Tech. Rep.). ETSI. Retrieved March, 6, 2015 from http://www.etsi.org/deliver/etsi_gs/NFV/001_099/001/01.01.01_60/gs_NFV001v010101p.pdf

ETSI-NFV-ISG. (2013d, Oct). *Network Function Virtualisation (NFV); Resiliency Requirements* (Tech. Rep.). ETSI. Retrieved March, 6, 2015 from http://www.etsi.org/deliver/etsi_gs/NFV/001_099/002/01.01.01_60/gs_NFV002v010101p.pdf

ETSI-NFV-ISG. (2014). *Network Functions Virtualisation (NFV); NFV Performance & Portability Best Practises* (Tech. Rep.). ETSI. Retrieved March, 6, 2015 from http://www.etsi.org/deliver/etsi_gs/NFV-PER/001_099/001/01.01.01_60/gs_NFV-PER001v010101p.pdf

Guichard, J., & Narten, T. (2013, Dec). *Service Function Chaining Charter* (Tech. Rep.). IETF. Retrieved March, 6, 2015 from http://datatracker.ietf.org/wg/sfc/charter

Loukides, M. (2012). *What is DevOps? Infrastructure as Code*. O'Reilly Media.

McKeown, N., Anderson, T., Balakrishnan, H., Parulkar, G., Peterson, L., Rexford, J., & Turner, J. et al. (2008, March). Openflow: Enabling innovation in campus networks. *SIGCOMM Comput. Commun. Rev.*, *38*(2), 69–74. doi:10.1145/1355734.1355746

Mell, P., & Grance, T. (2011, Sep). *The NIST Definition of Cloud Computing* (Special Publication No. 800-145). Computer Security Division, Information Technology Laboratory, National Institute of Standards and Technology. Retrieved March, 6, 2015 from http://csrc.nist.gov/publications/nistpubs/800-145/SP800-145.pdf

Open IMS Core. (n.d.). Retrieved March, 6, 2015 from http://www.openimscore.org/

OpenEPC - Open Evolved Packet Core. (n.d.). Retrieved March, 6, 2015 from http://www.openepc.net/index.html

Sato, Y., Fukuda, I., & Tomonori, F. (2013, Dec). Deployment of OpenFlow/SDN Technologies to Carrier Services. *IEICE Transactions, 96-B*(12), 2946–2952. Retrieved March, 6, 2015 from http://dblp.uni-trier.de/rec/bib/journals/ieicet/SatoFT13

TPM Main Specification. (2011, March). http://www.trustedcomputinggroup.org/resources/tpm_main_specification

Vollbrecht, J., Calhoun, P., Farrell, S., Gommans, L., Gross, G., & de Bruijn, B. ... Spence, D. (2000, August). *AAA Authorization Framework* (Tech. Rep. No. 2904). IETF Secretariat. RFC 2904.

Zong, N., Dunbar, L., Shore, M., Lóez, D., & Karagiannis, G. (2014, Jul). *Virtualized Network Function (VNF) Pool Problem Statement* (Internet-Draft No. draft-zong-vnfpool-problem-statement-06). IETF Secretariat. Retrieved March, 6, 2015 from http://tools.ietf.org/html/draft-zong-vnfpool-problem-statement-06

KEY TERMS AND DEFINITIONS

Carrier Cloud: A recently coined term referring to cloud infrastructures suitable to provide telco carrier services, able to bring the advantages of cloud computing to the telco environment by fulfilling the reliability requirements for critical infrastructures.

Composition: A technique for building complex elements by the (dynamic) composition of simpler ones. It requires components with well-known interfaces and verifiable service level agreements (SLA).

DevOps: Is a method for software development and management that integrates the development and deployment cycles to achieve a more agile, continuous evolution of software-based products and services.

NFV: (Network Functions Virtualization): A technology framework for the development and provisioning of network services, based on the separation of the functionality, implemented as software, and the capacity, provided by a homogeneous hardware infrastructure inspired on current cloud computing.

Orchestration: The process that governs the creation, instantiation, and composition of the different elements a service consists of. It includes a coordinated set actions at several supporting infrastructures (computing, storage, network…) and layers (local and WAN network).

SDN (Software Defined Networking): An architecture for building networks that advocates for a complete separation of the forwarding and control planes, and the definition of open interfaces between them. The control plane is implemented as a logically centralized programmable software element.

Virtualization: A technique common in computing, consisting in the creation of virtual (rather than actual) instance of any element, so it can be managed and used independently. Virtualization has been one of the key tools for resource sharing and software development, and now it is beginning to be applied to the network disciplines.

Chapter 18
Introducing Automation in Service Delivery Procedures:
An Overview

Isabel Borges
PT Inovação, Portugal

ABSTRACT

The combination of Software-Defined Networking (SDN) with Network Functions Virtualization (NFV) approaches is gaining momentum in the Industry as a new way of implementing, managing and controlling telecommunications networks. This chapter aims to go through SDN and lightly over NFV, presenting main characteristics and the standardization work on that technologies. SDN enables programming networks together with the ability to adapt to applications requirements and network dynamics. NFV aims at virtualizing network services by merging several network equipment types onto standard Information Technologies (IT) high volume virtualization technology (switches, servers and storage) located either in data centres, customer premises or network nodes. SDN and NFV interworking ambition is to bring on-demand resource provisioning, resource elasticity, among others with a centralized view of the overall network, able to automatically and dynamically honor service requirements.

INTRODUCTION

The Cloud Computing model began to be explored a few years ago and relies entirely upon basic distributed systems concepts (ITU-T, 2009). It was tackled for the first time in 1961 by John McCarthy, a computer scientist during a lecture under the celebration of the 1st centenary of Massachusetts Institute of Technology (MIT) foundation (Magoules, 2010). From a speech John McCarthy gave at MIT by that time he said: "If computers of the kind I have advocated become the computers of the future, then computing may someday be organized as a public utility just as the telephone system is a public utility… The computer utility could become the basis of a new and important industry." (Magoules, 2010). Cloud computing is, as mentioned above, based on the business model in which computational resources would be provided as a "Service". Providing computational resources or infrastructure as a service requires

DOI: 10.4018/978-1-4666-8371-6.ch018

virtualization. As a matter of fact, virtualization is the technological basis of the Cloud.

Surprisingly enough, virtualization techniques were also first investigated in the 60s by IBM where large mainframe hardware was logically partitioned in order to take advantage of idle processing capability, allowing mainframes to execute multiple applications and processes simultaneously, thereby optimizing the investment.

In the 80s and 90s three important factors put the virtualization in standby:

1. Intel x86 architecture enabling the microprocessor mass market debuting with the IBM Personal Computer (PC) (Intel 8088),
2. Client-server paradigm, and
3. Desktop applications.

The widespread adoption of Windows and the emergence of Linux as server Operating Systems, in the 90s, established x86 servers as the industry standard.

From that time the use of a PC becomes a commonplace and sharing a computing resource among many users by means of multiprogramming and multi-tasking was no more an issue.

In the 90s, based on the x86 architecture, computers have the same underutilization problems as mainframes had in the 60s. Again, as before, why not taking advantage of all the computational power possible? Following this idea, VMware has created, in the 90's, a virtualization for the x86 platform to deal with underutilization and other issues, overcoming many challenges in the process. The result is a virtual machine that is equivalent to the host hardware and maintains complete software compatibility. VMware pioneered this technique and today is the leader in virtualization technology that is the technological basis of the Cloud.

By the same time appears the concept of Grid Computing, where computer resources from multiple domains are shared to achieve a common goal. One example was the scientific initiative called SETI@home (SETI staff, 2014) that uses computers (resources) connected via the Internet to search for extraterrestrial intelligence.

Service utility, grid computing, virtualization and a broadband Internet access have created the Cloud computing momentum where the IT resources are available on-demand using the pay-as-you-go model.

Adherence to mobile communications has caused an exponential increase in existing mobile devices and mobile users demanding for better quality of service. This implies to have, among other considerations, better content delivery and self-organized networks due to the dynamic change of assets. This also encourages the use of automation techniques for accelerating service provisioning, but also for better mastering network evolution and dynamically enforcing service policies. Software-Defined Networking (SDN) are among those techniques that have emerged based on the promise to improve the efficiency of the overall service delivery procedure by means of programmable, centrally controlled networks, thereby providing an easy way to deploy new services according to specific user demands, as well as tuning network policies and performance.

Driven by operational savings and CAPEX budget constraints, operators are moving from proprietary hardware solutions to a more generic computing environment. Foreseen savings brought by lesser needs to proceed with periodic hardware replacement and lower integration costs, but also to overcome hardware obsolescence sometimes aggravated by heterogeneous proprietary systems, elasticity based on Software, Platform and Infrastructure as a Service (SPIaaS) are as many requirements that further encourage the use of NFV techniques.

1. SDN AND NFV PERSPECTIVES

This chapter will present a Strengths, Weaknesses, Opportunities, and Threats (SWOT) analysis that put in perspective the challenges and opportunities for operators relying on cloud technologies. It will also present SDN and a brief perspective of NFV approaches identifying main architectural aspects, standardization and the complementarity of both approaches, since SDN and NFV are many times associated as meaning the same thing, which is not true.

A. Cloud Challenges and Opportunities for Operators

Telecom Operators can be seen either as Cloud customers or as Cloud service provider. Being both a provider and a customer can bring customer requirements and functional specifications together, with a deeper knowledge on how to solve particular problems and evolve. The SWOT analysis for an operator providing Cloud services is:

Regarding the strengths:

- Strong market position with a significant customer's base. This means that the operator has already a previous knowledge of who may adhere and to which Cloud type (private, community or public as depicted in Figure 1).

The Cloud types could be (MSV, 2010).

- Private: only that specific enterprise has access to the servers on it – large I medium corporate customer (above 200 employees). (European Commission, 2014)
- Hybrid cloud: some data and services, due, for instance, to regulatory constraints, should stay in private servers, but others could be public.
- Community: where the services provided are shared among several organizations

Figure 1. Cloud types

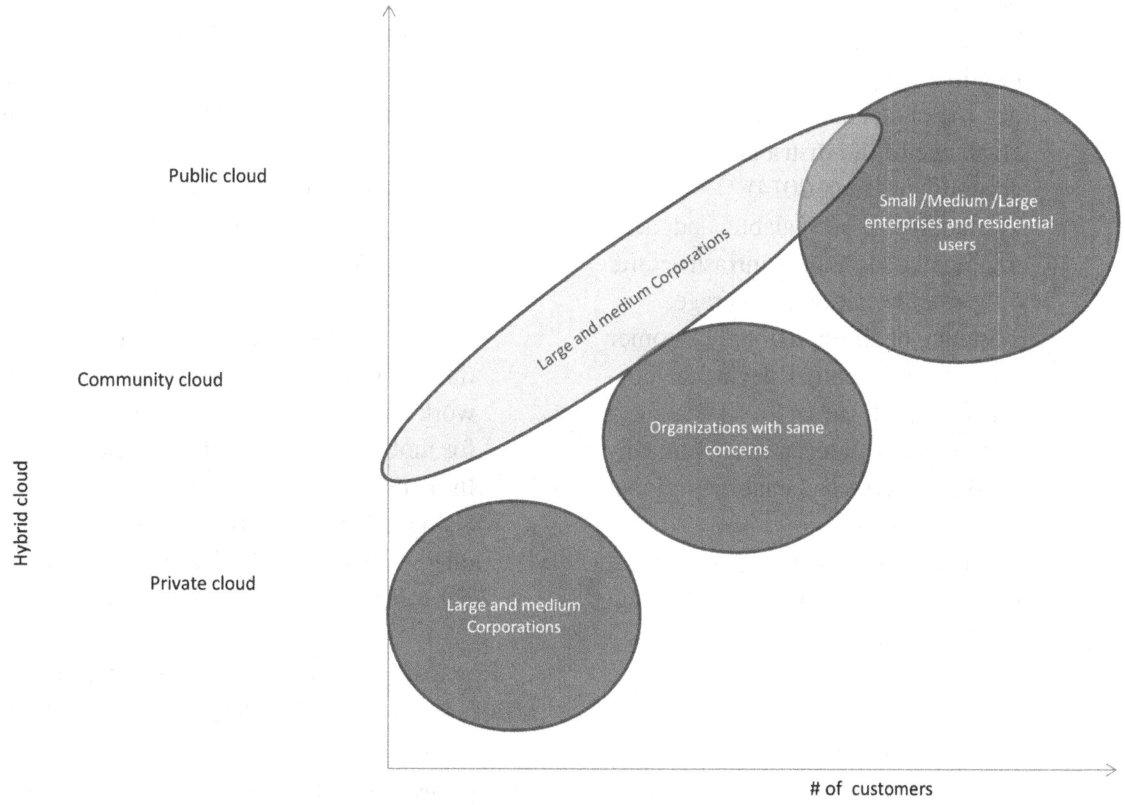

with the same areas of interest, requirements, etc.

- Public: where customers share resources and services. Public clouds needs a huge investment (that's why only few companies like Microsoft, Amazon and Google can afford to build them) and are implemented on different geographical locations (enhancing applications performance and being able to deal with disaster recovery). On each location (usually a country) there are several datacenters running hundreds or thousands of servers.
  - Resulting from having a strong market position, the knowledge of customers who share common interests can easily promote sets of services that could be replicated, since the operator already knows customer needs.
  - All processes associated with security, interconnection, billing, datacenters management are already in the place.
  - Availability of resources, up and running in a couple of minutes, answering to on-demand growth, taking advantage of the distribution chain – elasticity (Wayner, 2014)
  - Availability of a scalable and geographically distributed infrastructure, with, usually, national coverage.
  - Existence of an operational customer support (call centers, technical customer support, etc.).
  - National and International consolidated partnerships, enabling global service delivery.
  - Experience on end-to-end service offering, 3rd party storage and hosting, real-time charging and billing.
  - It is programmable

Looking at the weaknesses:

- Telecom operators have less skills in Information Technologies, namely those associated with virtualization and software as a service.
- Not very dynamic to address the need for new service provisioning due to complex environments and dependencies. If the operator could not rely in full automated OSS suites, all the process of service provisioning, or, even better, the self -provisioning process is difficult to achieve if there are several fulfillment systems that are not completely integrated with billing, assurance and performance management. Cost, particularly of storage: It is fundamental to deploy a model regarding the costs for volume and access cost storage. Today regarding cost is quite the same for data that has lots of accesses or for data with a small access rate. A statistical study on access behavior would be welcomed for data center cost efficiency. Regarding cloud computing services and apps delivered over the Internet, Microsoft (Microsoft Azure, 2014) and Google (Google Cloud Platform, 2014) has already billing customers on a per-minute basis and not on per-hour as Amazon.
- Having the same services and applications over any device requires computation power, memory, storage, and energy for mobile devices. Cloud could overcome some of those constraints but it needs bigger network capacity, which is a huge investment for mobile operators, since the spectrum is limited.
- Using advanced software in commercial off-the-shelf (COTS) hardware could imply some concerns on data speed.

Regarding opportunities, cloud potential resides on the capability that any device, from a sensor, a TV to a smartphone or a computer being able to reach the required cloud resources, requiring only an Internet access. It is fundamental to establish partnerships between operators, cloud providers and the industry in order to enable a seamless user experience. In this way, operators and providers can push for standardization in those meaningful technological areas leading to further industry research in areas as security, vertical (up and down) and horizontal (in and out) elasticity and reliability between, for example, mobile devices and Cloud servers.

Net neutrality's global acceptance reduces operator's mechanisms concerning traffic prioritization, since the intelligence is not under network nodes but rather at end devices that are not directly controlled by operators and is considered a threat, since operators may be exposed to the risk of becoming dumb pipe providers. Another threat is the existence of similar cloud services being provided by other service providers than operators, such as typical value-added services providers, who have a close relationship with customers. This fact could be an obstacle to interoperability, since many of those services are proprietary. System integrators are also offering customers with complex cloud configurations and customization solutions and other players are providing customer cloud services management.

B. Software-Defined Networking (SDN)

I. Definitions

SDN and NFV are many times seen as addressing the same issues. This section aims to define the meaning associating with of these terms.

SDN advocates the separation of the forwarding and control planes. This separation (beyond implementation considerations), allows an increase of flexibility in network operation. This flexibility is achieved through the dynamic adaptation to network behavior variations, allowing network and service providers to optimize resource usage.. Approaches relying on the separation of the control and data forwarding planes as proposed by SDN can enhance performance, simplify compatibility with existing deployments, and facilitate operation and maintenance procedures. (See Figure 2) According to (Boucadair and Jacquenet, 2014), Software-Defined Networking is the set of techniques used to facilitate the design, delivery, and operation of network services in a deterministic, dynamic, and scalable manner.

The NFV concept finds its origin in service provider communities that were looking to accelerate the deployment of new network services to support their revenue and growth objectives, by applying virtualization techniques to network services, trying to develop advanced computation logic mastered by service providers. Network services are extensively deployed and vital in many networks, providing a range of functions such as security, Wide Area Network (WAN) acceleration, virtual routing, Virtual Private Networks (VPN) functions and server load balancing among others. Service functions that form part of the overall service may be physically located at different points in the network infrastructure (WAN, data center, campus, etc.).

The above definitions lead us to the complementarity between SDN and NFV. Both use a software approach to bring networks more efficient, flexible, scalable, performant and agile.

So, both SDN and NFV can take advantage from each other. SDN will introduce a high level of automation in the overall service delivery procedure, while NFV will help structuring some services by means of combining virtualized functions.

II. SDN Architecture and functional blocks: The ONF Approach

This section will only focus on SDN, as NFV will be further detailed in ***Chapter "Network Functions Virtualization: Going Beyond the Carrier Cloud"***.

Figure 2. SDN view

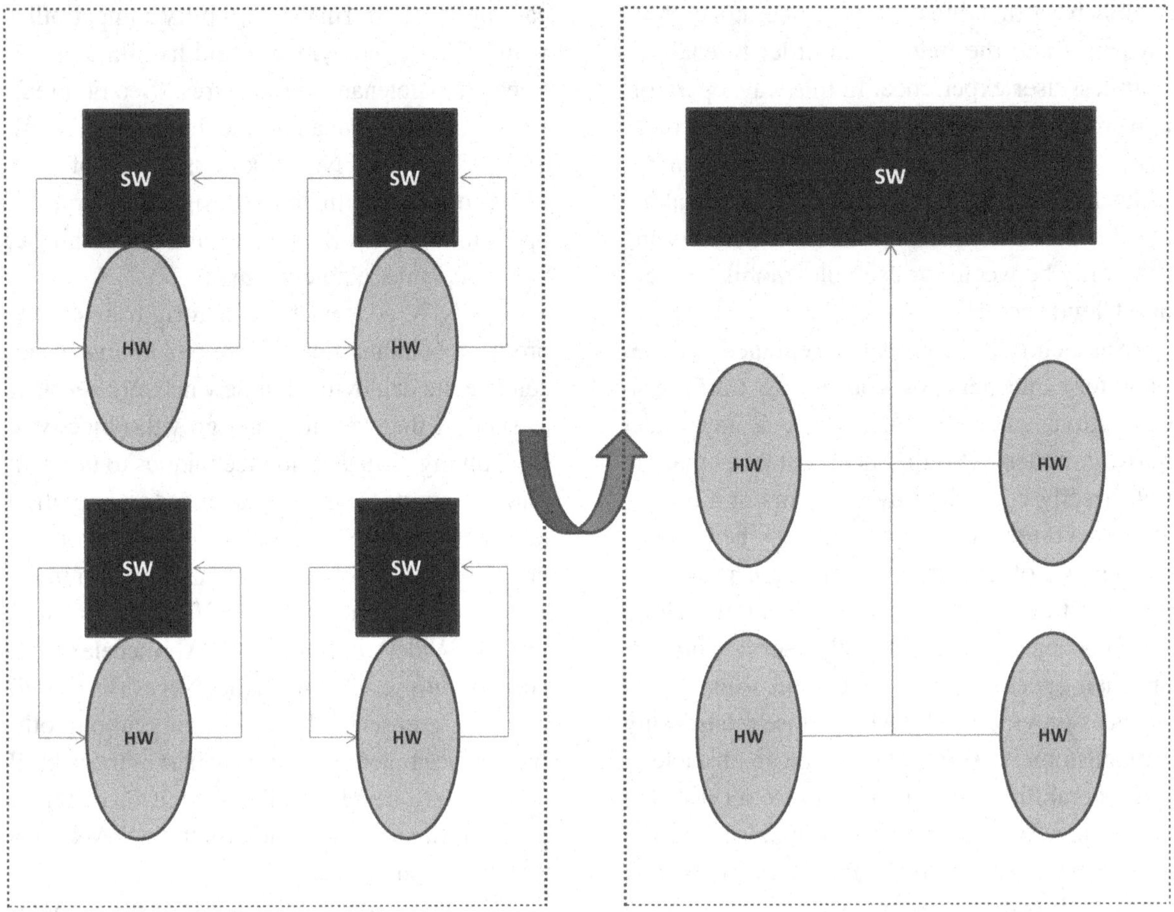

Figure 3 shows the basic blocks of the SDN architecture as defined by the Open Networking Foundation.

With SDN, applications can be network-aware, the control plane is logically centralized and decoupled from the data plane and has complete control of the SDN Data paths.

The data path segment exists in the forwarding engine, while high-level routing decisions are made by a separate controller. The OpenFlow forwarding engine and Controller communicate via the OpenFlow protocol.

The data path of an OpenFlow forwarding engine presents a flow table abstraction and each flow table entry contains a set of packet fields to match and an action to perform (output-port, modify-field, or drop). Also, it is the Controller that decides what happens to a packet received from the forwarding engine that was unable to deal with.

Network intelligence is (logically) centralized in software-based SDN controllers, which maintain a global view of the network. Network appears as a single, logical switch as depicted in Figure 2.

III. Automation

One of the most important claimed features of SDN is the dynamic ability to create network pathways according to application and data needs, being in line with user demands.

Figure 3. SDN architecture blocks (Bailey et all, 2013)

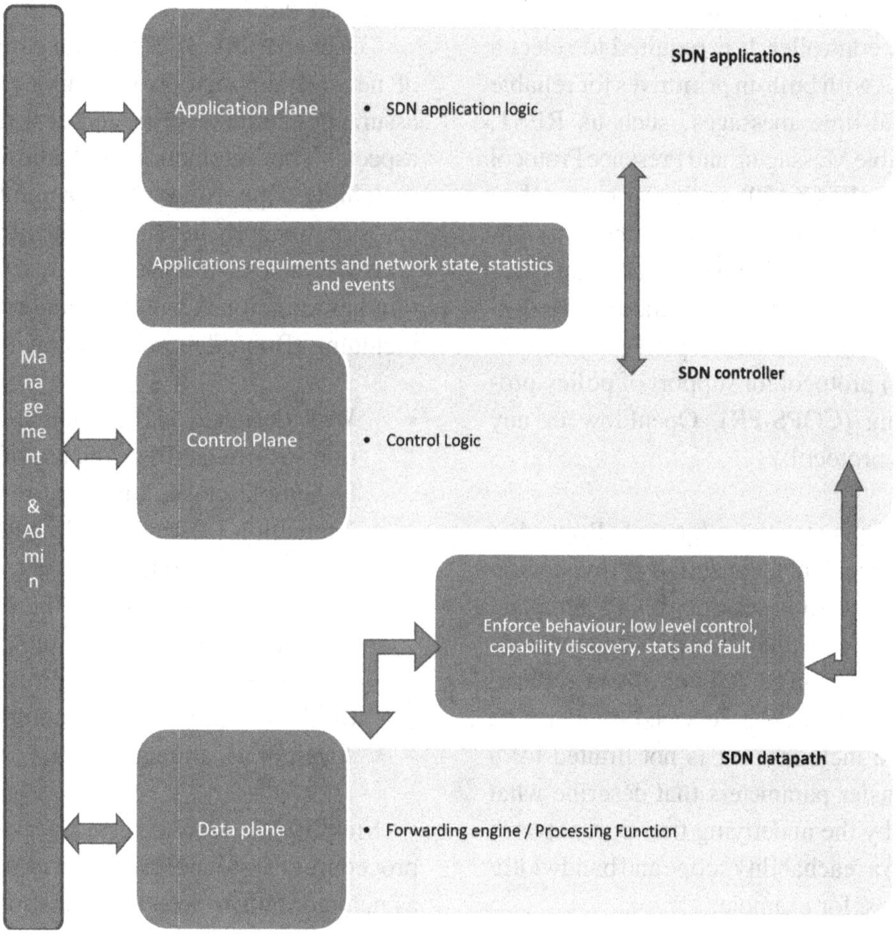

A centralized "controller-embedded", optimizing route computation scheme that selects routes which will then populate forwarding tables provides additional flexibility in how the network is operated, since the path computation logic can be fed with information that depicts a network-wise vision of the available resources, but also with information that reflects customer's expectations expressed as a set of service parameters (e.g., access bandwidth, traffic prioritization, etc.) that can be further translated into path computation metrics.. However this kind of flexibility cannot be reduced to the separation of the control and forwarding planes to facilitate forwarding decision-making processes.

Another approach to a SDN model is the application-enabled approach described at (Penno eta ll, 2013). Here, the end host has all the information required to make the correct service request. The architecture model is then divided into three main aspects:

1. SDN signaling, where the client host can signal flow characteristics to the network, and get the response from the network, regarding whether it is possible or not to accommodate that flow. The Port Control Protocol (PCP) is a candidate protocol to exchange corresponding information between the client host and the network.

2. Flow install request to share network availability information between network device and the controller. It is required to select a protocol with built-in primitives for reliable near-real-time messages, such us REST, Extensible Messaging and Presence Protocol (XMPP) (RFC6120) or similar protocol.
3. Flow install in routers and switches assigning a set of tasks. This can be accomplished by using Network Configuration Protocol (NETCONF), Common Open Policy Service (COPS) protocol for support of policy provisioning (COPS-PR), OpenFlow or any similar protocol.

Automation is also the subject of (Boucadair et all, 2014), where the Connectivity Provisioning Profile (CPP) model based upon a CPP template is meant to capture the IP/MPLS connectivity requirements that can be dynamically negotiated between a customer and a Service Provider. The CPP template includes (but is not limited to) a set of IP transfer parameters that describe what is requested by the underlying transport network together with a reachability scope and bandwidth/capacity needs, for example.

A PCE (Path Computation Element) is an entity that computes paths according to a set of requirements on behalf of routers, an Operation Support System or another PCE in a network. PCE could be seen as a cooperative operation between networking nodes implementing PCE providing a distributed functionality used to address path selection. This architecture provides an evolutionary approach to SDN that is especially suitable for WANs and telco networks. (Farrel et all, 2006)

As stated in (Boucadair and Jacquenet, 2014), further work needs to be done so that flexibility can be precisely defined in light of various criteria such as network evolution capabilities as a function of the complexity introduced by the integration of SDN techniques and seamless capabilities (i.e., the ability to progressively introduce SDN-enabled devices without disrupting network and service operation, etc.).

To achieve this, SDN must take full advantage of network automation regarding provisioning, assurance, fault, security and cost management aspects. The automation will allow growth in scalability supporting a higher number of users across public, private, and hybrid infrastructures.

Nevertheless, the path towards full automation has numerous challenges and requirements, including (Boucadair and Jacquenet, 2014):

- Well designed and implemented automation so as to facilitate the use of increasingly complex tasks that require less human interaction, testing (including validation checks) and troubleshooting. Simulation tools to accurately assess the impact of introducing a high level of automation in the overall service delivery procedure to get the global picture from control and QoS standpoints, among others.

Simplifying and fostering service delivery procedures, assurance, and fulfillment, as well as network failure detection, diagnosis, and root cause analysis for cost optimization. Logically centralized view of the network infrastructure (or a portion), yielding the need for highly automated topology, device and capabilities discovery means, and operational procedures. A detailed specification of the Policy Decision Point (PDP) function, including algorithms and behavioral state machineries that are based upon a complete set of standardized data and information models, is still missing.

According to (Pras and Schoenwaelder, 2003), the main purpose of an Information Model is to model managed objects at a conceptual level, independent of any specific implementations or protocols used to transport the data.

Data models are defined at a lower level of abstraction and include many details including protocol-specific constructs. Data models will enable applications to interpret and process the data. They apply not only to data stored and accessed by applications, but also to data passed in messages between applications allowing interoperability. While there are some standard data models (e.g., ITU-T X.500 standards for directories), most data models are specific for a particular application, what causes constraints in data portability for system integration and interoperability purposes. It is, therefore, important and valuable to standardize data models.

Most common data models are based on a relational database schema. Structured Query Language (SQL) standard applies to relational databases. Other types of data models are

eXtensible Markup Language (XML) schemas, designed to describe data readable both by machines and humans. Document Type Definitions (DTDs) defines the legal building blocks of an XML document. It defines the document structure with a list of legal elements and attributes.

Resource Description Framework (RDF) is a standard model for data interchange on the Web. It is mostly used as a data model describing web components at a conceptual level, using several syntax notations and data serialization formats based upon the idea of making statements about resources in the form of subject–verb–object expressions (triples). This model allows structured and semi-structured data to be mixed, exposed, and shared across different applications (World Wide Web Consortium staff, 2014). At (Kaoudi, Z., Manolescu, I., 2014)., it is proposed to describe and classify systems and proposals in Cloud are according to dimensions related to their capabilities and implementation techniques.

Processing large volumes of RDF data requires the optimization of native RDF stores and relational query engines for large-scale RDF processing. In parallel, a number of new data management systems known as NoSQL (not only SQL) represent today a popular alternative to classical databases and is being increasingly used to manage RDF data.

NoSQL presents advantages (Harrison, G., 2010) such as:

- Elastic scaling (move databases into the cloud or onto virtualized environments);
- Big data volumes of "big data" can be handled by NoSQL systems, such as Hadoop;
- NoSQL databases are generally designed to require less management (automatic repair, data distribution, etc.), lower administration and tuning requirement leading to be less dependent of database administrator;
- Economics – typically uses brand-less servers
- Data models flexibility allowing the application to store virtually any structure it wants in a data element

The Web Ontology Language (OWL) could be considered as an inference-based technique designed to improve the quality of data integration on the Web, by discovering new relationships, discovering possible inconsistencies in the (integrated) data, automatically analyzing the content of the data, or managing knowledge on the Web in general. OWL is designed for use by applications that need to process the content of information (and not just merely presenting it to humans), helping machines to interpret web content supported by XML, RDF and others by providing additional vocabulary along with a formal semantics. (W3C staff, 2014)

A data model is emerging in web services and cloud computing where data exists as a set of name-value pairs. This paradigm is assumed by many web service messages, and is the basis of some cloud SaaS (Software as a Service) "NoSQL" data stores. The Universal Data Element Framework (UDEF) is a framework for describing data to enable interoperability, supporting equivalent vocabularies in different languages as well as the possibility to include enterprise and standard specialist vocabularies. (The Open Group staff, 2014).

Multiple data models may exist for one information model. Information models should be independent of platforms and technologies, and are important to provide a consistent meaning to entities, their properties and inter-relationships allowing for interoperability in information exchange between services, between clients and services, and between services and resources. (Strassner, John C, 2004)

- DEN – next generation (DEN-ng) model is an initiative and specification for construct and store information in a central repository to bind services available in the network to clients using the network. This way, applications will automatically learn about user access privileges, bandwidth assignments and policies in use, and provide services accordingly. DEN-ng models are more focused on networking and implementation details.
- The IETF defined the Simple Network Management Protocol (SNMP) being the basis for the framework designed for Internet devices and making possible to write generic management systems that interoperate with vendor-specific products.
- Distributed Management Task Force (DMTF) maintains the information models created not only in the DMTF and OGF, but also in other standards bodies. DMTF defines management standards and among them the Common Information Model (CIM) that is an information model for describing computing and business entities in systems, networks, applications and services. It is an extensible; object oriented architecture that makes it simple to track and show interdependencies and associations that can be complex among different managed objects. The standard language used to define elements of CIM is Managed Object Format (MOF) and CIM is composed of a Specification and a Schema. The Schema provides the actual model descriptions, while the Specification defines the details for integration with other management models. (DMTF staff, 2014). DMTF is also working to address management interoperability for Cloud Systems. The Cloud Management Initiative is promoting work in several working groups as Cloud Management (CMWG), Cloud Auditing Data Federation (CADF), Open Virtualization, (OVF) and Software Entitlement (SEWG). (Cloud Management Initiative staff, 2014)
- The Information Framework (SID) (tmforum staff, 2014) provides a reference model and common vocabulary for all the information required to implement Business Process Framework (eTOM) processes. This model is more focused on business needs and on "business entity" definitions and their associated attributes and definitions.
- Distributed Computing Reference Model (DCRM) is defined by the Open Group, which is a global consortium enabling the achievement of business objectives through IT standards. (Open Group staff, 2014). This model applies to Cloud Computing Portability and Interoperability providing descriptions of the components of the model, and sections on performance and security and identifies the interfaces between the components.
- Open Applications Group is focused on building enterprise ready, process-based data exchange standards for Business-to-Business (B2B), Application.to-Application and Cloud integration. The current release available is the OAGIS® 10.1 covering eCommerce, Manufacturing, Logistics, Customer Relationship Management (CRM), Enterprise Resource Planning (ERP) and using XML to define a common business language for businesses

to use. (Open Applications Group staff, 2014)

The need for abstraction layers - clear interfaces between business actors and between layers. Such abstraction layers are invoked within the context of service structuring and packaging and are meant to facilitate:

- The emergence of IP connectivity service exposure to customers, peers, applications, content/service providers, etc.
- Solutions that accommodate IP connectivity service requirements with network engineering objectives.
- Dynamically adaptive decision-making processes, which can properly operate according to a set of input data and metrics, such as current resource usage and demand, traffic forecasts and matrices, etc., all for the sake of highly responsive dynamic resource allocation and policy enforcement schemes.
- Better accommodation of technologically heterogeneous networking environments through vendor-independent configuration procedures, tools for manageability and resource orchestration while privileging direct interaction with engines (e.g., routing and forwarding) and avoiding proxies.

IV. Operation

Implementing SDN cannot be at a glance. A service provider cannot simply replace all existing equipment from different vendors by others with SDN capabilities, since it is required to support current infrastructure while services stay running with compromised Service Level Agreements (SLA). Also there is limited availability of commercially available SDN-enabled equipment. Currently there are partnerships between solution and technology providers on SDN technology integration working on the provision of better service provider cloud architectures regarding dynamic service delivery with impacts on the user's quality of experience and costs. (Ericsson staff, 2014)

Implementing SDN is starting (Brandon, Jonathan, 2014; NTT Communications Corporation staff, 2014; Buckley, Sean, 2014) and as equipment evolves, there will be opportunities to deploy SDN capabilities aimed to provide flexibility by interacting with network service modules and invoking both connectivity and storage resources accordingly, in order to meet service-specific requirements (e.g., using CPP (Boucadair et all, 2014)). This will allow configuring and operating a whole range of devices at the scale of the network for automated service delivery, from service negotiation and creation to assurance and fulfillment (Boucadair and Jacquenet, 2014).

The migration for SDN will occur naturally from the data center to the network core, where there are less equipments to activate and configure and where SDN may enable some valuable automation and service innovation, but also where the most expensive equipments are.

Interestingly, from an enterprise point of view, the implementation of SDN or NFV solutions in the WAN should take precedence over data center (Leary, Mark, 2014), followed by Local Area Network (LAN) and wireless local area network.

However, as stated in (Boucadair and Jacquenet, 2014), one single SDN network-wide deployment is very unlikely and therefore, multiple instantiations of SDN techniques will be progressively deployed and adapted to various network and service segments. One example of SDN applicability is in dynamic private cloud services, where it offers the possibility of more dynamic private (VPN) connections to cloud services on a self-serve basis.

V. Core Intelligence

The ability to predict the network behavior as a function of the network running services and those to be delivered is crucial for service providers, so that they can assess the impact of introducing new services or activating additional network features or enforcing a given set of (new) policies from both financial and technical standpoints.

The SDN intelligence may reside in the control or the management planes (or both) and is typically represented by a Policy Decision Point (PDP) (Boucadair and Jacquenet 2014), which is one of the key functional components of the policy-based management framework. An abstract layer would allow for flexibility to configure, manage, secure, and optimize network resources via dynamic, automated SDN programs.

Typical policy-based techniques will interact with both provisioned services and the network and continuously assesses if the network behavior is compliant with the objectives set by the service characteristics and those that may have been dynamically negotiated with the customer.

PDP functions capable of processing various input data (traffic forecasts, outcomes of negotiation between customers and service providers, resource status, etc.) providing better decisions and scalable are the basis of SDN networking and are still in areas that need further investigation. Also an area of further research is the SDN architecture with the existence of multiple PDP instances per domain and inter-PDP communication preventing single points of failure and satisfying performance requirements.

C. On the Standardization Front

I. OpenFlow (OF)

The Open Networking Foundation (ONF) is a user-driven organization dedicated to the promotion and adoption of SDN through open standards development (ONF staff, 2014).

OpenFlow™, defined by Open Networking Foundation, is a protocol which structures communication between the control and data planes of supported network devices. It is a standard interface designed forproviding high-performance, granular traffic control across multiple vendors' network devices following a fully centralization of packet-forwarding decisions strategy (ONF staff, 2012).

Figure 4 shows the main components of an OpenFlow logical switch.

An OpenFlow Logical Switch consists of:

- One or more flow tables,
- A group table, which perform packet lookups and forwarding, and
- One or more OpenFlow channels to an external controller

The switch communicates with the controller and the controller manages the switch via the OpenFlow protocol.

OpenFlow allows adding, updating or removing entries in the switch internal flow-tables making possible to network react to real-time traffic demands. The ONF assumes the systematic support of OpenFlow to instruct devices about how they should forward traffic. Of course, the dynamic enforcement of traffic forwarding policies can rely upon other protocols such as NETCONF, COPS-PR or other similar protocols.

Although the OpenFlow controller determines how packets are forwarded between individual sources and destinations, it doesn't provide the configuration and management functions that are required to allocate IP addresses and ports. The OpenFlow Management and Configuration Protocol (OF-Config) (that relies upon NETCONF and a specific YANG module) is a special set of rules that defines a mechanism for OpenFlow controllers to access and modify configuration data on an OpenFlow switch. This way, OF-Config offers an overall view of the network and the ability to set forwarding policies and manage traffic across devices.

The OF-Config protocol is also being developed by the Open Networking Foundation.

An OpenFlow controller could have reactive or proactive operation behaviors with different results

Figure 4. Main components of an OpenFlow Switch

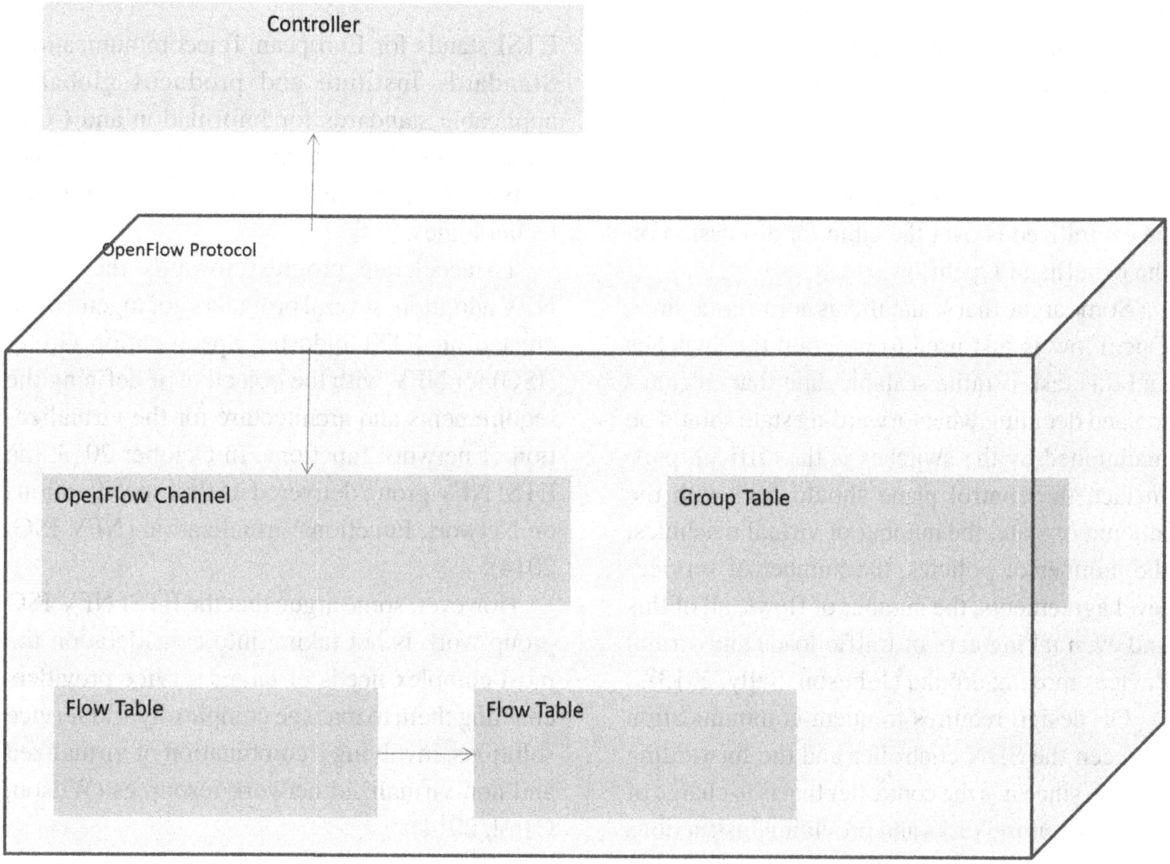

in scalability, since the controller's performance is different according to each operation mode. More precisely, in the reactive operation mode, the most common one, the first packet of the flow received by the switch triggers the controller in order to insert flow entries in each OpenFlow switch of the network. Every new flow needs a setup time. This approach is the most efficient in using flow table memory, but each new flow causes a small additional setup time, and this time could raise constraints in scalability. Moreover, if the switch loses the connection with the controller, it cannot forward the packet. In the Proactive approach, the controller populates the flow tables ahead of time for all traffic that may be processed by the switch. This approach doesn't introduce any additional flow setup times because the forwarding rule is pre-defined. In this case, if the switch loses the connection with the controller, it does not disrupt traffic forwarding. However, the network operation requires rules to cover all routes.

In fact it resembles the operation modes of a distance vector routing protocol, where if there is a failure the convergence time is significant when compared with link state routing protocols, where every router knows the overall topology and convergence time usually remains in the sub-second range . In the reactive mode which is the most common operation mode, the first packet of a flow received by a switch triggers the controller to propagate flow entries in each OpenFlow switch of the network.

The results of the work under (Fernandez, Marcial, 2013) shows that the controller is more performant when it uses the proactive approach, but in the reactive approach it facilitates the network operation and management.

It is also worthwhile to mention that besides reactive and proactive modes, it is possible to combine both, and the question of how much state should be distributed or how much should be centralized is over the table for discussion on the benefits of Openflow.

Some argue that scalability is not an issue since OpenFlow is just used to program the switches and this task is quite scalable, and that calculating and deciding what forwarding state should be maintained by the switches is the difficult part. In fact, the control plane should deal with the amount of state, the number of virtual machines, the number of policies, the number of service-level agreements, the number of flows, all of this and even taking care of traffic loads and virtual devices moving around (Johnson, Sally, 2013).

OF design requires frequent communication between the SDN controller and the forwarding engine, since it is the controller that is in charge of per flow routing tasks and providing instructions on how to handle new incoming packets. These procedures are demanding and the controller – forwarding engine connections could become congested, thereby raising scalability concerns.

Some studies about this topic referred in (Luo et all, 2012) advvocate the need to design a distributed control plane where some control functions returns back to forwarding engines or else to use multi-thread controllers

However, there is no consensus regarding the need to have yet another protocol, and which would be designed to address foreseen OF scalability issues. There is still a debate, having propositions towards analyzing the variety of existing signaling mechanisms and extensions before developing a new one.

II. ETSI

ETSI stands for European Telecommunications Standards Institute and produces globally-applicable standards for Information and Communications Technologies (ICT), including fixed, mobile, radio, converged, broadcast and internet technologies.

To accelerate progress towards the global NFV adoption, several providers got together and created an ETSI Industry Specification Group (ISG) for NFV with the objective of defining the requirements and architecture for the virtualization of network functions. In October 2013, the ETSI NFV group delivered its first specifications on Network Function Virtualization (NFV ISG, 2014).

However, some argue that the ETSI NFV ISG group work is not taking into consideration the most complex needs of larger service providers enabling them to manage complex hybrid service solutions, involving a combination of virtualized and non-virtualized network resources (Wilson, Carol, 2014).

III. TM Forum

The TM Forum is working together with leading providers in the ZOOM project, towards the definition of a vision of virtualized operations (tmforum ZOOM staff, 2014).

The ZOOM project stands for Zero-time Orchestration, Operations and Management, and aims to define a vision and architecture enabling the delivery and management of virtualized network and services. It's a framework that will define a vision of the new virtualized operations environment helping service providers to achieve flexibility and agility, enabling low cost operation.

TM Forum's ZOOM Program is organized along four key themes: Development and Operations (DevOps) Transformation Framework for Digital Ecosystem; Blueprint for End-to-End Management; Operations and Procurement Readiness and Open Source Direction (tmforum zoom program, 2014).

The ZOOM project will complement the work conducted by other standardization bodies, such as ETSI, by contributing to the development of a management platform to deploy NFV.

IV. IETF

IETF is working on SDN standards through a working group called the Interface to the Routing System (I2RS), created in November 2012. The interface to the routing system (IRS) is conceived as a programmatic, streaming interface for transferring state into and out of the Internet's routing system. The approach followed was to have decision points both at centrally located management and user applications but use the traditional routing protocols (OSPF, BGP, etc.). This strategy takes benefits of distributed routing, while it allows applications to overwrite routing decisions.

IETF is also working on Service Function Chaining (SFC) techniques, which are used to facilitate the enforcement of differentiated traffic forwarding policies within a network. This subject is also being discussed by the ETSI NFV group, as part of network function virtualization.

V. Open Source Initiatives: OpenDaylight

OpenDaylight is an open source project relying on a modular, pluggable, and flexible controller platform at its core. This controller is implemented strictly in software and is contained within its own Java Virtual Machine (JVM). As such, it can be deployed on any hardware and operating system platform that supports Java. (Project OpenDay-Light Technical Overview staff, 2014).

The controller supports the **OSGi** framework and bidirectional REST. Open northbound APIs that can be used by applications are also available. The southbound interface is capable of supporting multiple protocols (as separate plugins), e.g., OpenFlow, BGP-LS (Border Gateway Protocol – Link State), etc. (- (Project OpenDayLight Software staff, 2014 ; Gredler et all, 2014).

D. Interworking NFV / SDN

In the SDN architecture network intelligence is logically centralized at the control layer, and the underlying network infrastructure is abstracted from the applications, following a next generation network paradigm. This architecture is attractive to operators, since the control of network is on the operator's side, allowing to offer other services than merely bit transport without any added value service that can improve profits. This enables highly scalable and flexible networks that can adapt to dynamic changes in business world providing new offers, opportunities and operator differentiation.

NFV focuses on optimizing the network services themselves. Network functions like DNS, Caching, features such as Deep Packet Inspection (DPI), operation support systems (provisioning, mediation, etc.) are decoupled from hardware and fully implemented in software using cloud services, promoting service innovation, particularly within service provider environments (Pate, Prayson, 2013).

Network Function Virtualization objectives can be achieved using some Data Center techniques, however

As stated above, one can conclude that SDN and NFV are complementary to each other, but not dependent one from the other. When combined they can potentially improve the value for the operator.

NFV approach allows replacing expensive and proprietary appliances by generic hardware and advanced software running on commercial off-the-shelf servers. Second step is the virtualization of that software in an optimized location - datacenters, POPs or network edge. The third step is to take advantage of SDN throughout the decoupling of the control and data planes, allowing the evolution for network and application without the need for constant upgrades of network devices. Of course tradeoffs should be made in terms of maximizing performance, or flexibility, or scalability, since dynamic bandwidth-on-demand services for several millions of mobile customers lead to huge amounts of signaling traffic that can degrade the overall performance of the service.

Major developments are done by software. SDN aims at reducing the complexity of distributed networking control protocols with the simplicity of programming a central encyclopedic controller that administers networks optimally based upon policy decision and enforcement points supported by applications characteristics.

CONSIDERATIONS

According to (Signals and Systems Telecom staff, 2013) SDN, NFV and the network virtualization market will account for approximately $4 billion in 2014 and a foreseen growth at a CAGR of nearly 60% over the next 6 years. This means that service providers will consider migrating towards this kind of solution. From a variety of perspectives, it will be worth exploiting:

- Reducing costs: Reality or Pure Speculation?

Not only can SDN and NFV help address the dramatic traffic growth (particularly aggravated by mobile data services), but also this ecosystem can be interesting because of the likely reduction of CAPEX (Capital and Operational expenditure) by reducing the use of expensive proprietary hardware platforms and power consumption costs, also reducing the need of human resources, among others, while it improves experience for consumers.

Not only the service providers could decrease overall costs having higher margins but also they can offer better prices to customers because of easier per usage billing schemes, as other utility service (water, power, etc.) since machine-to-machine services using SDN could lead to new network management schemes, thereby improving performance and effectiveness. (Min et all, 2013)

Also industry-standard server hardware benefits from massive economies of scale and a highly competitive marketplace. It is cheaper to purchase computing cycles needed to drive network services.

- Impact of SDN and NFV on optical, Ethernet, IP networking technology:

The increase of mobile penetration, with the paradigm of all services always on, with customers always connected to social networks (Facebook, LinkedIn, Twitter,...) wherever they are, and also wired communications demanding higher and higher bandwidth put pressure on access and transport networks. Traffic patterns, also, are changing due to the adoption of cloud services, with customers exchanging high volumes of homemade data among friends and family taking advantage of cloud storage capability. This increases peering communications Using a combination of SDN and NFV techniques avoids the over provisioning of resources, since additional server-based capacity can be added whenever needed.

- Building service chains in NFV environments using SDN techniques

A service chain consists of an (ordered) set of service functions, such as firewalls or application delivery controllers (ADCs) that can be invoked for the delivery of a specific service.

The effort required to construct a service chain is high and lasts long, comprising many times the acquisition of specific hardware and corresponding deployment in the network with more or less complex configuration tasks. SDN and NFV moves management and network functions into software, meaning that building a service chain no longer requires acquiring hardware and that the entire service chains can be provisioned and constantly reconfigured from the controller. Network Functions virtualized in the cloud allow for on demand automated deployment and they could be moved on runtime to more convenient locations, or created when there are traffic peaks or during low traffic hours.

- NFV and SDN orchestration

On-demand infrastructure, meaning dynamically allocate or withdraw resources on demand, self service provisioning and virtualization could be answered by combining SDN and NFV to provide the required flexibility by full orchestration (replacing the concept of provisioning) of service performance and network domains automation and programmability with the required level of control and determinism.

Service orchestration allows the provision and management of customer services comprised of physical network elements and SDN/NFV-enabled virtual components across multiple domains over a relatively short period (near real-time). SDN/NFV will facilitate the development of cloud applications that will request resources at multiple points in networks breaking down management silos, allowing network operators to orchestrate end-to-end services.

- Impact of SDN on application delivery controllers (ADCs) in the data center

This is an issue that remains controversial and could be summarized as follows: whether the SDN controller should be standalone or integrated in other products as ADC devices, which have a better visibility of application execution. This last way will enable the operator to bypass those network functions that are not required for a particular service, improving network efficiency and granularly optimizing personalized service flows.

- Where complexity resides

SPs will need to assess the real benefits of SDN /NFV techniques and the major risks brought by the use of virtualization techniques. Virtualization is indeed exposed to several risks: the most visible risks concern security and the need to ensure that adequate measures are implemented at the IT infrastructure and operations (I&O) level in order to secure SP's customers information. Other important risks relate to performance, supportability, reliability, management and scalability. If an application or a virtual infrastructure is not properly designed and planned, it could impact the overall performance of the service delivery procedure. Moreover, hardware fine-tuning (application very specific requirement) or small modifications intended to improve performance are not possible in a virtualized environment. Supportability is another issue that deserves attention, since some applications including database applications could have specific requirements that may complicate the virtualization. Managing virtual environments with highly critical servers in a production environment is a demanding task that should be carefully executed, requiring special skills and knowledge. Reliability obliges to have redundancy in terms of servers and access and interconnection links (Fontana and Liebowitz, 2013.

Impacts of SDN/NFV techniques on organizations are likely to impact the operational level. The introduction of SDN/NFV will have a significant operational impact in Operators and Service Providers (SP), which will have to consider their management systems. OSS systems will have to migrate and the new management technologies will have to be integrated with the legacy management systems. This migration will be done according customer demand with the delivery of new Application Programming

Interfaces (APIs). Operators and SPs will move to an IT world that does not assume huge proprietary hardware units, with their specific alarms and operation, administration and maintenance, but with virtual machine user interfaces. From an industrial standpoint, it is difficult to abandon all their proprietary processes. Standardization procedures and specifications should come in advance to industry developments, and currently it comes with some delay concerning the required time to market. Standards and particularly in this case, service management standards should be ready well in advance to promote a common view across different technologies in delivering services to customers.

SDN and NFV introduce different network management models addressing legacy OSS. For SDN, two approaches are coming up: a physical network abstraction and automation layer (automating the configuration of physical and virtualized networks. Today there is a lot of manual operations); and a new set of SDN management applications that replace existing network management stacks. For NFV, the ETSI NFV group has also proposed an NFV Management and Orchestration (MANO) architecture that focuses on operational lifecycle needs of virtual network functions as they are deployed in the cloud. NFV needs to simplify (lots of complexity due to a high number of proprietary network adapters) and uniform network operations. Today's network complexity happens because there are multiple devices and management silos that have been used for many years. (Chappell 2004)

Another issue is about the SDN/NFV coexistence in an operational network. As mentioned above, the introduction of SDN / NFV should not disrupt existing SP business: these techniques will need to be introduced smoothly. A first step could consist in introducing a service orchestration layer able to automatically apply new configurations to network devices in a near real time and, at the same time, support traditional methods of service provisioning, like statically preparing configuration files to be downloaded to some devices within the context of minor or major software upgrade procedures. Open APIs that will take into consideration order management or assurance tools will allow that operators and SPs will eventually embrace SDN/NFV at their own pace.

FUTURE RESEARCH DIRECTIONS

Further research on this topic is the interconnection of cloud service providers and as a result, large scale interconnection of service providers over SDN and NFV. Research on business models that could potentiate CPU and storage applications on-demand anywhere from a chosen service provider is key (SDN resource optimization as a function of user location and mobility).

The possibility of having federations of SDN controllers working seamlessly (where a virtual service can bound endpoints together that are controlled by different controller clusters) also needs further investigation, since cloud providers will need federation between controllers for scalability reasons, because central controllers sooner or later are likely to become less performant.

Service provider's full virtualization (on the top of the cloud) and security are also important aspects to be further investigated. SDN resources should be armored against malicious procedures that could risk network and operating services. In particular, service providers should define procedures to assess the reliability of software modules embedded in SDN nodes.

CONCLUSION

This chapter presented an overview of SDN, discussed the complementarity of SDN and NFV, and also the major standardization efforts in these areas.

To summarize, SDN separates control and data planes, centralizing the control through the

SDN controller with the capability of network programmability. On the other hand, NFV relocates network functions from dedicated appliances into generic servers. SDN driver applications include cloud orchestration and networking, while NFV drivers include S/W router instances, firewalls, gateways, WAN accelerators, SLA assurance. Quality of experience at affordable prices is what customers ask for and they subscribe to a service according to their requirements. Service management platforms should take advantage of the capabilities provided by self-organizing networks (SON), dynamic restoration techniques, self-healing and anticipate problems impacting customers, by proactive provisioning of required virtualized resources (e.g., web acceleration), based on real-time service quality monitoring over the network, diagnosing and solving issues and maintaining quality of service. (ETSI NFV staff, 2012)

Regarding standardization, SDN includes the support of a new protocol called OpenFlow, specified by the Open Networking Forum. NFV is being standardized by the ETSI NFV ISG group. Operators are debating open systems and open source as a solution to lower involved costs while easing the development of interoperable implementations. SDN and NFV could be seen as complementary. SDN can act as an enabler for NFV, since the separation of control and data planes enables the virtualization of the separated control plane software. NFV can also act as an enabler for Software Defined Networks (SDN), since the separation between data plane and control plane implementations is simplified when one or both of them are implemented in software running on top of standard hardware.

Throughout this chapter several aspects were tackled as:

- Self-service functionality allowing dynamic service provisioning;
- Resources are shared with hardware virtualization, and being imperceptible for users;
- Broadband ubiquitous and constant network access – available at any time, from any device, anywhere using wired (fiber, copper) or wireless (LTE, Wi-Fi) networks
- Elasticity being easily up and down scalable pay as you consume just as another utility;
- Flexibility by continuous match to activity levels, with responsiveness capability to traffic peaks (up and down)
- Optimizes the costs with power consumption (see ***Chapter "Power-Aware Networking"***)
- Time-to-market – promotes a fast service provisioning and helps new entrants to be quickly and easily positioned in the market
- Cost reduction – it is not necessary to acquire, install and configure hardware and/or software. Tradeoff CAPEX and OPEX.

REFERENCES

Bailey, S., Bansal, D., Dunbar, L., Hood, D., Kis, Z. L., Mack-Crane, B, ... Varma. E. (2013). *SDN Architecture Overview, Version 1.0*. Retrieved from: https://www.opennetworking.org/images/stories/downloads/sdn-resources/technical-reports/SDN-architecture-overview-1.0.pdf

Boucadair, M. & Jacquenet, C. (2014). *Software-Defined Networking: A Perspective from within a Service Provider Environment*. IETF RFC7149.

Boucadair, M., Jacquenet, C., & Wang, N. (2014). *IP Connectivity Provisioning Profile (CPP)*. Retrieved from http://tools.ietf.org/html/rfc7297

Brandon, J. (2014). *Ericsson to help Telstra introduce SDN, NFV*. Retrieved from http://www.telecoms.com/278661/ericsson-to-help-telstra-introduce-sdn-nfv/

Buckley, S. (2014). *Verizon, Telus, China Mobile and China Telecom participate in transport SDN test*. Retrieved from: http://www.fiercetelecom.com/story/verizon-telus-china-mobile-and-china-telecom-participate-transport-sdn-test/2014-08-26

Chappell, C. (2004). *Managing the Virtualized Network: How SDN & NFV Will Change OSS*. Retrieved from: http://www.heavyreading.com/document.asp?doc_id=83218

Cloud Management Initiative. (2014). Retrieved from: http://www.dmtf.org/standards/cloud

DMTF. (2014). *Common Information Model*. Retrieved from: http://www.dmtf.org/standards/cim

Ericsson. (2014). *Ericsson White paper. The real-time cloud, Uen 284 23-3219 Rev B*. Retrieved from: http://www.ericsson.com/res/docs/whitepapers/wp-sdn-and-cloud.pdf

ETSI NFV. (2012). *Network Functions Virtualisation - An Introduction, Benefits, Enablers, Challenges & Call for Action*. Retrieved from: http://portal.etsi.org/nfv/nfv_white_paper.pdf

European Commission. (2003). *Enterprise and Industry. What is a SME?* Retrieved from: http://ec.europa.eu/enterprise/policies/sme/facts-figures-analysis/sme-definition/index_en.htm~

Farrel, A., Vasseur, J.P., & Ash, J. (2006). *A Path Computation Element (PCE)-Based Architecture*. IETF RFC 4655.

Fernandez, M. (2013). In Evaluating OpenFlow Controller Paradigms. *ICN 2013, The Twelfth International Conference on Networks*.

Fontana, A., & Liebowitz, M. (2013). *Introduction to Virtualizing Business Critical Applications*. Retrieved from: http://www.pearsonitcertification.com/articles/article.aspx?p=2121387&seqNum=3

Google Cloud Platform. (2014). *Pricing*. Retrieved from: https://cloud.google.com/products/compute-engine

Gredler, H., Medved, J., Previdi, S., Farrel, A., & Ray, S. (2014). *North-Bound Distribution of Link-State and TE Information using BGP, IETF draft-ietf-idr-ls-distribution-06*. IETF.

ITU-T. (2009). *ITU-T Technology Watch Report 9 Distributed Computing: Utilities, Grids & Clouds*. Retrieved from: http://www.itu.int/dms_pub/itu-t/oth/23/01/T23010000090001PDFE.pdf

Johnson, S. (2013). *OpenFlow scalability: The protocol*. Retrieved from http://searchtelecom.techtarget.com/feature/Exploring-OpenFlow-scalability-in-cloud-provider-data-centers

Kaoudi, Z., & Manolescu, I. (2014). RDF in the Clouds: A Survey. *The International Journal on Very Large Databases*.

Leary, M. (2014). *SDN, NFV, and open source: the operator's view*. Retrieved from http://bit.ly/1APDJKQ

Luo, T., Hwee-Pink, T., Quan, P. C., Law, Wei, Y., & Jiong, J. (2012). *Enhancing Responsiveness and Scalability for OpenFlow Networks via Control-Message Quenching*. Retrieved from: http://www1.i2r.a-star.edu.sg/~luot/pub/%5BICTC12%5D-OpenFlow-performance.pdf

Magoules, F. (2010). Future of grids resources management. In *Fundamentals of Grid Computing, Theory, Algorithms and Technologies* (p. 126). Taylor and Francis Group.

Microsoft Azure. (2014). *Cloud Services Pricing Details*. Retrieved from http://www.windowsazure.com/en-us/pricing/details/cloud-services/

MSV. J. (2010). The Tenets of the Cloud, In Demystifying the Cloud: An introduction to Cloud Computing. Zilmo Fash.

NTT Communications Corporation. (2014). Retrieved from: http://www.eu.ntt.com/about-us/press-releases/news/article/ntt-communications-launches-sdn-based-enterprise-cloud-in-germanyntt-europe.html

ONF. (2012). *ONF white paper (2012). In Software-Defined Networking, The New Norm for Networks*. Retrieved from http://bigswitch.com/sites/default/files/sdn_resources/onf-whitepaper.pdf

ONF. (2014). *ONF Overview*. Retrieved from https://www.opennetworking.org/about/onf-overview

Open Applications Group. (2014). *The Business Value of the OAGIS 10.1 Enterprise Edition*. Retrieved from: http://www.oagi.org/oagi/downloads/Presents/2014_BusinessValue_of_OAGIS_10.1_EnterpriseEdition.pdf

Open Group. (2014). *Cloud Computing Portability and Interoperability: Portability and Interoperability Interfaces*. Retrieved from: http://www.opengroup.org/cloud/cloud/cloud_iop/dcrm.htm#Figure_5

tmforum ZOOM. (2014). *Package: Overview, Z. O. O. M*. Retrieved from http://www.tmforum.org/KnowledgeDownloadDetail/9285/home.html?artf=artf4989

Park, S. M., Ju, S., Jonghun, K., & Lee, J. (2013). *Software-defined-networking for M2M services. ICT Convergence*. ICTC.

Pate, P. (2013). *NFV and SDN: What's the Difference?* Retrieved from http://www.sdncentral.com/technologynfv-and-sdn-whats-the-difference/2013/03/

Penno, R., Reddy, T., Boucadair, M., Wing, D., & Vinapamula, S. (2013). *Application Enabled SDN (A-SDN), IETF draft-penno-pcp-asdn-00*. Retrieved from http://tools.ietf.org/html/draft-penno-pcp-asdn-00)

Pras, A., & Schoenwaelder J. (2003). *On the Difference between Information Models and Data Models*. IETF RFC 3444.

Project OpenDayLight Software. (2014). Retrieved from: http://www.opendaylight.org/software

Project OpenDayLight Technical Overview. (2014). Retrieved from http://www.opendaylight.org/project/technical-overview

SETI. (2014). Retrieved from: http://setiathome.ssl.berkeley.edu/

Signals and Systems Telecom. (2013). *The SDN, NFV & Network Virtualization Bible: 2014–2020*. Retrieved from http://www.snstelecom.com/the-sdn-nfv-network-virtualization-bible

Strassner, J. C. (2004). *Policy-based Network Management: Solutions for the Next Generation* (1st ed.). Morgan Kaufmann.

The Open Group. (2014). *About the UDEF*. Retrieved from: http://www.opengroup.org/udef/

tmForum. (2014). *What is the Information Network?* Retrieved from: http://www.tmforum.org/InformationFramework/1684/home.html#

tmforum zoom program. (2014). *Making NFV Real*. Retrieved from: http://beta.tmforum.org/wp-content/uploads/2014/09/Toolkit-ZOOM2014.9.17.14.pdf

Wayner, P. (2014). *Amazon vs. Google vs. Windows Azure: Cloud computing speed showdown*. Retrieved from: http://www.computerworld.com.au/article/539633/amazon_vs_google_vs_windows_azure_cloud_computing_speed_showdown/

Wilson, C. (2014). *Report: NFV/SDN Standards 'Myopic' on Service Management*. Retrieved from http://www.lightreading.com/carrier-sdn/nfv-(network-functions-virtualization)/report-nfv-sdn-standards-myopic-on-service-management/d/d-id/708682

World Wide Web Consortium. (2014). *Resource Description Framework (RDF)*. Retrieved from: http://www.w3.org/RDF/

W3C. (2013). *OWL Web Ontology Language Current Status*. Retrieved from: http://www.w3.org/standards/techs/owl#w3c_all

KEY TERMS AND DEFINITIONS

Cloud Computing: Refers to the possibility of storing, processing and accessing data located somewhere in the Internet.

NFV: Network Function Virtualization is a set of virtualization techniques applied to network services.

OpenFlow Controller: Allows adding and removing flow-entries from the flow table maintained by an OpenFlow switch according to some implemented, controller-defined, policy.

OpenFlow: Is a protocol specified by the ONF and which enables to instruct switches about how traffic forwarding decisions should be made.

Programmability: Means the capability of a device or a network to accept a new set of instructions that may alter the device or network behavior.

SDN: Software-Defined Networking is as the set of techniques used to facilitate the design, delivery, and operation of network services in a deterministic, dynamic, and scalable manner.

Virtualization: Separation of software and hardware, where it is possible the creation of a virtual instantiation of a function (firewall, operating system, server, storage device or network resources).

Section 5

Advanced Service Delivery Solutions

Chapter 19
Optimizing the Delivery of Services Supported by Residential Gateways:
Virtualized Residential Gateways

Tiago Cruz
University of Coimbra, Portugal

Paulo Simões
University of Coimbra, Portugal

Edmundo Monteiro
University of Coimbra, Portugal

ABSTRACT

The Residential Gateway (RGW) is a key device, located on the customer premises, that stands between the home network and the access network. It imposes a considerable cost for the NSP and constitutes a single point of failure for all the services offered to residential customers – such as Internet access, VoIP, IPTV and Video-on-Demand. As such, the RGW constitutes an ideal candidate for virtualization, potentially relieving the NSP from such problems while also providing benefits to end-users. This chapter discusses the rationale and proposes an architecture for a virtualized Residential Gateway (vRGW) that physically removes the RGW from the customer premises, moving it into the operator data center or other logical point-of-presence, as a virtualized entity. This solution potentially reduces deployment, maintenance and operation costs, whilst improving overall performance, flexibility, reliability and manageability – both for the access network infrastructure and for the services provided over this infrastructure.

INTRODUCTION

As the access network gradually evolves towards a broad deployment of Fiber-To-The-Premises (FTTx) network topologies or cable (this is especially true, if considering the imminence of DOCSIS 3.1 (CableLabs, 2014) deployments), with DSL (Digital Subscriber Line) being progressively phased out. This trend spells the end of an era, where the decline of the old copper-based last mile paradigm with separated vertical service infrastructures gave place to a converged service

DOI: 10.4018/978-1-4666-8371-6.ch019

delivery model, with operators rethinking their service offers in order to reduce costs and improve flexibility and manageability, going well beyond the obvious performance benefits of upgrading the physical transport infrastructure.

Despite the evolution of the access network in terms of its role and underlying physical transport technologies, some components of the legacy access network model still persist, maintaining or even increasing their critical role in modern infrastructures. The Residential Gateway (RGW) is one of those components. Considering the present technology developments, the RGW starts to look like an anachronism, as it constitutes a device that mostly embodies the legacy access network model, surviving almost unchanged to the present day. As such, there is an opportunity to ponder alternative approaches. It is obviously impossible to completely remove the RGW physical device functionality from the customer premises, since it will always be necessary to bridge the local network devices (computers, set-top-boxes, telephones, etc.) with the access network. But beyond that, there is a whole array of RGW functionalities that can be moved outside the physical RGW and closer to the operator's infrastructure, thanks to advances in virtualization and access network technologies.

Virtualization technologies have become one of the main driving forces behind the evolution of the Network Service Provider (NSP) infrastructures, also proving instrumental for the introduction of cost-effective services to end-users, able to leverage the return on investment in the infrastructure. This is a natural outcome of the trend towards the convergence of technical advances in the field of virtualization, that has enabled the consolidation and scaling of resources in a cost-effective way and which has also found its way into the telecommunication operator infrastructure foundations, from data centers to networks alike. This evolution is slowly outgrowing the scope of the data center or the core network, as it reaches towards the edge of the infrastructure and into the access network (Xia, Wu & King, 2013). In this perspective, the vRGW (Virtual RGW) is a logical next step.

In this chapter we leverage the technical advances in the field of virtualization (from network to services) to propose a vRGW architecture that can be implemented on current NSP infrastructures. The proposed vRGW concept is also a departure from the conventional operator rationale about the customer premises network environment that considers it as a service consumer "island" populated by devices, going instead for an approach that extends the reach of the home network outside the physical boundaries of the home LAN. This means that the access network role might be somewhat converted from a simple connectivity pipe to an extension of the home LAN. This has a significant potential, especially considering how it can affect the way customers invoke services.

While recent developments in terms of Network Function Virtualization (NFV) and Software-Defined Networking (SDN) have prompted the industry to start developing standards and solutions to incorporate their benefits within NSP infrastructures, most of the work, including specifications, is still in its early stages. The vRGW solution hereby proposed was developed based on existing standards, namely Broadband Forum's (BBF) TR-101 (Anschutz, 2011) and TR-156 (Ooghe, 2013) broadband aggregation scenarios for DSL and GPON (Gigabit Passive Optical Networks) technologies and off-the-shelf hypervisor technologies, in order to enable a virtualized vRGW appliance that can be hosted on the NSP's network (e.g., in a data center). This deployment scenario is in line with use cases proposed by the main standardization bodies, including the NFV approach of replacing dedicated and proprietary hardware with virtual appliances implementing Virtualized Network Functions (VNF) with service chaining that allows the enforcement of differentiated traffic forwarding policies, as described in the European Telecommunications Standards Institute (ETSI) VNF-FG use case (ETSI NFV002, 2013), that can be leveraged to enable further evolutions of the baseline solution.

This chapter is organized as follows: the first section starts with an analysis of the rationale for virtualizing the RGW, also including a discussion of existing proposals, key technologies for its implementation and other aspects such as the infrastructure requirements and coexistence with the current RGW paradigm. This is followed by a section presenting and discussing a vRGW architecture proposal conceived to leverage the benefits of several virtualization technologies, while offering a compatibility strategy and migration path for the existing NSP infrastructure. Then, the management aspects of the vRGW proposal are presented, with a focus on vRGW instance management mechanisms. An evaluation-specific section is dedicated to an evaluation of the proposed vRGW, both in terms of performance and efficiency, also covering the management components. This chapter ends with a wrap-up section, providing conclusions and insights about the next developments of the vRGW concept.

THE CASE FOR VIRTUALIZING THE RGW

The expansion of high-speed broadband access networks, with an increasing growth in the number of connected households was one of the key factors that enabled a new breed of services, such as converged *n-play* offers or cloud services that are contributing to displace traditional split-medium communication and service delivery models in favour of an *everything-over-IP* approach (Royon, 2007; Smedt, Balemans, Onnegren, & Haeseleer, 2006). In line with those developments, the residential LAN ecosystem has evolved to become an environment where devices as diverse as PCs, set-top-boxes, VoIP (Voice over IP) telephones, smartphones, media players, smart TVs and storage devices cohabitate, providing access to a wide range of services to broadband customers. In fact, evolution has moved the role of the NSP towards a service-centric model where the RGW plays a crucial role, since it is placed in the nexus between three domains: connectivity delivery, services and the customer environment (Figure 1).

Standing on the customer premises, RGWs are standalone devices based on embedded system platforms that interface between the home network and the operator's access network. Their main role hasn't significantly changed over time. RGWs typically handle local network services such as DNS (Domain Name Service), DHCP (Dynamic Host Configuration Protocol), NAT (Network Address Translation), routing, firewalling, and wireless connectivity, while also providing direct support for added-value services such as IPTV – IGMP (Internet Group Management Protocol) proxying (Cain, Deering, Kouvelas, Fenner, & Thyagarajan, 2002) and VCI/VLAN management – and SIP (Session Initiation Protocol) gateways (Rosenberg et al., 2002) and/or analog terminal adapters.

Despite the current RGW deployment model is still successful, it is heavily influenced by the nature of current service distribution models and, to a certain extent, of the limited IPv4 address space. Besides, it may represent a significant burden for the operator in some contexts, due to several reasons.

To begin with, the RGW device is relatively expensive, representing a relevant share of the initial deployment costs. But initial acquisition costs are only part of the equation, as RGWs are a single point of failure, deployed right at the perimeter of the customer premises network. Malfunctioning or misconfigured RGWs may amount to a significant financial penalty for operators, both in terms of management, logistics (including on-site maintenance, in extreme cases) and customer loyalty. This situation is aggravated with consolidated service scenarios such as triple-play or quad-play, as the failure of a single RGW may lead to a complete media blackout on a household.

Additionally, the RGW can be an obstacle for remote diagnostic and troubleshooting of

Figure 1. The RGW role across different NSP service models

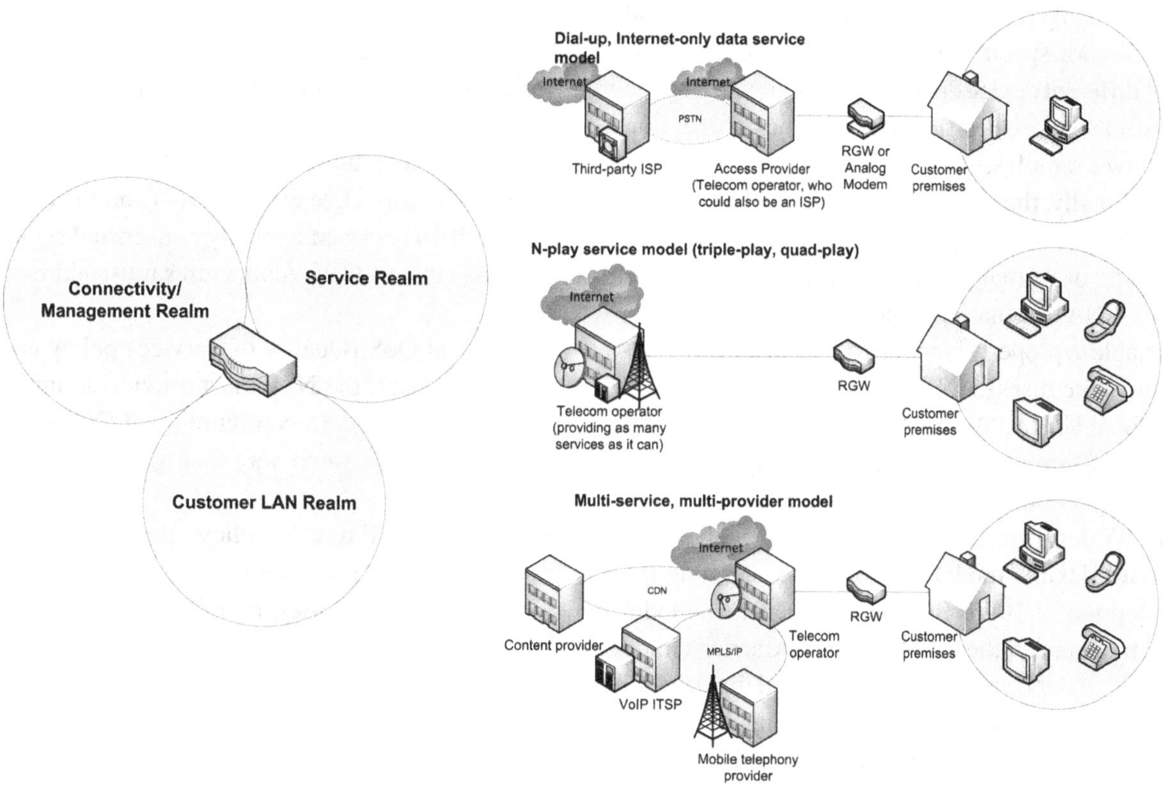

home LAN devices such as SIP phones or set-top-boxes, in order to solve problems within the customer LAN (for instance, the management/ diagnostics interfaces for certain devices within the home LAN may not be directly accessible without configuring port mappings on the RGW, because of NAT translation). The RGW might be an obstruction even for service introduction, as service time to market is often dependent on the device manufacturer to introduce support for new services which may depend on RGW support – this is often aggravated by the subsequent need to remotely upgrade thousands or millions of devices. In extreme cases, operators might be forced to consider mass replacement of RGWs to support new services, as they have reached the end of their lifecycle and cannot be further updated or simply because they have become too limited in terms of their embedded platform capabilities.

Furthermore, there is no uniform service set that a RGW vendor can integrate within some sort of "universal" device for all NSPs. Concretely, it is difficult for an operator to keep a homogeneous set of RGWs as even a single model from a single vendor may have minor firmware and hardware revisions that gradually compromise uniformity and hamper troubleshooting and management operations. This is due to several reasons such as the fact that even small hardware differences between revisions of the same RGW model may impose limitations from one model to another (for instance a smaller flash memory capacity on an older revision may limit the deployment of new services or even firmware upgrades), because of incompatibilities between firmware and hardware versions, the existence of heterogeneous feature sets between different models (or even different revisions of the same model), the risk of firmware upgrades (troublesome for a single RGW and even more dangerous for a mass roll-out) that depend on vendor-specific procedures or the management of different device data models (aggravated by the use of vendor-specific extensions), just to mention a few examples.

Finally, there is IPv6 migration, which has already started. IPv6 provides network transparency as one of its main advantages. Unlike the classic IPv4 NAT scenario, where a content provider is unable to properly identify a device within the customer premises LAN, IPv6 enables devices to have Global Unicast Addresses, enabling network and content providers to offer device specific services. This puts pressure on the current, IPv4-centric, RGW deployment model in order to evolve for a more flexible model capable of accelerating the adoption of IPv6. But the current RGW model hampers even the introduction of Carrier-Grade NAT (CGN), which is considered by several operators as part of a medium to long-term IPv4 service continuity during IPv6 migration stage.

Considering this situation, it is attractive to investigate alternative approaches in order to overcome or at least soften these problems. It is obviously impossible to completely remove the RGW physical device from the customer premises: it will always be necessary to bridge the local network devices (e.g., computers, set-top-boxes, telephones, etc.) with the access network. Still, and accordingly to the Network Functions Industry Specification Group (NFV ISG) of the ETSI (ETSI NFV ISG) and (Lee & Ghai, 2014), a considerable part of the functions currently hosted by the physical RGW device can be moved closer to the operator's infrastructure, thanks to advances in virtualization and access network technologies, namely in terms of: **Connectivity** (encompassing the DHCP Server, IPv4 NAT, NAT64, PPPoE client for BRAS connectivity or Application Level Gateways - like the ones used for dealing with the SIP NAT traversal); **Security** (including firewall, Intrusion Prevention System, parental control, port mapping or Virtual Private Network Server) and **Management** (including Web GUI, BBF CPE WAN Management Protocol (CWMP/TR-069) (Blackford & Digdon, 2013), Universal Plug and Play (eventually excluding the Internet Gateway Device profile, has it has been proven to raise security issues) and Statistics and Diagnostics). In line with this, (Lee & Xie, 2014) and the BBF (Alter, 2014) defined a mostly consensual set of use cases that vRGW architectures must address:

- Local QoS (Quality of Service) policy enforcement: the NSP must provide an interface for users to configure local QoS policies, in the same way that a conventional RGW;
- Personal Firewall policy: the NSP must provide an interface for users to configure local firewall rules, in the same way that is possible with a conventional RGW;
- NAT policy: port forwarding and other NAT features must be accessible to the end-user;
- IPv6 transition technology: as almost all IPv6 transition technologies require some functions defined in the RGW – virtualizing this functionality can ease the requirements on the RGW;
- M2M (Machine to Machine) gateway service: the vRGW must provide the same functionality as the M2M gateway of a classic RGW. As such, the NSP must provide an interface for M2M device provisioning and application management, to provide services to the users;
- Local storage: frequently, RGWs support local mass storage functionality for personal contents. The NSP might offer similar functionality to the end users (the BBF CWMP TR-140 (Kirksey, 2010) management interfaces might be of use in this case);
- VPN Service: some RGWs provide a VPN (Virtual Private Network) service for remote access (IPSec, Point-to-Point

Tunneling Protocol (PPTP), Layer 2 Tunneling Protocol (L2TP), etc.) – the NSP must be able to provision and manage VPN service for users;

- The extension of the customer premises LAN (implied by the vRGW concept) to the operator domain can be determinant to offer a new experience for browsing of private and public media, eventually using DLNA-like (DLNA, 2009) protocols for that purpose.
- Event notification: as virtualization moves the RGW outside the customer premises, it becomes tightly coupled with the NSP infrastructure. The RGW must be able to generate events to notify the NSP of relevant events – in this scope BBF's CWMP protocol support has the potential to play an important role (as it supports notifications, embedded up to the data model semantics messages as well as event subscription mechanisms);

One of the use cases benefits from the extension of the customer premises LAN up to the operator domain, something that may raise concerns about user privacy because it might lead to illegitimate probing of domestic network traffic, performed by the operator. Nevertheless, this risk already happens with current setups, where the operator remotely controls the physical RGW (which might be remotely used for illegitimate probing). Either with vRGWs or physical RGWs, if the user does not trust the operator his/her only option is to hide the home network behind an additional level of NAT/firewall – still, this is only true for network traffic that is restricted to the LAN boundaries, because every other network flow must traverse the NSP boundaries, where it can be monitored. For the latter case, end-to-end encryption may be the only available choice for privacy-conscious users.

There are several proposals describing how the vRGW might be actually implemented, differing on several aspects related to implementation, supported use cases and deployment. The next section discusses and analyses several proposals for vRGW implementation, as well as the work that is being developed within standardization bodies, working groups and organizations such as the BBF, ETSI, Eurescom or the IETF.

vRGW: One Concept, Several Perspectives

The evolution towards the virtualization of some of the RGW functions started with the first attempts to virtualize generic network router devices: (Egi et al., 2007) and (Egi et al., 2010) proposed a solution for RGW virtualization using the Xen Hypervisor (Barham et al., 2003), together with the click modular router and XORP extensible router platforms; (Pisa, Moreira, Carvalho, Ferraz, & Duarte, 2010), which studied virtual router migration scenarios on Xen hosts, with (Bazzi & Onozato, 2011) and (Zeng & Hao, 2009) discussing the virtualization-induced network performance penalty for virtualized network appliances; or (Basak, Toshniwal, Maskalik, & Sequeira, 2010) proposing a solution for implementing distributed firewalls using virtualized security appliances.

Later on, and specifically for mass virtualization of RGWs in NSP broadband access network environments, the Eurescom Project P2055 (Abgrall, 2011) provided a high-level discussion (and probably one of the first coordinated approaches to the problem, from an operator standpoint) of three alternative scenarios to remove the physical RGW from the customer's premises that claim to optimize operator's Capital Expenditure (CAPEX) and Operational Expenditure (OPEX):

- Pushing the RGW functionalities to the access nodes. This approach places packet processing near the subscribers and distributes the load across several geographically disperse nodes. However, it requires massive hardware upgrades of access nodes and fragments computing resources across the operators network – increasing complexity and costs.

- Integrating RGW functionalities on the BNG, keeping the network design unchanged (unlike the first one). However, the current BNG capabilities are not expected to support massive RGW virtualization, thus leading again to the need of hardware upgrade and fragmentation of computing resources across BNGs.
- As a stand-alone network element (NE) located somewhere in the operator's metro network. This option has the advantage of not interfering with already deployed network elements but introduces a new hardware component on the network, with inherent costs and maintenance requirements.

(Da Silva et al., 2011) discusses several alternatives to physical RGW replacement, embedding transport capabilities on the access node (OLT) and decoupling AAA, DHCP and NAT functionality. Some approaches, as those suggested by some Tier-1 equipment providers (Dustzadeh, 2013) favor the introduction of vRGW line cards in the OLT, as it is the case for Huawei's MA5600T OLT (Huawei, 2010) (which also integrates the aggregation switch and edge router functionality) – this technology is currently being evaluated by the Spanish operator *Telefonica* as of 2013 (see Figure 2).

Telefonica is also involved in another development of the vCPE concept, together with NEC (Matsumoto, 2013) which provides virtualization of RGW functionality supposedly using SDN and NFV technologies, moving virtualized functionality to the edge and data center – this solution is being evaluated in Brazil, as of October, 2014.

While those proposals paved the way for the first discussions on the vRGW concept, the introduction of new technologies, discussed in the next paragraph, have sparked again the interest in the concept as they bridge the missing gaps with existing operator infrastructures, providing much needed flexibility.

Introducing NFV and SDN

Nevertheless, as network applications and services scale and evolve (not only in sheer capacity requirements, but also in complexity), they impose an added burden to the supporting NSP infrastructure requiring the use of specific network management and traffic policies that cannot be provided by the network. In this perspective, NFV (Chiosi et al., 2012) (Chiosi et al., 2013) is a significant development as it enables the creation of flexible and on-demand network services though a, service chain-based, composition mechanism that uses

Figure 2. vRGW integrated within the OLT (simplified diagram)

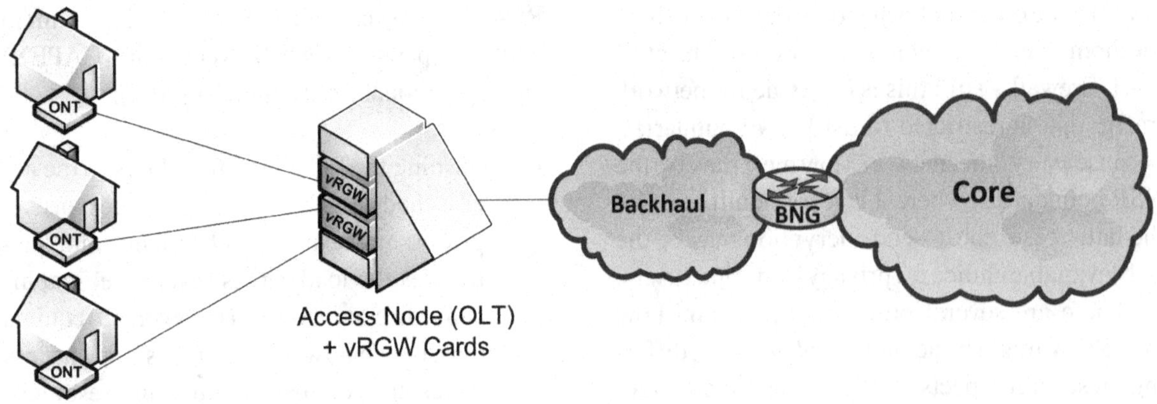

Figure 3. NFV Forwarding Graph example

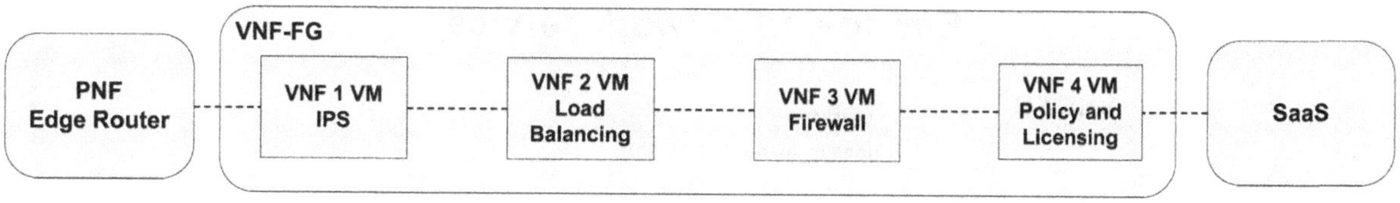

network functions implemented in VNF (Virtualized Network Functions, that can comprise functionality such as NAT, DHCP, BNGs, Firewalls, among many others) components, implemented as VM appliances.

The Network Functions Industry Specification Group of the ETSI (ETSI NFV ISG) is working on the standardization of NFV. The NFV vision attempts to decouple network capacity from functionality, by conceiving an end-to-end service as an entity that can be modeled and described by means of network function forwarding graphs involving interconnected VNFs and endpoints (also known as service chaining (IETF SFC WG)). This approach allows for creation of differentiated end-to-end services that can be provided by the (ordered) combination of elementary VNF or physical functions, chained together by a Forwarding Graph (FG), which models the service flow. Figure 3 shows an example of a FG.

Forwarding graphs chain VNFs together to define services. Furthermore, VNF FGs can be nested to define even more complex functions. VNFs are implemented in software and are interconnected through the logical links that are part of a virtualized network overlay, implemented with SDN technologies (next discussed) or network virtualization technologies such as VLANs (IEEE 802.1Q, 2011) or MPLS Pseudowires (Bryant & Pate, 2005), as depicted in Figure 4).

Eventually, even Physical Network Functions (conventional network devices with close coupled software and hardware that perform network functions) can be involved in a Network Forwarding Graph service chain (the concept of service chain is not exclusive of NFV). A virtualization layer abstracts the physical resources (computing, storage, and networking) on top of which the VNFs are deployed and implemented – the support infrastructure for such resources is the NFV Infrastructure (NFVI), which may be spread across different physical locations, called Points of Presence (NFVI PoPs).

The ETSI NFV architectural reference framework is depicted in Figure 5, being composed by several functional modules: the **Network Function Virtualization Infrastructure** (NFVI), providing the virtual resources (using COTS hardware, accelerators and software-based virtualization layer) on top of which the VNFs are supported; the **Virtual Network Function** domain, containing software implementation of VNFs (deployed on Virtual Machines, for instance) which run on top of the NFVI, also including the corresponding **Element Management Systems** (EMS) to ease integration with existing Operations Support Systems and Business Support Systems (OSS/BSS), when applicable; the **NFV Management and Orchestration** (MANO or M&O) domain deals with orchestration and lifecycle management of physical and/or software resources that support the infrastructure virtualization and the lifecycle management of VNFs and the service built using them.

The MANO domain focuses on the virtualization-specific tasks for the NFV framework, being composed by the following components: NFV Orchestrator, which is responsible for the lifecycle management of network services across the operator domain (data centers included); the VNF Manager(s) deal with the lifecycle management for the VNF instances and Virtualized Infra-

Figure 4. NFV end-to-end service with VNFs (adapted from (Ersue, 2013))

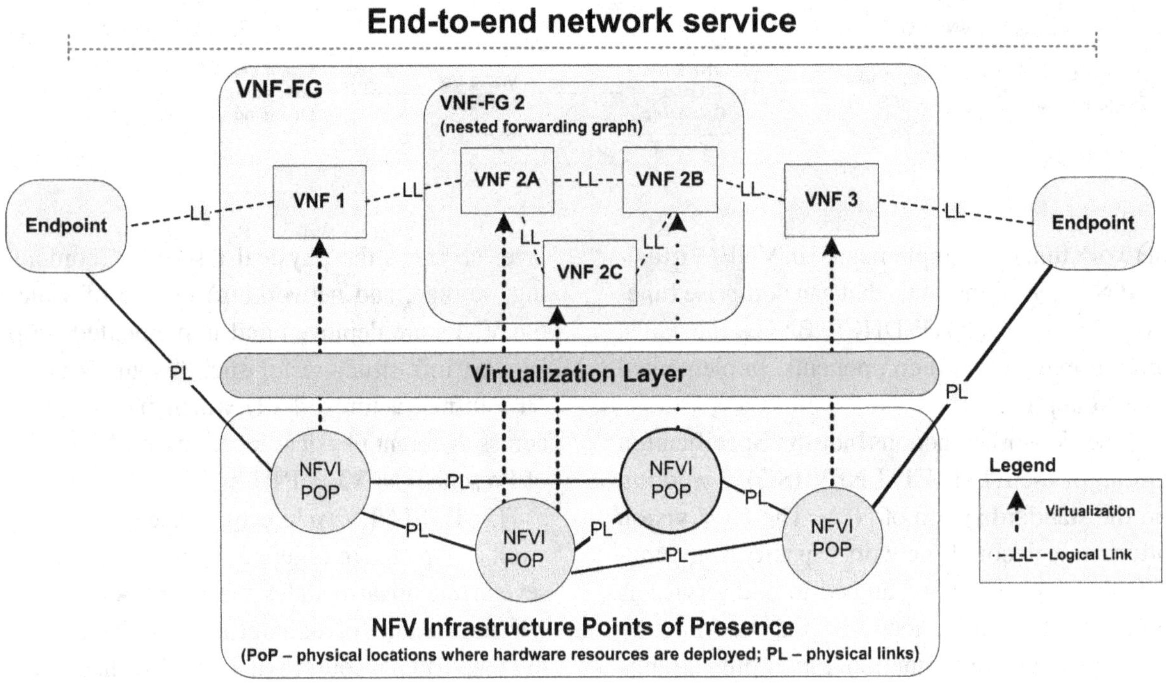

structure Manager (VIMs), which are responsible for NFVI computing, storage and networking resource management.

The entire NFV framework is driven by a set of metadata describing services, VNFs and Infrastructure requirements, feeding the MANO with the needed information about the resources it has to manage. This means that different resource providers (for instance, a VNF provider or an Infrastructure component provider, such as an hypervisor) can provide different solutions that fit within the same framework, provided they implement the APIs and descriptions for integration. This architecture also considers the relationship with existing operator OSS/BSS, defining their interfaces with the corresponding NFV domains.

SDN is an architecture that decouples forwarding functions (data plane) and network control (control plane), with the aim of introducing direct programmability into the network in such a way that it appears like a single logical switch to applications an policy engines alike. In an SDN infrastructure, there is an orchestration entity – the SDN controller – that is able to control SDN-capable switches and routers. This means that, for instance, the forwarding plane of an SDN-capable switch can be dynamically reconfigured over the network accordingly with the needs of network services and applications. Through decoupling of the data/control planes SDN allows for unprecedented flexibility and programmability in the networks. There are several SDN protocols, such as IETF FORCES (Forwarding and Control Element Separation) (FORCES, 2014) and OpenFlow (ONF, 2012).

NFV and SDN are complementary technologies: while the first one attempts to optimize and streamline the deployment of network functions (firewalls, load balancers, etc.), the second one targets the optimization of the network that supports such services. In the ETSI model, SDN can play a decisive role to implement the network virtualization mechanisms that support the logical links of a FG service chain, but also to provide

Figure 5. ETSI NFV reference architecture framework, based on (Chiosi et al. 2013)

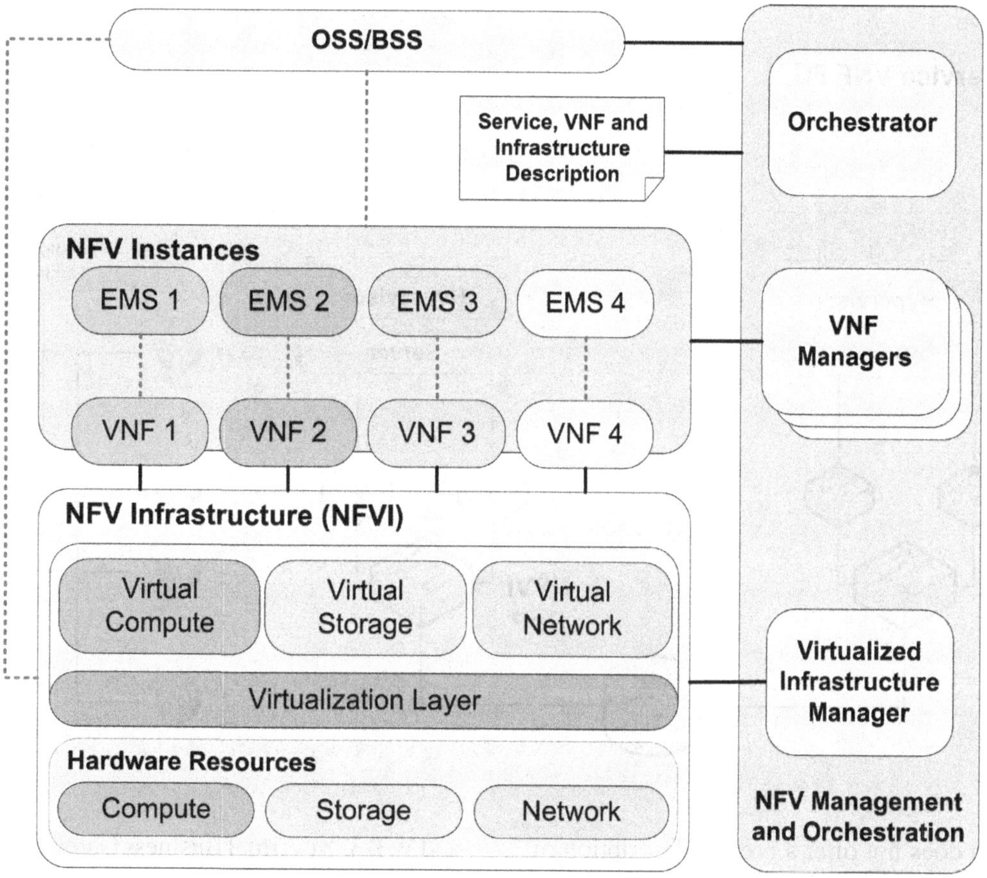

what the ETSI depicts as the NFVI as a Service use case: to provide operators with means to lease virtualized NFV Infrastructure support resources from other operators, to deploy their VNF in locations where they don't have a PoP.

Figure 6 shows an example of an OpenFlow SDN implementation for NFV, involving a service forward chain that interconnects two endpoints ("A" and "B"). This FG encompasses VNFs that are deployed across two NFVI PoPs – the M&O/MANO can interface with an OpenFlow controller, through its northbound interface to instruct network devices on how to make forwarding decisions accordingly with service function chain-specific information carried in packets, relaying the VNFs that are part of the service function chain.

Leveraging NFV and SDN to Support the vRGW Concept

It comes with no surprise that SDN, NFV and other developments in service and systems virtualization (such as commodity hypervisors) are recognized as key to realize the vRGW concept. In this line, the ETSI NFV Industry Specification Group has proposed a Virtualization of Home Environment use case (Figure 7) (ETSI NFV002, 2013) that describes how a RGW (and even a Set-Top Box) might be virtualized and migrated to the service platform located in the network, with benefits in terms of service simplification and integration.

In the ETSI vision, the vRGW still provides private addresses to the home devices, and mediates the delivery of services to home devices. However,

Figure 6. Example of an OpenFlow SDN implementation for a VNF service forward chain (adapted from (ONF, 2014)

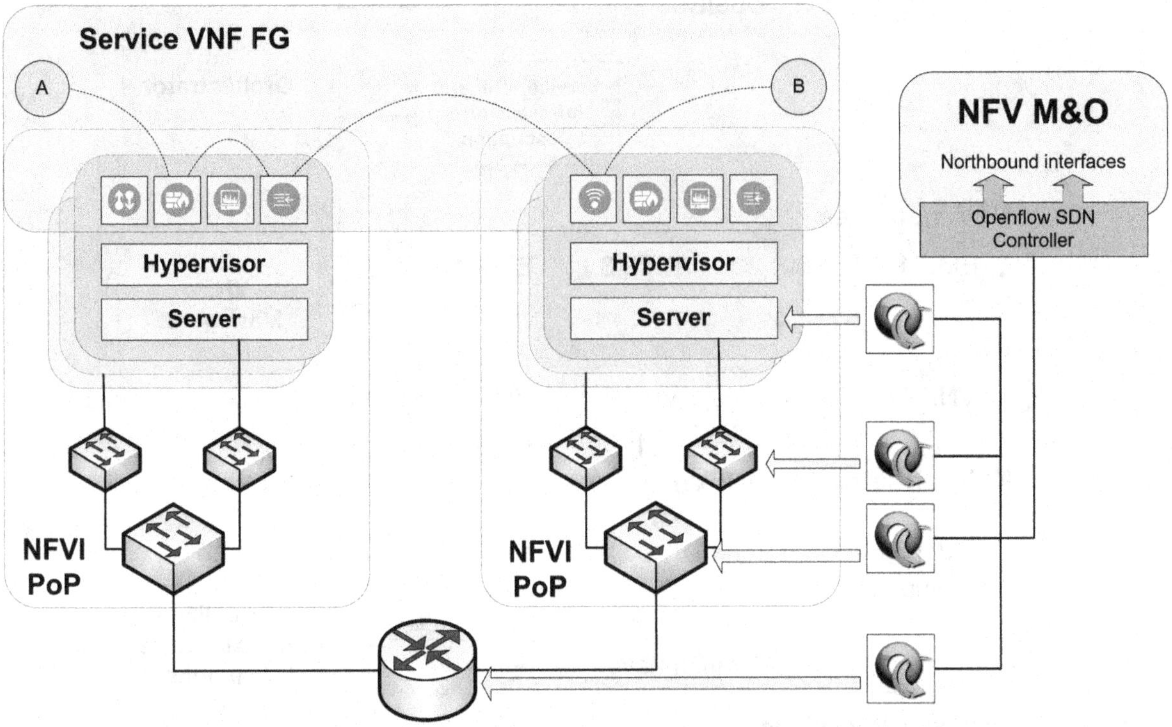

its vision does not offer a precise description of how nodal or functional distribution might be undertaken within the NSP infrastructure. This is because the introduction of NFV into carrier environments is still under definition, with several organizations and standard bodies working to evaluate existing options and propose adequate solutions.

Also, the Broadband Forum has been working since 2012 on several standards regarding the use of virtualization technologies for home and business gateway architectures. According to a liaison letter sent to the IETF, dated March 2014 (Alter 2014), the BBF became aware the IETF had interest for home and business gateway virtualization, as documented by recent drafts such as (Lee & Ghai, 2014) and (Lee & Xie, 2014). As a result, the BBF end-to-end architectures group started working on two documents (working texts), namely WT-317 (Network Enhanced Residential Gateway, NERG)) and WT-328 (Virtual Business Gateway, expected to be completed during 2015). The conceptual model for the NERG (Figure 8) explicitly follows an approach where the vG (virtual Gateway) is decoupled from the BRG (Bridged Residential Gateway). While the vG is in charge of service and network functions such as IP forwarding, routing, NAT, IP addressing, the forwarding plane is left at the customer premises, in the BRG (an ONT - Optical Network Terminal - with an integrated OpenFlow switch, for instance). Moreover, the NERG can make use of SDN (possibly based upon the use of OpenFlow) to make it control the BRG from the vG or another network controller. The fact that a SDN protocol is carried in-band means that a protection and fail-over schemes will have to be implemented to ensure security and availability.

Through WT-317, the BBF is analyzing several approaches to shift some of the functionalities of

Figure 7. ETSI NFV Virtualization of Home Environment use case (adapted from (ETSI NFV002, 2013))

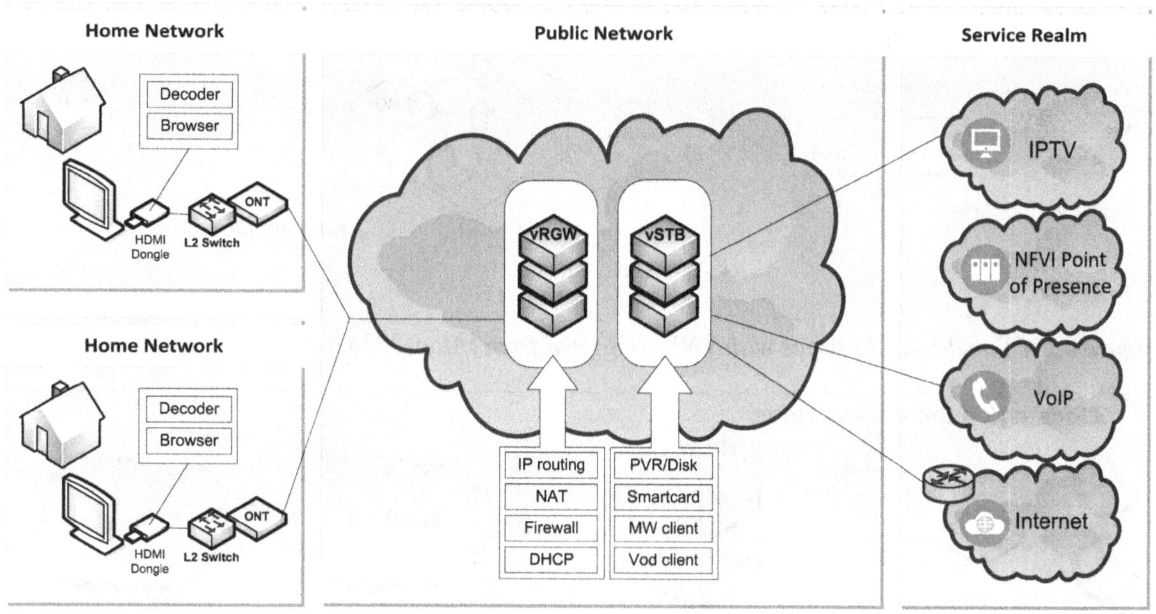

a RGW to the operator's network, through the use of NFV and SDN technologies. The main goal is to ease the deployment, maintenance and evolution of both existing and new capabilities while simplifying the RGW. WT-317 contemplates a series of nodal distribution scenarios (Figure 9), some of them evocative from the Eurescom proposals, contemplating the deployment of the vRGW within the access node, on the BNG or on a data center/cloud.

The BBF also introduces a new distribution model, called *Hybrid boxing* that splits the vRGW into two separate entities: the Service-vRG (which deals with services and SDN control) and the Network-vRG (that deals with the forwarding plane) – this allows to leverage the power of SDN to implement policy-based forwarding of subscriber traffic. Considering the ETSI model, it also becomes clear that the BBF proposals are compatible with the introduction of NFV and SDN elements.

Apart from the use generic vRGW use cases already discussed, the BBF foresees the NERG as a platform for leveraging the potential of commodity x86 virtualization advances for redundancy, elasticity and availability, supporting a wide range of applications and services. In fact, the BBF sees this as an opportunity to push an application store model for vRGW – this component-based model is not entirely new, as the BBF already envisioned such a business model through the use of TR-157 (Carey & Kirksey, 2011) component management for RGW embedded execution environments, such as OSGi (OSGi, 2012).

Also, since 2013 the BBF has been working on SDN-based use cases and their mapping to the BBF network architectures TR-101 and TR-145 (Cui & Hertoghs, 2012), in the form of working texts and study documents that are paving the way for future standardization efforts, such as WT-302 (Architecture and Connectivity of Cloud Services for Broadband Networks) and SD-313 (Business Requirements and Framework for SDN in Telecommunication Broadband Networks). The BBF is also working on the concept of flexible service chaining (this is also relevant in an NFV scenario, as it relates to the definition of chained Virtualized Network Function appliances within

Figure 8. The Broadband Forum NERG (adapted from (Alter 2014))

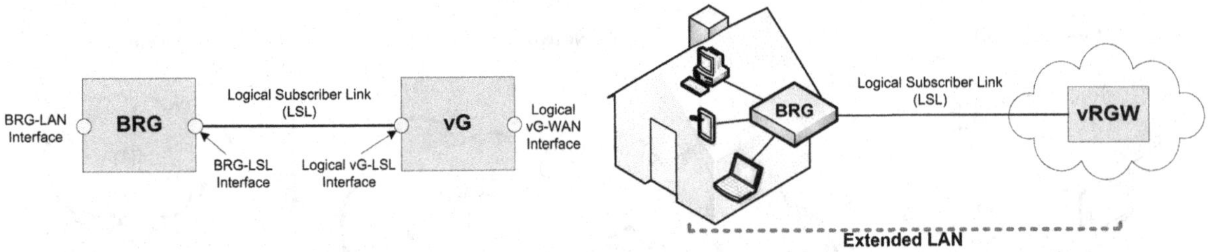

Figure 9. NFV end-to-end service with VNFs (adapted from (Alter 2014))

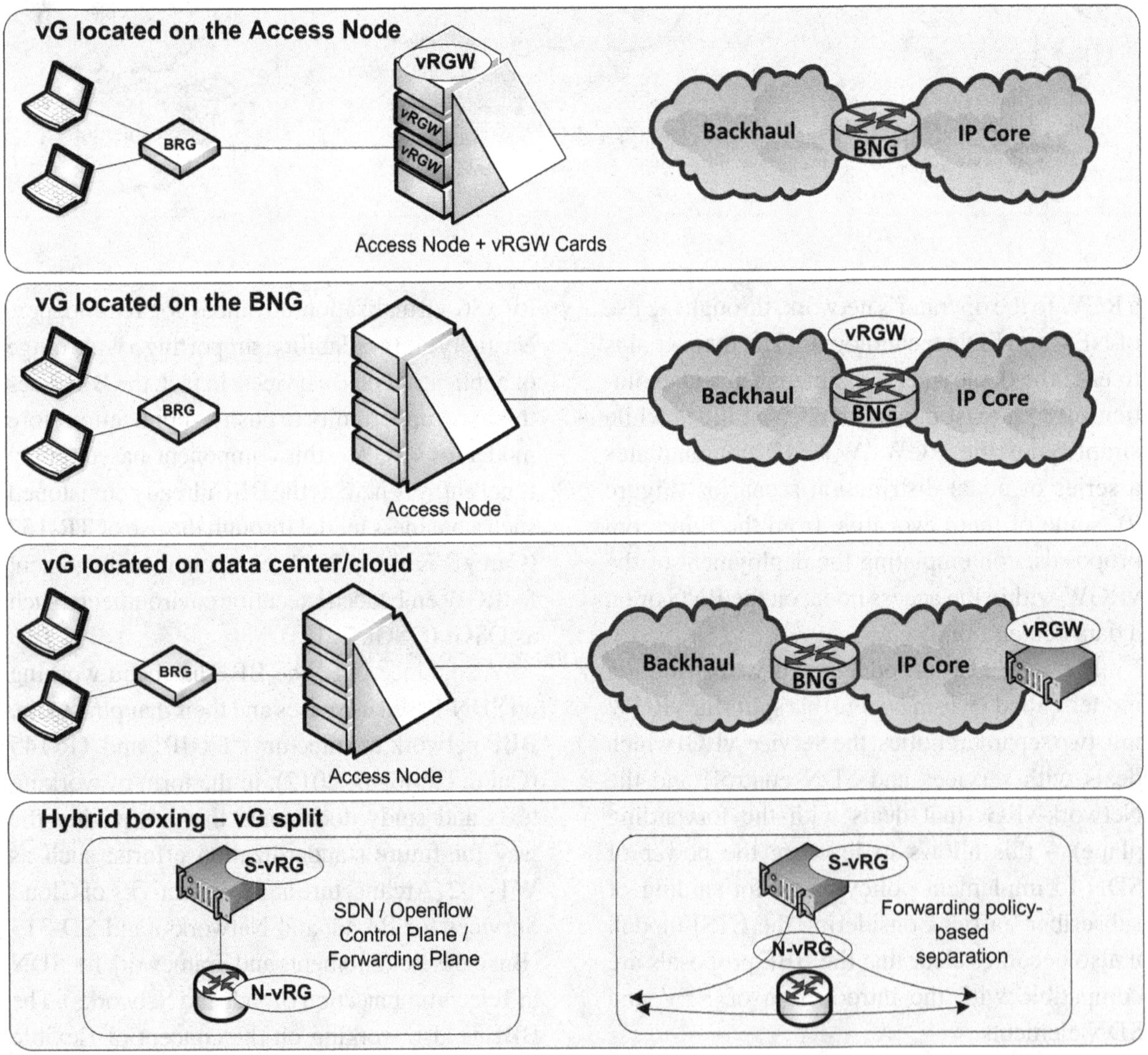

the ETSI NFV framework), as the study document SD-326 suggests (Alter & Daowood, 2014). This goes in line with the recent proposals from (Niu, Li, Jiang, & Yong, 2014), (Quinn & Nadeau, 2014), (Boucadair et. al., 2014), (Boucadair, Jacquenet, Parker, & Dunbar, 2014) and (Jiang & Li, 2014), that point towards the idea of using complex service composition for the creation of value-added service propositions by the chaining of advanced functions that go beyond basic routing or forwarding, such as differentiated forwarding, firewalling, Deep Packet Inspection, IPv6-to-IPv4 NAT, among others - it is important, however, to note that those proposals relate to Service Chaining in a generic perspective as it might involve PNFs as well as VNFs.

Also, (Lee & Ghai, 2014) and (Lee & Xie, 2014) document a proposal for virtualizing home services that contemplates an approach which decouples the RGW in a manner that is similar to the BBF hybrid boxing nodal distribution model (Figure 10), as it splits the RGW functionality into a Virtual CPE Packet Forwarder (VPF) and a Virtual CPE Controller (VC). It also maintains a simple bridge device on the customer premises, with no forwarding plane control capabilities, unlike the BBF NERG (such as an ONT).

The VPF is a network device that is optimized for packet processing, also including a northbound API for VC communications, to exchange control plane information (ACL rules and QoS parameters, for example). The Virtual CPE Controller embeds the control plane controller for the VPF, together with the Virtual Services (VS) available for the subscribers, also storing user service subscription rules used to provide the VSs for subscribers. Each VS contains the service definitions and the corresponding service logic: for instance, an IPS, a parental control service or a firewall. It is supposed for an NSP to be able to scale VS horizontally, also being able to allocate VS instances in a per-subscriber basis. The NSP provisioning system provides the information the VC needs about customer service activation and service-specific parameters.

Albeit those scenarios show promise in what regards to the development of a vRGW use case built using NFV and SDN technologies, they also pose some other questions. For instance, while the introduction of SDN and NFV into carrier environments could prove useful to the success of the vRGW concept, there are still several challenges to be tackled, even more so if we consider that the introduction of NFV into the NSP is still a work in progress. This means that some of the currently presented proposals are under evaluation and might be further developed with the introduction of standards and other reference documents.

vRGW Implementation Requirements

Both (Xia, Wu & King, 2013) and (ETSI NFV002, 2013) suggest a set of requirements that must be satisfied to make it possible to virtualize RGWs (and other Customer Premises Devices – CPE), as they raise several challenges regarding aspects such as bandwidth or computing resources:

- Scalability: functional migration from home devices (such as the vRGW) to the NSP infrastructure implies a considerable number of virtualized instances to be supported. This might raise scalability issues related with aspects such as: resource management, network bandwidth, fault detection and troubleshooting, among others. With estimations for the number of virtualized instances going up to the hundreds of thousands (ETSI NFV002, 2013) (Dustzadeh, 2013), means that a straightforward implementation of a VM-based vRGW would consume significant resources. As such, in order to manage cost and scale, an effort must be made towards the maximization of the number of virtualized instances and devices supported on a limited number of CPUs – this also calls for

Figure 10. High level architecture for a SDN-based split vRGW (adapted from (Lee & Xie, 2014))

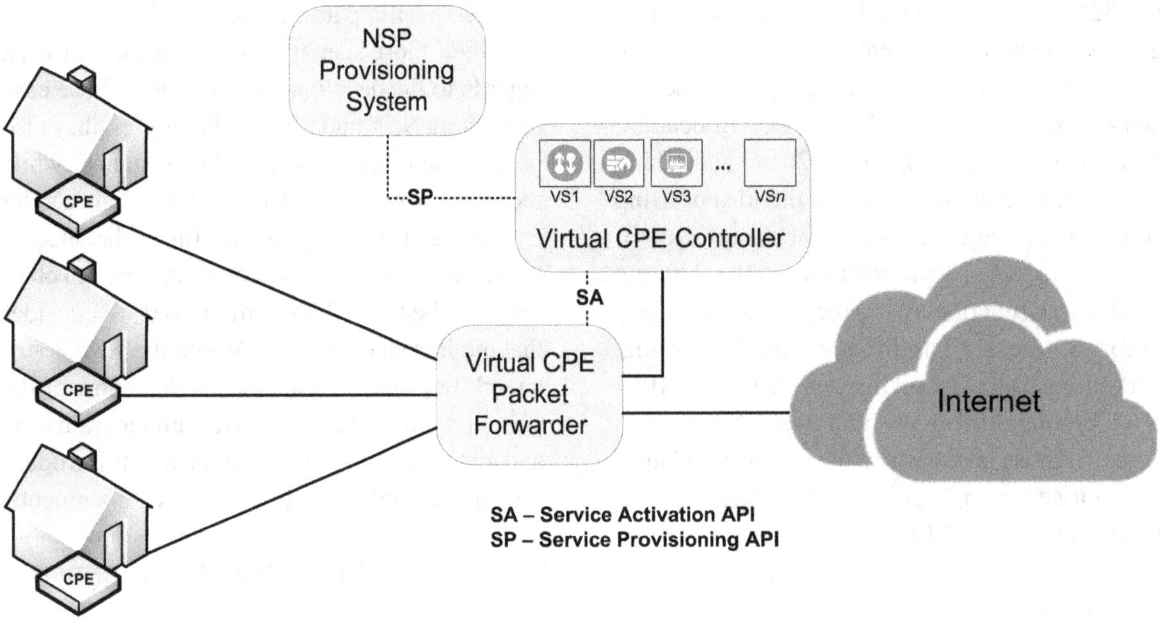

service consolidation to network located functions, horizontally scaled with server pools (such as DHCP) instead of using full virtual instances, but this also raises the problem of coordination as customer resources become scattered over different places – a question addressed by the next item.

- Service dynamics and elasticity: it must cope with the dynamics of the end user's applications and services, driving the virtual service node to be able to accommodate (through an alteration of topologies or functions). Also, the need for orchestration of scattered customer services means that the required per-user functionalities must be adequately instantiated, on-demand. Elasticity is also a key feature, as the ability for meeting demands depends on the capability to scale hardware resources as needed;
- Management and orchestration: regarding management, there are two perspectives to be considered – users and operators. Users do not want to relinquish a certain amount of control over their CPE devices, even if they are virtualized – this calls for some sort of "shared management" approach in which the CPE can be jointly shared by the end-user and the NSP that could eventually evolve towards some form of multi-tenancy, involving third-party content and service providers. As for operators, there are service coordination challenges when some functions are embedded in the vRGW while others are in the network (e.g., ACLs, security filtering rules): an example of this can be witnessed in the BBF NERG proposal or even the split-box approach that both the BBF and (Lee & Xie, 2014) have documented: these approaches do not (yet) account for the scalability, availability or security issues that arise with the decoupling of the forwarding and control plane in split topologies with the in-band introduction of an SDN protocol. This also calls for the integration of existing management and OSS technologies in the new manage-

ment paradigm, in order the cope with the lifecycle management and orchestration of software and virtualized functions as well as the infrastructure resources needed to support them – in this perspective, automation is also a vital feature to enable flexible and cost-effective, on-demand, operations;

- Stability, resiliency and continuity: service continuity and reliability during network or access link failures will remain a critical requisite. This means that the impact of service disruption must be limited, by avoiding single points of failure in the vRGW design (and also in the supporting infrastructure).
- Component portability: enabling the capability to load, execute and move software functions across different data centers. This is key for vRGW component migration (for instance, allowing components to move to a Point-of-Presence (PoP) closer to the customer geographic area) or recovery, but also to ease the introduction of VNFs or virtual components from third-party providers.
- Security: the evolution towards a vRGW paradigm must not compromise the home environment security. Also, the evolution towards a virtualized environment might expose the operator and/or customer to external attacks not foreseen or possible in legacy infrastructures;
- Energy efficiency: large scale virtualized infrastructures must be planned for energy efficiency. This transcends the data center energy efficiency issues (that are also important for the vRGW), also including the network infrastructure. For instance, in a vRGW embedded within an OLT or BNG there is the need to supply the power for new service cards, in opposition to the classic RGW model, where the customer supports the costs. While such costs might depend on several factors such as the nature of the deployment, the design of the support hardware and the specific characteristics of each site (power supply availability, reachability, etc.), the consolidation benefits should account for a significant part of the added expense. As an example, properly implemented power management and balancing within the same device (such as an OLT) can ensure that the vRGW cards sharing the same backplane can consume less energy than the corresponding standalone RGW devices altogether, and even if the energy costs are to be spread among costumers, it will amount to a negligible monetary overhead;
- Coexistence: coexistence of virtualized and legacy infrastructure components must be ensured. This will be discussed into more detail in the next section.
- Improved Quality of Experience (QoE): the end-user QoE must be significantly improved, as it is a driving factor for the acceptance and introduction of virtualized technologies, even if the end user might be unaware of its existence. This can be achieved, both by improving existing services and through the introduction of new, value-added services, discussed on the next point.
- Optimize the delivery of Value-Added Services (VAS): one of the key points for the vRGW proposal is the ability to deliver VAS in a flexible manner. The vRGW must improve the ability to deliver VAS per customer and/or per device in the home, providing enough flexibility to add new VAS from a self-care portal, for instance. The vRGW must ease the introduction of shared services such as parental control, advanced firewall, intrusion detection systems or antivirus, which can be shared among customers. This may also reduce the overhead

for VAS operation and maintenance, with an impact on OPEX.

Future developments of the vRGW use case must seriously address these requirements in order to succeed, leveraging a wealth of potential benefits in terms of CAPEX, OPEX and flexibility, while helping the RGW make the leap into the service-centric era.

Coexistence with the Existing Operator Infrastructure

As per (ETSI NFV002, 2013), coexistence between virtualized and non-virtualized functions is considered mandatory for the NSP infrastructure, mainly because the transition is expected to be a gradual and smooth procedure, implying that there will be a stage where legacy infrastructures will coexist along NFV infrastructures, and also because not all functions are eligible for virtualization (remaining as PNFs).

Specifically, the ETSI NFV *Virtualization of the Home Environment* use case addresses the virtualization of the RGW and Set-Top Box (the latter being outside the scope of this chapter), also accounting for coexistence issues – Figures 11 and 12 depict a scenario where conventional RGWs exist along with vRGWs. It must be noted that equipment such as optical splitters is not depicted, in order to remove unnecessary complexity from the figures.

Conventional RGWs (Figure 11) are connected to the BNG using a PPPoE tunnel or IPoE, which provides connectivity to the Internet or operator data centers or private cloud infrastructures (which might host parts of the NFVI), with IPTV and VoIP traffic bypassing the BNG (supported via BBF TR-101 and TR-156 aggregation scenarios for DSL and PON respectively, which are discussed in the next section and provide support for N:1 transport of Service VLANs into the customer network for Multicast IPTV and/or VoIP).

The same scenario can simultaneously support vRGWs (Figure 12), virtualized in private or public IP addresses (the figure only depicts the public IP case), which are deployed in the NFV network (or NFV front cloud), with the customer private LAN domain being extended up to that scope – for IPv4, the vRGW still provides private addresses to home devices and might communicate with a virtualized STB (not shown) by using a public or a private address. For IPv6, the vRGW provides the network prefix, received via stateless DHCPv6 RFC3633 (Troan & Droms, 2003) prefix delegation (or eventually via the method proposed by (Arkko, Lindem, & Paterson, 2013)), which is going to be assigned for internal hosts, using Stateless Address Auto-Configuration (SLAAC) and/or (stateless or stateful) DHCPv6. For all cases where a stateful DHCPv6 server is not used, hosts will generate their own IPv6 addresses by using the assigned network prefix.

As for the impact on OSS/BSS systems, the MANO components for the ETSI NVFI have been designed and laid out to interact with existing OSS/BSS systems (albeit it is recognized that NFV will most likely have a profound effect on current OSS/BSS architectures). However, the interfaces within the MANO domain and between it and the OSS still need to be standardized to reduce the integration effort in a heterogeneous multi-vendor infrastructure. In order to enable automation and agile management, the NFV MANO and OSS/BSS need to agree on interfaces and associated information and data models, as well as their business processes (such as Billing or Security). The impact on existing OSS will depend on its own nature – in some situations it may be as simple as configuring an integration agent, while in others it might imply profound configuration changes and even roll-out of new OSS components. The ETSI NFV is working to minimize the OPEX and complexity of integration but, once again, this is a work in progress as these aspects will need fur-

Figure 11. Operation of a conventional RGW within a vRGW-enabled scenario (adapted from (ETSI NFV002, 2013))

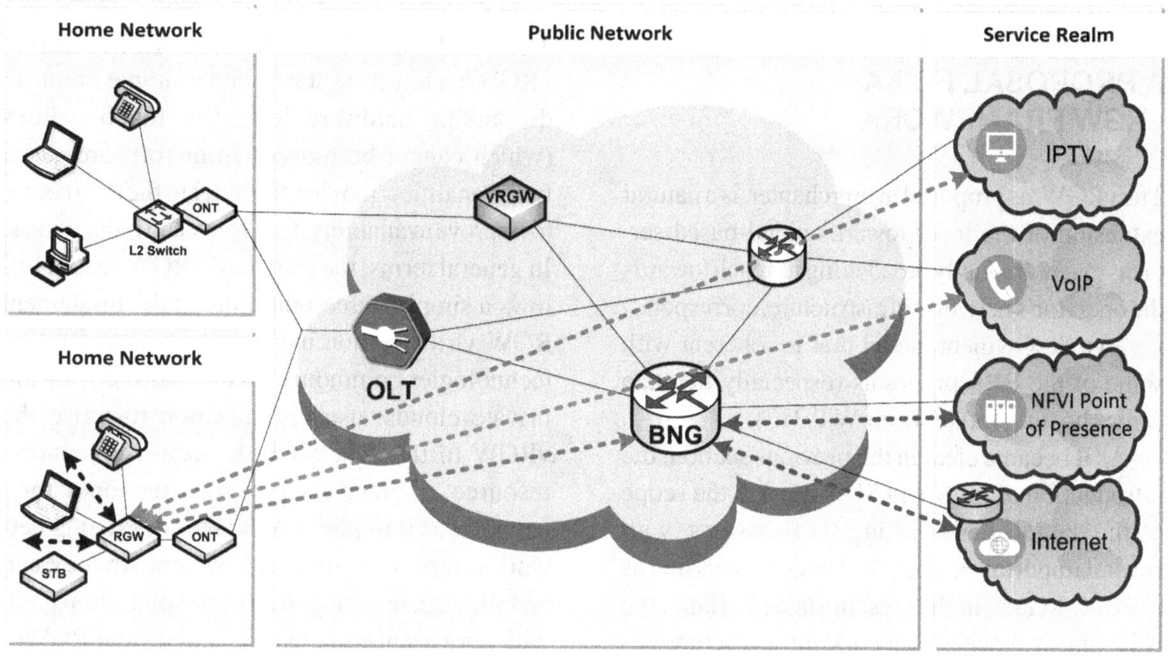

Figure 12. vRGW operation, as per the ETSI NFV vision (adapted from (ETSI NFV002, 2013))

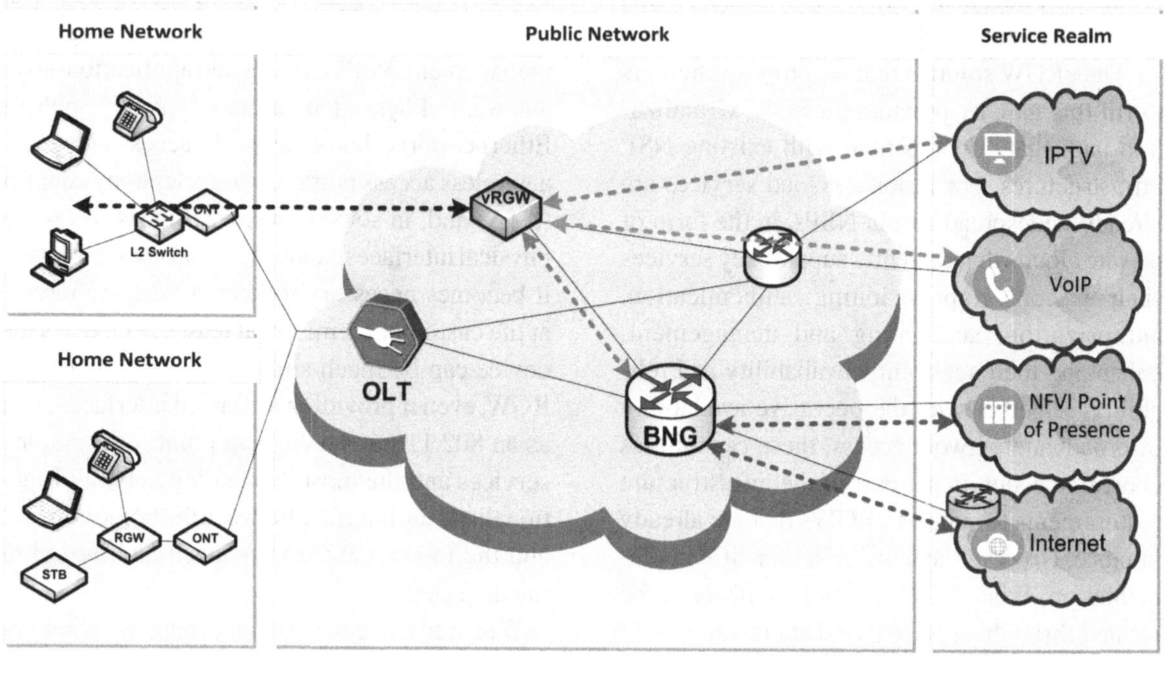

ther development, involving other standardization bodies and organisms.

A PROPOSAL FOR A vRGW FRAMEWORK

The vRGW, as proposed in this chapter, is a natural extension of the trend towards cloud-based services that is gradually broadening its reach towards the operator's network infrastructure, corresponding to a deployment model that is coherent with some of the BBF proposals (especially the data center hosting model from WT-317).

As it became clear in the previous section, the introduction of NFV and SDN outside the scope of the data center is taking its first steps, with several important aspects still under discussion as of 2014. In fact, in the present state of affairs, the NSP physical access network infrastructure has remained relatively excluded from the virtualization trend (the ETSI has proposed a use case for dealing with virtualization of the control plane for access nodes), since many of its components strongly depend on location.

The vRGW solution that we propose attempts to fill this gap, by providing a RGW virtualization path that is compatible with existing NSP infrastructures. For instance, cloud services are already widespread within NSPs, in the form of private clouds that currently support key services such as content provisioning, authentication, authorization, accounting and management, enhancing their scalability, availability and reliability. Together with the pervasive availability of broadband network access, these capabilities constitute a significant part of the infrastructure requirements to support vRGWs that are already in place. However, and due to its specific implementation, this vRGW solution is likely to be refined through an NFV-based approach.

Rationale for the Proposed vRGW Architecure

The fundamental rationale for the proposed vRGW architecture starts with a simple premise: decoupling hardware-dependent functionalities (which cannot be moved) from software-based functionalities, moving the latter to the data center to improve availability, flexibility and reduce costs. In general terms, the proposed vRGW model follows a simple, three-point, rationale: implement RGW virtualization using mature virtualization technologies commonly used in data centers and private clouds; use virtualization to move the vRGW to the data center to reduce computing resource fragmentation across the operator's network; as it implies no changes in existing network setups, a gradual deployment strategy can be followed, resulting in an easier migration path, with coexistence of physical and virtual RGWs.

RGWs typically consist of an embedded device based on specialized derivations of Unix (or a proprietary small-footprint OS, for that matter), including services such as NAT, routing, DHCP, firewalling, DNS, content filtering, QoS management, VoIP services and application-level gateways. Physical interfaces typically include Ethernet ports (home network, access network), a wireless access point, analog telephony adaptor (ATA) and, in some cases, USB ports. As some physical interfaces cannot be completely removed, it becomes necessary to keep a bridging device at the customer premises (at least the ONT). This device can be much simpler than a full-fledged RGW, even if providing advanced interfaces such as an 802.11 wireless access point: the complex services and the most demanding network functionality – the interface between the home network and the Internet – are virtualized and moved to the data center.

From a virtualization environment point-of-view, the RGW has modest computing requirements (embedded processors and a few hundred Mbytes of RAM), with the possible exception of the network interfaces between the access network and the home network. Overall, this means that virtualization of RGWs can be performed using off-the-shelf virtualization platforms, while further reducing their computing requirements. Even potential compatibility issues (due to the embedded hardware of RGWs) are also minimized by the fact that RGW firmware is usually based on Unix-derived software stacks ported to several hardware platforms, including the Intel x86 family, which is a popular platform for commoditized systems virtualization.

For the specific case of the vRGW, what we propose is a hybrid approach, decoupling hardware-based and software-based functionalities as much as possible, while extending the logical reach of the customer's "home network" to the data center so that it can include the virtualized RGW. This implies that, as already mentioned, there is a remaining device left at the customer's premises, mainly for simple bridging purposes. Figure 13 illustrates this approach.

It should be mentioned that the proposed approach is not a mere transfer of a handful of services from the (physical) RGW to the operator infrastructure: **first**, the remaining bridging device needs to be drastically simplified, in order to effectively reduce the associated capital expenditure (CAPEX) and operational expenditure (OPEX); **second**, the access network infrastructure (and the data center) needs to accommodate thousands or millions of logical networks, in order to link the home network of each customer with its vRGW; and **third**, the virtualization technologies at the data center need to efficiently support a large number of vRGWs. Whilst commodity virtualization platforms can be used, it should be noted that the proposed vRGW is different from the typical virtualized server instance, demanding less computing resources but more network performance (e.g., to support routing/bridging, NAT and/or firewalling).

It also must be mentioned that this approach makes sense for NSPs and/or service operators that are also involved in the cloud providing and or hosting businesses and are willing – for cases where operator data centers are only used for internally terminated services (such as OSS or IPTV), the absence of Internet pass through discourages the proposed approach. Such cases will be addressed into more detail later on, together with several other possible architectural optimizations.

Next we will present the key network virtualization technologies that enable the implementation of the proposed vRGW concept within existing operator infrastructures, therefore enabling its implementation before the mass introduction of NFV and SDN capabilities, which should be available in the medium-to-long term timeframe.

Network Virtualization Technologies for vRGW Support in Current Operator Infrastructures

Logically extending each customer's home network to the data center is a considerable challenge, due to the inherent scalability and manageability requirements. To the best of our knowledge, the proposals to address such a virtualization context are still being developed and discussed, as it was shown in the previous section. Nevertheless, two reference frameworks from the BBF for Ethernet-based broadband aggregation scenarios can be used for this purpose (even though they were not specifically developed with this objective in mind), namely TR-101 (Anschutz, 2011), which targets DSL technologies and TR-156 (Ooghe, 2013) for GPON scenarios.

Broadband Forum VLAN Aggregation Topologies

For GPON scenarios, the Optical Line Termination (OLT) and Optical Network Terminal (ONT) share the responsibility for Access Node VLAN requirements as specified by the Broadband Forum. TR-101 identifies three VLAN topologies:

Figure 13. Classic RGW vs. Virtualized RGW

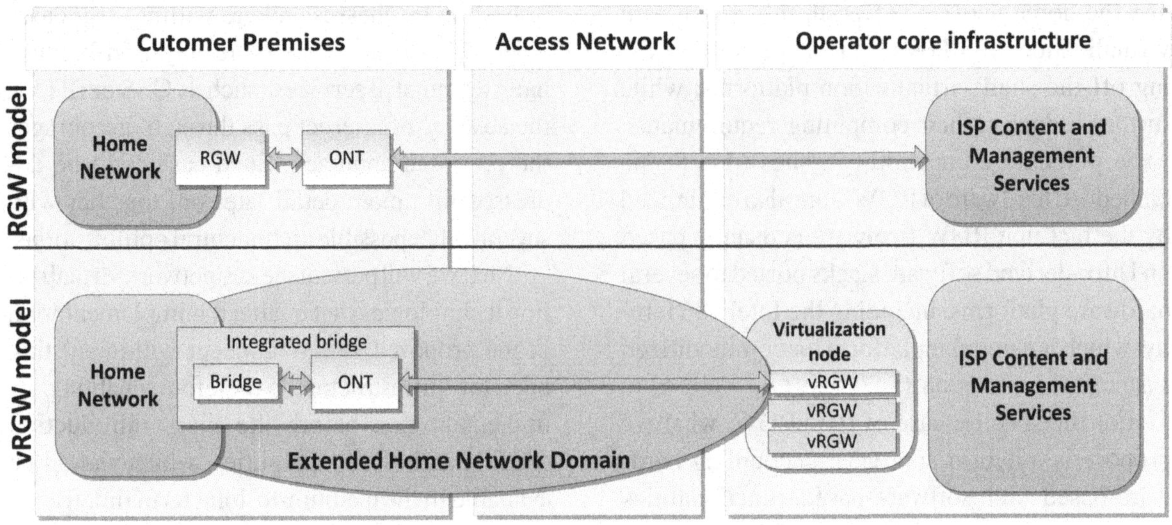

- **Service VLAN (N:1)**. This topology defines a single VLAN per service, which carries traffic to all subscribers. Each new service requires a dedicated VLAN (S-VLAN). This fits quite well into the IPTV model, where multicast IPTV is delivered in the same VLAN for all subscribers. Specifically considering GPON scenarios (TR-156 – Fig. 14), the ONT adds an S-VID (S-VLAN ID) or translates an incoming S-VID tag for upstream traffic – there is always an S-VID between the aggregation node and the access nodes. The aggregation node will allow any upstream frames with an S-VID to pass-through.
- **Customer VLAN (1:1)**. According to this topology, there is one VLAN per subscriber, which carries all its traffic. This topology implies a 1:1 mapping between services and Customer-VLANs (C-VLANs), trusting on the edge router to manage thousands of VLANs. Still, this topology is not efficient for IPTV, as streams for multiple subscribers would be carried several times across the network.
- Specifically considering GPON scenarios, the ONT maps each 1:1 VLAN into a unique U interface. Each U interface can map into one or more 1:1 VLANs. The ONT always adds a tag to untagged frames or translates an incoming Q-Tag in the upstream direction. Tag assignment at the V interface can follow two variations.
- The first variation corresponds to *single tagging*. For single-tagged VLANs at V, the ONT is provisioned to add an S-VID or translate an incoming tag into an S-VID, and the aggregation node passes through the tag. However, the 12-bit VLAN identifier only supports up to 4095 subscribers.
- *Double tagging* (depicted in Figure 15), using *Q-in-Q* VLAN stacking (IEEE 802.1Q, 2011), initially standardized by 802.1ad (IEEE 802.1ad, 2005) and later incorporated into the 802.1Q standard, makes it possible to increase VLAN capacity at the aggregation level. For double-tagged VLANs at V, the ONT is provisioned to assign a C-VID (C-VLAN ID) or translate an incoming tag into a C-VID, and the aggregation node adds the S-VID. The operator

core network will carry traffic with double-tagged, stacked VLAN headers, retaining the VLAN and Layer 2 protocol configurations of each subscriber.

- **Customer VLAN with Multicast VLAN**. This topology is a mixture, retaining the benefits from the two previous approaches, using a shared multicast VLAN (M-VLAN) to carry specific services such as IPTV traffic (Joseph & Mulugu, 2011) while the rest of the traffic is delivered using the 1:1 topology.

Nonetheless, there are other (even if only slightly) different approaches for this same purpose. For instance, on DOCSIS cable access networks, the CMTS (Cable Model Termination System, which provides many of the same functions as an xDSL Line Access Multiplexer) is not VLAN-aware. Instead, it receives client IP traffic as Ethernet frames within data streams modulated on a TV channel. In such cases, encapsulation can be used to create an overlay access network, with the BNG using the tunnel IP as part of its classifier. In fact, the use of overlay L2-over-L3 networks provides an alternative deployment model that is not described in the scope of this chapter and which has an impact on the BNG implementation.

Proposed Architecture for Support of vRGW in Existing Infrastructures

Figure 16 presents the proposed vRGW-enabling network architecture. According to this architecture, vRGW instances are hosted by virtualization nodes located at the operator's data centers (DC#1 and DC#2).

Each virtualization node is responsible for a set of vRGW instances. Each virtualization node is connected to the network by a mini VLAN trunk representing the I/O network traffic of every individual vRGW instance running in that specific virtualization node (i.e., the corresponding set of C-VLANs). Each mini VLAN trunk is aggregated into a larger sub-trunk representing all the C-VLANs on a specific data center. This sub-trunk is then encapsulated into MPLS Pseudo-Wires (PW, (Bryant & Pate, 2005)) at one of the MPLS edge routers of the operator core network. Those PW are then transported to other edge routers, also known as Broadband Network Gateways (BNGs).

At the existing BNGs, each PW is converted again into VLAN sub-trunks, each of them connected to the corresponding network access node. At each individual access node, each VLAN sub-trunk is divided into smaller C-VLAN trunks carrying the traffic of each individual subscriber (separated by one VLAN for each service being delivered). At the customer premises, on the ONT, each VLAN is untagged and mapped into a port in one unmanaged bridge with a wireless access point (the ONT and this bridge are not represented in Figure 16, for the sake of simplicity). At this point, all the equipment inside the subscriber LAN can connect to the stripped-down bridge and obtain a valid IP address from the DHCP daemon running on the vRGW.

This network architecture allows extending the logical reach of the subscriber LAN to the vRGW hosted at the operator's data center using the technologies already in place, with subscriber management, network attachment and policy enforcement being provided by the BNG (Authentication, Authorization and Accounting mechanisms were omitted, for the sake of simplicity). Moreover, the joint use of VLAN stacking, VLAN trunks and MPLS Pseudo-Wires make it possible to handle, aggregate and encapsulate in a scalable manner the high number of VLANs required by thousands or millions of subscribers. Considering the aforementioned Broadband Forum VLAN Aggregation mechanisms, the proposed architecture may fit both Customer VLAN (1:1) topologies and hybrid Customer VLAN with Multicast VLAN topologies.

Still, this proposal is based on the assumption that the home network is a flat Layer 2 network: with some NSPs considering the adoption of

Figure 14. VLAN per service model (adapted from (Young, 2009)).

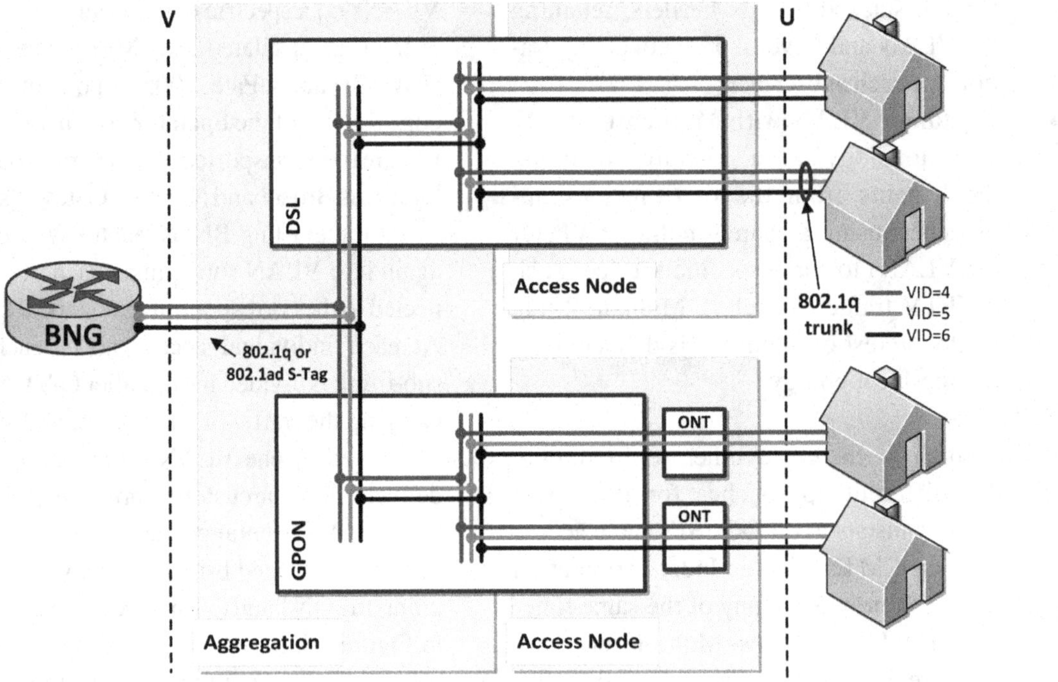

Figure 15. VLAN per subscriber model (adapted from (Young, 2009))

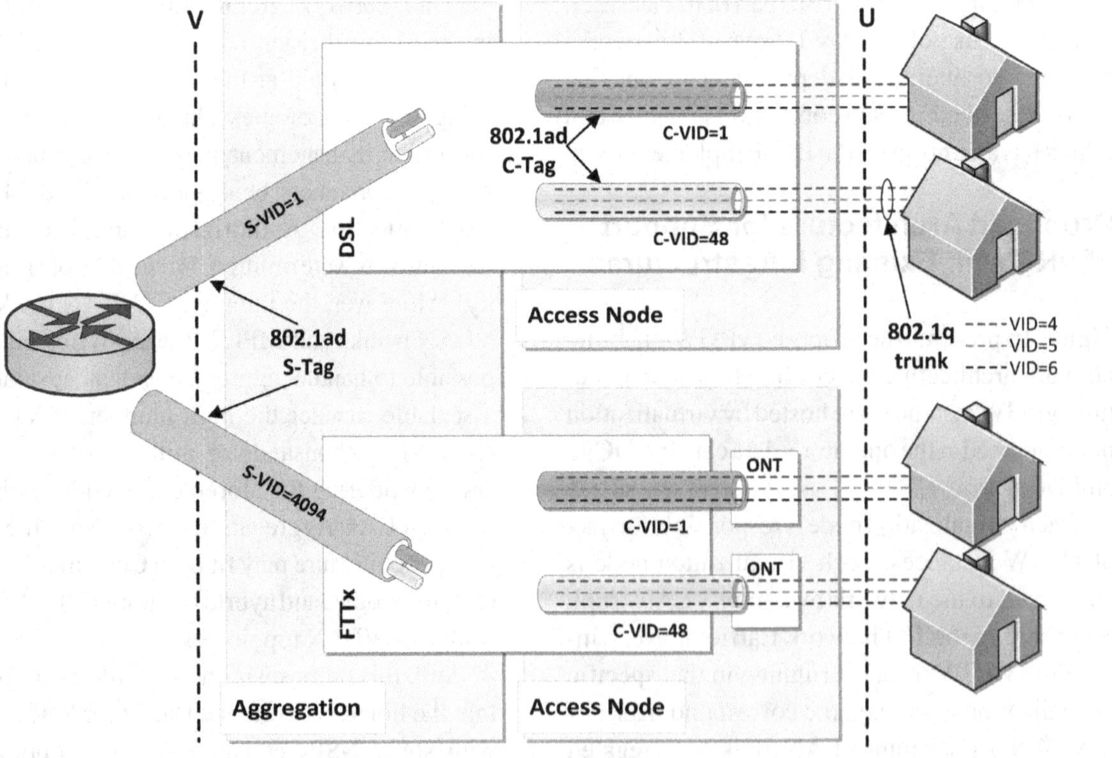

Figure 16. vRGW-enabling network architecture.

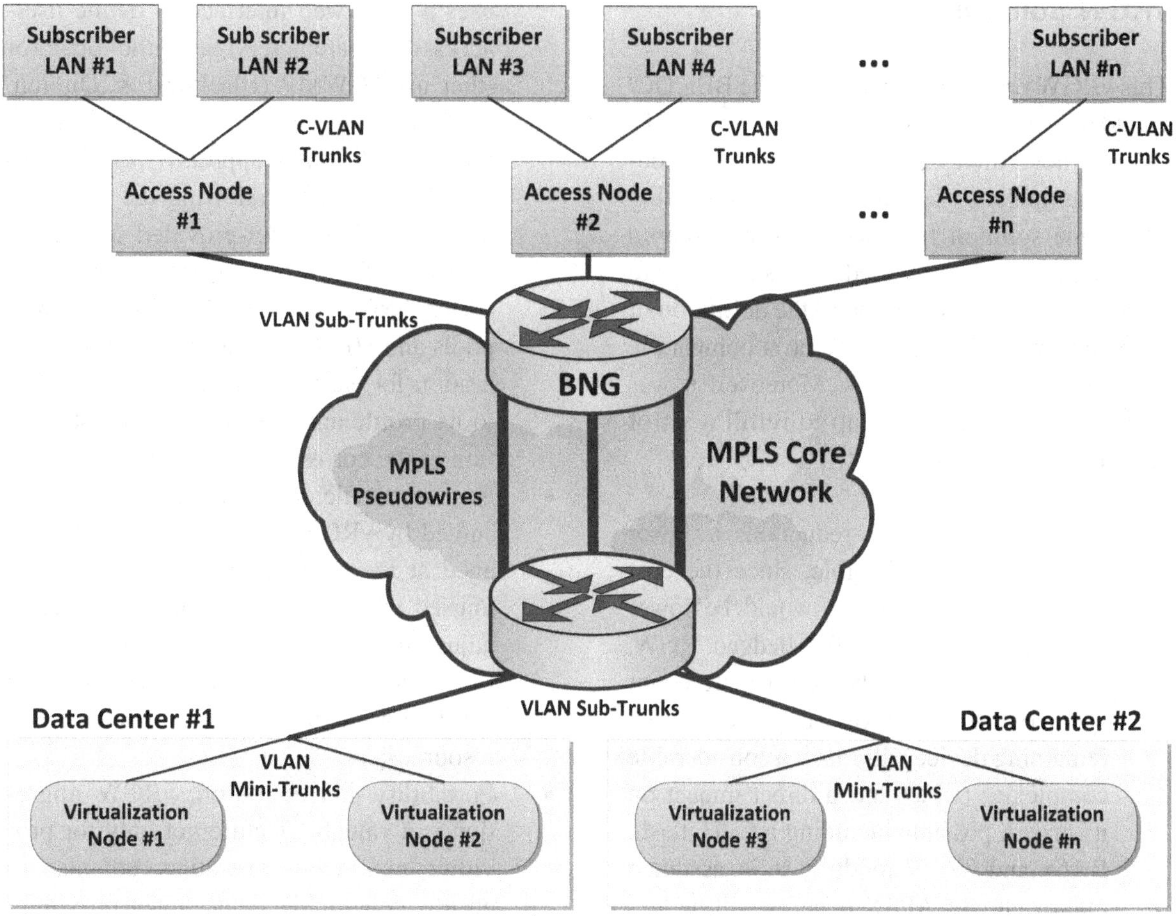

prefixes shorter than /64 in the scope of IPv6 migration, this means that the prefix needs to be subdivided so that every subnet is given its own /64 prefix. For instance, an 802.11 Access Point may provide "private" and "guest" SSIDs, placed in different network scopes, to provide Internet access to a visitor without placing him on a network with sensitive devices and/or information. Such networks may be isolated (physically or using VLANs) within the home network or routed at the RGW level (or eventually using other routers within the home network) – for such cases, the use of "overlayed" Layer 2 networks (such as Layer 2-over-3 tunnels) or VXLANs (Mahalingam et al., 2014) may provide an adequate solution that avoids the use of standard or stacked VLANs to bring the network traffic up to the BNG, where it can be classified accordingly. While the proposed solution requires the vRGW instance to eventually deal with multi-layer hone network traffic, this may be solved in future evolutions of the architecture, by separating the forwarding plane and providing decoupled virtual or physical routing functions closer to the access network, as part of an evolved (abstracted) vRGW. Also, replacing VLANs in the data center context with VXLANs (which scale better), could prove beneficial for the proposed architecture, reducing the overhead of bringing VLANs trunks up to the data center, with added flexibility.

Benefits of the Proposed vRGW Solution

This vRGW proposal is in line with the BBF DC/Cloud nodal distribution model from WT-317 (which, nevertheless, also suggests other deployment models – see Figure 9), also providing a baseline solution from which an NFV-based approach can be later refined. It was designed to constitute a first contribution to the definition of a gradual migration strategy that is compatible with existing infrastructures. Moreover, it was designed from the ground up to fulfill a set of critical requirements:

- OPEX and CAPEX reduction: a lower CAPEX may be possible, since the cost of the remaining device would be lower when compared to a full-fledged RGW, mainly because of the lower part count and reduced complexity. However, as the remaining device will retain a considerable complexity (which has a direct impact on its price), possibly including a CPU, flash, RAM and Wi-Fi module, it is assumed that eventual CAPEX benefits will be less significant when compared with OPEX – eventually, such device could be merged with the ONT to further reduce costs. OPEX would also be improved, since the need for on-site maintenance would be reduced (less hardware and misconfiguration problems), with the remaining device having an extended lifespan, not requiring any significant upgrade due to CPU or memory limitations (eventually only for improved wireless capabilities). Also, running some of the RGW functions in the operator data center can simplify service creation and support, improving the main issues of its high cost, when compared to the low margin of RGWs;
- User-driven customization capabilities: as the configuration of physical RGWs is typically shared between the customer (that uses a local web interface to define user-accessible parameters) and the operator (that uses CWMP (Blackford & Digdon, 2013) to remotely configure the other parameters). A similar approach might be followed for vRGWs, allowing the customer to access an operator-provided web interface to define user-accessible parameters of the vRGW (e.g. DHCP-based address pools and 802.11 credentials). The configuration for each customer might be added to its profile and activated upon instantiation of the corresponding vRGW;
- Resource efficiency: the resources consumed by vRGWs can be efficiently managed at the data center (e.g., suspending unused vRGW instances and dynamically adjusting the hosting hardware to effectively necessary resources), resulting in substantial savings of energy and hardware resources;
- Portability and migration: vRGW migration is a valuable feature not only for providing continuous operation, but also to ensure geographic data center proximity when a subscriber moves its location to a different household (specific operator data centers could be chosen accordingly to geographical proximity criteria). Also, this helps the operator become less dependent on hardware manufacturers (the virtual machine is, by nature, hardware independent). Also, the heterogeneity of RGWs is no longer an issue. The operator can keep a unified image for all virtual machines, using both VM templates and composition for increased flexibility – this also eases and accelerates the introduction of new services.

Live or cold migration of vRGWs inside the same data center is very similar to conventional VM migration in LAN environments, assuming the VLAN mini-trunks are mirrored across the virtualization nodes. However, migration across distinct data-centers is a different matter, since the C-VLAN for the customer must reach the new location. Using Layer 2 Generic Routing Encapsulation (GRE) tunnels from the bridged device up to the vRGW or VXLAN technologies in a scenario where C-VLANs are terminated at the BNG might be alternative solutions for this – however, this issue is out of scope for this chapter.

Cold migration across data centers can be achieved using two approaches: context-based, spawning or resuming a pooled vRGW instance on the destination data center, using context-specific mechanisms (discussed in the section of the chapter dedicated to the vRGW management capabilities) to transfer and activate service and device-specific configurations; or image-based, stopping and moving the VM instance across data centers, later resuming its operation.

Live vRGW migration across data centers (which may share common distributed storage capabilities) without disruption is a complex operation, demanding close cooperation between the network and VM layers. Coordination between the MPLS BNG and edge routers must ensure the correct C-VLAN is encapsulated within a MPLS PW connected to the data center that will host the vRGW.

An alternative to vRGW migration, inspired by Mobile IP techniques, is to create a virtual circuit between data centers to relay C-VLAN traffic (in Mobile IP, a "care-of" address that is temporarily used by a home agent router in the mobile node home network to tunnel and deliver data to a mobile node on a foreign network, through a foreign network agent). However, this approach is inefficient, introducing a series of path-related performance issues and unnecessary overhead;

- Reliability and resiliency: vRGW updates and replacement of defective instances (e.g., due to software and misconfiguration problems) are simple VM management operations at the operator data center, reducing downtime for the customer;
- Elasticity and flexibility: from the operators' perspective, the possibility of over-provisioning vRGW pools is a logical solution for resource optimization. By using a template-based mechanism with image composition capabilities, the system can easily assemble, customize and start pools of stateless vRGW instances, suspending the ones not immediately needed - this ensures a rapid starting time. Pooled vRGW reconfiguration is provided by a specific management component;

These requirements are in line with those outlined by (Xia, Wu & King, 2013) and (ETSI NFV002, 2013), which were discussed in the previous section. However, this vRGW proposal constitutes a straightforward implementation of a virtualized RGW that serves as the baseline for further development, for instance streamlining its service set through consolidation of functionality outside its own scope. These aspects will be next discussed.

Architectural Optimizations/ Developments and vRGW Evolution

The proposed vRGW solution makes use of a fully-virtualized instance that can be further optimized and streamlined as it evolves, moving functionality out of its scope into the NSP infrastructure (as it could be the case for the NAT function, which could be moved outside the vRGW, into a shared Carrier Grade NAT physical device, for instance) – however, the present proposal serves as a baseline study for a self-contained vRGW implementation created by migrating most of the functionality of a conventional RGW up to a Virtualization Node without extensive rearrangements of its architecture. As such, each vRGW remains isolated from the other vRGWs sharing the same private cloud.

Further developments of this vRGW concept open the possibility for more advanced solutions, where some services previously handled by the RGW can become consolidated outside the boundary of each individual RGW, on a context of shared functionality or functional distribution (see Figure 17), eventually resourcing to NFV and flexible service chaining approaches, for better integration and orchestration.

Application-level gateways such as SIP gateways, DNS cache servers and content caching mechanisms, for instance, could benefit from this approach to improve their manageability and functionality, as well as to reduce vRGW footprint. Also, heavy-duty network functionality such as NAT and firewalling could be moved outside the vRGW, being co-located or relocated to carrier-grade mechanisms. Also, DHCP can be moved outside the vRGW, being replaced by a relay agent (e.g., implementing DHCP option 82 (Patrick, 2001) for IPv4 or using prefix delegation through DHCPv6 relay agents (Droms et al., 2003)), located in the access node (i.e., in the OLT) or the vRGW.

Several RGW management functionalities could also be simplified if co-located at the virtualization node level (similarly to the vRGW management architecture proposed in the next section) or moved outside, to the operator infrastructure. In this perspective, and to improve scalability, the vRGW can eventually be trimmed down to a bare instance with minimal networking and management capabilities, an execution environment and a basic service set, retained for customer privacy or functional reasons. Ultimately, the vRGW might become an abstraction, formed by the bundle of services (integrated within a service FG), which are activated when a subscriber is activated, rather than dedicated entity for each subscriber.

Also, the introduction of SDN, together with NFV can easily make the proposed vRGW evolve into more sophisticated deployments. For instance, Figure 18 shows two examples: the first one inspired by (Lee & Ghai, 2014), makes use of SDN packet forwarding capabilities within the operator network (such as the Virtual CPE Packet forwarder), using OpenFlow to automate VLAN connectivity and forward user traffic from the house up to the vRGW, either deployed in a data center/private cloud or within the scope of the operator network, close to end-users, as suggested by (Xie et al. 2013); the second example makes use of a decoupled approach similar to the BBF NERG, as it leaves behind an OpenFlow switch at the customer premises, integrated with the ONT.

This decoupling of the forwarding plane is also interesting for several NSPs and/or service operators that are not involved in the cloud providing and/or hosting businesses and whose data centers usually handle internally terminated services such as OSS or IPTV – as such, Internet traffic normally doesn't flow across them, making them unsuitable for hosting vRGWs. In such cases, it is desirable to provide a way to separate the forwarding plane in a place where the packets aren't required to route to the data center, in line with the proposals from (Lee & Xie, 2014) or the split BBF NERG models suggest.

Also, the requirements for the management of the proposed vRGW VM instances for migration (live or cold migration), template composition and lifecycle management are in line with the NFV configuration northbound use cases, as described by (Deng, Song, Karagian, Haleplidis, & Martini,, 2014). This means that a NFV control and management plane should be able to manage pools of the proposed vRGW instances.

These scenarios do not exhaust the deployment possibilities for the proposed vRGW in an operator SDN or NFV scenario. For instance, the implementation of a migration strategy might dictate an incremental approach where an operator might start with the vRGW implemented in a scenario with legacy technologies, such as the BBF aggregation topology scenarios, which are not incompatible with the introduction of NFV. As NFV and SDN start being rolled out, first on the data center and then moving to the core,

Figure 17. Architectural Optimizations/Developments for vRGWs.

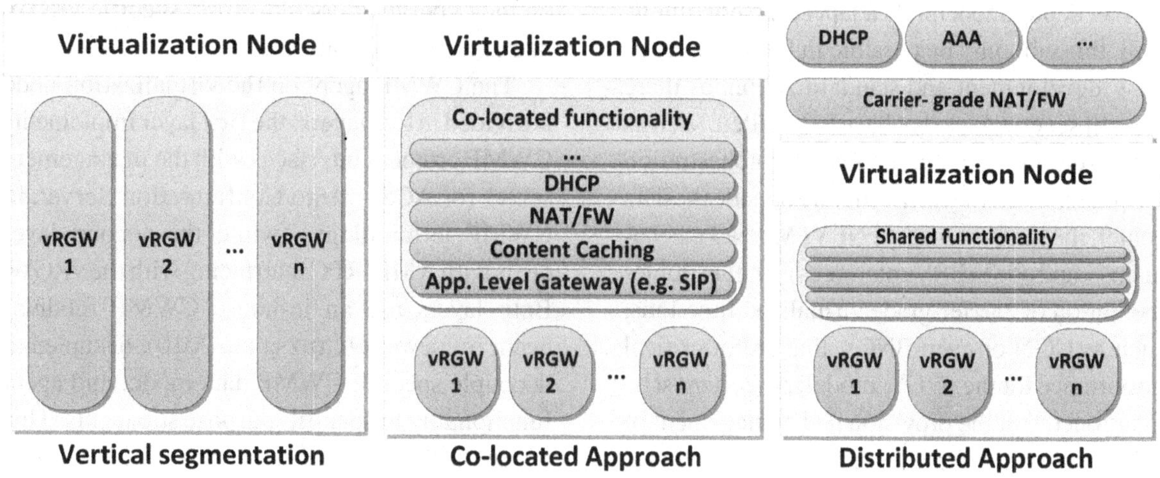

Figure 18. NFV/SDN vRGW deployment scenarios

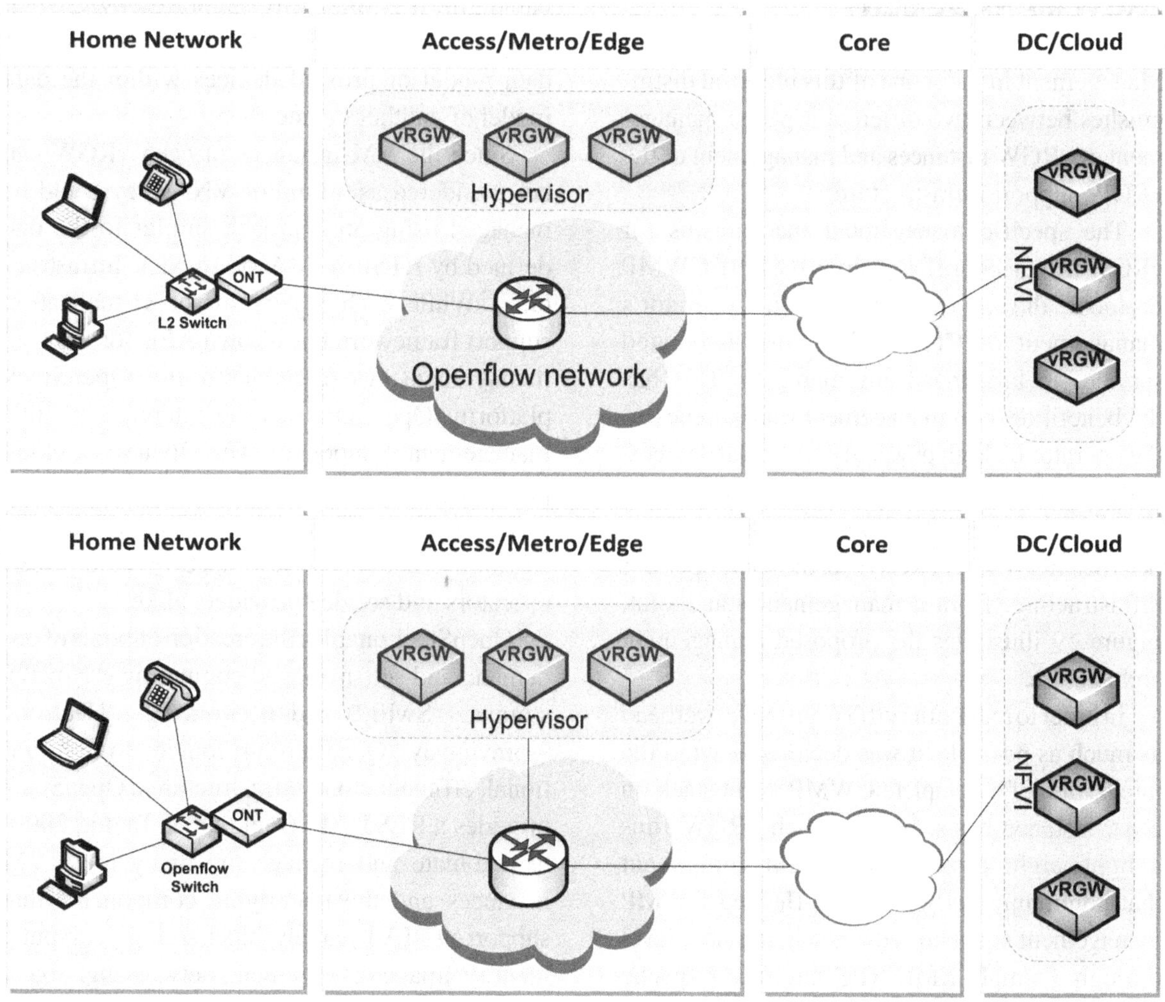

metro, aggregation and access networks, the vRGW deployment might adapt correspondingly. Still, this will only be possible in future stages of NFV development and standardization, as there are still several gaps that have to be filled, such as the development of comprehensive orchestration mechanisms for the infrastructure outside the data center, the improvement of NFVI MANO mechanisms (and OSS/BSS interfaces) or the implementation of carrier-grade virtualized functions, such as CGN or even BNGs, that are of critical importance for the vRGW model. Also, it must be mentioned that the provision and management of SDN controllers in the depicted scenarios is also a challenge that must be dealt with.

vRGW MANAGEMENT

Management in the scope of this proposal distinguishes between two different aspects: management of vRGW instances and management of the vRGW support infrastructure.

The specific management mechanisms for vRGW instances are based upon the BBF CWMP Protocol, the *de facto* standard for operator's management of CPE devices and associated services in broadband environments. This has the benefit of total management transparency to the operator on both physical and virtual devices, while using already existing Operations Support Systems (OSS) and, therefore, easing coexistence between RGWs and vRGWs, in the same operator infrastructure, from a management standpoint. Figure 19 illustrates the proposed management architecture.

In order to reduce the vRGW instance overhead as much as possible, it was decided to avoid the integration of a complete CWMP agent stack on a per-instance basis. Instead, each vRGW runs a lightweight proxy management component that communicates with a full-fledged CWMP management agent hosted at the hypervisor level through a simple XML-RPC interface (Apache XML-RPC), decoupling the CWMP logic (hosted on the hypervisor domain) from specific vRGW management mechanisms.

The CWMP agent on the virtualization node is divided in two layers: the first layer implements CWMP protocol interfaces with the management server (or ACS – Auto Configuration Server, in CWMP terminology), while the second layer deals with XML-RPC interfacing with the vRGW. Both layers use an in-house CWMP modular agent framework (Cruz et al., 2010), designed to decouple specific CWMP data model and agent functionality to specific-purpose subagents. This proxy-based approach departs from the vertical segmentation model used for physical device management, going instead for a solution that remains compatible with the CWMP management paradigm. It is implicitly supported by CWMP (Lupton, 2013), which allows for embedding the data model of proxied devices within the data model of another device.

Since the VM instances of each vRGW can be considered as a kind of VNF, they could be managed using an approach similar to the one defined by ETSI for MANO in NFV Infrastructures. While each hypervisor or virtualization support framework has its own APIs for external management, we considered the OpenStack platform (OpenStack) as the reference for this management component. The OpenStack cloud platform provides an approach to cloud management, focused on openness, interoperability and flexibility that can be leveraged by enterprises, operators and service providers alike.

OpenStack enables the creation of pools of on-demand and self-managed computing ("Nova"), storage ("Swift") and networking ("Neutron" – previously "Quantum") resources to build rational, efficient cloud infrastructures. OpenStack provides a REST API (Fielding & Taylor, 2000) to automate and manage the lifecycle of VM instances and the underlying components that support an NFVI, namely: block storage, compute, identity, image management, networking, object

Figure 19. vRGW management architecture

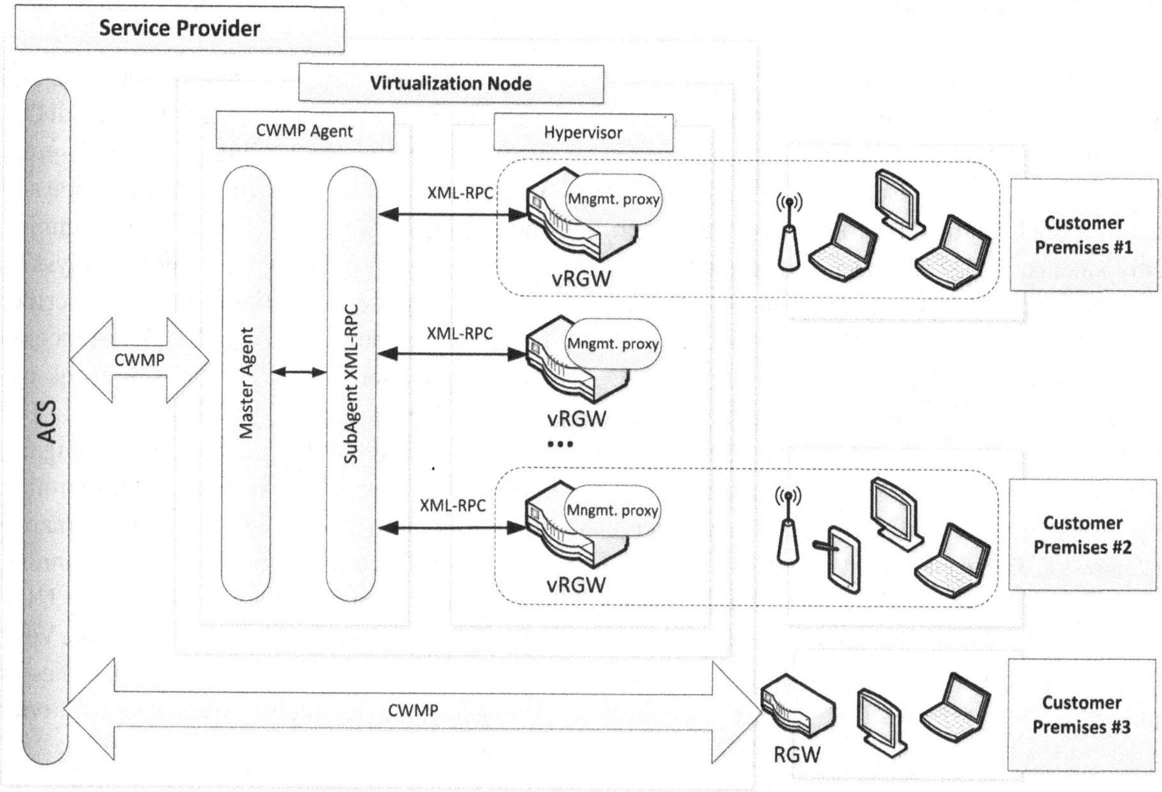

storage, orchestration and telemetry. Moreover, OpenStack Neutron supports a traffic steering abstraction that allows the specification of how traffic must be steered along a list of neutron ports, subject to different classification criteria. This abstraction can be leveraged to implement service function chaining (Gonçalves, 2014), allowing traffic to be forwarded between Neutron ports (network services and machines) according to traffic classification.

With reference to the ETSI NFV model, the capabilities of OpenStack (together with a plugin to support equipment outside the datacenter, such as OpenDayLight (OpenDayLight) to control edge routers, for example) make it adequate to support an NFVI and the Virtualized Infrastructure Manager from the ETSI MANO. Also, the OpenStack consortium is working on the support for NFV use cases, offering a test ground for new developments once they become standardized and implemented.

Nevertheless, while the proposed vRGW architecture accounts for the integration with existing OSS/BSS mechanisms, this will depend on the implementation of mediation modules capable of integrating the NFV MANO, which is outside the scope of this chapter.

EVALUATION AND PERFORMANCE ANALYSIS

This section discusses a proof-of-concept implementation of the proposed solution, the experimental validation process and obtained results. The validation process separately addresses two specific aspects of the proposed solution: vRGW performance and the management architecture.

Reference Testbed

In order to validate the proposed vRGW approach, a proof-of-concept testbed was built, illustrated in Figure 20, which emulates the data center environment and the home networks. This scenario does not include the infrastructure orchestration components, as it was conceived to study and analyze the performance of the proposed vRGW concept.

The virtualization node was based on an Intel server with 4GB of RAM, running CentOS Linux 6 x86 64 (CentOS) with KVM (Kernel-based Virtual Machine (Kivity, 2007)) as the virtualization hypervisor and *libvirt* (LibVirt) as management framework. The management server is a CentOS 6 Linux 6 x86 64 system with a Java-based CWMP ACS. The KVM virtualization node also hosts the Java-based CWMP Agent, incorporating the master agent and the XML-RPC layer for communication with the vRGW proxy management agents.

The link between the virtualization node and the home networks was based on a 1 Gbps Full Duplex Ethernet link, supporting one point-to-point VLAN trunk between the virtualization node and another CentOS 6 Linux x86 64 server running up to 30 OpenVZ Linux Containers (Kolyshin, 2006), to emulate up to 30 independent subscriber home environments (one per vRGW instance on the virtualization node). This VLAN Trunk aggregates the multiple C-VLANs involved. The virtualization node was connected to a Gigabit switch together with the CWMP ACS and two other Linux machines (needed for vRGW performance tests, being used as traffic generators) running *iperf* (IPerf), one of them configured as a UDP and UDP Multicast server source (to emulate VoIP and IPTV traffic, respectively) and the other as TCP generator (to emulate Internet connectivity and other general TCP traffic).

Figure 20. vRGW virtualization testbed.

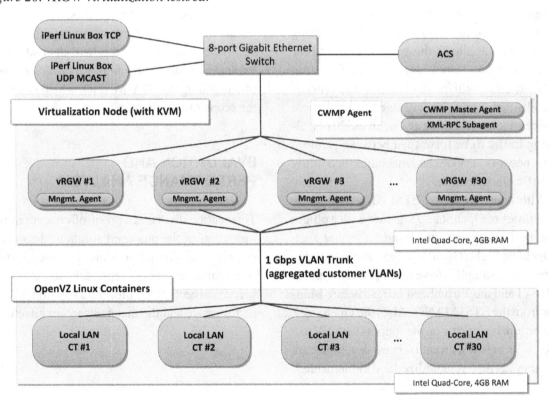

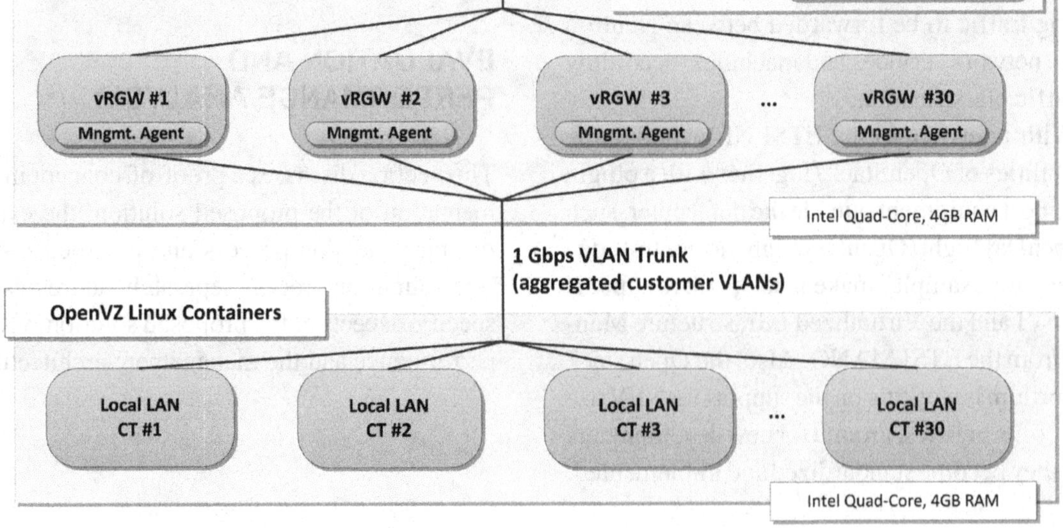

vRGW Implementation

The presented proof-of-concept testbed uses OpenWrt Backfire x86 RGW instances (OpenWrt), virtualized using the KVM hypervisor and the *libvirt* (LibVirt) management framework. Experimental measurements were collected using *virt-top* (Jones, 2009), which was used to monitor the vital statistics for virtualized domains. OpenWrt was chosen for practical reasons, since it is one of the most popular open-source RGW implementations, being a mature and well-organized project, easy to adapt and customize (selection and management of components, support for x86 architectures and customization). Besides, several commercial devices are using OpenWrt.

Also, the KVM virtualization infrastructure was chosen because of its capabilities and maturity, not being subject to any legal benchmarking/disclosure constraints. It is compatible with management frameworks such as Open Stack and Open Nebula (Open Nebula), supporting large-scale virtualization architectures.

As for the proxy management agent, the proof-of-concept implementation was written in Python (Python), in the form of a daemon listening to system call requests coming from the CWMP agent on the virtualization node. This agent is a simple XML-RPC server listening for system call requests on the OpenWrt operating system.

Evaluation of vRGW Performance

The vRGW performance tests were based on the Quality of Experience Requirements for IPTV Services proposed by ITU for "Average Users" and "High Users" (ITU FG IPTV-DOC-0184, 2007), according to the values presented in Table I. These requirements were used to configure the traffic generators for the testbed. Those requirements were used to model *iperf*-generated UDP traffic (IPTV and VoIP services). The "TCP Internet" traffic generator was not capped, using the remaining available bandwidth.

It should be noted that, despite the usage of UDP multicast for IPTV, a worst-case scenario was created by using 1:1 VLAN mapping between the virtualization node and the home networks. This is roughly representative of "Customer VLAN with Multicast VLAN" scenarios where each customer consumes distinct TV channels.

Measurements for the testbed scenario were conducted, varying the number of vRGWs and considering ITU-defined requirements for "Average Users" and "High Users" except for telephony, in which a requirement of 3 phone calls using the G.711a codec (exceeding the 0.1 Mb/s ITU recommendation) was established, for both profiles. Figure 21 presents the average throughput measured for each home network, with 1, 10, 15, 20, 25 and 30 vRGWs hosted by the virtualization node and the "Average User" scenario. Results show the ITU reference requirements to be easily surpassed, even for 30 vRGWs hosted on modest hardware.

The measured average throughput per home network achieved for the "High User" profile is presented in Figure 22. According to these results, our prototype should be able to support between 20 and 25 "High Users".

Table 1. Downstream rates for digital triple play

Service		Average User (Mbps)		High User (Mbps)
Internet	2 channels	5.0	2 channels	10.0
Telephony	1 channel	0.1	2 channels	0.1
SDTV (MPEG-4)		3.0		3.0
HDTV (MPEG-4)		8.0		16.0
Total		**16.1**		**29.1**

Figure 21. Measured Throughput per vRGW ("Average User").

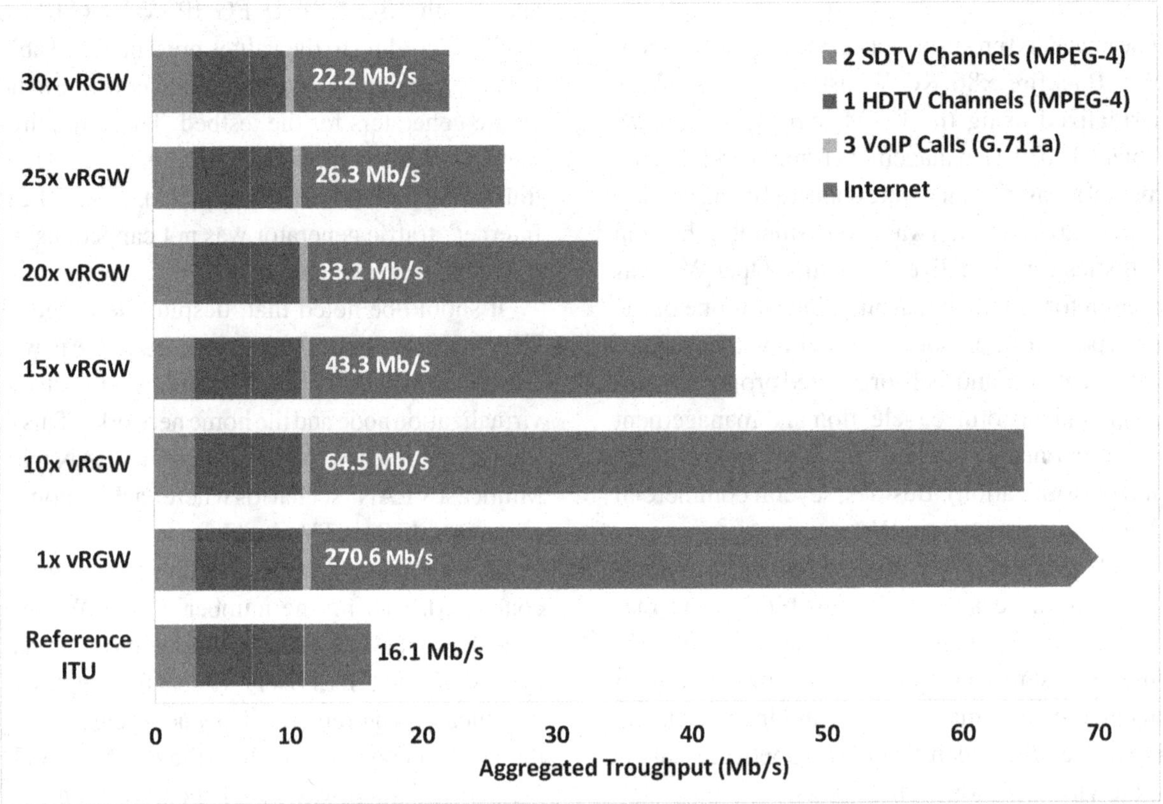

A small packet loss for UDP traffic in the most demanding scenarios (many vRGWs) was detected. The three worst cases were: 4.30% packet loss (30 vRGW and "High User" profile), 2.35% (25 vRGW, "High User") and 1.57% packet loss (30 vRGW, "Average User"). This can be partially justified by the fact that no traffic prioritization was used, an unlikely scenario in production environments. Furthermore, such packet loss ratios can be handled by the forward error correction (FEC) mechanisms employed by IPTV platforms without any noticeable degradation of quality (Ellis, Pezaros & Perkins, 2012) (Nagel et al., 2007).

CPU load and memory usage on the virtualization node were also monitored during the experimental tests. Figure 23 shows the total CPU load used by the hypervisor of the virtualization node (represented as a percentage of the maximum CPU capacity), for the "High User" scenario. Apart from the single vRGW case, the average CPU usage for 10, 15 and 30 vRGWs under load fits between 75% and 85%. This threshold could be explained by the fact that, besides running the virtualization hypervisor, the virtualization node also needs to handle the management of multiple VLANs with high load, running network I/O traffic on its VLAN trunk.

Figure 24 shows the average CPU load consumed by each individual vRGW instance (for the same "High User" scenario), represented as a percentage of the maximum CPU capacity of the virtualization node. These results are consistent with the hypervisor measurements of Figure 23, showing no sign of significant hypervisor-level overhead.

Each vRGW OpenWrt instance was configured with 32MB of RAM, totaling up to 960MB (30x32MB) of allocated memory on the hyper-

Figure 22. Measured Throughput per vRGW ("High User").

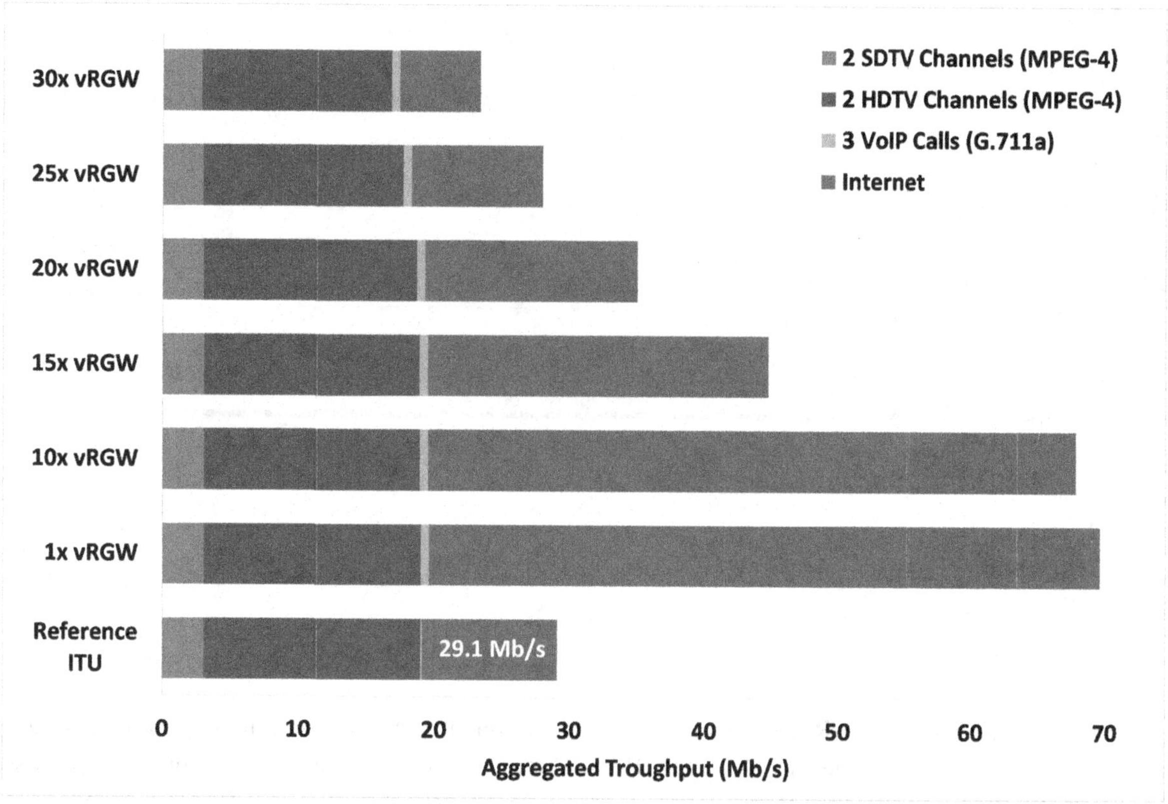

Figure 23. CPU used by the Hypervisor ("High User").

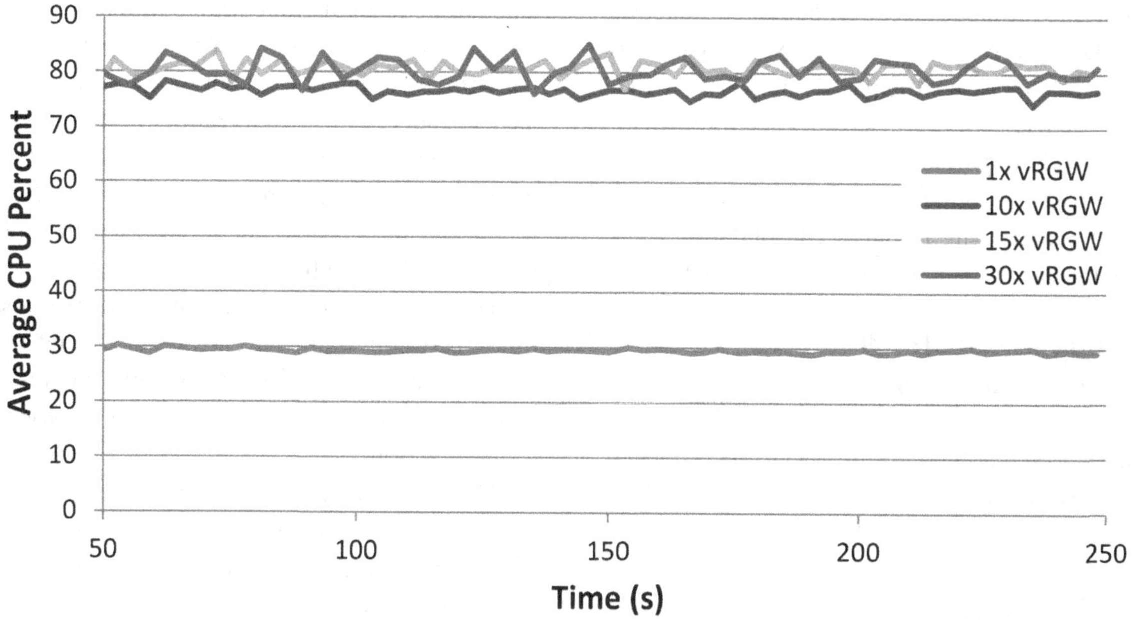

Figure 24. Average CPU used per vRGW ("High User").

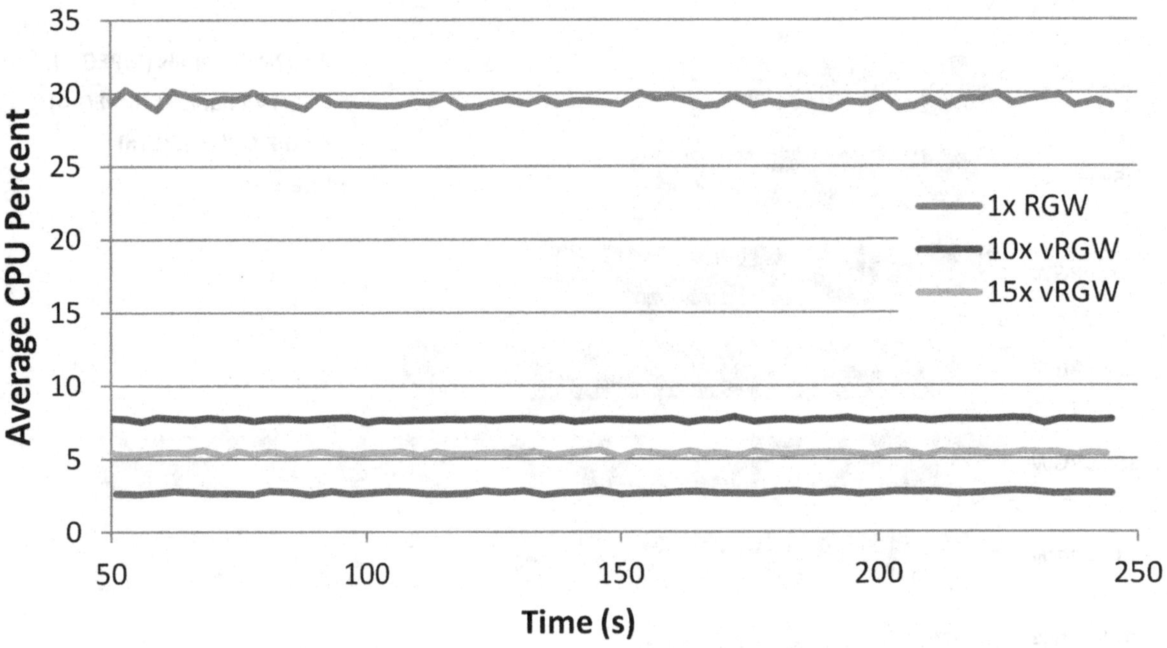

visor. During the tests each vRGW consistently used around 38% of available memory (12MB approximately), showing that RAM was not a key bottleneck in the specific system we used.

These results should be interpreted considering the limitations of the testbed. For instance, the vRGW capacity per virtualization node, as hinted by presented measurements, is constrained by modest hardware (outdated Intel Q8400 CPU, 4GB of RAM, entry-level network interfaces). Production deployments may achieve important capacity improvement by tuning hardware components and using resource consolidation tools provided by data center virtualization platforms.

Evaluation of vRGW Instance Management

The management architecture for vRGW instances was also subjected to experimental evaluation. Once again, the methodology consisted of performing measurements, varying the number of vRGWs from only 1 to 30 while registering operation latency times to a management operation (request for changing the LAN interface address on each vRGW), with each vRGW instance being assigned 1 CPU core and 32MB of RAM.

Measurements were performed using *top* (Unix Top) for recording the python CWMP proxy daemon CPU and memory utilization footprint at each vRGW instance and *tcpdump* (Tcpdump), on the virtualization node to capture traffic between the ACS server, the virtualization node and each running vRGW (see Figure 19). Moreover, to improve measurement resolution, both the ACS server and the CWMP agents were customized with a nanosecond timer.

The first round of tests compared response times between single vRGW requests and the average per-vRGW latency within bulk operations with 30 instances involved (see Figure 25), for 12 test interactions.

The error bars represent a 99% level of confidence for the mean on the 30x vRGW scenario and the standard deviation for single vRGW tests, respectively. We opted for working within the

Figure 25. Average CWMP operation latency

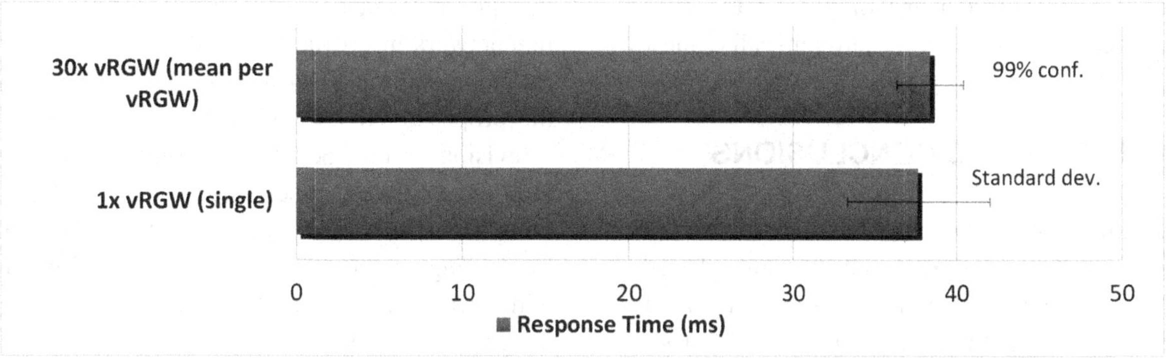

99% level of confidence for the mean, since it is a better representation of reality, thus avoiding sensitivity issues with standard deviation. Still, it doesn't make sense to use the same level of confidence in both cases, because the sample size for the 1x vRGW single requests was too small. Obtained values show no significant difference between the two test scenarios, with adequate performance in both cases.

As for management traffic, Figure 26 shows results for bulk operations involving 30 vRGWs.

Results show generated traffic between the ACS and CWMP agent (CWMP protocol exchanges only) to be quite significant in comparison to XML-RPC traffic (1620 bytes on average for each call). This situation leads to the conclusion that CWMP has inefficiencies in what relates to bulk management of vRGWs - the specific arrangement of several vRGW instances per virtualization node is partly to blame for this inefficiency, since CWMP was designed for the management of standalone physical devices. Thus, some sort of CWMP protocol optimizations for these operations should be considered.

Finally, vRGW proxy agent overhead was also measured, for batch samples (using *top*) performed every second during five minutes, to collect the daemon CPU and memory utilization footprint at each vRGW instance. Obtained results showed proxy agents to use an almost constant amount of 6.4MB RAM (20%) in each vRGW while CPU usage was near 0% at all times – this is due to the

Figure 26. CWMP vs. XML-RPC average traffic (bytes)

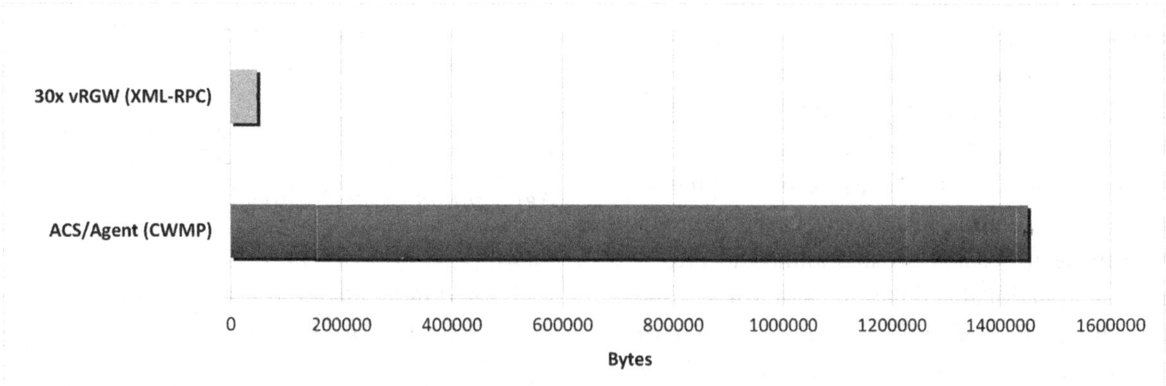

fact that the proxy agent daemon sleeps between each call request, using only the CPU cycles needed to accomplish each system call request.

WRAP-UP AND CONCLUSIONS

In this chapter we proposed a framework for virtualization of RGWs, with the aim of pushing the broadband home environment into the service-oriented era. Starting with a discussion on the rationale and state-of-the art regarding the virtualization of RGWs, it then presented a proposal for a vRGW architecture. This solution aims at CAPEX and OPEX reductions by making use of already existing technologies to logically extend each customer's home network up to the data center, relocating the RGW out of the customer premises, into a VM. This allows for decoupling the functionalities currently supported by physical RGWs, keeping a reduced set at the customer's premises (using a small bridge with minimum requirements) and moving most of them to the operator's data center. vRGW instance management mechanisms were also analyzed, then followed by the evaluation of a proof-of-concept implementation of the proposed vRGW, providing relevant insight about its capabilities.

This proposed RGW virtualization model was conceived as a starting point for the study of a vRGW migration strategy progressively rolled-out from the data center into the access network. While oriented towards integration within existing operator infrastructures, the proposed vRGW concept naturally fits the NFV paradigm. The baseline proposal hereby described provides a first approach to vRGWs as self-contained entities within isolated VM instances (vertical segmentation). The adoption of an NFV-based approach will make it possible to streamline the vRGW, moving functionality out of the VM instance into consolidated, chained VNFs, eventually with the help of SDN technologies, improving functionality, efficiency and manageability.

Future work will focus on the validation of this proposal on a larger scale scenario (with real network infrastructures). Also following the developments on SDN and NFV technologies, the proposed vRGW architecture will undergo a revision with a focus on splitting the vRGW into consolidated, functionally chained, VNF components, eventually coupled with SDN packet forwarding devices at the customer premises or within the NSP infrastructure. Development and integration of NFV MANO functionality (including an OSS/BSS interface layer), coupled with the OpenStack API is also a key development to improve the existing solution that will be pursued once the relevant interfaces and architectural details of the operator NFV reference framework are standardized and documented.

REFERENCES

Abgrall, D. (Ed.). (2011). Virtual Home Gateway: How can Home Gateway virtualization be achieved? *EURESCOM Study Report P2055 D1*, September 2011.

Alter, C. (2014), *Broadband Forum Work on "Network Enhanced Residential Gateway" (WT-317) and "Virtual Business Gateway"* (WT-328). Broadband Forum's liaison letter to the IETF, March 2014.

Alter, C., & Daowood, S. (2014). *Broadband Forum Work on Flexible Service Chaining (SD-326).* Broadband Forum's liaison letter to the IETF. February 2014.

Anschutz, T. (Ed.). (2011). *Broadband Forum TR-101: Migration to Ethernet-Based Broadband Aggregation, Issue 2*. Broadband Forum.

Apache, X. M. L.-R. P. C. (n.d.). *Apache XML-RPC Java Implementation*. Retrieved July 2014 from: http://ws.apache.org/xmlrpc

Arkko, J., Lindem, A., & Paterson, B. (2013). *Prefix Assignment in a Home Network (draft-arkko-homenet-prefix-assignment-04)*. IETF Internet Draft, May 2013.

Barham, P., Dragovic, B., Fraser, K., Hand, S., Harris, T., Ho, A., Neugebauer, R., … Warfield, A. (2003). Xen and the art of virtualization. *ACM SIGOPS Operating Systems Review, 37*(5), 164–177. DOI=10.1145/1165389.945462

Basak, D., Toshniwal, R., Maskalik, S., & Sequeira, A. (2010). Virtualizing networking and security in the cloud. *SIGOPS Operating Systems Review, 44*(4), 86-94. December 2010. DOI= http://doi.acm.org/10.1145/1899928.189993910.1145/1899928.1899939

Bazzi, A., & Onozato, Y. (2011, July). Feasibility Study of Security Virtual Appliances for Personal Computing. *IPSJ Journal of Information Processing, 19*(0), 378–388. doi:10.2197/ipsjjip.19.378

Blackford, J., & Digdon, M. (2013) *Broadband Forum, TR-069 – CPE WAN Management Protocol, Issue 1, Amendment 5*, November 2013.

Boucadair, M., Jacquenet, C., Jiang, Y., Parker, R., Pignataro, C., & Naito, K. (2014). *Requirements for Service Function Chaining (SFC) (draft-boucadair-sfc-requirements-05)*. IETF Internet Draft, February 2014.

Boucadair, M., Jacquenet, C., Parker, R., & Dunbar, L. (2014), *Service Function Chaining: Design Considerations, Analysis & Recommendations (draft-boucadair-sfc-design-analysis-02)*. IETF Internet Draft, February 2014.

Bryant, S., & Pate, P. (2005). *Pseudo Wire Emulation Edge-to-Edge (PWE3) Architecture.* IETF RFC 3985, March 2005.

CableLabs, Inc. (2014). *DOCSIS 3.1 Physical Specification*. CableLabs, July 2014.

Cain, B., Deering, S., Kouvelas, I., Fenner, B., & Thyagarajan, A. (2002). *Internet Group Management Protocol, Version 3.* IETF Standard RFC 3376, October 2002.

Carey, J., & Kirksey, H. (2011). *Component Objects for CWMP, TR-157 Issue 1 Amendment 5*, Broadband Forum Tech. Report, November 2011.

CentOS. (n.d.). *CentOS Project Website*. Retrieved July 2014 from: http://www.centos.org

Chiosi, M., Clarke, D., Willis, P., Donley, C., Johnson, L., & Bugenhagen, M. … Neil, A. (2013). *Network Functions Virtualization – Network Operator Perspectives on Industry Progress. Issue 1.* ETSI White Paper. October 2013. Retrieved July 2014 from http://portal.etsi.org/NFV/ NFV_White_Paper2.pdf

Chiosi, M., Clarke, D., Willis, P., Reid, A., Feger, J., Bugenhagen, M., … Sen, P. (2012). *Network Functions Virtualization – An Introduction, Benefits, Enablers, Challenges & Call for Action. Issue 1.* ETSI White Paper. October 2012. Retrieved July 2014 from http://portal.etsi.org/NFV/NFV_White_Paper.pdf

Corporation, N. E. C. (2013). *Telefónica and NEC start the first virtual customer premises equipment trial in Brazil. Press Release*, October 2013. Retrieved October 2014 from: http://www.nec.com/en/press/201310/global_20131010_01.html

Cruz, T., Simões, P., Batista, P., Almeida, J., Monteiro, E., Bastos, F., & Laranjeira, A. (2010). CWMP extensions for enhanced management of domestic network services. In *Proceedings of the 2010 IEEE 35th Conference on Local Computer Networks (LCN'2010)* (pp.180-183). Denver, CO: IEEE Computer Society. October 2010. doi:10.1109/LCN.2010.5735695

Cui, A., & Hertoghs, Y. (2012). *TR-145: Multi-service Broadband Network Functional Modules and Architecture, Issue 1.* Broadband Forum Technical Report, November 2012.

Da Silva, R., Fernandez, M., Gamir, L., & Perez, M. (2011). Home routing gateway virtualization: An overview on the architecture alternatives. In Proceedings of Future Network & Mobile Summit (FutureNetw 2011) (pp. 1-9). Warsaw, Poland: IEEE Computer Society. 15-17 June 2011.

Deng, L., Song, H., Karagian, G., Haleplidis, E., & Martini, B. (2014). *NFV configuration north bound use cases (draft-deng-nfvcon-nb-use-cases-00)*. IETF Internet Draft, June 2014.

DLNA (2009). *DLNA Networked Device Interoperability Guidelines*. DLNA Consortium Guidelines, 2009.

Droms, R., Bound, J., Volz, B., Lemon, T., Perkins, C., & Carney, M. (2003). *Dynamic Host Configuration Protocol for IPv6 (DHCPv6)*. IETF Internet Standard RFC 3315, July 2003.

Dustzadeh, J. (2013). *SDN: Time to Accelerate the Pace*. Keynote presentation at the Open Networking Summit 2013, Santa Clara, CA, US, April 4, 2013. Retrieved July 2014 from http://www.opennetsummit.org/pdf/2013/presentations/justin_dustzadeh.pdf

Egi, N., Greenhalgh, A., Handley, M., Hoerdt, M., Huici, F., Mathy, L., & Papadimitriou, P. (2010). A platform for high performance and flexible virtual routers on commodity hardware. *SIGCOMM Computer Communications Review, 40*(1), 127-128. DOI=10.1145/1672308.1672332

Egi, N., Greenhalgh, A., Handley, M., Hoerdt, M., Mathy, L., & Schooley, T. (2007). Evaluating Xen for Router Virtualization. In *Proceedings of 16th International Conference on Computer Communications and Networks (ICCCN 2007)* (pp. 1256-1261). Honolulu, HI: IEEE Computer Society. August 2007. doi:10.1109/ICCCN.2007.4317993

Ellis, M., Pezaros, D. P., & Perkins, C. (2012). Performance analysis of AL-FEC for RTP-based streaming video traffic to residential users. In *Proceedings of the 19th Int. Packet Video Workshop (PV)*. Munich, Germany: IEEE Computer Sociery. doi:10.1109/PV.2012.6229737

Ersue, M. (2013). ETSI NFV Management and Orchestration - An Overview. *Presentation at the IETF #88 Meeting*. Vancouver, Canada. Retrieved July 2014 from: http://www.ietf.org/proceedings/88/slides/slides-88-opsawg-6.pdf

ETSI NFV 002 (2013). *Network Functions Virtualization (NFV); Architectural Framework, version 1.1.1*. ETSI, October 2013.

ETSI NFV ISG. (n.d.) Website retrieved July 2014 from: http://www.etsi.org/about/how-we-work/industry-specification-groups

Fielding, R. T., & Taylor, R. N. (2000). Principled design of the modern Web architecture. In *Proceedings of the 22nd Int. Conf. on Software Engineering (ICSE'00)* (pp. 407-417). New York: ACM Press. Doi:10.1145/337180.337228

FORCES. (n.d.). *IETF Forwarding and Control Element Separation (forces) Working Group Website*. Retrieved July 2014 from: http://datatracker.ietf.org/wg/forces/charter/

Gonçalves, C. (2014). Traffic steering abstraction for Neutron. *OpenStack Project Blueprint*. Retrieved July 2014 from: https://blueprints.launchpad.net/neutron/+spec/traffic-steering-abstraction

Huawei Technologies Co. Ltd. (2010). *SmartAX MA5600T Series Product Website*. Retrieved October 2014 from: http://enterprise.huawei.com/en/products/network/access-network/olt/en_ma5600t.htm

IEEE 802.1ad. (2005). IEEE Standard 802.1ad-2005, *Virtual Bridged Local Area Networks Amendment 4: Provider Bridges*. IEEE 802.1 Working Group, 2005.

IEEE 802.1Q. (2011). *IEEE Standard 802.1Q-2011, Media Access Control Bridges and Virtual Bridged Local Area Networks*. IEEE 802.1 Working Group, 2011.

IETF SFC WG. (n.d.). Website retrieved October 2014 from: https://datatracker.ietf.org/wg/sfc/documents

Iperf. (n.d.). *Iperf Tool Website*. Retrieved July 2014 from: http://iperf.sourceforge.net

ITU FG IPTV-DOC-0184. (2007). *Quality of Experience Requirements for IPTV Services, FG IPTV-DOC-0184*. ITU IPTV Focus Group Output Document. December 2007.

Jiang, Y., & Li, H. (2014). *An Architecture of Service Function Chaining (draft-jiang-sfc-arch-01.txt)*. IETF Internet Draft. February 2014.

Jones, R. (2009). *Virt-top Package*. Retrieved July 2014 from http://people.redhat.com/rjones/virt-top

Joseph, V., & Mulugu, S. (2011). Deploying Next Generation Multicast-Enabled Applications: Label Switched Multicast for MPLS VPNs, VPLS, and Wholesale Ethernet (pp. 400-401). San Francisco, CA: Morgan-Kaufmann.

Kirksey, H. (2010). *TR-140 – TR-069 Data Model for Storage Service Enabled Devices, Issue: 1 Amendment 1*. April 2010.

Kivity, A. (2007). KVM, One Year On. *Keynote presentation delivered at the KVM Forum 2007, Tucson, USA, August 2007*. Retrieved July 2014 from: http://www.linux-kvm.org/wiki/images/6/61/KvmForum2007$kf2007-keynote.pdf

Kolyshin, K. (2006). *Virtualization in Linux*. Sept. 2006. Retrieved from http://download.openvz.org/doc/openvz-intro.pdf

Lee, Y., & Ghai, R. (2014). *Problem Statements of Virtualizing Home Services (draft-lee-vhs-ps-00)*. IETF Internet Draft, February 2014.

Lee, Y., & Xie, C. (2014). *Virtualizing Home Services Use Cases (draft-lee-vhs-usecases-00)*. IETF Internet Draft, February 2014.

Libvirt. (n.d.). *Libvirt Project Website*. Retrieved July 2014 from: http://libvirt.org

Lupton, W. (Ed.). (2013). Data Model Template for TR-069-Enabled Devices, Issue: 1 Amendment 7. Broadband Forum Technical Report, September 2013.

Mahalingam, M., Dutt, D., Duda, K., Agarwal, P., Kreeger, L., Sridhar, T., … Wright, C. (2014). *Virtual eXtensible Local Area Network (VXLAN): A Framework for Overlaying Virtualized Layer 2 Networks over Layer 3 Networks*. IETF RFC 7348, August 2014.

Nagel, B., Geilhardt, F., Gilon, E., Hoet, J., Peña, C., Maillet, A., & Le Mansec, G. … Simoens, P. (2007). Demonstration of TVoIP services in a multimedia broadband enabled access network. In Proceedings of BroadBand Europe 2007. Antwerp, Belgium. ISBN: 9789076546094.

Niu, L., Li, H., Jiang, Y., & Yong, L. (2014), *A Service Function Chaining Header and Forwarding Mechanism (draft-niu-sfc-mechanism-01.txt)*. IETF Internet Draft, April 2014

ONF (2012). *OpenFlow Switch Specification, version 1.3.0 (Wire Protocol 0x04)*, Open Networking Foundation, June 2012.

ONF (2014). Openflow-enabled SDN and Network Functions Virtualization, *ONF Solution Brief*, Open Networking Foundation, February 2014.

Ooghe, S. (Ed.). (2013). *Broadband Forum TR-156: Using GPON Access in the context of TR-101, Issue 3*. Broadband Forum.

Open Nebula. (n.d.). *Open Nebula Project Website*. Retrieved July 2014 from: http://opennebula.org

OpenDayLight. (n.d.). *OpenDayLight Project Website*. Retrieved October 2014 from: http://www.opendaylight.org

OpenStack. (n.d.). *OpenStack Project Website*. Retrieved July 2014 from: http://www.openstack.org

OpenWrt. (n.d.). *OpenWrt Project website*. Retrieved July 2014 from: https://openwrt.org

OSGi. (2012). *OSGI Service Compendium, Release 4, version 4.3. OSGi Alliance Specification*. Retrieved July 2014 from: http://www.osgi.org / Specifications/HomePage

Patrick, M. (2001). *DHCP Relay Agent Information Option*. IETF Internet Standard RFC 3046, January 2001.

Pisa, P., Moreira, M., Carvalho, H., Ferraz, L., & Duarte, O. (2010), Migrating Xen Virtual Routers with No Packet Loss. *First Workshop on Network Virtualization and Intelligence For Future Internet (WNetVirt'10)*, Búzios. April 2010.

Python. (n.d.). *Python Programming Language Website*. Retrieved July 2014 from: http://www.python.org

Quinn, P., & Nadeau, T. (2014). *Service Function Chaining Problem Statement (draft-ietf-sfc-problem-statement-07.txt)*. IETF Internet Draft. June 2014.

Rosemberg, J., Schulzrinne, H., Camarillo, G., Johnston, A., Peterson, J., Sparks, R., ... Schooler, E. (2002). *SIP: Session Initiation Protocol*. IETF Internet Standard. RFC 3261, June 2002.

Royon, Y. (2007). *Environments d'exécution pour paserelles domestiques*. (Doctoral Dissertation). Institut National des Sciences Apliquées (INSA/INRIA), Lyon, France.

Smedt, A., Balemans, H., Onnegren, J., & Haeseleer, S. (2006). The multi-play service enabled Residential Gateway. In Proceedings of Broadband Europe 2006. Geneva: Academic Press.

Tcpdump. (n.d.). *Tcpdump Project Website*. Retrieved july 2014 from: http://www.tcpdump.org

Troan, O., & Droms, R. (2003). *IPv6 Prefix Options for Dynamic Host Configuration Protocol (DHCP) version 6*. IETF Internet Standard RFC3633, December 2003.

Unix Top. (n.d.). *Unix Top Project Website*. Retrieved July 2014 from: http://www.unixtop.org

Xia, L., Wu, Q., & King, D. (2013). *Use cases and Requirements for Virtual Service Node Pool Management (draft-xia-vsnpool-management-use-case-01)*, IEFT Internet Draft, October 2013.

Xie, H., Li, Y., Wang, J., Lopez, D. R., Tsou, T., & Wen, Y. (2013). vRGW: Towards network function virtualization enabled by software defined networking. In *Proceedings of the International Conference on Network Protocols (ICNP 2013)*. Göttingen, Germany: IEEE Computer Society. Doi:10.1109/ICNP.2013.6733632

Young, G. (2009). Broadband Forum Overview with Focus on Next Generation Access. *Presentation delivered at the UKNOF event, September 2009*. Retrieved July 2014 from: http://www.uknof.org.uk/uknof14/Young-BroadbandForum.pdf

Zeng, S., & Hao, Q. (2009). Network I/O Path Analysis in the Kernel-based Virtual Machine Environment through Tracing. In *Proceedings of the 1st Int. Conf. on Information Science and Engineering (ICISE 2009)*. Nanjing, China: IEEE Computer Society. doi:10.1109/ICISE.2009.776

KEY TERMS AND DEFINITIONS

Broadband Access Networks: Access networks that provide high-speed network connectivity between customers and network service providers.

CWMP: Also known as Broadband Forum's CPE WAN Management Protocol, is a de facto standard for device and service management for customer equipment connected to broadband access network environments.

Network Function Virtualization: In NFV, network node functions, previously carried by dedicated hardware, are virtualized into blocks (Virtual Network Functions or VNFs) that can be chained together to create service abstractions.

Network Service Provider Infrastructures: It corresponds to the infrastructure elements, such as the networking structure or data centers, that support the operations of organizations that provide network access or converged services.

Service Delivery: This encompasses the delivery of converged services over IP networks, whether from the operator itself (as it is the case for Triple-Play offers) or from third parties.

Software-Defined Networking: This is a network architecture that decouples the network control and forwarding plane functions, making it possible to introduce flexible and dynamic, flow-oriented network control programmability.

Virtualized Residential Gateways (vRGWs): An alternative to conventional, physical gateway appliances, where the physical device is replaced by a simple bridge, with all functionality and services being moved to the operator infrastructure, as a virtualized entity.

Chapter 20
Context-Aware Content Delivery:
Architectures, Standards, and Transport

Hassnaa Moustafa
Intel Corporation, USA

V. Srinivasa Somayazulu
Intel Corporation, USA

Yiting Liao
Intel Corporation, USA

ABSTRACT

The huge changes in multimedia and video consumption styles are leading to different challenges for the current Internet architecture in order to support the required quality of experience. A comprehensive solution to these would help the service providers and over-the-top players (OTT) to differentiate their services and the network operators to handle ever growing demands on network resources in an era of slower growth in revenues. This chapter discusses the requirements for and approaches to enhanced content delivery architectures, video delivery standards and current and future content transport mechanisms. The chapter also discusses the Quality of Experience (QoE) metrics and management for video content and introduces context-awareness in the video delivery chain. It also provides several examples for context-aware content delivery and personalized services.

INTRODUCTION

Nowadays, we are living in a new era of huge growth in multimedia (especially video) content carried over communications networks, arising from the growth of cloud applications, a tremendous increase in the popularity and evolution of personal client devices such as smartphones, tablet devices, and ultrabooks. The ubiquity of wireless, including mobile networks, is also an important commodity in our daily life. Users' consumption style for multimedia content is strongly evolving as users tend to access and consume the content ANYWHERE, ANY TIME and through ANY DE-

DOI: 10.4018/978-1-4666-8371-6.ch020

VICE irrespective of the content location (home, office, cloud). Furthermore, users become active parts in the content area/business through User Generated Content (UGC) and interactive content sharing between friends and family members, for example. The personalization that these services need (in terms of matching different categories of users, different devices and different network characteristics and costs) presents a significant challenge to implement and a great opportunity as well for service providers and network operators to develop their business. At the same time, current content delivery network and service infrastructure does not fully meet the users' new consumption style in terms of delivering for the users' needs and function of the users' context. Also, the network resources are not optimized to handle the content delivery considering the device capabilities and content requirements. Up to now there is no standardized and broad consensus on efficient QoE provisioning for video."

The new challenges in managing content delivery over constrained networks (e.g., mobile and wireless networks) require video adaptation techniques to jointly enhance QoE, optimize network resource utilization and client devices' power consumption. Consequently, there is a requirement for adapted network and service infrastructures and advanced content delivery mechanisms better suited to today's emerging content types, consumption style and mobility needs.

This chapter discusses the limitations of the current Internet architecture, transport protocols, Quality of Service (QoS) ensuring and delivery mechanisms for video content and reviews the different literature and standardization work on advanced content delivery architectures, transport protocols and Quality of Experience (QoE) mechanisms. Finally, the chapter presents a cross-layer framework for the cooperation between the connectivity, transport and application layers aiming to deliver the video content in a network-aware, application-aware and device-aware adaptive manner.

BACKGROUND ON VIDEO DELIVERY ARCHITECTURES, PROTOCOLS, AND STANDARDS

Video traffic is dominating in the Internet, and is expected to continue growing (as much as 79% of global Internet traffic by 2018 (Cisco, 2014). Video traffic takes several forms including streaming premium content from content providers (e.g. NetFlix), web video (e.g. YouTube) and P2P video through various applications mainly for mobile devices. At the same time, a revolution is taking place in terms of how video and TV contents are consumed. While broadcast TV is still dominant for news and live events, there is a continuing tremendous growth of video on demand (VOD) and video streaming. Moreover, consumers are viewing this content on a much more diverse set of platforms than in the past – from big screen TVs, to PCs, tablets and smartphones, over fixed and mobile networks, and either managed or unmanaged service offerings. The growing sophistication of consumers' viewing habits is shown in data (Accenture,2014) that correlates the type of content being watched with the type of device. For example, full-length movies are mostly watched on TV, while user generated content (UGC) and short video clips are mostly associated with mobile devices. Tablets show the greatest growth in video viewing for all types of content, and also are associated with multi-screen viewing experiences, where viewers switch between screens, or view related content on one screen while watching video on another screen. It is therefore important for service and content providers to follow consumers across different devices, and offer a consistent user experience while the offering must be relevant to the device and the user exact needs. In addition, there are new opportunities for content and service providers to sustain and develop customer's fidelity by means of personalized services while exploring new monetization models, including target advertising.

These trends are paving a way towards online Internet video delivery architectures. Cable TV operators as well as Telcos are migrating to all-IP networks to lower their OPerational Expenditure (OPEX) as well as to provide a rich set of services, thereby increasing user's engagement and reducing churns. IPTV architectures have been deployed by service providers to deliver managed services including video on demand (VOD) to consumers. The IPTV architecture handles both multicast and unicast delivery, and deploys MPEG TS (International Telecommunications Union [ITU], 2012) streams over the Real-Time Transport Protocol (RTP) (Schulzrinne, Casner, Frederick, & Jacobson, 2002), using the Real-Time Streaming Protocol (RTSP) (Schulzrinne, Rao, & Lamphier, 1998) to enable the client to control the media server. Thus, for unicast RTSP streaming, the client addresses the server via a resource indicator or URL (Uniform Resource Locator), similar to HTTP(Fiedling & Resehre, 2014). However, RTSP is a stateful protocol, where the server maintains client state, and every message to the server contains a specific session identifier, which allows the server to correlate received messages to a specific multimedia session. The feedback from the client can be used by the server to adapt this correlation dynamically. Broadcast content from a national head-end is typically distributed to the service nodes using a multicast delivery scheme. The factors affecting service delivery include the compression quality, jitter and limited bandwidth as well as packet loss (itself caused by many factors including bandwidth limitations, congestion, link failures, etc.).

As mentioned above, over-the-top (OTT) video content has been steadily increasing its share in overall trafficin the Internet. Most of this content started out being served by the same HTTP protocol that underlies the World Wide Web. Content providers can in principle use the previously existing generic HTTP web server infrastructure to serve video content, rather than specialized streaming video servers needed for RTSP streaming, for example – thus providing a seamless, cost-effective and scalable deployment path for online video services. Internet Service Providers (ISPs) usually deploy content delivery networks (CDNs) – systems of web servers and caches that duplicate content and direct users to the nearest or least loaded server in order to rapidly serve large numbers of users –, and this architecture is particularly well suited for serving HTTP-based video. For very short video clips, the HTTP download approach for 'streaming' video could be acceptable. In classical streaming, when the viewer selects a video from a streaming server the video starts playing until its end. For this to happen, the data rate of the encoded video file must be smaller than the bandwidth capacity of the remote viewer; otherwise, the video will frequently stop playing (Examples are: SD video requires on average 700 kbps, HD video requires at least 2Mbps throughput and 4K video can require until 20Mbps for H.264 encoding).

With the growing popularity of content forms (ranging from User Generated Content "UGC" to Content Providers content), the ever-growing importance of mobile networks, and the need to provide a good quality of experience (QoE) for video, solutions for streaming video are increasingly needed.

The technologies such as Apple's HTTP Live Streaming (Pantos et al.,2014), Adobe's HTTP Dynamic Streaming (Adobe, Inc., n.d.) and Microsoft's Smooth Streaming (Microsoft, n.d.) are all proprietary or non-standard approaches to provide HTTP video streaming with client-driven adaptation features. All these approaches are based upon storing video content in small fragments, each of which is encoded at a range of quality settings (bitrates), as shown in Figure 1.

The player in the client is in full control of which fragment it wants to request and the quality at which it wants to request it. Thus, based upon various considerations such as playback buffer status, network congestion, CPU load, or user or device context information, the client can select

Figure 1. HTTP Adaptive Bit Rate (ABR) Streaming

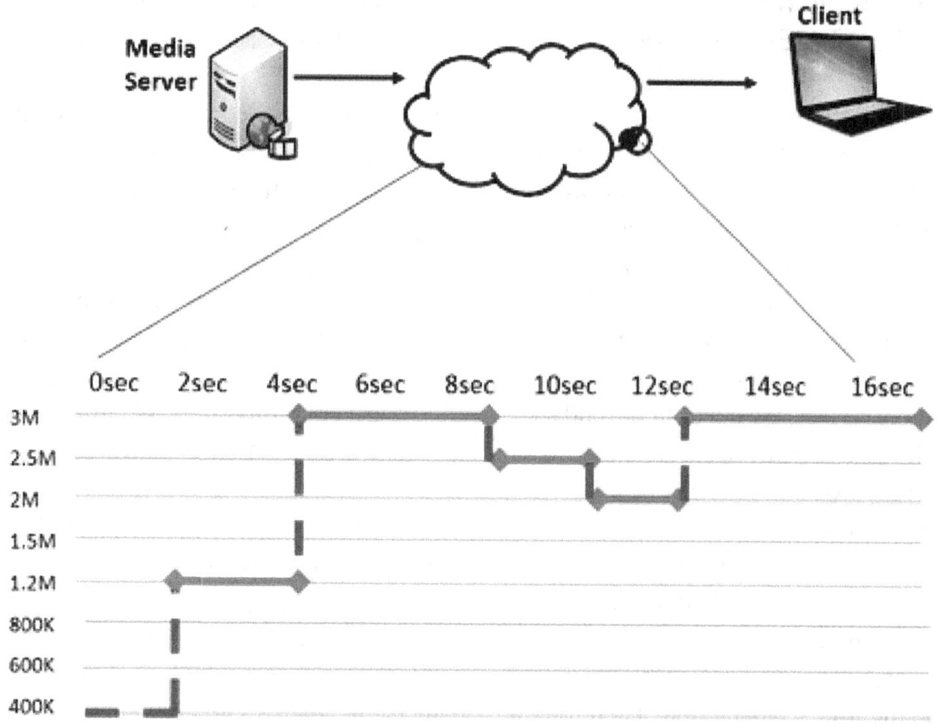

to deliver the best QoE for the video streaming application. This trend of client-driven adaptation, in keeping with stateless HTTP-based video servers becomes increasingly popular. One drawback is the proliferation of multiple approaches, which leads to a large number of formats and representations that must be stored (or dynamically generated) at the CDN servers. MPEG has developed a widely supported standard called Dynamic Adaptive Streaming over HTTP (MPEG-DASH) (International Standard Organization [ISO], 2014). As part of the collaboration with MPEG (3rd Generation Partnership Project [3GPP], 2014) has adopted DASH (with specific codecs and operating modes) for use over wireless networks. Furthermore, an industry group called the DASH Industry Forum (DASH-IF) is currently driving the effort to promote the adoption of MPEG-DASH and convert the specification into a commercial success (DASH Interoperability Forum [DASH IF], n.d.), including publishing interoperability guidelines, conformance and test.

This new model for video services consumption over mobile and wireless networks creates the need for feedback information between the end- user application, the network and the service platform in real-time. This helps optimizing the content for device/network resources on one hand and end-user QoE and battery experience on the other hand. In this view more intelligence needs to be considered in the network and in the service platform. A way to do that is through having context-based video delivery optimization and adaptation along the end-to-end delivery chain. This chapter presents examples of optimizations and adaptations to better manage the video delivery: TCP optimization, video optimization based on context information on the user, network and service, video controllers for content recommendation and personalization.

QUALITY OF EXPERIENCE (QOE): DEFINITION AND MANAGEMENT MECHANISMS

In the past years, network operators have been focusing on monitoring and developing mechanisms to provide efficient Quality of Service (QoS) to their consumers. Most QoS monitoring methods measure network level metrics such as bandwidth, delay, jitter, packet loss, etc., to determine the QoS and optimize network performance. For plain applications such as e-mail exchange or file transfer, QoS adequately reflects the needs of the end user and shows the ability of the network to provide a service at an assured service level (Soldani, Li, & Cuny, 2007). However, with the dramatically increasing multimedia content that emerged in the recent years, measuring and optimizing QoS become more than necessary on one hand and requires new user-centric approach on the other hand to guarantee the user's satisfaction. Therefore, a new concept called Quality of Experience (QoE) has rapidly gained interest and its definition has been discussed in many literature:

- ETSI has defined QoE as "a measure of user performance based on both objective and subjective psychological measures of using an ICT service or product" (European Telecommunications Standard Institute [ETSI], 2009). It considers both technical parameters and usage context variables, and measures effectiveness and efficiency of the communications as well as the user satisfaction and enjoyment of the services.
- (Lopez, Gonzalez, Bellido, & Allonso, 2006) described QoE as "an extension of the traditional QoS in the sense that QoE provides information regarding the delivered services from an end-user point of view"
- (Soldani, Li, & Cuny, 20070 claimed that "QoE is how a user perceives the usability of a service when in use – how satisfied he/she is with a service in terms of, e.g., usability, accessibility, retainability and integrity".
- The most commonly used definition of QoE comes from(ITU, 2007), in which QoE is "the overall acceptability of an application or services, as perceived subjectively by the end-user". As shown in Figure 2, it includes the complete end-to-end system effects (client, terminal, network, service infrastructure, etc.) and the overall acceptability may be influenced by user expectations and context.

Compared to QoS which focuses on the performance of the network, QoE is more concerned with the overall satisfaction of the consumer/user for the delivery of services. Despite the broad interest and agreement on QoE, the measurement of video's QoE remains very challenging due to its correlation to a number of subjective factors. Typically, QoE assessment methods can be categorized into three categories: subjective, objective and hybrid.

Subjective Video QoE Assessment

The most accurate way to assess video QoE is through subjective experiments since it best captures the human perceived quality. In a subjective experiment, a number of participants ranging from various ages and genders are asked to view a set of videos in a controlled environment and rate the quality in terms of mean opinion score (MOS) as shown in Table 1. Then, the MOS of a video clip is calculated by the arithmetic mean of all the individual participants' ratings of the images/videos under test (Bovik, 2013). Even though subjective experiments best reflect human perception of the video, it still cannot eliminate the variability of the ratings due to viewers' own expectations towards the video service. Therefore, various standards have defined test methods with

Figure 2. Definition of QoE

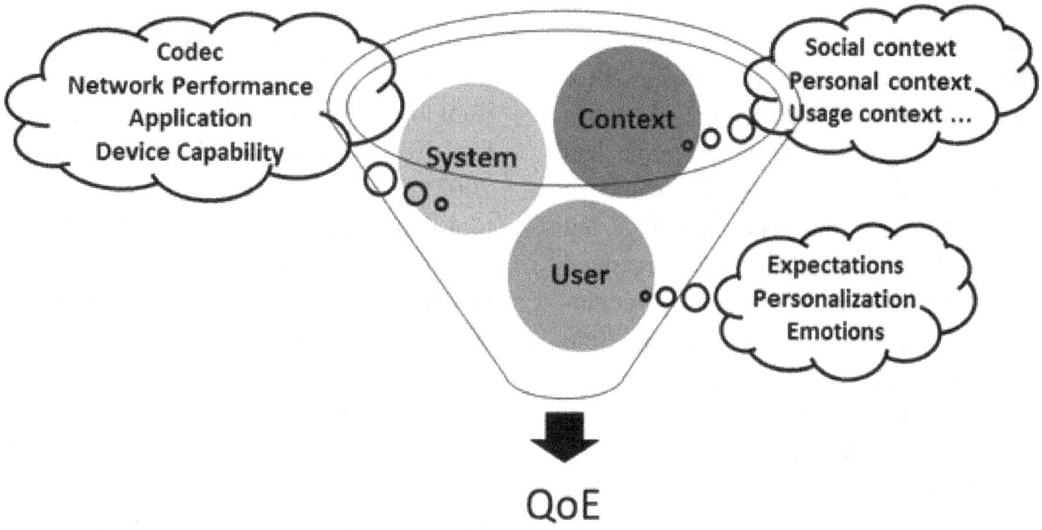

standard test environment, criteria for participant and test content selection, and precise assessment procedures to minimize the rating variations (ITU, 1998), (ITU, 1999) and (ITU, 2000). Some commonly used testing methods are single stimulus where participants rate the quality of impaired video stream without comparing to a reference. An example is Single Stimulus Continuous Quality Evaluation (SSCQE). Other methods are double stimulus where participants rate the quality or difference in quality between the references and impaired video streams. Some examples include Double Stimulus Impairment Scale (DSIS), Double Stimulus Continuous Quality Scale (DSCQS), and Simultaneous Double Stimulus for Continuous Evaluation (SDSCE).

Subjective tests are the most accurate method to find the ground truth of video's QoE. However, it is very expensive and time consuming due to the manpower requirements. Furthermore, it cannot be done in an automatic manner, the scale of the tests is often very limited.

Objective QoE Assessment

Due to the expensive and time-consuming nature of subjective approaches, many researchers have proposed objective metrics that make use of network and video information together with some algorithms to predict viewer's MOS (Younkin, Fernald, Deherty, Salskev, & Corriveau, 2007). Objective video quality assessment (VQA) methods can be generally divided into three categories: full-reference (FR), reduced-referenced (RR) and no-reference (NR):

Table 1. Mean Opinion Score

Value	Quality Anchor	Descriptor
5	Excellent	Imperceptible
4	Good	Perceptible but not annoying
3	Fair	Slightly annoying
2	Poor	Annoying
1	Bad	Very Annoying

- FR VQA metrics use algorithms to compare the pristine video with the distorted video and determine the quality. The most commonly used metric is peak-signal-to-noise ratio (PSNR) that measures the mean square error (MSE) between source and distorted videos. Its simplicity makes it one of the most popular VQA methods, but it doesn't correlate well to the perceptual video quality. Thus, other more perceptually relevant methods such as Structural Similarity Index (SSIM) (Weng, Bovik, Sheik, & Simeneelli, 2004) and Video Quality Metric (VQM) (Binsen and Welf, 2004) have been rapidly gaining popularity.

In an end-to-end video streaming system, the quality assessment may be conducted in the places where a high-quality reference video is not available. In those cases, RR or NR approaches are required for the quality assessment.

- RR approaches use an alternative channel to transmit a small portion of reference information to facilitate the quality assessment. For example, RRED (Reduced reference entropic differencing) indices (Sounararajan and Bovik, 2012) measure differences between the entropies of wavelet coefficients of reference and the distorted images to compute quality.
- NR approaches evaluate the video quality without any knowledge of the source content. Some of the representative methods include BLind Image Integrity Notator using DCT-Statistics (BLIINDS) (Saad, Bovik, & Charrier, 2012) and blind/referenceless image spatial quality evaluator (BRISQUE) index (Mittal, Meerthy, & Bovik, 2011).

A good review of the objective VQA methods can be found in Younkin, Fernald, Deherty, Salskev, & Corriveau, 2007) .

Hybrid QoE Assessment

Apart from the subjective and objective approaches introduced previously, a hybrid method called pseudo subjective quality assessment (PSQA) has also been proposed (Mohamed and Rubine, 2002). This approach uses a specific learning tool with random neural network (RNN) model to mimic the behaviors of real human observers and automatically provides real-time estimations of the quality. Since it requires some subjective evaluation in the training stage, it is considered as a hybrid method. The PSQA method has been applied to Voice over IP (VoIP) over wireless LANs (Robine, Varela, Bennin, 2006), video applications over DiffServ networks, IPTV over peer-to-peer networks (Cancela, Rudriguez, & Rubine, 2006) or generic video streaming applications over WLANs (Piamrat, Vihe, Bennine, & Ksentini, 2009) .

Another type of "hybrid" metrics use a combination of network QoS statistics, packet characteristics, decoded video signal and context information as an input to estimate the QoE. For example, a V-Factor metric inspects different sections of video streams such as the transport stream (TS) headers, the packetized elementary stream (PES) headers, and the decoded video signal to predict video quality subject to network and video impairments (Winkler and Mehandas, 2008). In (ITU, 2013), network performance as well as bitstream information is used to model multiple artifacts of the video and predict the MOS. Balachandran et al. developed a data-driven machine learning approach to capture the interactions between metrics and confounding effects on the QoE (Balachandran et al., 2013). Bitstream- and packet-based metrics appear particularly promising for practical use due to their lower computational complexity and better scalability(Winkler and Mehandas, 2008).

Due to the exponential growth of the video traffic over the internet and the subscription and advertisement-based business model, providing good QoE at the minimal storage/bandwidth/

power cost is fundamental to the success of video services. Therefore, video QoE assessment tools are critical to the stakeholders of the video services to evaluate competing solutions and improve services.

Figure 3 shows the main stakeholders in a video delivery ecosystem. In that system, video quality issues could be introduced during content generation, transcoding, transmission or display on a device. User-generated content may suffer from quality issues due to shaky cameras and poorly captured environments; video coding would introduce compression artifacts to the processed content; network impairments could lead to annoying issues such as video freezing and jerkiness; and a poor viewing device/software may cause unpleasant user experience. As a result, QoE assessment methods are widely used at the different checkpoints in the video delivery system to help stakeholders develop innovative technologies to improve their video solutions and inspire product development and strategy.

NETWORK TRANSPORT PROTOCOLS FOR VIDEO DELIVERY

As discussed in the earlier section on "Background on Video Delivery Architectures, Protocols and Standards", the rise of OTT video in particular is driving industry consolidation around DASH. In doing so, of course, the video content is being transported over IP networks using TCP (Transmission Control Protocol). Besides TCP out of order delivery and control overhead, the TCP/IP model needs to meet the challenges introduced by wireless access networks (e.g., bandwidth limitation, propagation delay, wireless link unreliability and mobility) and the delay requirements of real-time and video streaming services. Optimizing the performance of the transport layer in order to address these challenges has been an active and continuing area of research, and in particular a number of approaches have been considered that seek to improve HTTP and DASH video delivery over TCP. These can be roughly classified under several categories – including:

- Approaches which seek to modify the behavior of the TCP protocol itself;
- Approaches which seek to optimize TCP performance by introducing changes in the network delivery architecture;
- Approaches which introduce cross-layer optimization to exploit video and wireless network characteristics explicitly in the transport.

Figure 3. Video Delivery System

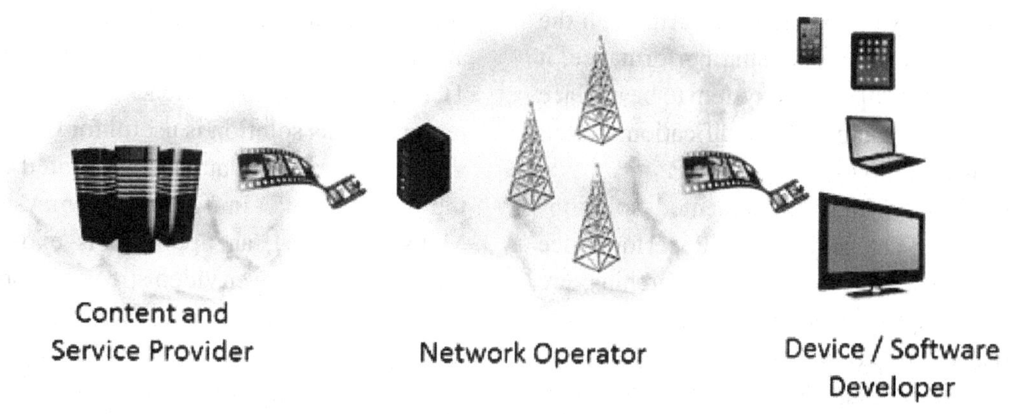

We discuss a few examples of each kind of approach next, in order to illustrate the point.

Modified TCP schemes in the first category include both sender-based as well as sender and receiver based approaches. In the former, existing congestion control mechanisms (e.g. slow start, congestion avoidance, etc.) are modified or new schemes are implemented, while in the latter sender and receiver side changes are also made to respond to the new changes at the other side. Among the experimental protocols being considered that require both sender and receiver side changes is the QUIC protocol (Reskind, 2013), which among other features, seeks to provide reliable stream support and congestion avoidance over UDP. To this end, QUIC employs FEC to provide lower latency and improved reliability at the expense of some increased bandwidth overhead. For congestion avoidance, various approaches can be supported including TCP Cubic-like algorithms augmented with packet pacing based upon inter-packet spacing and bandwidth estimation.

Another example is Minion (Iyengar et al., 2012), which presents a solution for out-of-order delivery TCP through an extension in the TCP stack for managing TCP sender's buffer and an extension to two application-level protocols (COBS "Consistent Overhead Byte Stuffing" and TLS "Transport Layer Security") yielding unordered datagram delivery. This retains TCP semantics and provides a datagram service to the application layer by embedding upper layer messages byte-stream and extracting messages at the receiver from the byte-stream considering the order. Although the solution of Minion shows better performance, it requires a whole supporting system to be in place due to the COBS and TLS modification as well as the OS-level modification in TCP.

Among the widely implemented solutions in the second category for TCP performance improvement based upon network architecture changes, are the so-called performance enhancing proxies (PEP) of which one example is the split-TCP proxy (Ivanovich et al., 2008)]. In split-connection TCP, the end-to-end TCP connection is split into two independent connections (transparent to the endpoints) in particular to isolate high RTT links, or wireless links that experience important packet loss, etc. By reducing the RTT in the individual split connections, the overall throughput is improved.

Finally, we consider a few examples in the third category, where cross-layer information is shared between the TCP congestion control and the application and the wireless MAC/PHY layers. A client-driven rate adaptation mechanism is presented in (Havey et al., 2012) to replace the congestion control mechanism in TCP by an application layer fairness mechanism. The flow of data from the server is managed according to an estimate for the Congestion Window "*cwnd*" size based on TCP's RTT clocking information at the application layer. A congestion detection mechanism is also used during the *cwnd* calculation by monitoring and analyzing the incoming packet streams from the network hardware. The deployment feasibility of this work remains unclear and the need for sniffing the incoming packet streams to derive round trip timeouts adds complexity. In (Gabale et al., 2012) the authors consider variable bit rate (VBR) video flows over TCP and bounded bandwidth egress interfaces of data centers between video servers and clients. The proposed solution provides an adjustment in video flow rates to maximize the QoE-fairness. Rate control is implemented looking continuously for the right TCP receiver window size for each flow to maximize the playback buffer sizes of all the clients. No modification is required to the TCP/IP stack and no feedback from the client is required. This solution is useful for Cloud-based video delivery and data centers shared between multiple tenants. In (Zheng, Somayazulu, & Moustafa, 2014), an approach is explored for providing cross-layer video streaming optimization opportunities within the TCP framework – by modifying the behavior of the TCP receiver alone, with no changes in the sender – to avoid triggering

TCP congestion control under a set of conditions derived from cross-layer context information. Important constraints placed on the design are that it should only require client side modifications, and also demonstrate fairness towards current and optimized models of TCP. In this work, gains obtained by integrating video and wireless network layers context information (e.g., frame type, playback buffer level, wireless network loss indication to distinguish from congestion, etc.) are demonstrated in terms of the video QoE impact.

Overall, the area of exploration for DASH optimizations considering the network layer transport protocols is an active and continuing area of research.

CONTEXT-AWARE CONTENT DELIVERY

The growth of new video services is resulting in a crowded market with many new players trying to maximize their market segment and a huge amount of video content consumption. However, without sufficient QoE consideration, service differentiation and resource optimization become hard to achieve. Consequently, new challenges are being encountered in managing media sessions and new capabilities are required on devices, content servers and edge routers to gather real-time information about the device capabilities, the network performance, and the video content requirements. This information allows context-aware video adaptation to enhance user's experience, optimize network resources and devices' power consumption.

Overview on Context-Awareness

A first step in context-awareness is to define the context in general and for audio-visual services, and then define the context information types in the audio-video delivery chain.

- Context definition started in 1991 by Mark Weiser who introduced the term 'pervasive' referring to seamless integration of devices into the users' daily life (Weiser, 1999) as a way to introduce environment information in computing systems.
- Then, "Context-aware computing" was defined in 1994 by Schilit & Theimer, describing context as "location of use, collection of nearby people and objects, as well as the changes to those objects over time" (Schilit and Theimer, 1994).
- Definition of context by enumeration of constituting parameters also appeared by Brown et al. in 1997 (Brown, Bevey, & Chen, 1997), enumerating "location, time of day, season of the year, and temperature".
- The general definition of context (and the most popular one) appeared in 1999, by Dey and Abowd (Dey et al., 1999) defining context as any information that can be used to characterize the situation of an entity. An entity is a person, place or object that is considered relevant to the interaction between the user and the application, including the user and the application themselves".
- Another general definition of context appeared by Chen and Kotz in 2000 (Chen and Ketz, 2000), focusing on the environment: "Context is the set of environmental states and settings that either determines an application's behaviour or in which an application event occurs and is interesting to the user".

Inspired from the different definitions of context in the literature, context for audio-visual services can be defined as any information that can be used to characterize the situation of an entity related to audio-visual services. An entity could be the user, device, network or the service itself. Context information can be either static information acquired in an offline manner or dynamic information gathered in real time while the session is active. Both static and dynamic context information can be "sensitive", and they should not be shared among applications without verifying and addressing privacy constraints.

Context information in the audio-visual delivery chain is gathered from the user, network and service domains and takes the following forms:

The following tables give examples different context information that can be static (gathered once at the beginning or the session) or dynamic (gathered continuously during the session). Table 2 shows examples of user context information and Table 3 shows examples of network context information. Examples of device context information and service/content context information are shown respectively in Table 4 and Table 5.

Overview on Context-Aware User Experience

Context-awareness is a valuable tool allowing rich user experience as follows:

- Knowing user's preferences, activity and location and use this information to enhance the user's perception quality and satisfaction during the access to the service (for example through content personalization and recommendation).
- Knowing the network characteristics (e.g., bandwidth availability, cost), the device connection to different networks and the content network requirement allows to enhance user's connectivity to networks (maximizing the always connected time, allowing seamless content transfer between different networks), content sharing between different devices (Multi-screen content), and providing richer battery life through power savings.
- Knowing the content context enables to create and share content with other users of same preference and context.
- Knowing a unique identity of the user without requiring typing password regularly and knowing the wireless interfaces characteristics allows seamless access to devices and services without passwords.

Although context-awareness is promising in enhancing user's experience for multimedia and video content and providing meaningful services to the user matching "and going beyond if possible"

Table 2. Examples of User Context Information

User Context Information	
Static	**Dynamic**
Unique ID "who is the user"	Environment information (e.g. ambient light and noise, population, density).
Address "useful for shopping"	Location: Indoor (including relative or annotated locations e.g. home, home/living-room), outdoor (geographical location) and network-related location (proximity to access routers, content servers, edge servers, caches, ..).
Age Category	Personal schedule/calendar: activity and availability.
Explicit Preferences (e.g. favorite content, actors, preferred devices and access network). These can be explicitly indicated by users	Implicit Preferences: preferred audio language and subtitle language, consumption history and watching habits such as watching news every evening and watching a movie every Friday night. These can be learnt from the user's interaction with the content.

Table 3. Examples of Network Context Information

Network Context Information	
Static	**Dynamic**
Security: security parameters and supported protocols	Access Network Information: stats (active, disables, not available), SSID and IP address
Location: network availability as a function of geographical location. This helps to appropriately manage network resources and content	Network and Quality: QoS parameters (e.g. nominal and effective transmission rate, latency, jitter, packet loss, available bandwidth, connection setup time) and link quality (Received Signal Strength Indicator "RSSI" indicates the strength of wireless connection)

Table 4. Examples of Device Context Information

Device Context Information	
Static	**Dynamic**
Device Identification: unique ID	Active Access Network: network interfaces and protocols and nominal bitrates and connections
Capabilities: audio/video codecs, touch screen, gesture recognition/control, control devices "e.g., keyboard", portability, audio/video processing capabilities	Power Resources: Battery level, remaining operation time and last charging time.
Screen: size & resolution, selected contrast, brightness and color saturation levels	Location: absolute/relative location (indoor/outdoor)
Loud Speakers Status: earphone, plugged in speakers, or internal speakers	Near-by Devices: information on devices in each other proximity. This enables utilizing those devices resources, e.g., displaying content on a nearby screen
Device Status: Shared or Private	Active Media Sessions/Applications: media sessions running on the device and information about them

Table 5. Examples of Service/Content Context Information

Service/Content Context Information	
Static	**Dynamic**
Content Identifier: unique identifier enables exclusive identification of content and content provider	User's Content Consumption History: views, purchases, ratings
Content Metadata: description, actors names, director name, type, content duration, studio, country of origin, date of recording, available languages, rating, reviews	Media session information: unique media session identifier
Content Characteristics: Format (Standard Definition "SD", High Definition "HD" or Ultra High Definition "UHD") and Codec (E.g. H.264, H.264)	Required or supported QoS: minimal supported bit rate, minimal and maximal supported resolution and required latency. This facilitates content presentation and session continuity and selecting the most appropriate device
Content Location: regional, national or international and content sources proximity to users	
Content Price: content/subscription price and offers	
Content Protection: Digital Right Management (DRM) type, recording limitations, content availability with respect to location. This evaluates whether session transfer between devices is possible	

his goals, needs and expectations, there remain several challenges to consider for the introduction of context-awareness in the audio-visual delivery chain. The following are some examples:

- Context-aware content delivery mechanisms: How the content delivery is adapted (codec, bitrate ....)? How the content is delivered through the network (unicast, multicast, applying network coding, from which server(s), from a Cloud, through which access network)? How to use the different context information about the user, device and service/content to enhance the network conditions (for example, resolving cases of congestion or bandwidth over/under utilization)?
- Context-aware capabilities: What are the technologies to implement in end-user devices, service platforms, maybe middle-boxes to enable context-awareness? How to collect context information and exchange them in the system? How to intelligently manage the vast amount of context information that can be gathered?
- Interoperable deployment: Is there any means to have standardized context-awareness features?

USER'S ACCEPTABILITY: ACCEPTANCE TO PRIVACY CONSTRAINT BY THE USER RESULTING FROM MANIPULATION OF PERSONAL INFORMATION.

Service Personalization and Content Recommendation

Gathering context information about the user, his environment and devices, the network conditions and the content metadata and the content bandwidth requirements allows the provisioning of personalized/customized content to the user. The following are some examples that could be considered in a mutual fashion:

- Content provision matching user's preferences.
- Providing different quality levels according to the users' subscription types (even if the bandwidth allows more quality levels).
- Session continuity when changing the terminals (content moving from terminal to terminal).
- Adapting the content according to the terminal capabilities.
- Session continuity when the terminal changes the network connectivity (for instance moving from Wi-Fi to 3G connection).
- Adapting the content according to the network capacity.
- Interactive service provision through introducing interactive means during users' access to services, as an example: Allowing each user to have metadata on each item of the content (e.g. a car used by an actor in the movie) which allows online purchase for any content item that the user likes (e.g., a scarf of a famous actor in a movie that the user is watching, ...).
- Context-based targeted advertisement depending on the user location and preferences.
- Context-based content recommendation, for example:
  - Recommending content matching the user's preference, age category, consumption style, location (in form of customized menus for example, for TV and Video on Demand).
  - Recommending content matching the characteristics of the device and network being used (e.g., in form of recommending only HD or SD content).

- Context-based content adaptation for optimizing device and network resources on one hand and end-user QoE and battery experience on the other hand. Examples are:
    - For a high display resolution, a video of high bitrate/resolution is sent if the user's application buffering level and the global network bandwidth conditions are sufficient and the battery level is sufficient.
    - If the battery level degrades during the session even if the user's application buffering level remains sufficient, then the video is continued to be streamed in lesser bitrate/ resolution to save battery and prevent video session interruption due to battery failure (keeping a threshold on the quality based on the remaining resources).
    - If the battery level is fine but the user's application buffering level and global network bandwidth conditions degrade, the video switches to lower bitrate (following the ordinary adaptive streaming approach), which in turn results in saving the battery level.
    - For small size display, the transmission errors are less observed by the user especially if the user is in motion and in a noisy environment. Therefore, video can be displayed with lower quality (bitrate) to save battery and network resources even if the buffering level and global network bandwidth conditions are not poor. This is very useful for content categories as news and content that is not Live, in which transmission errors have lesser impact on the user's perception.
    - If the user is in a bright/sunny environment and the battery level is not high, content can be sent with higher brightness but with lower bitrate to compensate the consumed power from content brightness.
    - If the user is in a dimly environment, no matter of the battery level and the global network bandwidth, the user can receive content with lower brightness. This has a dual benefit: allowing better perceived quality for the user and saving battery resources.
    - Users can receive content including targeted advertisement for regional services according to each user location, mobility status and battery level suitability. This saves network bandwidth and device resources (mainly battery resources) from the reception of bigger traffic volume if each user receives all the advertisements.

Multiscreen Experience

Multiscreen experience is increasing in home environments and is observing special attention from content providers (e.g. Netflix), equipment manufacturers and software manufacturers. However there remains some challenges and technical limitations preventing full adoption of multiscreen experience in the users' daily content consumption.

Multiscreen experience enables not only content for any device but also content transfer from device to device and content sharing across multiple devices. The following examples show scenarios for a multiscreen experience:

- A video session starts on device 1 (e.g., smartphone) and is transferred to device 2 (e.g., a tablet or TV screen) when it becomes available in the proximity of device 1.
- The same video is watched by multiple users with different device resources and under various network conditions (e.g., video for a lecture in a classroom).

Although WiDi (Wireless Display) (Wirless Display(WiDi), n.d.) and Miracast (Miracast, 2012) are two enabling technologies for content transfer from screen to screen, these solutions cannot always guarantee the best QoE especially with variable wireless links quality. Also, content protection is still a big challenge. Content providers cannot promote the secondary screen experience (e.g. TV content directly streamed to PC or tablet devices) without guaranteeing content protection for premium content.

Besides the device awareness (in terms of capabilities) and network awareness (in terms of available network interfaces for each device and available bandwidth) a number of challenges exist for multiscreen experience, as listed below:

- Content protection mechanisms per device for paid content.
- Session mobility through efficient session transfer mechanisms from device to device (Session Initiation Protocol (SIP) (Rosenberg, 2012) is a good candidate in this case).
- Efficient content delivery for sharing the same content across multiple devices (multicast is efficient in this case).
- Content quality on different screen sizes, which requires efficient content adaptation per device.
- Data plan sharing for multiple devices of the same user or for multiple users (multi-SIM is currently offered by different carriers).

CONTEXT-AWARE CROSS-LAYER FRAMEWORK FOR VIDEO DELIVERY ENHANCEMENT

Efficient content delivery is a key requirement for network operators and service providers on one hand and quality of experience is a key requirement for users on the other hand. Consequently, more intelligence is required in the service and the network infrastructure to better suit the network resources and to allow a differentiated treatment of user's consumption style.

In this context, the Next Generation Service Overlay Network (NGSON) within the IEEE P1903 (International Electrical and Electronic Engineering [IEEE], 2011PCP) is defining an intermediate layer between services and transport for seamless multimedia over wireless networks and video service personalization aiming at providing:

1. Service Control functions.
2. Discovery and execution of the requested service best satisfying the user requirements.
3. Enforcement of the QoS control of the underlying network according to the service requirements.
4. Support of context-awareness (context of users, services and networks).
5. Dynamic adaptability in the service control and delivery functions.
6. Content delivery caching/storage support especially for content-centric services.

Figure 4 introduces a context-aware cross-layer framework for video delivery optimization, allowing efficient utilization of network and device resources and providing better quality of experience for users. Cross-layer interaction takes place between the network and service layers to communicate in real-time context information about the network, the content and the user (and his/her device and environment). This provides: (i) knowledge to the network and service platforms about the available devices and network conditions for the end-user, (ii) knowledge to the network about the content requirements in terms of device capabilities and network resources and (iii) knowledge to the service platforms about the user and his/her environment.

Figure 4. Context-Based Cross-layer Optimization Framework

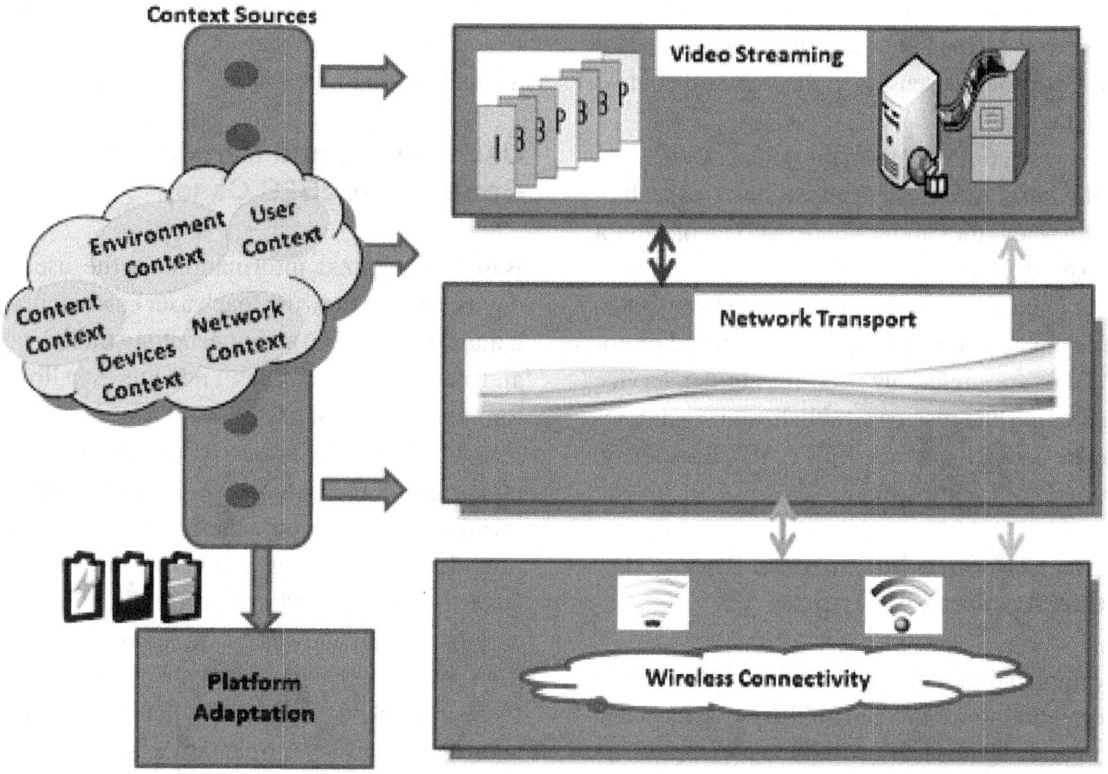

From an implementation perspective, the cross layer architecture considers three steps: i) Context Acquisition, ii) Context Data Transfer and iii) Context-Aware Multimedia and Video Applications Trigger.

Context Acquisition

Context detectors gather and pre-process raw context data. Context detector can be a physical sensor, e.g. biometric sensor or camera or can be a logical sensor (piece of software embedded in other architecture element (e.g. in the user device or Set Top Box "STB"). Context detectors can use different context gathering methods and protocols to gather context data from the following domains: i) User domain: environment sensors in the home sphere (e.g. for user location information), as well as information from user equipment (e.g. about available devices and their capabilities), ii) Network domain: network context information like bandwidth, QoS, etc. and iii) Service domain: content characteristics and metadata.

Context Data Storage and Transfer

There is a need for central or distributed repositories for context information acting as contextual databases. The main role for contextual database(s) is as follows: i) Aggregate, store and process context data from user, network and service domain, ii) Provide context to other modules in a unified way and iii) Trigger actions of other context-aware applications upon detection of changes in dynamic context information.

Context data storage needs to follow a standard context model and the contextual databased need to use well defined interfaces to: i) map information from context sensors to the standard context model and ii)

Expose context information to context-aware multimedia and video applications (respecting user privacy rules about which data can or cannot be exposed).

Context data transfer from context sensors to contextual databases need to use standard protocols that are preferably used during the service negotiation and session establishment (Examples that are not inclusive are: HTTP, SIP (Rosenberg, 2002), PCP (Wing, 2013)…).

Context-Aware Multimedia and Video Application Trigger

The application will dynamically use the context information stored in contextual databases to adapt and personalize services. Example of usage are the following: i) The video server can do real-time transcoding for the stored content to provide video bitrates matching the end-users available bandwidth and device screen sizes, ii) TCP can adapt its congestion window in a context-based manner for enhancing TCP performance over wireless networks, iii) Content servers can provide personalized content to users in a context based (e.g. targeted advertisement based on the user location) and iv) A video controller can adjust the resources reservation in cellular networks in a context-based manner (e.g. providing lesser resources for users having small screen sizes and/or fading batteries as they are not expected to have high video bitrate/resolution).

BUSINESS MODELS

From a business perspective, context-aware and personalized video services are expected to create new business opportunities allowing for B2B (Business to Business) and B2B2C (Business to Business to Client) opportunities presenting several business benefits as shown in the following subsections.

User-Centric and Personalized Content – (B2B2C Case)

Based on context information on the user, his device and the network, each user can receive the content and advertisement matching their devices and network capabilities and interest allowing for more users' satisfaction. This can be realized as follows: i) Service providers can provide monetized context information on the user (e.g. location, age category, preferences) to content providers for content adaptation and targeted advertisement according to different regions (locations). ii) Businesses can purchase air time for their advertisement from content providers for the local area or the category of clients they want to address, so that they can place their advertisements and reach the target audience. iii) Network operators could provide third parties with monetized useful information on the network context and the user context that allows these third parties to adapt the content (through choosing the most suitable compression mean) function of the network context (available bandwidth for example). iv) Users receive the content and advertisement matching their interest (more users' satisfaction) and their exact device capabilities and network bandwidth. Users in turn pay the service providers for personalized services.

Infrastructure as a Service (IaaS) – (B2B Case)

IaaS opens new market for network operators based on collaboration with third parties and letting them pay for the network infrastructure. This can be realized as follows: i) Network operators can open their networks to third parties for TV and VoD content diffusion (Youtube, Daily motion,

Apple, Google and the likes) providing them with useful information on the network context and user context and monetizing the services of providing the network. ii) Network operators owning CDNs (Content Delivery Networks) caching multimedia contents can be paid by content providers for delivering contents to clients in their local region. iii) Network operators can monetize the bandwidth offered by their infrastructures through making each actor pay for the bandwidth level used for his business (ex, advertisers can pay not only the content providers but also the operators).

Differentiated Network and Service Access – (B2B2C Case)

Context-aware service access can allow differentiated network and service access making use of different context information on the user to tailor the network and service access accordingly. This can be realized as follows: i) Service providers can populate caches according to the local clients' consumption style and are paid by content providers for delivering personalized contents to clients in their local region. And in turn clients pay the service providers for having personalized and tailored contents. ii) Network operators can provide differentiated access to users and monetize end-users directly by increasing the subscription price for offering personalized services with better QoE (premium clients) during video content transmission.

FUTURE RESEARCH DIRECTIONS

Context-aware video delivery is promising as it is meant to enhance user's experience on one hand and to optimize the network resources on the other hand. This chapter discusses how to introduce context-awareness in the video delivery chain, defines the context information to be considered in the user, network and service domains and presents a cross-layer framework sharing context information between the network and service domains for video delivery optimization and QoE enhancement.

Research Challenges

Several research challenges are still open to deploy context-aware services. The following are some examples showing future research directions in that area:

- Dealing with context-awareness during content delivery
    - What are the technologies to implement in end-user devices, service platforms, maybe middle-boxes to enable context information gathering? Do we need to evolve standardized technologies to cope with "context features"?
    - How to communicate context information through the network - proactive/on-demand approach, need for new protocols, ...?
- Managing context information
    - How to intelligently manage the vast amount of context information that can be gathered (big data analytics)?
    - How to manage user's acceptance of privacy constraints on use of user context information?
- Triggering context-aware content delivery
    - How to adapt the content being delivered based on context information (type, bitrate, resolution, etc.)?
    - How to deliver the content through the network in an optimized manner (unicast, multicast, applying network coding, from which server(s), from a Cloud, through which access network)?
- Quantifying the gain from context-awareness

- New usage models allowing new differentiation opportunities for content and service providers?
- Performance metrics (QoS, bandwidth/resources saving, QoE, ...)?
- Energy Savings (Power consumption, battery life, ..)?

Solution Example

Applying context-awareness for video and multimedia is being widely discussed in several research projects and appear in proprietary solutions for local applications in smartphones, smart TVs, smart homes (E.g. automatic screen luminosity setting in smartphones based on the ambient light, smart TVs detecting user's presence by hand gestures to re-start after pause, increasing speakers volume if a user is far from speakers). However, the main challenges that are still remaining are: i) How to enable context-awareness in non-local applications (e.g. Internet-based video and multimedia applications)? ii) How to provide a standard solution for context-information transfer from the user domain to the access network or the application server over the Internet?

To resolve these challenges, new capabilities are required to gather information during the video session on the user context (e.g. devices characteristics, buffering status "indicating the network conditions", location, environment light/noise, mobility status,...), network performance, and video content requirements in terms of processing power and network resources. This information can be notified to the network and service platform during session setup and also when the media session is already in place.

This subsection gives a potential standardized solution approach, making use of the IETF PCP (Port Control Protocol) specification (Wing, 2013), providing means to transfer context information from the user domain to the application servers over the Internet and/or the access networks. Consequently, this allows enabling context-aware video and multimedia applications over the Internet.

The use of PCP to signal context information from the user in real-time and to achieve the design goals for a standard context-aware signaling framework is motivated by the following:

- In PCP specification, PCP is viewed as a request/response protocol and also as a hint/notification protocol between a PCP client and a PCP server.
- Message flows in PCP are viewed as independent streams carrying information between the PCP client and the PCP server, in which the PCP client sends a stream of hints indicating to its server its mapping status and the PCP server sends to the client a notification informing the client on the actual state of its mapping. In this view of the protocol, PCP can be extended to carry more mapping information than the IP internal versus external addresses.
- PCP allows to learn and influence the mapping lifetime, which helps reducing network bandwidth, overload on application servers and middle boxes and battery resources on devices. This makes PCP suitable for conveying context information from the user in real-time in a resource wise way.

An example of a solution approach for a standard context-aware information signaling is found in the IETF draft (Moustafa, Moses, & Boucadair, 2014).

In (Moustafa, Moses, & Boucadair, 2014), PCP uses a "UserFeedback" to signal feedback information from the user to the application server and to the network to help optimizing the user's experience and the network and devices resources. This allows the end-user to signal in real-time to the network and application server information about the available device capabilities and network connectivity (e.g., support to different content bitrates, buffering status as an indication of the network connectivity level) as well as other useful context information (e.g., location, mobility status). The static information on the devices (e.g. screen size and screen resolution) needs to be signaled once at the beginning of the session initiated by the device, while the dynamic information on the devices (e.g. battery level and network connectivity) needs to be signaled at the beginning of the session and updated in real-time showing the variation in the battery level for the end-user device. In addition, the application server can signal, through PCP or other mechanism, in real-time to the network the requirement of the content it stores in terms of devices and network resources.

After signaling, the PCP server returns information in the UserFeedback option on the ability of providing matching content. The PCP server also decides on the best way of adapting the content to the end-user device based on the information indicated in the UserFeedback option.

To make use of the context information signaled through PCP UserFeedback option, the following are some examples on how to optimize the content for device and network resources on one hand and end-user QoE and battery experience on the other hand:

- For a high display resolution, a video of high bitrate/resolution is sent if the users application buffering level and the global network bandwidth conditions are sufficient and the battery level is sufficient.
- If the battery level degrades during the session even if the users application buffering level remains sufficient, then the video is continued to be streamed in lesser bitrate/resolution to save battery and prevent video session interruption due to battery failure (keeping a threshold on the quality based on the remaining resources). In this case, lesser resources can be allocated for cellular users to match the bandwidth required for the low bitrate video.
- If the battery level is fine but the users application buffering level and global network bandwidth conditions degrades, the video switches to lower bitrate (following the ordinary adaptive streaming approach), which in turns save in the battery level.
- For small size display, the transmission errors are less observed by the user especially if the user is mobile and is in a noisy environment and so video can be displayed with lesser quality (bitrate) to save battery resources and network resources even if the buffering level and global network bandwidth conditions are not poor. This is much useful for content categories as news and non-live content, in which transmission errors have lesser impact on the users' perception.

CONCLUSION

Video and multimedia applications are changing dramatically, coincident with a crowded market with many new players trying to maximize their market segment. On the other hand, users consumption styles for video and multimedia applications is strongly evolving. Users are heavily counting on wireless and mobile devices for video streaming and interactive video and multimedia applications. Although the amount of video content that is daily consumed is growing tremendously, there is no sufficient consideration for Quality of Experience (QoE), service differentiation and resource optimization. Several factors need consideration for better QoE and resource optimization, which are user dependent (e.g., user location, activity and preferences), application dependent (e.g., video codec, coding bit rate and content characteristics), device dependent (e.g., battery level, processing power and screen resolution) and network dependent (e.g., packet loss, delay and jitter).

This chapter discussed context-aware video content delivery and how to consider new capabilities to be supported by devices, content servers and edge routers to gather real-time information on device capabilities, network performance, and video content requirements. The need for context-aware video adaptation for enhancing user's experience, optimizing network resources and devices' power consumption is also outlined. Finally, a context-aware cross-layer framework is presented showing how to introduce context-awareness in the video delivery chain.

REFERENCES

Adobe, Inc. (n.d.). *HTTP Dynamic Streaming Features*. Retrieved from http://www.adobe.com/products/hds-dynamic-streaming/features.html

Balachandran, A., Sekar, V., Akella, A., Seshan, S., Stoica, I., & Zhang, H. (2013). Developing a predictive model of quality of experience for internet video. In *Proceedings of the ACM SIGCOMM*. doi:10.1145/2486001.2486025

Bovik, A. C. (2013). Automatic prediction of perceptual image and video quality. *Proceedings of the IEEE, 101*(9), 2008–2024.

Brown, P., Bovey, J., & Chen, X. (1997). Context-Aware Applications: from the Laboratory to the Market Place. *IEEE Personal Communication, 4*(5), 58-64.

Cancela, H., Rodriguez-Bocca, P., & Rubino, G. (2007). Perceptual quality in P2P multi-source video streaming policies. In *Proceedings of IEEE Global Telecommunications Conference* (pp. 2780-2785). IEEE.

Chen, G., & Kotz, D. (2000). A Survey of Context-Aware Mobile Computing Research. *Dartmouth Computer Science Technical Report*. TR2000-381.

Cisco Inc. Visual Networking Index. 2014. (n.d.). Retrieved from http://www.cisco.com/c/en/us/solutions/service-provider/visual-networking-index-vni/index.html

Dey, A., Abowd, G., Brown, P., Davies, N., Smith, M., & Steggles, P. (1999). Towards a better understanding of context and context-awareness. In *Proceedings of the 1st international symposium on Handheld and Ubiquitous Computing (HUC)*. London, UK: Springer-Verlag.

Display, I. W. (WiDi) Description. (n.d.). Retrieved from https://www-ssl.intel.com/content/www/us/en/architecture-and-technology/intel-wireless-display.html?

European Telecommunications Standards Institute (ETSI). (2009). Human factors (HF): Quality of experience (QoE) requirements for real-time communication services. *Technical Report T., 102*, 643.

Fielding, R., & Reschke, J. (2014). Hypertext Transfer Protocol (HTTP/1.1): Authentication. *IETF Standard,* RFC 7235.

Gabale, V., Dutta, P., Kokku, R., & Kalyanaraman, S. (2012). InSite: QoE-Aware Video Delivery from Cloud Data Centers. In *Proceeding of IWQoS*. doi:10.1109/IWQoS.2012.6245984

Havey, D., Chertov, R., & Almeroth, K. (2012). Receiver Driven Rate Adaptation for Wireless Multimedia Applications. *Proceeding of ACM MMSys'12*. doi:10.1145/2155555.2155582

International Standard Organization (ISO). (2014). Information technology -- Dynamic adaptive streaming over HTTP (DASH) -- Part 1: Media presentation description and segment formats. *ISO/IEC* 23009-1

International Telecommunication Union (ITU). (1998). *Subjective audiovisual quality assessment methods for multimedia applications* (p. 911). ITU-T Recommendation.

International Telecommunication Union (ITU). (1999). *Subjective video quality assessment methods for multimedia applications* (p. 910). ITU-T Recommendation.

International Telecommunication Union (ITU). (2002). Methodology for the subjective assessment of the quality of television pictures. *ITU-R Recommendation BT.*500-11.

International Telecommunication Union (ITU). (2007). Definition of Quality of Experience (QoE). *ITU-T SG 12.*

International Telecommunication Union (ITU). (2012). Information Technology – Generic coding of moving pictures and associated audio information – Systems. *Rec. ITU-T H222.0*

International Telecommunication Union (ITU). (2013). Parametric non-intrusive bitstream assessment of video media streaming quality – higher resolution application area. *ITU-T Recommendation P.1202.2.*

Interoperability Forum, D. A. S. H. (DASH-IF). (n.d.). Retrieved from http://dashif.org/white-papers/

Ivanovich, M., Bikerdike, P., & Li, J. (2008). On TCP performance enhancing proxies in a wireless environment. *IEEE Communications Magazine, 46*(9), 76–83. doi:10.1109/MCOM.2008.4623710

Iyengar, J., Amin, S., Ford, B., Ailawadi, D., Nowlan, M., & Tiwari, N. (2012). Minion: Unordered Delivery Wire-Compatible with TCP and TLS. *Technical Report.* ext. arXiv:1103.0463.

Lopez, D., Gonzalez, F., Bellido, L., & Alonso, A. (2006). Adaptive multimedia streaming over IP based on customer oriented metrics. In *Proceedings of IEEE International Symposium on Computer Networks.* IEEE. doi:10.1109/ISCN.2006.1662531

Lu, Z., Somayazulu, S., & Moustafa, H. (2014). Context-Adaptive Cross-Layer TCP Optimization for Internet Video Streaming. *Proceedings of the IEEE,* ICC.

Microsoft, Inc. (n.d.). *Smooth Streaming.* Retrieved from http://www.iis.net/downloads/microsoft/smooth-streaming

Mittal, A., Moorthy, A. K., & Bovik, A. C. (2011). Blind/referenceless image spatial quality evaluator. In *Proceedings of the IEEE Forty Fifth Asilomar Conference on Signals, Systems and Computers.* IEEE.

Mohamed, S., & Rubino, G. (2002). A study of real-time packet video quality using random neural networks. *IEEE Transactions on Circuits and Systems for Video Technology, 12*(12), 1071–1083. doi:10.1109/TCSVT.2002.806808

Moustafa, H., Moses, D., & Boucadair, M. (2014). PCP Extension for Signaling Feedback Information from the End-User Application to the Application Sever and to the Network. *IETF Internet draft.*

Pantos, R. P., & May, W. (2014). *HTTP Live Streaming.* Retrieved from http://tools.ietf.org/html/draft-pantos-http-live-streaming-14

Piamrat, K., Viho, C., Bonnin, J., & Ksentini, A. (2009). Quality of experience measurements for video streaming over wireless networks. In *Proceedings of IEEE Sixth International Conference on Information Technology: New Generations.* IEEE. doi:10.1109/ITNG.2009.121

Pinson, M. H., & Wolf, S. (2004). A new standardized method for objectively measuring video quality. *IEEE Transactions on Broadcasting*, *50*(3), 312–322. doi:10.1109/TBC.2004.834028

3rd Generation Partnership Project (3GPP). (2014). *Transparent end-to-end Packet-switched Streaming Service (PSS): Progressive Download and Dynamic Adaptive Streaming over HTTP Technical Specification TS26.247*. Accenture.

Rosenberg, J., Schlzrinne, H., Camarillo, G., Johnston, A., Peterson, J., Spark, R., … Schooler, E. (2002). SIP: Session Initiation Protocol. *IETF Standard, RFC* 3261.

Roskind, J. (2013). Quick UDP Internet Connections – Multiplexed Stream Transport over UDP. *IETF-88 TSV Area Presentation*. Retrieved from http://www.ietf.org/proceedings/88/slides/slides-88-tsvarea-10.pdf

Rubino, G., Varela, M., & Bonnin, J. M. (2006). Controlling multimedia QoS in the future home network using the PSQA metric. *The Computer Journal*, *49*(2), 137–155. doi:10.1093/comjnl/bxh165

Saad, M. A., Bovik, A. C., & Charrier, C. (2012). Blind image quality assessment: A natural scene statistics approach in the DCT domain. *IEEE Transactions on Image Processing*, *21*(8), 3339–3352. doi:10.1109/TIP.2012.2191563 PMID:22453635

Schilit, B., & Theimer, M. (1994). Disseminating Active Map Information to Mobile Hosts. *IEEE Network*, *8*(5), 22–32. doi:10.1109/65.313011

Schulzrinne, H., Casner, S., Frederick, R., & Jacobson, V. (2003). RTP: A Transport Protocol for Real-Time Applications. *IETF Standard RFC* 3550.

Schulzrinne, H., Rao, A., & Lanphier, R. (1998). Real Time Streaming Protocol (RTSP). *IETF Standard, RFC* 2326.

Soldani, D., Li, M., & Cuny, R. (Eds.). (2007). *QoS and QoE management in UMTS cellular systems*. John Wiley & Sons.

Soundararajan, R., & Bovik, A. C. (2012). RRED indices: Reduced reference entropic differencing for image quality assessment. *IEEE Transactions on Image Processing*, *21*(2), 517–526. doi:10.1109/TIP.2011.2166082 PMID:21878414

Spec, M. (2012). *WiFi Certified Miracst: Extending the Wi-Fi Experience to Seamless Video Display Industry*. Retrieved from http://www.wi-fi.org/file/wi-fi-certified-miracast-extending-the-wi-fi-experience-to-seamless-video-display-industry

Standard, I. E. E. E. (2011). *IEEE Standard for the Functional Architecture of Next Generation Service Overlay Networks* (pp. 1903–2011). SA.

Video over Internet Consumer Survey. (2013). Retrieved from http://www.accenture.com/SiteCollectionDocuments/PDF/Accenture-Video-Over-Internet-Consumer-Survey-2013.pdf

Wang, Z., Bovik, A. C., Sheikh, H. R., & Simoncelli, E. P. (2004). Image quality assessment: From error visibility to structural similarity. *IEEE Transactions on Image Processing*, *13*(4), 600–612. doi:10.1109/TIP.2003.819861 PMID:15376593

Weiser, M. (1991). The Computer for the 21st Century. *Scientific American, 3*(3), 3-11.

Wing, D. (2013). Port Control Protocol (PCP). *IETF Standard - RFC* 6887.

Winkler, S., & Mohandas, P. (2008). The evolution of video quality measurement: From PSNR to hybrid metrics. *IEEE Transactions on Broadcasting*, *54*(3), 660–668. doi:10.1109/TBC.2008.2000733

Younkin, A., Fernald, R., Doherty, R., Salskov, E., & Corriveau, P. (2007). Predicting an average end-user's experience of video playback. In *Third International Workshop on Video Processing and Quality Metrics for Consumer Electronics*.

ADDITIONAL READING

Choi, L. K., Liao, Y., & Bovik, A. C. (2013). Video QoE Models for the Compute Continuum. *IEEE E-Letter.*, *8*(5), 26–29.

Ciftci, S. (2011). Definition of QoE Interfaces for Virtual Networks.

Corriveau, P. (2006). Video quality testing. Digital video image quality and perceptual coding, 125-153.

Dabrowski, M., Gromada, J., & Moustafa, H. (2012). Context-awareness for IPTV Services Personalization. In *Proceedings of the Sixth International Conference on Innovative Mobile and Internet Services in Ubiquitous Computing (IMIS)* (pp. 37-44). Palermo, Italy, Conference Publishing Service (CPS). doi:10.1109/IMIS.2012.97

Dabrowski, M., Gromada, J., Moustafa, H., & Forestier, J. (2013). A context-aware architecture for IPTV services personalization. [JISIS]. *Journal of Internet Services and Information Security*, *3*(1), 49–70.

Diallo, M., Moustafa, H., Afifi, H., & Laghari, K. (2012). QoE for Audio-visual Services. In *Proceedings of UP-TO-US workshop associated with EuroiTV 2012 conference* (pp. 299-305). Berlin, ACM.

Diallo, M., Moustafa, H., Afifi, H., & Marechal, N. (2013). Adaptation of Audio-Visual Contents and their Delivery Means. Communications of the ACM (CACM) journal. 56(11), 86-93.

Diallo, M., Moustafa, H., Afifi, H., & Marechal, N. (2013). Context-aware QoE for audio-visual service groups. *IEEE Comsoc MMTC E-Letter.*, *8*(2), 9–11.

Ferguson, P., & Huston, G. (1998). *Quality of service: delivering QoS on the Internet and in corporate networks*. John Wiley & Sons, Inc.

Fiedler, M., Möller, S., & Reichl, P. (2012). Quality of Experience: From User Perception to Instrumental Metrics.

Flizikowski, A., Mateusz, M., Damian, P., & Moustafa, H. (2012). A concept of unobtrusive method for complementary emotive user profiling and personalization for IPTV platforms. In Proceedings of International Conference on Image Processing & Communication (IP&C) (pp. 269-281). Poland, Springer. doi:10.1007/978-3-642-32384-3_33

Liao, Y., Younkin, A., Foerster, J., & Corriveau, P. (2013). Achieving high QoE across the compute continuum: how compression, content, and devices interact. In the proceedings of 7th International Workshop on Video Processing and Quality Metrics for Consumer Electronics.

Lin, W., & Jay Kuo, C. C. (2011). Perceptual visual quality metrics: A survey. *Journal of Visual Communication and Image Representation*, *22*(4), 297–312. doi:10.1016/j.jvcir.2011.01.005

Lu, Z., Srinivasa, S., & Moustafa, H. (2014). Context-Adaptive Cross-Layer TCP optimization for Internet Video Streaming. In *Proceedings of International Conference on Communications (ICC)*. Sidney, Australia. doi:10.1109/ICC.2014.6883571

Moustafa, H., Marechal, N., & Zeadally, S. (2012). Mobile Multimedia Applications and Their Delivery. IEEE IT Professional Journal, special issue on Mobile and Wireless Technologies and Applications. 14(5), 12-21.

Reichl, P. (2010). From charging for quality of service to charging for quality of experience. annals of telecommunications-annales des télécommunications,65(3-4), 189-199.

Serral-Gracià, R., Cerqueira, E., Curado, M., Yannuzzi, M., Monteiro, E., & Masip-Bruin, X. (2010). An overview of quality of experience measurement challenges for video applications in IP networks. In Wired/Wireless Internet Communications (pp. 252-263). Springer Berlin Heidelberg. doi:10.1007/978-3-642-13315-2_21

Seshadrinathan, K., Soundararajan, R., Bovik, A. C., & Cormack, L. K. (2010). Study of subjective and objective quality assessment of video. *IEEE Transactions on Image Processing*, *19*(6), 1427–1441. doi:10.1109/TIP.2010.2042111 PMID:20129861

Song, S., Moustafa, H., Abid, M., & Afifi, H. (2011). Performance Evaluation of an Authentication Solution for IMS Services Access. Journal of Springer Telecommunication Systems – SI on Wireless and network Security. 52(4), 2205-2218.

Song, S., Moustafa, H., & Afifi, H. (2009). Context-Aware IPTV. In Proceedings of IFIP/IEEE Management of Multimedia & Mobile Network Service (MMNS) (pp. 189-194). Venice, Italy, Springer.

Song, S., Moustafa, H., & Afifi, H. (2010). Personalized TV Service through Employing Context-Awareness in IPTV/IMS Architecture. In *Proceedings of IEEE International Workshop on Future Multimedia networks (FMN)* (pp. 75-86). Krakow, Poland, Springer. doi:10.1007/978-3-642-13789-1_8

Song, S., Moustafa, H., & Afifi, H. (2012). IPTV Services Personalization Using Context-Awareness. International Journal of Informatica. *Special Issue on IPTV and Multimedia Services.*, *36*(1), 13–20.

Song, S., Moustafa, H., & Afifi, H. (2012). A Survey on Personalized TV & NGN Services through Context-Awareness. ACM Computing Surveys, 44(1):4, 1-18.

Song, S., Moustafa, H., & Afifi, H. (2012). Modeling an NGN authentication solution and improving its performance through clustering. In *Proceedings of IEEE Globecom* (pp. 2101-2106). Anaheim, CA. doi:10.1109/GLOCOM.2012.6503426

Song, S., Moustafa, H., & Afifi, H. (2012). Enriched IPTV services Personalization. In *Proceedings of IEEE International Conference on Communications (ICC)* (pp. 1911-1916). Ottawa, Canada.

Song, S., Moustafa, H., Afifi, H., & Forestier, J. (2012). Personalized TV Service through Employing Context-Awareness in IPTV NGN Architecture. In *Proceedings of UP-TO-US workshop associated with EuroiTV conference* (pp. 292-298). Berlin, ACM.

Song, S., Moustafa, H., & Afifi, H. (2012). Advanced IPTV Services Personalization through Context-Aware Content Recommendation. IEEE Transactions on Multimedia, SI on smart, social and converged TV. 14(6), 1528-1537.

Van Moorsel, A. (2001). Metrics for the internet age: Quality of experience and quality of business. In *Fifth International Workshop on Performability Modeling of Computer and Communication Systems, Arbeitsberichte des Instituts für Informatik*, Universität Erlangen-Nürnberg, Germany (Vol. 34, No. 13, pp. 26-31).

Winkler, S. (2005). *Digital video quality: vision models and metrics.* John Wiley & Sons. doi:10.1002/9780470024065

Zapater, M. N., & Bressan, G. (2007). A proposed approach for quality of experience assurance of IPTV. In *Proceedings of the First International Conference on the Digital Society*, 2007. (pp. 25-25). IEEE. doi:10.1109/ICDS.2007.4

Zeadally, S., Moustafa, H., & Siddiqui, F. (2011). Internet Protocol Television (IPTV): Architectures, Trends, & Challenges. Journal of IEEE Systems – special issue on Multimedia Communications Systems. 5(4), 518-527.

Zemek, R., Song, S., & Moustafa, H. (2012). *Context-Awareness for IPTV Services Personalization. Media Networks: Architectures, Applications and Standards book.* CRC Press Publisher.

Zeng, L., Benatallah, B., Ngu, A. H., Dumas, M., Kalagnanam, J., & Chang, H. (2004). QoS-aware middleware for web services composition. *IEEE Transactions on Software Engineering*, *30*(5), 311–327. doi:10.1109/TSE.2004.11

KEY TERMS AND DEFINITIONS

Battery Experience: The ability to enhance the battery life for the user during the service access (longer battery experience indicates more battery life).

Context: Is the information about the user and his environment (including his device, network and service).

Context-Awareness: Is the continuous knowledge of context information during the service access.

Multi-Screen Experience: The ability to access the same service on multiple devices (screens) by the same user or by different users.

Multi-SIM: The usage of multiple SIM-cards by the same cellular user to have data access on several devices or by multiple users sharing the data plan among their devices.

Quality of Experience (QoE): The perceived quality by the user for a certain service (e.g. video service).

User-Centric: The consideration of the user requirements, needs, profile and preferences during service provision.

Chapter 21
Recent Advances and Perspectives on Content Delivery Networks

Nathalie Amann
Orange, France

Valéry Bastide
Orange, France

Yiping Chen
Orange, France

Mateusz Dzida
Orange, France

Frédéric Fieau
Orange, France

Patrick Fleming
Orange, France

Ali Gouta
Orange, France

Yves L'Azou
Orange, France

Yannick Le Louédec
Orange, France

Nicolas Maréchal
Orange, France

Nathalie Omnès
Orange, France

Iuniana Oprescu
Orange, France

Vincent Thiebaut
Orange, France

ABSTRACT

This chapter provides an overview on the recent advances and perspectives on Content Delivery Networks. The first section, the introduction, sets the context. The second section identifies the different types of current CDNs and also insights on their evolution. The third section deals with CDN interconnection, reporting work status such as IETF and ETSI. The fourth section, on CDN and virtualization, describes the related initiatives in this area, in standardization bodies as well as in experimental deployments and evaluations. The fifth section focuses on the convergence of CDNs and clouds, presenting new business opportunities for the market players, as well as technical challenges. The sixth section addresses another trend, which is the extension of CDNs to home networking and terminal devices. The last section discusses content delivery for mobile, introducing solutions that operators can to optimize their networks and avoid being overwhelmed by ever growing traffic.

DOI: 10.4018/978-1-4666-8371-6.ch021

INTRODUCTION

A Content Delivery Network (CDN) is a set of servers specifically designed and deployed over one or several networks for optimizing the storage and delivery of content (e.g., web objects, audiovisual live or on-demand content, large files, etc.). From a high-level and functional perspective the main components of a CDN include request routing server(s) that handle and redirect content requests towards cache node servers, cache node servers that deliver the requested content, content ingestion server(s) that ingest content in the CDN, analytics and accounting server(s), and management server(s), as shown on Figure 1.

Today a large part of the Internet traffic is distributed via CDNs. As an illustration, the CDN market leader Akamai estimates that its infrastructure handles 20 percent of the world's total Web traffic (Akamai, 2014). The outstanding development of the CDNs since the late 90s has been driven by their intrinsic strengths: improved service latency thereby leading to a better quality of experience for end users, and better network resource utilization leading to a reduction of congestion risks and costs.

From a business perspective there is an increasing trend for "commoditization" in the CDN industry, with strong market competition and price decline. In this challenging context CDNs must evolve to meet the requirements of the supported applications. Among them, it is worth focusing on new promising areas such as CDN interconnection, network virtualization, convergence of CDNs and clouds, CDN extension in the home network, and content delivery for mobile users.

This chapter aims to provide an overview on these recent advances and perspectives on CDNs.

Given its strategic importance, the CDN market has attracted many new entrants these last years. Section 2 identifies the different types of current CDNs which have been deployed to address dif-

Figure 1. CDN Functional Model

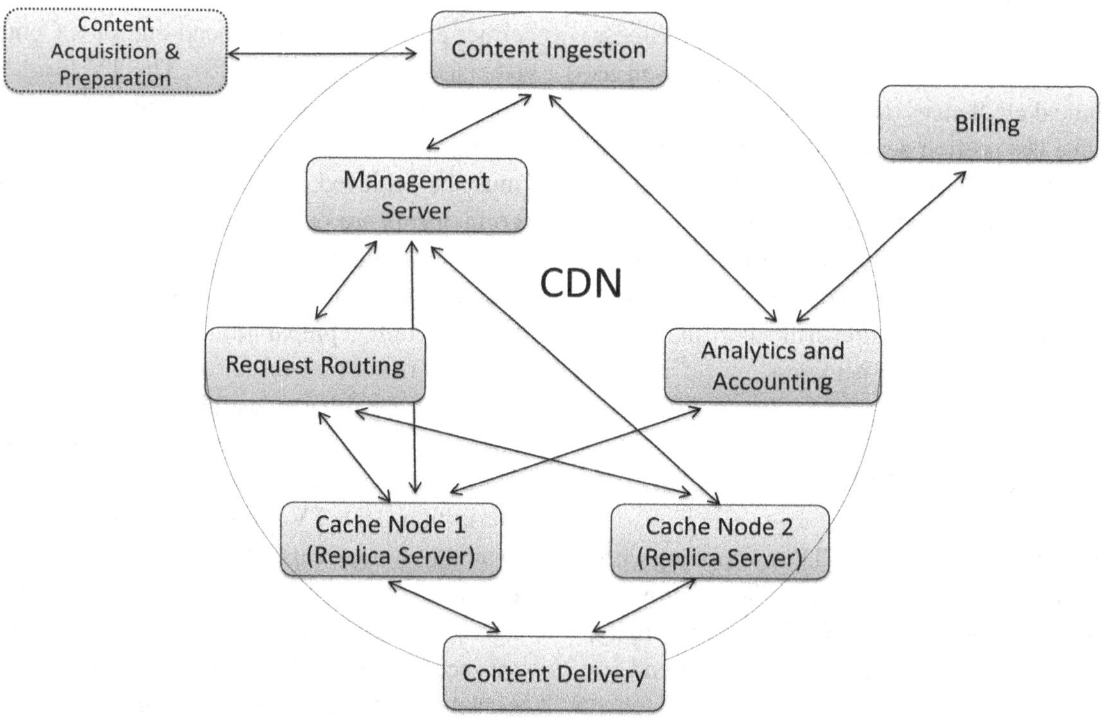

ferent CDN market segments, such as Internet Protocol Television (IPTV) service offers provided by Telecom operators (Telcos) and Over The Top (OTT) applications.

Section 3 deals with CDN interconnection, by presenting a status of the corresponding standardization effort. CDN interconnection techniques allow CDN service providers and Telcos to federate CDNs deployed in different countries, to scale up their CDN capacity and their CDN service portfolio.

Section 4 focuses on CDN and virtualization. Network Function Virtualization (NFV) is a major trend that emerged recently. The goals of NFV are to improve network capital and operational expenditures, flexibility, rapidity of service deployment and energy efficiency as compared to dedicated hardware implementations. Section4 describes the current initiatives in this area, in standardization bodies as well as in the field of experimental deployments and evaluations.

Sections 5 and 6 emphasize respectively on Cloud and CDN convergence, and on CDN extension in the home network and terminal devices. The converging and competitive landscape of online content delivery presents new business opportunities for the market players, as well as technical challenges these sections introduce.

The last section deals with CDN and mobile. Content distribution services are blooming on mobile networks and they are expected to be responsible for the majority of future mobile Internet traffic. This section introduces different solutions that operators may envision in the short and longer terms to optimize their networks.

CDN MARKET ECOSYSTEM

This section introduces the CDN positioning within a service delivery ecosystem. Then it provides an overview of the current CDN market. Finally, it presents an insight into the evolution trend.

CDNs in the Overall Technical Chain

CDNs can address different needs, audiovisual content delivery at large scale, but also others such as web acceleration. Yet audiovisual contents are by far the main types of contents delivered by CDNs in terms of traffic volume. So the design of the CDNs, notably the biggest ones, has been conditioned and adapted for audiovisual content delivery. Thus this section makes first a focus on the CDNs in the overall audiovisual technical chain before considering other applications like web acceleration. Before being delivered, contents have to be referenced and exposed for instance through web pages or applications, which are browsed by end users. In both cases, browsing is achieved by interacting with a service platform. This service platform redirects the end user to a content delivery component, which may be a CDN or an alternative content delivery solution.

In the technical chains dedicated to IPTV, before being delivered, contents have to be prepared and adapted to the different bandwidth constraints of the networks in which they have to be distributed. This preparation is achieved by either a Television (TV) head-end or a Content Management System (CMS). The TV head-end component is devoted to live content, and thus faces strong real-time constraints: video compression must be achieved on-the-fly. Conversely, CMS components are devoted to on-demand content. In this case, real-time constraints are released, and video compression is more efficient. These two types of content preparation may rely on different components optimized for one of these usages.

There are other constraints while preparing contents as they are delivered to a wide variety of devices, ranging from a Smartphone to a High Definition (HD) TV screen. The screen size, the available storage capacity, but also the supported encoding format, as well as Digital Rights Management (DRM) and protocols have to be taken into account before delivering the content. So each content can be translated into several media files.

Last but not least, right-owners can impose significant constraints depending on the type of content. Some contents such as royalty-free contents - including in particular User Generated Contents (UGCs) - face no constraints. This is not the case for Premium contents, which have to be encrypted during their preparation. The access to the contents also has to be protected, for example thanks to Uniform Resource Locator (URL) signing, and restricted to a specific geographical area (which is called geo-blocking).. Another major constraint is the concurrent stream limitations for a given household. This last constraint applies in particular when the household subscribed to an audiovisual service giving an unlimited access to a catalog of contents, on all registered devices and access networks. The CDN plays a major role in fulfilling all these constraints.

Once prepared, contents are ingested in the CDN architecture: the first copy of each content is made available within the CDN. Now the content is available on a service platform and on a content delivery component. So it can be selected by an end user. Then the media file has to be selected depending on the context, including the type of device and available bandwidth. As seen before, several media files can match the same content.

After content preparation and selection, there are several modes to deliver content: multicast, caching, transparent caching, CDN and a combination thereof.

- Multicast is the most efficient way to distribute the same content at the same time to different receivers, be they end user devices (for live content delivery), or even CDN edge servers (for feeding them with a content catalogue). Yet multicast necessitates protocols that are not all implemented on end user devices. Moreover there is a strong trend towards the individualization of the end users' consumption behavior. This has led the market players to favor CDN-based architectures;
- With caching, the most popular contents are stored locally, for example in a proxy. The management of the storage area is handled by the cache node itself thanks to an algorithm, typically Least Recently Used (LRU) or Least Frequently Used (LFU);
- With transparent caching, content requests are analyzed and diverted from their network path and redirected to a cache server, without the content service provider and client knowing anything about this redirection. It is to be highlighted that there are major differences between transparent caching and CDNs from both the technical and business model perspectives. Indeed, transparent caching is generally used by Telcos out of any business relationship with the content (delivery service) providers. And it mandates the transparent interception of traffic with systems such as Deep Packet Inspection (DPI). Besides, today more and more applications are using secured sessions with encrypted Transport Layer Security (TLS) tunnels (HTTPS, HTTP2.0) (Dierks, & Rescorla, 2008; Belshe, Peon, & Thomson, 2014). In this case, transparent caching no more applies, because TLS channels forbid man-in-the-middle interceptions;
- Some CDNs have been built as an evolution of a set of caches. In this case, the local storage is managed based on a caching algorithm such as LFU. The complexity of these CDNs is relatively low. Yet, content ingestion is in this case triggered by end users' requests, and these CDNs can hardly benefit from content provisioning before the peak hours. This behavior is well suited for contents with low popularity, also referred to as the "long tail". Other types of CDN lean on a global management of the

available storage areas and privilege content pre-provisioning, that is to say prior to end users' requests. These solutions are particularly well suited for the most popular contents.

Whatever the delivery mode, the media files can be delivered according to several protocols. In the case of CDN based delivery, if the available bandwidth is high enough, and more precisely higher than the content bitrate, content can be streamed with Real Time Streaming Protocol (RTSP). In this case, content can be instantaneously displayed by the end user. Another possibility is to use the HyperText Transfer Protocol (HTTP) download or progressive download. This can be achieved even if the bandwidth available is lower than the content bitrate, but in this case the end user must wait before displaying the content. Furthermore, the available bandwidth varies depending on many factors, including not only the number of simultaneous Transmission Control Protocol (TCP) connections on the access network, but also on the time of the day.

Adaptive streaming provides a disruptive solution, by cutting each content into chunks and providing each chunk in different qualities or bitrates. Chunks are further delivered using HTTP and the protocol dynamically adapts the format to the available bandwidth. Now available on almost any device, adaptive streaming has provided an efficient answer by letting the device itself select the media file.

For on-demand content, all these protocols can be considered. In contrast, because of the strong real-time constraints that have to be addressed, live content is mainly delivered using either RTSP (notably in IPTV environment), or RTMP (far more common in the OTT world), or even HTTP adaptive streaming.

The variation of the available bandwidth always includes a load peak during the busiest hours. Network and CDN dimensioning is based on these peak hours. It is important to notice that CDN servers placed close to end users and provisioned before the peak hours may lead to significant improvements.

The Current CDN Market

There are mainly four types of actors that are involved in the content delivery chain: CDN vendors, CDN operators, content service providers and network operators.

- CDN vendors specify content delivery products and sell them to other actors, such as content service providers or network operators. Cisco is for example positioned on this segment;
- CDN operators mainly sell services over their own managed CDNs. They offer a large range of services, including traffic optimization, web traffic acceleration, and/or some additional security functions such as geo-blocking and URL signing. CDN operators may also sell a licensed CDN to network operators. In this case, the network operator has to manage itself the CDN services provided by the CDN operator solution. Akamai and Level3 are examples of CDN operators. Currently, the main CDN operators provide a worldwide coverage for all types of contents, including non-audiovisual contents like software updates. They are currently negotiating with network operators to deploy their CDN servers closer to end users, thereby offering a better Quality of Experience (QoE) and reducing their delivery costs;
- Content service providers offer a catalog of contents to end users, ranging from Premium content to royalty-free content, representing a large part of the Internet traffic. For the corresponding content service providers, such as Google with YouTube,

this induces a steep invoice for their traffic at interconnection points. Some of them thus deploy their own caches as close to the end users as possible, such as Google with Google caches or Netflix with Open Connect. Others offer a turnkey solution including multi-format and multi-device content preparation, referencing and delivery, as well as analytics functions opened to third parties. Such is the case with DailyMotion Cloud of DailyMotion;

- Network operators offer network access bundled with audiovisual services. Having the network under their control, they can deploy delivery servers at different hierarchical levels as close to end users as possible, offering the highest content formats with the lowest delay so that perceived QoE is likely enhanced.

Network operators may play different business roles, such as:

- CDN operator role: by deploying a CDN within its network, for its own purpose or with the objective of reselling CDN services to third companies (which are thus called "Business-to-Business-to-Consumer" (B2B2C) services). It may further subscribe to a managed or licensed CDN offer to enrich its telecommunication infrastructure, and possibly resell CDN services to third parties;
- Content service provider role: by deploying a complete content delivery chain to expose, prepare and deliver contents. It may further contract with third parties' content service providers to either enrich its content offer or resell a content offer.

Current Trends: An Overview

Audiovisual architectures are currently evolving from multiple technical chains (e.g., IPTV, OTT) dedicated to specific access networks (e.g., fixed, mobile) or specific types of devices (e.g. Set-Top-Boxes, Personal Computers, smartphones) to a single convergent technical chain. This convergent architecture may address any kind of devices, including (but not limited to) Personal Computers (PCs), smart TVs, game consoles, tablets and Smartphones.

TV Everywhere is also a major trend. It allows displaying content on any type of device and from any access network, as long as the end user has acquired the right to access it. This new feature is becoming a must-have, and so is the fulfillment of the induced right-owners constraints.

Content metadata are crucial for a CDN operator to differentiate from its competitors. The management of these metadata highly varies from one actor to another. Yet, nobody can ignore the great success of Netflix, which claims an efficient combination of analytics, big data and content pre-provisioning. Content metadata pre-provisioning implies an efficient management of all metadata and illustrates their importance. More generally, the data model needs global and systemic thinking, together with the separation of products (which end users buy) from the service offers (through which the end users buy the content).

Each CDN actor has a different influence depending on its size. In order to reach a critical size or to gain more influence, partnership is necessary and currently represents a major trend. CDN operators contract partnerships with content service providers to deliver their contents, but also with network operators to deploy their CDN servers closer to end users (e.g., Akamai, 2012). Content service providers are interested in contracting with CDN operators to delegate the delivery of their contents, but they may also be interested in contracting directly with networks operators, in particular if their footprint is local to a region or a country. Network operators are interested by contracting with CDN operators, but not always for deploying the CDN operator's solution. Actually, if the network operator has deployed its own CDN infrastructure, he would rather have the CDN operator use it. Network operators are also interested in contracting with content service providers, but this is not straightforward with major worldwide content service providers. Within this global ecosystem, each actor tries to grow and gain more influence, either by leaning on its critical size or by trying to find a clever positioning.

Finally, it is to be noted that this section focuses on the CDN technical chain and market for audiovisual content delivery as this represents the majority of the traffic volumes carried by today's CDNs. But, next to audiovisual content services, CDN operators are now strongly expanding into CDN-based acceleration and security services. This trend is expected to grow and to represent a significant part of the CDN operators' revenues in the short to long term.

CDN INTERCONNECTION

When major entertainment events occur or any other flash crowd phenomenon, certain content items experience high popularity simultaneously in multiple regions of the world. Such contents need to be served to an extremely wide audience that is spread all over the planet. But the existing delivery infrastructures are often limited to a geographical area; very few CDNs have global coverage that can respond entirely to the end users' and Content Providers' demands.

Furthermore, other limitations of CDNs may include capacity constraints in terms of the number of available server instances to deliver the content, which might be a bottleneck in case of an overload event. When it comes to functionalities or specific delivery protocols, not all existing delivery infrastructures support a very diverse range of features. It might be useful for a content provider to be able to select and combine various delivery methods from multiple CDNs in order to reach the required performance.

Besides, smaller CDNs may want to cooperate in order to be able to compete against the traditional players that have extensive Points of Presence worldwide.

The reasons enumerated above should bring the need for scaling up the current architectures and for increasing the footprint of individual CDNs by leveraging CDN interconnection. The main objective is to allow several standalone CDNs to act together as a single delivery platform that can serve the end users on behalf of the Content Providers. These drivers have recently motivated significant work on CDN interconnection in standardization bodies, as well as different types of concrete deployment configurations.

Standardization of CDN Interconnection

Several standardization bodies have initiated the specification of interfaces for CDN interconnection, mainly the IETF (Internet Engineering Task Force) CDNI (Content Delivery Networks Interconnection) working group (IETF, 2014a), but also the ETSI (ETSI, 2013a), and ATIS (ATIS, 2011).

The IETF work is representative of these standardization initiatives on CDN interconnection. These activities have been focusing on defining interfaces between two CDNs, assuming that any more complex configuration (involving more than two CDNs) is the combination of several instances of this basic two CDN pattern. In this basic point-to-point relationship between CDNs, the CDN that has a contract with the Content Provider is the upstream CDN (uCDN). The uCDN settles an interconnection with another CDN called a downstream CDN (dCDN) in order to expand its initial (delivery) capabilities and be able to increase its footprint, thus reaching a bigger target of end users. The dCDN is the infrastructure that actually delivers the content to the end users. Note that there can be several cascaded CDNs, in this case the uCDN is always the one delegating the request and the dCDN is the one that receives the delegated request from the uCDN.

The CDNI framework defines two types of operations (Peterson, Davie, & van Brandenburg, 2014): synchronous and asynchronous. The synchronous operations happen "during the process of servicing a user request" and the asynchronous CDNI operations occur "independently of any given user request, such as advertisement of footprint information or pre-positioning of content for later delivery." The asynchronous operations are basically related to the management of content plus other peripheral actions required for being able to make informed decisions when it comes to redirecting the user to the correct cache node that will perform the delivery of the content.

The same framework assumes that the redirection of the end user's request can be either iterative or recursive. In the iterative mode, the request can be redirected by the uCDN to the dCDN's Request Router engine that can further decide to which cache node to redirect the request based on its internal knowledge of the dCDN. Conversely, in the recursive mode the dCDN can inform the uCDN through the CDNI Request Routing Redirection Interface on how to redirect the request. This means the initial request of the uCDN can be directly forwarded towards a cache node within the dCDN or even to another CDN node in a completely different CDN.

Figure 2 shows the five interfaces constituting the reference model of the IETF CDNI framework.

The Control Interface aims at bootstrapping and configuring the other CDNI interfaces, as well as handling operations such as pre-positioning, revalidation, purge of both metadata and content. The Request Routing interface is split in two distinct sub-interfaces, the Footprint and Capabilities Advertisement interface and the Request Routing Redirection Interface, which are used respectively for exchanging routing information and for redirecting the request. The Metadata interface governs how the content should be delivered (exchange of geo-blocking directives, availability windows, mechanisms for access control, purge instructions). The Logging interface exchanges logs about the relevant activities performed, both in real-time mode used for runtime traffic monitoring and offline information suitable for analytics and billing. These specification works are still on-going at the time this book is published, yet some sorts of CDN interconnections, not necessarily based on the aforementioned interfaces and building blocks, already exist in live networks. Note that some of the CDNI interface specifications are scheduled to be published before the end of 2014.

CDN Interconnection in Live Networks

CDN interconnection in live networks may take different forms beyond the basic pattern of the point-to-point relationship between two CDNs. Besides, the most common types of CDN interconnection in operational networks involve more than two CDNs (e.g., Conviva, 2011; Cedexis, 2014; Turbobytes, 2014; Broberga, Buyyaa, & Tarib, 2009; CDNTech, 2012). The goal of such more complex configurations is generally to allow a central entity to aggregate and benefit from the capabilities (geographical coverage, functional scope and capacities) of several CDNs and to provide a unified interface that exposes all these capabilities. This has opened the way to new specific business roles and market players such as CDN Brokers ([06]; Cedexis, 2014) and Multi-CDN Service Providers (Turbobytes, 2014; Broberga, Buyyaa, & Tarib, 2009; CDNTech, 2012).

The role of a CDN broker is to help content providers to dynamically forward at any time the end users' requests towards the best CDN in terms of delivery performances and/or delivery costs. Thanks to the CDN broker, the Content Providers

Figure 2. IETF CDNI Reference Model

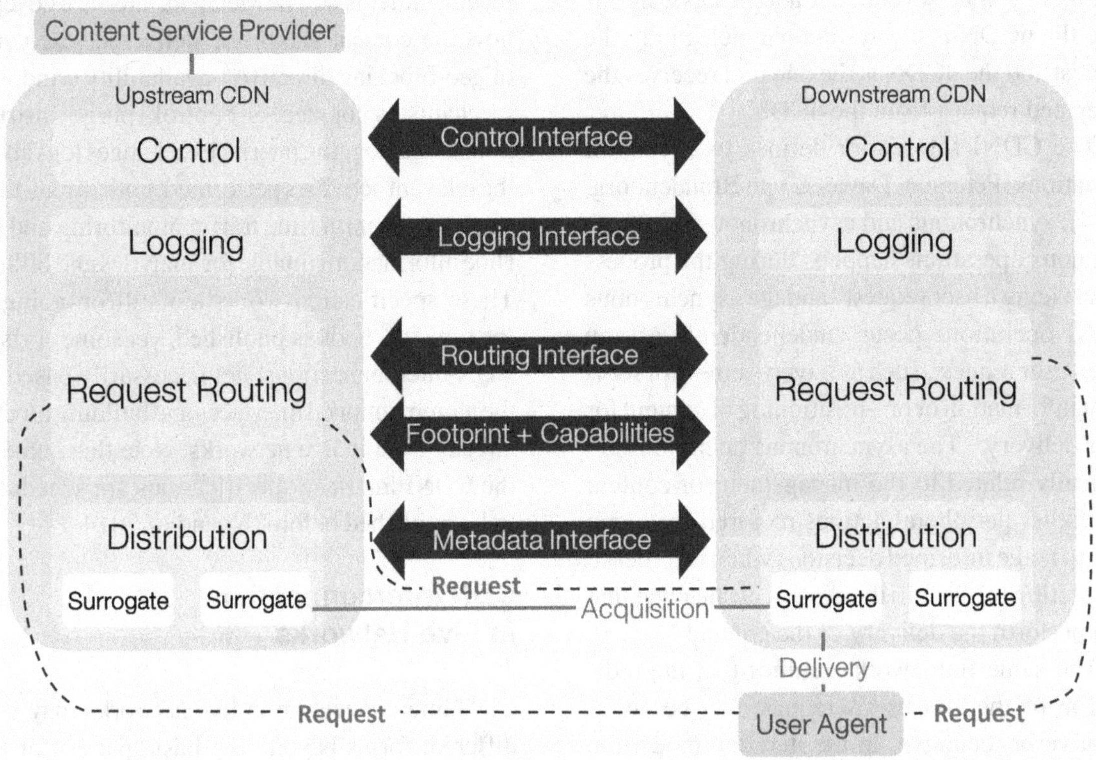

can be versatile and take advantage of the best delivery offer at any given time, thus improving the quality of experience of the end user (and/or reducing the risk of unreachable content) and augmenting its own revenues.

CDN brokers aggregate large amounts of data that reflect the global performances and the Quality of Experience (e.g., buffering ratio, startup time, average bitrate for video and round trip time delays for HTTP and DNS for websites) ensured by each of the CDNs they monitor. These data are typically collected per IP prefix and for each geographic zone of the considered area. The CDN brokers act from an OTT's standpoint: they retrieve the data as if they were the end-user, thus providing an end-to-end vision of the delivery chain, regardless of the underlying network infrastructure. This also means that the measured performance may sometimes be biased by the volatile behavior of the underlying network infrastructure, especially by the access network that might be faulty, independently from the CDN being used for the delivery. Based on the collected data, a performance matrix is established for each monitored CDN. These performance matrices can then be used to select the best suited CDN for a given end user request.

As shown in Figure 3, the Content Provider has to manage business relationships, that may be recorded in Service Level Agreements (SLA) with the CDN broker as well as with each of the monitored CDNs. To mitigate this complexity, the Content Providers may rely upon Multi-CDN Service Providers which offer a single point of contact for handling all the traffic delivery operations and interactions with the monitored CDNs, as shown in Figure 4.

Figure 3. CDN Broker

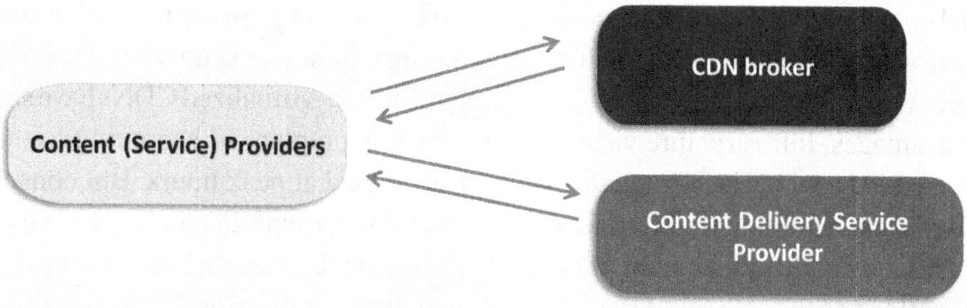

Figure 4. Multi-CDN Service Provider

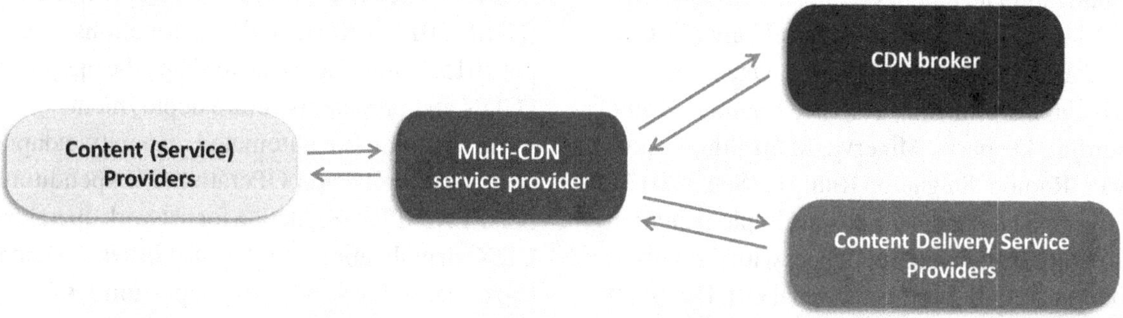

It is to be noted that, in the absence of complete CDNI standards, these interconnection models have been relying so far on proprietary interfaces and processes. These interfaces and processes are very different, yet very close functionally, from the aforementioned standards.

As a conclusion, it is worth mentioning that the need for aggregating and managing the capabilities of several CDNs is meant to address the issues experienced by content providers who have to deal with multiple CDNs in order to cover a very large footprint or diverse capabilities in terms of delivery. The main technical challenges raised by this kind of environment are related to the management of cascaded SLAs, the delegation of trust for encrypted traffic delivery (HTTPS) and the sheer interoperability on all required interfaces. From a business perspective, there has to be a clear model for revenue sharing that is profitable to all the involved parties willing to enter such interconnection schemes.

CDN AND VIRTUALIZATION

Introduction

Virtualization is a powerful technique to build isolated systems based on an abstracted view of underlying shared resources. It has recently received a lot of attention due to successful implementations in Information Technology (IT) datacenters (Faizul Bari, Boutaba, Esteves, Zambenedetti Granville, Podlesny, Golam Rabbani, Zhang, & Faten Zhani,

2013). Abstracted views of physical server resources together with software-based switching allow virtualized operating systems to share common server infrastructures. Clearly, infrastructure virtualization provides flexibility and portability to name a few advantages. Infrastructure virtualization has also enabled new business models of on-demand resource consumption (referred to as pay-as-you-go). Still, virtualization comes at the cost of reduced performance.

In addition to IT datacenter-oriented virtualization, the virtualization has also emerged these last years in the telecommunications field as a major trend with the emerging network function virtualization techniques (Chiosi, Clarke, Willis, Reid, Feger, Bugenhagen, Khan, el Fargano, Cui, Deng, Benitez, Michel, Damker, Ogaki, Matsuzaki, Fukui, Shimano, Delisle, Loudier, Kolia, Guardini, Demaria, Minerva, Manzalini, López, Javier Ramón Salguero, Ruhl, & Sen., 2012), whose goal is to replace hardware implementation and dedicated network appliances with virtualized functions running on Commercial Off-The-Shelf (COTS) servers. ETSI's Network Function Virtualization Industry Specification Group (NFV ISG) has defined a theoretical framework to organize virtualized resources (communication, management, etc.) (ETSI, 2013b). Such a framework is key for operators who may want to virtualize their infrastructures, in particular their CDNs.

The objective of this section is to discuss possible opportunities and challenges raised by building CDNs over virtualized infrastructures, and provide a preliminary analysis on CDN virtualization. The first parts of this section present some virtualized CDN (vCDN) business use cases and then the architectural design of the vCDN, including the NFV architecture and its possible implementation for the vCDN. The next part shows performance tests and their results to identify the performance bottlenecks. Finally, the last part shares some best practices for building virtual CDNs.

vCDN Use Cases

To handle fast growing network traffic, CDN has strong requirements on throughput. For example, current non-virtualized CDNs have static capacity, which is preplanned according to the maximum traffic load at peak hours. But considerations on scalability, flexibility and cost-efficiency are also important. CDNs can benefit from the infrastructure virtualization that offers more flexibility and automation, so that their capacity can dynamically scale to support unpredictable traffic demand such as live events or User Generated Content (UGC). Following this idea, CDN virtualization is identified by ETSI NFV as one of its target use cases (ETSI, 2013c). Technical specifications are, as per 2015, being elaborated to shape the upcoming vCDN and prepare its future deployment.

In addition to automated capacity adaptation and CApital and OPerational EXpenditures (CAPEX/OPEX) reduction for network operators, CDN virtualization enables also other advanced use cases and new business opportunities:

1. Infrastructure as a Service (IaaS) hosted by a CDN provider: in addition to content delivery service the spare resources of a CDN infrastructure can be used to host any other services that need computing, storage and network resources, for the same CDN provider or third party service providers ;
2. CDN footprint extension through third party IaaS offers: instead of deploying its own infrastructure, the CDN provider could deploy the content delivery service on the virtualized platform, hosted by another IaaS provider.

vCDN Architecture Design, Management and Orchestration (MANO)

The separation between software and infrastructure has implied the definition of NFV-MANO framework in ETSI NFV dedicated to support operation and management functions:

- Manage the NFV Infrastructure,
- Manage the VNFs,
- Orchestrate the resource allocation to deploy VNFs,
- Coordinate NFV infrastructure with the VNFs.

ETSI NFV ISG general architectural framework (ETSI, 2013b) includes layered functional blocks: NFV Infrastructure (NFVI) abstracts hardware resources such as storage, network and computing from the underlying infrastructure, and provides open interfaces for accessing virtualized resources. On top of the NFVI virtualization layer, Virtual Network Functions (VNFs) are the virtual instances of network functions in the sense of legacy non-virtualized networks. Typical examples of VNFs for CDN elements are cache nodes. As pure software components, they are deployed and executed in the NFVI virtual environment. Finally, traditional Operations Support System (OSS) / Business Support System (BSS) systems are deployed on top of the VNF instances.

In addition to these infrastructure and network oriented functional blocks, ETSI NFV is also specifying the Management and Orchestration (MANO) functional architecture (ETSI, 2014). These specifications, whose first release is planned for Q4 2014, are underway. They describe the three main functional blocks dedicated to the management operations deemed necessary to support the introduction of virtualization:

- The Virtualized Infrastructure Manager (VIM) manages the NFVI and is in charge of resource management and allocation at NFVI level, for example, Virtual Machine (VM) allocation by the hypervisor, VM monitoring, etc.;
- The VNF Manager (VNFM) is the management component located at the VNF layer. It is responsible for the instantiation, update, scaling and termination of different VNFs. VNFs can be theoretically managed by one or multiple VNF Managers;

One important role of the VNFM is to manage the scaling process. For example, VNFM monitors the state of its Caching VNFs. In case of heavy traffic load on the CDN, VNFM can choose to increase the resources (computing, storage, network) of the Caching VNFs (i.e., scale up), or to instantiate additional VNFs (i.e., scale out). However, the current management entity (the Management Server) supports basic features only (node configuration, monitoring, etc.) and many other MANO features are still missing (scaling, upgrading, etc.). One important question is: who is implementing and providing these missing features? Many scenarios are possible. The more likely scenario is that the CDN provider will implement dedicated VNFMs for its own CDN solution;

- At the top layer, the NFV Orchestrator (NFVO) is the central management entity of the entire NFV architecture, which ensures the orchestration of NFVI and software resources and the lifecycle management of different Network Services (NS), composed from one or several VNFs, deployed in the NFV architecture.

Figure 5 depicts a common implementation of vCDN based upon the NFV reference architecture. Note that other implementations for vCDN could be possible. A CDN is composed of functional blocks such as Caching, Request Routing, Analytics and Logging, and Management. In the NFV vCDN context, each of them can be virtualized and will be part of the virtualized infrastructure as a VNF. These VNFs will be then deployed on the virtualized infrastructure and interconnected in order to provide together the CDN functions.

From the architecture point of view, the main challenges for virtualizing a CDN are:

1. Cache nodes virtualization while keeping the same performance level as non-virtualized cache nodes. Fortunately, compared to low level network elements (switches, routers), cache nodes are running at the application layer and have less strict performance constraints in terms of forwarding delay and responsiveness. Also, they are distributed by design (a cache cluster is composed of multiple cache nodes), which makes their deployment easier in a virtualized environment.
2. Implementing the interfaces and metadata that are compliant with NFV definition. Each CDN vendor has its own components, interfaces and metadata. The challenge focuses here on having standards to interface NFV components from different vendors.
3. Clear separation of MANO responsibility of different components and different actors. Indeed some MANO functions of the CDN could be delegated to a third party, and the responsibility of each party shall be clearly defined.

Figure 5. vCDN Functional Architecture and its mapping to NFV

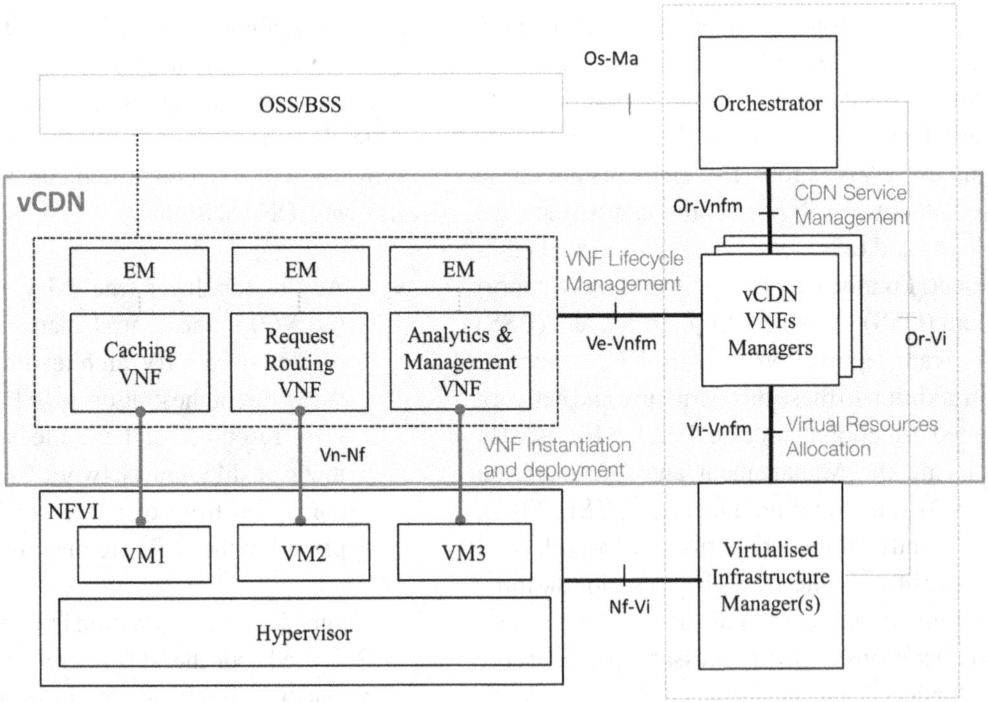

Performance Challenges

To address the ever-expanding and high uncertainty of content popularity, CDNs use high performance servers with optimized software. Using virtualized infrastructure, potentially limiting server performance, to host CDN nodes may seem to be in opposition to the high performance requirement. Therefore, assessing performance will help quantify and study resource usage in terms of Central Processing Unit (CPU) consumption, number of virtual CPUs (vCPU), memory size and virtual NICs (vNIC, virtual Network Interface Card) throughput. The objective is to ensure that a virtualized CDN still supports services with predictable and stable levels of quality and availability.

A testbed was set up by the authors of the present section to compare performances of CDN delivery application running on two servers: one physical server and one virtualized server.

In the latter case, this delivery application was running on a VM as a guest operating system located above the hypervisor. The hardware configuration for both machines was based on Intel Xeon processors. The same amount of memory (48 GB) was reserved to the delivery application, either on physical server or inside the VM.

A load generator was used to simulate end users, requesting in each scenario a specific content and then receiving the traffic. The tests simulated first users receiving traffic with progressive download using HTTP and second users using HTTP Adaptive Streaming (HAS) for on-demand or live contents. The load tests measured throughput and CPU consumption on each delivery server.

Although the same level of hardware resources was reserved and instantiated, performance degradations were detected in a virtualized environment. Theses degradations varied according to the type of traffic and other parameters (such as the total number of established sessions or the connection rate) but stayed always between 2 and 20 percent.

With optimization mechanisms such as "direct-path", also known as pass-through, it was possible to slightly lower these degradations. Direct-path is an optimization mechanism that allows guest systems to bypass the virtualization layer and to have exclusive access to the NIC (as if it was physically and directly attached to the guest operating system), and thus increasing throughput performances for high-speed network I/O devices such as 10 Gigabit Ethernet network interfaces. But the important point to notice is that in all the tests, the CPU consumption was always much higher with the virtualized server (Dzida, 2014).

As a result, to offer the same level of services with a virtual CDN, it is necessary to instantiate more VMs to compensate the loss of throughput. With more VMs, it would be possible to keep the CPU consumption at an acceptable level, and with a good knowledge of the sizing information needed for each component of the virtual CDN (number of virtual CPUs, memory capacity) it would be also possible to optimize the deployment. Then, achieving a comparable level of performance in virtualized environments may require to break this abstraction and to give to the most critical functions a direct access to physical resources.

Then, high and stable performance is achievable also on virtualized infrastructures by using existing advanced virtualization solutions supported by appropriately configured hardware (optimization mechanisms such as pass-through, Single Root I/O Virtualization, guaranteed memory reservation during VM allocation). Best practices, discussed in the next section, investigate how virtualization technology can be used to build efficient vCDN platforms.

Best Practices

OS virtualization may impact vCDN performance, this may cause resource bottlenecks. Hardware component bottlenecks typically refer to the overload of: processing unit, operational memory, storage, front-side bus or its equivalent, inter-socket bus, Network Interface Card (NIC). Software component bottlenecks typically refer to the poor efficiency of the OS/hypervisor modules: virtual switch, file subsystem, memory management subsystem, I/O subsystem, NIC driver, network socket pooling, context switching. Symptoms of bottlenecks in virtualized CDNs can be:

- Increased response times as an effect of insufficient computation capabilities;
- Intensive usage of virtual memory as a result of allocation of insufficient memory space;
- Small (byte) hit rate as a result of the allocation of insufficient storage space;
- Small throughput caused by software switch inefficiency;
- Packet drops resulting from the overload of internal data buses.

Memory virtualization, widely used in computer system architectures, may lead to efficiency limitations in case of virtualized OS. Contrary to OSes running on bare metal server, logical memory address space used by virtualized OS is translated into physical memory address space by the underlying hypervisor. So, in case of OS virtualization, memory page address from logical program space is translated twice: once by the guest OS, and then by the hypervisor. Thus, double memory address translation can limit performance of applications running over virtualized OS. To minimize the overhead associated with double memory address translation, two mechanisms can be proposed:

- Increased page size (so-called large pages) in the hypervisor memory management system;
- Efficient second-level translation caching (second level Translation Lookaside Buffer) implemented in hardware.

The performance of virtualized edge caches to the far end depends on the capabilities of physical resources, virtualized OS, underlying hypervisor and their proper configuration. To achieve stable and predictable performance, system designers shall consider the exclusive allocation of a subset of physical resources to edge cache VMs. This can help to minimize the influence of other VMs on edge caches. Furthermore, performance of virtualized edge caches can be limited by the OS and/or the hypervisor, such as vSwitch, and CPU and memory reservation. Thus, system designers shall identify whether the OS and/or the hypervisor components are most crucial for edge cache performance and shall possibly consider bypassing them by deploying alternative solutions, for instance by using Direct Memory Access (DMA), or Single Root I/O Virtualization (SRIOV) in order to grant VMs an exclusive access to physical NICs.

Conclusion

As a conclusion, the recent trend of network virtualization has received considerable attention from different actors, such as IT, Information System (IS) and telecom actors. In this context, the goal of ETSI NFV is to specify a standard virtualized platform for the sakes of interoperability and manageability. As a Network Service that requires both scalability and flexibility, CDN is a good candidate for *virtualization and is considered* as one of the promising use cases by the ETSI NFV initiative. Indeed, vCDNs can support relevant business use cases, such as scale in/out automation in live events, whose impact can differ from one actor to another depending on the infrastructure and the service-related parameters.

But CDN virtualization also raises new challenges for operators. The first challenge is to define a CDN architecture that can gracefully mix current deployments with future specifications and standards. Actually, this section presents a vCDN design, based on the ETSI/NFV reference architecture, where each CDN functional component is defined as a VNF. Such VNF is connected and managed by a multi-level management system, in order to achieve a content delivery service with flexible capability that dynamically adapts to traffic load. The second challenge is to identify bottlenecks of vCDNs, and to document best practices that can address these bottleneck issues: telecom operators are already organizing Proofs of Concept (PoCs) and trials to assess the proposed business case feasibility. The objectives for them are to assure stable and predictable performances and to identify the bottlenecks of the virtualization. The above text that discusses performance tests shows that this goal may be achieved under specific conditions. Some hardware optimization techniques could be applied in order to further improve the system performance at the cost of losing some flexibility, as far as virtualization is concerned.

The CDN transformation toward its fully virtualized version is still a long path. A key element of this transformation is the orchestration entity, which will eventually manage multiple Network Services and VNFMs from several vendors.

CONVERGENCE OF CDN AND CLOUDS

CDN operators have been improving content delivery and allowed widening audience on greedy contents. Those actors have been deploying geographically distributed servers to extend their footprint while locating them closer to the end users, i.e., on interconnection points. They still provide content delivery services to businesses or individuals. However, other actors like Telcos have been using CDN servers for their own services and their infrastructure is more regional-scoped, less extended.

On the other hand, more and more OTT actors like Amazon, Microsoft, provide cloud-based "X-as–a-Service" (XaaS) offers where X gradually includes Infrastructure, Platform or Software. It covers for instance mass storage, processing, grid computing, or development facilities. These offers are usually supported by centralized infrastructures, mainly datacenters connected somewhere to the Web. Cloud offers usually target Business-To-Business-To-Customer (B2B2C) markets, meaning that customers may be customers of other customers, which is the case of Netflix as a client of the Amazon S3 Cloud.

Today, CDN & Cloud services and infrastructures tend to converge, and two main trends are emerging:

- "Cloudification of CDN service offerings": trend towards CDNs and CDN service offerings relying on cloud offers, or directly via cloud infrastructures;
- "CDN-ization of cloud service offerings": trend towards cloud offerings relying on distributed (CDN based) infrastructure.

Cloudification of CDN Service Offerings

The cloudification of CDN service offerings is exemplified by some major CDN operators and content providers whose content delivery solutions (origin servers and/or CDN building blocks) are partly or fully based upon and/or deployed on top of cloud infrastructures. More precisely, this trend concerns in priority the control plane of CDNs (e.g., request routing operations, performance data collection and analysis), large storage required functions (Origin servers), Value Added Services (content preparation like multi-format/multi-rate video encoding or compression) rather than the data plane (e.g., content caching and delivery). From a business perspective, this trend brings stimulating opportunities to both the cloud service providers and their customers:

- For the former: the development of Infrastructure as a Service (IaaS) or Platform as a Service (PaaS) designs, thereby addressing the needs of content providers and content delivery service providers;

- For the latter: the optimization of their infrastructure and data analytics.

Until now CDN applications have been deployed mainly via dedicated, proprietary and distributed network nodes in order to provide the required performances and to control the quality experienced by the clients that use these applications. But CDNs are software systems in essence. This makes them potential candidates for being deployed in cloud infrastructures. The drivers for such a migration are to take advantage of cloud techniques when delivering contents:

- Scalability: content delivery service providers and content providers are traditionally heavy users of large content storage and content delivery capacities, and their needs grow as the evolution of their offerings (implementation of network Personal Video Recorder (PVR), time-shifting, Video On Demand (VoD) blockbusters, etc.), but they are also expanding massively into big data exploitation for various purposes - audience tracking, performance management, content recommendations, content placement, audience prediction, etc. -, which makes clouds relevant infrastructures for their business development;
- Auto-scaling: clouds ensure the possibility to use transport, storage and computing resources strictly dimensioned to the traffic, data and CPU load and to reallocate additional resources to absorb traffic peaks;
- Agility: the same servers can handle work tied to content delivery at peak hours and be reallocated to data analytics during idle hours.

This trend for cloud-ization of CDN service offerings has much in common with the so-called trend for NFV introduced in the above section on "CDN and Virtualization". In particular, these trends have in common that they all contribute to separate the CDN core functions (request routing, content caching, etc.) from an underlying commoditized hardware infrastructure (thus paving the way towards the "software-ization" of CDN infrastructures, so to speak).

This trend has been made conceivable by the dramatic increase of server performances. Nevertheless, CDN applications raise technical requirements that suggest tailored cloud services:

- Controlled performances to ensure the adequate QoE expected by the end user;
- Reservation of massive amounts of resources for special events (Olympics, etc.);
- Specific requirements about cache locations from end users; this looks easy to implement in a worldwide vision where the objective would be to cache content in data centers at the granularity of countries/states, yet high audience content delivery services may require to cache contents in Telcos' networks much closer to the end users.

A typical use case that illustrates this trend is the cloud-based infrastructure of Netflix. Netflix is a dominant player in the online content delivery market, accounting for 34 percent of North American Internet Traffic during peak times in the first half of 2014, according to Sandvine Inc. (Sandvine, 2014). Netflix is also one of the world's largest users of cloud computing, exploiting thousands of servers running in Amazon data centers (Amazon, 2014). Netflix has progressively built its cloud-based infrastructure with Amazon, first in the United States (US). Amazo Web Services (AWS) enables Netflix to quickly deploy thousands of servers and terabytes of storage within minutes. The type of tasks that can be managed in the cloud may include customer information, video recommendations, digital rights management, encoding of video files into different formats, security and monitoring of the performance of the systems, etc. This cloud technology allowed Netflix to quickly deploy outside of the US.

CDN-ization of Cloud Service Offerings

The CDN-ization of cloud service offerings is based upon the vision that centralized data centers and cloud computing infrastructures are not necessarily well suited for real-time decentralized and high processing / bandwidth consuming applications.

Besides, major CDN providers have been providing application acceleration services for quite some time, by exploiting the distributed topology of their decentralized infrastructures (Davis, Parikh, & Weihl, 2004). The purpose of such design is to improve the quality experienced by the end users, and to optimize transport and interconnection costs.

Today, several drivers contribute to the development of this trend. First, the massive adoption of cloud offers by both the enterprise and mass market segments fosters the storage of all types of data in the cloud; it becomes relevant to allow end users to more rapidly access these data by caching the most frequent/popular data closer to their location, like CDN infrastructures.

By the way, it is foreseeable that both these trends could merge in order to combine the best of existing CDN and cloud infrastructures.

Key Drivers for Convergence

Virtualization appears first as a determining enabler for simplifying and optimizing resource allocation and usage. The aforementioned initiatives on Network Function Virtualization are currently seeking to standardize and commoditize the use of network nodes' hardware. They will ease ultimately the expansion of cloud infrastructures inside Telcos' networks and closer to end users than they are today.

As mentioned before, the software aspects of CDN are particularly suited for virtualization. But virtualizing CDN will need to be done with respect to technical CDN constraints like performance and distributed organization. Please refer to the "CDN and virtualization" section for more details.

As far as heterogeneous (virtual and physical) resources are concerned, the orchestration logic will be needed to simplify the management and federation of resources. This top layer function will facilitate the commercialization of a new kind of Content Delivery XaaS services that take advantage of both CDN distributed servers and cloud centralized infrastructures.

To accomplish this, the orchestration logic will have to take into account several policies coming from actors involved in the value chain, such as for instance, the cloud operator, the content providers, the end users and the CDN operator. This policy should then take into account in particular the network bandwidth, content type, available resources, and SLA, as introduced in the above section on "CDN Interconnection".

Secondly, CDN and Cloud converged infrastructures should be rather "open" to the Web ecosystem. A means to the infrastructure is for instance to provide HTTP(S) APIs which is currently the case for cloud operators. They may allow a Web access from external components provided by third parties. For instance, front-end portals provided by content service providers, back-ends or databases will be able to trigger and chain services on the converged infrastructure. Such APIs may also allow service activation on the cloud (processing, transcoding), service chaining (capacity to chain several cloud services), service topology and request routing, creation of resources, management and configuration or analytics of the CDN and Cloud activity.

Finally, convergence of CDN and Cloud should be achieved thanks to a thorough and deeper knowledge of the network during the several stages of the lifecycle of cloud services.

For instance, cloud operators will be able to gather network information from Telcos about the configuration, management policies, and the status of their networks and services (e.g., is it possible to forward traffic to a given area?). If virtualization is involved, network information will allow the creation of new virtualized delivery or processing instances, taking into account real-time traffic bandwidth.

Cloud and CDN Challenges

While key drivers have been identified to empower Cloud and CDN trends, they raise challenges about:

- The interest in distributing caching locations;
- Storage, as deploying and managing high storage capacities closer to end users, so at a high capillarity, is more expensive compared to when it is achieved in centralized datacenters;
- The location of advanced features as a function of content caching design and data acceleration;
- Caching contents for encrypted customers' flows.

QoE assurance and the processing of high traffic volumes inside networks or at peering points are obviously key performance indicators for customers. While media services (volume-based services) strongly impact network dimensioning, a larger set of services simply requires short response times; improving these response times by some hundreds of milliseconds is key to a better business. In summary, understanding SLAs (performance requirements, reliability, usage) (Boucadair, 2014) and infrastructure costs will facilitate the assessment of distributing service delivery points. This assessment will help validate the interest of decentralizing caches in the network, and identify the best designs as a function of the network topology.

The solution to store content will depend on the considered services and audience (VoD catalogues, personal contents, etc.) but also on the required infrastructures that need to be deployed in central offices or regional PoPs. Also, it is directly linked to cost considerations and available bandwidth.

CDN and Cloud convergence gives also the opportunity to bring and decentralize value-added services. On-time transcoding or running third-party applications down to the caches are typical examples. The decentralization of such services should obviously take into account economical and performance questions.

Another important challenge relates to content access security requirements. This challenge will lead to deliver content through ciphered protocols (e.g., HTTPS) and design solutions in compliance with the brand new HTTP2.0 (Belshe, Peon, & Thomson, 2014). This trend on security and privacy needs is strongly linked to the growth of Internet for Business. But it also raises issues about CDN and caching infrastructures. Actually, ciphered flows prevent contents caching with respect to service agreements between partners.

The migration of applications towards secured sessions (HTTPS, HTTP2.0) hinders the efficiency of the traffic engineering mechanisms deployed inside the networks, especially the transparent caching systems, thereby impacting the quality experienced with the applications that were primarily taking advantage of transparent caching. CDN-izing these applications would help to compensate this impact.

Another technical solution relies upon the use of the trusted proxy approach which allows ciphered sessions (e.g., HTTPS) to be "split" in order to transit through a trusted intermediate between the end user and the server.

CDN EXTENSION IN THE HOME

Context and Stakes

In the present section CDN extension in the home means to partially or fully deploy CDN functions in one or several devices located in the end user's home network. The end user's home network designates the private local network deployed in the user's premises, including all the terminal devices connected to this network. The home network connects to the Internet via a Home Gateway. The Home Gateway is essentially a modem (Fiber To The Home (FTTH), Asymmetric Digital Subscriber Line (ADSL), Cable, etc.) embedded in a Home Gateway that provides routing and switching features.

Several strong drivers motivate the introduction of CDN functions into the home network. A first driver is to improve the scalability and cost efficiency of CDNs by exploiting the highly distributed infrastructure of home networks to achieve different CDN processes like CDN Operations, Administration and Management (OAM), as well as CDN request routing operations. A second driver is to go beyond the network bandwidth constraints and/or to optimize network costs, for example by deploying caching and prefetching functionality inside the home network. Caching aims here at storing temporarily into a local memory (inside the home network) pieces of data that were already requested and delivered, so that they can be delivered locally upon forthcoming requests. In contrast prefetching consists in predicting and pushing in a local memory at traffic off-peak periods and in advance to the users' requests pieces of data these users will probably request. A third driver is to improve latency in applications, hence the quality of experience of the end users.

This section provides four illustrative use cases of this trend, respectively on (i) request routing operations related to end user request processing, (ii) content delivery operations, (iii) ingestion and storage operations, and (iv) OAM. In all these use cases, the considered CDN functions are primarily supported by the Home Gateway. Yet, these functions can possibly be implemented into end user devices (Set Top Box (STB), PC player ...), either as an additional plug-in (at the application level or into a player) or as an optimization of the Operating System (network and transport stacks).

It is to be highlighted that, whatever the use cases, two major challenges must be addressed. First, all these use cases assume a close collaboration between the CDN operator and the telecom operator that manages the Home Gateway. Second, these use cases should not negatively impact the performances of the Home Gateways. For the time being, these use cases are being tested.

DELEGATING CDN REQUEST ROUTING FUNCTIONS TO THE HOME GATEWAY

Most of the CDNs rely on the Domain Name System (DNS) redirection and/or applicative redirection (e.g., HTTP redirection) to redirect the end user's requests for content to the most suited CDN cache node. It means that the end-user generates DNS and/or applicative requests (e.g., HTTP requests) that are handled by the CDN request routing servers. These messages do not represent a large amount of traffic, but traffic bursts may be experienced by the request routing server, which is often a centralized component of the CDN architecture.

As the Home Gateway processes all the traffic generated by the end user, it also processes the aforementioned requests for content generated by the end users. Involving the Home Gateway in the CDN request routing process could help decrease the traffic load both on the CDN request routing server and the network. Different options can be envisioned. A first option is that a DNS proxy in the Home Gateway increases the Time To Live values of DNS records to mitigate the burst impact on the request routing server. A second option is to transfer part of the CDN request routing logic from the CDN request routing server to a proxy located in the Home Gateway. Such options would not only mitigate the traffic burstiness experienced by the CDN request routing server, but also improve the latency, hence the QoE.

EXTENDING CDN CONTENT DELIVERY FEATURES INTO THE HOME NETWORK

The purpose here is to implement additional content delivery functions within the home network to improve network resource usage. The expected benefits are not only to increase network cost efficiency, but also to be able to support applications (e.g., 4K video content delivery) and needs (e.g., delivery of live events broadcast to large audiences) that could possibly be challenging, if not impossible, to provide without such additional functionality.

An example, already proposed by several CDN solution providers (BroadPeak, 2012; Octoshape, 2012; Law, 2013), consists in combining several content delivery schemes, including CDN with Multicast and Automatic Multicast Tunneling (AMT) (Bumgardner, 2014b). The goal is to provide the best possible network efficiency and quality of service when delivering live events broadcast to large audiences. The basic principles of such proposals are illustrated in Figure 6. A CDN cache node ingests the High Audience unicast live flow and uses one or more IP multicast group(s) for carrying flows into the core and access networks. The Home Gateway (or the end-user device) must embed a specific CDN extended agent. This CDN extended agent acts both as a multicast receiver that joins IP multicast groups (by means of Internet Group Management Protocol (IGMP) (Cain, Deering, Kouvelas, Fenner, & Thyagarajan, 2002) or Multicast Listener Discovery (MLD) (Vida, & Costa, 2004; Holbrook, Cain, & Haberman, 2006) Query messages and then receives the corresponding flows, and as a HTTP proxy for the player to receive the end user request and to deliver the requested content.

It is to be noted that such a delivery scheme can be enforced even over core and access networks where IP multicast is not enabled, as shown on the lower part of Figure 6. In such networks multicast traffic can be conveyed in AMT tunnels, for example (Bumgardner, 2014a). Yet, this assumes that the Home Gateway must also implement an AMT proxy.

EXTENDING CDN CONTENT INGESTION AND STORAGE FEATURES INTO THE HOME NETWORK

The goal here is to "smartly" ingest and store content inside the home network, either in advance of the user request or at the time of the content request and delivery. In the former case, the operation is called content prefetching, and in the latter content caching. The main objectives of these operations are to save on peak bandwidth and energy consumption during peak hours, and to ensure an adequate quality of experience for the end-user even in the case of adverse network conditions.

This domain has been widely investigated by the research community, for fixed and mobile networks as well as terminals, and by leveraging a high variety of technologies to feed content into the home networks and terminal devices: Peer-to-Peer (P2P), satellite, evolved Multimedia Broadcast Multicast Services (eMBMS), Digital terrestrial television (DTT), etc. (Nencioni, Sastry, Chandaria, & Crowcroft, 2013; Wang, Sun, Yang, & Zhu, 2011; Wang, Sun, Chen, Zhu, Liu, Chen, & Yang, 2012; Finamore, Mellia, Gilani, Papagiannaki, Erramilli, & Grunenberger, 2013; Lu, & de Veciana, 2013; Mohan, Nath, & Riva, 2013). Whatever the design choices, all the solutions in

Figure 6. Extending CDN content delivery features into the Home – Multicast based delivery scheme

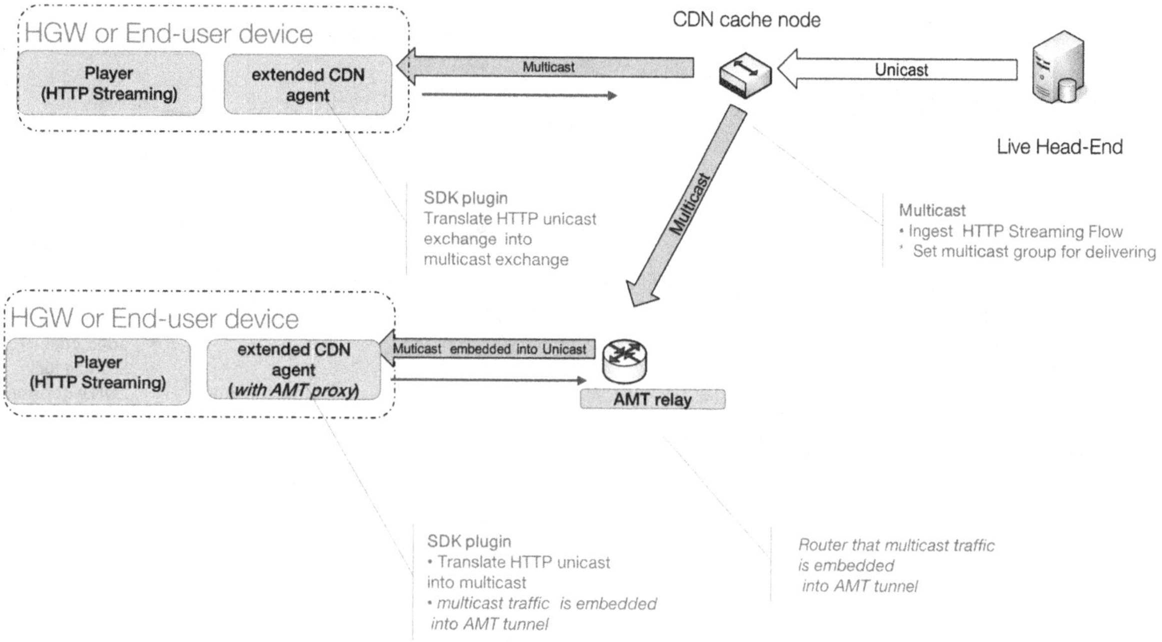

this domain have in common that they impose to implement specific content ingestion and storage logics on the considered home network device.

Figure 7 describes a proposal for implementing ingestion and storage functions into the Home Gateway. Note that prefetching can be achieved by many protocols such as P2P, File Transfer Protocol (FTP), Trivial File Transfer Protocol (TFTP) (or any other suitable protocol) on any access network (e.g., satellite, ADSL/FTTH, etc.)

EXTENDING CDN OAM FEATURES INTO THE HOME GATEWAY

This last example aims to illustrate that one could also envision to implement CDN OAM features on Home Gateways to measure accurate indicators inside the home network that could better help to supervise and troubleshoot the network and applications. The Home Gateway could also pre-process the collected traffic data (e.g., duration of video sessions, number of HAS chunks consumed in the different quality levels, etc.) in order to lower the pressure on the performance management and audience tracking systems of the CDN operators and content providers.

CONTENT DELIVERY FOR MOBILE

Mobile traffic has peaked up over the last decade and it is expected to continue to grow at amazing rates in the coming years. According to Cisco (2014) global mobile data traffic reached 1.5 exabytes per month at the end of 2013 and it will increase nearly 11-fold between 2013 and 2018, so at a compound annual growth rate (CAGR) of 61 percent from 2013 to 2018, reaching 15.9 exabytes per month by 2018.

Moreover, content distribution applications, especially video applications, are blooming on mobile networks. They are already responsible for the majority of future Mobile Internet traffic: Mobile video traffic was 53 percent of mobile traffic by the end of 2013 (Cisco, 2014).

Figure 7. Extending CDN content ingestion and storage features into the Home

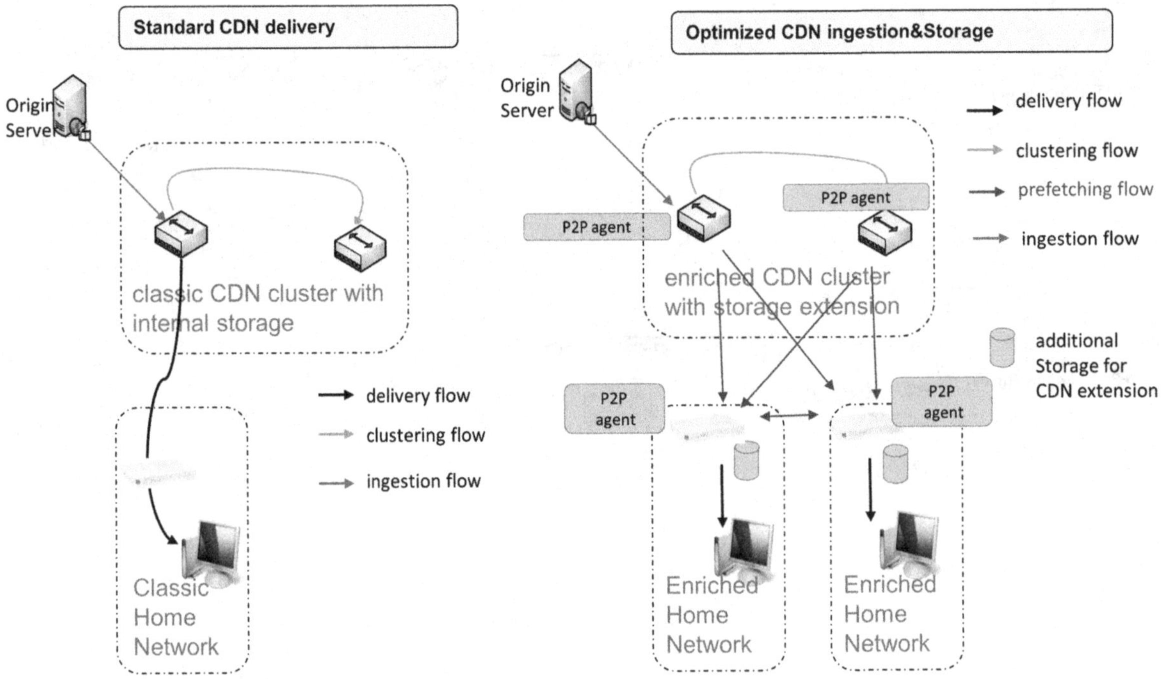

In addition, a specific trait of the mobile domain is the large diversity of existing mobile devices (feature phones, Smartphones, tablets, laptops, etc.), with heterogeneous hardware and software characteristics in terms of screen size, storage, CPU, graphic chipset, operating system and APIs. Each of these characteristics influences the way content are prepared, accessed, and delivered. For instance, different adaptive streaming solutions may have to be used depending on the terminal devices: Apple HLS for Apple iPad and iPhone, Microsoft Smooth Streaming for others. Nevertheless, there is a common clear trend towards a massive adoption of high-end devices which generate the majority of mobile traffic and drive the increase of the mobile connection speeds. Tablets will exceed 15 percent of mobile data traffic by 2016 and Smartphones will reach 66 percent of mobile data traffic by 2018 (Cisco, 2014).

These expected growths shall deeply impact current architectures of mobile cellular networks, as well as the associated content delivery systems.

Figure 8 represents the global end-to-end architecture typically involved in the delivery of a given content over 3G and 4G networks, from its originating server, also known as content source, to the end user's terminal. This architecture includes on the one side the mobile network the end user's terminal is connected to, and, on the other side, the Internet and/or the third parties' networks that connect the considered content source to the mobile network. The mobile network itself is composed of 3 parts:

- The RAN, Radio Access Network (UTRAN in 3G or E-UTRAN in 4G), connects the mobile devices to the Packet Core network and includes the radio interface;
- The Packet Core Network (GPRS Core Network in 3G or Evolved Packet Core (EPC) in 4G) performs all functional operations for data forwarding (mobility handling, routing toward/from Internet ...),

charging (online and offline), security handling, etc.;

- The (s)Gi PoP connects the (s)Gi Interface to the Internet and third networks. It may encompass additional IP-based equipments to provide features such as NAT and firewalls, content caching and compression, Deep Packet Inspection (DPI), legal filtering, etc. (non-exhaustive list).

For more detailed information on 3G and 4G mobile architectures, the reader may for instance refer to the 3GPP standard documents (3GPP, 2014a) or also to Cox (2012).

In this global end-to-end architecture, CDN nodes (often referred to as "streamers" in the case of video services) have typically been placed only between PGWs and the Origin Servers: on the (s)Gi PoP, on the Internet, or on any other 3rd party network involved in the delivery chain.

Indeed, in the past years, mobile telecommunication operators had little incentive to deploy CDNs in the Radio Access and Packet Core networks. First, the bandwidth consumed for content delivery in the mobile domain was relatively small in comparison to fixed broadband networks. Second, all data packets exchanged with the mobile device are encapsulated in GTP tunnels (GPRS Tunneling Protocol) (3GPP, 2014d; 3GPP, 2014e) between the (e)NodeB and the last gateway of the mobile Packet Core network, respectively the GGSN (Gateway GPRS Support Node) in 3G and the PGW (Packet Data Network GateWay) in 4G. And in most cases, there is only a few of such gateways in mobile operators' networks. Thus, cellular networks used to rely upon rather centralized topologies, and CDNs cannot be easily distributed in these networks.

In fact, these last years, the main network bottleneck being on the radio interface, the mobile operators have been focusing on addressing this issue with several answers. They answered commercially with the notion of fair-usage to rationalize heavy usages (pre-defined monthly data volume beyond which an extra charge is applied). From a technical perspective, they have been investing massively in several generations of mobile access technologies, each one improving significantly the performances of the previous one: GPRS (2.5G), EDGE (2.75G), UMTS (3G), HSDPA (3.5G), HSPA+ (3.75G), LTE (3.9G), LTE-Advanced (4G), as well as small cells (femtocells, picocells, microcells). Optimizing proxies, called "Mobile Internet Gateways" or "boosters", have been

Figure 8. Typical End-to-End Mobile Content Delivery Architecture

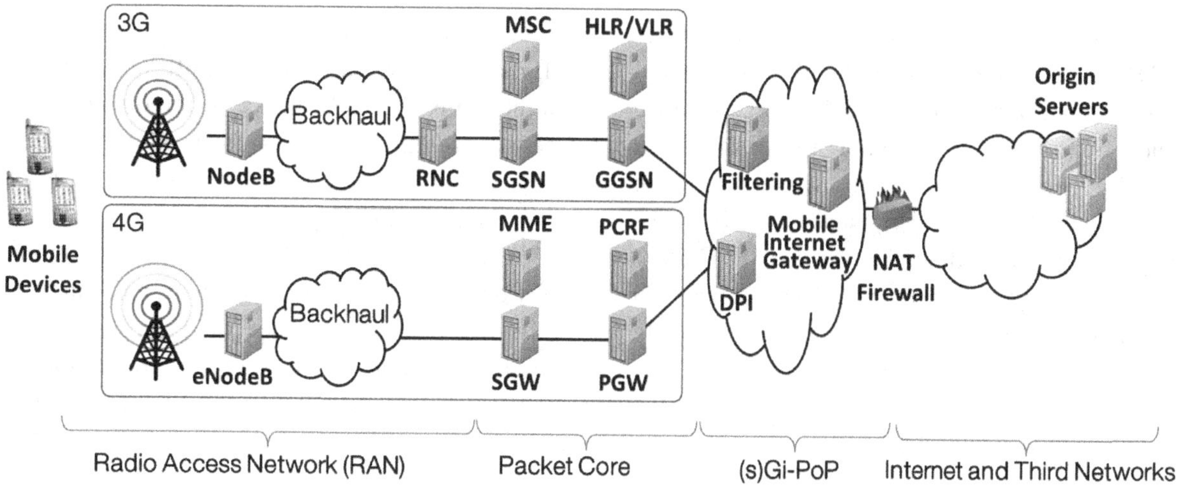

installed at the (s)Gi PoP to perform operations such as content caching and content compression. Multi-Path TCP (MPTCP) and eMBMS are also among the spectrum of solutions targeting this issue. MPTCP refers to a set of mechanisms that add the capability of simultaneously using multiple paths to forward traffic between two TCP peers, the objectives being to increase redundancy, network resource utilization and connection speed (IETF, 2014b). MBMS stands for Multimedia Broadcast Multicast Services and eMBMS is the LTE version of MBMS standardized by the 3GPP. As its name says, this technology relies upon broadcast and multicast delivery schemes to ensure an efficient use of the frequency spectrum (3GPP, 2014b).

By way of consequence, the average mobile network connection speed more than doubled in 2013 (1.387 Mbps) and it is expected to double, to exceed 2.5 Mbps by 2018 (Cisco, 2014). This will put a strong pressure on all the network segments above the radio interface. Deploying CDNs closer to end users should ease this traffic pressure. It would also reduce the latency by distributing at the edge of the mobile network both content and DNS resolutions, thus improving the quality experienced by end users. Moreover, if deployed on cell towers, CDN nodes could have access to information on terminal radio conditions and adapt the delivery to these conditions.

Different implementation options can be envisioned. In the short to medium terms, the GGSN/PDN gateways can be decentralized closer to end users, leaving more opportunities to distribute CDN nodes deeper in the network if a financial interest and/or business model emerge(s) from such opportunity. Any other approach would require to modify the mobile network protocol stack to enable the deployment of CDN nodes anywhere between the cell towers and the GGSN/PDN gateways. In the longer term, a new 5G architecture shall natively incorporate massively distributed content delivery systems.

It is expected that such 5G architectures will associate different wireless technologies, including device-to-device communication, cellular and WLAN networks (Osseiran, Boccardi, Braun, Kusume, Marsch, Maternia, Queseth, Schellmann, Schotten, Taoka, Tullberg, Uusitalo, Timus, & Fallgren, 2014). In this context, mobility management might have to be reviewed in-depth for at least two reasons. First, the network core of the 5G architecture shall be merged with fixed core networks, and this shall lead to reconsider the tunnel-based mobility model as enforced by 3G and 4G networks. Second, as terminal devices in mobility can possibly be connected to multiple very close CDN edge servers, each of these ones being behind different cells or (un)licensed small cells, this calls for innovative adequate content session continuity mechanisms between the CDN nodes.

Finally, a complementary solution to all the aforementioned ones is content prefetching and scheduling, possibly combined with content offloading exploiting network discovery and selection assistance systems like Access Network Discovery and Selection Function (ANDSF) (3GPP, 2014c). The prefetching approach consists in preloading a given content on the mobile device. This leads to the extension of the CDN infrastructure to the mobile device to some extent. The target benefits are to lessen the network traffic peaks and to enable the end user to consume this content, even when the network conditions are not sufficient for a correct experience. In order to be efficient, this approach must carefully take account of the status of mobile devices (including battery status), and this requires a good prediction of the consumption and mobility behaviors of the end user (Gautam, Petander, & Noel, 2013).

As a conclusion, in the next few years, mobile networks will experience great transformation driven by the convergence of usages between fixed and mobile. While the pressure on mobile operators' Average Revenue Per User (ARPU) motivated cost rationalization strategies in the past few years, the focus is now on the creation of synergies between networking and delivery functions. However, in order to benefit from this trend, mobile operators shall engage business partnerships with Over-The-Top players in order to propose advanced delivery services aligned with financial and marketing expectations.

CONCLUSION

CDNs play a strategic role today in the networks and the global ecosystem. As the latter evolves, so will the CDNs. The main drivers are to improve scalability, flexibility and cost efficiency of the content delivery infrastructures, as well as the Quality of Experience for the end users. This chapter focuses on a set of expected major trends: notably the convergence of CDN architectures, the interconnection of CDNs, the virtualization of CDNs, the convergence of CDNs and clouds, the extension of the CDNs towards the home networks and the evolution of content delivery over mobile networks. It also aims at highlighting the main associated challenges, from both the technical and business perspectives.

Audiovisual content dominates the traffic delivered by CDNs. The audiovisual architectures which used to be dedicated to specific access networks and services evolve towards a single convergent technical chain and aim at addressing the "any content, anytime, anywhere" paradigm. In this evolution, the management of the content metadata and the strategic positioning of the different types of market players will be decisive. Next to audiovisual content services, CDN-based acceleration and security services are also expected to pick up and to represent a significant part of the CDN operators' revenues in the short and long terms.

The need to scale up CDNs, in terms of functionality, volume and network coverage, is expected to stimulate CDN interconnection. This has motivated significant effort in standardization bodies on CDN interconnection interfaces, notably at IETF, as well as different types of concrete deployment contexts, involving CDN brokers and Multi-CDN Service Providers. The main technical challenges concern the management of cascaded SLAs, the delegation of trust for encrypted traffic delivery (HTTPS) and the sheer interoperability on all required interfaces. From a business perspective, there has to be a clear model for revenue sharing that is profitable to all the involved parties willing to enter such interconnection schemes.

The foreseen transformation of CDNs towards virtualized infrastructures is still ongoing, with the objective to assure stable and predictable performances. The key element of this transformation is the orchestration entity, which will have to manage multiple Network Services and Virtual Network Function Managers from different vendors, and then will have to deal with interconnection challenges. A closely related trend is the convergence of CDN and Cloud infrastructures, which involves the "cloud-ization of CDN service offerings" and the "CDN-ization of cloud service offerings". All this might significantly modify the competitive landscape of online content delivery, thus bringing new business opportunities for the different market players.

CDNs are also expected to expand towards the home network, so as to improve their scalability and cost efficiency, as well as the latency in applications, thus the Quality of Experience of the end users. Business and technical challenges must be addressed. First, this suggests a close collaboration between CDN and telecom operators, the latter managing the Home Gateway. Second, this must not negatively impact the performances of the Home Gateways.

In the mobile domain, different implementation options can be envisioned in the short to long term to decentralize content delivery infrastructures and to strengthen the convergence with fixed networks. The focus is now on the creation of synergies between networking and delivery functions. But mobile operators shall engage business partnerships with Over-The-Top players in order to propose advanced delivery services aligned with financial and marketing expectations.

REFERENCES

Akamai. (2012). *Press Release. November 20, 2012. Orange and Akamai form Content Delivery Strategic Alliance*. Retrieved October 23, 2014 from http://www.akamai.com/html/about/press/releases/2012/press_112012_1.html

Akamai. (2014). *Visualizing Akamai Web Page*. Retrieved October 23, 2014 from http://www.akamai.com/html/technology/dataviz3.html

Amazon. (2014). *AWS Case Study: Netflix*. Retrieved October 23, 2014 from http://aws.amazon.com/fr/solutions/case-studies/netflix/

ATIS. (2011). *ATIS Cloud Services Forum Releases Content Distribution Network Interconnection Specifications*. Retrieved October 23, 2014 from http://www.atis.org/PRESS/pressreleases2011/070511.html

Belshe, M., Peon, R., & Thomson, M. (2014). *Hypertext Transfer Protocol version 2, draft-ietf-httpbis-http2-14*. Retrieved July 30, 2014 from https://tools.ietf.org/html/draft-ietf-httpbis-http2-14

Boucadair, M., Jacquenet, C., & Wang, N. (2014). *IP Connectivity Provisioning Profile (CPP). Internet Engineering Task Force RFC 5246*. Retrieved from http://tools.ietf.org/html/rfc7297

BroadPeak. (2012). *nanoCDN*. Retrieved October 23, 2014 from http://www.broadpeak.tv/ en/technologies/nanocdn-25.php

Broberga, J., Buyyaa, R., & Tarib, Z. (2009). MetaCDN: Harnessing 'Storage Clouds' for high performance content delivery. *Journal of Network and Computer Applications*, *32*(5), 1012–1022. doi:10.1016/j.jnca.2009.03.004

Bumgardner, G. (2014a). *Automatic Multicast Tunneling, draft-ietf-mboned-auto-multicast-17*. Retrieved April 24, 2014 from http://tools.ietf.org/html/draft-ietf-mboned-auto-multicast-17

Bumgardner, G. (2014b). *Automatic Multicast Tunneling, draft-ietf-mboned-auto-multicast-17*. Retrieved April 24, 2014 from https://tools.ietf.org/html/draft-ietf-mboned-auto-multicast-17

Cain, B., Deering, S., Kouvelas, I., Fenner, B., & Thyagarajan, A. (2002). *Internet Group Management Protocol, Version 3. Internet Engineering Task Force RFC 3376*. Retrieved from https://tools.ietf.org/html/rfc3376

CDNTech. (2012). *White paper, "The acceleration of web and mobile content"*. Retrieved October 23, 2014 from http://www.cdn-tech.com/en/news/article/white-paper-the-acceleration-of-web-and-mobile-content

Cedexis. (2014). *Cedexis white paper. How (and why) to implement a Multi-CDN Strategy*. Retrieved October 23, 2014 from http://go.cedexis.com/Implementing-Multi-CDN.html

Chiosi, M., Clarke, D., Willis, P., Reid, A., Feger, J., Bugenhagen, M., . . . Sen, P. (2012). *Network Functions Virtualization— Introductory White Paper. ETSI. 22 October 2012*. Retrieved October 23, 2014 from http://portal.etsi.org/NFV/NFV_White_Paper.pdf

Cisco. (2014). *Cisco Visual Networking Index: Global Mobile Data Traffic Forecast Update, 2013–2018*. Retrieved June 5, 2014 from http://www.cisco.com/c/en/us/solutions/collateral/service-provider/visual-networking-index-vni/white_paper_c11-520862.html

Conviva. (2011). *Conviva Precision Video. Policy based Multi-CDN Optimization*. Retrieved October 23, 2014 from http://conviva.com/wp-content/uploads/Conviva-Precision-Video-Policy-based-Multi-CDN-Optimization.pdf

Cox, C. (2012). *An Introduction to LTE: LTE, LTE-Advanced, SAE and 4G Mobile Communications*. John Wiley & Sons. doi:10.1002/9781119942825

Davis, A., Parikh, J., & Weihl, W. E. (2004). Edge computing: extending enterprise applications to the edge of the internet. In *Proceedings of the 13th international World Wide Web conference on Alternate track papers & posters* (pp. 180-187). New York, NY: ACM. doi:10.1145/1013367.1013397

Dierks, T., & Rescorla, E. (2008). *The Transport Layer Security (TLS) Protocol. Version 1.2. Internet Engineering Task Force RFC 5246*. Retrieved from https://tools.ietf.org/html/rfc5246

Dzida, M. (2014). *Virtual CDN performance tests, ETSI GS NFV*. Retrieved October 23, 2014 from http://docbox.etsi.org/ISG/NFV/PER/05-CONTRIBUTIONS/2014//NFVPER(14)000032_Virtual_CDN_performance_tests.pptx

ETSI. (2013a). *CDN Interconnection Architecture. ETSI TS 182 032 V1.1.1 (2013-04)*. Retrieved October 23, 2014 from http://www.etsi.org/deliver/etsi_ts/182000_182099/182032/01.01.01_60/ts_182032v010101p.pdf

ETSI. (2013b). *Network Function Virtualization (NFV): Architectural Framework. ETSI GS NFV 002 V1.1.1 (2013-10)*. Retrieved October 23, 2014 from http://www.etsi.org/deliver/etsi_gs/nfv/001_099/002/01.01.01_60/gs_nfv002v010101p.pdf

ETSI. (2013c). *Network Function Virtualization (NFV): Use Cases. ETSI GS NFV 001 V1.1.1 (2013-10)*. Retrieved October 23, 2014 from http://www.etsi.org/deliver/etsi_gs/nfv/001_099/001/01.01.01_60/gs_nfv001v010101p.pdf

ETSI. (2014). *NFV Management and Orchestration. GS NFV-MAN 001 V0.6.1 (2014-07)*. Retrieved October 23, 2014 from http://docbox.etsi.org/ISG/NFV/Open/Latest_Drafts/NFV-MAN001v061-%20management%20and%20orchestration.pdf

Faizul Bari, M., Boutaba, R., Esteves, R., Zambenedetti Granville, L., Podlesny, M., Golam Rabbani, M., & Faten Zhani, M. et al. (2013). Data Center Network Virtualization: A Survey. *IEEE Communications Surveys and Tutorials*, *15*(2), 909–928. doi:10.1109/SURV.2012.090512.00043

Finamore, A., Mellia, M., Gilani, Z., Papagiannaki, K., Erramilli, V., & Grunenberger, Y. (2013). Is there a case for mobile phone content pre-staging? In *Proceedings of the ninth ACM conference on Emerging networking experiments and technologies* (pp. 321-326). New York, NY: ACM. doi:10.1145/2535372.2535414

Gautam, N., Petander, H., & Noel, J. (2013). A comparison of the cost and energy efficiency of prefetching and streaming of mobile video. In *Proceedings of the 5th Workshop on Mobile Video* (pp. 7-12). New York, NY: ACM. doi:10.1145/2457413.2457416

3GPP. (2014a). *3GPP Technologies Home*. Retrieved October 23, 2014 from http://www.3gpp.org/technologies/technologies

3GPP. (2014b). *LTE; Evolved Universal Terrestrial Radio Access Network (E-UTRAN); General aspects and principles for interfaces supporting Multimedia Broadcast Multicast Service (MBMS) within E-UTRAN (3GPP TS 36.440 version 12.0.0 Release 12). ETSI TS 136 440 V12.0.0 (2014-09)*. Retrieved October 23, 2014 from http://www.etsi.org/deliver/etsi_ts/136400_136499/136440/12.00.00_60/ts_136440v120000p.pdf

3GPP. (2014c). *Universal Mobile Telecommunications System (UMTS); LTE; Architecture enhancements for non-3GPP accesses (3GPP TS 23.402 version 12.6.0 Release 12). ETSI TS 123 402 V12.6.0 (2014-09)*. Retrieved October 23, 2014 from http://www.etsi.org/deliver/etsi_ts/123400_123499/123402/12.06.00_60/ts_123402v120600p.pdf

3GPP. (2014d). *Digital cellular telecommunications system (Phase 2+); Universal Mobile Telecommunications System (UMTS); General Packet Radio Service (GPRS); GPRS Tunnelling Protocol (GTP) across the Gn and Gp interface (3GPP TS 29.060 version 12.6.0 Release 12). ETSI TS 129 060 V12.6.0 (2014-10)*. Retrieved October 23, 2014 from http://www.etsi.org/deliver/etsi_ts/129000_129099/129060/12.06.00_60/ts_129060v120600p.pdf

Holbrook, H., Cain, B., & Haberman, B. (2006). *Using Internet Group Management Protocol Version 3 (IGMPv3) and Multicast Listener Discovery Protocol Version 2 (MLDv2) for Source-Specific Multicast. Internet Engineering Task Force RFC 4604*. Retrieved from https://tools.ietf.org/html/rfc4604

IETF. (2014a). *Cdni Status Pages*. Retrieved October 23, 2014 from http://tools.ietf.org/wg/cdni/

IETF. (2014b). *Mptcp Status Pages*. Retrieved October 23, 2014 from http://tools.ietf.org/wg/mptcp/

Law, W. (2013). *Maximizing the Pipe: Hybrid Protocols for Optimized OTT Delivery*. Retrieved October 23, 2014 from http://fr.slideshare.net/kfostervmx/multi-network-forum-ibcakamai-final

Lu, Z., & de Veciana, G. (2013). Optimizing Stored Video Delivery For Mobile Networks: The Value of Knowing the Future. In *Proceedings of the 32nd IEEE International Conference on Computer Communications* (pp. 2706-2714). IEEE. doi:10.1109/INFCOM.2013.6567079

Mohan, P., Nath, S., & Riva, O. (2013). Prefetching mobile ads: can advertising systems afford it? In *Proceedings of the 8th ACM European Conference on Computer Systems* (pp. 267-280). New York, NY: ACM. doi:10.1145/2465351.2465378

Nencioni, G., Sastry, N., Chandaria, J., & Crowcroft, J. (2013). Understanding and decreasing the network footprint of catch-up tv, In *Proceedings of the 22nd international conference on World Wide Web* (pp. 965-976). Geneva, Switzerland: International World Wide Web Conferences Steering Committee.

Octoshape. (2012). *Octoshape's Multicast Technology Suite: The Next-Gen CDN Alternative for Large-Scale, Cost-Optimized, Global HD Streaming*. Retrieved October 23, 2014 from http://www.octoshape.com/wp-content/uploads/2012/12/Multicast-Technical-Overview.pdf

Osseiran, A., Boccardi, F., Braun, V., Kusume, K., Marsch, P., Maternia, M., & Fallgren, M. et al. (2014). Scenarios for 5G Mobile and Wireless Communications: The Vision of the METIS Project. *IEEE Communications Magazine*, *52*(5), 26–35. doi:10.1109/MCOM.2014.6815890

Peterson, L., Davie, B., & van Brandenburg, R. (2014). *Framework for CDN Interconnection, draft-ietf-cdni-framework-14*. Retrieved June 6, 2014 from http://tools.ietf.org/html/draft-ietf-cdni-framework-14

3GPP. (2014e). *Universal Mobile Telecommunications System (UMTS); LTE; 3GPP Evolved Packet System (EPS); Evolved General Packet Radio Service (GPRS) Tunnelling Protocol for Control plane (GTPv2-C); Stage 3 (3GPP TS 29.274 version 12.6.0 Release 12). ETSI TS 129 274 V12.6.0 (2014-10)*. Retrieved October 23, 2014 from http://www.etsi.org/deliver/etsi_ts/129200_129299/129274/12.06.00_60/ts_129274v120600p.pdf

Sandvine. (2014). *Global Internet Phenomena Report - 1H2014*. Retrieved October 23, 2014 from https://www.sandvine.com/downloads/general/global-internet-phenomena/2014/1h-2014-global-internet-phenomena-report.pdf

Turbobytes. (2014). *Turbobytes Optimizer. How it works*. Retrieved October 23, 2014 http://www.turbobytes.com/products/optimizer/

Vida, R., & Costa, L. (2004). *Multicast Listener Discovery Version 2 (MLDv2) for IPv6. Internet Engineering Task Force RFC 3810*. Retrieved from https://tools.ietf.org/html/rfc3810

Wang, Z., Sun, L., Chen, X., Zhu, W., Liu, J., Chen, M., & Yang, S. (2012). Propagation-based social-aware replication for social video contents. In *Proceedings of the 20th ACM international conference on Multimedia* (pp. 29-38). New York, NY: ACM.

Wang, Z., Sun, L., Yang, S., & Zhu, W. (2011). Prefetching strategy in peer-assisted social video streaming, In *Proceedings of the 19th ACM international conference on Multimedia* (pp. 1233-1236). New York, NY: ACM. doi:10.1145/2072298.2071982

KEY TERMS AND DEFINITIONS

Caching: Caching is a special form of memory deployed in networks (on specific servers) as well as on computer architectures and web browsers. When the same object is requested several times, caching aims at avoiding this object to be accessed as many times from its origin location so as to minimize resource utilization and latency.

Cloud: Set of servers accessed remotely to manage, manipulate and store data.

Content Delivery Network Interconnection: A relationship between CDNs that enables one CDN to provide content delivery services on behalf of other CDNs.

Content Delivery Network: Set of servers specifically designed and deployed over one or several networks in order to optimize the storage and delivery of content objects (web objects, audiovisual live or on-demand content, large files, etc.).

Home Gateway: Equipment connecting the local area network of the home to a wide area network. It is essentially a modem (FTTH, ADSL, Cable, etc.) embedded in a box that provides routing and switching features.

Home Network: The private local network inside the end user's premises, including all the terminal devices connected to it. The home network is connected to the Internet via a Home Gateway.

HTTP Adaptive Streaming: Content delivery scheme based on HTTP. Content is segmented into small objects called chunks encoded at multiple bitrates. The client accesses the content by requesting one after the other the chunks that best fit the terminal and network conditions.

HTTP2.0: Network Protocol developed by the IETF Hypertext Transfer Protocol Bis (httpbis) Working Group as the next version of HTTP.

Over-The-Top: Designate a market player, application or service that does not rely upon telecom operators or Internet Service Providers, except for just getting connected to the end users via the Internet.

Prefetching: Process of prepositioning a content object closer to the entity that is expected to request it, and before this entity requests it.

Transparent Caching: Transparent caching is a special form of network caching, transparent for both the requesting and requested entities. The transparent caching node intercepts transparently the content request and delivers the requested content if its cache has a copy of it.

vCDN: Virtualization of the different components of the Content Delivery Network appliance.

Chapter 22
Future Networked Healthcare Systems:
A Review and Case Study

Rashid Mehmood
King Khalid University, Saudi Arabia

Muhammad Ali Faisal
COMSATS Institute of Information Technology, Pakistan

Saleh Altowaijri
Swansea University, UK

ABSTRACT

Future healthcare systems and organizations demand huge computational resources, and the ability for the applications to interact and communicate with each other, within and across organizational boundaries. This chapter aims to explore state-of-the-art of the healthcare landscape and presents an analysis of networked healthcare systems with a focus on networking traffic and architectures. To this end, the relevant technologies including networked healthcare architectures and performance studies, Health Level 7 (HL7), big data, and cloud computing, are reviewed. Subsequently, a study of healthcare systems, applications and traffic over local, metro, and wide area networks is presented using multi-hospital cross-continent scenarios. The network architectures for these systems are described. A detailed study to explore quality of service (QoS) performance for these healthcare systems with a range of applications, system sizes, and network sizes is presented. Conclusions are drawn regarding future healthcare systems and internet designs along with directions for future research.

1. INTRODUCTION

The Internet is going through rapid changes. We are seeing fundamental developments in the Internet design and the whole Internet landscape through technologies such as content delivery networks (CDNs), overlay networks, Internet radio, Internet television, Multicasting, P2PTV (peer-to-peer TV), etc. Devices, applications and traffic profiles that internet is to support are on

DOI: 10.4018/978-1-4666-8371-6.ch022

the rise. The Internet of Things (IoT) is driving the global adoption of IPv6. According to a 2011 report (Evans, 2011) by Cisco Internet Business Solutions Group (IBSG), the number of *things* connected to the Internet exceeded the world human population in 2008, the number almost doubled the human population in 2010, and it is predicted to reach 50 billion by 2020 with more than 6 devices connected to Internet per person in our world. These developments have the potential to transform and improve quality of life for all.

1.1 The Internet, Computing, and the Healthcare Industry

Cisco reports in a recent white paper (Cisco VNI, 2014), "Cisco Visual Networking Index: Forecast and Methodology, 2013–2018", 10 June 2014, that the global IP traffic has increased more than fivefold in the past 5 years, and will increase threefold over the next 5 years, surpassing the zettabyte threshold in 2016, reaching 1.6 zettabytes per year by 2018. Metro traffic will surpass long-haul traffic in 2015, and will account for 62 percent of total IP traffic by 2018. Metro traffic will grow nearly twice as fast as long-haul traffic from 2013 to 2018, due in part to the increasingly significant role of CDNs, which will carry 55% of Internet traffic by 2018, up from 36 percent in 2013. Global fixed broadband speeds will nearly triple by 2018, reaching 42 Mbps, up from 16 Mbps in 2013. IP video traffic (TV, video on demand (VoD), Internet, and P2P) globally will be 80% to 90% of global consumer traffic by 2018. Global mobile data traffic will grow three times faster than the fixed IP traffic from 2013 to 2018. Business IP traffic will grow by a factor of 2 between 2013 and 2018 due to the increasing adoption of video communications in enterprises.

The trends given above show a near-radical change in the Internet usage, applications, etc. and hence require fundamental changes in the Internet designs and appropriate deployment paths. Moreover, various industrial and government sectors, and other developments, such as transportation (see e.g. (TrafficLand, 2014)), healthcare (Microsoft, 2014), distance learning (Harvard Extension School, 2014), smart cities ('Smart Cities', 2014) are increasingly relying on the Internet for communications. Healthcare is now considered the largest global industry (McKinsey & Company, 2014) with an increasing ICT penetration rate. Big data and Internet of Things (IoT) are also set to drive radical changes in the healthcare systems landscape. The emerging technologies of big data, IoT, and broader ICT, in healthcare will enhance and accelerate the convergence between the activities of the healthcare professional and stakeholders, including patients, clinicians, administrators, healthcare providers, payers, researchers, and policy makers (Piai & Claps, 2013). They all try to coordinate their activities with the aim to provide personalized and preventive healthcare to patients, reduced healthcare risks, improve systems and operational efficiencies, and reduce healthcare costs. Patients particularly will benefit from this convergence because the healthcare data that they produce can help them in making more informed decisions about their health, preventing diseases and staying healthy. Moreover they can play a more proactive role in managing their health throughout their clinical pathways. Indeed with the emerging concepts in urban developments such as smart cities, a coordinated healthcare approach like the one described above can manage health for the whole society at city, country or global levels.

In brief, the future healthcare systems will leverage the technologies such as big data and IoT to provide personalized and preventive healthcare. It substantiates our view that the future healthcare systems and organizations will demand huge computational resources, and the ability for the applications to interact and communicate with each other, within and across organizational boundaries. Internet, that provides connectivity for healthcare systems, would hence have to support a growing network traffic generated by an increasing plethora of mobile and fixed healthcare applications.

1.2 Aims, Objectives, and Contributions

The aim of this chapter is to explore state-of-the-art of the healthcare landscape and present an analysis of future healthcare systems with a focus on networking traffic and architectures. We are particularly interested in tracing the developments in healthcare systems as well as broader ICT technologies that are shaping the future of healthcare. Our objective here is also to analyze the behavior of future healthcare systems particularly related to networking and applications generated traffic. The contributions of this chapter fall within two areas. Firstly, a review of the state-of-the-art of the healthcare landscape is given. The relevant literature is reviewed to trace the evolution of healthcare systems from earlier times to the current status, and the broader directions that the healthcare industry is taking to move towards personalized and preventive healthcare. The technologies and developments that are shaping the future of healthcare systems are described. The first area of contributions collectively provides the motivation and requirements for the future healthcare systems, as well as for the design of the Internet that will provide the connectivity for these systems. Secondly, a simulation based case study is presented in order to analyze the behavior of future healthcare systems. The case study is designed using the requirements and findings gained from the literature review. The focus of the case study is on healthcare systems, applications, traffic and networks. A range of configurations for healthcare systems, applications, traffic profiles, and networks are used.

The rest of the Chapter is organized as follows. Section 2.1 provides a review of the changing landscape of healthcare, healthcare systems, and healthcare applications. A review of architectures and performance studies of networked healthcare systems is given Section 2.2. The role of (Health Level 7) HL7 in improving interoperability of networked healthcare systems is explored in Section 2.3. The role of big data, grid computing and cloud computing in the evolution of healthcare systems is examined in Sections 2.4, 2.5.1, 2.5.2, respectively. Requirements for healthcare-related networking come from collaborative and distributed healthcare applications. A major part of the collaborative and distributed healthcare applications was started by the grid computing community. Moreover, computing requirements and other properties of networked healthcare systems are important to be considered for Internet architectures because, though exchange of healthcare messages (such as those based on HL7) may seem an insignificant network loads, these are going to grow in size as well as the frequency of messages. Particularly for High Performance Computing (HPC) applications, there will be a need for very low latency network support. We have therefore reviewed literature on high performance computing applications of healthcare with grid computing. Cloud computing and big data are the current technologies for high performance computing in healthcare and hence the literatures on these are reviewed as well. The network and system architectures for the healthcare systems that we have simulated are described in Section 3. We use multi-hospital scenarios spread across continents including Asia, Europe and North America. A detailed study to explore quality of service (QoS) performance for these healthcare systems with a range of applications, system sizes, and network sizes is presented in Section 4. Finally, in Section5, conclusions are drawn from the study regarding future healthcare systems and Internet designs along with directions for future research.

2. STATE OF THE ART

2.1 The Changing Landscape of Healthcare Systems and Applications

The healthcare sector and generally many other areas such as transportation, finance industry, etc. have gone through a rapid growth recently due to the exponential growth in ICT. The increasing role and benefits of ICT in healthcare are becoming visible in the enhancement and emergence of technologies such as healthcare telematics, health informatics, epidemiology, bioengineering and Healthcare Information Systems (HIS). We can now imagine a near future where healthcare providers can port powerful analytics and decision support tools to mobile computing devices (smartphones, tablets, laptops, etc.) aiding clinicians at the point of care helping them with synthesis of data from multiple sources, optimization of clinical workflows, and context-aware decision making. The crowdsourcing technologies are also coming to healthcare augmenting people in their decision making processes for their wellbeing though the complexity of such a setting in healthcare domain, including appropriate models (reimbursement, who holds the liability), are posing challenges (Fluckinger, 2014).

The major drivers for ICT-based healthcare include demands for increased access to and quality of healthcare, rising healthcare costs, system inefficiencies, variations in quality of care, high prevalence of medical errors, greater public analysis of government spending, ageing population, and the fact that patients and the public want a greater say in decisions about their health and healthcare. The scientific developments that are yet to reach their required potential for providing personalized healthcare include genetic and molecular research, translation of knowledge into clinical practice, new processes and relationships in product development, and health information technology and knowledge management (United States Department of Health and Human Services, 2007). However, we believe that the major hurdles for the healthcare industry in realizing the full potential of ICT include the social reasons (e.g. sensitivity of health-related issues and data, privacy and public trust) and lack of business models (Mitton & Donaldson, 2004), and (Roth, Lim, Pevnick, Asch, & McGlynn, 2009). Though the efforts for the realization of networked healthcare systems are being made for long (see e.g. (Kaihara, 1994)), the vision of personalized healthcare is yet to be realized fully.

Goldstein et al. (2007) in their book "Medical Informatics 20/20", published in 2007, state that the key management strategies that healthcare executives should be focused on over the coming years include Collaboration, Open Systems, and Innovation (COSI). The key health information technologies (HIT), according to them (Goldstein et al.) to be deployed over the next decade include Electronic Health Record (EHR), Personal Health Record (PHR), and Health Information Exchange (HIE) systems. Goldstein et al. projected that by 2020, 80% of health care provider organizations will have implemented EHR systems in the US; 80% of the general population will have started using PHR systems in the US; and 80% of EHR and PHR systems in the U.S. will be linked via HIE networks. Groen and Goldstein (2009) present their vision of Medical Informatics 2040 and believe that transformation of healthcare will be enabled through the implementation of technologies including genomic information systems & bio-repositories integrated with EHR systems; nanotechnology & implantable health IT systems interfaced to EHR and PHR systems, advanced user interface solutions, e.g. wearable systems, health apps, and eGame technologies; health information exchange (HIE) with other industries/sectors, e.g. banking, security, manufacturing, pharma, etc; Televideo & Home-based TeleHealth solutions interconnecting patients with health care providers; medical robotic devices interfaced to health IT (HIT) systems; and complementary & alternative medicine (CAM) information systems modules integrated with EHR systems.

The United States Department of Health and Human Services (2007) envisions Personalized health care and gives a perspective on how far and how quickly we have come by comparing treatment strategies of diseases (cancer, diabetes and heart attacks) used by physicians in the 1940s with the contemporary times. The times are changing. At the Apple Worldwide Developers Conference, WWDC 2014, June 2–6, Apple introduced the mobile health platform HealthKit, a cloud API which will be available for iOS 8 later during 2014 (Carr, 2014; Chouffani, 2014). HealthKit would benefit by the Apple's partnership on this enterprise with Mayo Clinic and software company Epic Systems. The HealthKit API will provide the users with an interface for accessing to and sharing of their personal health records (PHRs). The HealthKit will use the patient education research done by the Mayo Clinic. The information collected through the Apple Health App will be integrated with the Epic's EHR systems allowing the use of Epic's software tools. The Apple Health app provides a convenient entry point to personalized health services. Apple has also provided information for developers and extended an invitation to discuss the possibilities for interaction of various devices with the system. Potentially the Apple mHeath App will be able to unite feeds from many health monitors and interact with a hospital's HER systems allowing real time personalized healthcare. Samsung has already released its S Heath app for Android platform that helps to "become healthier and happier by helping you manage four basic areas of your life: Heart rate, Food, Exercise, and Sleep" (Samsung Electronics Co, 2013). These are an important milestone in actualizing the vision of personalized healthcare. We would like to see more applications and collaborations coming particularly from the Open Source community and it appears that revolution in personalized healthcare space is coming.

2.1.1 Advanced Video Communications and Healthcare

The Cisco VNI forecast paper (Cisco VNI, 2014) states that the IP video traffic will continue to dominate the global consumer traffic (80% to 90%). Healthcare industry is also adopting video communications to provide a range of novel usages such as video consultations where hospitals and healthcare authorities need to cover large geographical areas with low population density, training for faculty, coordination and administration of staff, patient education and training etc. For example, Vidyo provides video conferencing solutions telehealth and critical care telemedicine applications, such as for specialists in the field of neurology to schedule virtual office visits with patients in rural areas where hospitals and clinics may not have an on-staff neurologist (Vidyo, 2014). Polycom through its telemedicine video conferencing system is also providing better healthcare options to passengers and crew onboard ships in remote locations linking the medical expertise of a major city hospital through video communications (Polycom, 2014). Citrix solutions for healthcare are aimed at empowering patient-centered care by providing clinicians and staff anywhere, any device access to the healthcare resources, and increasing operational efficiency while ensuring patient privacy and compliance (Bitpipe, 2014). Cisco HealthPresence software, using the network as a platform, integrates high-definition video, advanced audio, third-party medical devices, and collaboration tools. It provides highly secure and scalable deployment for collaboration, a choice of interoperable video endpoints to flexibly support HealthPresence sessions from any location, and integrated workflow features such as appointment queuing, presence, and access to electronic medical records (Cisco HealthPresence, 2014).

2.2 Networked Healthcare System Architectures and Performance Studies

This section presents a review of the literature of the various works on the architecture of networked healthcare systems and the studies to understand networked systems performance. In discussing the architectures of networked healthcare systems, we will also highlight on the various networked healthcare applications being used and developed. Concepts of connected systems for healthcare have been envisioned for long time. For example, Kaihara (1994) reported on a networked workstation system for (international) exchange of characters and images that was being built at the University of Tokyo Hospital. He discussed the circumstances where physicians would like to exchange information with each other, workstation specifications (e.g. to display images and videos), the location of data. Kaihara used the discussions on these system requirements to report on a networked system of approximately 300 workstations and a mainframe that was supposed to be installed in November 1993 and operational in July 1994. He reported on the healthcare networked system architecture that the system will be connected to the University campus LAN (with a gateway to the Internet) through which any system user will have access to the library databases as well as to the Internet. He reported that the coordination of the campus LAN and UMIN to provide medical community with dedicated data exchange was underway. The University Medical Information Network (UMIN) was a private network linking 35 national university hospitals through a special communication protocol called N-l. He stated the possibility for outside general practitioners to have access to this system, the need for service level agreements for this access to healthcare information, the need for the standardization of data exchange, and the administrative issues related to the access and charging of data to external users. More works of similar nature and from similar era include (Buffone & Beck, 1994; Hammond et al., 1991; Lemke et al., 1994; Orthner, Scherrer, & Dahlen, 1994; Patil, Silva, & Swartout, 1994).

Aminian and Naji (2013) propose a hospital healthcare monitoring system based on wireless sensor networks. Specifically, the monitoring system monitors physiological parameters from multiple patient bodies through a coordinator node attached to the patient's body that collects the signals from the wireless sensors and sends them to the base station. Continuous monitoring of physiological parameters is an important application area of healthcare and has major implication on the design of network that connects sensors, analysis applications, physicians, healthcare systems and providers. For example, as exemplified in this paper, monitoring of blood pressure and heart rate of a pregnant woman, and the heart rate/movement of the fetus, is a vital requirement for managing her health. The sensors attached to a patient's body form a wireless body sensor network (WBSN) and provide information related to heart rate, blood pressure and other health related parameters. A framework for a unified middleware based on SIP (Session Initiation Protocol) to enable mobile healthcare applications over heterogeneous networks is proposed in (Soomro & Schmitt, 2011). Their motivation is the need for anytime anywhere delivery of healthcare services that will in turn require operation over heterogeneous networks. Their approach is to use the proposed unified middleware to isolate applications from mobility management and other transport/discovery related tasks. Zhang et al. (2013), motivated by the need for lower delays and reliable communications for healthcare applications, propose a Best-fit Carrier Dial-up (BCD) algorithm for LTE-A (Long Term Evolution-Advanced) mobile networks that can dynamically schedule demanded bandwidth for GBR-oriented (Guaranteed Bit Rate) healthcare applications. Their proposed algorithm is compared with Carrier Aggregation (CA) by analyzing performance of medical images and consulting videos transmission over LTE. Results in terms of average delays and satisfaction rate for images and video against the number of UEs (User Equipment) are compared.

Alemdar and Ersoy provide a survey of wireless sensor networks (WSNs) for healthcare in (Alemdar & Ersoy, 2010). An overview of the design issues for healthcare monitoring systems using WSNs is provided along with a discussion of the benefits of these systems. Several applications and prototypes of WSN healthcare monitoring systems are reviewed from the literature, as well as challenges and open research problems for the design of these systems. Dolezel et al. (2011) presented a study on transmission of large volumes of image data over low capacity links considering response times using the OPNET modeler. They used a hospital with 8 nodes producing images. They also considered the influence of controlled queue management, namely WFQ (Weighted Fair Queuing). They looked at the FTP response times for the transfer of these images over the network with different link bitrates (5Mbps, 10Mbps and 20 Mbps), with and without WFQ. Assaad and Fayek (2006) presented a study of end-to-end network performance within and between three hospitals in the Central-West region of Ontario with the aim to examine the healthcare applications requirements. The OPNET modeler is used to study the network performance. Five applications were used in this study; database, HTTP, FTP, email, and videoconferencing (see OPNET modeler documentation for specification of each of these applications). Results were presented and discussed for throughput and queuing delays for servers and the main router.

2.3 The HL7 Standards and Networked Healthcare

HL7, Health Level Seven International, is a not-for-profit organization that was formed in 1987. It is accredited by ANSI (American National Standards Institute) and its aim is to "create the best and most widely used standards in healthcare" (HL7, 2014). HL7 is "dedicated to providing a comprehensive framework and related standards for the exchange, integration, sharing, and retrieval of electronic health information that supports clinical practice and the management, delivery and evaluation of health services" (HL7, 2014). "Level Seven" refers to the seventh layer (the application layer) of the International Organization for Standardization (ISO) seven-layer communications model for Open Systems Interconnection (OSI).

A number of works on HL7 middleware and the developments of relevant mappings have been reported in the literature, see e.g. (Alam et al., 2011; Calamai & Giarre, 2012; Cuenca et al., 2012; Liu & Huang, 2012; Nie et al., 2013; Sharma at al., 2012). A multi-agent system to support patients in their search of healthcare services was presented by De Meo et al. (2011). The information about the patients and services was embedded in the system using HL7 directives. Bender and Sartipi (2013) look at the potential of HL7 FHIR (Fast Health Interoperable Resources) to provide interoperability for healthcare systems. Yuksel and Dogac (2011) address the interoperability problems between medical devices and diverse healthcare applications by using the ISO/IEEE 11073 Domain Information Model, DIM, to derive an HL7 v3 Refined Message Information Model (RMIM) of the medical device domain from the HL7 v3 Reference Information Mode (RIM). This enables the medical device data in their developed RMIM format to be transformed into HL7-based standard interfaces. However, none of these works have looked at the performance and architecture of the networks that will support future communications based on HL7 or otherwise. The literature provides increasing evidence that healthcare information exchange over network using HL7 or similar future standards is rapidly growing due to the need for interoperability between healthcare data, applications and systems. Consequently, the information exchange would impact the network architectural requirements in the near future.

2.4 Big Data and Networked Healthcare Systems

The cost of healthcare, according to World Health Organization is mostly due to system and operational inefficiencies, and missed disease-prevention opportunities. Big data analytics can minimize these efficiencies and improve the clinical processes resulting in better, preventive, personalized healthcare; estimated to save billions in the healthcare sector alone with virtually unquantifiable impact (PRETZ, 2014).

IDC, International Data Corporation, defines Big Data technologies as "a new generation of technologies and architectures, designed to economically extract value from very large volumes of a wide variety of data produced every day, by enabling high velocity capture, discovery, and/or analysis" (Piai & Claps, 2013). These four Vs (value, volume, variety, velocity) would have a key impact on the future architectures of global networks and healthcare systems. In terms of variety, we have around 15% structured data such as transactional data in databases, and 85% unstructured data coming from social media, tweets, videos blogs, emails, physicians notes, sensor feeds, etc. The velocity of big data is concerned with production and capture of data, which in turn affect the analysis, discovery and decision process. The future applications and systems would work in increasingly dynamic environments hence velocity of incoming and outgoing data streams is an important design dimension for networks and systems. Consider that decoding the human genome took 10 years the first time it was done. It can now be done in one week. The value of big data is the driver; it can potentially transform the whole social and economic landscape, such as the industries including healthcare, operations management, risk management, and sustainability (Piai & Claps, 2013). Therefore, big data is set to affect the future network traffic and hence the network architecture. Particularly, a class of distributed HPC applications that require access to data spread across the globe will demand low network latencies and this may become a class of priority traffic over metro and wide area networks.

2.5 Networked Healthcare with Grid and Cloud Computing

Healthcare applications demand increasingly large amounts of computational and communication resources. Moreover, these applications require access to large amounts of data within and outside the boundaries of the organization. The access patterns are typically dynamic and this dynamic nature of data and computational interaction (e.g. service orchestration, service access) is to grow; it is being only limited by the granularity of interaction that the current applications and systems are able to provide and sustain. We have already seen in Section 2.4 the motivations for big data in healthcare sector. In this section, we look briefly look at grid computing and cloud computing, the two technologies that are providing foundations for networked healthcare.

2.5.1 Grid Computing and Networked Healthcare

The next generation healthcare infrastructure will have to support a diverse range of applications and their ability to communicate with each other within and across the organizational boundaries. Moreover, increasing requirements on compliance with environmental and economic sustainability demand efficient and green use of resources by the infrastructure. Grid computing we believe was the first widely used technology to address such large-scale interaction of applications and data across organizational boundaries. It provided (economic and environmental) efficiency through its ability to harness the idle power of disparate resources to dynamically provide high performance and throughput to large computing applications, as well as gradual and smooth technology deployment options that it may provide with minimum disruption. At the heart of this endeavor was the concept of virtual organizations (VOs), i.e., coordinated resource sharing and problem solving in dynamic, multi-institutional virtual organizations. This is not meant simply to be a file exchange between applications across organizational boundaries, but it is rather a direct access to data, computational and other resources as may be required by a range of collaborative problem-solving and resource brokering strategies emerging in industry, science, and engineering (Foster, Kesselman, & Tuecke, 2001).

Grid computing has played a key role in the rapid growth of healthcare and other sectors that require large processing power, data storage and retrieval. However, the most important characteristic of grid computing that has fostered this rapid growth in healthcare (and other sectors) is its ability to facilitate collaborations between various stakeholders and enable dynamic interactions between various applications beyond organizational boundaries. The deployment of grid computing has enabled researchers to examine diseases and rare conditions. Additionally, grid computing has provided healthcare professionals with new ways to analyze and treat patients. Moreover, by integrating the medical data available, specialists have been able to start personalizing treatments for patients. Grid computing has shaped the future of healthcare, collaborative research and business between healthcare organizations and other stakeholders. See (Altowaijri et al., 2010), for further details and references on grid-based healthcare.

2.5.2 Cloud Computing and Networked Healthcare

NIST defines Cloud computing (Mell & Grance, 2011) as "a model for enabling ubiquitous, convenient, on-demand network access to a shared pool of configurable computing resources (e.g., networks, servers, storage, applications, and services) that can be rapidly provisioned and released with minimal management effort or service provider interaction." Note the emphasized words in the definition such as shared, configurable, rapidly provisioned/released, minimal management effort. Grid computing allows sharing of resources which is adopted by cloud computing vendors who own the resources and allow their sharing by their customers. It is possible to create VOs by multiple individuals or organizations by renting computational resources from the same cloud computing vendor. In this case, in contrast to grid computing, the administrations and interoperability issues may be dealt by the cloud computing vendor.

A whitepaper by Cisco (Macias & Thomas, 2011) looks at how cloud computing is benefitting the government, education and healthcare organizations. A whitepaper (Hitachi Data Systems, 2012) by Hitachi Data Systems examines the different aspects of cloud adoption and how healthcare providers can move forward with a cloud-based solution. A number of other white papers/works have also discussed cloud computing in healthcare including Cloud Computing for Healthcare Organizations: Is there a Silver Lining (Advisors, 2010) by Aspen Advisors, Cloud Computing: Building a New Foundation for Healthcare (IBM, 2011) by IBM, Impact of Cloud Computing on Healthcare (Cloud Standards Customer Council, 2012) by Cloud Standards Customers Council, and Your Cloud in Healthcare (VMware, Inc, 2014) by VMware.

Now that we have completed the background and literature review, it is useful to mention here our earlier work relevant to this chapter, i.e. healthcare related and general network modeling and analysis. Performance analysis of multimedia traffic (video, voice and text) over wireless ad hoc networks was presented in (Alturki et al., 2008). End to end Service Modeling of multimedia (video, voice and text) over Wi-Fi networks within metropolitan area network environments was explored in (Alturki et al., 2009). This work was extended in (Mehmood et al., 2011) where we focused on VoIP and presented a novel analysis methodology combining simulations and Markov modeling. A Markovian study of healthcare organizations and a review of solution methodologies for Markov chains was presented in (Mehmood & Lu, 2011). A scalable multimedia QoS architecture for ad hoc networks was introduced in (Mehmood et al., 2009) and later extended in (Mehmood & Alturki, 2011). Cross-Layer QoS and provisioning for multimedia applications (video, voice and text) over wireless Ad hoc Networks was reported in (Alturki et al., 2012). An overview of our work on multimedia communications over wireless networks, both infrastructure and ad hoc networks, was reported in (Mehmood et al., 2013); a classification (based on an extensive literature) of ad hoc networks design and QoS for multimedia communications into ten dimensions was also reported.

3. NETWORK ARCHITECTURE AND METHODOLOGY

In this section, we detail our methodology for the analysis of healthcare systems. Our focus is to explore the network behavior and requirements of future healthcare systems. The analysis is carried out through simulations in OPNET (Riverbed, 2014). From now on, we will refer to it as the OPNET modeler.

3.1 The Network Architecture

Figure 1 depicts the high-level diagram of the healthcare system that we have simulated in this chapter. The simulations include a total of 12 hospitals located in four cities around the world. The intercity hospital networks are connected through high speed IP-based links. The OPNET modeler provides models for a range of communication technologies, components and devices. For the links between cities, we have used OC-48 links, synchronous optical networking (SONET) fiber optic networks, which provide 2488.32 Mbps data rates.

The cities that we have used in the simulations are Abha and Riyadh (Kingdom of Saudi Arabia, KSA), Birmingham (UK) and Washington DC (USA). There is a total of three hospitals in each city, making a total of 12 hospitals in the whole healthcare systems network. Figure 2 depicts the IntraCity network for the Abha City. The Saudi-German Hospital, the Abha General Hospital, and Aseer Hospital are connected to each other, and to the Abha City Data Center, via routers and 44.736 Mbps links. The three hospitals and the Abha City Data Center are connected to the hospitals in the other cities via the InterCity links via a separate router called the "Abha City Healthcare Systems Router". These InterCity (or InterCountry) links connect Abha city hospital network to the three other cities via OC-48 SONET links (Riyadh, Birmingham and Washington DC: see Figure 1). Figure 2 depicts that the Abha City Data Centre is also connected to the other cities via an OC-48 link, so to provide other cities access to the data held by the Abha City Data Center. The IntraCity networks for the other three cities are the same as for the Abha city (the three hospitals, routers and the data center). The Abha hospitals named in this paper are actual hospitals. However, the network and the applications as well as the data are developed by the authors to explore healthcare systems behavior and performance. The hospital names are used for demonstration purposes; the hospitals have no liability whatsoever and cannot be held responsible for anything in this chapter. The setup with separate data centers for each city allows the cities to have their own data spaces and permission to access the data through SLAs. These data centers may have local replicas in multiple cities, for example, to allow lower communication latencies and higher quality of service (QoS).

Each hospital is designed to have similar application and network environments. There are three buildings in each hospital. Each building has two floors. The details of the network for each floor are the same. The clients running various applications (video, FTP, and database) on each floor

Figure 1. The high-level diagram of the healthcare system network

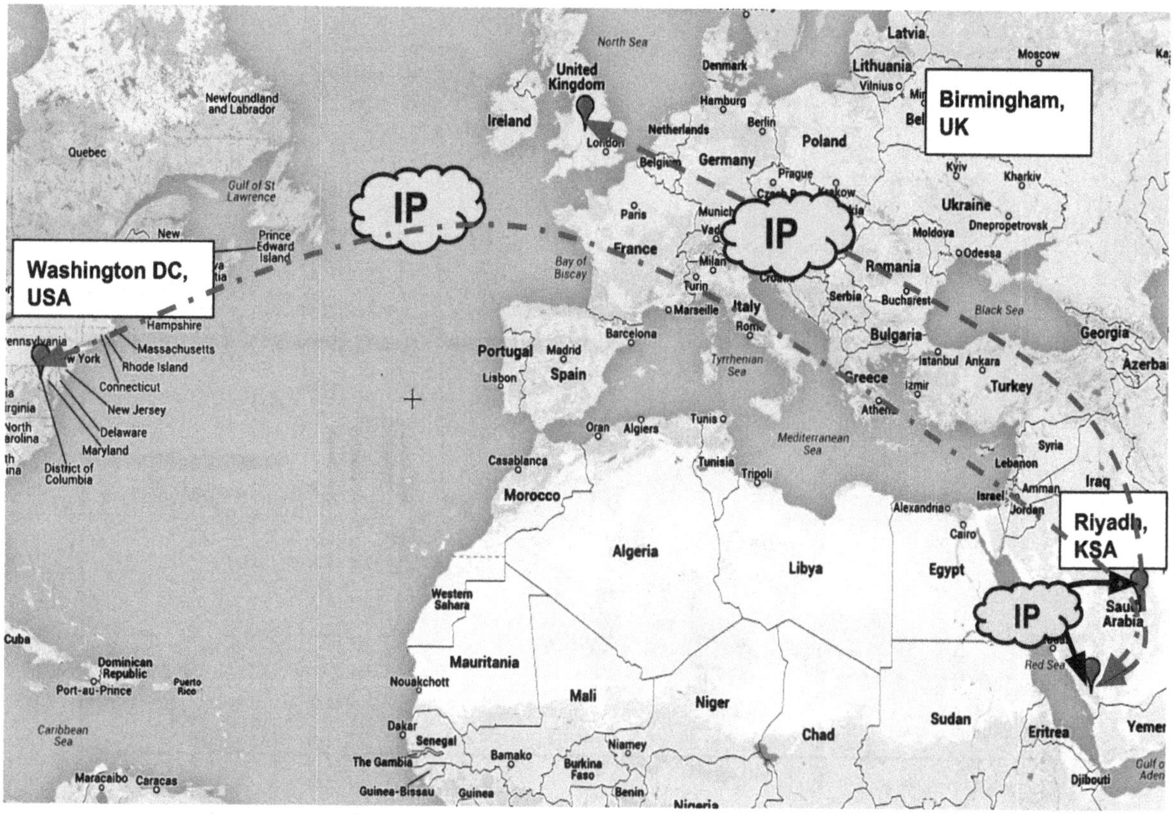

are connected through 100BASE-T to the Floor1 and Floor2 switches. These floor switches then connect to the Intra-Hospital networks through separate building switches. The number of clients and applications vary according to various simulation scenarios and these will become apparent later on when we discuss application scenarios. The IP network behavior for the three InterCity / InterCountry networks between the four cities is captured using the IP Cloud model provided by the OPNET modeler. Specifically, we use the "ip32_cloud" node model which represents an IP cloud supporting up to 32 serial line interfaces at a selectable data rate through which IP traffic can be modeled. Finally, Figure 3 shows the Inter-Country network between Abha and Washington DC. The networks between Abha and other cities are similar except that their behavior depends on various characteristics including the distance between the cities.

3.2 Methodology for the Analysis of the Healthcare Systems

We have created a range of applications and networking scenarios to explore the network behavior and requirements of future healthcare systems. The details of these scenarios are discussed in this section. For the analysis purposes, we can think of our overall study to have three dimensions: (a) mix of healthcare applications and respective traffic loads/bitrates; (b) size of the system in terms of nodes involved in healthcare networked applications; and (c) type and geographical size of the system networks.

Table 1 lists the details of the first two dimensions (applications/bitrates and network sizes in

Figure 2. IntraCity Network for Abha with three hospitals and a data centre

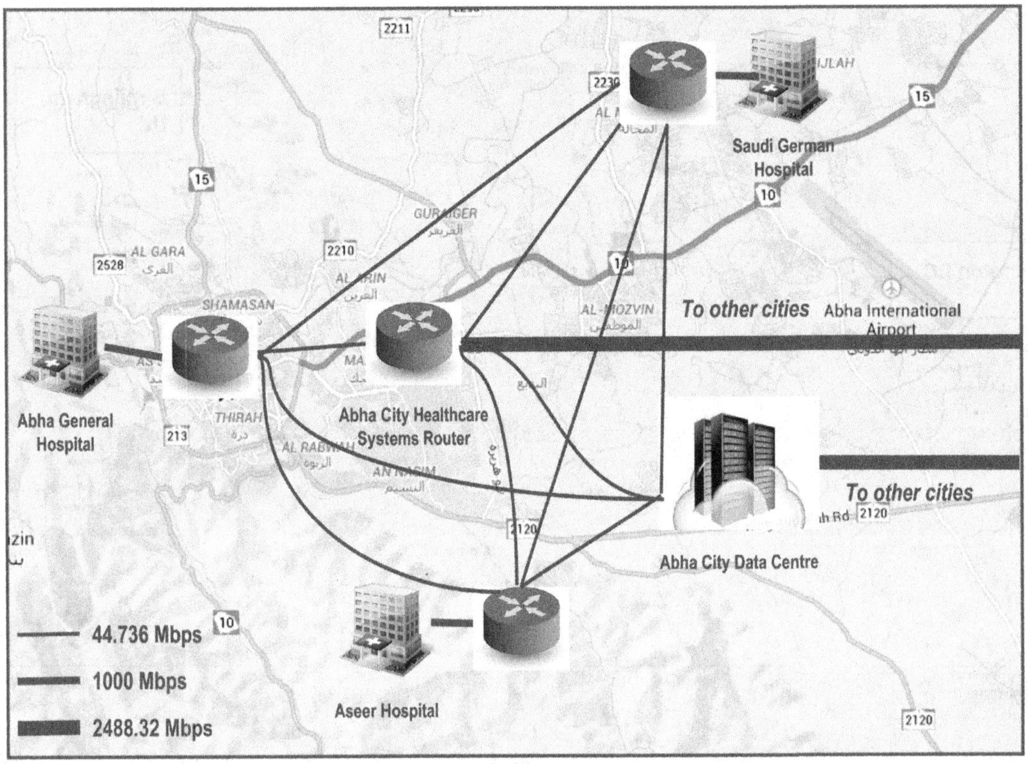

Figure 3. InterCountry network between Abha and Washington DC

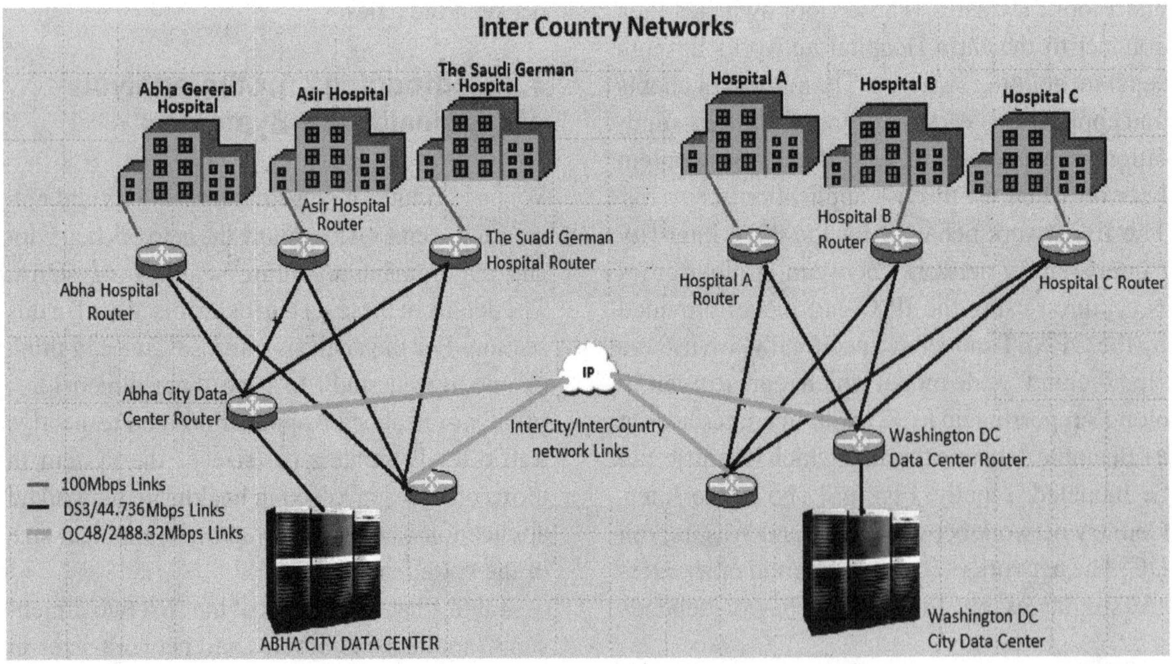

nodes). The third dimension (type and geographical size of the system networks) relates to the Wide Area Network (WAN) characteristics of the network and it will become apparent as we discuss the details of networks and application traffic in this section. The first column gives the number of nodes in the network (96, 192, 384, 768 and 1248). The sizes increase in multiples of 2 except for the network with 1248 nodes. The top row gives details of the data types as follows. There are five Traffic Profiles that we have used in these simulations: Low (L), Medium (M), High (H), Very High (VH), and Ultra High (UH). Each Traffic Profile has three types of applications (database, FTP and video) but with different bitrates. We have used exponential distribution for the arrival processes of these applications with one second arrival time.

Table 2 gives additional (general) details for the Traffic Profiles. The Low (L) profile (see Table 2) comprises one database transaction per second (each transaction comprises 512 bytes of request communication and 100 bytes of reply communication), one FTP transaction per second (512 bytes of file request and 50 bytes of file reply), and 2 way video stream (each-way stream containing 10 frames with 500 bytes per frame). The bitrates for the other four general traffic profiles are detailed in the table (Table 2). The VH and UH traffic profiles are determined by the H traffic profile as follows:

$$UH \cong 4 \times VH \cong 16 \times \mathrm{H}$$

See Table 1, the VH96 profiles generate almost 4 times the traffic load of each of the database, FTP and video applications (note that the database and FTP traffic includes requests which is fixed at 500 bytes; see Table 2). The UH96 profile generates four times the traffic load of VH96 and 16 times the traffic load of H96. Column 2 (Traffic Profiles) of Table 1 lists the details for traffic profiles specific to the networks of different sizes; L96 refers to the L traffic profile for the network with 96 nodes, M192 refers to M traffic profile for the network with 192 nodes, H1248 refers to the H traffic for the network with 1248 nodes, and so on. Column 3 to Column 5 list details for database, FTP and video bitrates, respectively, for specific traffic profiles. Column 6 and Column 7 list the total traffic load for the traffic profiles in Bytes per seconds (Bps) and Megabits per seconds (Mbps), respectively. Let us explain the (specific) traffic profile by taking a couple of examples. The L192 traffic profile includes (a) database applications running one transaction (600 bytes each) per second between 72 client nodes and the database servers, (b) FTP applications running one file request and transfer (550 bytes each) per second between 72 client nodes and the FTP servers, (c) video conferencing connection of 10 frames (of 500 bytes each) per second between 48 client nodes and the video servers. For each application, half of the clients are located in Abha and the other half in one of the other cities (either of Riyadh, Birmingham or Washington DC). Half of the clients in the Abha city access the servers (database, FTP and video servers) located in the Abha City Data Center (we call it IntraCity Communications) while the other half of the clients in Abha city hospitals access the servers (database, FTP and video servers) located in the data center of one of the other cities (we call it InterCity or InterCountry communications). This is because in any one scenario or simulation the networks between only two cities are considered. The total traffic inclusive of all applications and nodes is 5.64 Mbps. This distribution of applications and nodes for the network between Abha and Washington DC cities with 768 nodes is given in Table 3 (also see Figure 3 that depicts the InterCountry network between Abha and Washington DC). Similarly half of the nodes in the hospitals in (e.g.) Birmingham are communicating with the Data Center in Washington DC while the other half of the nodes are communicating with the Abha City Data Center.

Table 1. Network Traffic Profiles, Their Respective Attributes and Traffic Intensities

Nodes	Traffic Profiles	Database Query	FTP	Video Conferencing	Total Traffic	
	(Bytes/s)	(Bytes/s)	(Bytes/s)	(Bytes/s)	(Bytes/s)	(Mbps)
96	**L96**	612×36	562×36	500×10×24×2		
		22032	20232	240000	282264	2.82
	M96	662×36	587×36	800×10×24×2		
		23832	21132	384000	428964	4.28
	H96	712×36	612×36	1000×10×24×2		
		25632	22032	480000	527664	5.27
	VH96	1312×36	912×36	4000×10×24×2		
		47232	32832	1920000	2000064	20.00
	UH96	3712×36	2112×36	16000×10×24×2		
		133632	76032	7680000	7889664	78.89
192	**L192**	612×72	562×72	500×10×48×2		
		44064	40464	480000	564528	5.64
	M192	662×72	587×72	800×10×48×2		
		47664	42264	768000	857928	8.57
	H192	712×72	612×72	1000×10×48×2		
		51264	44064	960000	1055328	10.5
384	**L384**	612×144	562×144	500×10×96×2		
		88128	80928	960000	1129056	11.29
	M384	662×144	587×144	800×10×96×2		
		95328	84528	1536000	1715856	17.15
	H384	712×144	612×144	1000×10×96×2		
		102528	88128	1920000	2110656	21.10
768	**L768**	612×288	562×288	500×10×192×2		
		176256	161856	1920000	2258112	22.58
	M768	662×288	587×288	800×10×192×2		
		190656	169056	3072000	3431712	34.31
	H768	712×288	612×288	1000×10×192×2		
		205056	176256	3840000	4221312	42.21
1248	**L1248**	612×624	562×624	500×10×288×2		
		381888	350688	2880000	3612576	36.12
	M1248	662×624	587×624	800×10×288×2		
		413088	366288	4608000	5387376	53.87
	H1248	712×624	612×624	1000×10×288×2		
		444288	381888	5760000	6586176	65.86

Table 2. General Traffic Profiles and respective bitrates

	Database (Bps)	FTP (Bps)	Video (Bps)
L	512 + 100	512 + 50	500×10×2
M	512 + 150	512 + 75	800×10×2
H	512 + 200	512 + 100	1000×10×2
VH	512 + 800	512 + 400	4000×10×2
UH	512 + 3200	512 + 1600	16000×10×2

4. NETWORKED HEALTHCARE APPLICATIONS: SIMULATIONS AND ANALYSIS

We now present an analysis of the results collected from simulations. The results are analyzed according to the three dimensions that we had mentioned in the previous section (see Page 24). The results are presented for each application for their IntraCity, InterCity/InterCountry, and Global performance. The results are grouped into each traffic profile, L92, M92 and so on (see Table 1). Each network is analyzed for their application based performance (database, FTP and video). Note that though we analyze performance for applications one at a time (database followed by FTP and video), the various configurations of healthcare system are loaded simultaneously with all three applications (see Table 1). We are short of space in this chapter and therefore have not provided the definitions of network related statistics (database query response time, jitter, etc.); see relevant RFCs and the OPNET documentation.

4.1 Abha – Riyadh Networked System

Figure 4 shows results of IntraCity, InterCity and global database response times for all the five network sizes and all five traffic profiles. Let us explain the results for the network with 96 nodes. The amount of traffic sent by the nodes for L96 network is listed in Table 1. Figure 4 shows that the database IntraCity Response Time is 0.4825 milliseconds (ms) (see 'IntraCity', the top of the three rows at the bottom). It is supposed to be

Table 3. Distribution of clients and applications for a network of 768 nodes between Abha and Washington DC cities

Washington DC				Abha			
Hospital	Application			Hospital	Application		
	FTP Clients	Database Clients	Video Clients		FTP Clients	Database Clients	Video Clients
A	48	48	32	Abha General	48	48	32
B	48	48	32	Asir	48	48	32
C	48	48	32	Saudi German	48	48	32
Total (Apps)	144	144	96		144	144	96
Total (City)	384				384		
Total (All)	768 Clients						

the blue color bars in the figure but most of the IntraCity response times are not visible due to the small values. The IntraCity response time is relatively small because the propagation delay in the network and processing delay at the nodes and servers is relatively small. The InterCity Response Time for the database query of L96 profile is 200.8 ms. The InterCity (between Abha and Riyadh) results relate to the networked applications among hospitals and data centers of the two cities. A half of the overall communications between applications is within the Abha city and the other half is between Abha and Riyadh (see Section 3). The latency of the IP Cloud that connects Abha and Riyadh is 100 ms. Since Response Time includes the time for sending a request and receiving the response, the response time for InterCity communications is dominated by the value twice the latency cost. The response time in this case is relatively high, however, acceptable for database networked applications.

The global (combined IntraCity and InterCity) database response time for the L96 network traffic profile is 100.6 ms, approximately half of the InterCity response times. The IntraCity database response times are close to zero (0.48 ms), half of the nodes are involved in the IntraCity communications, and therefore the average over all the IntraCity and InterCity response times (200.8 ms and 0.48 ms) is approximately 100.6 ms. The results for M96, H96, VH96 and UH96 network traffic profiles show a similar trend. The IntraCity times increase slightly (0.55, 0.64, 1.5, and 4.3 ms) as we move towards higher traffic loads. The InterCity database response times for M96, H96, VH96 and UH96 network traffic profiles (200.9, 201, 202.4, and 269.2 ms, respectively) also show similar trends as for IntraCity. Similarly, as explained earlier, the global response times for these four traffic profiles are average of the IntraCity and InterCity response times: 100.7, 100.8, 102.6 and 130.9 ms, respectively. The rest of the

Figure 4. Database response times: All Abha – Riyadh Networks

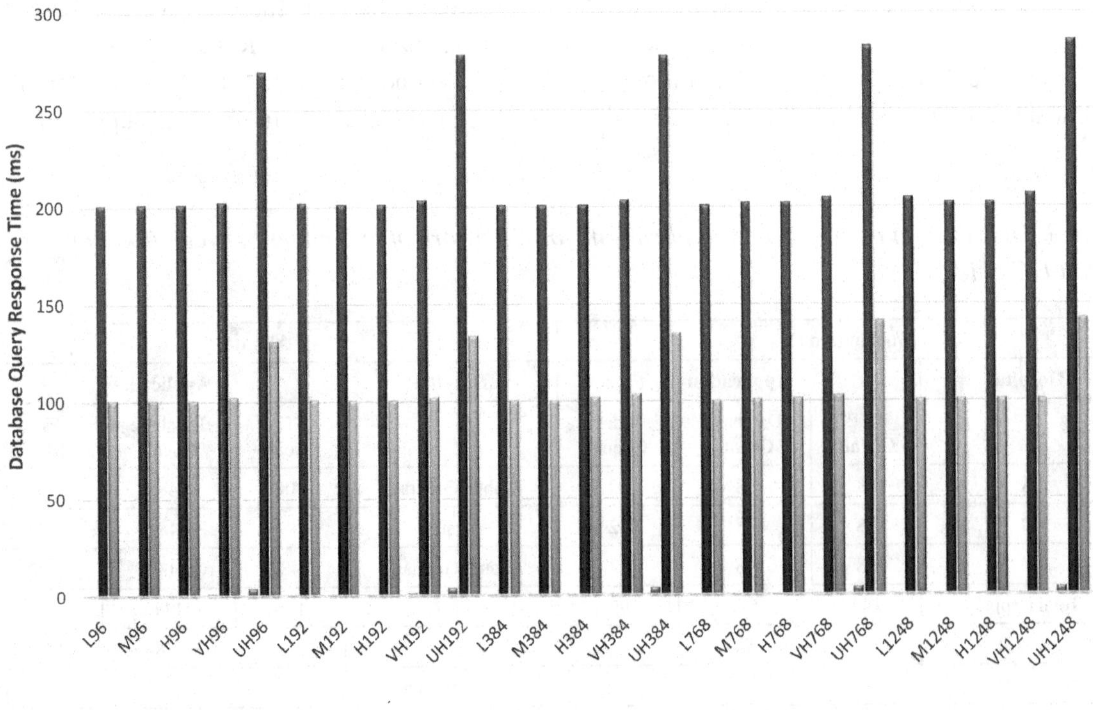

results in Figure 4 can be explained similarly. For each network size (96, 192, 384, 768, and 1248), we see results for 5 network profiles (L, M, H, VH and UH). The results for each network size show similar trend: database response times increase slightly as we move towards higher traffic loads. Similarly, a general pattern can be noted among all the results presented in Figure 4. The IntraCity, InterCity and global database response times increase as we move towards higher number of nodes, applications and higher traffic loads. This increase is relatively small for L, M, and H profiles which we believe is due to the relatively small (i.e., relative to the network and system capacity) increase in traffic load. The increase in the response times is higher towards VH and UH traffic profiles because the network and system load is reaching closer to the network and system capacity. Obviously, increasing the system and network capacity will help scale the system; i.e., the response times can be kept low by running the system below some system utilization threshold.

Figure 5 shows results of IntraCity, InterCity and global FTP response times for all the five network sizes and all five traffic profiles. As for Figure 4, the results are grouped into each traffic profile, L92, M92 and so on. Let us first look at the results for the network with 96 nodes. The figure shows that the IntraCity FTP Response Time is 0.6245 milliseconds (ms). The InterCity FTP Response Time of L96 profile is 601.2 ms. FTP uses TCP and therefore for each file transfer, a TCP connection has to be established (3 way handshake). Subsequently, the file is sent over the network (1 way communication), and finally the connection is closed (2 way communication). FTP applications therefore involve 3 roundtrip communications. The response time for the FTP applications for this network therefore is approximately 600 ms. The global FTP response times of L96 profile is 303.4 ms; average over all the IntraCity and InterCity response times (601 ms and 0.6 ms) is approximately 303 ms. The rest of the FTP results in Figure 5 can be explained similarly. A general pattern can be noted among all the FTP results. The IntraCity, InterCity and global FTP response times increase as we move towards higher number of nodes, applications and higher traffic loads. The InterCity response times are dominated by the InterCity network latency. The global response times are average of the IntraCity and InterCity times. Slight variations of few milliseconds can be caused by the random application behavior and can be ignored.

Figure 6 shows video end-to-end delay results. Let us first look at the results for the network with 96 nodes. The figure shows that the IntraCity video end-to-end delay is 0.2781 milliseconds (ms). As for the database and FTP, the video delay in the IntraCity case is relatively small because the propagation delay in the network and processing delay at the nodes and servers is relatively small. The InterCity video delay of L96 profile is 100.5 ms due to the 100ms latency for the Abha – Riyadh network. The global video end-to-end delay of L96 profile is 47.6 ms; average over all the IntraCity and InterCity response times (100.5 ms and 0.278 ms), approximately 47.6 ms. The rest of the video results in Figure 6 can be explained similarly. A general pattern can be noted among all the video results. The IntraCity, InterCity and global video delays increase as we move towards higher number of nodes, applications and higher traffic loads. The InterCity delays are dominated by the InterCity network latency. The global delays are average of the IntraCity and InterCity times.

Finally, Figure 7 provides video packet delay variation results for all the networks and traffic profiles. These are plotted in picoseconds (ps). The delay variations for the L, M, and H profiles are relatively small, less than 100 ps, and hence can be ignored for the video applications in this use case environment. The delay variations increase considerably for the VH and UH traffic profiles, reaching near 1010 ps (10 ms). The increase in network traffic and system load increase the uncertainty of communication and computing, increasing the variations in video end-to-end

Figure 5. FTP response times: All Abha – Riyadh Networks

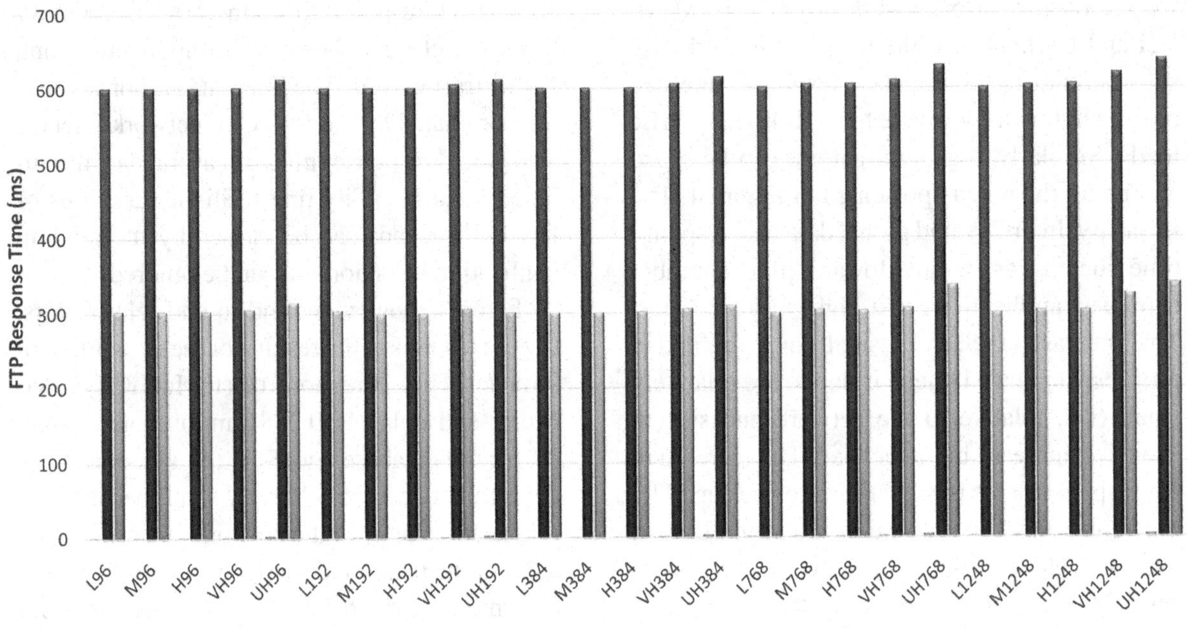

Figure 6. Video end-to-end delay: All Abha – Riyadh Networks

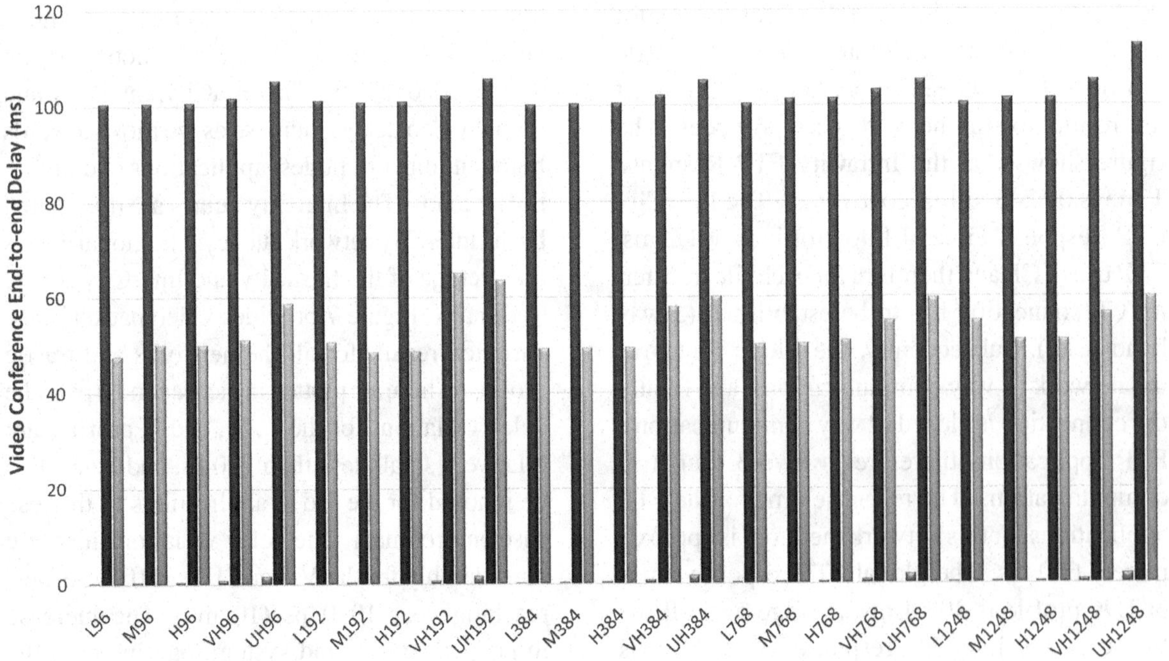

delays. These values are quite high, however, generally 20 ms is considered an acceptable value for videoconferencing delay variation. Moreover, the delay variations can be kept low by increasing the system and network capacity, and hence running the system below some system utilization threshold.

4.2 Abha – Birmingham Networked System

We now give a summary of the results for the Abha – Birmingham healthcare system. To save space and efforts, in this section and the next section, we will present results for three traffic profiles (L, M, and H) and will exclude VH and UH profiles. Figure 8 shows results of IntraCity, InterCity and global database response times for all the five network sizes and three traffic profiles (as provided in Table 1). The IntraCity results are same as for Abha – Riyadh network because the IntraCity networked system is symmetric for both cities. Minor differences in city geography and size will make little difference in the results if the number of applications and number of nodes are the same. Note a general pattern among all the network sizes that the database response time increases slightly respective to the increase in traffic load (L, M and H). The response times for InterCountry communications for the different network sizes are the same, approximately 600 ms, due to the latency of the IP Cloud which is 300 ms for the Abha – Birmingham network. This latency value includes the propagation delay (consider the distance between the two cities is over 6000 km), congestion due to background traffic, etc. The global response time for all the networks is around 300 ms, half of the InterCity response times. The response times in these cases are relatively large, however, may be acceptable for database networked applications. A large number of database accesses across networks can allow the latencies to be hidden by overlapping communications and computing.

Figure 9 shows results of the Abha – Birmingham FTP response times for all the five network sizes and three traffic profiles. The response times for InterCity communications for the different network sizes are same – 1.8 seconds - due to the roundtrip latency (600 ms) of the Abha – Birmingham network. The global response time value for the three networks is 900 ms, half of the InterCity

Figure 7. Video packet delay variation: All Abha – Riyadh Networks

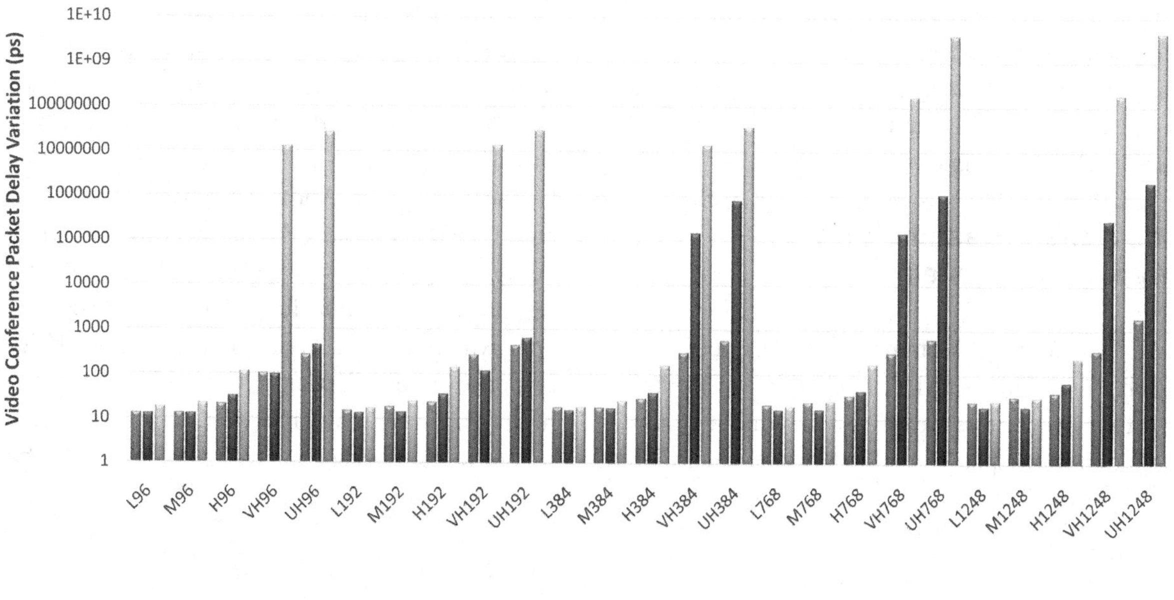

Figure 8. Database response times: All Abha – Birmingham Networks

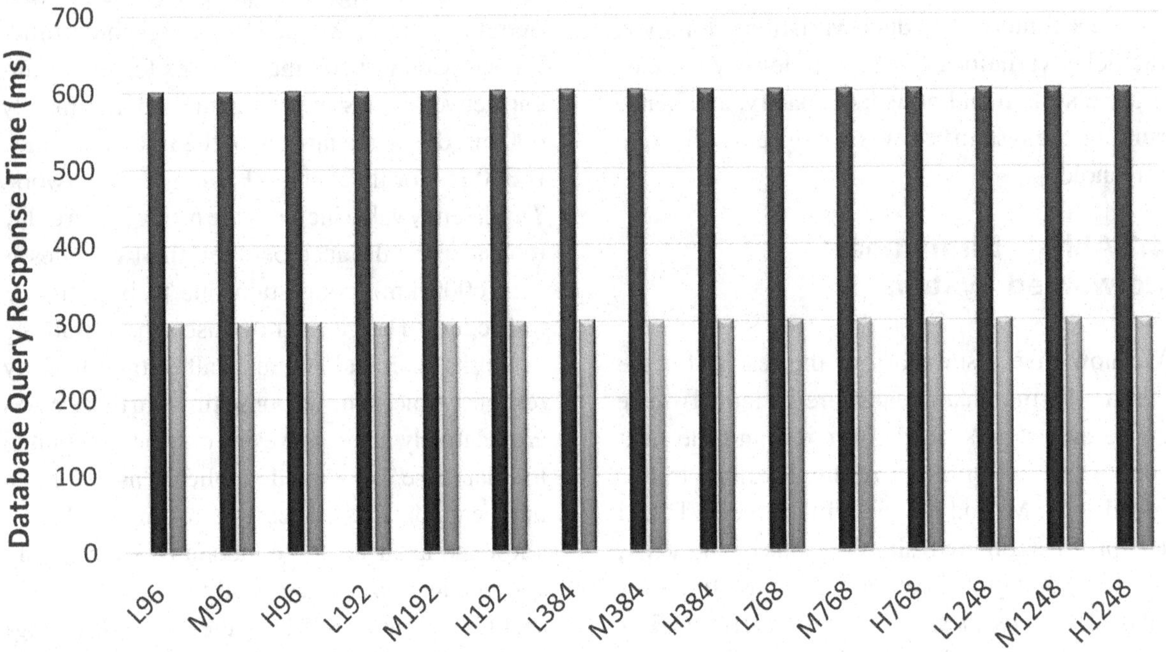

response times. Figure 10 shows video end-to-end delay results. The InterCity results for the different network sizes are the same – 300 ms - due to the communication latency (300 ms) of the Abha – Birmingham network. The global response time value for the three networks is between 142 ms to 161.9 ms, around half of the InterCity response times. A delay of 150 ms to 300 ms is generally considered to give acceptable QoS for video conferencing though 150 ms is more widely accepted as the acceptable delay bound. The video delays in these Abha – Birmingham networks therefore are hardly acceptable.

4.3 Abha – Washington DC Networked System

We analyze in this section the performance of the Abha – Washington DC healthcare networked system. The results are discussed without graphs due to lack of space. The IntraCity results for all three applications are similar to the Abha – Riyadh and Abha – Birmingham networks due to the symmetric nature of the IntraCity networked systems for all cities. The database response times for InterCountry communications for the different network sizes are similar, approximately 1200 ms (twice the latency of the Abha – Washington DC communications link). The global response time for all the networks is approximately 600 ms, half of the InterCity response times. Similarly, the FTP response times for InterCity communications for the different network sizes are approximately same – 3.6 seconds - due to the roundtrip latency (1.2 seconds) of the Abha – Birmingham network, and the reason that FTP requires 3 roundtrips to complete a file transfer process. The global FTP response times value for the three networks is approximately 1.8 seconds, half of the InterCity response times. Certainly, these results are too high to be acceptable, however, these results are for one request per second per node; results can be

Figure 9. FTP response times: All Abha – Birmingham Networks

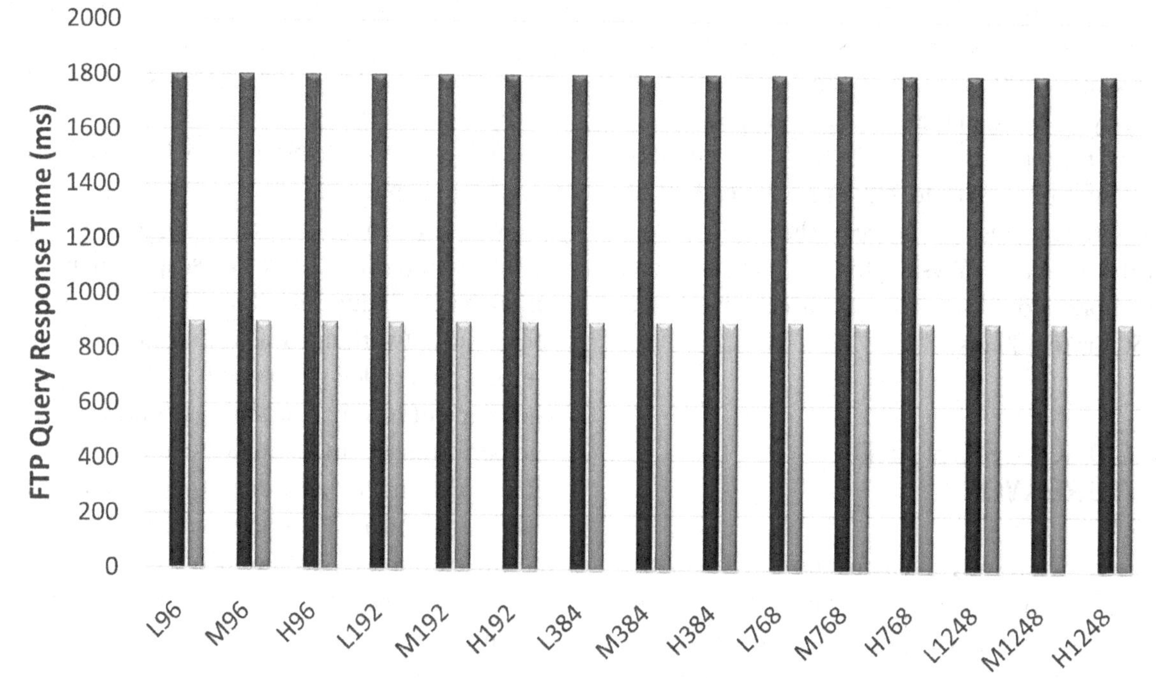

Figure 10. Video end-to-end delay: All Abha – Birmingham Networks

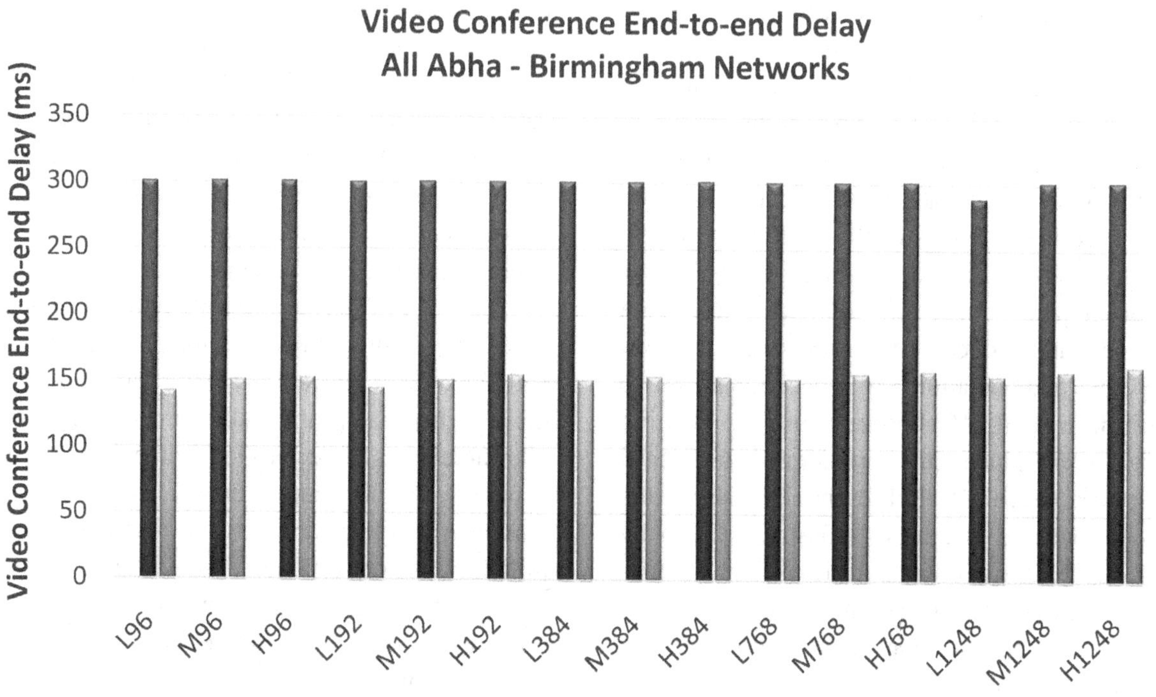

improved through large files transfers. The video end-to-end delay for InterCity communications for the different network sizes are approximately the same – 600 ms - due to the communication latency (600 ms) of the network. As expected, the global response time value for the three networks is between 277.3 ms to 323.8 ms, around half of the InterCity response times. The video delays in these Abha – Washington DC networks are therefore poor, considering the acceptable range (150 ms to 300 ms).

5. CONCLUSION AND FUTURE WORK

We are witnessing fundamental developments in the Internet design and the whole Internet landscape. Devices, applications and traffic that Internet is to support are on the rise. The trends show a near-radical change in the Internet usage, applications, etc., and hence require fundamental changes in the Internet designs and appropriate deployment paths. Healthcare is now considered the largest global industry with an increasing ICT penetration rate. Big data and IoT are also set to drive radical changes in the healthcare systems landscape. The emerging technologies of big data, IoT, and broader ICT, in healthcare will enhance and accelerate the convergence between the activities of the healthcare professional and stakeholders resulting in the provision of personalized and preventive healthcare to patients, reduced healthcare risks, improve systems and operational efficiencies, and reduce healthcare costs. Healthcare industry is adopting video communications to provide a range of novel services. Cisco's HealthPresence emphasizes the importance of healthcare industry, as seen by market leaders in communications. The material presented in this chapter demonstrated that the future healthcare systems and organizations demand huge computational resources, and the ability for the applications to interact and communicate with each other, within and across organizational boundaries. Therefore, the Internet that provides connectivity for healthcare systems would have to support a growing network traffic generated by an increasing plethora of mobile and fixed healthcare applications.

With our aim in this chapter to explore state-of-the-art of the healthcare landscape and present an analysis of future healthcare systems with a focus on networking traffic and architectures, we provided a detailed review of the changing landscape of healthcare, healthcare architectural and performance studies, and the role of big data, HL7, grid and cloud computing in emerging healthcare domain. The literature review provided the motivation and requirements for the future Internet designs and we built a study of healthcare systems, applications and traffic over local, metro, and wide area networks. The network architectures for these healthcare systems were described and a detailed study to explore quality of service (QoS) performance for these healthcare systems with a range of applications, system sizes, and network sizes was presented. The key takeaways of this study are that the requirements of a wide range of applications can well be met by a wired network and system as proposed in this chapter provided that the traffic is kept within the capacity of the network. The problems start appearing once the network traffic and system load reach the overall capacity. The higher network traffic loads (VHTL and UHTL) start impacting the response times and end-to-end delays for database, FTP and video communications. Delay variations for these higher load profiles also start reaching the allowable limits for decent QoS. Latencies for long haul networks also impact the quality of service, particularly FTP applications due to its 3 roundtrip time for one connection. FTP therefore may not be a good option for healthcare systems where transmissions of a large number of small files are required between distinct users or distinct connections. The FTP response times can be improved for large file transfers, possibly by combining multiple FTP requests at IntraSystem level into large file requests. This will be explored in our future work. Therefore, network latencies over larger geographic distances would be a challenge for low-latency healthcare applications such as real-time simulations and analytics requiring access to data spread over larger geographical areas.

This chapter exclusively focuses on conventional data transfer schemes and how they can be adapted to healthcare networking environments. In particular, the simulation activities presented in the chapter have been the opportunity to assess the applicability of legacy transfer techniques such as FTP to healthcare applications. Obviously, this work needs to be complemented so that new challenges raised by connected healthcare environments can be better addressed by emerging techniques, such as advanced, multi-metric, path computation schemes adapted to specific healthcare traffic patterns. A typical example of such traffic patterns is the dynamic monitoring of biometric data that suggests the selection of robust, privacy-friendly, low latency paths. Tuning the underlying routing and forwarding logics to improve the reliability of traffic delivery is therefore one of the key challenges of emerging healthcare systems.

The symmetric nature of the healthcare system that we have used in this chapter is to make the results easier to analyze and understand. We believe that this study is the first of its kind and it is better to make the networks and applications scenarios symmetric. We plan to use this study as the basis for future studies where we will use heterogeneous and asymmetric system environments. Similarly, minor differences in city geography and size will make little difference in the results if the number of applications and nodes are the same. Our future will also consider these differences. In all our networked systems scenarios, the transaction traffic is generated with exponential inter-arrival times of one second per node. We will consider lower inter-arrival times per node and this we believe would reduce the latencies subject to some bounds on congestion. Moreover, more efforts are needed to extract requirements for future healthcare systems (and hence simulations) including the range of applications and traffic profiles, including IoT. There is also a need to include other dimensions related to healthcare computing systems such as monitoring of biometric data at various geographic scales, effects due to primary, secondary and tertiary healthcare centers, remote monitoring of patients, computationally intensive analytics applications, healthcare policy related studies, situations arising from the use of cloud computing (e.g., virtual machine migration, data mirroring), etc. Privacy and security would be of major concern in future healthcare systems and these need to be considered. We will look at these in our future work.

ACKNOWLEDGMENT

We are thankful to the editors and the reviewers for their insight in our work and their valuable comments. These have greatly helped us in improving the quality of our chapter.

REFERENCES

Advisors, A. (2010). *Cloud Computing for Healthcare Organizations: Is There a Silver Lining?* Retrieved 26 September 2014, from http://www.techrepublic.com/resource-library/whitepapers/cloud-computing-for-healthcare-organizations-is-there-a-silver-lining/

Alam, M., Hussain, M., Afzal, M., Maqbool, M., Ahmad, H. F., & Razzaq, S. (2011). Design and Implementation of HL7 V3 Standard-Based Service Aware System. In *2011 10th International Symposium on Autonomous Decentralized Systems (ISADS)* (pp. 420–425). doi:10.1109/ISADS.2011.62

Alemdar, H., & Ersoy, C. (2010). Wireless sensor networks for healthcare: A survey. *Computer Networks*, *54*(15), 2688–2710. doi:10.1016/j.comnet.2010.05.003

Altowaijri, S., Mehmood, R., & Williams, J. (2010). A Quantitative Model of Grid Systems Performance in Healthcare Organisations. In *ISMS '10 Proceedings of the 2010 International Conference on Intelligent Systems, Modelling and Simulation* (pp. 431 –436). Liverpool, UK: IEEE Computer Society, Washington, DC, USA. doi:10.1109/ISMS.2010.84

Alturki, R., & Mehmood, R. (2008). Multimedia Ad Hoc Networks: Performance Analysis. In *Second UKSIM European Symposium on Computer Modeling and Simulation, 2008. EMS '08* (pp. 561–566). doi:10.1109/EMS.2008.9

Alturki, R., & Mehmood, R. (2012). *Chapter 19: Cross-Layer Multimedia QoS Provisioning over Ad Hoc Networks - Using Cross-Layer Techniques for Communication Systems*. Retrieved 27 September 2014, from https://www.safaribooksonline.com/library/view/using-cross-layer-techniques/9781466609600/978-1-4666-0960-0.ch019.xhtml

Alturki, R., Nwizege, K., Mehmood, R., & Faisal, M. (2009). End to End Wireless Multimedia Service Modelling over a Metropolitan Area Network. In *11th International Conference on Computer Modelling and Simulation, 2009. UKSIM '09* (pp. 532–537). doi:10.1109/UKSIM.2009.90

Aminian, M., & Naji, H. (2013). A Hospital Healthcare Monitoring System Using Wireless Sensor Networks. *Journal of Health & Medical Informatics*, *04*(02), 1–6. doi:10.4172/2157-7420.1000121

Assaad, A., & Fayek, D. (2006). General Hospitals Network Models for the support of E-Health Applications. In *Network Operations and Management Symposium, 2006. NOMS 2006. 10th IEEE/IFIP* (pp. 1–4). doi:10.1109/NOMS.2006.1687619

Bender, D., & Sartipi, K. (2013). HL7 FHIR: An Agile and RESTful approach to healthcare information exchange. In *2013 IEEE 26th International Symposium on Computer-Based Medical Systems (CBMS)* (pp. 326–331). doi:10.1109/CBMS.2013.6627810

Bitpipe. (2014). *Citrix solutions for healthcare*. Retrieved from http://www.bitpipe.com/detail/RES/1403881767_417.html

Buffone, G. J., & Beck, J. R. (1994). Facilitation of health care delivery through enhanced communications. *International Journal of Bio-Medical Computing*, *34*(1-4), 349–355. doi:10.1016/0020-7101(94)90035-3 PMID:8125649

Calamai, R., & Giarre, L. (2012). Enabling Primary and Specialist Care Interoperability Through HL7 CDA Release 2 and the Chronic Care Model: An Italian Case Study. *IEEE Transactions on Systems, Man, and Cybernetics. Part A, Systems and Humans*, *42*(6), 1364–1384. doi:10.1109/TSMCA.2012.2210205

Carr, D. F. (2014). *Apple Partners With Epic, Mayo Clinic For HealthKit - InformationWeek* [online community for business technology professionals]. Retrieved 26 September 2014, from http://www.informationweek.com/healthcare/mobile-and-wireless/apple-partners-with-epic-mayo-clinic-for-healthkit/d/d-id/1269371

Chouffani, R. (2014). *Apple's HealthKit mHealth platform linked with Mayo Clinic, Epic* [health care technology professional's how-to guide]. Retrieved 26 September 2014, from http://searchhealthit.techtarget.com/opinion/Apples-HealthKit-mHealth-platform-linked-with-Mayo-Clinic-Epic

Cisco, V. N. I. (2014). *Cisco Visual Networking Index: Forecast and Methodology, 2013–2018*. Retrieved 27 September 2014, from http://cisco.com/c/en/us/solutions/collateral/service-provider/ip-ngn-ip-next-generation-network/white_paper_c11-481360.html

Cisco HealthPresence. (2014). *Cisco HealthPresence - Industry Solutions - Cisco Systems: Transforming the elivery of Healthcare Telehealth Collaboration Software*. Retrieved 28 September 2014, from http://www.cisco.com/web/strategy/healthcare/cisco_healthpresence_solution.html

Cloud Standards Customer Council. (2012). *Impact of Cloud Computing on Healthcare*. Cloud Standards Customer Council.

Cuenca, T. C., Gomez, T. J. G., & Scotti, S. S. (2012). Design an architecture that allows the interoperability between information systems, software or medical device adopting the standard HL7 V2.x. In *Communications Conference (COLCOM), 2012 IEEE Colombian* (pp. 1–7). doi:10.1109/ColComCon.2012.6233647

De Meo, P., Quattrone, G., & Ursino, D. (2011). Integration of the HL7 Standard in a Multiagent System to Support Personalized Access to e-Health Services. *IEEE Transactions on Knowledge and Data Engineering*, *23*(8), 1244–1260. doi:10.1109/TKDE.2010.174

Dolezel, R., Dostal, O., Hosek, J., Molnar, K., & Rucka, L. (2011). Data-Rate and Queuing Method Optimization for Internetworking Medical Applications. In R. Szabó, H. Zhu, S. Imre, & R. Chaparadza (Eds.), *Access Networks* (pp. 141–152). Springer Berlin Heidelberg. doi:10.1007/978-3-642-20931-4_11

Evans, D. (2011). *Cisco Internet of Things White Paper - How the Next Evolution of the Internet Is Changing Everything*. Cisco Internet Business Solutions Group (IBSG). Retrieved from http://postscapes.com/cisco-internet-of-things-white-paper-how-the-next-evolution-of-the-internet-is-changing-everything

Fluckinger, D. (2014). *pulse Strategic insight for health IT leaders. As clinicians push to make mobile devices the standard in healthcare facilities, the communications badge—a technology throwback to some—proves newly relevant*. TechTarget Inc.

Foster, I., Kesselman, C., & Tuecke, S. (2001). The Anatomy of the Grid: Enabling Scalable Virtual Organizations. *International Journal of High Performance Computing Applications*, *15*(3), 200–222. doi:10.1177/109434200101500302

Goldstein, D., Groen, P. J., Ponkshe, S., & Wine, M. (2007). *Medical Informatics 20/20: Quality And Electronic Health Records Through Collaboration, Open Solutions, And Innovation* (1st ed.). Sudbury, MA: Jones & Bartlett Learning.

Groen, P. J., & Goldstein, D. (2009). Medical Informatics 2040: Reengineering & Transforming Healthcare in the 21st Century. *ePractice.eu*, (8), 1–4.

HL7. (2014). *Health Level Seven International*. Retrieved 23 September 2014, from http://www.hl7.org/

Hammond, J. E., Berger, R. G., Carey, T. S., Rutledge, R., Cleveland, T. J., Kichak, J. P., & Ayscue, C. F. (1991). Making the transition from information systems of the 1970s to medical information systems of the 1990s: The role of the physician's workstation. *Journal of Medical Systems*, *15*(3), 257–267. doi:10.1007/BF00996555 PMID:1804927

Harvard Extension School. (2014). *Distance Education | Harvard Distance Learning Courses* [Education]. Retrieved 21 November 2014, from http://www.extension.harvard.edu/distance-education

Hitachi Data Systems. (2012). *How to Improve Healthcare with Cloud Computing*. Hitachi Data Systems.

IBM. (2011). *Cloud Computing: Building a New Foundation for Healthcare*. IBM Corporation.

Kaihara, S. (1994). Workstation network system which enables international exchange of characters and images at the University of Tokyo Hospital. *International Journal of Bio-Medical Computing*, *34*(1-4), 357–361. doi:10.1016/0020-7101(94)90036-1 PMID:8125650

Lemke, H. U., Faulkner, G., & Krauss, M. (1994). Development towards multimedia medical workstations. *Computerized Medical Imaging and Graphics: The Official Journal of the Computerized Medical Imaging Society*, *18*(2), 67–71. doi:10.1016/0895-6111(94)90015-9 PMID:8168052

Liu, L., & Huang, Q. (2012). An extensible HL7 middleware for heterogeneous healthcare information exchange. In *2012 5th International Conference on Biomedical Engineering and Informatics (BMEI)* (pp. 1045–1048). doi:10.1109/BMEI.2012.6513196

Macias, F., & Thomas, G. (2011). *Cloud Computing Advantages in the Public Sector: How Today's Government, Education, and Healthcare Organizations Are Benefiting from Cloud Computing Environments*. White Paper, Cisco Systems, Inc.

McKinsey & Company. (2014). *Healthcare Systems & Services Practice* [Management Consulting Firm]. Retrieved 21 November 2014, from http://www.mckinsey.com/client_service/healthcare_systems_and_services

Mehmood, R., & Alturki, R. (2011). A scalable multimedia QoS architecture for ad hoc networks. *Multimedia Tools and Applications*, *54*(3), 551–568. doi:10.1007/s11042-010-0569-0

Mehmood, R., & Alturki, R. (2013). Video QoS Analysis over Wi-Fi Networks. In *Advanced Video Communications over Wireless Networks* (pp. 439–480). CRC Press. doi:10.1201/b13746-16

Mehmood, R., Alturki, R., & Faisal, M. (2009). A Scalable Provisioning and Routing Scheme for Multimedia QoS over Ad Hoc Networks. In A. Mauthe, S. Zeadally, E. Cerqueira, & M. Curado (Eds.), *Future Multimedia Networking* (pp. 131–142). Springer Berlin Heidelberg. doi:10.1007/978-3-642-02472-6_12

Mehmood, R., Alturki, R., & Zeadally, S. (2011). Multimedia applications over metropolitan area networks (MANs). *Journal of Network and Computer Applications*, *34*(5), 1518–1529. doi:10.1016/j.jnca.2010.08.002

Mehmood, R., & Lu, J. A. (2011). Computational Markovian analysis of large systems. *Journal of Manufacturing Technology Management*, *22*(6), 804–817. doi:10.1108/17410381111149657

Mell, P., & Grance, T. (2011). *The NIST Definition of Cloud Computing: Recommendations of the National Institute of Standards and Technology* (Technical Report No. 800-145). Gaithersburg, MD: NIST.

Microsoft. (2014). *Revolutionize Healthcare with the Internet of Things: Achieve new levels of health technology interoperability* [Software]. Retrieved 21 November 2014, from http://www.microsoft.com/windowsembedded/en-us/internet-of-things-health.aspx

Mitton, C., & Donaldson, C. (2004). Health care priority setting: Principles, practice and challenges. *Cost Effectiveness and Resource Allocation, 2*(1), 1–8. doi:10.1186/1478-7547-2-3 PMID:15104792

Nie, H., Li, S., Lu, X., & Duan, H. (2013). From Healthcare Messaging Standard to Semantic Web Service Description: Generating WSMO Annotation from HL7 with Mapping-Based Approach. In *2013 IEEE International Conference on Services Computing (SCC)* (pp. 470–477). doi:10.1109/SCC.2013.74

Orthner, H. F., Scherrer, J. R., & Dahlen, R. (1994). Sharing and communicating health care information: Summary and recommendations. *International Journal of Bio-Medical Computing, 34*(1-4), 303–318. doi:10.1016/0020-7101(94)90030-2 PMID:8125644

Patil, R. S., Silva, J. S., & Swartout, W. R. (1994). An architecture for a health care provider's workstation. *International Journal of Bio-Medical Computing, 34*(1-4), 285–299. doi:10.1016/0020-7101(94)90029-9 PMID:8125640

Piai, S., & Claps, M. (2013). *Bigger Data for Better Healthcare*. IDC Health Insights. Retrieved from http://www.intel.com/content/www/us/en/healthcare-it/bigger-data-better-healthcare-idc-insights-white-paper.html

Polycom. (2014). *New Healthcare Vision, Collaborative video solutions improving care and reducing cost.* Polycom, Inc.

Pretz, K. (2014). *Better Health Care Through Data How health analytics could contain costs and improve care.* Retrieved 26 September 2014, from http://theinstitute.ieee.org/technology-focus/technology-topic/better-health-care-through-data

Riverbed. (2014). *SteelCentral for Performance Management and Control | Riverbed application and network performance management solutions | Riverbed* [Communications Hardware, Technology, Software]. Retrieved 19 November 2014, from http://www.riverbed.com/products/performance-management-control/opnet.html

Roth, C. P., Lim, Y.-W., Pevnick, J. M., Asch, S. M., & McGlynn, E. A. (2009). The Challenge of Measuring Quality of Care From the Electronic Health Record. *American Journal of Medical Quality, 24*(5), 385–394. doi:10.1177/1062860609336627 PMID:19482968

Samsung Electronics Co. (2013). *S Health* [Electronics]. Retrieved 26 September 2014, from http://content.samsung.com/us/contents/aboutn/sHealthIntro.do

Sharma, M., Bai, Y., Chung, S., & Dai, L. (2012). Using Risk in Access Control for Cloud-Assisted eHealth. In *2012 IEEE 14th International Conference on High Performance Computing and Communication 2012 IEEE 9th International Conference on Embedded Software and Systems (HPCC-ICESS)* (pp. 1047–1052). doi:10.1109/HPCC.2012.153

Smart Cities. (2014). Retrieved 21 November 2014, from ec.europa.eu//digital-agenda/en/smart-cities

Soomro, A., & Schmitt, R. (2011). A framework for mobile healthcare applications over heterogeneous networks. In *2011 13th IEEE International Conference on e-Health Networking Applications and Services (Healthcom)* (pp. 70–73). doi:10.1109/HEALTH.2011.6026789

TrafficLand. (2014). *TrafficLand.com - Traffic Cameras, Traffic Video, Live Traffic Cams.* Retrieved 28 September 2014, from http://www.trafficland.com/

United States Department of Health and Human Services. (2007). Personalized Health Care: Opportunities, Pathways [Health and Human Services]. *Resources*, 1–69.

Vidyo. (2014). *Personalized Healthcare Without Borders*. Retrieved 28 September 2014, from http://www.vidyo.com/solutions/healthcare/

VMware, Inc. (2014). *Your Cloud in Healthcare*. VMware, Inc.

Yuksel, M., & Dogac, A. (2011). Interoperability of Medical Device Information and the Clinical Applications: An HL7 RMIM based on the ISO/IEEE 11073 DIM. *IEEE Transactions on Information Technology in Biomedicine*, *15*(4), 557–566. doi:10.1109/TITB.2011.2151868 PMID:21558061

Zhang, Y., Huang, A., Wang, D., Duan, X., Jiao, B., & Xie, L. (2013). To enable stable medical image and video transmission in mobile healthcare services: A Best-fit Carrier Dial-up (BCD) algorithm for GBR-oriented applications in LTE-A networks. In *2013 IEEE International Conference on Communications (ICC)* (pp. 4368–4372). doi:10.1109/ICC.2013.6655253

KEY TERMS AND DEFINITIONS

Big Data: It refers to the emerging technologies that are designed to extract value from data having four Vs characteristics; volume, variety, velocity and veracity. Big data is set to affect the future network traffic and hence the network architectures.

Cloud Computing: Cloud computing is an approach to provide computing as a utility making it easy to acquire, manage, and release ICT infrastructure. A formal definition is given by NIST and is included in this chapter. Cloud Computing is set to affect the future network traffic and hence the network architectures.

Database Response Time: It is the time elapsed between the Database Entry Application sending a request to the server and receiving the response from the server.

FTP Response Time: It is the time elapsed between a client application sending a request to the FTP server and receiving the response packet. The response time includes the 3 way TCP handshake.

Smart Cities: Smart cities: or future cities, are emerging mainstream approaches for urbanisation. Environmental and economic sustainability, digital inclusion and high quality of life are considered important elements in smart cities design. Healthcare systems discussed in this chapter will be an important dimension of smart cities.

Video End-To-End Delay: It is the time taken to send a video application packet to a destination node application layer.

Video Packet Delay Variation: It is the variance among end-to-end delays for video packets.

Compilation of References

Abbott, K. W., & Snidal, D. (1998). Why States Act through Formal International Organizations. *The Journal of Conflict Resolution*, *42*(1), 3–32. doi:10.1177/0022002798042001001

Abgrall, D. (Ed.). (2011). Virtual Home Gateway: How can Home Gateway virtualization be achieved? *EURESCOM Study Report P2055 D1*, September 2011.

Aboba, B., Simon, D., & Eronen, P. (2008, August). *Extensible Authentication Protocol (EAP) Key Management Framework*. Retrieved from http://tools.ietf.org/html/rfc5247

Aboba, B., Zorn, G., & Mitton, D. (2001, August). *RADIUS and IPv6*. Retrieved from http://tools.ietf.org/html/rfc3162

Abts, D., Marty, M. R., Wells, P. M., Klausler, P., & Liu, H. (2010). Energy Proportional Datacenter Networks. In *Proceedings of the 41st International Symposium on Computer Architecture (ISCA '10)*. New York, NY: ACM.

Achmawi, R. (2009). Brazil Wants Bigger Role for Emerging Nations in Internet's Management. *Brazzilmag.com*. Retrieved from: http://www.brazzilmag.com/index2.php?option=com_content&task=view&id=10204&pop=1&page=0&Itemid=1

Adaptive Streaming, H. T. T. P. (n.d.). *Wikipedia*. Retrieved November 25, 2014, from http:// https://en.wikipedia.org/wiki/Adaptive_bitrate_streaming

Adobe, Inc. (n.d.). *HTTP Dynamic Streaming Features*. Retrieved from http://www.adobe.com/products/hds-dynamic-streaming/features.html

Advisors, A. (2010). *Cloud Computing for Healthcare Organizations: Is There a Silver Lining?* Retrieved 26 September 2014, from http://www.techrepublic.com/resource-library/whitepapers/cloud-computing-for-healthcare-organizations-is-there-a-silver-lining/

Ahmed, J., Cavdar, C., Monti, P., & Wosinska, L. (2012). A dynamic bulk provisioning framework for concurrent optimization in PCE-based WDM networks. *Journal of Lightwave Technology*, *30*(14), 2229–2239. doi:10.1109/JLT.2012.2195296

Aiscaler. (2014). *Product overview*. Retrieved from http://aiscaler.com/product-overview#ADN

Akamai. (2012). *Akamai and AT&T Forge Global Strategic Alliance to Provide Content Delivery Network Solutions*. Retrieved from http://www.akamai.com/html/about/press/releases/2012/press_120612.html

Akamai. (2012). *Press Release. November 20, 2012. Orange and Akamai form Content Delivery Strategic Alliance*. Retrieved October 23, 2014 from http://www.akamai.com/html/about/press/releases/2012/press_112012_1.html

Akamai. (2013). *KT and Akamai Expand Strategic Partnership*. Retrieved from http://www.akamai.com/html/about/press/releases/2013/press_032713.html

Akamai. (2013). *Swisscom and Akamai Enter Into a Strategic Partnership*. Retrieved from http://www.akamai.com/html/about/press/releases/2013/press_031413.html

Akamai. (2014). *Visualizing Akamai Web Page*. Retrieved October 23, 2014 from http://www.akamai.com/html/technology/dataviz3.html

Akamai. (2014). *Akamai and Telefonica Enter into Global Content Delivery Alliance*. Retrieved from http://www.akamai.com/html/about/press/releases/2014/press-032514.html

Akamai. (2014). *Web Application Accelerator*. Retrieved from http://www.akamai.com/html/solutions/web_application_accelerator.html

Akko, J., & Farrel, S. (2014, April 7). *Pervasive Monitoring*. Retrieved from http://www.internetsociety.org/sites/default/files/IETF%20Update-Pervasive%20Monitoring.pdf

Alaettinoglu, C., Villamizar, C., Gerich, E., Kessens, D., Meyer, D., Bates, T., . . . Terpstra, M. (1999). Routing policy specification language (RPSL) (pp. 1-56). RFC 2622.

Alam, M., Hussain, M., Afzal, M., Maqbool, M., Ahmad, H. F., & Razzaq, S. (2011). Design and Implementation of HL7 V3 Standard-Based Service Aware System. In *2011 10th International Symposium on Autonomous Decentralized Systems (ISADS)* (pp. 420–425). doi:10.1109/ISADS.2011.62

Alemdar, H., & Ersoy, C. (2010). Wireless sensor networks for healthcare: A survey. *Computer Networks*, *54*(15), 2688–2710. doi:10.1016/j.comnet.2010.05.003

Al-Fares, M., Radhakrishnan, S., Raghavan, B., Huang, N., & Vahdat, A. (2010). *Hedera: Dynamic flow scheduling for data center networks*. Academic Press.

Alim, M., & Griffin, T. (2011). On the interaction of multiple routing algorithms. In *Proceedings of ACM CoNEXT*. New York, NY: ACM. doi:10.1145/2079296.2079303

Alter, C. (2014), *Broadband Forum Work on "Network Enhanced Residential Gateway" (WT-317) and "Virtual Business Gateway"* (WT-328). Broadband Forum's liaison letter to the IETF, March 2014.

Alter, C., & Daowood, S. (2014). *Broadband Forum Work on Flexible Service Chaining (SD-326)*. Broadband Forum's liaison letter to the IETF. February 2014.

Alternative reality - The internet in China. (2008, February 2). *The Economist*.

Altowaijri, S., Mehmood, R., & Williams, J. (2010). A Quantitative Model of Grid Systems Performance in Healthcare Organisations. In *ISMS '10 Proceedings of the 2010 International Conference on Intelligent Systems, Modelling and Simulation* (pp. 431 –436). Liverpool, UK: IEEE Computer Society, Washington, DC, USA. doi:10.1109/ISMS.2010.84

Alturki, R., & Mehmood, R. (2012). *Chapter 19: Cross-Layer Multimedia QoS Provisioning over Ad Hoc Networks - Using Cross-Layer Techniques for Communication Systems*. Retrieved 27 September 2014, from https://www.safaribooksonline.com/library/view/using-cross-layer-techniques/9781466609600/978-1-4666-0960-0.ch019.xhtml

Alturki, R., & Mehmood, R. (2008). Multimedia Ad Hoc Networks: Performance Analysis. In *Second UKSIM European Symposium on Computer Modeling and Simulation, 2008. EMS '08* (pp. 561–566). doi:10.1109/EMS.2008.9

Alturki, R., Nwizege, K., Mehmood, R., & Faisal, M. (2009). End to End Wireless Multimedia Service Modelling over a Metropolitan Area Network. In *11th International Conference on Computer Modelling and Simulation, 2009. UKSIM '09* (pp. 532–537). doi:10.1109/UKSIM.2009.90

Amazon. (2014). *AWS Case Study: Netflix*. Retrieved October 23, 2014 from http://aws.amazon.com/fr/solutions/case-studies/netflix/

Aminian, M., & Naji, H. (2013). A Hospital Healthcare Monitoring System Using Wireless Sensor Networks. *Journal of Health & Medical Informatics*, *04*(02), 1–6. doi:10.4172/2157-7420.1000121

Anderson, L. AB, A., Minei, I, Thomas, B. (2007) LDP Specification, RFC5036.

Andersson, L., & Rosen, E. (2006). Framework for Layer 2 Virtual Private Networks (L2VPNs). RFC 4664.

Andriolli, N., Giorgetti, A., Valcarenghi, L., & Castoldi, P. (2007). Idle protection capacity reuse in multiclass optical networks. *Journal of Lightwave Technology*, *25*(5), 1152–1162. doi:10.1109/JLT.2007.893928

Anschutz, T. (Ed.). (2011). *Broadband Forum TR-101: Migration to Ethernet-Based Broadband Aggregation, Issue 2*. Broadband Forum.

Apache, X. M. L.-R. P. C. (n.d.). *Apache XML-RPC Java Implementation*. Retrieved July 2014 from: http://ws.apache.org/xmlrpc

Apple. (2014, October). *iOS: Multipath TCP Support in iOS 7*. Retrieved March 16, 2015 from http://support.apple.com/kb/ht5977

Aranda Gutiérrez, P., & Zitterbart, M. (Eds.). (2010). Final Architectural Framework. 4WARD. In *Architecture and Design for the Future Internet FP7-ICT-2007-1-216041-4WARD Deliverable D-2.3.1*. Retrieved from http://www.4ward-project.eu/

Arkko, J., Lindem, A., & Paterson, B. (2013). *Prefix Assignment in a Home Network (draft-arkko-homenet-prefix-assignment-04)*. IETF Internet Draft, May 2013.

Arzani, B., Gurney, A., Cheng, S., Guerin, R., & Loo, B. T. (2014). Impact of Path Characteristics and Scheduling Policies on MPTCP Performance. *The 4th International Workshop on Protocols and Applications with Multi-Homing Support (PAMS 2014)*. Victoria/Canada: IEEE CS Conference Publishing Service.

Assaad, A., & Fayek, D. (2006). General Hospitals Network Models for the support of E-Health Applications. In *Network Operations and Management Symposium, 2006. NOMS 2006. 10th IEEE/IFIP* (pp. 1–4). doi:10.1109/NOMS.2006.1687619

AT&T. (2014). *Products & services*. Retrieved from http://www.business.att.com/enterprise/business-solutions/

ATIS. (2011). *ATIS Cloud Services Forum Releases Content Distribution Network Interconnection Specifications*. Retrieved October 23, 2014 from http://www.atis.org/PRESS/pressreleases2011/070511.html

Atkinson, R. D., Ezell, S. J., & Stewart, L. A. (2012). *The Global Innovation Policy Index. Rep. N.p.* Information Technology and Innovation Foundation and the Kauffman Foundation.

Atlas, A., & Zinin, A. (2008). *IP fast re-route*. Retrieved March 15, 2015 from https://datatracker.ietf.org/doc/rfc5286/

Atlas, A., Kebler, R., Bowers, C., Enyedi, G., Csaszar, A., Tantsura, J., & White, R. (2015). *Maximally Redundant Trees (MRT)*. Retrieved March 15, 2015 from https://datatracker.ietf.org/doc/draft-ietf-rtgwg-mrt-frr-architecture/

Audet, F., & Jennings, C. (2007, January). *Network Address Translation (NAT) Behavioral requirements for Unicast UDP*. Retrieved from http://tools.ietf.org/html/rfc4787

Awduche, D., Berger, L., Gan, D., Li, T., Srinivasan, V. (2001) RSVP-TE: Extensions to RSVP for LSP Tunnels, RFC3209.

Awduche, D., Berger, L., Gan, D., Li, T., Srinivasan, V., & Swallow, G. (2001). RSVP-TE: Extensions to RSVP for LSP Tunnels. *IETF*. Retrieved November 25, 2014, from https://tools.ietf.org/html/rfc3209

Awduche, D.; Berger, L., Gan, D., Li, T., Srinivasan, V., & Swallow, G. (2001). *RSVP-TE: extensions to RSVP for LSP tunnels*. RFC 3209.

Awduche, D.; Malcom, J.; Agogbua, J.; O'Dell, M.; McManus, J. (1999). *Requirements for traffic engineering over MPLS*. RFC 2702.

Bagnulo, M., Paasch, C., Gont, F., Bonaventure, O., & Raiciu, C. (2013). *Analysis of MPTCP residual threats and possible fixes*. Academic Press.

Bailey, S., Bansal, D., Dunbar, L., Hood, D., Kis, Z. L., Mack-Crane, B, ... Varma. E. (2013). *SDN Architecture Overview, Version 1.0*. Retrieved from: https://www.opennetworking.org/images/stories/downloads/sdn-resources/technical-reports/SDN-architecture-overview-1.0.pdf

Bai, T., & Heath, R. W. (2013). Coverage in dense millimeter wave cellular networks.*Asilomar Conference on Signals, Systems and Computers* (pp. 2062-2066). Asilomar.

Balachandran, A., Sekar, V., Akella, A., Seshan, S., Stoica, I., & Zhang, H. (2013). Developing a predictive model of quality of experience for internet video. In *Proceedings of the ACM SIGCOMM*. doi:10.1145/2486001.2486025

Barham, P., Dragovic, B., Fraser, K., Hand, S., Harris, T., Ho, A., Neugebauer, R., ... Warfield, A. (2003). Xen and the art of virtualization. *ACM SIGOPS Operating Systems Review, 37*(5), 164–177. DOI=10.1145/1165389.945462

Bartley, T. (2014). *Orange is Glad they Chose Akamai for Live Video & Events*. Retrieved from https://blogs.akamai.com/2014/06/orange-is-glad-they-chose-akamai-for-live-video-events.html?utm_source=feedburner&utm_medium=feed&utm_campaign=Feed%3A+TheAkamaiBlog+%28The+Akamai+Blog%29

Basak, D., Toshniwal, R., Maskalik, S., & Sequeira, A. (2010). Virtualizing networking and security in the cloud. *SIGOPS Operating Systems Review, 44*(4), 86-94. December 2010. DOI= http://doi.acm.org/10.1145/1899928.189993910.1145/1899928.1899939

Basta, A., Kellerer, W., Hoffmann, M., Hoffmann, K., & Schmidt, E. D. (2013, November). A Virtual SDN-enabled LTE EPC Architecture: a case study for S-/P-Gateways functions. In Future Networks and Services (SDN4FNS), 2013 IEEE SDN for (pp. 1-7). IEEE.

Basta, A., Kellerer, W., Hoffmann, M., Morper, H. J., & Hoffmann, K. (2014). Applying NFV and SDN to LTE Mobile Core Gateways, the Functions Placement Problem. In *Proceedings of the 4th workshop on all things cellular: Operations, applications, & challenges* (pp. 33–38). New York, NY, USA: ACM; http://doi.acm.org/10.1145/2627585.2627592 doi:10.1145/2627585.2627592

Bauman, Z. (2009). *Intervista sull'identità*. Roma: Laterza.

Bazzi, A., & Onozato, Y. (2011, July). Feasibility Study of Security Virtual Appliances for Personal Computing. *IPSJ Journal of Information Processing, 19*(0), 378–388. doi:10.2197/ipsjjip.19.378

Bejarano, O., Knightly, E. W., & Park, M. (2013). IEEE 802.11ac: From channelization to multi-user MIMO. *IEEE Communications Magazine, 51*(10), 84–90. doi:10.1109/MCOM.2013.6619570

Belshe, M., Peon, R., & Thomson, M. (2014). *Hypertext Transfer Protocol version 2, draft-ietf-httpbis-http2-14*. Retrieved July 30, 2014 from https://tools.ietf.org/html/draft-ietf-httpbis-http2-14

Bender, D., & Sartipi, K. (2013). HL7 FHIR: An Agile and RESTful approach to healthcare information exchange. In *2013 IEEE 26th International Symposium on Computer-Based Medical Systems (CBMS)* (pp. 326–331). doi: doi:10.1109/CBMS.2013.6627810

Benson, T., Akella, A., & Maltz, D. (2009). *Unraveling the complexity of network management*. In *Proceedings of USENIX NSDI*. Berkeley, CA: USENIX Association.

Berger, L. (2003, January). *Generalized Multi-Protocol Label Switching (GMPLS) Signaling Functional Description*. Retrieved from https://tools.ietf.org/html/rfc3471

Bergkvist, A., Burnett, D. C., Jennings, C., & Narayanan, A. (2013). WebRTC 1.0: Real-time Communication Between Browsers. *World Wide Web Consortium*. Retrieved November 25, 2014, from www.w3.org/TR/webrtc/

Bernardos, C. J., de la Oliva, A., Serrano, P., Banchs, A., Contreras, L. M., Jin, H., & Zúñiga, J. C. An Architecture for Software Defined Wireless Networking. IEEE Wireless Communications Magazine. doi:10.1109/MWC.2014.6845049

Bernardos, C. J., Zunniga, J.C., & Reznik, A. (2012). Towards flat and distributed mobility management: A 3GPP evolved network design. In *Communications (ICC),2012IEEE International Conference on*. IEEE.

Bernardos, C. J., De Domenico, A., Ortin, J., Rost, P., & Wübben, D. (2013). *Challenges of designing jointly the backhaul and radio access network in a cloud based mobile network*. Lisbon, Portugal: Future Networks Summit.

Bertrand, G., Stephan, E., Burbridge, T., Eardley, P., Ma, K., & Watson, G. (2012). Use Cases for Content Delivery Network Interconnection. *IETF*. Retrieved November 25, 2014, from https://tools.ietf.org/html/rfc6770

Bhaumik, S., Chandrabose, S. P., Jataprolu, M. K., Kumar, G., Muralidhar, A., Polakos, P., . . . Woo, T. (2012). CloudIQ: A Framework for Processing Base Stations in a Data Center. ACM MobiCom, August 22-26, Istanbul, Turkey.

Bing, H., He, C., & Jiang, L. (2003), Performance analysis of vertical handover in a UMTS-WLAN integrated network. *Personal, Indoor and Mobile Radio Communications, PIMRC, 14th IEEE Proceedings on.*

Biswas, J., Lazar, A. A., Huard, J. F., Lim, K., Mahjoub, S., Pau, L. F., & Weinstein, S. et al. (1998). The IEEE P1520 standards initiative for programmable network interfaces. *Communications Magazine, IEEE, 36*(10), 64–70. doi:10.1109/35.722138

Bitpipe. (2014). *Citrix solutions for healthcare.* Retrieved from http://www.bitpipe.com/detail/RES/1403881767_417.html

Black, D., Hudson, J., Kreeger, L., Lasserre, M., Narten, T. (2015) An Architecture for Overlay Networks (NVO3), draft-ietf-nvo3-arch-01.

Blackford, J., & Digdon, M. (2013) *Broadband Forum, TR-069 – CPE WAN Management Protocol, Issue 1, Amendment 5*, November 2013.

Bocci, M., Bryant, S., Frost, D., Levrau, L., & Berger, L. (2010). *MPLS-TP Framework.* Retrieved March 15, 2015 from https://datatracker.ietf.org/doc/rfc5921/

Bolla, R., Bruschi, R., Carrega, A., & Davoli, F. (2011). Green Network Technologies and the Art of Trading-Off. In *Proceedings of the 30th IEEE Conference on Computer Communications Workshops on Green Communications and Networking (INFOCOM WKSHPS '11).* New York, NY: IEEE. doi:10.1109/INFCOMW.2011.5928827

Bonaventure, O., & Paasch, C. (2014). *Experience with Multipath TCP*. Academic Press.

Bonomi, F., Milito, R., Zhu, J., & Addepalli, S. (2012). Fog computing and its role in the internet of things. In *Proceedings of the first edition of the mcc workshop on mobile cloud computing* (pp. 13–16). New York, NY, USA: ACM. doi:10.1145/2342509.2342513

Bosshart, P., Daly, D., Izzard, M., McKeown, N., Rexford, J., Talayco, D., . . . Walker, D. (2013). Programming protocol-independent packet processors. *arXiv preprint arXiv:1312.1719.*

Boucadair, M, & Jacquenet, C. (2014). Software-Defined Networking: A Perspective from within a Service Provider Environment, *RFC 7149.*

Boucadair, M. & Jacquenet, C. (2014). *Software-Defined Networking: A Perspective from within a Service Provider Environment.* IETF RFC7149.

Boucadair, M., & Jacquenet, C. (2014). *Software-Defined Networking: A Perspective from within a Service Provider Environment, RFC 7149, March 2014.* Retrieved from http://www.rfc-editor.org/rfc/rfc7149.txt

Boucadair, M., & Jacquenet, C. (2014). Software-Defined Networking: A Perspective from within a Service Provider Environment. *IETF*. Retrieved November 25, 2014, from https://tools.ietf.org/html/rfc7149

Boucadair, M., & Jacquenet, C. (2014). *Software-Defined Networking: A Perspective from within a Service Provider Environment.* RFC7149.

Boucadair, M., Jacquenet, C., & Wang, N. (2014). IP Connectivity Provisioning Profile (CPP). *IETF*. Retrieved November 25, 2014, from https://tools.ietf.org/html/rfc7297

Boucadair, M., Jacquenet, C., & Wang, N. (2014). *IP Connectivity Provisioning Profile (CPP). Internet Engineering Task Force RFC 5246.* Retrieved from http://tools.ietf.org/html/rfc7297

Boucadair, M., Jacquenet, C., & Wang, N. (2014). *IP Connectivity Provisioning Profile (CPP).* Retrieved from http://tools.ietf.org/html/rfc7297

Boucadair, M., Jacquenet, C., & Wang, N. (2014). IP Connectivity Provisioning Profile (CPP). RFC 7297.

Boucadair, M., Jacquenet, C., Jiang, Y., Parker, R., Pignataro, C., & Naito, K. (2014). *Requirements for Service Function Chaining (SFC) (draft-boucadair-sfc-requirements-05).* IETF Internet Draft, February 2014.

Boucadair, M., Jacquenet, C., Parker, R., & Dunbar, L. (2014), *Service Function Chaining: Design Considerations, Analysis & Recommendations (draft-boucadair-sfc-design-analysis-02).* IETF Internet Draft, February 2014.

Boucadair, M., Jacquenet, C., & Wang, N. (2014). *IP Connectivity provisioning Profile (CPP), RFC 7297.* IETF. doi:10.17487/rfc7297

Boulianne, S. (2009). Does Internet Use Affect Engagement? A Meta-Analysis of Research. *Political Communication, 26*(2), 193–211. doi:10.1080/10584600902854363

Bovik, A. C. (2013). Automatic prediction of perceptual image and video quality. *Proceedings of the IEEE, 101*(9), 2008–2024.

Braden, R., Zhang, L., Herzog, S., Berson, S., & Jamin, S. (1997). Resource ReSerVation Protocol (RSVP). *IETF*. Retrieved November 25, 2014, from https://tools.ietf.org/html/rfc2205

Bradford, R., Vasseur, J. P., & Farrel, A. (2009). Preserving Topology Confidentiality in Inter-Domain Path Computation Using a Path-Key-Based Mechanism. RFC5520.

Brams, S. J. (2004). *Game Theory and Politics*. Mineola, NY: Dover Publications.

Brandon, J. (2014). *Ericsson to help Telstra introduce SDN, NFV*. Retrieved from http://www.telecoms.com/278661/ericsson-to-help-telstra-introduce-sdn-nfv/

BroadPeak. (2012). *nanoCDN*. Retrieved October 23, 2014 from http://www.broadpeak.tv/ en/technologies/nanocdn-25.php

Broberga, J., Buyyaa, R., & Tarib, Z. (2009). MetaCDN: Harnessing 'Storage Clouds' for high performance content delivery. *Journal of Network and Computer Applications*, *32*(5), 1012–1022. doi:10.1016/j.jnca.2009.03.004

Brodkin, J. (2012, May 30). WiFi, cellular data to account for 60% of all Internet traffic by 2016. *Ars Technica*. Retrieved from http://arstechnica.com/information-technology/2012/05/wifi-cellular-data-to-account-for-60-all-internet-traffic-by-2016/

Brown, P., Bovey, J., & Chen, X. (1997). Context-Aware Applications: from the Laboratory to the Market Place. *IEEE Personal Communication*, *4*(5), 58-64.

Brustein, J. (2014, Sep 18). Wi-Fi Should Scare the Hell out of Verizon and AT&T. *Business Week*. Retrieved from http://www.businessweek.com/articles/2014-09-08/wi-fi-should-scare-the-hell-out-of-verizon-and-at-and-t

Bryant, S., & Pate, P. (2005). *Pseudo Wire Emulation Edge-to-Edge (PWE3) Architecture*. IETF RFC 3985, March 2005.

Bryant, S., Filsfils, C., Previdi, S., Shand, M., & So, N. (2014). *Remote-LFA (RLFA)*. Retrieved March 15, 2015 from https://datatracker.ietf.org/doc/draft-ietf-rtgwg-remote-lfa/

Bryskin, I., Papadimitriou, D., Berger, L., & Ash, J. (2008). *Policy-Enabled Path Computation Framework, RFC5394*. IETF.

Buckley, S. (2014). *Verizon, Telus, China Mobile and China Telecom participate in transport SDN test*. Retrieved from: http://www.fiercetelecom.com/story/verizon-telus-china-mobile-and-china-telecom-participate-transport-sdn-test/2014-08-26

Buffone, G. J., & Beck, J. R. (1994). Facilitation of health care delivery through enhanced communications. *International Journal of Bio-Medical Computing*, *34*(1-4), 349–355. doi:10.1016/0020-7101(94)90035-3 PMID:8125649

Bumgardner, G. (2014). *Automatic Multicast Tunneling, draft-ietf-mboned-auto-multicast-17*. Retrieved April 24, 2014 from http://tools.ietf.org/html/draft-ietf-mboned-auto-multicast-17

Bumgardner, G. (2014). *Automatic Multicast Tunneling, draft-ietf-mboned-auto-multicast-17*. Retrieved April 24, 2014 from https://tools.ietf.org/html/draft-ietf-mboned-auto-multicast-17

Bush, R. (2011). *The Address plus Port (A+P) Approach to the IPv4 Address Shortage (RFC 6346)*. IETF. doi:10.17487/rfc6346

Buttarelli, V. (1997). *Banche dati e tutela della riservatezza*. Milano: Giuffrè.

Buyya, R., Pathan, M., & Vakali, A. (Eds.). (2008). *Content Delivery Networks*. Berlin: Springer-Verlang. doi:10.1007/978-3-540-77887-5

CableLabs, Inc. (2014). *DOCSIS 3.1 Physical Specification*. CableLabs, July 2014.

Caesar, M., Caldwell, D., Feamster, N., Rexford, J., Shaikh, A., & van der Merwe, J. (2005, May). Design and implementation of a routing control platform. In *Proceedings of the 2nd conference on Symposium on Networked Systems Design & Implementation-Volume 2* (pp. 15-28). USENIX Association.

Cain, B., Deering, S., Kouvelas, I., Fenner, B., & Thyagarajan, A. (2002). *Internet Group Management Protocol, Version 3*. IETF Standard RFC 3376, October 2002.

Cain, B., Deering, S., Kouvelas, I., Fenner, B., & Thyagarajan, A. (2002). *Internet Group Management Protocol, Version 3. Internet Engineering Task Force RFC 3376.* Retrieved from https://tools.ietf.org/html/rfc3376

Cai, Y., Wei, L., Ou, H., Arya, V., & Jethwani, S. (2012). *Protocol Independent Multicast Equal-Cost Multipath (ECMP).* Redirect. doi:10.17487/rfc6754

Calamai, R., & Giarre, L. (2012). Enabling Primary and Specialist Care Interoperability Through HL7 CDA Release 2 and the Chronic Care Model: An Italian Case Study. *IEEE Transactions on Systems, Man, and Cybernetics. Part A, Systems and Humans*, *42*(6), 1364–1384. doi:10.1109/TSMCA.2012.2210205

Callon, R. & Suzuki, M. (2005). A Framework for Layer 3 Provider-Provisioned Virtual Private Networks (PPVPNs). RFC 4110.

Campbell, A., & Gomez, J. (2002). IP Micromobility Protocols. *ACM SIGMOBILE Mobile Computer and Communication Review (MC2R)*, 45–54.

Campbell, T. (2014). *Orange: "OTT services bring new revenue growth opportunities".* Retrieved from http://www.iptv-news.com/2014/06/orange-ott-services-bring-new-revenue-growth-opportunities/

Campbell, A. T., De Meer, H. G., Kounavis, M. E., Miki, K., Vicente, J. B., & Villela, D. (1999). A survey of programmable networks. *Computer Communication Review*, *29*(2), 7–23. doi:10.1145/505733.505735

Canadian Internet Registration Authority. (n.d.). *Open letter to the Internet Corporation for Assigned Names and Numbers (ICANN) from the Canadian Internet Registration Authority (CIRA).* Retrieved from www.cira.ca

Cancela, H., Rodriguez-Bocca, P., & Rubino, G. (2007). Perceptual quality in P2P multi-source video streaming policies. In *Proceedings of IEEE Global Telecommunications Conference* (pp. 2780-2785). IEEE.

Capone, A., Filippini, I., Gloss, B., & Barth, U. (2012). Rethinking cellular system architecture for breaking current energy efficiency limits. IEEE Sustainable Internet and ICT for Sustainability (SustainIT), Pisa, Italy.

Carey, J., & Kirksey, H. (2011). *Component Objects for CWMP, TR-157 Issue 1 Amendment 5*, Broadband Forum Tech. Report, November 2011.

Carpenter, B. & Jung, C. (1999). Transmission of IPv6 over IPv4 Domains without Explicit Tunnels, *Internet Engineering Task Force (IETF) RFC 2529.*

Carr, D. F. (2014). *Apple Partners With Epic, Mayo Clinic For HealthKit - InformationWeek* [online community for business technology professionals]. Retrieved 26 September 2014, from http://www.informationweek.com/healthcare/mobile-and-wireless/apple-partners-with-epic-mayo-clinic-for-healthkit/d/d-id/1269371

Carrel, D. (1997, January). *The TACACS+ Protocol - Work in Progress.* Retrieved from http://tools.ietf.org/html/draft-grant-tacacs-02

Casado, M., Freedman, M. J., Pettit, J., Luo, J., McKeown, N., & Shenker, S. (2007). Ethane: Taking control of the enterprise. *Computer Communication Review*, *37*(4), 1–12. doi:10.1145/1282427.1282382

Case, J., Fedor, M., Schoffstall, M., & Davin, J. (1990, May). *A Simple Network Management Protocol (SNMP).* Retrieved from https://tools.ietf.org/html/rfc1157

Casellas, R., Martinez, R., Munoz, R., Vilalta, R., Liu, L., Tsuritani, T., & Morita, I. (2013). Control and management of flexi-grid optical networks with an integrated stateful path computation element and OpenFlow controller. *Optical Communications and Networking, IEEE/OSA Journal of, 5*(10).

Casellas, R., Munoz, R., Fabrega, J.M., Moreolo, M.S., Martinez, R., Liu, L., … Morita, I. (2013). Design and Experimental Validation of a GMPLS/PCE Control Plane for Elastic CO-OFDM Optical Networks. *Selected Areas in Communications, IEEE Journal on, 31*(1), 49-61.

Caviglione, L. (2013). A first look at traffic patterns of Siri. *Transactions on Emerging Telecommunications Technologies.*

CDN Planet. (2011). *Telefonica.* Retrieved from http://www.cdnplanet.com/cdns/telefonica/

CDNTech. (2012). *White paper, "The acceleration of web and mobile content".* Retrieved October 23, 2014 from http://www.cdn-tech.com/en/news/article/white-paper-the-acceleration-of-web-and-mobile-content

Cedexis. (2014). *Cedexis Radar.* Retrieved from http://www.cedexis.com/radar/

Cedexis. (2014). *Cedexis white paper. How (and why) to implement a Multi-CDN Strategy.* Retrieved October 23, 2014 from http://go.cedexis.com/Implementing-Multi-CDN.html

Center for Strategic and International Studies (CSIS). (2008). *Securing cyberspace for the 44th presidency.* Retrieved from http: //csis.org/files/media/csis/pubs/081208_securingcyberspace_44.pdf

CentOS. (n.d.). *CentOS Project Website.* Retrieved July 2014 from: http://www.centos.org

Chan, H., Liu, D., Seite, P., Yokota, H., & Korhonen, J. (2014). Requirements for Distributed Mobility Management, *Internet Draft: draft-ietf-dmmrequirements-15 (work-in-progress).* IETF. [Online]. Available: http://datatracker.ietf.org/doc/draft-ietf-dmm-requirements/

Chan, K., Seligson, J., Durham, D., Gai, S., McCloghrie, K., Herzog, S., & Smith, A. (2001). *COPS usage for policy provisioning* (COPS-PR). RFC3084.

Chan, K., Seligson, J., Durham, D., Gai, S., McCloghrie, K., Herzog, S., . . . Smith, A. (2001). COPS Usage for Policy Provisioning (COPS-PR). *IETF.* Retrieved November 25, 2014, from https://tools.ietf.org/html/rfc3084

Chander, A. (2003). The new, new property. *Texas Law Review, 81*(3), 715–797.

Chan, G. (2005). Domain name protection in Hong Kong: Flaws and proposals for reform. *International Journal of Law and Information Technology, 13*(2), 206–242. doi:10.1093/ijlit/eai009

Channegowda, M., Nejabati, R., & Simeonidou, D. (2013). Software-defined optical networks technology and infrastructure: enabling software-defined optical network operations [Invited]. *Optical Communications and Networking, IEEE/OSA Journal of, 5*(10), A274-A282.

Chappell, C. (2004). *Managing the Virtualized Network: How SDN & NFV Will Change OSS.* Retrieved from: http://www.heavyreading.com/document.asp?doc_id=83218

Chen, G., & Kotz, D. (2000). A Survey of Context-Aware Mobile Computing Research. *Dartmouth Computer Science Technical Report.* TR2000-381.

Chen, Y., Griffith, R., Liu, J., Katz, R.H., & Joseph, A.D. (2009). *Understanding TCP Incast Throughput Collapse in Datacenter Networks.* Academic Press.

Cheng, D., Boucadair, B., Retana, A. (2013) Routing for IPv4-Embedded IPv6 Packets, RFC6992.

China's Internet users total 162 mln by end-June. (2007, July 18). *Xinhua Financial Network (XFN) News.*

Chiosi, M., Clarke, D., Willis, P., Donley, C., Johnson, L., & Bugenhagen, M. ... Neil, A. (2013). *Network Functions Virtualization – Network Operator Perspectives on Industry Progress. Issue 1.* ETSI White Paper. October 2013. Retrieved July 2014 from http://portal.etsi.org/NFV/ NFV_White_Paper2.pdf

Chiosi, M., Clarke, D., Willis, P., Reid, A., Feger, J., Bugenhagen, M., . . . Sen, P. (2012). *Network Functions Virtualization— Introductory White Paper. ETSI. 22 October 2012.* Retrieved October 23, 2014 from http://portal.etsi.org/NFV/NFV_White_Paper.pdf

Chiosi, M., Clarke, D., Willis, P., Reid, A., Feger, J., Bugenhagen, M., ... Sen, P. (2012). *Network Functions Virtualization – An Introduction, Benefits, Enablers, Challenges & Call for Action. Issue 1.* ETSI White Paper. October 2012. Retrieved July 2014 from http://portal.etsi.org/NFV/NFV_White_Paper.pdf

Chiosi, M., Clarke, D., Willis, P., Reid, A., López, D., ... A. M. (2012, October). *Network Functions Virtualisation. An Introduction, Benefits, Enablers, Challenges and Call for Action.* Retrieved March, 6, 2015 from http://portal.etsi.org/NFV/NFV_White_Paper.pdf

Chochlidakis, G., & Friderikos, V. (2014). Hybrid Distributed Mobility Management for Next-Generation Wireless Networks. *International Conference on the Network of the Future (NoF'14),* Paris, France.

Chouffani, R. (2014). *Apple's HealthKit mHealth platform linked with Mayo Clinic, Epic* [health care technology professional's how-to guide]. Retrieved 26 September 2014, from http://searchhealthit.techtarget.com/opinion/Apples-HealthKit-mHealth-platform-linked-with-Mayo-Clinic-Epic

Chown, T. (2006). Use of VLANs for IPv4-IPv6 Coexistence in Enterprise Networks, *Internet Engineering Task Force (IETF) RFC 4554.*

Chu, Y. H. (2013, September). *SDN Architecture and Service Trend.* Retrieved from http://event.nchc.org.tw/2013/sdn/upload/content_file/525770e4007ba.pdf

Cisco HealthPresence. (2014). *Cisco HealthPresence - Industry Solutions - Cisco Systems: Transforming the elivery of Healthcare Telehealth Collaboration Software.* Retrieved 28 September 2014, from http://www.cisco.com/web/strategy/healthcare/cisco_healthpresence_solution.html

Cisco Inc. Visual Networking Index.2014. (n.d.). Retrieved from http://www.cisco.com/c/en/us/solutions/service-provider/visual-networking-index-vni/index.html

Cisco Security Advisory. (2013, August 1). *OSPF LSA Manipulation Vulnerability in Multiple Cisco Products.* Retrieved from http://tools.cisco.com/security/center/content/CiscoSecurityAdvisory/cisco-sa-20130801-lsaospf

Cisco, V. N. I. (2014). *Cisco Visual Networking Index: Forecast and Methodology, 2013–2018.* Retrieved 27 September 2014, from http://cisco.com/c/en/us/solutions/collateral/service-provider/ip-ngn-ip-next-generation-network/white_paper_c11-481360.html

Cisco. (2009). *Power Management for the Cisco 12000 Series Router.* Retrieved from http://www.cisco.com/c/en/us/td/docs/ios/12_0s/feature/guide/12spower.html

Cisco. (2013). *Cisco EnergyWise Suite.* Retrieved from http://www.cisco.com/c/en/us/products/switches/energywise-technology/index.html

Cisco. (2014). *Cisco Technology Radar Trends.* Retrieved from http://www.cisco.com/c/dam/en/us/solutions/collateral/trends/tech-radar/tech-radar-trends-infographics.pdf

Cisco. (2014). *Cisco Visual Networking Index: Global Mobile Data Traffic Forecast Update, 2013–2018.* Retrieved June 5, 2014 from http://www.cisco.com/c/en/us/solutions/collateral/service-provider/visual-networking-index-vni/white_paper_c11-520862.html

Claise, B. (Ed.). (2004). *Cisco Systems NetFlow Services Export Version 9, RFC 3954, October 2004.* Retrieved from http://www.rfc-editor.org/rfc/rfc3954.txt

Clark, D., Sollins, K., Wroclawski, J., & Braden, R. (2005). Tussle in Cyberspace: Defining Tomorrow's Internet[TON]. *IEEE/ACM Transactions on Networking, 13*(3), 462–475. doi:10.1109/TNET.2005.850224

Clarke, R. (1994). The digital persona and its application to data surveillance. *The Information Society, 10*(2), 77-92.

Clemm, A. (2007). Network Management Fundamentals (1 ed.). CiscoPress.

Cloud Management Initiative. (2014). Retrieved from: http://www.dmtf.org/standards/cloud

Cloud Standards Customer Council. (2012). *Impact of Cloud Computing on Healthcare.* Cloud Standards Customer Council.

Conboy, C. (2014). *Front End Optimization for Developers.* Retrieved from https://developer.akamai.com/stuff/Optimization/Front_End_Optimization.html

Condoluci, A., Dohler, M., Araniti, G., Molinaro, A., & Zheng, K. (2014, August). (accepted). Towards 5G DenseNets: Architectural Advances For Effective Machine-Type Communications over Femtocells. *IEEE Communications Magazine.*

Cong, G., & Wen, H. (2013). (2013). Mapping Applications for High Performance on Multithreaded, NUMA Systems. In *Proceedings of the acm international conference on computing frontiers* (pp. 7:1–7:4). New York, NY: ACM. http://doi.acm.org/10.1145/2482767.2482777

Conviva. (2011). *Conviva Precision Video. Policy based Multi-CDN Optimization.* Retrieved October 23, 2014 from http://conviva.com/wp-content/uploads/Conviva-Precision-Video-Policy-based-Multi-CDN-Optimization.pdf

Cooper, A. (2012). *Report from the Internet Privacy Workshop (RFC 6462).* IETF.

Cooper, A., Tschofenig, H., Aboba, B., Peterson, J., Morris, J., Hansen, M., & Smith, R. (2013, July). *Privacy Considerations for Internet Protocols.* Retrieved from http://tools.ietf.org/html/rfc6973

Cordeiro, C., Akhmetov, D., & Park, M. (2010). *IEEE 802.11ad: introduction and performance evaluation of the first multi-gbps wifi technology. ACM international workshop on mmWave communications: from circuits to networks (mmCom '10)*. New York, NY, USA: ACM.

Cormode, G., Krishnamurthy, B., & Willinger, W. (2010). A Manifesto for modelling and measurement in a social media. *First Monday*, *15*(9). doi:10.5210/fm.v15i9.3072

Corporation, N. E. C. (2013). *Telefónica and NEC start the first virtual customer premises equipment trial in Brazil. Press Release*, October 2013. Retrieved October 2014 from: http://www.nec.com/en/press/201310/global_20131010_01.html

Costa-Perez, X., Swetina, J., Guo, T., Mahindra, R., & Rangarajan, S. (2013, July). Tao Guo; Mahindra, R.; Rangarajan, S., "Radio access network virtualization for future mobile carrier networks. *Communications Magazine, IEEE*, *51*(7), 27–35. doi:10.1109/MCOM.2013.6553675

Cox, C. (2012). *An Introduction to LTE: LTE, LTE-Advanced, SAE and 4G Mobile Communications*. John Wiley & Sons. doi:10.1002/9781119942825

Crabbe, E., Minei, I., Medved, J., Varga, R. (2014) PCEP Extensions for Stateful PCE, draft-ietf-pce- stateful-pce-10.

Crabbe, E., Minei, I., Sivabalan, S., Varga, R. (2014) PCEP Extensions for PCE Initiated LSP Setup in a Stateful PCE Model, draft-ietf-pce-pce-initialed-lsp-03.

Crabbe, E., Minei, I., Medved, J., & Varga, R. (2014). *PCEP Extensions for Stateful PCE, draft-ietf-pce-stateful-pce-10*. IETF.

Cranor, L. F., & Greenstein, S. (2002). *Communications Policy and Information Technology: Promises, Problems, Prospects*. The MIT Press.

Crispin, M. (2003, March). *Internet message access protocol - Version 4rev1*. Retrieved from http://tools.ietf.org/html/rfc3501

Cruz, T., Simões, P., Batista, P., Almeida, J., Monteiro, E., Bastos, F., & Laranjeira, A. (2010). CWMP extensions for enhanced management of domestic network services. In *Proceedings of the 2010 IEEE 35th Conference on Local Computer Networks (LCN'2010)* (pp.180-183). Denver, CO: IEEE Computer Society. October 2010. doi:10.1109/LCN.2010.5735695

Cuenca, T. C., Gomez, T. J. G., & Scotti, S. S. (2012). Design an architecture that allows the interoperability between information systems, software or medical device adopting the standard HL7 V2.x. In *Communications Conference (COLCOM), 2012 IEEE Colombian* (pp. 1–7). doi:10.1109/ColComCon.2012.6233647

Cugini, F., Meloni, G., Paolucci, F., Sambo, N., Secondini, M., Gerardi, L., & Castoldi, P. et al. (2012, March1). Demonstration of flexible optical network based on path computation element. *Journal of Lightwave Technology*, *30*(5), 727–733. doi:10.1109/JLT.2011.2180361

Cugini, F., Paolucci, F., Meloni, G., Berrettini, G., Secondini, M., Fresi, F., & Castoldi, P. et al. (2013). Push-pull defragmentation without traffic disruption in flexible grid optical networks. *Journal of Lightwave Technology*, *31*(1), 125–133. doi:10.1109/JLT.2012.2225600

Cui, A., & Hertoghs, Y. (2012). *TR-145: Multi-service Broadband Network Functional Modules and Architecture, Issue 1*. Broadband Forum Technical Report, November 2012.

Czernich, N. (2012). Broadband Internet and Political Participation Evidence for Germany. *Kyklos*, *65*(1), 31–52. doi:10.1111/j.1467-6435.2011.00526.x

Da Silva, R., Fernandez, M., Gamir, L., & Perez, M. (2011). Home routing gateway virtualization: An overview on the architecture alternatives. In Proceedings of Future Network & Mobile Summit (FutureNetw 2011) (pp. 1-9). Warsaw, Poland: IEEE Computer Society. 15-17 June 2011.

DailyMail. (2008). Retrieved November 14, 2008, from http://www.dailymail.co.uk/news/article-1085412/Revealed-The-woman-Second-Life-divorce--whos-engaged-web-cheat-shes-met.html

Daqupta, D. (2014) Segment Routing. Retrieved from https://conference.apnic.net/data/37/apnic2014-segment-routing_santanu_v5_1393404956.pdf

Darwiche, A. (2010). Bayesian Networks. *Communications of the ACM*, *53*(12), 80–90. doi:10.1145/1859204.1859227

Davis, A., Parikh, J., & Weihl, W. E. (2004). Edge computing: extending enterprise applications to the edge of the internet. In *Proceedings of the 13th international World Wide Web conference on Alternate track papers & posters* (pp. 180-187). New York, NY: ACM. doi:10.1145/1013367.1013397

De Meo, P., Quattrone, G., & Ursino, D. (2011). Integration of the HL7 Standard in a Multiagent System to Support Personalized Access to e-Health Services. *IEEE Transactions on Knowledge and Data Engineering*, *23*(8), 1244–1260. doi:10.1109/TKDE.2010.174

de Mesquita, B. B. (2004). Decision-Making Models, Rigor and New Puzzles. *European Union Politics*, *5*(1), 125–138. doi:10.1177/1465116504040448

De Santis, F., & Liguori, L. (2011). *The "right to be forgotten" privacy and online news*. Retrieved March 8, 2011, from http://www.portolano.it/2011/03/the-"right-to-be-forgotten"-privacy-and-online-news

Deering, S. & Hinden, R. (1998). Internet Protocol, Version 6 (IPv6) Specification, *Internet Engineering Task Force (IETF) RFC 2460.*

Deering, S., & Hinden, R. (1998) Internet Protocol, Version 6 (IPv6) Specification. RFC2460

DeKok, A., & Lior, A. (2013, April). *Remote Authentication Dial-In User Service (RADIUS) Protocol Extensions*. Retrieved from http://tools.ietf.org/html/rfc6929

Dely, P., Kassler, A., & Bayer, N. (2011, July). Openflow for wireless mesh networks. In *Computer Communications and Networks (ICCCN), 2011 Proceedings of 20th International Conference on* (pp. 1-6). IEEE. doi:10.1109/ICCCN.2011.6006100

DeNardis, L. (2009). *Protocol Politics: The Globalization of Internet Governance*. Cambridge, MA: MIT. doi:10.7551/mitpress/9780262042574.001.0001

Deng, L., Song, H., Karagian, G., Haleplidis, E., & Martini, B. (2014). *NFV configuration north bound use cases (draft-deng-nfvcon-nb-use-cases-00)*. IETF Internet Draft, June 2014.

Deutsche Telekom. (2012). *Strategic partnership for Cloud Computing: T-Systems to offer customers VMware vCloud Datacenter Services*. Retrieved from http://www.telekom.com/media/enterprise-solutions/129772

Deutsche Telekom. (2014). *CDN solution*. Retrieved from http://www.telekom-icss.com/cdnsolution

Devarapalli, V., Wakikawa, R., Petrescu, A., & Thubert, P. (2005). *Network Mobility (NEMO) Basic Support Protocol (RFC 3963)*. IETF. doi:10.17487/rfc3963

Devaraplli, V., Wakikawa, R., Petrescu, A., & Thubert, P. (2005). Network Mobility (NEMO) Basic Support Protocol, *Internet Engineering Task Force (IETF) RFC 3963.*

Dey, A., Abowd, G., Brown, P., Davies, N., Smith, M., & Steggles, P. (1999). Towards a better understanding of context and context-awareness. In *Proceedings of the 1st international symposium on Handheld and Ubiquitous Computing (HUC)*. London, UK: Springer-Verlag.

Dharwadkar, P. (2011). *Network Positioning System, Cisco on-line presentation*. Retrieved from http://www.ausnog.net/sites/default/files/ausnog-05/presentations/ausnog-05-d02p01-pranav-dharwdkar-cisco.pdf

Dhody, D., & Wu, Q. (2014). *Path Computation Element communication Protocol extensions for relationship between LSPs and Attributes, draft-dhody-pce-association-attr-01, IETF*. PCE Working Group.

Di Ciommo, F. & Pardolesi, R. (2012). Dal diritto all'oblio alla tutela dell'identità dinamica. *Danno e Responsabilità*, 703-715

Dierks, T. (2008). *The transport layer security (TLS) protocol version 1.2*. RFC5246.

Dierks, T., & Rescorla, E. (2008). The Transport Layer Security (TLS) Protocol Version 1.2. *IETF*. Retrieved November 25, 2014, from https://tools.ietf.org/html/rfc5246

Dierks, T., & Rescorla, E. (2008). *The Transport Layer Security (TLS) Protocol. Version 1.2. Internet Engineering Task Force RFC 5246*. Retrieved from https://tools.ietf.org/html/rfc5246

Dierks, T., & Rescorla, E. (2008, August). *The Transport Layer Security (TLS) Protocol Version 1.2*. Retrieved from http://tools.ietf.org/html/rfc5246

DiMaggio, P., Hargittai, E., Neuman, W. R., & Robinson, J. P. (2001). W. Russell Neuman, and John P. Robinson. "Social Implications of the Internet. *Annual Review of Sociology*, *27*(1), 307–336. doi:10.1146/annurev.soc.27.1.307

Display, I. W.(WiDi) Description. (n.d.). Retrieved from https://www-ssl.intel.com/content/www/us/en/architecture-and-technology/intel-wireless-display.html?

Dixit, A., Prakash, P., & Kompella, R. (2011). *On the Efficacy of Fine-Grained Traffic Splitting Protocols in Data Center Networks*. Academic Press.

Djarallah, N. B., Pouyllau, H., Le Sauze, N., & Douville, R. (2011). Business-driven PCE for inter-carrier QoS connectivity services. In *Future Network & Mobile Summit*. FutureNetw.

D-Link. (2007). *D-link first company to offer 'green ethernet™' technology for network connectivity, embrace energy-saving initiatives*. Retrieved from http://www.dlinkgreen.com/press.asp?pressrelease_id=6

DLNA (2009). *DLNA Networked Device Interoperability Guidelines*. DLNA Consortium Guidelines, 2009.

DMTF. (2014). *Common Information Model*. Retrieved from: http://www.dmtf.org/standards/cim

Dogliotti, M. (1980). Tutela dell'onore, identità personale e questioni di compatibilità. *Giustizia Civile*, 965-974.

Dolezel, R., Dostal, O., Hosek, J., Molnar, K., & Rucka, L. (2011). Data-Rate and Queuing Method Optimization for Internetworking Medical Applications. In R. Szabó, H. Zhu, S. Imre, & R. Chaparadza (Eds.), *Access Networks* (pp. 141–152). Springer Berlin Heidelberg. doi:10.1007/978-3-642-20931-4_11

Donadio, P., Russo, S., Canonico, R., & Ventre, G. (2013). O-Gene: Towards an Open Green Network Control Plane. In *Proceedings of the 8th IEEE symposium on Computers and Communications (ISCC '13)*. New York, NY: IEEE. doi:10.1109/ISCC.2013.6754941

Doppler K., Rinne M., Wijting C., Ribeiro C.B., Hugl, K. (2009). Device-to-device communication as an underlay to LTE-advanced networks. *IEEE Communications Magazine, 47*(12).

DOTCOM Act of 2014, H.R. H.R. 4342, 113th Cong. (2014).

Droms, R., Bound, J., Volz, B., Lemon, T., Perkins, C. & Carney, M. (2003). Dynamic Host Configuration Protocol for IPv6 (DHCPv6), *Internet Engineering Task Force (IETF) RFC 3315*.

Droms, R., Bound, J., Volz, B., Lemon, T., Perkins, C., & Carney, M. (2003). *Dynamic Host Configuration Protocol for IPv6 (DHCPv6)*. IETF Internet Standard RFC 3315, July 2003.

Dunahee, M. (2012). *World Internet Project International Report. Rep. Center for the Digital Future, 2012*. Retrieved from www.worldinternetproject.net

Dustzadeh, J. (2013). *SDN: Time to Accelerate the Pace*. Keynote presentation at the Open Networking Summit 2013, Santa Clara, CA, US, April 4, 2013. Retrieved July 2014 from http://www.opennetsummit.org/pdf/2013/presentations/justin_dustzadeh.pdf

Dutta, S., & Bilbao-Osorio, B. (2012). *The Global Information Technology Report 2012, Living in a Hyperconnected World. Insight Report*. Geneva: World Economic Forum and INSEAD.

Dutta, S., Dutton, W. H., & Law, G. (2011). *The New Internet World: A Global Perspective on Freedom of Expression, Privacy, Trust and Security Online*. INSEAD Working Paper No. 2011/89/TOM. Retrieved from: http://ssrn.com/abstract=1916005

Dzida, M. (2014). *Virtual CDN performance tests, ETSI GS NFV*. Retrieved October 23, 2014 from http://docbox.etsi.org/ISG/NFV/PER/05-CONTRIBUTIONS/2014//NFVPER(14)000032_Virtual_CDN_performance_tests.pptx

Eardley, P. (2013). *Survey of MPTCP Implementations*. Academic Press.

Edgecast. (2014). *Application delivery network*. Retrieved from http://www.edgecast.com/services/adn/

Egi, N., Greenhalgh, A., Handley, M., Hoerdt, M., Huici, F., Mathy, L., & Papadimitriou, P. (2010). A platform for high performance and flexible virtual routers on commodity hardware. *SIGCOMM Computer Communications Review, 40*(1), 127-128. DOI=10.1145/1672308.1672332

Egi, N., Greenhalgh, A., Handley, M., Hoerdt, M., Mathy, L., & Schooley, T. (2007). Evaluating Xen for Router Virtualization. In *Proceedings of 16th International Conference on Computer Communications and Networks (ICCCN 2007)* (pp. 1256-1261). Honolulu, HI: IEEE Computer Society. August 2007. doi:10.1109/ICCCN.2007.4317993

Ellis, M., Pezaros, D. P., & Perkins, C. (2012). Performance analysis of AL-FEC for RTP-based streaming video traffic to residential users. In *Proceedings of the 19th Int. Packet Video Workshop (PV)*. Munich, Germany: IEEE Computer Sociery. doi:10.1109/PV.2012.6229737

Elshaer, H., Boccardi, F., Dohler, M., & Irmer, R. (2014). Downlink and Uplink Decoupling: a Disruptive Architectural Design for 5G Networks. IEEE Globecom 2014, Austin, TX.

Enck, W., McDaniel, P., Sen, S., Sebos, P., Spoerel, S., Greenberg, A., & Aiello, W. et al. (2007). Configuration management at massive scale: System design and experience. In *Proceedings of USENIX Annual Technical Conference*. Berkeley, CA: USENIX Association.

Energy Efficient Ethernet Study Group. (2007). *IEEE 802.3 EEESG Objectives* [PDF document]. Retrieved from http://www.ieee802.org/3/eee_study/eee_objectives.pdf

Enns, R., Bjorklund, M., Schoenwaelder, J., & Bierman, A. (2011). Network Configuration Protocol (NETCONF). *IETF*. Retrieved November 25, 2014, from https://tools.ietf.org/html/rfc6241

Enns, R., Bjorklund, M., Schoenwaelder, J., & Bierman, A. (2011). *Network configuration protocol* (NETCONF). Internet Engineering Task Force, RFC6241.

Enyedi, G., Csaszar, A., Atlas, A., Bowers, C., Gopalan, A. (2015) Algorithms for computing Maximally Redundant Trees for IP/LDP Fast-Reroute, draft-ietf-rtgwg-mrt-frr-algorithm-03.

Erickson, D. (2013, August). The beacon openflow controller. In *Proceedings of the second ACM SIGCOMM workshop on Hot topics in software defined networking* (pp. 13-18). ACM. doi:10.1145/2491185.2491189

Ericsson. (2014). *Ericsson White paper. The real-time cloud, Uen 284 23-3219 Rev B*. Retrieved from: http://www.ericsson.com/res/docs/whitepapers/wp-sdn-and-cloud.pdf

Ermert, M. (2011). UN And Internet Governance, Next Four Years: Better Cooperation Or Bigger Role?. *Intelectual Property Watch*.

Ersue, M. (2013). ETSI NFV Management and Orchestration - An Overview. *Presentation at the IETF #88 Meeting*. Vancouver, Canada. Retrieved July 2014 from: http://www.ietf.org/proceedings/88/slides/slides-88-opsawg-6.pdf

ETSI - I. (2012). Intelligent Transport Systems (ITS); Security; Trust and Privacy Management. *ETSI TS 102 941 V1.1.1*. Retrieved from http://www.etsi.org/deliver/etsi_ts/102900_102999/102941/01.01.01_60/ts_102941v010101p.pdf

ETSI - II. (2012). Security and privacy requirements for collaborative cross domain network monitoring. *ETSI GS INS 009 V1.1.1*. Retrieved from http://www.etsi.org/deliver/etsi_gs/INS/001_099/009/01.01.01_60/gs_ins009v010101p.pdf

ETSI NFV 002 (2013). *Network Functions Virtualization (NFV); Architectural Framework, version 1.1.1*. ETSI, October 2013.

ETSI NFV ISG. (n.d.) Website retrieved July 2014 from: http://www.etsi.org/about/how-we-work/industry-specification-groups

ETSI NFV Wiki. (2014). *Ongoing PoCs*. Retrieved from http://nfvwiki.etsi.org/index.php?title=On-going_PoCs

ETSI NFV. (2012). *Network Functions Virtualisation - An Introduction, Benefits, Enablers, Challenges & Call for Action*. Retrieved from: http://portal.etsi.org/nfv/nfv_white_paper.pdf

ETSI. (2013). *Network Function Virtualisation: Architectural Framework. ETSI GS NFV 002, V1.1.1*. Sophia Antipolis, France: ETSI.

ETSI. (2013). *CDN Interconnection Architecture. ETSI TS 182 032 V1.1.1 (2013-04)*. Retrieved October 23, 2014 from http://www.etsi.org/deliver/etsi_ts/182000_182099/182032/01.01.01_60/ts_182032v010101p.pdf

ETSI. (2013). *Network Function Virtualization (NFV): Architectural Framework. ETSI GS NFV 002 V1.1.1 (2013-10)*. Retrieved October 23, 2014 from http://www.etsi.org/deliver/etsi_gs/nfv/001_099/002/01.01.01_60/gs_nfv002v010101p.pdf

ETSI. (2013c). *Network Function Virtualization (NFV): Use Cases. ETSI GS NFV 001 V1.1.1 (2013-10)*. Retrieved October 23, 2014 from http://www.etsi.org/deliver/etsi_gs/nfv/001_099/001/01.01.01_60/gs_nfv001v010101p.pdf

ETSI. (2014). *NFV Management and Orchestration. GS NFV-MAN 001 V0.6.1 (2014-07)*. Retrieved October 23, 2014 from http://docbox.etsi.org/ISG/NFV/Open/Latest_Drafts/NFV-MAN001v061-%20management%20and%20orchestration.pdf

ETSI. Network Function Virtualization: Architectural Framework, white paper (available online) 2013

ETSI-NFV-ISG. (2013a, Oct). *Network Functions Virtualisation (NFV); Architectural Framework* (Tech. Rep.). ETSI. Retrieved March, 6, 2015 from http://www.etsi.org/deliver/etsi_gs/NFV/001_099/002/01.01.01_60/gs_NFV002v010101p.pdf

ETSI-NFV-ISG. (2013b, Oct). *Network Functions Virtualisation (NFV); NFV Security; Problem Statement* (Tech. Rep.). ETSI. Retrieved March, 6, 2015 from http://docbox.etsi.org/ISG/NFV/Open/Latest_Drafts/NFV-SEC001v021-NFV_Security_Problem_Statement.pdf

ETSI-NFV-ISG. (2013c, Oct). *Network Functions Virtualisation (NFV); Use Cases* (Tech. Rep.). ETSI. Retrieved March, 6, 2015 from http://www.etsi.org/deliver/etsi_gs/NFV/001_099/001/01.01.01_60/gs_NFV001v010101p.pdf

ETSI-NFV-ISG. (2013d, Oct). *Network Function Virtualisation (NFV); Resiliency Requirements* (Tech. Rep.). ETSI. Retrieved March, 6, 2015 from http://www.etsi.org/deliver/etsi_gs/NFV/001_099/002/01.01.01_60/gs_NFV002v010101p.pdf

ETSI-NFV-ISG. (2014). *Network Functions Virtualisation (NFV); NFV Performance & Portability Best Practises* (Tech. Rep.). ETSI. Retrieved March, 6, 2015 from http://www.etsi.org/deliver/etsi_gs/NFV-PER/001_099/001/01.01.01_60/gs_NFV-PER001v010101p.pdf

European Commision. (2012, January 25). *The protection of individuals with regard to the processing of personal data and on the free movement of such data (General Data Protection Regulation)*. Retrieved from http://ec.europa.eu/justice/data-protection/document/review2012/com_2012_11_en.pdf

European Commission. (2003). *Enterprise and Industry. What is a SME?* Retrieved from: http://ec.europa.eu/enterprise/policies/sme/facts-figures-analysis/sme-definition/index_en.htm~

European Telecommunications Standards Institute (ETSI). (2009). Human factors (HF): Quality of experience (QoE) requirements for real-time communication services. *Technical Report T.*, *102*, 643.

European Telecommunications Standards Institute. (2012). *Network Functions Virtualisation*. white paper. Retrieved March 12, 2015, from http://portal.etsi.org/NFV/NFV_White_Paper.pdf

European Telecommunications Standards Institute. (2014). *ETSI ES 203 237 V1.1.1*. [PDF document]. Retrieved from http://www.etsi.org/deliver/etsi_es/203200_203299/203237/01.01.01_60/es_203237v010101p.pdf

Evans, D. (2011). *Cisco Internet of Things White Paper - How the Next Evolution of the Internet Is Changing Everything*. Cisco Internet Business Solutions Group (IBSG). Retrieved from http://postscapes.com/cisco-internet-of-things-white-paper-how-the-next-evolution-of-the-internet-is-changing-everything

Facca, F. M., Salvadori, E., Karl, H., López, D. R., Gutiérrez, P. A. A., Kostic, D., & Riggio, R. (2013, October). NetIDE: First steps towards an integrated development environment for portable network apps. In *Software Defined Networks (EWSDN), 2013 Second European Workshop on* (pp. 105-110). IEEE.

Faizul Bari, M., Boutaba, R., Esteves, R., Zambenedetti Granville, L., Podlesny, M., Golam Rabbani, M., & Faten Zhani, M. et al. (2013). Data Center Network Virtualization: A Survey. *IEEE Communications Surveys and Tutorials*, *15*(2), 909–928. doi:10.1109/SURV.2012.090512.00043

Fajardo, V., Arkko, J., Loughney, J., & Zorn, G. (2012, October). *Diameter Base Protocol*. Retrieved from http://tools.ietf.org/html/rfc6733

Fang, L., Bita, N., Le Roux, J. L., & Miles, J. (2005). Inter-provider IP-MPLS services: Requirements, implementations, and challenges. *Communications Magazine, IEEE*, *43*(6), 119–128. doi:10.1109/MCOM.2005.1452840

Farinacci, D., Li, T., Hanks, S., Myer, D., Traina, P. (2000) Generic Routing Encapsulation (GRE), RFC2784.

Farrel, A., Vasseur, J.P., & Ash, J. (2006). *A Path Computation Element (PCE)-Based Architecture*. IETF RFC 4655.

Farrel, A., Vasseur, J.P., & Ash, J. (2006). A Path Computation Element (PCE)-Based Architecture. RFC 4655.

Farrel, A., Drake, J., Bitar, N., Swallow, G., Ceccarelli, D., & Zhang, X. (2014). *Problem Statement and Architecture for Information Exchange Between Interconnected Traffic Engineering Networks, draft-farrel-interconnected-te-info-exchange-07, Network Working Group*. IETF.

Farrel, A., Vasseur, J. P., & Ash, J. (2006). *A Path Computation Element (PCE)-based Architecture, RFC 4655*. IETF. doi:10.17487/rfc4655

Feamster, N., Rexford, J., Shenker, S., Clark, R., Hutchins, R., Levin, D., & Bailey, J. (2013). *SDX: A software-defined internet exchange*. Open Networking Summit.

Feamster, N., Rexford, J., & Zegura, E. (2013). The road to SDN. *Queue*, *11*(12), 20–40. doi:10.1145/2559899.2560327

Fernandez, M. (2013). In Evaluating OpenFlow Controller Paradigms. *ICN 2013, The Twelfth International Conference on Networks*.

Fettweis, G. (2013). 5G What Will it Be: The Tactile Internet. *Keynote talk at ICC 2013*. Retrieved from http://goo.gl/DJhg8E

Fettweis, G. P. (2014). The Tactile Internet: Applications and Challenges. *IEEE Vehicular Technology Magazine*, *9*(1), 64–70. doi:10.1109/MVT.2013.2295069

Fielding, R., & Reschke, J. (2014). Hypertext Transfer Protocol (HTTP/1.1): Authentication. *IETF Standard*, RFC 7235.

Fielding, R., & Reschke, J. (2014, June). *Hypertext Transfer Protocol (HTTP/1.1):Message Syntax and Routing*. Retrieved from http://tools.ietf.org/html/rfc7230

Fielding, R. T., & Taylor, R. N. (2000). Principled design of the modern Web architecture. In *Proceedings of the 22nd Int. Conf. on Software Engineering (ICSE'00)* (pp. 407-417). New York: ACM Press. Doi: doi:10.1145/337180.337228

Filsfils, C., Francois, P., Previdi, S., Decraene, B., Litkowski S., Horneffer, M., … Crabbe, E. (2014). Segment Routing Use Cases, draft-filsfils-spring-segment-routing-use-cases-01.

Filsfils, C., Previdi, S., Bashandy, A., Decraene, B., Litkowski S., Horneffer, M., … Crabbe, E. (2014) Segment Routing Architecture, draft-ietf-spring-segment-routing-mpls-00.

Filsfils, C., Previdi, S., Decraene, B., Litkowski, S., Horneffer, H., Milojevic, I., . . . Crabbe, E. (2014). Segment Routing Architecture. *IETF*. Retrieved November 25, 2014, from https://tools.ietf.org/html/draft-filsfils-spring-segment-routing-04

Finamore, A., Mellia, M., Gilani, Z., Papagiannaki, K., Erramilli, V., & Grunenberger, Y. (2013). Is there a case for mobile phone content pre-staging? In *Proceedings of the ninth ACM conference on Emerging networking experiments and technologies* (pp. 321-326). New York, NY: ACM. doi:10.1145/2535372.2535414

Finseth, C. (1993, July). *An Access Control Protocol, Sometimes Called TACACS*. Retrieved from http://tools.ietf.org/html/rfc1492

Fischer, A., Botero, J. F., Till Beck, M., de Meer, H., & Hesselbach, X. (2013). Virtual Network Embedding: A Survey. Communications Surveys & Tutorials, IEEE, 15(4), 1888-1906.

Fluckinger, D. (2014). *pulse Strategic insight for health IT leaders. As clinicians push to make mobile devices the standard in healthcare facilities, the communications badge—a technology throwback to some—proves newly relevant*. TechTarget Inc.

Fontana, A., & Liebowitz, M. (2013). *Introduction to Virtualizing Business Critical Applications*. Retrieved from: http://www.pearsonitcertification.com/articles/article.aspx?p=2121387&seqNum=3

FORCES. (n.d.). *IETF Forwarding and Control Element Separation (forces) Working Group Website*. Retrieved July 2014 from: http://datatracker.ietf.org/wg/forces/charter/

Ford, A., Raiciu, C., Handley, M., & Bonaventure, O. (2013). *TCP Extensions for Multipath Operation with Multiple Addresses*. Academic Press.

Ford, A., Raiciu, C., Handley, M., & Bonaventure, O. (2013). *TCP Extensions for Multipath Operation with Multiple Addresses (RFC 6824)*. IETF. doi:10.17487/rfc6824

Foster, N., Harrison, R., Freedman, M. J., Monsanto, C., Rexford, J., Story, A., & Walker, D. (2011, September). Frenetic: A network programming language. ACM SIGPLAN Notices, 46(9), 279-291. doi:10.1145/2034773.2034812

Foster, I., Kesselman, C., & Tuecke, S. (2001). The Anatomy of the Grid: Enabling Scalable Virtual Organizations. *International Journal of High Performance Computing Applications*, *15*(3), 200–222. doi:10.1177/109434200101500302

Francois, P., Filsfils, C., Decraene, B., Shakir, R. (2014) Use-cases for Resiliency in SPRING, draft-ietf-spring-resiliency-use-cases-00.

Frank, B., Poese, I., Lin, Y., Smaragdakis, G., Feldmann, A., Maggs, B., & Weber, R. et al. (2013). Pushing CDN-ISP Collaboration to the Limit. *SIGCOMM Computer Communications Review*, *43*(3), 34–44. doi:10.1145/2500098.2500103

Freier, A., Karlton, P., & Kocher, P. (2011, August). *The Secure Sockets Layer (SSL) Protocol Version 3.0*. Retrieved from http://tools.ietf.org/html/rfc6101

Future Internet REsearch (FIRE). (n.d.). Retrieved March 12, 2015, from http://www.ict-fire.eu/home.html

Gabale, V., Dutta, P., Kokku, R., & Kalyanaraman, S. (2012). InSite: QoE-Aware Video Delivery from Cloud Data Centers. In *Proceeding of IWQoS*. doi:10.1109/IWQoS.2012.6245984

Gao, P. X., Curtis, A. R., Wong, B., & Keshav, S. (2012). It's not Easy Being Green. In *Proceedings of the ACM Special Interest Group on Data Communication (SIGCOMM) on the applications, technologies, architectures, and protocols for computer communication (SIGCOMM '12)*. New York, NY: ACM.

Garg, P., Wang, Y. (2014) NVGRE: Network Virtualization using Generic Routing Encapsulation, draft-sridharan-virtualization-nvgre-07.

Garroppo, R. G., Giordano, S., & Tavanti, L. (2010). A survey on multi-constrained optimal path computation: Exact and approximate algorithms. *Computer Networks*, *54*(17), 3081–3107. doi:10.1016/j.comnet.2010.05.017

Gautam, N., Petander, H., & Noel, J. (2013). A comparison of the cost and energy efficiency of prefetching and streaming of mobile video. In *Proceedings of the 5th Workshop on Mobile Video* (pp. 7-12). New York, NY: ACM. doi:10.1145/2457413.2457416

Gharbaoui, M., Paolucci, F., Giorgetti, A., Martini, B., & Castoldi, P. (2013). Effective Statistical Detection of Smart Confidentiality Attacks in Multi-Domain Networks. *Network and Service Management, IEEE Transactions on, 10*(4), 383-397.

Ghodsi, A., Shenker, S., Koponen, T., Singla, A., Raghavan, B., & Wilcox, J. (2011). Information-centric networking: seeing the forest for the trees. In *Proceedings of the 10th ACM Workshop on Hot Topics in Networks (HotNets-X)* (pp. 1-6). New York: ACM. doi:10.1145/2070562.2070563

Gifre, L., Paolucci, F., Velasco, L., Aguado, A., Cugini, F., Castoldi, P., & Lopez, V. (2014). First Experimental Assessment of ABNO-driven In-Operation Flexgrid Network Re-Optimization. *IEEE Journal of Lightwave Technology*.

Giorgetti, A., Valcarenghi, L., Cugini, F. & Castoldi, P. (2010). PCE-based dynamic restoration in wavelength switched optical networks. *ICC conference, 2010.*

Giorgetti, A., Paolucci, F., Cugini, F., & Castoldi, P. (2011). Hierarchical PCE in GMPLS-based multi-domain Wavelength Switched Optical Networks. *OFC Conference.* doi:10.1364/NFOEC.2011.NTuC4

Giorgetti, A., Paolucci, F., Cugini, F., & Castoldi, P. (2012). Impact of intra-domain information in GMPLS-based WSONs with hierarchical PCE. *OFC Conference.* doi:10.1364/NFOEC.2012.NTu2J.2

Gleick, J. (1988). *Chaos: Making a New Science*. New York: Penguin.

Global Environment for Network Innovations (GENI). (n.d.). Retrieved March 12, 2015, from http://www.geni.net/

Gojmerac, I., Ziegler, T., Ricciato, F., & Reichl, P. (2003). *Adaptive Multipath Routing for Dynamic Traffic Engineering*. Academic Press.

Goldstein, D., Groen, P. J., Ponkshe, S., & Wine, M. (2007). *Medical Informatics 20/20: Quality And Electronic Health Records Through Collaboration, Open Solutions, And Innovation* (1st ed.). Sudbury, MA: Jones & Bartlett Learning.

Golrezaei, N., Shanmugam, K., Dimakis, A. G., Molisch, A. F., & Caire, G. (2012). *FemtoCaching: Wireless video content delivery through distributed caching helpers.* Orlando, FL: IEEE INFOCOM.

Gonçalves, C. (2014). Traffic steering abstraction for Neutron. *OpenStack Project Blueprint.* Retrieved July 2014 from: https://blueprints.launchpad.net/neutron/+spec/traffic-steering-abstraction

Gont, F. (2011). *Security Assessment of the Internet Protocol Version 4 (RFC 6274).* IETF. doi:10.17487/rfc6274

Gonzalez de Dios, O.; et al., (2014). *Framework and Requirements for GMPLS based control of Flexi-grid DWDM, draft-ietf-ccamp-flexi-grid-fwk-01, Feb 2014.* IETF.

Google Cloud Platform. (2014). *Pricing*. Retrieved from: https://cloud.google.com/products/compute-engine

Gredler, H., Medved, J., Previdi, S., Farrel, A., & Ray, S. (2014). *North-Bound Distribution of Link-State and TE Information using BGP, IETF draft-ietf-idr-ls-distribution-06.* IETF.

Gredler, H., Medved, J., Previdi, S., Farrel, A., & Ray, S. (2014). *North-Bound Distribution of Link-State and TE Information using BGP, draft-ietf-idr-ls-distribution-06, IDR Working Group*. IETF.

Green, I. C. N. (2013). *Architecture and Applications of Green Information Centric Networking*. Retrieved from http://www.greenicn.org/

Greenberg, A., Hjalmtysson, G., Maltz, D. A., Myers, A., Rexford, J., Xie, G., & Zhang, H. et al. (2005). A clean slate 4D approach to network control and management. *Computer Communication Review, 35*(5), 41–54. doi:10.1145/1096536.1096541

GreenTouch. (2014). *Global Study by Greentouch Consortium Reveals How Communications Networks Could Reduce Energy Consumption by 90 Percent by 2020.* Retrieved from http://www.greentouch.org/index.php?page=green-meter-research

Gringeri, S., Bitar, N., & Xia, T. J. (2013). Extending software defined network principles to include optical transport. *Communications Magazine, IEEE, 51*(3), 32–40. doi:10.1109/MCOM.2013.6476863

Groen, P. J., & Goldstein, D. (2009). Medical Informatics 2040: Reengineering & Transforming Healthcare in the 21st Century. *ePractice.eu*, (8), 1–4.

Gross, G. (2012). Critic's: EU's proposed data protection rules could hinder Internet. *Computer World.* Retrieved September 5, 2012 from http://www.computerworld.com/article/2492101/data-privacy/u-s--privacy--consumer-groups-back-eu-s-proposed-privacy-rules.html

Gross, J., Sridhar, T., Garg, P., Wright, C., Ganga, I., Agarwal, P., … Hudson, J. (2014) Geneve: Generic Network Virtualization Encapsulation, draft-gross-geneve-02.

Guan, H., Kolding, T., & Merz, P. (2010). *Discovery of Cloud RAN.* C-RAN International Workshop, Bejing, China.

Gude, N., Koponen, T., Pettit, J., Pfaff, B., Casado, M., McKeown, N., & Shenker, S. (2008). NOX: Towards an operating system for networks. *ACM SIGCOMM Computer Communications Review*, *38*(3), 105–110. doi:10.1145/1384609.1384625

Guha, A., Reitblatt, M., & Foster, N. (2013). *Formal Foundations For Software Defined Networks.* Open Net Summit.

Guichard, J., & Narten, T. (2013, Dec). *Service Function Chaining Charter* (Tech. Rep.). IETF. Retrieved March, 6, 2015 from http://datatracker.ietf.org/wg/sfc/charter

Guichard, J., Faucheur, F. L., & Vasseur, J. P. (2005). *Definitive MPLS Network Designs.* Indianapolis, IN: Cisco Press.

Guillen, M. F., & Suarez, S. L. (2005). Explaining the Global Digital Divide: Economic, Political and Sociological Drivers of Cross-National Internet Use. *Social Forces*, *84*(2), 681–708. doi:10.1353/sof.2006.0015

Guimaraes, D., Corujo, R. L., Aguiar, F., Silva, & Rosa. (2013),. Empowering Software Defined Wireless Networks Through Media Independent Handover Management. IEEE Globecom, Atlanta, GA.

Gulbrandsen, A., Vixie, P., & Esibov, L. (2000). *A DNS RR for specifying the location of services (DNS SRV) (RFC 2782).* IETF. doi:10.17487/rfc2782

Gunaratne, C., Christensen, K., Nordman, B., & Suen, S. (2008). Reducing the Energy Consumption of Ethernet with Adaptive Link Rate (ALR). *IEEE Transactions on Computers*, *4*, 447–461.

Gundavelli, S., Devarapalli, V., Chowdhury, K., & Patil,B. (2008). Proxy Mobile IPv6, *Internet Engineering Task Force (IETF) RFC 5213.*

Gundavelli, S., Leung, K., Devarapalli, V., Chowdhury, K., & Patil, B. (2008). *Proxy Mobile IPv6," RFC 5213 (Proposed Standard), IETF, updated by RFC 6543.* Retrieved from: http://www.ietf.org/rfc/rfc5213.txt

Gundavelli, S., Leung, K., Devarapalli, V., Chowdhury, K., & Patil, B. (2008). *Proxy Mobile IPv6.* Academic Press.

Gundavelli, S., Leung, K., Devarapalli, V., Chowdhury, K., & Patil, B. (2008). *Proxy Mobile IPv6 (RFC 5213).* IETF. doi:10.17487/rfc5213

Guo, T., & Arnott, R. (2013), Active LTE RAN Sharing with Partial Resource Reservation, *Vehicular Technology Conference (VTC Fall), 2013 IEEE 78th*, pp.1-5 doi:10.1109/VTCFall.2013.6692075

Guo, T., Ul Quddus, A., Wang, N., & Tafazolli, R. (2013a, January). Local Mobility Management for Networked Femtocells Based on X2 Traffic Forwarding, *Vehicular Technology. IEEE Transactions on*, *62*(1), 326–340.

Guttman, E., Perkins, C., Veizades, J., & Day, M. (1999). *Service Location Protocol, Version 2 (RFC 2608).* IETF. doi:10.17487/rfc2608

Hadi Salim, J., Joachimpillai, D., Martin, J., Lopez, D., & Haleplidis, E. (2014). *ForCES applicability for NFV and integrated SDN, ETSI NFV PoC,April2014.* Retrieved March 12, 2015, from http://docbox.etsi.org/ISG/NFV/PER/05CONTRIBUTIONS/2014//NFVPER(14)000046r2_ForCES_Applicability_for_NFV_and_integrated_SDN.docx

Hahn, W. (2011). 3GPP Evolved Packet Core support for distributed mobility anchors: Control enhancements for GW relocation. *ITS Telecommunications (ITST), 2011 11th International Conference on.*

Hahn, W. (2011). Flat 3GPP Evolved Packet Core. *Wireless Personal Multimedia Communications (WPMC), 2011 14th International Symposium on.*

Hakiri, A., Gokhale, A., Berthou, P., Schmidt, D. C., & Thierry, G. (2014). Software-defined Networking: Challenges and Research Opportunities for Future Internet. *Computer Networks*, *75*, 453–471. doi:10.1016/j.comnet.2014.10.015

Haleplidis, E., Pentikousis, K., Denazis, S., Salim, J. H., Meyer, D., & Koufopavlou, O. (2014). *RFC 7426 Software Defined Networking: Layers and Architecture Terminology*. IRTF SDNRG.

Haleplidis, E., Salim, J. H., Denazis, S., & Koufopavlou, O. (2014). Towards a Network Abstraction Model for SDN. *Journal of Network and Systems Management*, 1–19.

Hallam-Baker, P. (2009). *RE: Last Call Comment on Draft-weiler-dnssec-dlv-iana-00.txt*. The Internet Engineering Task Force (IETF®).

Halpern, J., & Pgnataro, C. (2015) Service Function Chaining (SFC) Architecture, draft-ietf-sfc-architecture-07.

Halpern, J., & Pignataro, C. (2015) Service Function Chaining (SFC) Architecture, draft-quinn-sfc-arch-07.

Hammond, J. E., Berger, R. G., Carey, T. S., Rutledge, R., Cleveland, T. J., Kichak, J. P., & Ayscue, C. F. (1991). Making the transition from information systems of the 1970s to medical information systems of the 1990s: The role of the physician's workstation. *Journal of Medical Systems*, *15*(3), 257–267. doi:10.1007/BF00996555 PMID:1804927

Handbook on European Data Protection Law. (2014). Luxembourg: Publications Office of the European Union.

Handigol, N., Heller, B., Jeyakumar, V., Mazières, D., & McKeown, N. (2012, August). Where is the debugger for my software-defined network? In *Proceedings of the first workshop on Hot topics in software defined networks*(pp. 55-60). ACM. doi:10.1145/2342441.2342453

Hao, W., Yong, L., Li, Y., Shao, W., Liu, V. (2014) NVO3 Anycast Layer 3 Gateway, draft-hao-nvo3-anycast-gw-00.

Hao,W., Yong, L., Hares, S., Fang, L., Davari, S. (2014) Inter-AS Option B between NVO3 and BGP/MPLS IP VPN network, draft-hao-l3vpn-inter-nvo3-vpn-01.

Hardt, D. (2012, October). *The OAuth 2.0 Authorization Framework*. Retrieved from http://tools.ietf.org/html/rfc6749

Hartman, S., & Zhang, D. (2013, March). *Analysis of OSPF Security According to the Keying and Authentication for Routing Protocols (KARP) Design Guide*. Retrieved from http://tools.ietf.org/html/rfc6863

Hart, T., & Rolletschek, G. (2003). The challenges of regulating the web. *The Journal of Policy, Regulation and Strategy for Telecommunications*, *5*(5), 6–24. doi:10.1108/14636690310500420

Harvard Extension School. (2014). *Distance Education | Harvard Distance Learning Courses* [Education]. Retrieved 21 November 2014, from http://www.extension.harvard.edu/distance-education

Havey, D., Chertov, R., & Almeroth, K. (2012). Receiver Driven Rate Adaptation for Wireless Multimedia Applications.*Proceeding of ACM MMSys'12*. doi:10.1145/2155555.2155582

Hawksley, H. (2006). Chinese influence in Brazil worries US. *BBC News*. Retrieved from http://news.bbc.co.uk/go/pr/fr/-/2/hi/americas/4872522.stm

Hinden, R. (2004) Virtual Router Redundancy Protocol, RFC2004.

Hirshleifer, J. (1980). Privacy: Its origin, function and future. *The Journal of Legal Studies*, *9*(4), 649–664. doi:10.1086/467659

Hitachi Data Systems. (2012). *How to Improve Healthcare with Cloud Computing*. Hitachi Data Systems.

HL7. (2014). *Health Level Seven International*. Retrieved 23 September 2014, from http://www.hl7.org/

Ho, K. H., & Cheung, C. C. (2010). Green Distributed Routing Protocol for Sleep Coordination in Wired Core Networks. In *Proceedings of the 6th International Conference on Networked Computing (INC '10)*. New York, NY: IEEE.

Holbrook, H., Cain, B., & Haberman, B. (2006). *Using Internet Group Management Protocol Version 3 (IGMPv3) and Multicast Listener Discovery Protocol Version 2 (MLDv2) for Source-Specific Multicast. Internet Engineering Task Force RFC 4604*. Retrieved from https://tools.ietf.org/html/rfc4604

Homma, S., Naito, K., Lopez, D. R., Stiemerling, M., Dolson, D. (2015) Analysis on Forwarding Methods for Service Chaining, draft-homma-sfc-forwarding-methods-analysis-01.

Hood, D. (2014). *SDN Architecture. Issue 1. Open Networking Foundation*. ONF.

Hopps, C. (2000). *Analysis of an Equal-Cost Multipath Algorithm*. Academic Press.

Howarth, M., Boucadair, M., Flegkas, P., Wang, N., Pavlou, G., Morand, P., & Georgatsos, P. et al. (2006). End-to-end Quality of Service Provisioning through Inter-provider Traffic Engineering. *Computer Communications (Elsevier)*, *29*(6), 683–702. doi:10.1016/j.comcom.2005.07.022

Huawei Technologies Co. Ltd. (2010). *SmartAX MA5600T Series Product Website*. Retrieved October 2014 from: http://enterprise.huawei.com/en/products/network/access-network/olt/en_ma5600t.htm

Huawei. (2013). *5G: A Technology Vision*. Retrieved from http://www.huawei.com/5gwhitepaper/

Huitema, C. (1995). *Multi-homed TCP*. Academic Press.

Huitema, C. (1993). *IAB Recommendation for an Intermediate Strategy to Address the Issue of Scaling (RFC 1481)*. IETF. doi:10.17487/rfc1481

Humphreys, L., Gill, P., & Krishnamurthy, B. (2013). Twitter: A content analysis of personal information. *Information Comunication and Society Journal*, *17*(7), 843–857. doi:10.1080/1369118X.2013.848917

Hunter, D. (2003, Spring). ICANN and the Concept of Democratic Deficit. *Loyola of Los Angeles Law Review*, *36*, 1149–1183.

Huston, G., Lord, A., & Smith, P. (2004). IPv6 Address Prefix Reserved for Documentation, *Internet Engineering Task Force (IETF) RFC 3849*.

IBM. (2011). *Cloud Computing: Building a New Foundation for Healthcare*. IBM Corporation.

ICNRG. (2014). *Information-Centric Networking Research Group (ICNRG)*. Retrieved from https://irtf.org/icnrg

IEEE 802.1ad. (2005). IEEE Standard 802.1ad-2005, *Virtual Bridged Local Area Networks Amendment 4: Provider Bridges*. IEEE 802.1 Working Group, 2005.

IEEE 802.1Q. (2011). *IEEE Standard 802.1Q-2011, Media Access Control Bridges and Virtual Bridged Local Area Networks*. IEEE 802.1 Working Group, 2011.

IEEE. (2011). IEEE Standard for the Functional Architecture of Next Generation Service Overlay Networks. In *IEEE Std. 1903-2011*. New York, NY: IEEE.

IEEE. (2012, January). *Bridges and Virtual Bridged Local Area Networks – Amendment 9: Shortest Path Bridging*. Academic Press.

IETF Handover Keying WG (hokey). (2006). Retrieved from Handover Keying (hokey): http://datatracker.ietf.org/wg/hokey/history/

IETF Seamless Mobility (seamoby) Working Group. (2000). *Context Transfer, Handoff Candidate Discovery, and Dormant Mode Host Alerting (seamoby) charter*. IETF.

IETF SFC WG. (n.d.). Website retrieved October 2014 from: https://datatracker.ietf.org/wg/sfc/documents

IETF. (1992). *IP Routing for Wireless/Mobile Hosts (mobileip)*. IETF.

IETF. (2014). *Cdni Status Pages*. Retrieved October 23, 2014 from http://tools.ietf.org/wg/cdni/

IETF. (2014). *Mptcp Status Pages*. Retrieved October 23, 2014 from http://tools.ietf.org/wg/mptcp/

Incapsula. (2014). *Application delivery from the cloud*. Retrieved from http://www.incapsula.com/cloud-based-application-delivery.html

Index, D. (2011). (n.d.). Rep. N.p. *Economist Intelligence Unit*.

Information Science Institute. (1981, September). *Transmission Control Protocol*. Retrieved from http://tools.ietf.org/html/rfc793

International Monetary Fund, World Economic Outlook Database. (n.d.). International Monetary Fund. Retrieved from http://www.imf.org/external/pubs/ft/weo/2012/01/weodata/weoselgr.aspx

International Standard Organization (ISO). (2014). Information technology -- Dynamic adaptive streaming over HTTP (DASH) -- Part 1: Media presentation description and segment formats. *ISO/IEC* 23009-1

International Telecommunication Union (ITU). (1998). *Subjective audiovisual quality assessment methods for multimedia applications* (p. 911). ITU-T Recommendation.

International Telecommunication Union (ITU). (1999). *Subjective video quality assessment methods for multimedia applications* (p. 910). ITU-T Recommendation.

International Telecommunication Union (ITU). (2002). Methodology for the subjective assessment of the quality of television pictures. *ITU-R Recommendation BT.*500-11.

International Telecommunication Union (ITU). (2007). Definition of Quality of Experience (QoE). *ITU-T SG 12.*

International Telecommunication Union (ITU). (2012). Information Technology – Generic coding of moving pictures and associated audio information – Systems. *Rec. ITU-T H222.0*

International Telecommunication Union (ITU). (2013). Parametric non-intrusive bitstream assessment of video media streaming quality – higher resolution application area. *ITU-T Recommendation P.1202.2.*

Internet Engineering Task Force, Energy Management Working Group. (2010). *Charter for "Energy Management" WG (charter-ietf-eman-01).* Retrieved from https://datatracker.ietf.org/wg/eman/charter/

Internet Governance Project. (2004). *Internet Governance: The State of Play.* Retrieved from www.internetgovernance.org

Internet Governance Project. (2005). *Internet Governance: Quo Vadis? A Reponse to the WGIG Report.* Retrieved from http://www.internetgovernance.org/pdf/igp-quovadis.pdf

Internet Governance Project. (2005). *The Future US Role in Internet Governance: 7 Points in Response to the US Commerce Dept.'s "Statement of Principles"*. Retrieved from www.internetgovernance.org

Internet Governance Project. (2005). *What to Do About ICANN: A Proposal for Structural Reform.* Retrieved from www.internetgovernance.org

Interoperability Forum, D. A. S. H.(DASH-IF). (n.d.). Retrieved from http://dashif.org/white-papers/

Ioannidis, J. (1993). *Protocols for Mobile Internetworking* (PhD Thesis). New York: Columbia University.

Ioannidis, J., & Maguire, G. Q. (1993). The design and implementation of a Mobile Internetwork Architecture. *USENIX Winter 1993 Technical Conference* (pp. 491-502). USENIX Association.

Ioannidis, J., Maguire, G. Q., Ben-Shaul, I. Z., Levedopoulos, M., & Liu, M. (1990). *Porting AIX onto the Student Electronic Notebook.* New York: Columbia University Computer Science Technical Reports.

Iperf. (n.d.). *Iperf Tool Website.* Retrieved July 2014 from: http://iperf.sourceforge.net

ISO. IEC 10589. (2002, November 15). *Information technology -Telecommunications and information exchange between systems — Intermediate System to Intermediate System intra-domain routeing information exchange protocol for use in conjunction with the protocol for providing the connectionless-mode network service (ISO 8473).* Retrieved November from http://webstore.iec.ch/preview/info_isoiec10589%7Bed2.0%7Den.pdf

ITU FG IPTV-DOC-0184. (2007). *Quality of Experience Requirements for IPTV Services, FG IPTV-DOC-0184.* ITU IPTV Focus Group Output Document. December 2007.

ITU-T Study Group 13. (2014). *Y.3300, Framework of software-defined networking.* Retrieved March 12, 2015, from http://www.itu.int/ITU-T/recommendations/rec.aspx?rec=12168

ITU-T. (2009). *ITU-T Technology Watch Report 9 Distributed Computing: Utilities, Grids & Clouds.* Retrieved from: http://www.itu.int/dms_pub/itu-t/oth/23/01/T23010000090001PDFE.pdf

Ivanovich, M., Bikerdike, P., & Li, J. (2008). On TCP performance enhancing proxies in a wireless environment. *IEEE Communications Magazine*, *46*(9), 76–83. doi:10.1109/MCOM.2008.4623710

Iyengar, J., Amin, S., Ford, B., Ailawadi, D., Nowlan, M., & Tiwari, N. (2012). Minion: Unordered Delivery Wire-Compatible with TCP and TLS. *Technical Report*. ext. arXiv:1103.0463.

Jackson, P. (2007). News fuels Russian internet boom. *BBC News*. Retrieved from http://news.bbc.co.uk/go/pr/fr/-/2/hi/europe/4880540.stm

Jacob, P., & Davie, B. (2005). Technical challenges in the delivery of interprovider QoS. *Communications Magazine, IEEE*, *43*(6), 112–118. doi:10.1109/MCOM.2005.1452839

Jain, S., Kumar, A., Mandal, S., Ong, J., Poutievski, L., Singh, A., & Vahdat, A. et al. (2013, August). B4: Experience with a globally-deployed software defined WAN. In *Proceedings of the ACM SIGCOMM 2013 conference on SIGCOMM* (pp. 3-14). ACM. doi:10.1145/2486001.2486019

Jammal, M., Singh, T., Shami, A., Asal, R., & Li, Y. (2014). Software-Defined Networking: State of the Art and Research Challenges. *Computer Networks*, *72*, 74–98.

Jensen, F. B., & Graven-Nielsen, T. (2010). *Bayesian Networks and Decision Graphs (Information Science and Statistics)*. Springer.

Jiang, Y., & Li, H. (2014). *An Architecture of Service Function Chaining (draft-jiang-sfc-arch-01.txt)*. IETF Internet Draft. February 2014.

John, W., Pentikousis, K., Agapiou, G., Jacob, E., Kind, M., Manzalini, A., . . . Meirosu, C. (2013, November). Research directions in network service chaining. In Future Networks and Services (SDN4FNS), 2013 IEEE SDN for (pp. 1-7). IEEE. doi:10.1109/SDN4FNS.2013.6702549

Johnson, S. (2013). *OpenFlow scalability: The protocol*. Retrieved from http://searchtelecom.techtarget.com/feature/Exploring-OpenFlow-scalability-in-cloud-provider-data-centers

Jones, R. (2009). *Virt-top Package*. Retrieved July 2014 from http://people.redhat.com/rjones/virt-top

Joseph, V., & Mulugu, S. (2011). Deploying Next Generation Multicast-Enabled Applications: Label Switched Multicast for MPLS VPNs, VPLS, and Wholesale Ethernet (pp. 400-401). San Francisco, CA: Morgan-Kaufmann.

Juniper Network. (2008). *What's behind network downtime? Proactive Steps to Reduce Human Error and Improve Availability of Networks*. Retrieved from https://www-935.ibm.com/services/au/gts/pdf/200249.pdf

Kaihara, S. (1994). Workstation network system which enables international exchange of characters and images at the University of Tokyo Hospital. *International Journal of Bio-Medical Computing*, *34*(1-4), 357–361. doi:10.1016/0020-7101(94)90036-1 PMID:8125650

Kalt, C. (2000, April). *Internet Relay Chat: Server Protocol*. Retrieved from http://tools.ietf.org/html/rfc2813

Kandula, S., Sengupta, S., Greenberg, A., Patel, P., & Chaiken, R. (2009). *The Nature of Data Center Traffic: Measurements and Analysis*. Academic Press.

Kaoudi, Z., & Manolescu, I. (2014). RDF in the Clouds: A Survey. *The International Journal on Very Large Databases*.

Karlsson, M. (2008, Oct). *Access Network Discovery and Selection Function (ANDSF)*. Retrieved from 3GPP TS 24.312: http://www.3gpp.org/dynareport/24312.htm

Katz, D., Kompella, K., & Yeung, D. (2003). *Traffic engineering (TE) extensions to OSPF version 2*. RFC 3630.

Kauffman, S. A. (1996). *At Home in the Universe: The Search for Laws of Self-organization and Complexity*. New York: Oxford UP.

Kawamura, S., & Kawashima, M. (2010). A Recommendation for IPv6 Address Text Representation, *Internet Engineering Task Force (IETF) RFC 5952*.

Kent, S., & Seo, K. (2005, December). *Security Architecture for the Internet Protocol*. Retrieved from http://tools.ietf.org/html/rfc4301

Kent, S., Lynn, C., Mikkelson, J., & Seo, K. (2000). Secure Border Gateway Protocol (S-BGP)—Real World Performance and Deployment Issues. In *Proceedings of the Network and Distributed System Security Symposium (NDSS 2000)*. Retrieved from http://users.ece.cmu.edu/~adrian/731-sp04/readings/KLMS-SBGP.pdf

Keohane, R. O. (2005). *After Hegemony: Cooperation and Discord in the World Political Economy*. Princeton, NJ: Princeton UP.

Kerravala, Z. (2004). *As the value of enterprise networks escalates, so does the need for configuration management*. The Yankee Group Report.

Khalili, R., Gast, N., Popovic, M., & Le Boudec, J.Y. (2012). *Non-Pareto Optimality of MPTCP: Performance Issues and a Possible Solution*. Academic Press.

Khalili, R., Gast, N., Popovic, M., & Le Boudec, J.Y. (2014). *Opportunistic Linked-Increases Congestion Control Algorithm for MPTCP*. Academic Press.

Khan, A., Kellerer, W., Kozu, K., & Yabusaki, M. (2011, October). Network sharing in the next mobile network: TCO reduction, management flexibility, and operational independence. *Communications Magazine, IEEE, 49*(10), 134–142. doi:10.1109/MCOM.2011.6035827

King, D., & Farrel, A. (2012). *The Application of the Path Computation Element Architecture to the Determination of a Sequence of Domains in MPLS and GMPLS*. RFC6805.

King, D.; Farrel, A.; (2014). A *PCE-based Architecture for Application-based Network Operations, IETF draft, draft-farrkingel-pce-abno-architecture-13, Oct 2014*. IETF.

Kirksey, H. (2010). *TR-140 – TR-069 Data Model for Storage Service Enabled Devices, Issue: 1 Amendment 1*. April 2010.

Kittilson, M. C., & Dalton, R. J. (2012). Virtual Civil Society: The New Frontier of Social Capital? *Political Behavior, 33*(4), 625–644. doi:10.1007/s11109-010-9143-8

Kivity, A. (2007). KVM, One Year On. *Keynote presentation delivered at the KVM Forum 2007, Tucson, USA, August 2007*. Retrieved July 2014 from: http://www.linux-kvm.org/wiki/images/6/61/KvmForum2007$kf2007-keynote.pdf

Klein, H. (2001). ICANN and the feasibility of global democracy: Understanding ICANN's at-large elections. *The Journal of Policy, Regulation and Strategy for Telecommunications Information and Media, 3*(4), 333–345. doi:10.1108/14636690110801996

Kleinwächter, W. (2000). ICANN as the 'United Nations' of the Global Information Society? The Long Road towards Self-Regulation of the Internet. *Gazette, 62*(6), 451–476. doi:10.1177/0016549200062006001

Kleinwächter, W. (2001). ICANN the silent subversive: ICANN and the new global governance. *The Journal of Policy, Regulation and Strategy for Telecommunications Information and Media, 3*(4), 259–278. doi:10.1108/14636690110801950

Kleinwächter, W. (2003). From Self-Governance to Public-Private Partnership: The Changing Role of Governments in the Management of the Internet's Core. *Loyola of Los Angeles Law Review, 36*, 1103–1126.

Klensin, J. (2008, October). *Simple Mail Transfer Protocol*. Retrieved from http://tools.ietf.org/html/rfc5321

Knight, S. (1998) Virtual Router Redundancy Protocol, RFC2338.

KOF Index of Globalization. (n.d.). *Eidgenössische Technische Hochschule Zürich*. Retrieved from http://globalization.kof.ethz.ch/

Kokku, R., Mahindra, R., Zhang, & Rangarajan, S. (2013). CellSlice: Cellular wireless resource slicing for active RAN sharing. *Communication Systems and Networks (COMSNETS), 2013 Fifth International Conference on.*

Kolkman, O., Mekking, W., & Gieben, R. (2012, December). *DNSSEC Operational Practices, Version 2*. Retrieved from https://tools.ietf.org/html/rfc6781

Kolyshin, K. (2006). *Virtualization in Linux*. Sept. 2006. Retrieved from http://download.openvz.org/doc/openvz-intro.pdf

Kompella, K., Drake, J., Amante, S., Henderickx, W., Yong, L. (2012) The Use of Entropy Labels in MPLS Forwarding, RFC6790.

Koodli, R. (2008). *Fast Handovers for Mobile IPv6', RFC 5268 (Proposed Standard)*. IETF.

Koodli, R. (2009). *Mobile IPv6 Fast Handovers (RFC 5568)*. IETF. doi:10.17487/rfc5568

Kreutz, D., Ramos, F., & Verissimo, P. (2013, August). Towards secure and dependable software-defined networks. In *Proceedings of the second ACM SIGCOMM workshop on Hot topics in software defined networking* (pp. 55-60). ACM. doi:10.1145/2491185.2491199

Krevat, E., Vasudevan, V., Phanishayee, A., Andersen D. G., Ganger, G. R., Gibson, G. A., & Seshan, S. (2007). *On Application-level Approaches to Avoiding TCP Throughput Collapse in Cluster-Based Storage Systems*. Academic Press.

La Due Lake, R., & Huckfeldt, R. (1998). Social Capital, Social Networks, and Political Participation. *Political Psychology, 19*(3), 567–584. doi:10.1111/0162-895X.00118

Lance, W. (2015). *Google advisers: Limit 'right to be forgotten' to Europe*. Retrieved February 6, 2015, from http://www.cnet.com/news/google-advisers-limit-right-to-be-forgotten-to-europe/

Lasserre, M., Balus, F., Morin, T., Bitar, N., Rekhter, Y. (2014) Framework for DC Network Virtualization, RFC7365.

Latour, B. (2005). *Reassembling the Social: An Introduction to Actor-network-theory*. Oxford: Oxford UP.

Law, W. (2013). *Maximizing the Pipe: Hybrid Protocols for Optimized OTT Delivery*. Retrieved October 23, 2014 from http://fr.slideshare.net/kfostervmx/multi-network-forum-ibcakamai-final

Lawrence, R. Z., Hanouz, M. D., & Doherty, S. (2012). *The Global Enabling Trade Report 2012 Reducing Supply Chain Barriers. Insight Report*. Geneva: World Economic Forum.

Le Roux, J. L. (2006). *Requirements for Path Computation Element (PCE) Discovery, RFC 4674*. IETF.

Le Roux, J. L., & Papadimitriou, D. (2008). *Evaluation of Existing GMPLS Protocols against Multi-Layer and Multi-Region Networks (MLN/MRN), RFC 5339*. IETF. doi:10.17487/rfc5339

Le Roux, J. L., Vasseur, J. P., & Lee, Y. (2009). *Encoding of Objective Function in the Path Computation Element Communication Protocol (PCEP), RFC 5541*. IETF. doi:10.17487/rfc5541

Leary, M. (2014). *SDN, NFV, and open source: the operator's view*. Retrieved from http://bit.ly/1APDJKQ

Lebo, H. (2012). *World Internet Project International Report. Rep* (3rd ed.). Los Angeles: University of Southern California.

Lee, J., Bonnin, J.-M., Seite, P., & Chan, H.A. (2013). Distributed IP mobility management from the perspective of the IETF: motivations, requirements, approaches, comparison, and challenges. *IEEE Wireless Communications, 20*(5), 159-168.

Lee, Y., & Ghai, R. (2014). *Problem Statements of Virtualizing Home Services (draft-lee-vhs-ps-00)*. IETF Internet Draft, February 2014.

Lee, Y., & Xie, C. (2014). *Virtualizing Home Services Use Cases (draft-lee-vhs-usecases-00)*. IETF Internet Draft, February 2014.

Lee, Y., Bernstein, G., Dhody, D., & Choi, T. (2014). ALTO Extensions for Collecting Data Center Resource Information. In IETF draft-lee-alto-ext-dc-resource-03.

Lee, D. H., Choi, K. W., Jeon, W. S., & Jeong, D. G. (2013). *Resource Allocation Scheme for Device-to-Device Communication for Maximizing Spatial Reuse*. IEEE Wireless Communications and Networking. doi:10.1109/WCNC.2013.6554548

Lee, S., & Kang, S. (2012). NGSON: Features, state of the art, and realization. *IEEE Communications Magazine, 50*(1), 54–61. doi:10.1109/MCOM.2012.6122533

Lee, Y., Bernstein, G., & Imajuku, W. (2011). *Framework for GMPLS and Path Computation Element (PCE) Control of Wavelength Switched Optical Networks (WSONs), RFC 6163*. IETF. doi:10.17487/rfc6163

Lee, Y., Le Roux, J. L., King, D., & Oki, E. (2009). *Path Computation Element Communication Protocol (PCEP) Requirements and Protocol Extensions in support of Global Concurrent Optimization, RFC 5557*. IETF. doi:10.17487/rfc5557

Le, F., Xie, G., & Zhang, H. (2007). Understanding route redistribution. In *Proceedings of International Conference on Network Protocols*. Piscataway, NJ: IEEE.

Le, F., Xie, G., & Zhang, H. (2008). Instability free routing: Beyond one protocol instance. In *Proceedings of ACM CoNEXT*. New York, NY: ACM. doi:10.1145/1544012.1544021

Lemke, H. U., Faulkner, G., & Krauss, M. (1994). Development towards multimedia medical workstations. *Computerized Medical Imaging and Graphics: The Official Journal of the Computerized Medical Imaging Society*, *18*(2), 67–71. doi:10.1016/0895-6111(94)90015-9 PMID:8168052

Leung, K., Dommety, G., Narayanan, V., & Petrescu, A. (2008). *Network Mobility (NEMO) Extensions for Mobile IPv4 (RFC 5177)*. IETF. doi:10.17487/rfc5177

Li, Q.C., Niu, Wu, & Hu, R.Q. (2013). Anchor-booster based heterogeneous networks with mmWave capable booster cells. *Globecom Workshops (GC Wkshps), 2013 IEEE.*

Li, R., Zhao, Q., Yang, T., Raszuk, R. (2014) MPLS Global Label Use Cases, draft-li-mpls-global-label-usecases-03.

Li, T. & Smith, H. (2008). *IS-IS Extensions for Traffic Engineering*. RFC5305.

Libvirt. (n.d.). *Libvirt Project Website*. Retrieved July 2014 from: http://libvirt.org

Limelight. (2014). *Orchestrate performance*. Retrieved from http://www.limelight.com/services/orchestrate-performance.html

Lindsay, D. (2007). *International Domain Name Law: ICANN and the UDRP*. Oxford: Hart Pub.

Liu, D., Zuniga, J., Seite, P., Chan, H., & Bernandos, C. (2014), Distributed Mobility Management: Current practices and gap analysis. *Internet Draft: draft-ietf-dmm-best-practices-gap-analysis- 03, IETF, 2014.* Retrieved From: http://datatracker.ietf.org/doc/draft-ietf-dmm-best-practices-gap-analysis

Liu, L., & Huang, Q. (2012). An extensible HL7 middleware for heterogeneous healthcare information exchange. In *2012 5th International Conference on Biomedical Engineering and Informatics (BMEI)* (pp. 1045–1048). doi:10.1109/BMEI.2012.6513196

Liu, X., & Xiao, L. (2007). A Survey of Multihoming Technology in Stub Networks: Current Research and Open Issues. *IEEE Network*, *21*(3), 32–40. doi:10.1109/MNET.2007.364256

Lockwood, J. W., McKeown, N., Watson, G., Gibb, G., Hartke, P., Naous, J., . . . Luo, J. (2007, June). NetFPGA--An Open Platform for Gigabit-Rate Network Switching and Routing. In *Microelectronic Systems Education, 2007. MSE'07. IEEE International Conference on* (pp. 160-161). IEEE.

Lopez, D., Gonzales De Dios, O., Wu, Q., & Dhody, D. (2014). *Secure Transport for PCEP, draft-ietf-pce-pceps-00, IETF draft*. IETF.

Lopez, D., Gonzalez, F., Bellido, L., & Alonso, A. (2006). Adaptive multimedia streaming over IP based on customer oriented metrics. In *Proceedings of IEEE International Symposium on Computer Networks*. IEEE. doi:10.1109/ISCN.2006.1662531

Loukides, M. (2012). *What is DevOps? Infrastructure as Code*. O'Reilly Media.

Luo, T., Hwee-Pink, T., Quan, P. C., Law, Wei, Y., & Jiong, J. (2012). *Enhancing Responsiveness and Scalability for OpenFlow Networks via Control-Message Quenching*. Retrieved from: http://www1.i2r.a-star.edu.sg/~luot/pub/%5BICTC12%5D-OpenFlow-performance.pdf

Lupton, W. (Ed.). (2013). Data Model Template for TR-069-Enabled Devices, Issue: 1 Amendment 7. Broadband Forum Technical Report, September 2013.

Lu, Z., Somayazulu, S., & Moustafa, H. (2014). Context-Adaptive Cross-Layer TCP Optimization for Internet Video Streaming. *Proceedings of the IEEE*, ICC.

Lu, Z., & de Veciana, G. (2013). Optimizing Stored Video Delivery For Mobile Networks: The Value of Knowing the Future. In *Proceedings of the 32nd IEEE International Conference on Computer Communications* (pp. 2706-2714). IEEE. doi:10.1109/INFCOM.2013.6567079

Macias, F., & Thomas, G. (2011). *Cloud Computing Advantages in the Public Sector: How Today's Government, Education, and Healthcare Organizations Are Benefiting from Cloud Computing Environments*. White Paper, Cisco Systems, Inc.

Magoules, F. (2010). Future of grids resources management. In *Fundamentals of Grid Computing, Theory, Algorithms and Technologies* (p. 126). Taylor and Francis Group.

Mahalingam, M., Dutt, D., Duda, K., Agarwal, P., Kreeger, L., Sridar, T., … Wright, C. (2014) VXLAN: A Framework for Overlaying Virtualized Layer 2 Networks over Layer 3 Networks, RFC7348.

Mahalingam, M., Dutt, D., Duda, K., Agarwal, P., Kreeger, L., Sridhar, T., … Wright, C. (2014). *Virtual eXtensible Local Area Network (VXLAN): A Framework for Overlaying Virtualized Layer 2 Networks over Layer 3 Networks.* IETF RFC 7348, August 2014.

Mahy, R., Matthews, P., & Rosenberg, J. (2010). *Traversal Using Relays around NAT.* TURN.

Maltz, D., & Bhagwat, P. (1998). MSOCKS: An Architecture for Transport Layer Mobility. *INFOCOM '98. Seventeenth Annual Joint Conference of the IEEE Computer and Communications Societies.* (pp. 1037 - 1045). IEEE.

Mannie, E. (2004). *Generalized multi-protocol label switching (GMPLS) architecture.* RFC3945.

Manning, R. (n.d.). Obama's Internet Giveaway Threatened in House. *Breitbart.* Retrieved from: http://www.breitbart.com/Big-Government/2014/05/27/Obamas-Internet-GiveAway-Threatened-in-House

Mathis, M. & Heffner, J. (2007). Packetization Layer Path MTU Discovery, *Internet Engineering Task Force (IETF) RFC 4821.*

Matsumoto, A., Kozuka, A., Fujikawa, K., & Okabe, Y. (2003). *TCP Multi-Home Options.* Academic Press.

McCann, J., Deering, S., & Mogul, J. (1996). Path MTU Discovery for IP version 6, *Internet Engineering Task Force (IETF) RFC 1981.*

McCann, P. (2012). Authentication and Mobility Management in a Flat Architecture. *Internet Engineering Task Force Internet Draft: draft-mccann-dmm-flatarch-00.* Retrieved from: http://tools.ietf.org/html/draft-mccann-dmm-flatarch-00

McKeown, N., Anderson, T., Balakrishnan, H., Parulkar, G., Peterson, L., Rexford, J., & Turner, J. et al. (2008). Openflow: Enabling innovation in campus networks. *ACM SIGCOMM Computer Communications Review, 38*(2), 69–74. doi:10.1145/1355734.1355746

McKinsey & Company. (2014). *Healthcare Systems & Services Practice* [Management Consulting Firm]. Retrieved 21 November 2014, from http://www.mckinsey.com/client_service/healthcare_systems_and_services

Medved, J., Varga, R., Tkacik, A., & Gray, K. (2014, June). OpenDaylight: Towards a Model-Driven SDN Controller architecture. In *A World of Wireless, Mobile and Multimedia Networks (WoWMoM), 2014 IEEE 15th International Symposium on* (pp. 1-6). IEEE.

Mehmood, R., & Alturki, R. (2011). A scalable multimedia QoS architecture for ad hoc networks. *Multimedia Tools and Applications, 54*(3), 551–568. doi:10.1007/s11042-010-0569-0

Mehmood, R., & Alturki, R. (2013). Video QoS Analysis over Wi-Fi Networks. In *Advanced Video Communications over Wireless Networks* (pp. 439–480). CRC Press. doi:10.1201/b13746-16

Mehmood, R., Alturki, R., & Faisal, M. (2009). A Scalable Provisioning and Routing Scheme for Multimedia QoS over Ad Hoc Networks. In A. Mauthe, S. Zeadally, E. Cerqueira, & M. Curado (Eds.), *Future Multimedia Networking* (pp. 131–142). Springer Berlin Heidelberg. doi:10.1007/978-3-642-02472-6_12

Mehmood, R., Alturki, R., & Zeadally, S. (2011). Multimedia applications over metropolitan area networks (MANs). *Journal of Network and Computer Applications, 34*(5), 1518–1529. doi:10.1016/j.jnca.2010.08.002

Mehmood, R., & Lu, J. A. (2011). Computational Markovian analysis of large systems. *Journal of Manufacturing Technology Management, 22*(6), 804–817. doi:10.1108/17410381111149657

Melakessou, F. (2014). *Towards a New Way of Reliable Routing: Multiple Paths over ARCs*. Retrieved March 15, 2015 from https://www.scilab.org/content/download/1718/15085/file/UniversityLuxembourg_ScilabTEC2014.pdf

Melakessou, F., Palatella, M., & Engel, T. (2014). *Towards-a-new-way-of-reliable-routing-multiple-paths-over-arcs*. Retrieved March 15, 2015 from http://www.iot-butler.eu/news/towards-a-new-way-of-reliable-routing-multiple-paths-over-arcs

Mell, P., & Grance, T. (2011). *The NIST Definition of Cloud Computing: Recommendations of the National Institute of Standards and Technology* (Technical Report No. 800-145). Gaithersburg, MD: NIST.

Mell, P., & Grance, T. (2011, Sep). *The NIST Definition of Cloud Computing* (Special Publication No. 800-145). Computer Security Division, Information Technology Laboratory, National Institute of Standards and Technology. Retrieved March, 6, 2015 from http://csrc.nist.gov/publications/nistpubs/800-145/SP800-145.pdf

Mendonca, M., Nunes, B. A. A., Nguyen, X. N., Obraczka, K., & Turletti, T. (2013). *A Survey of software-defined networking: past, present, and future of programmable networks*. hal-00825087.

Menychtas, A. (Ed.). (2010). Updated Final version of IRMOS Overall Architecture. In *Interactive Realtime Multimedia Applications on Service Oriented Infrastructures Deliverable D3.1.4*. Retrieved from http://www.irmosproject.eu/Files/IRMOS_WP3_D3_1_4_NTUA_v1_0.pdf

METIS Consortium. (2013). *METIS 2020*. Retrieved from https://www.metis2020.com/

Microsoft Azure. (2014). *Cloud Services Pricing Details*. Retrieved from http://www.windowsazure.com/en-us/pricing/details/cloud-services/

Microsoft, Inc. (n.d.). *Smooth Streaming*. Retrieved from http://www.iis.net/downloads/microsoft/smooth-streaming

Microsoft. (2014). *Revolutionize Healthcare with the Internet of Things: Achieve new levels of health technology interoperability* [Software]. Retrieved 21 November 2014, from http://www.microsoft.com/windowsembedded/en-us/internet-of-things-health.aspx

Milton, L. (2008, Mar). *3GPP Evolved Packet System (EPS); Evolved General Packet Radio Service (GPRS) Tunnelling Protocol for Control plane (GTPv2-C); Stage 3*. Retrieved from 3GPP TS 29.274: http://www.3gpp.org/DynaReport/29274.htm

Mishra, A., Shin, M., & Arbaugh, W. (2003). An Empirical Analysis of the IEEE 802.11 MAC Layer Handoff Process. *SIGCOMM Comput. Commun. Rev*, 93-102.

Mittal, A., Moorthy, A. K., & Bovik, A. C. (2011). Blind/referenceless image spatial quality evaluator. In *Proceedings of the IEEE Forty Fifth Asilomar Conference on Signals, Systems and Computers*. IEEE.

Mitton, C., & Donaldson, C. (2004). Health care priority setting: Principles, practice and challenges. *Cost Effectiveness and Resource Allocation*, *2*(1), 1–8. doi:10.1186/1478-7547-2-3 PMID:15104792

Mockapetris, P. (1987). Domain names - Implementation and specification, *Internet Engineering Task Force (IETF) RFC 1035*.

Mockapetris, P. (1987). *RFC 1035 - Domain Names - Implementation and Specification*.

Mockapetris, P. (1987, November). Domain names - Concepts and facilities. *RFC*. Retrieved November 1987, from http://www.ietf.org/rfc/rfc1034.txt

Mockapetris, P. (1987, November). Domain names - Implementation and specification. *RFC*. Retrieved November 1987, from http://www.ietf.org/rfc/rfc1035.txt

Mogul, J., & Deering, S. (1990). Path MTU Discovery, *Internet Engineering Task Force (IETF) RFC 1191*.

Mohamed, S., & Rubino, G. (2002). A study of real-time packet video quality using random neural networks. *IEEE Transactions on Circuits and Systems for Video Technology*, *12*(12), 1071–1083. doi:10.1109/TCSVT.2002.806808

Mohan, P., Nath, S., & Riva, O. (2013). Prefetching mobile ads: can advertising systems afford it? In *Proceedings of the 8th ACM European Conference on Computer Systems* (pp. 267-280). New York, NY: ACM. doi:10.1145/2465351.2465378

Monsanto, C., Foster, N., Harrison, R., & Walker, D. (2012). A compiler and run-time system for network programming languages. *ACM SIGPLAN Notices*, *47*(1), 217–230. doi:10.1145/2103621.2103685

Monsanto, C., Reich, J., Foster, N., Rexford, J., & Walker, D. (2013, April). *Composing Software Defined Networks*. NSDI.

Moskowitz, R., Nikander, P., Jokela, P., & Henderson, T. (2008, April). *Host Identity Protocol*. Retrieved from http://tools.ietf.org/html/rfc5201

Moustafa, H., Moses, D., & Boucadair, M. (2014). PCP Extension for Signaling Feedback Information from the End-User Application to the Application Sever and to the Network. *IETF Internet draft*.

Moy, J. (1998, April). *OSPF Version 2*. Retrieved from http://tools.ietf.org/html/rfc2328

MSV. J. (2010). The Tenets of the Cloud, In Demystifying the Cloud: An introduction to Cloud Computing. Zilmo Fash.

Mueller, M. (2007). The Politics of DNSSEC: The Light. *Internet Governance Project Blog*. Retrieved from http://blog.internetgovernance.org/blog/_archives/2007/9/9/3217425.html

Mueller, M. (1999). ICANN and Internet Governance: Sorting through the debris of 'self-regulation'. *The Journal of Policy, Regulation and Strategy for Telecommunications Information and Media*, *1*(6), 497–520.

Mueller, M. (1999b, June). "ICANN and Internet Regulation." Association for Computing Machinery. *Communications of the ACM*, *42*(6), 41–43. doi:10.1145/303849.303860

Mueller, M. (2010). *Networks and States: The Global Politics of Internet Governance*. Cambridge, MA: MIT. doi:10.7551/mitpress/9780262014595.001.0001

Mueller, M. L. (2004). *Ruling the Root*. The MIT Press.

Mueller, M., Mathiason, J., & McKnight, L. W. (2004). Making Sense of "Internet Governance:" Defining Principles and Norms in a Policy Context. *Internet Governance: Principles and Norms*, 2, 1–22.

Multipath Networks, M. P. N. (2012). Retrieved from http://multipathnetworks.com/

Munoz, R., Casellas, R., & Martinez, R. (2010). Experimental evaluation of dynamic PCE-based path restoration with centralized and distributed wavelength assignment in GMPLS-enabled transparent WSON networks. *ECOC Conference*, 2010. doi:10.1109/ECOC.2010.5621587

Nagel, B., Geilhardt, F., Gilon, E., Hoet, J., Peña, C., Maillet, A., & Le Mansec, G. … Simoens, P. (2007). Demonstration of TVoIP services in a multimedia broadband enabled access network. In Proceedings of BroadBand Europe 2007. Antwerp, Belgium. ISBN: 9789076546094.

Nakamura, T., Nagata, S., Benjebbour, A., Kishiyama, Y., Hai, T., Xiaodong, S., & Nan, L. et al. (2013). Trends in small cell enhancements in LTE advanced. *IEEE Communications Magazine*, *51*(2), 98,105. doi:10.1109/MCOM.2013.6461192

Nakao, A. (2012). *Flare: Open deeply programmable network node architecture*. Author.

Named Data Networking. (2013). *What is NDN?* Retrieved from http://named-data.net/2013/07/03/what-is-ndn/

Named Function Networking. (2013). Retrieved from http://named-function.net

Narain, S. (2005). Network configuration management via model finding. In *Proceedings of USENIX LISA*. Berkeley, CA: USENIX Association.

Narten, T., Gray, E., Black, D., Fang, L., Kreeger, L., Napierala, M. (2013) Problem Statement: Overlays for Network Virtualization, draft-narten-nov3-overlay-problem-statement-04.

Narten, T., Nordmark, E., Simpson, W. & Soliman, H. (2007). Neighbor Discovery for IP version 6 (IPv6), *Internet Engineering Task Force (IETF) RFC 4861*.

Nasdas, S. (2010) Virtual Router Redundancy Protocol (VRRP) Version 3 for IPv4 and IPv6, RFC5798.

National Telecommunications and Information Administration (NTIA). (n.d.). *United States Department of Commenrce. NTIA Announces Intent to Transition Key Internet Domain Name Functions*. Author.

Neil, M., Malcolm, B., & Shaw, R. (2003). *Modeling an Air Traffic Control Environment Using Bayesian Belief Networks*. Paper presented at the 21st International System Safety Conference, Ottawa, Canada.

Nencioni, G., Sastry, N., Chandaria, J., & Crowcroft, J. (2013). Understanding and decreasing the network footprint of catch-up tv, In *Proceedings of the 22nd international conference on World Wide Web* (pp. 965-976). Geneva, Switzerland: International World Wide Web Conferences Steering Committee.

NGO and Academic ICANN Study. (2001). *ICANN, Legitimacy, and the Public Voice: Making Global Participation and Representation Work*. Report of the NGO and Academic ICANN Study.

Nie, H., Li, S., Lu, X., & Duan, H. (2013). From Healthcare Messaging Standard to Semantic Web Service Description: Generating WSMO Annotation from HL7 with Mapping-Based Approach. In *2013 IEEE International Conference on Services Computing (SCC)* (pp. 470–477). doi:10.1109/SCC.2013.74

Nikander, P., & Laganier, J. (2008, April). *Host Identity Protocol (HIP) Domain Name System (DNS) Extension*. Retrieved from http://tools.ietf.org/html/rfc5205

Nikander, P., Laganier, J., & Dupont, F. (2007, April). *An IPv6 Prefix for Overlay Routable Cryptographic Hash Identifiers (ORCHID)*. Retrieved from http://tools.ietf.org/html/rfc4843

Niu, L., Li, H., Jiang, Y., & Yong, L. (2014), *A Service Function Chaining Header and Forwarding Mechanism (draft-niu-sfc-mechanism-01.txt)*. IETF Internet Draft, April 2014

Norris, P. (2001). *Digital Divide: Civic Engagement, Information Poverty, and the Internet Worldwide*. Cambridge, UK: Cambridge UP. doi:10.1017/CBO9781139164887

Notes. (2013, November). Retrieved from http://www.ietf.org/proceedings/88/minutes/minutes-88-mptcp

NTT Communications Corporation. (2014). Retrieved from: http://www.eu.ntt.com/about-us/press-releases/news/article/ntt-communications-launches-sdn-based-enterprise-cloud-in-germanyntt-europe.html

Octoshape. (2012). *Octoshape's Multicast Technology Suite: The Next-Gen CDN Alternative for Large-Scale, Cost-Optimized, Global HD Streaming*. Retrieved October 23, 2014 from http://www.octoshape.com/wp-content/uploads/2012/12/Multicast-Technical-Overview.pdf

Oki, E., Takeda, T., Le Roux, J. L., & Farrel, A. (2009). *Framework for PCE-based Inter-Layer MPLS and GMPLS Traffic Engineering, RFC 5623*. IETF. doi:10.17487/rfc5623

Olsson, M., Rommer, S., Mulligan, C., Sultana, S., & Frid, L. (2009). *SAE and the Evolved Packet Core: Driving the mobile broadband revolution*. Academic Press.

OneAPI. (n.d.). *GSM Association*. Retrieved November 25, 2014, from http://www.gsma.com/oneapi/

ONF (2012). *OpenFlow Switch Specification, version 1.3.0 (Wire Protocol 0x04)*, Open Networking Foundation, June 2012.

ONF (2014). Openflow-enabled SDN and Network Functions Virtualization, *ONF Solution Brief*, Open Networking Foundation, February 2014.

ONF. (2012). *ONF white paper (2012). In Software-Defined Networking, The New Norm for Networks*. Retrieved from http://bigswitch.com/sites/default/files/sdn_resources/onf-whitepaper.pdf

ONF. (2014). *ONF Overview*. Retrieved from https://www.opennetworking.org/about/onf-overview

Ooghe, S. (Ed.). (2013). *Broadband Forum TR-156: Using GPON Access in the context of TR-101, Issue 3*. Broadband Forum.

Open Applications Group. (2014). *The Business Value of the OAGIS 10.1 Enterprise Edition*. Retrieved from: http://www.oagi.org/oagi/downloads/Presents/2014_Business-Value_of_OAGIS_10.1_EnterpriseEdition.pdf

Open Group. (2014). *Cloud Computing Portability and Interoperability: Portability and Interoperability Interfaces*. Retrieved from: http://www.opengroup.org/cloud/cloud/cloud_iop/dcrm.htm#Figure_5

Open IMS Core . (n.d.). Retrieved March, 6, 2015 from http://www.openimscore.org/

Open Nebula. (n.d.). *Open Nebula Project Website*. Retrieved July 2014 from: http://opennebula.org

Open Networking Foundation. (2012). *Software-Defined Networking: The New Norm for Networks*. ONF White Paper.

Open Networking Foundation. (2013). *SDN Architecture Overview*. Retrieved March 12, 2015, from https://www.opennetworking.org/images/stories/downloads/sdn-resources/technical-reports/SDN-architecture-overview-1.0.pdf

Open Networking Foundation. (2014). *OpenFlow Table Type Patterns Version 1.0*. Retrieved March 12, 2015, from https://www.opennetworking.org/images/stories/downloads/sdn-resources/onf-specifications/openflow/OpenFlow%20Table%20Type%20Patterns%20v1.0.pdf

Open Networking Foundation. (2014). *SDN Architecture, Issue 1*. Retrieved March 12, 2015, from https://www.opennetworking.org/images/stories/downloads/sdn-resources/technical-reports/TR_SDN_ARCH_1.0_06062014.pdf

OpenDayLight. (n.d.). *OpenDayLight Project Website*. Retrieved October 2014 from: http://www.opendaylight.org

OpenEPC - Open Evolved Packet Core. (n.d.). Retrieved March, 6, 2015 from http://www.openepc.net/index.html

OpenFlow. (2013). OpenFlow Switch Specification Version 1.4. *OpenNetworking Foundation*. Retrieved November 25, 2014, from https://www.opennetworking.org/images/stories/downloads/sdn-resources/onf-specifications/openflow/openflow-spec-v1.4.0.pdf

OpenStack. (n.d.). *OpenStack Project Website*. Retrieved July 2014 from: http://www.openstack.org

OpenWrt. (n.d.). *OpenWrt Project website*. Retrieved July 2014 from: https://openwrt.org

Oppenheime, P. (2010). *Top-Down Network Design* (3rd ed.). Indianapolis, IN: Cisco Press.

Orange. (2012). *Orange and Akamai form Content Delivery Strategic Alliance*. Retrieved from http://www.orange.com/en/press/press-releases/press-releases-2012/Orange-and-Akamai-form-Content-Delivery-Strategic-Alliance

Orthner, H. F., Scherrer, J. R., & Dahlen, R. (1994). Sharing and communicating health care information: Summary and recommendations. *International Journal of Bio-Medical Computing*, *34*(1-4), 303–318. doi:10.1016/0020-7101(94)90030-2 PMID:8125644

OSGi. (2012). *OSGI Service Compendium, Release 4, version 4.3. OSGi Alliance Specification*. Retrieved July 2014 from: http://www.osgi.org /Specifications/HomePage

Osseiran, A., Boccardi, F., Braun, V., Kusume, K., Marsch, P., Maternia, M., & Fallgren, M. et al. (2014). Scenarios for 5G Mobile and Wireless Communications: The Vision of the METIS Project. *IEEE Communications Magazine*, *52*(5), 26–35. doi:10.1109/MCOM.2014.6815890

Osseiran, A., Braun, V., Hidekazu, T., Marsch, P., Schotten, H., Tullberg, H., & Schellman, M. et al. (2013). The Foundation of the Mobile and Wireless Communication System for 2020 and Beyond. In *Proc. IEEE Vehic. Tech Conf.* Dresden, Germany: IEEE.

Paasch, C., Detal, G., Duchene, F., Raiciu, C., & Bonaventure, O. (2012). *Exploring Mobile/WiFi Handover with Multipath TCP*. Academic Press.

Panchal, J. S., Yates, R. D., & Buddhikot, M. M. (2013, September). Mobile Network Resource Sharing Options: Performance Comparisons. *Wireless Communications, IEEE Transactions on*, *12*(9), 4470–4482. doi:10.1109/TWC.2013.071913.121597

Panda, A., Scott, C., Ghodsi, A., Koponen, T., & Shenker, S. (2013, August). CAP for Networks. In *Proceedings of the second ACM SIGCOMM workshop on Hot topics in software defined networking* (pp. 91-96). ACM. doi:10.1145/2491185.2491186

Pantos, R. P., & May, W. (2014). *HTTP Live Streaming*. Retrieved from http://tools.ietf.org/html/draft-pantos-http-live-streaming-14

Paolucci, F., Cugini, F., Iovanna, P., Bottari, G., Valcarenghi, L., Castoldi, P. (2010). Delay-Bandwidth-aware Metric Abstraction Schemes for OIF E-NNI Multidomain Traffic Engineering. *IEEE/OSA Journal of Optical Communication and Networking*, *2*(10), 782-792.

Paolucci, F., Sambo, N., Cugini, F., Giorgetti, A, & Castoldi, P. (2011). Experimental Demonstration of Impairment-Aware PCE for Multi-Bit-Rate WSONs. *Optical Communications and Networking, IEEE/OSA Journal of, 3*(8).

Paolucci, F., Cugini, F., Giorgetti, A., Sambo, N., & Castoldi, P. (2013). A survey on the path computation element (PCE) architecture. *IEEE Communications Surveys and Tutorials, 15*(4), 1819–1841. doi:10.1109/SURV.2013.011413.00087

Park, S. M., Ju, S., Jonghun, K., & Lee, J. (2013). *Software-defined-networking for M2M services. ICT Convergence.* ICTC.

Parkvall S., Furuskar A., Dahlman E. (2011). Evolution of LTE toward IMT-advanced. *IEEE Communications Magazine, 49*(2), 84-91.

Parniewicz, D., Doriguzzi Corin, R., Ogrodowczyk, L., Rashidi Fard, M., Matias, J., Gerola, M., & Pentikousis, K. et al. (2014, August). Design and implementation of an OpenFlow hardware abstraction layer. In *Proceedings of the 2014 ACM SIGCOMM workshop on Distributed cloud computing* (pp. 71-76). ACM. doi:10.1145/2627566.2627577

Pate, P. (2013). *NFV and SDN: What's the Difference?* Retrieved from http://www.sdncentral.com/technology-nfv-and-sdn-whats-the-difference/2013/03/

Patil, R. S., Silva, J. S., & Swartout, W. R. (1994). An architecture for a health care provider's workstation. *International Journal of Bio-Medical Computing, 34*(1-4), 285–299. doi:10.1016/0020-7101(94)90029-9 PMID:8125640

Patrick, M. (2001). *DHCP Relay Agent Information Option.* IETF Internet Standard RFC 3046, January 2001.

Pearl, J. (2000). *Causality: Models, Reasoning, and Inferences.* Cambridge University Press.

Penno, R., Reddy, T., Boucadair, M., & Wing, D. (2013). Application Enabled SDN (A-SDN). *IETF.* Retrieved November 25, 2014, from http://tools.ietf.org/html/draft-penno-pcp-asdn-00

Penno, R., Reddy, T., Boucadair, M., Wing, D., & Vinapamula, S. (2013). *Application Enabled SDN (A-SDN), IETF draft-penno-pcp-asdn-00.* Retrieved from http://tools.ietf.org/html/draft-penno-pcp-asdn-00)

Pentikousis, K., Wang, Y., & Hu, W. (2013). Mobileflow: Toward software-defined mobile networks. Communications Magazine, IEEE, 51(7).

Perkins, C. (2010). *IP Mobility Support for IPv4, Revised, RFC 5944 (Proposed Standard), IETF.* Retrieved From: http://www.ietf.org/rfc/rfc5944.txt

Perkins, C. (2010). *IP Mobility Support for IPv4.* Academic Press.

Perkins, C., Johnson, D., & Arkko, J. (2011). Mobility Support in IPv6, RFC 6275 (Proposed Standard). *IETF.* Retrieved from: http://www.ietf.org/rfc/rfc6275.txt

Perkins, C., Johnson, D., & Arkko, J. (2013). Mobility Support in IPv6, *Internet Engineering Task Force (IETF) RFC 6275.*

Perkins, C. (1996). *IP Mobility Support (RFC 2002).* IETF. doi:10.17487/rfc2002

Perkins, C. (1996). *Minimal Encapsulation within IP (RFC 2004).* IETF. doi:10.17487/rfc2004

Perkins, C. (2010). *IP Mobility Support for IPv4, Revised (RFC 5944).* IETF. doi:10.17487/rfc5944

Perkins, C., Johnson, D., & Arkko, J. (2011). *Mobility Support in IPv6.* IETF. doi:10.17487/rfc6275

Pershad, R. (2000). *A Bayesian Belief Network for Corporate Credit Risk Assessment.* (M.A.Sc. Thesis). University of Toronto.

Pescatore, J. (2003). *Taxonomy of software vulnerabilities.* The Gartner Group Report.

Peterson, L., Davie, B., & van Brandenburg, R. (2014). *Framework for CDN Interconnection, draft-ietf-cdni-framework-14.* Retrieved June 6, 2014 from http://tools.ietf.org/html/draft-ietf-cdni-framework-14

Pfister, H., & Zalewski, J. (n.d.). *Bayesian Belief Networks.* Academic & Event Technology Services. Florida Gulf Coast University. Retrieved from http://itech.fgcu.edu/faculty/zalewski/CEN4935/BBN_Pfister_Zalewski.pdf

Piai, S., & Claps, M. (2013). *Bigger Data for Better Healthcare*. IDC Health Insights. Retrieved from http://www.intel.com/content/www/us/en/healthcare-it/bigger-data-better-healthcare-idc-insights-white-paper.html

Piamrat, K., Viho, C., Bonnin, J., & Ksentini, A. (2009). Quality of experience measurements for video streaming over wireless networks. In *Proceedings of IEEE Sixth International Conference on Information Technology: New Generations*. IEEE. doi:10.1109/ITNG.2009.121

Pieterse, J. N. (2002). Globalization, Kitsch and Conflict: Technologies of Work, War and Politics. *Review of International Political Economy*, *9*(1), 1–36. doi:10.1080/09692290110102549

Pinheiro, M. (2014). *Brazil Assumes Leadership in Future of Internet Governance*. Inter Press Service News Agency. Retrieved from http://www.ipsnews.net/2014/04/brazil-assumes-leadership-future-internet-governance/

Pinson, M. H., & Wolf, S. (2004). A new standardized method for objectively measuring video quality. *IEEE Transactions on Broadcasting*, *50*(3), 312–322. doi:10.1109/TBC.2004.834028

Pisa, P., Moreira, M., Carvalho, H., Ferraz, L., & Duarte, O. (2010), Migrating Xen Virtual Routers with No Packet Loss.*First Workshop on Network Virtualization and Intelligence For Future Internet (WNetVirt'10)*, Búzios. April 2010.

Ploberger, C. (2012). Analyzing Complex Political Change by Applying the Concept of Regime Change: Identifying the Transformations within the Japanese Political-bureaucratic-business Regime. *Asian Social Science*, *8*(15), 12–23. doi:10.5539/ass.v8n15p12

Pluntke, C., Eggert, L., & Kiukkonen, N. (2011). *Saving Mobile Device Energy with Multipath TCP*. Academic Press.

Poese, I., Frank, B., Ager, B., Smaragdakis, G., Uhlig, S., & Feldmann, A. (2012). Improving Content Delivery with PaDIS. *IEEE Internet Computing*, *16*(3), 46–52. doi:10.1109/MIC.2011.105

Poese, I., Frank, B., Smaragdakis, G., Uhlig, S., & Feldmann, A. (2012). Enabling content-aware traffic engineering. *SIGCOMM Computer Communications Review*, *42*(5), 21–28. doi:10.1145/2378956.2378960

Polito, S.G., Zaghloul, S., Chamania, M., & Jukan, A. (2011). Inter-Domain Path Provisioning with Security Features: Architecture and Signaling Performance. *Network and Service Management, IEEE Transactions on*, *8*(3).

Polycom. (2014). N*ew Healthcare Vision, Collaborative video solutions improving care and reducing cost.* Polycom, Inc.

Postel, J. (1980). User Datagram Protocol, *Internet Engineering Task Force (IETF) RFC 768.*

Postel, J. (Ed.). (1981). Internet Protocol, Internet Engineering Task Force (IETF) RFC 791.

Postmes, T., & Brunsting. (2002). Collective Action in the Age of the Internet. *Social Science Computer Review*, *20*(3), 290-301.

Powell, G. (2007). Promoting unique China Internet. *China Economic Review - Industries Updates*. Retrieved from: http://www.chinaeconomicreview.com

Pras, A., & Schoenwaelder J. (2003). *On the Difference between Information Models and Data Models*. IETF RFC 3444.

Presuhn, R., Case, J., McCloghrie, Rose, M., K., & Waldbusser, S. (2002). Version 2 of the Protocol Operations for the Simple Network Management Protocol (SNMP). RFC 3416.

Pretz, K. (2014). *Better Health Care Through Data How health analytics could contain costs and improve care.* Retrieved 26 September 2014, from http://theinstitute.ieee.org/technology-focus/technology-topic/better-health-care-through-data

Project OpenDayLight Software. (2014). Retrieved from: http://www.opendaylight.org/software

Project OpenDayLight Technical Overview. (2014). Retrieved from http://www.opendaylight.org/project/technical-overview

Proust, C. (2004). *An approach for Routing at Flow level*. Academic Press.

Pudney, C. (2006, Dec). *General Packet Radio Service (GPRS) enhancements for Evolved Universal Terrestrial Radio Access Network (E-UTRAN) access*. Retrieved from 3GPP TS 23.401: http://www.3gpp.org/DynaReport/23401.htm

Python. (n.d.). *Python Programming Language Website*. Retrieved July 2014 from: http://www.python.org

Qiang, D., Yuhong, Y., & Vasilakos, A. V. (2012). A Survey on Service-Oriented Network Virtualization Toward Convergence of Networking and Cloud Computing. *IEEE eTransactions on Network and Service Management*, *9*(4), 373–392. doi:10.1109/TNSM.2012.113012.120310

Qin, Z., Denker, G., Giannelli, C., Bellavista, P., & Venkatasubramanian, N. (2014) A Software Defined Networking Architecture for the Internet-of-Things.*Network Operations and Management Symposium (NOMS)*. IEEE. doi:10.1109/NOMS.2014.6838365

Quadros, C., Cerqueira, E., Neto, A., Riker, A., Immich, R., & Curado, M. (2012). *A mobile QoE Architecture for Heterogeneous Multimedia Wireless Networks*. Anaheim, CA: IEEE Globecom Workshops. doi:10.1109/GLOCOMW.2012.6477724

Quinn, P., & Nadeau, T. (2014) Service Function Chaining Problem Statement, draft-ietf-sfc-problem-statement-13.

Quinn, P., & Nadeau, T. (2014). *Service Function Chaining Problem Statement (draft-ietf-sfc-problem-statement-07.txt)*. IETF Internet Draft. June 2014.

Quittek, J. (Ed.). (2013). *Requirements for Energy Management, RFC 6988, September 2013*. Retrieved from http://www.rfc-editor.org/rfc/rfc6988.txt

Rafiee, H., & Meinel, C. (2013). A Secure, Flexible Framework for DNS Authentication in IPv6 Autoconfiguration. In *Proceedings of IEEE Conference on Network Computing and Applications (NCA 2013)* (pp. 165 – 172). IEEE. doi:10.1109/NCA.2013.37

Raiciu, C., Handley, M., & Wischik, D. (2011). *Coupled Congestion Control for Multipath Transport Protocols*. Academic Press.

Raiciu, C., Paasch, C., Barre, S., Ford, A., Honda, M., Duchene, F., … Handley, M. (2012). *How Hard Can It Be? Designing and Implementing a Deployable Multipath TCP*. Academic Press.

Raiciu, C., Pluntke, C., Barre, S., Greenhalgh, A., Wischisk, A., & Handley, M. (2010). *Data center networking with multipath TCP*. Academic Press.

Raiciu, C., Pluntke, C., Barre, S., Greenhalgh, A., Wischisk, A., & Handley, M. (2011). *Improving datacenter performance and robustness with Multipath TCP*. Academic Press.

Ramjee, R., Porta, T., Thuel, S., & Varadhan, K. (2002). HAWAII: A Domain-based Approach for Supporting Mobility in Wide-area Wireless Networks. *IEEE/ACM Transaction on Networking*.

Rapoport, A. (1960). *Fights, Games, and Debates*. Ann Arbor, MI: University of Michigan.

Rappaport, T. S., Sun Shu, R., Mayzus, Z. H. Z., Azar, Wang, Wong, Schulz, Samimi, & Gutierrez. (2013). Millimeter Wave Mobile Communications for 5G Cellular: It Will Work!. IEEE Access, 1.

Reich, J., Monsanto, C., Foster, N., Rexford, J., & Walker, D. (2013). Modular SDN Programming with Pyretic. *USENIX Login, 38*(5), 128-134.

Rekhter, R., Li, T., Hares, S. (2006) A Border Gateway Protocol 4 (BGP-4), RFC4271.

Rekhter, Y., Li, T., & Hares, S. (2006). A Border Gateway Protocol 4 (BGP-4), *Internet Engineering Task Force (IETF) RFC 4271*.

Rekhter, Y., Li, T., & Hares, S. (2006, January). *A Border Gateway Protocol 4 (BGP-4)*. Retrieved from http://tools.ietf.org/html/rfc4271

Relay Extensions to Session Traversal Utilities for NAT (STUN). (n.d.). *IETF*. Retrieved November 25, 2014, from https://tools.ietf.org/html/rfc5766

Rescorla, E. (2000, May). *HTTP Over TLS*. Retrieved from http://tools.ietf.org/html/rfc2818

Rescorla, E., & Modadugu, M. (2012, January). *Datagram Transport Layer Security Version 1.2*. Retrieved from http://tools.ietf.org/html/rfc6347

Review, H. L. (1999). Developments in the Law. *The Law of Cyberspace*, *112*(7), 1574–1704.

Ricci, A. (2008). Il diritto al nome. In Diritto dell'anonimato. Anonimato, nome e identità personale. Torino: Utet.

Rijsman, B., & Moisand, J. (2014). Metadata Considerations, draft-rijsman-sfc-metadata-considerations-00.

Riverbed. (2014). *SteelCentral for Performance Management and Control | Riverbed application and network performance management solutions | Riverbed* [Communications Hardware, Technology, Software]. Retrieved 19 November 2014, from http://www.riverbed.com/products/performance-management-control/opnet.html

Rivest, R. (1992, April). *The MD5 Message-Digest Algorithm*. Retrieved from https://tools.ietf.org/html/rfc1321

Rodotà, S. (1997). Persona, riservatezza e identità personale. Prime note sistematiche sulla protezione dei dati personali. *Rivista critica di diritto private*, 605-619.

Rodotà, S. (2014). *Il mondo nella rete. Quali diritti, quali I vincoli*. Roma: Laterza.

Rodrigues, R. J., Wilson, P., & Schanz, S. J. (2002). The Regulatory Framework. In *The Regulation of Privacy and Data Protection in the Use of Electronic Health Information* (pp. 34–38). Washington, DC: Pan American Health Org.

Rooney, S., van der Merwe, J. E., Crosby, S. A., & Leslie, I. M. (1998). The Tempest: A framework for safe, resource assured, programmable networks. *Communications Magazine, IEEE, 36*(10), 42–53. doi:10.1109/35.722136

Rosemberg, J., Schulzrinne, H., Camarillo, G., Johnston, A., Peterson, J., Sparks, R., … Schooler, E. (2002). *SIP: Session Initiation Protocol*. IETF Internet Standard. RFC 3261, June 2002.

Rosen, E., Rekhter, Y. (2006) BGP/MPLS IP Virtual Private Networks (VPNs), RFC 4364.

Rosen, E., Viswanatan, A., Callon, R. (2001) Multiprotocol Label Switching Architecture, RFC 3031.

Rosen, E., Viswanathan, A., & Callon, R. (2001, January). *Multiprotocol Label Switching Architecture*. Retrieved from http://tools.ietf.org/html/rfc3031

Rosenberg, J. (2010). Interactive Connectivity Establishment (ICE): A Protocol for Network Address Translator (NAT) Traversal for Offer/Answer Protocols. *IETF*. Retrieved November 25, 2014, from https://tools.ietf.org/html/rfc5245

Rosenberg, J., Mahy, R., & Wing, D. (2008). Session Traversal Utilities for NAT (STUN). *IETF*. Retrieved November 25, 2014, from https://tools.ietf.org/html/rfc5389

Rosenberg, J., Schlzrinne, H., Camarillo, G., Johnston, A., Peterson, J., Spark, R., … Schooler, E. (2002). SIP: Session Initiation Protocol. *IETF Standard, RFC* 3261.

Roskind, J. (2013). Quick UDP Internet Connections – Multiplexed Stream Transport over UDP. *IETF-88 TSV Area Presentation*. Retrieved from http://www.ietf.org/proceedings/88/slides/slides-88-tsvarea-10.pdf

Rost, P., Bernardos, C. J., De Domenico, A., Di Girolamo, M., Lalam, M., Maeder, A., & Wübben, D. et al. (2014). Cloud technologies for flexible 5G radio access networks. *IEEE Communications Magazine, 52*(5), 68–76. doi:10.1109/MCOM.2014.6898939

Roth, C. P., Lim, Y.-W., Pevnick, J. M., Asch, S. M., & McGlynn, E. A. (2009). The Challenge of Measuring Quality of Care From the Electronic Health Record. *American Journal of Medical Quality, 24*(5), 385–394. doi:10.1177/1062860609336627 PMID:19482968

Royon, Y. (2007). *Environments d'exécution pour passerelles domestiques*. (Doctoral Dissertation). Institut National des Sciences Apliquées (INSA/INRIA), Lyon, France.

Rubino, G., Varela, M., & Bonnin, J. M. (2006). Controlling multimedia QoS in the future home network using the PSQA metric. *The Computer Journal, 49*(2), 137–155. doi:10.1093/comjnl/bxh165

Saad, M. A., Bovik, A. C., & Charrier, C. (2012). Blind image quality assessment: A natural scene statistics approach in the DCT domain. *IEEE Transactions on Image Processing, 21*(8), 3339–3352. doi:10.1109/TIP.2012.2191563 PMID:22453635

SAIL - Scalable and Adaptive Internet Solutions. (2011). *Network of Information.* Retrieved from http://www.sail-project.eu/about-sail/netinf/

Saint-Andre, P. (2011). Extensible Messaging and Presence Protocol (XMPP): Core. *IETF*. Retrieved November 25, 2014, from https://tools.ietf.org/html/rfc6120

Sakaguchi, K., Sampei, S., Shimodaira, H., Rezagah, R., Tran, G. K., & Araki, K. (2013). *Cloud cooperated heterogeneous cellular networks.* Intelligent Signal Processing and Communications Systems (ISPACS), 2013 International Symposium on.

Samsung Electronics Co. (2013). *S Health* [Electronics]. Retrieved 26 September 2014, from http://content.samsung.com/us/contents/aboutn/sHealthIntro.do

Samuels, J. M., & Linda, B. (2003, Summer). Samuels "Internet domain names – The uniform dispute resolution policy.". *American Business Law Journal, 40*(4), 885–904. doi:10.1111/j.1744-1714.2003.tb00312.x

Sandvine. (2014). *Global Internet Phenomena Report - 1H2014.* Retrieved October 23, 2014 from https://www.sandvine.com/downloads/general/global-internet-phenomena/2014/1h-2014-global-internet-phenomena-report.pdf

Sato, Y., Fukuda, I., & Tomonori, F. (2013, Dec). Deployment of OpenFlow/SDN Technologies to Carrier Services. *IEICE Transactions, 96-B*(12), 2946–2952. Retrieved March, 6, 2015 from http://dblp.uni-trier.de/rec/bib/journals/ieicet/SatoFT13

Scharf, M., & Ford, A. (2013). *Multipath TCP (MPTCP).* Application Interface Considerations. doi:10.17487/rfc6897

Scharf, M., Voith, T., Roome, W., Gaglianello, B., Steiner, M., Hilt, V., & Gurbani, V. K. (2012). Monitoring and Abstraction for Networked Clouds. In *Proceedings of the 16th International Conference on Intelligence in Next Generation Networks (ICIN)* (pp. 80-85). Berlin: IEEE.

Schilit, B., & Theimer, M. (1994). Disseminating Active Map Information to Mobile Hosts. *IEEE Network, 8*(5), 22–32. doi:10.1109/65.313011

Schomberger, V. M. (2009). *Delete: The virtue of forgetting in the digital age.* USA: Princeton University Press.

Schulzrinne, H., Casner, S., Frederick, R., & Jacobson, V. (2003). RTP: A Transport Protocol for Real-Time Applications. *IETF Standard RFC* 3550.

Schulzrinne, H., Rao, A., & Lanphier, R. (1998). Real Time Streaming Protocol (RTSP). *IETF Standard, RFC* 2326.

Seedorf, J., & Burger, E. (2009). Application Layer Traffic Optimization (ALTO) Problem Statement. In IETF RFC 5693.

SETI. (2014). Retrieved from: http://setiathome.ssl.berkeley.edu/

Sezer, S., Scott-Hayward, S., Chouhan, P. K., Fraser, B., Lake, D., Finnegan, J., . . . Rao, N. (2013). Are we ready for SDN? Implementation challenges for software-defined networks. Communications Magazine, IEEE, 51(7).

Shacham, R., Schulzrinne, H., Thakolsri, S., & Kellerer, W. (2009). *Session Initiation Protocol (SIP) Session Mobility (RFC 5631).* IETF.

Sharma, M., Bai, Y., Chung, S., & Dai, L. (2012). Using Risk in Access Control for Cloud-Assisted eHealth. In *2012 IEEE 14th International Conference on High Performance Computing and Communication 2012 IEEE 9th International Conference on Embedded Software and Systems (HPCC-ICESS)* (pp. 1047–1052). doi:10.1109/HPCC.2012.153

Sherwood, R., Gibb, G., Yap, K. K., Appenzeller, G., Casado, M., McKeown, N., & Parulkar, G. (2009). Flowvisor: A network virtualization layer. *OpenFlow Switch Consortium, Tech. Rep.*

Shimanek, A., (2001). Do you Want Milk with those Cookies?: Complying with Safe Harbor Privacy Principles. *Iowa J. Corp. L., 455*, 462–463.

Shin, S., & Gu, G. (2013). Attacking Software-Defined Networks: A First Feasibility Study. *Proceedings of HotSDN'13 Conference in China.* Retrieved from http://conferences.sigcomm.org/sigcomm/2013/papers/hotsdn/p165.pdf

Shiomoto, K., Papadimitriou, D., Le Roux, J. L., Vigoreaux, M., & Brungard, D. (2008). *Requirements for GMPLS-based Multi-Region and Multi-Layer Networks (MRN/MLN), RFC 5212.* IETF. doi:10.17487/rfc5212

SiciliaToday. (2009). Retrieved December 10, 2009, from http://siciliatoday.net/quotidiano/news/Rubata-identit-su-Badoo-a-ragazza-siciliana_17980.shtml

Signals and Systems Telecom. (2013). *The SDN, NFV & Network Virtualization Bible: 2014 – 2020*. Retrieved from http://www.snstelecom.com/the-sdn-nfv-network-virtualization-bible

Simpson, W. (1994, July). *The Point-to-Point Protocol (PPP)*. Retrieved from http://tools.ietf.org/html/rfc1661

Simpson, W. (1996, August). *PPP Challenge Handshake Authentication Protocol (CHAP)*. Retrieved from http://tools.ietf.org/html/rfc1994

Singh, V., Karkkainen, T., Ott, J., Ahsan, S., & Eggert, L. (2013). *Multipath RTP*. Academic Press.

Sivabalan, S., Medved, J., Filsfils, C., Crabbe, E., Raszuk, R., Lopez, V., Tantsura, J. (2014) PCEP Extension for Segment Routing, draft-sivabalan-pce-segment-routing-03.

Sivalaban, S., Parker, J., Boutros, S., & Kumaki, K. (2009). *Diffserv-Aware Class-Type Object for the Path Computation Element Protocol*. RFC 5455.

Small, C. F. R. (2013). *Market status statistics Q1 2013*. Author.

Smart Cities. (2014). Retrieved 21 November 2014, from ec.europa.eu//digital-agenda/en/smart-cities

Smedt, A., Balemans, H., Onnegren, J., & Haeseleer, S. (2006). The multi-play service enabled Residential Gateway. In Proceedings of Broadband Europe 2006. Geneva: Academic Press.

Smith, D. (2014). *Four things we've learned from the EU Google judgment*. Retrieved May 20, 2014, from https://iconewsblog.wordpress.com/2014/05/20/four-things-weve-learned-from-the-eu-google-judgment/

Smith, M., Dvorkin, M., Laribi, Y., Pandey, V., Garg, P. & Weidenbacher, N. (2014). OpFlex Control Protocol. *IETF individual draft, draft-smith-opflex-00*.

Snidal, D. (1985). Coordination versus Prisoners' Dilemma: Implications for International Cooperation and Regimes. *The American Political Science Review*, *79*(4), 923–942. doi:10.2307/1956241

Snoeren, A. C., & Balakrishnan, H. (2000). *TCP Connection Migration*. IETF Internet Draft.

Soldani, D., Li, M., & Cuny, R. (Eds.). (2007). *QoS and QoE management in UMTS cellular systems*. John Wiley & Sons.

Soliman, H., Castelluccia, C., El-Malki, K., & Bellier, L. (2008). Hierarchical Mobile IPv6 (HMIPv6) Mobility Management, RFC 5380 (Proposed Standard). *IETF*. Retrieved from: http://www.ietf.org/rfc/rfc5380.txt

Soliman, H. (2009). *Mobile IPv6 Support for Dual Stack Hosts and Routers (RFC 5555)*. IETF. doi:10.17487/rfc5555

Song, H. (2013) Protocol-Oblivious Forwarding: Unleash the Power of SDN through a Future-Proof Forwarding Plane. In proceeding of sigcomm 2013.

Song, H. (2013, August). Protocol-oblivious forwarding: Unleash the power of SDN through a future-proof forwarding plane. In *Proceedings of the second ACM SIGCOMM workshop on Hot topics in software defined networking* (pp. 127-132). ACM. doi:10.1145/2491185.2491190

Soomro, A., & Schmitt, R. (2011). A framework for mobile healthcare applications over heterogeneous networks. In *2011 13th IEEE International Conference on e-Health Networking Applications and Services (Healthcom)* (pp. 70–73). doi:10.1109/HEALTH.2011.6026789

Sotirov, A., Stevens, M., Appelbaum, J., Lenstra, A., Molnar, D., Osvik, D. A., & Weger, B. D. (2008, December). *MD5 considered harmful today*. Retrieved from http://www.win.tue.nl/hashclash/rogue-ca/

Soundararajan, R., & Bovik, A. C. (2012). RRED indices: Reduced reference entropic differencing for image quality assessment. *IEEE Transactions on Image Processing*, *21*(2), 517–526. doi:10.1109/TIP.2011.2166082 PMID:21878414

Spec, M. (2012). *WiFi Certified Miracst: Extending the Wi-Fi Experience to Seamless Video Display Industry*. Retrieved from http://www.wi-fi.org/file/wi-fi-certified-miracast-extending-the-wi-fi-experience-to-seamless-video-display-industry

Spurgeon, C. E., & Joann, Z. (2014). *Ethernet: The Definitive Guide*. Sebastopol, CA: O'Reilly Media.

Srinivasan, C., Viswanathan, A., & Nadeau, T. (2004). *Multiprotocol label switching (MPLS) label switching router (LSR) management information base (MIB)*. RFC 3813.

Standard, I. E. E. E. (2011). *IEEE Standard for the Functional Architecture of Next Generation Service Overlay Networks* (pp. 1903–2011). SA.

Starr, C., & Shi, P. (2004). *An Introduction to Bayesian Belief Networks and their Applications to Land Operations*. Land Operations Division, Systems Sciences Laboratory – Australian Government Department of Defense.

Status of implementation of Directive 95/46 on the Protection of Individuals with regard to the Processing of Personal Data. (2013, July 16). Retrieved from http://ec.europa.eu/justice/data-protection/law/status-implementation/index_en.htm

Sterman, J. D. (2000). *Business Dynamics: Systems Thinking and Modeling for a Complex World*. Irwin/McGraw-Hill.

Stewart, R., Xie, Q., Morneault, K., Sharp, C., Schwarzbauer, H., & Taylor, T. (2000). *Stream Control Transmission Protocol (RFC 2960)*. IETF. doi:10.17487/rfc2960

Stewart, R., Xie, Q., Tuexen, M., Maruyama, S., & Kozuka, M. (2007). *Stream Control Transmission Protocol (SCTP)*. Dynamic Address Reconfiguration. doi:10.17487/rfc4960

Strassner, J. C. (2004). *Policy-based Network Management: Solutions for the Next Generation* (1st ed.). Morgan Kaufmann.

Sung, E., Sun, X., Rao, S., Xie, G., & Maltz, D. (2011). *Towards systematic design of enterprise networks*. IEEE/ACM Trans. *Networking*, *19*(3), 695–708. doi:10.1109/TNET.2010.2089640

Sunshine, C. (1980). *Addressing Mobile hosts in the ARPA Unternet Environment*. J. P.: IETF.

Sushant, J., & Alok, A. (2013) B4: Experience with a Globally-Deployed Software Defined WAN. In *Proc. SIGCOMM* (2013), 3-14.

Tamijetchelvy, R., & Sivaradje, G. (2012). An optimized fast vertical handover strategy for heterogeneous wireless access networks based on IEEE 802.21 media independent handover standard. *Fourth International Conference on Advanced Computing (ICoAC)*. doi:10.1109/ICoAC.2012.6416817

Tamura, T. (1999, Apr). *General Packet Radio Service (GPRS); GPRS Tunnelling Protocol (GTP) across the Gn and Gp interface*. Retrieved from 3GPP TS 29.060: http://www.3gpp.org/DynaReport/29060.htm

Tcpdump. (n.d.). *Tcpdump Project Website*. Retrieved july 2014 from: http://www.tcpdump.org

Telecommunication Standardization sector of ITU. (1990). *CCITT Recommendation 1.361, B-ISDN ATM Layer Specification*, Geneva, Switzerland: Author.

Telecommunication Standardization sector of ITU. (1993). *ITU, Q.700: Introduction to CCITT Signalling System No. 7*. Geneva, Switzerland: Author.

Telecompetitor. (2011). *AT&T Intros New Cloud Based CDN Services*. Retrieved from http://www.telecompetitor.com/att-intros-new-cloud-based-cdn-services/

Templin, F. (2011). The Internet Routing Overlay Network (IRON), *Internet Engineering Task Force (IETF) RFC 6179*.

Templin, F. (2012). Asymmetric Extended Route Optimization (AERO), *Internet Engineering Task Force (IETF) RFC 6706*.

Templin, F. (2013). Operational Guidance for IPv6 Deployment in IPv4 Sites Using the Intra-Site Automatic Tunnel Addressing Protocol (ISATAP), *Internet Engineering Task Force (IETF) RFC 6964*.

Templin, F. (2014). Asymmetric Extended Route Optimization (AERO) (Second Edition), Internet Engineering Task Force (IETF) work-in-progress (draft-templin-aerolink).

Templin, F., Gleeson, T., & Thaler, D. (2005). Intra-Site Automatic Tunnel Addressing Protocol (ISATAP), *Internet Engineering Task Force (IETF) RFC 5214*.

Tennenhouse, D. L., Smith, J. M., Sincoskie, W. D., Wetherall, D. J., & Minden, G. J. (1997). A survey of active network research. *Communications Magazine, IEEE*, *35*(1), 80–86. doi:10.1109/35.568214

The Internet Society. (2000). *IAB Technical Comment on the Unique DNS Root*. Retrieved from http://www.ietf.org/rfc/rfc2826.txt

The Open Group. (2014). *About the UDEF*. Retrieved from: http://www.opengroup.org/udef/

The World Bank. (n.d.). *Data*. Retrieved from http://data.worldbank.org/

Thomas, L. (1978). *The Lives of a Cell: Notes of a Biology Watcher*. New York: Penguin.

Thubert, P., & Bellagamba, P. (2014). *Available Routing Construct (ARC)*. Retrieved March 15 2015, from https://datatracker.ietf.org/doc/draft-thubert-rtgwg-arc/

tmforum zoom program. (2014). *Making NFV Real*. Retrieved from: http://beta.tmforum.org/wp-content/uploads/2014/09/ToolkitZOOM2014.9.17.14.pdf

tmforum ZOOM. (2014). *Package:Overview, Z. O. O. M.* Retrieved from http://www.tmforum.org/KnowledgeDownloadDetail/9285/home.html?artf=artf4989

tmForum. (2014). *What is the Information Network?* Retrieved from: http://www.tmforum.org/Information-Framework/1684/home.html#

Tornatore, M., De Grandi, F., Munoz, R., Martinez, R., Casellas, R., & Pattavina, A. (2009). Effects of outdated control information in control-plane enabled optical networks with path protection. *IEEE /OSA Journal of Optical Communication and Networking, 1* (2), A194-A204.

Touch, J., & Perlman, R. (2009). *Transparent Interconnection of Lots of Links (TRILL): Problem and Applicability Statement*. Academic Press.

TPM Main Specification . (2011, March). http://www.trustedcomputinggroup.org/resources/tpm_main_specification

TrafficLand. (2014). *TrafficLand.com - Traffic Cameras, Traffic Video, Live Traffic Cams*. Retrieved 28 September 2014, from http://www.trafficland.com/

Troan, O. & Droms, R.. (2003). IPv6 Prefix Options for Dynamic Host Configuration Protocol (DHCP) version 6, *Internet Engineering Task Force (IETF) RFC 3633.*

Troan, O., & Droms, R. (2003). *IPv6 Prefix Options for Dynamic Host Configuration Protocol (DHCP) version 6.* IETF Internet Standard RFC3633, December 2003.

Trossen, D. (Ed.). (2011). Conceptual Architecture: Principles, Patterns and Sub-components Descriptions. In *Publish Subscribe Internet Technology FP7-INFSO-ICT-257217 Deliverable D2.2*. Retrieved from http://www.fp7-pursuit.eu/PursuitWeb/

Tuan, A. L., Kyung, H., Choong, S.E., Razzaque, M.A., & Sungwon, L. (2012). *ecMTCP: An Energy-Aware Congestion Control Algorithm for Multipath TCP*. Academic Press.

Tuner, S., & Chen, L. (2011, March). *Updated Security Considerations for the MD5 Message-Digest and the HMAC-MD5 Algorithms*. Retrieved from https://tools.ietf.org/html/rfc6151

Turbobytes. (2014). *Turbobytes Optimizer. How it works*. Retrieved October 23, 2014 http://www.turbobytes.com/products/optimizer/

Turkle, S. (2011). *Alone together: Why we expect more from technology and less from each other*. Cambridge: MIT Press.

Twomey, P. (2006). *ICANN letter to CIRA – Ref.* Retrieved from http://www.icann.org

UNESCO Institute for Statistics. (n.d.). Retrieved from http://www.uis.unesco.org/

Unit, E. I. Democracy Index 2011, Democracy Under Stress. Rep. (2011). *The Economist*. Retrieved May 2012 from: www.eiu.com

United Nations E-Government Survey 2012. (n.d.). United Nations, Economic & Social Affairs, United Nations. Retrieved from www.unpan.org/e-government

United States Department of Health and Human Services. (2007). Personalized Health Care: Opportunities, Pathways[Health and Human Services]. *Resources*, 1–69.

Unix Top. (n.d.). *Unix Top Project Website*. Retrieved July 2014 from: http://www.unixtop.org

Valdivieso Caraguay, Á. L., Benito Peral, A., Barona López, L. I., & García Villalba, L. J. (2014). SDN: Evolution and Opportunities in the Development IoT Applications. *International Journal of Distributed Sensor Networks*, 2014.

Van der Pol, R., Boele, S., Dijkstra, F., & Barczyk, A. (2012). *Multipathing with MPTCP and Openflow*. Academic Press.

Van der Pol, R., Bredel, M., Barczyky, A., Overeinder, B., Van Adrichem, N., & Kuipers, F. (2013). *Experiences with MPTCP in an intercontinental multipathed OpenFlow network*. Academic Press.

Van Duijnhoven, J. (2003). *Knowledge Assessment using Bayesian Networks – A case study in the domain of algebraic expectation*. Master's Thesis.

Vasseur, J., Ayyangar, A., & Zhang, R. (2008). *A per-domain path computation method for establishing inter-domain traffic engineering (TE) label switched paths (LSPs)*. RFC5152.

Vasseur, J.P., Zhang, R., Bitar, N., & Le Roux, J.L. (2009). *A Backward-Recursive PCE-based Computation (BRPC) Procedure to Compute Shortest Constrained Inter-Domain Traffic Engineering Label Switched Paths, RFC 5441*. IETF.

Vasseur, J. P., & Le Roux, J. L. (2009). *Path Computation Element (PCE) Communication Protocol (PCEP), RFC 5440*. IETF. doi:10.17487/rfc5440

Vasseur, J. P., & Le Roux, J. L. (2009). *Path Computation Element (PCE) Communication Protocol (PCEP). RFC 5440. Crabbe, E., Minei, I., Medved, J., Varga, R. (2014), PCEP Extensions for Stateful PCE, draft-ietf-pce-stateful-pce-10*. IETF.

Vasseur, J. P., Le Roux, J. L., & Ikejiri, Y. (2010). *A set of Monitoring Tools for Path Computation (PCE)-based Architecture, RFC 5886*. IETF. doi:10.17487/rfc5886

Veizades, J., Guttman, E., Perkins, C., & Kaplan, S. (1997). *Service Location Protocol (RFC 2165)*. IETF. doi:10.17487/rfc2165

Vercellone, P. (1959). *Il diritto sul proprio ritratto*. Torino: Utet.

Vestin, J., Dely, P., Kassler, A., Bayer, N., Einsiedler, H., & Peylo, C. (2013). CloudMAC: Towards software defined WLANs. *ACM SIGMOBILE Mobile Computer Communications Review*, *16*(4), 42–45. doi:10.1145/2436196.2436217

Vida, R., & Costa, L. (2004). *Multicast Listener Discovery Version 2 (MLDv2) for IPv6. Internet Engineering Task Force RFC 3810*. Retrieved from https://tools.ietf.org/html/rfc3810

Video over Internet Consumer Survey. (2013). Retrieved from http://www.accenture.com/SiteCollectionDocuments/PDF/Accenture-Video-Over-Internet-Consumer-Survey-2013.pdf

Vidyo. (2014). *Personalized Healthcare Without Borders*. Retrieved 28 September 2014, from http://www.vidyo.com/solutions/healthcare/

Villamizar, C. (1999). *OSPF Optimized Multipath*. OSPF-OMP.

Vixie, P., Gudmundsson, O., Eastlake, D., III, & Wellington, B. (2000, May). Secret Key Transaction Authentication for DNS (TSIG). *RFC*. Retrieved May 2000, from http://www.ietf.org/rfc/rfc2845.txt

VMware, Inc. (2014). *Your Cloud in Healthcare*. VMware, Inc.

Voellmy, A., Kim, H., & Feamster, N. (2012, August). Procera: a language for high-level reactive network control. In *Proceedings of the first workshop on Hot topics in software defined networks* (pp. 43-48). ACM. doi:10.1145/2342441.2342451

Vollbrecht, J., Calhoun, P., Farrell, S., Gommans, L., Gross, G., & de Bruijn, B. …Spence, D. (2000, August). *AAA Authorization Framework* (Tech. Rep. No. 2904). IETF Secretariat. RFC 2904.

Volpano, D., Sun, X., & Xie, G. (2014). *Towards Systematic Detection and Resolution of Network Control Conflicts. In Proceedings of ACM HotSDN*. New York, NY: ACM.

W3C. (2013). *OWL Web Ontology Language Current Status*. Retrieved from: http://www.w3.org/standards/techs/owl#w3c_all

Wang, R., & Mukherjee, B. (2013). Provisioning in elastic optical networks with non-disruptive defragmentation. *Journal of Lightwave Technology, 31*(15), 2491–2500. doi:10.1109/JLT.2013.2268535

Wang, Z., Bovik, A. C., Sheikh, H. R., & Simoncelli, E. P. (2004). Image quality assessment: From error visibility to structural similarity. *IEEE Transactions on Image Processing, 13*(4), 600–612. doi:10.1109/TIP.2003.819861 PMID:15376593

Wang, Z., Sun, L., Chen, X., Zhu, W., Liu, J., Chen, M., & Yang, S. (2012). Propagation-based social-aware replication for social video contents. In *Proceedings of the 20th ACM international conference on Multimedia* (pp. 29-38). New York, NY: ACM.

Wang, Z., Sun, L., Yang, S., & Zhu, W. (2011). Prefetching strategy in peer-assisted social video streaming, In *Proceedings of the 19th ACM international conference on Multimedia* (pp. 1233-1236). New York, NY: ACM. doi:10.1145/2072298.2071982

Wannstrom, J., (2013). *Carrier Aggregation Explained.* Academic Press.

Warman, M. (2012). Government minister Ed Vaizey questions EU's "right to be forgotten" regulations. *The Telegraph.* Retrieved February 28, 2012, form http://www.telegraph.co.uk/technology/news/9109669/Government-minister-Ed-Vaizey-questions-EU-right-to-be-forgotten-regulations.html

Wayner, P. (2014). *Amazon vs. Google vs. Windows Azure: Cloud computing speed showdown.* Retrieved from: http://www.computerworld.com.au/article/539633/amazon_vs_google_vs_windows_azure_cloud_computing_speed_showdown/

Web. (2014). *World Wide Web Consortium.* Retrieved from http://www.w3.org/Consortium/

Wedlund, E., & Schulzrinne, H. (1999). Mobility Support using SIP. In *WOWMOM '99 Proceedings of the 2nd ACM international workshop on Wireless mobile multimedia* (pp. 76-82). New York: ACM.

Weiler, S., & Blacka, D. (2013, February). *Clarifications and Implementation Notes for DNS Security (DNSSEC).* Retrieved from tools.ietf.org/html/rfc6840

Weinberg, J. (2000). ICANN and the Problem of Legitimacy. *Duke Law Journal, 50*(187), 187–260. doi:10.2307/1373114

Weiser, M. (1991). The Computer for the 21st Century. *Scientific American, 3*(3), 3-11.

Wen, S., Zhu, X., Lin, Z., Zhang, X., & Yang, D. (2013). Distributed Resource Management for Device-to-Device (D2D) Communication Underlay Cellular Networks. *IEEE 24th International Symposium on Personal Indoor and Mobile Radio Comm. (PIMRC).*

Wendt, A. E. (1987, Summer). The agent-structure problem in international relations theory. *International Organization, 41*(03), 335–370. doi:10.1017/S002081830002751X

Wetherall, D. J., Guttag, J. V., & Tennenhouse, D. L. (1998, April). ANTS: A toolkit for building and dynamically deploying network protocols. In Open Architectures and Network Programming, 1998 IEEE (pp. 117-129). IEEE. doi:10.1109/OPNARC.1998.662048

Wilson, C. (2014). *Report: NFV/SDN Standards 'Myopic' on Service Management.* Retrieved from http://www.lightreading.com/carrier-sdn/nfv-(network-functions-virtualization)/report-nfv-sdn-standards-myopic-on-service-management/d/d-id/708682

Wing, D. (2013). Port Control Protocol (PCP). *IETF Standard - RFC* 6887.

Wing, D., Cheshire, S., Boucadair, M., Penno, R., & Selkirk, P. (2013). Port Control Protocol (PCP). *IETF.* Retrieved November 25, 2014, from https://tools.ietf.org/html/rfc6887

Wing, D., Penno, R., Reddy, T., & Selkirk, P. (2013). PCP Flowdata Option. *IETF.* Retrieved November 25, 2014, from https://tools.ietf.org/html/draft-wing-pcp-flowdata-00

Winkler, S., & Mohandas, P. (2008). The evolution of video quality measurement: From PSNR to hybrid metrics. *IEEE Transactions on Broadcasting, 54*(3), 660–668. doi:10.1109/TBC.2008.2000733

Winter, T., Thubert, P., Brandt, A., Hui, J., Kelsey, R., Levis, P., … Vasseur, J. P. (2012). *RPL: IPv6 Routing Protocol for Low-Power and Lossy Networks*. Retrieved March 15, 2015 from https://datatracker.ietf.org/doc/rfc6550/

Wobker, L. J. (2012). *Power consumption in high-end routing systems* [PDF document]. Retrieved from http://www.nanog.org/meetings/nanog54/presentations/Wednesday/Wobker.pdf

Woodyatt, J. (2011) Recommended Simple Security Capabilities in Customer Premises Equipment (CPE) for Providing Residential IPv6 Internet Service, RFC6092.

World Wide Web Consortium. (2014). *Resource Description Framework (RDF)*. Retrieved from: http://www.w3.org/RDF/

Wubben, D., Rost, P., Bartelt, J., Lalam, M., Savin, V., Gorgoglione, M., & Fettweis, G. et al. (2014, May). Benefits and impact of cloud computing on 5G signal processing, *IEEE Signal Processing Magazine, Special Issue on 5G. Signal Processing.*

Xenakis, D., Passas, N., Merakos, L., & Verikoukis, C. (2014). Mobility Management for Femtocells in LTE-Advanced: Key Aspects and Survey of Handover Decision Algorithms. Communications Surveys & Tutorials, IEEE, 16(1), 64-91.

Xia, L., Wu, Q., & King, D. (2013). *Use cases and Requirements for Virtual Service Node Pool Management (draft-xia-vsnpool-management-use-case-01)*, IEFT Internet Draft, October 2013.

Xie, H., Li, Y., Wang, J., Lopez, D. R., Tsou, T., & Wen, Y. (2013). vRGW: Towards network function virtualization enabled by software defined networking. In *Proceedings of the International Conference on Network Protocols (ICNP 2013)*. Göttingen, Germany: IEEE Computer Society. Doi: doi:10.1109/ICNP.2013.6733632

Xu, M., Cao, Y., & Fu, X. (2014). *Delay-based Congestion Control for MPTCP*. Academic Press.

Xylomenos, G., Ververidis, C., Siris, V., Fotiou, N., Tsilopoulos, C., Vasilakos, X., & Polyzos, G. et al. (2013). A Survey of Information-Centric Networking Research. *IEEE Communications Surveys and Tutorials*, *16*(2), 1024–1049. doi:10.1109/SURV.2013.070813.00063

Yap, K. K., Kobayashi, M., Sherwood, R., Huang, T. Y., Chan, M., Handigol, N., & McKeown, N. (2010). OpenRoads: Empowering research in mobile networks. *Computer Communication Review*, *40*(1), 125–126. doi:10.1145/1672308.1672331

Yavatkar, R., Pendarakis, D., & Guerin, R. (2000). A Framework for Policy-based Admission Control. *IETF*. Retrieved November 25, 2014, from https://tools.ietf.org/html/rfc2753

Yong, L., Hao, W., Eastlake, D., Qu, A., Hudson, J., Chunduri, U. (2014) ISIS Protocol Extension For Building Distribution Trees, draft-yong-isis-ext-4-distribution-tree-02.

Young, G. (2009). Broadband Forum Overview with Focus on Next Generation Access. *Presentation delivered at the UKNOF event, September 2009*. Retrieved July 2014 from: http://www.uknof.org.uk/uknof14/ Young-BroadbandForum.pdf

Younkin, A., Fernald, R., Doherty, R., Salskov, E., & Corriveau, P. (2007). Predicting an average end-user's experience of video playback. In *Third International Workshop on Video Processing and Quality Metrics for Consumer Electronics*.

Yousaf, F. Z., Lessmann, J., Loureiro, P., & Schmid, S. (2013). SoftEPC Dynamic Instantiation of Mobile Core Network Entities for Efficient Resource Utilization. *IEEE International Conference on Communications*, Budapest, Hungary.

Yuksel, M., & Dogac, A. (2011). Interoperability of Medical Device Information and the Clinical Applications: An HL7 RMIM based on the ISO/IEEE 11073 DIM. *IEEE Transactions on Information Technology in Biomedicine*, *15*(4), 557–566. doi:10.1109/TITB.2011.2151868 PMID:21558061

Zaidi, Z., Friderikos, V., & Ali Imran, M. (2014). An integrated approach for future mobile network architecture. *IEEE International Symposium on Personal, Indoor and Mobile Radio Communications (PIMRC)*, Washington, DC.

Zeng, S., & Hao, Q. (2009). Network I/O Path Analysis in the Kernel-based Virtual Machine Environment through Tracing. In *Proceedings of the 1st Int. Conf. on Information Science and Engineering (ICISE 2009)*. Nanjing, China: IEEE Computer Society. doi:10.1109/ICISE.2009.776

Zeus News. (2009). Retrieved February 9, 2009, from http://www.zeusnews.it/n.php?c=9393

Zgurovsky, M. Z., Boldak, A. A., & Pomerantseva, T. N. (2010). Analysis of the influence of global threats on the sustainable development of countries and regions of the world using Bayesian Belief Networks. *Cybernetics and Systems Analysis*, *46*(5), 822–832. doi:10.1007/s10559-010-9264-4

Zhang, J., Ren, F., & Lin, C. (2013). *Survey on Transport Control in Data Center Networks*. Academic Press.

Zhang, F., & Farrel, A. (2014). *Conveying Vendor-Specific Constraints in the Path Computation Element Communication Protocol, RFC 7150*. IETF. doi:10.17487/rfc7150

Zhang, M., Cheng, Y., Liu, B., & Zhang, B. (2010). GreenTE: Power-Aware Traffic Engineering, In *Proceedings of the 18th IEEE International Conference on Network Protocols (ICNP '10)*. New York, NY: IEEE. doi:10.1109/ICNP.2010.5762751

Zhang, Y., Huang, A., Wang, D., Duan, X., Jiao, B., & Xie, L. (2013). To enable stable medical image and video transmission in mobile healthcare services: A Best-fit Carrier Dial-up (BCD) algorithm for GBR-oriented applications in LTE-A networks. In *2013 IEEE International Conference on Communications (ICC)* (pp. 4368–4372). doi:10.1109/ICC.2013.6655253

Zhang, Y., Roughan, M., Duffield, N., & Greenberg, A. (2003). Fast Accurate Computation of Large-Scale IP Traffic Matrices from Link Loads. In *Proceedings of the ACM Special Interest Group on Performance Evaluation (SIGCOMM '03)*. New York, NY: ACM. doi:10.1145/781027.781053

Zhao, Q., Raza, K., Zhou, C., Fang, L., Li, L., King, D. (2014) LDP Extensions for Multiple Topology, RFC7307.

Zhao, Q., Zhao, K., Li, R., Dhuody, D., Palle, U., Zhang, B. (2015) PCEP Procedures and Protocol Extensions for Using PCE as a Central Controller (PCECC) of LSPs, draft-zhao-pce-pcep-extension-for-pce-controller-01.

Zhao, Q., Zhao, K., Li, R., Ke, K. (2014) The Use Cases for Using PCE as the Central Controller (PCECC) of LSPs, draft-zhao-pce-central-controller-user-cases-01.

Zhao, Y., et al. (2012). Routing and wavelength assignment problem in PCE-based wavelength-switched optical networks. *Optical Communications and Networking, IEEE/OSA Journal of* 2(4), 196-205.

Zhao, Q., King, D., Verhaeghe, F., Takeda, T., Ali, Z., & Meuric, J. (2010). *Extensions to the Path Computation Element Communication Protocol (PCEP) for Point-to-Multipoint Traffic Engineering Label Switched Paths, RFC 6006*. IETF. doi:10.17487/rfc6006

Zheng, K., Hu, F., Wang, W., Xiang, W., & Dohler, M. (2012). Radio Resource Allocation in LTE-Advanced Cellular Networks with M2M Communications. *IEEE Communications Magazine*, *50*(7), 184–192. doi:10.1109/MCOM.2012.6231296

Zong, N., Dunbar, L., Shore, M., Lóez, D., & Karagiannis, G. (2014, Jul). *Virtualized Network Function (VNF) Pool Problem Statement* (Internet-Draft No. draft-zong-vnfpool-problem-statement-06). IETF Secretariat. Retrieved March, 6, 2015 from http://tools.ietf.org/html/draft-zong-vnfpool-problem-statement-06

Zuniga, J.C., Bernardos C. J., De La Oliva A, Melia, T., Costa, R., Reznik, A, (2013). Distributed mobility management: A standards landscape. *IEEE Communications Magazine, 51*(3).

About the Contributors

Mohamed Boucadair is a Senior IP Architect with France Telecom. He has worked for France Telecom R&D and has been part of the team working on VoIP services. He is now working at the France Telecom corporate division responsible for making recommendations on the evolution of IP/MPLS core networks. He has been involved in IST research projects, working on dynamic provisioning and inter-domain traffic engineering. He has also worked as an R&D engineer in charge of dynamic provisioning, QoS, multicast and intra/inter-domain traffic engineering. He has published many journal articles and written extensively on these subject areas. Mr. Boucadair holds several patents on VoIP, IPv4 service continuity, IPv6, etc.

Christian Jacquenet graduated from the Ecole Nationale Supérieure de Physique de Marseille, a French school of engineers. He joined Orange in 1989, and he's currently the Director of the Strategic Program Office for advanced IP networking within Orange Labs. In particular, he's responsible of Orange's IPv6 Program that aims at defining and driving the enforcement of the Group's IPv6 strategy and conducts development activities in the area of Software-Defined Networking (SDN) and service function chaining. He authored and co-authored several Internet drafts and RFC documents in the field of dynamic routing protocols and resource allocation techniques, as well as multiple papers and books in the areas of IP multicast, traffic engineering and automated IP service delivery techniques.

* * *

Laura Abba graduated in mathematics in 1979, Technical Executive of the Institute of Informatics and Telematics of the Italian National Research Council (CNR) . She is committed in the field of Global Internet Governance as a new interdisciplinary research field. Her main activity is in supporting the process of interaction between the Research networks and the Internet in Italy. She has participated in projects introducing the Internet in Italy at CNR-CNUCE, collaborating, within the GARR Italian Academic and Research Network framework, in the establishment of research networks and in the development of the information society. Since 2003 she is a member of the Board of ISOC Italy, the Italian Chapter of Internet Society. She is a member of the promoting committee of IGF Italy. She participated, since the beginning, in the Internet Governance Forums promoted by the United Nations. She has continuously worked for the dissemination of the Internet culture and technologies (training, conventions, editorials).

Maid Aghvami is a Professor at King's College London, Centre for Telecommunications Research. He was a member of the Board of Governors of the IEEE Communications Society in 2001-2003, was a Distinguished Lecturer of the IEEE Communications Society in 2004-2007, and has been member, Chairman, and Vice-Chairman of the technical programme and organising committees of a large number of international conferences. He has published over 550 conference and journal papers. He has been awarded the IEEE Technical Committee on Personal Communications (TCPC) Recognition Award in 2005 for his outstanding technical contributions to the communications field, and for his service to the scientific and engineering communities. Professor Aghvami is a Fellow of the Royal Academy of Engineering, Fellow of the IET, Fellow of the IEEE, and in 2009 was awarded a Fellowship of the Wireless World Research Forum in recognition of his personal contributions to the wireless world, and for his research achievements as Director at the Centre for Telecommunications Research at King's.

Saleh Altowaijri is the Deputy Head of the Academic Monitoring Section at the Saudi Arabian Cultural Bureau in London. He has obtained his PhD from Swansea University in the area of cloud computing. He has over 6 years of research experience and has published several book chapters, conference and journal papers. He is a reviewer of several international conferences and journals. His research interests include grid and cloud computing, database management systems, data mining, information systems, information technology risk management, and emerging ICT systems in healthcare and transportation sectors.

Nathalie Amann obtained an engineering degree in telecommunications from the ESIGETEL, Fontainebleau in 1997. She started in development activities on intranet and Internet applications in Société Générale. She then worked during four years in Siemens Research and Development, prominently on vocal applications. For ten years, she has been working for Orange Labs on traffic analysis, IP Network architectures and on Content Delivery research activities. She is currently in charge of anticipation activities on Content Delivery Networks.

Valentina Amenta, Degree in Economics, Ph.D. in public and economics law, during which she focused the research on the right of access to the Internet. Since 2012 collaborates with the Institute of Informatics and Telematics of the CNR in Pisa. Currently with research grant for activities in the field of Internet Governnace. Participate in the process of the Internet Governance Forum of the United Nations. Member of Internet Society Italy. Subject Expert in Information Technology Law at the University of Pisa and contract ciollaborazione teaching for the course of Private Law.

Valéry Bastide obtained a degree level of telecommunication from Lille 1 University in 1987. He started as technical team manager on voice telephony and cable network in France Telecom. He worked during 5 years in Orange Labs on broadband access server and IP ADSL Networks. For ten years, he has been working on Content delivery activities for Orange Labs and he is currently in charge of integration and validation activities on Content Delivery Networks.

Patrice Bellagamba is a Distinguished System Engineer working for Cisco Systems in Europe. He is mainly in charge of the technical introduction of new routing or transport protocols like LISP, VPLS, OTV or VXLAN and others. Patrice has been in the industry of networking since 1984, and on IP since 1991 and MPLS in 1998 working with large Enterprises or Services-Providers. Patrice is the co-inventor of the ARC (Available Route Construct) protocol that intend to enable SDN for routing with fast convergence.

David Binet is graduated from Telecom-Lille 1 and senior expert on inter access mobility technologies in France Telecom. He first worked on IPv6 technologies mainly in Home Networking context. He has contributed on several French and European collaborative projects in mobility area and convergence issues. Involved in Research and pre-deployment projects, he is the author of several patents and he has contributed to the writing of papers for international conferences. Besides the leading of IPv6 projects, he was responsible for several research contracts with universities and contribute to IETF activities on mobility topics. He participated in several collaborative projects funded by French government and European commission on IPv6 and mobility topics. He currently chairs Mobile WG in France Telecom IPv6 program and is an IP architect involved in IP/MPLS core networks architectures deployment in Orange affiliates.

Maria Isabel Borges received both her degrees in Electronics and Telecommunications engineering from Aveiro University, where she also accomplished a post-graduation work on the microwave systems. She worked at TEKA Portuguesa and joined PT Inovação, S.A. (PTIN) former Centro de Estudos de Telecomunicações, in 1991. Since then she worked on applied research and, since then, has been involved in several national and international R&D programs, namely in the area of development and integration of broadband access networks' technologies, IP networking and Services and VoIP systems. Recently, she has been promoting partnerships, and engaged in consultancy and training programs, in Portugal and abroad in PALOPs (Brasil, Angola, Moçambique, Cabo Verde, Timor, S. Tomé e Príncipe, Guiné) and in Norway, Namibia and Dubai. She was a key member in the creation of the certification area at PT Inovação and she is currently responsible for the technology and services training and certification division. She is author or co-author of several publications on the above-mentioned subjects and a reviewer of IEEE Communications Magazine.

Dariusz Bursztynowski graduated as M.Sc. and Ph.D. in Telecommunications from Warsaw University of Technology in 1982 and 1992, respectively. Since 1983 to 1990 he worked for several telecom companies continuing his research in the field of performance evaluation in distributed systems. Since 1990 to 1991 he worked for Alcatel SESA, Madrid, under a contract related to the deployment of S12 system in Poland. He has been with Orange Polska (formerly TPSA) since 1998, participating to a number of internal and collaborative projects in the field of network planning (including the deployment of network planning tools for the core and access), network management, traffic engineering, and network architecture evolution. His current research interests include content and service centric architectures, cloud networking solutions based on SDN and NFV, and the application of these concepts in the telco domain. He serves as a member to Network of the Future community in Orange. He is also a lecturer at the Warsaw University of Technology, and has served as a TPC member to a number of international conferences.

Daniele Ceccarelli is an SDN senior system architect at Ericsson with 10+ years of experience in centralized and distributed control plane. He has been a key contributor in several working groups of the IETF routing area and has recently been appointed as co-chairman of the CCAMP WG. He is one of the proponent of the ACTN BoF in IETF.

Yiping Chen prepared his PhD in Computer Science between 2006 and 2010 at Telecom Bretagne (Brest, France) on the topic of locality-awareness of Peer-to-Peer applications. After that He worked as postdoctoral researcher at CNRS-LaBRI (Bordeaux, France), on the EU FP7 project Alicante aiming at the deployment of networkedMedia Ecosystem. Then he joined Orange Labs as research engineer, working on mobile traffic optimization and network virtualization.

Giorgios Chochlidakis graduated from the school of Electrical and Computer Engineering of the National Technical University of Athens (NTUA). Since 2013 he is a member of the Centre for Telecommunications Research (CTR) of the Informatics department of King's College London (KCL). He, also, participates to the European Initial Training Networks (ITN) Marie Curie action project named CROSSFIRE (unCooRdinated netwOrk StrategieS for enhanced interFerence, mobIlity, radio Resource, and Energy saving management in LTE-Advanced networks). His research interests focus on network virtualization, mobility management for next-generation networks, virtual network embedding and network sharing.

Denis Collange is Research & Development Engineer in Orange Labs. He graduated from Telecom ParisTech. His research interests include modelling and performance evaluation of network protocols, traffic analysis and modelling, performance measurements and network troubleshooting. He manages projects to develop tools and algorithms to optimize the performance of France Telecom data services. He has produced a number of papers on these subjects. He has been involved in the Network of Excellence EuroNF, and in many european projects and national co-operations.

Tiago Cruz is Assistant Professor at the University of Coimbra (Portugal), from where he got his PhD in Informatics Engineering, in 2012. He is also a researcher at the Centre for Informatics and Systems of the University of Coimbra. His research interests include (but are not restricted to) Broadband Network Architectures, Systems, Network Management, Security and Embedded Systems Design and Critical Infrastructure Security.

Filippo Cugini received the M.S. degree in Telecommunication Engineering from the University of Parma, Italy. Since 2001, he has been with the National Laboratory of Photonic Networks, CNIT, Pisa, Italy. His main research interests include theoretical and experimental studies in the field of optical communications and networking. He served as co-chair of several international symposia and he serves as Editorial Board Member of the Elsevier Optical Switching and Networking journal. He is co-author of twelve international patents and more than 130 IEEE publications.

Spyros Denazis received his B.Sc. in Mathematics from the University of Ioannina, Greece, in 1987, and in 1993 his Ph.D. in computer science from the University of Bradford, UK. He worked in European industry for eight years, and is now an associate professor in the Department of Electrical and Computer Engineering, University of Patras, Greece. His current research interests include P2P, SDN, and Future Internet. He is currently the technical manager of STEER EU project. He has co-authored more than 50 papers.

Mischa Dohler is full Professor in Wireless Communications at King's College London, Head of the Centre for Telecommunications Research, co-founder and member of the Board of Directors of the smart city pioneer Worldsensing, Fellow and Distinguished Lecturer of the IEEE, and Editor-in-Chief of the Transactions on Emerging Telecommunications Technologies. He is a frequent keynote, panel and tutorial speaker. He has pioneered several research fields, contributed to wireless broadband, IoT/M2M and cyber security standards, holds a dozen patents, organized and chaired numerous conferences, has >200 publications, and authored several books. He acts as policy, technology and entrepreneurship adviser, examples being Richard Branson's Carbon War Room, House of Lords UK, UK Ministry BIS, EPSRC ICT Strategy Advisory Team, European Commission, and various start-ups. He is also an entrepreneur, pianist and fluent in 6 languages. He has talked at TEDx and his contributions have featured on BBC News and the Wall Street Journal.

Mateusz Dzida, Ph.D, is a graduate of Institute of Telecommunications at Warsaw University of Technology. He graduated master studies in 2003 on the basis of a thesis, which received the first prize in the contest for best master's thesis in the field of telecommunications, organized by Stowarzyszenie Inżynierów Telekomunikacji in 2003. In years 2003-2008 he completed doctoral studied at Faculty of Electronics and Information Technology WUT. In January 2009 Mateusz Dzida with distinction defended his doctoral dissertation titled „Optimization models. During work at Warsaw University of Technology, i.e., in 2003-2009 Mateusz Dzida actively participated in realization of many (national and international) research projects conducted in Department of Computer Networks and Switching. Since 2005 Mateusz Dzida actively participates in R&D projects at Orange Labs. Mateusz Dzida is an author and coauthor of over 35 scientific publications. Twice awarded the Rector of WUT for research.

Muhammad Ali Faisal has been working as an Assistant Professor at COMSATS Institute of Information Technology (CIIT), Abbottabad, Pakistan since 2008. Earlier, he has gained over 12 years industrial experience at Pakistan Telecommunication Limited (PTCL), the largest telecommunication organization in Pakistan. His research interests lie in future intelligent networks and applications for wired and wireless technologies.

Frédéric Fieau is a R&D engineer in Orange Labs. He received his engineer's degree from Telecom Bretagne, France. He is now working as a network architect on Cloud and Content Delivery Networks, video quality of experience and infrastructures virtualization.

Patrick Fleming is a network architect for Orange S.A. He is an expert in the routing and delivery aspects of audiovisual services deployment and regularly delivers training courses to audiences drawn from operational and business units of the company, universities and french engineering schools. He has a degree in mathematics and computing from the University of Pierre et Marie Curie (Paris VI) and earned a master in telecommunication and network at Telecom ParisTech.

Michael Franke, born 1984, studied Game Design at Mediadesign Hochschule in Munich. After that he worked as a software development consultant with focus on media, web and mobile applications for different customers. After having several contract assignments at Spinor he joined the company as a software engineer in 2012.

Vasilis Friderikos is a Senior Lecturer at King's College London, Centre for Telecommunications Research. His research interests lie broadly within the closely overlapped areas of wireless networking, mobile computing, and architectural aspects of the Future Internet. He has written more than 120 research papers in the aforementioned research scope areas and has been co-chairing, organizing and programme committee member in numerous flagship IEEE international conferences and workshops, examples being IEEE Globecom, IEEE ICC and IEEE PIMRC. He has been a British Telecom Fellow, a visiting researcher at the WinLab at Rutgers University USA and received two times Best Paper Award in IEEE ICC and WWRF conferences.

Vincent Gouraud has been an R&D engineer at Orange labs since 1995.

Ali Gouta is a phd and R&D engineer. His research interests include TCP/IP, traffic measurements and modeling, content delivery networks, caching algorithms and social networks.

David Griffin is a Principal Research Associate in the Department of Electronic and Electrical Engineering, UCL. He has a BSc from Loughborough University and a PhD from UCL, both in Electrical Engineering. Before joining UCL he was a Systems Design Engineer at GEC-Plessey Telecommunications (now part of Ericsson) before joining the Foundation for Research and Technology, Institute of Computer Science, Greece as a Research Associate in Telecommunications. He has had a significant involvement in EU research programmes in RACE, ACTS, IST and ICT projects with both technical research contributions and project management activities. His research interests are in the planning, management and dynamic control for providing QoS in multiservice networks, p2p networking and novel routing paradigms for the future Internet.

Karine Guillouard received her MS and PhD degrees from INSA, France, in 1994 and 1997 respectively. Joining Orange Labs, she was successively involved in techno-economic, wireless home network and IP-based mobility protocol studies. She was in charge of the French RNRT Cyberté project (2001-2004) relative to multi-access IPv6 terminal architecture and conducted research contracts. Orange expert since 2010 in the Future Networks Community, her research activities evolved towards dynamic and adaptive network architectures applied in the context of fixed and mobile convergence, network function virtualization and network programmability.

Pedro Andres Aranda Gutierrez obtained his Telecommunications Engineering degree in 1988 at the Universidad Politécnica de Madrid and his PhD in 2013 at the Universität Paderborn. He joined Telefónica, Investigación y Desarrollo in 1989, where he started designing hardware modules for Telefónica's experimental ATM demonstrator. He then moved on design inter-domain IP networks for the Telefónica group. During all his professional life he has been involved in different international collaborative projects of the different framework programmes of the E.U. Currently he is working at the Network Innovation & Virtualisation directorate at the GCTO Unit of Telefónica I+D in the Technology Exploration Group. He is acting as Technical Manager of the EU-funded FP7 NetIDE project and overlooks control plane evolutions like OpenFlow and SDN in general as well as their interaction with Cloud Management frameworks.

Evangelos Haleplidis received his B.Eng. in Electrical and Computer Engineering from the University of Patras, Greece in 2002. He is actively involved in the standardization work in the IETF and IRTF, specifically in the ForCES working group and the SDN research group. His current research interests inlcude SDN and NFV. He has co-authored several papers in this area as well as a number of RFCs and drafts in the IETF and IRTF.

Tirumaleswar Reddy Konda received his Bachelor of Engineering in Computer Science and Engineering from PES College of Engineering, Mysore University in 2000 and Master of Computer Science from Illinois institute of Technology, Chicago in 2004. He is currently as Technical Leader in Cisco systems. He worked on Bluetooth, SIP, Firewall, IPS, Identity and Cloud based security as a Service. He has 22 pending patents, co-authored three RFC and several IETF working group documents. His recent work and interests include SFC, WebRTC, STUN, TURN and PCP.

Odysseas Koufopavlou received the Diploma of Electrical Engineering in 1983 and the Ph.D. degree in Electrical Engineering in 1990, both from University of Patras, Greece. From 1990 to 1994 he was at the IBM Thomas J. Watson Research Center, Yorktown Heights, NY, USA. He is currently Professor with the Department of Electrical and Computer Engineering, University of Patras. He has co-authored more than 200 papers in his field.

Yves L'Azou is an engineer for Orange, France, whose body of work includes: IT infrastructures environmental sustainability; Networks and internet services design & expertise; development of new services, in various environments from cooperative university research to large operational rollouts; cutting-edge technologies; Project and technical implementation management; Team management Specialties; IT infrastructure platforms (DataCenter, hardware, software); virtualization; OTT, VoD and Live TV solutions for mobile and fixed networks (IPTV, Web based); Content Management Networks (CDN); Networking (IP, routing, probe & survey, design); Management, head of R&D team (20 p), and of development team (18 p).

Adriana Lazzaroni, University degree in Political Science. Specialised in International Relations she begins working in the network environment in 1992. She starts her carrier at the Italian National Research Council (CNR) working on projects for the development of computer infrastructures in developing countries and on pilot projects for the Information Society. In this field she gives her contribution to the evolution of the Internet in Italy and she enhances her competences in the field of network services for the academic users, in technology transfer and in promoting scientific data by means of web technologies. From 2001 to 2003 she is a member of the Executive Board of ISOC Italy, the Italian Chapter of Internet Society, contributing to the start up activities of the Chapter. Since 1992 she is head of the Scientific Affairs Unit of the Institute of Informatics and Telematics of the Italian National Research Council (www.iit.cnr.it). She is in charge with the International Relations of IIT. Expert in Internet Governance, since 2009 she participates in the dialogue on the international regulations for the Internet and she works in promoting the global Internet governance as a new interdisciplinary research field.

Young Lee is currently Technical Director of Network Architecture and SDN at Huawei Technologies USA Research Center, Plano, Texas since 2006. He is leading optical transport control plane technology research and development and standard work in IETF and ONF. He served as co-chair of ACTN BoFs in IETF and New Transport Discussion Group in ONF. He has led GMPLS and PCE standardization to enable new capability like WSON and global concurrent optimization. His research interest includes SDN, cloud computing architecture, cross stratum optimization, network virtualization, distributed path computation architecture, multi-layer traffic engineering methodology, and network optimization modeling and new concept development in optical control plane signaling and routing. Prior to joining to Huawei Technologies, he was a co-founder and a Principal Architect at Ceterus Networks (2001-2005) where he developed topology discovery protocol and control plane architecture for optical transport core product. Prior to joining to Ceterus Networks, he was Principal Technical Staff Member at AT&T/Bell Labs in Middletown/Holmdel, New Jersey (1987-2000). Young Lee received B.A. degree in applied mathematics from the University of California at Berkeley in 1986, M.S. degree in operations research from Stanford University, Stanford, CA, in 1987, and Ph.D. degree in decision sciences and engineering systems from Rensselaer Polytechnic Institute, Troy, NY, in 1996.

Zhenbin Li, Principal Engineer, Network Solution, Huaiwei Technologies. He has been worked in MPLS field for 14 years and been responsible for the design and development of MPLS LDP, MPLS TE, MPLS L2VPN, MPLS L3VPN, BFD, MPLS OAM, Seamless MPLS, P2MP MPLS, GMPLS, EVPN, PCE, etc. Currently, he is in charge of the innovation and standard development of Huawei IP software platform, focusing on SDN, mobile backhaul, data center, etc.

Yiting Liao is a research scientist in Wireless Communications Lab at Intel Labs in Hillsboro, OR, focusing on multimedia communication technologies and wireless body area networks. She received her Ph.D. in Electrical and Computer Engineering from University of California, Santa Barbara and M.S. and B.S. degrees in Electrical Engineering from Tsinghua University, China. She has published 20 journal/conference papers and book chapters, and holds 10+ pending patents. Her research interests include image and video quality assessment, video optimization techniques and QoE enhancement over wireless networks, machine learning and protocol design for wearables and body area networks.

Diego R. Lopez joined Telefonica I+D in 2011 as a Senior Technology Expert on network middleware and services. He is currently in charge of the Technology Exploration activities within the GCTO Unit of Telefónica I+D. Before joining Telefónica he spent some years in the academic sector, dedicated to research on network service abstractions and the development of APIs based on them. During this period he was appointed as member of the High Level Expert Group on Scientific Data Infrastructures by the European Commission. Diego is currently focused on identifying and evaluating new opportunities in technologies applicable to network infrastructures, and the coordination of national and international collaboration activities. His current interests are related to network virtualization, infrastructural services, network mamagement, new network architectures, and network security. Diego is actively participating in the ETSI ISG on Network Function Virtualization (chairing its Technical Steering Committee), the ONF, and the IETF WGs connected to these activities. Apart from this, Diego is a more than acceptable Iberian ham carver, and extremely fond of seeking and enjoying comics, wines, and cheeses.

Yannick Le Louédec holds an engineering degree in telecommunications from theEcole Nationale Supérieure des Telecommunications de Bretagne. He has been working for Orange Labs for fourteen years where he has been successively in charge of research activities on Optical Networks, IP Networks and Content Delivery Networks.

Nicolas Marechal has a MSc and a PhD in Computer Sciences from the University of Lyon (France). He his R&D Project Manager for Orange Labs since 2010 and is driving technical anticipation studies related to service/content delivery over mobile networks.

Rashid Mehmood is the Professor of Networked Information Systems and the Head of Research at the College of Computer Science, King Khalid University, Saudi Arabia. He has gained qualifications and academic work experience from universities in the UK including Huddersfield, Swansea, Cambridge, Birmingham and Oxford. Rashid has over 15 years of research experience in computational modelling and simulation systems coupled with his expertise in high performance computing. His broad research aim is to develop multi-disciplinary science and technology to enable better quality of life and Smart Economy with a focus on real-time intelligence and dynamic system management. He has published over 70 research papers including 4 edited books. He has chaired international conferences and workshops in his areas of expertise. He has led and contributed to academia-industry collaborative projects funded by EPSRC, EU, UK regional funds, and Technology Strategy Board UK. He is a member of ACM, OSA, Senior Member IEEE and former Vice-Chairman of IET Wales SW Network.

Christoph Meinel is a professor and director at the Hasso-Plattner-Institut at the University of Potsdam, where he leads the Internet Technologies and Systems research group. He is a member of acatech, the GermanNational Academy of Science and Engineering, and numerous scientific committees and supervisory boards. He is a member of the Security Advisory board at SAP SE, advisory committee chairman of the SAP Meraka UTD advisory board in South Africa, and works closely with a number of other supervisory boards. Since 2007 Christoph Meinel has been chairman of the German IPv6 Council. His research interests include security and trust engineering, Web 3.0, and eLearning. Meinel has a Ph.D. in computer science from the Humboldt-University in Berlin. Contact him at meinel@hpi.uni-potsdam.de.

Edmundo Monteiro is Full Professor at the Department of Informatics Engineering (DEI) of the University of Coimbra (UC), Portugal. He is also a Senior Member of the research Centre for Informatics and Systems of the University of Coimbra (CISUC). He graduated in Electrical Engineering (Informatics Specialty) from the University of Coimbra in 1984, and received his PhD in Informatics Engineering (Computer Communications) and the Habilitation in Informatics Engineering from the same university in 1996 and 2007 respectively. He has near 30 years of research and industry experience in the field of Computer Communications, Wireless Technologies, Quality of Service and Experience, Network Management, and Computer Security. He participated in many Portuguese and European research projects and initiatives. His publications include 6 books (authored and edited), several book chapters and journal publications, and over 200 papers in national and international refereed conferences. He is also co-author of 9 international patents. He is member of the Editorial Board of Elsevier Computer Communication and Springer Wireless Networks journals, and involved in the organization of many national and international conferences and workshops. Edmundo Monteiro is member of Ordem dos Engenheiros (the Portuguese Engineering Association), and senior member of IEEE Communication Society, and ACM Special Interest Group on Communications.

Hassnaa Moustafa is a Senior Research Scientist in Intel PC Client Division, leading innovations in user's experience for multimedia and video applications. Her research interests include wireless networks (including WPANs and IoT), optimized video delivery and context-awareness. She previously worked in France Telecom (Orange), where she led projects on low-cost wireless networks and services convergences in next generation networks. Hassnaa is a senior IEEE member and is qualified as a research director by the University of Paris XI in 2010. She is contributing to the IETF standardization and has over 70 publications in international conferences and journals and she is a co-author of two books published by the CRC press. Hassnaa obtained a PhD in Computer and Networks from Telecom ParisTech in 2004, a Master degree in distributed systems from the University of Paris XI in 2001.

Luca Muscariello received the Dr Ing degree in telecommunication engineering in 2002 and the Ph.D. in electronics and communications engineering in 2006 both from Politecnico di Torino, Italy. He is a senior research scientist at Orange Labs working on future networks. He was program co- chair of Valuetools 2013, program co-chair of ACM ICN 2014 and general co-chair of ACM ICN 2014. He is a member of the ACM and a senior member of the IEEE and SEE.

Martin A. Negron has over fifteen years of technical program management experience in areas related to defense, national security, biological threat reduction and energy policy. He has collaborated in multiple programs in the United States and also participated in programs in the United Kingdom, Saudi Arabia, Azerbaijan and Puerto Rico. He obtained a bachelor's degree in mechanical engineering from the University of Puerto Rico, a master's degree in engineering from the Johns Hopkins University and a doctorate degree in engineering management from the George Washington University. He recently lead an effort to reform the energy infrastructure of Puerto Rico while working as a senior advisor to the president of the Puerto Rico Senate.

Nathalie Omnès obtained a PhD in applied probability in 2001. She then joined Mitsubishi Electric ITE TCL in Rennes (France) where she worked until 2006 on mathematical models for QoS-enabled wireless networks, including several mechanisms at PHY and MAC layers. She then studied computer systems networking and telecommunications at Telecom Bretagne in Brest (France) and obtained an award for her internship on hybrid CDN/P2P content delivery networks. She continued her work on content delivery architectures in Devoteam, before joining Orange Labs in 2010. She has been working since then on audiovisual architectures, highlighting architecture recommendations based on Orange strategy and marketing requirements, in close relationship with existing components.

Iuniana Oprescu, after obtaining a double engineering degree in computer networks from the Polytechnic University of Bucharest and the ENSEEIHT from Toulouse, Iuniana went on to pursuing a Ph. D. diploma working jointly in the Orange Labs and the LAAS-CNRS. Her main topics of interest switched from global routing in the Internet and improving BGP to content delivery networks. Recently, she has been directing her attention towards web acceleration techniques, traffic optimization on mobile networks and evolutions of HTTP.

Francesco Paolucci received the Laurea degree in Telecommunications Engineering in 2002 from the University of Pisa, Italy and the Ph.D. degree in 2009 from the Scuola Superiore Sant'Anna, Pisa, Italy. In 2008 he was granted a research Merit Scholarship at the Istitut National de le Recherche Scientifique (INRS), Montreal, Quebec, Canada. Currently, he is Postdoctoral Research Fellow at the TeCIP Institute of Scuola Superiore Sant'Anna, Pisa, Italy. His main research interests are in the field of optical networks control plane, including Generalized Multi Protocol Label Switching (GMPLS) and Software Defined Networking (SDN) protocol extensions, impairment-aware routing based on Path Computation Element (PCE), inter-domain traffic engineering and flexible optical node architectures. Other research activities include network services for Grid/Cloud Computing applications, optical network fault tolerance, inter-domain security and confidentiality.

Prashanth Patil received his Bachelor degree in Computer Science and Engineering from VTU, Bangalore in 2004. He is currently a Technical Leader at Cisco Systems, working in the Security Business Group. He has designed and developed solutions around identity based firewall, policy based networking, network admission control and cloud web security. He actively contributes to the IETF, in the areas of security, port control, and NAT traversal. He has over 15 patents, pending USPTO.

Charles Perkins is a senior principal engineer at Futurewei, investigating mobile wireless networking and dynamic configuration protocols, in particular various IETF, IEEE, and ONF efforts. He has continued strong involvement with performance issues related to Internet access for billions of portable wireless devices as well as actitivies for ad hoc networking and scalability. Charles has authored and edited books on Mobile IP and Ad Hoc Networking, and has published a number of papers and award winning articles in the areas of mobile networking, ad-hoc networking, route optimization for mobile networking, resource discovery, and automatic configuration for mobile computers. He has served as general chair and Program Committee chair for MobiHoc, MASS 2006, ICWUS 2010, and other conferences and workshops. Charles has served on the Internet Architecture Board (IAB) of the IETF and, at last count, has authored or co-authored at least 25 RFCs. He has made numerous inventions and been awarded dozens of patents, including nomination for Inventor of the Year by the European Patent Office. He has served on various committees for the National Research Council, as well as numerous technical assessment boards for Army Research Lab and the Swiss MICS program. He has also served as associate editor for Mobile Communications and Computing Review, the official publication of ACM SIGMOBILE, and has served on the editorial staff for IEEE Internet Computing magazine.

Hosnieh Rafiee is a senior security researcher at Huawei Technologies Duesseldorf GmbH. Her research interests are security and privacy in networks and applications. She focuses on network virtualizations (SDN/NFV) and clouds security (Including software that communicates with the hardware and OpenFlows). Rafiee has several years of experience in developments and security related topics. She has more than 3 years of experience in teaching technical topics to others as technical seminars at universities. She has practical knowledge of Standards (IETF) and standard protocols and active in standardization communities. She has a Ph.D. inSecurity in Internet Technologies from the University of Potsdam.

Laurent Reynaud is a senior research engineer and expert for the Future Networks research community at Orange. Specialized into the performance of agile infrastructures for challenging environments, his topics of interest include wireless multi-hop, multipath and large scale routing techniques as well as the various issues related to QoS in wireless networks. After receiving his engineering degree from ESIGETEL at Fontainebleau, France in 1996, he acquired a significant experience regarding the development and deployment of distributed software in the context of telecommunications, through successive positions in the French Home Department in 1997, in Alcatel-Lucent from 1998 to 2000, and in Orange since 2000. He participated to many French, European and international cooperative research projects. He co-authored many conference and journal articles, and holds a dozen international patents.

Miguel Rio is a Senior Lecturer in the Department of Electronic and Electrical Engineering where he researches and lectures on Internet technologies. He helps to coordinate the Networks and Services Research Laboratory where he leads research projects on real-time overlay streaming, network support for interactive applications, Quality of Service routing and network monitoring and measurement. He has been the Principal Investigator in several EPSRC projects and he currently helps coordinating the EU FP7 FUSION project. He has published more than 50 articles in conference and high impact journals. Previously he worked as a PhD graduate in the University of Kent and, as a post-doctoral fellow in EPSRC and EU funded projects: Promile, MB-NG and DataTAG. His research interests also include Multimedia and peer-to-peer networks, quality of service, distributed information retrieval and gossip based search systems. See also http://www.ee.ucl.ac.uk/~mrio/.

Folker Marten Schamel is founder and managing director of Spinor GmbH, provider of the Shark 3D software for creating interactive virtual worlds for PC, mobile and consoles gaming, virtual production and previz of movies and series, broadcasting graphics, virtual reality and simulations. The software initiated by Folker Schamel powers various award winning products and productions, including for example several E3 awards for world- wide best video game of the year or the children's media award-Der weiße Elefant for contributing to the quality of media services for children. Users of the software include Intel, ATI, Funcom, Siemens, Volkswagen, Ravensburger Digital, ARD, ZDF, and Pro7Sat1. Folker Schamel is credited for contributing to the specification of the OpenGL standard, the world-wide leading cross-platform 3d graphics API. He was selected as jury member for allocating government funding for ambitious collaborative multi-year high-tech projects of companies and universities. He is a teacher about 3d engine development and has talked at various conferences, including for example the Games Convention Developers Conference (GCDC), Future Internet Assembly (FIA), and Microsoft Gamefest. He is an expert on software product design, product management and software development methodologies, especially agile development. Folker Schamel has a Diploma in theoretical physics with mathematics as minor.

Pierrick Seite received the Ph.D in electronic and digital communications from the university of Metz (France) in 1995. He joined France Telecom in 2001 being in charge of architecture studies dealing with mobility management over heterogeneous access systems. He is currently focusing on network-controlled mobility management and convergent fixed/mobile as well as distributed a network architectures. He was involved in European collaborative projectsand is an active contributor to IETF standardization since 2007, being editor, co-author or contributor of standards in the area of IP mobility and multiple-interfaces terminals (RFC 6418, RFC 6419, RFC 7222, RFC7233, etc...). His working interests include IP mobility management, mobile network evolution and connectivity management in heterogeneous networks.

Pieter Simoens is an assistant professor at Ghent University, Belgium. He received a Ph.D. in Computer Science Engineering from the same university. His research activity focuses on mobile cloud computing and cloud networking. He has been involved in several national and European research projects (FP6 MUSE, FP7 MobiThin, FP7 FUSION).

Paulo Simões is Assistant Professor at the Department of Informatics Engineering of the University of Coimbra, Portugal, from where he obtained his doctoral degree in 2002. He regularly collaborates with Instituto Pedro Nunes as senior consultant, leading technology transfer projects for industry partners such as telecommunications operators and energy utilities. His research interests include Future Internet, Network and Infrastructure Management, Security, Critical Infrastructure Protection and Virtualization of Networking and Computing Resources. He has over 150 publications in refereed journals and conferences and he is member of the IEEE Communications Society.

V. Srinivasa Smayazulu (Zulu) is a Senior Research Scientist with the Wireless Communication Research Lab within Intel Labs. His research interests are in the areas of multimedia communications over wireless networks, low-power wireless body area and personal area networks (WBAN/WPAN), as well as platform architecture optimizations in the areas of energy efficiency and QoE improvements for multimedia communications. He has previously contributed to the development of cross-layer optimized solutions for real-time video conferencing, wireless display solutions over WiFi and WiGiG interfaces, Wimedia (UWB) PHY/MAC specifications and UWB spectrum regulations.

Piet Smet graduated from his M.Sc. degree in Engineering Informatics in July 2012 at Hogeschool Ghent. He started a PhD on 'Service-Centric Networking' at Ghent University in August 2012 and is involved as researcher in the FP7 FUSION project.

Xin Sun received his Ph.D. in 2012 from Purdue University, and B.E. in 2005 from University of Science and Technology of China, both in Computer Engineering. Since 2012 he has been an assistant professor in the School of Computing and Information Sciences at Florida International University, Miami. In 2014 he was a visiting researcher at IBM T.J. Watson Center from June to August. His research interests are in computer networks and networked systems, with current focus on network design and management, and network function virtualization.

Fred L. Templin is a computer networking R&D professional with focus on Internet protocol and data link specifications, operating system networking internals, networked applications, and programming languages. He has in-depth experience in Internet networking and security architectures for civil aviation, tactical military, space-based systems and enterprise network applications. Mr. Templin has been an active contributor to the Internet Engineering Task Force (IETF) since 1999. He is currently a senior research engineer in Boeing Research & Technology (BR&T) since May 2005, where he is an Associate Technical Fellow of the Boeing Company.

Vincent Thiebaut, graduated in Engineering, in Telecommunication and Electronics Worked for 12 years for network deployments of IPTV services Today team leader on CDN solutions.

Pascal Thubert has been involved in research, development, and standards efforts for evolving Internet and wireless technologies since joining Cisco in 2000. He currently works within Cisco's Chief Technology and Architecture Office (CTAO), where he focuses on industrial and other deterministic networks and products in the general context of the Internet of Everything. He is co-leading 6TiSCH, the IETF standard for IPv6 over the 802.15.4e TSCH deterministic MAC, and DetNet, a new joined effort with IEEE for cross layer deterministic networks. Earlier, he specialized in IPv6 as applied to mobility and wireless devices and worked in Cisco's core IPv6 product development group. In parallel with his R&D missions, he has authored multiple IETF RFCs and draft standards dealing with IPv6, mobility and the Internet of Things. In particular, Pascal participated as co-editor to the ISA100.11a specification, as well as the NEMO, 6LoWPAN and RPL IETF standards, and participated actively to the introduction of the IT/OT convergence for an Industrial Internet.

Frederik Vandeputte is a research engineer in the IP Platforms Research Program in Bell Labs in Antwerp, Belgium. He obtained his master's degree in Computer Science in 2003 at Ghent University, Belgium, developing a link-time optimizer for the IA64 architecture during his master's thesis. In 2008, he obtained his PhD in Computer Science at Ghent University for doing research on characterizing and exploiting the time-varying behavior of applications on multi-configuration processor architectures. In 2008, he did a joint research project with Alcatel-Lucent Bell Labs at Ghent University, focusing on software parallelization, and evaluating the real-time capabilities, scheduling efficiency and performance of the Linux operating system. He joined Alcatel-Lucent Bell Labs in 2009, continuing his work on software parallelization for many-core as well as heterogeneous architectures for media processing applications. During this work, he created a graph-based description and processing framework for efficiently developing and deploying real-time media applications on modern hardware. From 2012 onwards, he started working on efficiently deploying media processing applications in the network and studying the feasibility and impact of using hardware accelerators in such environments. His current research topics include heterogeneous clouds, network functions virtualization and performance optimization. He is currently also work package leader of the FUSION FP7 project involving service-oriented networking for demanding real-time media applications, and is author or co-author of over a dozen papers in international conferences and journals.

Luc Vermoesen is a research scientist with the Alcatel-Lucent Bell Labs Bearer Plane Virtualization Technology Dept, Antwerp, Belgium. He received his master's degree in industrial sciences from KIH DeNayer, Sint-katelijne Waver, Belgium. As a workstudent he joined the masters program in Applied Computer Science at University of Brussels (VUB), Belgium. For several years, he was involved in the architecture and design of various Alcatel-Lucent Mobile, DSL and IP products, prior to joining the Research and Innovation Dept. His main long-standing research interests are in computer sofware engineering, embedded software, novel cloud, virtualization, overall system performance and multimedia distribution techniques.

Hongfang Yu received her B.S. degree in Electronic Engineering in 1996 from Xi'dian University, her M.S. degree and Ph.D. degree in Communication and Information Engineering in 1999 and 2006 from University of Electronic Science and Technology of China, respectively. From 2009 to 2010, she was a visiting scholar in Department of Computer Science and Engineering, University at Buffalo (SUNY). From 2011 to 2012, she was a visiting scholar in Department of Computer Science and Engineering, City University of Hong Kong. She is currently a professor at School of Communication and Information Engineering, University of Electronic Science and Technology of China. Her research has been supported by NSFC, National Grand Fundamental Research 973 Program, China Mobile and Huawei Company et.al. She submitted 10 international and national-wide patent applications (among 8 patents have got the license). She has authored/coauthored over 70 papers on international journals and conferences. Her current research interest includes network virtualization, SDN/NFV, cloud computing, network survivability and Next Generation Internet, etc.

Anca Livovschi Zamfir received her Bachelor and M.Sc. Engineering degrees in Computer Science and Engineering from the Polytechnic Institute of Bucharest (PUB), Bucharest, Romania, in 1986. She is currently a Technical Leader at Cisco Systems and has been working in different roles since 1999, being involved in software development for several technologies such as MPLS, GMPLS, L2VPN, Metro Ethernet, ISSU, routing and autoIPv6 for enterprise transition to IPv6. Her recent work and interests include Application Enabled Collaborative Networking, specifically the signaling and information encoding aspects. Before 1999 she worked at the National Research Institute for Telecommunications in Bucharest, Romania, was a Lecturer at the Department of Computer Science at the University of Brasov, Romania, and worked on SVC signaling and NNI routing protocols at Nortel Networks in Ottawa, Canada.

Mingui Zhang is a research engineer in Huawei. He had been working for protocol standardization in IETF (Internet Engineering Task Force) in Huawei since he received his PhD degree from Tsinghua University in 2010. His research interest includes Power Aware Networks and Data Center Networks.

Quintin Zhao is a principal engineer in the IP software group of Huawei Technologies USA IP Lab. He mainly focuses on IP Routing and MPLS technology. Quintin currently leads the network virtualization through Multiple Topology technology projects and SDN transition through PCE+ technology projects. With more than twenty years' experience in networking, Quintin has been involved in the architecture design/implementation at Huawei's VRP, Cisco's IOS/IOX, and Ericsson's AXE. Quintin is an active contributor in IETF. He has co-authored multiple RFCs and Internet Drafts in the MPLS, L2/L3 VPN and PCE Working Groups. Quintin also holds more than a dozen patents in the area of multicast traffic engineering, traffic engineering protection, network virtualization and SDN. He joined Huawei Technologies USA in 2006, and he worked in the MPLS technology area at Cisco Systems before he joined Huawei Technologies USA. Prior to Cisco, he worked in the VoIP technology area at Ericsson. He received BS degree in Systems Engineering from Beijing Institute of Technology and MS degree in Computer Science from Iowa State University.

Index

E

F

G

H

I

J

L

M

N

O

P

Q

R

S

T

U

V

W

Printed in the United States
By Bookmasters